9976

P9-EDF-109

(Continued on back endsheets)

Nineteenth-Century German Writers, 1841-1900

Nineteenth-Century German Writers, 1841-1900

Edited by
James Hardin
University of South Carolina
and
Siegfried Mews
University of North Carolina at Chapel Hill

A Bruccoli Clark Layman Book
Gale Research Inc.
Detroit, London

Printed in the United States of America

Published simultaneously in the United Kingdom
by Gale Research International Limited
(An affiliated company of Gale Research Inc.)

The paper used in this publication meets the minimum requirements
of American National Standard for Information Sciences–Permanence
Paper for Printed Library Materials, ANSI Z39.48-1984. ∞ ™

Library of Congress Catalog Card Number 92-44546
ISBN 0-8103-5388-1

I⟨T⟩P™

The trademark ITP is used under license.

10 9 8 7 6 5 4 3 2 1

Contents

Plan of the Series

. . . Almost the most prodigious asset of a country, and perhaps its most precious possession, is its native literary product — when that product is fine and noble and enduring.

Mark Twain*

The advisory board, the editors, and the publisher of the *Dictionary of Literary Biography* are joined in endorsing Mark Twain's declaration. The literature of a nation provides an inexhaustible resource of permanent worth. We intend to make literature and its creators better understood and more accessible to students and the reading public, while satisfying the standards of teachers and scholars.

To meet these requirements, *literary biography* has been construed in terms of the author's achievement. The most important thing about a writer is his writing. Accordingly, the entries in *DLB* are career biographies, tracing the development of the author's canon and the evolution of his reputation.

The purpose of *DLB* is not only to provide reliable information in a convenient format but also to place the figures in the larger perspective of literary history and to offer appraisals of their accomplishments by qualified scholars.

The publication plan for *DLB* resulted from two years of preparation. The project was proposed to Bruccoli Clark by Frederick C. Ruffner, president of the Gale Research Company, in November 1975. After specimen entries were prepared and typeset, an advisory board was formed to refine the entry format and develop the series rationale. In meetings held during 1976, the publisher, series editors, and advisory board approved the scheme for a comprehensive biographical dictionary of persons who contributed to North American literature. Editorial work on the first volume began in January 1977, and it was published in 1978. In order to make *DLB* more than a reference tool and to compile volumes that individually have claim to status as literary history, it was decided to organize volumes by topic, period, or genre. Each of these freestanding volumes provides a biographical-bibliographical guide and overview for a particular area of literature. We are convinced that this organization – as opposed to a single alphabet method – constitutes a valuable innovation in the presentation of reference material. The volume plan necessarily requires many decisions for the placement and treatment of authors who might properly be included in two or three volumes. In some instances a major figure will be included in separate volumes, but with different entries emphasizing the aspect of his career appropriate to each volume. Ernest Hemingway, for example, is represented in *American Writers in Paris, 1920–1939* by an entry focusing on his expatriate apprenticeship; he is also in *American Novelists, 1910–1945* with an entry surveying his entire career. Each volume includes a cumulative index of the subject authors and articles. Comprehensive indexes to the entire series are planned.

With volume ten in 1982 it was decided to enlarge the scope of *DLB*. By the end of 1986 twenty-one volumes treating British literature had been published, and volumes for Commonwealth and Modern European literature were in progress. The series has been further augmented by the *DLB Yearbooks* (since 1981) which update published entries and add new entries to keep the *DLB* current with contemporary activity. There have also been *DLB Documentary Series* volumes which provide biographical and critical source materials for figures whose work is judged to have particular interest for students. One of these companion volumes is entirely devoted to Tennessee Williams.

We define literature as the *intellectual commerce of a nation:* not merely as belles lettres but as that ample and complex process by which ideas are generated, shaped, and transmitted. *DLB* entries are not limited to "creative writers" but extend to other figures who in their time and in their way influenced the mind of a people. Thus the series encompasses historians, journalists, publishers, and screenwriters. By this means readers of *DLB* may be aided to perceive literature not as cult scripture in the keeping of intellectual high priests but firmly po-

From an unpublished section of Mark Twain's autobiography, copyright by the Mark Twain Company

sitioned at the center of a nation's life.

DLB includes the major writers appropriate to each volume and those standing in the ranks immediately behind them. Scholarly and critical counsel has been sought in deciding which minor figures to include and how full their entries should be. Wherever possible, useful references are made to figures who do not warrant separate entries.

Each DLB volume has a volume editor responsible for planning the volume, selecting the figures for inclusion, and assigning the entries. Volume editors are also responsible for preparing, where appropriate, appendices surveying the major periodicals and literary and intellectual movements for their volumes, as well as lists of further readings. Work on the series as a whole is coordinated at the Bruccoli Clark Layman editorial center in Columbia, South Carolina, where the editorial staff is responsible for accuracy of the published volumes.

One feature that distinguishes DLB is the illustration policy – its concern with the iconography of literature. Just as an author is influenced by his surroundings, so is the reader's understanding of the author enhanced by a knowledge of his environment. Therefore DLB volumes include not only drawings, paintings, and photographs of authors, often depicting them at various stages in their careers, but also illustrations of their families and places where they lived. Title pages are regularly reproduced in facsimile along with dust jackets for modern authors. The dust jackets are a special feature of DLB because they often document better than anything else the way in which an author's work was perceived in its own time. Specimens of the writers' manuscripts are included when feasible.

Samuel Johnson rightly decreed that "The chief glory of every people arises from its authors." The purpose of the *Dictionary of Literary Biography* is to compile literary history in the surest way available to us – by accurate and comprehensive treatment of the lives and work of those who contributed to it.

The *DLB* Advisory Board

Introduction

In 1814–1815 delegates from all the European powers participated in the Congress of Vienna. The congress signified the end of the Napoleonic era and the beginning of the Restauration (restoration), a period that was characterized by the attempt to restore the European political order that had prevailed before the French Revolution of 1789. The Restauration is also known as the Metternichsches System (Metternich System) after the Austrian chancellor Prince Klemens von Metternich. Metternich, the leading figure of the Congress of Vienna, was chiefly responsible for the repressive measures passed by the federal diet of the Deutscher Bund, the federation of thirty-nine German states set up by the congress. The Metternichsches System was in effect until 1848, when revolutions broke out in many European countries; although the bourgeois revolutions in Berlin and Vienna — the respective capitals of Prussia and Austria, the two dominant powers in the Deutscher Bund — were unsuccessful, they heralded changes that influenced the cultural climate and resulted in shifting literary directions.

A fairly widely accepted view holds that the period from 1815 to 1848 was essentially dominated by two major tendencies that may be defined in political terms: the conservative Biedermeier, on the one hand, and the liberal Junges Deutschland (Young Germany) and Vormärz (Pre-March), on the other. The writers and poets of the so-called Biedermeier generally abstained from engagement in politics and emphasized middle-class values and virtues such as family, home, and community. Although a definition of the period in purely political terms gives short shrift to literary criteria such as style and technique, for the period from 1815 to 1848 the distinction between conservative Biedermeier writers and their progressive counterparts offers a valid pattern of interpretation. There have been attempts to subsume all liberal, bourgeois writers under one rubric; it is appropriate, however, to distinguish between Junges Deutschland and the writers of the Vormärz proper, the latter term encompassing the period that began around 1840 and ended with the March 1848 Revolution. The writers of the two groups were united by their opposition to the Metternichsches System and their propensity for voicing their opinions on topical issues.

An 1835 decree declared the writings of Junges Deutschland to be an attack on Christianity and on existing social conditions as well as a denigration of manners and morals; the further printing and distribution of all writings by Heinrich Heine, Karl Gutzkow, Heinrich Laube, Theodor Mundt, and Ludolf Wienbarg were prohibited. But writers who came to the fore in the 1840s, including Georg Herwegh and Ferdinand Freiligrath, tended to scorn the wittily polemical style of Junges Deutschland as playful and subjective; they opted for an unambiguously tendentious mode of representation and turned to topics that had been neglected by Junges Deutschland, including criticism of the anachronistic feudal system and the apolitical stance of much of the German middle class, the idea of German national unity, and such social issues as the uprisings of the Silesian weavers. The Vormärz poets used as their favorite means of expression the political and topical poem, which was suitable for quick dissemination via broadsides, posters, or oral delivery. These poems were designed to speak directly to the masses and to appeal to their emotions by invoking concepts such as freedom and justice, which lacked specific content.

Three reasons are usually cited for considering 1840 as the actual beginning of the Vormärz — the reemergence of patriotic, anti-French feelings; the ascension to the Prussian throne of Friedrich Wilhelm IV, who was erroneously considered a liberal; and the appearance of the Left or Young Hegelians. The Left Hegelians set out to apply the encyclopedic system of the preeminent idealist philosopher of his age, Georg Wilhelm Friedrich Hegel, to religion and to politics and, in the process, to radicalize those fields. In 1835–1836 the highly influential and controversial study by the theologian David Friedrich Strauß, *Das Leben Jesu, kritisch betrachtet* (The Life of Jesus, Critically Examined; translated as *The Life of Christ*, 1843), appeared. Strauß's critical examination of the Bible, which viewed Jesus as a human being rather than as the son of God, went through five editions by 1840. The demythologizing of Christianity continued with *Das Wesen des Christenthums* (1841; translated as *The Essence of Christianity*, 1854), by the philosopher Ludwig Feuerbach, and *Das entdeckte Christenthum*

(Christianity Discovered, 1843), by the theologian Bruno Bauer. This criticism of religion constituted an attack on the state itself, particularly Protestant Prussia, which, since the Reformation, depended on the alliance of Thron und Altar (throne and altar) — a phrase coined by Voltaire.

Max Stirner in *Der Einzige und sein Eigenthum* (1845; translated as *The Ego and His Own*, 1907) vehemently attacked the protection that the state extended to the financially privileged bourgeoisie and drew attention to a potentially formidable weapon of the workers — the strike; but Karl Marx and his collaborator Friedrich Engels developed a systematic criticism of capitalism. In his "Kritik des hegelschen Staatsrechts" (1927; translated as *Critique of Hegel's "Philosophy of Right,"* 1970), written in 1843, Marx used the then-current metaphor of religion as "Opium des Volks" (opium of the people) to argue that religion prevented true emancipation by offering palliatives to the people rather than genuine solutions to their problems. In elaborating on and taking issue with Feuerbach, Marx radically redefined the task of philosophers in his "Thesen über Feuerbach" (1932; translated as "Theses on Feuerbach," 1964), written in 1845. Marx's famed eleventh thesis reads: "Die Philosophen haben die Welt nur verschieden *interpretiert*, es kömmt darauf an, sie zu *verändern*" (Philosophers have merely *interpreted* the world in different ways; the point is to *change* it). This desire to change the world culminates in the *Manifest der kommunistischen Partei* (1848; translated as *Manifesto of the Communist Party,* 1888), by Marx and Engels, which appeals to the international proletariat rather than to the middle class, the main ideological and political force in the March 1848 Revolution.

The *Manifest der kommunistischen Partei* also served to propagate the ideas of "scientific" socialism, as opposed to "utopian" socialism such as that promulgated by Wilhelm Weitling. His social origins made Weitling a genuine Arbeiterschriftsteller (working-class writer) during the Vormärz. Weitling broke with Marx in 1847, and he later immigrated to the United States and turned away from politics. The first viable workers' association did not originate until 1863, when Ferdinand Lassalle, author of the historical tragedy *Franz von Sickingen* (1859; translated, 1904), founded the Allgemeiner Deutscher Arbeiterverein (General German Workers' Association), which in 1875 merged with the Sozialdemokratische Arbeiterpartei (Social Democratic Workers' Party) to form the Sozialistische Arbeiterpartei Deutschlands (Socialist Workers' Party of Germany).

The literary and intellectual ferment generated during the Vormärz culminated in a major revolutionary effort. The March 1848 Revolution in Germany followed the Paris revolution in February, which resulted in France temporarily becoming a republic. Mass meetings and demonstrations were held in southern Germany, but the most important events took place in Vienna, Berlin, and Frankfurt am Main. Liberal demands such as the institution of constitutional governments, freedom of the press (one of the most serious grievances during the Vormärz), the appointment of reform-minded governments (in Austria, Chancellor Metternich was forced to resign), and the arming of the people were granted almost immediately by most German governments.

The freely elected Frankfurter Nationalversammlung (Frankfurt National Assembly), which convened in the Frankfurt Paulskirche (Saint Paul's Church) in May 1848, counted among its members university professors and Vormärz writers who sought to contribute to the shaping of Germany's future. Their political positions ranged from the conservative patriotism of the poet Ernst Moritz Arndt to the liberalism of the poet Ludwig Uhland to the left radicalism of Arnold Ruge, who with Marx had coedited the Paris-based *Deutsch-französische Jahrbücher* (German-French Yearbooks) in the mid 1840s. Herwegh, who in the course of an 1842 literary feud with Freiligrath had expressed his conviction that poets should assume an active role in the revolutionary struggle, acted according to his beliefs by leading an expeditionary corps of German workers living in Paris exile into the southwestern state of Baden with the goal of establishing a German republic. But the corps was quickly defeated in April, and Herwegh fled to Switzerland.

The Frankfurter Nationalversammlung voted for a constitution and elected King Friedrich Wilhelm IV of Prussia emperor, thereby virtually excluding multinational Austria from German affairs. In April 1849, however, Friedrich Wilhelm IV rejected the crown for fear of offending Austria and of weakening the sovereign rights of monarchs. This abortive attempt to establish German unity marked, in effect, the failure of the March Revolution. Because of the involvement of writers and poets in the Frankfurter Nationalversammlung, one critic commented that these efforts constituted the last attempt "die Zeitfragen von den Dichtern und Denkern her zu lösen" (to resolve relevant contemporaneous issues through poets and thinkers). Although the revolution was eventually crushed by military force, some of its achievements — for example, freedom of the press and the abolition of feudal privileges in Prussia – remained in effect. Although constitutional government, one of the chief political objectives that many Vormärz writers had supported, survived in several German states, the most important goal – German unity – was not attained until 1871. German unity was not achieved through a democratic movement; instead, the Reichsgründung (founding of the empire) took place under Prussian hegemony as a consequence of the Franco-Prussian War of 1870–1871.

One of the results of the failed March Revolution was the growing awareness among the middle class that it was difficult if not impossible to achieve liberal reforms and political unity in opposition to the prevailing order. As a consequence, a withdrawal from politics and a concentration on economic issues ensued. This change in the intellectual climate is also reflected in literature; if one exempts the late poetry of Heine, both the engaged prose writings of Junges Deutschland and the political poetry of the Vormärz tend to disappear in the postrevolutionary era. Lyric poetry in the 1850s came to be regarded as a vehicle for affording the reader access, via the sensibilities and emotions that found expression in the poem, to the realm of ideas that was thought to exist behind the manifestations of external reality. There was a renewed emphasis on Erlebnislyrik (the poetry of immediate and intense emotions), on the one hand, and the finely crafted – albeit somewhat ornamental – poem, on the other. The chief representative of the latter type of poetry was Emanuel Geibel, by far the best-known poet of the second half of the nineteenth century. His collection *Gedichte* (Poems) was first published in 1840 but did not achieve its impact until after the March Revolution; it went through 127 editions by 1900. Unlike the Vormärz poets, whose politically tendentious poetry he attacked, Geibel was a staunchly conservative promoter of national unity. Also, unlike the writers of Junges Deutschland and the Vormärz, who, for the most part, sought to make a living by means of their pen, Geibel, the son of a Protestant pastor, deliberately cultivated contacts with the aristocracy and with royalty. In 1852 he was appointed reader to King Maximilian II of Bavaria and honorary professor at the University of Munich. He soon became the central figure of the Münchner Dichterkreis (Munich Circle of Poets) and the Krokodil (Crocodile Society), a private association of Munich poets that was named after the title of a poem by Hermann Lingg. The Munich poets included the prolific writer of novellas and future Nobel Prize winner Paul Heyse;

the poet Friedrich von Bodenstedt; the poet and dramatist Count Adolf Friedrich von Schack; the writer and director from 1851 to 1857 of the Munich Hoftheater (court theater) Franz von Dingelstedt; and the future novelist Felix Dahn. In general, the Munich poets hewed to the ideal of an apolitical, classicistic, art and attributed great significance to formal perfection; the depiction of social problems was considered aesthetically offensive. They stressed the dignity of the artist and the artist's aesthetic responsibilities. Geibel, especially, cultivated the image of a König Dichter (royal poet) who both represented art and celebrated it in a quasi-religious fashion.

Although Geibel and his Munich colleagues are today considered epigones, they were quite popular in the second half of the nineteenth century; a host of family magazines, anthologies, and almanacs contributed to the wide dissemination to a middle-class audience of their noncontroversial, harmonious, and aesthetically pleasing poetry. The middle class's appreciation of poetry is also attested to by the firm place occupied by poetry at festive and convivial occasions; the public reading of poems both lent dignity to such events and served entertainment purposes.

Less popular, but on a significantly higher plane artistically, was the poetry by Theodor Storm, Gottfried Keller, Theodor Fontane, and Conrad Ferdinand Meyer. These poets and writers are generally considered the chief representatives of realism, the style that dominated the second half of the nineteenth century. Originally derived from French painting, which around 1850 developed a style of representation based on the close observation of external phenomena, the term *realism* was appropriated by contemporaneous literary critics and writers. Contributions to the theory of realism include those by Fontane in his essay "Unsere lyrische und epische Poesie seit 1848" (Our Lyric and Epic Poetry since 1848, 1853); by Julian Schmidt, coeditor with the novelist Gustav Freytag of the influential literary-cultural review *Die Grenzboten* (The Border Messenger); and, above all, by Otto Ludwig, who gave the term *Poetischer Realismus* (Poetic Realism) wide currency. The common denominator of these attempts to define realism is the postulate that the literary text should reflect objective reality in a plausible fashion, which means that there should be no endeavor to make an exact copy of reality. Rather, as Fritz Martini, author of one of the standard works on the literature of German realism, *Deutsche Literatur im bürgerlichen Realismus 1848-1898* (German Literature during

Middle-Class Realism 1848-1898, 1962) put it, in their subject matter and themes literary texts tended to be limited by the empirical boundaries of time, place, causality, and the psychological and societal conditioning the authors shared with their readers because of their common middle-class origins. Although these texts included the depiction of human beings in their social contexts and class relations, they generally avoided the treatment of social conflict and political crises; in contrast to the Vormärz, tendentiousness was shunned. Freytag wrote in *Die Grenzboten* in 1853 that authors should infuse their portrayals of daily life with poetry and beauty and, by implication, should move and elevate the reader. This didactic intention was formulated by Keller, an active participant in the life of the Swiss democracy, who wrote in a letter of June 1860 that it was not sufficient to glorify the past but that it was important to strengthen and beautify the seeds of the future so as to induce readers to recognize themselves in fictional guise and realize their constructive potential. Keller also pointed out the role of humor as a means of overcoming the tension between realistic fiction tinged with idealism and the real as evident in readers' daily experiences.

This tension was also to be perceived in lyric poetry, next to the novella the preferred genre of the major writers of realism. The preponderance of nature poetry in the postrevolutionary period may be construed as signifying the poets' search for a refuge removed from the unsatisfactory political reality and encroaching technical progress and industrialization. Storm, Keller, and Fontane were essentially liberals, and Storm and Keller served their respective communities in official functions – Storm in his native Schleswig-Holstein, and Keller in his hometown of Zurich. Although Switzerland had been an independent state for centuries, authors from German-speaking Switzerland participated fully in the literary life of Germany, a country that did not exist as a political entity until 1871. Switzerland served as a haven for exiles and refugees during the repressive Restauration period and in the postrevolutionary decades. The impulses that literary life in Switzerland received from the German exiles are evident in Keller, who began his career as a writer in 1846 with the publication of *Gedichte* and was encouraged in his poetic efforts by German exiles in Zurich, especially Herwegh. Thus Keller's early poetry shows an affinity with that of the Vormärz. But in his "Abendlied" (Evening Song, 1879) he gives poetic expression to his rejection of religion and the Christian concept of immortality – views he had acquired under the influence of

Feuerbach during his studies at the University of Heidelberg in 1848–1849.

The lack of political unity and of an undisputed political-cultural center comparable to Paris or London for all of Germany brings into focus the close ties to specific regions – particularly of Storm, but also of Keller, and to a lesser extent of Fontane, who came from the former Prussian border region, the Mark Brandenburg. One of Storm's most renowned poems, "Die Stadt" (The Town, 1851) is a glorification of and declaration of love for his small hometown of Husum. The concept of home as a sanctuary is also evident in "Oktoberlied" (October Song), the opening poem of Storm's first collection, *Gedichte* (1852). The poem originated during the revolutionary year of 1848 and posits the contrast between a happy, contented, private domestic sphere and "draußen," the external world of commotion and political strife. Storm indicated that he wanted the poem to be understood as a protest against the political poetry of the Vormärz. Poems such as "Abseits" (Apart, 1847) evoke the natural scenery so familiar to the poet – in this instance the deserted but idyllic heath near the North Sea that is not yet threatened by the turmoil of the world outside.

The pronounced preference of Storm and other writers for Heimat (home), which was defined in regional terms, and the absence in the German-speaking countries of a genuine literary and cultural center led the French literary historian Claude David, in his *Geschichte der deutschen Literatur: Zwischen Romantik und Symbolismus 1820–1885* (History of German Literature: Between Romanticism and Symbolism 1820–1885, 1966) to use a geographical structuring device for his discussion of post-1848 writers. David's distinction between the "inner German space," northern Germany, the Swiss, and the Austrians draws attention to the centrifugal forces dominating the literary scene, but this distinction may prove an insufficient criterion for an understanding of works that are devoid of pronounced regional characteristics.

Yet provincialism favored the German propensity for Innerlichkeit (inwardness or introspection). For instance, it has been suggested that German realism in general and Poetic Realism in particular were not suitable for the novel, in that authors tended to concentrate on the personal, private development of individuals or on the interaction of the members of small groups rather than on the relationship of the individual to society as a whole, as French and English novelists were accustomed to doing. The influential critic Erich Auerbach defined literary realism as "a serious representation of contemporary everyday social reality against the background of a constant historical movement" – a criterion that German novels generally failed to meet on account of the special socioeconomic and political conditions that prevailed in Germany and that retarded the development of a self-confident middle class. Although there was no dearth of novels, the novella, a tightly constructed form of prose fiction that has generated a substantial body of theoretical disquisitions, was and is regarded as the most significant genre of realism in terms of artistic merit. In contrast to the novel, which, according to the professor of aesthetics Friedrich Theodor von Vischer, offers "ein umfassendes Bild der Weltzustände" (an encompassing portrayal of the condition of the world), the novella, according to the novelist and theoretician Friedrich Spielhagen, deals with fully developed characters who are forced to reveal their true essences when confronted with major crises. The novella's emphasis on the individual and its concentration on a particular moment in that individual's life suggest its affinity to the drama rather than to the novel.

Yet novels continued to be written and published. The Goethean tradition of the humanistic bildungsroman was upheld, notably by Adalbert Stifter in *Der Nachsommer* (1857; translated as *Indian Summer,* 1985), Keller in *Der grüne Heinrich* (1854–1855; revised, 1879–1880; translated as *Green Henry,* 1960), and Wilhelm Raabe in *Der Hungerpastor* (1864; translated as *The Hunger-Pastor,* 1885). But the bildungsroman in the second half of the nineteenth century tended to center on the intellectual and spiritual maturing of the male protagonist rather than on the protagonist's relation to contemporaneous social developments. Whereas the bildungsroman has occupied a privileged position in much of twentieth-century scholarship, the novels by Freytag and Spielhagen proved immediately popular; Freytag's *Soll und Haben* (1855; translated as *Debit and Credit,* 1855) quickly went through several editions. The novel's appeal may be attributed to its depiction of the middle-class protagonist's rise from humble beginnings to a position of responsibility in a commercial firm. The protagonist thus provided a model of identification for its male readers, who saw their values of hard work, loyalty, reliability, and punctuality confirmed and rewarded. Freytag extols the middle class at the expense of both the rising proletariat, deemed socially inferior, and the aristocracy, for the most part viewed as morally corrupt. In contrast to Freytag's positive depiction of middle-class commercial activities, the Vormärz

writer Georg Weerth, sometime collaborator of Marx and Engels at the *Neue Rheinische Zeitung* (New Rhenish Newspaper) in 1848, provides a scathing satire of the exploitative practices of commercial establishments in his *Humoristische Skizzen aus dem deutschen Handelsleben* (Humorous Sketches from German Business Life; serialized 1847–1848, published 1949). Freytag – although hardly a rabid anti-Semite himself – created a disquieting literary racial stereotype in the figure of the Jew Veitel Itzig, in all respects the opposite of the protagonist of *Soll und Haben,* Anton Wohlfart. This stereotype contributed to subverting the hopes of Jewish emancipation and assimilation. Conversely, authentic Jewish life is in the foreground in the novels of Karl Emil Franzos, who was intimately familiar with the Jewish communities of eastern Europe that, for the most part, belonged to the Hapsburg Empire.

Several authors of novels have been classified as Unterhaltungsschriftsteller – writers providing pure entertainment rather than striving to produce an uplifting reading experience. Unterhaltungsschriftsteller – or, to use a term that has pejorative connotations, the practitioners of Trivialliteratur (trivial literature) – became a semirespectable subject of study in the 1960s and 1970s as a consequence of the democratic widening of the literary canon, which no longer concentrated exclusively on works deemed to be of superior artistic quality.

Literary realism did not preclude the treatment of faraway lands. Friedrich Gerstäcker, whose works began to be published in the 1840s, based his travel accounts and novels on his own adventuresome travels in the United States and other parts of the world. Titles such as *Die Flußpiraten des Mississippi* (1848; translated as *The Pirates of the Mississippi,* 1856) convey the exotic flavor Gerstäcker's works had for German readers. The prolific Balduin Möllhausen, author of forty-five novels and eighty novellas, also traveled extensively in the United States, the favorite place of action in his fiction. In contrast to the interest in exotic places stimulated by Gerstäcker and Möllhausen, the liberal Austrian writer and journalist Ferdinand Kürnberger depicted in his first novel, *Der Amerika-Müde* (Disenchanted with America, 1855), the negative experiences of the Austrian poet Nikolaus Lenau, who had returned from America in 1833. Lenau was disappointed by uncongenial living conditions and his failure to establish a farm in Pennsylvania.

The most extraordinary literary phenomenon among the writers of adventure fiction was Karl May. His novels about the Indians in the Wild West gained immense popularity in Germany and

Europe – but not in the United States – even though he had not set foot on American soil when he wrote them. May's novels are indicative of the nationalistic spirit that was generated by the Franco-Prussian War and remained dominant throughout the empire in that they feature an invincible German hero who is physically, intellectually, and morally superior to his adversaries.

A further instance of the wide range of fiction during the period of realism is provided by Fritz Reuter, a contemporary of Junges Deutschland and the Vormärz who, however, did not begin to have his works published until the 1850s owing to his long incarceration for political reasons. Reuter, born in rural Mecklenburg, wrote in a Low German dialect that is not easily accessible to speakers of standard German. Yet his novels – for example, *Ut mine Festungstid* (From My Time in the Fortress, 1862), a work that rarely alludes to the harshness of prison life – found an appreciative audience.

Women writers were usually excluded from literary histories, but they have recently attracted increased scholarly attention. Louise von François, by virtue of the praise bestowed on her historical novel *Die letzte Reckenburgerin* (1871; translated as *The Last von Reckenburg*, 1887) by Freytag, has attracted a modicum of critics' attention, but feminist tendencies are not pronounced in her work. Other women writers, however – among them Fanny Lewald, Louise Aston, Louise Mühlbach, and Louise Otto-Peters – wrote novels that advocated women's social and sexual emancipation. Most of these female authors wrote in the 1840s and were attuned to the liberal ideas promulgated by Junges Deutschland and the Vormärz – ideas that did not specifically stress women's advancement. But in the 1860s the novelist Otto-Peters cofounded the Allgemeiner deutscher Frauenverein (General German Women's Association), and, beginning in 1866, she coedited the association's journal *Neue Bahnen* (New Ways). Her pioneering activities paved the way for an organized women's movement – a movement that was supported by the Social Democrat August Bebel, whose widely read book *Die Frau und der Sozialismus* (translated as *Woman under Socialism*, 1904) was published in 1883.

Although the novels of Mühlbach and especially those of E. Marlitt (pseudonym of Eugenie John) rely on sentimentality and trivial plots in which true love emerges victorious in the face of a hostile social environment, it has been argued that they drew attention to the plight and vulnerability of women in society. But the fact that Marlitt's novels were frequently serialized in the weekly *Die Gar-tenlaube* (The Garden Arbor), the most popular German family magazine during the second half of the nineteenth century and one dedicated to upholding conservative values, does not inspire much confidence in the alleged emancipatory thrust of her writing.

The true forte of realism is generally held to be the novella, an artistically demanding prose form favored by Storm, Keller, Raabe, and Meyer. Lesser lights such as the extraordinarily productive Heyse, coeditor with Hermann Kurz of *Deutscher Novellenschatz* (Treasury of German Novellas, 1871–1876) and theorist of the novella, also contributed to the popularity of the genre. The comparative brevity of these works made them well suited for publication in the family magazines and similar periodicals that constituted the prime reading matter for the middle-class public. Heyse is less remembered for his fictional writings than for his vaunted Falkentheorie (theory of the falcon), the postulate that each novella should incorporate a "falcon." Heyse derived the idea of the falcon from the *Decameron* (1349–1351), the cycle of novellas by Giovanni Boccaccio. The falcon has been defined as a leitmotiv or as a Dingsymbol (distinct object with a symbolic function) that reappears at important junctures of the novella, thereby forcing the author to concentrate on one central conflict.

The theory and practice of the novella did not always coincide, however. A case in point is Storm's "Immensee" (1851; translated, 1863), which has remained one of his most popular works. The novella is less a tightly constructed narrative than a Stimmungsbild, the creation of a lyrical mood by the protagonist/narrator Reinhard through a series of vignettes. Reinhard is prompted by the picture of his lost childhood sweetheart, Elisabeth, to reminisce about the past and missed opportunities. The novella does have a social component in its contrast of the materialistic orientation of Elisabeth's mother, according to whose wishes Elisabeth marries a well-to-do suitor, with the artistic inclinations of the impecunious Reinhard. The theme of the heightened sensibilities of the artist versus the narrow materialistic preoccupation of the bourgeois was noted by Thomas Mann, who acknowledged Storm as a literary precursor. Storm's last novella and masterpiece, *Der Schimmelreiter* (1888; translated as "The Rider of the White Horse," 1914) features an intricate narrative situation that was intended to lend plausibility to the events involving a supernatural creature, the white horse mentioned in the novella's title. Despite its strong regional characteristics and its rootedness in the landscape of the

North Sea coast, the novella takes cognizance of the changes wrought as a consequence of the Reichsgründung in 1871. The protagonist, the dikegrave and dike builder Hauke Haien, exhibits traits of the new Machtmensch (a man enamored of the exercise of power). His imperiousness, detestation of the superstitious workers, and reliance on rational, innovative thinking that is unhampered by ethics are indicative of his elevated status – a status akin to that of great historical figures. At the same time, Haien's virtual suicide at the novella's conclusion resembles a sacrificial death, an atonement for his hubris. This ending emphasizes Storm's ambivalent attitude and characterizes him as a writer who essentially belongs to the preimperialist period of realism.

Just as Storm's novellas are infused with the atmosphere of his native northern German region, so Keller's prose works are evocative of Switzerland and, in particular, of his native city of Zurich, after which he named his cycle of novellas *Züricher Novellen* (Zurich Novellas, 1878). In contrast to Storm, it is the spirit of the people and their sometimes quaint characteristics that are important to Keller; in further contrast to Storm, Keller's fiction shows a decidedly didactic tendency that is attributable to his belief in Swiss democracy, which deserved both criticism to eliminate undesirable tendencies and praise to strengthen its positive traits. This didactic intent is evident in the novellas of Keller's cycle *Die Leute von Seldwyla* (The People of Seldwyla, 1856; enlarged, 1874).

Keller's didacticism is tempered by his humor; his imaginary Seldwyla, a small town peopled for the most part by odd inhabitants, receives a broadly humorous treatment that occasionally borders on the satirical and grotesque. But Keller usually allows gentle humor to prevail; most of his misguided protagonists who adhere to fanciful, unrealistic notions become reintegrated into society in the end. For example, in "Pankraz, der Schmoller" (Pankraz the Sulker) and "Kleider machen Leute" (Clothes Make the Man) the protagonists are cured of their egotistical behavior and romantic illusions, respectively, and become useful members of their communities. Yet in one of the crowning achievements of the nineteenth-century novella, "Romeo und Julia auf dem Dorfe" (translated as "Romeo and Juliet of the Village," 1919), Keller transplants Shakespeare's "star-cross'd lovers" into a contemporaneous rustic Swiss milieu in which the narrow-minded greed of their fathers and their own clinging to a hollow concept of bourgeois respectability and honor lead to their suicides.

The rural milieu of "Romeo und Julia auf dem Dorfe" relates Keller's novella to a subgenre that had been flourishing since the 1840s, the so-called Dorfgeschichte (village tale). The Dorfgeschichte was represented by Keller's compatriot Jeremias Gotthelf; the Germans Berthold Auerbach and Otto Ludwig; and the Austrians Ludwig Anzengruber and Peter Rosegger. The Dorfgeschichte typically deals with the everyday problems of common people in a specific region or locality. It appealed primarily to readers with less discerning literary tastes; hence, there tended to be a correspondence between protagonists and readers. Rosegger, the son of a poor, illiterate peasant, was intimately familiar with the social milieu he depicted – a familiarity that in his case proved to be a drawback. In his autobiographical *Die Schriften des Waldschulmeisters* (1875; translated as *The Forest Schoolmaster,* 1901) Rosegger, under the pressure of publishers' deadlines, reiterated and varied basic situations that had proved effective in his earlier works to satisfy the public's hunger for entertaining fiction. Rosegger's prose writings feature dialect for greater authenticity, and they display an awareness of the social consequences of encroaching industrialization. Anzengruber's novels *Der Schandfleck* (The Blot of Shame, 1877) and *Der Sternsteinhof* (The Star-Stone Farm, 1885) take a critical look at social differentiation among the rural population and the harsh treatment of outsiders; in the end, however, love prevails and obliterates all antagonisms.

The drama, traditionally considered the pinnacle of poetic accomplishment, was not a major genre in the period of realism. Friedrich Hebbel, the foremost dramatist of the 1840s and 1850s, sought to adapt the eighteenth-century genre of the bürgerliches Trauerspiel (bourgeois tragedy) to the middle of the nineteenth century. His first significant drama, *Maria Magdalene* (1844), first performed in 1846, is based on the lower middle class's inherent contradictions, notably its members' inability to rise above narrowly conceived moral conventions, and not on the external conflict between the middle class and the aristocracy, as in the bourgeois tragedies of Gotthold Ephraim Lessing and Friedrich Schiller. Thus, in accordance with Hebbel's concept of the tragic, both the victim (Klara, who is expecting a child out of wedlock) and the victimizers (especially Klara's father, the master carpenter Anton, whose rigid moral code drives her to suicide) are guilty of transgressing against the universally valid idea of ethics. Hebbel does not offer a solution to the problems he presents; Anton remains unbending and fails to comprehend the tragedy he has caused. Yet *Maria Magdalene* may be viewed as an indictment of the patriarchally dominated lower middle class of artisans that, threatened by extinction through the advancement of industrialization, fails to provide even a modest degree of female emancipation. In his subsequent dramas, which dealt with historical and mythological subjects, Hebbel repeatedly used female characters as central figures.

Although the period of realism has a clearly demarcated beginning in the aftermath of the 1848 Revolution, its end is less well defined. In terms of literary and theater history 1889, the year in which the seminal "social drama" *Vor Sonnenaufgang* (translated as *Before Dawn*, 1909), by the young Gerhart Hauptmann, premiered in Berlin, signaled the breakthrough of the new style of naturalism. Two of the preeminent realists died around this time – Storm in 1888 and Keller in 1890 – and Meyer, who died in 1898, ceased writing during the last decade of his life. Hence a persuasive case may be made for realism having come to an end around 1890. Moreover, in 1890 the Prussian and imperial chancellor Otto von Bismarck was dismissed from office by the young emperor Wilhelm II. Bismarck was the dominant figure of the 1870s and 1880s, a veritable culture hero who had accomplished, through the proclamation of the German Empire in Versailles on 18 January 1871, what many writers and intellectuals had longed for: German unification. The wave of national euphoria generated by the Prussian victory in the Franco-Prussian War engulfed erstwhile liberal and democratically minded writers such as the Vormärz poet Freiligrath. The conservative Geibel's patriotic *Heroldsrufe* (Calls of a Herald) in 1871 celebrated the newly founded Reich as the fulfillment of the Germans' aspirations.

Since the new Reich did not correspond in all respects to the dreams and expectations of poets, in that it was neither democratic nor the political home of all the German-speaking people – it excluded Austria – writers intent on legitimating the empire derived from the past elements that lent grandeur to the present. Conversely, they projected into the past contemporaneous events of dramatic quality such as Bismarck's fight against the Catholic church, the so-called Kulturkampf of the 1870s, and his attempts to suppress the political party of the workers, the Social Democrats. In this fashion they endowed Bismarck's pragmatic policies with greater dignity by establishing false historical precedents. The latter tendency is quite noticeable in the historical novels and dramas of the unabashed Bismarck admirer Felix Dahn, although not necessarily in

Dahn's major historical novel, *Ein Kampf um Rom* (1876; translated as *A Struggle for Rome*, 1878). But in its focus on larger-than-life individuals and in its endeavor to embrace an entire historical period the novel shows the monumental quality that is also characteristic of the visual arts and architecture of the Reichsgründung era.

The fascination with Bismarck extended beyond the borders of the empire. The Swiss author Meyer also subscribed to the notion that history was the province of great men. In his only novel, *Jürg Jenatsch* (originally published as *Georg Jenatsch*, 1876; translated, 1976), Meyer portrays a ruthless individual from seventeenth-century Swiss history who resembles Bismarck in his single-minded devotion to the pursuit of political goals. But unlike Dahn, who uncritically supports Bismarck's policies, Meyer poses the question of moral responsibility and its place in the political arena. Meyer's eleven novellas, published between 1873 and 1891, deal with historical figures and epochs, above all the Renaissance. Meyer's historical settings in conjunction with his narrative stance serve as a distancing device to veil experiences of his own troubled life. In masterful and complex form these novellas explore the conflicts between legality and morals and between politics and ethics with which the protagonists are confronted. Meyer conforms to the mode of historicism prevalent in the last third of the nineteenth century in that he views history as determined by great men – a view that gives his figures their monumental quality.

A monumental quality of a different kind was promulgated by Richard Wagner. Wagner, who as a young man had fought on the barricades of Dresden, the capital of Saxony, during the 1848 Revolution and had had to flee Germany, was able in the 1870s to put his idea of the Festspiel (festive theatrical event) into practice. The Festspiel idea had served during the nineteenth century to emphasize German cultural unity in the absence of political nationhood, but Wagner opened the Bayreuth Festspielhaus (theater for festive occasions) in August 1876 with a performance of his tetralogy *Der Ring des Nibelungen* (1863; translated as *The Nibelung's Ring*, 1877) with the support of the romantically inclined King Ludwig II of Bavaria. The literary historian Klaus Günther Just calls Wagner's unrelenting dedication to his Gesamtkunstwerk (work fusing all elements of the arts), which included staging it in an appropriate setting, a "künstlerische Großtat" (artistic accomplishment of the highest degree) comparable in aesthetic terms to Bismarck's founding of the empire. Wagner's Gesamtkunstwerk, however, continues to endure whereas Bismarck's creation perished at the end of World War I.

Wagner's complex tetralogy was viewed in nationalistic terms. Somewhat superficially, the youthful, heroic character Siegfried, who is opposed to the intellectualizing supreme god Wotan, was perceived as a guarantor of the empire's strength in conquering its enemies. Such an optimistic interpretation is subverted by Wagner's pessimism, which finds prominent expression in the world catastrophe of *Götterdämmerung* (translated as *The Twilight of the Gods*), the final part of the tetralogy. This pessimism is in strong contrast to the facile optimism of the Gründerzeit, a time of rapid economic expansion during the early 1870s, and does not lend support to the belief in unlimited progress and a glorious future. The criticism of the philosopher Friedrich Nietzsche, the erstwhile friend and admirer of Wagner who turned into a formidable anti-Wagnerite, that Wagner had betrayed his revolutionary origins and had become a pessimist under the influence of philosopher Arthur Schopenhauer, had little effect on the profound influence that Wagner exerted and was unable to prevent the exploitation of his work for nationalistic purposes.

Literary efforts on a large scale did not generate the same degree of recognition and controversy as Wagner's monumental operatic work. In the manner of Dahn, Freytag wrote a series of six historical novels titled *Die Ahnen* (The Ancestors, 1872–1880s) in which he traced the fates of two fictional German families from 357 to 1848. Unlike Dahn's essentially affirmative stance, which tends to legitimate the Reich as the realization of past historical strivings, Freytag implicitly draws attention to the fact that in important respects the hopes of the 1848 Revolution had not been fulfilled.

In the late 1870s Fontane emerged as the most prominent critic in fiction of the Bismarckian period. Fontane is generally credited with creating that anomaly in nineteenth-century German realism, the Gesellschaftsroman (social novel), which was flourishing in other European countries but eluded his contemporaries in the German-speaking areas. Specifically in his Berlin novels, which reflect the growing political and cultural eminence of the empire's capital, Fontane critically examines social conditions such as the impossibility of overcoming class barriers in *Irrungen, Wirrungen* (1888; translated as *Trials and Tribulations*, 1917) and the excessive materialistic orientation of the wealthy bourgeoisie in *Frau Jenny Treibel* (1893; translated as *Jenny Treibel*, 1976). Yet Fontane's criticism appears muted; it is tempered by the irony and wit that usually surface in the extensive dialogues that are a hallmark of Fontane's fiction.

The role that society plays in Fontane's fiction becomes obvious when one recalls that Raabe's first novel is also a Berlinroman (Berlin novel) of sorts. *Die Chronik der Sperlingsgasse* (The Chronicle of Sparrow Alley, 1856) is not devoid of allusions to current events, but the narrator's prevailing view is that from the window of his flat — hence, greater significance is attributed to the domestic, private sphere than to the public arena. After Raabe's withdrawal from the literary scene in the late 1860s because of his disappointment with his bourgeois reading public, who increasingly abandoned their liberal and humanitarian ideals, his protagonists tended to be outsiders with tenuous connections to society. These outsiders are usually given to contemplation rather than action. For instance, Heinrich Schaumann in *Stopfkuchen* (1891; translated as "Tubby Schaumann," 1983) represents humanistic values but lives as an outsider in virtual physical isolation. Yet by dint of superior insight into and knowledge of human nature, he solves a murder case. The protagonists of Raabe's last novels, which are overshadowed by resignation and pessimism, are generally not capable of such activity.

Raabe, who died in 1910, was the last of the major writers of realism. But new literary impulses that were promoted by a new generation of writers, who were born in the 1860s and 1870s, had begun to assert themselves at least twenty years earlier. Fontane, who in his theater reviews had greeted the naturalistic plays by Hauptmann and Henrik Ibsen, was not prepared to share the social commitment of the naturalists and their preoccupation with representing the seamier side of life. In essence, then, Fontane, the astute but gentle critic of societal conditions in Bismarckian Germany, remained indebted to the tenets of realism — the dominant literary style of the second half of the nineteenth century.

– Siegfried Mews with the cooperation
of James Hardin

ACKNOWLEDGMENTS

This book was produced by Bruccoli Clark Layman, Inc. Karen L. Rood is senior editor for the *Dictionary of Literary Biography* series. Philip B. Dematteis was the in-house editor.

Photography editors are Edward Scott and Timothy C. Lundy. Layout and graphics supervisor is

Penney L. Haughton. Copyediting supervisor is Bill Adams. Typesetting supervisor is Kathleen M. Flanagan. Samuel Bruce is editorial associate. Systems manager is George F. Dodge. The production staff includes Rowena Betts, Steve Borsanyi, Barbara Brannon, Patricia Coate, Rebecca Crawford, Margaret McGinty Cureton, Denise Edwards, Sarah A. Estes, Joyce Fowler, Robert Fowler, Brenda A. Gillie, Bonita Graham, Jolyon M. Helterman, Ellen McCracken, Kathy Lawler Merlette, John Myrick, Pamela D. Norton, Thomas J. Pickett, Patricia Salisbury, Maxine K. Smalls, Deborah P. Stokes, and Wilma Weant.

Walter W. Ross and Suzanne Burry did library research. They were assisted by the following librarians at the Thomas Cooper Library of the University of South Carolina: Linda Holderfield and the interlibrary-loan staff; reference librarians Gwen Baxter, Daniel Boice, Faye Chadwell, Cathy Eckman, Rhonda Felder, Gary Geer, Qun "Gerry" Jiao, Jackie Kinder, Laurie Preston, Jean Rhyne, Carol Tobin, Carolyn Tyler, Virginia Weathers, Elizabeth Whiznant, and Connie Widney; circulation-department head Thomas Marcil; and acquisitions-searching supervisor David Haggard.

Nineteenth-Century German Writers, 1841-1900

Dictionary of Literary Biography

Ludwig Anzengruber
(29 November 1839 – 10 December 1889)

Calvin N. Jones
University of South Alabama

BOOKS: *Der Pfarrer von Kirchfeld: Volksstück mit Gesang in vier Akten*, as Ludwig Gruber (Vienna: Rosner, 1871);

Der Meineidbauer: Volksstück mit Gesang in drei Akten, as Gruber, music by A. Müller (Vienna: Rosner, 1872); translated by Adolf Busse as *The Farmer Forsworn*, in *The German Classics of the Nineteenth and Twentieth Centuries*, volume 16, edited by Kuno Francke and W. G. Howard (New York: German Publishing Society, 1914), pp. 112–188;

Die Kreuzelschreiber: Bauernkomödie mit Gesang in drei Akten, as Gruber (Vienna: Rosner, 1872);

Elfriede: Schauspiel in drei Akten (Vienna: Rosner, 1873);

Die Tochter des Wucherers: Schauspiel mit Gesang in fünf Akten (Vienna: Rosner, 1873);

Der Gwissenswurm: Bauernkomödie mit Gesang in drei Akten (Vienna: Rosner, 1874);

Hand und Herz: Trauerspiel in vier Akten (Vienna: Rosner, 1875);

Doppelselbstmord: Bauernposse mit Gesang in drei Akten (Vienna: Rosner, 1876);

Der ledige Hof: Schauspiel in vier Akten (Vienna: Rosner, 1877);

Der Schandfleck: Roman (Vienna: Rosner, 1877; revised edition, Leipzig: Breitkopf & Härtel, 1884);

Ein Faustschlag: Schauspiel in drei Akten (Vienna: Rosner, 1878);

Das vierte Gebot: Volksstück in vier Akten (Vienna: Rosner, 1878);

's Jungferngift: Bauernkomödie mit Gesang in fünf Abtheilungen (Vienna: Rosner, 1878);

Alte Wiener: Volksstück mit Gesang in vier Akten (Vienna: Rosner, 1879);

Die Trutzige: Bauernkomödie mit Gesang in drei Akten (Vienna: Rosner, 1879);

Ludwig Anzengruber (photograph by Raoul Korty)

Dorfgänge: Gesammelte Bauerngeschichten, 2 volumes (Vienna: Rosner, 1879) — comprises, in volume 1, "Eine Plauderei," "Die Polizze," "Gänseliesel," "Diebs-Annerl," "Eine Begegnung"; in volume 2, "Eine Plauderei"; "Wie der Huber ungläubig ward"; "Der gottüberlegene Jakob," translated by William Metcalfe as "How Jacob Prevailed," in *The 12 Best Short*

3

Stories in the German Language, edited by R. M. Meyer (London: Gowans & Gray, 1926); "Die fromme Katrin' "; "Das Sündkind";

Aus'm gewohnten Gleis: Posse mit Gesang in fünf Abtheilungen (Vienna: Rosner, 1880);

Bekannte von der Straße: Genrebilder (Leipzig: Albrecht, 1881);

Feldrain und Waldweg (Stuttgart: Spemann, 1882);

Launiger Zuspruch und ernste Red': Kalender-Geschichten (Lahr: Schauenburg, 1882);

Kleiner Markt: Studien, Erzählungen, Märchen und Gedichte (Breslau: Schottländer, 1883);

Die Kameradin: Eine Erzählung (Dresden: Minden, 1883);

Allerhand Humore: Kleinbäuerliches, Großstädtisches und Gefabeltes (Leipzig: Breitkopf & Härtel, 1883);

Der Sternsteinhof: Eine Dorfgeschichte, 2 volumes (Leipzig: Breitkopf & Härtel, 1885);

Stahl und Stein: Volksstück mit Gesang in drei Akten (Dresden: Pierson, 1887);

Wolken und Sunn'schein: Gesammelte Dorfgeschichten (Berlin & Stuttgart: Spemann, 1888);

Der Fleck auf der Ehr': Volksstück mit Gesang in drei Akten (Dresden & Leipzig: Pierson, 1889);

Gesammelte Werke, 10 volumes, edited by Anton Bettelheim, Vincenz Chiavacci, and V. K. Schembera (Stuttgart: Cotta, 1890);

Brave Leut' vom Grund: Volksstück mit Gesang in drei Abteilungen (Stuttgart: Cotta, 1892);

Letzte Dorfgänge: Kalendergeschichten und Skizzen aus dem Nachlaß, edited by Bettelheim and Chiavacci (Stuttgart: Cotta, 1894);

Werke, 14 volumes, edited by Bettelheim (Berlin: Bong, 1920);

Ludwig Anzengrubers sämtliche Werke, 17 volumes, edited by Rudolf Latzke and Otto Rommel (Vienna: Schroll, 1920–1922; reprinted, Nendeln, Liechtenstein: Kraus, 1976);

Ausgewählte Werke, 2 volumes, edited by Erwin Heinzel (Vienna: Kremayr & Scheriau, 1966);

Werke, 2 volumes, edited by Manfred Kuhne (Berlin & Weimar: Aufbau, 1971) – comprises, in volume 1, *Die Kreuzelschreiber, Der Gwissenswurm, Hand und Herz, Das vierte Gebot, Die Märchen des Steinklopferhanns*; in volume 2, *Der Sternsteinhof,* "Der Einsame," "Zu fromm," "Der gottüberlegene Jakob," "Nit gehn tan tat's," "Örtler."

OTHER: *Die Heimat,* edited by Anzengruber (1 April 1882–1 May 1885).

Ludwig Anzengruber, a Viennese writer who set most of his works in the Austrian provinces, received equal acclaim as a playwright and as an author of stories and novels. In championing liberal causes and opposing clerical influence in the lives of the populace, he provided a different perspective on the rural milieu from that of many of his contemporaries and successors, who employed local color for its own sake and tended to idealize country life in a conservative way. Anzengruber's enlightened and critical observation of the society in which his characters lived made him a favorite of the naturalists, who became prominent shortly after his death. His influence also extended to the Bavarian playwright and novelist Ludwig Thoma and, indirectly, to other twentieth-century writers who concentrate on rural regions but refuse to accept the notion of a timeless status quo. Anzengruber's use of dialect has made translation difficult and has limited his influence abroad, but in German-speaking countries his works remain in print and his plays are still performed.

Anzengruber was born in Vienna on 29 November 1839 to Johann Anzengruber, a bureaucrat who had grown up on a farm in Upper Austria, and Maria Herbich Anzengruber, who was from a middle-class Viennese family. Anzengruber's father wrote unpublished poems and plays in the theatrically rhetorical style of the time; they had no influence on his son's writing except as an inspiration to take up the profession. The elder Anzengruber died when Ludwig was five; the boy was brought up by his mother, who remained his closest companion throughout her life. Until the age of sixteen Anzengruber attended the Realschule, which he later said he left with "mehr Wissensdurst als Wissen" (more thirst for knowledge than knowledge); he was essentially an autodidact. An apprenticeship in a bookstore ended when he realized that he enjoyed reading books more than selling them; Friedrich Schiller, William Shakespeare, and Franz Grillparzer were among his favorite authors. In 1859 he gave up a job as a copyist at an insurance firm to become a traveling actor in the Austrian provinces. The troupes that employed him were poor in both quality of performance and remuneration, and he was often in financial difficulty. He wrote much during these years, which he later called his "prähistorische Zeit" (prehistoric period), though he subsequently destroyed most of it. Many ideas for novels and stories arose at this time, however, that he found time years later to put to paper. A half-dozen stories published in magazines during the 1860s point to later themes, but they lack the aesthetic unity of his mature works. Only one of the thirteen plays that he wrote during this period sur-

Anzengruber at his desk (drawing by Ernst Juch)

vives; another was performed on the road and received critical acclaim. Accounts of these years are contained in a few satirical pieces, autobiographical essays, and letters. In one letter he expresses the didactic conception of his task as an author that would drive much of his later work: he recounts a dream in which he descends from a tribune to the people, reaching out his hand to help them improve their lot.

When Anzengruber was laid off in 1865, he returned to Vienna and found a job in the police directorate. One of the few works that he did not destroy at this time was *Der Pfarrer von Kirchfeld* (The Parish Priest of Kirchfeld, 1871). The performance of this "Volksstück mit Gesang" (popular drama with songs) at the Theater an der Wien on 5 November 1870 marks the major turning point in Anzengruber's career. The play is set against the background of the Roman Catholic church's concordat with the government of Austria in 1885, which gave church courts authority over broad

areas of life, including education and marriage, until the liberals brought it to an end in 1870. The play depicts the conflict between a dogmatic nobleman and an enlightened young priest who approaches his congregation with a flexible, humane Christianity. The names of these two characters contain the words for dark and light, respectively; the opposition between the two forces is such a dominant guiding idea that it hampers the dramatic development. For this reason *Der Pfarrer von Kirchfeld* has often been dismissed as a mere tendentious play, but its topicality increased its popularity. By calling the play a "Volksstück" Anzengruber specified its audience as the lower-middle-class craftsmen and tradesmen for whom the Volkstheater provided an alternative form of entertainment to the upper-class court theater. Although much of the fare offered there was characterized by sentimentality or coarse comedy, playwrights such as Ferdinand Raimund and Johann Nestroy had written sophisticated plays that provided critical insight, and

Anzengruber followed in their tradition. The play became a hit not only in Vienna but also throughout German-speaking areas; it even reached Detroit in 1872 and New York in 1881. The young Viennese publisher L. Rosner acquired the rights to Anzengruber's works and would publish them through 1880.

Encouraged by this success, Anzengruber gave up his clerk's job to devote more time to his true calling and also to avoid the professional conflict between civil servant and critical author. In quick succession he wrote several more plays, most of which showed similarities in setting, conflict, and treatment to *Der Pfarrer von Kirchfeld*. *Der Meineidbauer* (1872; translated as *The Farmer Forsworn*, 1914) deals with greed and hypocrisy. In the comedy *Die Kreuzelschreiber* (The Cross-Makers, 1872) the most powerful landowner in the village, a conservative Catholic, convinces the men to sign a petition against the newly proclaimed doctrine of papal infallibility; adopting a strategy reminiscent of that of Aristophanes' Lysistrata, their wives rally behind the pope and the village priest and renounce sex to try to make the men recant, until the freethinking stonecutter Steinklopferhanns convinces them all to follow a more enlightened path.

In 1873 Anzengruber married Adelinde Lipka, the eighteen-year-old sister of a boyhood friend, and moved to the country with his wife and mother. After the failure of *Elfriede* (1873) and *Die Tochter des Wucherers* (The Usurer's Daughter, 1873), Anzengruber had success with the comedy *Der Gwissenswurm* (Pangs of Conscience, 1874). The hypocritical Dusterer exploits the old farmer Grillhofer's regret over a youthful transgression in an attempt to gain possession of his land, but Grillhofer discovers that the love of his youth is happily married after all and that their daughter, Horlacher-Lies, has also turned out well. Dusterer is banished, and the joy of life exemplified by Horlacher-Lies prevails. *Doppelselbstmord* (Double Suicide, 1876), a peasant comedy with music that contrasts the erotic expectations of the younger generation with the traditional morality of their parents, was the last of Anzengruber's successful plays of this half decade.

During this period Anzengruber continued writing stories, many of which are considered among his best. His experiences on provincial stages and his appreciation of Berthold Auerbach's popular *Schwarzwälder Dorfgeschichten* (1843–1854; translated as *Black Forest Village Stories,* 1869) account for his preference for rural settings for both his prose and dramatic works. Dorfgeschichten

such as Auerbach's combined a Romantic esteem for a simple, natural life with an Enlightenment belief in improvement through education; Anzengruber's self-proclaimed mission of enlightening the common people by stressing reason over dogma further explains his predilection for the village tale. The verisimilitude of his portrayals encouraged the performance of his plays by the naturalists a few years later, yet his works are not naturalistic; for example, he mixed several Alpine dialects to increase the aesthetic appeal of his works. He employed a poetic realism that does not endorse sociological or biological determinism and forms at most a precursor of naturalism. The chief target of Anzengruber's message – the people's subservience to superstition, ignorance, authoritarian dogma, and belief in an afterlife – is countered with a liberating, affirmative humanity that is based on the materialistic atheism of Ludwig Feuerbach and is most explicitly represented by Steinklopferhanns.

Anzengruber's first attempts at prose narration often relied on literary models, and his notes reveal his struggle to find a weltanschauung as well as the poetic means to express it. The story "Die Polizze" (The Police, 1879), written before the success of *Der Pfarrer von Kirchfeld* but first published in 1872 in the annual *Wiener Rothbuch* (Viennese Redbook), is a Kalendergeschichte (brief moral tale) within a realistic frame and indicates the roots of his prose in the village tales of Auerbach and Johann Peter Hebel. Although similar to other stories from his "prehistoric period," it indicated the beginning of Anzengruber's development in the genre of the Dorfgeschichte and displayed enough maturity to be included in his first published collection of stories, *Dorfgänge* (Village Strolls, 1879). This two-volume work contains eight stories, most of which had been published in magazines between 1872 and 1878 and which treat village characters confronted by problems of daily life. In "Der gottüberlegene Jakob" (translated as "How Jacob Prevailed," 1926) the title character regrets not having sold a cow before it got sick and promises to light candles for the saints if they will intercede on the cow's behalf. When the animal recovers Jakob sells it to a wealthy farmer; later he says that the farmer owes him for the candles. The farmer complies, filled with both annoyance and admiration at Jakob's cleverness. In its use of straightforward narration that deftly characterizes the principals and portrays village life without indulging in unnecessary description, combined with large amounts of conversation in dialect similar to that in his dramas, this tale is typical of Anzengruber's handling of the

Scene from a performance of Anzengruber's Das vierte Gebot *at the Vienna Volkstheater in 1890*

genre: he treats his characters with both respect and criticism, using humor and irony to condemn those aspects of religion that he regards as repressive superstition. "Wie der Huber ungläubig ward" (How Huber Lost His Faith), a frequently reprinted story from this collection, has a similar treatment and theme.

The preface to the second volume of *Dorfgänge*, "Eine Plauderei" (Small Talk), is one of Anzengruber's most explicit theoretical statements. He argues for an art that remains true to daily life as opposed to one that provides a refuge from life by transfiguring the objects of its portrayal through fantasy and idealism. He says that art must arise from its material rather than from the author's preconceived notions; such art depicts the lower classes, sex, and negative aspects of life and employs humor. His belief in the unity of the aesthetic and the ethical underlies his argument for poetic realism, which is found not just in these stories but in most of his writings. *Dorfgänge* was praised by liberal critics and condemned by the conservatives.

In 1876 Anzengruber completed the novel *Der Schandfleck* (The Blot of Shame), which was published the following year and takes as its theme the duty that parents have to their children and that is the precondition for filial devotion. Although the farmer Reindorfer consents to raise Magdalena, the product of a neighbor's seduction of his wife, he is so overcome with shame that he at first ignores the child, as does Magdalena's natural father. But as Reindorfer's own son and daughter turn away from him, he treats Magdalena with increasing fatherly affection. When Magdalena learns that she cannot marry the neighbor boy because they share the same father, she seeks her fortune in the city. Anzengruber could not duplicate his success with rural settings when he portrayed an urban locale, and the second half of the novel also suffers from too many episodes and a hurried conclusion. In 1881 Anzengruber began a revised version, published in 1884, in which Magdalena goes to work for a wealthy farmer rather than moving to the city. She eventually marries him, and Reindorfer, driven from his farm by his son and rejected by his natural daughter, is taken in by Magdalena and her husband. The fatherly treatment is repaid, and Reindorfer considers that "the blot of shame" has removed itself. *Der Schandfleck* resembles the village tales in using a peasant milieu to express a belief in people's ability to work out humane solutions in opposition to inflexible tradition and morality.

Several factors contributed to Anzengruber's decision to devote less attention to the drama in the second half of the 1870s. Competition from the increasingly popular operetta and a rise in ticket prices affected the development of the Volkstheater at this time. Although Anzengruber had a contract to provide a play a year for the Theater an der Wien, the director did not always produce them. The critics had praised *Der Gwissenswurm* and *Doppelselbstmord*; but the public was smaller than for the earlier plays, and Anzengruber had even less success with *Ein Faustschlag* (A Blow with the Fist, 1878), *Die Trutzige* (The Obstinate One, 1879), and *Aus'm gewohnten Gleis* (Out of the Usual Path, 1880). An important exception was *Das vierte Gebot* (The Fourth Commandment, 1878), a Viennese Lokalstück (play intended for a popular audience, set in the rural or urban environment of the audience, and employing authentic or modified dialect) that received thirty consecutive performances in 1877. Like *Der Schandfleck* it deals with the duties of parents to their children; interweaving plots about three families, it is a good example of Anzengruber's realism. The unsuccessful first performance of *Aus'm gewohnten Gleis* in 1879 marked the last premiere of an Anzengruber play in Vienna for ten years. By 1880 he was completely disillusioned: feeling that the public had failed him and that he had written in vain, he decided to give up the Volksstück and turn to narrative prose.

In 1875 he suffered what he called the bitterest blow of his life when his mother died. He had also begun to realize that he had made a poor choice in marriage, since his wife, who had wed Anzengruber only to please her mother, did not understand his concerns and was not able to manage on his uncertain income. The couple's first child was stillborn, and the second died shortly after birth. Two sons and a daughter (Karl, Hans, and Marie) survived, but three other pregnancies resulted in miscarriages or infant death. Neither the children nor their common sorrows brought the couple closer together. When Anzengruber learned that his wife was unfaithful, he held up stoically on the outside while committing his bitterness to paper. He found some consolation in his circle of tavern friends and fellow authors, including Peter Rosegger, and in his continued critical success at home and in northern Germany. Anzengruber received a stipend from the ministry of education and shared the Schiller Prize of Vienna in 1878.

It was during this period that Anzengruber wrote his most widely read novel, *Der Sternsteinhof* (The Star-Stone-Farm, 1885). Although he con-

ceived the plot in the 1860s, he did not begin writing the work until 1882, after he had completed the revised version of *Der Schandfleck*. In this same year he assumed the editorship of the family magazine *Die Heimat* (The Homeland); this position assured him financial security for the first time, but its demands interfered with work on the novel. He completed it in 1884; its publication the following year was greeted by restrained though positive reviews. Helene Zinshofer is a beautiful village girl whose ambition is to escape from her humble beginnings to a life on the wealthy farm that gives the novel its title. When her plan to marry Toni, the only son at the Sternsteinhof, is foiled, she hastily weds her childhood sweetheart to save her honor, for she is carrying Toni's child. Toni later marries a wealthy farmer's daughter. The relationship between Toni and Helene is gradually rekindled, but they are unable to fulfill it openly until the deaths of their respective spouses. Although marriage to Toni brings Helene to the station that she always thought she deserved, her triumph is clouded by her failure to gain the respect of Toni's father and by the memory of the deaths of those who once stood in the way of her goal. After Toni is killed in military service, Helene is reconciled with her father-in-law and lives out her life as a good mother to her son and stepdaughter, as a proper mistress of the farm, and as a good citizen of the community.

Der Sternsteinhof is similar to Anzengruber's other narrative and dramatic creations. The rural milieu is carefully described and related to the development of character, and dialect is a prominent feature. The novel has a strong plot line and many dramatic scenes, as well as several comic interludes. Although much of the story is advanced through dialogue, less is used here than in the dramas or even the short stories. At some points an omniscient narrator reveals Helene's motivations, but more frequently readers have to come to their own conclusions from accounts of her actions or from other characters' opinions about her. This technique makes an evaluation of Helene more difficult, but also more interesting. Interior monologue, conveyed in dialect without quotation marks, also provides glimpses into characters' thoughts. *Der Sternsteinhof* has sentimental scenes, although restraint is usually employed. Many of these elements of composition reveal an affinity between this novel and the beginnings of naturalism. The targets of Anzengruber's criticism are not as precisely defined as they are in his stories and plays, nor is his message as clearly explained. His main characters are not exemplary figures who are unjustly kept apart;

they are not totally sympathetic. Yet his implicit criticism of their shortcomings does not focus on premarital sex and adultery but on deeper ethical concerns involving the effects on others of the pursuit of personal goals.

Anzengruber continued to write village tales but also shifted his attention to the city and the suburbs in stories in journals such as *Wiener Leben* (Viennese Life) and in collections such as *Bekannte von der Straße* (Acquaintances from the Street, 1881) and *Allerhand Humore* (Various and Sundry Humors, 1883). Many of these stories show influences of Anzengruber's predecessors in the genre of the feuilleton. His city stories tend to be marked by satire, whereas his village tales contain a more comic sense of humor. Anzengruber also frequently employed the Märchen (fairy tale) to get social criticism past the censors. One of his most successful attempts in this vein is "Die Märchen des Steinklopferhanns" (The Fairy Tales of Steinklopferhanns), written for journals between 1872 and 1875 and first published in book form in 1882 in *Launiger Zuspruch und ernste Red'* (Humorous Exhortation and Serious Talk), in which contemporary rural characters reveal their everyday problems to the stonecutter who was introduced in *Die Kreuzelschreiber*. With his characteristic insightful simplicity, Steinklopferhanns tells tales that illustrate similar problems and from which his hearers — and the reader — should draw certain conclusions. His lessons are taught through practical experience in self-enlightenment rather than through preaching. Even though Steinklopferhanns represents a philosophy of reason, compassion, and happiness, he is not an advocate of a saccharine harmony for its own sake. He is an outsider, aware and quite critical of the conditions that put him in that position.

In the last years of Anzengruber's life recognition was again paid to his dramatic talents. Although he did not write plays in the early 1880s, revivals of his works saved the 1883–1884 season at the Vienna Stadttheater. He felt that a performance of his *Stahl und Stein* (Steel and Stone, 1887) at the Burgtheater rehabilitated him in the eyes of the public, and there were successful performances of at least four of his dramas on north German stages in the following two years. He was awarded the Grillparzer Prize in 1887 and the prize of the Peter Wilhelm Müller Foundation in Frankfurt am Main in 1888. The Deutsches Volkstheater was established in Vienna to replace the popular institutions that had fallen into decline a few years before; Anzengruber agreed to write the opening play, *Der*

Fleck auf der Ehr' (The Blot on the Honor, 1889), which premiered on 14 September 1889.

In the fall of 1889 Anzengruber divorced his wife, from whom he was already separated. His health declined rapidly; two operations for a hip infection were unsuccessful, and he died of blood poisoning on 10 December 1889, less than two weeks after his fiftieth birthday. A monument was erected beside the Deutsches Volkstheater, and the Cotta publishing house brought out his collected works in 1890.

Letters:

Briefe, 2 volumes, edited by Anton Bettelheim (Stuttgart & Berlin: Cotta, 1902).

Biographies:

Anton Bettelheim, *Ludwig Anzengruber: Der Mann — sein Werk — seine Weltanschauung* (Berlin: Hofmann, 1898);

Alfred Kleinberg, *Ludwig Anzengruber: Ein Lebensbild* (Stuttgart & Berlin: Cotta, 1921);

Otto Rommel, "Ludwig Anzengrubers Leben und Werke," in *Ludwig Anzengrubers sämtliche Werke*, edited by Rommel and Rudolf Latzke, volume 15, part 3 (Vienna: Scholl, 1922), pp. 273–455.

References:

Hugo Aust, "Ludwig Anzengruber," in *Volksstück: Vom Hanswurstspiel zum sozialen Drama der Gegenwart*, by Aust, Peter Haida, and Jürgen Hein (Munich: Beck, 1989), pp. 204–220;

Rainer Baasner, "Anzengrubers *Sternsteinhof*," *Zeitschrift für deutsche Philologie*, 102, no. 4 (1983): 564–583;

J. G. Blankenagel, "Naturalistic Tendencies in Anzengruber's *Das vierte Gebot*," *Germanic Review*, 10 (January 1935): 26–34;

Walter Dietze, "Ludwig Anzengruber," in *Erbe und Gegenwart: Aufsätze zur vergleichenden Literaturwissenschaft* (Berlin: Aufbau, 1972), pp. 58–134;

Patricia Howe, "End of a Line: Anzengruber and the Viennese Stage," in *Viennese Popular Theatre: A Symposium*, edited by W. E. Yates and John R. P. McKenzie (Exeter, U.K.: University of Exeter Press, 1985), pp. 139–152;

Calvin N. Jones, "Poetry or Realism: Ludwig Anzengruber's *Die Kreuzelschreiber*," in his *Negation and Utopia: The German Volksstück from Raimund to Kroetz* (New York: Lang, 1993), pp. 87–107;

Jones, "Variations on a Stereotype: The Farmer in the Nineteenth Century *Volkskomödie*," *Maske und Kothurn*, 27, nos. 2–3 (1981): 155–162;

A. H. J. Knight, "Prolegomena to the Study of Ludwig Anzengruber," in *German Studies Presented to W. H. Bruford* (London: Harrap, 1962), pp. 207–217;

Rudolf Latzke, "Anzengruber als Erzähler," in *Ludwig Anzengrubers sämtliche Werke*, edited by Latzke and Otto Rommel, volume 15, part 1 (Vienna: Schroll, 1922), pp. 403–697;

Hubert Lengauer, "Anzengrubers realistische Kunst," *Österreich in Geschichte und Literatur*, 21 (1977): 386–404;

Werner Martin, "Anzengruber und das Volksstück," *Neue Deutsche Literatur*, 9, no. 2 (1961): 110–121;

Edward McInnes, "Das vierte Gebot," in his *Das deutsche Drama des 19. Jahrhunderts* (Berlin: Schmidt, 1983), pp. 134–140;

McInnes, "Ludwig Anzengruber and the Popular Dramatic Tradition," *Maske und Kothurn*, 21, nos. 2–3 (1975): 131–152;

Gerd Müller, *Das Volksstück von Raimund bis Kroetz* (Munich: Oldenbourg, 1979), pp. 42–56;

Paul Reimann, "Ludwig Anzengruber," *Weimarer Beiträge*, 6 (1960): 532–550;

Otto Rommel, "Die Philosophie des Steinklopferhanns: Ludwig Anzengruber und seine Beziehungen zur Philosophie Ludwig Feuerbachs," *Zeitschrift für den deutschen Unterricht*, 33 (1919): 19–25;

Karlheinz Rossbacher, "Ludwig Anzengruber: *Die Märchen des Steinklopferhanns* (1875–79): Poesie der Dissonanz als Weg zur Volksaufklärung," in *Romane und Erzählungen des bürgerlichen Realismus*, edited by Horst Denkler (Stuttgart: Reclam, 1980), pp. 231–245;

Adalbert Schmidt, "Ludwig Anzengruber: 'Das vierte Gebot,' " in *Das österreichische Volksstück*, edited by Alfred Doppler (Vienna: Hirt, 1971), pp. 59–76;

Wendelin Schmidt-Dengler, "Die Unbedeutenden werden bedeutend. Anmerkungen zum Volksstück nach Nestroys Tod: Kaiser, Anzengruber und Morre," in *Die andere Welt: Aspekte der österreichischen Literatur des 19. und 20. Jahrhunderts. Festschrift für Hellmuth Himmel*, edited by Kurt Barsch, Dietmar Goltschnigg, Gerhard Melzer, and Wolfgang Heinz Schober (Bonn: Francke, 1979), pp. 133–146;

W. E. Yates, "Nestroysche Stilelemente bei Anzengruber: Ein Beitrag zur Wirkungsgeschichte der Possen Nestroys," *Maske und Kothurn*, 14, nos. 3–4 (1968): 287–296;

Wilhelm Zentner, "Ludwig Anzengruber," in *Reclams Schauspielführer*, edited by Otto C. A. zur Nedden (Stuttgart: Reclam, 1970), pp. 433–445.

Papers:

Ludwig Anzengruber's literary remains are at the Stadtbibliothek, Vienna. Additional letters are at the Schiller-Nationalmuseum und Deutsches Literaturarchiv, Marbach, Germany.

Otto von Bismarck

(1 April 1815 - 30 July 1898)

Otto Pflanze
Bard College

BOOKS: *Die politischen Reden des Fürsten Bismarck: Historisch-kritische Gesammtausgabe*, 14 volumes, edited by Horst Kohl (Stuttgart: Cotta, 1892–1905);

Gedanken und Erinnerungen, 2 volumes, edited by Kohl (Stuttgart: Cotta, 1898; reprinted, 1900; reprinted, 1920); translated by A. J. Butler as *Bismarck, the Man and the Statesman: Being the Reflections and Reminiscences of Otto Prince von Bismarck, Written and Dictated by Himself after His Retirement from Office* (2 volumes, London: Smith-Elder, 1898; reprinted, 1899; New York: Harper, 1898; reprinted, 1899; 3 volumes, Leipzig: Tauchnitz, 1899; 2 volumes, New York: Fertig, 1966);

Anhang zu den Gedanken und Erinnerungen von Otto Fürst von Bismarck, 2 volumes, edited by Kohl (Stuttgart: Cotta, 1901);

Gedanken und Erinnerungen: Volksausgabe, 2 volumes, edited by Kohl (Stuttgart: Cotta, 1905; reprinted, 1911; reprinted, 1913; reprinted, 1919; reprinted, 1922);

Gedanken und Erinnerungen, 4 volumes, edited by Kohl (Stuttgart: Cotta, 1911) – includes as volumes 3–4, *Anhang zu den Gedanken und Erinnerungen von Otto Fürst von Bismarck;*

Gedanken und Erinnerungen: Schulausgabe, 2 volumes, edited by Gottlob Egelhaaf (Stuttgart: Cotta, 1912);

Otto Prince von Bismarck: New Chapters of Bismarck's Autobiography, translated by Bernard Miall (London: Hodder & Stoughton, 1920; reprinted, 1921); republished as *The Kaiser versus Bismarck: Suppressed Letters by the Kaiser and New Chapters from the Autobiography of the Iron Chancellor* (New York & London: Harper, 1920; reprinted, 1921; New York: AMS Press, 1971); German version published as *Erinnerung und Gedanke* (Stuttgart: Cotta, 1921; reprinted, 1922);

Otto von Bismarck

Gedanken und Erinnerungen: Neue Ausgabe, 3 volumes (Stuttgart: Cotta, 1921; reprinted, 1922; reprinted, 1925; reprinted, 1928);

Gedanken und Erinnerungen: Taschenausgabe, 2 volumes (Stuttgart: Cotta, 1921; reprinted, 1926);

Bismarck: Die gesammelten Werke, 15 volumes, edited by Herman von Petersdorff and others (Berlin: Deutsche Verlagsgesellschaft, 1923–1933) – includes as volume 15 (1932), *Erinnerung und Gedanke: Kritische Neuausgabe auf Grund des gesamten schriftlichen Nachlasses,* edited by Gerhard Ritter and Rudolf Stadelmann, republished as *Gedanken und Erinnerungen* (Munich: Herbig, 1982);

Bismarck, Deutscher Staat: Ausgewählte Dokumente, edited by Hans Rothfels (Munich: Drei Masken, 1925); republished as *Bismarck und der Staat: Ausgewählte Dokumente* (Stuttgart: Kohlhammer, 1953; reprinted, 1954; reprinted, 1958; reprinted, 1964; reprinted, 1969);

Gedanken und Erinnerungen: Taschenausgabe (Stuttgart: Cotta, 1932; reprinted, 1938; reprinted, 1941);

Gedanken und Erinnerungen: An Abbreviated and Critically Annotated Edition, edited by A. M. Gibson (Cambridge: Cambridge University Press, 1940);

Gedanken und Erinnerungen, Reden und Briefe, edited by Kurt L. Walter-Schomburg (Berlin: Safari, 1942);

Gedanken und Erinnerungen, Reden und Briefe, edited by Reinhard Jaspert, introduction by Theodor Heuss (Berlin: Safari, 1951);

Gedanken und Erinnerungen, edited by Hermann Proebst (Munich: Droemer, 1952);

Gedanken und Erinnerungen, with appendix by Ernst Friedlaender (Stuttgart: Cotta, 1959; reprinted, 1965).

Otto von Bismarck was in his lifetime Europe's most prominent statesman. From 1862 to 1890 he was minister-president of Prussia; from 1867 to 1871, chancellor of the North German Confederation; and from 1871 to 1890, chancellor of the German Reich. As first minister of the king of Prussia and German kaiser he was in charge of both domestic and foreign affairs, but his fame rests chiefly on his achievements in the latter field. At the cost of three brief wars – against Denmark in 1864, Austria in 1866, and France in 1870–1871 – he unified Germany (excluding Austria, which before 1866 had been a part of Germany geographically, politically, and psychologically) under the leadership of an expanded Prussia. Afterward he strove successfully for nearly two decades to preserve peace in Europe to give Germany time to consolidate and fortify its new union. In domestic affairs he had less success. His attacks on political Catholicism and the socialist movement were failures, and the same was also largely true of his attempts to reform German fiscal policy. Bismarck's claim to literary significance rests on his memoirs, his letters, and a host of brilliantly crafted state (chiefly diplomatic) papers.

Bismarck was born at Schönhausen on the Elbe on 1 April 1815. Through his father, Ferdinand, he belonged to a Junker family of long lineage with estates in the Altmark and Pomerania. His mother, Wilhelmine Mencken Bismarck, was the daughter of a cabinet secretary to King Friedrich der Große (Frederick the Great) and his successors. Her paternal ancestors included several Leipzig university professors, from whom the American journalist and critic H. L. Mencken was also descended. Contrary to the norm, his mother was the dominant partner in the marriage, both in intellect and in force of character. "Meine Mutter," he wrote in 1847, "war eine schöne Frau, die äußre Pracht liebte, von hellem lebhaften Verstande, aber wenig von dem was der Berliner Gemüth nennt. Sie wollte, daß ich viel lernen und viel werden sollte, und es schien mir oft, daß sie hart, kalt gegen mich sei" (My mother was a beautiful woman who loved outward pomp, with a bright, lively intelligence but with little of what the Berliner calls soul. She wanted me to learn much and become much, and it often seemed to me that she was hard, cold toward me).

Bismarck seems to have had a disturbed oedipal relationship with his mother; in later years he mentioned her only with aversion. When he was five she sent him to boarding school at the Plamann Anstalt in Berlin, which had been founded by a disciple of the Swiss educator Johann Heinrich Pestalozzi and of which the naturalist and statesman Wilhelm von Humboldt was a patron. Afterward he attended the Friedrich Wilhelm Gymnasium and the Graues Kloster Gymnasium, also in Berlin. Except for the two years at the Graues Kloster he remembered his early schooling with great distaste. His six years at the Plamann Anstalt were for him like a prison, with harsh discipline and poor food. His three semesters at the University of Göttingen were spent in the usual manner of a corps student (twenty-five duels with one loss, and uncounted gallons of beer), his two years at the University of Berlin in cramming for the state service examination.

His marks were fair, and yet Bismarck seems to have been little affected by the humanistic education he received at his mother's insistence. For him, as for so many other students, classical languages were formal intellectual exercises rather than keys to a philosophy of life. What he read provided him with quotations that later adorned his speech and writing but did not form his character or mold his mind. He retained some knowledge of Latin, the language of philosophy and aesthetics. His intellectual life began late in the great productive years of German idealistic philosophy, but the systems of Immanuel Kant, Johann Gottfried von Herder, Johann Gottlieb Fichte, and Georg Wilhelm Friedrich Hegel did not interest him. From the lectures and historical works of Arnold Heeren at Göttingen he

"Bismarck takes aim at the Liberals": caricature from the satirical Berlin weekly Kladderadatsch

may have acquired some historical understanding of the interest of state and the balance of power, subjects that informed his future career, but for the most part he ended his formal education with a contempt for the academic mind. Ideas that he found unrealistic he dismissed as "Doktorfragen" (academic issues) or "Professorenweisheit" (professorial wisdom).

Yet Bismarck was not uncultured. His training in French began in the nursery. English he apparently learned from American university students, including the future historian and diplomat John Lothrop Motley, and from two Englishwomen (and their families) whom he successively and unsuccessfully courted at Aachen in 1836. Later he acquired some conversational Polish from Kaschuben farmers in Pomerania and a smattering of Russian during his residence in Saint Petersburg as a diplomat from 1859 to 1861.

Bismarck was baptized in the Protestant faith and confirmed by Friedrich Schleiermacher at the Dreifaltigkeitskirche in Berlin. Later he could remember nothing that the great theologian taught him, and soon after his confirmation he ceased the childhood practice of nightly prayer. He graduated from the gymnasium with religious views that he described variously as deistic, atheistic, and pantheistic. After failing in a halfhearted attempt at a civil service career in Aachen and Potsdam, he retired to the country to manage estates at Kniephof and Schönhausen in 1839. There he engaged in religious discussions with pietistic Junkers, one of whom was Marie von Thadden, whose sudden death in 1846 was a shattering experience for him. From that time onward prayer and devotion were integral parts of his daily life. In the following year he married Marie's close friend, Johanna von Puttkamer, with whom he had three children: Herbert, Wilhelm, and Marie. Pietism attracted him because of its lack of dogmatism and its faith in the human capacity to reach God

without the mediation of the clergy. Bible reading became a daily habit, but he was not a churchgoer. His marriage and religious conversion ended a period of inner turmoil in his personal life and gave him a new sense of responsibility and steadiness of purpose.

Bismarck's cultural interests were primarily literary. His parliamentary speeches of later years, which were extemporaneous, contain frequent quotations, usually from Johann Wolfgang von Goethe, Friedrich Schiller, and William Shakespeare, but on occasion from Christian Gellert, Joseph von Scheffel, Ludwig Uhland, Friedrich Kind, Horace, and Thomas Moore. Baroness Hildegard von Spitzemberg, a family friend and frequent houseguest in later years, reported that Bismarck acquired the works of Uhland, Adelbert von Chamisso, Heinrich Heine, and Friedrich Rückert for each of his residences. "Wenn ich dann so recht verärgert und abgemattet bin, lese ich am liebsten diese deutschen Lyriker, das erquickt mich" (When I get very exasperated and exhausted, I prefer to read these German lyricists; that revives me), he said. Among the classic authors he preferred Schiller to Goethe as a personality. Goethe, he asserted, was "ein echter Bureaukrat, stolzer auf seine Ministerwürde als auf sein Dichtertalent" (a genuine bureaucrat, prouder of his ministerial dignity than of his poetic talent). He knew the first part of *Faust* (1808) intimately; the second part (1832) he considered "unverständlich und darum ungenießbar" (incomprehensible and therefore unenjoyable).

Guests were surprised at how well-read Bismarck appeared to be in contemporary belles lettres. One evening during the war against France he discussed with dinner companions Friedrich Spielhagen's *Problematische Naturen* (1861; translated as *Problematic*

Bismarck in uniform

journalist and feuilletonist. During the revolution of 1848–1849 he wrote for the conservative *Kreuzzeitung* (Cross Newspaper), and in later years he dictated hundreds of articles for publication by favored journalists. Many of his letters to family and friends are masterpieces of epistolary art and reflect his swiftly shifting moods and purposes – they are alternately witty, tender, ironic, sardonic, descriptive, and expository. Throughout his career he fought against the tendencies toward official jargon, pomposity of phrase, and contradiction in content that affect every bureaucracy. His state papers are notable for their clear, unadorned style; often lengthy, they are seldom verbose. Two are well enough known to have been given titles – "Das kleine Buch" (The Small Book, 1858) and "Die Baden-Badener Denkschrift" (The Baden-Baden Memorandum, 1861). He avoided foreign words and insisted on German typography in preference to Latin. Above all, the state papers demonstrate his extraordinary capacity for persuasion: he marshals evidence to overcome the objections and resistance of the recipient and shapes and reshapes the context without outright deceit or undue distortion of the facts.

Bismarck's only book was his memoirs, *Gedanken und Erinnerungen* (Reflections and Reminiscences, 1898–1921; translated as *Bismarck, the Man and the Statesman*, 1898, and *The Kaiser versus Bismarck*, 1920). The work was written after his departure from office and was heavily influenced by the circumstances of that event. After twenty-eight years as the monarchy's first minister he was dismissed as chancellor of the German Reich and minister-president of Prussia by Kaiser Wilhelm II. The kaiser had ascended the throne in 1888, following the deaths in fast succession of his grandfather, Wilhelm I, and father, Friedrich III. By January 1890 he was thirty-one years old and eager to establish his "persönliche Regierung" (personal government). Bismarck, despite his nearly seventy-five years and bad health, was reluctant to surrender his offices. At issue between the two men were also substantial matters of foreign and domestic policy. Bismarck left Berlin seething with anger over his dismissal, not only against the kaiser but also against those he believed had influenced it. From Friedrichsruh, his estate near Hamburg, he launched attacks in the newspapers on his successors and their policies – and by inference on the kaiser himself. Begun as a weapon in this struggle, the memoirs became a tool for molding the author's image in the public mind and, hence, in the historical memory of the nation.

Characters, 1869), Gustav Freytag's *Soll und Haben* (Debit and Credit, 1855), and Fritz Reuter's "Ut de Franzosentid" (From My Time in France, 1860; translated as *In the Year '13*, 1868) and *Ut mine Stromtid* (From My Time as an Agricultural Apprentice, 1863–1864; translated as *Seed-Time and Harvest*, 1871). Houseguests in 1880 found him acquainted with the feuilletonist Paul Lindau's monthly *Nord und Süd* (North and South) and the recently published memoirs of Louis Schneider, reader to Kings Friedrich Wilhelm IV and Wilhelm I, and of Karoline Bauer, a leading actress. In later years he remembered with nostalgia the hours he had spent reading the songs of Pierre-Jean de Béranger on warm summer days under a tree in the park at Schönhausen. George Eliot he admired, having read *Adam Bede* (1859), but he did not care for Victor Hugo; he considered Ivan Turgenev the most gifted of all living authors. Among Shakespeare's plays his favorite appears to have been *Coriolanus*, considering the frequency with which he cited it. He judged Hippolyte Taine's history of the origins of modern France superior to comparable works by contemporary German historians.

Bismarck's letters and dispatches show that he was a master of the German language. His native literary talent would have enabled him, if circumstances had required it, to become a highly effective

In July 1890 Bismarck signed a contract with the firm of J. G. Cotta at Stuttgart. Founded in the seventeenth century, Cotta had published the works of Schiller, Herder, Goethe, Fichte, Friedrich Hebbel, Ludwig Tieck, and many other eminent authors. Following the death of Karl von Cotta in 1888 the firm had been purchased by Adolf and Paul Kröner, who contracted with Bismarck to publish six volumes with a royalty of one hundred thousand marks each. The royalty was meager compared with the millions the publisher could expect, but the agreement also relieved Bismarck of any liability if the work were never finished. Indeed, the brothers Kröner had a long wait. Bismarck dallied with the dictations; his secretary and collaborator, Lothar Bucher, died in 1892; and a surface reconciliation with Wilhelm II in 1894 made the project less urgent.

The book was set in type in late 1893, but Bismarck held on to the galleys until his death on 30 July 1898. His heir, Prince Herbert, engaged an editor, Horst Kohl, who added documents, made corrections (some dubious), and converted the enlarged work into two volumes, which were published in late 1898. The manuscript for a third volume, containing Bismarck's version of his quarrel with Wilhelm II, remained in the safe at Friedrichsruh. Herbert had decreed that its publication should await the kaiser's death; but the monarchy fell in 1918, Wilhelm fled to Holland, and Herbert's widow authorized publication in 1919. A lawsuit by the exiled kaiser, who contested the inclusion of a few of his own letters, delayed release of the new volume until 1921.

Volume three was titled *Erinnerung und Gedanke*, apparently to differentiate it from the two volumes already in print; later the editors who prepared the scholarly edition of the memoirs for Bismarck's collected works (1923–1933) revived that title for all three volumes in the conviction that it was the title Bismarck himself had approved. Manfred Hank has established that this assumption was probably erroneous; in any case, the reversed and plural form of the title has been used with such regularity by publishers and historians that it is now indelible.

Bismarck's *Gedanken und Erinnerungen* has been regarded as the first modern political autobiography, a genre that has become commonplace and, some might argue, even a plague. The work has enjoyed a popularity that has justified many editions and translations. Friedrich Nietzsche, a severe critic of Bismarck, was once asked whether he could recommend any good German books; with a blush he replied, "Ja, Bismarcks." Ludwig Bamberger, one of

Bismarck's liberal opponents, described the work as "ein höchst inhaltreiches, historisches, politisches und psychologisches Denkmal menschlichen Geistes und menschlicher Charakterstärke" (a most meaningful, historical, political, and psychological monument to the human spirit and strength of character). It was, he declared, a contribution to world literature that would have been even more effective had it been objectively written: "Weder Caesar, noch Friedrich der Große, noch Napoleon haben in so eigenartigen, blendenden, schriftstellerisch vollkommenen Schilderungen ihrer Person und ihrer Thaten ein so weit- und tiefgehendes Bild hinterlassen" (Neither Caesar, nor Frederick the Great, nor Napoleon left behind so wide-ranging and penetrating a portrait of himself sketched in such unique, brilliant, and literarily complete accounts of his person and his deeds). In a survey of political autobiographies beginning with that of Babur, the founder of the Mogul empire in the sixteenth century, and ending with Adolf Hitler's *Mein Kampf* (1925–1926; translated as *My Struggle*, 1933), the British historian George Peabody Gooch concluded that Bismarck's "stands at the top of the list . . . not merely because he is the greatest man who ever wrote a full-length narrative of his life, and not merely because the events he records are of world-wide significance, but because [the work's] value as a manual of statecraft is unsurpassed." Another British historian, A. J. P. Taylor, was more acerbic: "*Gedanken und Erinnerungen* ranks with the most remarkable political memoirs ever written, not least for its artistic inaccuracy of detail."

Letters:

Bismarckbriefe, 1844–1870: Originalbriefe Bismarcks an seine Gemahlin, seine Schwester und andere (Bielefeld & Leipzig: Velhagen & Klasing, 1876); translated by Fitzhardinge Maxse as *Prince Bismarck's Letters to His Wife, His Sister, and Others, from 1844 to 1870* (New York: Scribners, 1878);

Politische Briefe Bismarcks aus den Jahren 1849–1889, 3 volumes (Berlin: Steinitz, 1889);

Bismarck-Briefe: Neue Folge, 3 volumes, edited by Heinrich von Poschinger (Berlin: Hennig & Eigendorf, 1889–1891);

Fürst Bismarcksbriefe, 2 volumes, edited by Bruno Walden (pseudonym of Florentine Galliny) (Berlin & Leipzig: Fried, 1892–1893);

Briefwechsel des Generals Leopold von Gerlach mit dem Bundestagsgesandten Otto von Bismarck (Berlin: Hertz, 1893);

Bismarcks Briefe an den General Leopold von Gerlach, edited by Horst Kohl (Berlin: Häring, 1896);

Bismarckbriefe, 1836–1872, edited by Kohl (Bielefeld & Leipzig: Velhagen & Klasing, 1897); enlarged as *Bismarckbriefe, 1836–1873* (Bielefeld & Leipzig: Velhagen & Klasing, 1898);

Fürst Bismarcks Briefe an seine Braut und Gattin, edited by Herbert von Bismarck (Stuttgart: Cotta, 1900); translated by Charlton T. Lewis and others as *The Love Letters of Bismarck* (New York & London: Harper, 1901); German version enlarged, 2 volumes, edited by Kohl (Stuttgart: Cotta, 1914);

Kaiser- und Kanzler-Briefe: Briefwechsel zwischen Kaiser Wilhelm I. und Fürst Bismarck, edited by Johannes Penzler (Leipzig: Fiedler, 1900); translated by J. A. Ford as *The Correspondence of William I & Bismarck, with Other Letters from and to Prince Bismarck* (London: Heinemann, 1903; New York: Stokes, 1903);

Bismarcks Briefwechsel, 1851–1861 (Stuttgart: Cotta, 1905);

Bismarcks Briefwechsel mit dem Minister Freiherrn von Schleinitz, 1858–1861 (Stuttgart: Cotta, 1905);

Vom jungen Bismarck: Briefwechsel Otto von Bismarcks mit Gustav Scharlach, edited by A. Zeising (Weimar: Duncker, 1912);

Briefe Otto von Bismarcks an Schwester und Schwager, Malwine von Arnim geb. von Bismarck und Oskar von Arnim-Kröchlendorff, 1843–1897, edited by Kohl (Leipzig: Weicher, 1915); republished as *Bismarcks Briefe an Schwester und Schwager,* edited by Erich Brandenburg (Leipzig: Insel, 1934);

Bismarcks Briefwechsel mit Kleist-Retzow, edited by Herman von Petersdorff (Stuttgart: Cotta, 1919);

Bismarcks Briefe an seinen Sohn Wilhelm, edited by Wolfgang Windelband (Berlin: Verlag für Politik und Wirtschaft, 1922);

Briefe, edited by Wolfgang Windelband and Werner Frauendienst, volume 14 of *Bismarck: Die gesammelten Werke,* edited by Petersdorff and others (Berlin: Deutsche Verlagsgesellschaft, 1933);

Bismarck-Briefe, edited by Hans Rothfels (Göttingen: Vandenhoeck & Ruprecht, 1955).

Bibliographies:

Karl Erich Born, ed., *Bismarck-Bibliographie: Quellen und Literatur zur Geschichte Bismarcks und seiner Zeit* (Cologne: Grote, 1966);

Klaus Tenfelde and Gerhard A. Ritter, eds., *Bibliographie zur Geschichte der deutschen Arbeiterschaft und Arbeiterbewegung, 1863–1975* (Bonn: Neue Gesellschaft, 1981).

Biographies:

Erich Marcks, *Bismarck: Eine Biographie* (Stuttgart: Cotta, 1909);

Erich Eyck, *Bismarck: Leben und Werk,* 3 volumes (Erlenbach & Zurich: Rentsch, 1941–1944);

Arnold Oskar Meyer, *Bismarck: Der Mensch und der Staatsmann* (Stuttgart: Koehler, 1949);

Lothar Gall, *Bismarck: Der Weiße Revolutionär* (Frankfurt am Main: Propyläen, 1980); translated by J. A. Underwood as *Bismarck: The White Revolutionary,* 2 volumes (London: Allen & Unwin, 1986);

Ernst Engelberg, *Bismarck: Urpreusse und Reichsgründer,* 2 volumes (Berlin: Siedler, 1985–1990);

Otto Pflanze, *Bismarck and the Development of Germany,* 3 volumes (Princeton: Princeton University Press, 1990).

References:

Ludwig Bamberger, "Bismarck Posthumus," *Die Nation,* 16 (1899): 145–147;

George Peabody Gooch, "Bismarck's Legacy," *Foreign Affairs,* 30 (July 1952): 517–530;

Gooch, "Political Autobiography," in his *Studies in Diplomacy and Statecraft* (London: Longmans, Green, 1942), pp. 261–263;

Manfred Hank, *Kanzler ohne Amt: Fürst Bismarck nach seiner Entlassung, 1890-1898* (Munich: Tuduv, 1977);

William L. Langer, "Bismarck as a Dramatist," in *Studies in Diplomatic History and Historiography in Honour of G. P. Gooch, C. H.,* edited by A. O. Sarkissian (London: Longmans, 1961), pp. 199–216;

Robert Pahncke, *Die Parallel-Erzählungen Bismarcks zu seinen Gedanken und Erinnerungen* (Halle: Niemeyer, 1914);

A. J. P. Taylor, *The Struggle for Mastery in Europe, 1848–1918* (Oxford: Clarendon Press, 1954), p. 585;

Rudolf Vierhaus, ed., *Das Tagebuch der Baronin Spitzemberg* (Göttingen: Vandenhoeck & Ruprecht, 1961), pp. 212, 229.

Papers:

Otto von Bismarck's correspondence is in the family archive at Friedrichsruh, near Hamburg. His state papers are in the archives of the German Federal Republic at Bonn, Berlin-Dahlem, Koblenz, Merseburg, and Potsdam. The papers of the Cotta publishing house are in the Deutsches Literaturarchiv at Marbach am Neckar.

Friedrich von Bodenstedt

(22 April 1819 - 18 April 1892)

William H. McClain
Johns Hopkins University

BOOKS: *Die Völker des Kaukasus und ihre Freiheitskämpfe gegen die Russen: Ein Beitrag zur neuesten Geschichte des Orients* (Frankfurt am Main: Keßler, 1848; revised and enlarged edition, 2 volumes, Berlin: Decker, 1855);

Tausend und Ein Tag im Orient, 2 volumes (Berlin: Decker, 1849-1850); translated by Richard Waddington as *The Morning-Land; or, A Thousand and One Days in the East,* 2 volumes (London: Bentley, 1851); German version enlarged, 3 volumes (Berlin: Decker, 1853-1854);

Die Einführung des Christenthums in Armenien: Eine Vorlesung, gehalten am 2. März 1850 im Wissenschaftlichen Verein zu Berlin (Berlin: Decker, 1850);

Die Lieder des Mirza-Schaffy, mit einem Prolog von Friedrich Bodenstedt (Berlin: Decker, 1851); translated by Elsa d'Esterre as *The Songs of Mirza Schaffy: With a Prologue* (Hamburg: Grädener, 1880);

Die neuen Nibelungen oder Der auferstandene Sigfried, as M. Reckenlob (Leipzig: Haessel, 1851);

Gedichte (Bremen: Schlodtmann, 1852);

Ada die Lesghierin: Ein Gedicht (Berlin: Decker, 1853);

Demetrius: Historische Tragödie in fünf Aufzügen (Berlin: Decker, 1856);

Gedichte, 2 volumes (Berlin: Decker, 1856-1859) – comprises volume 1, *Aus der Heimat und Fremde;* volume 2, *Altes und Neues;*

Festspiel zur Jubelfeier des hundertjährigen Geburtstages Friedrich Schiller's in München (Berlin: Decker, 1860);

König Authari's Brautfahrt: Dramatisches Gedicht in drei Aufzügen (Berlin: Decker, 1860);

Aus Ost und West: Sechs Vorlesungen (Berlin: Decker, 1861);

Epische Dichtungen (Berlin: Decker, 1862);

Erzählungen, 2 volumes (Munich: Rieger, 1863);

Ausgewählte Dichtungen (Berlin: Decker, 1864);

Gesammelte Schriften: Gesammt-Ausgabe, 12 volumes (Berlin: Decker, 1865-1869);

Zeitgedichte (Berlin: Lipperheide, 1870);

Friedrich von Bodenstedt

Neun Kriegslieder (Bielefeld & Leipzig: Velhagen & Klasing, 1870);

Erzählungen und Romane, 7 volumes (Jena: Costenoble, 1871-1872) – comprises volumes 1-2, *Aus deutschen Gauen: Erzählungen;* volumes 3-4, *Vom Hofe Elisabeth's und Jakob's: Erzählungen;* volumes 5-7, *Das Herrenhaus im Eschenwalde: Ein Roman;*

Shakespeares Frauencharaktere (Berlin: Hofmann, 1874);

Aus dem Nachlasse Mirza-Schaffy's: Neues Liederbuch (Berlin: Hofmann, 1874);

Alexander in Corinth: Schauspiel in drei Akten (Hannover: Helwing, 1876);

Einkehr und Umschau: Neueste Dichtungen (Jena: Costenoble, 1876);

Theater (Berlin: Grote, 1876) – comprises *Kaiser Paul: Drama; Wandlungen: Lustspiel;*

Aus meinem Leben: Erinnerungsblätter. I. Bd. Eines Königs Reise: Erinnerungsblätter an König Max (Leipzig: Albrecht, 1879);

Szegedin: Prolog zu der Sonntag, 30. März stattfindenden Matinée zum Besten Szegedins (Wiesbaden: Jurany & Hensel, 1879);

Gräfin Helene: Novelle (Stuttgart: Richter & Kappler, 1880);

Vom Atlantischen zum Stillen Ocean (Leipzig: Brockhaus, 1882; New York: Steiger, 1882);

Aus Morgenland und Abendland: Neue Gedichte und Sprüche (Leipzig: Brockhaus, 1882);

Neues Leben: Gedichte und Sprüche (Breslau: Schottländer, 1886);

Die letzten Falkenburger: Roman (Berlin: Janke, 1887);

Sakuntala: Eine Dichtung in fünf Gesängen (Leipzig: Titze, 1887);

Eine Mönchsliebe: Das Mädchen von Liebenstein (Berlin: Janke, 1887);

Lady Penelope: Erzählung (Berlin: Janke, 1887);

Erinnerungen aus meinem Leben, 2 volumes (Berlin: Allgemeiner Verein für deutsche Litteratur, 1888–1890);

Feona; Ein Mißverständnis: Zwei Erzählungen (Berlin: Janke, 1889);

Priuthina; Hugo und Hulda: Zwei Erzählungen (Berlin: Janke, 1889);

Thamar und ihr Kind; Die geheimnisvolle Sängerin; Oheim und Neffe: Drei Erzählungen (Berlin: Janke, 1889);

Die Zigeunerherberge; Die feindlichen Nachbarn: Zwei Erzählungen (Berlin: Janke, 1889);

Theodora: Ein Sang aus dem Harzwald (Leipzig: Fischer, 1891).

OTHER: *Journal des Österreichischen Lloyd,* edited by Bodenstedt (1848);

Deutsche Reform, edited by Bodenstedt (1848–1851);

Die Weserzeitung, edited by Bodenstedt (1851–1854);

Russische Fragmente: Beiträge zur Kenntnis des Staats- und Volkslebens in seiner historischen Entwicklung, 2 volumes, edited by Bodenstedt (Leipzig: Brockhaus, 1862);

Shakespeare-Jahrbuch, edited by Bodenstedt (1864–1865);

Album deutscher Kunst und Dichtung, edited by Bodenstedt (Berlin: Grote, 1867);

Kunst und Leben: Ein neuer Almanach für das deutsche Haus, 3 volumes, edited by Bodenstedt (Stuttgart: Spemann, 1877–1880);

Verschollenes und Neues: Ein Dichterbuch aus Deutschland und Österreich, edited by Bodenstedt (Hannover: Helwing, 1878);

Die tägliche Rundschau, edited by Bodenstedt (circa 1881–1892);

Liebe und Leben: Eine Sammlung deutscher Lyrik, edited by Bodenstedt (Leipzig: Fischer, 1892).

TRANSLATIONS: *Kaslow, A. Puschkin, M. Lermontoff: Eine Sammlung aus ihren Gedichten* (Leipzig: Kollmann, 1843);

Die poetische Ukraine: Eine Sammlung kleinrussischer Volkslieder (Stuttgart: Cotta, 1845);

Michaïl Lermontoff's poetischer Nachlaß: Zum ersten Mal in den Versmaßen der Urschrift aus dem Russischen übersetzt, 2 volumes (Berlin: Decker, 1852);

Alexander Puschkin's poetische Werke aus dem Russischen übersetzt, 3 volumes (Berlin: Decker, 1854–1855);

Shakespeare's Zeitgenossen und ihre Werke: In Charakteristiken und Übersetzungen, 3 volumes (Berlin: Decker, 1858–1860);

William Shakespeare's Sonette in deutscher Nachbildung (Berlin: Decker, 1862);

Turgenjew's Erzählungen, 2 volumes (Munich: Rieger, 1864–1865);

Shakespeare's König Lear (Berlin: Decker, 1865);

Shakespeare's dramatische Werke übersetzt, by Bodenstedt, Nikolaus Delius, Otto Gildemeister, Georg Herwegh, Paul Heyse, Hermann Kurz, and Adolf von Wilbrandt (Leipzig: Brockhaus, 1866–1872);

Kleine Geschichten aus fernem Land (Jena: Costenoble, 1872);

Der Sänger von Schiras: Hafisische Lieder verdeutscht (Berlin: Hofmann, 1877);

Die Lieder und Sprüche des Omar Chajjâm, verdeutscht (Breslau: Schletter, 1881).

Obituaries by prominent contemporaries who praise Friedrich von Bodenstedt as a sensitive translator and knowledgeable mediator of Russian, Middle Eastern, and Elizabethan literature; as a journalist of considerable stature; and as a poet who gave pleasure to millions of readers make it difficult to imagine that he was, for a time, headed toward a career in business. Even as a youngster growing up in the Hannoverian town of Peine, where he was born on 22 April 1819, Bodenstedt demonstrated in the verses he composed for birthdays, holidays, and other occasions verbal skills of a high order. His practical-minded father, however, while proud of his son's poetic ability, continually reminded him that no German writer had ever been able to live by his pen alone, enrolled him in a commercial school, and made him promise to stop writing. For a time Bodenstedt tried to obey his father, but he finally gave in to temptation and secretly composed poems and essays. He also read widely and learned English and French. At sixteen he made his first translation from English into German: a metrical version of Shakespeare's *Macbeth*.

After commercial school Bodenstedt was apprenticed to a business firm in Brunswick. In his leisure hours he continued to write. At considerable financial sacrifice he attended lectures on history, philosophy, and literature at the University of Göttingen. As his intellectual horizons widened he became ever more eager to travel. The chance came when a German friend, whose father was a cavalry officer stationed in Moscow, invited him to Russia.

Early in 1840 Bodenstedt sailed from Lübeck to Saint Petersburg and traveled from there to Moscow by coach. While staying with his German friends he studied Russian intensively. At the University of Moscow he passed an examination that qualified him to teach in Russia, and with the help of a Russian friend he secured a position as tutor of the two sons of Prince Gallitzyn. During his two and a half years as a member of the Gallitzyn household he met prominent Muscovites, intellectuals, and writers. The journals in which he recorded his conversations with his new acquaintances formed the basis for his accounts, later published in Germany, of contemporary Russian political, social, and cultural conditions. Mikhail Lermontov became a close friend, and Bodenstedt was named his literary executor after the poet's death in a duel in 1841.

In the summer of 1843 Bodenstedt received an offer to teach German at a gymnasium in Tiflis (today Tbilisi, Ukraine). The month-long journey by troika, on which he embarked in mid October, took him through the Cossack territories in the Kirghiz Steppes and through the regions farther south where the Russians were attempting to subjugate Lesghistan and Dagestan. The impressions he gathered on this epic journey furnished subject matter for several of Bodenstedt's later travel accounts and fictional and dramatic works.

In Tiflis, Bodenstedt found the poetry, art, and customs of the region intriguing and decided to learn Tatar so as to be able to read the poetry in the original language. The teacher he engaged, Mirza Schaffy (*Mirza* is not a name but a title meaning "man of letters"), also enlightened him concerning local folkways and Sufism, a mystical religious movement that emerged among Shiite Muslims in the late tenth century. The ideal of some Sufis, including the renowned Persian poets Hafez and Omar Khayyám, is mystical union of the soul with Allah. Mirza Schaffy, according to Bodenstedt, was a Sufi in a more limited sense: "ein nach Wahrheit und Selbstveredelung strebender Mensch, dem es als höchstes Ziel der Weisheit galt: mit Gott, den Menschen und sich selbst in Frieden und Einklang zu leben" (a man who strove for truth and self-improvement and for whom the highest goal of human wisdom was to learn to live in peace and harmony with God, one's fellowmen, and oneself). Bodenstedt was soon able to translate poetry from Tatar into German and to imitate in German the verse forms employed by the regional poets.

An opportunity to travel south into the mountainous regions of Armenia presented itself when Georg Rosen, a Berlin Orientalist about to embark on a research project in that remote part of the Caucasus, invited Bodenstedt to come along. In the course of the long journey by coach, horseback, and on foot the two had several adventures that Bodenstedt recorded in his travel diary along with his impressions of the landscapes, the people, and their customs. He also eagerly collected regional folk songs and translated some of them into German.

Before leaving Germany, Rosen had promised to forward excerpts from his travel diary for publication in the Stuttgart publisher Georg von Cotta's *Morgenblatt* (Morning News). Finding himself unable to meet this commitment because of the pressure of his scientific work, he suggested that Cotta print Bodenstedt's accounts instead. Bodenstedt suddenly had an outlet for his work in one of the most prestigious German periodicals. Cotta asked Bodenstedt to submit enough of his translations of Ukrainian poetry to make up a small volume. This collection, Bodenstedt's first major literary publication, appeared in 1845 under the title *Die poetische Ukraine* (Poetry of Ukraine).

Although strongly attracted to Caucasia and its peoples, Bodenstedt found the rugged climate unhealthful and reluctantly left in April 1845, returning to Peine by way of Odessa, Constantinople, the Aegean Islands, Trieste, Vienna, Prague, Dresden, and Leipzig. Not long after his return Cotta offered him a position as a roving reporter for the *Allgemeine Zeitung* (Universal News). Bodenstedt declined so that he could complete some of his writing projects. After trying to work in Peine he moved to Munich, where the sources he might need would be readily available and where he could enjoy the company of friends and colleagues, in May 1846. By the summer of 1847 he had completed *Die Völker des*

Bodenstedt with the Sufi poet Mirza Schaffy (frontispiece for the first edition of Bodenstedt's Tausend und ein Tag im Orient)

Kaukasus und ihre Freiheitskämpfe gegen die Russen (The Peoples of the Caucasus and Their Struggle for Freedom against the Russians, 1848), which he offered to Cotta. Before he and Cotta reached an agreement concerning the honorarium, however, a friend persuaded him to offer the manuscript to a publishing house in Frankfurt am Main.

On his way back to Munich from Frankfurt, Bodenstedt stopped for several days at Schloß (Castle) Escheberg, the country estate of his friend Baron Karl Otto von der Malsburg, a well-to-do Hessian official and devotee of the arts. The baron enjoyed a certain renown because of his well-crafted translations of Spanish dramas of the Golden Age; Johann Wolfgang von Goethe had spoken well of his translations of the works of Pedro Calderón de la Barca. At Schloß Escheberg, Bodenstedt met and fell in love with an author of children's books, Mathilde Osterwald.

Early in 1848, seeking relief from a nagging throat ailment, Bodenstedt went to Italy. He spent a few weeks in Rome with the journalists Levin

Schücking and Willibald Alexis, who had begun to make their reputations as novelists. In Rome he witnessed the first stirrings of the revolutionary upheavals of 1848 and sent a firsthand account back to Germany. In Bologna, Italian revolutionaries mistook him for an Austrian spy and detained him until a German friend negotiated his release. Not long after this episode he received the news that his publisher in Frankfurt had declared bankruptcy and the Lizius publishing house had purchased the stock of the bankrupt firm. The transaction meant that Bodenstedt had no hope of receiving the anticipated and sorely needed income from *Die Völker des Kaukasus.* Eduard Kolb, the editor of the *Allgemeine Zeitung,* came to Bodenstedt's rescue by recommending him for the editorship of the journal published by the Austrian Lloyd marine insurance company in Trieste. Bodenstedt did not realize an income from *Die Völker des Kaukasus* until 1855, when the Decker publishing house brought out a revised edition of the work.

When the Austrian Lloyd relocated the headquarters of its journal to Vienna later in 1848, Bodenstedt was invited to continue as editor. In Vienna, Bodenstedt renewed old friendships. Especially congenial was the small circle of journalists and writers who met regularly at the home of Heinrich Landesmann, an astute chronicler of the contemporary scene whom his readers knew by his pseudonym Heironymus Lorm. Bodenstedt often regaled the group with his reminiscences of Mirza Schaffy and recited some of Mirza Schaffy's poetry. At their urging he began to compose a manuscript based on his experiences.

Work on this project had to be suspended temporarily toward the end of 1848 when Bodenstedt accepted an offer to become editor in chief of Decker's periodical *Deutsche Reform* (German Reform) in Berlin. He then completed the manuscript, and Decker brought it out in two volumes in 1849 and 1850 under the title *Tausend und Ein Tag im Orient* (A Thousand and One Days in the East); the second volume appeared a few weeks after Bodenstedt's marriage to Mathilde Osterwald.

Although Bodenstedt's intention, as he explains in the final chapter of volume 1, is to provide an objective account of the countries between the Caspian and Black seas, the personal nature of the reminiscences on which it is based gives it a strongly subjective tone. It offers a lively medley of fairly short, eminently readable essays on the history, customs, and outlook of the Caucasus peoples, interspersed with examples of popular poetry from the regions described. Prominent are poems and sayings that are attributed to Mirza Schaffy but were, as he acknowledged in 1854, actually Bodenstedt's own creations.

Popular response to *Tausend und Ein Tag im Orient* was enthusiastic; readers especially liked "Mirza Schaffy's" easily understandable and quotable verses. A separate edition of the poems appeared in 1851 as *Die Lieder des Mirza-Schaffy*. By the time of Bodenstedt's death in 1892 the collection had gone through 142 printings and had made his name known throughout the German-speaking world.

To many of those who made *Die Lieder des Mirza-Schaffy* a best-seller, Bodenstedt's cleverly crafted, catchy, and easily memorizable verses on the evils of oppression, the importance of striving toward self-betterment, and the desirability of learning to live in harmony with oneself, one's fellows, and the natural world seemed to be expressions of their own longings in a period of political, social, and economic changes. Readers also found refreshing the antiascetic, life-affirming religious outlook expressed in some of the poems, for example in the tenth poem in the section "Lieder zum Lobe des Weins und irdischer Glückseligkeit" (Songs in Praise of Wine and Earthly Bliss):

> Verbittre Dir das junge Leben
>   nicht,
> Verschmähe, was Dir Gott ge-
>   geben nicht!
> Verschließ Dein Herz der Liebe
>   Offenbarung
> Und Deinen Mund dem Trank der
>   Reben nicht!
> Sieh, schönern Doppellohn als
>   Wein und Liebe
> Beut Dir die Erde für Dein Streben
>   nicht!
> Drum ehre sie als Deine Erden-
>   götter
> Und andern huldige daneben nicht!
>
> (Let not your young life turn
>   sour,
> Scorn not what God has given
>   you!
> Close not your heart to love's
>   revelation
> Or your mouth to the drink
>   from the fruit of the vine!
> Behold, fairer double reward
>   than wine and love
> Earth does not offer as reward
>   for your striving!
> Honor these, therefore, as
>   your earthly gods
> And do homage to no others!)

In this exhortation to enjoy the beauties and pleasures of earthly life both the theme and the verse form – the ghasel (in Arabic, Persian, and Turkish poetry a poem of five to twelve couplets, all of which have the same end rhyme) – recall the poetry of Hafez and Omar Khayyám. Literary historians often refer to this style of poetic writing in Germany as "Orientlyrik" and cite as main exponents Goethe, Friedrich Rückert, August Graf von Platen, and Bodenstedt, and most agree that Goethe, Rückert, and Platen are superior to Bodenstedt in artistry. None, however, has surpassed him in popular appeal.

Bodenstedt's first child, a daughter named Henny, was born in September 1850. In 1851 Bodenstedt accepted an editorial position with the *Weserzeitung* in Bremen. A second child, Paula, was born in December 1851; a son, Gotthardt, was born in March 1853; and another daughter, Frieda, was born in 1856. Bodenstedt's responsibilities left him little time with his wife and children, but they loved him dearly. After his death Frieda said of him, "er ließ uns immer im Sonnenschein des Glücks" (he always left us in the sunlight of happiness).

In a letter of 13 October 1851 to the Decker firm Bodenstedt mentions for the first time the work that was to be one of his major contributions as an interpreter of contemporary Russian literature to the German reading public: his translations of the posthumous poems of Lermontov, which were unknown in Russia as well as in Germany. In the letter he offers the collection to Decker, which immediately accepted. In the letter accompanying the manuscript Bodenstedt reveals that he is also in possession of Lermontov's complete posthumous writings and offers these to Decker as well as the poems. Again, the response was quick and affirmative. The two volumes of *Michaïl Lermontoff's poetischer Nachlaß* (Mikhail Lermontov's Posthumous Poems) appeared in 1852, with an introductory biographical sketch and a short essay on contemporary Russian literature.

The other work that established Bodenstedt's reputation as an interpreter of Russian literature is his edition of his translations of major poetic, dramatic, and prose works of Aleksandr Pushkin. Bodenstedt's plan was to include only works that had not been previously translated into German or that had been ineptly translated. Volume one of *Alexander Puschkin's poetische Werke* came out in 1854 with a short biographical sketch and a generous sampling of Pushkin's lyric poetry. Volume two, which appeared later the same year, offers a new translation of *Eugene Onegin* (1831), and volume three (1855) includes several of Pushkin's dramatic fragments.

Early in 1853 Bodenstedt received a letter from King Maximilian II of Bavaria expressing great admiration for his writings and extending an invitation to move to Munich. The stipend offered and the prospect of participating in the sessions of the group of nobles, scientists, scholars, and artists who met with the king on a weekly basis were tempting, but Bodenstedt hesitated to accept the invitation because of the cost of moving to Munich. This difficulty was overcome when the Decker firm gave him a generous advance and Maximilian offered to reimburse him for his moving expenses.

A letter to Decker shortly after Bodenstedt's arrival in Munich expresses disappointment with the city but great satisfaction with King Maximilian's "Tafelrunde" (round table), which he characterizes as "außerordentlich anregend, genußvoll und lehrreich" (extremely stimulating, enjoyable and profitable). On 17 July 1854 Bodenstedt proudly announced to Decker that Maximilian had appointed him professor of Slavic studies at the University of Munich. With the new post came new responsibilities, and soon the letters from Munich were reflecting the pressure of attempting to fulfill a variety of obligations while revising old works for new editions and preparing new works for publication.

One of the new projects was a multivolume work, along the lines of Ludwig Tieck's *Altenglisches Theater* (Early English Theater, 1811), on the most important contemporaries of Shakespeare. Decker proposed that he also consider preparing a new edition of German translations of Shakespeare's dramas for the forthcoming tercentenary of Shakespeare's birth. Contracts for the two projects were signed in April 1857. In spite of a protracted and debilitating illness and a long interruption of work occasioned by King Maximilian's invitation to join the royal party on a trip to the Bavarian mountains, by mid June 1858 Bodenstedt completed the first volume of his series on Shakespeare's contemporaries while also readying a collection of his own poems for publication. The first volume, on John Webster, was published in 1858; volume 2, on John Ford, and volume 3, on John Lilly, Robert Greene, and Christopher Marlowe, were in print by 1860. The collection of Bodenstedt's poems, *Gedichte: Altes und Neues* (Poems: Old and New), came out in 1859.

In the fall of 1859 the committee planning the Munich celebration of the centennial of Friedrich Schiller's birth commissioned Bodenstedt to write a piece for the occasion. His Festspiel (festival play) in verse was presented before an enthusiastic audience at the Odeon on 10 November. The Decker firm, which published the Festspiel the following year, donated all proceeds from the sale to the Schiller Fund for indigent artists and their families. The first volume of Bodenstedt's Shakespeare translations, comprising the sonnets, appeared in 1862 and was praised by the critics.

In the spring of 1864 Bodenstedt and other eminent German Shakespeare scholars were invited to take part in a conference sponsored by the Grand Duke Karl Alexander of Weimar to commemorate the three hundredth anniversary of Shakespeare's birth. A signal accomplishment of the scholarly sessions was the founding of the Deutscher Shakespeare-Verein (German Shakespeare Association), which later became the Deutsche Shakespeare-Gesellschaft (German Shakespeare Society). One of the association's first official actions was to establish a journal, the *Shakespeare-Jahrbuch* (Shakespeare Yearbook), of which Bodenstedt was general editor during the first two years.

On 10 March 1864 King Maximilian died. His nineteen-year-old son Ludwig, who succeeded him, had high esteem for Bodenstedt and even had a framed copy of one of his poems over his bed; but it soon became evident that the only artist who truly mattered to the young king was Richard Wagner, whom he invited to Munich in May 1864. Ludwig appointed Bodenstedt director of classical productions at the Hoftheater the following year, but Bodenstedt soon saw that all final decisions concerning productions were made by the general director. Accordingly, when the theater-loving Georg, Duke of Saxe-Meiningen, offered him the directorship of his highly acclaimed court theater two years later, Bodenstedt eagerly accepted. The duke even raised Bodenstedt to the peerage; but the association that began with high hopes on the part of both patron and director soon deteriorated when it became evident that Bodenstedt had no real theatrical talent. In early 1870 Bodenstedt received an inquiry from the publisher Hermann Costenoble in Jena, and by late June Bodenstedt was under contract with Costenoble.

Many illnesses afflicted Bodenstedt in his later years, including vision problems, intense headaches, and gout. The Bodenstedts moved from Meiningen to Hannover in 1875, and two years later to Wiesbaden. There were no great literary successes in those last years, but during a trip to the United States between October 1879 and September 1880 he met Carl Schurz and was received in the White House by President Rutherford B. Hayes; in cities with large German-American populations banquets and concerts were given in his honor, and singing societies performed musical settings of his poems. In Milwaukee there was a torchlight parade, and he was crowned with a laurel wreath. His account of his American experiences was titled *Vom Atlantischen zum Stillen Ocean* (From the Atlantic to the Pacific, 1882).

On Bodenstedt's seventieth birthday the city of Wiesbaden honored him with an official tribute, and letters and telegrams poured in from all parts of the world. By then his health had deteriorated and his productive hours were quite limited. What energies he was able to summon he devoted to his responsibilities as editor of the *Tägliche Rundschau* (Daily Observer) and to revising old works for new editions. The spirit that sustained him during those last years is poignantly expressed in one of his last letters to the Decker firm (23 February 1892): "Ich weiß nur, daß ich täglich älter und schwächer werde und bei meinem hohen Alter auf kein langes Leben mehr rechnen darf. Um so ernster mahnt mich die Pflicht meine Interessen zu wahren, so lange es noch möglich ist . . ." (I know only that I grow older and weaker each day and that at my advanced age I can no longer count on a long life. Duty accordingly exhorts me all the more earnestly to watch over my interests as long as I possibly can . . .).

The obituaries after Bodenstedt's death on 18 April 1892 cited the human qualities that had endeared him to so many, his poetic insights and skills, and the self-discipline that had enabled him to work productively until his last days. In 1894 the city of Wiesbaden erected a monument in his memory. During World War II the metal parts of the monument were melted down for the war effort, but it has been restored to its original state.

Letters:

"Friedrich Bodenstedts Nachlaßbriefe von 1859 an seine Gattin," *Westermanns illustrierte deutsche Monatshefte,* 75 (1887): 115–137;

Friedrich von Bodenstedt: Ein Dichterleben in seinen Briefen 1850–1892, edited by Gustav Schenck (Berlin: Decker, 1893);

"Friedrich von Bodenstedts Briefe an Hermann Costenoble," edited by Lieselotte E. Kurth-Voigt and William H. McClain, *Archiv für Geschichte des Buchwesens,* 18 (1977): cols. 799–962.

Biographies:

Karl Engelmann, *Friedrich von Bodenstedt: Ein Dichterleben* (Munich: Privately printed, 1958);

Theodor Engelmann, *Friedrich von Bodenstedt: Persönliche Erinnerungen an den Dichter-Großvater* (Munich: Privately printed, 1958).

References:

William Rounsville Alger, Reviews of *Tausend und Ein Tag im Orient* and *Die Lieder des Mirza-Schaffy, North American Review,* 75 (April 1857): 291–311;

Hugo Bieber, *Der Kampf um die Tradition: Die deutsche Dichtung im europäischen Geistesleben 1830–1880* (Stuttgart: Metzler, 1928), pp. 496–497;

Konrad Burdach, "Goethes West-Östlicher Divan," *Goethe-Jahrbuch,* 17 (1896): 1–46;

Carl Busse, *Neuere deutsche Lyrik* (Halle: Hendel, 1895), pp. 2–84;

Issa Chehabi, "Friedrich Bodenstedts Verdeutschung der Hafischen Lieder," Ph.D. dissertation, University of Cologne, 1967;

Elsa D'Esterre-Keeling, "Friedrich von Bodenstedt," *Eclectic Magazine of Foreign Literature, Science and Art,* new series 55 (June 1892): 825–826;

Adolf Endler, "Drei Herren im alten Tbilisi," *Neue deutsche Literatur,* 24 (1976): 125–135;

Edward Payson Evans, "Texts and Translations of Hafiz," *Atlantic Monthly,* 53 (March 1884): 309–320;

Rudolf Gregor, "Friedrich Bodenstedts Beitrag zum deutschen Lermontovbild," *Zeitschrift für Slawistik,* 14 (1969): 224–232;

Max Grube, *Aus der Geschichte der Meininger* (Stuttgart: Deutsche Verlags-Anstalt, 1926); translated by Ann Marie Koller as *Max Grube's "The Story of the Meininger"* (Coral Gables, Fla.: University of Miami Press, 1963);

Gerta Heinrich, "Friedrich Bodenstedts Bemühungen um Shakespeares Zeitgenossen," Ph.D. dissertation, University of Vienna, 1950;

Heinz Kindermann, *Theatergeschichte Europas,* volume 7 (Salzburg: Müller, 1974), p. 39;

Robert Koenig, "Zur Erinnerung an den Sänger Mirza-Schaffy," *Daheim,* 38 (May 1892): 536–539;

W. Kreiten, S. J., "Die Lieder des Mirza-Schaffy," *Stimmen aus Maria Laach,* 45 (1892): 496–507;

Alexander Meyer, "Friedrich Bodenstedt," *Jahrbuch der deutschen Shakespeare-Gesellschaft,* 28 (1893): 338;

Richard Meyer, *Die deutsche Literatur des 19. und 20. Jahrhunderts* (Berlin: Bondi, 1923), pp. 315–318;

Johannes Mundhenk, *Friedrich Bodenstedt und Mirza Schaffy in der aserbeidschanischen Literaturwissenschaft* (Hamburg: Buske, 1971);

Robert Prutz, *Die deutsche Literatur der Gegenwart 1848–1858,* volume 1 (Leipzig: Günther, 1870), pp. 220–226;

Horst Rappich, "Bemerkungen über I. S. Turgenevs und F. Bodenstedts Beziehungen zu Shakespeare und zur 'Deutschen Shakespeare-Gesellschaft,' " *Zeitschrift für Anglistik und Amerikanistik,* 11 (1963): 386–394;

Rappich, "Friedrich Bodenstedt: Ein Bahnbrecher für die Kenntnis Rußlands in Deutschland," *Wissenschaftliche Zeitschrift der Humboldt-Universität zu Berlin,* 12 (1963): 697–703;

Rappich, "Friedrich Bodenstedts Bedeutung als Vermittler russischen Kulturgutes in Deutschland," *Forschungen und Fortschritt,* 37 (1963): 280–283;

Rappich, "Friedrich Bodenstedts literarische Beziehungen zu Rußland," *Zeitschrift für Slawistik,* 8 (1963): 582–594;

Mária Rózsa, "Friedrich Bodenstedts Mittlerrolle in der ersten ungarischen Onegin-Übertragung von Károly Bérczy," *Germanistisches Jahrbuch DDR-UVR,* 8 (1989): 166–179;

Eduard Stemplinger, ed., *Der Münchener Kreis* (Leipzig: Reclam, 1933);

Stemplinger, ed., *Nachromantiker: Kinkel, Redwitz, Roquette, Carrière, Bodenstedt, Schack* (Leipzig: Reclam, 1938), pp. 5–10, 88–91;

Kurt Sundermeyer, *Friedrich Bodenstedt und die "Lieder des Mirza-Schaffy"* (Wilhelmshaven: Stecker, 1930);

Alfred von der Heydt, "Friedrich Bodenstedt in Amerika und sein Buch 'Vom Atlantischen zum Stillen Ozean,' " Ph.D. dissertation, Cornell University, 1949;

Bertha von Suttner, *Memoirs of Bertha von Suttner: The Records of an Eventful Life,* volume 1 (Boston & London: Ginn, 1910), pp. 308–309;

Aubertine Woodward [pseudonym of Auber Forestier], "The Songs of Mirza Schaffi," *Lippincott's,* 17 (March 1876): 367–378;

Eugen Zabel, "Krim und Kaukasus in literarischer Beleuchtung," *Deutsche Rundschau,* 116 (July–September 1903): 99–120;

Ernst Ziel, "Friedrich Bodenstedt," in *Literarische Reliefs: Dichterportraits* (Leipzig: Hoppe, 1895), pp. 195–212.

Papers:

The Volksbildungsamt (National Education Office) in Peine has Friedrich von Bodenstedt's calendar for 1880, with copious notes on his tour of America, and his Munich diary from February 1855 to April 1865. The Hessische Landesbibliothek (Hessian Provincial Library) in Wiesbaden has letters to the editors of the *Tägliche Rundschau* and the *Wacht am Rhein,* a manuscript for the first three cantos of *Sakuntala,* and a photograph of Bodenstedt with an autograph. The Milton Stover Eisenhower Library of Johns Hopkins University has 102 letters from Bodenstedt to his publisher Hermann Costenoble and photostatic copies of letters to various individuals.

Felix Dahn

(9 February 1834 – 3 January 1912)

Siegfried Mews
University of North Carolina at Chapel Hill

BOOKS: *Entgegnung auf die Schrift, "Das anthropologische
System der Philosophie, von Carl Prantl: In seinem
historischen und innern Zusammenhang, sowie in Bezug
auf die Religion gewürdigt. Augsburg, 1852"*
(Munich: Kaiser, 1852);

Harald und Theano: Gedicht (Berlin: Herbig, 1855);

*Über die Wirkung der Klagverjährung bei Obligationen:
Inaugural-Dissertation* (Munich: Kaiser, 1855);

Gedichte (Berlin: Herbig, 1857); republished as *Jugend-
Gedichte* (Leipzig: Breitkopf & Härtel, 1891);

*Studien zur Geschichte der germanischen Gottes-Urtheile:
Habilitations-Schrift* (Munich: Kaiser, 1857);

*Fest-Hymne zur Feier der Gründung Münchens im 700.
Jahre der Stadt* (Munich: Franz, 1858);

Die Könige der Germanen, 12 volumes (volumes 1–2,
Munich: Fleischmann, 1861; volumes 3–5,
Würzburg: Stuber, 1866–1871; volumes 6–12,
Leipzig: Breitkopf & Härtel, 1894–1909) –
comprises volume 1, *Die Zeit der Wanderung;
Die Vandalen* (1861); volume 2, *Die kleineren
gothischen Völker, Die Ostgothen* (1861); volume
3, *Verfassung des ostgothischen Reiches in Italien*
(1866); volume 4, *Die Edicte der Könige Theoderich und Athalarich; das gothische Recht im gothischen Reich* (1866); volume 5, *Die politische
Geschichte der Westgothen* (1878); volume 6, *Die
Verfassung der Westgothen; Das Reich der Sueven in
Spanien* (1870); volume 7, *Die Franken unter den
Merovingern*, 3 volumes (1894–1895); volume
8, *Die Franken unter den Karolingern*, 6 volumes
(1897–1900); volume 9, part 1, *Die Alamannen*
(1902); part 2, *Die Baiern* (1905); volume 10,
Die Thüringe (1907); volume 11, *Die Burgunden*
(1908); volume 12, *Die Langobarden* (1909);

*Prokopius von Cäsarea: Ein Beitrag zur Historiographie
der Völkerwanderung und des sinkenden Römerthums*
(Berlin: Mittler, 1865);

*Das Kriegsrecht: Kurze, volksthümliche Darstellung für
Jedermann zumal für den deutschen Soldaten*
(Würzburg: Stuber, 1870);

Felix Dahn

Macte Imperator! Heil dem Kaiser: Gedicht (Berlin: Mittler, 1871);

Die Schlacht von Sedan: Gedicht (Würzburg: Stahel,
1871);

*Alma Mater! Gedicht zum vierhundertjährigen Jubiläum
der Hochschule München* (Munich: Kaiser, 1872);

Gedichte: Zweite Sammlung, 2 volumes (Stuttgart:
Cotta, 1873);

*Sind Götter? Die Halfred Sigskaldsaga: Eine nordische
Erzählung aus dem zehnten Jahrhundert* (Stuttgart:

25

Cotta, 1874); translated by Sophie F. E.
Veitch as *Saga of Halfred the Sigskald: A Northern
Tale of the Tenth Century* (Paisley: Gardner,
1886);

*Westgothische Studien: Entstehungsgeschichte, Privatrecht,
Strafrecht, Civil- und Straf-Proceß und Gesammt-
kritik der Lex Visigothorum* (Würzburg: Stahel,
1874);

*Deutsche Treue: Ein vaterländisches Schauspiel in fünf
Aufzügen* (Leipzig: Breitkopf & Härtel, 1875);

Handelsrechtliche Vorträge (Leipzig: Breitkopf & Härtel, 1875);

König Roderich: Ein Trauerspiel in fünf Aufzügen (Leipzig: Hartknoch, 1875);

*Markgraf Rüdeger von Bechelaren: Ein Trauerspiel in 5
Aufzügen* (Leipzig: Breitkopf & Härtel, 1875);

Zwölf Balladen (Leipzig: Breitkopf & Härtel, 1875);

Die Amalungen: Ein Gedicht (Leipzig: Breitkopf & Härtel, 1876);

Ein Kampf um Rom: Historischer Roman (4 volumes,
Leipzig: Breitkopf & Härtel, 1876; 2 volumes,
New York: Munro, 1882); translated by Lily
Wolffsohn as *A Struggle for Rome*, 3 volumes
(London: Bentley, 1878);

Langobardische Studien, 2 volumes (Leipzig: Breitkopf
& Härtel, 1876) — comprises volume 1, *Paulus
Diaconus*; volume 2, *Des Paulus Diaconus Leben
und Schriften*;

*Deutsches Rechtsbuch: Ein Spiegel des heutigen bürgerli-
chen Rechts in Deutschland* (Nördlingen: Beck,
1877);

Fehde-Gang und Rechts-Gang der Germanen (Berlin:
Habel, 1877);

Die Staatskunst der Frau'n: Ein Lustspiel in 3 Aufzügen
(Leipzig: Breitkopf & Härtel, 1877);

Balladen und Lieder (Leipzig: Breitkopf & Härtel,
1878);

*Deutsches Privatrecht (mit Lehen-, Handels-, Wechsel- und
Seerecht): Grundriß* (Leipzig: Breitkopf & Härtel, 1878);

Kämpfende Herzen: Drei Erzählungen (Berlin: Janke,
1878); translated by Joseph B. Hare as "Goodhearts," in *Goodhearts; Schoolteacher's Marie: A
Delineation of a Rural Romance* (Louisville, Ky.:
Standard Printing Co., 1935);

Bausteine: Gesammelte kleine Schriften, 8 volumes (Berlin: Janke, 1879–1884);

Sühne: Schauspiel in fünf Aufzügen (Leipzig: Breitkopf
& Härtel, 1879);

Die Vernunft im Recht: Grundlagen der Rechtsphilosophie
(Berlin: Janke, 1879);

*Die Alamannenschlacht bei Straßburg, 357 n. Chr.: Eine
Studie* (Brunswick: Westermann, 1880);

Armin: Operndichtung in 4 Aufzügen, music by Heinrich
Carl Johann Hofmann (Leipzig: Breitkopf &
Härtel, 1880)

Der Fremdling: Operndichtung in 4 Aufzügen (Leipzig:
Breitkopf & Härtel, 1880);

Harald und Theano: Operndichtung in 4 Aufzügen (Leipzig: Breitkopf & Härtel, 1880);

*Odhin's Trost: Ein nordischer Roman aus dem elften Jahr-
hundert* (Leipzig: Breitkopf & Härtel, 1880);

*Der Schmied von Gretna-Green: Operndichtung in drei
Aufzügen* (Leipzig: Breitkopf & Härtel, 1880);

Urgeschichte der germanischen und romanischen Völker, 4
volumes (Berlin: Grote, 1881–1889);

Kleine Romane aus der Völkerwanderung, 13 volumes
(Leipzig: Breitkopf & Härtel, 1882–1901) —
comprises volume 1, *Felicitas: Historischer
Roman (a. 476 n. Chr.)* (1882); translated by
M.A.C.E. as *Felicitas: A Tale of the German
Migrations, A.D. 476* (London: Macmillan,
1883); translated by Mary J. Safford as *Felicitas: A Romance* (New York: Gottsberger, 1883);
volume 2, *Bissula: Historischer Roman aus der Völkerwanderung (a. 378 n. Chr.)* (1883); translated
by Safford as *A Captive of the Roman Eagles* (Chicago: McClurg, 1902); volume 3, *Gelimer:
Historischer Roman aus der Völkerwanderung (a.
534 n. Chr.)* (1883); translated by Safford as
The Scarlet Banner (Chicago: McClurg, 1903);
volume 4, *Die schlimmen Nonnen von Poitiers:
Historischer Roman aus der Völkerwanderung*
(1885); volume 5, *Fredigundis: Historischer
Roman aus der Völkerwanderung* (1886); volume
6, *Attila: Historischer Roman aus der Völkerwanderung (a 453 n. Chr.)* (1886); translated anonymously as *Attila the Hun: A Novel* (New York:
Minerva, 1891); volume 7, *Die Bataver: Historischer Roman aus der Völkerwanderung (a. 69 n.
Chr.)* (1887); volume 8, *Chlodovech: Historischer
Roman aus der Völkerwanderung* (1895); volume
9, *Vom Chiemgau: Historischer Roman aus der Völkerwanderung (a. 596 n. Chr.)* (1896); volume
10, *Ebroin: Historischer Roman aus der Völkerwanderung* (1896); volume 11, *Am Hof Herrn Karls:
Vier Erzählungen* (1900); volume 12, *Stilicho:
Historischer Roman aus der Völkerwanderung*
(1900); volume 13, *Der Vater und die Söhne:
Historischer Roman aus der Völkerwanderung*
(1901);

Skalden-Kunst: Schauspiel in drei Aufzügen (Leipzig:
Breitkopf & Härtel, 1882);

Das Weib im altgermanischen Recht und Leben (Prague:
Deutscher Verein, 1882);

Deutsche Geschichte, 2 volumes (Gotha: Perthes,
1883–1888);

Der Kurier nach Paris: Lustspiel in 5 Aufzügen (Leipzig: Breitkopf & Härtel, 1883);

Eine Lanze für Rumänien: Eine völkerrechtliche und geschichtliche Betrachtung (Leipzig: Breitkopf & Härtel, 1883);

Die Kreuzfahrer: Erzählung aus dem dreizehnten Jahrhundert, 2 volumes (Berlin: Janke, 1884; New York: Munro, 1885);

Walhall: Germanische Götter- und Heldensagen. Für alt und jung am deutschen Herd erzählt, by Dahn and Therese Dahn (Kreuznach: Voigtländer, 1884);

Bis zum Tode getreu: Erzählung aus der Zeit Karls des Großn (Leipzig: Breitkopf & Härtel, 1887);

Was ist die Liebe? Erzählung (Leipzig: Breitkopf & Härtel, 1887); translated by Kannida as *What is Love?* (Chicago, 1892);

Frigga's Ja: Erzählung (Leipzig: Breitkopf & Härtel, 1888);

Vale Imperator! Leb wohl nun, Kaiser Wilhelm! und Heil Dir, mein Kaiser Friedrich! 2 Gedichte (Leipzig: Breitkopf & Härtel, 1888);

Die Landnot der Germanen (Leipzig: Duncker & Humblot, 1889);

Skirnir: Erzählung (Leipzig: Breitkopf & Härtel, 1889);

Prüfungsaufgaben aus dem deutschen Privatrecht, Handels-, See- und Wechselrecht: Anhang zum Grundriß des deutschen Privatrechts, Handels-, See- und Wechselrechts (Leipzig: Breitkopf & Härtel, 1889);

Welt-Untergang: Geschichtliche Erzählung aus dem Jahre 1000 nach Christus (Leipzig: Breitkopf & Härtel, 1889);

Erinnerungen, 5 volumes (Leipzig: Breitkopf & Härtel, 1890–1895);

Die letzten Goten: Geschichtliche Erzählung (Frankfurt am Main: Diesterweg, 1890); translated anonymously as *The Last of the Vandals* (New York: Minerva, 1891);

Moltke: Festspiel zur Feier des 90. Geburtstags des Feldmarschalls Grafen Hellmuth Moltke (Leipzig: Breitkopf & Härtel, 1890);

Moltkelied: Dichtung von Felix Dahn. Deutsch-patriotisches Volkslied für einstimmigen Massenchor mit charakteristischem Vor- und Nachspiel, music by Hinrich N. Hoft (Munich: Hoft, 1890);

Odhins Rache: Erzählung (Leipzig: Breitkopf & Härtel, 1891);

Rolandin: Erzählung in Versen (Leipzig: Breitkopf & Härtel, 1891);

Der Entwurf eines Gesetzes über die Volksschule in Preußen: Betrachtungen (Breslau: Schlesische Buchdruckerei, 1892; New York: Stechert, 1892);

Fürst Bismarck: Rede gegeben bei'm Bismarck-Commers der national liberalen Vereinigung Nordwest zu Frankfurt am Main am 31. März 1892 (Leipzig: Breitkopf & Härtel, 1892);

Gedichte: Vierte Sammlung, by Dahn and Therese Dahn (Leipzig: Breitkopf & Härtel, 1892);

Gedichte, fünfte Sammlung: Vaterland (Leipzig: Breitkopf & Härtel, 1892);

Moltke als Erzieher: Allerlei Betrachtungen. Nebst Anhang: Betrachtungen über den Entwurf eines Volksschulgesetzes in Preußen (Breslau: Schlesische Buchdruckerei, 1892);

Die Finnin: Erzählung (Leipzig: Breitkopf & Härtel, 1893);

Julian der Abtrünnige: Geschichtlicher Roman, 3 volumes (Leipzig: Breitkopf & Härtel, 1893);

Gratulationsgedichte gelegentlich der fünfzigjährigen Jubelfeier der Altherthumsgesellschaft Prussia 1844–1894, by Dahn, Ernst Wichert, and L. Goldoni (Königsberg: Beyer, 1894);

Macte senex consiliator! Heil Dir, alter Rathschlag-Finder! Gedicht (Leipzig: Breitkopf & Härtel, 1894);

Über den Begriff des Rechts: Ein Beitrag zur Rechtsphilosophie (Leipzig: Breitkopf & Härtel, 1895);

Zum achtzigsten Geburtstag des Fürsten Bismarck (Breslau: Schlesiche Buchdruckerei, 1895);

Sämtliche Werke poetischen Inhalts, 21 volumes (Leipzig: Breitkopf & Härtel, 1898–1899);

Sigwalt und Sigridh: Eine nordische Erzählung (frei erfunden) (Leipzig: Breitkopf & Härtel, 1898);

Fünfzig Jahre: Ein Festspiel in 3 Bildern (Leipzig: Breitkopf & Härtel, 1902);

Herzog Ernst von Schwaben: Erzählungen aus dem elften Jahrhundert (Leipzig: Breitkopf & Härtel, 1902);

Meine wälschen Ahnen: Kleine Erzählungen (Leipzig: Breitkopf & Härtel, 1903);

Sämtliche Werke poetischen Inhalts: Neue Folge, 4 volumes (Leipzig: Breitkopf & Härtel, 1903);

Die Germanen: Volkstümliche Darstellungen aus Geschichte, Recht, Wirtschaft und Kultur (Leipzig: Breitkopf & Härtel, 1905);

Zur Kunde deutscher Vorzeit: Aufsätze, by Dahn and Gustav Freytag (Berlin: Neelmeyer, 1906);

Armin der Cherusker: Erinnerungen an die Varusschlacht im Jahre 9 nach Christus (Munich: Lehmann, 1909);

Gesammelte Werke: Erzählende und poetische Schriften. Neue wohlfeile Gesamtausgabe, 16 volumes (Leipzig: Breitkopf & Härtel, 1912);

Gesammelte Werke: Erzählende und poetische Schriften. Neue Gesamtausgabe, 10 volumes (Leipzig: Breitkopf & Härtel, 1921–1924).

OTHER: Johann Kaspar Bluntschli, *Deutsches Privatrecht*, third edition, enlarged by Dahn (Munich & Stuttgart: Cotta, 1864);

Eduard Karl August Wilhelm von Wietersheim, ed., *Geschichte der Völkerwanderung*, 2 volumes, revised by Dahn (Leipzig: Weigel, 1880–1881);

Karl August von Hase, *Liederbuch des deutschen Volkes*, edited by Dahn, Carl Hase, and Carl Reinecke (Leipzig: Breitkopf & Härtel, 1883);

Ludwig Steub, *Mein Leben*, afterword by Dahn (Breslau: Schottländer, 1884);

Therese Dahn, *Kaiser Karl und seine Paladine: Sagen aus dem Kerlingischen Kreise der deutschen Jugend erzählt*, introduction by Dahn (Leipzig: Breitkopf & Härtel, 1887);

Carl Count Brandis, *Die Blumen-Monde: 12 Bilder nach der Natur photographiert*, poems by Dahn and Therese Dahn (Vienna: Lechner, 1891);

Germanistische Abhandlungen zum LXX. Geburtstag Konrad von Maurers, edited by Dahn, Oskar Brenner, Carl Gareis, Wolfgang Golther, K. B. M. Olsen, Axel Petersen, Vilhelm Adolf Secher, and Philipp Zorn (Göttingen: Dieterich, 1893);

"Mein Erstling: 'Harald und Theano,'" in *Die Geschichte des Erstlingswerks: Selbstbiographische Aufsätze* (Berlin: Concordia, 1894);

Allgemeines Reichs-Commersbuch für deutsche Studenten, edited by Dahn, Max Rauprich, and Reinecke (Leipzig: Breitkopf & Härtel, 1895);

Bruno Garlepp, *Unseres Bismarck Heimgang: Ein Trauertag All-Deutschlands*, introductory poem by Dahn (Akron, Ohio & New York: Werner, 1898);

Wandbilder zur deutschen Götter- und Sagenwelt, 2 volumes, texts by Dahn and Therese Dahn (Halle: Buchhandlung des Waisenhauses, 1904–1906).

SELECTED PERIODICAL PUBLICATIONS – UNCOLLECTED: "Haus und Wohnung," by Dahn and Josef Lentner, *Bavaria: Landes- und Volkskunde des Königreichs Bayern*, 2 (1863): 777–784;

"Reinhardt und Fatme: Erzählung aus der Zeit der Kreuzzüge," *Deutsche-Roman-Zeitung*, 15, no. 3 (1878).

Felix Dahn is traditionally considered one of the chief representatives of the Professorenroman (archaeological novel), a subgenre of the historical novel that flourished briefly during the latter half of the nineteenth century. Unlike the American and British campus, college, or university novel (terms used synonymously), the Professorenroman derives its designation not from the college milieu, the place of action in college novels, but from the profession of its practitioners, who wrote fiction on topics based on their academic research and scholarly pursuits. Although frequently dismissed by critics as overly pedantic and lacking in imagination, Professorenromane generally proved popular with the German reading public. *Ein Kampf um Rom* (1876; translated as *A Struggle for Rome*, 1878), Dahn's major work, has been in print since its publication and has attracted readers ranging from teenagers of both sexes thirsting for adventure and heroic deeds to such eminent authors as Nobelist Gerhart Hauptmann and perennial Nobel Prize-candidate Günter Grass. To dismiss Dahn as a merely popular author and a literary lightweight also is to ignore another dimension of his voluminous output of fiction. Dahn made use of the contradictory impulses of the historical novel in that he both offered a reconstruction of the past and infused his texts with nineteenth-century ideology. This ideology has been characterized as a variant of "politischer Germanismus" (political Germanism), an intellectual current that Dahn shared with illustrious contemporaries such as Richard Wagner and that sought, especially after the Reichsgründung (founding of the empire) in 1871, both to justify and to promote nationalistic goals by implicitly or explicitly postulating an unbroken historical continuity extending from the Völkerwanderung (migration of the Germanic tribes) to the Bismarckian national state, the Reich.

Felix Ludwig Sophus Dahn was born on 9 February 1834 in Hamburg as the first child of Friedrich and Constanze Dahn, née Le Gaye, both of whom were actors at the Hamburg Stadttheater. In March 1834 the family moved to Munich, where both parents became pillars of the Hoftheater, the theater of the Bavarian royal court. A precocious child, Dahn received his initial schooling from a private tutor; his voracious reading in world history, which he began at an early age, later enabled him to achieve in his novels a high degree of authenticity with regard to the historical milieu in general and the details of battles in particular. In the first volume of his *Erinnerungen* (Memoirs, 1890–1895) Dahn fondly recalls the Ritterspiele (knights' games) that he and his playmates staged in the large garden of the Dahns' first Munich residence near the Englische Garten, a vast park in the English garden style. These games, Dahn claims, were imaginative re-creations of battles he had read about. In 1842 the eight-year-old Dahn entered the Lateinschule, the first stage of secondary school. After an undistinguished beginning that was marred by his fear of failure, Dahn proved to be an excellent student at the gymnasium, the second stage of secondary school. He attended the gymnasium from 1845 to 1850 and left with the Zeugnis der Reife (certificate of maturity), the prerequisite for enrolling at a university.

The sixteen-year-old Dahn's joy over leaving school was spoiled by the death of his best friend, Julius Grieß, in August 1850 and the divorce of his parents in September of the same year. Dahn remained with his father. The divorce had a profound effect on his outlook and reinforced his solitary, ascetic study habits and rigorous work ethic. The separation also robbed the budding writer, who had begun composing poems in his early teens, not only of his protected environment but also of an immediate source of inspiration for his future poetry and fiction; he was particularly attracted by the pathos of Friedrich Schiller's dramas, which were frequently produced at the Hoftheater. Dahn's father, an actor in the solemn and idealistic Schillerian mold, and his vivacious mother had tended to rehearse their roles at home, providing lessons for Dahn on how to present a text effectively onstage.

At the University of Munich Dahn studied law, history, and philosophy. In 1851 his beloved philosophy professor Karl Eduard von Prantl was attacked in a pamphlet by a Catholic priest who denounced Prantl's anthropological system as incommensurable with Catholic dogma, morality, and loyalty to the Bavarian king. The seventeen-year-old Dahn rose to Prantl's defense with *Entgegnung auf die Schrift, "Das anthropologische System der Philosophie, von Carl Prantl: In seinem historischen und innern Zusammenhang, sowie in Bezug auf die Religion gewürdigt. Augsburg, 1852"* (Response to the Treatise "The Anthropological System of Carl Prantl's Philosophy: Considered in Its Historical and Internal Connections, as well as in Reference to Religion. Augsburg, 1852"), published in 1852, which expressed his vehement opposition to what he considered the Catholic church's insatiable ambition to dominate nations and states. This opposition inspired many of Dahn's subsequent works of fiction.

To remove his son from the center of the Prantl controversy, the elder Dahn insisted that he continue his studies in Berlin, the capital of Prussia. In Berlin, where Dahn studied from 1852 to 1853, he was invited to attend the meetings of the literary society "Tunnel über der Spree" (Tunnel above the [River] Spree); its participants included Theodor

Fontane, a balladeer and a future novelist of the first rank. Under Fontane's influence Dahn developed a preference for the heroic-historical ballad. He also frequented the salon of Charlotte Birch-Pfeiffer, a well-known actress and author of popular sentimental plays; he was briefly engaged to her daughter Minna, who, as Wilhelmine von Hillern, was to attract considerable attention as the author of suspenseful and sentimental novels.

After his return to Munich, Dahn passed his law examinations with distinction in 1854 and served his two-year internship at lower courts, first at the königliches Landgericht (Royal Provincial Court) and then at the königliches Stadtgericht (Royal City Court) in Munich. In 1855 he successfully defended his doctoral dissertation; in the same year his first literary publication, *Harald und Theano*, appeared. Dedicated to Friedrich Rückert, whom Dahn considered one of his chief models in the use of poetic language, the verse epic was not successful in terms of sales. *Harald und Theano* displays several characteristic Dahnian thematic features: set in Cyprus, then an East Roman territory, at the beginning of the fourth century A.D., the epic depicts the struggle between the hedonism prevalent in Greco-Roman antiquity on the one hand and the denial of the flesh characteristic of Christianity on the other. The general context of the Völkerwanderung provides the background for the clash between the forces of the declining Roman Empire and the barbaric but heroic and morally superior Germanic tribes. Harald and his band of Saxon marauders land on Cyprus and nobly save the persecuted Christians. Harald falls in love with Theano, the sister of the island's governor; as a consequence he is treacherously murdered by her brother. The Saxons wreak terrible revenge on the Greco-Romans and return home with the corpse of their leader; Theano turns Christian and sets out for the far north to do missionary work.

In December 1856 Dahn passed his bar examination with such excellent results that he felt encouraged to pursue an academic career. After completing his inaugural dissertation, *Studien zur Geschichte der germanischen Gottes-Urtheile* (Studies on the History of Germanic Divine Judgments), in the following year, he became a Privatdozent (unsalaried university lecturer) with little prospect of obtaining a salaried professorship. The necessity of making a living by means of hackwork — particularly after his 1858 marriage to Sophie Fries, a painter and daughter of a wealthy Munich family — and the desire to establish a publishing record to boost his scholarly credentials impeded his literary

Manuscript for Dahn's hymn praising the emperor (Volk und Wissen Archiv, Berlin)

efforts from approximately the late 1850s to the late 1860s. The publication in 1857 of Dahn's *Gedichte* (Poems), a collection of love lyrics addressed to a youthful platonic love, ballads on historical topics, and didactic poems, did nothing to alleviate his financial woes. As a consequence, he suspended work on what was to become his magnum opus, *Ein Kampf um Rom.*

Yet Dahn was not devoid of literary contacts. He exchanged ideas with his friend Josef Viktor von Scheffel, a fellow jurist and an author of popular historical novels. He also attended the meetings of the literary association Das Krokodil (The Crocodile), whose most prominent members were the poet Emanuel Geibel, acknowledged by Dahn as one of his models in matters of poetic form, and the future Nobelist Paul Heyse. Dahn's scholarly endeavors bore fruit in 1861, when the first two volumes of his work on the historical development of the constitutional law of the Germanic tribes, *Die Könige der Germanen* (The Kings of the Germanic Tribes), were published.

In part as a result of his unenviable financial situation, in 1862 Dahn began suffering from physical and mental exhaustion; he took an extended journey to northern Italy to restore his health. During this journey he was exposed to the fervor of Italian nationalism and the Italian unification movement, and his own nationalist feelings came to the fore. As a southern German – albeit the son of a Prussian father – Dahn initially supported Austria as the power most likely to accomplish German unification. But in view of Austria's opposition to Italian unification in 1861, Dahn's position gradually changed to favor Prussia. In 1863 he was appointed außerordentlicher Professor (university lecturer) at the University of Würzburg; two years later he was promoted to ordentlicher Professor (professor). While in Würzburg, Dahn witnessed a battle between the Austrians and the Prussians during the 1866 war; the defeat of Austria and allied Bavaria in that war constituted a further element that induced Dahn to shift from "großdeutsch" (supporting German unification including Austria) to "kleindeutsch" (advocating unification under the leadership of Prussia and excluding Austria). The latter position necessarily involved acceptance of Prussian chancellor Otto von Bismarck's unification policy, to be carried out "mit Eisen und Blut" (with iron and blood).

In 1867 Dahn met Therese von Droste-Hülshoff, a niece of the writer Annette von Droste-Hülshoff. He fell in love with her and underwent a painful separation in 1869 from his wife. At the outbreak of the Franco-Prussian War, Dahn volunteered, but he was turned down by both the Bavarian and Prussian armies. Dahn, who repeatedly expressed in *Erinnerungen* his preference for the career of an officer rather than that of a scholar and writer, was not content with aiding the war effort by writing patriotic poems but longed to serve his country in the heroic mode of his fictional protagonists, and he joined the campaign as a Red Cross nurse. The centrality Dahn attributed to his participation in the Franco-Prussian War may be gathered from his devoting nearly four hundred pages in *Erinnerungen*, which covers the years from 1834 to 1888, to a time span of less than two months (August to September 1870). Dahn frequently polemicizes against the anti-German sentiments allegedly expressed in Emile Zola's *La Débâcle* (1892; translated as *The Debacle*, 1972), a fictional account of the war, and endeavors to set the record straight. Dahn briefly became a combatant in the Battle of Sedan on 1 September 1870. He compared this battle, which ended with the surrender of the French army and the capture of French emperor Napoleon III by the Germans, to the grandeur of a Shakespearean drama; he celebrated it in an independently published poem, *Die Schlacht von Sedan* (The Battle of Sedan, 1871). The second volume of Dahn's *Gedichte* (1873) and his *Balladen und Lieder* (Ballads and Songs, 1878) also include poems on the battle.

In 1873 Dahn's divorce became final, he was appointed professor of law at the University of Königsberg (today Kaliningrad, Russia), and he married Therese von Droste-Hülshoff. The vivacious Bavarian Dahn's first impression of Königsberg — whose claim to scholarly fame derived from its former lifelong resident, the philosopher Immanuel Kant — and East Prussia were hardly flattering. He called the province on Germany's border with Russia and its inhabitants "recht undeutsch, barbarisch und Kulturarm" (rather un-German, barbaric, and lacking in culture). Yet the fifteen years Dahn was to spend at Königsberg were among the most productive in his life: he had approximately twenty volumes of schol-

arly writings published and wrote or completed most of his major literary works — including his dramas, which frequently premiered at the Königsberg Stadttheater — during his tenure at the East Prussian university.

In 1874 *Sind Götter? Die Halfred Sigskaldsaga* (Do Gods Exist? The Saga of Halfred Sigskald), subtitled *Eine nordische Erzählung aus dem zehnten Jahrhundert* (Nordic Story from the Tenth Century), appeared. This short prose text offers an expression of what Dahn termed his tragic-heroic and anti-Christian weltanschauung in fictional guise, a weltanschauung that he had begun developing in the 1850s. Despite the fairy-tale elements used, Dahn implicitly suggests the authenticity of the saga by introducing two scribes as narrators. The first narrator records the deeds of his father, Halfred, a hero and poet-singer, or Skalde (skald). Halfred increasingly doubts the existence of the heathen gods because they do nothing to prevent the suffering and deaths of innocents. Ultimately he denies the gods' existence; he carries his loss of faith to the extreme of becoming an outcast and murdering those who continue to profess their religion. He dies from wounds inadvertently inflicted by his own son, a Christian. The son adopts Halfred's stance of disbelief and writes the story of his father's life. The second narrator, the abbot of the monastery in which Halfred's son was brought up, completes the latter's manuscript as a cautionary tale for godless sinners. The abbot relates that Halfred's son became a formidable leader in battle who fiercely fought the spreading of Christianity; he died proclaiming his heroic self-reliance and rejecting the rites of both heathen and Christian priests. *Sind Götter?*, attacked by Christian critics as the work of an atheist, pertains to the complex of Nordic mythology that, next to the Völkerwanderung, provided an important source of inspiration for Dahn.

The tragedy *König Roderich* (King Roderic, 1875) deals with the baleful influence of the Catholic church on affairs of state. Roderich, eighth-century king of the Visigoths in Spain, is thwarted in his efforts to defeat the invading Moors by the treasonous activities of the kingdom's bishops who, fearing for their privileges, have allied themselves with the Moors. Roderich dies on the battlefield; but in an act of poetic justice the victorious Moors sentence the bishops to death for their treachery. Although Dahn denies any connection of his drama with the so-called Prussian Kulturkampf (Bismarck's efforts, beginning in 1872, to suppress or reduce the influence of the Catholic church in the civic sphere in general and in educational policy in particular), the tragedy's dedication "Dem Deutschen Reiche" (To the German Empire) enhanced rather than dispelled the impression of its partisan tendentiousness. Because of its topicality the drama had successful runs in many Protestant cities in Germany, but its success proved to be ephemeral.

A more optimistic outlook concerning the future of the Reich is evident in the tragedy *Markgraf Rüdeger von Bechelaren* (Margrave Rüdeger of Bechelaren, 1875), a treatment of the second part of the anonymous twelfth-century *Nibelungenlied* (translated as *The Nibelungenlied*, 1965, 1984), then considered the German national epic. Margrave Rüdeger is torn between his affection for the Burgundians and his obligations toward his lieges Krimhild, the widow of Siegfried, and Attila, the king of the Huns. He perishes in the general slaughter that ensues after the Huns' insidious attack on the valiant Burgundians. In the end Dietrich von Bern, the king of the Ostrogoths (who in *Ein Kampf um Rom* appears as Theodoric the Great), restores peace by delivering the evil but heroic Hagen, the murderer of Siegfried, into Krimhild's hands. In his most radical departure from the *Nibelungenlied* Dahn added a "heldenhaft-germanisch-patriotisch" (heroic-Germanic-patriotic) ending: Dietrich von Bern liberates the Germanic tribes from the yoke of the Huns and becomes uncontested ruler "für der Germanen Volk" (for the Germanic people). This patriotic ending establishes Dietrich von Bern as a kind of precursor of the newly established Reich. Although the play was staged repeatedly – in the Munich production Dahn's father and his father's second wife, Marie Dahn-Hausmann, played major roles – it ultimately suffered from comparison with more comprehensive and complex treatments of the subject: Friedrich Hebbel's three-part tragedy *Die Nibelungen* (1862; translated as *The Niebelungs*, 1903) and, above all, Richard Wagner's tetralogy *Der Ring des Nibelungen* (1853; translated as *The Ring of the Nibelung*, 1976). Dahn – who was invited by King Ludwig II of Bavaria to be present at the 1876 Bayreuth premiere of the *Ring* – considered Wagner's work highly evocative of the German spirit, even if he found fault with its dramatic structure.

Deutsche Treue (German Loyalty, 1875) is another drama in a patriotic vein. It takes place in 920, at the beginning of the reign of Heinrich I. The powerful dukes of Bavaria and Suebia refuse to recognize Heinrich; as a consequence the dangers of fratricidal fighting and foreign invasion loom large. Heinrich prevails in the end and achieves both internal unity and victory against external enemies – a policy that, in essence, had been followed by Bismarck during the Franco-Prussian War. While the play clearly reflects the patriotic sentiments of the day, it was not universally acclaimed. Theodor Fontane noted the play's tendentiousness and remarked that the predictability of its positive outcome and the absence of genuine human conflict detracted from its artistic merit.

None of Dahn's works achieved the popular success of *Ein Kampf um Rom*, his most voluminous and significant novel. Dahn began to write *Ein Kampf um Rom* in Munich in 1859, continued it during his 1862 stay at Ravenna, the site of Theodoric the Great's mausoleum, and completed it in Königsberg after his wife persuaded him not to toss the manuscript into the fire in a bout of depression over his skills as an author. In epic breadth but with a keen eye for dramatic effects, Dahn depicts the Ostrogoths' struggle against the Romans and Byzantines from the death of Theodoric in 526 to their defeat and expulsion from Italy in 553.

Dahn essentially follows the sources he used for *Die Könige der Germanen* and his treatise on the Byzantine historian Procopius, *Prokopius von Cäsarea* (Procopius of Caesarea, 1865), but he concentrates on diplomatic and military history to the virtual exclusion of social and economic developments. The external structuring device is formed by the seven books that are named after the six Gothic kings and one queen who reigned from 526 to 552: Theoderich (Theodoric), Athalarich (Athalaric), Amalaswintha (Amalsuintha), Theodahad, Witichis (Vitigis), Totila, and Teja. Under Theoderich's benevolent rule the native population of Italy and the Goths live in peaceful coexistence; but this coexistence is threatened after Theoderich's death. Amalaswintha, Theoderich's daughter, governs the realm for her young son Athalarich. The true Goths oppose her policy of romanization; they are led by the mythic figure of old Hildebrand, who rejects assimilation as weakening the moral fiber and sapping the strengths of the Goths. The kingdom of the Goths is also threatened by the ambitious Cethegus, a fictional figure and a Machiavellian before his time, who is consumed by the desire to restore the grandeur of the Roman Empire. A masterful schemer, he has ingratiated himself with the proud Amalaswintha. He arranges the murder of pro-Gothic king Athalarich and persuades Amalaswintha to relinquish her crown in favor of her cousin Theodahad. Amalaswintha is drowned in a Roman bath by the vengeful, monstrous Gothelindis, Theodahad's wife.

The murder of Amalaswintha, who had been in contact with the Byzantine emperor Justinian, serves as a pretext for the latter to declare war on the Goths. The Byzantine army under the brave and strong but impetuous Belisarius lands in Sicily preparatory to invading the Italian mainland. Belisarius is accompanied by his secretary Prokopius, Dahn's main source, whose reports and letters, quoted by the author, are designed to lend authenticity to the novel and to bear witness to the heroic feats of the Goths. Theodahad is deposed at the Ding, the assembly of the free Goths that is governed by law. The people (that is, the male part of the population) assert their sovereignty in the face of the king's treasonous selling out to the Byzantines and elect as their new king Witichis, a man of humble origins but brave in battle and circumspect in politics. In the interest of legitimating his position and uniting his people in the fight against the combined forces of Belisarius and Cethegus, Witichis consents to separation from his wife, Rauthgundis, and marriage to Mataswintha (Matasuntha), who is Theoderich's granddaughter and, hence, of royal blood. Whereas Rauthgundis, in her devotion to the domestic sphere, to children and husband, represents the Dahnian ideal of womanhood, the beautiful Mataswintha, like many of the novel's major figures, is a one-dimensional character whose hatred of Witichis knows no bounds once she realizes that he still loves his first wife. Mataswintha's treasonous collaboration with Cethegus forces Witichis to lift the siege of Rome, and her burning of the granaries in Ravenna, capital of the Goths, results in Witichis's surrender to Belisarius. After Witichis's perfidious capture and death at the hands of Cethegus, Totila is proclaimed king.

Totila, a blond, blue-eyed young man who is associated with the color white, is by far the most appealing among the figures representing the Goths. He not only restores the Goths' kingdom in Italy by defeating the Byzantines and Cethegus but surpasses Theoderich by extending the boundaries of the realm. Victorious in war, he is magnanimous in peace. Adored as a sun-god whose mild and just rule contrasts strongly with the oppressiveness and exploitation practiced by the Byzantines, he follows Theoderich's policy of reconciliation between the Goths and the native population. This policy finds its symbolic expression in his engagement to Valeria, a noblewoman of Roman extraction. The beautiful and innocent Miriam, a young Jewish woman modeled after Rebecca in Sir Walter Scott's *Ivanhoe* (1819), has paved the way for Totila's happiness by sacrificing her life for him out of unrequited love. Cethegus's scheming at the Byzantine court has succeeded; Empress Theodora, evil incarnate but the real power behind the throne, has persuaded her husband, Justinian, to send a new army, which vastly outnumbers that of the Goths, to Italy. The physically handicapped but brilliant Byzantine general Narses methodically destroys all Gothic strongholds. Totila is forced to retreat; finally, he is defeated in battle and killed through the treachery of a jealous suitor whose advances Valeria had spurned.

Faced with certain defeat, the Goths turn to Teja, who is prepared to lead them to their deaths in a blaze of glory. The dark and sorrowful Teja is in all respects the opposite of the radiant Totila; as a poet-singer he also propounds Dahn's tragic-heroic — but not pessimistic, Dahn insists — worldview that finds its rationale and ultimate justification in the individual's heroic and selfless service to his people and his state. Teja carefully selects the final battleground on Mount Vesuvius, where "der letzte Akt einer großartigen Tragödie der Geschichte" (the last act of a grandiose tragedy of history) takes place. He fights with superhuman effort but is killed by Cethegus. Cethegus also succumbs to his wounds, his utopian dream of restoring Rome's former glory shattered. Yet the remaining Goths' plan to commit mass suicide by jumping into the crater of Mount Vesuvius does not take place, and the novel ends on a positive note of sorts: unexpectedly, and contrary to Dahn's sources, a fleet of Viking ships appears. The battle-weary Narses gives in to the Vikings' demands for the surviving Goths' safe conduct, and the defiant Goths return to northern Europe. They carry with them their dead kings — Teja, on whom Narses deferentially bestows his laurel wreath, and Theoderich, the originator of the Ostrogoths' greatness. Among the survivors are old Hildebrand and the noble young Adalgoth, the respective representatives of the glorious pagan past and the promising future; they provide an indication that despite their crushing defeat the Goths' spirit is unbroken.

Ein Kampf um Rom can be read on various levels. The fast-paced action, the rapid succession of theatrically staged scenes which include many battles, the larger-than-life characters with their single-minded devotion or destructive passions, and the novel's underlying black-and-white pattern that pits the good Goths against the evil Romans and Byzantines appealed to young readers. But Dahn also exploits the potential of the historical novel to endow topical issues with greater significance.

When Dahn began writing the novel in 1858, the constellation of European powers paralleled that of the contending forces in *Ein Kampf um Rom*. In the 1850s Napoleon III supported Italian unification to weaken Austria; Austria was opposed to Italian unification because of its territorial possessions in northern Italy. Thus, the Austrians correspond to the Goths – although, as Dahn remarked, the former lacked the stature of the latter – and Napoleon III corresponds to Justinian, who wants to rid Italy of the Goths so as to reestablish his rule over that country. The driving force behind Justinian's war effort is his wife, Theodora; she is motivated by religious zealotry in that she hopes to be granted forgiveness for her long list of sins through the infidel Goths' annihilation. She is supported by the archdeacon and subsequent pope Silverius, whose aspirations to secular power bring him into conflict with both the Goths and Cethegus, both of whom claim control over Rome and Italy. In the 1850s Pope Pius XI, ruler of a secular state, resisted Italian unification. Just as Silverius was dependent on the support of Justinian and Theodora, so Pius XI relied on Napoleon and his religious wife Eugénie's backing for the autonomy of his territorial possessions.

The initial historical parallel Dahn established between the Austrians and the Goths could not account for the new state of affairs that obtained after the Franco-Prussian War. As an enthusiastic student and scholar of German history and a selfprofessed German patriot, Dahn participated fully in the attempt to legitimate the newly founded Reich by suggesting a questionable historical continuity that extended from the distant, venerable, and heroic Germanic past to the 1870s. The use of a literary text that portrays disunity and ends with the Goths' defeat to lend ideological support to the newly established national unity seems less paradoxical in view of the novel's quasi-optimistic ending. This ending provides an indication that *Ein Kampf um Rom*, according to Dahn, presents merely one phase in the necessary and inevitable struggle between the Germanic and Roman peoples and their successors. Although this struggle, the major theme of Dahn's novels after *Ein Kampf um Rom*, seemed to have been decided in 1870–1871, the unity of the Reich continued to be threatened by ideological and religious divisiveness. Dahn's anachronistic introduction of the Donation of Constantine clearly reveals his partisan stance during the Kulturkampf: the Donation, a forged document from the eighth century allegedly issued by the Roman emperor Constantine the Great in the fourth century, transferred power over Rome and the western half of Constantine's empire to the pope. In the novel the Donation buttresses Silverius's illegitimate claims on Rome; *Ein Kampf um Rom* conveys the implicit message that during the Kulturkampf the Catholic church operated with equally fraudulent claims and that its universalism constituted a threat to national unity.

Dahn's anti-Catholic sentiments result from his militant nationalism, which had its philosophical underpinnings in the fatalistic worldview explicated by Teja. Such a worldview, which substitutes blind fate for the Christian God and declares unstinting service to one's people to be the ultimate goal, is contradicted, however, by Totila's belief in a just God and his policy of reconciling Goths and the native Italian population. These irreconcilable positions may have contributed to the novel's popular success: it afforded readers the possibility of choosing between xenophobic nationalism that demanded sacrifice and heroism, on the one hand, and youthful optimism that posited the gradual overcoming of cultural and national differences, on the other.

Such an ambivalent message is far less evident in Dahn's other works, especially those that originated after 1871. His desire to create "deutsche, nationale Kunst" (German, national art) for the stage is evident in two works dealing with the historical figure of Arminius or Hermann der Cherusker, who defeated the Roman legions in the Teutoburg Forest in A.D. 9 but was subsequently murdered by rival Germanic tribes. Arminius's rise to the status of national symbol had begun in the sixteenth century when secular humanist thought and the Reformation fostered the awakening of German national consciousness. But the literary exploitation of the Arminius figure intensified after the Reichsgründung: fifty-five dramatic treatments have been recorded for the period from 1871 to 1914. Dahn's tragedy *Sühne* (Atonement, 1879) drives home the point that the voluntary acceptance of one ruler by competing Germanic tribal princes was the prerequisite for Arminius's victory. Defining the monarch, albeit a monarch subject to the rule of law, as the force capable of vanquishing a foreign power recalls the subtext of the Franco-Prussian War; the anachronistic imitation of a Germanic Heerkaiserwahl (election of a leader in battle) in January 1871 at Versailles, where the assembled German princes proclaimed the king of Prussia German emperor, is characteristic of the 1870s' tendency to bestow glory on the present by shrouding it in the trappings of the past. Thus, Dahn's operatic libretto *Armin* (Arminius, 1880) ends with Arminius's apotheosis. The stage directions stipulate that a replica of the Teutoburg Forest monument to Arminius, which was dedicated in 1875, appear onstage. Arminius is claimed as the guarantor of imperialist goals in the name of a vaguely defined pan-Germanism: "Und die Welt, sie gehört den

Germanen" (And the world belongs to the Germanic tribes).

Neither *Armin* nor Dahn's other librettos achieved great success; Dahn blamed the changing taste of an audience that, under the influence of a younger generation of writers, was no longer interested in historical subjects. Voices critical of Dahn's historical fiction began to be heard with increasing frequency. Authors and critics affiliated with naturalism, who endeavored to create a socially relevant novel that dealt with contemporaneous subjects on a scientific basis, especially scorned Dahn's outmoded preoccupation with the Germanic and Nordic past. Dahn fully reciprocated the naturalists' sentiments; his *Erinnerungen* are replete with diatribes against the aesthetic abominations of naturalism, the naturalistic bias of Berlin critics, and the naturalists' sympathies for the Social Democratic party, the proponent of an international workers' movement. Criticism of a different sort came from Dahn's professorial colleagues, who deemed his literary pursuits unacademic. But such criticism had comparatively little effect on Dahn's career; in 1877–1878 he served as rector of the university, and in 1887 he received a medal from the Hohenzollerns, the Prussian royal family.

In his libretto *Der Fremdling* (The Stranger, 1880) Dahn returned to the realm of Nordic myths, endeavoring to imitate Wagner in fusing the fates of human beings and the Germanic gods. The novel *Odhin's Trost* (Odin's Solace, 1880) is fraught with tortuous disquisitions in prose and alliterative verse on Dahn's weltanschauung. Curiously, Dahn preferred *Odhin's Trost* to the far more popular *Ein Kampf um Rom* and regarded it as his most important work in terms of intellectual content. Like *Sind Götter?*, the work is based on Germanic mythology, the love of which Dahn derived from his study of the works of Jacob Grimm. In eleventh-century Iceland an old man, who has been baptized but clings to the pagan beliefs of his forefathers, writes down the Sage (saga) of "Odhin's Trost" as his legacy to his absent warrior son. The saga tells of the struggle between gods and giants: after his favorite son, Baldur, the sun-god, is mortally wounded, the supreme god Odin begins to have doubts about the gods' immortality and the permanence of his reign. From the three Norns, who determine the fate of gods and humans, he learns that the existence of the gods and of humanity is subject to eternal necessity, without hope of an afterlife or of a benevolent fate. Yet the heroic individual may derive solace from the recognition that in devoting himself to the life-affirming principle of service to his people he will

contribute to the perpetuation of the species. The narrator acts according to the message of "Odhin's Trost"; he accepts humanity's essentially tragic condition and dies bravely in battle. His son and granddaughter prosper; they likewise confirm the validity of Odin's solace for exceptional individuals.

In 1882 *Kleine Romane aus der Völkerwanderung* (Minor Novels from the Migration of Germanic Tribes) began to appear; the series was to comprise thirteen volumes by 1901. These novels are a continuation and variation of the themes Dahn developed in *Ein Kampf um Rom;* they take place in diverse locations, and chronologically they span, albeit not in sequential order, the period from A.D. 69 to the reign of Charlemagne (768 to 814). *Felicitas* (1882; translated as *Felicitas: A Tale of the German Migrations, A.D. 476,* 1883) deals with Dahn's favorite topic, the clash between Romans and Germanic tribes in the border region of today's Salzburg, Austria. *Felicitas* has its share of the requisite battle scenes and duels, but there are humorous touches and a happy ending: the protagonist's domestic bliss is restored after the disruptions caused by war. The novel proved to be a minor popular success and was praised by the Swiss authors Gottfried Keller and Conrad Ferdinand Meyer. *Bissula* (1883; translated as *A Captive of the Roman Eagles*, 1902) takes place toward the end of the fourth century on the northern shore of Lake Constance. The novel is reminiscent of *The Taming of the Shrew* in that the young Suebian protagonist is freed from Roman captivity by a noble and heroic countryman whom she previously rejected but whose wooing she can no longer resist.

The Dahns' common literary interests gradually evolved into cooperation; in 1884 their first joint work, the collection *Walhall: Germanische Götter- und Heldensagen* (Valhalla: Germanic Sagas of Gods and Heroes), was published. In contrast to *Felicitas* and *Bissula*, the third novel in the *Kleine Romane aus der Völkerwanderung* series, *Gelimer* (1883; translated as *The Scarlet Banner*, 1903), ends tragically. The novel is an extension of *Ein Kampf um Rom* and depicts the decline of the Vandals and the overthrow of their North African kingdom by the Byzantine army under Belisarius in 534–535. The Vandals, who conquered the Roman province of North Africa fifty years before Theoderich founded his Italian kingdom, have become degenerate beyond saving because of their intermingling with the hedonistic native population. Hence the efforts of their last king, Gelimer, to resist the invading Byzantines are doomed to failure. Although not physically unfit and morally corrupt like most of his countrymen, Gelimer, a former monk, exhibits the fatal flaw of indecision at decisive moments in battle – a flaw that is attributable both to his religious upbringing and to the pernicious influence of a scheming and treasonous priest, one of the many who populate Dahn's novels. The Vandals' ignominious defeat is distinctly different from the heroism displayed by the Goths in *Ein Kampf um Rom;* the thrust of *Gelimer* is clearly directed against acculturation and miscegenation as detrimental to national self-preservation and greatness.

Two further novels of the series, *Die schlimmen Nonnen von Poitiers* (The Naughty Nuns of Poitiers, 1885) and *Fredigundis* (1886), both of which are based on the history of the Franks by Gregory of Tours, offer contrasting perspectives. The fate of the Merovingian king Chilperich's wife, the beautiful but profoundly evil Fredigundis, hardly lent itself to a treatment in terms of poetic justice since her unspeakable crimes went unpunished. But Dahn sought, albeit not too successfully, to impose meaning on Fredigundis's murderous activities by reverting to his basic pattern of historical interpretation: the bloody, romanized Merovingians, represented by Fredigundis, are going to be replaced by the youthful, heroic, Germanic Arnulfings, predecessors of the Carolingians. *Die schlimmen Nonnen von Poitiers* is in a lighter vein and lacks profound historical significance. It deals with the rebellion of young girls against the pedantic and narrow-minded mother superior of the nunnery in which they receive their education. Other representatives of the clergy, notably Dahn's source, Gregory of Tours, appear exceptionally benevolent. Instead of becoming nuns, most of the girls eventually get married.

In 1888 Dahn, instead of returning to an environment more congenial to someone accustomed to the artistic and intellectual climate of Munich, accepted for patriotic reasons an appointment as professor of law in Breslau (today Wroclaw, Poland) in the Prussian province of Silesia. As he had done in Königsberg, he felt called upon to strengthen the German element in Breslau through his activities as a teacher and a writer of fiction with a nationalistic slant.

The publication of *Kleine Romane aus der Völkerwanderung* continued with *Attila* (1886; translated as *Attila the Hun,* 1891), a novel that – despite Dahn's claim to the contrary – provides vivid, suspenseful, gory, and melodramatic scenes rather than a psychological analysis of the protagonist. Dahn's propensity for using clichés in characterization is in evidence in his embellishment of the sparsely documented mode of Attila's death: an in-

nocent Germanic maiden strangles the drunk Attila in self-defense with her long blond hair. Attila's death in 453 signals the beginning of the liberation of the Germanic tribes that had been held in thralldom by the savage Huns. The novel concludes, in almost mandatory fashion, by pointing to a future dominated by the Germanic tribes. The novel *Die Bataver* (The Batavians, 1887) takes the reader to the year A.D. 69, the beginning of the Germanic tribes' struggle to shake off the yoke of Rome in the post-Arminian period. The leader of this struggle, Claudius Civilis, is severely hampered by the inability of the Germanic tribes to conceive of themselves as one army and one people and to form one state. But there is hope: implausibly, the severely wounded Claudius Civilis makes a long pilgrimage to Arminius's grave to die; before he succumbs, his son vows to continue the fight against the Romans and to work for the unification of the Germanic tribes. The novel is dedicated to Bismarck – "Otto dem Großen" (Otto the Great) – whom Dahn revered as the founder of the German Reich. He deplored Bismarck's ouster as chancellor in 1890 as a national disaster and, in a dubious historical analogy, attributed the failure of the Germanic tribes to unite against the crumbling Roman Empire to their lack of a leader of Bismarck's stature. Not surprisingly, Dahn considered his day-long visit with Bismarck in 1892 one of the highlights of his life.

Although the publication of *Kleine Romane aus der Völkerwanderung* as well as verse epics, poems, and prose narratives continued in the twentieth century, Dahn's last major work of fiction was *Julian der Abtrünnige* (Julian the Apostate, 1893), about the fourth-century Roman emperor who endeavored to reintroduce the cult of the Greek gods and persecuted Christians. The subject of the three-volume novel, which Dahn had begun after the completion of *Ein Kampf um Rom,* proved irresistible to him for several reasons: Julian reigned during a time when the declining Roman Empire was in danger of losing its preeminence to the invading Germanic tribes; furthermore, the subject matter offered ample opportunity to indulge in the depiction of saber-rattling and bloodcurdling battle scenes – including those in faraway Persia; finally, because of the central conflict between the adherents of the pagan gods of antiquity and the representatives of Christianity, Dahn was again in a position to formulate his much-vaunted tragic-heroic worldview. The spokesperson for this view is Merowech (Serapion), a Germanic prince whom Dahn's sources mention only in passing. Defeated and captured by Julian, Merowech becomes the emperor's friend and accompanies him on his campaigns against the Persian ruler. Indifferent to both pagan and Christian beliefs, he acknowledges only historical necessity as the ultimate rationale in the "weltgeschichtlichen Ringen zweier Völker" (world-historical struggle of two peoples), the Romans and the Germanic tribes. In the final analysis, he argues, it is "Not" (need), specifically "Landnot" (lack of arable land), that forces the Germanic tribes to continue attacking the Roman Empire. To be sure, Dahn's spokesperson pays tribute to Roman accomplishments, particularly to the legal system and the creation of a state and an empire that the Germanic tribes are unable to construct because of their fratricidal feuds, their limitless imbibing, and their disinclination to conceive of themselves as part of a greater entity, a Volk. Nevertheless, the postulated historical mission of the Germanic tribes on the basis of their genetic superiority conveyed a disquieting imperialist message.

During their more than two decades in Breslau, Dahn and his wife became popular figures. The author was publicly honored on his sixtieth and seventieth birthdays as well as the fiftieth anniversary of receiving his Ph.D. Although he continued to find his reading public, he did not provide any new literary impulses. After 1900 his productivity decreased markedly; around the turn of the century collections of his and his wife's works appeared that attested both to the demand for his writings and the fact that no more major works were to be expected. The last decade of his life Dahn devoted to the completion of his major scholarly work, *Die Könige der Germanen;* the first volumes had been published in 1861, and the twelfth and last volume came out in 1909. Despite his impressive output — at least in quantitative terms — in two fields of endeavor, Dahn tended to be modest about his accomplishments; he viewed himself as a scholar of the second rank and a writer of the third. To be sure, Dahn's historical fiction appears of lesser quality when compared, for example, to that of his contemporary Conrad Ferdinand Meyer, whose depiction of the complex relationship between ethics and politics transcends Dahn's essentially dichotomous view of history.

In 1910 Dahn asked to be relieved of his teaching duties for health reasons; after a brief illness he died on 3 January 1912. His widow died in 1929.

Biography:

Herbert Meyer, *Felix Dahn* (Leipzig: Breitkopf & Härtel, 1913).

References:

Heinrich Eckenroth, "Felix Dahn als Dramatiker," Ph.D. dissertation, University of Würzburg, 1921;

Mark A. Hovey, "Felix Dahn's *Ein Kampf um Rom*," Ph.D. dissertation, State University of New York at Buffalo, 1981;

Otto Kraus, *Der Professorenroman* (Heilbronn: Henninger, 1884);

Michael Limlei, "Geschichtspessimismus und Destruktion der Romanform im tragischen Heroismus. Felix Dahn: *Ein Kampf um Rom*," in his *Geschichte als Ort der Bewährung. Menschenbild und Gesellschaftsverständnis in den deutschen historischen Romanen (1820–1890)* (Frankfurt am Main: Lang, 1988), pp. 203–217, 342–343;

Albert Ludwig, "Dahn, Fouqué, Stevenson," *Euphorion*, 17 (1910): 606–613;

George L. Mosse, "The Image of the Jew in German Popular Culture: Felix Dahn and Gustav Freytag," *Yearbook of the Leo Baeck Institute*, 2 (1952): 218–227;

Alfons Schindler, "Geschichte als tragisches Schicksal: Dahn," in Josef Jansen and others, *Einführung in die deutsche Literatur des 19. Jahrhunderts,* volume 2: *März-Revolution, Reichsgründung und die Anfänge des Imperialismus* (Opladen: Westdeutscher Verlag, 1984), pp. 243–261;

Theodor Siebs, *Felix Dahn und Viktor Scheffel: Mit zehn noch unbekannten Briefen Scheffels an Dahn* (Breslau: Korn, 1914);

Johanna Spitaler, "Die poetische Namengebung bei Felix Dahn," Ph.D. dissertation, University of Graz, 1946;

Clemens Taesler, ed., *Felix Dahn: Festschrift zum 75. Geburtstage* (Charlottenburg: Verlag freistudentischer Schriften, 1909);

Hermann Tepper, "Felix Dahns Balladenkunst," Ph.D. dissertation, University of Breslau, 1930;

Romuald Walter, ed., *Felix Dahn als Erzieher: Deutsche Worte aus seinen Werken* (Leipzig: Breitkopf & Härtel, 1911);

Josef Weisser, "Studien zu den germanischen Romanen Dahns," Ph.D. dissertation, University of Cologne, 1922;

Eugen Wohlhaupter, "Felix Dahn," in his *Dichterjuristen*, volume 3, edited by Horst Gerhard Seifert (Tübingen: Mohr, 1957), pp. 285–343.

Papers:

Felix Dahn's papers are in the library of the University of Münster.

Wilhelm Dilthey

(19 November 1833 – 30 September 1911)

Jill Anne Kowalik
University of California, Los Angeles

BOOKS: *De principiis ethices Schleiermacheri* (Berlin: Schade, 1864);

Grundriß der Logik und des Systems der philosophischen Wissenschaften: Für Vorlesungen (Berlin: Mittler, 1865);

Das Leben Schleiermachers, 2 volumes (Berlin: Reimer, 1867–1870);

Einleitung in die Geisteswissenschaften: Versuch einer Grundlegung für das Studium der Gesellschaft und der Geschichte (Leipzig: Duncker & Humblot, 1883); translated by Ramon B. Betanzos as *Introduction to the Human Sciences* (Detroit: Wayne State University Press, 1988); translated and edited by Rudolf A. Makkreel and Frithjof Rodi as *Introduction to the Human Sciences* (Princeton: Princeton University Press, 1989);

Dichterische Einbildungskraft und Wahnsinn: Rede, gehalten zur Feier des Stiftungstages der militär-ärztlichen Bildungsanstalten am 2. Aug. 1886 (Leipzig: Duncker & Humblot, 1886);

Das Erlebnis und die Dichtung: Lessing, Goethe, Novalis, Hölderlin. Vier Aufsätze (Leipzig: Teubner, 1906; enlarged, 1907; enlarged, 1910); section on Goethe translated by Christopher Rodie as "Goethe and the Poetic Imagination," section on Hölderlin translated by Joseph Ross as "Friedrich Hölderlin," in *Poetry and Experience,* edited by Makkreel and Rodi (Princeton: Princeton University Press, 1985), pp. 233–383;

Über die Möglichkeit einer allgemeingültigen pädagogischen Wissenschaft, edited by Herman Nohl (Langensalza: Beltz, 1930);

Von deutscher Dichtung und Musik: Aus den Studien zur Geschichte des deutschen Geistes, edited by Nohl and Georg Misch (Leipzig & Berlin: Teubner, 1933 [i.e., 1932]);

Die Philosophie des Lebens: Eine Auswahl aus Diltheys Schriften 1867–1910, edited by Nohl (Frankfurt am Main: Klostermann, 1946; revised edition,

Wilhelm Dilthey

Stuttgart & Göttingen: Teubner & Vandenhoeck & Ruprecht, 1961);

Grundriß der allgemeinen Geschichte der Philosophie, edited by Hans-Georg Gadamer (Frankfurt am Main: Klostermann, 1949);

Die große Phantasiedichtung und andere Studien zur vergleichenden Literaturgeschichte, edited by Nohl (Göttingen: Vandenhoeck & Ruprecht, 1954);

Schiller, edited by Nohl (Göttingen: Vandenhoeck & Ruprecht, 1959);

Der Aufbau der geschichtlichen Welt in den Geisteswissenschaften, edited by Manfred Riedel (Frankfurt am Main: Suhrkamp, 1970).

Collection: *Gesammelte Schriften,* 32 volumes projected, 22 volumes published (volumes 1–12, Leipzig & Berlin: Teubner, 1914–1958; volumes 13–32, Göttingen: Vandenhoeck & Ruprecht, 1966–   ) – comprises volume 1: *Einleitung in die Geisteswissenschaften* (1922), edited by Bernhard Groethuysen; volume 2: *Weltanschauung und Analyse des Menschen seit Renaissance und Reformation: Abhandlungen zur Geschichte der Philosophie und Religion* (1914), edited by Georg Misch; volume 3: *Studien zur Geschichte des deutschen Geistes: Leibniz und sein Zeitalter; Friedrich der Große und die deutsche Aufklärung; Das achtzehnte Jahrhundert und die geschichtliche Welt* (1929), edited by Paul Ritter; volume 4: *Die Jugendgeschichte Hegels und andere Abhandlungen zur Geschichte des deutschen Idealismus* (1921), edited by Herman Nohl; volume 5: *Die geistige Welt: Einleitung in die Philosophie des Lebens, Erste Hälfte: Abhandlungen zur Grundlegung der Geisteswissenschaften* (1924), edited by Misch; volume 6: *Die geistige Welt: Einleitung in die Philosophie des Lebens: Zweite Hälfte: Abhandlungen zur Poetik, Ethik und Pädagogik* (1924), edited by Misch; volume 7: *Der Aufbau der geschichtlichen Welt in den geisteswissenschaften* (1927), edited by Groethuysen; excerpts translated by H. P. Rickman as *Meaning in History: W. Dilthey's Thoughts on History and Society* (London: Allen & Unwin, 1961); republished as *Pattern and Meaning in History: Thoughts on History and Society* (New York: Harper, 1962); volume 8: *Weltanschauungslehre: Abhandlungen zur Philosophie der Philosophie* (1931), edited by Groethuysen; volume 9: *Pädagogik* (1934), edited by Otto Friedrich Bollnow; volume 10: *System der Ethik* (1958), edited by Nohl; volume 11: *Vom Aufgang des geschichtlichen Bewußtseins: Jugendaufsätze und Erinnerungen* (1936), edited by Erich Weniger; volume 12: *Zur preußischen Geschichte* (1936), edited by Weniger; volume 13, part 1: *Leben Schleiermachers* (1970), edited by Martin Redeker; volume 13, part 2: *Leben Schleiermachers* (1970), edited by Redeker; volume 14, part 1: *Leben Schleiermachers: Schleiermachers System als Philosophie und Theologie* (1966), edited by Redeker; volume 14, part 2: *Leben Schleiermachers: Schleiermachers System als Philosophie und Theologie* (1966), edited by Redeker; volume 15: *Zur Geistesgeschichte des 19. Jahrhunderts: Portraits und biographische Skizzen,* edited by Ulrich Herrmann; volume 16: *Zur Geistesgeschichte des 19. Jahrhunderts: Aufsätze und Rezensionen aus Zeitungen und Zeitschriften, 1859–1874* (1972), edited by Herrmann; volume 17: *Zur Geistesgeschichte des 19. Jahrhunderts: Aus "Westermanns Monatsheften." Literaturbriefe, Berichte zur Kunstgeschichte, Verstreute Rezensionen, 1867–1884* (1974), edited by Herrmann; volume 18: *Die Wissenschaft vom Menschen, der Gesellschaft und der Geschichte: Vorarbeiten zur Einleitung in die Geisteswissenschaften (1865–1880)* (1977), edited by Helmut Johach and Rodi; volume 19: *Grundlegung der Wissenschaften vom Menschen, der Gesellschaft und der Geschichte: Ausarbeitungen und Entwürfe zum zweiten Band der Einleitung in die Geisteswissenschaften* (1982), edited by Johach and Rodi; volume 20: *Logik und System der philosophischen Wissenschaften: Vorlesungen zur erkenntnistheoretischen Logik und Methodologie* (1990), edited by Rodi and Hans-Ulrich Lessing.

OTHER: *Aus Schleiermachers Leben in Briefen: Schleiermachers Briefwechsel mit Freunden bis zu seiner Übersiedlung nach Halle, namentlich der mit Friedrich und August Wilhelm Schlegel,* 3 volumes, edited by Dilthey and Ludwig Jonas (Berlin: Reimer, 1861; revised, 1863);

"Die Einbildungskraft des Dichters: Bausteine für eine Poetik," in *Philosophische Aufsätze, Eduard Zeller zu seinem fünfzigjährigen Doctor-Jubiläum gewidmet* (Leipzig: Reisland, 1877), pp. 301–482; translated by Louis Agosta and Rudolf A. Makkreel as "The Imagination of the Poet: Elements for a Poetics," in *Poetry and Experience,* edited by Makkreel and Rodi (Princeton: Princeton University Press, 1985), pp. 29–173;

"Über die Möglichkeit einer allgemeingültigen pädagogischen Wissenschaft," in *Sitzungsberichte der königlich preußischen Akademie der Wissenschaften* (Berlin: Reimer, 1888), pp. 807–832;

Archiv für Geschichte der Philosophie, edited by Dilthey, Hermann Diels, Benno Erdmann, Eduard Zeller, and others, volumes 1–11 (1888–1909);

"Beiträge zur Lösung der Frage vom Ursprung unseres Glaubens an die Realität der Außenwelt und seinem Recht," *Sitzungsberichte der königlich preußischen Akademie der Wissenschaften* (Berlin: Reimer, 1890), pp. 977–1022;

"Friedrich Daniel Ernst Schleiermacher," in *Allgemeine Deutsche Biographie,* volume 31 (Leipzig: Duncker & Humblot, 1890), pp. 422–457;

"Ideen über eine beschreibende und zergliedernde Psychologie," in *Sitzungsberichte der königlich preußischen Akademie der Wissenschaften* (Berlin: Reimer, 1894), pp. 1309–1407;

"Beiträge zum Studium der Individualität," in *Sitzungsberichte der königlich preußischen Akademie der Wissenschaften* (Berlin: Reimer, 1896), pp. 295–335;

"Übersicht meines Systems," in *Friedrich Überwegs Grundriß der Geschichte der Philosophie,* part 3, volume 2, edited by Max Heinze (Berlin: Mittler, 1897), pp. 277–279;

"Die Entstehung der Hermeneutik," in *Philosophische Abhandlungen, Christoph Sigwart zu seinem 70. Geburtstag 28. März 1900 gewidmet* (Tübingen: Mohr, 1900), pp. 185–202; translated by Fredric Jameson as "The Rise of Hermeneutics," *New Literary History,* 3 (Winter 1972): 229–244;

"Drei Briefe Schleiermachers an Gaß," in *Litterarische Mitteilungen: Festschrift zum zehnjährigen Bestehen der Litteraturarchiv-Gesellschaft in Berlin* (Berlin: Litteraturarchiv-Gesellschaft, 1901), pp. 37–50;

"Die Funktion der Anthropologie in der Kultur des 16. und 17. Jahrhunderts," in *Sitzungsberichte der königlich preußischen Akademie der Wissenschaften* (Berlin: Reimer, 1904), pp. 2–33, 316–347;

"Studien zur Grundlegung der Geisteswissenschaften," in *Sitzungsberichte der königlich preußischen Akademie der Wissenschaften* (Berlin: Reimer, 1905), pp. 322–343;

"Das Wesen der Philosophie," in *Die Kultur der Gegenwart,* edited by Paul Hinneberg, part 1, section 6 (Berlin & Leipzig: Teubner, 1907), pp. 1–72; translated by Stephen A. Emery and William T. Emery as *The Essence of Philosophy* (Chapel Hill: University of North Carolina Press, 1954);

Kants gesammelte Schriften, edited by the Preußische Akademie der Wissenschaften, section 1, volume 1: *Vorkritische Schriften I (1747–1756),* preface by Dilthey (Berlin: Reimer, 1910);

"Die Typen der Weltanschauung und ihre Ausbildung in den metaphysischen Systemen," in *Weltanschauung, Philosophie und Religion,* edited by Max Frischeisen-Köhler (Berlin: Reichl, 1911), pp. 3–51; translated by William Kluback and Martin Weinbaum as "The Types of World Views and Their Unfoldment within the Metaphysical Systems," in their *Dilthey's Philosophy of Existence: Introduction to Weltanschauungslehre* (New York: Columbia University Press, 1956; London: Vision, 1960).

SELECTED PERIODICAL PUBLICATIONS – UNCOLLECTED: "Johann Georg Hamann," *Deutsche Zeitschrift für christliche Wissenschaft und christliches Leben,* new series 1, no. 40 (1858): 315–320; no. 41 (1858): 323–327; no. 44 (1858): 347–354;

"Satan in der christlichen Poesie," as Wilhelm Hoffner, *Westermanns Monatshefte,* 8, no. 45 (1860): 321–329; no. 46 (1860): 434–439;

"Goethe als Naturforscher, besonders als Anatom," *Preußische Zeitung,* 10 February 1861, pp. 1–3;

"Ein Brief A.W. Schlegels an Huber," anonymous introduction by Dilthey, *Preußische Jahrbücher,* 8 (1861): 225–235;

"Schleiermachers politische Gesinnung und Wirksamkeit," anonymous, *Preußische Jahrbücher,* 10 (1862): 234–277;

"Arthur Schopenhauer," as Hoffner, *Westermanns Monatshefte,* 16, no. 90 (1864): 634–651;

"Novalis," *Preußische Jahrbücher,* 15 (1865): 596–650;

"Deutsche Geschichtsschreiber I: Johannes von Müller," as Hoffner, *Westermanns Monatshefte,* 19, no. 111 (1865): 245–255;

"Deutsche Geschichtsschreiber II: Barthold Georg Niebuhr," as Hoffner, *Westermanns Monatshefte,* 19, no. 112 (1866): 363–371;

"Deutsche Geschichtsschreiber III: Friedrich Christoph Schlosser," as Hoffner, *Westermanns Monatshefte,* 19, no. 113 (1866): 484–491;

"Deutsche Geschichtsschreiber IV: Friedrich Christoph Dahlmann," as Hoffner, *Westermanns Monatshefte,* 20, no. 115 (1866): 24–33;

"Phantastische Gesichtserscheinungen von Goethe, Tieck und Otto Ludwig," as Hoffner, *Westermanns Monatshefte,* 20, no. 117 (1866): 258–265;

"Die neuesten literarhistorischen Arbeiten über das klassische Zeitalter unsrer Dichtung," as Hoffner, *Westermanns Monatshefte,* 20, no. 119 (1866): 482–491;

"Eduard Gibbon," as Hoffner, *Westermanns Monatshefte,* 21, no. 122 (1866): 135–149;

"Über Gotthold Ephraim Lessing," *Preußische Jahrbücher,* 19 (1867): 117–161;

"Hölderlin und die Ursachen seines Wahnsinns," as Hoffner, *Westermanns Monatshefte,* 22, no. 128 (1867): 155–165;

"Zu Lessings Seelenwanderungslehre," *Preußische Jahrbücher,* 20 (1867): 439–444;

"Die romantischen Dichter I: Ludwig Tieck," as Hoffner, *Westermanns Monatshefte,* 25, no. 145 (1868): 25–42;

"Die romantischen Dichter II: Novalis," as Hoffner, *Westermanns Monatshefte,* 25, no. 147 (1868): 272-280;

"Die Reorganisatoren des preußischen Staates (1807-1813), I: Der Freiherr von Stein," as Hoffner, *Westermanns Monatshefte,* 31, no. 184 (1872): 366-376;

"Die Reorganisatoren des preußischen Staates (1807-1813), II: Karl August von Hardenberg," as Hoffner, *Westermanns Monatshefte,* 31, no. 186 (1872): 599-607;

"Die Reorganisatoren des preußischen Staates (1807-1813), III: Wilhelm von Humboldt," as Hoffner, *Westermanns Monatshefte,* 32, no. 188 (1872): 140-155;

"Die Reorganisatoren des preußischen Staates (1807-1813), IV: Neithardt von Gneisenau," as Hoffner, *Westermanns Monatshefte,* 32, no. 191 (1872): 470-479;

"Die Reorganisatoren des preußischen Staates (1807-1813) V: Scharnhorst," as Hoffner, *Westermanns Monatshefte,* 33, no. 193 (1872): 18-132;

"Die römische Cultur auf ihrer Höhe im Kaiserreiche," as Hoffner, *Westermanns Monatshefte,* 34, no. 204 (1873): 660-668;

"Die Literatur der Niederlande," as Hoffner, *Westermanns Monatshefte,* 35, no. 207 (1873): 320-331;

"Voltaire," as Hoffner, *Westermanns Monatshefte,* 36, no. 212 (1874): 171-178;

"Mohamed," as Hoffner, *Westermanns Monatshefte,* 37, no. 220 (1875): 444-447;

"Die Fürstin Galitzin," as Hoffner, *Westermanns Monatshefte,* 37, no. 222 (1875): 588-593;

"Vittorio Alfieri," *Westermanns Monatshefte,* 38, no. 225 (1875): 324-335; no. 226 (1875): 425-443;

"Neue Mitteilungen über G. A. Bürger," as Hoffner, *Westermanns Monatshefte,* 38, no. 226 (1875): 443-448;

"Über das Studium der Geschichte der Wissenschaften vom Menschen, der Gesellschaft und dem Staat," *Philosophische Monatshefte,* 11, no. 3 (1875): 118-132; no. 6 (1875): 241-267;

"Richard Wagner," as Karl Elkan, *Westermanns Monatshefte,* 39, no. 232 (1876): 421-432;

"Balzac," as Hoffner, *Westermanns Monatshefte,* 39, no. 233 (1876): 476-483;

"Goethe und Corona Schröter," as Hoffner, *Westermanns Monatshefte,* 40, no. 235 (1876): 71-75;

"Ein Beitrag zu unserer Erkenntnis der ersten französischen Revolution," anonymous, *Westermanns Monatshefte,* 40, no. 235 (1876): 75-77;

"Heinrich Heine," as Elkan, *Westermanns Monatshefte,* 40, no. 236 (1876): 147-155; no. 237 (1876): 311-320; no. 239 (1876): 478-491;

"Japanesische Novellen," as Hoffner, *Westermanns Monatshefte,* 40, no. 240 (1876): 577-587;

"John Stuart Mill," as Elkan, *Westermanns Monatshefte,* 41, no. 243 (1876): 255-260;

"Charles Dickens und das Genie des erzählenden Dichters," *Westermanns Monatshefte,* 41, no. 245 (1877): 482-499; no. 246 (1877): 586-602;

"George Sand, eine biographische Skizze," as Hoffner, *Westermanns Monatshefte,* 42, no. 247 (1877): 93-98;

"Über die Einbildungskraft der Dichter," *Zeitschrift für Völkerpsychologie und Sprachwissenschaft,* 10 (1878): 42-104;

"Schleiermachers Weihnachtsfeier," *Westermanns Monatshefte,* 47, no. 279 (1879): 343-364;

"Wilhelm Scherer zum persönlichen Gedächtnis," *Deutsche Rundschau,* 49 (1886): 132-146;

"Zu Goethes Philosophie der Natur," *Archiv für Geschichte der Philosophie,* 2, no. 1 (1889): 45-48;

"Die Rostocker Kanthandschriften I: Acht Briefe Kants an Jakob Sigismund Beck," introduction and afterword by Dilthey, *Archiv für Geschichte der Philosophie,* 2, no. 4 (1889): 592-650;

"Aus den Rostocker Kanthandschriften II: Ein ungedruckter Aufsatz Kants über Abhandlungen Kästners," introduction by Dilthey, *Archiv für Geschichte der Philosophie,* 3, no. 1 (1890): 79-90;

"Der Streit Kants mit der Zensur über das Recht freier Religionsforschung: Drittes Stück der Beiträge aus den Rostocker Kanthandschriften," introduction by Dilthey, *Archiv für Geschichte der Philosophie,* 3 (1890): 418-450;

"Thomas Carlyle," *Archiv für Geschichte der Philosophie,* 4, no. 2 (1891): 260-285;

"Auffassung und Analyse des Menschen im 15. und 16. Jahrhundert," *Archiv für Geschichte der Philosophie,* 4, no. 4 (1891): 604-651; 5 (1892): 337-400;

"Die drei Epochen der modernen Aesthetik und ihre heutige Aufgabe," *Deutsche Rundschau,* 72 (1 August 1892): 200-236; translated by Michael Neville as "The Three Epochs of Modern Aesthetics and Its Present Task," in *Poetry and Experience,* edited by Makkreel and Rodi (Princeton: Princeton University Press, 1985), pp.175-222;

"Das natürliche System der Geisteswissenschaften im siebzehnten Jahrhundert," *Archiv für Geschichte der Philosophie,* 5, no. 4 (1892): 480-502; 6, no. 1 (1893): 60-127; no. 2 (1893):

225–256; no. 3 (1893): 347–379; no. 4 (1893): 509–545;

"Die Autonomie des Denkens, der konstruktive Rationalismus und der pantheistische Monismus nach ihrem Zusammenhang im 17. Jahrhundert," *Archiv für Geschichte der Philosophie,* 7, no. 1 (1893): 28–91;

"Giordano Bruno und Spinoza," *Archiv für Geschichte der Philosophie,* 7, no. 2 (1893): 269–283;

"Die Glaubenslehre der Reformatoren, aufgefaßt in ihrem entwicklungsgeschichtlichen Zusammenhang," *Preußische Jahrbücher,* 75 (1894): 44–86;

"Aus der Zeit der Spinozastudien Goethes," *Archiv für Geschichte der Philosophie,* 7, no. 3 (1894): 317–341;

"Ein Gutachten Wilhelm von Humboldts über die Staatsprüfung der höheren Verwaltungsbeamten," edited by Dilthey and Alfred Heubaum, *Jahrbuch für Gesetzgebung, Verwaltung und Volkswirtschaft im Deutschen Reich,* new series 23 (1899): 245–261;

"Urkundliche Beiträge zu Herbarts praktischer pädagogischer Wirksamkeit," edited by Dilthey and Heubaum, *Neue Jahrbücher für das klassische Altertum, Geschichte und deutsche Litteratur und für Pädagogik,* 6 (1900): 325–350;

"Die Berliner Akademie der Wissenschaften, ihre Vergangenheit und ihre gegenwärtigen Aufgaben," *Deutsche Rundschau,* 103 (June 1900): 416–444; 104 (July 1900): 81–118;

"Der entwicklungsgeschichtliche Pantheismus nach seinem geschichtlichen Zusammenlang mit de älteren pantheistischen Systamen," *Archiv fur Geschichte der Philosophie,* 13, no. 3 (1900): 307–360; no. 4 (1900): 445–482;

"Die deutsche Aufklärung im Staat und in der Akademie Friedrich's des Großen," *Deutsche Rundschau,* 107 (April 1901): 21–58; (May 1901): 210–235.

Wilhelm Dilthey, a man of extraordinary erudition even by nineteenth-century standards, made significant contributions to the fields of philosophy, cultural history, literary theory, psychology, and aesthetics. He is often viewed as the founder of the German school of thought known as *Geistesgeschichte* (intellectual history; sometimes inaccurately translated as "history of ideas"), but in fact Dilthey based his scholarly career on a vehement critique of post-Hegelian notions of history. He believed that the various "philosophies of history" written in the wake of the works of Georg Wilhelm Friedrich Hegel were predicated on an essentially metaphysi-

cal concern for locating a single principle of historical development. This endeavor impressed him as a reductive activity whose roots could be found in the teleologically inspired universal histories of the medieval period. Instead of looking for what he felt was a nonexistent mainspring of history, Dilthey embarked on a lifelong enterprise that he called the "Kritik der historischen Vernunft" (critique of historical reason). The phrase echoes the titles of Immanuel Kant's major works, which Dilthey admired. But he argued that Kant had not provided an adequate framework for understanding human experience in its totality because he had not sufficiently accounted for the role of volition and affect in the formation of consciousness. Such a formative process is, according to Dilthey, fundamentally historical in nature and operates on several levels: individual, social, and cultural. Moreover, these levels exist in a state of "Wechselwirkung" (interdeterminacy). Individuals both influence and are influenced by the social, historical, and cultural settings in which they live. Biography plays a central role in the human sciences because it not only documents an individual life but also illuminates an entire cultural context. The task of the historian – especially the literary historian – is to explicate the historically acquired mental structures of individuals and societies, which are uniquely preserved in their literary and artistic productions, and to recognize the fundamentally temporal nature, the "historicity," of these structures.

It is ironic that no formal biography has been written of a man for whom biography was such a significant genre. The outlines of his life have to be reconstructed from statements made by his daughter, his students, and other contemporaries and from the small fraction of his correspondence that has been published. Dilthey was born on 19 November 1833 in Biebrich, a part of present-day Wiesbaden. Like so many German philosophers and poets before him, he was the son of a pastor: Maximilian Dilthey, the court preacher to the duke of Nassau and a dedicated Calvinist, was intensely interested in history and politics. He also had a large private library in which his son was allowed to browse. Dilthey's mother, Laura, née Heuschkel, was the daughter of a conductor. From her, Dilthey acquired his abiding love of music. As a student in Berlin he would often play the piano as a way of resting from his work.

After attending the local elementary school, Dilthey was enrolled in a private gymnasium that also admitted girls; coeducation was unusual at that time. He was subsequently sent to the regular gymnasium in Wiesbaden, where he studied from 1847 to 1852. On graduating as valedictorian of his class, he gave an address titled "Über den Einfluß des griechischen Altertums auf die Jugend" (Concerning the Influence of Greek Antiquity on Our Youth). Although he had planned to study law, he enrolled at the University of Heidelberg as a student of theology, apparently at the insistence of his father. After three semesters he transferred to the University of Berlin to enjoy the advantages of a larger city, including the more sophisticated musical program that it offered. Dilthey's letters to his family from Berlin indicate how absorbed he was in his academic pursuits: he repeatedly writes of working twelve to fourteen hours a day. His main area of research was early Church history and Neoplatonism, a project for which he read voraciously in several original languages. All of his friendships at this period appear to have been based strictly on intellectual rapport, a pattern that was to prevail throughout his life. In addition to his regular university courses he participated in informal reading circles on Plato, Aristotle, William Shakespeare, and other classical authors. He was most influenced in his early student years by the philosopher Friedrich Trendelenburg, but he also took courses from Friedrich Schleiermacher's student Karl Immanuel Nitzsch and from the historian Leopold von Ranke.

He took his first examination in theology in the summer of 1856, followed in November by the state examination qualifying him to teach at a gymnasium. He tried his hand as a school instructor for about a year, hoping to become financially independent from his father, but he found that teaching Latin, Hebrew, religion, and history to adolescents was deathly tedious. He turned to journalism, producing – usually anonymously or under a pseudonym – scores of book reviews and short articles, primarily for *Westermanns Monatshefte* (Westermann's Monthlies) and for the distinguished *Preußische Jahrbücher* (Prussian Yearbooks). By 1859 he was working on an edition of Schleiermacher's letters (published in 1861), and he immersed himself in the study of the philosopher's life and times to compose an appropriate introduction. During this year the Schleiermacher Foundation sponsored a contest for the best essay on Schleiermacher's hermeneutics in its historical context; when the prize was awarded to Dilthey, it was doubled in view of the unusual breadth and thoroughness of his analysis. Dilthey did not have the work published, hoping to bring it out later in a more complete form. *Das Leben Schleiermachers* (The Life of Schleiermacher) ap-

Dilthey as a young man

peared in two volumes in 1867 and 1870; but Dilthey labeled both of them volume one, insisted that the work was incomplete, and worked on the sequel intermittently for the rest of his life. Volume two was never published.

In January 1864 Dilthey submitted a dissertation to the philosophical faculty of the University of Berlin on Schleiermacher's ethics; six months later he produced a short Habilitationsschrift (dissertation that would allow him to teach on the university level) titled "Versuch einer Analyse des moralischen Bewußtseins" (Attempt to Analyze the Moral Sense). He then began to lecture as a docent in Berlin on logic and on Schleiermacher's work.

In 1866 Dilthey was invited to join the faculty of the University of Basel. Although he was hesitant to leave his beloved Berlin, the position meant that he would no longer have to ask his father for financial support. Before leaving for Basel he wrote an essay on Gotthold Ephraim Lessing for the *Preußische Jahrbücher;* it would later form part of his book *Das Erlebnis und die Dichtung: Lessing, Goethe, Novalis, Hölderlin* (Experience and Poetry: Lessing,

Goethe, Novalis, Hölderlin, 1906). The eminent historian Jakob Burckhardt, who knew Dilthey in Basel, wrote of him: "Die Studenten faßten Feuer für Dilthey . . . Seine Bildung ist, nach seinem Gespräch und seiner Antrittsvorlesung zu urteilen, höchst solid, und dabei hat er eine superbe literarhistorische Ader" (The students were terribly excited by Dilthey . . . His intellectual development, judging from conversations with him and from his inaugural lecture, is absolutely solid, and he has a superb literary-historical sense).

The inaugural lecture mentioned by Burckhardt was delivered in 1867 and bore the title "Die dichterische und philosophische Bewegung in Deutschland 1770–1800" (The Poetic and Philosophic Movement in Germany from 1770 to 1800). Mainly an excerpt from his introduction to the Schleiermacher volume, it explains Dilthey's fascination with and intellectual indebtedness to a particular phase of German literary history. Dilthey thought that the philosophic systems of Hegel, Schleiermacher, and Friedrich von Schelling were extensions of a Weltansicht (worldview) developed by Lessing, Friedrich Schiller, and Johann Wolfgang von Goethe. Not since the days of the Greeks, he argued, had literature and philosophy been so closely connected; indeed, they were organically related in this period in that poetry had deep philosophic origins and implications, and philosophy was conducted as a poetic-creative activity. This statement is a brief indication of Dilthey's critique, to be expanded in his major manuscripts, of his own time: he saw the latter nineteenth century as threatened by the proliferation of disciplines, the fragmentation of knowledge, and general confusion about the purpose of the Geisteswissenschaften (human sciences), especially vis-à-vis the natural sciences. (The term *Geisteswissenschaften* first occurred in 1849 as a translation of John Stuart Mill's phrase *moral sciences*.) Dilthey's critique appears to be inspired in some respects by Schiller's cultural criticism, but his elaboration of a new method of historical research goes far beyond the remedies that Schiller had proposed.

Dilthey came to feel isolated and bored in Basel and wanted to return to Germany. In 1868 he began lecturing at the University of Kiel. He became engaged to Marianne von Witzleben on 21 November 1870 but dissolved the engagement a few days later after learning that his fiancée had an illegitimate child. It has been reported that von Witzleben was devastated by the break, was bedridden for a time afterwards, and never married; she died in 1924.

In 1871 Dilthey accepted an appointment at the University of Breslau. In November 1873 he announced his engagement to Katharine ("Käthe") Püttmann, whom he had met the previous August. They married in March 1874 and had three children: Clara, Dilthey's favorite child, born in 1877; Max, born in 1884; and Helene, born in 1888. Clara later said that her parents were not happily married: her father insisted on spending nearly sixteen hours a day with his books, while her mother wanted him to devote some time to her and the children. The frequent quarrels appear to have caused Dilthey to retreat even more into his study, where students presented him with additional research material for incorporation into his work and took dictation from him.

In Breslau Dilthey met Count Paul Yorck von Wartenburg, who had read *Das Leben Schleiermachers* and had sought out its author. A representative of the educated nobility, he became Dilthey's primary intellectual companion, a veritable "soul mate" with whom Dilthey could work out his ideas in conversation or in letters; Dilthey was a frequent guest at Yorck's estate. Their friendship was perhaps the most important relationship that Dilthey ever maintained. "Sie sind der Leser, an den ich immer denke, wenn ich mich zum Schreiben niedersetze" (You are the reader who is always in my mind when I begin to write), he once wrote to Yorck. Dilthey's *Einleitung in die Geisteswissenschaften* (1883; translated as *Introduction to the Human Sciences,* 1988) is dedicated to Yorck. And in 1897, a few months before Yorck's death, he told his friend: "Ich leide mit Ihnen als begegnete es mir selbst; denn ich kann mein Lebensgefühl von Ihnen nicht sondern, wir sind durch eine innere Verwandtschaft verwachsen, welche so fest hält und einigt als jede physische vermag" (I am suffering with you as if the pain were my own because I cannot separate my own feeling for life from you; we have grown together through an inner relation that binds and unites just as strongly as any physical one would).

As with the Schleiermacher book, Dilthey considered *Einleitung in die Geisteswissenschaften* to be unfinished and intended to produce a second volume; despite years of further research, however, he was never able to do so. He produced a staggering amount of manuscript material that he viewed as "work in progress" and therefore as unpublishable. Most of his major pieces were not accessible until his students Georg Misch (who married Dilthey's daughter Clara), Paul Ritter, Bernhard Groethuysen, and Herman Nohl began an edition of his *Gesammelte Schriften* (Collected Writings). The first eight volumes appeared between 1914 and 1931. In 1934 volume nine, edited by Otto Friedrich Bollnow, appeared, followed in 1936 by volumes eleven and twelve, edited by Erich Weniger. In 1958 Nohl completed the long-planned volume ten. With the publication of these twelve volumes Dilthey's students seemed to feel that their work was complete; but a younger generation of philosophers and social scientists began to take renewed interest in Dilthey's ideas, and in 1962 the publishing house of Vandenhoeck and Ruprecht (which had acquired the publication rights from Teubner) began negotiations with Georg and Clara Misch (who died in 1965 and 1967, respectively) regarding a continuation of the collected works. Eventually thirty-two volumes will make up this collection; the last three will contain a portion of Dilthey's large correspondence.

Dilthey's inability, or unwillingness, to finish any of his major projects was the result of his approach to the human sciences. He viewed all historical knowledge as tentative and merely probable and, therefore, subject to revision as one acquires more information and insight into the period under consideration. Dilthey's considerable manuscript production and relatively short list of major publications in his lifetime attest to the distress that his theory caused him: hoping desperately to achieve closure to studies that he himself had defined as open-ended, he held back most of what he wrote in order to "complete" it. This ambivalence may reflect a more fundamental problem in Dilthey's philosophic position. Hans-Georg Gadamer argues in *Wahrheit und Methode* (1960; translated as *Truth and Method,* 1975) that Dilthey remained unwittingly indebted to a Hegelian notion of universal history even as he criticized Hegel on this score. Thus Dilthey continued to view history as a meaningful totality free of discontinuities, as the manifestation of "objective mind." If Gadamer is correct, the later reduction of Dilthey's philosophy to a theory of "Zeitgeist" may have been facilitated by unresolved aspects in Dilthey's own work.

In *Einleitung in die Geisteswissenschaften* Dilthey sets forth his view of the intellectual crisis of his period. Cultural studies such as psychology, sociology, history, and anthropology had, he believed, fallen under the sway of the natural sciences. Thus these disciplines used their observations of singular phenomena as "Rohstoff für ihre Abstraktionen" (raw material for their abstractions). Furthermore, they operated independently of each other, with research in one field left unconnected to the results achieved in another. This state of affairs meant that no one discipline would ever be able to capture the "Gesamtzusammenhang" (total context) of the human historical experience. But the particulars of experience could only be fully understood with reference to the total context.

For "die geschichtlich-gesellschaftliche Wirklichkeit" (the historical-social reality) to be understood, a methodology of the human sciences per se had to be developed. Dilthey's "critique of historical reason" was intended to create an epistemology that would define the nature of historical knowledge, which includes knowledge of the historically generated present. This epistemology would allow one to specify how such a field of knowledge is or ought to be constructed – that is, how the methodology of the human sciences operates.

Dilthey's concept of historical reality is explicitly indebted to the philosopher Gottfried Wilhelm von Leibniz's concept of the monad. Dilthey viewed reality as a system of "Lebenseinheiten" (experiencing individuals) constantly interacting with each other socially, psychologically, linguistically, economically, religiously, politically, and in other respects. The historical world is a ceaselessly changing constellation of individual experiences. Whereas Leibniz speaks of the monad as a microcosm of the universe, Dilthey maintains that individual lives are typical or representative of their milieu; from this concept follows the significance he assigned to biography as a means of understanding a particular period or culture. Dilthey's notion of biography was, in some cases, distorted by his followers, but Dilthey himself did not usually conceive of an individual life as significant in proportion to the "heroic" stature of the person. When Dilthey says that individuals influence their world and are influenced by it, he means all individuals all of the time. Life is an interactive system of "Wechselwirkungen."

Against this ceaselessly changing historical system Dilthey posited a historically constant capacity of human beings to make sense of their experience. He called this process "Selbstbesinnung" (self-reflection). Whereas Aristotle had defined man as the political animal, Dilthey thought of man as the interpreting animal. The human mind is continuously involved in a process of symbol formation. Moreover, each culture, age, and individual has a characteristic way of organizing its experience with the help of symbols. The analysis of the particulars of individual existence is possible precisely because both the object of understanding and the interpreting individual have participated in the construction of meaning. Knowledge of history is, thus, the reconstruction of the form that experience takes in any given historical context.

Dilthey further argued that interpreters stand on a specific historical horizon from which it is impossible entirely to free themselves. Their understanding of the historical world is determined by the context in which they currently operate. Conversely, their understanding of their present world is structured by their historical experience. "Absolute" historical knowledge is a theoretical impossibility because interpreters can never free themselves from the historically generated context out of which their interpretation arises. Understanding of both the past and the present is subject to the principle of "Geschichtlichkeit" (historicity). While such an assertion left Dilthey open to the charges of relativism and skepticism, his goal in writing *Einleitung in die Geisteswissenschaften* was to extricate historical knowledge from its dependence on metaphysics and to argue for an interactive approach to historical research in multiple disciplines so as to grasp the interactive nature of experience itself. His project anticipates the current scholarly interest in discourse analysis, and it also offers the first important rationale for the necessity of interdisciplinary studies in the humanities and social sciences.

In 1882 Dilthey received an appointment to the chair in philosophy once occupied by Hegel at the University of Berlin. He and his family lived in a comfortable apartment with several servants in a good district of the city. In addition to his generous academic salary, Dilthey drew income from book reviews and scholarly articles for journals. (By the end of his life he had reviewed more than one thousand books.) A thorough study of Dilthey's political opinions in relation to his philosophy remains to be done, largely because his entire correspondence has never been published; the existing collections of his letters have been so heavily edited that they are unusable for reconstructing his thoughts on many of the issues of his day. It is known, however, that even before becoming an established member of the Prussian university system Dilthey supported Chancellor Otto von Bismarck's political goals. In 1870 he wrote to his friend, the historian Heinrich von Treitschke, that Prussia should remain a military state with a strong monarch. He also believed, like Treitschke, that the Franco-Prussian War was a political necessity. In 1881, five years before Treitschke was appointed Prussian state historiographer, Dilthey wrote a letter of support to him following Theodor Mommsen's attack on Treitschke's anti-Semitism. Although Dilthey complained that Treitschke's historical methodology had been mis-

interpreted by Mommsen, his letter may also have been prompted by some emotional kinship with Treitschke: Dilthey's own correspondence contains anti-Semitic remarks. But as Max Horkheimer has observed, the conservative (if not reactionary) attitudes that Dilthey shared with many intellectuals of his time should not blind one to his progressive ideas and achievements.

In his "Die Einbildungskraft des Dichters: Bausteine für eine Poetik" (1887; translated as *The Imagination of the Poet: Elements for a Poetics,* 1985) Dilthey extends the argument of *Einleitung in die Geisteswissenschaften* to cover literary production and interpretation. Just as history can no longer be seen as operating according to a single metaphysical principle, so too must literature be viewed independently of a timeless standard of perfection. All literary production is historically conditioned, and all literary standards are temporal. Once again, Dilthey opens himself to the charge of relativism: if literary standards are in continual flux, how is it possible to make aesthetic judgments at all? Worse, Dilthey seems to be caught in the skeptical circle: the claim that all literary standards are temporal must itself be temporal or historically relative.

Dilthey attempted to work his way out of this logical cul-de-sac by specifying a historically constant function of literature that could accommodate the multiplicity of historical manifestations of literary production. Literature, Dilthey argued, has always had a unique capacity to constitute and convey the "erworbener Zusammenhang des Seelenlebens" (historically acquired structure of intellectual-emotional experience). Therefore, it is the most important source of historical knowledge, including knowledge of the historically formed world of the present. Here Dilthey differs from modern practitioners of discourse analysis in that he privileges literature as the primary mode of grasping social-historical reality. Yet he also seems to relegate literature to the historian's toolbox. Given his interest in a multidisciplinary approach to understanding human experience, why would Dilthey assign literature this paradoxical double status of privilege and apparent subservience? This antinomy in his thought is the probable source of many misapprehensions of his work.

Dilthey's justification for the importance of literature is that experience is the essence of literature. But experience is also the essence of all lives. What, then, distinguishes literature from nonliterary expressions? Dilthey suggests two answers. First, literature, more than other historical documents, is less the expression than the construction of experience.

The literary text does not simply represent an already formed "inner" life of poets; rather its production is an organizing mechanism by which manifold perceptions are brought into a context and given significance. But this historically characteristic manner of structuring experience is shared by poets and their particular social-historical reality. In addition, the relationship between poet and world is interactive. A poetic work does not "reflect" the structure of the poet's historical reality, nor does this structure "determine" how the poet organizes experience in the literary work. Instead, poets both contribute to and draw upon the organization of experience that is characteristic of their age. Dilthey is suggesting a kind of "limited autonomy" for poets, whereby they are granted the ability to influence their environment even as their creative powers are shaped by their historical standpoint. Failure to understand this interaction led later literary scholars to distort Dilthey's theory in two opposite directions. On the one hand, he was said to have proposed that all literary works of a given age are simple reflections of the "spirit" of the age. On the other hand, Dilthey was said to have defended a notion of the omnipotent author whose works create the "Zeitgeist."

Dilthey's second justification for privileging literary discourse is its high degree of typicality, a quality it shares with all artistic creations. The typical is not to be confused with the ideal, Dilthey stressed; it is instead the embodiment of the principles of "Notwendigkeit" (necessity) and "Allgemeingültigkeit" (generality). By the former term Dilthey means that the organization of experience the work undertakes is equally applicable to or "zwingend" (binding) for artist and recipient; the latter term means that the structure of the work can be reconstituted by any adequately sensitive recipient. *Necessity* and *generality* are, of course, the key categories in Aristotle's analysis of *poesis,* but Dilthey differs from Aristotle in the historical significance he assigns to these terms: grasping literary structures means the apprehension of the entire historical milieu that they represent.

Dilthey defines literary reception as the process of "nachbilden" (reconstructing), a word that is easily misconstrued, as he was well aware. Thus, in "Die Einbildungskraft des Dichters" he was careful to point out that reconstruction is neither simple identification with the author nor recollection of an experience similar to that represented in the work. Relying on identification or recollection was the error, he felt, of the writers of German middle-class drama in the eighteenth century, for they based

their effects on "Mitleid" (sympathy). The audience was merely drawn into the work in a passive identificatory moment without being asked to reflect actively on the significance of the experience captured in the representation. Dilthey's "nachbilden" involves both the intellect and the emotions in an imaginative interplay whereby recipients are able to "sich hineinversetzen" (place themselves into) experience opened up in the poetic work, versus the naive assumption that they feel what the poet feels. In the subsequent reception of Dilthey's theories, this process was often reduced to a quasi-mystical act of empathy wherein recipients abandon their own historical situation in an escapist act of identification with the poet. But such an act is precisely what Dilthey did not mean by *nachbilden* and *sich hineinversetzen.* To be sure, the poet's biography provides an essential element in interpretation, but Dilthey felt that the goal of interpretation was the understanding not of the poet but of the text.

During the 1890s Dilthey was concerned primarily with studies in German history and philosophy. In 1906 *Das Erlebnis und die Dichtung: Lessing, Goethe, Novalis, Hölderlin,* which had enormous influence on literary scholars, appeared. The essays on Lessing, Goethe, and Novalis had been composed in 1867, 1877, and 1865, respectively, and were slightly revised for the volume; the Hölderlin section, with the exception of a few paragraphs, was new material. An introductory essay, "Gang der neueren europäischen Literatur" (The Course of Modern European Literature), was added to the 1910 edition to show how the four authors fit into a larger developmental pattern.

The purpose of the book was to illustrate the relationship between biography, literary interpretation, and historical understanding by explicating the interdependence of "Erlebnis" (experience), "Ausdruck" (expression), and "Verstehen" (understanding). Each author is shown to have had a characteristic way of experiencing and understanding the world that affected his literary production and that must be taken into consideration by those who seek to interpret that production. The impact of Dilthey's book stemmed in part from his attempt to place the work of these authors in context, as opposed to the positivistic biography of his day, which merely provided detailed chronological information. Thus, Lessing's writings are described in terms of the conflict among theology, philosophy, and criticism in the Enlightenment; Goethe's work is related to his unusual gift for observation; Novalis and Hölderlin are discussed as members of the Romantic generation. The Novalis essay also addresses the significance of the death of his fiancée, Sophie von Kühn, and the Hölderlin essay focuses on his poetic confrontation with Greek culture.

The centerpiece of the book is the essay on Goethe, whom Dilthey deemed the first German author to have recognized the importance of biography and autobiography in the production of literature. The source of all he wrote is "Leben und dessen Auslegung" (life and its interpretation). "Persönlichkeit" (character) is the "Mittelpunkt" (focus) of his oeuvre. Goethe had a talent for finding the general in the particular: "Jedes Erlebnis wird ihm zu einer Belehrung über das Leben selbst" (every experience becomes for him a lesson in life itself), and he was convinced of the typicality of his own experience: "Er lauscht den Bewegungen in den heimlichen Tiefen seiner Seele und versteht aus ihnen Menschendasein und menschliche Entwickelung" (He listens to the movements in the secret depths of his soul and recognizes therein human existence and human development). Goethe's belief in his own typicality extended even to the past: "Überall fand er dieselben Modifikationen der menschlichen Natur, dieselben seltsamen Wendungen in der Entwickelung der Charaktere, dieselben Seelenzustände wieder, die er erlebt hatte. So hatte jede Gestalt und jedes Erlebnis der Vergangenheit für ihn Bedeutung durch etwas, das in seine eigene Erfahrung fiel" (Everywhere he found the same modifications in human nature, the same curious turns in the development of character, the same spiritual conditions that he experienced. Hence every figure and every experience of the past was significant for him because it could be found in his own experience).

These are troubling statements because they describe Goethe as a solipsist. They also controvert many of Dilthey's insights in "Die Einbildungskraft des Dichters" regarding the dangers of naive identification with authors of the past – dangers of which Goethe, in these lines at least, is said not to have been aware. But Dilthey goes on to observe that Goethe had the capacity to place himself in the position of the other without contaminating this transposition with his own experience. Goethe's genius lay in his ability to use his work to gain access to experiences that would otherwise have remained closed to him. His field of experience is thus expanded, albeit vicariously. Less gifted individuals are only capable of recognizing similarities between their own lives and those of others. When they find no similarities, no understanding is possible. The construction of a false similarity, as in escapist forms of reception, constitutes naive identification.

Goethe avoided such pseudoconstructions. Nonetheless, he was able to understand, through the productive use of his imagination, many more modes of existence than those which merely reduplicated – or appeared to reduplicate – his own.

Another quality that distinguishes Goethe or any great poet from nonpoetic minds is the ability to translate self-reflection into expression. Poets are able to express fully their inner experience because they are faced with relatively little resistance from the unconscious. From the standpoint of psychoanalytic theory one must characterize Dilthey's notion as somewhat inaccurate, for he exempts poets from universal processes of repression that may be ameliorated by the composition of a literary work or autobiography but are never completely suspended. Furthermore, from the perspective of semiotic theory, he can be criticized for failing to account for the resistance to expression offered by language itself, and for the linguistically creative work of poets who find the idiom of their day inadequate for their artistic statement.

Although *Das Erlebnis und die Dichtung* is Dilthey's most widely read book among literary scholars, it disappoints the reader who is familiar with his philosophical writing. Dilthey is keenly analytical in the latter genre, but these qualities are less evident in the book for which he is best known; recent reception of Dilthey's work is, for this reason, more concerned with his epistemology of the human sciences than with his literary historiography. The book is actually disturbing because it idealizes the authors under discussion as heroes of German culture, thereby overturning the important distinction Dilthey had drawn between the ideal and the typical. And Dilthey does not always follow his own advice for conducting historical analysis. For example, he refers to the happy and carefree years Lessing spent in Berlin in the 1750s – a characterization that is not substantiated by Lessing's correspondence, which was available to Dilthey and from which he quotes elsewhere in his essay. One must wonder whether Dilthey is violating his own precepts by naively identifying with Lessing so that his own affection for Berlin is transferred onto that author. The idealizing tone of Dilthey's presentation would be carried forth by his student Friedrich Gundolf, whose interpretive assumptions influenced several generations of German literary scholars.

In his eight-hundred-page biography *Goethe* (1916), Gundolf praises his subject as a singularly heroic figure in the history of the German spirit. Goethe's greatness is said to derive from the fact that he created his work independently of social, political, and economic realities. Indeed, artists are distinguished from all other men, according to Gundolf, to the degree that they can divorce their creative production from a base social reality. Goethe's poetic power was an especially stunning example of this poetic autonomy. It makes no sense to Gundolf to examine the facts of Goethe's life to get at his work, for the work is not a simple expression of the life. Work and life are inseparable. Dilthey, Gundolf says, has taught us that the goal of history is the development or objectification of "Geist" (mind or spirit), a Hegelian distortion of his teacher's project. Goethe, he goes on to say, knew that poetry was the manifestation of spirit, that the spirit is constituted in the poetic act. Here Gundolf strays from Dilthey, who would never have discounted the essential role played by the poet's milieu in the creative process. Gundolf plays lip service to the fusion of life and work, but he ignores the significance of life in the production of literature. Absent from his analysis is his teacher's fine sense of the interdependence between poetry and the social-historical world. Experience, or life, in Gundolf's conception is completely self-contained and internally generated; it has nothing to do with the poet's interactive relationship to his environment. Gundolf speaks partly in Dilthey's idiom, but he negates the latter's insightful insistence on a multidisciplinary approach to the understanding of human expression. Unfortunately, these distinctions have not always been kept in mind by literary historians of the twentieth century who have written critiques of Dilthey's work.

In his last years Dilthey devoted considerable effort to clarifying the process of historical and poetic understanding. In 1910 his treatise *Der Aufbau der geschichtlichen Welt in den Geisteswissenschaften* (The Construction of the Historical World in the Human Sciences, 1970) was published in the *Abhandlungen der Preußischen Akademie der Wissenschaften* (Proceedings of the Prussian Academy of Sciences). Here he recapitulates, in particularly lucid fashion, many of his earlier formulations. Life expressions can only be understood in the context of their milieu, but the milieu can only be grasped by analyzing specific life expressions. The historian brings to every interpretive situation a certain "Vorurteil" (prejudgment), not to be confused with "prejudice." This prejudgment may simply be a capacity to recognize a generic human aspect of the represented experience, or it may be based on more extensive historical information. Repeated investigation of any given historical context through a careful examination of the particulars of that context will bring the significance of these very particulars into better focus. But historical understanding is an endless procedure because as one's knowledge of a milieu improves, one's appreciation of its complexity intensifies, thereby resulting in the continuous need for further study of its particulars.

Historical understanding is not a matter of collecting information but rather of placing information into a context, lending it significance. But because all interpreters occupy specific historical standpoints and live within their own historically acquired psychic structures, the construction of significance is a historically determined enterprise. The irrational cannot be excluded from the interpretive process because experience is a combination of "denken, fühlen, wollen" (thinking, feeling, desiring). Dilthey therefore asserted – following Schleiermacher and other Romantics – that interpretation of historical documents, including literature, is ultimately "divinatorisch" (a matter of divination) and not subject to demonstrative certainty.

Dilthey's critique of historical reason was meant to ground and legitimize historical knowledge, but divination, the inclusion of the irrational in historical understanding, would seem to defeat this endeavor. His dilemma was profound. As a possible remedy he proposed, but never developed, a science of the fantasy – a new psychology that would explicate the role of affect and desire in the construction and interpretation of historical experience. Such a project would have involved an investigation of the unconscious, an investigation Dilthey was unwilling to undertake. While he suspected that interpretation is as much a matter of the will as of the intellect, he refused to consider the possibility that the will might sometimes have the upper hand, as Friedrich Nietzsche was arguing. Dilthey's inability to solve the problem of the relationship between unconscious will and conscious intellect in the interpretive process expressed itself as an enduring hostility toward Nietzsche, whom he dismissed as a brilliant man obsessed with "subjectivity." Nietzsche, he claimed, was lost in a narrow and fruitless pondering of individual experience without reference to its general historical aspect. Like so many of his neo-Romantic contemporaries, Dilthey confused the unconscious with the individual and the subjective. This confusion prevented him from appreciating the significance of Nietzsche's historical exploration of the unconscious dynamics at work in the Western tradition.

Since about 1890 Dilthey had been feeling overburdened by his professorial duties. In 1900, at the age of sixty-seven, he ceased holding seminars; in 1903 he ended his university lectures. He was increasingly plagued by nervousness, fatigue, and related complaints, which his students felt originated in his anxiety that he would never finish his major studies. He died on 30 September 1911, a few weeks before his seventy-eighth birthday, while vacationing in Tirol. It was the same year that Thomas Mann was writing *Der Tod in Venedig* (1912; translated as *Death in Venice,* 1925), a work that provides an uncanny demonstration of Dilthey's theory that literature paradigmatically captures life. Dilthey, who resembles Mann's protagonist Gustav von Aschenbach in several ways, was apparently so absorbed in his work that he, like Aschenbach, did not notice that an infection was claiming the lives of the guests in the hotel where he was staying. While others fled, Dilthey succumbed.

Letters:

"Zwei Briefe an Richard Adalbert Lipsius," in *Kieler Professoren: Briefe aus drei Jahrhunderten zur Geschichte der Universität Kiel,* edited by Moritz Liepmann (Stuttgart & Berlin: DVA, 1916), pp. 380–382;

Briefwechsel zwischen Wilhelm Dilthey und dem Grafen Paul Yorck von Wartenburg 1877–1897, edited by Sigrid von der Schulenburg (Halle: Niemeyer, 1923);

"Brief an Hermann Baumgarten vom 5.5.1862," in *Deutscher Liberalismus im Zeitalter Bismarcks: Eine politische Briefsammlung,* edited by Julius Heyderhoff (Bonn & Leipzig: Schroeder, 1925), pp. 89–90;

Der junge Dilthey: Ein Lebensbild in Briefen und Tagebüchern 1852–1870, edited by Clara Dilthey Misch (Leipzig: Teubner, 1933);

Briefe Wilhelm Diltheys an Bernhard und Luise Scholz 1859–1864, edited by Sigrid von der Schulenburg (Berlin: De Gruyter, 1934);

Briefe an Rudolf Haym 1861–1873, edited by Erich Weniger (Berlin: De Gruyter, 1936);

"Jugendfreundschaft Teichmüllers und Diltheys: Briefe und Tagebücher," *Archiv für spiritualistische Philosophie und ihre Geschichte,* 1 (1939): 385–412;

"Vier Briefe Wilhelm Diltheys an Erich Adickes Winter 1904–1905," edited by Gerhard Lehmann, in *Deutsche Akademie der Wissenschaften zu Berlin 1946–1956,* edited by the Deutsche Akademie der Wissenschaften zu Berlin (Berlin: Akademie Verlag, 1956), pp. 429–434;

"En torno a la Filosofia como ciencia estricta y al alcance del historicismo: Correspondencia entre Dilthey y Husserl de 29-junio, 5/6-julio y 10-julio de 1911," edited by Walter Biemel, *Revista de Filosofia de la Universidad de Costa Rica,* 1 (1957): 101–124.

Bibliography:

Ulrich Herrmann, *Bibliographie Wilhelm Dilthey: Quellen und Literatur* (Weinheim: Beltz, 1969).

References:

Karl-Otto Apel, "Dilthey's Distinction between 'Explanation' versus 'Understanding' and the Possibility of Its 'Mediation,'" *Journal of the History of Philosophy,* 25 (January 1987): 131–149;

Joseph Bleicher, *Contemporary Hermeneutics* (London: Routledge & Kegan Paul, 1980);

Otto Friedrich Bollnow, *Dilthey: Eine Einführung in seine Philosophie* (Leipzig: Teubner, 1936);

Bollnow, *Das Verstehen: Drei Aufsätze zur Theorie der Geisteswissenschaften* (Mainz: Kirchheim, 1949);

R. G. Collingwood, *The Idea of History* (New York: Oxford University Press, 1946);

Stanley Corngold, "Dilthey's Essay 'The Poetic Imagination': A Poetics of Force," *Interpretation: A Journal of Political Philosophy,* 9 (September 1981): 301–337;

Michael Ermarth, *Wilhelm Dilthey: The Critique of Historical Reason* (Chicago: University of Chicago Press, 1978);

Horace Freiss, "Wilhelm Dilthey, a Review of his Collected Works as an Introduction to a Phase of Contemporary German Philosophy," *Journal of Philosophy,* 26 (January 1929): 5–25;

Hans-Georg Gadamer, *Wahrheit und Methode: Grundzüge einer philosophischen Hermeneutik* (Tübingen: Mohr, 1960); translated by Garrett Barden and John Cumming as *Truth and Method* (London: Sheed & Ward, 1975);

Jürgen Habermas, *Erkenntnis und Interesse* (Frankfurt am Main: Suhrkamp, 1968); translated by Jeremy J. Shapiro as *Knowledge and Human Interests* (Boston: Beacon Press, 1971);

Herbert Hodges, *The Philosophy of Wilhelm Dilthey* (London: Routledge & Kegan Paul, 1952);

Hodges, *Wilhelm Dilthey: An Introduction* (New York: Oxford University Press, 1944);

Hajo Holborn, "Wilhelm Dilthey and the Critique of Historical Reason," *Journal of the History of Ideas,* 11 (January 1950): 93–118;

Max Horkheimer, "The Relation between Psychology and Sociology in the Work of Wilhelm Dilthey," *Studies in Philosophy and Social Science,* 8 (1939): 430–443;

Henry Stuart Hughes, *Consciousness and Society: The Re-orientation of European Social Thought 1890–1930* (New York: Knopf, 1958);

William Kluback, *William Dilthey's Philosophy of History* (New York: Columbia University Press, 1956);

Ludwig Landgrebe, *Philosophie der Gegenwart* (Frankfurt am Main: Ullstein, 1958);

Landgrebe, "Wilhelm Diltheys Theorie der Geisteswissenschaften: Analyse ihrer Grundbegriffe," *Jahrbuch für Philosophie und phänomenologische Forschung,* 9 (1928): 237–366;

Gerhard Lehmann, "Zur Geschichte der Kant-Ausgabe 1896–1955," *Deutsche Akademie der Wissenschaften zu Berlin 1946–1956,* edited by the Deutsche Akademie der Wissenschaften zu Berlin (Berlin: Akademie-Verlag, 1956), pp. 422–434;

Rudolf A. Makkreel, *Dilthey: Philosopher of the Human Studies* (Princeton: Princeton University Press, 1975);

Maurice Mandelbaum, *The Problem of Historical Knowledge: An Answer to Relativism* (New York: Liveright, 1938);

Georg Misch, *Lebensphilosophie und Phänomenologie: Eine Auseinandersetzung der Diltheyschen Richtung mit Heidegger und Husserl* (Leipzig & Berlin: Teubner, 1931);

Kurt Müller-Vollmer, *Towards a Phenomenological Theory of Literature: A Study of Wilhelm Dilthey's "Poetik"* (The Hague: Mouton, 1963);

Beate Pinkerneil, "Trennung von Geist und Politik: Literaturwissenschaft im Bann der Geistesgeschichte," in *Am Beispiel "Wilhelm Meister": Einführung in die Wissenschaftsgeschichte der Germanistik,* volume 1, edited by Klaus L. Berghahn and Beate Pinkerneil (Königstein: Athenäum, 1980), pp. 54–74;

H. P. Rickman, *Dilthey Today: A Critical Appraisal of the Contemporary Relevance of His Work* (New York: Greenwood Press, 1988);

Rickman, *Wilhelm Dilthey: Pioneer of the Human Studies* (Berkeley: University of California Press, 1979);

Frithjof Rodi, *Morphologie und Hermeneutik: Diltheys Ästhetik* (Stuttgart: Kohlhammer, 1969);

Rodi, Bollnow, Makkreel, Ulrich Dierse, Karlfried Gründer, Otto Pöggeler, and Hans-Martin Sass, eds., *Dilthey-Jahrbuch für Philosophie und Geschichte der Geisteswissenschaften,* 1- (1983-   );

Karol Sauerland, *Diltheys Erlebnisbegriff: Entstehung, Glanzzeit und Verkümmerung eines literaturhistorischen Begriffs* (Berlin: De Gruyter, 1972).

Papers:

Most of Wilhelm Dilthey's manuscripts are in the central archive of the Akademie der Wissenschaften (Academy of Sciences) in Berlin. A collection of his letters, some working notes, and – most important – a draft for the continuation of *Einleitung in die Geisteswissenschaften* known as the "Breslauer Ausarbeitung" (Breslau version) are in the Handschriftenabteilung der Niedersächsischen Staatts- und Universitätsbibliothek (Manuscript Division of the State and University Library of Lower Saxony) in Göttingen. Archives of the Georg Westermann Verlag contain Dilthey's correspondence with this publishing firm from 1874 to 1883.

Friedrich Engels

(28 November 1820 – 5 August 1895)

Helen G. Morris-Keitel
Bucknell University

SELECTED BOOKS: *Schelling und die Offenbarung: Kritik des neuesten Reaktionsversuchs gegen die freie Philosophie,* anonymous (Leipzig: Binder, 1842);

Schelling, der Philosoph in Christo, oder Die Verklärung der Weltweisheit zur Gotteswelt: Für gläubige Christen denen der philosophische Sprachgebrauch unbekannt ist, anonymous (Berlin: Eyssenhardt, 1842);

Die frech bedräute, jedoch wunderbar befreite Bibel. Oder: Der Triumph des Glaubens. Das ist: Schreckliche, jedoch wahrhafte und erkleckliche Historia von dem weiland Licentiaten Bruno Bauer; wie selbiger vom Teufel verführet, vom reinen Glauben abgefallen, Oberteufel geworden und endlich kräftiglich entsetzt ist. Christliches Heldengedicht in vier Gesängen, anonymous (Neumünster: Heß, 1842);

Die heilige Familie, oder Kritik der kritischen Kritik: Gegen Bruno Bauer und Consorten, by Engels and Karl Marx (Frankfurt am Main: Literarische Anstalt [J. Rütten], 1845); translated by Richard Dixon and Clemens Dutt as *The Holy Family; or, Critique of Critical Critique* (Moscow: Foreign Languages Publishing House, 1956);

Die Lage der arbeitenden Klasse in England: Nach eigner Anschauung und authentischen Quellen (Leipzig: Wigand, 1845); translated by Florence Kelley Wischnewetzky as *The Condition of the Working Class in England in 1844* (New York: Lovell, 1887; London: Sonnenschein, 1892);

Manifest der kommunistischen Partei, by Engels and Marx (London: Office der "Bildungsgesellschaft für Arbeiter" von J. E. Burghard, 1848; Chicago: Hofmann, 1871); translated by Samuel Moore, edited by Engels as *Manifesto of the Communist Party* (London: Reeves, 1888; Chicago: Kerr, 1902);

Po und Rhein, anonymous (Berlin: Duncker, 1859);

Savoyen, Nizza und der Rhein, anonymous (Berlin: Behrend, 1860);

Essays Addressed to Volunteers (London: Smith, 1861);

Friedrich Engels

Die preußische Militärfrage und die deutsche Arbeiterpartei (Hamburg: Meissner, 1865);

Der deutsche Bauernkrieg (Leipzig: Verlag der Expedition des "Volksstaats," 1870); translated by Moissaye J. Olgin as *The Peasant War in Germany* (London: Allen & Unwin, 1926; New York: International Publishers, 1926);

Zur Wohnungsfrage (Leipzig: Verlag der Expedition des "Volksstaats," 1872); translated as *The Housing Question,* edited by Dutt (London: Lawrence, 1935; New York: International Publishers, 1935);

L'Alliance de la Démocratie Socialiste et l'Association Internationale des Travailleurs: Rapport et documents publiés par ordre du Congrès International de la Haye, by Engels, Marx, and Paul Lafargue (London: Darson / Hamburg: Meissner, 1873);

Herrn Eugen Dührings Umwälzung der Wissenschaft: Philosophie; Politische Oekonomie; Sozialismus (Leipzig: Genossenschafts-Buchdruckerei, 1878); translated by Emile Burns, edited by Dutt as *Herr Eugen Dühring's Revolution in Science (Anti-Dühring)* (London: Lawrence & Wishart, 1934; Chicago: Kerr, 1935);

Die Entwicklung des Sozialismus von der Utopie zur Wissenschaft (Hottingen-Zurich: Schweizerische Genossenschaftsdruckerei, 1882); translated by Edward Aveling as *Socialism, Utopian and Scientific* (London: Sonnenschein / New York: Scribners, 1892);

Der Ursprung der Familie, des Privateigenthums und des Staats: Im Anschluß an Lewis H. Morgan's Forschungen (Hottingen-Zurich: Schweizerische Volksbuchhandlung, 1884); translated anonymously as *The Origin of the Family, Private Property and the State* (Moscow: Foreign Languages Publishing House, 1891); translated by Ernest Untermann as *The Origin of the Family, Private Property and the State* (Chicago: Kerr, 1902); translated by Alick West, revised by Dona Torr as *The Origin of the Family, Private Property and the State, in the Light of the Researches of Lewis H. Morgan* (London: Lawrence & Wishart, 1940);

Ludwig Feuerbach und der Ausgang der klassischen deutschen Philosophie (Stuttgart: Dietz, 1888); translated as *Ludwig Feuerbach and the Outcome of Classical German Philosophy,* edited by Dutt (London: Lawrence, 1934; New York: International Publishers, 1934);

In Sachen Brentano contra Marx, wegen angeblicher Citatsfälschung (Hamburg: Meissner, 1891);

Revolution and Counter-Revolution; or, Germany in 1848, by Engels and Marx, edited by Eleanor Marx Aveling (London: Sonnenschein / New York: Scribners, 1896);

Aus dem literarischen Nachlaß von Karl Marx, Friedrich Engels und Ferdinand Lassalle, 4 volumes, edited by Franz Mehring (Stuttgart: Dietz, 1902) – includes in volume 2, "Die deutsche Reichsverfassungskampagne," pp. 289–383;

Feuerbach, the Roots of the Socialist Philosophy, translated by Austin Lewis (Chicago: Kerr, 1903);

The Essentials of Marx: The Communist Manifesto, by Karl Marx and Friedrich Engels; Wage-Labor and Capital; Value, Price and Profit, and Other Selections, by Karl Marx, edited by Algernon Lee (New York: Vanguard, 1926);

Karl Marx, Friedrich Engels: Historisch-kritische Gesamtausgabe, Werke, Schriften, Briefe, 12 volumes, edited by David Rjazanov (David Borisovich Goldendach) and Vladimir Viktorovich Adoratskij (Frankfurt am Main: Marx-Engels-Archiv, 1927–1935) – includes in volume 5 (1932), "Die deutsche Ideologie: Kritik der neuesten deutschen Philosophie in ihren Repräsentanten, Feuerbach, B. Bauer und Stirner, und des deutschen Sozialismus in seinen verschiedenen Propheten 1845–1846," by Engels and Marx, pp. 3–532; translated by S. Ryazanskaya as *The German Ideology* (Moscow: Progress Publishers, 1964); in volume 6 (1932), "Grundsätze des Kommunismus," pp. 503–522; translated by Max Bedacht as *Principles of Communism* (Chicago: Workers' Party of America, 1925);

The Fourteenth of March 1883: Frederick Engels on the Death of Karl Marx (New York: International Publishers, 1933);

Konspekt über "Das Kapital," edited by the Marx-Engels-Lenin-Institut, Moscow (Moscow: Verlagsgenossenschaft ausländischer Arbeiter in der UdSSR, 1933);

The British Labour Movement: Articles from the Labour Standard (London: Lawrence, 1934; New York: International Publishers, 1940);

Dialektik der Natur (Moscow: Verlagsgenossenschaft ausländischer Arbeiter in der UdSSR, 1935); translated by Dutt as *Dialectics of Nature* (New York: International Publishers, 1940; London: Lawrence & Wishart, 1941);

Engels on Capital: Synopsis, Reviews, Letters and Supplementary Material, translated and edited by Leonard E. Mins (New York: International Publishers, 1937; London: Lawrence & Wishart, 1938);

The Civil War in the United States, by Engels and Marx (London: Lawrence & Wishart, 1938);

Revolution in Spain, by Engels and Marx (New York: International Publishers, 1939);

Über den Verfall des Feudalismus und das Aufkommen der Bourgeoisie (Moscow: Verlag für fremdsprachige Literatur, 1941);

Über die Gewaltstheorie: Gewalt und Ökonomie bei der Herstellung des neuen Deutschen Reiches (Berlin: Neuer Weg, 1946);

Über Kunst und Literatur, by Engels and Marx, edited by Michail Lifschitz (Berlin: Henschel, 1948);

Die Revolution von 1848: Auswahl aus der "Neuen Rheinischen Zeitung," by Engels and Marx (Berlin: Dietz, 1949); translated by Ryazanskaya as *The Revolution of 1848–49: Articles from the Neue Rheinische Zeitung* (New York: International Publishers, 1972);

Women and Communism: Selections from the Writings of Marx, Engels, Lenin, and Stalin (London: Lawrence & Wishart, 1950);

Die Bauernfrage in Frankreich und Deutschland (Berlin: Dietz, 1951); translated anonymously as *The Peasant Question in France and Germany* (Moscow: Foreign Languages Publishing House, 1955);

Zur Geschichte und Sprache der deutschen Frühzeit: Ein Sammelband (Berlin: Dietz, 1952);

Karl Marx and Friedrich Engels on Britain (Moscow: Foreign Languages Publishing House, 1953);

Marx and Engels on Malthus: Selections from the Writings of Marx and Engels Dealing with the Theories of Thomas Robert Malthus, translated by Dorothea L. Meek and Ronald L. Meek, edited by Ronald L. Meek (London: Lawrence & Wishart, 1953);

Über die Gewerkschaften, by Engels and Marx (Berlin: Tribüne, 1953);

Karl Marx, Friedrich Engels: Werke, 43 volumes (Berlin: Dietz, 1956–1968);

K. Marx and F. Engels on Religion (Moscow: Foreign Languages Publishing House, 1957);

Basic Writings on Politics and Philosophy, by Engels and Marx, edited by Lewis S. Feuer (Garden City, N.Y.: Doubleday, 1959);

On Colonialism, by Engels and Marx (Moscow: Foreign Languages Publishing House, 1960);

Marx/Engels über Erziehung und Bildung, edited by Pavel N. Gruzdev (Berlin: Volk und Wissen, 1960);

Auf Reisen: Reiseskizzen aus einem halben Jahrhundert, edited by R. Schack (Berlin: Dietz, 1966);

Karl Marx, Friedrich Engels, 4 volumes, edited by Iring Fetscher (Frankfurt am Main: Fischer, 1966);

Über Kultur, Ästhetik, Literatur: Ausgewählte Texte, by Engels, Marx, and Vladimir I. Lenin, edited by Hans Koch (Leipzig: Reclam, 1969);

The Bakuninists at Work: Review of the Uprising in Spain in the Summer of 1873, translated by Bryan Bean (Moscow: Progress Publishers, 1971);

Birth of the Communist Manifesto: Full Text of the Manifesto, All Prefaces by Marx and Engels, Early Drafts by Engels and Other Supplementary Material, edited by Dirk J. Struik (New York: International Publishers, 1971);

The Cologne Communist Trial, by Engels and Marx, translated and edited by Rodney Livingstone (London: Lawrence & Wishart, 1971; New York: International Publishers, 1971);

Ireland and the Irish Question, by Engels and Marx, compiled by Lev Isaakovich Golman, V. E. Kunina, and M. A. Zhelnova, translated by Angela Clifford, K. Cook, R. Bean, and others, edited by Richard Dixon (Moscow: Progress Publishers, 1971; New York: International Publishers, 1972);

Anarchism and Anarcho-Syndicalism, by Engels, Marx, and Lenin (New York: International Publishers, 1972);

The Marx-Engels Reader, edited by Robert C. Tucker (New York: Norton, 1972);

Die russische Kommune: Kritik eines Mythos, by Engels and Marx, edited by Maximilien Rubel (Munich: Hanser, 1972);

Karl Marx, Friedrich Engels Gesamtausgabe [MEGA] (Berlin: Dietz, 1972–);

Marx, Engels on Literature and Arts: A Selection of Writings, edited by Lee Baxandall and Stefan Morawski (Saint Louis: Telos Press, 1973; enlarged edition, New York: International General, 1974);

Cola di Rienzi: Ein unbekannter dramatischer Entwurf, edited by Michael Knieriem (Wuppertal: Hammer, 1974);

Über Sprache, Stil und Übersetzung, by Engels and Marx, edited by Heinz Ruschinski and Bruno Retzlaff-Kresse (Berlin: Dietz, 1974);

Karl Marx, Friedrich Engels: Collected Works, 12 volumes, translated by Dixon and others (London: Lawrence & Wishart, 1975–1977; New York: International Publishers, 1975–1979);

Der Bürgerkrieg in den Vereinigten Staaten, by Engels and Marx, edited by Günter Wistozki and Manfred Tetzel (Berlin: Dietz, 1976);

Marx, Engels, Lenin: Über die Frau und die Familie, edited by the Bundesvorstand des Demokratischen Frauenbundes Deutschlands (Leipzig: Verlag für die Frau, 1976);

Marx and Engels on Ecology, edited by Howard L. Parsons (Westport, Conn.: Greenwood Press, 1977);

On Literature and Art, by Engels and Marx (Moscow: Progress Publishers, 1978);

Über Deutschland und die deutsche Arbeiterbewegung, by Engels and Marx (Berlin: Dietz, 1978);

Karl Marx, Friedrich Engels, the Collected Writings in "The New York Daily Tribune," edited by A. Thomas Ferguson and Stephen J. O'Neil (New York: Urizen Books, 1980);

Droht der gemeinsame Untergang?: Marxismus und Ökologie. Originaltexte von Marx und Engels in Gegenüberstellung zu ihren aktuellen Kritikern (Hamburg: Buntbuch, 1980);

Marx und Engels über die sozialistische und kommunistische Gesellschaft: Die Entwicklung der marxistischen Lehre von der kommunistischen Umgestaltung, edited by Rolf Dlubek and Renate Merkel (Berlin: Dietz, 1981);

Unbekanntes von Friedrich Engels und Karl Marx, edited by Bert Andreas, Jacques Grandjonc, and Hans Pelger (Trier: Karl-Marx-Haus, 1986);

Über die Liebe, by Engels and Marx, edited by Heinrich and Hilde Gemkow (Berlin: Dietz, 1986);

Heiteres und Bissiges von Marx und Engels, edited by Käte Schubert (Berlin: Dietz, 1987);

Über den Kampf um Frieden und sozialen Fortschritt, by Engels, Marx, and Lenin (Berlin: Dietz, 1987);

Über den Sozialismus, by Engels, Marx, and Lenin (Berlin: Dietz, 1987).

OTHER: Karl Marx, *Der Bürgerkrieg in Frankreich: Adresse des Generalraths der Internationalen Arbeiter-Association an alle Mitarbeiter in Europa und den Vereinigten Staaten,* translated by Engels (Leipzig: Verlag der Expedition des "Volksstaats," 1871);

Marx, *Das Kapital: Kritik der politischen Ökonomie. Zweiter Band. Buch II: Der Circulationsprocess des Kapitals,* edited by Engels (Hamburg: Meissner, 1885); translated by Ernest Untermann as *Capital: A Critique of Political Economy. Volume 2: The Process of Circulation of Capital* (Chicago: Kerr, 1907);

Marx, *Capital: A Critical Analysis of Capitalist Production,* translated by Moore and Edward Aveling, edited by Engels (2 volumes, London: Sonnenschein, Lowrey, 1887; 1 volume, New York: Appleton, 1889);

Marx, *Free Trade: A Speech Delivered before the Democratic Club, Brussels, Belgium, Jan. 9, 1848. With Extract from La misère de la philosophie,* translated by Florence Kelley Wischnewetzky, preface by Engels (Boston: Lee & Shepherd / New York: Dillingham, 1888);

Marx, *Das Kapital: Kritik der politischen Ökonomie. Dritter Band. Buch III: Der Gesamtprocess der kapitalistischen Produktion,* edited by Engels (Hamburg: Meissner, 1894); translated by Untermann as *Capital: A Critique of Political Economy. Volume 3: The Process of Capitalist Production as a Whole* (Chicago: Kerr, 1909);

Marx, *Die Klassenkämpfe in Frankreich 1848 bis 1850,* introduction by Engels (Berlin: Grote, 1895);

translated by Henry Kuhn as *The Class Struggles in France, 1848–1850* (New York: New York Labor News Co., 1924);

Marx, *The Paris Commune, Including the "First Manifesto of the International on the Franco-Prussian War," the "Second Manifesto of the International on the Franco-Prussian War," "The Civil War in France,"* introduction by Engels, edited by Lucien Sanial (New York: New York Labor News Co., 1902).

Friedrich Engels is most often seen in the shadow of his friend and collaborator, Karl Marx — a position he himself did not contest: "Es ist mein Schicksal, daß ich den Ruhm und die Ehre einernten muß, deren Saat ein Größerer als ich, Karl Marx, ausgestreut hat. Und so kann ich nur geloben, den Rest meines Lebens im aktiven Dienst des Proletariats so zu verbringen, daß ich womöglich mich jener Ehren noch nachträglich würdig mache" (It is my fate that I must harvest the fame and the honor, the seed of which was sown by one greater than I, Karl Marx. And so I can only pledge to spend the rest of my life in the active service of the proletariat in such a way that I will yet make myself worthy of these honors wherever possible), he said on his seventieth birthday. Theoretician, writer, propagandist, and adviser of the nascent working-class movement and its associated political parties that developed in Europe and the United States, Engels, it can be argued, had an influence during his lifetime that equaled or even surpassed that of Marx. This influence was due to his ability to "translate" Marx's economic and social theories into a language more accessible to workers and to his application of dialectical materialism to such diverse fields as military science, linguistics, natural science, and history.

Engels was born on 28 November 1820 in Barmen, near Wuppertal — an important center of the textile industry that was technologically advanced in comparison to the rest of the German states at the time. He was the oldest of eight children of Friedrich and Elisabeth Franziska Mauritia Engels (née van Haar). His father ran a bleaching and spinning works and was also in partnership with Godfrey and Peter Ermen, who ran a similar factory in Manchester, England. An adroit businessman, the elder Engels was influenced by Pietism, the predominant religious movement in that part of Germany, which emphasized industriousness and the notion that the masses deserved to suffer because of their "sinful" ways. Sent to the gymnasium in Elberfeld in 1834, the young Engels became enthralled with

Engels in 1845

humanistic and liberal ideas. Friedrich, senior, removed his son from school before he could take his Abitur (the examinations necessary for entrance to the university) and began training him to help run the family business.

In July 1838 Engels was sent to Bremen as an intern with the firm of Heinrich Leupold. There he spent his free time reading the works of the Young German movement, including those of Heinrich Heine and Ludwig Börne. Influenced by the Young Germans' notion of freedom, he wrote the anonymous "Briefe aus dem Wuppertal" (Letters from Wuppertal) in 1839 for the *Telegraph für Deutschland,* in which he indicted the Pietists for their treatment of the workers. The articles were Engels's first public expression of concern for the working class.

Reading the works of David Friedrich Strauß and then of Georg Wilhelm Friedrich Hegel, Engels became a self-declared Young Hegelian and placed his hope in revolutionary thought and action. In September 1841 he went to Berlin – the center of Young Hegelianism – to serve a mandatory year of

military service. There he spent his free time attending lectures at the university and in debate with the most renowned Young Hegelians such as Edgar and Bruno Bauer and Max Stirner. Eventually, however, due to the influence of Ludwig Feuerbach's *Das Wesen des Christenthums* (1841; translated as *The Essence of Christianity,* 1854), he rejected the subjectivity of the Young Hegelians and adopted a materialist position.

After he finished his military service in September 1842, Engels went to Manchester to work for his father's partners. On the way he stopped in Cologne to meet Marx, who was editing the *Rheinische Zeitung* (Rhenish Newspaper); Engels had contributed a few articles to the paper. This first meeting was rather cool, as Marx was suspicious of Engels's connections to the Young Hegelians.

In Manchester the pace and level of industrialization were much greater than anything Engels had experienced in Germany. Appalled at the destitution of the English working class, Engels searched for an explanation and a solution in the works of such utopian socialist writers as Robert Owen,

Charles Fourier, and Claude-Henri de Rouvroy, Comte de Saint-Simon, and of such bourgeois political economists as Adam Smith and David Ricardo. He established contacts with the Chartists – the leading English labor movement of the day – and with the League of the Just, a group of mostly German exiled utopian socialists. Through his relationship with Mary Burns, an Irish working-class woman, he was able to establish direct contact with the workers. His article "Umrisse zu einer Kritik der Nationalökonomie" (Critical Essays in Political Economy) appeared in 1844 in the first number of the *Deutsch-Französische Jahrbücher* (German-French Yearbooks), the exile version of the *Rheinische Zeitung* edited by Marx in Paris. In this article Engels attacks the effects of private property on the working class: "der Arbeiter muß arbeiten, um zu leben, während der Grundbesitzer von seinen Renten und der Kapitalist von seinen Zinsen, im Notfall von seinem Kapital oder dem kapitalisierten Grundbesitz leben kann. Die Folge davon ist, daß dem Arbeiter nur das Allernotdürftigste, die nackten Subsistenzmittel zufallen, während der größte Teil der Produkte sich zwischen dem Kapital und dem Grundbesitz verteilt" (the worker has to work to live, while the landowner is able to live off his rents and the capitalist off his interest or, if the need arises, off his capital or capitalized landed property. The result is that only the absolute necessities, the bare means of subsistence, accrue to labor while the major proportion of the products fall to the share of capital and landed property). Engels concludes that private property must be abolished, and that the workers will rise to this task. Marx's concurrence with many of Engels's insights and conclusions opened the door to a lifelong friendship that began at their second meeting, which took place in Paris in August 1844.

Engels gathered as much empirical knowledge of the condition of the English workers as he could. This material was organized and analyzed in his *Die Lage der arbeitenden Klasse in England* (1845; translated as *The Condition of the Working Class in England in 1844*, 1887), which was written after his return to Barmen. With this work Engels laid the foundations for modern sociology and urban geography. He begins with a description of the rise of industrialization in England and the growing rift between the bourgeoisie and the industrial proletariat. He then focuses on the squalor of large industrial centers and its effects – disease, illiteracy, crime, alcoholism, sexual abuse, and the exploitation of women and children as sources of cheap labor. As Marx wrote seventeen years later: "Wie frisch, leiden-

Engels in 1856

schaftlich, kühn vorausgreifend und ohne gelehrte und wissenschaftliche Bedenken wird hier noch die Sache gefaßt!" (How freshly, passionately, with what bold anticipation and no learned and scientific doubts, the thing is dealt with here!). The work is the testament of a young man newly converted to communism, and it is in this light that its predictions of the speedy collapse of capitalist society and the rise of the working class must be seen. It was, however, the first work to analyze the social conditions of the English working class as a whole. Its publication in late May 1845 helped fuel the ideological debate surrounding the social question in Germany, which had received increased attention since the Silesian weaver uprisings of 1844.

In April 1845 Engels went to Brussels, the center of the international socialist movement in the 1840s, to join Marx, who had been forced to flee Paris in January. In early 1846 Marx and Engels wrote their first joint treatise, "Die deutsche Ideologie" (translated as *The German Ideology*, 1964), which was not published until 1932. The work took issue with the various strands of post-Hegelian philosophy, including the "true" socialism of Karl Grün, Wilhelm Weitling, and others. Engels's and Marx's criticism was aimed at the unscientific premise of these movements: that social and economic conditions were the product of ideas. According to Marx and Engels, the reverse was true: social and economic conditions produced ideas. This line of thought formed the basis of what is known today as Marxism.

Engels spent much of his time between 1846 and 1848 working to disseminate the goals of "scientific" communism, especially among the members of the League of the Just. These activities required him to make several trips to Paris, where the league was headquartered. His efforts led the league to decide at its first international congress in London from 2 to 9 June 1847 to change its name to the Communist League and its motto from "All Men are Brothers" to "Working Men of All Countries, Unite!" The delegates also debated a document by Engels, "Grundsätze des Kommunismus" (1932; translated as *Principles of Communism,* 1925), which served as a first draft for Marx and Engels's *Manifest der kommunistischen Partei* (1848; translated as *Manifesto of the Communist Party,* 1888).

Engels was in Paris when he heard about the March 1848 revolution in Berlin. His early assessment was that the working people had won but that rule had passed not into their hands but into those of the haute bourgeoisie. Hence, Engels considered the revolution unfinished. On the night of 5–6 April 1848 Engels left for Cologne, where he and Marx, with the help of writers such as Ernst Dronke, Georg Weerth, and Wilhelm Wolff, established a daily newspaper, the *Neue Rheinische Zeitung* (New Rhenish Newspaper), to help the revolution to a successful end. In addition to securing financial backing for the paper, Engels was the specialist on foreign policy and military affairs. He argued strongly against German imperialism, insisting that with every country Germany set free it would be freeing itself.

By the end of September 1848 the counterrevolutionary forces were regaining strength, and Engels fled to Switzerland. He returned to Germany on 26 January 1849 to serve as a military adviser to the troops in Elberfeld and in the Palatinate during the last two months of the revolution. On 6 October 1849 he left Germany for London, where Marx was awaiting him.

In the following years Engels produced three major works analyzing past German revolutionary struggles. "Die deutsche Reichsverfassungskam-

pagne" (The Campaign for a German Constitution, 1902) and *Der deutsche Bauernkrieg* (1870; translated as *The Peasant War in Germany,* 1926) appeared in the *Neue Rheinische Zeitung: Politisch-ökonomische Revue* (New Rhenish Newspaper: Political-Economic Review), published in Hamburg from March to November 1850. *Revolution and Counter-Revolution; or, Germany in 1848* (1896) was a series of articles published under Marx's name in the *New York Daily Tribune* in 1852. Engels's goal was twofold: to apply the new theoretical position defined by himself and Marx, and to demonstrate the necessity of a worker-peasant alliance for a successful revolution.

In November 1850 Engels had moved back to Manchester to manage the spinning factory of Ermen and Engels. He thereby secured a steady income for himself as well as for Marx and Marx's family. For the next twenty years Engels led a double life — attending to his business duties by day and refining and disseminating the theory of scientific communism after work. Although he kept a residence in town to fulfill his social obligations as a member of the firm, he considered his real home to be the house of Mary Burns and her younger sister, Lizzie. There he often spent his evenings and weekends writing or meeting with representatives of workers' organizations.

A major effort of the Communist League was to establish contact with nascent labor movements all over Europe and in the United States. Engels's proficiency with languages — by the end of the 1860s he spoke and wrote twelve and read eight more — meant that a large share of the correspondence fell to him. A major focus of Engels's studies in these years was military science and military history. His interest in those subjects was stimulated by the Crimean War, the American Civil War, and other armed struggles around the world. Engels tried to demonstrate in articles in such publications as *Putnam's Monthly,* the *New American Cyclopedia,* the *Allgemeine Militär-Zeitung* (Universal Military Newspaper), and the *Volunteer Journal* that capitalism and warfare are closely linked.

During the 1850s Engels was constantly encouraging Marx to complete the first volume of *Das Kapital: Kritik der politischen Ökonomie* (1867; translated as *Capital: A Critical Analysis of Capitalist Production,* 1887). Although they only saw one another a few times a year, they corresponded almost daily. Engels assisted Marx with the collection and organization of the empirical data that Marx incorporated into the work and served as his friend's most insightful critic.

In May 1863 the General Association of German Workers was established, and Ferdinand Lassalle was elected its president. Although Marx and Engels were skeptical about Lassalle's reformist rhetoric, they were glad that the German working class was beginning to organize. After Lassalle's death in September 1864 Engels joined the correspondent staff of the *Social-Demokrat,* the newspaper of the association, with the explicit intent of combating Lassallean ideology. In his pamphlet *Die preußische Militärfrage und die deutsche Arbeiterpartei* (The Prussian Military Question and the German Workers' Party, 1865), which outgrew its intended proportions as an article for the *Social-Demokrat,* Engels assesses what he considered the dual purpose behind Prussia's military buildup under Chancellor Otto von Bismarck: to achieve hegemony over other German states and to suppress any democratic movements. At this point in Germany's history, he argues, the bourgeoisie and the workers must fight together for democracy against the Prussian Junkers and the military. This alliance could only be effective, however, if the workers were represented by their own revolutionary party.

During the 1860s tensions between Engels and the Ermen brothers grew steadily. He left the firm on 30 June 1869, which he called his "first day of freedom." On 20 September 1870 he moved to London to devote his entire attention to the quickly growing socialist movement. He joined Marx on the General Council of the International Working Men's Association, which had been formed in September 1864. The association was constantly threatened by factionalization; of particular concern were the anarchists, led by Mikhail Bakunin. Marx and Engels collaborated on many articles attacking the anarchists' putschist concepts and their rejection of every form of state power.

In May 1875 the German Socialist Workers' party was formed at the Unity Congress in Gotha. Although the ideas of Marx and Engels had the support of two of its key leaders, Wilhelm Liebknecht and August Bebel, the party was not devoid of Lassallean reformist influences. One reformist was Karl Eugen Dühring, a Berlin university lecturer. At the request of Liebknecht and at Marx's urging, Engels attacked Dühring in a series of articles in the Social Democratic party organ *Vorwärts* (Forward) between January 1877 and June 1878 that were collected as *Herrn Eugen Dührings Umwälzung der Wissenschaft* (1878; translated as *Herr Eugen Dühring's Revolution in Science [Anti-Dühring],* 1934). Engels outlines dialectical and historical materialism, Marxist political economy, and scientific socialism. For the first time, the Marxist theory was written in a lan-

Cover for Engels's anthropological study of the origin of the family, private property, and the state

guage that could be understood by the workers. While working on his own projects, Engels was encouraging Marx to finish the second volume of *Das Kapital.* Marx died on 14 March 1883, however, leaving the editorial work on the volume to Engels; it was published in July 1885.

For the rest of his life Engels was an adviser to working-class movements and parties around the world. He was always concerned to maintain and clarify his and Marx's theories in opposition to the reformists, opportunists, and anarchists who, he felt, threatened to defuse the revolutionary spirit of the socialist movement. Letters, pamphlets, articles, and the publication and republication of Marx's writings were his weapons in this struggle.

One of the few longer works Engels completed during this period, *Der Ursprung der Familie, des Privateigenthums und des Staats* (1884; translated as *The Origin of the Family, Private Property and the State,* 1891), is a critique of Lewis Henry Morgan's *Ancient Society; or, Researches in the Lines of Human Progress from Savagery, through Barbarism to Civilization* (1877). Engels tries to show that the family, property relations, and the state are historically determined and, therefore, subject to change. Modern social anthropologists and feminists have found oversimplifications in the work, but it is one of the first attempts – together with August Bebel's *Die Frau und der Sozialismus* (1883; translated as *Woman under Socialism,* 1904) – to link patriarchy and capitalism.

Engels played a leading role at the second International Workers' Congress in Paris, with 407 delegates from twenty-two countries, in July 1889. Resolutions were passed to establish 1 May as International Labor Day, to demonstrate for an eight-hour workday, and to demand improved and safer working conditions.

After the antisocialist laws were abolished in Germany in 1890 Engels helped Liebknecht, Bebel, and Karl Kautsky develop a new program for the Social Democratic party. He made his last trip to the Continent from 1 August to 29 September 1893, meeting with leaders of the party in Zurich, Munich, Vienna, Berlin, and Hannover. The third volume of *Das Kapital,* edited by Engels from Marx's notes, was published in December 1894.

Even though his health was deteriorating and his doctor had forbidden him to read or work by artificial light, Engels continued to advise the fledgling socialist movement. On 5 August 1895 he died in London of cancer of the throat. He left behind an uncompleted work, *Dialektik der Natur* (1935; translated as *Dialectics of Nature,* 1940), in which he tried to apply dialectical materialism to the physical sciences.

Letters:

Briefwechsel Karl Marx–Friedrich Engels, 4 volumes (Berlin: Dietz, 1949-1950);

Karl Marx and Frederick Engels: Letters to Americans, 1848–1895, a Selection, translated by Leonard E. Mins (New York: International Publishers, 1953);

Briefe über "Das Kapital": Karl Marx–Friedrich Engels, edited by the Marx-Engels-Lenin-Stalin Institut (Berlin: Dietz, 1954);

Zwischen 18 und 25: Jugendbriefe, edited by Hannes Skambraks (Berlin: Dietz, 1965).

Bibliographies:

Robert J. Usher, "The Bibliography of the *Communist Manifesto,*" *Bibliographical Society of America,* 5 (1910): 109–114;

Institut für Marxismus-Leninismus, *Die Erstdrucke der Werke von Marx und Engels: Bibliographie der Einzelausgaben* (Berlin: Dietz, 1955);

Maximilien Rubel, *Bibliographie des œuvres de Karl Marx* (Paris: Rivière, 1956);

Rubel, *Supplément à la Bibliographie des œuvres de Karl Marx* (Paris: Rivière, 1960);

R. L. Prager, *Marx, Engels, Lassalle: Eine Bibliographie des Sozialismus* (London: Slienger, 1977);

Franz Neubauer, *Marx-Engels Bibliographie* (Boppard: Boldt, 1979);

Dieter Zirnstein, *Verzeichnis der Werke von Karl Marx und Friedrich Engels: Herausgegeben von Verlagen nichtsozialistischer Länder in den Jahren 1945–1981* (Berlin, 1982);

Inge Kiesshauer, *Lebendiges Erbe der Klassiker: Auswahlbibliographie zum Karl-Marx-Jahr 1983* (Leipzig: Deutsche Bücherei, 1982);

Cecil L. Eubanks, *Karl Marx and Friedrich Engels: An Analytical Bibliography,* second edition (New York: Garland, 1984);

Hal Draper, *The Marx-Engels Register: A Complete Bibliography of Marx and Engels' Individual Writings* (New York: Schocken Books, 1985).

Biographies:

Gustav Mayer, *Friedrich Engels. Eine Biographie,* 2 volumes (The Hague: Nijhoff, 1934); translated by Gilbert and Helen Highet as *Friedrich Engels: A Biography,* edited by Richard H. S. Crossman (New York: Fertig, 1969);

J. B. Coates, *The Life and Teachings of Friedrich Engels* (New York: Universal Distributors, 1946);

Grace Carleton, *Friedrich Engels: The Shadow Prophet* (London: Pall Mall Press, 1965);

Karl Kupisch, *Vom Pietismus zum Kommunismus: Zur Jugendentwicklung von Friedrich Engels* (Berlin: Lettner, 1965);

Leonid F. Ilyichov and others, *Frederick Engels – A Biography* (Moscow: Progress Publishers, 1974);

William Otto Henderson, *Life of Friedrich Engels,* 2 volumes (London: Cass, 1976);

David McLellan, *Friedrich Engels* (New York: Viking, 1978);

Terrell Carver, *Engels* (New York: Hill & Wang, 1981);

Jenny Marx, *Ein bewegtes Leben,* edited by Renate Schack (Berlin: Dietz, 1989);

Eugene Kamenka, *Friedrich Engels: His Life, His Works, His Writings* (Chicago: Kerr, n.d.).

References:

Martin Berger, *Engels, Armies and Revolution: The Revolutionary Tactics of Classical Marxism* (Hamden, Conn.: Archon, 1977);

Ernst Bloch, *Das Prinzip Hoffnung* (Frankfurt am Main: Suhrkamp, 1959);

Theodore Brameld, *A Philosophic Approach to Communism* (Chicago: University of Chicago Press, 1933);

Willy Brandt, *Friedrich Engels und die sozialen Demokratie: Rede zum 150. Geburtstag von Friedrich Engels in Wuppertal* (Bonn & Bad Godesberg: Neue Gesellschaft, 1970);

Anthony Brewer, *Marxist Theories of Imperialism: A Critical Survey,* second edition (New York: Routledge, 1990);

Kenneth N. Cameron, *Marx and Engels Today: A Modern Dialogue on Philosophy and History* (Hicksville, N.Y.: Exposition Press, 1976);

Terrell Carver, *Marx & Engels: The Intellectual Relationship* (Bloomington: Indiana University Press, 1983);

Ian Cummings, *Marx, Engels, and National Movements* (New York: St. Martin's Press, 1980);

Peter Demetz, *Marx, Engels and the Poets: Origins of Marxist Literary Criticism,* revised and enlarged edition, translated by Jeffrey L. Sammons (Chicago: University of Chicago Press, 1967);

Herwig Förder, *Marx und Engels am Vorabend der Revolution; die Ausarbeitung der politischen Richtlinien für die deutschen Kommunisten (1846–1848)* (Berlin: Akademie-Verlag, 1960);

W. B. Gallie, *Philosophers of Peace and War: Kant, Clausewitz, Marx, Engels, and Tolstoy* (London & New York: Cambridge University Press, 1978);

Richard F. Hamilton, *The Bourgeois Epoch: Marx and Engels on Britain, France, and Germany* (Chapel Hill: University of North Carolina Press, 1991);

Oscar J. Hammen, *The Red '48ers: Karl Marx and Friedrich Engels* (New York: Scribners, 1969);

Mick Jenkins, *Friedrich Engels in Manchester* (Manchester, U.K.: Lancashire and Cheshire Communist Party, 1964);

Linda Jenness, ed., *Feminism and Socialism* (New York: Pathfinder Press, 1972);

Steven Marcus, *Engels, Manchester, and the Working Class* (New York: Random House, 1974);

Marx-Engels-Jahrbuch, 1– (1978–);

Fritz Nova, *Friedrich Engels: His Contributions to Political Theory* (New York: Philosophical Library, 1967);

Hans Pelger, ed., *Friedrich Engels, 1820–1970; Referate, Diskussionen, Dokumente,* Schriftenreihe des Forschungsinstituts der Friedrich-Ebert-Stiftung, no. 85 (Hannover: Verlag für Literatur und Zeitgeschehen, 1971);

Edward E. Rice, *Marx, Engels and the Workers of the World* (New York: Four Winds Press, 1977);

Janet Sayers, Mary Evans, and Nanneke Redclift, eds., *Engels Revisited: New Feminist Essays* (New York: Tavistock, 1987);

Manfred Schneider, *Die kranke schöne Seele der Revolution: Heine, Börne, das "Junge Deutschland," Marx und Engels* (Frankfurt am Main: Syndikat, 1980);

Frank Trommler, *Sozialistische Literatur in Deutschland* (Stuttgart: Kröner, 1976).

Papers:

Friedrich Engels's personal and political documents, correspondence, manuscripts, and notes are collected with those of Karl Marx at the International Institute of Social History in Amsterdam. The Institute for Marxism-Leninism in Moscow has the largest part of the Marx-Engels papers, with photocopies of the Amsterdam collection. Other letters are among the papers of August Bebel at the International Institute of Social History. Copies of letters to Engels's brother, Hermann, are at the Stadtarchiv (City Archive) in Wuppertal.

Theodor Fontane

(30 December 1819 – 20 September 1898)

Glenn A. Guidry
Nashville, Tennessee

BOOKS: *Männer und Helden: Acht Preußenlieder* (Berlin: Hayn, 1850);

Von der schönen Rosamunde: Gedicht (Dessau: Katz, 1850);

Gedichte (Berlin: Reimarus, 1851; enlarged edition, Berlin: Hertz, 1875; enlarged, 1889; enlarged, 1891; enlarged edition, Berlin: Besser, 1898);

Ein Sommer in London (Dessau: Katz, 1854);

Aus England: Studien und Briefe über Londoner Theater, Kunst und Presse (Stuttgart: Ebner & Seubert, 1860);

Jenseit des Tweed: Bilder und Briefe aus Schottland (Berlin: Springer, 1860); translated by Brian Battershaw as *Across the Tweed: A Tour of Mid-Victorian Scotland* (London: Phoenix House, 1965);

Balladen (Berlin: Hertz, 1861);

Wanderungen durch die Mark Brandenburg: Die Grafschaft Ruppin; Barnim-Teltow (Berlin: Hertz, 1862);

Wanderungen durch die Mark Brandenburg: Zweiter Teil. Das Oderland; Barnim; Lebus (Berlin: Hertz, 1863);

Deutsche Inschriften an Haus und Gerät: Zur epigrammatischen Volkspoesie, anonymous, attributed to Fontane (Berlin: Hertz, 1865);

Der Schleswig-Holsteinische Krieg im Jahre 1864 (Berlin: Decker, 1866);

Der deutsche Krieg von 1866, 3 volumes (Berlin: Decker, 1870–1871);

Kriegsgefangen: Erlebtes 1870 (Berlin: Decker, 1871);

Aus den Tagen der Occupation: Eine Osterreise durch Nordfrankreich und Elsaß-Lothringen, 1871, 2 volumes (Berlin: Decker, 1872);

Wanderungen durch die Mark Brandenburg: Dritter Teil. Havelland; die Landschaft um Spandau, Potsdam, Brandenburg (Berlin: Hertz, 1873);

Der Krieg gegen Frankreich, 1870–1871, 2 volumes (Berlin: Decker, 1873–1876);

Vor dem Sturm: Roman aus dem Winter 1812 auf 13, 4 volumes (Berlin: Hertz, 1878); translated by

Theodor Fontane

R. J. Hollingdale as *Before the Storm: A Novel of the Winter of 1812–13* (Oxford: Oxford University Press, 1985);

Grete Minde: Nach einer altmärkischen Chronik (Berlin: Hertz, 1880);

Ellernklipp: Nach einem Harzer Kirchenbuch (Berlin: Hertz, 1881);

Wanderungen durch die Mark Brandenburg: Vierter Teil. Spreeland; Beeskow-Storkow und Barnim-Teltow (Berlin: Hertz, 1882);

L'Adultera: Novelle (Breslau: Schottländer, 1882); translated by Gabriele Annan as *The Woman*

Taken in Adultery, in *The Woman Taken in Adultery and The Poggenpuhl Family* (Chicago: University of Chicago Press, 1979);

Schach von Wuthenow: Erzählung aus der Zeit des Regiments Gensdarmes (Leipzig: Friedrich, 1883); translated by E. M. Valk as *A Man of Honor* (New York: Ungar, 1975);

Graf Petöfy: Roman (Dresden & Leipzig: Dürselen, 1884);

Christian Friedrich Scherenberg und das literarische Berlin von 1840 bis 1860 (Berlin: Hertz, 1885);

Unterm Birnbaum (Berlin: Grote, 1885);

Cécile: Roman (Berlin: Dominik, 1887);

Irrungen, Wirrungen: Roman (Leipzig: Steffens, 1888); translated by Katherine Royce as *Trials and Tribulations,* in *German Fiction: J. W. von Goethe, Gottfried Keller, Theodor Fontane, Theodor Storm* (New York: Collier, 1917); translated by Sandra Morris as *A Suitable Match* (London & Glasgow: Blackie, 1968);

Fünf Schlösser: Altes und Neues aus der Mark Brandenburg (Berlin: Hertz, 1889);

Gesammelte Romane und Novellen, 12 volumes (volumes 1-5, Berlin: Deutsche Verlagshandlung; volumes 6-12, Berlin: Fontane, 1890-1891);

Stine (Berlin: Fontane, 1890); translated by Harry Steinhauer as *Stine,* in *Twelve German Novellas* (Berkeley: University of California Press, 1977);

Quitt: Roman (Berlin: Hertz, 1891);

Unwiederbringlich: Roman (Berlin: Hertz, 1892); translated by Douglas Parée as *Beyond Recall* (London & New York: Oxford University Press, 1964);

Frau Jenny Treibel oder "Wo sich Herz zum Herzen find't": Roman (aus der Berliner Gesellschaft) (Berlin: Fontane, 1893); translated by Ulf Zimmermann as *Jenny Treibel* (New York: Ungar, 1976);

Meine Kinderjahre: Autobiographischer Roman (Berlin: Fontane, 1894);

Von, vor und nach der Reise: Plaudereien und kleine Geschichten (Berlin: Fontane, 1894);

Effi Briest: Roman (Berlin: Fontane, 1895); translated by William A. Cooper as "Effi Briest," in *The German Classics of the Nineteenth and Twentieth Centuries,* volume 12, edited by Kuno Francke and William Guild Howard (New York: German Publication Society, 1914), pp. 217-451;

Die Poggenpuhls: Roman (Berlin: Fontane, 1896); translated by Annan as *The Poggenpuhl Family,* in *The Woman Taken in Adultery and The Poggen-*

puhl Family (Chicago: University of Chicago Press, 1979);

Von Zwanzig bis Dreißig: Autobiographisches (Berlin: Fontane, 1898);

Der Stechlin: Roman (Berlin: Fontane, 1899);

Causerien über Theater, edited by Paul Schlenther (Berlin: Fontane, 1905); enlarged as *Plaudereien über Theater: 20 Jahre Königliches Schauspielhaus 1870-1890),* edited by Theodor and Friedrich Fontane (Berlin: Fontane, 1926);

Gesammelte Werke, 22 volumes (Berlin: Fontane, 1905-1911);

Aus dem Nachlaß von Theodor Fontane, edited by Josef Ettlinger (Berlin: Fontane, 1908) — comprises "Mathilde Möhring: Roman," "Gedicht-Nachlese," "Literarische Studien und Eindrücke," "Das Märker und das Berlinertum: Ein kulturhistorisches Problem";

Theodor Fontanes engere Welt: Aus dem Nachlaß, edited by Mario Krammer (Berlin: Collignon, 1920);

Gesammelte Werke: Jubiläumsausgabe, 10 volumes, edited by Schlenther (Berlin: Fischer, 1920);

Gesamtausgabe der erzählenden Schriften, 9 volumes, edited by Schlenther (Berlin: Fischer, 1925);

Allerlei Gereimtes, edited by Wolfgang Rost (Dresden: Reißner, 1932);

Kritische Jahre — Kritikerjahre: Autobiographische Brüchstücke aus den Handschriften, edited by Conrad Höfer (Eisenach: Kühner, 1934);

Bilderbuch aus England, edited by Hanns Martin Elster (Berlin: Grote, 1938);

Aus meiner Werkstatt: Unbekanntes und Unveröffentlichtes, edited by Albrecht Gaertner (Berlin: Das Neue Berlin Verlags-Gesellschaft, 1949);

Sämtliche Werke, 28 volumes, edited by Edgar Gross (Munich: Nymphenburger Verlagshandlung, 1959-1962);

Schriften zur Literatur, edited by Hans-Heinrich Reuter (Berlin: Aufbau, 1960);

Sämtliche Werke, 6 volumes, edited by Walter Keitel (Munich: Hanser, 1962);

Gesamtausgabe, 10 volumes, edited by Reuter (Berlin: Aufbau, 1970).

Edition in English: *Journeys to England in Victoria's Early Days,* translated by Dorothy Harrison (London: Massie, 1939).

OTHER: *Deutsches Dichter-Album,* edited by Fontane (Berlin: Jancke, 1852);

Argo Belletristisches Jahrbuch für 1854, edited by Fontane and Friedrich Kugler (Dessau: Katz, 1854);

Wilhelm von Merckel, *Kleine Studien,* preface by Fontane (Berlin: Enslin, 1863).

SELECTED PERIODICAL PUBLICATIONS –
UNCOLLECTED: "Das schottische Hochland und
seine Bewohner," *Europa,* 16, no. 2 (1860):
509;

"Die alten englischen und schottischen Balladen,"
Morgenblatt für Gebildete Leser, 10 January 1861,
pp. 6–10;

"Reisebrief aus Jütland," *Neue Preußische Zeitung,*
6 March 1864, pp. 3–5;

"Paul Heyse: Ein Liebling der Musen," *Gartenlaube,*
15, no. 36 (1867): 9–34;

"Gustav Freytag: *Die Ahnen,*" *Vossische Zeitung,*
21 February 1875, pp. 8–9;

"Heinrich Seidel: *Aus der Heimat,*" *Vossische Zeitung,*
14 March 1875, pp. 4–5;

"Zwei Bilder in der Commandantenstraße," *Die
Gegenwart,* 5, no. 51 (1876): 406–412;

"Gesammelte Schriften von Theodor Storm," *Vossische Zeitung,* 14 January 1877, pp. 13–14;

"Baltisches Leben in Romanen von Thomas H. Pantenius," *Die Gegenwart,* 7, no. 27 (1878): 198–217;

"Julius Rodenberg: *Die Grandidiers,*" *Vossische Zeitung,* 22 November 1879, pp. 26–29;

"Über Wilhelm Raabes Roman *Das Horn von
Wanza,*" *Magazin,* 50, no. 27 (1881): 411–423;

"Wilhelm Raabe: *Fabian und Sebastian,*" *Magazin,* 51,
no. 25 (1882): 339–351;

"Otto Brahm: *Gottfried Keller,*" *Vossische Zeitung,*
8 April 1883, p. 14;

"Cafés von heute und Konditoreien von ehemals,"
Das neue Berlin, 20, no. 12 (1886): 8–16;

"Die Märker und die Berliner und wie sich das Berlinerthum entwickelte," *Deutsches Wochenblatt,*
2, no. 47 (1889): 560–564;

"Die gesellschaftliche Stellung der Schriftsteller,"
Magazin, 60, no. 52 (1891): 818–842;

"Das Schlachtfeld von Groß-Beeren," *Deutsche Dichtung,* 16, no. 3 (1894): 60–72;

"Adolph Menzel," *Zukunft,* 3, no. 10 (1895): 441–444.

Theodor Fontane is generally considered the
most significant realistic novelist of the German-speaking countries. For these lands Fontane consummated the development of the type of novel, the
Gesellschaftsroman (novel of society), that is characteristic of such great European realists as Charles
Dickens, Gustave Flaubert, and Leo Tolstoy. Fontane also paved the way for modernist trends in the
novel genre: as the plots of his novels became more
and more spare, he placed them more and more in
the background and emphasized conversations
among characters, who are grouped in socially and
symbolically significant constellations. Thomas
Mann, who acknowledged his debt to Fontane, developed this form of the novel with even greater
complexity and profundity, summing up the epoch-making intellectual and political movements of the
early twentieth century in his *Der Zauberberg* (1924;
translated as *The Magic Mountain,* 1927) and *Doktor
Faustus* (1947; translated as *Doctor Faustus,* 1948).
But Fontane's conversational scenes reflect and
comment on political, philosophical, and aesthetic
preoccupations of his time without abandoning a
style and tone of simple spontaneity, natural charm,
and engaging wit. He also placed increasing emphasis on the device of the interior monologue, a tendency that was furthered in the twentieth century
with the development of the literary technique of
"stream of consciousness."

Fontane was descended from French Huguenots, Protestants who were driven from France by
the revocation of the Edict of Nantes in 1685. Encouraged by Friedrich Wilhelm, the Great Elector,
to come to Prussia, many Huguenots settled in Berlin and made an important contribution to the city's
economy, notably through their proficiency in silk
weaving.

Henri Théodor Fontane – it was not until
much later that he shed his first name and germanized his second – was born in Neuruppin, a small
town in the Brandenburg March of Prussia, on
30 December 1819 to Louis Henri and Emilie
Labry Fontane. His father, the owner of a small
apothecary store, sold the shop in 1827 and moved
to Swinemünde, where Fontane studied at the public school and later received instruction from his father as well as from tutors of families with whom
the Fontanes were acquainted. With an awakening
interest in history, he began writing historical tales
in a school notebook. In 1832 he was sent back to
Neuruppin to attend secondary school. There he
began to write poems, mostly of a lyrical nature,
and joined literary clubs dedicated to the poets
Nikolaus Lenau and August von Platen.

These alternating residencies in Neuruppin
and Swinemünde had a formative influence on
Fontane that he recognized and attested to in the autobiographical novel *Meine Kinderjahre* (My Childhood Years, 1894). Whereas Neuruppin was narrowly bourgeois and dull but practical and realistic,
Swinemünde was a romantic city whose population
consisted largely of bankrupt merchants. Similarly
contrasting traits were presented by Fontane's parents: his mother was strong-willed, principled, and
practical, his father congenial, whimsical, but impractical. Fontane vacillated between these poles in

his personal life but brought them into a complementary, mutually enhancing relationship in the style of his best novels, which is often termed "poetic realism."

From 1836 until 1840 Fontane served his apothecary apprenticeship in Berlin; he was then an apothecary's assistant in Burg in 1840, in Leipzig in 1841, in Dresden in 1842, and in Leipzig again in 1843. He performed his military service in a grenadier regiment in Berlin in 1844; on a two-week furlough he made his first visit to England. He then practiced pharmacy in Berlin. Although he pursued the profession of his father to support himself, Fontane's first love was still lyric poetry; but as the political climate among the poets of Fontane's generation became increasingly revolutionary, his poetry echoed more and more the rhetorical, heroic tone of others. Finally, toward the end of 1847 Fontane wrote to a friend that he had renounced lyric poetry because he realized that he lacked the gift for it.

Although he was an active member of the conservative literary club "Tunnel über der Spree" (Tunnel over the Spree), Fontane always observed his society with a critical eye. As he tried to establish himself as a free-lance writer he accommodated himself to the status quo; but as the bourgeois revolution became imminent he went along with the changing tide and participated in the street fights of 18 March 1848. With the failure of the revolution, Fontane adapted to the ensuing conservative ambience.

Fontane gave up the practice of pharmacy in October 1849. By this time he had become thoroughly familiar with the English ballad tradition, and he turned to writing his own ballads in German. It was in this genre that Fontane first achieved a reputation. The historical and romantic-heroic elements of ballads fit his own interests as well as those of readers during the Prussian ascendancy. His ballads on figures from Prussian history in *Männer und Helden: Acht Preußenlieder* (Men and Heroes: Eight Prussian Songs, 1850) attracted a wide audience. Fontane continued to write ballads for the rest of his life; during his lifetime he was known primarily as a balladeer. Though many of his ballads and some of his lyric poems are still familiar in German-speaking countries, his poems are mostly conventional. The small body of poetry written much later, after he had become a novelist, contains some notable exceptions.

On 16 October 1850 he married Emilie Rouanet-Kummer; that same year he secured a position in the newly founded press headquarters of the

Fontane in 1844; pencil drawing by J. W. Burford (Preußischer Kulturbesitz, Bildarchiv)

Prussian government. The Fontanes' first child was born in November 1851 and named George (the English form, rather than the German *Georg*) Emile. Continued participation in the Tunnel über der Spree brought Fontane into contact with many prominent writers, including the poet and realist fiction writer Theodor Storm.

In 1855 the Prussian press headquarters took advantage of Fontane's Anglophilia by making him the leader of a group of foreign correspondents assigned to London. His wife and son accompanied him, and a second son, Theodor, was born in November 1856. Fontane wrote reports and feuilletons for German and English newspapers and magazines and also began to write theater reviews. The love of the theater that Fontane acquired at this time is reflected in the settings and characters of some of his novels and the predominance of dialogue over narrative and the theatrical metaphors throughout his novelistic oeuvre.

Fontane resigned his position as foreign correspondent and returned to his homeland in 1859; homesickness and bad health contributed to his decision. The Fontanes had a daughter, Martha, in 1860, and a third son, Friedrich, in 1864. Aside from covering the war in Schleswig-Holstein in 1864 and 1866 and the Franco-Prussian War in 1870–1871 (during which he spent October to December 1870 as a prisoner of war) and two trips with his family to Italy in 1874 and 1875, the only other travels Fontane undertook were a series of journeys through Prussia's Brandenburg March from 1859 to 1882. From 1860 to 1870 he was the editor of the English section of *Kreuz-Zeitung* (Cross Newspaper), and from 1870 until 1889 he was theater critic for the *Vossische Zeitung* (Voss's Newspaper). During the period of his Brandenburg wanderings Fontane stopped writing ballads; it was not until after he had firmly developed his talents as a novelist that he returned to the genre — but with a change of material from the romantic-historical to the realistic-contemporary.

Fontane's *Wanderungen durch die Mark Brandenburg* (Wanderings through the Brandenburg March) appeared in four volumes, in 1862, 1863, 1873, and 1882; in 1889 a fifth volume was published titled *Fünf Schlösser: Altes und Neues aus der Mark Brandenburg* (Five Castles: Old and New from the Brandenburg March). These volumes were Fontane's second most popular works after the ballads; they also signified a shift from a primary interest in the past, imagined as heroic and romantic, to a concern for the present, viewed critically, and the everyday, transformed into art with subtle symbolism, irony, and humor. Fontane's raconteur style and detailed yet ironic observations, developed in his travel books, laid the foundation for his novels. Berlin and much of the rest of the Brandenburg landscape and its lore play significant roles in Fontane's fiction.

The idea of journeying through Brandenburg and describing it had occurred to Fontane earlier; but it was not until his 1858 visit to Scotland — the native country of Sir Walter Scott, whose ballads and novels Fontane had long admired — that he had resolved to carry out his plan. During a trip across Loch Leven, Fontane had had a vision of the Rheinsberg Lake in his homeland. His identification with Scott seems to have stimulated in Fontane an almost mystical merging of Prussia and Scotland, and the rest of his literary career seems to imitate Scott's: after reestablishing a connection with his geographical roots and abandoning the composition of ballads, Fontane turned to writing novels, just as Scott wrote novels after having begun his literary career by composing ballads.

The *Wanderungen* volumes are affectionate yet critical portrayals of the topography, economy, ethnography, history, and politics of the Prussian province. Fontane begins the first volume with the Ruppin landscape from which he hails, sketching the biographies of Prussian generals who also came from the area and recounting the history of his hometown, Neuruppin. As in all of his travel books, historical chronicles alternate with narration of and commentary on current events and scenes, suggesting parallels and contrasts between Prussia's past and present. The second volume opens with a description of a steamboat ride from Frankfurt to Schwedt an der Oder. The area's settling, its sagas, and its legends are treated. The third volume tells of the founding of several historically and culturally important cloisters by Cistercian monks and nuns, followed by a portrayal of the landscape around Potsdam and Spandau. The fourth volume relates a series of journeys through the Spree forest to Teltow and from Cöpenick to Teupitz. The final volume contains essays on five castles located throughout Brandenburg. Fontane's intention, expressed in the preface, is to sum up emblematically the five hundred years of Brandenburg history in the histories of these castles. Fontane's affection for the old Prussian aristocracy mingles with criticism of its less admirable contemporary representatives and with an awareness of its gradual obsolescence through quickly growing industrialization.

After serving as secretary of the Academy of the Arts in 1876, Fontane devoted most of his time to writing novels. His career as a novelist began with *Vor dem Sturm: Roman aus dem Winter 1812 auf 13* (1878; translated as *Before the Storm: A Novel of the Winter of 1812–13*, 1985), a panorama of the Prussian aristocracy, bourgeoisie, and peasantry just before the outbreak of the Wars of Liberation against Napoleon. Despite the obvious parallels, it does not merit being called a German *War and Peace* (1864–1869) — even though it is one of the best historical novels in German literature. It is characteristic of Fontane's approach that he avoids the "storm" itself and portrays the less dramatic events that preceded the great campaign of 1813. The plot is rather slender for a novel of six hundred pages. Since Fontane was a writer of long experience yet a novice in the field of the novel, it is not surprising that his first effort should demonstrate his skill as a writer while revealing narrative and structural inadequacies. The novel's sketches of cultural history, similar to those in the Brandenburg *Wanderungen,* as well as character analyses that appear as ends in themselves lessen the work's artistic effect.

Three more historical novels followed *Vor dem Sturm* in fairly rapid succession: *Grete Minde* (1880); *Ellernklipp* (1881), whose title is the name of a cliff in the Harz mountains; and *Schach von Wuthenow* (1883; translated as *A Man of Honor,* 1975). The first two are based on historical chronicles Fontane had discovered in Brandenburg and

Fontane in 1883; painting by Carl Breitbach (from Fontane's Briefe an Julius Rodenberg, *edited by Hans-Heinrich Reuter, 1969)*

the Harz mountain region; both examine crimes of past ages and explore with insight the state of mind of the criminal. The third work, which discloses the hollowness of the Prussian military code of honor, is set in 1806; Fontane's historical and topographical studies for *Vor dem Sturm* provided the background.

Grete Minde and *Ellernklipp* are usually referred to as Fontane's balladesque novels, implying not only that they have a structural and stylistic affinity to the ballads Fontane wrote but also that they have less merit than his later Gesellschaftsromane. It is true that in these early fictional works the romantic, balladic elements impose themselves rather ungracefully, and that there is a development in Fontane's oeuvre from a highly colored poetic or balladic mode to a more complex, realistic treatment of social relations. Nonetheless, the novels of society also benefit from the lessons Fontane learned in his long apprenticeship to the ballad form. They, too, contain such elements as the refrain, or leitmotivic repetition of words, phrases, and symbols; the tendency of the story to return to its beginnings; narrative leaps that leave much unsaid and engage the reader's imagination; presentiment or prefiguration; exposition through conversation; and a colloquial manner. On a thematic level, the motif of infidelity that is so often paired in Fontane's works with the themes of guilt and retribution can be traced back to the author's own ballads as well as to the English ballads that served him as models. These balladic elements contribute to the transformation of reality Fontane called "Verklärung" (transfiguration) – the essential ingredient in his poetic realism, one Fontane found lacking in the fiction of Ivan Turgenev and the works of the naturalistic playwright Gerhart Hauptmann. The real distinction in regard to the balladic elements in Fontane's oeuvre is that they are not interwoven subtly and seamlessly into the narrative fabric until his novels of society.

The first of Fontane's novels of society, which have as their background the Berlin of the Bismarckian era, was *L'Adultera* (1882; translated as *The Woman Taken in Adultery,* 1979); like his *Cécile* (1887), *Unwiederbringlich* (1892; translated as *Beyond Recall,* 1964), and *Effi Briest* (1895; translated, 1914), it portrays the gradual decay of a marriage between

Fontane in 1890; crayon drawing by Fritz Weaver (from Kurt Schober, Theodor Fontane in Freiheit dienen, *1980)*

people who are unequally matched in temperament and age. Each novel is based on an actual scandal in the respectable bourgeois society of contemporary Berlin.

With *Irrungen, Wirrungen* (Confusions, Entanglements, 1888; translated as *Trials and Tribulations*, 1917) Fontane produced his first true masterpiece of fiction: it has no superfluous sentence; its critical vision is clear and steady, its style is relaxed and fluent, and its plot avoids the romantic and melodramatic tendencies to which the author gave partial or complete rein in other works. Unlike his earlier novels, it was long in the making: after drafting the

first few chapters in 1882, Fontane picked it up again in the spring of 1884; it reached its final polished form in 1887, appeared as a serial in the *Vossische Zeitung* in July and August of that year, and was published in book form early in 1888. The writing of it overlapped the composition of five other novels, all of which have tragic climaxes; *Irrungen, Wirrungen* is the odd one out. It may wring the heart, but its ending is neither tragic nor happy. The element of resignation in the tone stems from Fontane's reading of the philosophy of the great pessimist Arthur Schopenhauer. The synthesis of resignation, irony, and humor in the novel is characteristic of all of Fontane's greatest works.

Irrungen, Wirrungen is set in Berlin in the 1870s. Lene Nimptsch, the daughter of a washerwoman, has a summer love affair with the young Baron Botho von Rienäcker. The lovers know that their relationship cannot become permanent because of their class differences. Lene is the stronger and more realistic of the pair and does not yield to even the most fleeting of illusions. The two live for their present happiness, the high point of which is a journey up the Spree. Botho's family reminds him of his duties to them and their class, which he is to fulfill by marrying a wealthy distant cousin. Botho and Lene are convinced that they cannot and should not defy the existing social order – reflecting Fontane's conviction of the necessity of order and respect even for its imperfect realization in contemporary social conditions. Botho's marriage to his cheerful but superficial cousin is conventional, yet not unhappy. Lene also marries someone of her own class, a lay preacher whose love for her is strong enough to help her overcome the past – about which she tells her husband everything – but not to forget it. Botho and Lene's short-lived happiness and the sorrow of their separation remain with them for the rest of their lives.

Cut down to these essentials, the plot may seem rather trivial. The achievement in each of Fontane's major novels recalls that of Flaubert's *Madame Bovary* (1857). Flaubert claimed that he deliberately chose the most trivial and mundane subject to highlight the skill of his writing and the aesthetic quality of his prose; in emphasizing the writer's virtuosity and form over content, Flaubert and Fontane point ahead to the modernist and postmodernist writers of the twentieth century. The content of *Irrungen, Wirrungen* was, however, more important to its first readers than stylistic or formal considerations. The novel met with fierce criticism from the reading public.

Many took offense at the positive portrayal of a love affair between a nobleman and a woman from the lower class – especially at the author's description of her feelings as simple, true, and natural, which gave them as well as the lovers' relationship a value the reigning middle-class morality would not attribute to what was called a "ghastly whore story." Fontane's social criticism, camouflaged by his acknowledgment of the class hierarchy, is aimed precisely at this moral code that forces people to sacrifice their personal happiness to popular prejudices and social conventions.

George, Fontane's first son, had died at the age of thirty-six in 1887. The following year his youngest son, Friedrich, founded the English-named Fontane and Company, which published Fontane's next work, *Stine* (1890; translated, 1977); *Irrungen, Wirrungen* had made Fontane too controversial for most other publishers. *Stine,* which also deals with the subject of lovers from different social classes, is one of the least well constructed of his novels.

During the three years that followed *Irrungen, Wirrungen,* Fontane wrote important reviews of Hauptmann's first two dramas. These extensive pieces, which are more like formal essays than newspaper reviews, reveal many of Fontane's own artistic principles in expressing his antipathy for the movement of naturalism that was then gaining ascendancy. At the same time, Fontane produced two novels that seemed to confirm what he had been saying in letters to friends after his recent setbacks: that he was finished with novels set in contemporary Berlin. *Quitt* (A Settling of Accounts, 1891) is set in Silesia and in the United States, while *Unwiederbringlich* alternates between Danish-ruled Schleswig and Denmark. The first novel begins promisingly but breaks down in the latter half; the tragic conclusion of the second falls short on motivation.

Each of these works is a tragedy, and neither takes place in Berlin; but Fontane's next novel is a comedy set in the capital. *Frau Jenny Treibel* (1893; translated as *Jenny Treibel,* 1976) rates for many as an even greater masterpiece than *Irrungen, Wirrungen, Effi Briest,* or *Der Stechlin* (1899). It is appropriate to use the dramatic terms *comedy* and *tragedy* in describing Fontane's novels, particularly *Frau Jenny Treibel:* including the letters and interior monologues in the text, approximately three quarters of the novel is in direct speech; and the work is easily divided into three "acts." (A dramatization by Christian Hammel was produced in East Berlin in 1964 and in Darmstadt in 1976.) Besides linguis-

Fontane in 1896; lithograph by Max Liebermann

tic brilliance and versatility, the novel has a plot that is deceptively simple yet perfectly contrived for its comic purpose and a range of comic characters presented for the most part without caricature. It satirizes middle-class hollowness, pretentiousness, falseness, arrogance, and hardheartedness with incisive urbanity.

The exponent of the middle-class standpoint is the titular figure. Jenny Treibel is a social climber, a grocer's daughter who is married to a Berlin industrialist. A self-styled lover of poetry and a romantic idealist, Jenny never forgets that material security is the only value to be taken seriously. She is not a hypocrite but is unaware of the contradiction between her attitudes and behavior. At the beginning of the novel she invites Corinna Schmidt, the daughter of Professor Willibald Schmidt – who was romantically involved with Jenny in their youth – to dinner. The intelligent and witty Corinna displays her charm ostensibly for the benefit of the guest of honor, the young Englishman Mr. Nelson; in actuality, she is trying to capture the heart of Leopold Treibel, the hosts' son. Corinna's cousin, Marcell Wedderkopp, observes the execution of her strategy with painful jealousy, for he is deeply in love with her. On the way home, Corinna admits to Marcell that she is determined to marry Leopold, who she knows is weaker and less intelligent than she, simply to gain entrée to the affluence and ease of the bourgeoisie.

A few weeks later, on a country outing sponsored by the Treibels, Jenny promenades on the arm of Willibald Schmidt, who views his former lover with characteristically good-humored irony. She sentimentally recalls past times, claiming that she probably would have been happier if she had married a man devoted to the world of ideas and ideals. Meanwhile, Corinna skillfully evokes from Leopold a confession of love and a proposal of marriage. That evening, when Leopold informs his mother of the engagement, Jenny recognizes Corinna's motives and expresses indignation. A tug-of-war between the two pertinacious women ensues; Jenny wins, but only at the price of accepting as a daughter-in-law Helga Monk, a young woman of a wealthy banking family whom Jenny has always disliked. By this time Corinna is happy to relinquish Leopold: she has gained a new perspective on her own motives by seeing them reflected in her opponent. Rather than become another Jenny Treibel, Corinna agrees to marry Marcell, an archaeologist. The Treibel and Schmidt families, their long-standing friendship restored, hold a double wedding; all is forgiven and forgotten.

From March through September 1892 Fontane suffered from anemia of the brain, which caused him to despair of all further artistic creation; his family thought that he was beginning to show signs of mental derangement. He gradually recovered, however, and began to write *Meine Kinderjahre*. This novel became his only narrative work to attain widespread success during his lifetime.

It was also during this time that Fontane resumed writing ballads and lyric poetry. This late poetry is quite different from the poems Fontane had written before. As he points out in the poem "Auch ein Stoffwechsel" (Even a Change of Material), he began his literary career in the land of legends and knights but is finishing it in the everyday world. In his late poems Fontane creates a decidedly unconventional lyric poetry, one that is matter-of-fact, humorous, and ironic in tone – a lyric poetry that is self-consciously unlyrical. In 1894 he was

awarded an honorary doctorate by the University of Berlin.

In 1895 *Effi Briest* was published. Effi, who lives with her parents in the Havelland district of Brandenburg, is sought in marriage by an ambitious civil servant, the thirty-eight-year-old Geert von Innstetten. He had once wished to marry Effi's mother, but she had married an older man of more adequate means. Effi scarcely knows Innstetten but accepts him because the offer flatters her and her parents favor the match. Married at seventeen, she moves to Kessin on the Baltic, where her husband is Landrat (prefect). There is no social life, the house is reputed to be haunted, and Innstetten, intent on his career, does not give her much attention. The new territorial district commander, Major von Crampas, has a reputation for success with women and for recklessness in pursuit of them. Mainly out of loneliness and boredom, Effi enters into a brief liaison with him. To her relief the dangerous link with Crampas is broken when Innstetten is promoted to a post in Berlin.

After six pleasant years Innstetten discovers a bundle of old letters from Crampas. Though inclined to forgive his wife and her former lover, Innstetten yields to the Prussian code of honor, kills Crampas in a duel, and divorces Effi. She receives financial support from her parents, though they will not permit her to live with them until illness compels her doctor to urge the Briests that she be allowed to return home. Innstetten, though once again promoted, finds that his career has lost its flavor and is led to question the rightness of his past conduct. A reconciliation with Effi is impossible, even though she has forgiven him; he is, she says, as good as anyone who does not really know how to love could have been. After a serene year at her parents' home, Effi dies of consumption.

Effi Briest is unique among Fontane's masterpieces. Considered the German equivalent of *Madame Bovary* and Leo Tolstoy's *Anna Karenina* (1873–1876) both in subject and in artistic achievement, it is Fontane's only narrative to contain a richly woven plot. There is a corresponding dearth of dialogue. This is a novel of significant silences: things that should be critically examined – above all, the social values and norms the characters allow to dictate their behavior – are never brought up for discussion. As is true even in the novels where Fontane's art of dialogue shines forth, what is not said is always of equal importance to, and sometimes of greater importance than, what is openly stated. In *Effi Briest* Fontane poses a series of problems, leaving the reader to supply possible solutions.

Die Poggenpuhls (translated as *The Poggenpuhl Family,* 1979), Fontane's small-scale portrayal of the dying Prussian aristocracy which he was to portray on a large scale in his last novel, appeared in book form in 1896. During its serialization Fontane finished the first draft of a work that remained unpublished during his lifetime; "Mathilde Möhring," a character study of an emancipated woman, did not appear until 1908. His second autobiographical work, *Von Zwanzig bis Dreißig* (From Twenty to Thirty, 1898), was published in the year of his death. The following year brought the publication of what many consider his greatest work, *Der Stechlin.* According to Thomas Mann (in *Theodor Fontane* [1973], edited by Wolfgang Preisendanz), this work artistically extends far beyond its epoch; yet in content *Der Stechlin* is a summation of its epoch. An extended conversation piece in which virtually nothing "happens," it is a novel of matchless humanity and remarkable technical achievement.

The minimal action of the novel is largely set in a country house and a Berlin residence. The work focuses on the aristocracy, but a wider world — especially that of the growing proletariat — is visible in the background. Dubslav von Stechlin runs for a parliamentary seat, which is won by a member of the recently founded Social Democratic party. Dubslav's son, Woldemar, is faced with a choice between two sisters, daughters of Count Barby in Berlin. He opts for Armgard's youth and simplicity in preference to Melusine's maturity and sophistication. Fontane's position seems to be represented most closely in the Christian Socialism of Pastor Lorenzen, Woldemar's mentor. Dubslav represents "eine aus dem Herzen kommende Humanität" (a humaneness that comes from the heart) incorporated (according to Fontane) in the best examples of the old Brandenburg nobility; the pastor nourishes this trait in himself while at the same time propagating the political ideas and social reforms of socialism.

Dubslav lives on the shore of Lake Stechlin, a small body of water that is reputed to possess an amazing property: whenever some abnormal seismic happening occurs anywhere in the world, Lake Stechlin, in mysterious communication, becomes turbulent; if the event is truly sensational a waterspout forms, at the summit of which a flaming red rooster appears. The lake appealed to Fontane, who had visited it during his Brandenburg travels, as a symbol; Fontane termed it the "Leitmotif" of the

Memorial to Fontane in Neuruppin

novel. It figures sparingly in the work, being inspected twice, discussed twice, and mentioned in the final words of the final sentence, spoken by Pastor Lorenzen at Dubslav's burial: "Es ist nicht nötig, daß die Stechline weiterleben, aber es lebe *der* Stechlin" (It is not necessary that the Stechlins live on, but long live *the* Stechlin). Although once, in jest, one of the characters calls it "ein richtiger Revolutionäre" (a real revolutionary), thus touching the political spheres, the lake's exact symbolic significance is never defined — consistent with Fontane's usual practice of leaving symbols ambiguous.

The Fontanes spent a month at a spa near Dresden, returning to Berlin for the publication of *Von Zwanzig bis Dreißig.* They then went to the spa at Karlsbad, where the author made final corrections for the book edition of *Der Stechlin.* On their return to the capital the Fontanes celebrated their daughter Martha's engagement. Martha was with Fontane when he died around nine o'clock in the evening of 20 September 1898. He was buried in the cemetery of the French Reformed Congregation in Berlin.

Two months later, the book edition of *Der Stechlin* was put out by Fontane.

Letters:

Theodor Fontane's Briefe an seine Familie, 2 volumes, edited by K. E. O. Fritsch (Berlin: Fontane, 1905);

Der Briefwechsel von Theodor Fontane und Paul Heyse, 1850–1897, edited by Erich Petzet (Berlin: Weltgeist-Bücher, 1929);

Theodor Fontane und Bernhard von Lepel: Ein Freundschafts-Briefwechsel, 2 volumes, edited by Julius Petersen (Munich: Beck, 1940);

Theodor Fontane: Briefe an seine Freunde, 2 volumes, edited by Friedrich Fontane and Hermann Fricke (Berlin: Fontane, 1943);

Storm – Fontane: Briefe der Dichter, edited by Erich Gülzow (Bern: Lang, 1948);

Theodor Fontane: Briefe an Friedrich Paulsen, edited by Fricke (Bern: Lang, 1949);

Theodor Fontane: Briefe an Georg Friedlaender, edited by Kurt Schreinert (Heidelberg: Quelle & Meyer, 1954);

Theodor Fontane: Von Dreißig bis Achtzig. Sein Leben in seinen Briefen, edited by Hans-Heinrich Reuter (Leipzig: Steffens, 1959);

Fontane: Unbekannte Briefe, edited by Schreinert (Berlin: Aufbau, 1964);

Briefe an Julius Rodenberg, edited by Reuter (Berlin & Weimar: Aufbau, 1969).

Bibliography:

Charlotte Jolles, *Theodor Fontane* (Stuttgart: Metzler, 1976).

Biographies:

Conrad Wandrey, *Theodor Fontane* (Munich: Beck, 1919);

Mario Krammer, *Theodor Fontane* (Berlin: Fontane, 1922);

Gustav Radbruch, *Theodor Fontane oder Skepsis und Glaube* (Leipzig: Steffens, 1945);

Herbert Roch, *Fontane, Berlin und das 19. Jahrhundert* (Berlin: Schöneberg, 1962);

Elisabeth Moltmann-Wendel, *Hoffnung – jenseits von Glaube und Skepsis: Theodor Fontane und die bürgerliche Welt* (Munich: Nymphenburger, 1964);

Hans-Heinrich Reuter, *Fontane* (Munich: Nymphenburger, 1968);

Helmut Ahrens, *Das Leben des Romanautors, Dichters und Journalisten Theodor Fontane* (Düsseldorf: Droste, 1985);

Gustav Sichelschmidt, *Theodor Fontane: Lebensstationen eines großen Realisten* (Munich: Heyne, 1986).

References:

John S. Andrews, "The Reception of Fontane in Nineteenth-Century Britain," *Modern Language Review,* 52 (July 1957): 403–406;

Hugo Aust, ed., *Fontane aus heutiger Sicht: Analysen und Interpretationen seines Werkes* (Munich: Nymphenburger, 1980);

George C. Avery, "The Language of Attention: Narrative Technique in Fontane's *Unwiederbringlich,*" in *Formen realistischer Erzählkunst: Festschrift für Charlotte Jolles,* edited by Jörg Thunecke and Eda Sagarra (Nottingham, U.K.: Sherwood Press, 1979), pp. 526–534;

Ehrhard Bahr, "Fontanes Verhältnis zu den Klassikern," *Pacific Coast Philology,* 11 (1976): 15–22;

Marianne Bonwit, "Effi Briest und ihre Vorgängerinnen Emma Bovary und Nora Helmer," *Monatshefte,* 40 (December 1948): 445–456;

Richard Brinkmann, *Über die Verbindlichkeit des Unverbindlichen* (Munich: Piper, 1967);

W. H. Bruford, "Theodor Fontane: *Frau Jenny Treibel,*" in his *The German Tradition of Self-Cultivation: "Bildung" from Humboldt to Thomas Mann* (London: Cambridge University Press, 1975), pp. 190–205;

T. E. Carter, "A Leitmotif in Fontane's *Effi Briest,*" *German Life and Letters,* 10 (October 1956): 38–42;

Harry E. Cartland, "The 'Old' and the 'New' in Fontane's *Stechlin,*" *Germanic Review,* 54 (Winter 1979): 20–28;

Cartland, "The Prussian Officers in Fontane's Novels: A Historical Perspective," *Germanic Review,* 52 (May 1977): 183–193;

Ernst Correll, "Theodor Fontane's *Quitt,*" *Mennonite Quarterly Review,* 16 (1942): 221–222;

Arthur Davis, "Fontane and the Revolution of 1848," *Modern Language Notes,* 50 (January 1935): 1–9;

Peter Demetz, *Formen des Realismus: Theodor Fontane* (Munich: Hanser, 1964);

Henry B. Garland, *The Berlin Novels of Theodor Fontane* (Oxford: Clarendon Press, 1980);

Glenn A. Guidry, "Fontane's *Frau Jenny Treibel* and 'Having' a Conversation," *Germanic Review,* 64 (Winter 1989): 2–9;

Guidry, *Language, Morality, and Society: An Ethical Model of Conversation in Fontane and Hofmannsthal*

(Berkeley: University of California Press, 1989);

Guidry, "Myth and Ritual in *Effi Briest*," *Germanic Review*, 59 (Winter 1984): 19–25;

Henry C. Hatfield, "Realism in the German Novel," *Comparative Literature*, 3 (Summer 1951): 234–252;

Peter Uwe Hohendahl, "Bemerkungen zum Problem des Realismus," *Orbis Litterarum*, 23, no. 3 (1968): 183–191;

Charlotte Jolles, "Zu Fontanes literarischer Entwicklung im Vormärz," *Jahrbuch der Deutschen Schillergesellschaft*, 13 (1969): 419–425;

Mark Lehrer, "The Nineteenth-Century 'Psychology of Exposure' and Theodor Fontane," *German Quarterly*, 58 (1985): 501–518;

Ingrid Mittenzwei, *Die Sprache als Thema: Untersuchungen zu Fontanes Gesellschaftsromanen* (Bad Homburg: Gehlen, 1970);

Katharina Mommsen, *Hofmannsthal und Fontane* (Bern: Lang, 1978);

Walter Müller-Seidel, *Theodor Fontane: Soziale Romankunst in Deutschland* (Stuttgart: Metzler, 1975);

Wolfgang Paulsen, "Zum Stand der heutigen Fontane-Forschung," *Jahrbuch der Deutschen Schiller-Gesellschaft*, 25 (1981): 474–508;

Wolfgang Preisendanz, ed., *Theodor Fontane* (Darmstadt: Wissenschaftliche Buchgesellschaft, 1973);

Karl Richter, *Resignation: Eine Studie zum Werk Theodor Fontanes* (Stuttgart: Kohlhammer, 1966);

Kurt Schober, *Theodor Fontane in Freiheit dienen* (Herford: Mittler, 1980);

Lambert A. Shears, *The Influence of Walter Scott on the Novels of Theodor Fontane* (New York: Columbia University Press, 1922);

J. P. M. Stern, " 'Effi Briest': 'Madame Bovary': 'Anna Karenina,' " *Modern Language Review*, 52 (July 1957): 363–375;

Erika Swales, "Private Mythologies and Public Unease: On Fontane's 'Effi Briest,' " *Modern Language Review*, 75 (January 1980): 114–123;

Reinhard H. Thum, "Symbol, Motif, and Leitmotif in Fontane's *Effi Briest*," *Germanic Review*, 54 (Summer 1979): 115–124;

Hans Rudolf Vaget, "Schach in Wuthenow: 'Psychographie' und 'Spiegelung' im 14. Kapitel von Fontanes 'Schach von Wuthenow,' " *Monatshefte*, 61 (Spring 1969): 1–14;

Marianne Zerner, "Zur Technik von Fontanes 'Irrungen, Wirrungen,' " *Monatshefte*, 45 (January 1953): 25–34.

Papers:

The Theodor Fontane Archive is at the Landes- und Hochschulbibliothek (Provincial and University Library) in Potsdam. In addition, the Märkisches Museum, Berlin, has novel manuscripts; the Handschriftenabteilung (Manuscript Department) of the Deutsche Staatsbibliothek (German State Library), Berlin, has drafts and notebooks; the Deutsches Literaturarchiv at the Schiller-Nationalmuseum, Marbach, has letters and manuscripts of poems; the Cotta-Archiv at the Schiller-Nationalmuseum has letters; the Universitäts-Bibliothek (University Library), Berlin, has manuscripts of novels and poems and magazine and newspaper articles; and the Stiftung Preußischer Kulturbesitz (Foundation for Prussian Cultural Property), Berlin, has letters, manuscripts of poems, and school notebooks.

Louise von François

(27 June 1817 – 25 September 1893)

Tiiu V. Laane
Texas A&M University

BOOKS: *Ausgewählte Novellen*, 2 volumes (Berlin: Duncker, 1868) – comprises in volume 1, "Das Jubiläum," "Der Posten der Frau," "Die Sandel"; as volume 2, *Judith, die Kluswirtin*;

Erzählungen, 2 volumes (Brunswick: Westermann, 1871) – comprises in volume 1, "Geschichte einer Häßlichen," "Glück"; in volume 2, "Der Erbe von Saldeck," "Florentine Kaiser," "Hinter dem Dom";

Die letzte Reckenburgerin: Roman, 2 volumes (Berlin: Janke, 1871); translated by J. M. Percival (Mary Joanna Safford) as *The Last von Reckenburg* (Boston: Cupples & Hurd, 1887; Paisley & London: Gardner, 1888);

Frau Erdmuthens Zwillingssöhne: Roman, 2 volumes (Berlin: Janke, 1873);

Geschichte der preußischen Befreiungskriege in den Jahren 1813 bis 1815: Ein Lesebuch für Schule und Haus (Berlin: Janke, 1874);

Hellstädt und andere Erzählungen, 3 volumes (Berlin: Janke, 1874) – comprises in volume 1, "Hellstädt," "Die Schnakenburg, erster Teil"; in volume 2, "Die Schnakenburg, Schluß," "Die goldene Hochzeit, erster Teil"; in volume 3, "Die goldene Hochzeit, Schluß," "Eine Formalität," "Die Geschichte meines Urgroßvaters";

Natur und Gnade, nebst anderen Erzählungen, 3 volumes (Berlin: Janke, 1876) – comprises in volume 1, "Natur und Gnade," "Eine Gouvernante, erster Teil"; in volume 2, "Eine Gouvernante, Schluß," "Ein Kapitel aus dem Tagebuche des Schulmeisters Thomas Luft in Matzendorf," "Des Doctors Gebirgsreise, erster Teil"; in volume 3, "Des Doctors Gebirgsreise, Schluß," "Fräulein Muthchen und ihr Hausmaier," "Die Dame im Schleier";

Stufenjahre eines Glücklichen: Roman, 2 volumes (Leipzig: Breitkopf & Härtel, 1877);

Der Katzenjunker (Berlin: Paetel, 1879);

Phosphorus Hollunder; Zu Füßen des Monarchen, Deutsche Hand- und Hausbibliothek, volume 1 (Berlin & Stuttgart: Spemann, 1881);

Louise von François

Der Posten der Frau: Lustspiel in fünf Aufzügen (Stuttgart: Spemann, 1881);

Das Jubiläum und andere Erzählungen, Deutsche Hand- und Hausbibliothek, volume 94 (Berlin & Stuttgart: Spemann, 1886) – comprises "Das Jubiläum," "Der Posten der Frau," "Die Sandel";

Gesammelte Werke, 5 volumes (Leipzig: Insel, 1918) – comprises in volume 1, *Die letzte Reckenburgerin*; in volume 2, *Frau Erdmuthens Zwillingssöhne*; in volume 3, *Stufenjahre eines Glücklichen*; in volume 4, *Novellen* ("Judith, die Kluswirtin," "Der Posten der Frau," "Fräulein Muthchen und ihr Hausmeier," "Die goldene Hochzeit," "Phosphorus Hollunder"); in volume 5, *Novellen* ("Der Katzenjunker," "Die Geschichte meines Urgro ßvaters," "Zu Füßen des Monarchen," "Hinter dem Dom"); volumes 4 and 5 republished as *Ausgewählte Novellen*, 2 volumes (Leipzig: Insel, 1918);

Judith, die Kluswirtin und andere Novellen (Berlin: Gesellschaft deutscher Literaturfreunde, 1927);

Aus einer kleinen Stadt: Erzählungen, edited by Albert Schröder and Karl Stork, Heimatkundliche Schriften, no. 2 (Weißenfels: Kell, 1937) – comprises "Aus einer kleinen Stadt," "Potsdam: Ein Frühlingsbrief," "Die Krippe," "Die Benneckensteiner Marlene," "Von einem lustigen Nönnlein";

Vergessene Geschichte(n): Aus der Provinz Sachsen und Thüringen, edited by Joachim Jahns (Querfurt: Dingda, 1991).

OTHER: "Etwas von Brauch und Glauben in sächsischen Landen," in *Leipziger Volkskalender*, edited by the Leipziger Zweigverein der Gesellschaft für Verbreitung von Volksbildiung (Leipzig: Seemann, 1876).

SELECTED PERIODICAL PUBLICATIONS – UNCOLLECTED: "Potsdam: Weihnachten 1854," as V. L., *Morgenblatt für gebildete Leser*, no. 3 (14 January 1855): 68–70;

"Aus dem Leben meines Urgroßvaters: Eine bürgerlich deutsche Geschichte von F. von L.," *Europa, Chronik der gebildeten Welt*, nos. 28–31 (1855);

"Aus dem preußischen Herzogthum Sachsen," anonymous, *Morgenblatt für gebildete Leser*, no. 14 (6 April 1856): 330–333;

"Der Erbe von Saldeck," as F. v. L., *Morgenblatt für gebildete Leser*, no. 7 (17 February 1856): 145–150; no. 8 (24 February 1856): 181–184; no. 9 (2 March 1856): 202–208; no. 10 (9 March 1856): 226–233; no. 11 (16 March 1856): 250–257; no. 12 (23 March 1856): 269–276; no. 13 (30 March 1856): 289–296;

"Das Leben der George Sand," as einer Dame, *Deutsches Museum: Zeitschrift für Literatur, Kunst and öffentliches Leben*, 6, no. 45 (1856): 680–693;

"Aus Mitteldeutschland," anonymous, *Morgenblatt für gebildete Leser*, no. 35 (31 August 1856): 839–840; no. 36 (7 September 1856): 856–859;

"Eine Formalität," as F. von L., *Morgenblatt für gebildete Leser*, no. 8 (22 February 1857): 169–174; no. 9 (1 March 1857): 202–208; no. 10 (8 March 1857): 217–223;

"Das Jubiläum: Anekdote," anonymous, *Morgenblatt für gebildete Leser*, no. 12 (22 March 1857): 272–277; no. 13 (29 March 1857): 299–305;

"Aus dem Tagebuche des Schulmeisters Thomas Luft; Eine Geistergeschichte," anonymous, *Morgenblatt für gebildete Leser*, no. 15 (12 April 1857): 344–350; no. 16 (19 April 1857): 375–379; no. 17 (26 April 1857): 390–397; no. 18 (3 May 1857): 421–426;

"Aus Thüringen," anonymous, *Morgenblatt für gebildete Leser*, 19 July 1857, pp. 692–695;

"Der Posten der Frau," anonymous, *Morgenblatt für gebildete Leser*, no. 42 (18 Ocotber 1857): 992–997; no. 43 (25 October 1857): 1005–1015; no. 44 (1 November 1857): 1041–1047; no. 45 (8 November 1857): 1057–1063;

"Phosphorus Hollunder," 25 F. von L., *Novellenzeitung: Eine Wochenchronik für Literatur, Kunst, schöne Wissenschaften und Gesellschaft*, third series, nos. 4–5 (1857);

"Die Dame im Schleier," as F. von L., *Allgemeine Modenzeitung*, 2, nos. 35–39 (1857);

"Aus der Provinz Sachsen," anonymous, *Morgenblatt für gebildete Leser*, no. 2 (10 January 1858): 48; no. 3 (17 January 1858): 67–72;

"Geschichte einer Häßlichen," anonymous, *Morgenblatt für gebildete Leser*, no. 47 (21 November 1858): 1105–1111; no. 48 (28 November 1858): 1138–1144; no. 49 (5 December 1858): 1154–1162; no. 50 (12 December 1858): 1177–1184; no. 51 (19 December 1858): 1208–1215; no. 52 (26 December 1858): 1223–1231;

"Hinter dem Dom," anonymous, *Morgenblatt für gebildete Leser*, no. 23 (5 June 1859): 534–541; no. 24 (12 June 1859): 560–568;

"Eine Gouvernante," anonymous, *Morgenblatt für gebildete Leser*, no. 28 (10 July 1859): 649–657; no. 29 (17 July 1859): 682–689; no. 30 (24 July 1859): 697–705; no. 31 (31 July 1859): 728–734;

"Die goldene Hochzeit," anonymous, *Morgenblatt für gebildete Leser*, no. 38 (18 September 1859): 889–894; no. 39 (25 September 1859): 924–928; no. 40 (2 October 1859): 938–945;

"Fräulein Mutchen und ihr Hausmaier," *Hausblätter von F. W. Hackländer und Edmund Hoefer*, 4 (1859): 161–194;

"Des Doktors Gebirgsreise," anonymous, *Morgenblatt für gebildete Leser*, no. 24 (10 June 1860): 553–559; no. 25 (17 June 1860): 589–593; no. 26 (24 June 1860): 610–616; no. 27 (1 July 1860): 625–632; no. 28 (8 July 1860): 660–

664; no. 29 (15 July 1860): 680–684; no. 30 (22 July 1860): 707–712;

"Natur und Gnade," anonymous, *Morgenblatt für gebildete Leser,* no. 18 (30 April 1861): 409–416; no. 19 (7 May 1861): 438–443; no. 20 (14 May 1861): 457–465; no. 21 (21 May 1861); 487–494;

"Judith, die Kluswirthin," *Hausblätter von F. W. Hackländer und Edmund Hoefer,* 3 (1862): 321–390, 402–453;

"Die Schnakenburg," *Allgemeine Modenzeitung,* 1, nos. 13–25 (1865);

"Die letze Reckenburgerin," *Deutsche Romanzeitung,* 4 (1870): 581–624, 663–704, 743–784, 821–864, 905–938;

"Frau Erdmuthens Zwillingssöhne," *Deutsche Romanzeitung,* 3 (1872): 513–546, 589–620, 667–696, 743–776, 825–856, 913–930; 4 (1872): 41–64, 117–140;

"Hellstädt," *Deutsche Romanzeitung,* 4 (1873);

"Teplitz," *Salon für Literatur, Kunst und Gesellschaft,* 1 (1873): 591–599;

"Ein Plauderbrief aus Chamounix," *Salon für Literatur, Kunst und Gesellschaft,* 2 (1874): 541, 712;

"Stufenjahre eines Glücklichen," *Daheim,* 13, nos. 1–26 (1877);

"Ein deutscher Bauernsohn," *Nation,* no. 11 (1878);

"Der Katzenjunker," *Deutsche Rundschau,* 19 (April–June 1879): 167–201, 335–360; 20 (July–September 1879): 21–50;

"Maria und Joseph, nach einer kalabresischen Volkssage," *Vom Fels zum Meer,* 1 (October 1881–March 1882): 1–8;

"Schauen und Hörensagen: Aus meinen Kindertagen," *Deutsche Revue* (January 1920): 55–79.

Louise von François is one of the three major female German-language writers of the nineteenth century, along with Marie von Ebner-Eschenbach and Annette von Droste-Hülshoff. Her reputation rests primarily on *Die letzte Reckenburgerin* (1871; translated as *The Last von Reckenburg,* 1887), one of the most innovative novels of the century. Prominent literary critics and writers of François's era praised it as a classic of the historical novel; the noted man of letters Fritz Reuter kept a copy of *Die letzte Reckenburgerin* on his desk, while Ebner-Eschenbach proclaimed that she would have exchanged all her works for the honor of having written it. Her other works were lauded for their careful craftsmanship and psychological detail. By the time of her death, however, François had fallen into obscurity; her works remain largely unread, and even *Die letzte Reckenburgerin* is not part of the academic canon.

Blame for her eclipse can be placed on the difficulty of her prose and on the overemphasis of nineteenth-century literary criticism on the bildungsroman at the expense of sociopolitical novels such as François's. Feminist critics have generally ignored François since they have failed to find a radical champion in her. Recognition for her work has suffered along with that of other nineteenth-century women writers whose literary creation has been relegated to the secondary status of the Frauenroman (women's novels) or to trivial literature.

Marie Louise von François was born on 27 June 1817 in Herzberg. Her father, Maj. Ernst Christian Otto Friedrich von François, a nobleman of Huguenot descent, was commandant of the Prussian garrison there. Her mother, Amalie Henriette Hohl François, came from a wealthy bourgeois family in Weißenfels. François's father died in 1818, shortly after the birth of François's brother, Ernst. A man of profound social compassion, his final wish was that he be buried in his army overcoat so that his casket might be reused by the poor. François's mother moved back to Weißenfels shortly after her husband's death; in 1819 she married the Kriegsgerichtsrat (judge advocate) Adolf August Herbst, with whom she had two sons, Bernhard and Arthur Herbst. The family led a comfortable life in a large house on the marketplace.

François's father had willed his wife only a small annuity because he anticipated that she would remarry. His estate, Niemegk, was deeded to his children, to be managed by two guardians. When Louise's guardian declined the responsibility, both guardianships fell to a distant relative, a Herr von Raschkau. Niemegk was sold in 1819, and Raschkau squandered the proceeds. A long court battle began. During this time Raschkau showed little interest in his ward, noting only that her education was inferior and insisting that she take harp lessons.

As befit her class and her gender François received only private tutoring; she was taught French by the daughter of a local family. François acquired the nickname "Fräulein Grundtext" (Miss Rudimentariness) because of her intellectual curiosity and endless questions. Her best instruction came from the schoolmaster – later superintendent – Gustav Heinrich Heydenreich, who fostered her love of history. She augmented her knowledge of the subject by reading accounts of Saxon and Prussian history to her stepfather, who had poor eyesight; they concentrated on the Wars of Liberation, which were to serve as the backdrop for many of François's narratives. The battlefields of Lützen and Roßbach near Weißenfels also stirred François's imagination, and the tales told by her grandmothers Hohl and Herbst inspired her interest in the late eighteenth and early nineteenth centuries. Her narratives repeatedly herald the glories of Prussia and call for a strong and unified German nation to be brought about through the hegemony of Prussia.

François also absorbed the influence of Weißenfels's literary figures. Johann Gottfried Seume came from Poserna, near Weißenfels; François dedicated the essay "Ein deutscher Bauernsohn" (A German Country Lad, 1878) to him. The Romantic poet Novalis had died in Weißenfels in 1801 and was buried there. The second stanza of his poem "An Adolf Selmnitz" (To Adolf Selmnitz) was to echo as the "Bundeslied" (Confederation Song) in François's second novel, *Frau Erdmuthens Zwillingssöhne* (Mrs. Ermuthe's Twin Sons, 1873), and the first stanza provided mottos that recur in leitmotiv fashion throughout the novel. A more important influence was the playwright Adolf Müllner, who wrote Schicksalstragödien (tragedies of fate) and worked as a lawyer in Weißenfels. François's mother had played Elvira in an amateur production of Müllner's *Die Schuld* (Guilt, 1816). The young François served as a companion to Müllner's sickly son Alfred, cheering him with her sunny personality. She was a frequent guest at dinner at Müllner's home and was the only person permitted to enter Müllner's study when he worked. Müllner made his library available to François and guided her reading, fostering her interest especially in Sir Walter Scott. Müllner sharpened François's critical sense for literature by demanding that she analyze the works that she read; he also had her learn passages by heart to develop her sense of language and rhythm, and she memorized his *Die Schuld* in its entirety. Beauty and variety of language were to become some of the strongest features of François's writing. Inspired by Müllner she wrote a bloody nine-act play, which is now lost.

The most important mentor in François's early years was the family physician and friend, Johann Friedrich Traugott Schütze, whose rationalist bias steered her away from the Romantic tendencies of her era. François's composed, unsentimental, and disciplined style reflects his influence. Schütze introduced François to the humanistic concepts of the Enlightenment and instilled in her a reliance on reason. Under his tutelage François developed an inclination for critical and independent thinking, along with a rationalistic stance toward religion that stressed the ethic of social love and the obligation of people to help each other. On the occasion of his

death in 1850 François acknowledged Schütze as the decisive influence in her life. She honored him in her story "Glück" (Happiness, 1871) in the character of the enlightened physician Dr. Bastian, who serves as the voice of reason. Again and again her writings lance vaporous and sentimental thinking, often with barbs of satire.

François's tendency toward independent thinking is evident from her reaction to society, which she entered at sixteen. Her cousin Clotilde von Schwarzkoppen reports that François, an unusually beautiful young woman, participated in parties and dancing but with little interest; she viewed empty social conventions with a sense of critical humor beyond her years. This ironic stance was to find expression in François's works, which make frequent use of social satire.

In the 1830s François was invited to the literary salon of the novelist and feminist Fanny Tarnow, who had moved to Weißenfels in 1828. Tarnow was known for her translations from English and French literature, including the works of George Sand. François copied pages of Sand's works and absorbed the French feminist's thinking. In 1856 she was to review Sand's *Histoire de ma vie* (Story of My Life, 1854–1855) for the periodical *Deutsches Museum*; "Das Leben der George Sand" (The Life of George Sand) endorses Sand's social ethic of active love, describes the difficulties encountered by women authors, and explains their reluctance to become writers. In Tarnow's salon François became acquainted with the works of Jean-Jacques Rousseau and Johann Wolfgang von Goethe, the latter becoming her lifelong authority on literary and philosophical matters. Tarnow introduced François to the liberal world of the writers of the Vormärz (the period from 1815 to the March 1848 revolution) such as Theodor Mundt and Karl Gutzkow. François was also introduced to English Romantic literature and immediately began to learn English. She developed a special passion for George Gordon, Lord Byron, and subsequently lost what little taste she had for dancing since, as she pointed out, no suitor could match Childe Harold.

In Tarnow's literary circle François also made her first acquaintance with the works of principal writers of the women's movement in addition to George Sand; she rated George Eliot as a favorite. Subsequent contact with Tarnow, which was to persist until Tarnow's death in 1862, expanded this initial exposure. Letters from Tarnow to François mention most of the important women writers of the 1840s and 1850s: Ida Hahn-Hahn, Fanny Lewald, Luise Mühlbach, Elise von Hohenhausen,

François circa 1850; crayon drawing by an unknown artist
(Museum Weißenfels)

Betti Paoli, Amalie Bölte, Henriette Paalzow, Ludmilla Assing, Ottilie Wildermuth, and Amalie Schoppe. François was committed to feminist causes throughout her life, although she never participated actively in the women's movement and avoided tendentious literature; she chose to veil her social commentary behind the polished veneer of a well-told tale and to leave the interpretation to the reader. Also, the majority of François's narratives were written in the 1850s, a time of political repression after the failed revolution of 1848, during which the women's movement in Germany was at its nadir; to avoid censorship François had to avoid broaching women's issues too forthrightly. Her stance remained that of moderate German feminists such as Lewald, Louise Otto-Peters, and Luise Büchner: François believed in the sacrosanct role of a woman as wife and mother and affirmed that men and women had gender-based characteristics; at the same time, she argued for the right of women to self-development. Her narratives, essays, and letters call for improved education for women, argue

against the marriage of convenience, and reiterate the right of women to meaningful work and self-expression. Her progressive message, however, is always submerged in a broader artistic and philosophical framework and includes a traditional call for women to perform "womanly" deeds of social service.

It was at Tarnow's salon that François met and fell in love in 1834 with Count Alfred von Görtz, an officer stationed at the Weißenfels garrison. Although Görtz had no money, the couple, hoping for a positive resolution to François's protracted court proceedings, became engaged. As the litigation dragged on, however, Görtz became impatient and began to long for his freedom, and François released him from his promise in 1840. Although she was only twenty-three years old, the dissolution of the engagement represented to her the end of her youth, and she withdrew from society. Her mother's family went bankrupt in the 1840s, and her mother lost her inheritance. The Herbsts continued to live beyond their means, even though they were dependent on the modest inheritance of François's stepfather. François's mother suffered a nervous breakdown from which she never completely recovered. François's despair during this period was profound. Tarnow attempted to find work for François, but plans for François to become a tutor at the court of Dessau fell through when François became ill, and the idea of becoming a governess in England was rejected because François considered the position no better than slavery. François was not accepted as a lady-in-waiting at court nor into the Rotherstiftung, a foundation for unmarried noblewomen, probably because of the bourgeois background of her mother. François wanted to become a physician, but women were not permitted to study at a university until the early 1900s.

In 1848 François's uncle, the widowed Gen. Karl von François, called her to Minden to manage his household and serve as a companion to his daughter, Clotilde. The social and intellectual life of Minden refreshed François and expanded her horizons. She met von Hohenhausen, a Hessian writer known for her translations of Byron and Scott, and her daughter Elise Rüdiger von Hohenhausen, a friend of Droste-Hülshoff. François, in turn, brought intellectual stimulation to her uncle's home. Clotilde, who was to become the writer Clotilde von Schwarzkoppen, recounts how the two discussed their favorite writers, Goethe, Sand, Heinrich Heine, and deep into the night, they talked about art, love, and religion and even debated about politics, a subject considered to be out-side the domain of nineteenth-century women. François's uncle had been a soldier in the Wars of Liberation, during which German troops under the leadership of Prussia, together with allied armies from Russia, Austria, and Britain, forced Napoleon to retreat from German territory. His tales aug-mented François's fascination with the military and reinforced her belief in the concepts of honor and duty.

The happy years in Minden ended in 1850 after the court decided against François and her brother. François returned to Weißenfels to arrange legal matters; since her brother and stepbrothers were in the military, the total burden seems to have fallen on her. She sold the family's house, and they moved into an apartment. Her mother became pro-gressively more ill. François later burned all letters and other memoirs which originated from this dis-couraging time except those from Tarnow. In 1851 she returned to Minden to care for her aging uncle. They moved to Halberstadt and in 1852 to Pots-dam, where François observed at first hand the pro-found social changes in a society that was shifting from feudalism to industrialism. Themes of class conflict and social injustice were to form the core of many of her narratives.

When her uncle died in 1855, François re-turned to live with her parents in Weißenfels. Her mother had broken a hip and was bedridden; her stepfather was becoming progressively more blind. François herself was in bad health and was an "old maid," a lowly status in nineteenth-century society. On her return home François had brought along her first essay, "Potsdam: Weihnachten 1854" (Potsdam: Christmas 1854), which depicts class prejudice and the poverty and humiliation of the nobility in the new industrial society. Tarnow and Rüdiger von Hohenhausen – who was later to claim that she had been the grandmother of François's spiritual children (Tarnow proclaimed herself the godmother) – sent the essay to Hermann Hauff, the editor of Cotta's *Morgenblatt für gebildete Leser* (Morn-ing Paper for Cultured Readers). Hauff published it in 1855 and requested further materials. François's first story, "Aus dem Leben meines Urgroßvaters" (From the Life of My Great-Grandfather), appeared in 1855 in the weekly *Europa, Chronik der gebildeten Welt* (Europe, Chronicle of the Cultured World). Based on the tales of François's Grandmother Hohl, it takes up the theme of duty versus inclination that was to be a leitmotiv of François's oeuvre. The great-grandfather, David Haller, sacrifices his own happiness to carry out his responsibilities to his family. His son Joseph, in contrast, succumbs to Storm and Stress longings. While giving approba-tion to the middle-class values of the father, François balances her call for socially responsible behavior with compassion for those who lose their personal freedom. The story concludes on a note of sympathy for Joseph, who returns home with his spirit broken. François's narratives show that fulfill-ing the demands of conscience necessitates resigna-tion, pain, and sacrifice, but they reflect a sympa-thetic understanding of psychology and never casti-gate human failings. The story serves also as an early example of François's ability to capture the tone of past eras, here that of the late eighteenth century.

In becoming a writer, François was aware that she was entering into a somewhat disreputable pro-fession for a woman; both male and female writers, in fact, were considered dubious characters in the 1850s, but she needed the income from her writing to support her family. She kept her literary activities secret from her family, writing at night or in the early morning, and all of her early works were pub-lished either anonymously or under such pseud-onyms as "F. v. L.," "V. L.," "L. v. F.," and "C. v. François." Painfully shy, François was repulsed by the thought of public scrutiny; she did not even seem to care if her works were attributed to men. Her self-effacement led her to condemn her works with inordinate harshness, although contradictory statements point to a deeply felt authorial pride. The majority of François's narratives appeared in the *Morgenblatt*. "Der Erbe von Saldeck" (The Heir of Saldeck), published in 1856, depicts the social up-heaval resulting from the Stein-Hardenberg reforms of 1807 to 1811, which brought about the break-down of feudal social structures and allowed owner-ship of land by nonaristocrats. The story recounts the conflict between the déclassé nobility and the rising peasant class, proposes that the nobility reju-venate itself through productive activity and fulfill-ment of duty, and condemns class prejudice. Two cultural-historical essays, "Aus dem preußischen Herzogthum Sachsen" (From the Prussian Duke-dom of Saxony) and "Aus Mitteldeutschland" (From Middle Germany), published in 1856, further underscore François's awareness of the changing so-cial patterns in a time of transition. "Der Posten der Frau" (The Wife's Post, 1857), which shows the in-fluence of Gotthold Ephraim Lessing's *Minna von Barnhelm* (1767), has been criticized by feminists for depicting the willingness of women to guard the hearth and home at the expense of personal free-dom. François also submitted work to other journals, adapting the tone of her narratives to suit the character of the periodical. "Phosphorus Hollunder," which appeared in 1857 in the *Novellenzeitung* (Novella Paper), spoofs the self-centered Phosphorus, a dilettante and dabbler in sentimental poetry who is tempered by hardship to become a productive member of society. The novella, which treats the relationship between the rich bourgeoisie and the impoverished aristocrats, reveals François's warm sense of humor and ability to satirize her characters without humiliating them. The melodramatic "Die Dame im Schleier" (The Lady in the Veil) is written in a more sentimental style to suit the readership of the *Allgemeine Modenzeitung* (Universal Fashion Magazine), where it appeared in 1857. It was not until 1859, after prolonged urging by Tarnow, that François allowed the story "Fräulein Muthchen und ihr Hausmaier" (Miss Muthchen and Her Chief Steward) to be published under her full name in the *Hausblätter* (House Papers). Uneasy at displaying her own authorial persona, François distanced herself from her creation through the use of the memoir technique, a feigned autobiography in which a fictional character recounts his or her recollections of significant events. François also favored the frame story, a tale within a tale with one or more first-person narrators. The frame-story technique enabled her to give her works a warm personal style as well as to evoke the illusion of reality.

Since François began to write at the age of thirty-nine, her early narratives exhibit the firmly formulated philosophical stance of a mature woman. They also reveal the principal artistic tenets that characterize her later prose. Although François's works belong to the poetic realist tradition, they evade any single stylistic description. Her narratives show indebtedness to classical and sentimental literary forebears, especially Goethe; share traits of the eighteenth-century novel; and reflect the influence of Jean Paul, Karl Leberecht Immermann, Reuter, Scott, Charles Dickens, Eliot, and Sand. The majority of François's stories are set in the period from the late eighteenth century to the revolution of 1848. Her language has an archaic ring that suits that period. Written in an unsentimental yet intimate style that blends irony with affectionate humor, they take up sociopolitical themes and emphasize psychological detail. François's contemporaries praised her style as "manly," a term meant to laud the objectivity and intellectual quality of her writing. Her stories are characterized by a strong sense of foreboding, and suspense is created through the skillful withholding and revelation of information. Antithetical characters exemplify opposing ethical and social value systems; they serve as symbols of duty and frivolity, conscience and guilt, and reason and feeling. Philosophically, François's narratives are aligned with the bourgeois writers of the ethically sensitive second half of the nineteenth century in Germany. Drawing on the humanistic currents of the Enlightenment, François's didactic stories give approbation to the bourgeois values of duty, moral behavior, the work ethic, and social conscience. None of the bitterness of François's own life is reflected in her stories, which are colored by an idealistic optimism. The stories fall into two categories: those that deal with the relationship between the classes and those that depict the fate of a heroine. Tall, strong, and "manly," François's female protagonists proclaim the dignity of all human beings and exhibit the characteristics of the "new woman" who emerged in the 1850s. The feminist message in her narratives is carefully veiled through the use of contradictory thematic patterns, innuendos, and ambiguities.

Having overcome her reserve, François began productive years of literary activity; her stories were published first in serialized form in periodicals and then in book editions. Some take up the theme of duty to family, friends, or the fatherland: "Geschichte einer Häßlichen" (The Story of an Ugly Woman, 1858), "Eine Gouvernante" (A Governess, 1859), and "Des Doctors Gebirgsreise" (The Doctor's Trip to the Mountains, 1860). Others deliberate about the religious concerns of her day such as anti-Semitism and zealotry: "Hinter dem Dom" (Behind the Cathedral, 1859), "Die goldene Hochzeit" (The Golden Wedding Anniversary, 1859), "Natur und Gnade" (Nature and Grace, 1861). Of the early stories, "Judith, die Kluswirtin" (Judith, the Keeper of the Klus Inn, 1862) was François's favorite. Late in life she sent a copy of it to the Swiss writer Conrad Ferdinand Meyer, enclosing a letter that both derides the story as a piece of old-fashioned, rewarmed pumpernickel that is hard to digest and simultaneously praises it as one of her best-composed stories. A mystery story that begins with the presentation of a seemingly impenetrable secret – a typical plot configuration for François – the narrative uses nature symbolism to depict human passions. The strong and independent Judith's sense of duty and self-discipline is contrasted to the weak will of Simon Lauter, whose alcoholism reflects his self-indulgence.

François's most emotional story, "Geschichte einer Häßlichen" incorporates motifs from Goethe's *Die Wahlverwandtschaften* (Elective Affinities, 1809) and Friedrich Maximilian Klinger's *Die Zwillinge* (The Twins, 1776). It exemplifies how François buried a covert feminist message within her stories. The misfit Laurentia, who is painfully ugly and ostracized by society, is wrapped up in her own ego, a slave to romantic fantasies and temper tantrums. François resolves Laurentia's plight by having her put an end to her immature longings; she must learn unselfishness and set her inner life in order before she can become a respected member of society. While the surface content of the story emphasizes rationalism and demands that women adhere to the rigorous ethical and social standards expected of men, an ironic undercurrent condemns the abuse of women in a patriarchal society that valued women only for their physical attributes. François both illuminates and hides this liberal message through skillfully constructed masking devices: no progressive statement is made in "Die Geschichte einer Häßlichen" without being countered or veiled in some manner. Laurentia is also contrasted to a wide array of subordinate characters who typify other modes of female behavior and who argue lucidly on behalf of traditional nineteenth-century social concepts. The story ends on a note of ambiguity, as do the majority of François's narratives having female protagonists. In a letter to François, Meyer describes her narratives as a curious yet homogeneous blend of conservative and liberal viewpoints. His words sum up the elusive quality of François's writing and help to explain why critics have generally missed the feminist impulses in her writings. Finding no overt feminist challenge to social norms in François's narratives, her contemporaries praised her work as that of a "noble lady" who did not overstep the bounds of feminine dignity.

Although François remained productive during the 1850s and 1860s, her honoraria were meager. She wrote her masterpiece, *Die letzte Reckenburgerin*, in the 1860s. *Morgenblatt* accepted it; but due to the death of its editor, Hauff, the journal ceased publication in 1865, and the manuscript was returned. François's supporters began a search for a publisher, and the novel was finally published in 1870 by Otto Janke's *Deutsche Romanzeitung* (German Novel Newspaper). François received the negligible sum of 150 gulden (300 marks) for the work. A year later Janke brought it out in book form in a two-volume edition. The novel found little recognition until the noted writer Gustav Freytag reviewed it in 1872, calling it the best German novel of recent decades. The work was reprinted four times during her lifetime and was published in translation in England, Holland, Denmark, and America. Between

sixteen and twenty thousand copies had been printed by 1918, a remarkable triumph at a time when there was still strong bias against women writers.

Die letzte Reckenburgerin depicts the fates of two women, the aristocratic Eberhardine von Reckenburg and the bourgeois Dorothee Müller, whose lives intertwine against the historical canvas of the time between the French Revolution and the Wars of Liberation. The work is a probing analysis of the class tension in eighteenth- and nineteenth-century society, as well as a perceptive psychological study of the conflict of duty and inclination. François's preference for antithetical character configurations is developed painstakingly in the story. The tall, rational Eberhardine, a prototype of François's strong and stern "manly" women, argues for a staunchly post-Romantic philosophy, affirming the humanistic bourgeois ethos of duty, work, and social conscience. She anchors her life in her family's motto, "in Recht und Ehren" (according to justice and honor), and becomes embroiled in a moral dilemma when she is forced to evade the truth to protect her childhood friend Dorothee, the daughter of a pub worker. In contrast to Eberhardine, the frivolous Dorothee, the prototype of a nineteenth-century child-woman, gives in to her every inclination. Aware that she is transgressing accepted class boundaries, she falls in love with a prince and becomes pregnant with his child even though she is engaged to Faber, a studious and sober-minded physician away at war. After the prince is killed in battle she bears a son out of wedlock and places him in an orphanage for soldiers' children – a step carried out with Eberhardine's help, despite the latter's deep misgivings. Dorothee marries Faber when he returns home, but she is afraid to tell him of her son. Tormented by her secret and racked by guilt, she eventually becomes mad and finally dies. The novel has a positive resolution when Eberhardine adopts Dorothee's granddaughter, Hardine, and makes her heiress to the Reckenburg estate.

Told by alternating narrators, the work exemplifies François's mastery of prose form. The events move forward and back in time in a complicated pattern as Eberhardine's story connects at critical junctures with the life of Dorothee. François's use of irony, repetition, and symbolism – including color symbolism and imagery making use of light and dark and the refractive quality of mirrors – reflects a high degree of artistic self-consciousness. A wealth of subordinate characters brings to life a past era: Eberhardine's aunt, the Black Reckenburgerin, symbolizes aristocratic arrogance as she clings to outmoded social patterns; stalwart burghers engaged in productive activity are contrasted with frivolous aristocrats who are anachronisms in a bourgeois society. The novel proposes a reorganization of society, exemplified in the marriage of the aristocratic Hardine to a bourgeois husband. The story suggests that the nobility should reform itself, using the entrepreneurial Eberhardine's renovation of her estate as a model of aristocratic productivity. François affirms the validity of conscience, represented in the novel by Eberhardine, but she tempers Eberhardine's moral sternness through a call for love, which alone gives life its meaning: in the end Eberhardine makes a child, Dorothee's granddaughter, the focal point of her life. The novel's complexity is augmented by an undercurrent of feminist criticism: using the motifs of freedom and entrapment, François depicts the victimization of Dorothee by a patriarchal society that robs her of her chance for self-development and condemns her to perpetual childhood. The subtext undercuts the seemingly positive resolution of the novel.

A collection of François's prose works had appeared in 1868; a second was published in 1871 that includes two new stories, "Glück," written before 1860, and "Florentine Kaiser," probably written in 1858. A second novel, *Frau Erdmuthens Zwillingssöhne*, was published in the *Deutsche Romanzeitung* in 1872 and in book form the following year. Narrated by the chronicler Gottfried Bleibtreu, the novel in the story of two brothers whose personal fates intertwine with historical events between 1790 and 1813. Born to a father of French descent and a German mother, the sons display antithetical racial characteristics: the darkly hued Raul, who favors his French father, is passionate, volatile, lighthearted, and elegant and develops an idealistic adoration of Napoleon; his blond and solidly built brother, Hermann, is characterized by Germanic sober-mindedness, lives stalwartly according to the dictates of conscience, and devotes himself to the liberation of Germany from Napoleonic rule. In conflict because of their political viewpoints, the brothers also clash over a Polish girl, Liska, who is engaged to Hermann but betrays him for Raul. The brothers meet on opposite sides at the battle of Dennewitz, where Raul is mortally wounded; they are reconciled only at Raul's death. By equating the welfare of the brothers to the fates of the countries they represent, François depicts the growth of German political strength and final liberation. While the novel shares the ardent nationalism of other German historical novels published between 1850 and 1875, François ends the story with a call for universal brotherhood that will surmount nationalistic hatreds.

Although the depiction of national race characteristics makes the novel somewhat unpalatable to post–World War II readers, it serves as the best example of François's superb control of language. Using finely hued satire that ranges from the macabre to lighthearted hilarity, François spoofs the eras of German classicism and romanticism through painstakingly drawn subordinate characters. The anachronistic rococo language of the narrator, Bleibtreu, who is schooled in the poetry of Friedrich Gottlieb Klopstock, lampoons the sweet sentimentality of the poets of the Göttinger Hainbund of the early 1770s. Bleibtreu barely escapes the clutches of a "schöne Seele" (beautiful soul) who introduces him to Goethe's *Die Leiden des jungen Werthers* (1774; translated as *The Sorrows of Werther,* 1779), presented in a tear-soaked book wrapped up in pink ribbons. François reveals her fondness for eccentrics, and thus her indebtedness to Dickens and Jean Paul, in the character of Dr. Bär, a Fichtean who thrashes out his viewpoints with the teacher Gustel Hecht, an ardent Hegelian. The two match wits in the philosophical style of their mentors. If one considers that François was self-educated, her feat as a linguist and her ability to play a sophisticated intellectual game with her readers are remarkable. In spite of its many merits, *Frau Erdmuthens Zwillingssöhne* did not achieve the success of François's first novel.

François's mother died on 1 July 1871. François herself was in poor health but continued to care for her stepfather, who was totally helpless from 1872 until his death in 1874. She had her *Geschichte der preußischen Befreiungskriege in den Jahren 1813 bis 1815: Ein Lesebuch für Schule und Haus* (History of the Prussian Wars of Liberation in the Years 1813–1815: A Reader for School and Home, 1874), which she had written between 1855 and 1874, published under the name L. von François because she believed that a history written by a woman would not be taken seriously. The work was used as a textbook by officers at the Prussian military academy. After her stepfather's death François moved to smaller quarters, her beloved "Mansardenstube" (attic room), overlooking the river Saale. Relieved of her caretaker role, François enjoyed some of her happiest years there. Between 1875 and 1877 she wrote her lengthiest novel, the bildungsroman *Stufenjahre eines Glücklichen* (Steps through the Years of a Lucky Fellow, 1877). While it has serious structural flaws and thus does not equal François's other novels technically, it is a moving summation of her ethical approach to life. Set against the events leading up to the 1848 revolution, the story is told by the peasant Dezimus Frey and depicts his pathway to learning and inner nobility. The novel echoes the Swiss pedagogue Johann Pestalozzi's call for education for all classes as the means to the moral elevation of society. Dezimus is guided by the kindly pedagogue Pastor Blümel, who presides over a country village, a type of agrarian romantic idyll envisioned by Pestalozzi and also portrayed in the Swiss rural novels of Jeremias Gotthelf. Using a broad array of subordinate characters who represent the sociopolitical trends of the era, François affirms the right of the individual to self-development and advocates moral and productive behavior. The principal planks of the women's movement once again form a subtext, incorporating demands for women's right to education, meaningful work, dignity, and self-fulfillment. Dezimus is also guided by a woman, the aristocratic Lydia; the two ultimately marry, since their love bridges all class boundaries. The novel recognizes free will and the ability of all to rise above the poorest of circumstances. François ends her novel with a refutation of the pessimism of her era, embodied by the philosophy of Arthur Schopenhauer.

Stufenjahre eines Glücklichen received little recognition in François's day, the first edition never selling out. François remained indifferent; she took little interest in the business aspect of her publications, not even knowing where some of her works were published and often receiving copies only as presents from relatives. The powerfully written *Der Katzenjunker* (The Cat Junker, 1879) carries one of François's strongest indictments of the abuse of female vulnerability in a patriarchal society. "Zu füßen des Monarchen" (At the Foot of the Monarch, 1881), based on a trip François made to the valley of Chamounix at the foot of Mont Blanc, is her only admitted self-portrait. The female protagonist's desire to adopt a child reflects François's greatest regret, not having had a child. François poured her maternal love onto her nephew Leo Herbst, the son of her half-brother Arthur, who had died in 1876.

After completing *Der Katzenjunker*, which was written after "Zu füßen des Monarchen" even though it was published earlier, François felt no more urge to write. She continued her life of solitude in Weißenfels, taking long walks and reading voraciously. Dr. Otto Hartwig, the librarian at the University of Halle, provided her with works of French and German literature, especially those of Goethe, and studies by the historians Ferdinand Gregorovius, Theodor von Bernhardi, Jacob Burckhardt, Victor Hehn, Leopold von Ranke, Heinrich Treitschke, Thomas Carlyle, and Karl Hillebrand. She pursued her lifelong interest in Immanuel Kant's *Kritik der reinen Vernunft* (Critique of Pure Reason, 1781) and professed at age fifty-eight to have mastered it. Contact with the wider world came through friendships with Ebner-Eschenbach and Meyer, both of whom approached her through letters. Enraptured by *Die letzte Reckenburgerin*, Ebner-Eschenbach sent an admiring letter in 1880, enclosing a copy of her own *Aphorismen* (1880; translated as *Aphorisms*, 1883) dedicated to François. This introduction developed into a correspondence that continued until François's death. Four months after their initial contact they met at Bad Nauheim; the following year they spent several weeks together in Bad Reichenhall in Upper Bavaria, after which François traveled to Bolzano and Merano. They met again in 1883 in Sankt Zeno, near Bad Reichenhall.

In 1881 François was approached by Meyer, who had been impressed by "Zu füßen des Monarchen" and sought her opinion of his works. Since the *Deutsche Rundschau* (German Review), in which many of Meyer's stories were published, was not available in Weißenfels, François had not heard of Meyer – even as she had never heard of Ebner-Eschenbach until the Austrian introduced herself to her. A lengthy correspondence between Meyer and François ended in 1891, when Meyer had a mental breakdown. François lacked understanding of Meyer's pessimistic and ambiguous narrative world, and Meyer soon ceased soliciting her opinion about his works, but their letters shed valuable light on the breadth of François's reading in history, literature, and philosophy. François's letters condemn the pessimism of Nordic and Slavic literature and the ugliness and negativism of naturalism. Being highly disciplined herself, she had little use for torn characters such as Heinrich von Kleist.

After several grants initiated at the secret request of François's friends Charlotte Duncker and Mathilde Thümmel, the German Schiller Foundation awarded François a lifetime pension in 1880. She attended concerts and exhibits in Leipzig, Berlin, Bayreuth, and Halle; visited friends and relatives in Naumburg, Erfurt, and Wiesbaden; and attended the annual meetings of the Goethe Society in Weimar. In 1883 she began an autobiography, "Schauen und Hörensagen: Aus meinen Kindertagen" (Observations and Hearsay: From My

Childhood), but broke off after the description of her father's death. The fragment was published in the *Deutsche Revue* in 1920. Encouraged by Ebner-Eschenbach, but against the advice of other friends, she permitted the performance of *Der Posten der Frau: Lustspiel in fünf Aufzügen* (The Wife's Post: Comedy in Five Acts, 1881), which she had adapted in 1880 from her short story. It received a prize from the Grillparzer Fund of the Viennese Schiller Foundation and was performed in 1881 in Meiningen at the request of Duke Georg II and his wife, but was not successful. It was never repeated since François did not feel up to making revisions. François declined to attend the performance because of her intense shyness. In 1884 she took a trip to Switzerland, visiting Meyer in Kilchberg, followed by a second trip to Switzerland the following year.

As friends and relatives died, François became more and more alone. Other friends and relatives invited her to move to Halle or Wiesbaden, but she refused to leave Weißenfels. She shared her modest pension with the poor and with her nephew Leo, who seemed to be in continual bad health. She was remembered on her seventieth birthday in 1887 by congratulations and a monetary gift from the German Schiller Foundation and by an album of greetings in prose and verse from Austrian writers including Paoli and Ebner-Eschenbach. In 1888 François became blind in her right eye due to a cataract; she spent seven months in a semidark room to protect the sight in her other eye. In the spring of 1889 she was able to undertake a trip to Switzerland, where she visited Meyer for the second and last time. Shorter trips included one to Wiesbaden, where she met the feminist Amalie Bölte. At a meeting of the Goethe Society in 1891 she met the writers Karl Emil Franzos, Julius Rodenberg, Friedrich Spielhagen, and Ernst von Wildenbruch and was surprised that they knew her work. Suffering from what may have been stomach cancer, she became bedridden in August 1893 and died on 25 September.

Letters:

"Marie von Ebner-Eschenbach und Louise von François," edited by Anton Bettelheim, *Deutsche Rundschau*, 27, no. 1 (1900): 104–119; enlarged as "Marie von Ebner-Eschenbach, ein Briefwechsel mit Louise von François," *Biographische Blätter*, volume 5 (Berlin: Paetel, 1900), pp. 102–125, 138, 213;

Louise von François und Conrad Ferdinand Meyer: Ein Briefwechsel, edited by Bettelheim (Berlin: Reimer, 1905);

Briefe deutscher Frauen, edited by Fedor von Zobeltitz (Berlin & Vienna: Ullstein, 1910), pp. 511–537;

"Briefe von Louise von François und Julius Rodenberg," edited by Hermann Hoßfeld, *Thuringen: Monatsheft für alte und neue Kultur*, 6 (1930): 166–177;

"Louise von François und Eisenach: Drei Briefe der Dichterin an Hedwig Bender und an Frau Oberstleutnant Bender, Adelheid, geb. von François in Eisenach," edited by Hermann Hoßfeld, *Der Bergfried, Eisenach*, 2 (1924);

"Aus den Briefen von Fanny Tarnow an Louise von François," edited by Adolf Thimme, *Deutsche Rundschau*, 53 (1927): 223–234;

Die Akte von Louise von François, edited by Helmut Motekat, Veröffentlichungen aus dem Archiv der Deutschen Schillerstiftung, 7 (Weimar: Aufbau, n.d.).

Bibliographies:

Fritz Oeding, *Bibliographie der Louise von François*, Heimatkundliche Schriften, 1 (Weißenfels: Kell, 1937);

Hermann Hoßfeld, "Zur François-Forschung," *Geistige Arbeit*, 4 (20 October 1937): 9.

Biography:

Ernst Schroeter, *Louise von François: Die Stufenjahre der Dichterin. Zur Erinnerung an die 100. Wiederkehr ihres Geburtstags am 27. Juni 1917* (Weißenfels: Lehmstedt, 1917).

References:

Gertrud Bäumer, "Louise von François," in her *Gestalt und Wandel: Frauenbildnisse* (Berlin: Herbig, 1939), pp. 456–468;

Hedwig Bender, "Louise von François: Ein Nachruf," *Neue Bahnen*, 15 January 1894, pp. 9–11;

Marie von Ebner-Eschenbach, "Louise von François," *Neue freie Presse*, 23 February 1894, pp. 1–3;

Ebner-Eschenbach, "Louise von François: Erinnerungsblätter," *Velhagen und Klasings Monatshefte*, 8 (March 1894): 18–30;

Georg Ellinger, "Louise von François," *Die Nation*, 11 (4 October 1893): 59–61;

Hans Enz, *Louise von François* (Zurich: Rascher, 1918);

Thomas C. Fox, *Louise von François and "Die letzte Reckenburgerin": A Feminist Reading* (New York: Lang, 1988);

Adolf Frey, "Louise von François und Conrad Ferdinand Meyer," *Deutsche Rundschau*, 32 (April 1906): 146–149;

Gustav Freytag, "Ein Roman von Louise von François," *Im Neuen Reich*, 8, no. 2 (1872): 295–300;

Otto Hartwig, "Zur Erinnerung an Louise von François," *Deutsche Rundschau*, 20, no. 3 (1893): 456–461;

Hermann Hoßfeld, "Louise von François," *Westermanns Monatshefte*, 61 (1917): 679–684;

Elisabeth Krause, "Louise von François," *Mitteilungen der literarhistorischen Gesellschaft Bonn*, 10, nos. 5–6 (1915–1916): 117–155;

Tiiu V. Laane, "The Incest Motif in Louise von François's 'Der Katzenjunker': A Veiled yet Scathing Indictment of Patriarchal Abuse," *Orbis Litterarum*, 47 (1992): 11–30;

Gertrud Lehmann, *Louise von François: Ihr Roman "Die letzte Reckenburgerin" als Ausdruck ihrer Persönlichkeit* (Greifswald: Abel, 1918);

Sigrid Meinecke, "Louise von François: Die dichterischen und menschlichen Probleme in ihren Erzählungen," Ph.D. dissertation, University of Hamburg, 1984;

Walter Reichle, "Studien zu den Erzählungen der Louise von François," Ph.D. dissertation, University of Freiburg, 1952;

Uta Scheidemann, *Louise von François: Leben und Werk einer deutschen Erzählerin des 19. Jahrhunderts*, Europäische Hochschulschriften, Reihe I, volume 973 (Frankfurt am Main: Lang, 1987);

Ronald M. Schoeffel, "The Ethical Thought of Louise von François," Ph.D. dissertation, University of Toronto, 1963;

Ernst Schroeter, "Das Modell und seine Gestaltung in den Werken der Louise von François," in *Bilder aus der Weißenfelser Vergangenheit*, edited by the Weißenfelser Verein für Natur- und Altertumskunde (Weißenfels: Selbstverlag des Vereins, 1925), pp. 187–252;

Clotilde Schwarzkoppen, "Louise von François: Ein Lebensbild," *Vom Fels zum Meer*, 2, no. 10 (1894): 193–198;

Paul von Szczepanski, "Luise von François," *Daheim*, 30, no. 6 (1894): 92–94;

Emil Staiger, "Vorwort," in *Frau Erdmuthens Zwillingssöhne,* by François (Zurich: Manesse, 1954), pp. 7–28;

Lionel Thomas, "Luise von François: 'Dichterin von Gottes Gnaden,'" *Proceedings of the Leeds Philosophical and Historical Society*, 11 (1964): 7–27;

Till Urech, *Louise von François. Versuch einer künstlerischen Würdigung* (Zurich: Juris, 1955);

Edith Wendel, "Frauengestalten und Frauenprobleme bei Louise von François," Ph.D. dissertation, University of Vienna, 1959;

Linda Kraus Worley, "Louise von François: A Reinterpretation of Her Life and Her 'Odd-Women' Fiction," Ph.D. dissertation, University of Cincinnati, 1985.

Papers:
Louise von François's papers are in the Museum Weißenfels.

Karl Emil Franzos

(25 October 1848 – 28 January 1904)

Mark H. Gelber
Ben-Gurion University

BOOKS: *Aus Halb-Asien: Culturbilder aus Galizien, der Bukowina, Südrußland und Rumänien,* 2 volumes (Leipzig: Duncker & Humblot, 1876; revised, 1878; enlarged and revised edition, Stuttgart: Bonz, 1889);

Die Juden von Barnow: Novellen (Stuttgart & Leipzig: Hallberger, 1877; enlarged edition, Leipzig: Duncker & Humblot, 1880); translated by M. W. Macdowall as *The Jews of Barnow: Stories* (Edinburgh & London: Blackwood, 1882; New York: Appleton, 1883); German version enlarged (Stuttgart: Bonz, 1887);

Vom Don zur Donau: Neue Culturbilder aus "Halb-Asien," 2 volumes (Leipzig: Duncker & Humblot, 1878);

Junge Liebe: Zwei Geschichten (Breslau: Schottländer, 1879);

Die Hexe: Novelle (Leipzig: Reclam, 1880);

Moschko von Parma: Geschichte eines jüdischen Soldaten (Leipzig: Duncker & Humblot, 1880; New York: Munro, 1882);

Stille Geschichten (Dresden: Minden, 1881);

Ein Kampf um's Recht: Roman, 2 volumes (Breslau: Schottländer, 1882; New York: Munro, 1882); translated by Julie Sutter as *For the Right* (New York: Harper, 1888; London: Clarke, 1889);

Mein Franz: Novelle in Versen (Leipzig: Breitkopf & Härtel, 1883);

Der Präsident: Erzählung (Breslau: Trewendt, 1884); translated by Miles Corbet as *The Chief Justice* (New York: Lovell, 1890; London: Heinemann, 1891);

Die Reise nach dem Schicksal: Erzählung (Stuttgart: Bonz, 1885; New York: Munro, 1885);

Tragische Novellen (Stuttgart: Bonz, 1886);

Aus der großen Ebene: Neue Kulturbilder aus Halb-Asien, 2 volumes (Stuttgart: Bonz, 1888);

Die Schatten: Erzählung (Stuttgart: Bonz, 1888);

Judith Trachtenberg: Erzählung (Breslau: Trewendt, 1891); translated by L. P. and Charlton Thom-

as Lewis as *Judith Trachtenberg: A Novel* (New York: Harper, 1891);

Der Gott des alten Doktors: Erzählung (Berlin: Fontane, 1892);

Der Wahrheitsucher: Roman, 2 volumes (Jena: Costenoble, 1893);

Ein Opfer: Erzählung (Stuttgart: Engelhorn, 1893);

Ungeschickte Leute: Geschichten (Jena: Costenoble, 1894);

Der kleine Martin: Erzählung (Berlin: Concordia, 1896);

Leib Weihnachtskuchen und sein Kind: Erzählung (Berlin: Concordia, 1896);

Allerlei Geister: Geschichten (Berlin: Concordia, 1897);

Konrad Ferdinand Meyer: Ein Vortrag (Berlin: Concordia, 1899);

Heines Geburtstag (Berlin: Concordia, 1900);

Mann und Weib: Novellen (Berlin: Concordia, 1900);

Deutsche Fahrten: Reise- und Kulturbilder, 2 volumes (Berlin & Stuttgart: Cotta, 1903–1905) — comprises volume 1, *Aus Anhalt und Thüringen;* volume 2, *Aus den Vogesen;*

Neue Novellen (Stuttgart & Berlin: Cotta, 1905);

Der Pojaz: Eine Geschichte aus dem Osten (Stuttgart & Berlin: Cotta, 1905);

Der alte Damian und andere Geschichten (Stuttgart & Berlin: Cotta, 1905);

OTHER: *Buchenblätter: Ein Jahrbuch für deutsche Literaturbestrebungen in der Bukowina,* volume 1, edited by Franzos (Czernowitz: Buckowcki, 1870);

Georg Büchner, *Sämmtliche Werke und handschriftlicher Nachlaß: Erste kritische Gesammt-Ausgabe,* edited by Franzos (Frankfurt am Main: Sauerländer, 1879);

Deutsches Dichterbuch aus Österreich, edited by Franzos (Leipzig: Breitkopf & Härtel, 1883);

Deutsche Dichtung, 1–35 edited by Franzos (October 1886–March 1904);

Karl Emil Franzos (photograph by E. Bieber)

Die Suggestion und die Dichtung: Gutachten über Hypnose und Suggestion, edited by Franzos (Berlin: Fontane, 1892);

Die Geschichte des Erstlingswerks: Selbstbiographische Aufsätze, edited, with a contribution, by Franzos (Leipzig: Titze, 1894);

Aus dem neunzehnten Jahrhundert: Briefe und Aufzeichnungen, 4 volumes, edited by Franzos (Berlin: Concordia, 1897–1900).

Although Karl Emil Franzos has been largely forgotten, during the last two decades of his life he was an imposing figure on the Austro-German and central European literary scenes. His novellas, novels, and travelogues were translated into almost twenty languages, and his influence and prestige as an editor, critic, essayist, and journalist were considerable. Franzos's place in literary history has been secured by his role as the editor of Georg Büchner's works (1879), for it was Franzos who rescued Büchner's writings from near oblivion. Franzos was also important as an educator and as a mediator between the East and the West.

Born on 25 October 1848 in Podolia, Russia, near the eastern Galician town of Czortkow, in the midst of the revolutionary events of that year, Franzos remained committed throughout his life to the liberal and democratic, if nationalistic, values of the revolution. He was influenced by his father, Heinrich, in this regard. After having studied medicine at German universities, where he had been affiliated with German nationalist groups, Heinrich Franzos had settled in Czortkow as district physician with his bride, Karoline Klarfeld Franzos, who was from Odessa.

Eastern Galicia was inhabited by Ruthenians (Ukrainians), Poles, Jews, and German-speaking Austrians. An "enlightened," partially assimilated, and highly acculturated Jew, Heinrich was alienated from the various social circles in Czortkow; he appeared to relish this "outsider" status, perhaps believing that it allowed him access to the various groups on his own terms. This independence of spirit seems to have been inherited by his son. The youngest child in the family, Karl was raised for the most part in isolation from the Jewish community of Czortkow as a German national of Jewish faith. His Jewish allegiance was inculcated by his father as an unhappy duty, whereas the German component of his education, including a strong love of German language and culture, was instilled with genuine enthusiasm. His father's sympathy for the Ruthenian peasants, whom he apparently treated irrespective of remuneration, was likewise transmitted to the son and appears as a constant feature in Franzos's writings. Although Franzos claimed later that Deutschtum (German nationality) and Judentum (Judaism) came together in harmonious unity in his being, he remained alienated from the traditional forms of Jewish life characteristic of eastern European Jewry.

After the death of Heinrich Franzos in 1858, his widow moved with the children to Czernowitz (now Chernovtsy, Ukraine), the culturally Germanized capital of the eastern Austrian province of Bukovina. While distinguishing himself at the gymnasium Franzos helped to support his family by tutoring his fellow students, mostly in classical languages. He read voraciously in German and other literatures and began to write poems and short stories that were published in Czernowitz. Despite a strong interest in classical philology, Franzos eventually chose a more practical career path. From 1867 to 1871 he studied law at the University of Vienna and the University of Graz. He continued to write verse and stories, some of which attested to his enthusiasm for Bukowina and its German culture. In Vienna, Franzos joined Teutonia, the German nationalist fraternity; in Graz he became president of the German nationalist society Orion. These organizations were hotbeds of the Pan-German movement, which gained momentum and intensity in Austria after the Franco-Prussian War and German unification in 1871, despite attempts by the Habsburg monarchy to control and limit its spread. As the anti-Semitic strain in Pan-Germanism became more pronounced, as in the rhetoric of its most dynamic Austrian spokesman, Georg von Schönerer, Jewish students with German nationalist sympathies were alienated and eventually excluded from its activities. Like his father, Franzos committed himself to Pan-Germanic public activity, often traveling and speaking before large audiences, and some of his activities caused complications with the Austrian authorities. An indictment against him ended any hopes he may have had for a career in the civil service. But he had never been happy with his legal studies, and be-

fore receiving a degree he decided to embark on a career as a journalist and writer in Vienna.

A disastrous love affair served as the inspiration for his first acclaimed novella, "Das Christusbild" (translated as "The Picture of Christ"), a tale in which an intense love affair is terminated when the woman, a Christian, learns of her lover's Jewish background. The work, which was first published in the periodical *Westermanns Monatshefte* in 1869, was reprinted in 1877 in Franzos's first novella collection, *Die Juden von Barnow* (translated as *The Jews of Barnow*, 1882). In his fiction the tragic termination of love relationships because of religious or ethnic barriers is a recurrent theme.

The novellas of *Die Juden von Barnow* are complex aesthetic structures with subtle alterations in narrative perspective, synchronic shifts, and intertextual correspondences among the stories. In "Der Shylock von Barnow" (translated as "The Shylock of Barnow") an omniscient narrator sets the scene: the small, filthy streets and dilapidated houses of the Jewish ghetto in the fictional town of Barnow. Attention is drawn to the wealthy but unhappy Moses Freudenthal. The narrator disappears; a dialogue ensues between two representatives of the Barnow German-Austrian elite, a judge and an actuary; and some details of the tragic story of Freudenthal's daughter are revealed. The narrator returns, and the scene shifts to Freudenthal, who, in conversation with an elderly workman, mentions his daughter. A synchronic break brings the reader back to the judge, who has just finished relating the story of Freudenthal's daughter, blaming the father and characterizing the Jews as heartless people. Further shifts carry the reader back and forth among the various circles and interested parties in the town until the narrative of the girl is completed. Little sympathy is aroused for the father, while the benighted conditions of eastern European Jewish social life are condemned for thwarting the girl's attempts to acquire a secular German education and driving her to a tragic love affair with a dashing hussar and, ultimately, to her death. Satire of insensitive and simplistic attitudes toward Jews on the part of the German-Austrian elite is included in the form of the ignorant criticism of the girl by the wives of the Austrian bureaucrats. The most stringent satire is reserved for the legal recipient of Freudenthal's prodigious estate, the Hassidic Wunderrabbi (wonder rabbi) of Sadagora, the enemy of Western enlightenment and implacable defender of Jewish superstition.

According to Franzos's omniscient narrators, antiquated and destructive Jewish customs and the narrow-mindedness and insularism of the Jewish community are to blame for creating the conditions that allow such terrible occurrences to transpire. This pattern is followed in the novellas in *Die Juden von Barnow* and in most of Franzos's works that treat eastern European life. Jewish characters who persist and acquire a semblance of German education and culture move inexorably to their tragic fates after they break with the Jewish community. The highly idealized model of German education and the promulgation of secularized German bourgeois values remain intact.

In the 1870s Franzos contributed articles and stories to a wide range of German-language newspapers and magazines, the most important being the Viennese *Neue Freie Presse* (New Free Press), Budapest's *Pester Lloyd,* and the prestigious *Westermanns Monatshefte*. Between 1874 and 1876 he traveled in Europe, Russia, the Orient, and Egypt. His most important success was a bulky collection of vignettes and travel pieces, *Aus Halb-Asien* (From Half-Asia, 1876). The work was translated into many languages, giving Franzos an international reputation. *Half-Asia* became a popular designation for eastern European life, conveying the sense of a variegated society characterized by the backward customs of recalcitrant and uneducated Slavic groups — especially the benighted Poles — together with the superstitious and unenlightened religious practices of Hassidic Jews, all in the face of the bright social and economic opportunities afforded by the penetration of civilized and rational German cultural possibilities in the East. Franzos's *Vom Don zur Donau* (From the Don to the Danube, 1878) contains the same kind of material as *Aus Halb-Asien*. In 1888 a third collection *Aus der großen Ebene* (From the Great Plain), appeared, and in some subsequent editions the three works were published as a massive six-volume trilogy titled *Halb-Asien*.

In 1877 Franzos married Ottilie Benedikt, a writer (under the pseudonym F. Ottmer) of novellas and the daughter of a socially prominent Viennese Jewish businessman. He continued his literary activity in Vienna while also lecturing throughout Europe. His first novel *Moschko von Parma* (Moschko of Parma, 1880) is the story of Moses (Moschko) Veilchenduft. Unlike most of his Jewish playmates, the young Moschko is able to stand up to Christian boys and defend physically his human dignity. His desire to become a soldier, a fate normally avoided at all costs in the eastern European Jewish communities, distances him even further from his Jewish cultural environment. Apprenticed to a Ruthenian blacksmith, he proves that Jews can also excel at hard physical labor. He falls in love with a Ruthenian woman, whom he cannot marry because of the Jewish opposition to intermarriage, and a child is born to them. At about this time he is drafted into the army. Twenty years later, after being wounded in battle, he returns home an invalid. The mother of his child has married in the meantime, and his son has been raised by a former friend. Isolated from the various societal circles and dependent on charity, he becomes a well-known local personality. Although he does not reveal his true identity to his son, he fosters a close relationship with him before he dies stoically and without compromising his moral beliefs.

Several long narratives followed the positive reception of *Moschko von Parma,* including *Ein Kampf um's Recht* (1882; translated as *For the Right,* 1888), a stirring defense of the Ruthenian cause that has been compared to Heinrich von Kleist's *Michael Kohlhaas* (1810); *Der Präsident* (1884; translated as *The Chief Justice,* 1890); *Die Reise nach dem Schicksal* (The Journey toward Fate, 1885); and *Die Schatten* (The Shadows, 1888). From 1884 to 1886 Franzos edited the *Neue Illustrierte Zeitung* (New Illustrated Newspaper).

In 1886 Franzos and his wife moved to Berlin. There he founded the literary magazine *Deutsche Dichtung* (German Poetry), which he managed and edited single-handedly until his death. He also founded the Concordia publishing company, which published many of his own works. The magazine and the publishing company enabled Franzos to promote his favorite writers and to provide a forum for the exponents of the liberal, democratic, and humane traditions of European civilization. Franzos edited *Die Geschichte des Erstlingswerks* (The History of the First Publication, 1894), which contains the autobiographical context and genesis of the first publications of some major literary figures of the day.

During his years in Berlin, Franzos wrote some of his best-known works, including *Judith Trachtenberg* (1891; translated, 1891); *Leib Weihnachtskuchen und sein Kind* (Leib Weihnachtskuchen and His Child, 1896); and *Der Pojaz* (The Clown, 1905). He was a major contributor to *Deutsche Dichtung,* with essays on Heinrich Heine, Ludwig Börne, Conrad Ferdinand Meyer, and the Young Germans. He also published previously unknown letters from such authors as Ludwig Uhland, Friedrich Hebbel, Friedrich Rückert, Johann Wolfgang von Goethe, Fritz Reuter, Karl Gutzkow, and Berthold Auerbach. The increasingly anti-Semitic atmosphere in the 1890s brought him into conflict with several members of the Berlin literary community, and the disputes sometimes found their way into court. By the end of his life he was somewhat estranged from the literary circles in Berlin, although he remained an imposing personality and a guide for aspiring young writers. He was dismayed by the rise of German racial and chauvinistic ideologues and political parties, which portended the exclusion of Jews and other "outsiders" from enfranchisement in German political and cultural life. Yet Franzos, while continuing to play a modest part in Jewish community life, distanced himself from Jewish nationalist expression.

Franzos died in Berlin on 28 January 1904 and was buried in the Jewish Cemetery in Weissensee. His widow moved back to Vienna and arranged over the following years for the publication of some of his unpublished or uncollected writings. She died in 1932. In 1905 *Der Pojaz* was published, and it has proven to be his most enduring work. Although it was completed more than a decade before his death, Franzos may not have wished to see it in print for fear that it might add to the anti-Semitic feelings that were in ascendancy in Germany at the time. In truth, though, this novel is not significantly more critical of eastern European Jewish life than are many of his other works. *Der Pojaz* is a bildungsroman about Sender Glatteis, a Jewish orphan of low birth from fictional Barnow. He has some natural talents, such as a gift for imitation, which he manages to develop despite the abusive environment of the Cheder, the traditional Jewish elementary school. (The Cheder and its pitifully backward approach to education are standard objects of vicious satire in Franzos's works.) Sender eventually leaves school and decides to become an actor. To do so, he must master German and acquire the basic secular education that is anathema to the orthodox Jewish community. Various Christians aid him in his endeavor. Severe setbacks, as well as the deprivations of his childhood, result in his developing consumption. He dies, having only glimpsed his dream in feverish hallucinations.

Although Franzos enjoyed wide popularity in the late nineteenth century, the rise of modernist schools of literature and literary criticism has led to the virtual disappearance of his writings from the canon of German literature. Furthermore, his commitment to secularism and to Jewish acculturation has caused many Jewish readers to reject him. His fate anticipated the disappearance of eastern European Jewry as an ethnic group, a process that was almost completed by the end of the twentieth century. Nevertheless, Franzos deserves to be remembered for the role he played in mediating eastern European life to the West and for promoting a humane conception of Germanic letters in a time characterized by rising nationalism and racism.

Biography:

Carl Steiner, *Karl Emil Franzos, 1848–1904: Emancipator and Assimilationist* (New York: Lang, 1990).

References:

Ludwig Geiger, "Karl Emil Franzos," in his *Die deutsche Literatur und die Juden* (Berlin: Reimer, 1910), pp. 250–304;

Mark H. Gelber, "Ethnic Pluralism and Germanization in the Works of Karl Emil Franzos (1848–1904)," *German Quarterly,* 56 (May 1983): 376–385;

Dietmar Goltschnigg, "Die Wiederentdeckung Georg Büchners durch Karl Emil Franzos," in *Die Bukowina: Studien zu einer versunkenen Literaturlandschaft,* edited by Goltschnigg and Anton Schwab (Tübingen: Francke, 1990), pp. 75–88;

Jost Hermand, "Nachwort," in *Der Pojaz,* by Franzos (Königstein: Athenäum, 1979), pp. 353–369;

Günther A. Höfler, *Psychoanalyse und Entwicklungsroman: Karl Emil Franzos "Der Pojaz"* (Munich: Verlag des Südostdeutschen Kulturwerks, 1987);

Höfler, "Das Recht als 'Poesie des Charakters' – Ödipus als Partisan: Zu Karl Emil Franzos' Roman 'Ein Kampf um's Recht,'" in *Die Bukowina: Studien zu einer versunkenen Literaturlandschaft,* pp. 63–73;

Dieter Kessler, *Ich bin vielleicht kein genügend moderner Mensch: Notizen zu Karl Emil Franzos (1848–1904)* (Munich: Verlag des südostdeutschen Kulturwerks, 1984);

Maria Klanska, "Drei deutschsprachige Schriftsteller im nationalen Spannungsfeld Galizien," *Österreich in Geschichte und Literatur,* 34 (January–February 1990): 26–39;

Jong-Dae Lim, "Das Leben und Werk des Schriftstellers Karl Emil Franzos," Ph.D. dissertation, University of Vienna, 1981;

Mary Lynn Martin, "Karl Emil Franzos: His Views on Jewry, as Reflected in His Writings on the Ghetto," Ph.D. dissertation, University of Wisconsin, 1968;

Margarita Pazi, "Die frühen Erzählungen von Karl Emil Franzos," in *Die Bukowina: Studien zu einer versunkenen Literaturlandschaft,* pp. 49–62;

Pazi, "Der Gefühlspluralismus im Werk Karl Emil Franzos," in *Galizien – eine literarische Heimat,* edited by Stefan H. Kaszynski (Poznan: Naukowe Uniwersytet Imenia Adama Mickiewicza, 1987), pp. 77–113;

Pazi, "Karl Emil Franzos' Assimilationsvorstellung und Assimilationserfahrung," in *Conditio Judaica: Judentum, Antisemitismus und deutschsprachige Literatur vom 18. Jahrhundert bis zum ersten Weltkrieg. Zweiter Teil,* edited by Hans Otto Horch and Horst Denkler (Tübingen: Niemeyer, 1989), pp. 218–233;

Ritchie Robertson, "Western Observers and Eastern Jews: Kafka, Buber, Franzos," *Modern Language Review,* 83 (January 1988): 87–105;

Miriam M. W. Roshwald, "The Shtetl in the Works of Karl Emil Franzos, Sholom Aleichem, and Shmuel Yosef Agnon," Ph.D. dissertation, University of Minnesota, 1972;

Egon Schwarz and Russell A. Berman, "Karl Emil Franzos: Der Pojaz," in *Romane und Erzählungen des Bürgerlichen Realismus,* edited by Klaus Peter Denkler (Stuttgart: Reclam, 1980), pp. 378–392;

Fred Sommer, *"Halb–Asien": German Nationalism and the Eastern European Works of Karl Emil Franzos* (Stuttgart: Heinz, 1984);

Wilhelm Stoffers, *Juden und Ghetto in der deutschen Literatur bis zum Ausgang des Weltkrieges* (Graz: Stiasny, 1939);

Andrea Wodenegg, *Das Bild der Juden Osteuropas: Ein Beitrag zur komparatistischen Imagologie an Textbeispielen von Karl Emil Franzos und Leopold von Sacher-Masoch* (Frankfurt am Main, Bern & New York: Lang, 1987);

Stefan Zweig, "Karl Emil Franzos," *Jung-Deutschland,* 3 (1900): 37–41.

Papers:

Karl Emil Franzos's literary remains are at the Stadt- und Landesbibliothek (City and Provincial Library), Vienna.

Gustav Freytag

(13 July 1816 – 30 April 1895)

Nancy Kaiser
University of Wisconsin – Madison

BOOKS: *De initiis scenicae poesis apud Germanos* (Berlin: Nietack, 1838);

De Hrosuitha poetria: Adjecta est comoedia Abraham inscripta (Breslau: Aderholz, 1839);

Die Brautfahrt oder Kunst von der Rose: Lustspiel in fünf Akten (Breslau: Schuhmann, 1844);

In Breslau: Gedichte (Breslau: Kern, 1845);

Deutsche Geister: Festspiel. Zur Feier der 9. Versammlung deutscher Land- und Forstwirthe am 8. September 1845 aufgeführt auf dem Stadttheater von Breslau (Breslau: Kern, 1845);

Die Valentine: Schauspiel in fünf Aufzügen (Leipzig: Verlagsbureau, 1847);

Graf Waldemar: Schauspiel in fünf Akten (Leipzig: Herbig, 1850);

Die Journalisten: Lustspiel in vier Akten (Leipzig: Hirzel, 1854); translated anonymously as *The Journalists: Comedy in Four Acts* (Cambridge, Mass.: Sever, 1888);

Soll und Haben: Roman in sechs Büchern, 3 volumes (Leipzig: Hirzel, 1855); translated by L. C. C. as *Debit and Credit,* 2 volumes (New York & London: Harper, 1855);

Dramatische Werke (Leipzig: Hirzel, 1858) – comprises *Die Brautfahrt, Der Gelehrte, Die Valentine, Graf Waldemar, Die Journalisten;*

Die Fabier: Trauerspiel in fünf Acten (Leipzig: Hirzel, 1859);

Bilder aus der deutschen Vergangenheit, 2 volumes (Leipzig: Hirzel, 1859); translated by Georgiana Malcolm as *Pictures of German Life in the XVth, XVIth, and XVIIth Centuries,* 2 volumes (London: Chapman & Hall, 1862) and *Pictures of German Life in the XVIIIth and XIXth Centuries: Second Series,* 2 volumes (London: Chapman & Hall, 1863);

Ein Haus-A.B.C. zum 6. Februar 1861 (Leipzig: Breitkopf & Härtel, 1861);

Neue Bilder aus dem Leben des deutschen Volkes (Leipzig: Hirzel, 1862);

Die Technik des Dramas (Leipzig: Hirzel, 1863; revised, 1872); translated by Elias J. MacEwan as *The Technique of the Drama: An Exposition of*

Gustav Freytag

Dramatic Composition and Art (Chicago: Griggs, 1895);

Die verlorene Handschrift: Roman in fünf Büchern, 3 volumes (Leipzig: Hirzel, 1864); translated by Malcolm as *The Lost Manuscript: A Novel* (3 volumes, London: Chapman & Hall, 1865; 1 volume, New York: Appleton, 1869);

Was wird aus Sachsen, anonymous (Leipzig: Wigand, 1866);

Bilder aus der deutschen Vergangenheit, 5 volumes (Leipzig: Hirzel, 1867) – comprises volume 1, *Aus dem Mittelalter;* volume 2, part 1, *Vom Mittelalter zur Neuzeit (1200 bis 1500);* volume 2, part 2,

Aus dem Jahrhundert der Reformation (1500–1600); volume 3, *Aus dem Jahrhundert des großen Krieges (1600–1700);* volume 4, *Aus neuer Zeit (1700–1848);*

Karl Mathy: Geschichte seines Lebens (Leipzig: Hirzel, 1870);

Die Fahnenweih in Siebleben: Ein Bild aus der deutschen Gegenwart (Leipzig: Breitkopf & Härtel, 1871);

Vom ersten Reichstage: Brief an die Wähler des Wahlkreises Erfurt-Schleusingen-Ziegenrück (Leipzig: Wigand, 1871);

Die Ahnen: Roman, 6 volumes (Leipzig: Hirzel, 1872–1880) – comprises volume 1, *Ingo und Ingraban* (1872); translated by Malcolm as *Ingo: The First Novel of a Series Entitled "Our Forefathers"* (New York: Holt & Williams, 1873) and *Ingraban: The Second Novel of a Series Entitled Our Forefathers* (New York: Holt, 1873); volume 2, *Das Nest der Zaunkönige* (1873); volume 3, *Die Brüder vom deutschen Hause* (1874); volume 4, *Marcus König* (1876); volume 5, *Die Geschwister* (1878); volume 6, *Aus einer kleinen Stadt* (1880);

Doktor Luther: Eine Schilderung (Leipzig: Hirzel, 1883); translated by Henry E. O. Heinemann as *Martin Luther* (Chicago: Open Court, 1897);

Gesammelte Werke, 22 volumes (Leipzig: Hirzel, 1887–1888) – includes as volume 1, *Erinnerungen aus meinem Leben* (1887); translated by Katharine Chetwynd as *Reminiscences of My Life,* 2 volumes (London: White, 1890);

Der Kronprinz und die deutsche Kaiserkrone: Erinnerungsblätter (Leipzig: Hirzel, 1889); translated by George Duncan as *The Crown Prince and the German Imperial Crown: Reminiscences* (London: Bell, 1890);

Vermischte Aufsätze aus den Jahren 1848 bis 1894, 2 volumes, edited by Ernst Elster (Leipzig: Hirzel, 1901–1903) – comprises volume 1, *Aufsätze zur Kunst und Literatur, Philologie und Alterthumskunde;* volume 2, *Aufsätze zur Geschichte und Kulturgeschichte;*

Über den Antisemitismus: Eine Pfingstbetrachtung, edited by the Central-Verein Deutscher Staatsbürger Jüdischen Glaubens (Berlin: Lewent, 1910);

Erzählungen und Geschichten aus schwerer Zeit: Bilder und Dichtungen, edited by Wilhelm Rudeck (Leipzig: Fiedler, 1911);

Deutsche Lebensführung: Lebensbilder und Leitworte, edited by Rudeck (Leipzig: Fiedler, 1912);

Auf der Höhe der Vogesen: Kriegsberichte von 1870/71 (Leipzig: Hirzel, 1914);

Das Vermächtnis: Eine Erzählung, edited by Ernst von Otto (Leipzig: Seeman, 1925).

Gustav Freytag was a noted author, journalist, and cultural historian whose works are a useful source of cultural and historical information about the second half of the nineteenth century. His novel *Soll und Haben* (1855; translated as *Debit and Credit,* 1855) remained a best-seller long into the twentieth century, and his multivolume cultural history *Bilder aus der deutschen Vergangenheit* (Pictures from the German Past, 1859–1867; excerpts translated as *Pictures of German Life,* 1862–1863) remains a treasure trove of historical fact and anecdote. In both his writings and his life, Freytag was a typical representative of the bourgeois liberal nationalism in German lands after the unsuccessful revolutionary upheavals of 1848. He was a political moderate and a strong advocate of a Germany unified under Prussian leadership and excluding Austria. This agenda was realized in 1871 with the founding of the German Empire.

Freytag was born on 13 July 1816 in Kreuzburg, Silesia, to Gottlob Ferdinand and Henriette Albertine (Zebe) Freytag. His father was a doctor and long-standing mayor of Kreuzburg; his mother was the daughter of a pastor. A brother, Reinhold, was born in 1820. According to Freytag's memoirs, his reading as a youth included popular novels by Sir Walter Scott and James Fenimore Cooper, and he began writing a novel himself at age ten. In 1829 Freytag left home to attend a gymnasium in Öls, where he lived with his paternal uncle. His diploma, which he received in 1835, attests especially to his talents and achievements in Latin and Greek. In the spring of 1835 Freytag began studying philology at the University of Breslau (now Wroclaw, Poland), where he acquired the skill of reading manuscripts from Hoffmann von Fallersleben.

In the fall of 1836 Freytag moved on to Berlin, where he attended lectures on ancient and medieval literature by Karl Lachmann and resumed his studies in philology under the linguist Franz Bopp. His dissertation, *De initiis scenicae poesis apud Germanos* (On the Beginnings of Dramatic Poetics among the Germans, 1838), traced the origin of German drama. His habilitation thesis, *De Hrosuitha poetria* (On the Poetic Work of Hrotsvitha, 1839), dealt with the works of an early-medieval woman writer. The completion of the habilitation certified Freytag to hold lectures after his return to the University of Breslau in the spring of 1839. Freytag offered lectures on German grammar, literary history, and the mythology of Germanic tribes; his colloquium topics included epic folk literature of the Middle Ages, literature of the twelfth century, and heathen traces in older Germanic literatures. The study of German literature was just becoming legitimate during this period, and Freytag was an enthusiastic supporter of the discipline.

During his Breslau years Freytag composed historical dramas as well as poetry with a dramatic tone. In a manner that was to remain characteristic of his writings throughout his life, Freytag's early literary endeavors evince a commitment to middle-class values, even when the setting is feudal society.

Freytag's dramatic efforts during this period include *Die Brautfahrt* (The Bridal Voyage, 1844), written in 1841. The play shared a prize with three other dramas at the Hoftheater (Court Theater) in Berlin in 1842, but it never enjoyed great success. (Nevertheless, it was this drama that the great director Franz Dingelstedt was reportedly working on at the time of his death in 1881.) A historical comedy dramatizing the marital politics of the Hapsburg Empire in the fifteenth century, the play owes much to similar period pieces such as Johann Wolfgang von Goethe's *Götz von Berlichingen* (1773; translated, 1799). It depicts the union of Maria of Burgundy with the archduke Maximilian of Hapsburg, who became Kaiser Maximilian I. The couple takes five acts to come together, with Maria enduring trials and tribulations in Ghent and her betrothed, Maximilian, struggling to reach her side. Unrest accompanied the engagement, which was regarded by the French court as the loss of Burgundy to the Hapsburgs. Although she has never laid eyes on him, Maria remains steadfast in her engagement to Maximilian, rejecting all other offers and arguments. Her only moment of hesitation comes in the final act, when she is misinformed that her fiancé is a hunchback. Meanwhile, Maximilian and his trusty court fool Kunz encounter scoundrels and rivals for the hand of Maria on their journey to Ghent. Kunz is rewarded at the end with the love of a young woman who had accompanied them disguised in male clothing.

Among Freytag's other dramatic works from this period is a one-act fragment in iambic verse, *Der Gelehrte* (The Scholar, 1858). Freytag's comments on the play in his memoirs and the existence in his unpublished papers of a fragmentary comedy from the early 1840s titled *Der Schulmeister* (The Schoolmaster) have led his biographer Hans Lindau to speculate that *Der Gelehrte* was distilled from the earlier work. Compared by Lindau to Goethe's *Torquato Tasso* (1790; translated, 1861), the play concerns the archivist Walter's thwarted love for the baroness Leontine; the temptation offered him to compromise his intellectual integrity in the service of the state or of contemporary politics; and his

final decision to work for an abstractly defined "Volk" (people), a decision that may heal his broken heart. The dialogue between Walter and the political journalist Romberg juxtaposes the humanist intellectual and the activist, and Freytag's sympathies lie clearly with the former.

Further dramatic texts from this period exist only in manuscript form among Freytag's papers. In the political farce *Dornröschen* (Snow White), written in 1842, a sleeping princess is the embodiment of freedom; she and her court awaken for five minutes every hundred years. Figures representing France, England, and Russia attempt unsuccessfully to free her from the spell. Germany is represented by the youthful Michael, who is guided by his tutor Philosophus and the good spirit Fantel. The other three national representatives succumb to various temptations and themselves fall under the spell of eternal sleep, as does Philosophus. Michael alone withstands all lures and kisses and thereby awakens the princess. The final scene shows the joy of Europe that has been effected by German effort.

Concurrently, Freytag was writing the libretto for a ballet titled *Die Tscherkessin* (The Circassian Woman) or, alternatively, *Russen und Tscherkessen* (Russians and Circassians). Its plot is the familiar one of forbidden love between leading figures of two feuding peoples. As the piece begins, Suleika is mourning the death of her brother at the hands of the Russians and planning revenge through a sleeping potion to be administered to the enemy troops. Predictably, she falls in love with their leader, Iwan, prevents his execution, abets his escape, and tends to his wounds. In the final scene she hides him in the cave where ammunition and powder are stored. Discovering that he is the murderer of her brother, she shoots him, igniting the munitions. Although Freytag's correspondence reveals that Duke Ernst von Coburg once considered composing the score, there is no record of the work having been printed or produced.

Passed over for promotion to a full professorship in 1843, Freytag left the teaching profession in the summer of 1844. The poetry in his collection *In Breslau* (1845) is generally regarded as derivative. Much of the collection consists of poems written for various social occasions or celebrations. The best pieces are generally deemed to be the ballads, a poetic form that incorporates elements of the two genres in which Freytag possessed literary talent: the narrative and the drama.

Freytag wrote *Die Valentine* (1847) in the spring of 1846. In five acts, this romantic comedy snarls and then untangles the fates of Baroness Valentine and Georg, a commoner who has just returned from political exile. From the beginning of the first act it is clear that Valentine and Georg are meant for each other, despite class differences. The baroness becomes the unwilling object of a night visit by a prince in act 3. Wishing to explain the silken ladder dangling from her window to Georg, who was passing by, she invites him to her room, and he rescues her from burglars. Georg himself is taken for an intruder and seized, and he saves Valentine's honor by pretending to be a thief. It would endanger his safety if his political past were discovered in a police investigation, so Valentine publicly announces that she had invited him to her quarters. Dismissed from the court for such impropriety, she is free to marry for love. The play is amusing, and the themes are fairly clear: the irrelevance of class distinctions to human emotion, the immorality of the petty princes in German lands, and the political conditions that created exiles in the 1840s.

In 1847 Freytag moved to Dresden following a visit to Leipzig, where he had contacts in literary and cultural circles. Leipzig at that time was home to the composers Richard Wagner and Robert and Clara Schumann; the writers Berthold Auerbach, Karl Gutzkow, Heinrich Laube, and Ludwig Richter; the theater director Eduard Devrient; and the sculptor Ernst Riechel. Also in 1847 Freytag married Emilie Scholz, a wealthy Silesian divorced from a count. Finally, that year he completed the play *Graf Waldemar* (Count Waldemar, 1850), which again takes up the theme of the unimportance of social class. Hans, the illegitimate child of Count Waldemar Schenk, is raised by the lowly gardener's daughter Gertrud Hiller. Princess Georgine Udaschkin, who is attempting to win the count's heart, is revealed as a former lover of Waldemar's and the biological mother of the boy. Both she and the count show distinct signs of the weltschmerz portrayed by many writers of the 1840s, and Georgine's unhappiness is connected by Freytag to her denial for so many years of the supposedly natural female role of mother. Gertrud, on the other hand, represents the revitalizing force of nature and is an instinctive mother. Georgine ultimately relinquishes her claims to both father and son in the face of the human bond between Waldemar, Gertrud, and Hans. In the penultimate act she attempts to force Gertrud to choose between the boy and the count. In the final act, on the verge of shooting Waldemar, she undergoes a change of heart at the sight of her son. In the last scene Waldemar and Gertrud are preparing to marry

without regard for class difference. *Die Valentine* and *Graf Waldemar* extol the merit of human sentiment over social class in a manner typical of German middle-class ideology of the period.

It would seem that Freytag's career as a dramatist had finally been launched; but between these two plays and his next, history intervened in the form of the revolutionary upheavals of 1848. Together with Julian Schmidt, Freytag took over the editorship of the journal *Die Grenzboten* (The Border Messengers) in July of that year. The journal became an influential forum for the national-liberal politics advocating a united Germany under Prussian leadership. Although deeply disappointed by the actions of Friedrich Wilhelm IV in the spring of 1848, Freytag never tended toward radical politics. The journal remained a primary occupation for Freytag until 1870. The acquisition of a country home in the village of Siebleben near Gotha allowed him to divide his time between rural summers of relative tranquillity and winters of hectic activity in Leipzig. Schmidt left *Die Grenzboten* in 1861; his position was taken over by Moritz Busch until 1866 and then by Julius Eckardt. Not only a political medium for national-liberal ideology, the journal was also the forum for discussions of literary realism. Contributing to both functions with many articles and essays, Freytag also wrote character sketches of cultural and literary personalities of the time.

In the early 1850s Freytag began a friendship with Ernst II, Duke of Saxe-Coburg-Gotha. The duke was a strong proponent of national liberalism and was a founder of the National-liberaler Verein (National-Liberal Union) in 1853. Freytag headed the press committee for the National-liberaler Verein, and a feature series that he established as a service to German newspapers earned him the ire of the Prussian authorities. In 1854 he got wind of a secret order for his arrest, but Duke Ernst secured his immunity by granting him citizenship in Saxe-Coburg-Gotha and the title of Hofrat (councillor).

In 1852 Freytag again turned his energies to drama, writing *Die Journalisten* (1854; translated as *The Journalists*, 1888) during a sojourn in his summer residence. Performed with enormous success in 1853 under the direction of Devrient in Karlsruhe, the play is a comedy about the ideological conflicts between the conservative and liberal parties of the period as embodied in the press. The rivalry between the fictional newspapers *Coriolan* and *Union* hinders the love of Ida Berg and Professor Oldendorf: Oldendorf is the editor of the liberal *Union,* and the retired Colonel Berg, Ida's father, is allied with the conservative *Coriolan.* Abetted

Scene 2 from the second act of Freytag's comedy Die Journalisten *(etching by Herbert, 1853)*

by her friend Adelheid Runeck, who is in love with Oldendorf's colleague Konrad Bolz, Ida finally gains the permission of her father to marry his rival. Adelheid secretly buys the *Union,* but she willingly signs her rights over to Bolz in the final scene. With engaging characters and sprightly dialogue, the play endured well into the twentieth century as one of the few successful German comedies.

Freytag also turned his hand to narrative fiction in the 1850s. The novel *Soll und Haben* was intended as an example of the literary realism being advocated by *Die Grenzboten.* Dedicated to Duke Ernst, the novel enjoyed critical acclaim and popular success. The latter has been of long duration; by the time the copyright expired in 1925 more than a half million copies had been sold. By 1960 the total exceeded a million, and in the late 1970s there were two additional paperback editions and plans for a ten-segment television film by the German director Rainer Werner Fassbinder. The film project was canceled after public controversy over the suitability of an anti-Semitic, chauvinistic novel for the West German Radio and Television Network. Much of the scholarly attention accorded the book

in the 1970s and 1980s analyzed the ideological content of the novel, which was acclaimed at the time of its publication as the first flowering of German realism and as the first truly German novel. *Soll und Haben* is a novel of commerce and character development with an emphasis on solid middle-class values and Prussian nationalism. It is realistic to the extent that its value system reflects the retrenchment of the German bourgeoisie after the political setbacks of 1848. There was a compensatory emphasis on the economic strength of the middle classes in the 1850s. In Freytag's novel the work ethos of the German middle classes is contrasted to the self-seeking speculation of the aristocracy and the frenzied activity of the Jewish financial manipulators. Germans are also contrasted with Poles, and the superior national characteristics of the former are emphasized.

The German middle-class hero, Anton Wohlfart, is apprenticed to the firm of T. O. Schröter. Based on the company of Theodor Molinari in Breslau, this establishment represents disciplined order, a diligent work ethic, and a patriarchal yet benevolent structure of authority. These middle-class values stand in contrast to the irresponsible financial speculations of the von Rothsattel family and to the dishonest schemes of the Jew Veitel Itzig. After bringing the von Rothsattels to the brink of ruin and murdering an accomplice, Itzig drowns while fleeing the police. The proud yet increasingly impoverished von Rothsattels had made various attempts to salvage their social status and fortune, and for a time Wohlfart leaves the Schröter firm to assist them on their estate in Poland. He is motivated partly by his infatuation with Lenore von Rothsattel, but her affections finally settle on Fritz von Fink. Fink is an engaging yet aberrant young nobleman who at the beginning of the novel was an intern in the Schröter firm, where he was unable to abide by the rules of decency and order. Wohlfart is rewarded for his steadfast service and loyalty with the hand of Sabine Schröter and ownership of the firm. The motto on the novel's title page was provided by Schmidt: "Der Roman soll das deutsche Volk da suchen, wo es in seiner Tüchtigkeit zu finden ist, nämlich bei seiner Arbeit" (The novel should search for the German people where they may be found in diligence — at work). *Soll und Haben* was Freytag's first novel and his most successful one. His influences are generally assessed to be Charles Dickens and Walter Scott.

In the writings of his friend, the historian Theodor Mommsen, Freytag found the inspiration for *Die Fabier* (The Fabii, 1859), a tragedy about the struggle between the family of Fabius and the populace of Rome. Written in iambic verse, the play met with little critical enthusiasm and was Freytag's last dramatic effort.

Based on essays that had appeared in *Die Grenzboten* since 1849, Freytag's *Die Technik des Dramas* (1863; translated as *The Technique of the Drama,* 1895) outlines the structure and components of successful tragedy. Drawing on plays by the great tragedians of antiquity, Aeschylus, Sophocles, and Euripides; William Shakespeare; and the German dramatists Goethe, Gotthold Ephraim Lessing, Friedrich Schiller, and Heinrich von Kleist, Freytag says that a properly structured tragedy has five sections and three moments. The sections, which form a pyramid, are the introduction, rising action, the climax (at the apex of the pyramid), falling action or reversal, and the catastrophe. The three moments are the incipient moment between the introduction and the rising action leading to the climax; the tragic moment, which often coincides with the climax and begins the falling action; and the moment of final suspense, which heightens the impending catastrophe, often by a brief retardation of the fall-

Freytag surrounded by characters from his novel Soll und Haben; *this etching by S. Loeffler, commemorating Freytag's fortieth birthday, was published in the Leipzig* Illustrierte Zeitung *in 1856.*

ing action. Freytag's structural model of the tragedy has often been quoted.

His next novel, *Die verlorene Handschrift* (1864; translated as *The Lost Manuscript,* 1865), takes his erstwhile profession as its subject. The main character is a professor of philosophy, Felix Werner, and the title refers to a previously unknown manuscript by Tacitus. Intently following references to the whereabouts of the manuscript, Werner first makes an unexpected find — Ilse, the lovely daughter of a country squire. With Ilse as his wife, Werner continues his quest. The promised patronage of one of the ubiquitous despots in German lands prior to unification lures them to the prince's court. The contrast of values between Ilse and the court could not be clearer, and the prince has equally clear intentions on her honor. Werner, blinded by his scholarly quest and by a cleverly constructed fake manuscript, fails to realize

Ilse's unhappiness and endangerment. The novel ends happily and with a moral – Werner realizes the treasure he has in Ilse when he finds her in a cave, next to the cover of the long-sought manuscript. Ilse has been rescued through the loyal efforts of Werner's servant, Gabriel, and his landlord, Mr. Hummel; the manuscript itself never turns up. In a subplot, Hummel's daughter finds happiness with the son of her father's archenemy. The bourgeois values emphasized in the novel are similar to those of *Soll und Haben,* even though the hero is a scholar and not a merchant. *Die verlorene Handschrift* offers a cross section of social classes of the time, with finely drawn character sketches, particularly of the academic world. Although it presents the dangers of extreme preoccupation with historical artifacts, such preoccupations were to absorb Freytag's energies for most of his remaining publications. An emphasis on the German past accompanied the withdrawal of many German writers from contemporary issues and politics in the 1860s and 1870s.

Freytag's next major publication was a multivolume cultural history of the Germans, *Bilder aus der deutschen Vergangenheit.* Again based on essays in *Die Grenzboten,* the work appeared in two stages. The initial two volumes, covering the period from the sixteenth to the mid nineteenth centuries, were published in 1859; the final part appeared in 1862 as *Neue Bilder aus dem Leben des deutschen Volkes* (New Pictures from the Life of the German Nation) and encompassed the period from the beginnings of Germanic culture through the Middle Ages. The five-volume combined version of 1867 is regarded as the definitive edition. The volumes depict the economy, social conditions, and culture of each successive epoch of German history; the unique value of Freytag's cultural history lies in the interspersed sketches and anecdotes. Combining biographical reports with autobiographical accounts, mixing famous historical figures and ordinary people, *Bilder aus der deutschen Vergangenheit* provides insight into a broad sweep of German history. The work is meant to instruct the German people and encourage the establishment of a unified German state. While writing *Bilder aus der deutschen Vergangenheit* Freytag compiled a large collection of political pamphlets, mainly from the Reformation through the Thirty Years' War. This collection is now housed in the Municipal and University Library of Frankfurt am Main.

Freytag's next book, *Karl Mathy: Geschichte seines Lebens* (Karl Mathy: The Story of His Life, 1870), is a carefully written, admiring biography of the liberal thinker and journalist from the state of Baden in the progressive southwest area of Germany. Freytag and Mathy had worked together in Gotha and Leipzig in the late 1850s and early 1860s, and Freytag wanted to preserve the story of his friend after his death in 1868.

In 1867 Freytag was a representative for one session of the North German Parliament, and during the Franco-Prussian War of 1870–1871 he accompanied Crown Prince Friedrich on his campaigns. But Freytag found himself consistently at odds with Otto von Bismarck, the architect of German unification. In articles in *Die Grenzboten* Freytag disparaged Bismarck's politics and policies throughout the 1860s. After the publisher, Hans Grunow, abruptly reassigned the editorship of *Die Grenzboten* in 1870, Freytag began to write for the newly founded weekly *Im neuen Reich* (In the New Empire), edited by Alfred Dove. The founding of the German Empire in 1871 was the fulfillment of a lifelong dream for Freytag. He continued to work for *Im neuen Reich* until 1873. His wife died in 1875 after a lengthy illness; his second wife, Marie Dietrich Freytag, whom he married in 1876, gave birth to two sons: Gustav in 1876 and Waldemar in 1877.

Freytag's six-volume cycle of historical novels, *Die Ahnen* (The Ancestors, 1872–1880), is a fictional companion to *Bilder aus der deutschen Vergangenheit* that traces the development of a German family from the middle of the fourth century through the revolutionary year of 1848. The first volume contains two tales, as does the fifth volume; each of the remaining four volumes adds a further story, and the last volume appends an additional brief narrative as a finale. The reception of the cycle was mixed, with more enthusiasm for the earlier volumes. Freytag said at the completion of the project that it had cost him dearly and that he was uncertain whether he would ever write anything again.

The initial volume is titled *Ingo und Ingraban* (translated as *Ingo,* 1873, and *Ingraban,* 1873). The story of Ingo begins with the battle of the Vandals against the Romans in A.D. 357 and follows the travels of the title figure and his wife Irmgard to Thuringia. Both perish in a fire, but their young son is saved to found a ruling dynasty. Centuries later Ingraban, a scion of that family, serves as a guide to Bonifatius, the Christian missionary to the Germanic tribes. The first volume of *Die Ahnen* ends with Ingraban's death. In *Das Nest der Zaunkönige* (The Wrens' Nest, 1873) his descendant Immo intervenes in the struggles for the accession to the German throne in the early eleventh century and finally marries the daughter of Heinrich II. In the third volume, *Die Brüder vom deutschen Hause* (The Brothers of the German House, 1874), the hero, Ivo, accompanies Emperor Friedrich II on the Crusade of 1228-1229. Ivo's tribulations include the dissension among the ranks of the Teutonic Order. With the fourth volume the lineage of Ingo, Ingraban, Immo, and Ivo gives way to the König family. In *Marcus König* (1876) the hero is a merchant of the early sixteenth century. *Die Geschwister* (The Siblings, 1878) consists of two tales, each following a set of siblings in the König family. Toward the end of the Thirty Years' War, Regine takes over the care of her brother Bernhard's son after Bernhard and his wife, Judith, die; the latter has been accused of witchcraft. The second story takes place a century later: when August König falls in battle in 1745, his brother Friedrich assumes responsibility for August's widow and children. The final volume of *Die Ahnen, Aus einer kleinen Stadt* (From a Small Town, 1880), brings the historical cycle up to Freytag's own lifetime. The physician Ernst König marries the daughter of a country pastor and settles in a small Silesian town after the Wars of Liberation in 1813-1814. In the final episodes, their son Viktor becomes a writer and founds a literary-cultural journal with a friend after the revolution of 1848. The biographical overtones of the final volume are unmistakable.

For health reasons, Freytag switched his winter residence from Leipzig to the gentler climate of Wiesbaden in 1881. In 1883 his slender volume *Doktor Luther: Eine Schilderung* (Doctor Luther: A Description; translated as *Martin Luther*, 1897) was published. A contribution to the celebrations surrounding the five-hundredth anniversary of the reformer's birth, it was mostly a reworking of a section of *Bilder aus der deutschen Vergangenheit*. Freytag's younger son died of diphtheria in 1884; Marie Freytag was committed to an asylum later that year. The first volume of Freytag's *Gesammelte Werke* (Collected Works, 1887-1888) was his memoirs, *Erinnerungen aus meinem Leben* (1887; translated as *Reminiscences of My Life*, 1890).

Freytag's last publications included a somewhat controversial memorial to Crown Prince Friedrich, who died after a brief reign as Friedrich III in 1888. *Der Kronprinz und die deutsche Kaiserkrone* (1889; translated as *The Crown Prince and the German Imperial Crown*, 1890) repeated some of his initial reservations from 1871 about the title and function of an emperor and also captured the character of Friedrich III, who some historians believe would have given German history a more liberal course than did Wilhelm II. Freytag was divorced from

Freytag in 1887 (engraving by Karl Stauffer-Bern)

Marie in 1890, and he married Anna Götzel Strakosch in March 1891.

Freytag's final years brought him several honors: in 1886 the title of Geheimer Hofrat (privy councillor); in 1893 the additional title of Exzellenz (excellency) and the Ordens pour le mérite der Friedensklasse (Order of Merit for Peace). Freytag was an active member of the jury for the Schiller Prize. In March 1895 he caught a cold while traveling to a conference regarding the construction of a monument for Duke Ernst. The cold turned into a lung inflammation, and Freytag died in Wiesbaden on 30 April 1895. He is buried in the village cemetery in Siebleben. The Gustav-Freytag-Gesellschaft (Gustav Freytag Society) was founded in Kreuzburg in 1908 and existed until 1934. In 1953 the Deutsche Gustav-Freytag-Gesellschaft (German Gustav Freytag Society) was founded; since 1957 it has published the *Gustav-Freytag-Blätter: Mitteilungen der Deutschen Gustav-Freytag-Gesellschaft Wiesbaden und des Gustav-Freytag-Archivs und "Museums"* (Gustav Freytag Pages: Communications of the German Gustav Freytag

Society of Wiesbaden and the Gustav Freytag Archives and "Museum").

Letters:

Gustav Freytag und Heinrich von Treitschke im Briefwechsel, edited by Alfred Dove (Leipzig: Hirzel, 1900);

Gustav Freytag an Salomon Hirzel und die Seinen, edited by Dove (Leipzig: Breitkopf & Härtel, 1903);

Gustav Freytag und Herzog Ernst von Coburg im Briefwechsel 1853 bis 1893, edited by Eduard Tempeltey (Leipzig: Hirzel, 1904);

Briefe an seine Gattin, edited by Hermance Strakosch-Freytag and Curt L. Walter van der Bleek (Berlin: Lehmann, 1912);

Briefe an Albrecht von Stosch, edited by Hans Ferdinand Helmolt (Stuttgart: Deutsche Verlags-Anstalt, 1913).

Biographies:

Conrad Alberti, *Gustav Freytag: Sein Leben und Schaffen* (Leipzig: Schloemp, 1885);

Friedrich Seiler, *Gustav Freytag* (Leipzig: Voigtländer, 1898);

Hans Lindau, *Gustav Freytag* (Leipzig: Hirzel, 1907);

Hans Zuchhold, *Gustav Freytag: Ein Buch von deutschem Leben und Wirken* (Breslau: Goerlich, 1926).

References:

T. E. Carter, "Freytag's *Soll und Haben*: A Liberal National Manifesto as a Best-Seller," *German Life and Letters,* 21 (July 1968): 320–329;

Mark H. Gelber, "An Alternate Reading of the Role of the Jewish Scholar in Gustav Freytag's *Soll und Haben,*" *Germanic Review,* 58 (Spring 1983): 83–88;

Gelber, "Die literarische Umwelt zu Gustav Freytags *Soll und Haben* und die Realismustheorie der *Grenzboten,*" *Orbis Litterarum,* 39 (Spring 1984): 38–53;

Gelber, "Teaching 'Literary Anti-Semitism': Dickens' *Oliver Twist* and Freytag's *Soll und Haben,*" *Comparative Literature Studies,* 16 (March 1979): 1–11;

Claus Holz, *Flucht aus der Wirklichkeit: "Die Ahnen" von Gustav Freytag. Untersuchungen zum realistischen historischen Roman der Gründerzeit 1872–1880* (Frankfurt am Main: Lang, 1983);

Herbert Kaiser, "Gustav Freytag: *Soll und Haben.* Poesie des Geschäfts – Kunst der bürgerlichen Bedürfnisse," in his *Studien zum deutschen Roman nach 1848* (Duisburg: Braun, 1977), pp. 57–106;

Nancy Kaiser, "Cohesion and Integration: Reading as Reaffirmation (*Soll und Haben*)," in her *Social Integration and Narrative Structure: Patterns of Realism in Auerbach, Freytag, Fontane, and Raabe* (Bern: Lang, 1986), pp. 35–86;

Ernst Kohn Bramstedt, *Aristocracy and the Middle-Classes in Germany: Social Types in German Literature 1830–1900* (London: King, 1937; Chicago: University of Chicago Press, 1964);

Edward McInnes, " 'Die Poesie des Geschäfts': Social Analysis and Polemic in Freytag's *Soll und Haben,*" in *Formen realistischer Erzählkunst. Festschrift für Charlotte Jolles,* edited by J. Thunecke (Nottingham, U.K.: Sherwood Agencies, 1979), pp. 99–107;

George Mosse, "The Image of the Jew in German Popular Culture: Felix Dahn and Gustav Freytag," *Publications of the Leo Baeck Institute,* 2 (1957): 218–227;

Claus Richter, "Freytag's *Soll und Haben,*" in his *Leiden an der Gesellschaft: Vom literarischen Liberalismus zum poetischen Realismus* (Kronberg: Athenäum, 1978);

Jeffrey L. Sammons, "The Evaluation of Freytag's *Soll und Haben,*" *German Life and Letters,* 22 (July 1969): 315–324;

Michael Schneider, *Geschichte als Gestalt: Gustav Freytags Roman "Soll und Haben"* (Stuttgart: Akademischer Verlag, 1980);

Hartmut Steinecke, "Gustav Freytag: *Soll und Haben* (1855): Weltbild und Wirkung eines deutschen Bestsellers," in *Romane und Erzählungen des bürgerlichen Realismus: Neue Interpretationen,* edited by Horst Denkler (Stuttgart: Reclam, 1980), pp. 138–152;

Lynne Tatlock, "Realist Historiography and the Historiography of Realism: Gustav Freytag's *Bilder aus der deutschen Vergangenheit,*" *German Quarterly,* 63 (Winter 1990): 59–74;

Lionel Thomas, "Bourgeois Attitudes: Gustav Freytag's Novels of Life in Nineteenth-Century Germany," *Proceedings of the Leeds Philosophical and Literary Society. Literary and Historical Section,* 15 (June 1973): 59–74.

Papers:

Gustav Freytag's papers are in the Westdeutsche Bibliothek (West German Library), Marburg; the Goethe- und Schillerarchiv, Weimar; the Gustav Freytag Archiv, Wangen/Allgäu; the Landesbibliothek (Provincial Library), Wiesbaden; and the Stadt- und Universitätsbibliothek (Municipal and University Library), Frankfurt am Main.

Emanuel Geibel

(17 October 1815 – 6 April 1884)

Wulf Koepke
Texas A&M University

Gedichte (Berlin: Duncker, 1840; enlarged, 1843);

Zeitstimmen: Zwölf Gedichte (Lübeck: Asschenfeldt, 1841; enlarged, 1843; enlarged, 1846);

König Roderich: Eine Tragödie in fünf Aufzügen (Stuttgart & Tübingen: Cotta, 1844);

Ein Ruf von der Trave: Gedicht (Lübeck: Asschenfeldt, 1845);

König Sigurds Brautfahrt: Eine nordische Sage (Berlin: Besser, 1846); translated by Ellen Cook as *The Wooing of King Sigurd, and the Ballad of the Page and the King's Daughter* (London: Bell & Daldy, 1864);

Zwölf Sonette für Schleswig-Holstein (Lübeck: Asschenfeldt, 1846);

Auf Felix Mendelssohn-Bartholdy's Tod (Hamburg: Perthes-Besser & Mauke, 1847);

Juniuslieder (Stuttgart: Cotta, 1848);

Meister Andrea: Lustspiel in zwei Aufzügen (Stuttgart: Cotta, 1855);

Neue Gedichte (Stuttgart & Augsburg: Cotta, 1856);

Brunhild: Eine Tragödie aus der Nibelungensage (Stuttgart: Cotta, 1857); translated by George Theodore Dippold as *Brunhild: A Tragedy from the Nibelung Saga* (Boston: Ginn & Heath, 1879);

Die Loreley (Hannover: Rümpler, 1860);

Gedichte und Gedenkblätter (Stuttgart: Cotta, 1864);

Morgenländischer Mythus: Mit Randverzierungen von Luise Kugler und Albertine von Hochstetter (Berlin: Behr, 1865);

Sophonisbe: Tragödie in fünf Aufzügen (Stuttgart: Cotta, 1868);

Heroldsrufe: Ältere und neuere Zeitgedichte (Stuttgart: Cotta, 1871);

Am 13. Juli 1874: Ode (Elberfeld: Baedeker, 1874);

Spätherbstblätter: Gedichte (Stuttgart: Cotta, 1877);

Echtes Gold wird klar im Feuer: Ein Sprichwort (Schwerin: Hildebrand, 1882);

Gesammelte Werke, 8 volumes (Stuttgart: Cotta, 1883);

Emanuel Geibel (photograph by Franz Hanfstaengl)

Gedichte: Aus dem Nachlaß (Stuttgart: Cotta, 1896);

Ausgewählte Gedichte (Stuttgart: Cotta, 1904);

Geibels Werke, 3 volumes, edited by Wolfgang Stammler (Leipzig: Bibliographisches Institut, 1918);

Gedichte für Cäcilie Wattenbach aus dem Jahre 1835: Erstdruck zum 18. X. 1940, dem 125. Geburtstag des Dichters (Lübeck: Coleman, 1940);

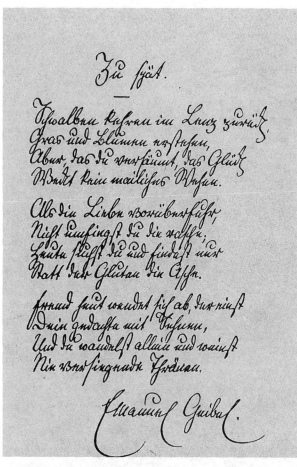

Manuscript for a poem by Geibel (from Karl Theodor Gaedertz, Emanuel Geibel: Sänger der Liebe, Herold des Reiches, 1897)

Die Truhe: Ein Lübecker Heft mit unveröffentlichten Dichtungen Emanuel Geibels, edited by Robert Ludwig (Lübeck: Schmidt-Römhild, 1940).

Editions in English: Adaptations from the German of Emanuel Geibel, by the Late Henry John Dayrell Stowe (London: Bowden, Hudson, 1879);

The White Snake, and Other Poems, translated by Julius Madison Cawein (Louisville: Morton, 1895);

"The Watchman's Song," "The Call of the Road," "Autumn Days," "The Death of Tiberius," translated by Alexis Irenee du P. Coleman, in The German Classics of the Nineteenth and Twentieth Centuries, volume 7, edited by Kuno Francke and William Guild Howard (New York: German Publication Society, 1913), pp. 521–528.

OTHER: Übersetzungen aus griechischen Dichtern, translated by Geibel and Ernst Curtius (Bonn: Weber, 1840);

Volkslieder und Romanzen der Spanier im Versmaße des Originals verdeutscht, translated by Geibel (Berlin: Duncker, 1843);

Spanisches Liederbuch, translated by Geibel and Paul Heyse (Berlin: Hertz, 1852);

Romanzero der Spanier und Portugiesen, translated by Geibel and Adolf Friedrich von Schack (Stuttgart: Cotta, 1860);

Fünf Bücher französischer Lyrik vom Zeitalter der Revolution bis auf unsere Tage in Übersetzungen, translated by Geibel and Heinrich Leuthold (Stuttgart: Cotta, 1862);

Ein Münchner Dichterbuch, edited by Geibel (Stuttgart: Kröner, 1862);

Classisches Liederbuch: Griechen und Römer in deutscher Nachbildung, translated by Geibel (Berlin: Hertz, 1875; enlarged, 1879).

Emanuel Geibel was one of the most celebrated and popular poets of the nineteenth century. His first collection, Gedichte (Poems, 1840), went into one hundred editions during his lifetime. He won the acclaim of kings, aristocrats, and students; leading scholars of German literature, such as Karl Goedeke, wrote respectful biographies. His reputation, however, did not last far into the twentieth century. Recent histories of German literature, if they mention him at all, characterize his work with one or two pejorative sentences. No attempt has yet been made to assess this extraordinary reception history.

The seventh of eight children of Johannes and Elisabeth Luise Ganslandt Geibel, Franz Emanuel August Geibel was born in Lübeck a few minutes before midnight on 17 October 1815; since 18 October was the anniversary of the decisive victory over Napoleon near Leipzig in 1813, the patriotic Geibel family liked to celebrate both occasions together. Geibel's father was the pastor of the Reformed church in Lübeck; Reformed parishes had a high percentage of Huguenot refugees among their members, and Geibel's mother, the daughter of a wealthy merchant, had a French mother. Geibel's father came from Hanau, near Frankfurt am Main; thus, the family was not a typical northern German one. The father won respect from the community through his fervent sermons and his exemplary demeanor, but also as a courageous patriot during the crisis years 1806–1807 and 1813.

Geibel attended the Katharineum, the traditional gymnasium founded during the Reformation that was to receive unwelcome attention through Thomas Mann's Buddenbrooks (1901; translated,

1924). The Katharineum instilled in Geibel a love of classical antiquity. Geibel was a good but not very diligent student who, in his last school years, was equally attracted to writing poetry, the conviviality of his social circle, and his studies. He fell in love with Cäcilie Wattenbach, the sister of a friend; they remained close for many years, until it became clear that he would not soon be in a position to support a family. The *Deutscher Musenalmanach* (German Almanac of the Muses) for 1834, published in the fall of 1833, included Geibel's first published poem, "Vergessen" (Forgotten).

Geibel studied at the University of Bonn in 1835–1836 and at the University of Berlin from 1836 to 1838. It was intended that he become a minister like his father, but he soon abandoned theology for classical philology. His real occupation, however, was writing poems. It was in Berlin that he was first introduced to literary circles. In the writers' club "Tunnel über der Spree" (Tunnel over the Spree) he met Adelbert von Chamisso, Willibald Alexis, and his idol, Joseph von Eichendorff. Bettina von Arnim helped him to obtain the post of tutor for the children of Prince Katakazis, the Russian ambassador in Athens, and Geibel spent 1838 to 1840 in Greece. After his North German homeland and the Rhineland, Greece became the third source of inspiration for his poetry. Although his friend from Lübeck, Ernst Curtius, who was to become a prominent archaeologist, philologist, historian, and educator of princes, was living nearby, Geibel was unhappy as a tutor: he disliked his dependence and unwanted social obligations, and when the Katakazis family moved back to Russia, he resigned his post. After a trip to the Greek islands with Curtius, he returned home.

He never finished a planned doctoral dissertation on Roman poetry, and his professional future seemed bleak. But 1840 brought his first book publications: a volume of translations from the classical Greek by Geibel and Curtius and *Gedichte*, which Geibel rewrote after the original manuscript was destroyed in a fire at the printing shop. Initially *Gedichte* attracted little attention, but its popularity grew rapidly a few years later. It remained his chief claim to fame. After a passing phase of influence by Heinrich Heine and George Gordon, Lord Byron, Geibel developed a style that included elements of those of Friedrich Rückert, Ludwig Uhland, and especially August Graf von Platen-Hallermünde, who impressed Geibel with his metric discipline and his use of antique and Italian models.

Geibel's poetry evokes the German scenery and society of around 1830, before the advent of railroads and heavy industry. His unfulfilled love for Wattenbach became the source of some of his most authentic poems. A dominant theme was that of Wanderschaft (wandering), in which the wanderer experiences the succession of the seasons as a metaphor for life. The transitional seasons, spring and fall, provided the setting for most such poems. These poems of Wanderschaft were his most popular ones, and some of them, set to music, have survived in the German collective memory. "Der Mai ist gekommen" (May Has Come) captures the carefree atmosphere of student life in its first two stanzas:

> Der Mai ist gekommen, die Bäume schlagen aus,
> Da bleibe wer Lust hat mit Sorgen zu Haus;
> Wie die Wolken wandern am himmlischen Zelt,
> So steht auch mir der Sinn in die weite weite Welt.
>
> Herr Vater, Frau Mutter, daß Gott euch behüt!
> Wer weiß, wo in der Ferne mein Glück mir noch blüht!
> Es gibt so manche Straße, die nimmer ich marschiert,
> Es gibt so manchen Wein, den ich nimmer noch probiert.
>
> (May has come, the trees are covered with buds,
> Now may stay home with worries whoever feels like it;
> Like the clouds that are wandering on the heavenly
>   sky,
> My longing goes, too, into the wide, wide world.
>
> Dear father and mother, may God protect you!
> Who knows where in the distant land I may find my
>   luck!
> There are many highways where I have not yet marched,
> There are many wines that I have not yet tasted.)

The hiking and drinking are followed in the next stanzas by a love affair with an innkeeper's daughter. (Many years after writing this poem Geibel was traveling on the Rhine near Sankt Goar when another boat passed by with students drinking and singing this very song. Moved by this sign of the passage of time, Geibel expressed his feelings in another poem, "Ich fuhr von Sankt Goar" [I Went on the River from Saint Goar]). "Der Mai ist gekommen" ends with praise of God's wonderful world, reinforcing the religious subtext of the poem. Landscape and other details are realistic yet nonspecific, the tone is upbeat, and the verses are easy to memorize. It is a song for the young, and Geibel remained predominantly a poet for young people, especially students.

In "Morgenwanderung" (Wandering in the Morning), written in Athens, the religious feelings are much more explicit:

Wer recht in Freuden wandern will,
Der geh' der Sonn' entgegen;
Da ist der Wald so kirchenstill,
Kein Lüftchen mag sich regen.
 Noch sind nicht die Lerchen wach,
 Nur im hohen Gras der Bach
Singt leise den Morgensegen.

Die ganze Welt ist wie ein Buch,
Darin uns aufgeschrieben,
In bunten Zeilen manch ein Spruch,
Wie Gott uns treu geblieben;
 Wald und Blumen nah und fern
 Und der helle Morgenstern
Sind Zeugen von seinem Lieben.

Da zieht die Andacht wie ein Hauch
Durch alle Sinne leise,
Da pocht ans Herz die Liebe auch
In ihrer stillen Weise.
 Pocht und pocht, bis sich's erschließt
 Und die Lippe überfließt
Von lautem, jubelndem Preise.

Und plötzlich läßt die Nachtigall
Im Busch ihr Lied erklingen,
In Berg und Tal erwacht der Schall
Und will sich aufwärts schwingen.
 Und der Morgenröte Schein
 Stimmt in lichter Glut mit ein:
Laßt uns dem Herrn lobsingen!

(Who wants to walk with joy,
He should go and meet the rising sun;
The forest is still like a church,
And no wind is stirring.
 The larks are not yet up,
 Only in the high grass the brook
Is quietly murmuring the morning blessing.

The entire world is like a book,
In which is written down,
In colorful lines so many a saying,
How God remained true to us;
 Forest and flowers near and far
 And the shining morning star
Are witnesses to his loving.

Devotion is moving like a breath
Quietly through all the senses,
And love is knocking on the heart's door
In its quiet manner.
 Knocks and knocks, until it opens up
 And the lip flows over
With loud, jubilant praise.

And suddenly the nightingale
Begins its song in the bush,
Sound is awakening in mountain and valley
And wants to swing upward.
 And the shine of sunrise
 Joins in with its brightening glow:
Let us sing praise to the Lord!)

Geibel, the minister's son, had early become alienated from church dogma and the disputes of theologians. He adhered to a nonsectarian religiosity that propounded a belief in God's goodness and providence and found the divine greatness in nature. Many of his contemporaries also preferred the "church" of the forest to the buildings designated as such. Geibel echoes the experience of nature shared by many readers. "Morgenwanderung" is a painting in words in which forms, colors, and sounds blend harmoniously, and nothing disturbs the perfect peace, least of all the unfolding urbanization and industrialization of Germany. Quite a few of Geibel's poems have a nostalgic if not escapist quality.

In this poem time seems to stand still, but most of Geibel's poems describe the passage of time. Geibel stays within the tradition of the German folk song, retaining some of the folk song's awkwardness and simple tone. Detractors have found skill in various meters and rhyme schemes but not enough substance in his poetry. Geibel, however, was not just a traditionalist; he was no innovator, but he did experiment, especially with form. His *Gedichte,* with its subsequent revisions, contains the liveliest and most popular of his poems. In later years political poetry and translations dominated.

In 1841 Freiherr Karl von der Malsburg invited Geibel, who was stranded in Lübeck, to live at his castle, Escheburg, near Kassel. While there he learned Spanish; his translations of Spanish poems were published in 1843 as *Volkslieder und Romanzen der Spanier* (Folksongs and Romances of the Spanish). In 1842 King Friedrich Wilhelm IV of Prussia awarded him an annual pension of three hundred talers; the king, it seems, was not so much impressed by Geibel's serious poetry as by a modest, humorous poem about a statue of the naked god Mercurius on a bridge in Lübeck – a poem still known to the locals. In 1843 Geibel spent some time in Sankt Goar with the poet Ferdinand Freiligrath and then with the poet Justinus Kerner in Weinsberg. In Stuttgart, where he spent the winter of 1843, he established his lifelong association with the publisher Johann Cotta.

Cotta published Geibel's first play, *König Roderich* (King Roderich), in 1844. Geibel would never abandon his theatrical ambitions, although he could not claim a single success on the stage; but he soon realized that this first experiment was a failure, and he never had it reprinted. *König Roderich* takes place

A meeting of the Munich writers' club Krokodil. Geibel is standing, center, with a glass in his left hand and his right hand extended toward the stuffed crocodile (engraving from a drawing by Theodor Pixis for the periodical Die Gartenlaube, *1866).*

in Spain during the Moorish conquest in the eighth century and intertwines conflicts of love and loyalty; the plot is similar to the legend of the Cid. The Weimar theater presented the play on 3 October 1846; it was unsuccessful.

The 1840s were a time of political turmoil. The accession of Friedrich Wilhelm IV to the Prussian throne in 1840 raised the hopes of German patriots who were longing for a new Reich (empire) and who, like Geibel, preferred a traditional monarchy to a constitutional democracy. Geibel was among the first to advocate German unification under Prussian leadership. Tensions were also high in the Rhineland, where France seemed to threaten a new invasion. Finally, the constitutional problems in Danish-ruled Schleswig-Holstein were mounting; and Schleswig-Holstein was right outside Lübeck. Denmark's hostility exacerbated the economic problems of this smallest of the Free Cities. Geibel spoke out in *Zeitstimmen* (Voices of the Time, 1841) and in *Ein Ruf von der Trave* (A Call from the [River] Trave, 1845). Geibel was a citizen of the Free City and thus of a republic; but as Mann was to remind the world

in *Buddenbrooks,* the ruling class of the city – the merchants – was aristocratic. While Geibel spoke of "Freiheit" (liberty) and "Einheit" (unity), he was not a champion of equality; he expressed aversion to the Pöbel (rabble). He favored law and order and a hierarchical social structure. Geibel was attacked by Georg Herwegh, a champion of liberal causes and the working class, but such polemics only endeared Geibel even more to the ruling classes.

Geibel tried his hand at writing epic poetry with a fairly short verse narrative, *König Sigurds Brautfahrt* (1846; translated as *The Wooing of King Sigurd, and the Ballad of the Page and the King's Daughter,* 1864). He used the Nordic setting and mood then in fashion for the tale, in which an old king wants to marry a young maid; she kills herself after a fight between the king's warriors and her brothers ends with the brothers' deaths. For King Sigurd nothing is left but to die. There is a superabundance of death and tragedy and Nordic gloom, but such was the taste of the times.

Some of Geibel's unfinished works show that he might have developed in more-innovative directions. An example is the fragment of the verse narrative "Julian," published in the second volume of Geibel's collected works in 1883. Julian's German father and Russian mother meet during Napoleon's invasion of Russia in 1812, when she saves his life. They move to the Rhineland and live happily until they are killed by lightning when Julian is sixteen. Julian goes to Russia to live with his Uncle Paul, an aristocratic landowner who turns out to be an unfeeling despot who mistreats his serfs. The tale breaks off before the idealistic, liberal-minded Julian can become involved in the conflicts between the uncle and his subjects. Geibel's innate inertia, and in later years his frequent illnesses, usually stifled such large projects; he remained the master of the short form.

The composer Felix Mendelssohn-Bartholdy asked Geibel to write a libretto for an opera based on the legend of the Lorelei. Geibel responded with enthusiasm. In his version of the legend the Lorelei is a femme fatale who destroys the marriage of a prince and thus becomes a danger to the stability of society. Supernatural elements are used for heightened theatrical effect but are not essential to the plot. Mendelssohn had sketched some of the music and had planned a meeting with Geibel to complete the project when he died suddenly on 4 November 1847. Geibel refused to allow *Die Loreley* to be published until 1860; in 1861 he assented to a composition by Max Bruch. The opera was first performed in 1863.

Geibel collected his political poetry in *Juniuslieder* (Junius Songs, 1848). Initially the revolution of 1848 seemed to Geibel to offer the chance for a unified Germany under the rule of a high-minded liberal elite, but these hopes were disappointed. The Schleswig-Holsteiners rose up against the Danish administration, which had tried to centralize the government, eliminate old privileges and cultural autonomy, and divide the two provinces; the badly armed and trained volunteers were defeated by the Danish army.

In 1848–1849 Geibel served as a substitute teacher at his old school, the Katharineum. In 1852 King Maximilian II of Bavaria nominated him for a professorship in aesthetics at the University of Munich. Geibel hesitated before accepting the offer, and he never felt completely at home in Munich; but he became the center of a circle of poets and writers there, among them Heinrich Leuthold, Wilhelm Heinrich Riehl, and especially Paul Heyse, the prolific poet and novelist with whom he had been in contact since 1848. Geibel was a founder of the writers' club Krokodil (Crocodile) in Munich.

On 26 June 1852 Geibel married Amanda Luise Trümmer, who was eighteen years younger than her husband. Their only child, Ada, was born on 10 May 1853. Geibel's happiness did not last long: a severe illness left his wife bedridden, and she died on 21 November 1855. Geibel's daughter was brought up by one of his sisters in Lübeck.

Geibel continued writing for the stage. His comedy *Meister Andrea* (Master Andrea, 1855), set in Renaissance Florence, is a character study of an absent-minded sculptor and an obsessed musician that offers stock characters and comedy situations. He worked for years on a large-scale tragedy about the Albigenses, adherents of a heretical creed in southern France in the twelfth and thirteenth centuries who rejected the worldly power and riches of the Catholic church; Pope Innocent III called for a crusade against them, and they were exterminated between 1209 and 1229. Geibel was attracted by the issue of fanaticism versus tolerance but finally abandoned the play. A "prelude," *Die Jagd von Beziers* (The Hunt at Beziers), was published in volume seven of his collected works (1883).

The next tragedy, which he completed, was *Brunhild: Eine Tragödie aus der Nibelungensage* (1857; translated as *Brunhild: A Tragedy from the Nibelung Saga,* 1879). Unlike the tetralogy by Richard Wagner (1853) and the trilogy by Friedrich Hebbel (1862) that are also based on the Nibelung saga but focus on Siegfried and Kriemhild, Geibel makes Brunhild his heroine. Geibel considered Brunhild the most interesting character because she comes from a foreign civilization and is sensitive to rejection, has a strong sense of honor, and does not know until well into the play that it is Siegfried whom she loves. The weddings of Gunther with Brunhild and Siegfried with Chriemhild (sic) have taken place; Gunther won his victory over Brunhild under false pretenses, and on the wedding night he needs Siegfried's help once more, this time to overcome Brunhild in the bedroom. Siegfried reluctantly obliges but commits the fatal error of telling his wife about the scheme. When the two queens quarrel over who has precedence, the secret comes to light. Gunther refuses to fight his friend Siegfried to restore Brunhild's honor, so Brunhild induces Hagen to murder Siegfried. When Brunhild sees the dead hero she confesses her love for him and kills herself, a psychologically motivated act that is not part of any of the medieval versions of the saga. Chriemhild vows revenge for her husband's assassination.

King Maximilian II died in 1864; his successor, Ludwig II, had little use for Geibel. Moreover,

Geibel at his desk (engraving after a portrait by an unknown artist)

in the war between Prussia and Austria in 1866 Bavaria was allied with Austria, and Geibel was on the Prussian side. This allegiance served the Bavarian administration as a pretext to strip him of all appointments and pensions. In 1868 Geibel left Munich; he soon received a pension from the king of Prussia.

Geibel wrote one more tragedy in blank verse: *Sophonisbe* (1868) won a share of a Prussian prize of one thousand talers in gold in 1869, but the prize did not help the play's fortunes on the stage. Sophonisbe, a Carthaginian princess of Hannibal's family, is married to a much older Numidian king, Syphax; in her youth she and Massinissa had been in love. Massinissa, feeling that he has been cheated out of his kingdom, becomes an ally of the Romans under Scipio. Syphax wages war against the Romans and nearly wins, but a surprise night attack deprives him of the victory. Too proud to become a prisoner of war, he commits suicide. Sophonisbe continues the fight against the Romans and tries to win Massinissa over to her side. Scipio wins the battle and takes her prisoner. He endeavors to overcome Sophonisbe's enmity through generosity and respect for her dignity. A feeling evolves between them that goes beyond mutual respect; but, like her husband, Sophonisbe realizes she has no place in a Roman-dominated Africa, and she, too, kills herself. The characters, while human and complex, are in the heroic, larger-than-life mold of *Brunhild;* Sophonisbe's motivations would hardly be believable to a bourgeois audience.

The Franco-Prussian War of 1870-1871 and the founding of the German Reich brought forth Geibel's last lyrical outburst of patriotism, *Heroldsrufe* (Calls of a Herald, 1871). His political goals had been achieved: Schleswig-Holstein had been liberated from the Danes in 1864, and Germany was reunited under Prussian leadership. Lübeck saw a modest economic recovery.

Geibel, suffering from frequent illnesses, spent most of his time in Lübeck and the nearby seaside resort Travemünde, except for occasional trips to see friends. The wanderer, whose life and poetry had been identified with the theme of Wanderschaft, had come home. He became an institution in his native city: the memory of the poet during the time Heinrich and Thomas Mann were growing up there is preserved in the character of Heines in Heinrich Mann's novel *Eugénie oder der Bürgerzeit* (Eugénie; or The Bourgeois Age, 1928; translated as *The Royal Woman,* 1930). Geibel collected and revised decades of work on translating the poetry of antiquity in *Classisches Liederbuch* (Classical Song Book, 1875). New production was slow and intermittent, more "occasional verses" than true inspiration. There is an echo of his love for the theater in a last one-act play, *Echtes Gold wird klar im Feuer* (Genuine Gold Becomes Shining through Fire, 1882). A prince returning from the war of 1870–1871 visits an actress to declare his love; but she convinces him, in a feat of heroic generosity, that he does not really love her but his estranged former fiancée. When Geibel died on 6 April 1884 he was mourned not only by his native city, not only by monarchs and aristocrats, but by millions of readers and admirers.

While Geibel felt the occasional urge to write verse epics, and while he dreamed of gaining fame on the stage, his love and talent were for poetry. Besides his lieder – his most popular genre – he wrote ballads, sonnets, odes and elegies in the Greek form, blank-verse narratives, and epigrammatic verses. He was adept at the formal intricacies of the sonnet. Following the model of Friedrich Rückert, he used the sonnet for political messages; like the Romantics, he employed it as a vehicle for reflection on the arts, on poetry, and on himself. He seldom missed a chance to rebut criticism and to restate his poetic and political convictions. From an emotional poet of love and nature he grew to be a commentator on his age and society, a dominant voice between 1848 and 1871.

Geibel was heir to the Romantic tradition of world literature. Besides Greek and Roman antiquity and German folk song he adopted Spanish forms and some Oriental elements. His formal skills were considerable; his vocabulary was rich; his manner was decorous yet familiar. He always remained accessible and hardly ever became pompous.

Geibel shared the taste of his audience for such topics and themes as the Nibelungen, Charlemagne, and the Kyffhäuser – the cave in Thuringia where Emperor Frederick Barbarossa is said to sleep until the German empire is restored. He sang of the Rhineland, an area of major political concern to German patriots between 1830 and 1870. He celebrated the heritage of Greece, a country on the mind of many Germans because of its recent war of liberation.

Geibel's professional existence was somewhat contradictory. He was a free-lance poet but published little. He praised the lonely wanderer in songs that were sung in groups. He sang of freedom and observed the conventions. He praised hard work but led a leisurely life. He had too much pride and good taste to write trivial literature, but in an age of mass culture he would have written hit songs. Geibel exemplifies the post-Romantic German middle class between 1830 and 1880.

Letters:

Emanuel Geibel's Briefe an Karl Freiherr von der Malsburg und Mitglieder seiner Familie, edited by Albert Duncker (Berlin: Paetel, 1885);

Emanuel Geibels Jugendbriefe: Bonn – Berlin – Griechenland, edited by E. F. Fehling (Berlin: Curtius, 1909);

Der Briefwechsel von Emanuel Geibel und Paul Heyse, edited by Erich Petzet (Munich: Lehmann, 1922);

Briefwechsel: Emanuel Geibel und Karl Goedeke, edited by Gustav Struck, Veröffentlichungen der Bibliotheken der Hansestadt Lübeck, new series, no. 1 (Lübeck: Selbstverlag der Stadtbibliothek, 1939);

Briefe an Henriette Nölting, 1838–1855, edited by Hans Reiss and Herbert Wegener (Lübeck: Schmidt-Römhild, 1963).

Biographies:

Karl Goedeke, *Emanuel Geibel* (Stuttgart: Cotta, 1869);

Wilhelm Scherer, *Emanuel Geibel* (Berlin: Weidmann, 1884);

Karl Theodor Gaedertz, *Geibel-Denkwürdigkeiten* (Berlin: Friedrich, 1886);

Gaedertz, *Emanuel Geibel: Sänger der Liebe, Herold des Reiches. Ein deutsches Dichterleben* (Leipzig: Wigand, 1897);

Karl Ludwig Leimbach, *Emanuel Geibels Leben, Werke und Bedeutung für das deutsche Volk,* revised by Max Trippenbach (Wolfenbüttel: Zwißler, 1915);

Ernst Curtius, *Erinnerungen an Emanuel Geibel* (Berlin: Curtius, 1915).

References:

Ute Druvius, "Propreußische Propaganda: Zu Emanuel Geibels Herrscherlob *An König Wilhelm,*" in *Gedichte und Interpretationen,* volume 4: *Vom Biedermeier zum Bürgerlichen Realismus,* edited by Günter Häntzschel (Stuttgart: Reclam, 1983), pp. 346–356;

Hans Norbert Fügen, "Geibel und Heyse: Elemente und Strukturen des literarischen Systems im 19. Jahrhundert. Dokumentation und Analyse," in his *Dichtung in der bürgerlichen Welt* (Bonn: Bouvier, 1972), pp. 28–50;

Véronique de la Giroday, *Die Übersetzertätigkeit des Münchener Dichterkreises* (Wiesbaden: Athenaion, 1978);

Walter Hinck, "Epigonendichtung und Nationalidee: Zur Lyrik Emanuel Geibels," in his *Von Heine zu Brecht: Lyrik im Geschichtsprozeß* (Frankfurt am Main: Suhrkamp, 1978), pp. 60–82;

Arno Holz and Klaus Groth, eds., *Emanuel Geibel: Ein Gedenkbuch* (Berlin & Leipzig: Parrisius, 1884);

Herbert Kaiser, "Die ästhetische Einheit der Lyrik Geibels," *Wirkendes Wort,* 27 (1977): 244–257;

Jürgen Link, "Was heißt: 'Es hat sich nichts geändert'?: Ein Reproduktionsmodell literarischer Evolution mit Blick auf Geibel," in *Epochenschwellen und Epochenstrukturen im Diskurs der Literatur- und Sprachhistorie,* edited by Hans Ulrich Gumbrecht and Ursula Link-Heer (Frankfurt am Main: Suhrkamp, 1985);

Johannes Mahr, ed., *Die Krokodile: Ein Münchner Dichterkreis. Texte und Dokumente* (Stuttgart: Reclam, 1987);

Hilde Meinardus, "Emanuel Geibel und die deutsche Dichtung seiner Zeit," Ph.D. dissertation, University of Münster, 1952;

Bettina Plett, "Die Emanuel-Geibel-Situation und die Theodor-Fontane-Situation: Anmerkungen zu Stellung und Selbstverständnis zweier Schriftsteller im 19. Jahrhundert," in *Theodor Fontane im literarischen Leben seiner Zeit: Beiträge zur Fontane-Konferenz vom 17. bis 20. Juni 1986 in Potsdam* (Berlin: Deutsche Staatsbibliothek, 1987), pp. 466–495;

Beatriz Brinkmann Scheiking, *Spanische Romanzen in der Übersetzung von Diez, Geibel und von Schack: Analyse und Vergleich* (Marburg: Elwert, 1975);

Friedrich Winterscheidt, "Deutschlands deutschester Dichter," in his *Deutsche Unterhaltungsliteratur der Jahre 1850–1860* (Bonn: Bouvier, 1970), pp. 220–227.

Papers:
Emanuel Geibel's papers are at the Stadtbibliothek (City Library), Lübeck.

Friedrich Gerstäcker
(10 May 1816 – 31 May 1872)

Jeffrey L. Sammons
Yale University

BOOKS: *Streif- und Jagdzüge durch die Vereinigten Staaten Nord-Amerikas*, 2 volumes (Dresden & Leipzig: Arnold, 1844); translated anonymously as *Wild Sports in the Far West* (London & New York: Routledge, 1854);

Die Regulatoren in Arkansas: Aus dem Waldleben Amerika's, 3 volumes (Leipzig: Wigand, 1846); chapters 1–13 translated anonymously as *The Regulators of Arkansas: A Thrilling Tale of Border Adventure* (New York: Dick & Fitzgerald, 1857); chapters 13–25 translated anonymously as *Bill Johnson; or, The Outlaws of Arkansas* (New York: Dick & Fitzgerald, 1857); translated as *The Feathered Arrow; or, The Forest Rangers* (London: Routledge, 1857);

Der Kinderspiegel (Leipzig: Wigand, 1847);

Der deutschen Auswanderer Fahrten und Schicksale, volume 4 of *Volks-Bibliothek* (Leipzig: Brockhaus, 1847); translated by David Black as *The Wanderings and Fortunes of Some German Emigrants* (London: Bogue, 1848; Philadelphia: Appleton, 1848);

Mississippi-Bilder: Licht- und Schattenseiten transatlantischen Lebens, 3 volumes (Leipzig: Arnold, 1847–1848); excerpts translated anonymously as *Western Lands and Western Waters* (London: Beeton, 1864); "Eine Gerichtsscene in Arkansas" and "Frauen in den Backwoods," translated by James William Miller as "Courtroom Scenes" and "Women of the Backwoods," in *In the Arkansas Backwoods: Tales and Sketches*, edited by Miller (Columbia & London: University of Missouri Press, 1991), pp. 30–61;

Reisen um die Welt: Ein Familienbuch, 6 volumes (Leipzig: Schlicke, 1847);

Die Flußpiraten des Mississippi, 3 volumes (Leipzig: Costenoble, 1848); translated as *The Pirates of the Mississippi* (London: Routledge, 1856);

Friedrich Gerstäcker

Schießwaffen: Einige Worte über den Gebrauch und die Behandlung der Büchsen und Flinten (Leipzig: Wigand, 1848);

Amerikanische Wald- und Strombilder, 2 volumes (Dresden & Leipzig: Arnold, 1849); includes "Schulen in den Backwoods," translated by Miller as "Schools in the Backwoods," in *In the Arkansas Backwoods: Tales and Sketches*, pp. 62–73;

Pfarre und Schule: Eine Dorfgeschichte, 3 volumes (Leipzig: Wigand, 1849);

Wie ist es denn nun eigentlich in Amerika?: Eine kurze Schilderung dessen, was der Auswanderer zu thun und dafür zu hoffen und zu erwarten hat (Leipzig: Wigand, 1849);

Der Wahnsinnige: Eine Erzählung aus Süd-Amerika (Berlin: Allgemeiner deutscher Volksschriftenverein, 1853);

Reisen, 5 volumes (Stuttgart: Cotta, 1853–1854) — comprises volume 1, *Südamerika*; volume 2, *Californien*; volume 3, *Die Südsee-Inseln*; volume 4, *Australien*; volume 5, *Java*; translated anonymously as *Narrative of a Journey round the World: Comprising a Winter-Passage across the Andes to Chili; with a Visit to the Gold Regions of California and Australia, the South Sea Islands, Java, &c.* (3 volumes, London: Hurst & Blackett, 1853; 1 volume, New York: Harper, 1853);

Aus zwei Welttheilen: Gesammelte Erzählungen, 2 volumes (Leipzig: Arnold, 1854); selections translated anonymously as *Tales of the Desert and the Bush: From the German* (Edinburgh: Constable, 1854);

Fritz Wildau's Abenteuer zu Wasser und zu Lande (Munich: Braun & Schneider, 1854); translated and revised by Lascelles Wraxall as *Frank Wildman's Adventures on Land and Water* (London & New York: Routledge, 1855);

Tahiti: Roman aus der Südsee, 4 volumes (Leipzig & Jena: Costenoble, 1854);

Aus der See: Drei Erzählungen (Prague, Vienna & Leipzig: Kober & Markgraf, 1855);

Nach Amerika!: Ein Volksbuch, 3 volumes (Leipzig: Costenoble, 1855);

Californische Skizzen (Leipzig: Arnold, 1856); translated by George Cosgrave from the 1859 French translation by Gustave Revilliod as *Scenes of Life in California* (San Francisco: Howell, 1942);

Der kleine Wallfischfänger: Erzählung für die Jugend (Leipzig: Costenoble, 1856); translated anonymously as *The Little Whaler; or, The Adventures of Charles Hollberg* (London & New York: Routledge, 1857);

Aus dem Matrosenleben (Leipzig: Arnold, 1857); translated as *A Sailor's Adventures* (London: Routledge, 1859);

Das alte Haus: Erzählung (Jena: Costenoble, 1857); translated anonymously as *The Haunted House: A Tale* (London: Routledge, 1857);

Die beiden Sträflinge: Australischer Roman, 3 volumes (Leipzig: Costenoble, 1857); translated as *The Two Convicts* (London: Routledge, 1857);

Der kleine Goldgräber in Californien: Erzählung für die Jugend (Jena: Costenoble, 1857); translated anonymously as *The Young Gold-Digger; or, A Boy's Adventures in the Gold Regions* (London & New York: Routledge, Warne & Routledge, 1860);

Eine Gemsjagd in Tyrol (Leipzig: Keil, 1857);

Herrn Mahlhuber's Reiseabenteuer: Erzählung (Leipzig: Brockhaus, 1857);

Waidmanns Heil!: Ein Buch für Jäger und Jagdfreunde (Munich: Braun & Schneider, 1857);

Die Welt im Kleinen für die kleine Welt, 7 volumes (Leipzig: Schlicke, 1857–1861) — comprises volume 1, *Allgemeine Einleitung*; volume 2, *Europa*; volume 3, *Nord-Amerika*; volume 4, *Süd-Amerika*; volume 5, *Polynesien und Australien*; volume 6, *Asien*; volume 7, *Afrika*;

Blau Wasser: Skizzen aus See- und Inselleben (Leipzig: Arnold, 1858);

Der erste Christbaum: Ein Märchen (Leipzig: Costenoble, 1858);

Gold! Ein californisches Lebensbild aus dem Jahre 1849, 3 volumes (Leipzig: Costenoble, 1858); translated as *Each for Himself, or, The Two Adventurers* (London: Routledge, 1859);

Der Flatbootmann: Amerikanische Erzählung (Prague & Leipzig: Kober, 1858; New York: Steiger, 1866);

Hell und Dunkel: Gesammelte Erzählungen, 2 volumes (Leipzig: Arnold, 1859) — includes "Ein berühmter Name" and "John Wells," translated by Miller as "Fame" and "John Wells," in *In the Arkansas Backwoods: Tales and Sketches*, pp. 87–118;

Inselwelt: Gesammelte Erzählungen, 2 volumes (Leipzig: Arnold, 1860);

Der Kunstreiter: Erzählung, 3 volumes (Leipzig & Jena: Costenoble, 1861);

Unter dem Aequator: Javanisches Sittenbild, 3 volumes (Leipzig: Costenoble, 1861); translated by Edmund Routledge as *A Wife to Order* (London: Routledge, Warne & Routledge, 1860);

Die Deutschen im Ausland: Vorlesung (Rio de Janeiro: Winter, 1861);

18 Monate in Süd-Amerika und dessen deutschen Colonien, 3 volumes (Jena: Costenoble, 1862);

Heimliche und unheimliche Geschichten: Gesammelte Erzählungen, 2 volumes (Leipzig: Arnold, 1862) — includes "Germelshausen," translated anonymously as *Germelshausen* (Cambridge, Mass.: Sever, 1888); translated by C. W. Bell as *Germelshausen* (London: Harrap, 1919);

Aus meinem Tagebuch: Gesammelte Erzählungen, 2 volumes (Leipzig: Arnold, 1863) — includes "Ein

Nachmittag in Cincinnati," translated by
Ralph Walker as "A Cincinnati Afternoon,"
Early American Life, 8, no. 3 (1977): 42–45;
"Der getaufte Baptistenprediger," "Der Hei-
ratsantrag," "Der Fremde," "Das Postbureau
in Arkansas," "Die schwarze Kuh," translated
by Miller as "The Baptism of the Baptist
Preacher," "The Marriage Proposal," "The
Stranger," "A Post Office in Arkansas," "The
Black Cow," in *In the Arkansas Backwoods: Tales
and Sketches*, pp. 74–86, 119–137;

Die Colonie: Brasilianisches Lebensbild, 3 volumes
(Jena: Costenoble, 1864);

Im Busch: Australische Erzählung, 3 volumes (Jena:
Costenoble, 1864);

*Das Märchen von dem Schneider, der Bauchschmerzen
hatte, oder Woher die Schneider-Vögel kommen*
(Leipzig: Schlicke, 1864);

Der Wilderer: Drama in 5 Aufzügen (Jena: Costenoble,
1864);

*Reise des Herzogs Ernst von Sachsen-Coburg-Gotha nach
Ägypten und den Ländern der Habab, Mensa und
Bogos*, as Duke Ernst II of Saxe-Coburg-Gotha
(Leipzig: Arnold, 1864);

*"Pätz und Putz" oder die Lebensgeschichte zweier Bären:
Ein Märchen* (Leipzig: Schlicke, 1865);

Zwei Republiken, 6 volumes (Jena & Leipzig: Coste-
noble, 1865) – comprises *General Franco:
Lebensbild aus Ecuador*, 3 volumes; *Sennor
Aguila: Peruanisches Lebensbild*, 3 volumes;

Unter Palmen und Buchen: Gesammelte Erzählungen, 3
volumes (Leipzig: Arnold, 1865–1867);

Wilde Welt: Gesammelte Erzählungen, 3 volumes (Leipzig: Arnold, 1865–1867) – includes "Wolfs-
Benjamin," translated by Miller as "Wolf-Ben-
jamin," in *In the Arkansas Backwoods: Tales and
Sketches*, pp. 138–165;

Eine Mutter: Roman im Anschluß an "Die Colonie," 3
volumes (Jena: Costenoble, 1867);

Der Erbe: Roman, 3 volumes (Jena: Costenoble,
1867);

Unter den Penchuenchen: Chilenischer Roman, 3 volumes
(Jena: Costenoble, 1867); translated by Francis Jordan as *How a Bride Was Won; or, A Chase
across the Pampas* (New York: Appleton, 1869);

Hüben und Drüben: Neue gesammelte Erzählungen, 3
volumes (Leipzig: Arnold, 1868) – includes
"Martin," translated by Miller in *In the Arkansas Backwoods: Tales and Sketches*, pp. 201–225;

Die Missionäre: Roman aus der Südsee, 3 volumes
(Jena: Costenoble, 1868);

*Neue Reisen durch die Vereinigten Staaten, Mexiko, Ecua-
dor, Westindien und Venezuela*, 3 volumes (Jena:
Costenoble, 1868) – comprises volume 1,

Nord-Amerika; volume 2, *Mexiko, der Isthmus und
Westindien*; volume 3, *Venezuela*;

Das sonderbare Duell (Berlin: Goldschmidt, 1869);

Irrfahrten (Berlin: Goldschmidt, 1869);

Kreuz und Quer: Neue gesammelte Erzählungen, 3 volumes (Leipzig: Arnold, 1869);

*Ein Parcerie-Vertrag: Erzählung zur Warnung und Beleh-
rung für Auswanderer und ihre Freunde. Volksbuch*
(Leipzig: Keil, 1869);

*Die Blauen und Gelben: Venezuelanisches Charakterbild
aus der letzten Revolution von 1868*, 3 volumes
(Jena: Costenoble, 1870);

Buntes Treiben: Neue gesammelte Erzählungen, 3 volumes (Leipzig: Arnold, 1870) – includes "Eine
Pfauen- und Schweine-Jagd auf Java," "Im
alten Kloster," "Durch die Pampas," translated by Felix L. Oswald as *Adventures in the Tro-
pics* (New York: Allison, 1898); "Der junge
Lehrmeister," translated by Miller as "The
Young Schoolteacher," in *In the Arkansas Backwoods: Tales and Sketches*, pp. 166–200;

Das Wrack des Piraten (Jena: Costenoble, 1870);

Nach dem Schiffbruch (Jena: Costenoble, 1870);

In Mexico: Charakterbild aus den Jahren 1864–1867, 4
volumes (Jena: Costenoble, 1871);

Verhängnisse (Berlin: Goldschmidt, 1871);

Ein Plagiar: Mexicanische Erzählung (Berlin: Goldschmidt, 1872);

Im Eckfenster: Roman, 4 volumes (Jena: Costenoble,
1872);

*In Amerika: Amerikanisches Lebensbild aus neuer Zeit. Im
Anschluß an "Nach Amerika!,"* 3 volumes (Jena:
Costenoble, 1872);

Der Tolle (Jena: Costenoble, 1872);

Gesammelte Schriften: Volks- und Familien-Ausgabe, 43
volumes (Jena: Costenoble, 1872–1879);

Das Hintergebäude: Erzählung (Leipzig: Günther,
1873);

Kleine Erzählungen und nachgelassene Schriften, 3 volumes (Jena: Costenoble, 1879) – includes
"Unberufene Gäste" and "In den Backwoods,"
translated by Miller as "Uninvited Guests"
and "In the Backwoods," in *In the Arkansas
Backwoods: Tales and Sketches*, pp. 226–242;

Reiseromane und Schriften, 45 volumes, edited by Dietrich Theden, Carl Döring, and Max Bauer
(Berlin: Neufeld & Henius, 1903–1910);

Der Freischütz: Scene aus dem Dresdner Leben, edited by
Thomas Ostwald (Brunswick: Friedrich Ger-
stäcker-Gesellschaft, 1979);

Erzählungen für die "Fliegenden Blätter," edited by Ostwald (Brunswick: Friedrich Gerstäcker-
Gesellschaft, 1991);

Erzählungen für die "Hausblatter," edited by Ostwald (Brunswick: Friedrich Gerstäcker–Gesellschaft, 1991);

"Arbeiten für die *"Gartenlaube,"* edited by Ostwald (Brunswick: Friedrich Gerstäcker–Gesellschaft, 1991).

TRANSLATIONS: Charles Rowcroft, *Die Abenteuer eines Auswanderers: Erzählungen aus den Colonien von Van Diemansland*, 3 volumes (Leipzig: Wigand, 1845);

Anonymous [Ann Sophia Stephens], *Jonathan Slick oder Leben und Treiben der vornehmen Welt in New York*, 2 volumes (Leipzig: Wigand, 1845);

Charles Fenno Hoffman, *Wilde Scenen in Wald und Prärie mit Skizzen amerikanischen Lebens*, 2 volumes (Dresden: Arnold, 1845);

Rowcroft, *Der Buschrähndscher: Erzählungen aus den Colonien von Van Diemensland*, 3 volumes (Leipzig: Wigand, 1846);

G. Poulett Cameron, *Reiseabenteuer in Georgien, Circassien und Russland*, 2 volumes (Dresden & Leipzig: Arnold, 1846);

William Gilmore Simms, *"Wigwam und Hütte" — Erzählung aus dem Westen Amerikas* (Leipzig: Arnold, 1846);

Douglas Jerrold, *Madame Kaudel's Gardinenpredigten* (Leipzig: Wigand, 1846);

Seba Smith, *Der Indianerhäuptling und die Gefangene des Westens: Eine Erzählung aus dem letzten amerikanische Kriege*, 2 volumes (Grimma: Verlag-Comptoir, 1847);

Herman Melville, *Omoo, oder Abenteuer im Stillen Ocean mit einer Einleitung, die sich den "Marquesas-Inseln" anschließt und Toby's glückliche Fahrt enthält* (Leipzig: Mayer, 1847);

China, das Land und seine Bewohner (Leipzig: Wigand, 1848);

Edward Bulwer-Lytton, *Harold — der letzte der Sachsenkönige* (Leipzig: Weber, 1849);

J. Tyrwhitt-Brooks, *Vier Monate unter den Goldfindern in Obercalifornien* (Leipzig: Weber, 1849);

Tyrwhitt-Brooks, *Kaliforniens Gold- u. Quecksilber-District: Nach the California-Herald* (Leipzig: Jurany, 1849).

OTHER: Thomas Ostwald, ed., *Die Hazardspieler in Californien*, contributions by Gerstäcker (Brunswick: Graff, 1976).

Friedrich Gerstäcker was the major German author of fiction and reportage about America in the mid nineteenth century. One of the most adventurous and intrepid German travelers of his time, he ranged through North and South America and the South Seas from the Sandwich Islands (Hawaii) and Tahiti to Australia, Java, and Egypt, writing unremittingly. He produced not only fiction and memoirs about these experiences but also social novels set in Germany, stories of fantasy and mystery, and even drama and some verse. In the third quarter of the nineteenth century he had an international reputation; in the United States his works were widely read in both German and English. After that, he gradually declined to the status of a children's writer and otherwise came to be forgotten except in connection with so-called ethnographic literature. Attention to him has, however, been reviving.

Friedrich Wilhelm Christian Gerstäcker was born on 10 May 1816 in Hamburg, where his father, Karl Friedrich Gerstäcker, an opera singer of some prominence, was performing. His mother, Luise Friederike Gerstäcker, née Herz, was a singer and actress. For a time the family lived in Dresden, then in Kassel. After the father died in 1825 the mother settled in Leipzig in straitened circumstances, but Gerstäcker was sent to live with relatives in Brunswick. He began to train for a commercial career in Leipzig, but it did not suit him, so he was sent as an apprentice to an estate near Grimma in Saxony to learn agriculture. Thus, he had no real hometown. This lack may account for the uncommon restlessness characteristic of his whole life; when he was traveling he was subject, particularly at times of inconvenience, discomfort, or danger, to attacks of homesickness — not so much for a particular place as for Germany in general and for his family; but when he was domestically settled, he would become uneasy and begin to make arrangements for further travel.

In 1837 he went to New York, where a partner cheated him out of an investment in a tobacco shop on Broadway — an experience he always valued as an archetypal lesson in American commerce. He traveled through New York, Ontario, the upper Midwest, Illinois, Arkansas, Louisiana, and Texas. He lived off and on in Cincinnati, where he passed a schoolteacher's examination without ever practicing, worked for a chocolate maker, assisted a silversmith, constructed pillboxes for an apothecary, and sold cane that he had cut on the banks of the Mississippi for pipestems. He worked briefly as a fireman on a Mississippi riverboat and as a woodcutter in Memphis, and at the end of his stay in the United States he was manager of a hotel in Louisiana. But the largest block of time he spent as a backwoodsman in Arkansas, living primarily from hunting. Thus, in contrast to most

Gerstäcker in 1844 (daguerreotype by Carl Weniger)

other German writers about America who were observers or travelers (if they bothered to go there at all), he lived an authentic American life at several levels and was able to make a realistic assessment of the myths of the wilderness that he had absorbed from assiduous reading of the works of James Fenimore Cooper.

Gerstäcker has written that when he returned to Germany in 1843 he found to his surprise that he was a published writer: he had been sending his diary to his mother, who had had excerpts published in the journal *Rosen* (Roses). Modern scholars have not been able to verify this account, as there are no extant copies of those issues of *Rosen;* but there is no reason to doubt it, as Gerstäcker is exceptionally trustworthy. This unexpected success encouraged him to submit for publication his first

book, *Streif- und Jagdzüge durch die Vereinigten Staaten Nord-Amerikas* (Wanderings and Hunts through the United States of North America, 1844; translated as *Wild Sports in the Far West*, 1854). The book displays from the beginning his major assets as a writer: a descriptive skill and instinctive sense of narrative structure that make the reader feel almost as if he or she were experiencing the events directly, and an extraordinary memory for detail. It is evident from this work and elsewhere that the passion that drew him to America and sustained him there was hunting, at which he became highly skilled. He was particularly fond of hunting bear, since it was the most dangerous game. In his homeland he became a hunting companion of Duke Ernst IV of Saxe-Coburg-Gotha and Archduke Johann of Austria. In 1857 he produced what today would be called a coffee-table book, *Waidmanns Heil!* (Huntsman's Health!), containing hunting stories; a hunter's calendar in verse; and an illustrated alphabet of game animals, accompanied by poems, apparently intended for children.

To earn a living after his return to Germany, Gerstäcker put the English-language skills he had acquired to use by translating English and American books, including Herman Melville's *Omoo* (1847). As he translated this work, he began to wonder if he might have a talent for creative writing himself, and he was soon launched on his busy literary career. He turned out to be a natural magazine-story writer. His descriptive and mimetic skills were complemented by a fluent, undemanding style; an ability to give a story an unexpected twist that sometimes reminds one of O. Henry; and a well-developed sense of humor. He regularly collected his stories in book form, beginning with *Mississippi-Bilder* (Mississippi Images, 1847–1848; excerpts translated as *Western Lands and Western Waters,* 1864) and *Amerikanische Wald- und Strombilder* (American Forest and River Images, 1849). He also achieved early success with two wild and woolly novels of crime and adventure, *Die Regulatoren in Arkansas* (The Regulators in Arkansas, 1846; translated as *The Regulators of Arkansas,* 1857, and *Bill Johnson; or, The Outlaws of Arkansas,* 1857) and its sequel, *Die Flußpiraten des Mississippi* (1848; translated as *The Pirates of the Mississippi,* 1856). As with other of his works, abridged segments of these books appeared as dime novels in the United States, and they contributed to his reputation as a writer of children's entertainments. Gerstäcker did write books for young readers, among them *Fritz Wildau's Abenteuer zu Wasser und zu Lande* (1854; translated as *Frank Wildman's Adventures on Land and Water,* 1855), a novel that combines South Sea adventure with nautical and anthropological information. But his more significant contribution lay in another area.

Emigration from Germany to America had been gaining momentum since the 1820s; by the 1840s it had become a major social issue, and the emigration manual had become a ubiquitous publishing genre. Gerstäcker, giving as his reason that he had grown tired of answering the same questions over and over, wrote one of the best and wittiest of them: *Wie ist es denn nun eigentlich in Amerika?* (How Is It after All in America?, 1849). Here and in all his writing about and for emigrants he reiterates the same points: America is not a land of ease and plenty but is rude and dangerous, full of crooks and swindlers – not a few of them among the German-Americans themselves; dimwits, loafers, and fortune seekers are doomed; those who cannot give up European ways of doing things and learn from those with experience, who cannot change course or profession, or who cannot live without class status and the deference of inferiors will have a difficult time. He never encouraged his readers to emulate his own adventures as a frontiersman, warning emigrants that the frontier and the wilderness were full of hardship and advising them to seek cleared, settled land. His memoirs suggest that he himself was less heroic than dogged: they are full of the miseries of heat, cold, hunger, mosquitoes, swamp fevers, apparently hopeless situations, and dangers real and imagined; with wry self-irony he sometimes implies that only a moron would have gotten into such scrapes. He was anxious not to lead his readers into delusions, as he believed other writers who romanticized the wilderness or treated America as paradise regained had done. But he holds out the prospect that with a level head, hard work, and a decent amount of luck the emigrant might hope to achieve a life of modest prosperity and political freedom well beyond what was available to him in Germany.

Gerstäcker always kept a sorrowfully patriotic eye on the impoverished, oppressive, and static German social and political conditions and wrote about them in social novels such as *Pfarre und Schule* (Parsonage and School, 1849), designed to expose the deleterious effect of clerical oversight of the schools, and *Im Eckfenster* (In the Corner Window, 1872), which measures the liberated, egalitarian spirit of a nobleman returned from America against the rigidities and secret depravities of German aristocratic society. In the essay "Der Klöppeldistrikt des sächsischen Erzgebirges" (The Lacemakers' District of the Saxon Ore Mountains), published in his *Aus zwei Welttheilen* (From Two Parts of the World,

1854), he reports movingly on the abject poverty of the technologically obsolescent lace makers and proposes a government initiative to move the entire community to America. Other people in Gerstäcker's time could and did write such things; his special contribution was his writings about emigrants.

In 1845 Gerstäcker married Anna Aurora Sauer. They had three children: Alexander Georg Friedrich, born in 1847; Marie Betty Sophie, born in 1853; and Ernst Alexander Friedrich, born in 1857. After commanding a company of Leipzig sharpshooters in the revolution of 1848, Gerstäcker persuaded the short-lived postrevolutionary Frankfurt Parliament to grant him five hundred talers to report on German settlements abroad – an acquaintance said that Gerstäcker was the only German to have had any advantage from the provisional government. With an additional modest advance from the publisher Johann Georg von Cotta, he set out in 1849. He traveled to Brazil, then to Argentina, crossed the Cordilleras to Chile in winter because everyone told him it could not be done (which almost proved to be true), then sailed to San Francisco, arriving in time for the gold rush. He mined gold to scrape a little money together, then sailed to Honolulu; from there he voyaged on a whaling ship to the island of Moorea and in a fragile native vessel to Tahiti, where he was thrilled to find himself in Melville territory. He went on to Australia, where he determined to paddle the length of the Murray River in a handmade canoe because, again, everyone told him it could not be done. This time everyone was right; the canoe and most of his belongings were lost, and he continued on foot to Adelaide across seven hundred miles of hardscrabble outback through tribes of hostile aborigines. From Sydney he sailed to Java, where he was finally able to find some decent hunting, and he returned home around the tip of Africa; he had been away for three years. From his itinerary it is obvious that viewing German settlements was not the only purpose he had in mind; but he did do so, and he refers to them from time to time in one of the best travel books ever written in German, the five-volume *Reisen* (Travels, 1853–1854; translated as *Narrative of a Journey round the World*, 1853).

His concern about emigration remained constant; among his many writings on this topic three novels stand out. *Nach Amerika!* (To America!, 1855), which may be his best work of fiction, follows a large and differentiated cast of characters from their first thought of emigrating through their voyage and their various destinies throughout the

Gerstäcker at his desk in his exotically decorated study (engraving after a drawing by Herbert König, from the magazine Gartenlaube*)*

up the Nile from Cairo to Luxor and Karnak. Gerstäcker wrote a memoir of this journey, which, to his disappointment, the duke had published under his own name. In 1863 Gerstäcker married a Dutch woman, Marie Louise Fischer van Gaasbeek, whom he had met as a girl in Java. They had two daughters: Elisabeth Alexandrine Charlotte Ida, born in 1865, and Margarethe Adeline Ricarda, born in 1871.

In 1867 he set out on another journey, landing in New York thirty years after his first visit. He traveled by train to the oil fields of Pennsylvania; later he visited Cincinnati, Louisville, and Saint Louis. In Saint Louis he heard of a meeting that Gen. William Tecumseh Sherman was to hold with Indian chiefs at Council Bluffs, Iowa, and he set off via Chicago to observe it. Gerstäcker probably had more direct experience of native Americans than any other German writer of his time; he sympathized with their plight but thought it inevitable, and his portrayal of them, especially those who had fallen victim to civilization, was more realistic than ennobling. After the conference he returned to Arkansas, finding it much changed. He then traveled by steamboat to New Orleans and sailed to Vera Cruz, where he commenced a leisurely journey through Mexico and present-day Panama, Ecuador, and Venezuela, returning home via Trinidad. This journey generated another of his elaborate travel memoirs, *Neue Reisen durch die Vereinigten Staaten, Mexiko, Ecuador, Westindien und Venezuela* (New Travels through the United States, Mexico, Ecuador, the West Indies, and Venezuela, 1868), and several works of fiction and nonfiction about Central and South America. In 1868 Gerstäcker brought controversy on himself with a new novel of the South Seas, *Die Missionäre* (The Missionaries). Gerstäcker held highly liberal and, as he thought, "natural" religious views and was hostile to what he regarded as irrational or fanatical religious expression. Like many German observers he was scornful of popular religion in America, and he satirized Baptists, Methodists, and Mormons; every American clergyman in his fiction is either a knave or a lunatic. He regarded missionary activity in the South Seas as bringing repression and denominational strife into the lives of the natives and accused it of existing primarily for the benefit of the missionaries themselves. He had been saying such things for many years, but this time a representative of the missionary movement, Gustav Jahn, struck back in a pamphlet – practically the only unpleasant reaction from the public in his entire career and one that he could afford to ignore.

United States. In *Gold!* (1858; translated as *Each for Himself*, 1859), as elsewhere, he tried to explain to a potentially crazed public that there really was gold in California, that with extreme hard work and much luck one might find enough to meet one's expenses while doing so, and that any excess would be skimmed off by gamblers and gouging merchants. *In Amerika* (1872) picks up the characters of *Nach Amerika!* and continues their stories.

The novel *Die Colonie* (The Colony, 1864), dealing with immigrant conditions in the Brazilian south, and the story *Ein Parcerie-Vertrag* (A Parceria Contract, 1869), warning against indentured servitude in conditions approaching slavery on plantations in northern Brazil, were the consequence of a year-and-a-half journey to South America, primarily Peru and Ecuador, beginning in 1860. On his return he found that his wife had died. Partly as a distraction from his sorrow, in 1862 he accompanied the duke of Saxe-Coburg-Gotha to Africa, traveling

One oddity of that career is that Gerstäcker, who was the epitome of the rationalistic, commonsensical realist, liked to write stories of the supernatural, sometimes in a humorous vein. In 1862 two volumes of them were published as *Heimliche und unheimliche Geschichten* (Secret and Eerie Stories); one of the stories in the collection, "Germelshausen" (translated, 1888), about a village that appears for one day every hundred years, served as a textbook for generations of American and English schoolchildren learning German and is reputed to have been the inspiration for the musical *Brigadoon* (1947). Another story of the supernatural, *Das alte Haus* (The Old House, 1857; translated as *The Haunted House*, 1857), is one of Gerstäcker's most intriguingly constructed novels, largely because the mystery remains partly unresolved.

By the time of the Franco-Prussian War in 1870–1871 Gerstäcker was one of the most beloved and admired German writers, and this high repute gained him easy access as a war correspondent to the royal and noble commanders at the siege of Paris. He took the Prussian line on the conflict, portraying France as an unprovoked aggressor that had received its just deserts and exulting at the unification of the German nation. The lifelong, patriotic democrat who dreamed that the liberty enjoyed by Americans might one day be available to his people did not live to see these dreams unfulfilled by the new Reich, for he died of a stroke on 31 May 1872 in Brunswick, where he had moved in 1869. At his death he was in the midst of plans for a journey to the Far East.

Gerstäcker has occupied an insecure place on the periphery of literary history. At times he has been counted among the German anti-American writers, but his acerbic critical perspective in no way diminishes the affection and respect he felt for the United States and its liberties; he once remarked that only in America could Germans become truly themselves, with a sense of self-worth and equality unfettered by oppression and stagnation. The very range of his adventurous life has so far foiled attempts at a full-scale biography. What has been untangled of his exceptionally confusing bibliography has been the achievement of devoted amateurs; not all of his periodical contributions have been identified, and his reception history in translation, mostly in pirated editions or dime-novel adaptations, has not been exhaustively researched. Sometimes he has been of more interest to historians than to literary scholars, especially in Arkansas; it was a historian, Clarence Evans, who instigated a posthumous grant of honorary citizenship of the state of Arkan-

sas to Gerstäcker in 1957. But, among literary historians, as a writer about America he has fallen into a crack between the ideologue Charles Sealsfield and the fantasist Karl May. Intermittently he has been of interest to those studying literary reflections of Australia; otherwise, his writings about the South Seas, like those about Latin America, have been largely neglected, as has his role early in his career as a mediator of American literature to the German public. Thus, there are many opportunities for learning more about this remarkable life that combined adventure with prolific writing.

Letters:

Friedrich Gerstäckers Briefe an Hermann Costenoble, edited by William H. McClain and Liselotte E. Kurth-Voigt (Frankfurt am Main: Buchhändler-Vereinigung, 1974);

Mein lieber Herzensfreund!: Briefe an seinen Freund Adolph Hermann Schultz 1835–1854. Briefe I, edited by Thomas Ostwald (Brunswick: Friedrich Gerstäcker–Gesellschaft, 1982);

Mein guter Herr von Cotta: Friedrich Gerstäckers Briefwechsel mit dem Stuttgarter Cotta Verlag — eine Briefedition. Briefe II, edited by Karl Jürgen Roth (Brunswick: Friedrich Gerstäcker–Gesellschaft, 1992).

Bibliographies:

Gerstäcker-Verzeichnis: Erstausgaben, Gesammelte Werke und Sekundärliteratur mit Nachweis im Stadtarchiv und in der Stadtbibliothek Braunschweig, edited by Manfred R. W. Garzmann, Thomas Ostwald, and Wolf-Dieter Schuegraf (Brunswick: Stadtarchiv und Städtische Bibliotheken, 1986);

James William Miller, "Bibliography," in Gerstäcker's *In the Arkansas Backwoods: Tales and Sketches*, edited and translated by Miller (Columbia & London: University of Missouri Press, 1991), pp. 243–253.

Biography:

Thomas Ostwald and Armin Stöckhert, *Friedrich Gerstäcker: Leben und Werk*, second edition (Brunswick: Graff, 1977).

References:

Evan Burr Bukey, "Friedrich Gerstaecker and Arkansas," *Arkansas Historical Quarterly*, 31 (Spring 1972): 3–14;

Alan Corkhill, " 'At Home in Foreign Climes': Friedrich Gerstäcker's Australian Writings," in his *Antipodean Encounters: Australia and the German Literary Imagination 1754–1918* (Bern, Frankfurt am Main, New York & Paris: Peter Lang, 1990), pp. 73–102;

Corkhill, " 'Das unbekannte Südland' – Australien im deutschen Überseeroman des 19. Jahrhunderts," *Exotische Welt in populären Lektüren*, edited by Anselm Maler (Tübingen: Niemeyer, 1990), pp. 35–48;

Karl W. Doerry, "Three Versions of America: Sealsfield, Gerstäcker, and May," *Yearbook of German-American Studies*, 16 (1981): 39–49;

Manfred Durzak, "Nach Amerika. Gerstäckers Widerlegung der Lenau-Legende," in *Amerika in der deutschen Literatur: Neue Welt – Nordamerika – USA*, edited by Sigrid Bauschinger and others (Stuttgart: Reclam, 1975), pp. 135–153;

Harald Eggebrecht, *Sinnlichkeit und Abenteuer: Die Entstehung des Abenteuerromans im 19. Jahrhundert* (Berlin & Marburg: Guttandin & Hoppe, 1985), pp. 91–124;

Clarence Evans, "Friedrich Gerstäcker, Social Chronicler of the Arkansas Frontier," *Arkansas Historical Quarterly*, 6 (Winter 1947): 440–449;

Evans, "Gerstaecker and the Konwells of White River Valley," *Arkansas Historical Quarterly*, 10 (Spring 1951): 1–36;

Werner Paul Friederich, *Australia in Western Imaginative Prose Writings 1600–1900: An Anthology and a History of Literature* (Chapel Hill: University of North Carolina Press, 1967), pp. 143–171;

Erwin G. Gudde, "Friedrich Gerstaecker: World Traveller and Author, 1816–1872," *Journal of the West*, 7 (July 1968): 345–350;

Erich Hofacker, "Über die Entstehung von Gerstäckers 'Germelshausen,' " *Germanic Review*, 3 (January 1928): 23–33;

Amanda Hume, "F. W. C. Gerstäcker: An Overlooked Informant on Language in Mid-19th Century Australia," *AUMLA: Journal of the Australasian Universities Language and Literature Association*, 66 (November 1986): 272–285;

Gustav Jahn, *Gerstäcker und die Mission: Ein Gespräch über den Roman aus der Südsee "Die Missionäre" von Fr. Gerstäcker, allen Freunden der Wahrheit mitgetheilt* (Halle: Mühlmann, 1869);

Sonja Karsen, "Friedrich Gerstäcker in South America," *Modern Language Studies*, 5 (Fall 1975): 55–62;

Alfred Kolb, "Friedrich Gerstäcker and the American Dream," *Modern Language Studies*, 5 (Spring 1975): 103–108;

Kolb, "Friedrich Gerstäcker and the American Frontier," Ph.D. dissertation, Syracuse University, 1966;

John T. Krumpelmann, "Gerstaecker's 'Germelshausen' and Lerner's 'Brigadoon,' " *Monatshefte*, 40 (1948): 396–400;

Hartmut Kugler, "Rohe Wilde: Zur literarischen Topik des Barbarenbildes in Gerstäckers Roman 'Unter den Pehuenchen,' " in *Exotische Welt in populären Lektüren*, pp. 146–163;

Bjarne Emil Landa, "The American Scene in Friedrich Gerstäcker's Works of Fiction," Ph.D. dissertation, University of Minnesota, 1952;

Anselm Maler, "Deutsche Südseebilder: Von der arkadischen Vision zum ethnographischen Realismus," in *Galerie der Welt: Ethnographisches Erzählen im 19. Jahrhundert*, edited by Maler and Sabine Schott (Stuttgart: Belser, 1988), pp. 83–96;

Maler, *Der exotische Roman: Bürgerliche Gesellschaftsflucht und Gesellschaftskritik zwischen Romantik und Realismus* (Stuttgart: Klett, 1975), pp. 33–43;

William H. McClain, "Die Gerstäcker-Briefe in der Kurrelmeyer-Sammlung," *Modern Language Notes*, 82 (October 1967): 428–434;

Juliane Mikoletzky, *Die deutsche Amerika-Auswanderung des 19. Jahrhunderts in der zeitgenössischen fiktionalen Literatur* (Tübingen: Niemeyer, 1988);

Günter Moltmann, "Überseeische Siedlungen und weltpolitische Spekulationen: Friedrich Gerstäcker und die Frankfurter Zentralgewalt 1849," in *Russland – Deutschland – Amerika. Russia – Germany – America. Festschrift für Fritz T. Epstein zum 80. Geburtstag*, edited by Alexander Fischer, Moltmann, and Klaus Schwabe (Wiesbaden: Steiner, 1978), pp. 56–72;

Jürgen Ockel, *Nach Amerika! Die Schilderung der Auswanderer-Problematik in den Werken Friedrich Gerstäckers*, Beiträge zur Friedrich Gerstäcker-Forschung, no. 3 (Brunswick: Friedrich Gerstäcker–Gesellschaft, 1983);

George H. R. O'Donnell, "Gerstäcker in America, 1837–1843," *Publications of the Modern Language Association of America*, 42 (December 1927): 1036–1043;

Thomas Ostwald, "Friedrich Gerstäckers ethnographische Realien," in *Galerie der Welt: Ethnographisches Erzählen im 19. Jahrhundert*, pp. 12–23;

Andrea Pagni, "Friedrich Gerstäckers 'Reisen' zwischen Ferne und Heimat: Überlegungen zum Reisebericht im literarischen Feld Deutschlands um 1850," in *Studien zur Literatur des Frührealismus*, edited by Günter Blumberger, Manfred Engel, and Monika Ritzer (Frankfurt am Main, Bern, New York & Paris: Lang, 1991), pp. 276–288;

Augustus J. Prahl, "America in the Works of Gerstäcker," *Modern Language Quarterly*, 4 (June 1943): 213–224;

Prahl, "Gerstäcker über zeitgenössische Schriftsteller," *Modern Language Notes*, 49 (May 1934): 302–309;

Karl Jürgen Roth, *Die Darstellung der deutschen Auswanderung in den Schriften Friedrich Gerstäckers* (Brunswick: Friedrich Gerstäcker–Gesellschaft, 1989);

Roth, "Gerstäckers 'Jugend- und Volksschriften' in einer Kritik des 19. Jahrhunderts," *Mitteilungen der Friedrich-Gerstäcker-Gesellschaft*, 16 (1985): 7–18;

Roth, "Herr v. Sechingen auf Gerstäckers Spuren in Arkansas: Eine Erzählung und ihre Hintergründe," *Mitteilungen der Friedrich-Gerstäcker-Gesellschaft*, 14 (1984): 7–20;

Jeffrey L. Sammons, "Friedrich Gerstäcker: American Realities Through German Eyes," in *Germans in America: Aspects of German-American Relations in the Nineteenth Century*, edited by E. Allen McCormick (New York: Brooklyn College Press, 1983), pp. 79–90; reprinted in his *Imagination and History: Selected Papers on Nineteenth-Century German Literature* (New York: Lang, 1988), pp. 249–263;

H. Schutz, "Friedrich Gerstäcker's Image of the German Immigrant in America," in *Deutschlands literarisches Amerikabild: Neue Forschungen zur Amerikarezeption der deutschen Literatur*, edited by Alexander Ritter (Hildesheim & New York: Olms, 1977), pp. 319–337;

Erich Seyfarth, *Friedrich Gerstäcker: Ein Beitrag zur Geschichte des exotischen Romans in Deutschland* (Freiburg: Waibel, 1930);

Bernd Steinbrink, *Abenteuerliteratur des 19. Jahrhunderts in Deutschland: Studien zu einer vernachlässigten Gattung* (Tübingen: Niemeyer, 1983), pp. 131–145.

Papers:

Manuscripts and relics of Friedrich Gerstäcker are in the museum of the Friedrich-Gerstäcker-Gesellschaft (Friedrich Gerstäcker Society) in Brunswick; biographical and reception materials are at the Stadtarchiv und städtische Bibliothek (Municipal Archive and Library), Brunswick, and in the Archives of the University of Arkansas at Little Rock. Letters are in the Literaturarchiv of the Staats- und Universitätsbibliothek (State and University Library), Hamburg.

Klaus Groth

(24 April 1819 – 1 June 1899)

Reinhard K. Zachau
University of the South

BOOKS: *Quickborn: Volksleben in plattdeutschen Gedichten dithmarscher Mundart nebst Glossar* (Hamburg: Perthes, Besser & Mauke, 1853; enlarged, 1853; enlarged again, 1854; enlarged again, 1856; enlarged again, 1856);

Hundert Blätter: Paralipomena zum Quickborn (Hamburg: Perthes, Besser & Mauke, 1854);

Vertelln: Plattdeutsche Erzählungen, 2 volumes (Kiel: Schwers, 1855–1859);

Briefe über Hochdeutsch und Plattdeutsch (Kiel: Schwers, 1858);

Voer de Goern: Kinderreime alt und neu (Leipzig: Wigand, 1858);

Vertelln II: Trina (Kiel: Homann, 1859);

Festgedichte zum Kranzbinden für Adolph Koop und Charlotte Finke am 2. März 1860 (Bremen: Schünemann, 1860);

Zum Kranzbinden für Johanna Finke und Jennings Blow am 29. April 1861 (Bremen: Schünemann, 1861);

Festspiel zum letzten April 1861 (Bremen: Schünemann, 1861);

Rothgeter Meister Lamp un sin Dochder: Plattdeutsches Gedicht (Hamburg: Perthes, Besser & Mauke, 1862);

En Geschichte vun min Vetter voer min Herzog to sin Geburtsdag den Juli 1864 (Kiel: Schwers, 1864);

Fiv nie Leder ton Singn un Beden voer Schleswig-Holsteen (Hamburg: Perthes, Besser & Mauke, 1864);

Zur silbernen Hochzeit von Onkel Heinrich und Tante Emilie, den 16. Mai 1868 (Kiel: Jensen, 1868);

Quickborn: Zweiter Teil. Volksleben in plattdeutschen Dichtungen dithmarscher Mundart (Leipzig: Engelmann, 1871);

Über Mundarten und mundartige Dichtung (Berlin: Stilke, 1873);

Ut min Jungsparadies: Dree Vertelln (Berlin: Stilke, 1876);

Zur Hochzeits-Feier des Herrn Carl Finke mit Fräulein Henny Geyer am 14. November 1877 (Bremen: Hunckel, 1877);

Klaus Groth, circa 1865

Dietsche Beweging: Eene keerzijde omgekeerd (Antwerp: Dela Montagne, 1882);

Emanuel Geibel: Ein Gedenkbuch, by Groth and Arno Holz (Berlin & Leipzig, 1884);

Lebenserinnerungen, edited by Eugen Wolff (Kiel: Lipsius & Tischer, 1891);

Gesammelte Werke, 4 volumes (Kiel & Leipzig: Lipsius & Tischer, 1893);

Die patriotische Wirksamkeit eines schleswig-holsteinischen Privatmannes (Neumünster: Wachholtz, 1930);

Eine Lebensskizze von ihm selbst, edited by the Dithmarsche Landesschule in Lunden (Heide: Westholsteinische Verlags-Druckerei, 1932);

Sämtliche Werke, 8 volumes, edited by Friedrich Pauly, Ivo Braak, and Richard Mehlem (Flensburg: Wolff, 1952–1965);

Mien Jungsparadies, edited by Magdalena Weihmann (Heide: Boyens, 1977);

Sämtliche Werke, 6 volumes, edited by Braak and Mehlem (Heide: Boyens, 1981).

OTHER: Karl Tannen, ed., *Reineke Voss: Plattdeutsch nach der Lübecker Ausgabe von 1498,* foreword by Groth (Bremen: Strack, 1861);

Ferdinand Weber, *Plattdeutsche Gedichte,* edited by Groth (Kiel: Homann, 1861);

Lieder aus und für Schleswig-Holstein, edited by Groth (Hamburg: Perthes, Besser & Mauke, 1864);

J. Dorr, *De lostgen Wiewer von Windsor en't Plattdietsche äwersett,* foreword by Groth (Liegnitz, 1877);

Emanuel Geibel: Ein Gedenkbuch, edited by Groth and Arno Holz (Berlin & Leipzig: Parrisius, 1884).

SELECTED PERIODICAL PUBLICATION – UNCOLLECTED: "Um de Heid," *Westermanns Illustrierte deutsche Monatshefte,* 18 (1870): 523–569.

Klaus Groth was highly acclaimed during his lifetime as a re-creator of a Low German literary language that had been virtually extinct since the late Middle Ages. A late Romantic, he showed his fellow Schleswig-Holsteiners their cultural identity, eventually strengthening their resistance against the Danish occupation. Groth later shifted his allegiance to Otto von Bismarck's vision of a unified Germany.

Klaus Johann Groth was born on 24 April 1819 in Heide, the capital of the Schleswig-Holstein province of Dithmarschen, to Hartwig Groth and Anna Christina Groth, née Lindemann. His father owned a windmill, a carpentry shop, a small farm, and a grain store. Groth's industrious father was the model for the steadfast Dithmarschen citizen portrayed in his poems. Groth's brother, Johannes,

Title page for Groth's first collection of Low German poems

was born on 22 December 1822. Groth's grandfather instilled in him an appreciation of his native region by reciting local poetry and folklore.

In 1825 Groth attended Mrs. Meinung's elementary school in Heide, moving on to a private middle school for boys of the upper class. Groth's father, a proud member of Heide's petty bourgeoisie, did not want his family to move too far away from their roots; thus, Groth was not allowed to attend the school's last grade, where he would have learned foreign languages – a limitation he came to regret. When Groth was sixteen his father got him a position as scribe to the parish administrator in Heide. During his work there, Groth continued his reading and his self-education.

In 1838 Groth enrolled in the teacher's seminary in Tondern, North Schleswig. He graduated in 1841 second in his class and in April 1842 became a teacher at the public girls' school in his hometown of Heide. He also got involved in community politics, became a leader in a singing club, participated in a volunteer fire company, and joined an agricultural society. In 1847 he requested a two-year leave to study under the great Germanist Jacob Grimm at Berlin University.

In 1845 Groth had fallen in love with Mathilde Ottens, one of Heide's most beautiful girls, and he wrote his first poems about her. As a member of Heide's ruling class, however, Mathilde had to marry her cousin. It was at this time that Groth first understood the consequences of insurmountable class barriers, and the unhappy love affair sent him into a deep depression. He was unable to pursue his studies at the university.

At this low point a friend from the seminary, Leonhard Selle, invited Groth to spend some time with him in Landkirchen on the island of Fehmarn, where Selle was the church organist. Groth was in such poor health that he had to interrupt his trip to Landkirchen and rest in Preetz for several weeks. The intended short visit with Selle developed into a six-year stay, from June 1847 until April 1853, that comprised Groth's most productive years as a poet.

He became interested in English Romantic literature, especially the work of Sir Walter Scott, Lord Byron, and Robert Burns. In translating Burns's poem "Tam o'Shanter" into Low German as "Hans Schander" in July 1849 Groth began to find his own poetic language, even creating his own spelling based on Dutch. His first collection of poems in Low German, *Quickborn* (Fountain of Youth, 1853), was highly praised by Johann Wolfgang von Goethe's assistant Johann Peter Eckermann, the historian Theodor Mommsen, and the scientist Alexander von Humboldt; compared to Johann Peter Hebel's Swabian dialect poetry; and described as one of the most important books of German literature. The Kiel professor of Low German language and literature, Karl Müllenhoff, regarded *Quickborn* as true folk literature that closed the gap between the educated and the common people. The poems in *Quickborn* present a nostalgic view of home, family, and early love in re-creating Groth's childhood. The poem "Min Jehann" (My John), modeled after an American folk song, is a good example of the sentimental and nostalgic feelings Groth's poetry tries to evoke: "Ik wull, we weern noch kleen, Jehann, / Do weer de Welt so grot! / Weest noch, wa still dat weer, Jehann . . . / Dar röhr keen Blatt an Bom. / So is dat nu ni mehr Jehann, / As höchstens noch in Drom. . . . / Doch allens, wat ick finn, Jehann, / Dat is – ik sta un ween" (I wish we were still small, John, / The world was then so big! / Do you remember how quiet everything was, John. . . . / Not a leaf moved on the tree. / It is

no longer that way, John, / Only in our dreams. . . . / But all I still find, John, / Is – I stand and cry). Other poems in the work include "Dat Gewitter" (The Thunderstorm), "Unruh Hans, der letzte Zigeunerkönig" (Restless John, the Last Gypsy King), "Peter Plumm," and "Rumpelkamer" (Attic Room).

Soon after the publication of *Quickborn,* Groth was invited by Müllenhoff to be a guest at the Schleswig-Holstein University in Kiel. In June 1854 Groth and Müllenhoff brought out an enlarged edition of *Quickborn* with a glossary. Among the twenty-seven new poems in this edition was the popular "Matten Has" (Matten the Rabbit): "Lütt Matten de Has; / De mak sik en Spaß, / He weer bi't studeern, / Dat Danzen to lehrn" (Little Matten the Rabbit / Was Having Fun; / He was studying / To learn to dance). Groth composed the poem in his garden while watching a friend come up from the street to visit him. Groth knew he had to finish the poem before his friend saw him; otherwise, the inspiration would be lost. Thus, "Matten Has" was written down in a couple of minutes, as were most of Groth's poems. In 1854 Groth's collection of High German poems, *Hundert Blätter* (One Hundred Pages), was published. The following year brought the publication of his first collection of Low German stories, *Vertelln* (To Tell). In the best known of these stories, "Detelf," the hero is a blend of a school friend of Groth's and Groth's favorite brother, Johann, who died from wounds received in the 1848–1849 campaign to free Schleswig-Holstein from Danish rule. Groth does not show Danish soldiers as monsters but as victims of the war like the Schleswig-Holstein soldiers. The popularity of the story was due to the tender love story of Detelf and Anna.

In April 1855 Groth left Kiel in a nervous fever similar to the condition that had sent him to Fehmarn in 1847; he went to his uncle's house in Hamburg. As had been the case eight years earlier, the cause of Groth's breakdown was a love affair. Theone Henningsen had inspired Groth to write twenty sonnets; but her parents had opposed her relationship with Groth, and she had gotten engaged to a reputable Kiel citizen. Groth returned to Kiel in June. In 1855 he received a travel stipend from the Danish king, with which he traveled to Hamburg, Hannover, Bad Pyrmont, and Bonn. Groth's main interest in Bonn was to learn from such German liberals as the critic Karl Simrock; the educator Friedrich L. Jahn; the classical linguist and archaeologist Gottlieb Welcker; the scientist Hermann von Helmholtz; the historian Friedrich C.

Dahlmann; and the law professor Eduard Böcking, with whom he traveled to Switzerland in September 1855. Groth soon came to realize that a unified Germany would not be built by intellectuals but by businessmen. His time in Bonn laid the foundation for Groth's shift to Bismarck's idea of achieving German unification through capitalism.

On 2 February 1856 Groth was given an honorary doctorate by the Friedrich Wilhelm University in Bonn. That year the sixth edition of *Quickborn* was printed; it contained Groth's translation of the poems into High German in an attempt to suppress the illegal translations that were appearing everywhere. In September 1856 Groth went to Eisenach, Weimar, Dresden, and Leipzig; in Leipzig he met the writer Gustav Freytag and the painter Adolf Hölterhoff. In July 1857 he moved back to Kiel.

A second volume of *Vertelln* (1859) comprised the long story "Trina." Once again Groth wrote a popular love story about life in a small Dithmarschen village. By this time Groth had become an established authority on Schleswig-Holstein and Low German literature. He was visited in Kiel by a continuous succession of admirers, among them the painter Ludwig Richter and the writer Berthold Auerbach. Groth's poems were translated in Holland and Denmark; in the United States, North German immigrants founded cultural societies to support Groth's poetry. According to Groth's biographer Heinrich Siercks, Groth was the most popular German in the United States in the nineteenth century after Bismarck. But when Groth wanted to take over Müllenhoff's vacated position as professor of modern philology at Kiel in 1859, Müllenhoff opposed his application. Even though Groth traveled to Copenhagen to apply directly to the king, he was denied the position. Groth saw himself as a self-made man of letters who was ridiculed by members of the upper classes. His sensitivity in this matter resulted in occasional outbursts of anger.

On 24 August 1859 Groth married Doris Finke, the daughter of a wealthy Bremen merchant, and in this way finally became a member of the upper middle class. The Groths had four sons: Detmar, Albert, Carl, and August. In the summer and fall of 1863 the family took an extended trip to England, where the Groths had distant relatives; they returned to England in 1872–1873. In 1863 Groth got directly involved in the political arena by speaking out for the claim of Friedrich, Duke of Augustenburg, to Schleswig-Holstein. After the Danes were defeated by Prussia and Austria in 1864, Schleswig was occupied by Prussia and Holstein by

Groth with his wife, Doris Finke Groth, and one of their four sons, circa 1861 (photograph by J. E. Feilner, Bremen)

Austria. In 1866 Groth was finally appointed professor at Kiel by the Austrian governor; this was a new position, however, not the one Müllenhoff had held. Müllenhoff and other pro-Schleswig-Holsteiners criticized Groth for his ties with the Danish and Austrian crowns. After Austria was defeated by Prussia in 1866 and Schleswig-Holstein was annexed as a Prussian province, Groth shifted his allegiance to Prussia and supported the Prussian drive for German unification. Two of Groth's sons predeceased him – Detmar died in 1866; August, who became an engineer, died in 1889 of appendicitis – and Groth's wife died in Kiel on 19 January 1878. When Groth died on 1 June 1899, he was celebrated as North Germany's most important dialect poet.

Groth's poetry is based on his deeply felt resentment of the Danish occupation of Schleswig-Holstein. Against the young Germans' claim that a common High German language was needed as a vehicle for political unification, Groth showed that a love of local language could strengthen cultural identity. Such a love is epitomized in his poem "Min Modersprak, wat klingst du schön!" (My mother tongue, how pretty you are!).

Letters:

Klaus Groth: Briefe an seine Braut Doris Finke, edited by Hermann Krumm (Brunswick: Westermann, 1910);

Klaus Groth: Briefe, edited by Walther Schröder (Heide: Boyens, 1931);

Klaus Groths Briefe an Joachim Mähl, edited by Werner Eberhardt (Kiel: Wissenschaftliche Gesellschaft für Literatur und Theater, 1936);

Um den Quickborn: Briefwechsel zwischen Klaus Groth und Karl Müllenhoff, edited by Volquart Pauls (Hamburg: Wachholtz, 1938);

Briefe der Freundschaft: Johannes Brahms – Klaus Groth, edited by Pauls (Heide: Boyens, 1956);

Klaus Groth und Johannes Kneppelhout: Ein Briefwechsel 1868–1883 (nebst dazu gehörigen Dokumenten), edited by U. Henry Gerlach (Stuttgart: Heinz, 1986).

Bibliographies:

Joachim Hartig, Ulf Bichsel, and Willy Sanders, *Die Klaus-Groth-Arbeitsstelle: Planung, Projekte, Arbeitsbericht 1978/79,* 2 volumes (Kiel: Klaus-Groth-Forschungsstelle in der Niederdeutschen Abteilung des Germanistischen Seminars an der Christian-Albrechts-Universität Kiel, 1979–1982);

Rudolf Cauer, *Verzeichnis der Bibliotheksbestände im Klaus-Groth-Museum zu Heide,* 2 volumes (Heide: Klaus-Groth-Gesellschaft, 1987–1988).

Biographies:

Heinrich Siercks, *Klaus Groth: Sein Leben und seine Werke. Ein deutsches Volksbuch* (Kiel & Leipzig: Lipsius & Tischer, 1899);

Timm Kröger, *Klaus Groth* (Berlin & Leipzig: Schuster & Loeffler, 1905);

Gottfried Seelig, *Klaus Groth: Sein Leben und Werden* (Hamburg: Alster, 1924);

Friedrich Pauly, *Klaus Groth: Bedeutung und Persönlichkeit* (Rendsburg: Möller, 1949);

Ivo Braak and Richard Mehlem, *Klaus Groth: Sein Leben in Bild und Wort* (Flensburg: Wolff, 1965);

Joachim Hartig, ed., *Das Leben Klaus Groths, von ihm selbst erzählt* (Heide: Boyens, 1979).

References:

Kurt Batt, "Untersuchungen zur Auseinandersetzung zwischen Klaus Groth und Fritz Reuter," Ph.D. dissertation, University of Leipzig, 1958;

Rudolf Bülck, "Die literarische Tätigkeit Klaus Groths während des Jahres 1864," *Jahrbuch des Vereins für niederdeutsche Sprachforschung,* 69/70 (1947): 83–89;

Doris Groth, *Wohin das Herz uns treibt: Die Tagebücher der Doris Groth geb. Finke,* edited by Elvira and Joachim Hartig (Boyens: Heide, 1985);

Hildegard Binder Johnson, "The Claus Groth Guild of Davenport, Iowa," *American German Review,* 11 (December 1944): 26–29;

Peter Jørgensen, *Die dithmarsische Mundart von Klaus Groths "Quickborn"* (Hamburg: Buske, 1981);

Frithjof Löding, *Theodor Storm und Klaus Groth in ihrem Verhältnis zur Schleswig-Holstein Frage: Dichtung während einer politischen Krise* (Neumünster: Wachholtz, 1985);

Volquart Pauls, *Klaus Groth und Emil Kuhs Hebbel-Biographie* (Heide: Boyens, 1934);

Friedrich Pauly, *Die geschichtlichen und geistigen Grundlagen des "Quickborn": Jahresgabe der Klaus-Groth-Gesellschaft* (Heide: Boyens, 1955);

Jochen Schütt, "Robert Burns' 'Tam O'Shanter' – Klaus Groths 'Hans Schander' – Ein Vergleich," in *Festschrift für Gerhard Cordes zum 65. Geburtstag,* edited by Friedrich Debus and Joachim Hartig (Neumünster: Wachholtz, 1973), pp. 186–200;

Gerhard Seehase, "Verskundliche Studien zur niederdeutschen Lyrik Klaus Groths," Ph.D. dissertation, University of Hamburg, 1959.

Papers:

Most of Klaus Groth's papers are at the Schleswig-Holsteinische Landesbibliothek (Provincial Library) in Kiel and at the Niederdeutsche Abteilung (Low German Division) of the Germanistisches Seminar at the Christian-Albrechts-Universität Kiel. Some letters and an extensive Klaus Groth library are at the Klaus Groth Museum in Heide.

Rudolf Haym
(5 October 1821 – 27 August 1901)

Kurt R. Jankowsky
Georgetown University

BOOKS: *Gesenius: Eine Erinnerung für seine Freunde*
(Berlin: Gaertner, 1842);
*De rerum divinarum apud Aeschylum conditione: Particula
1* (Berlin: Amelang, 1843);
*Lessing, Bernardin de Saint-Pierre und ein Dritter: Eine
Trilogie von Bekenntnissen. Zur Verständigung in
dem religiösen Streite der Gegenwart* (Berlin: Ame-
lang, 1846);
*Die Autorität, welche fällt und die, welche bleibt: Ein
populär-philosophischer Aufsatz* (Halle: Heyne-
mann, 1846);
*Selbstgespräche: Ein Versuch des philosophischen
Bewußtseins sich mit den populären Bewegungen der
Gegenwart zu vermitteln* (Berlin: Amelang,
1846);
*Feuerbach und die Philosophie: Ein Beitrag zur Kritik Bei-
der* (Halle: Heynemann, 1847);
Die Krisis unserer religiösen Bewegung (Halle: Heyne-
mann, 1847);
*Die deutsche Nationalversammlung bis zu den Septembere-
reignissen: Ein Bericht aus der Partei des rechten
Centrums* (Frankfurt am Main: Jügel, 1848);
*Die deutsche Nationalversammlung von den Septemberereig-
nissen bis zur Kaiserwahl: Ein weiterer Parteibericht*
(Berlin: Amelang, 1849);
*Die deutsche Nationalversammlung von der Kaiserwahl bis
zu ihrem Untergange: Ein Schlußbericht* (Berlin:
Amelang, 1850);
De pulchri atque artis notione: Particula 1 (Halle:
Gebauer, 1850);
Wilhelm von Humboldt: Lebensbild und Charakteristik
(Berlin: Gaertner, 1856);
*Hegel und seine Zeit: Vorlesungen über Entstehung und
Entwickelung, Wesen und Werth der Hegel'schen
Philosophie* (Berlin: Gaertner, 1857); enlarged
edition, edited by Hans Rosenberg (Leipzig:
Heims, 1927);
Arthur Schopenhauer (Berlin: Reimer, 1864);
*Die romantische Schule: Ein Beitrag zur Geschichte des
deutschen Geistes* (Berlin: Gaertner, 1870);
Die Hartmann'sche Philosophie des Unbewußten (Berlin:
Reimer, 1873);

Rudolf Haym

Wiedergefundene Blätter zu Herders Schriften (Leipzig,
1873);
Herder, nach seinem Leben und seinen Werken dargestellt,
2 volumes (Berlin: Gaertner, 1877–1885) —
comprises in volume 1, "Herder in Preußen,"
"Herder in Riga," "Reiseleben," "Das Bücke-
burger Exil"; in volume 2, "Die ersten sieben
Weimarer Jahre," "Herder auf dem Höhe-
punkt seines Wirkens," "Nach der italienischen Reise";
Das Leben Max Dunckers, erzählt (Berlin: Gaertner,
1891);

Rede bei der Gedächtnissfeier des Fürsten Bismarck in der Aula der Königlichen Vereinigten Friedrichs-Universität Halle-Wittenberg am 2. November 1898 (Halle: Gebauer-Schwetschke, 1898);

Aus meinem Leben: Erinnerungen. Aus dem Nachlaß herausgegeben (Berlin: Gaertner, 1902);

Gesammelte Aufsätze, edited by Wilhelm Schrader (Berlin: Weidmann, 1903);

Zur deutschen Philosophie und Literatur, edited by Ernst Howald (Zurich & Stuttgart: Artemis, 1963).

OTHER: *Reden und Redner des ersten Vereinigten Preussischen Landtags,* edited by Haym (Berlin: Duncker & Humblot, 1847);

Preussische Jahrbücher, 14 volumes, edited by Haym (Berlin: Reimer, 1858-1864);

Briefe von Wilhelm von Humboldt an Georg Heinrich Ludwig Nicolovius, edited by Haym (Berlin: Felber, 1894).

SELECTED PERIODICAL PUBLICATIONS – UNCOLLECTED: Review of *Geschichte des englischen Deismus,* by Gotthard V. Lechler, *Allgemeine Literaturzeitung* (Halle), 3 (1842): 41-44, 49-72, 79-80;

"Die protestantischen Freunde in Halle," *Jahrbücher der Gegenwart,* 74 (1846): 799-800, 814-819;

"Philosophie," *Ersch- und Grubers Allgemeine Enzyklopädie,* 24, no. 3 (1848): 1-231;

"Gentz," *Ersch- und Grubers Allgemeine Enzyklopädie,* 58, no. 1 (1854): 325-392;

"Der preussische Landtag während der Jahre 1851 bis 1857," *Preussische Jahrbücher,* 1 (1858): 186-213;

"Ulrich von Hutten," *Preussische Jahrbücher,* 1 (1858): 487-532;

"Zu den Wahlen in Preussen," *Preussische Jahrbücher,* 2 (1858): 457-468;

"Die Fabier," *Preussische Jahrbücher,* 3 (1859): 657-682;

"Schiller an seinem hundertjährigen Jubiläum," *Preussische Jahrbücher,* 4 (1859): 516-544, 626-664;

"Ernst Moritz Arndt," *Preussische Jahrbücher,* 5 (1860): 470-511;

"Thomas Babington Macaulay," *Preussische Jahrbücher,* 6 (1860); 353-396;

"Eine Erinnerung an Johann Gottlieb Fichte," *Preussische Jahrbücher,* 7 (1861): 244-259;

"Politische Korrespondenz," *Preussische Jahrbücher,* 9 (1862): 467-477;

"Varnhagen von Ense," *Preussische Jahrbücher,* 11 (1863): 445-515;

"Die Verordnung vom 1. Juni und die Presse," *Preussische Jahrbücher,* 11 (1863): 627-643;

"Ein Artikel der Grenzboten," *Preussische Jahrbücher,* 12 (1863): 62-72;

"Ästhetisch-politische Wahlverwandtschaften," *Preussische Jahrbücher,* 18 (1866): 235-240;

"Die Vollendung von Kobersteins Geschichte der deutschen Literatur," *Preussische Jahrbücher,* 19 (1867): 238-244;

"An G. W. Friedrich Hegels hundertstem Geburtstag," *Die Grenzboten,* 1 (1870/1872): 377-387;

Review of Klaus Groth's *Quickborn II,* in *Preussische Jahrbücher,* 27 (1871): 479-486; reprinted in *Jahresgabe der Klaus-Groth Gesellschaft,* 21 (1979/1980): 30-42;

"Ein deutsches Frauenleben aus der Zeit unserer Literaturblüthe," *Preussische Jahrbücher,* 28 (1871): 457-506;

"Herder," *Allgemeine Deutsche Biographie,* 12 (1880): 55-100;

"Otto Nasemann," *Deutsch-evangelische Blätter,* 20 (1895): 785-817.

Rudolf Haym practiced, more or less simultaneously, at least three professions, and he did well in all three of them. As a student he developed a keen interest in politics that soon led to active participation and remained undiminished all his life. His second profession was that of a scholar, specializing in three major disciplines – philosophy, literary history, and political science – without suffering a loss of focus or depth in any of his chosen fields. Finally, he spent a large portion of his time writing political pamphlets and literary biographies, neither of which was directly part of his political or scholarly professions.

Haym was born on 5 October 1821 in Grünberg, Silesia. His father, Johann Gottlieb Haym, was a teacher at the public primary school; his mother, Henriette, née Gaertner, was descended on her own mother's side from a Huguenot family. When he was about six years old Haym tried to carve some "ornaments" into the frame of the kitchen door; his pocketknife slipped and stabbed him in the left eye. In spite of the best medical treatment, the sight in the eye was permanently lost.

Both father and mother took a great interest in the education of their son. Piano lessons and instruction in French were the domain of his mother, but it was his father who exerted the most decisive influence. In his posthumously published *Aus meinem Leben: Erinnerungen* (From My Life: Memoirs, 1902) Haym leaves no doubt as to how powerful and comprehensive that influence was: "seine Sinnesweise [wurde] durchaus die meinige. Er war in Allem, was für die letzte Richtung des Geistes entscheidend ist, mein alleiniger Lehrer" (his mental disposition [became] altogether my own. In all matters that are decisive for the ultimate direction of the intellect, he was my exclusive teacher).

In 1834 Haym began high school at the Köllnische Gymnasium in Berlin. After passing his Abitur (the required examination for admission to a university) in 1839 he started studying theology at the University of Halle. As a result of exposure to Arnold Ruge's *Hallesche Jahrbücher für deutsche Wissenschaft und Kunst* (Halle Yearbooks for German Science and Art), the main organ of the young radical followers of the philosopher Georg Wilhelm Friedrich Hegel, and David Friedrich Strauss's *Das Leben Jesu, kritisch bearbeitet* (The Life of Jesus, Critically Examined, 1835–1836), Haym switched from theology to philosophy and classical philology. He obtained his doctorate in 1843 and took the state board examination required for high-school teachers in 1844. The following two years he spent as a teacher in training at his former high school.

In 1845 he tried to get the *venia legendi* (permission to give lectures on the university level), but his application was rejected for political rather than academic reasons. Political activism had become an important part of Haym's life, and the government authorities responsible for the universities were reluctant to allow an appointment that was likely to add to the general turmoil in the troubled years immediately preceding the revolution of 1848. Also, Haym had started out as one of the most fervent followers of Hegel; his enthusiasm had been absorbed in Halle, the "stronghold of Hegelianism." This passion had reigned until about 1842 but then wore off rapidly, to some extent because of the influence of Ludwig Feuerbach. His disenchantment with Hegel soon gave way to adamant opposition. When he applied to have his *venia legendi* approved, he pointed out that he regarded it as the most important task of his life to fight against and, if possible, to destroy the Hegelian philosophy. To what extent his opposition to Hegel – launched in Halle, of all places – was responsible for the rejection of his application is open to conjecture. His 231-page article "Philosophie" in *Ersch- und Grubers Allgemeine Enzyklopädie* (General Encyclopedia edited by Ersch and Gruber, 1848) contains a section on Hegel that is almost an outline for his Hegel book of 1857.

Haym was elected to the Frankfurt National Parliament in 1848. He produced three outstanding volumes of reports on the parliamentary proceedings under the title *Die deutsche Nationalversammlung* (The German National Assembly, 1848–1850) that reaped praise from various quarters, above all from his fellow members of parliament. In 1850 he obtained the second doctorate, required for university teachers, in philosophy at the University of Halle. On 1 July he assumed the duties of managing editor of the *Konstitutionelle Zeitung* (Constitutional Newspaper), the newly founded organ of the Partei der Konstitutionellen (Party of the Constitutionalists) in Berlin. For five months he mounted a forceful publicity campaign against certain aspects of the domestic and foreign policy of Prussia, at the end of which time the chief of police ordered him expelled from Berlin for alleged infractions of the law.

Haym embarked on his teaching career at the University of Halle in the summer of 1851. Due to enemies he had acquired through his political activities, he moved up the academic ladder rather slowly. It took him ten years to attain appointment as außerordentlicher Professor (professor without tenure) of modern literary history and eight more years to be promoted to a full professorship in philosophy and literary history. In both cases he encountered considerable opposition from the faculty.

In the foreword to his *Wilhelm von Humboldt: Lebensbild und Charakteristik* (Wilhelm von Humboldt: Short Biography and Character Sketch, 1856) Haym outlines the procedure he followed in all his biographical writings: "Eine Charakteristik Wilhelm's von Humboldt . . . konnten wir nicht versuchen, ohne zugleich ein möglichst vollständiges und genaues Bild seines Lebens zu zeichnen, und ein solches Lebensbild nicht zeichnen, ohne es in die Entwicklung des deutschen Geistes und Lebens mitten hineinzustellen" (We could not attempt a characterization of Wilhelm von Humboldt . . . without at the same time presenting a comprehensive and precise picture of his life, and could not present such a biography without placing it within the development of the German intellectual life). He depicts the unfolding of Humboldt's personality "aus dem Kern seines eigenen Wesens" (from the nucleus of his own nature) through a succession of historical events that shaped Humboldt without his full awareness. Haym traces to its most likely origin every detail of Humboldt's life that he could verify. The result was quite unusual for the time. Rather than focusing on the results of his subjects' endeavors, as other biographers did, Haym discovered the causal factors to which they owed their achievements. But at the same time Haym was able to show that the human intellect is the mover behind all historical developments. This notion is a manifestation of the "Geist des Historismus" (spirit of historicism)

Haym as a young man

Die romantische Schule: Ein Beitrag zur Geschichte des deutschen Geistes (The Romantic Movement: A Contribution to the History of German Thought, 1870) took Haym ten years to complete. It is still the most authoritative guide for those interested in this area. Few books in historical scholarship are written with as much thoroughness, critical insight, and well-balanced judgment. Haym claimed as his goal to supersede all previously written works on German Romanticism. He achieved this goal by treating literature in its interrelationship with philosophy and all other areas of the intellectual life of the nation.

In 1871 Haym was invited to join the faculty of the University of Breslau; a year later he received an offer from the newly established German University of Strasbourg. He rejected both offers out of loyalty to the University of Halle. He was elected rector of the university in 1873.

Writing *Herder, nach seinem Leben und seinen Werken dargestellt* (Herder, according to His Life and Works, 1877–1885) was, in all likelihood, the most challenging task of Haym's life; it took him fourteen years to complete the project. The difficulty lay in the seemingly unfathomable, extremely complex and contradictory nature of Johann Gottfried Herder. Haym's proven approach of explaining his subject's development through causal analysis was especially onerous in this case because Herder's personality had been shaped by circumstances and influences that seemed to be accidental. The Herder book was praised as yielding an image of a man that had no match in German literature. Haym, however, felt that a synoptic view of Herder's thought was still required. He intended to produce such a work, but the plan was never carried out.

During the last two decades of Haym's life the activism of his earlier years was gone, though not his keen interest in following political developments. In his correspondence he felt quite comfortable criticizing the actions of the government, including those of Emperor Wilhelm I; he was increasingly concerned about "unser Vorwagen in die Weltpolitik" (our venturing into world politics) and expressed uneasiness about the prospect of disastrous consequences. Haym, nevertheless, refrained from participating in the public debate, preferring to live the private life of a scholar. The reason for this change of attitude was his deep frustration with the disappearance of liberalism from German politics. He had little interest in Chancellor Otto von Bismarck's attempts to improve the economic situation of the working class, and what he considered the "zest for power" of the proletariat, even if only

that originated in the first half of the nineteenth century and grew in strength during the second half.

In his *Hegel und seine Zeit: Vorlesungen über Entstehung und Entwickelung, Wesen und Werth der Hegel'schen Philosophie* (Hegel and His Time: Lectures on Origin and Development, Nature and Value of the Hegelian Philosophy, 1857) Haym's presentation suffers from his barely concealed eagerness to dismantle Hegel's philosophy because, in his opinion, it did not correspond to the necessities of the time and would prove detrimental to the state. He occasionally carries his criticism too far, leaving himself open to the charge of interpreting subjectively rather than objectively – a flaw that is absent from any of his other biographical studies. The main virtue of the book is its attempt to place Hegel's philosophy in its historical context. No author writing on Hegel before Haym had used such a historical approach.

In 1858 Haym founded the *Preussische Jahrbücher* (Prussian Yearbooks), serving as editor for the first six years of its existence. Also in 1858 he married Wilhelmine (Minna) Dzondi, the daughter of a prominent Halle ophthalmologist. They had one son, Hans.

in the direction of obtaining the right to vote, disgusted him.

In November 1898 Haym was invited to deliver, as the representative of the University of Halle, a memorial lecture on Bismarck, who had died on 30 July. Although others were favorably impressed by his last public lecture, he was not satisfied with it and refused to allow it to be printed. Haym's modesty grew with age; in 1898 he confessed to a friend that "das wenige, was ich kann, weder Gelehrtheit noch Erfinden, sondern ein bißchen Kritik, ein bißchen Lehrgeschick und rhetorische Lebhaftigkeit ist" (this little bit that I know is neither learnedness nor inventiveness, but just some critique, some ability to teach and some rhetorical vivacity). Neither his colleagues nor his students would have agreed with this vast underestimation.

The true passion of Haym's last decades was teaching. At the age of sixty-five a German professor may retire but is not required to do so; the right to hold lectures continues as long as the professor pleases and as long as he or she can attract students. Haym held lectures until 1901; he died on 27 August of that year while vacationing in the mountain village of Sankt Anton am Arlberg, Austria.

Letters:

Julius Heyderhoff, "R. Haym und Karl Twesten: Briefwechsel über politische Philosophie und Fortschrittspolitik 1859–63," *Preussische Jahrbücher,* 161 (1915): 232–256;

Ausgewählter Briefwechsel Rudolf Hayms, edited by Hans Rosenberg (Stuttgart: Deutsche Verlagsanstalt, 1930).

Bibliography:

Wilhelm Kosch, "Rudolf Haym," in *Deutsches Literatur-Lexikon,* edited by Heinz Rupp and Carl Ludwig Lang, volume 7 (Bern: Francke, 1979), pp. 578–579.

References:

Hugo Bieber, "Rudolf Haym," *Schlesische Lebensbilder,* 2 (1926): 263–271;

Berthold Delbrück, "Rudolf Haym," *Euphorion,* 8 (1901): 842–849;

Ludwig Feuerbach, "Entgegnung an R. Haym," in his *Sämtliche Werke,* volume 7, edited by Wilhelm Bolin and Friedrich Jodl (Stuttgart: Frommann-Holzboog, 1903), pp. 506–520;

Gerhart von Graevenitz, "Geschichte aus dem Geist des Nekrologs: Zur Begründung der Biographie im 19. Jahrhundert," *Deutsche Vierteljahrsschrift für Literaturwissenschaft und Geistesgeschichte,* 54 (March 1980): 105–170;

Wolfgang Harich, "Rudolf Haym, seine politische und philosophische Entwicklung," *Sinn und Form,* 6 (1954): 482–527;

Harich, *Rudolf Haym und sein Herderbuch: Beiträge zur kritischen Aneignung des literaturwissenschaftlichen Erbes* (Berlin: Aufbau, 1955);

Justus Hashagen, "G. Freytag, Treitschke, H. Baumgarten, R. Haym," *Deutsche Monatsschrift für das gesamte Leben der Gegenwart,* 5 (1906): 625–632, 763–771;

Wolfgang Hessler, *Die philosophische Persönlichkeit Rudolf Hayms* (Würzburg: Mayr, 1935);

Wolfgang Hock, *Liberales Denken im Zeitalter der Paulskirche: Droysen und die Frankfurter Mitte* (Münster: Aschendorff, 1957);

Ernst Howald, "Der Literarhistoriker Rudolf Haym," in his *Deutschfranzösisches Mosaik* (Zurich: Artemis, 1962), pp. 199–216;

Marie Joachimi-Dege, *Die Weltanschauung der deutschen Romantik* (Jena: Diederichs, 1905);

Günter Klieme, "Rudolf Hayms 'Romantische Schule': Historiographische und methodische Betrachtungen," Ph.D. dissertation, University of Leipzig, 1969;

Alfred Edwin Lussky, *Tieck's Approach to Romanticism* (Borna & Leipzig: Noske, 1925);

Michael John Maher, "Hegel Rejected: Ludwig Büchner, Rudolf Haym, and Eduard von Hartmann: The Retreat from German Idealism, 1855–1870," Ph.D. dissertation, University of Minnesota, 1974;

Leonard von Renthe-Fink, *Geschichtlichkeit: Ihr terminologischer und begrifflicher Ursprung bei Hegel, Haym, Dilthey und Yorck* (Göttingen: Vandenhoeck & Ruprecht, 1964);

Alois Riehl, "Rudolf Haym," in *Führende Denker und Forscher* (Leipzig: Quelle & Meyer, 1922), pp. 150–170;

Riehl, *Rudolph Haym: Rede zu seinem Gedächtnis in der Aula der Universität Halle-Wittenberg am 14. Dezember 1901, gehalten von Alois Riehl* (Halle: Niemeyer, 1902);

Frithjof Rodi, "Die Romantiker in der Sicht Hegels, Hayms und Diltheys," in *Kunsterfahrung und Politik im Berlin Hegels,* edited by Otto Pögeler and Annemarie Gethmann-Siefert (Bonn: Bouvier, 1983), pp. 73–103;

Hans Rosenberg, *Politische Denkströmungen im deutschen Vormärz* (Göttingen: Vandenhoeck & Ruprecht, 1972);

Rosenberg, *Rudolf Haym und die Anfänge des klassischen Liberalismus* (Munich: Oldenbourg, 1933);

Rosenberg, "Zur Geschichte der Hegelauffassung," in *Hegel und seine Zeit,* by Haym, edited by Rosenberg (Leipzig: Heims, 1927), pp. 510–550;

Karl Rosenkranz, *Apologie Hegels gegen Dr. R. Haym* (Berlin: Duncker & Humblot, 1858);

Erich Rothacker, *Einleitung in die Geisteswissenschaften* (Tübingen: Mohr, 1920; revised, 1930);

Fritz Schalk, "Zu den Erinnerungen Hayms," *Philosophische Perspektiven,* 5 (1973): 227–237;

Aloys Schmid, *Entwicklungsgeschichte der hegelschen Logik: Ein Hilfsbuch zu einem geschichtlichen Studium derselben, mit Berücksichtigung der neuesten Schriften von R. Haym und K. Rosenkranz* (Regensburg: Manz, 1858);

Siegfried Schmidt, "Zum historisch-politischen Standort der bürgerlichen Hegel-Rezeption im 19. Jahrhundert: Rudolf Hayms Hegelbuch von 1857," *Wissenschaftliche Zeitschrift der Friedrich Schiller-Universität Jena, Gesellschafts- und sprachwissenschaftliche Reihe,* 21 (1972): 91–96;

Wilhelm Schrader, "Rudolf Haym," *Biographisches Jahrbuch,* 6 (1901): 33–47;

Eberhard Günter Schulz, "Rudolf Haym und seine Grünberger Jugendjahre," *Schlesien,* 10 (1965): 21–27;

Hans Vaihinger, *Dem Andenken an Rudolf Haym* (Halle: Kaemmerer, 1901);

Erich Weniger, ed., *Briefe Wilhelm Diltheys an Rudolf Haym, 1861–1873* (Berlin: Verlag der Akademie der Wissenschaften, Phil.-Hist. Klasse, 1936);

Robert M. Wernaer, *Romanticism and the Romantic School in Germany* (New York: Haskell House, 1966);

Otto Westphal, *Welt- und Staatsauffassung des deutschen Liberalismus: Eine Untersuchung über die Preussischen Jahrbücher und den konstitutionellen Liberalismus in Deutschland von 1858 bis 1863* (Munich: Oldenbourg, 1919);

Ottomar Wichmann, "Rudolf Haym," in *Lebensbilder des 19. Jahrhunderts,* edited by the Historische Kommission für die Provinz Sachsen (Magdeburg: Verlag der Landesgeschichtlichen Forschungsstelle, 1927), pp. 307–312.

Papers:

Rudolf Haym's papers are at the Universitäts- und Landesbibliothek (University and Provincial Library), Halle, and the Deutsche Staatsbibliothek (German State Library), Berlin.

Friedrich Hebbel

(18 March 1813 – 13 December 1863)

A. Tilo Alt
Duke University

BOOKS: *Judith: Eine Tragödie in fünf Acten* (Hamburg: Hoffmann & Campe, 1841); translated by Carl van Doren as *Judith: A Tragedy in Five Acts* (Boston: Badger, 1914);

Gedichte (Hamburg: Hoffmann & Campe, 1842);

Genoveva: Tragödie in fünf Acten (Hamburg: Hoffmann & Campe, 1843);

Mein Wort über das Drama!: Eine Erwiderung an Professor Heiberg in Copenhagen (Hamburg: Hoffmann & Campe, 1843); translated by Moody Campbell as "My View on the Drama," in his *Hebbel, Ibsen and the Analytic Exposition* (Heidelberg: Winter, 1922), pp. 78–85;

Maria Magdalene: Ein bürgerliches Trauerspiel in drei Acten. Nebst einem Vorwort, betreffend das Verhältnis der dramatischen Kunst zur Zeit und verwandte Puncte (Hamburg: Hoffmann & Campe, 1844); translated by Paul Bernard Thomas as *Maria Magdalena*, in *The German Classics of the Nineteenth and Twentieth Centuries*, volume 9, edited by Kuno Francke and William Guild Howard (New York: German Publication Society, 1914), pp. 22–80;

Der Diamant: Eine Komödie in fünf Acten (Hamburg: Hoffmann & Campe, 1847);

Neue Gedichte (Leipzig: Weber, 1848);

Herodes und Mariamne: Eine Tragödie in fünf Acten (Vienna: Gerold, 1850); translated by Edith J. R. Isaacs and Kurt Rahlson as *Herod and Mariamne: A Tragedy in Five Acts*, in *Drama: A Quarterly Review of Dramatic Literature*, no. 6 (May 1912): 3–168;

Schnock: Ein niederländisches Gemälde (Leipzig: Weber, 1850);

Ein Trauerspiel in Sicilien: Tragicomödie in einem Act, nebst einem Sendschreiben an H. T. Rötscher (Leipzig: Geibel, 1851);

Friedrich Hebbel; painting by Karl Rahl, 1851 (*Freies Deutsches Hochstift, Frankfurter Goethemuseum*)

Julia: Ein Trauerspiel in drei Akten. Nebst einer Vorrede und einer Abhandlung: "Abfertigung eines ästhetischen Kannegießers" (Leipzig: Weber, 1851);

Der Rubin: Ein Märchen-Lustspiel in drei Acten (Leipzig: Geibel, 1851);

Agnes Bernauer: Ein deutsches Trauerspiel in fünf Aufzügen (Vienna: Tendler, 1855); translated by

131

Loueen Pattee as *Agnes Bernauer (a German Tragedy in Five Acts)*, in *Poet Lore,* 20, no. 1 (1909): 1–60;

Erzählungen und Novellen (Pest: Heckenast, 1855) – comprises "Matteo," "Herr Haidvogel und seine Familie," "Anna," "Pauls merkwürdige Nacht," "Die Kuh," "Der Schneidermeister Nepomuk Schlägel auf der Freudenjagd," and "Eine Nacht im Jägerhaus"; "Anna" translated by Frances H. King in *The German Classics of the Nineteenth and Twentieth Centuries,* volume 9, pp. 166–173;

Michel Angelo: Ein Drama in zwei Akten (Vienna: Tendler, 1855);

Gyges und sein Ring: Eine Tragödie in fünf Acten (Vienna: Tendler, 1856); translated by L. H. Allen as *Gyges and His Ring,* in *Three Plays by Friedrich Hebbel* (London: Dent / New York: Dutton, 1914);

Gedichte: Gesamt-Ausgabe, stark vermehrt und verbessert (Stuttgart & Augsburg: Cotta, 1857);

Mutter und Kind: Ein Gedicht in sieben Gesängen (Hamburg: Hoffmann & Campe / New York: Westermann, 1859);

Die Nibelungen: Ein deutsches Trauerspiel in drei Abtheilungen, 2 volumes (Hamburg: Hoffmann & Campe, 1862); translated by G. H. McCall as *The Niebelungs: A Tragedy in Three Acts* (London: Siegle, 1903);

Demetrius: Eine Tragödie (Hamburg: Hoffmann & Campe, 1864);

Sämmtliche Werke, 12 volumes, edited by Emil Kuh (Hamburg: Hoffmann, 1865–1867);

Tagebücher, 2 volumes, edited by Felix Bamberg (Berlin: Grote, 1885, 1887); excerpts translated by King as "Extracts from the Journals of Friedrich Hebbel," in *The German Classics of the Nineteenth and Twentieth Centuries,* volume 9, pp. 253–267;

Sämtliche Werke: Historisch-Kritische Ausgabe, 24 volumes, edited by Richard Maria Werner (Berlin: Behr, 1901–1907);

Friedrich Hebbel: Sämtliche Werke nebst Tagebüchern und einer Auswahl der Briefe, 6 volumes, edited by Paul Bornstein (Munich: Müller, 1911–1925);

Werke, 5 volumes, edited by Gerhard Fricke, Werner Keller, Karl Pörnbacher (Munich: Hanser, 1963–1967).

Edition in English: *Three Plays, by Friedrich Hebbel* (London: Dent / New York: Dutton, 1914) – comprises *Gyges and His Ring,* translated by L. H. Allen; *Herod and Mariamne,* translated by Allen; and *Maria Magdalena,* translated by Barker Fairley.

OTHER: *Ernst Freiherrn von Feuchtersleben's sämtliche Werke: Mit Ausnahme der rein medicinischen,* edited by Hebbel (Vienna: Gerold, 1853).

SELECTED PERIODICAL PUBLICATIONS – UNCOLLECTED: "Über den Styl des Dramas," *Jahrbücher für dramatische Kunst und Literatur,* 1 (1847): 35–40;

"Wie verhalten sich im Dichter Kraft und Erkenntnis zu einander?," *Jahrbücher für dramatische Kunst und Literatur,* 1 (1847): 310–313;

"Aus meiner Jugend," *Unterhaltungen am häuslichen Herd,* 2, no. 40 (1854): 625–626; translated by Frances H. King as "Recollections of My Childhood (1846–1854)," in *The German Classics of the Nineteenth and Twentieth Centuries,* volume 9, edited by Kuno Francke and William Guild Howard (New York: German Publication Society, 1914), pp. 221–254.

Friedrich Hebbel had to overcome formidable odds to achieve greatness. Not only did he have a most difficult start in life, but he also lived in an epoch that regarded greatness as dangerous and modesty and moderation as virtues. At the beginning of the age of science and technology, the idealistic and spiritual side of life had been replaced with materialistic concerns.

Although Hebbel's misappropriation by the Nazis as a "Nordic" poet and dramatist on the one hand and his rejection by Marxist critics on the other have made him a controversial figure, there is agreement among admirers and critics alike that he was the most significant playwright to follow Johann Wolfgang von Goethe and Friedrich Schiller. His poetry, too, though to a lesser degree, commands a place of high regard in the annals of German letters, and a good deal of it is part of the canon. Hebbel has been labeled a poet of the conservative Biedermeier restoration period between 1815 and 1848, a neoclassicist, an early realist, a prophet of German national unity, as well as an advocate of a league of nations. These contradictory classifications make Hebbel a difficult but fascinating figure in German cultural history.

Hebbel's posthumous road to fame proved as rocky as the reception of his work during his lifetime. His friend Emil Kuh hoped to publicize Hebbel's work by bringing out an edition of his collected works (1865–1867) shortly after the writer's death in 1863; in 1877 Kuh's biography of Hebbel was published in two volumes. Neither effort produced the desired result. Interest in Hebbel's works was not to gather momentum until Felix Bamberg, Hebbel's friend and admirer from his Paris days, edited Hebbel's diaries (1885, 1887) and letters (1890–1892). Bamberg's commentaries, his article on the poet in the *Allgemeine Deutsche Biographie* (Universal German Biography) of 1880, and his publication of the correspondence between Hebbel and Theodor Rötscher, a disciple of the philosopher Georg Wilhelm Friedrich Hegel, alerted academicians that here was a man of both artistic and philosophical significance. Finally, after the completion of Richard Maria Werner's critical edition of Hebbel's works (1901–1907), the poet gained admission to the pantheon of German literature. The Hebbel centenary in 1913 brought the unveiling of his monument in Wesselburen and the publication of new editions of his works, including diaries. Hebbel had become a "classic," part of the curriculum of schools and universities and of the repertory of most important theaters in the German-speaking countries.

Christian Friedrich Hebbel was born on 18 March 1813 in Wesselburen, a small town near the North Sea in the region of Dithmarschen in Holstein. Since the duchies of Schleswig and Holstein belonged to Denmark, Hebbel was a Danish citizen by birth and remained so throughout his life. His father, Claus Friedrich, was a poor bricklayer; his mother, Antje Margarete Schubert, worked as a domestic. Hebbel's "Aus meiner Jugend" (translated as "Recollections of my Childhood, 1846–1854]," 1914), published in 1854 in Karl Gutzkow's popular magazine *Unterhaltungen am häuslichen Herd* (Fireside Chats) as the first part of a planned but soon abandoned autobiography, is the main source of information about his youth. Most critics, including the author himself, have regarded this fragment as his best prose work; his forte was dramatic dialogue and verse. His account passes over the unhappy moments of his youth in favor of experiences that had a positive effect on him and that might inspire others. In this effort Hebbel's ambition to be a classical writer asserted itself.

Hebbel's father died in 1827 at the age of thirty-seven, leaving Hebbel and his brother Johann to be brought up by their mother. On the recommendation of Hebbel's schoolteacher, the fourteen-year-old was hired as an errand boy and clerk by J. J. Mohr, the magistrate of the parish of Wesselburen. Without this stroke of good fortune Hebbel would not have had the opportunity to continue his education. In later years he complained bitterly

about Mohr's treatment of him – he had to share a bed under the stairs with Mohr's coachman, even when the latter was sick, and he had to take his meals with the servants – but Hebbel's duties were light, and he was permitted to use the magistrate's library. Although Mohr's library lacked Goethe's works, those of Schiller, Heinrich von Kleist, Friedrich Klopstock, E. T. A. Hoffmann, and – momentously – Ludwig Uhland were well represented. After Hebbel made some poetic attempts in the manner of Schiller's reflective lyric, Uhland's natural simplicity struck the boy as a revelation. As late as 1857 Hebbel would dedicate his collected poems to Uhland, "dem ersten Dichter der Gegenwart" (premier poet of the present). By the time Uhland died in 1862, however, Hebbel had come to recognize the poet's mediocrity.

During his self-education Hebbel also became acquainted with Immanuel Kant's ethical theory, Hegel's dialectic, and Ludwig Feuerbach's materialism. The vehicles for these ideas were Christoph Tiedge's poem "Urania: Über Gott, Unsterblichkeit und Freiheit" (Urania: Of God, Immortality, and Freedom, 1800), Gotthilf H. Schubert's "Ansichten von der Nachtseite der Naturwissenschaft" (Views on the Dark Side of Natural Science, 1808) and "Symbolik des Traums" (Dream Symbolism, 1814), and Feuerbach's "Gedanken über Tod und Unsterblichkeit" (Reflections on Death and Immortality, 1830). These texts did not come to light as sources of his philosophical ideas until nearly a century later. The philosophy of Friedrich Wilhelm Joseph von Schelling and Hegel's aesthetics also exercised a lasting but unacknowledged influence on the poet. With the exception of Friedrich Theodor von Vischer's *Ästhetik oder Wissenschaft des Schönen* (Aesthetics; or, the Science of the Beautiful, 1847–1858), he endeavored to conceal the sources of his ideas.

In 1832 Amalie Schoppe, a popular writer of trivial novels, published some poems and stories Hebbel had sent her in the two Hamburg journals she edited: *Iduna: Eine Zeitschrift für die Jugend beiderlei Geschlechts, belehrenden, erheiternden und geistbelebenden Inhalts* (Iduna: A Journal of Didactic, Amusing and Stimulating Contents for the Youth of Both Sexes) and *Neue Pariser Modeblätter* (New Parisian Fashion Journal). One of the poems he sent her subsequently, the patriotic "Die Schlacht bei Hemmingstedt" (The Battle of Hemmingstedt, 1833), was timely because the 1830s were a period of unrest in the duchies, where the populace sought to free itself from Danish rule in the wake of uprisings in Poland and France. The poem commemorates the victory of the Dithmarschen peasants over Danish and German troops in the sixteenth century. It prompted Schoppe to invite Hebbel to come to Hamburg to prepare himself for admission to a university. One of the requirements for admission was proficiency in Latin, and Schoppe arranged for Latin lessons for him. Hebbel arrived in Hamburg in February 1835. He was given free room and board in the home of a ship's carpenter, whose step-daughter, Elise Lensing, a seamstress, became his lover, even though she was eight and a half years his senior. In March 1835 Hebbel began to keep a journal, a practice he continued until his death.

Hebbel failed his Latin examinations; furthermore, Schoppe disapproved of his liaison with Lensing, and his relationship with his benefactress became strained. Therefore, after collecting the funds she had set aside for his studies, on 27 March 1836 he left for the University of Heidelberg. He arrived in Heidelberg on 3 April. Shortly thereafter he began attending lectures without matriculating.

Hebbel remained in Heidelberg until September 1836. The most important aspect of his life then was his friendship with Emil Rousseau, a law student. After Rousseau's death in 1838 Hebbel remarked that Rousseau had been the only real friend he had ever had. He was to keep up a regular correspondence with Rousseau's father and sister.

From Heidelberg, Hebbel traveled to Munich on foot to continue his studies. To supplement his meager resources he had accepted a position as correspondent for the *Morgenblatt für gebildete Leser* (Morning Paper for Educated Readers). On the way to Munich he visited his revered poetic mentor Uhland, but he came away disappointed in what he regarded as Uhland's banal nature. In Munich he stayed with the family of the master joiner Schwarz. He and Schwarz's daughter Beppi became lovers.

In March 1839 Hebbel ran out of money and returned to Hamburg on foot. There he took a job as correspondent for the *Telegraph für Deutschland* (German Telegraph).

At the end of 1839 Hebbel began writing his first drama, *Judith* (1841; translated, 1914), based on the apocryphal Book of Judith. The play depicts the clash between paganism, represented by the mighty general Holofernes, and Judaism, represented by Judith of Bethulia. Since, according to Hebbel, the nature of woman is to love rather than to hate, the virgin Judith faces a tragic conflict when she is called on by the deity to kill Holofernes, the enemy of her people. In the end she has a personal reason to kill Holofernes: she stabs him to death for raping her even though she longed for the encounter with Holofernes, a man of imposing physical attributes and great power. If she should become pregnant, she tells her people, they must kill her. Hegel's dialectic is visible here in that Judith functions as the guilty tool of history: she produces the downfall of Holofernes, which results in the rise of monotheism. The play premiered on 6 July 1840 at the Berlin court theater and was a great success.

Hebbel summarized his ideas about drama in the essay *Mein Wort über das Drama!* (1843; translated as "My View on the Drama," 1922) and in the preface to his tragedy *Maria Magdalene* (1844; translated as *Maria Magdalena,* 1914). They reveal Hebbel's near total dependence on Hegel's aesthetic paradigm, despite his repeated denials of any Hegelian influence. With Hegel, Hebbel accepts the need to "regenerate" Western tragedy as the highest form of poetic expression and as the vehicle for establishing a divine presence in the world, the original raison d'être of tragedy. Hebbel opposed the view of history as an objective phenomenon, as the concrete result of human activity. For Hebbel and Hegel, history has a religious source that manifests itself in ethical values. Hebbel claimed that his historical dramas had a higher, more universal purpose than the historical tragedies of his contemporaries, which served narrow nationalistic interests. Hebbel sought to establish a synthesis of the cultural achievements of the West in a symbolic way. In Hebbel's concept of tragic guilt, guilt arises not by accident but by necessity, because life exists only individually while – at the same time – the individual remains a part of the Whole. Through separation from the Whole, the individual unavoidably incurs guilt. Tragic guilt is part of what is known as Hebbel's concept of pantragedy. Finally, Hebbel says that the task of drama is to help overcome the alienation that he saw taking place between the individual and social institutions, such as the emerging metropolis and the state.

In the summer of 1840 Hebbel had a brief affair with Emma Schröder, the daughter of a Hamburg senator. Lensing, who knew of the affair, was expecting a child by him. He was beset by feelings of guilt and remorse, and the figure of Golo in the drama *Genoveva* (1843), which he had begun writing, reflects those feelings. On 5 November 1840 Lensing gave birth to a son, Max. Hebbel's financial situation had become desperate despite the royalties he received from *Judith*. He decided to petition King Christian VIII of Denmark, who was known for his support of the arts, for a professorship at the University of Kiel or some other position. In the winter of 1842 he journeyed to Copenhagen, where the poet Adam Oehlenschläger was his advocate at court. In the spring of 1843 Hebbel obtained from the king a two-year travel grant of twelve hundred talers, a stipend that was larger than customary and that entailed no obligation on his part. He returned to Hamburg and gave Lensing half of the grant to help support herself and their child. After completing *Genoveva,* one of his lesser plays, he set sail for France on 9 September 1843. His knowledge of French was poor, and he came to depend on the services and the subsequent friendship of Bamberg, the Prussian consul in Paris. During his stay in Paris Hebbel met the poet Heinrich Heine and, through Heine, the philosopher and socialist Arnold Ruge, coeditor with Karl Marx of the *Deutsch-Französische Jahrbücher* (German-French Annuals). Hebbel lived extremely frugally in Paris, and he felt inadequate because of his poverty, his humble origins, and his lack of social graces.

His stay in Paris was marred even further when he learned of his son's death on 2 October 1843 and Lensing's despondency over the loss. She was expecting their second child, and Hebbel feared for her life. He despaired over her inability to put the loss behind her. For Hebbel, pain caused by the state of the world outweighs pain suffered because of the loss of an individual; the death of the individual is necessary for the preservation and progress of humanity as a whole. At one point, however, he was so gripped by guilt and remorse that he offered to marry her and share the rest of his stipend with her. Bamberg prevented him from doing so by reminding him of his creative mission. In May 1844 she gave birth to their second son, Ernst.

In September 1844 Hebbel's *Maria Magdalene,* a "bürgerliches Trauerspiel" (middle-class tragedy) in the tradition of Gotthold Ephraim Lessing's *Miß Sara Sampson* (1755) and *Emilia Galotti* (1772), was published. It was to become his most influential and most frequently staged tragedy. In many ways Hebbel's most personal work, it depicts the misery of an individual in social and economic circumstances not unlike those of the playwright's youth. He modeled the characters Klara and Meister Anton on the Schwarzes, the family with whom he had stayed when he was a student in Munich. The tragedy arises not from conflict between social classes but from conflict within the same class. The destruction of the family is the re-

sult of the harshness of Meister Anton, the master joiner and father of Klara. Klara becomes pregnant by her fiancé, the villainous clerk Leonhard, whom she does not love and who wants to marry her only for her dowry. She commits suicide so as not to "disgrace" her father. When it is explained to her father that he and the secretary Friedrich – Klara's former fiancé, who had neglected her – must bear the guilt for her death, Meister Anton is moved to utter the final and often-quoted line of the play: "Ich verstehe die Welt nicht mehr" (I no longer understand the world). Not only do the men in Klara's environment fail to understand her, but, in the last analysis, she agrees with their assessment because she has internalized the values of her father's patriarchal world. Hebbel's interest in character and environment and his keen psychological insight make *Maria Magdalene* an unusual middle-class tragedy. Anticipating the naturalists, Hebbel depicts the social milieu as the reason for the actions of his characters: the rigid moral standards of his class make Meister Anton a tyrant, even though he loves his children. A dramatic technique that Hebbel employs with great success and that had been used by Lessing, Schiller, and Kleist is that of analytic exposition: opening the drama not long before the catastrophe and then showing the events that led up to it.

Because he was afraid he had represented the everyday milieu of a contemporary small-town family too graphically, Hebbel, at Bamberg's urging, added to the play a preface in which he asserts his noble intentions and great regard for the drama as the highest form of artistic expression. The Greeks had as their purpose the representation of fate; Shakespeare showed the destruction of the individual through the individual's inherently demonic nature. The drama of Hebbel's time is to make visible the struggle of the extraordinary individual with God or history. Drama must serve the highest and truest interests of its own time, even if the plot is taken from ancient myths. Hebbel came to regret adding the preface because it was frequently used to attack him by pointing to the contradiction between his idealistic goals and naturalistic results.

On 26 September 1844 Hebbel left Paris for Italy. His stays in Rome and Naples yielded some poems, epigrams, and the plot for his tragicomedy *Ein Trauerspiel in Sicilien* (A Tragedy in Sicily, 1851), about the rape and murder of a young woman by two policemen who are convicted on the testimony of a witness. In Rome he met the painter Louis Gurlitt, with whom he was to enter into a lengthy correspondence, and the literary historian Hermann Hettner. And he broke with Lensing in harsh and uncompromising letters from Rome.

In October 1845, after the Danish king sent him additional money for his return home – Hebbel had spent every penny of his grant – he left for Berlin via Vienna. The author of three tragedies, he was no longer unknown, and the papers in Vienna reported his arrival in early November. The wealthy brothers Julius and Wilhelm Zerboni, admirers of Hebbel's work, organized a grand party in his honor and showered him with attention and presents. Book dealers began to order his works, and Christine Enghaus, the leading actress at the Vienna Burgtheater, let it be known that she was interested in playing the roles of Judith and Klara. Like Hebbel, Christine was from northern Germany and was the parent of a child born out of wedlock. On 26 May 1846 she and Hebbel were married. Vienna, which was to have been a stop on his way to Berlin and an uncertain future, had become his home. That same year, through the good offices of his deceased friend Rousseau's father, who advanced him the money for the fee, Hebbel was granted a doctorate in philosophy by the University of Erlangen. He had submitted *Mein Wort über das Drama!* in lieu of a dissertation.

Christine's relative financial security enabled Hebbel to concentrate on his writing and her generosity allowed him to resolve his relationship with Elise Lensing in an amicable if unconventional way. The couple invited Elise to visit them in Vienna; the death of Ernst, Hebbel and Elise's second son, on 12 May 1847 was the immediate reason for the invitation. Hebbel's marriage had caused Elise much bitterness at first, but her good nature prevailed over her rancor; she accepted the invitation and stayed with the Hebbels for more than a year in an innocent menage à trois. Christine's illegitimate son, Carl, whom Hebbel had adopted but whom he had come to resent, was placed in Elise's care as a substitute for Ernst. Christine and Hebbel's first child, Emil, was born on 27 December 1846 and died a few months later. On Christmas Eve of 1847 their second child, Christine (Titi), was born; she was Hebbel's only child to grow to adulthood. Elise and Christine kept up a correspondence until Elise's death in 1854.

Hebbel's *Herodes und Mariamne* (1850; translated as *Herod and Mariamne,* 1912) was based on Flavius Josephus's history of the Jewish people (circa A.D. 65); Hebbel knew nothing of the previous dramatic treatments of the story by Hans Sachs (1552), Pedro Calderón de la Barca (1637), Voltaire (1730), and Friedrich Rückert (1844). Herodes (Herod), an Edomite forcibly converted to Judaism, marries Mariamne, a descendant of the royal house of the Maccabees. With the help of the Romans, Herodes becomes king of Judea. Josephus reports that Herod's love for Mariamne was directly proportionate to her hatred for him, but in Hebbel's tragedy Mariamne loves Herodes as passionately as he loves her. But Mariamne learns that Herodes has twice given orders that she is to be killed should he fail to return from Alexandria, where he fears death at the hands of his Roman superiors. She is hurt and outraged at his lack of trust in her to take her own life out of devotion to him, and she decides to force him to execute her. When he returns from his second journey, he finds her celebrating his supposed death. She is tried and sentenced to die. Above all, the tragedy is another variant of Hebbel's representation of the battle of the sexes. The reduction of Mariamne to the status of an object is a sin, and a world that permits it to happen is doomed. Mariamne reveals her true feelings to the Roman captain Titus not long before her death; she has resolved that Herodes should be her executioner. Titus must promise not to reveal Mariamne's reasons for acquiescing in her death sentence. When Herodes learns of his wife's innocence after her execution, it is the Roman, Titus, who steadies the fainting king, thus symbolizing the greater stability represented by imperial Rome. After the arrival of the three wise men and their announcement of the birth of the King of Kings, Herodes issues his infamous order to have all the male infants of Bethlehem killed.

In keeping with Hegel's dialectics of history and aesthetics, the drama ends on a hopeful note: the arrival of the three kings from the Orient heralds the dawning of a more humane age. The three wise men symbolize the Christian gospel of love, forgiveness, and redemption. This new age is a synthesis that was produced by the clash of the antithetical cultures of paganism and Judaism and is a stage in the inevitable progress of history toward its ultimate goal of reunion with the Absolute. Hebbel was criticized for superimposing this conciliatory and idealistic perspective on the tragic events rather that having it flow naturally from them; this criticism seems justified.

Hebbel felt that he had to subordinate realistic psychological details, such as those in *Maria Magdalene,* to his abstract view of history: the spectator was to ponder the subordination of the individual to the general tragic order of the universe. The open-ended, relativistic tragedies of the realists and naturalists no longer admitted of such cosmic vistas; it was Hebbel's ambition to renew the ancient Attic tragedy. The price he had to pay for his untimely ambition was the slight theatrical success of the drama. *Herodes und Mariamne* premiered in April 1849 at the Burgtheater in Vienna. Hebbel's wife played Mariamne, a role he had written for her; despite a stellar performance by Christine, the play did not meet with a warm reception and to this day lags far behind *Maria Magdalene* as a stage success.

With his tragedy *Agnes Bernauer* (1855; translated, 1909) Hebbel hoped to gain access to the circle of literary neoclassicists around King Maximilian II of Bavaria and his flourishing Hoftheater (court theater) in Munich under the direction of Franz Dingelstedt. As Friedrich Sengle has pointed out, Hebbel sought to overwhelm the king and his coterie with a tragedy that was to demonstrate his sympathy with the restoration of aristocratic rule in the sense of medieval feudalism. But he was naive in his assumption that Munich was the residence of a feudal king rather than that of an enlightened constitutional monarch.

The play is based on actual events from the fifteenth century. Albrecht, the son of Duke Ernst of Bavaria, marries Agnes Bernauer, the beautiful daughter of a barber-surgeon in Augsburg. Ernst fears that Agnes's beauty and rightful claims as the wife of the heir to the Bavarian throne will drive a wedge between the people and the dynasty, and during Albrecht's absence the duke signs her death warrant in the name of the widows and orphans that would be created and the cities and towns that would be reduced to cinders if civil war broke out. She is drowned in the Danube. When Albrecht learns of this legal murder he goes to war against his father. They meet on the battlefield, and the duke offers to acknowledge the dead Agnes as his son's legitimate wife and to establish a requiem to commemorate her sacrifice for all time. Ernst abdicates the throne and retires to a monastery, and father and son are reconciled.

Ludwig of Bavaria, who had been forced to abdicate in 1848 because of the scandal that arose from his attempt to have his mistress, Lola Montez, elevated to the peerage, granted Hebbel an audience after the drama's premiere in Munich on 25 March 1852. Horror-struck by the cruelty of his medieval ancestor, the former king said that he himself could never have contemplated such an act. Hebbel replied that the king would have had to act in this manner if he had been in power at that time. The Munich audience responded favorably to the play because of the historical pomp and colorful setting provided by Dingelstedt and because of the parallels it drew between Agnes and Lola Montez.

In *Gyges und sein Ring* (1856; translated as *Gyges and His Ring*, 1914) Hebbel sought to revive the tradition of French classical theater in Germany. He based the plot on the account of Herodotus; the ring episode was taken from Plato's *Republic;* and the source of the oriental customs depicted was a book on Indian legends that Hebbel had reviewed in 1848. In a note appended to the list of characters Hebbel points out that his drama has a prehistoric and mythical plot and that it observes the Aristotelian unities by taking place within a period of two days. It was Hebbel's ambition to prove that, like Schiller and Goethe, he could produce a synthesis of antiquity and modernity.

Rhodope, the wife of Kandaules, King of Lydia, comes from a place where Indian and Greek customs blend and where women, on pain of death, must not be seen except by their fathers and husbands. Gyges, a young Greek who is Kandaules' guest, gives the king a magic ring that has the power to make its wearer invisible. Kandaules boasts to Gyges of Rhodope's beauty and urges Gyges to enter her chamber with the help of the magic ring. On glimpsing Rhodope, Gyges is overwhelmed by her beauty and falls in love with her. Rhodope senses that something is amiss, and she sends for Gyges the next day. He confesses his love for her. The breach of time-honored custom cannot be forgiven, and Rhodope insists that Kandaules and Gyges fight a duel. Gyges prevails, and Rhodope pledges herself to be his consort. She demands the ring from Gyges, who replies that it is still on the dead king's finger. She says that the ring has found its proper place and continues: "Ich bin entsühnt, / Denn Keiner sah mich mehr, als dem es ziemte, / Jetzt aber scheide ich mich so von Dir!" (I have been cleansed, / For no one has seen me except the one who had a right to, / But now I am leaving you, thus!). She then stabs herself to death. By ignoring what custom and tradition demand of Rhodope and by attempting to be "modern" before the time is ripe, Kandaules has violated what he calls the "Schlaf der Welt" (sleep of the world). The world needs its "sleep" in order to "digest" previous changes, to recover from and to consolidate them. By the same token, Hebbel did not think that the Austrian revolution of 1848 should have demanded a republic; he felt that the radical changes advocated by the communists and socialists were premature. He believed that, at

Page from the manuscript for Hebbel's tragedy Die Nibelungen *(Goethe and Schiller Archive, Weimar)*

most, Austria should become a constitutional monarchy, and he had been a member of the delegation of Viennese writers dispatched to Innsbruck, where the royal family had fled, to persuade Archduke Johann to accept the office of constitutional monarch. In Hebbel's view the new does not have the right to supplant the old unless it is stronger than the old. In the case of Austria, he felt that neither the educational level of the populace nor the influence of the educated was sufficient to allow for a form of government more liberal than a constitutional monarchy. In Hegelian terms the clash between the forces of absolutism (thesis) and democracy (antithesis) results in a synthesis in which the rights and privileges of the ruling classes are preserved while being limited through a new constitution. King Kandaules has no new and better values with which to replace the old customs; hence, he should have respected the old values.

Gyges und sein Ring could not be performed in the age of realism, and the playwright had to be content with giving a public reading of the drama in April 1855. The play was not staged until 1889.

Hebbel purchased a modest summer home on the Traunsee in Gmunden, Upper Austria, in 1855. Grand Duke Karl Alexander of Saxe-Weimar awarded him a high decoration for his dramas in 1858, as did the Bavarian king in 1860. His plays were staged at the court theaters in Munich and Weimar. On his fiftieth birthday Hebbel was awarded the honorary title of private librarian to the grand duke.

At the Weimar court he befriended Princess Caroline Sayn-Wittgenstein, the wife of the Russian ambassador, and their daughter Marie. Through the Wittgensteins, Hebbel met Franz Liszt. Marie Wittgenstein became Hebbel's confidante and was the first person to read the manuscript for his *Die Nibelungen: Ein deutsches Trauerspiel in drei Abtheilungen* (1862; translated as *The Niebelungs: A Tragedy in Three Acts,* 1903).

In addition to royal patronage, Hebbel enjoyed friendships with the leading liberal Jewish journalists and writers in Vienna. His relations with such great Austrian writers of his day as Franz Grillparzer, Adalbert Stifter, and Johann Nepomuk Nestroy and the German composer Richard Wagner were fraught with hostility and mutual lack of understanding, but the poets Ludwig Tieck and Eduard Mörike and the composers Liszt and Robert Schumann thought highly of the playwright.

Hebbel's lengthy epic poem *Mutter und Kind* (Mother and Child, 1859) is composed in the manner of Goethe's *Hermann und Dorothea* (1798), which,

in turn, harks back to the tradition of the Greek idyll. While still in manuscript, the poem was awarded the Tiedge Prize in December 1857. It concerns motherly love, economic hardship, and the tendency of the wealthy to regard their wishes as everyone else's command. A poor couple is offered land in exchange for their infant son by a wealthy childless couple, but in the end they are allowed to keep both. The two couples are not portrayed in simplistic terms of good and evil but are represented with all their weaknesses.

Hebbel's first collection of lyrics, *Gedichte* (Poems), had appeared in 1842, followed by *Neue Gedichte* (New Poems) in 1848; his own rearrangement of all his poetry into cycles was published in 1857. The critical evaluation of his poetry has, by and large, focused on a comparison with the lyrical tradition begun by Goethe, the lyric of the private experience, and the mid-century realism exemplified by Theodor Storm and Gottfried Keller. There is little in Hebbel's lyrics that can be called realistic; his shorter verse reflects a Romantic and Goethean orientation in keeping with the residual romanticism of the Biedermeier period as well as the residual classicism (in a formal sense) typical of this prerealistic period. He experimented with many sounds and rhythms; his emotional palette ranged from happy to serene to sad to sarcastic, from the folk song to the intellectual and reflective lyric. Metrically, the classical, stately, occasionally somber measures of trochees and dactyls predominate; among the strophic forms the sonnet and distich are the most frequent.

In 1857 Hebbel traveled to Frankfurt am Main to meet the philosopher Arthur Schopenhauer and to Stuttgart to meet Mörike. While Mörike was an admirer of Hebbel's works, Schopenhauer did not reciprocate Hebbel's enthusiasm for the philosopher's ideas. The poet and herald of a metaphysics of pain and suffering expected his cycle of poems "Dem Schmerz sein Recht" (The Legitimacy of Pain) to strike a responsive chord in the philosopher. Instead, Schopenhauer argued with Hebbel about his preface to *Maria Magdalene,* which Schopenhauer regarded as unnecessary.

Hebbel also traveled to Kraków, Poland, with his friend and future biographer Kuh to gather Slavic material for the drama *Demetrius* (1864) — which, however, like Schiller's play of the same title, was to remain a fragment. In January 1861 Hebbel and his wife went to Weimar, where the first two parts of his most ambitious and impressive project, *Die Nibelungen,* were performed. Christine played Brunhild on the first evening and Kriemhild

Hebbel in 1858 (detail from a lithograph by J. Kriehuber)

on the second. More than any of his other works, this German heroic epic in new and typically Hebbelian guise helped establish his fame among the educated throughout Germany. It received acclaim during a time of rising nationalism, even though Hebbel was a Danish subject and wished to remain so.

Hebbel's interest in this most German of all legends, *Das Nibelungenlied* (The Lay of the Nibelungs), had begun in 1847, when he saw his wife in the role of Kriemhild in Ernst Raupach's dramatization of the epic. He had started working on his own version in earnest in October 1855 and, with many interruptions, completed the drama at the end of 1860. The great success of the Weimar performance helped thaw the icy atmosphere at the Burgtheater (Hebbel and Heinrich Laube, the director at the Burgtheater, had had differences concerning Hebbel's dramas as well as his wife, who in

Hebbel's opinion had consistently been slighted by Laube in the roles she was given), and the first two parts were staged there in February 1863. Its success was attributable to the popularity of the national myth, which continued into the Nazi period. In post–World War II Germany *Die Nibelungen* has rarely been staged; it received an avant-garde and "denationalized" treatment in 1973, when it was performed in Cologne under the direction of Hansgünther Heyme.

In keeping with Hebbel's Hegelian view of history, the drama brings into relief a point of crisis when barbaric German paganism yields to the more civilized Christian view of the world. As in *Gyges und sein Ring,* Hebbel sought to create an entirely human tragedy on the foundation of a mythical subject. The heroic pagan figures – Siegfried, Brunhild, Kriemhild, Frigga, the Burgundians, and the Huns – are governed by an ethic of loyalty, bravery, and revenge that inevitably leads to their downfall. Rüdeger, Dietrich von Bern, and the chaplain represent the emerging norms of Christianity: self-control, compassion, and forgiveness.

Hebbel's major change from the epic revolves around the conflict between the sexes. After her betrothal to Gunther, Brunhild wonders why Siegfried, destined by a prophecy to be hers, has married Kriemhild instead. Siegfried explains to the kings of Burgundy that when he first saw Brunhild in her castle on Isenland he was unmoved by her beauty, and he felt that he must not court one whom he could not love. In the world of human conventions Siegfried's attitude is praiseworthy, but in the irrational, primordial, mythical sphere he has committed a grave sin. Siegfried should have recognized Brunhild as preordained for him and should have loved her.

He compounds his sin of omission with one of commission by using his mysterious powers to subdue Brunhild for Gunther. Again, the cardinal sin of the male – of Siegfried, Holofernes, Herod, Kandaules, and of Hebbel himself in his relationship with Elise Lensing – is to degrade a woman to the status of an object. Only in the abdication of Etzel (Attila), the king of the Huns, in favor of Dietrich von Bern is the chain of revenge broken.

In March 1863 Hebbel became ill with what was misdiagnosed as rheumatism; his real ailment was osteoporosis. At the end he could not walk or even hold his head erect. On 7 November 1863 the king of Prussia awarded him the Schiller Prize for *Die Nibelungen*. The prize had been established in 1859 but had never been awarded; Hebbel was the first writer considered worthy of what was to become Germany's most prestigious literary award. Later that month he contracted pneumonia, and on 13 December he died. He was buried in Vienna's Protestant cemetery at Matzleinsdorf.

Letters:

Briefwechsel mit Freunden und berühmten Zeitgenossen, 2 volumes, edited by Felix Bamberg (Berlin: Grote, 1890–1892);

Aus Friedrich Hebbels Korrespondenz, edited by Friedrich Hirth (Munich & Leipzig: Müller, 1913);

Neue Hebbel-Dokumente, edited by Dietrich Kralik and Fritz Lemmermayer (Berlin: Schuster & Loeffler, 1913);

Hebbel-Dokumente: Unveröffentlichtes aus dem Nachlaß, edited by Rudolf Kardel (Heide: Westholsteinische Verlagsanstalt, 1931);

Neue Hebbel-Briefe, edited by Anni Meetz (Neumünster: Wachholtz, 1963);

Friedrich Hebbel: Briefe, edited by Henry Gerlach (Heidelberg: Winter, 1975);

Briefe von und an Friedrich Hebbel, edited by Gerlach (Heidelberg: Winter, 1978);

Hebbel-Briefe, edited by A. Tilo Alt (Berlin: Schmidt, 1989).

Bibliographies:

Hans Wütschke, *Hebbel-Bibliographie: Ein Versuch* (Berlin: Behr, 1910);

Henry Gerlach, *Hebbel-Bibliographie 1910–1970* (Heidelberg: Winter, 1973);

Gerlach, "Hebbel-Bibliographie 1970–1980," *Hebbel Jahrbuch* (1983): 157–189.

Biographies:

Emil Kuh, *Biographie Friedrich Hebbels,* 2 volumes (Vienna: Braumüller, 1877);

Thomas Campbell, *The Life and Works of Friedrich Hebbel* (Boston: Badger, 1919);

Paul Bornstein, *Friedrich Hebbels Persönlichkeit,* 2 volumes (Berlin: Propyläen, 1924);

Edna Purdie, *Friedrich Hebbel: A Study of His Life and Work* (London: Oxford University Press, 1932);

Anni Meetz, *Friedrich Hebbel* (Stuttgart: Metzler, 1962);

Friedrich Sengle, "Friedrich Hebbel," in his *Biedermeierzeit,* volume 3: *Die Dichter* (Stuttgart: Metzler, 1980), pp. 332–414;

Heinz Stolte, *Friedrich Hebbel – Leben und Werk* (Husum: Druck- und Verlagsgesellschaft, 1987);

Barbara Wellhausen, *Friedrich Hebbel: Sein Leben in Texten und Bildern. Eine Bildbiographie* (Heide: Boyens, 1988).

References:

A. Tilo Alt, "Hebbel's 'Die Muschel im Ozean' as Metaphor and Motto," in *Essays in Honor of Clifford Albrecht Bernd on the Occasion of His Sixtieth Birthday,* edited by John Fetzer and others (Stuttgart: Heinz, 1989), pp. 11–21;

Alt, "Die kritische Rezeption Friedrich Hebbels in den USA," *Hebbel Jahrbuch* (1978): 163–180;

Alt, "Zum Humanismus Friedrich Hebbels," *Monatshefte,* 76 (Winter 1984): 441–456;

Patricia Boswell, "The Hunt as a Literary Image in Hebbel's 'Die Nibelungen,' " *Hebbel Jahrbuch* (1977): 163–194;

Otfrid Ehrismann, "Tod und Erkenntnis. Hebbels Polenbild," *Hebbel Jahrbuch* (1983): 9–40;

Sten Flygt, *Friedrich Hebbel* (New York: Twayne, 1968);

Paul G. Graham, "Hebbel's Study of King Lear," *Smith College Studies in Modern Languages,* 21 (October 1939): 81–90;

Graham, "The Principle of Necessity in Hebbel's Theory of Tragedy," *Germanic Review,* 15 (December 1940): 258–262;

Graham, *The Relation of Drama to History in the Works of Friedrich Hebbel* (Northampton, Mass.: Smith College, 1934);

Hilmar Grundmann, ed., *Friedrich Hebbel: Neue Studien zu Werk und Wirkung* (Heide: Boyens, 1982);

A. E. Hammer, "The Comic Element in Hebbel's Plays," *German Life and Letters,* new series 26 (April 1973): 192–201;

Elisabeth Heptner, "Two Nineteenth-Century Conceptions of Womanhood: A Comparison of the Attitudes of Kleist and Hebbel," Ph.D. dissertation, Washington University, 1975;

Harvey W. Hewitt-Thayer, "Ludwig Tieck and Hebbel's Tragedy of Beauty," *Germanic Review,* 2 (January 1927): 16–25;

Edith Isaacs, "Concerning the Author of *Herod and Mariamne,*" *Theatre Arts Monthly,* 22 (December 1938): 886–890;

Lee B. Jennings, "Treasure and the Quest for the Self in Wagner, Grillparzer, and Hebbel," in *Myth and Reason: A Symposium,* edited by Walter Wetzels (Austin: University of Texas Press, 1973), pp. 71–100;

Herbert Kaiser, *Friedrich Hebbel: Geschichtliche Interpretation des dramatischen Werks* (Munich: Fink, 1983);

Ida Koller-Andorf and Hilmar Grundmann, eds., *Hebbel: Mensch und Dichter im Werk. Neue Wege zu Hebbel. Internationales Hebbel Symposium in Wien* (Vienna: VWGÖ, 1990);

Helmut Kreuzer, ed., *Hebbel in neuer Sicht* (Stuttgart: Kohlhammer, 1963);

Wolfgang Liepe, "Ideology Underlying the Writings of Friedrich Hebbel," *American Philosophical Society Year Book 1953* (1954): 221–225;

Alfred D. Low, *Jews in the Eyes of the Germans. From Enlightenment to Imperial Germany* (Philadelphia: Institute for the Study of Human Issues, 1979), pp. 217–218, 234–240;

Ludger Lütkehaus, *Friedrich Hebbel, "Maria Magdalene"* (Munich: Fink, 1983);

Ludwig Marcuse, "Der Hegelianer Friedrich Hebbel – gegen Hegel," *Monatshefte,* 39 (December 1947): 506–514;

W. John Niven, *The Reception of Friedrich Hebbel in Germany in the Era of National Socialism* (Stuttgart: Heinz, 1984);

Hannelore and Heinz Schlaffer, *Studien zum ästhetischen Historismus* (Frankfurt am Main: Suhrkamp, 1975), pp. 121–139;

Betty Nance Weber, "Bertolt Brecht and Friedrich Hebbel: A Study in Literary Influence and Vandalism," Ph.D. dissertation, University of Wisconsin – Madison, 1973;

Benno von Wiese, *Die deutsche Tragödie von Lessing bis Hebbel,* 2 volumes (Hamburg: Hoffmann & Campe, 1948), II: 334–461;

James D. Wright, "Hebbel's Klara: The Victim of a Division in Allegiance and Purpose," *Monatshefte,* 38 (May 1946): 304–316;

Klaus Ziegler, *Mensch und Welt in der Tragödie Friedrich Hebbels* (Darmstadt: Wissenschaftliche Buchgesellschaft, 1966).

Papers:

The Hebbel Archives are at the University of Kiel; the Hebbel Museum in Wesselburen, Schleswig-Holstein; and the Goethe and Schiller Archive in Weimar.

Paul Heyse

(15 March 1830 – 2 April 1914)

Charles H. Helmetag
Villanova University

BOOKS: *Frühlingsanfang 1848* (Berlin: Schade, 1848);

Der Jungbrunnen: Neue Märchen von einem fahrenden Schüler, anonymous (Berlin: Duncker, 1850) — comprises "Das Märchen von der guten Seele," "Glückspilzchen," "Das Märchen von Musje Morgenroth und Jungfer Abendbrod," "Veilchenprinz," "Das Märchen von Blindekuh," "Fedelint und Funzifudelchen"; revised edition (Berlin: Paetel, 1878);

Francesca von Rimini: Tragödie in fünf Akten (Berlin: Hertz, 1850);

Die Brüder: Eine chinesische Geschichte in Versen (Berlin: Hertz, 1852);

Studia romanensia: Particula I. Dissertatio inauguralis (Berlin: Schade, 1852);

Urica: Novelle in Versen (Berlin: Hertz, 1852);

Hermen: Dichtungen (Berlin: Hertz, 1854) — comprises "Margherita Spoletina," "Urica," "Idyllen von Sorrent," "Die Furie," "Die Brüder," "Michel-Angelo Buonarotti," "Perseus: Eine Puppentragödie";

Meleager: Eine Tragödie (Berlin: Hertz, 1854);

Novellen (Berlin: Hertz, 1855) — comprises "Die Blinden," "Marion," "L'Arrabbiata," "Am Tiberufer";

Die Braut von Cypern: Novelle in Versen. Mit einem lyrischen Anhang (Stuttgart & Augsburg: Cotta, 1856);

Thekla: Ein Gedicht in neun Gesängen (Stuttgart: Cotta, 1858);

Neue Novellen: 2. Sammlung (Stuttgart: Cotta, 1858) — comprises "Erkenne dich selbst"; "Das Mädchen von Treppi," translated by A. W. Hinton as *The Maiden of Treppi; or, Love's Victory* (New York: Hinton, 1874); "Der Kreisrichter"; "Helene Morten";

Vier neue Novellen: 3. Sammlung (Berlin: Hertz, 1859) — comprises "Die Einsamen," translated anonymously as "The Lonely Ones," in *Eugenie Marlitt, Magdalena; Paul Heyse, The Lonely Ones* (Philadelphia: Lippincott, 1869);

Paul Heyse

"Anfang und Ende"; "Maria Franziska"; "Das Bild der Mutter";

Die Sabinerinnen: Tragödie in fünf Akten (Berlin: Hertz, 1859);

Die Grafen von der Esche: Schauspiel in fünf Akten (Munich: Deschler, 1861);

Neue Novellen: 4. Sammlung (Berlin: Hertz, 1862) — comprises "Annina"; "Im Grafenschloß"; "Andrea Delfin," translated anonymously as

Andrea Delfin (Boston: Burnham, 1864); "Auf der Alm";

Ludwig der Bayer: Schauspiel in fünf Akten (Berlin: Hertz, 1862);

Rafael: Eine Novelle in Versen (Stuttgart: Kröner, 1863);

Elisabeth Charlotte: Schauspiel in fünf Akten (Berlin: Hertz, 1864);

Gesammelte Novellen in Versen (Berlin: Hertz, 1864) — comprises "Die Braut von Cypern," "Die Brüder," "König und Magier," "Margherita Spoletina," "Urica," "Die Furie," "Rafael," "Michel-Angelo Buonarotti," "Die Hochzeitsreise an den Walchensee"; enlarged (1870) — includes "Thekla," "Syritha," "Der Salamander," "Schlechte Gesellschaft," "Das Feenkind";

Meraner Novellen: 5. Sammlung (Berlin: Hertz, 1864) — comprises "Unheilbar," translated by Mrs. H. W. Eve as *Incurable* (London: Nutt, 1890); "Der Kinder Sünde der Väter Fluch"; "Der Weinhüter";

Maria Moroni: Trauerspiel in fünf Akten (Berlin: Hertz, 1865);

Hadrian: Tragödie in fünf Akten (Berlin: Hertz, 1865);

Hans Lange: Schauspiel in fünf Akten (Berlin: Hertz, 1866);

Fünf neue Novellen: 6. Sammlung (Berlin: Hertz, 1866) — comprises "Franz Alzeyer," "Die Reise nach dem Glück," "Die kleine Mama," "Kleopatra," "Die Witwe von Pisa";

Die glücklichen Bettler: Morgenländisches Märchen in drei Akten, frei nach Carlo Gozzi (Berlin: Hertz, 1867);

Novellen und Terzinen: 7. Sammlung der Novellen (Berlin: Hertz, 1867) — comprises "Syritha: Novelle in Versen," "Mutter und Kind: Novelle," "Auferstanden: Novelle," "Der Salamander: Novelle in Versen," "Beatrice: Novelle";

Colberg: Historisches Schauspiel in fünf Akten (Berlin: Hertz, 1868);

Der Rothmantel: Komische Oper in drei Aufzügen nach Musäus' Volksmärchen (Munich: Wolf, 1868);

Moralische Novellen: 8. Sammlung (Berlin: Hertz, 1869) — comprises "Die beiden Schwestern," "Lorenz und Lore," "Vetter Gabriel," "Am toten See," "Der Thurm von Nonza";

Die Göttin der Vernunft: Trauerspiel in fünf Akten (Berlin: Hertz, 1870);

Adam und Eva: Operette in 1. Aufzuge, music by Robert von Hornstein (Munich: Straub, 1870);

Ein neues Novellenbuch: 9. Sammlung (Berlin: Hertz, 1871) — comprises "Barbarossa," "Die Sticke-rin von Treviso," "Lottka," "Der letzte Centaur," "Der verlorene Sohn," "Das schöne Käthchen," "Geoffroy und Garcinde," "Die Pfadfinderin";

Die Franzosenbraut: Volksschauspiel in fünf Akten (Munich: Straub, 1871);

Der Friede: Ein Festspiel für das Münchener Hof- und National-Theater, music by Baron von Perfall (Munich: Oldenbourg, 1871);

Gesammelte Werke, 38 volumes (volumes 1–29, Berlin: Hertz; volumes 30–38, Stuttgart & Berlin: Cotta, 1872-1914) — includes in volume 9 (1872), *Die Pfälzer in Irland: Trauerspiel in fünf Akten;*

Kinder der Welt: Roman in sechs Büchern, 3 volumes (Berlin: Hertz, 1873); translated anonymously as *Children of the World: A Novel* (London: Chapman & Hall, 1882; New York: Munro, 1883);

Neue Novellen: Der Novellen 10. Sammlung (Berlin: Hertz, 1875) — comprises "Er soll dein Herr sein," "Die ungarische Gräfin," "Ein Märtyrer der Phantasie," "Judith Stern," "Nerina";

Ehre um Ehre: Schauspiel in fünf Akten (Berlin: Hertz, 1875);

Im Paradiese: Roman in sieben Büchern, 3 volumes (Berlin: Hertz, 1875); translated anonymously as *In Paradise,* 2 volumes (New York: Appleton, 1878);

Skizzenbuch: Lieder und Bilder (Berlin: Hertz, 1877);

Graf Königsmark: Trauerspiel in fünf Akten (Berlin: Hertz, 1877);

Elfride: Trauerspiel in fünf Akten (Berlin: Hertz, 1877);

Neue moralische Novellen: 11. Sammlung der Novellen (Berlin: Hertz, 1878) — comprises "Jorinde," "Getreu bis in den Tod," "Die Kaiserin von Spinetta," "Das Seeweib," "Die Frau Marchesa";

Zwei Gefangene: Novelle (Leipzig: Reclam, 1878); translated anonymously as *Two Prisoners* (London: Simpkin, 1893);

Das Ding an sich und andere Novellen: 12. Sammlung der Novellen (Berlin: Hertz, 1879) — comprises "Das Ding an sich," "Zwei Gefangene," "Die Tochter der Excellenz," "Beppe der Sternseher";

Die Madonna im Oelwald: Novelle in Versen (Berlin: Hertz, 1879);

Verse aus Italien: Skizzen, Briefe und Tagebuchblätter (Berlin: Hertz, 1880);

Die Weiber von Schorndorf: Historisches Schauspiel in vier Akten (Berlin: Hertz, 1880);

Frau von F. und römische Novellen: 13. Sammlung der Novellen (Berlin: Hertz, 1881) – comprises "Frau von F."; "Die talentvolle Mutter"; "Romulusenkel"; "Die Hexe vom Korso," translated by George W. Ingraham as *The Witch of the Corso* (New York: Munro, 1882);

Das Glück von Rothenburg: Novelle (Augsburg: Reichel, 1881); translated by C. L. Townsend as "The Spell of Rothenburg," in *The German Classics of the Nineteenth and Twentieth Centuries*, volume 13, edited by Kuno Francke and William Guild Howard (New York: German Publication Society, 1914), pp. 105–152;

Troubadour-Novellen: 14. Sammlung der Novellen (Berlin: Hertz, 1882; New York: Munro, 1883) – comprises "Der lahme Engel," "Die Rache der Vizgräfin," "Die Dichterin von Carcassonne," "Der Mönch von Montaudon," "Ehre über alles," "Der verkaufte Gesang";

Alkibiades: Tragödie in drei Akten (Berlin: Hertz, 1883);

Das Recht des Stärkeren: Schauspiel in drei Akten (Berlin: Hertz, 1883);

Don Juan's Ende: Trauerspiel in fünf Akten (Berlin: Hertz, 1883); translated anonymously as *The Last Days of Don Juan* (London, n.d.);

Unvergeßbare Worte und andere Novellen: 15. Sammlung der Novellen (Berlin: Hertz, 1883) – comprises "Unvergeßbare Worte," "Die Eselin," "Das Glück von Rothenburg," "Geteiltes Herz";

Buch der Freundschaft: Novellen. 16. Sammlung der Novellen (Berlin: Hertz, 1883) – comprises "David und Jonathan"; "Grenzen der Menschheit"; "Nino und Maso," translated by Alfred Remy as "Nino and Maso: A Tale Drawn from a Sienese Chronicle," in *The German Classics of the Nineteenth and Twentieth Centuries*, volume 13 (1914), pp. 74–104;

Siechentrost: Novelle (Augsburg: Reichel, 1883);

Buch der Freundschaft: Neue Folge. 17. Sammlung der Novellen (Berlin: Hertz, 1884) – comprises "Siechentrost," "Die schwarze Jakobe," "Gute Kameraden," "Im Bunde der Dritte";

Drei einaktige Trauerspiele und ein Lustspiel (Berlin: Hertz, 1884) – comprises *Ehrenschulden, Frau Lukrezia, Simson, Unter Brüdern: Lustspiel in einem Akt*;

Spruchbüchlein (Berlin: Hertz, 1885);

Gedichte (Berlin: Hertz, 1885; enlarged, 1889);

Himmlische und irdische Liebe – F.V.R.I.A. – Auf Tod und Leben: Novellen. 18. Sammlung der Novellen (Berlin: Hertz, 1886; New York: Munro, 1886);

Getrennte Welten: Schauspiel in vier Akten (Berlin: Hertz, 1886);

Die Hochzeit auf dem Aventin: Trauerspiel in fünf Akten (Berlin: Hertz, 1886);

Die Weisheit Salomo's: Schauspiel in fünf Akten (Berlin: Hertz, 1887);

Der Roman der Stiftsdame: Eine Lebensgeschichte (Berlin: Hertz, 1887); translated by "J. M. Percival" (Mary Joanna Safford) as *The Romance of the Canoness: A Life-History* (New York: Appleton, 1887);

Villa Falconieri und andere Novellen: 19. Sammlung der Novellen (Berlin: Hertz, 1888) – comprises "Villa Falconieri," "Doris Sengeberg," "Emerenz," "Die Märtyrerin der Phantasie";

Gott schütze mich vor meinen Freunden: Lustspiel in drei Akten (Berlin: Hertz, 1888);

Prinzessin Sascha: Schauspiel in vier Akten (Berlin: Hertz, 1888);

Weltuntergang: Volksschauspiel in fünf Akten (Berlin: Hertz, 1889);

Kleine Dramen: Erste Folge (Berlin: Hertz, 1889) – comprises *Im Bunde der Dritte, Der Venusdurchgang, Nur keinen Eifer, In sittlicher Entrüstung*;

Kleine Dramen: Zweite Folge (Berlin: Hertz, 1889) – comprises *Eine erste Liebe, Eine Dante-Lektüre, Zwischen Lipp und Bechersrand, Die schwerste Pflicht*;

Liebeszauber: Orientalische Dichtung (Munich: Hanfstaengl, 1889);

Novellen: Auswahl fürs Haus, 3 volumes (Berlin: Hertz, 1890) – comprises "L'Arrabbiata," "Anfang und Ende," "Andrea Delfin," "Unheilbar," "Vetter Gabriel," "Die beiden Schwestern," "Er soll dein Herr sein," "Der verlorene Sohn," "Nerina," "Unvergeßbare Worte," "Die Dichterin von Carcassonne," "Das Glück von Rothenburg," "Siechentrost";

Ein überflüssiger Mensch: Schauspiel in vier Akten (Berlin: Hertz, 1890);

Die schlimmen Brüder: Schauspiel in vier Akten und einem Vorspiel (Berlin: Hertz, 1891);

Weihnachtsgeschichten (Berlin: Hertz, 1891) – comprises "Eine Weihnachtsbescherung," "Das Freifräulein," "Die Geschichte von Herrn Wilibald und dem Frosinchen," "Die Dryas";

Merlin: Roman in sieben Büchern, 3 volumes (Berlin: Hertz, 1892);

Marienkind (Stuttgart: Engelhorn, 1892);

Wahrheit?: Schauspiel in drei Akten (Berlin: Hertz, 1892);

Ein unbeschriebenes Blatt: Lustspiel in vier Akten (Berlin: Hertz, 1893);

Jungfer Justine: Schauspiel in vier Akten (Berlin: Hertz, 1893);

Aus den Vorbergen: Novellen (Berlin: Hertz, 1893) – comprises "Vroni," "Marienkind," "Xaverl," "Dorfromantik";

In der Geisterstunde und andere Spukgeschichten (Berlin: Hertz, 1894) – comprises "In der Geisterstunde: Die schöne Abigail," translated by Frances A. Van Santford as *At the Ghost Hour: The Fair Abigail* (New York: Dodd, Mead, 1894); "In der Geisterstunde: Mittagszauber," translated by Van Santford as "Mid-Day Magic," in *At the Ghost Hour: Mid-Day Magic* (New York: Dodd, Mead, 1894); "In der Geisterstunde: 's Lisabethle," translated by Van Santford as "Little Lisbeth," in *At the Ghost Hour: Mid-Day Magic*; "In der Geisterstunde: Das Waldlachen," translated by Van Santford as *At the Ghost Hour: The Forest Laugh* (New York: Dodd, Mead, 1894); "Martin der Streber"; "Das Haus 'Zum unglaubigen Thomas' oder des Spirits Rache," translated by Van Santford as *At the Ghost Hour: The House of the Unbelieving Thomas* (New York: Dodd, Mead, 1894);

Wolfram von Eschenbach: Ein Festspiel (Munich: Knorr & Hirth, 1894);

Melusine und andere Novellen (Berlin: Hertz, 1895) – comprises "Hochzeit auf Capri," translated anonymously as "The Wedding at Capri," *Cosmopolitan,* 16 (January 1894): 318–331; "Fedja"; "Donna Lionarda"; "Die Rächerin"; "Melusine";

Über allen Gipfeln: Roman (Berlin: Hertz, 1895);

Roland's Schildknappen oder Die Komödie vom Glück: Volksmärchen in drei Akten und einem Vorspiel (Berlin: Hertz, 1896);

Vanina Vanini: Trauerspiel in vier Akten (Berlin: Hertz, 1896);

Die Fornarina: Trauerspiel in fünf Akten (Leipzig: Naumann, 1896);

Das Goethe-Haus in Weimar (Berlin: Hertz, 1896);

Verrathenes Glück; Emerenz: Zwei Geschichten (Stuttgart: Krabbe, 1896);

Einer von Hunderten und Hochzeit auf Capri (Stuttgart: Franckh, 1896);

Abenteuer eines Blaustrümpfchens (Stuttgart: Krabbe, 1897); translated anonymously as "Adventures of a Little Blue-Stocking," *International,* 1 (1896): 329–338;

Das Räthsel des Lebens und andere Charakterbilder (Berlin: Hertz, 1897) – comprises "Der Dichter und sein Kind," "Der Siebengescheite," "Ehrliche Leute," "Einer von Hunderten," "Ein

Mädchenschicksal," "Das Steinchen im Schuh," "Das Räthsel des Lebens";

Männertreu; Der Sohn seines Vaters: Zwei Novellen (Stuttgart: Krabbe, 1897);

Drei neue Einakter (Berlin: Hertz, 1897) – comprises *Der Stegreiftrunk: Drama in einem Akt, Schwester Lotte: Lustspiel in einem Akt, Auf den Dächern: Dramatischer Scherz in einem Akt;*

Neue Gedichte und Jugendlieder (Berlin: Hertz, 1897);

Der Sohn seines Vaters und andere Novellen (Berlin: Hertz, 1898) – comprises "Der Sohn seines Vaters," "Verratenes Glück," "Medea," "Männertreu," "Abenteuer eines Blaustrümpfchens";

Der Bucklige von Schiras: Komödie in vier Akten (Berlin: Hertz, 1898);

Martha's Briefe an Maria: Ein Beitrag zur Frauenbewegung (Stuttgart: Cotta, 1898);

Neue Märchen (Berlin: Hertz, 1899) – comprises "Holdrio, oder Das Märchen vom wohlerzogenen Königssohn," "Das Märchen vom Herzblut," "Die vier Geschwister," "Der Jungbrunnen," "Lilith," "Die gute Frau," "Die Nixe," "Das Märchen von Niels mit der offenen Hand," "Johannisnacht," "Die Dryas";

Das literarische München: 25 Porträtskizzen (Munich: Bruckmann, 1899);

Die Macht der Stunde; Vroni: Zwei Novellen (Stuttgart: Krabbe, 1899); "Die Macht der Stunde" translated anonymously as "The Power of the Hour," *English Illustrated Magazine,* 31 (May 1904): 155–183;

Maria von Magdala: Drama in fünf Akten (Berlin: Hertz, 1899); translated by A. I. Coleman as *Mary of Magdala* (New York: Lederer, 1900);

Fräulein Johanne; Auf der Alm: Zwei Novellen (Stuttgart: Krabbe, 1900);

Der Schutzengel: Novelle (Leipzig: Keil, 1900);

Jugenderinnerungen und Bekenntnisse (Berlin: Hertz, 1900; revised and enlarged edition, 2 volumes, Stuttgart: Cotta, 1912);

Das verschleierte Bild zu Sais: Drama in drei Akten (Stuttgart & Berlin: Cotta, 1901; New York: Lederer, 1901);

Tantalus; Mutter und Kind: Zwei Novellen (Stuttgart: Krabbe, 1901);

Ninon und andere Novellen (Stuttgart & Berlin: Cotta, 1902) – comprises "Ninon," "Zwei Seelen," "Der Blinde von Dausenau," "Fräulein Johanne," "Tantalus," "Ein Mutterschicksal";

Der Heilige: Trauerspiel in fünf Akten (Berlin & Stuttgart: Cotta, 1902);

Novellen vom Gardasee (Stuttgart & Berlin: Cotta, 1902) – comprises "Gefangene Singvögel," "Die Macht der Stunde," "San Vigilio," "Entsagende Liebe," "Eine venezianische Nacht," "Antiquarische Briefe";

Romane und Novellen, 42 volumes (Stuttgart: Cotta, 1902–1912);

Moralische Unmöglichkeiten und andere Novellen (Stuttgart & Berlin: Cotta, 1903) – comprises "Moralische Unmöglichkeiten," "Er selbst," "Zwei Wittwen," "Ein Idealist";

Ein Wintertagebuch (Gardone 1901–1902) (Stuttgart: Cotta, 1903);

Mythen und Mysterien (Stuttgart: Cotta, 1904) – comprises "Lilith: Ein Mysterium," "Kain: Ein Mysterium," "Perseus: Puppentragödie in vier Akten," "Am Thor der Unterwelt," "Der Waldpriester: Ein Satyrspiel," "Gespräche im Himmel";

Crone Stäudlin: Roman (Stuttgart: Cotta, 1905);

Die thörichten Jungfrauen: Lustspiel in drei Akten (Stuttgart & Berlin: Cotta, 1905);

Ein Canadier: Drama in drei Akten (Stuttgart & Berlin: Cotta, 1905);

Sechs kleine Dramen (Stuttgart & Berlin: Cotta, 1905) – comprises *Eine alte Geschichte: Familienszene in einem Akt, Die Zaubergeige: Drama in einem Akt, Zu treu: Genrebild in einem Akt, Horaz und Lydia, Der Stern von Mantua: Schauspiel in zwei Akten, Die Tochter der Semiramis: Tragödie in einem Akt;*

Victoria Regia und andere Novellen (Stuttgart & Berlin: Cotta, 1906) – comprises "Victoria Regia," "Lucile," "Tante Lene," "Die Ärztin," "Der Hausgeist," "Ein Ring";

Gegen den Strom: Eine weltliche Klostergeschichte (Stuttgart: Cotta, 1907);

Menschen und Schicksale: Charakterbilder (Stuttgart: Cotta, 1908) – comprises "Das Karussell," "Das Unglück, Verstand zu haben," "Lottchen Täppe," "Verfehlter Beruf," "Die gute Tochter," "Ein Luftschiffer," "Mei Bübche," "Fromme Lüge," "Florian," "Iwan Kalugin," "Ein Christuskopf," "Ein Menschenfeind," "Ein literarischer Vehmrichter";

Helldunkles Leben: Novellen (Stuttgart: Cotta, 1909) – comprises "Unüberwindliche Mächte," "Rita," "Ein unpersönlicher Mensch," "Eine Collegin," "Clelia";

Die Geburt der Venus: Roman (Stuttgart & Berlin: Cotta, 1909);

König Saul: Biblische Historie in fünf Akten (Leipzig: Reclam, 1909);

Mutter und Tochter: Drama in fünf Akten (Leipzig: Reclam, 1909);

Das Ewigmenschliche: Erinnerungen aus einem Alltagsleben von ***; Ein Familienhaus: Novelle (Stuttgart: Cotta, 1910);

Plaudereien eines alten Freundespaares (Stuttgart: Cotta, 1912) – comprises "Faustrecht," "Das schwächere Geschlecht," "Altruismus," "Don Juan," "Erste Liebe," "Oliva von Planta," "Vendetta," "Der Jubilar";

Letzte Novellen (Stuttgart: Cotta, 1914) – comprises "Die bessere Welt," "Fanchette," "Unwiederbringlich";

Ausgewählte Gedichte, edited by Erich Petzet (Stuttgart & Berlin: Cotta, 1920);

Gesammelte Novellen, 5 volumes, edited by Petzet (Stuttgart & Berlin: Cotta, 1921);

Italienische Novellen, 2 volumes (Stuttgart: Cotta, 1924);

Gesammelte Werke, 15 volumes (Stuttgart: Cotta, 1924; reprinted, Hildesheim, Zurich & New York: Olms, 1984);

Die Reise nach dem Glück: Eine Auswahl aus dem Werk, selected by Gerhard Mauz (Stuttgart: Cotta, 1959);

Das Mädchen von Treppi: Italienische Liebesgeschichten (Berlin: Der Morgen, 1965);

Andrea Delfin und andere Novellen (Berlin & Weimar: Aufbau, 1966);

Die Hexe vom Corso und andere Novellen mit der Novellentheorie (Munich: Goldmann, 1969);

L'Arrabbiata; Das Mädchen von Treppi, edited by Karl Pörnbacher (Stuttgart: Reclam, 1969);

Novellen, introduction by Manfred Schunicht (New York & London: Johnson Reprint, 1970) – comprises "L'Arrabbiata," "Andrea Delfin," "Kleopatra," "Beatrice," "Der letzte Zentaur," "Der lahme Engel," "Das Glück von Rothenburg," "Die Kaiserin von Spinetta," "Siechentrost," "Einleitung zu *Deutscher Novellenschatz,*" "Meine Novellistik";

Werke, mit einem Essay von Theodor Fontane, 2 volumes, edited by Bernhard and Johanna Knick, Hildegard Korth (Frankfurt am Main: Insel, 1980);

Novellen, Die Große Erzähler-Bibliothek der Weltliteratur, volume 54 (Dortmund: Harenberg, 1986) – comprises "L'Arrabbiata," "Helene Morten," "Andrea Delfin," "Der letzte Zentaur," "Judith Stern," "Victoria Regia."

Editions in English: *Four Phases of Love,* translated by G. H. Kingsley (London: Routledge, 1857) – comprises "Eye-Blindness and Soul-Blindness," "Marion," "La Rabbiata," "By the Banks of the Tiber";

L'Arrabiata and Other Tales, translated by Mary Wilson (Leipzig: Tauchnitz / New York: Leypoldt & Holt, 1867) – comprises "L'Arrabiata," "Count Ernest's Home," "Blind," "Walter's Little Mother";

The Dead Lake and Other Tales, translated by Wilson (Leipzig: Tauchnitz / New York: Low, Marston, Searle & Rivington, 1870) – comprises "A Fortnight at the Dead Lake," "Doomed," "Beatrice," "Beginning and End";

Barbarossa and Other Tales, translated by L. C. S. (Leipzig: Tauchnitz / London: Low, Marston, Low & Searle, 1874) – comprises "Barbarossa," "The Embroideress of Treviso," "Lottka," "The Lost Son," "The Fair Kate," "Geoffroy and Garcinde";

Tales from the German of Paul Heyse (New York: Appleton, 1879) – comprises "Count Ernest's Home," "The Dead Lake," "The Fury (L'Arrabiata)," "Judith Stern";

Selected Stories, from the German of Paul Heyse (Chicago: Schick, 1886) – comprises "L'Arrabiata," "Beppe, the Star-Gazer," "Maria Francisca";

La Marchesa, a Tale of the Riviera and Other Tales, translated by John Philips (London: Stock, 1887) – comprises "La Marchesa," "Her Excellency's Daughter," "A Divided Heart";

Words Never to Be Forgotten and The Donkey: Two Novellettes from the German of Paul Heyse, translated by A. E. Fordyce (Union Springs, N.Y.: Hoff, 1888);

A Divided Heart, and Other Stories, translated by Constance Stewart Copeland (New York: Brentano's, 1894) – comprises "A Divided Heart," "Minka," "Rothenburg on the Tauber."

OTHER: "Frohe Botschaft," "Freischarenlied," "Hurrah!," "Unser Wahlspruch," "An die deutschen Frauen," "Morgenandacht," "Hurrah!," "Einen Mann!," in *fünfzehn neue deutsche Lieder zu alten Singweisen: Den deutschen Männern Ernst Moritz Arndt und Ludwig Uhland gewidmet,* edited by Franz Kugler (Berlin: 1848), pp. 5-6, 13-14, 22-25, 27-30;

Spanisches Liederbuch, translated and edited and with contributions by Heyse and Emanuel Geibel (Berlin: Hertz, 1852);

Romanische inedita auf Italiänischen Bibliotheken gesammelt, edited by Heyse (Berlin: Hertz, 1856);

José Caveda, *Geschichte der Baukunst in Spanien,* edited by Kugler, translated by Heyse (Stuttgart: Ebner & Seubert, 1858);

Italienisches Liederbuch, edited and translated by Heyse (Berlin: Hertz, 1860);

William Shakespeare, *Antonius und Kleopatra,* translated by Heyse (Leipzig: Brockhaus, 1867);

Shakespeare, *Timon von Athen,* translated by Heyse (Leipzig: Brockhaus, 1868);

Antologia dei moderni poeti italiani, edited by Heyse (Stuttgart: Hallberger, 1869);

Deutscher Novellenschatz, 24 volumes, edited by Heyse and Hermann Kurz (Munich: Oldenbourg, 1871-1876);

Novellenschatz des Auslandes, 14 volumes, edited by Heyse and Kurz, (Munich: Oldenbourg, 1872-1875);

Kurz, *Gesammelte Werke: Mit einer Biographie des Dichters,* 10 volumes, edited by Heyse (Stuttgart: Kröner, 1874);

Giuseppe Guisti, *Gedichte,* edited and translated by Heyse (Berlin: Hofmann, 1875);

Italienische Novellisten, 6 volumes, edited by Heyse (Leipzig: Grunow, 1877-1878);

Giacomo Leopardi, *Werke,* translated by Heyse (Berlin: Hertz, 1878);

Lodovico Ariosto, *Rasender Roland,* 2 volumes, translated by Kurz, edited by Heyse (Breslau: Schottlaender, 1880-1881);

Neues Münchener Dichterbuch, edited, with contributions, by Heyse (Stuttgart: Kröner, 1882);

Neuer deutscher Novellenschatz, 24 volumes, edited by Heyse and Ludwig Laistner (Munich: Oldenbourg, 1884-1887);

Italienische Dichter seit der Mitte des 18. Jahrhunderts: Übersetzungen und Studien, 5 volumes, translated by Heyse (volumes 1-4, Berlin: Hertz; volume 5, Stuttgart & Berlin: Cotta, 1889-1905);

"Meine Erstlingswerke," in *Die Geschichte des Erstlingswerkes,* edited by Karl Emil Franzos (Leipzig: Titze, 1894), pp. 53-63;

Lodovico Ariostos Satiren, translated by Otto Gildemeister, edited by Heyse (Berlin: Behr, 1904);

Hermann Lingg, *Ausgewählte Gedichte,* edited by Heyse (Stuttgart & Berlin: Cotta, 1905);

Italienische Volksmärchen, translated by Heyse (Munich: Lehmann, 1914);

Drei italienische Lustspiele aus der Zeit der Renaissance, translated by Heyse (Jena: Diederichs, 1914) – comprises *Die Cassaria,* by Ariosto; *Die Aridosia,* by Lorenzino de' Medici; *Mandragola,* by Niccolò Machiavelli.

SELECTED PERIODICAL PUBLICATIONS – UNCOLLECTED: "Die Geister des Rheins: Ein Märchenschwank," *Süddeutsche Monatshefte,* 7 (1910): 417-441;

"Luco de Grimaud: Eine ungedruckte Versnovelle von Paul Heyse," *Euphorion,* 29 (1928): 471–479.

Paul Heyse, author of novellas, novels, poetry, and dramas, editor, translator, and essayist, was revered by the German middle class throughout much of his life as Johann Wolfgang von Goethe's successor. He was such a prominent and prolific author that some of his contemporaries maintained that the second half of the nineteenth century would be remembered as the "Age of Heyse." Others accused him of endangering morality through the glorification of the nonconformist in his works, although twentieth-century critics tend to regard his novellas as compromising tributes to the very social order they seem to attack. The naturalists criticized his novels and novellas for their lack of realism, and his works were quickly forgotten after his death. Although his accomplishments as a translator and editor and his theory of the novella have endured, his stories, novels, plays, and poems are of interest today primarily as a reflection of the literary taste of his time.

Heyse was born in Berlin on 15 March 1830, the second of two sons of Karl Wilhelm Ludwig and Julie Saaling Heyse. Both his father and his grandfather Johann Christian August Heyse were well-known philologists. Prior to his appointment to the faculty at the University of Berlin, Karl Heyse had been a tutor to Felix Mendelssohn-Bartholdy. There was a connection to Mendelssohn on Heyse's mother's side, as well: her mother and Mendelssohn's mother were cousins. Julie Heyse came from a prominent banking family, was fluent in French and English, and was a member of Rahel Varnhagen von Ense's literary salon. In imitation of Goethe, Heyse attributed his own balanced personality to the contrasting natures of his conscientious Germanic father and his witty, irrepressible "Oriental" mother.

Heyse excelled as a pupil at the Friedrich-Wilhelms-Gymnasium, especially in classical languages and French. While still in school he helped his father proofread the dictionary he was preparing; wrote his first play, a tragedy titled "Don Juan de Pedillo" that was never published or performed; and began writing nature and love poems. In 1845 he established a poets' society, the "Club," with his classmates Bernhard Endrulat, Richard Göhde, and Felix von Stein, the great-grandson of Goethe's friend Charlotte von Stein. In poems written between 1845 and 1847 he described his feelings for Stein's sister Anna, a love thwarted by class differ-

ences. Heyse's early poems were clearly influenced by Heinrich Heine and Joseph Freiherr von Eichendorff, two of the favorite models of the Club's young poets. Except for Endrulat, Göhde, and Stein, Heyse had little rapport with his classmates; eventually, he realized that he would have to compromise with the values of his peers. Some critics have regarded this attitude as the basis for the immense popularity of his stories – he gave his readers what they wanted – and, at the same time, the reason for the disturbing lack of realism in his works.

In 1846 the poet Emanuel Geibel saw some poems Heyse had written in school and arranged a meeting with him. Under Geibel's influence Heyse's inclination toward an emphasis on form over content was further cultivated.

In March 1847 Heyse matriculated at the University of Berlin to study classical philology. As a student he wrote political poetry in support of the revolution of 1848, including his first published poem, *Frühlingsanfang 1848* (The Beginning of Spring 1848, 1848) and the seven poems he contributed to Franz Kugler's *Fünfzehn neue deutsche Lieder zu alten Singweisen* (Fifteen New German Songs for Old Singing Styles, 1848). The events of 1848 made a great impact on the eighteen-year-old Heyse. Seeing his contemporaries die in the streets probably helped inspire the central theme in his works, the conflict between the individual and the inflexible forces of society. The events he witnessed may also be responsible for the nonrevolutionary tendency in his works.

In the various cultured Berlin homes and salons the young Heyse came in contact with artists, musicians, and writers such as Mendelssohn, Wilhelm Hensel, Peter Cornelius, Franz Liszt, and Theodor Fontane. Especially important for Heyse's development were the associations formed in the home of the art historian Franz Kugler. There he met his future wife – Kugler's daughter Margarethe – as well as Fontane and the historian Jakob Burckhardt, who inspired his love for Italy and the Renaissance. Fontane, well known at the time for his ballads, inspired Heyse's competitive spirit. Heyse regarded the older poet as a worthy opponent, and, despite some friction at first, they became lifelong friends and carried on a correspondence until Fontane's death in 1898.

In the spring of 1849, at Burckhardt's suggestion, Heyse transferred to the University of Bonn. During his summer vacation in 1849 he visited Burckhardt in Basel and began a correspondence with him that would continue until 1890.

Title page for Heyse's 1852 verse novella

Burckhardt encouraged and cultivated Heyse's veneration of harmonious beauty, a veneration that colored Heyse's works and his perception of reality. Before returning to Bonn he went hiking in the Swiss Alps, where a chambermaid in his hotel fell in love with him. A girl of classical Roman beauty and elemental passion, she was possibly the earliest inspiration for a character type that appears in many of his stories.

In January 1850 Heyse changed his major to Romance languages and literatures, a field that complemented his literary talents. His first published play, *Francesca von Rimini* (Francesca of Rimini), and the fairy-tale collection *Der Jungbrunnen* (The Fountain of Youth) were published the same year. The inspiration for *Francesca von Rimini* was Heyse's love affair with Sophie Ritschl, the young wife of a Bonn professor. The tragic situation of lovers who go against conventional morality was repeated again and again in his works.

Heyse returned to Berlin in 1851 to complete his doctoral dissertation on the poetry of the troubadours. His preoccupation with Italian, Spanish, and French literature resulted in many translations, several of which were set to music. It also left its mark on his literary works, which frequently have southern European settings, characters, flavor, and form.

While writing his dissertation, Heyse immersed himself again in the social life of the Berlin artists and writers. He had joined the literary group "Der Tunnel über der Spree" (The Tunnel over the River Spree) in January 1849. Most of the group's members were would-be writers from the Prussian military and bureaucracy, but Kugler, Fontane, and Geibel were also members. Everyone in the group had a special "Tunnel" name; Heyse's was "Hölty II," after the eighteenth-century author of love and nature poetry Ludwig Heinrich Christoph Hölty. Every member's literary endeavors were subject to the others' criticism, which made the "Tunnel" a valuable apprenticeship for a young writer. Heyse became a celebrity in the "Tunnel" as well as in its offshoot, "Rütli," to which Geibel, Fontane, Kugler, and Theodor Storm also belonged. He wrote his verse novella *Die Brüder* (The Brothers, 1852) during this period. In Berlin literary circles a Heyse cult developed that compared his form-conscious works to those of the young Goethe.

In June 1852 Heyse was awarded a doctorate in Romance philology. The same year brought the publication of his and Geibel's *Spanisches Liederbuch* (Book of Spanish Songs), a collection of translations of Spanish poems and folk songs, many of which were later set to music and remain popular today. The *Spanisches Liederbuch* also contains original poems by Heyse and Geibel under Spanish pseudonyms. Heyse continued his activity as a translator and editor throughout his life.

In the fall of 1852 Heyse received a grant from the Prussian Ministry of Culture to study unpublished Provençal manuscripts in Italy. He traveled with Otto Ribbeck, a former classmate in Bonn, who was consulting manuscripts in Italian libraries for an edition of the works of Virgil. In Rome, Heyse stayed with his uncle Theodor Heyse, who had translated the works of Catullus. There was a sizable German colony in Rome, and Heyse became acquainted with Arnold Böcklin and many other artists and sculptors. He found ample opportunity to make sketches of dark-haired, dark-eyed Italian girls who epitomized his idea of "classical" Mediterranean beauty. The high point of his Italian journey was the spring of 1853, which he spent in Naples and Sorrento, enthusiastically observing the life of the people. He eventually did publish a volume of old manuscripts, *Romanische inedita* (1856), but the main product of the trip was a series of poems and

Heyse (seated at center, facing left, with hand inside waistcoat) and other members of the Munich literary club "Krokodil" celebrating the centenary in 1859 of Friedrich Schiller's birth. Emanuel Geibel is seated next to Heyse, with his hand on Heyse's shoulder (woodcut after a drawing by Theodor Pixis).

stories with Italian settings and passionate female characters, works that would be associated with Heyse in the mind of the German middle-class reading public for the rest of his life.

Heyse shared two weeks of his stay in the Rosa magra, an inn in Sorrento frequented by artists, with Josef Viktor von Scheffel, the author of historical novels such as *Der Trompeter von Säckingen* (1854; translated as *The Trumpeter of Säkkingen,* 1877). Nearly twenty-five years later he would send a poem to Scheffel in which he recalled an incident with a servant girl at the inn who inspired his first published novella, "L'Arrabbiata" (translated as "La Rabbiata," 1857). He portrayed her in these lines as a tan, uninhibited fifteen-year-old who scurried about the dining room and nearly bit him with her sharp, white cat's teeth when he grabbed her by the hair. In 1854 the novella appeared in *Argo,* the literary yearbook edited by Fontane, and established Heyse's reputation. It went through fourteen editions between 1857 and 1914, in addition to ten editions in the first collection of Heyse's novellas (1855) and many textbook editions for American students.

"L'Arrabbiata" opens with Sorrento fishermen casting off at dawn in the Bay of Naples. In one of the boats sit the young fisherman Antonio and the local priest, Father Curato, who is taking Holy Communion to a wealthy patroness in Capri. The two men are joined by a striking young woman named Laurella, barely eighteen, who has a habit of tossing her head in a wild and somewhat imperious manner. Externally she is the typical Heyse Italian female with her brown face, black hair, full lips, fine nose, and flashing black eyes. Laurella's coyness and reserve result from her father's abusive treatment of his wife. Laurella is wary of suitors since she fears that they might treat her the same way, but she accepts Antonio's invitation to return to Sorrento with him in the afternoon while the priest remains on the island. The young fisherman declares his love for her; when she rejects him, he tries to drown her and himself. She bites his hand, jumps overboard, and starts swimming for shore. When Antonio rows after her and apologizes, she climbs back on board. That evening she brings him herbs to stop the bleeding and reveals that she has been in love with him for a long time but was afraid to trust

Heyse circa 1867, the year of his second marriage

her emotions. When Father Curato hears her confession, he is secretly delighted that Laurella's stubbornness has been overcome by true love. Laurella's encounter with Antonio makes her realize that she cannot act contrary to her inmost nature. The theme of self-realization through love is repeated again and again in Heyse's stories.

Heyse returned to Berlin in September 1853. During the following months his lifelong friendship with Storm began. Heyse corresponded with most of the major German literary figures of the second half of the nineteenth century, but his correspondence with Storm reveals the closest personal relationship. In 1853 Heyse also began writing for Friedrich Eggers's *Literaturblatt des deutschen Kunstblattes* (Literary Journal of the German Art Journal). He contributed perceptive essays on Storm and Eduard Mörike to the journal and would serve as its editor in 1858.

In March 1854, at Geibel's recommendation, Heyse received an invitation to live in Munich on a stipend from King Maximilian II of Bavaria with no obligation except to write and participate in the symposia of authors and artists sponsored by the court. The appointment also gave Heyse the right to lecture at the University of Munich, but he preferred to devote his time and energy to writing. Storm, with a tinge of envy, compared Heyse's position to that of Goethe at the court at Weimar. Heyse enjoyed and encouraged being compared to Goethe.

On 15 May 1854 Heyse married Margarethe Kugler. They settled in Munich and had two sons, one of whom died at the age of twelve, and two daughters. The Berliner Heyse quickly adjusted to Munich, where the life-style reminded him of Italy, and resisted repeated invitations from Grand Duke Carl Alexander of Saxony to move to Weimar.

Maximilian wanted to make Munich a cultural and scientific capital, and Heyse and Geibel quickly became the nucleus of the literary branch of this endeavor. In 1856 Heyse and the Thuringian poet Julius Grosse founded the literary group "Der heilige Teich der Krokodile" (the Holy Pond of the Crocodiles), generally known as "Krokodil," in an attempt to reconcile the native Bavarian authors with the predominantly North German writers whom Maximilian had brought in for his symposia. The founding members included Geibel; the Munich poet Hermann Lingg, from whose poem "Das Krokodil zu Singapur" (The Crocodile of Singapore, 1854) the group's name was derived; Friedrich Bodenstedt; Felix Dahn; Heinrich Leuthold; the journalist Adolf Wilbrandt, who later became director of the Vienna Burgtheater; and the medievalist and translator Wilhelm Hertz. Scheffel was an honorary member. Unlike the "Tunnel" membership, most of the Crocodiles, who also became known as the "Münchner Dichterkreis" (Munich Poets' Circle), were professional writers or academics who wrote on the side. Heyse was the president of the group, Geibel the spiritual leader. The Crocodiles met weekly in various coffeehouses for twenty-seven years.

Heyse wrote more than forty plays, including historical dramas and plays dealing with classical antiquity and biblical themes. The tragedy *Hadrian* (1865), considered by some to be Heyse's best play, deals with the relationship between the first-century Roman emperor Hadrian and the Greek youth Antinous, representatives respectively of the insufficiency of wealth and power and the contentment to be found in a life of simplicity and freedom. *Hans Lange* (1866), a theatrically effective Prussian patriotic play, was performed on every major German stage. *Colberg* (1868), a historical drama commemorating the defense of the Prussian harbor town Colberg against superior French forces in 1807, was performed in Berlin more than 139 times through the end of World War I and sold 180,000 copies during Heyse's lifetime, assisted by the patriotic fervor of 1870–1871 and 1914.

Heyse's wife had died on 30 September 1862; in 1867 he married Anna Schubart, a beautiful, dark-haired seventeen-year-old from Munich society. Near the Glyptothek Museum he built a splendid villa, which became a center of Munich cultural life; he and his wife spent the winters in a second home in Gardone on Italy's Lake Garda. The son and daughter from Heyse's second marriage both died in childhood. In the 1860s Heyse openly supported the struggles for freedom in Italy and Schleswig-Holstein; in 1868 he gave up his stipend from Ludwig II, who had succeeded Maximilian in 1864, to preserve his political independence.

The collection *Novellen und Terzinen* (Novellas and Terza Rimas) appeared in 1867. The narrator in one of these stories, "Beatrice," introduces the concept of the tragic conflict between the norms of society and the instinctive desires of those nonconformists whom Heyse refers to elsewhere as "Ausnahmemenschen" (exceptional individuals). He calls this phenomenon "der Streit der Pflichten" (the conflict of duties). His most extensive statement of the concept is contained in the introduction to his *Moralische Novellen* (Moral Novellas, 1869), an essay titled "Brief an Frau Toutlemonde in Berlin" (Letter to Mrs. Everybody in Berlin) and written in response to the criticism provoked by the *Novellen und Terzinen*. He regards conventional morality as a universal code of conduct which, in attempting to guarantee the general welfare, sometimes infringes on the rights of the exceptional individual. The latter is justified in acting in harmony with his or her instinctive personal morality, although such action inevitably leads to conflict with the forces of society and convention and frequently to the death or lifelong unhappiness of the exceptional individual. The conflict of duties provided Heyse, by his own account, with many of his most interesting and challenging themes.

"Die Stickerin von Treviso" (The Embroideress of Treviso, 1871) was one of Heyse's favorite stories. In fourteenth-century Italy the knight Attilio Buonfigli helps his fellow townsmen regain the city of Treviso from the soldiers of Vicenza. Recovering from a neck wound at the home of Emilia Scarpa, a citizen of Vicenza, he agrees to marry her in an attempt to end the feud that has separated their cities for years. When he returns to Treviso, however, he falls in love with the embroideress Gianna. As so often is the case in Heyse's works, true love is accompanied by self-realization. Attilio asks why his eyes were opened too late, why he did not come to know himself until after he had made a vow to Emilia. He and Gianna resolve to spend each night together until his wedding and then never to see each other again. When he is mortally wounded in a tournament held in honor of his fiancée's arrival in Treviso, however, Gianna sacrifices her reputation by claiming the right to be at her lover's side during his last moments alive. For the Ausnahmemensch the supreme obligation is fidelity to oneself.

The novella "Himmlische und irdische Liebe" (Heavenly and Earthly Love, 1886), another of Heyse's favorites, justifies adultery when one partner is unworthy or inimical to the personal development of the other. Professor Chlodwig commits suicide when, for the sake of public opinion, his poetess wife refuses to let him leave her for the simple and emotionally honest seamstress Traud. Before he met Traud, Chlodwig had defended German bourgeois morality, even philistinism, as potentially beneficial; afterward he rejects convention as restrictive and destructive. Heyse implies that it is each partner's duty to promote the other's potential; where there is no mutual support, the individual has the right to be unfaithful to a spouse rather than deny his or her own inner voice. In a letter to Fontane of 2 January 1879 Heyse said that he preferred a tragic resolution to such conflicts rather than a life founded on halfhearted relationships and wretched compromises.

Occasionally Heyse lets the conflict with society end in resignation rather than tragedy. In the novella "Der letzte Centaur" (The Last Centaur, 1871) he selected his friend Bonaventura Genelli, who was known for his paintings of centaurs and who had died in 1868, to represent the strong personality in conflict with the conservative society around him. In an elaborate story-within-a-story-within-a-story Genelli relates his encounter with the mythical creature, which suddenly appeared in the philistine milieu of a Bavarian village. The artists to whom he tells the story are lonely outsiders like himself who would have admired the classical beauty of the centaur.

One August, Genelli relates, he went to a mountain village outside Munich to escape the heat of the city. As he sat at an inn drinking Tirolean wine, the giant centaur approached, followed by a crowd of curious children and old people. The crea-

Heyse in 1885

When the musicians began to play, he set the voluptuous Nanni on his bare back and enthusiastically joined the townsfolk in a dance. The festivities were interrupted, however, by the concessionaire and the village police, who had been called by Nanni's fiancé. Genelli explained to the centaur that these men were hunters who wanted to lock him in a stall to reflect on the benefits of the law and the progress of civilization. The creature jumped over the heads of the crowd, Nanni still on his back, and ran away. High on a mountainside he released the girl to return to her fiancé and jumped into a gorge, never to be seen again.

The story implies that Genelli and his artist friends cannot be at home in the bourgeois Catholic society of nineteenth-century Bavaria, since their ideals and appetites are those of classical antiquity. Genelli has accepted ostracism as the price of his creativity.

In an age that paralleled the Victorian era in England, Heyse was considered by many a dangerously immoral writer, a reputation that contributed to his immense popularity during his lifetime. Most of Heyse's novellas either portray Italy – or young Italian women – as an idealized model of natural beauty or depict the psychological problems of characters living in nineteenth-century Germany. Heyse tended to portray exceptional cases rather than timeless human conflicts and problems; nevertheless, some of his novellas still make for diverting reading because of their cosmopolitan style and exotic subject matter, especially those set in pre-nineteenth-century Italy or France such as "Die Stickerin von Treviso"; "Andrea Delfin" (1862; translated, 1864), a story of failed revenge in eighteenth-century Venice; and "Geoffroy und Garcinde" (1871), a troubadour novella dealing with conflict between filial piety and personal happiness in medieval Provence. Of those set in Germany, "Der letzte Centaur" offers a contrast of nineteenth-century Bavaria with the naturalness of classical antiquity.

Heyse coedited two important collections of German novellas, the twenty-four-volume *Deutscher Novellenschatz* (Treasury of German Novellas, 1871–1876) and *Neuer deutscher Novellenschatz* (New Treasury of German Novellas, 1884–1887), likewise in twenty-four volumes. He also edited an anthology of works of modern Italian poets, *Antologia dei moderni poeti italiani* (1869); the fourteen-volume *Novellenschatz des Auslandes* (Treasury of Foreign Novellas, 1872–1875); and the six-volume *Italienische Novellisten* (Italian Short-Story Writers, 1877–1878). He edited and translated two collections of Italian

ture grabbed two bottles of wine from the pretty waitress Nanni, drank the contents, and asked Genelli – in Greek, of course – where he was. He explained that he had been making his rounds as a country doctor to shepherds and bear hunters, had become intoxicated from the homemade concoctions with which they paid for his services, and had gone into an ice grotto to sleep it off. When he awakened, he had found the forests thinner, the wine more sour, and the women (except for Nanni) less graceful and shapely than before. On the outskirts of the village he had been moved by the sight of a crucifix and had offered to help the man on the cross. Attracted by the sounds emanating from a church, he had been struck by the beauty of a statue of a blue-eyed, blond Virgin Mary. The village priest had dissuaded the curious villagers from associating with the creature, who surely had never been baptized and was probably immoral; only Genelli was friendly to the centaur.

Genelli, the centaur, and Nanni left the inn together. At a church carnival the centaur partook of more Tirolean wine and stole customers from the concession where a two-headed calf was on display.

Heyse in 1910

poetry: *Italienisches Liederbuch* (Book of Italian Songs, 1860) and *Italienische Dichter seit der Mitte des 18. Jahrhunderts: Übersetzungen und Studien* (Italian Poets since the Middle of the Eighteenth Century: Translations and Studies, 1889–1905), as well as selected works of Giuseppe Guisti (1875) and Giacomo Leopardi (1878). He also translated William Shakespeare's *Antony and Cleopatra* (1867) and *Timon of Athens* (1868) and a collection of comedies by Ludovico Ariosto, Niccolò Machiavelli, and Lorenzo de Medici (1914).

Heyse's statements on the German novella in his introduction to *Deutscher Novellenschatz* were embraced by his and later generations as one of the most important theories of the genre. Each of the stories in the collection, Heyse maintained, possesses a "Grundmotif" (basic motif) that can be summarized in a few lines. He compares the basic motif to a "starke Silhouette" (strong silhouette) in painting and cites as an example the story from

Giovanni Boccaccio's *Decamerone* (1351–1353) of the impoverished nobleman who prepares his prized falcon as a meal for his lady. Heyse suggests that a storyteller ask himself at the outset "wo 'der Falke' sei, das Spezifische, das diese Geschichte von tausend anderen unterscheidet" (where "the falcon" is, the specific thing that distinguishes this story from a thousand others). Heyse's idea soon became known as the "falcon theory," a designation he himself eventually adopted. Many scholars have misinterpreted the demand for a "falcon" as a requirement that every "true" novella contain a symbol, a requirement that Heyse never mentions in his comments on the novella.

As the novel became the dominant form of fiction in Germany, Heyse turned to the genre. Between 1873 and 1906 he produced seven novels. The best known are *Kinder der Welt* (1873; translated as *Children of the World,* 1882) and *Im Paradiese* (1875; translated as *In Paradise,* 1878). Although both were best-sellers, Heyse never attained the level of technical skill in the novel that he had in the more concentrated form of the novella.

Kinder der Welt deals with artists and academics in Berlin during the forming of the Second German Empire. Heyse divides the characters into the children of God and the children of the world. The former group includes the artist König; his daughter, the young artist Lea; and the theology student Lorinser. The children of the world are the young philosopher and freethinker Edwin; his sickly brother Balder; Toinette Marchand, the mistress of a count; the music teacher Christiane Falk; and the poet Heinrich Mohr. Edwin is attracted to Toinette, who marries the count although she does not love him. After Balder's death Edwin suffers from a severe fever and is consoled by reading the diary of his former pupil Lea, which was entrusted to him by her father, König. He falls in love with her. They get married and move to a city in Thuringia, where he works as a mathematics teacher. Several years later Edwin visits his friend Mohr and learns that Toinette has become estranged from her husband after bearing him a child and that she is mentally ill. At Mohr's urging, Edwin visits Toinette and tries to help her. She declares her love for him, but now it is he who cannot return her affection because he loves Lea. Soon thereafter Toinette dies as a result of a fall from a horse. A few years later Edwin, who is now a contented husband and father, takes his family back to Berlin, where he visits his old haunts and the friends of his youth.

Both *Kinder der Welt* and *Im Paradiese,* which deals with the artists' world in Munich, aroused controversy for advocating free love. In Heyse's conception of love and marriage, which owes much to German romanticism, a relationship derives its sanctity not from the external bonds of marriage but from a balance of physical and spiritual attraction. Even so, Edwin marries and remains faithful to Lea, and the lovers in *Im Paradiese* feel required to have their union sanctified by church and state once they have children.

Beginning with *Die Weisheit Salomo's* (The Wisdom of Solomon, 1887), Heyse wrote several plays based on biblical themes. *Maria von Magdala* (1899; translated as *Mary of Magdala,* 1900), which was later adapted by Maurice Maeterlinck, provoked scandals both in Germany and in New York for its portrayal of Judas as a Hebrew patriot, disillusioned follower of Jesus, and lover of Mary Magdalene. Next to "L'Arrabbiata," it appears to be the work of Heyse most frequently translated into En-

glish. Its banning by the Prussian censors in 1903 created so much interest in the play that it went through twenty-eight editions in that year alone.

Heyse's works seldom deviate from the theme of the exceptional individual in conflict with the forces of society. He has been placed among such representatives of the Gründerzeit (the years of reckless financial speculation following the Franco-Prussian War) as Conrad Ferdinand Meyer, Friedrich Nietzsche, and the mature Storm, portrayers of larger-than-life figures who live according to their own rules. During the 1880s and 1890s Heyse was the object of severe personal attacks from critics who considered his works immoral and from the naturalists, for whom his oeuvre represented everything that was artificial and untrue in the works of the older generation. Heyse responded with the novel *Merlin* (1892), about an idealistic young dramatist who stages his last play in an insane asylum and then commits suicide.

Heyse never hesitated to take a stand against any form of censorship or prejudice. On his eightieth birthday he was elevated to the nobility, was made an honorary citizen of Munich, and had a street in the city named after him. The same year he was awarded the Nobel Prize for Literature, the first German literary author to be so honored. (The first German to receive the Nobel Prize for Literature was the historian Theodor Mommsen in 1902, followed in 1908 by the philosopher Rudolf Eucken.) Heyse died on 2 April 1914 and was buried, with no religious ceremony, in the Waldfriedhof Cemetery in Munich.

Letters:

"Paul Heyse und Heinrich Leuthold: Aus unveröffentlichten Briefen Heyses," edited by Georg J. Plotke, *Das Literarische Echo,* 16 (1 May 1914): columns 1034–1036;

"Briefe von Paul Heyse und seinen Angehörigen an die Hahnsche Buchhandlung, Hannover," edited by G. Schmidt, *Börsenblatt für den Deutschen Buchhandel,* 81 (1914): 793–797;

Der Briefwechsel von Jakob Burckhardt und Paul Heyse, edited by Erich Petzet (Munich: Lehmann, 1916);

Der Briefwechsel zwischen Paul Heyse und Theodor Storm, 2 volumes, edited by Plotke (Munich: Lehmann, 1917–1918);

Paul Heyse und Gottfried Keller im Briefwechsel, edited by Max Kalbeck (Braunschweig: Westermann, 1919);

"Aus dem Briefwechsel zwischen Paul Heyse und Hermann Kurz," edited by Hugo Falkenheim,

Der schwäbische Bund, 1 (November 1919): 218–229; (December 1919): 346–352;

"Der Briefwechsel von Paul Heyse und Fanny Lewald," edited by Rudolf Göhler, *Deutsche Rundschau,* 183 (May 1920): 274–285; (June 1920): 410–441;

Der Briefwechsel von Emanuel Geibel und Paul Heyse, edited by Petzet (Munich: Lehmann, 1922);

"Freundesbriefe an Richard Voß," edited by Paul Weiglin, *Velhagen & Klasings Monatshefte,* 38 (September 1923): 89–94;

"Briefe von Paul Heyse an Otto und Emma Ribbeck," edited by Petzet, *Euphorion,* 27 (1926): 424–462;

"Aus dem Briefwechsel Paul Heyse – Ernst Wichert, 1900–1902," edited by Paul Wichert, *Deutsche Rundschau,* 207 (April / June 1926): 35–44;

Der Briefwechsel von Theodor Fontane und Paul Heyse, 1850–1897, edited by Petzet (Berlin: Weltgeist-Bücher Verlags-Gesellschaft, 1929);

"Der Briefwechsel zwischen Albert Dulk und Paul Heyse," edited by Ernst Rose, *Germanic Review,* 4 (January 1929): 1–32; (April 1929): 131–152;

Briefwechsel zwischen Joseph Victor von Scheffel und Paul Heyse, edited by Conrad Höfer (Karlsruhe: Gräff, 1932);

"Briefwechsel von Paul Heyse und Marie von Ebner-Eschenbach," in *Die Lebens- und Weltanschauung der Freifrau Marie von EbnerEschenbach,* by Mechtild Alkemade, Deutsche Quellen und Studien, volume 15 (Würzburg & Graz: Wächter, 1935), pp. 257–398;

"Sieben Briefe von Paul Heyse an Feodor Löwe, 1859–1862," edited by Claire Strube Schradieck, *PMLA,* 52 (March 1937): 261–271;

Monika Walkhoff, *Der Briefwechsel zwischen Paul Heyse und Hermann Kurz in den Jahren 1869–1873 aus Anlaß der Herausgabe des "Deutschen Novellenschatzes"* (Munich: Foto-Druck Frank, 1967);

Theodor Storm – Paul Heyse: Briefwechsel. Kritische Ausgabe, 3 volumes, edited by Clifford Albrecht Bernd (Berlin: Schmidt, 1969–1974);

Der Briefwechsel zwischen Theodor Fontane und Paul Heyse, edited by Gotthard Erler (Berlin & Weimar: Aufbau, 1972);

"Emilie Fontane und Paul Heyse: Brief um Fontane," edited by Joachim Krueger, *Fontane Blätter,* 5, no. 3 (1983): 280–286;

"Du hast alles, was mir fehlt . . . ": Gottfried Keller im Briefwechsel mit Paul Heyse, edited by Fridolin Stähli (Stafa: Gut, 1990).

Bibliographies:

Charles H. Helmetag, "Paul Heyse-Bibliographie (Sekundärliteratur)," *Börsenblatt für den Deutschen Buchhandel,* 25 (14 October 1969): 2557–2564;

Werner Martin, *Paul Heyse: Eine Bibliographie seiner Werke* (Hildesheim: Olms, 1978);

Helmetag, "Paul Heyse-Bibliographie: Sekundärliteratur 1968–1978," *Börsenblatt für den Deutschen Buchhandel,* 26 (28 March 1980): A116–A120.

Biographies:

Helene Raff, *Paul Heyse* (Stuttgart: Cotta, 1910);

Michail Krausnick, *Paul Heyse und der Münchner Dichterkreis* (Bonn: Bouvier, 1974).

References:

E. K. Bennett, "The Novelle as a Literary Genre," and "The Psychological Novelle" in his *A History of the German Novelle,* revised and continued by H. M. Waidson (Cambridge: Cambridge University Press, 1961), pp. 1–19, 206–240;

Clifford Albrecht Bernd, "Paul Heyse, 1910" in *The Nobel Prize Winners: Literature,* volume 1, edited by Frank N. Magill (Pasadena, Cal.: Salem Press, 1987), pp. 145–155;

Genevieve Bianquis, "The Life and Works of Paul Heyse," in *Nobel Prize Library: André Gide, Karl Gjellerup, Paul Heyse* (New York: Gregory / Del Mar, Cal.: CRM Publishing, 1971), pp. 347–353;

Georg Brandes, "Paul Heyse," in his *Creative Spirits of the Nineteenth Century,* translated by Rasmus R. Anderson (New York: Crowell, 1923), pp. 54–105;

Gerhard Friedrich, "Theodor Fontanes Kritik an Paul Heyse und seinen Dramen," in *Fontane aus heutiger Sicht,* edited by Hugo Aust (Munich: Nymphenburger, 1980), pp. 81–117;

Hans Norbert Fügen, "Geibel und Heyse: Elemente und Strukturen des literarischen Systems im 19. Jahrhundert. Dokumentation und Analyse," in his *Dichtung in der bürgerlichen Gesellschaft: Sechs literatursoziologische Studien* (Bonn: Bouvier, 1972), pp. 28–50;

Véronique de la Giroday, *Die Übersetzertätigkeit des Münchner Dichterkreises* (Wiesbaden: Athenaion, 1978);

Friedrich Hammer, "Die Idee der Persönlichkeit bei Paul Heyse," Ph.D. dissertation, University of Tübingen, 1935;

Charles Hugh Helmetag, "Love and the Social Morality in the Novellen of Paul Heyse," Ph.D. dissertation, Princeton University, 1968;

Jost Hermand, "Zur Literatur der Gründerzeit" and "Hauke Haien: Kritik oder Ideal des gründerzeitlichen Übermenschen?," in *Von Mainz nach Weimar (1937–1919): Studien zur deutschen Literatur* (Stuttgart: Metzler, 1969), pp. 211–249, 250–268;

Annemarie von Ian, "Die zeitgenössische Kritik an Paul Heyse 1850–1914," Ph.D. dissertation, University of Munich, 1965;

Donald LoCicero, "Paul Heyse: 'Falkentheorie,' " in his *Novellentheorie: The Practicality of the Theoretical* (The Hague: Mouton, 1970), pp. 66–83;

Warren R. Maurer, *The Naturalist Image of German Literature* (Munich: Fink, 1972);

J. A. Michielsen, "Paul Heyse and Three of His Critics: Theodor Fontane, Gottfried Keller and Theodor Storm," Ph.D. dissertation, University of Toronto, 1970;

Robert McBurney Mitchell, *Heyse and His Predecessors in the Theory of the Novelle* (Frankfurt am Main: Baer, 1915);

Sigrid von Moisy, ed., *Paul Heyse, Münchner Dichterfürst im bürgerlichen Zeitalter: Ausstellung in der Bayerischen Staatsbibliothek, 23. Januar bis 11. April 1981* (Munich: Beck, 1981);

Kenneth Negus, "Paul Heyse's *Novellentheorie*: A Revaluation," *Germanic Review,* 40 (May 1965), 173–191;

Brigitte Schader, "Paul Heyse: 'Unheilbar,' " in her *Schwindsucht – Zur Darstellung einer tödlichen Krankheit in der deutschen Literatur vom poetischen Realismus bis zur Moderne* (Frankfurt am Main & Bern: Lang, 1987), pp. 8–45;

Manfred Schunicht, "Der 'Falke' am 'Wendepunkt': Zu den Novellentheorien Tiecks und Heyses," *Germanisch-romanische Monatsschrift,* new series 10 (1960): 44–56;

Margaret G. Sleeman, "Variations on Spanish Themes: The *Spanisches Liederbuch* of Emanuel Geibel and Paul Heyse and Its Reflection in the Songs of Hugo Wolf," *Proceedings of the Leeds Philosophical and Literary Society,* 18, part 2 (1982): 159–274;

Martin Swales, *The German Novelle* (Princeton: Princeton University Press, 1977);

Christiane Ullmann, "Form and Content of Paul Heyse's Novelle *Andrea Delfin,*" *Seminar,* 12 (May 1976): 109–120;

Roland A. Wolff, "Der *Falke* am *Wendepunkt* Revisited: Some Thoughts on Schunicht's Theory and on the German *Novelle* in General," *New German Studies,* 5 (1977): 157–168.

Papers:

The Heyse Archive of the Bayerische Staatsbibliothek (Bavarian State Library) includes unpublished early works and fragments, letters, diaries, newspaper reviews, school and university records, works of German and Italian literature from Heyse's personal library, and a considerable amount of material on his dramas. The Schiller National Museum in Marbach has an extensive collection of letters, poems, drama manuscripts, and other materials.

Gottfried Keller

(19 July 1819 – 15 July 1890)

Gail K. Hart
University of California, Irvine

BOOKS: *Gedichte* (Heidelberg: Winter, 1846);
Neuere Gedichte (Brunswick: Vieweg, 1851; enlarged, 1854);
Der grüne Heinrich: Roman, 4 volumes (Brunswick: Vieweg, 1854–1855; revised edition, Stuttgart: Göschen, 1879–1880); translated by A. M. Holt as *Green Henry* (London: Calder, 1960; New York: Grove, 1960);
Die Leute von Seldwyla: Erzählungen (Brunswick: Vieweg, 1856) – comprises "Pankraz, der Schmoller," "Frau Regel Amrain und ihr Jüngster," "Romeo und Julia auf dem Dorfe," "Die drei gerechten Kammacher," "Spiegel, das Kätzchen"; enlarged edition, 2 volumes (Stuttgart: Göschen, 1874) – volume 2 comprises "Kleider machen Leute," "Der Schmied seines Glückes," "Die mißbrauchten Liebesbriefe," "Dietegen," "Das verlorene Lachen"; excerpts translated by Wolf von Schierbrand as *Seldwyla Folks: Three Singular Tales by the Swiss Poet Gottfried Keller* (New York: Brentano's, 1919) – comprises "Three Decent Combmakers," "Dietegen," "Romeo and Juliet of the Village";
Sieben Legenden (Stuttgart: Göschen, 1872); translated by Martin Wyness as *Seven Legends* (London & Glasgow: Gowans & Gray, 1911);
Züricher Novellen, 2 volumes (Stuttgart: Göschen, 1878);
Das Sinngedicht: Novellen (Berlin: Hertz, 1882 [i.e., 1881]);
Gesammelte Gedichte (Berlin: Hertz, 1883);
Martin Salander: Roman (Berlin: Hertz, 1886); translated by Kenneth Halwas as *Martin Salander* (London: Calder, 1964);
Gesammelte Werke, 10 volumes (Berlin: Hertz, 1889);
Sämtliche Werke, 22 volumes, edited by Jonas Fränkel and Carl Helbling (Bern & Leipzig: Benteli, 1926–1949);
Sämtliche Werke und ausgewählte Briefe, 4 volumes, edited by Clemens Heselhaus, fourth edition (Munich: Hanser, 1978–1979);

Gottfried Keller in 1886 (photograph by Karl Stauffer-Bern)

Sämtliche Werke, 6 volumes, edited by Thomas Böning, Gerhard Kaiser, and Dominik Müller (Frankfurt am Main: Deutscher Klassiker Verlag, 1985–1990);
Die Jugenddramen, edited by Laurence A. Rickels (Zurich: Ammann, 1990).

Editions in English: *Legends of Long Ago* ("Sieben Legenden"), translated by Charles Hart Handschin (Chicago: Abbey, 1911; reprinted, Freeport, N.Y.: Books for Libraries Press, 1971);

"The Governor of Greifensee," translated by Paul Bernard Thomas; "The Company of the Upright Seven," "Ursula," translated by Bayard Quincy Morgan, in *The German Classics of the Nineteenth and Twentieth Centuries,* volume 14, edited by Kuno Francke and William Guild Howard (New York: German Publication Society, 1914), pp. 96–319;

The People of Seldwyla and Seven Legends, translated by M. D. Hottinger (London & Toronto: Dent / New York: Dutton, 1929) – comprises "The People of Seldwyla: 'Spiegel the Cat,' 'A Village Romeo and Juliet,' 'The Three Righteous Combmakers,' 'Clothes Make the Man'; Seven Legends: 'Eugenia,' 'The Virgin and the Devil,' 'The Virgin as Knight,' 'The Virgin as Nun,' 'Vitalis, the Holy Rogue,' 'Dorothea's Rose-Basket,' 'A Little Legend of the Dance' ";

The Misused Love Letters, translated by Michael Bullock, and Regula Amrain and Her Youngest Son, translated by Anne Fremantle: Two Novellas (New York: Ungar, 1974);

Gottfried Keller: Stories, edited by Frank Ryder (New York: Continuum, 1982).

Gottfried Keller – poet, critic, and Switzerland's most prominent writer of fiction – aspired initially to be a landscape painter; it was only after his reluctant and costly determination that he lacked the talent to support himself as such that he began to produce the moderately successful poems and the great novels and novellas that have established him as one of the major figures of German "poetic realism," as the dominant style of the period from approximately 1850 to 1880 is known. Though his subject matter was wide-ranging, he consistently focused on themes of individual development, paying close attention to the role of childhood experience in the formation of character. As Heinrich Lee, the hero of Keller's autobiographical novel *Der grüne Heinrich* (1854–1855; revised, 1879–1880; translated as *Green Henry,* 1960), explains: "Wenn ich nicht überzeugt wäre, daß die Kindheit schon ein Vorspiel des ganzen Lebens ist und . . . schon die Hauptzüge der menschlichen Zerwürfnisse im Kleinen abspiegele . . . so würde ich mich nicht so weitläufig mit den kleinen Dingen jener Zeit beschäftigen" (If I were not convinced that childhood is a foretaste of the rest of life and . . . that it reflects the main characteristics of human struggle in miniature . . . I would not occupy myself to such an

extent with the minor matters of childhood). This conviction, as well as a tendency to represent the movements of the unconscious mind in symbols and images strikingly similar to those recognized by psychoanalysis, endeared Keller's neurotic prose to Sigmund Freud, who cites him twice in *Die Traumdeutung* (1900; translated as *The Interpretation of Dreams,* 1913), and to psychoanalytic critics.

Another conspicuous aspect of Keller's output is its educational mission. Keller, who regularly affirmed his morally or socially didactic intentions in letters and essays, wrote mainly of errant souls and dreamers who blunder into situations that force a confrontation with a reality that contradicts their desires. Those who are enlightened by such confrontations tend to prosper, whereas those who persist in erring or dreaming suffer some sort of punishment. Poetic justice generally prevails, and the recommendation is that the reader avoid lingering in a subjectively or selfishly defined world of dreams and emerge as an active member of the family or social community. Thus, Keller's thematics fit the general pattern of nineteenth-century realism, which pits individual fantasy against an overwhelming "objective reality" that negates it; but Keller's texts tend to undercut this process with ironic humor. A lingering regret at the loss of the dream or of the dreamer colors the apparently conventional conclusion of most of Keller's prose works and reflects the author's own experience as a man caught between self-involvement and social responsibility. Unfortunately, Keller's irony does not always survive translation, and this circumstance may account for the relative obscurity of this important author in the English-speaking world.

Keller was born on 19 July 1819 in Zurich to Elisabeth Scheuchzer Keller, a pious woman from Glattfelden with a sharp mind and conservative values, and Rudolf Keller, a master lathe turner. Rudolf, also from Glattfelden, was a farmer's son, but he was, by Glattfelden standards, well traveled and cosmopolitan in his tastes. As a journeyman he had lived for four years in Vienna, and he spoke High German rather than Swiss dialect. He was an astute businessman who devoted long hours to community service, an ardent supporter of public education who favored national unity over cantonal sovereignty, and a relatively cultured man who wrote poetry and organized amateur theatrical presentations in his spare time. Always overextended and often working himself to exhaustion, he died in 1824, leaving Elisabeth with Gottfried and a daughter, Regula, who was two. The only one of Keller's

Keller, age eighteen; sketch by Johann Müller (Zurich Central Library)

five siblings to survive early childhood, Regula would live her entire life in the shadow of her brother, working as a seamstress and later as a salesclerk to replenish family funds spent on his prolonged professional training; after the death of Elisabeth in 1864 Regula would keep house for her brother. Neither Gottfried nor Regula ever married.

Keller always felt that the early death of his father deprived him of a role model who might have taught him steadfast devotion to duty and helped him make more rational career choices. Though his mother's second marriage, to a journeyman worker named Hans Heinrich Wild, lasted from 1826 to 1834, Keller only once mentions his stepfather in his writings and then as "ein fremder Mann, der bei uns wohnt" (a strange man who lives in our house). His intense possessiveness of his mother, who, like Regula, devoted her life and savings to him, seems to have resulted in the absolute effacement of the challenger. Nowhere in Keller's largely autobiographical fiction does a stepfather occur, though "Frau Regel Amrain und ihr Jüngster" (1856; translated as

"Regula Amrain and Her Youngest Son," 1951) contains a scene in which the heroine, deserted by her husband, must fend off the advances of the foreman of the family stone quarry; at the moment she considers yielding, her youngest son, Fritz, emerges from the bedroom armed with a curtain rod, calls the intruder a thief, clobbers him with the rod, and repossesses his mother. She resolves to devote all her energies to raising this son, choosing him over his colorless brothers, who slept through the attack, because of his resemblance to his father. Keller extracted similar loyalty from his mother after her divorce.

The other major setback of Keller's childhood occurred in 1834, when he was permanently expelled from the cantonal trade school. Keller, who already had been disciplined for lack of concentration in class – when asked to name the capital of Italy he had answered, "camera obscura" – was singled out for punishment for his role in a student demonstration against an unpopular teacher. Since his family did not possess the means to send him to private or boarding school, his formal education was at an end for the time being. Keller never recovered from the insult and the exclusion. In *Der grüne Heinrich,* where the hero suffers the same fate, Keller uses the word *köpfen* (decapitate) to describe the effect on Heinrich's spiritual development.

After his expulsion Keller began the serious study of painting, repairing to rural Glattfelden to sketch the natural scenery. Through the efforts of his mother he was eventually apprenticed to the lithographer Peter Steiger in Zurich. Steiger, who emphasized rapid reproduction over sound composition and refinement, failed to impart the basic principles of landscape art to his pupil, and in 1838 Elisabeth Keller engaged the talented but mentally unbalanced artist Rudolf Meyer to tutor her son. Meyer was an effective teacher who expanded Keller's horizons in many directions; but he soon succumbed to paranoid delusions, and the relationship ended bitterly when Keller and his mother demanded a refund. Steiger and Meyer have their fictional counterparts in *Der grüne Heinrich* in Meister Habersaat and Römer, respectively.

In 1840, after demanding and obtaining a large part of the money that had been held in trust for him from his grandfather's estate, Keller enrolled at the great art academy in Munich. Though the stay in a large urban center with a thriving artistic and literary culture augmented the young man's store of experience, he was unable to lay the foundations of a painting career – largely because of a strong inclination to drink and socialize. Like many students who find themselves on their own for the first time in a big city, Keller spent beyond his means and neglected his training. His letters to his mother from this period, each containing a request for more money, recount the factors that impeded his study: from a four-week bout with typhus to the need to get out and enjoy himself (lest his spirit become impoverished) to lack of funds for proper food, shelter, and artistic supplies – a problem that resulted in part from a decision to eat in better restaurants (for the sake of his health). The German word *Schuld* means both monetary debt and personal guilt, and it sums up the legacy of Keller's Munich years: he incurred vast debts and drained his family's finances while refusing to take available work as a colorist, causing his mother great worry and sorrow. That Keller recognized the extent of his callousness is suggested by the ending of the first version of *Der grüne Heinrich*: the hero returns to Switzerland after spending several years in a German urban art center at great cost to his overindulgent mother, whom he has, as it turns out, literally worried to death. Heinrich arrives as his mother's funeral is in progress, and his guilt over her death

and his failure is so great that he himself dies a short time afterward.

Frau Keller was alive when her dejected son returned in November 1842. He spent the winter in the kitchen reading, sulking, and writing. While in Munich, Keller had had brief articles and essays published in a local newspaper for Swiss residents; in Zurich he continued writing poems and occasional pieces, ultimately coming to the conclusion that he could express himself "rascher und bequemer" (more quickly and easily) in words than in pictorial images.

Having made his choice, Keller, inspired by the revolutionary ferment in post-Restoration Europe and by the large group of illustrious political refugees who had come to live in liberal Zurich, began writing political poetry as well as occasional and nature poems. One of the refugees, A. A. L. Follen, published a selection of Keller's poems in two issues of his *Deutsches Taschenbuch* (German Notebook) in 1845 and 1846 under the heading "Lieder eines Autodidakten" (Songs of an Autodidact) to the resounding approval of critics and readers. Keller was greeted as "das bedeutendste lyrische Talent, das in der Schweiz laut geworden" (the most important poetic talent to be heard from in Switzerland). The enthusiastic reception led to the publication of a volume of his poetry, *Gedichte* (Poems), in Heidelberg in 1846. A second volume, *Neuere Gedichte* (Recent Poems), appeared in Brunswick in 1851, and an enlarged edition of that collection came out in 1854.

Keller's poetry encompasses a broad range of themes, from brief reflections on love, patriotism, lost youth, and nature to extended narrative poetry such as the parody of Heinrich Heine, "Der Apotheker von Chamounix" (The Pharmacist of Chamonix) and the long poem "Gedanken eines Lebendig-Begrabenen" (Thoughts of One Buried Alive), which realistically records the thoughts of a man who finds himself in this situation. Though formally flawed, Keller's poems are appreciated for their immediacy of expression and the humor and irony with which he often treats his subject matter. One further volume, *Gesammelte Gedichte* (Collected Poems, 1883), appeared during Keller's lifetime, and many other poems from his personal papers have been published in critical editions since his death.

In Zurich, Keller experienced the first of a series of demoralizing rejections by women. By most standards unattractive – gruff, diminutive, and oddly proportioned – he was awkward and resentful toward the women he loved, almost as if he mis-

Keller in Munich; drawing by Johann Salomon Hegi (Zurich Central Library)

trusted or feared them for the influence they exerted on his feelings. He repeatedly chose tall, beautiful women, and they consistently rebuffed this small, impecunious, and unpleasant suitor. The first documented case is that of Luise Rieter, to whom Keller confessed his love in a letter of 16 October 1847: "Ich bin noch gar nichts und muß erst werden, was ich werden will, und bin dazu ein unansehnlicher armer Bursche, also habe ich keine Berechtigung, mein Herz einer so schönen und ausgezeichneten jungen Dame anzutragen, wie Sie sind, aber wenn ich einst denken müßte, daß Sie mir doch ernstlich gut gewesen wären und ich hätte nichts gesagt, so wäre das ein sehr großes Unglück für mich, und ich könnte es nicht wohl ertragen. . . . Wollen Sie so gütig sein und mir mit zwei Worten sagen, ob Sie mir gut sind oder nicht?" (I am as yet nothing at all and still have to become what I wish to become, and besides that I am a poor unattractive lad and therefore I have no right to offer my heart to such a beautiful and distinguished young lady, but if I had to think someday that you really had liked me and that I

had said nothing, that would be a very great misfortune for me and I would not be able to bear it. . . . Would you please be so kind and tell me plainly whether you love me or not?). She did not, nor did Johanna Kapp in 1849 or Betty Tendering in 1855. Finally, in 1866 Keller became engaged to a much younger woman, the twenty-three-year-old Luise Scheidegger; but Scheidegger, depressed by tales of his drinking escapades, drowned herself in July of that year to avoid marrying him. As far as can be determined, he never again proposed to a woman.

In 1848 several Zurich politicians who had taken an interest in Keller's poetry awarded him a scholarship to help him acquire a university education. Keller chose the University of Heidelberg and left Zurich in October. In Heidelberg, Keller attended the lectures of the atheist philosopher Ludwig Feuerbach, an experience that permanently altered his worldview. In *Das Wesen des Christentums* (The Essence of Christianity, 1841) Feuerbach sought to expose the Christian God as a mere projection of the virtues and talents of

Keller in 1854; pastel drawing by Ludmilla Assing (Zurich Central Library)

human beings: "Die Religion zieht die Kräfte, Eigenschaften, Wesensbestimmungen des Menschen vom Menschen ab und vergöttert sie als selbstständiges Wesen" (Religion draws the strengths, qualities, and essential determinations of man away from mankind and deifies them as an independent being). Thus, in worshiping their own good qualities, abstracted and reconstituted as God, men and women failed to recognize the value of humanity; and in their yearning for heaven and immortality – a second, superior "reality" beyond experience – they devalued their own finite lives. Feuerbach, best known today for the observation "Der Mensch ist, was er ißt" (You are what you eat), preached a doctrine of "Diesseitigkeit" (this-worldliness), exhorting his listeners and readers to find fulfillment in the material world and to abandon the distractions of preparing for an imagined eternity. Over the course of the Heidelberg lectures Keller enjoyed frequent personal contact with Feuerbach and grew ever more convinced of the truth of the philosopher's message, though he rarely dis-

played the quasi-religious zeal with which Feuerbach proclaimed the new materialism.

Keller left Heidelberg in 1850 for Berlin, where he hoped to establish himself as a tragedian. Though he never completed a drama that was worthy of being published or produced, his five years in Berlin, during which he produced *Der grüne Heinrich,* the first volume of *Die Leute von Seldwyla* (1856; excerpts translated as *Seldwyla Folks,* 1919), and many sketches for later novellas, were the most fruitful of his career.

Der grüne Heinrich, which is regarded as one of the most important works in the genre of the bildungsromane after Johann Wolfgang von Goethe's *Wilhelm Meisters Lehrjahre* (1795–1796; translated as *Wilhelm Meister's Apprenticeship,* 1824), begins as the twenty-year-old Heinrich Lee, described as an ungrateful child, leaves Switzerland for Germany and the art academy. The "green" of the title derives from Heinrich's green coat and refers to the hero's youth and inexperience as well as to hope for the future. Heinrich has written a lengthy account of his youth, "Eine Jugendgeschichte," and the third-person narrator of the novel's first four chapters suggests that "wir" (we) read it while Heinrich is getting settled in Germany. The first-person account follows the adventures of the child Heinrich, who enlivens mundane events with flourishes of fantasy while resisting assimilation into the social order that threatens to overwhelm him. When he cannot grasp the spiritual nature of God as described by his mother, Heinrich selects the weathercock on top of the church steeple and later a drawing of a tiger from one of his picture books to serve as the material objects of his worship: "Es waren ganz innerliche Anschauungen und nur wenn der Name Gottes genannt wurde, so schwebte mir erst der glänzende Vogel und nachher der schöne Tiger vor" (These were entirely subjective perceptions and when someone spoke the name of God, first the image of the shimmering bird came to me and later that of the beautiful tiger). His habit of appropriating and personalizing elements of the external order persists and has a dual and contradictory purpose in the novel as a regrettable retardant of his socialization and as a compelling demonstration of his imagination.

A later incident allows Heinrich actually to shape objective events. When caught uttering profanities, he spontaneously invents a tale of four older boys, whom he names, luring him into the forest and forcing him to use foul language. This testimony results in severe punishment of the alleged offenders and in great satisfaction for

Heinrich: "ich fühlte . . . eine Befriedigung in mir, daß die poetische Gerechtigkeit meine Erfindung so schön und sichtbarlich abrundete, daß etwas auffallendes geschah, gehandelt und gelitten wurde und das infolge meines schöpferischen Wortes" (I felt . . . great satisfaction that poetic justice had completed my invention so palpably and so well, that something remarkable had happened and that suffering had occurred and that it was all a consequence of my creative words). Heinrich's participation in the schoolboys' heckling of their least favorite teacher (a close parallel to Keller's own experience, as are many of the events in "Eine Jugendgeschichte") does not turn out as he might have wished: he is reprimanded and expelled from school by a teachers' committee.

As Heinrich matures, his dualistic worldview finds corroboration in his two loves, the fragile and ethereal Anna and the wise, frank, and earthy Judith, who appeal, respectively, to his soul and his body. When the delicate Anna dies of consumption, Heinrich, like Feuerbach's Christian, swears eternal allegiance to the departed and lives in anticipation of joining her after death. When he rejects Judith on the grounds that he cannot have a harem in eternity, she asks slyly whether he is sure that there is such a thing as eternity. "Eine Jugendgeschichte," which is the heart of the novel, ends as Heinrich and Judith separate, and the third-person narrator returns to chronicle Heinrich's failure as a painter, his subsequent reflections on vocation and the purpose of life, and his conversion to atheism shortly before his departure from Germany. While making his way home Heinrich encounters a liberal-minded count and his adopted daughter, Dortchen Schönfund, both of whom are disciples of Feuerbach and patrons of the arts. With their help and encouragement he produces and exhibits paintings and earns money that is augmented by an unexpected inheritance. Heinrich returns too late to benefit his long-suffering mother. Having botched his personal life, despairing of becoming an asset to his community through public service, and knowing he cannot encounter his mother in an afterlife, Heinrich dies. His corpse is found clutching a slip of paper on which Dortchen had written a poem about hope. Beautiful green grass grows on his grave.

Keller's first novel was well received by contemporary critics and writers; they enjoyed the many ancillary narratives, such as the child who could not pray and the family of readers, that punctuate Heinrich's life story, though most complained that Heinrich's death was unmotivated and incongruous. Keller initially defended his "tragic" conclusion as preferable to a tidy ending in which the hero finds love and marries; but he ultimately relented and in 1878 – after buying and burning all remaining copies of the original printing, which had not sold well – set about rewriting his great novel. The second version of *Der grüne Heinrich,* which was published in 1879–1880, is considered the standard version, and it is the one that has been translated into English. The second version has the author's endorsement as the definitive one, and it contains certain improvements in style and organization. Nonetheless, many critics believe that Keller traded the frank immediacy of the original language for a more polished and less expressive idiom. The second version of *Der grüne Heinrich* begins with the account of Heinrich's youth, in which Keller made few significant changes. The rest of the novel is also related in the first person by Heinrich. Significantly, Heinrich now returns just as his mother is dying – she is able to give her son a single "fragenden Blick" (questioning look) before expiring. In his deep despair over the death of his mother and his inability to rid his office of corruption – he has been managing the chancery of a small district near his hometown – Heinrich takes to a mountain path, where he casts to the winds the paper containing Dortchen's hope verses. At this moment Judith appears, having returned from America because she has heard that Heinrich is in trouble, and becomes his guide, his platonic friend, and his companion for life. It is her death many years later that inspires Heinrich to review the account of his youth and to record the further course of his life, "die alten grünen Pfade der Erinnerung zu wandeln" (to wander down the old green paths of memory).

While finishing the first version of *Der grüne Heinrich* Keller conceived a collection of novellas set against the backdrop of life in the fictional town of Seldwyla. *Die Leute von Seldwyla* describes Seldwyla as a pleasant sunny spot, home to a community of fun-loving, failure-prone fools. Seldwyla men all go bankrupt between the ages of thirty and thirty-six, and the major local "product" is Gemütlichkeit, an untranslatable German word that indicates good fellowship or conviviality. The first of the five novellas, "Pankraz, der Schmoller" (Pankraz, the Sulker), describes a lazy, bitter boy who deserts the widowed mother and the sister who supported him and travels the world learning to work and to adjust to "eine feste außer mir liegende Ordnung" (a fixed order external to me). He returns to relate his adventures to his mother and sister, but the women hear only the beginning and end of his tale: how he ran away and was ultimately socialized during a

Part of the desk blotter Keller used during the writing of Der grüne Heinrich *(Zurich Central Library)*

standoff with a man-eating lion. They mysteriously fall asleep during Pankraz's narration of the central experience of his life: the baffling encounter with Lydia, a beautiful woman who appeared to be kind, wise, and sincerely interested in him but was actually a crass and indifferent flirt who solicited a declaration of love for the sake of ego gratification. Pankraz neither solves nor comes to terms with "das Rätsel der Schönheit" (the mystery of beauty), but he does stop sulking and becomes a good son and brother.

"Romeo und Julia auf dem Dorfe" (translated as "Romeo and Juliet of the Village," 1919) is the most widely read and the most controversial of Keller's works. The narrator stresses that the adaptation of Shakespeare's theme to village life is the fictional reflection of a real occurrence — Keller had read of two young peasants who shot themselves because their feuding families refused to let them marry — and evidence that the great plots of fiction derive from human behavior rather than detached imaginings or literary borrowings. Sali and Vrenchen are the children of farmers whose dispute over property rights results in the ruin of both families. When they fall in love and can find no socially acceptable means of marrying, they spend a festive day together and drown themselves rather than separate when the day is over. The tale closes with a report of a newspaper article deploring their "gottverlassene" (godless) action. The fairy-tale romanticism of the lovers' idylls seems to enshrine them in the starry firmament of fantasy, but it coexists — eerily at times — with a realistic rendering of the families' debasement, an unappealing social portrait, and reminders of the grim finality of suicide. Such unresolved tensions, as well as the suicide and the richly symbolic character of the narrative, have made it unusually popular with scholars, who have produced more than fifty essays on "Romeo und Julia auf dem Dorfe." Most of these essays undertake to demonstrate that the suicide was inevitable, suggesting that critics are still uncomfortable with Keller's harsh conclusion.

"Frau Regel Amrain und ihr Jüngster" follows Fritz Amrain's exemplary upbringing, which culminates in Fritz's overcoming his errant father and ejecting him from the family business. "Die drei gerechten Kammacher" (The Three Righteous Combmakers; translated as "Three Decent Combmakers," 1919) is the humorous history of three ascetic journeyman combmakers who lead lives they consider to be beyond reproach, even though they hoard all their money and benefit no one. Each hopes to purchase the master's workshop when the latter predictably goes bankrupt, but they end grotesquely when forced to race each other for the privilege. The final tale, "Spiegel, das Kätzchen" (Mirror, the Cat; translated as "Spiegel the Cat," 1929), features a Faustian cat who strikes a bargain with the evil sorcerer Pineiß. Pineiß will give Spiegel a life of perfect ease and abundance, and in return the cat will deliver up his skin at the end of a specified period so that the sorcerer can use the attached fat in his spells. When the day of reckoning comes, Spiegel becomes Scheherezade and literally saves his skin by entangling the sorcerer in a lengthy tall tale. As a consequence of his gullibility, Pineiß blunders into marriage with a domineering witch, and Spiegel regains his freedom.

Though Keller had already finished two more Seldwyla novellas by 1855 and had composed significant parts of another three by the early 1860s, it was not until 1874 that he submitted final revisions of a second volume to the publisher. The town has changed drastically since the first volume appeared. Along with industrialization, a capitalist economy has taken hold in Seldwyla, and the citizens, as born speculators, are ideally suited to this kind of economic system because of their love of empty activity and their abhorrence of honest work. Prosperity, however, has taken its toll: the Seldwylers laugh less frequently, and they are too busy to play pranks on each other. In other words, nothing happens there anymore, so the narrator proposes to return to the old days for narrative material and offers five tales from the past.

"Kleider machen Leute" (translated as "Clothes Make the Man," 1929) was inspired by various contemporary reports of commoners masquerading as nobles for profit. Wenzel Strapinski, a well-dressed but impoverished journeyman tailor whose master has gone bankrupt, hitches a ride to the next town, Goldach, with a coachman who is delivering an elegant carriage to its aristocratic pur-

Keller circa 1870. The inscription, to his friend Marie Exner, reads "Bildnis des frommen Jünglings aber ungerechten Kammachers Gottfried Keller" (Portrait of the pious youth but unrighteous combmaker Gottfried Keller) (Private Collection).

chaser. When Wenzel emerges from the coach in his fine clothes, the Goldachers take him for a Polish count, and every awkward move he makes reinforces this perception. Eventually Wenzel catches on and plays along, providing the Goldachers with the excitement their dreary lives lack. Inevitably, Wenzel is unmasked by the merry Seldwylers; but his fiancée, Nettchen, who had fallen in love with *Count* Strapinski, decides that she loves the man and not the clothes, and the two marry and move to Seldwyla to make clothes for the Seldwylers. In the end, Wenzel proves to be as much a Philistine as any Goldacher – he works hard and drains the Seldwylers' pockets without reinvesting in the town's economy. "Kleider machen Leute" is one of Keller's signature pieces and has often been cited for its "Sein und Schein" (essence and appearance) thematics, which many believe are central to Keller's program as a writer.

Anthologies and single editions have helped to popularize individual Seldwyla stories, such as "Romeo und Julia auf dem Dorfe," "Die drei gerechten Kammacher" and "Kleider machen Leute." "Der Schmied seines Glückes" (The Smith of His Own Fortune) is rarely singled out, but it has one of the most interesting plots. John Kabys, determined to become rich without working, agrees to be "adopted" by Adam Litumlei, a rich old man who fears that he will die without an heir and will thus appear to have been impotent. It is agreed that Kabys will act as if he were a long-lost illegitimate son of Litumlei and inherit the latter's riches. The plan backfires because Kabys cannot resist the charms of Litumlei's young wife. When she becomes pregnant by him, her "stepson" is displaced by a "true" heir; Kabys realizes that he has collaborated in the manufacture of his *mis*fortune. When he claims to be the father of his "father's" son, he is cast out and forced to make his living as a nailsmith.

"Die mißbrauchten Liebesbriefe" (translated as "The Abused Love Letters," 1891) and "Dietegen" (translated, 1919) are less compelling than the other Seldwyla tales. The first is a graceless and immoderate literary satire, taking broad stabs at contemporary writers who wish to recapture the ferment of the Sturm und Drang (Storm and Stress) years; "Dietegen" is an endless and intricately plotted fifteenth-century period piece about concealment and revelation of emotions, wealth, and truth. The final tale, "Das verlorene Lachen" (translated as "The Lost Smile," 1982), is a compendium of Keller's social-didactic concerns into which is woven the love and marriage of Justine Glor and Jukundus Meyenthal, whose suitedness to one another is indicated by their identical smiles. "Das verlorene Lachen" attempts to shore up declining values by demonstrating the shallowness of caste consciousness, the dangers of religious orthodoxy, the fragility of the natural environment in an age of increasing industrialization, the folly of ignoring tradition, the vanity of faith in progress, and the destructive effects of greed. At least one of these factors threatens the lovers' relationship at any given time, and they must navigate a treacherous course and learn many lessons before they come to a true and lasting understanding. "Das verlorene Lachen," which begins at a folk festival, is a tapestry of Swiss life.

In 1855 Keller left Berlin for Zurich. There he made his living as a free-lance writer, contributing articles and essays to journals and writing patriotic and political poems and essays that were widely praised — especially by those in the government. In 1861 cantonal officials encouraged him to apply for the position of "Erster Staatsschreiber" (first secretary) of Zurich, and on 14 September he was elected to that prestigious and demanding post. He was forty-two, and it was his first job. On 22 September, the evening before he was to take office, he attended a party for the German socialist agitator Ferdinand Lassalle. After much drinking and a lengthy demonstration of magic tricks by Lassalle, Keller lost his temper and attacked the guest of honor with a stool. He was seized and ejected before he could do any damage, and Lassalle was not offended; but Keller did not show up at eight the next morning at his office, where accounts of his drunken brawling were already circulating. Finally, at ten, one of Keller's supporters went to his house, woke him up, and brought him in. Since Keller's excesses had been an issue in the discussion of his application, his future in government did not look bright; but the reprimand he received his first day on the job was the last. For the next fifteen years he was a model civil servant. When he stepped down in 1876, it was to return to his fiction, which he had neglected as Staatsschreiber.

Sieben Legenden (translated as *Seven Legends,* 1911), which appeared in 1872, was conceived during the Berlin years and, like the second volume of Seldwyla stories, took final form during Keller's years in office. It was intended as an ironic counterpart or profane rejoinder to *Legenden* (1804), a book of sentimental legends of the saints by Ludwig Kosegarten. The first piece, "Eugenia," concerns an early Christian bluestocking whose intellectual vanity leads her to masquerade as a man – Keller's prose abounds with women in men's clothing and men in women's clothing – so as to become a monk. She is saved from this folly by the man who loves her. The next three legends relate the adventures of the Virgin Mary in medieval times: she wrestles with the devil in "Die Jungfrau und der Teufel" (translated as "The Virgin and the Devil"); wins a jousting contest disguised as a knight in "Die Jungfrau als Ritter" (translated as "The Virgin as Knight"); and substitutes in a cloister for a nun who goes out to enjoy civilian life in "Die Jungfrau als Nonne" (translated as "The Virgin as Nun"). "Der schlimm-heilige Vitalis" (translated as "The Naughty Saint Vitalis) describes a monk who tries to convert prostitutes by paying for their time and praying for them. "Dorotheas Blumenkörbchen" (translated as "Dorothea's Flower-Basket") follows two lovers who forgo happiness on earth to spend eternity together in heaven. Postponement of pleasure is also the theme of the final piece, "Das

Tanzlegendchen" (translated as "A Legend of the Dance"), where King David convinces the young Musa to take a vow to cease dancing on earth so that she may dance forever in the afterlife. She achieves sainthood by denying herself her favorite pleasure and arrives in heaven, where she finds that the souls long for earthly music and dancing. Keller renders his parodies of saints' legends with great control and finesse. Barely touched by the author's will to educate readers to social utility, they are among the most subtle examples of his narrative style.

By the time Keller stepped down from office he had also finished his *Züricher Novellen* (Zurich Novellas, 1878), a collection of tales from Zurich history; most of the stories deal with themes of originality and the belatedness of the epigone writer. The frame narrative of the first cycle follows the career of Herr Jacques, a young boy who understands the strange stirrings of puberty to be "der unbewußte Trieb, ein Original zu sein oder eines zu werden" (the unconscious drive to be an original or to become one). Jacques wishes to write highly original literature but fails to produce anything, and his well-meaning godfather finds it necessary to tell him several didactic tales so that he might recognize that "good" originality is exemplary behavior or conduct that deserves imitation.

"Hadlaub" is the account of an epigone minnesinger of late medieval times, Johannes Hadlaub, whose legendary contribution to culture was his copying of old minnesongs to compile the Codex Manesse — a secondary phenomenon that is original as well. "Der Narr auf Manegg" (The Fool of Manegg) depicts the negative originality of the deranged and cruel Buz Falätscher, for whom death is a relief. "Der Landvogt von Greifensee" (translated as "The Governor of Greifensee," 1914) chronicles the romantic life of the historical Salomon Landolt, whose fruitful bachelorhood would never have been if he had married one of the five women whose stories he relates. Keller's tendency to embed stories within stories within stories is especially apparent in "Der Landvogt von Greifensee." Jacques, who had been bidden to copy "Der Landvogt von Greifensee" from a manuscript his godfather had written, is ultimately unaffected by the tales offered as tonic for his disturbance. He continues to pursue the arts as a patron or cocreator and renounces his aspirations only after his shocking discovery that a sculptor he had sponsored in Rome has produced an illegitimate child rather than the marble statue Jacques had expected. The tale closes with the suggestion that the recently married Jacques will imitate the sculptor and produce or originate progeny.

Two more tales are appended to the "Jacques" cycle. "Ursula" (translated, 1914) is the account of a victim of religious fanaticism and the loyal lover who rescues her amid post-Reformation factional strife. "Das Fähnlein der sieben Aufrechten" (The Banner of the Upright Seven; translated as "The Company of the Upright Seven," 1914) remains one of Keller's most popular tales. Seven patriotic master craftsmen prepare for a great folk festival at which they will arrive under their own banner and present a silver cup. One of them must make a speech for the presentation, but none of them has a gift for oratory. This situation and the developing romance between the son of one of the craftsmen and the daughter of another — which the fathers oppose — constitute the plot, but the main intent of the novella is to convey vignettes of exemplary citizenship and admirable social behavior.

Less tendentious and more pluralistic in its appeal to the educated reader was Keller's last collection of tales, *Das Sinngedicht* (The Epigram), which appeared in late autumn of 1881 with the publication date 1882 on the title page. His contemporaries greeted it as the finest of his works, and even today it is considered the best example of Keller's mature writing. The philosopher Friedrich Nietzsche praised it in a letter to the author of 14 October 1886 ("so rein, frisch und körnig schmeckte uns dieser Honig" [so pure, fresh, and crystalline does this honey taste to us]), and *Das Sinngedicht* does have the quality of an elegantly wrought refreshment.

Das Sinngedicht, the frame story of which is essentially a battle of the sexes leading to reconciliation and betrothal, is free of the social-didactic theme of the earlier works and also of the unrelenting misogyny that Keller had up to this point displayed in his authorial comments on women and in his characterizations of them. Though many have praised Keller for his "strong woman characters," closer inspection reveals that the few "strong women" he produced — Judith in *Der grüne Heinrich* is an example — are pure projections of the needs of male protagonists, who suffer from existential problems that the strong women cannot fathom. Their "strength" thus derives from their relative ignorance. Yet Lucie seems to have full rights and privileges in *Das Sinngedicht* — that is, she has strengths *and* weaknesses. Her past is as troubled and error-ridden as that of any man in Keller's works, and she often appears to be the wiser of the two protagonists.

The premise of *Das Sinngedicht* is playful and "aesthetic" to the highest degree. A young scientist, Herr Reinhart, notices one day that he has been pursuing the study of light (in the dark) to excess and that his eyes need a rest; light is the dominant metaphor of the collection, and Lucie, whose nickname is "Lux," is the light the myopic Reinhart seeks. As a first step toward reentering the world of human concerns he seeks advice in a volume of Karl Lachmann's edition of Gotthold Ephraim Lessing's edition of Friedrich Logau's epigrams and finds: "Wie willst du weiße Lilien zu roten Rosen machen? / Küß eine weiße Galathee: sie wird errötend lachen!" (How do you turn white lilies to red roses? / Kiss a white Galatea: she will laugh and blush!). Reinhart vows to enact this imperative and sets off on a quest for his Galatea. The circumstances of his discovery of the epigram and the multiply mediated nature of the text (Logau edited by Lessing edited by Lachmann) make it clear that his is a purely fanciful mission that has less to do with the epigram itself than with a frivolous urge to experiment outside the walls of his laboratory. Reinhart is thus able to kiss several of the women he encounters without arousing their anger – but also without eliciting the combined reaction predicted by Logau. But when he stumbles on Lucie in a white gown, next to a marble fountain, sorting roses, he betrays his purpose; and she, angered by the presumption of a man seeking his Galatea, enters into a round of competitive storytelling with him. All the tales they tell are loosely related to the Pygmalion theme: "Regine" depicts a wealthy man who educates a servant girl to be his wife; "Die arme Baronin" (The Poor Baroness) concerns the efforts of a young boarder to revive his sullen, aristocratic landlady to life's joys; and "Don Corea" relates the adventures of a Portuguese admiral who finds happiness with an African woman, whom he grooms to be his good Catholic wife. These tales are told by Reinhart. Lucie's tales are more inclined to show the failure of the Pygmalion projects and the losses incurred by those who attempt them. In "Die Berlocken" (The Trinkets), for example, Thibaut, a French soldier and rake, spends many years acquiring a superb collection of trinkets, only to lose them to an Indian woman in America. Trusting in her savage simplicity, Thibaut gives his treasures to the woman, whom he wishes to marry, only to find them dangling from the nose of her fearsome Indian fiancé the next day. Thibaut's colonialist construction of a naive and artless Indian maiden is a delusion of superiority that makes him her dupe. The analogy to

Reinhart, hoping to breathe life into his blushing Galatea, is subtly established.

Whereas Reinhart strives to preserve an objective historical style in his narratives, Lucie favors empathic penetration of her figures' states of mind. These differences give rise to many methodological arguments that deepen their knowledge of one another and fuel their growing affection. Eventually they join hands, Lucie laughs and blushes when Reinhart kisses her, and he professes to have forgotten his original purpose.

Keller, who acknowledged that his collection might appear "leer und skurril" (empty and farcical) to some, defended in letters to his publisher and friends his right to produce something that was purely poetic and unrelated to social utility. Despite his protests, he seems to have had compensatory intentions when, in 1881, the same year in which *Das Sinngedicht* appeared, he began writing a "relevant" novel. *Martin Salander* (1886; translated, 1964) represents an emphatic return to social themes. Keller's last work (he never wrote the intended sequel), it reflects all of the aging author's bitterness about the political and social changes wrought by industrial capitalism in Switzerland. Martin Salander, an upstanding merchant, is legally swindled out of his fortune by an old friend, Louis Wohlwend. To rebuild, Salander goes off to work in Brazil for seven years, leaving his wife and children behind. The poignancy of their difficult separation is nicely rendered and becomes all the more heartbreaking when Martin, having returned with ample funds, is again swindled by Wohlwend and must again go off to work in South America. He returns and establishes a healthy business; but he suffers great disappointment when his indistinguishable daughters, Setti and Netti, marry the worthless and unscrupulous Weidelich twins. Figures who are profoundly dull or nearly subhuman tend to occur in twos or threes in Keller's works; the Weidelichs "haben keine Seelen" (have no souls) because, like the three combmakers, they are motivated by personal gain and make no contribution to the society that sustains them.

Martin suffers further during his brief fascination with the beautiful Myrrha Glawicz, who turns out to be mindless, but he remains with his loyal Marie after learning that appearances can be deceiving. He must also learn to accept that the democratic system, which he supports so passionately, makes no distinction between a Salander and a Wohlwend and thus abets the destructive dishonesty of the latter and his ilk. With the exception of Marie, the only positive force in the novel is their

Keller in 1889; tempera-on-wood portrait by Arnold Böcklin (Kunsthaus Zürich)

son, the upstanding Arnold Salander, who was to be the subject of the sequel.

Though it has a few bright moments, *Martin Salander* is flat and disappointing. It lacks humor, and Keller himself admitted that there was too little poetry in it. The great socialist literary critic Georg Lukács wrote that Keller's poetic vein dried up with his increasing awareness of and disappointment in the capitalistic industrialization of Switzerland, and *Martin Salander* tends to confirm this suspicion. Keller was extremely worried about economic trends and suspicious of those in power. He saw the world of his youth deteriorating in his later years, but instead of returning to the past, as in the second volume of Seldwyla stories, he brooded about the present. Emil Ermatinger, the preeminent biographer of Keller, notes that the effects of aging as well as having to write *Martin Salander* in new lodgings above a lively tavern on a noisy street may have also taken their toll on Keller's poetic vein.

Keller spent his final years reaping the benefits of his poetic labors. He had attained widespread fame in German-speaking lands by the mid 1870s

and spent much of his time corresponding with critics, publishers, and other authors – notably with Theodor Storm and Conrad Ferdinand Meyer, two other important realist writers. He also received distinguished visitors and accepted awards as befitted a writer of his renown and advancing age. By the early 1880s his beloved sister was ill with heart disease, and he began to care for her as she had once cared for him. He was deeply shaken by her death in 1888.

In 1889 Keller began arrangements for the publication of his collected works in ten volumes, a great achievement for a living poet and confirmation of his stature. His seventieth birthday brought further confirmation. Along with trophies, medals, awards, telegrams, books, and paintings came official recognition from the German government and a proclamation from the Swiss legislature declaring Keller the best living German-language writer and recognizing him for his many contributions to Swiss society and culture. Keller was by then too feeble to attend the celebrations or respond energetically to the panegyrics. He received only the representatives of the legislature, preferring to be alone for most of the day. When he was honored with a gold medal in September, he wept and told those present that the award signified the end for him. In January 1890 he contracted influenza; he never recovered from its complications. Several strokes followed. Keller seems to have been barely alert during his last months; though he was attended by many friends and literary acquaintances, they report no profound deathbed conversations. There is testimony from his nurses that Keller asked them to read to him from the Bible and to say the Lord's Prayer, but one is tempted to take these reports with a grain of salt. A return to the Christian faith would have pleased most of Keller's admirers, inasmuch as it would have rounded out the popular image of a benign, humorous, happy – and by this time religious – man that so many of his readers cherished. It is, however, unclear how Keller stood on theological matters at the time of his death on 15 July 1890, and his posthumous "deification" (as one critic puts it) tends to distort the record of Keller's life and achievement by effacing his dark side. The dual image of Keller as benevolent, pious national poet, on the one hand, and bitter, misogynistic, alcoholic atheist, on the other, cannot be resolved by forcing a choice. Keller's brave recognition of his limits – including his difficult personality – and his passionate wish that these limits did not exist constitute a contradiction that was mediated time and again by his unique ironic humor. Only in the experience of this contradiction, or tension, between the desired and the available did Keller's genius emerge, enabling him to produce some of the finest poetic fiction of the nineteenth century.

Letters:

Gottfried Keller und und J. V. Widmann: Briefwechsel, edited by Max Widmann (Zurich: Füßli, 1922);

Gesammelte Briefe, 4 volumes, edited by Carl Helbling (Bern: Benteli, 1950–1954);

Der Briefwechsel zwischen Theodor Storm und Gottfried Keller, edited by Peter Goldammer, second edition (Berlin: Aufbau, 1967);

Aus Gottfried Kellers glücklicher Zeit: Der Dichter im Briefwechsel mit Marie und Adolf Exner, edited by Irmgard Smidt (Stafa: Gut, 1981);

Kellers Briefe, edited by Goldammer, second edition (Berlin: Aufbau, 1982);

Mein lieber Herr und bester Freund: Gottfried Keller im Briefwechsel mit Wilhelm Petersen, edited by Smidt (Stafa: Gut, 1984);

Gefährdete Künstler: Der Briefwechsel zwischen Gottfried Keller und Johann Salomon Hegi, edited by Fridolin Stahli (Zurich: Artemis, 1985);

Gottfried Keller – Emil Kuh Briefwechsel, edited by Smidt and Erwin Streitfeld (Stafa: Gut, 1988).

Bibliographies:

Jakob Baechthold, *Gottfried Keller Bibliographie (1844–1897)* (Berlin: Hertz, 1897);

Charles Zippermann, *Gottfried Keller Bibliographie* (Zurich: Rascher, 1935);

Hermann Boeschenstein, *Gottfried Keller* (Stuttgart: Metzler, 1969).

Biographies:

Jakob Baechthold, *Gottfried Kellers Leben: Seine Briefe und Tagebücher* (Berlin: Hertz, 1894–1897);

Marie Hay, *The Story of a Swiss Poet: A Study of Gottfried Keller's Life and Works* (Bern: Wyss, 1920);

Emil Ermatinger, *Gottfried Kellers Leben,* eighth revised edition (Zurich: Artemis, 1950);

James Lindsay, *Gottfried Keller: Life and Works* (London: Wolff, 1968);

Adolf Muschg, *Gottfried Keller,* second edition (Munich: Kindler, 1977);

Bernd Breitenbruch, *Gottfried Keller in Selbstzeugnissen und Bilddokumenten,* third edition (Reinbek: Rowohlt, 1983);

Hans Wysling, ed., *Gottfried Keller 1819–1890* (Zurich: Artemis, 1990).

References:

Walter Benjamin, "Gottfried Keller: Zu Ehren einer kritischen Gesamtausgabe seiner Werke," in his *Angelus Novus: Ausgewählte Schriften,* volume 2 (Frankfurt am Main: Suhrkamp, 1966), pp. 384–395;

John M. Ellis, "Die drei gerechten Kammacher," in his *Narration in the German Novelle* (Cambridge, U.K.: Cambridge University Press, 1974), pp. 136–154;

William Harrison Faulkner, *Keller's Der grüne Heinrich: Anna and Judith and Their Predecessors in Rousseau's Confessions* (Charlottesville: University of Virginia, 1912);

Gail K. Hart, *Readers and Their Fictions in the Novels and Novellas of Gottfried Keller* (Chapel Hill: University of North Carolina Press, 1989);

Eduard Hitschmann, *Gottfried Keller: Psychoanalyse des Dichters, seiner Gestalten und Motive* (Leipzig: Internationaler psychoanalytischer Verlag, 1919);

Hugo von Hofmannsthal, "Unterhaltung über die Schriften von Gottfried Keller," in his *Gesam-*

melte Werke, volume 2 (Berlin: Fischer, 1924), pp. 266–275;

T. M. Holmes, "Poetry Against Realism: The Divided Structure of Gottfried Keller's *Das verlorene Lachen*," *Forum for Modern Language Studies*, 19 (July 1983): 249–260;

Robert C. Holub, "Realism, Repetition, Repression: The Nature of Desire in *Romeo und Julia auf dem Dorfe*," *Modern Language Notes*, 100 (April 1985): 461–497;

David Jackson, "*Pankraz, der Schmoller* and Gottfried Keller's Sentimental Education," *German Life and Letters*, 30 (October 1976): 52–64;

Lee B. Jennings, "The Model of the Self in Gottfried Keller's Prose," *German Quarterly*, 56 (March 1983): 196–230;

Gerhard Kaiser, *Gottfried Keller: Das gedichtete Leben* (Frankfurt am Main: Insel, 1981);

Kaiser, *Gottfried Keller: Eine Einführung* (Munich: Artemis, 1985);

Lucie Karcic, *Light and Darkness in Gottfried Keller's "Der grüne Heinrich"* (Bonn: Bouvier, 1976);

Priscilla Kramer, *The Cyclical Method of Composition in Gottfried Keller's Sinngedicht* (New York: Ottendorfer, 1939);

Victor Lemke, "The Deification of Gottfried Keller," *Monatshefte*, 48 (1956): 119–126;

Kaspar T. Locher, *Gottfried Keller: Der Weg zur Reife* (Bern: Francke, 1969);

Rätus Luck, *Gottfried Keller als Literaturkritiker* (Bern: Francke, 1970);

Georg Lukács, *Gottfried Keller: Mit einer Einleitung* (Berlin: Aufbau, 1946);

Bernd Neumann, *Gottfried Keller: Eine Einführung in sein Werk* (Königstein: Athenäum, 1982);

Wolfgang Preisendanz, *Poetischer Realismus als Spielraum des Grotesken in Gottfried Kellers "Der Schmied seines Glückes"* (Constance: Universitätsverlag Konstanz, 1989);

Herbert W. Reichert, *Basic Concepts in the Philosophy of Gottfried Keller*, second edition (New York: AMS Press, 1966);

Heinrich Richartz, *Literaturkritik als Gesellschaftskritik: Darstellungsweise und politisch-didaktische Intention in Gottfried Kellers Erzählkunst* (Bonn: Bouvier, 1975);

B. A. Rowley, *Keller: Kleider machen Leute* (London: Arnold, 1960);

Richard Ruppel, *Gottfried Keller: Poet, Pedagogue, and Humanist* (New York: Lang, 1988);

Bruno Weber, *Gottfried Keller: Landschaftsmaler* (Zurich: Neue Zürcher Zeitung, 1990);

Kurt Wenger, *Gottfried Kellers Auseinandersetzung mit dem Christentum* (Bern: Francke, 1971);

Hans Wysling, ed., *Gottfried Keller: Elf Essays zu seinem Werk* (Munich: Fink, 1990).

Papers:

Gottfried Keller's papers are in the Zentralbibliothek (Central Library) in Zurich, the Goethe- und Schiller-Archiv in Weimar, and the Cotta-Archiv in the Schiller Nationalmuseum in Marbach.

Friederike Kempner

(25 June 1836 – 23 February 1904)

Tiiu V. Laane
Texas A&M University

BOOKS: *Denkschrift über die Nothwendigkeit einer gesetzlichen Einführung von Leichenhäusern* (Breslau: Korn, 1856; enlarged, 1867);

Berenize: Tragödie in fünf Aufzügen und in Jamben (Breslau: Morgenstern, 1860);

Novellen (Leipzig: Schrag, 1861) – comprises "Eine Frage Friedrichs des Großen: Humoristische Novelle," "Roger Bacon: Eine historische Novelle";

Rudolf der Zweite oder Der Majestätsbrief: Ein Trauerspiel (Leipzig: Fritsch, 1867);

Nettelbeck oder Patriot und Kosmopolit (Dresden: Dietze, 1868);

Gegen die Einzelhaft oder das Zellengefängnis (Breslau: Heidenfeld, 1869);

Gedichte (Leipzig: Lorber, 1873; enlarged edition, Breslau: Trewendt & Granier, 1882; enlarged edition, Berlin: Stuhr, 1884; enlarged, 1885; enlarged edition, Berlin: Siegismund, 1888; enlarged, 1891; enlarged, 1895; enlarged, 1903);

Antigonos: Trauerspiel in drei Aufzügen (Berlin: Hermann, 1880);

Das Büchlein von der Menschheit. Mit einem Anhang: Gegen die Einzelhaft oder das Zellengefängnis (Berlin: Grüger, 1885);

Jahel: Drama (Berlin: Siegismund, 1886);

Der faule Fleck im Staate Dänemark oder Eine lustige Heirath: Lustspiel in einem Aufzuge (Namslau: Opitz, 1888);

Ein Wort in harter Zeit (Namslau: Opitz, 1899);

Unfreiwilliger Humor. Mit zwei Bildnissen: Joh. Gg. Aug. Galletti und Friederike Kempner, edited by Ernst Heimeran (Munich, 1935);

Friederike Kempner, der schlesische Schwan, edited by Gerhart Herrmann Mostar (Heidenheim: Heidenheimer Verlagsanstalt, 1953);

Die Nachtigall im Tintenfaß: Die erste originalgetreue Sammlung schönster Gedichte der schlesischen Nachti-

gall, edited by Walter Meckauer (Munich: Pohl, 1956);

"An der Tugend nur genippet . . . ": Aus dem Liederschatz der "Schlesischen Nachtigall." Mit einem ganz diskreten Blick in Friederikes "Denkschrift über die Nothwendigkeit einer gesetzlichen Einführung von Leichenhäusern," selected by Percy Eichbaum (Zurich: Sanssouci, 1961);

Meister des unfreiwilligen Humors, volume 3: *Die erlesensten Gesänge von Friederike Kempner, genannt der Schlesische Schwan,* edited by Alfred Weitnauer (Kempten: Verlag für Heimatpflege, 1963);

Die sämmtlichen Gedichte der Friederike Kempner, Sammlung Dieterich, 291 (Bremen: Schünemann, 1964);

Das Leben ist ein Gedicht, edited by Horst Drescher, fourth edition (Leipzig: Reclam, 1986);

Friederike Kempner: Dichterleben, Himmelsgabe. Sämtliche Gedichte, edited by Nick Barkow and Peter Hacks (Berlin: Rütten & Loening, 1989).

OTHER: *Auszüge aus den berühmtesten Philosophen von Plato bis auf unsere Zeit in beliebiger Zeit und Reihenfolge. 1. Lieferung: Kant. Locke. Cartesius. Friedrich der Große. Marc Aurel. Rousseau,* edited by Kempner (Namslau: Opitz, 1883);

Auszüge aus den berühmtesten Philosophen von Plato bis auf unsere Zeit in beliebiger Zeit und Reihenfolge. 2. Lieferung: Plato. Leibnitz. Wolf. Cicero. Haller. Garwe. Bernhard v. St. Pierre. Reimarus. Bayle, edited by Kempner (Namslau: Opitz, 1886).

Friederike Kempner occupies a unique place in nineteenth-century German literature through being a bad poet. Her poems are so bad that they are hilariously funny. Kempner has been dubbed "der schlesische Schwan" (the Silesian Swan), "die schlesische Nachtigall" (the Silesian Nightingale), and "das Genie der unfreiwilligen Komik" (the Ge-

Friederike Kempner

nius of Involuntary Humor). She is regarded as the archetype of the dilettante poet who naively brutalizes grammar, rhyme, and logic in a dogged attempt to bless the world with his or her message. Written in the latter half of the nineteenth century, one of the less original periods of lyric production in German literature, her poems can also be read as caricatures of the imitative, clichéd, and pompously tendentious lyrics of the post-Romantic and post-Goethe era. Convinced of her calling to art, Kempner never intended her poems to be travesties. She seemed totally unaware of her own lack of talent. Kempner's poems would have fallen into oblivion had not the notable editor and literary critic Paul Lindau discovered them in 1880. With biting irony he encouraged his readers to savor Kempner's acrobatics with the German language, and her poems have had a loyal following ever since. Kempner's family, mortified by her dubious fame, systematically destroyed her lyric works during her lifetime and did not permit further publications after her death; consequently, her collections of poems found their way onto the

shelves of rare-book dealers, where they even surpassed the prices of works by Johann Wolfgang von Goethe. Her lyrics were copied, parodied, published illegally, and read aloud in homes. In the twentieth century new editions of Kempner's poems have appeared regularly. Not generally known, however, is her work as a social activist or as the author of narratives and plays. An idealistic woman with a profound social conscience, Kempner worked and wrote with dogged determination on behalf of the downtrodden and maligned of her society. She cried out against prejudice, injustice, and anti-Semitism and argued tirelessly against any form of brutality, from war to vivisection. Although she was maligned and made fun of because of her bombastic and painfully naive poems, her idealism and courage never flagged, nor did her efforts to help her fellow citizens.

Kempner was born on 25 June 1836 in Opatow in the province of Posen, an area that had belonged to Poland before Poland was partitioned by Austria, Russia, and Prussia in 1815; it was the poorer and more backward of the two provinces allotted to Prussia. Kempner's parents were Jewish.

Her father, Joachim Kempner, a capable and diligent man from Silesia, was a well-to-do tenant farmer on the lands of Count Maltzahn in Opatow. Kempner's mother, Marie Aschkenasy Kempner, came from a Polish family. Kempner had an older brother, David, and an older sister, Luise, who both became writers, and a younger sister, Helene. Sometime after Helene's birth Joachim Kempner bought his own manor in the village of Droschkau, near Breslau, in Silesia. Kempner never attended public school; she was taught primarily by her mother, a dignified, humane, and well-educated woman who must have been a thorough and capable teacher, for Kempner knew French, English, and Latin well enough to quote in those languages. She was also well versed in history and philosophy. Her literary references indicate that she had a good command of German, English, and French literature and was familiar with the classics. Kempner's scholarly bent is evident most clearly from the learned footnotes in her treatises, plays, narratives and even her poems.

The Kempner family associated with the academic circles at the Friederich Wilhelm University in Breslau. In her teens Kempner came in contact with such intellectual luminaries as the philologist Philipp August von Böckh, an expert in the classics, and the botanist Ferdinand Julius Cohn, the president of the Academy of Sciences and the director of the Botanical Gardens in Breslau. It was to Cohn that Kempner rushed to ask for an appraisal of her first poems. The distinguished scientist and philosopher Christian Nees von Esenbeck was the primary force in shaping Kempner's budding liberal thinking. When Esenbeck was dismissed from the university in 1851 because of his political activities, Kempner recognized with bitterness "den Undank und die Ungerechtigkeit der Welt" (the ingratitude and injustice of the world). Contact with academics instilled in Kempner an enduring love for science and faith in reason. Poetry was regarded in these circles as something noble, and Kempner became convinced that she had a calling to become a writer.

In addition to leading a stimulating intellectual life, the Kempner family was committed to philanthropy. When she was barely fifteen years old Kempner began helping to care for sick peasants. Kempner's first published work resulted from her sense of social commitment: while she was in her midteens Kempner learned to her horror that people were at times buried alive because they were in a trancelike state resembling death. This subject, which was to become Kempner's obsession, was much in circulation at the end of the eighteenth century, and Kempner soon discovered that prominent physicians such as Christoph Wilhelm Hufeland and well-known writers such as Jean Paul and Goethe had been concerned about the matter. Characteristically, Kempner began to explore the problem with gusto. She pored methodically through books, manuscripts, newspapers, and journals and discovered that many scholars, statesmen, and scientists had called for a longer waiting period between death and burial and for the establishment of mortuaries. Kempner persuaded her parents to build a small mortuary in their village; it was dedicated by the pastors of both Christian confessions on 31 July 1853. She also began personally to examine the dead to ascertain the onset of decay, which she believed was the only proof of death, and to note the degree of decay at the time of burial. For those areas that did not have public mortuaries Kempner prescribed the use of a special coffin, developed by a Mr. Lowden in Warsaw, with a pipe that could bring air into the coffin. The buried person, if awaking from a state of seeming death, could pull a string wrapped around his or her hands to open the ventilation hole. The pipe would also serve as a means of communication.

Kempner's efforts culminated in a scholarly book, *Denkschrift über die Nothwendigkeit einer gesetzlichen Einführung von Leichenhäusern* (Memorandum Concerning the Necessity of Legal Establishment of Mortuaries, 1856). In the introduction she stated that this was the fifth printing of the work and that she had written the treatise in 1850; no record exists of these earlier editions. The thirty-four-page treatise of 1856 is now generally held in medical libraries. Relying on medical books, it makes an impassioned plea against the brutality of burying people alive and demands that the seemingly dead should be laid in state for at least eight days so that doctors could determine whether they were actually dead. The work points out the hygienic and aesthetic advantages of cremation and calls for public mortuaries. Kempner appends a list of carefully documented cases describing the results of her own examinations of the dead in gruesome detail. By the time the work reached its sixth edition in 1867 she was able to document seventy-seven cases. Kempner's treatise did not go unnoticed: newspapers took up the topic with vigor, societies were founded to prevent overhasty burial, and a public mortuary was constructed in Breslau in 1863. Kempner was bold enough to send her work to heads of state and to the most prominent scientists and clergymen in Europe. In the introduction to the sixth edition, she was proud to acknowledge the recognition of her book by Wilhelm I of Prussia, Napoleon III of France, Alexander II of Russia, Leopold I of Belgium, and Queen Victoria of England. The distinguished German scientist Alexander von Humboldt had also sent his congratulations, as had the Catholic Prince-Bishop Henry of Breslau and the Protestant High Court Chaplain Bödeker from Hannover. On 7 March 1871 Wilhelm I, who had become emperor of Germany, mandated a waiting period of five days between the time of death and burial. Kempner had won her cause.

Encouraged by the success of her first publication, Kempner turned to historical drama as the next vehicle for her social message. *Berenize: Tragödie in fünf Aufzügen und in Jamben* (Berenize: Tragedy in Five Acts and in Iambic Meter, 1860) is based on careful studies of the works of the Jewish historian and warrior Flavius Josephus and depicts the battle of Jotapata, the last Jewish battle against the legions of Rome, which led to the destruction of Jerusalem. As in all of Kempner's dramas, the characters are depicted with sharp antithesis. Josephus is a humane leader, a man of virtue and reason. The Roman commander, Titus Flavius Vespasianus, in contrast, is an egotistical and arrogant ruler. The Jewish princess Berenize, torn between her passion for Titus and her love for her homeland, attempts to mediate between the Jewish and Roman nations; but Titus does not keep his promise to negotiate with Josephus and attacks the Jewish army. The drama displays a curious blend of historical veracity and fiction typical of Kempner. The historical events of *Berenize* are painstakingly researched. Citing *L'Histoire par Flavius Josephus* (History by Flavius Josephus, 1681), a French translation from the original Greek by Arnauld d'Andilly, as her principal source, Kempner adds copious footnotes to the drama to attest to the accuracy of the historical detail. The introduction, however, asserts that a poet has every right to fill in gaps in history as long as the changes are within the realm of possibility and help bring history to life. Taking poetic license with abandon, she offers her own interpretation of the events, which were left unclear, she claims, by the Roman historian Tacitus in his history of Rome. Why did Princess Berenize suddenly flee from Rome, where she was taken by Titus after the battle? Kempner gives her variant of the story, which she says will be different from that presented by Jean Racine in his play *Bérénice* (1670). In Kempner's drama, Berenize flees to Pompeii when Titus

wants to make her his queen because she is repulsed by Titus's betrayal. Pulling out all the stops of melodrama, Kempner has Berenize commit suicide by jumping into an erupting volcano. Full of pathos and fire and storm imagery, the play makes a plea for tolerance between nations and calls for loyalty and humane behavior. *Berenize* was never staged, but it did come into a second edition in 1865.

In 1861 Kempner's first volume of narrative fiction, *Novellen* (Novellas), was published; it contained two stories. "Eine Frage Friedrichs des Großen" (A Question by Frederick the Great) is designated as a "Humoristische Novelle" (Humorous Novella). It is introduced by mottos from Goethe's *Hermann und Dorothea* (1798; translated as *Hermann and Dorothea,* 1801) and Gotthold Ephraim Lessing's *Nathan der Weise* (1779; translated as *Nathan the Wise,* 1791). Kempner announces that the story will depict the roots of human misery through the viewpoint of luminaries whose names are set in the stars. The novella begins with a lighthearted frame story that introduces the young poet Ferdinand and his beloved Gertrude. Gertrude promises to marry Ferdinand if he recounts a story he has written. Ferdinand's story – the novella proper – is decidedly earnest, even though it has light moments and ironic touches. On a distant star that serves as the congregating place for the most noble deceased of all humankind, a group of poets, philosophers, statesmen, scientists, physicians, and pedagogues of all eras are starved to hear news from earth. They flood a new arrival, still dazed by his death, with questions. Each spirit explains his or her greatest achievement on earth on behalf of humanity, whether in the realm of science, art, or human welfare, and wishes to know whether his or her efforts have borne fruit. Lessing and Moses Mendelssohn, leaders of the Enlightenment, hear that their appeals for tolerance have been heeded in wide areas of the earth, while the theologian Christian Thomasius, who worked to do away with torture and the death penalty, finds out that his efforts have been in vain. Kempner's list of the achievements of the dedicated men and women of all ages is an impressive show of her erudition. The spirits recount their efforts to stamp out slavery, witch-hunts, anti-Semitism, injustice toward women, and the Inquisition; they tell how they sought to enact prison reform and to establish institutes for the deaf and blind and humane mental institutions. Frederick the Great, the king of Prussia, who has been moderating the discussion, poses the final question: what is the greatest evil on earth today? Not surprisingly, the international ghostly brain trust answers that it is being buried alive. A curtain opens up to reveal a picture of a person waking up from seeming death. The spirits conclude that the world needs public mortuaries, and they laud the advantages of cremation.

While the novella is strongly tendentious, it contains lively dialogue and clever ironic interplay among the characters. The work reveals Kempner's fascination with science, which she, like her contemporaries, viewed as the means to stamp out ignorance. The story also shows her fascination with the idea of travel into outer space. She envisions interstellar flight to the glowing star and depicts a sense of release from the bonds of Earth. The spirits wear their hearts outside their bodies, and the newcomer must adjust to the rarefied air on the strangely beautiful star. Here nightingales bellow with a volume that is almost unbearable for the newcomer. Kempner vividly describes the multitudes of suns circling the star at sunrise and the rose-colored night. The star shimmers with iridescent color and is bathed in flowers.

The second story is a revision of a novella written by Kempner's sister, Luise Stadthagen, which Kempner found in her sister's posthumous estate. "Roger Bacon: Eine historische Novelle" (Roger Bacon: A Historical Novella) lacks the vivid color of "Eine Frage Friedrichs des Großen" but shares the serious intention of the first story. Set in the late thirteenth century in Wales and based loosely on historical events, it depicts a battle between good and evil rulers. The ruthless and power-hungry King Edward I of England usurps the lands of the young Count Mortimer of Lewellyn, a lover of the arts and beauty who uses his lofty position to help his subjects. Lewellyn is married to Roger Bacon's idealistic daughter, Lucie. Morality and justice ultimately win, but not before Lewellyn is starved to death by Edward and his honest brother David is murdered. Kempner depicts a ruthless world in which goodness must continually battle evil. In addition to Lewellyn, she makes the philosopher and physicist Bacon, the epitome of the noble man of science, a symbol of humaneness and reason. The novella argues forcefully that people of power must use their lofty positions to advance human progress and goodness. While often moving, the novella suffers from occasional awkward shifts in tense that point to Kempner's inexperience with narrative structure.

In 1864 Kempner's father bought her an estate in Reichthal, near Breslau. Kempner called it "Friederikenhof" (Friederike's Court). Her best drama, the five-act *Rudolf der Zweite oder Der*

Majestätsbrief (Rudolf II; or, The Letter of Majesty, 1867), was performed in Berlin, the only play by Kempner to reach the stage. It is loosely based on historical events. In 1606 Emperor Rudolf II issued a conciliatory royal charter proclaiming religious freedom to the people of Silesia and Bohemia, including the Jews. The topic of religious persecution was timely, for anti-Semitism was still prevalent in Prussia despite the inroads made against it by decrees in the first half of the nineteenth century. The play again makes a man of science the voice of reason and enlightenment: this time it is the astronomer and mathematician Johannes Kepler who speaks on behalf of religious tolerance. Set in 1612 in Prague, the play shows how the noble Rudolf II, Kepler's benefactor, is forced to engage in a civil war against his mean-spirited and jealous brother, Prince Matthias. Kempner supplies Kepler with a sister, Johanna, who loves Rudolf and is loved by him. Prince Matthias takes Johanna hostage and demands that Rudolf give him Bohemia and Hungary in return for her freedom. Recognizing that Matthias is a demonic ruler who will brutalize his subjects, Johanna foils his plan by committing suicide. Broken by grief and outmaneuvered politically by Matthias, Rudolf abdicates after making Matthias promise to carry out the terms of the Letter of Majesty proclaiming religious freedom. Rudolf is haunted by guilt for lacking the courage to marry the bourgeois Johanna; he has realized too late that her integrity would have made her worthy to be a queen.

The aim of her novella *Nettelbeck oder Patriot und Kosmopolit* (Nettelbeck; or, Patriot and Cosmopolitan, 1868), Kempner declares in the introduction, is to present "den Fortschritt in der Humanität" (the progress in humanity). The novella deals with the slave trade. The title character is the honorable and patriotic Joachim Nettelbeck, the Prussian hero of the 1807 battle of Kolberg, which humiliated France. An equally idealistic force in the story is the British philosopher and politician William Wilberforce, who brought about the suppression of the slave trade in England in 1807. In Kempner's story Wilberforce is married to Nettelbeck's daughter Louise, who in actuality was married to a clergyman. In the introduction Kempner clarifies why she prefers the novella to the novel: novels, she says, were meant to be read for entertainment by people who had time to spare; Kempner preferred to get to the point quickly.

Her treatise *Gegen die Einzelhaft oder das Zellengefängnis* (Against Solitary or Cellular Confinement, 1869) labels the practice of solitary confinement a perversion coming from America, a land that also produced slavery. Solitary confinement, Kempner insists, is spiritual torture, worse than capital punishment and a shame for all humanity. She denies that prisoners will learn the tricks of the criminal trade from each other if they are placed together in cells. Anticipating modern thinking, she suggests that the state provide education and psychological counseling for prisoners. Again Kempner's voice was heard: lifelong solitary confinement of criminals was eliminated in the revision of penal laws in Germany in 1879.

Kempner requested permission to go to the battlefront during the Franco-Prussian War of 1870–1871 to help determine whether the fallen were actually dead and to prevent overhasty burial. Her request was denied because she was a civilian. Kempner consequently set up a hospital on her estate, where she cared for the wounded.

While pursuing her humanitarian activities and her fiction, Kempner never forgot her first love, poetry. Kempner's literary heroes were Goethe, Friedrich Schiller, Heinrich Heine, and Lord Byron. She also revered the pathetic and exotic lyrics of Ferdinand Freiligrath and the sweetly romantic verses of Joseph Viktor von Scheffel. The minor poet Otto Roquette was another of her favorites, and she admired the glowingly passionate lyrics of the Swiss poet Heinrich Leuthold. Accustomed to the generally uninspired lyrics of the latter nineteenth century, such as those of the immensely popular Emanuel Geibel, Kempner seemed unable to distinguish between the imitative verse produced by dilettantes and true poetic creation. She completed a 164-page volume of poems in July 1872 that was published in 1873, largely at her own expense. The book contains ballads, mottos, songs, and exhortations to society to stamp out all forms of evil. Full of pathos and sentiment, the poems speak of violets, fragrant roses, and bubbling springs, or they burst with images of thunder, roaring waves, and shattering lightning. When the poems gained little attention, Kempner, with characteristic determination, began to solicit reviews by sending copies of her bright red volume to prominent personalities, newspapers, and journals.

In 1880 the book fell into the hands of Lindau, an influential literary critic and the editor of the magazine *Gegenwart* (The Present Time) in Berlin. Lindau's review, which appeared in the magazine on 26 June 1880, recommended the book most highly to all readers who wished to be thoroughly amused. Kempner was suddenly in vogue. The book sold well in 1881, and jokes abounded about the "Nachtigall im Tintenfaß" (Nightingale in the Inkwell). Important men of letters facetiously offered encouragement, which Kempner took at face value. Kempner's family was mortified. Since the dedication included Kempner's mother's maiden name, Aschkenasy, a clearly Jewish name, the Kempners felt that the Jewish community would be humiliated; they also feared their daughter would become a laughingstock. Consequently, they secretly bought up the remainder of the first edition and destroyed it. A new edition, to which Kempner added new poems, came out in 1882. In the introduction she thanked her public for its support. Once again, readers hungry for amusement bought the edition avidly, and the family quietly acquired the remaining volumes. Thus a cycle was born that lasted until the eighth edition in 1903. The public found Kempner's lyrics exquisitely funny, but she did not intend them to be funny. Like her social tracts and her longer fiction, they were written for deadly earnest purposes.

The entire chorus of Kempner's thematic material echoes in her lyrics: calls for tolerance, peace, woman's rights, love, and justice. Kempner pays tribute to noble rulers, pleads for the maligned and hungry, and defends the innocent. Animals, including her dog Nero, her parrot Jakob (nicknamed Koberle), and her beloved canary, serve as symbols of loyalty and trust; slithering snakes symbolize evil. Kempner trumpets against war, vivisection, and, not to be forgotten, the horror of being buried alive: in the ballad "Logik" (Logic) a brave warrior lets out a heartrending cry demanding mortuaries. The humor of Kempner's poems derives from their soul-wrenching pathos and their naive sentimentality. Kempner has an uncanny ability to just miss the mark in a poem, or to break the tone at the last moment – often in the last line. A single word with an unintended innuendo can cause the entire lyrical edifice to collapse. Kempner falls unwittingly into every possible grammatical trap offered by the German language: subjects and objects become mercilessly confused, and pronouns suddenly lose their antecedents. Hopelessly mixed metaphors result in delightful confusion. If a line is too short Kempner simply adds extra letters, creating words such as *mite* instead of *mit* (with). If the line is too long, contractions solve the problem. Cases are abandoned at will; syntax is eclipsed to the point that the reader must create his own sentence structure. Words are repeated mindlessly to express deeply held sentiment: "Woge rollst zum Meer, / Und so rollst du, rollst" (Wave rolls to the ocean / And so you roll, roll). Kempner's poetic world echoes with literary allusions: one hears snatches of Schiller, Goethe, and the Romantics in grotesque imitations. Kempner's most original poems share the spirit of the exotic poems by Freiligrath. They speak of her vision of utopia, which she locates in America or in a desert oasis with emerald green palm trees and caravans of camels.

Kempner's third play, *Antigonos,* was published in 1880, followed in 1883 by the anthology *Auszüge aus den berühmtesten Philosophen von Plato bis auf unsere Zeit in beliebiger Zeit und Reihenfolge* (Excerpts from the Most Famous Philosophers from Plato to Our Time in Arbitrary Time Sequence and Order). The aim of the anthology was twofold, according to the introduction: she wanted to prove to the materialistic world that important philosophers believed in God and in the eternal life of the spirit, and she wanted to pick out the most important passages in the philosophers' works for ordinary readers who might have difficulty finding the pertinent passages on their own. The book contains excerpts from the works of Immanuel Kant, John Locke, René Descartes, Frederick the Great, and Jean-Jacques Rousseau. She documents the work with learned footnotes. Her *Büchlein von der Menschheit* (Little Book about Humanity, 1885) continues in a similar philosophical vein. Drawing on the ideas of philosophers, Kempner proves that human beings are basically good. She then details her proposals for the establishment of the ideal state. It should be "die Mutter unser aller" (the mother of us all) and should provide a secure existence for all its citizens. It should furnish free education, training for teachers, and training for jobs. It should build public kitchens so that no one need go hungry, and have health insurance or a sick fund so that no one would be dependent on private charity. Kempner insists that this social system will not be abused because people are basically honest and wish to be independent, and she points out the danger that the recipients of social welfare might begin to feel envious, humiliated, and degraded. She also suggests that universities should be moved to the countryside so that the students will have contact with nature. While urging that war is to be avoided if at all possible, Kempner, like many of her contemporaries, sees the battlefield as a testing ground for ideals such as self-sacrifice, bravery, and honor. Kempner's book closes with an appendix of her previously published arguments against solitary confinement.

In 1886 Kempner put forth a historical drama, *Jahel,* and a second compilation of the thoughts of great philosophers. A one-act comedy, *Der faule Fleck im Staate Dänemark oder Eine lustige Heirath* (The Rotten Spot in the State of Denmark; or, A Merry Marriage), was published in 1888. Set in 1887 in Berlin, the play takes a humorous, though seriously intended look at nineteenth-century marriage conventions. Women at that time had to pay suitors to marry them; a deal would be struck between the woman's family and her suitor through a marriage broker. Kempner's play depicts the efforts of the well-to-do banker Mr. Müller and his wife to marry off their daughter, Bella. Bella, however, is already in love with her impoverished cousin Siegmund. The lovers hit on a plan to trick Bella's parents into giving them permission to marry. They disguise Siegmund as a rich suitor from America; at first ecstatic that their daughter will make a superb match, the parents quickly learn that the "American" is a married man with children. They come to realize that the noble-minded Siegmund, although without financial means, is the proper husband for Bella. The message is that marriages should be based on love and the moral worth of the individual and not entered into for the sake of money. Kempner makes a clear statement on behalf of women's rights and chastises society for holding women in a state of slavery. The play is interspersed with songs performed by the main characters, and the lively dialogue shows Kempner's considerable talent for comedy. Kempner's final plea for social justice, the essay *Ein Wort in harter Zeit* (A Word in Hard Times, 1899), is an emotional appeal to humanity to stamp out the "Unkraut" (weeds) of all forms of prejudice, including anti-Semitism. Kempner calls for a world of goodness and beauty and ends on an optimistic note by saying that human beings are capable of moral and noble behavior and of bringing about a golden age in the twentieth century.

By the eighth edition of 1903, Kempner's volume of lyrics had increased to more than three hundred pages. Each edition had a new introduction. The introductions became increasingly bitter because Kempner was receiving more and more derogatory letters. She swore that the day would come when her name would be etched in bronze; it was, but not for the reason that she had expected. Kempner died of a stroke on 23 February 1904. In her will she had requested that an electrical device be placed in her coffin that she could ring for help if she should wake up. The device proved unnecessary, since Kempner was cremated.

References:

Nick Barkow, "Kerrs Tante oder Die Rache des Germanischen Volksgefühls," in *Friederike Kempner: Dichterleben, Himmelsgabe. Sämtliche Gedichte,* edited by Barkow and Peter Hacks (Berlin: Rütten & Loening, 1989), pp. 251–274;

Peter Hacks, "Vorwort zur 9. Auflage: Die Kempner wäre nicht so komisch, wenn sie nicht so gut wäre," in *Friederike Kempner: Dichterleben, Himmelsgabe. Sämtliche Gedichte,* pp. 7–34;

Bruno Kaiser, *Echte und falsche Moritaten: Vom Bänkelsang zu Friederike Kempner* (Berlin: Rütten & Loening, 1962);

Kaiser, "Poesie auf Abwegen oder vom Gesangbuch zu Friederike Kempner," in *Buch-Bibliothek-Leser. Festschrift für Horst Kunze zum 60. Geburtstag,* edited by Werner Dube, Othmar Feyl, Gotthard Rückl, and Hans-Erich Teitge (Berlin: Akademie, 1969), pp. 539–549;

Margot Krohn, "Friederike Kempner, die 'schlesische Nachtigall,' als Kämpferin für Menschenrecht," *Jahrbuch der Schlesischen-Friedrich-Wilhelms Universität zu Breslau,* 8 (1962): 233–246;

Arno Lubos, *Geschichte der Literatur Schlesiens,* volume 2 (Munich: Korn, 1967), pp. 34–38;

Walter Meckauer, "Ernst besinnliches Nachwort über heiter unsinnige Verse," in *Die Nachtigall im Tintenfaß: Die erste originalgetreue Sammlung schönster Gedichte der schlesischen Nachtigall,* edited by Meckauer (Munich: Pohl, 1956), pp. 163–191;

Gerhart Herrmann Mostar, "Friederike Kempner: Genie der unfreiwilligen Komik," *Frankfurter Hefte: Zeitschrift für Kultur und Politik,* 7 (September 1952): 692–700;

Christa Niesel-Lessenthin, "Die Friederike Kempner," *Schlesische Monatshefte: Blätter für Kultur und Schrifttum der Heimat,* 9 (1932): 58;

Fritz Nötzoldt, *Johanna gewappnet mit bannendem Blick, oder Du dunkelgrüner Lorbeer bists: Im vergnüglichen Gedenken an Friederike Kempner, die Königin im Reich der unfreiwillig-komischen Poesie* (Munich: Ehrenwirth, 1964).

Ferdinand Kürnberger

(3 July 1821 – 14 October 1879)

Karl Ludwig Stenger
University of South Carolina — Aiken

BOOKS: *Epilog bey Gelegenheit der öffentlichen Vertheilung der Schulpreise am k.k. Schotten-Gymnasium in Wien am 7. August 1839* (Vienna: Ueberreiter, 1839);

Catilina: Drama in fünf Aufzügen (Hamburg: Hoffmann & Campe, 1855);

Der Amerika-Müde: Amerikanisches Kulturbild (Frankfurt am Main: Meidinger, 1855);

Ausgewählte Novellen (Prague: Bellmann, 1857) — comprises "Das Kind mit dem Briefe," "Die Versuchungen der Armen," "Das große und das kleine Los," "Giovanna," "Ein Brautpaar in Polen," "Der Drache," "Die Braut des Gelehrten," "Der Windfall";

Das Goldmärchen (Pest, Vienna & Leipzig: Hartleben, 1857);

Novellen, 3 volumes (Munich: Fleischmann, 1861–1862) — comprises in volume 1, "Spieler und Bettler," "Flucht und Fund," "Die Opfer der Börse," "Die Göttin"; in volume 2, "Drei Tage in Pyrmont," "Der Dichter des Don Juan," "Amor im Felde," "Der Kuß"; in volume 3, "Am Abend: Ein Idyll," "Ein Abenteuer in Venedig," "Novelletten," "Humoreske Charakterbilder";

Aufruf für Schleswig-Holstein: Epistel an den Kaiser von Oesterreich (Munich: Fleischmann, 1864);

Das Pfand der Treue: Bürgerliches Schauspiel in fünf Aufzügen (Vienna: Daberkow, 1873);

Siegelringe: Eine ausgewählte Sammlung politischer und kirchlicher Feuilletons (Hamburg: Meissner, 1874);

Der Haustyrann: Roman (Vienna: Rosner, 1876);

Literarische Herzenssachen: Reflexionen und Kritiken (Vienna: Rosner, 1877);

Novellen (Berlin: Hertz, 1878) — comprises "Künstlerbräute," "Bergschrecken," "Der Erbe," "Die Last des Schweigens," "Liebesschuld," "Alimek und der Derwisch";

Löwenblut: Novelle. Aus dem Nachlaß, edited by Wilhelm Lauser (Dresden: Minden, 1892);

Ferdinand Kürnberger

Novellen: Aus dem Nachlaß des Dichters, edited by Lauser (Stuttgart: Deutsche Verlagsanstalt, 1893);

Eis; Aus Liebe sterben: Zwei Novellen. Aus dem Nachlasse (Leipzig: Reclam, 1898);

Quintin Messis: Schauspiel (Vienna: Daberkow, 1900);

Aug und Ohr: Novelle (Vienna: Daberkow, 1900);

Die Kinder der Vornehmen: Novelle (Vienna: Daberkow, 1900);

Die Sängerin von Augsburg: Ein mittelalterliches Frauenbild; Der Schulmeister Krachenberger: Novellette (Vienna: Daberkow, 1900);

Firdusi: Drama (Vienna: Daberkow, 1902);

Das Trauerspiel: Lustspiel in drei Aufzügen (Vienna: Daberkow, 1902);

Das Schloß der Frevel: Roman, 2 volumes, edited by Karl Rosner (Leipzig & Berlin: Seemann, 1903);

Fünfzig Feuilletons: Mit einem Präludium in Versen (Vienna: Daberkow, 1905);

Dramen, 5 volumes (Vienna: Daberkow, 1907) — comprises *Quintin Messis, Catilina, Firdusi, Das Trauerspiel, Das Pfand der Treue;*

Novellen, 12 volumes (Vienna: Daberkow, 1907);

Über das antik und modern Tragische: Acht Vorlesungen. Aus dem Nachlaß, edited by Otto Erich Deutsch (Munich & Leipzig: Müller, 1910);

Gesammelte Werke, 4 volumes, edited by Deutsch (Munich: Müller, 1910–1914) — comprises *Siegelringe, Literarische Herzenssachen, Der Amerika-Müde, Das Schloß der Frevel; Löwenblut;*

Die deutsche Schillerstiftung: Aufsätze, Literaturberichte und Gutachten, edited by Deutsch (Munich: Müller, 1912);

Aufsätze über Fragen der Kunst und des öffentlichen Lebens, edited by Adolf Watzke (Vienna: Tempsky, 1913);

Adulis: Roman (Vienna: Seidl, 1925);

Novellen (Vienna: Österreichischer Bundesverlag für Unterricht, Wissenschaft & Kunst, 1925);

Das denkende Herz: Eine Auswahl (Klagenfurt: Kaiser, 1947);

Spiegelungen, edited by Rudolf Holzer (Graz & Vienna: Stiasny, 1960);

Feuilletons, edited by Karl Riha (Frankfurt am Main: Insel, 1967).

Ferdinand Kürnberger has been called the "Stammvater" (founding father) of Viennese critical journalism, and his fanatical pursuit of the truth earned him the appellation of "Vienna's Cato." Kürnberger elevated the feuilleton, which had been considered the poor cousin of the serious essay, by infusing it with political and cultural criticism. Feuilletons, which were printed "unter dem Strich" (below the line) — that is, separated from the serious news and editorials — were generally considered lightweight, even frivolous, and were regarded by many readers as a pleasant respite from the frequently disturbing news accounts. Kürnberger used the feuilleton as a vehicle to express his liberal views and to oppose the repressive tendencies of the Austrian government and the Catholic church. He subverted this heretofore benign genre with masterly skill and turned it into a political weapon while maintaining a satirical guise to distract the powerful censors.

It was Kürnberger's expressed goal "die Leute zu inkommodieren" (to incommode people), a credo he borrowed from Friedrich Schiller. One of Kürnberger's favorite targets was the abuse of language at the hands of politicians and journalists. In this respect he was the direct forerunner of the influential Viennese satirist Karl Kraus, who acknowledged Kürnberger's achievement by publishing more than thirty essays by or about Kürnberger in his periodical *Die Fackel* (The Torch).

Kürnberger himself thought of his essays as a mere means of livelihood; he considered himself a journalist by circumstance but a poet by calling. He was certain that his fame would rest on his novellas, his novels, and, above all, his plays, and it was his greatest disappointment that these works never received the recognition he thought they deserved. Only some of his short stories and the novel *Der Amerika-Müde* (Disenchanted with America, 1855) gained a certain amount of popularity, the latter mainly because it was considered to be a roman à clef about the Romantic poet Nikolaus Lenau's disillusioning trip to America. Kürnberger's plays, however, were not deemed theatrical enough to be performed and his magnum opus, the novel *Das Schloß der Frevel* (The Castle of Sacrilege, 1903), which Kürnberger called the "Schatz meines Lebens" (treasure of my life), was not published in its entirety during his lifetime. Kürnberger was a forward-looking and innovative journalist but a derivative writer of fiction and plays.

Kürnberger was born on 3 July 1821 in Vienna as the fourth of five children of the lantern lighter Ferdinand Kürnberger and Barbara Kürnberger, née Girner, who sold fruit, vegetables, and flowers from a stand at the Naschmarkt. In elementary and high school Kürnberger became known for his ability to memorize poetry, and his serious demeanor earned him the nickname "heiliger Mann" (Holy Man). As the most industrious and talented pupil, he was given a stipend. An elaborate poem Kürnberger composed, *Epilog bey Gelegenheit der öffentlichen Vertheilung der Schulpreise am k.k. Schotten-Gymnasium in Wien am 7. August 1839* (Epilogue on the Occasion of the Public Distribution of School Prizes at the Royal Schotten Gymnasium in Vienna on 7 August 1839, 1839), was publicly recited and published, and it bestowed minor celebrity status on its author.

When he graduated from secondary school in 1841, a low grade in mathematics prevented him from being admitted to the University of Vienna; he was permitted only to audit courses, and he soon decided to forego lectures in favor of symphony

Kürnberger in 1851 (from Briefe eines politischen Flüchtlings, *edited by Otto Erich Deutsch, 1920)*

concerts and museums. Kürnberger educated himself, and he earned his living by giving private lessons and selling articles to Viennese newspapers. One of these essays, "Ein Votum über die Literatur der Dorfgeschichten" (A Vote on the Literature of the Village Tales), published in January 1848 and republished in the second volume of Kürnberger's collected works (1911), criticized the fashionable genre of village tales and its leading proponents, Berthold Auerbach and Joseph Rank; it caused a storm of outrage and indignation. Kürnberger's play *Quintin Messis* (1900), completed at the beginning of 1848, portrays the artistic development of a Belgian painter in the sixteenth century. The play's lack of theatricality and its excessive reliance on coincidence as a plot device prevented it from being staged at Vienna's Burgtheater.

When revolution broke out in the spring of 1848, Kürnberger became a chronicler of the rapidly developing events and had more than fifty articles published in support of the uprising. He also participated actively in the revolution. Falsely charged with complicity in the assassination of the Austrian minister of war, he fled Vienna on 10 November. Using a false passport, he traveled to Breslau and then to Dresden, where he again became embroiled in revolutionary events and was ar-

rested in May 1849. He spent nine months in prison awaiting trial, for a time together with the Russian anarchist Mikhail Bakunin. Kürnberger plotted an escape, only to be pardoned by the king one day before he was able to execute his plan. After his release on 17 February 1850 Kürnberger, instead of obeying orders to return to Austria, traveled under an assumed name to Hamburg by way of Leipzig and Magdeburg. In Hamburg he made the acquaintance of several political fugitives who were about to immigrate to America. Witnessing the despair of these men, who had to leave their homeland because of their beliefs and hoped to find freedom in the New World, may have given Kürnberger the idea for *Der Amerika-Müde.*

Kürnberger moved to Bremen at the beginning of 1851. There he contributed essays to the liberal newspaper *Tageschronik* (Daily Chronicle). His employment, however, was short-lived, since the paper's publisher, a freethinking pastor, immigrated to America soon after Kürnberger's arrival. Kürnberger left Bremen in May 1851, and his whereabouts cannot be traced for almost a year; while it was Kürnberger's custom to keep his family informed about his well-being by sending frequent and detailed letters, he was not able to contact them during this period. At the beginning of 1852 he resurfaced in Frankfurt am Main, where he remained for four years. During this period Kürnberger barely eked out a living by contributing essays and novellas to German and Austrian newspapers and magazines.

Repeated attempts to have his early plays staged failed, but Kürnberger continued to pursue his calling as a dramatist. In 1851 he wrote *Catilina* (1855), an expansive five-act drama with an enormous cast of characters. While the first century B.C. Roman patrician and rebel Catiline, who conspired to overthrow the government, had been depicted as a monstrous villain by Sallust and Cicero, Kürnberger portrays him as an idealistic revolutionary and champion of the disenfranchised. A similar interpretation can be found in Henrik Ibsen's first play, *Catiline* (1850). Since Kürnberger insisted on the originality of his concept, it appears that the two playwrights happened on the same subject at approximately the same time and, inspired by political events, turned the much maligned title figure into a hero. In spite of extensive revisions and Kürnberger's tenacious negotiations with Heinrich Laube, director of Vienna's prestigious and influential Burgtheater, *Catilina* never made it to the stage. In November 1852 Kürnberger entered his novella "Das große und das kleine Los" (The

Great and the Small Lot, 1857) in a competition sponsored by a Viennese journal and won thirty gold ducats.

Kürnberger's novel *Der Amerika-Müde* was considerably more successful. Ten thousand copies of the book were sold within a few years, and it made its author's name widely known. Burgeoning anti-American sentiments contributed to the novel's popularity, as did the fact that the majority of readers saw in its protagonist, Dr. Moorfeld, a thinly veiled portrait of the Hungarian-Austrian poet Lenau. Kürnberger did rely on accounts of Lenau's disappointing journey to America. He integrated some of these details into his novel, altered some, and discarded others altogether. It was not his intention to present an accurate depiction of a key event in Lenau's life; rather, he hoped that his audience's intense interest in the tragic fate of the poet, who had died in an insane asylum in 1850, would entice them to buy and read his tendentious book. It was conceived as the counterpart to Ernst Willkomm's popular novel *Die Europamüden* (Disenchanted with Europe, 1838), a paean to the New World. In Kürnberger's novel the hopes and expectations of the idealistic protagonist are thwarted soon after his arrival in America, and, having witnessed the corruption and inequities of American society, he returns to Europe a disillusioned man.

Kürnberger, who never visited the United States and based his descriptions of the country on contemporary travelogues and novels, used Moorfeld as his mouthpiece to voice a scathing condemnation of American mores, culture, education, religion, politics, and business practices. His main target was the materialism of American society. Some scholars have interpreted the novel not as an indictment of a particular country but rather as a critique of capitalism in general. Whether one agrees with this reading or not, Kürnberger's novel represents an important step in the development of the United States as a literary subject.

While Kürnberger was completing *Der Amerika-Müde* in Frankfurt, his father died of a cerebral disease in January 1855. Kürnberger stepped up his efforts to obtain a passport so that he could join his aging mother in Vienna. He was granted permission to return to Austria but was denied a passport. On 29 March 1856 Kürnberger arrived in Vienna, where he was kept under clandestine surveillance by the police. The subsequent four years he spent in the city he both loved and hated proved to be disappointing ones. Kürnberger did not attain the recognition he craved, and his mother died in 1858.

The only ray of sunshine during this period was Kürnberger's close friendship with Isabella Wendelin, a married woman. Their relationship, which has been documented in a volume of intense letters (1907), was to last until Kürnberger's death.

In 1860 the Schiller Foundation offered Kürnberger a stipend for a stay in Germany. He joyfully accepted and traveled illegally to Munich, where he struck up a friendship with the historical painter Wilhelm von Kaulbach. He was soon expelled by the Bavarian authorities at the instigation of the Austrian government and traveled to Coburg, Stuttgart, Salzburg, and Graz. Faced with a subpoena, he spent almost a year in seclusion at the Hungarian country estate of his friend Samuel Engländer. Kürnberger used this period of involuntary leisure to immerse himself in his writing. In addition to several long essays he began the play *Firdusi* (1902) and wrote the psychological novella "Die Last des Schweigens" (The Burden of Silence, 1878) and parts of *Das Schloß der Frevel*.

Firdusi, (1902) completed in 1865, dramatizes the conflict between its title character, Firdawsi, Persia's first great poet of the Islamic era and author of the national epic *Shah-Nameh* (Book of Kings, 1010), and the ambitious Shah Mahmud. The play suffers from the same weaknesses as Kürnberger's earlier dramas: it is too didactic, and its plot is too contrived. It was staged by the Munich Residenztheater in 1871, but for only two performances.

"Die Last des Schweigens," one of Kürnberger's most successful works, was translated into Hungarian and published in various newspapers and magazines. Its protagonist is a murderer who feels compelled to confess his crime. On the eve of his execution, the condemned man does not regret having committed the murder but rather having felt the urge of owning up to it. Critics have found the work remarkable for anticipating psychoanalytical ideas and have compared its protagonist to Raskolnikov in Fyodor Dostoyevski's masterpiece, *Crime and Punishment* (1866).

Das Schloß der Frevel is set in nineteenth-century Italy and depicts the adventurous travels of Balm, a journalist. Balm witnesses the raging "Kulturkampf" (struggle between state and church) and becomes involved with the deformed and mysterious painter Zuppa, the representative of sensuality, and the Marchese Santafiore, the advocate of spirituality. Kürnberger used this Zeitroman (novel analyzing the historical period in which it was written) to voice his liberal views and to vent his intense dis-

Lithograph of Kürnberger by Carl von Stur

like of the Catholic church. The negative portrayal of organized religion as well as the inclusion of erotic material prevented the publication of the complete text during Kürnberger's lifetime. The Viennese newspaper *Deutsche Zeitung* (German Newspaper) began publishing the work in the middle of 1875, but the project was abandoned after Austrian censors seized several issues. Kürnberger tried unsuccessfully to secure an American publisher, and it was twenty-seven years before the entire novel was published in ninety-seven installments by the Viennese newspaper *Die Zeit* (Time). At the end of 1903 *Das Schloß der Frevel* appeared for the first time as a book, and in 1914 it was published in the fifth volume of Kürnberger's collected works. The colorful and gripping novel has received little attention since then and deserves to be rediscovered.

After leaving Hungary, Kürnberger spent several years in Munich and Graz before returning to Vienna in 1865. Repeated efforts to resolve his passport problems and to clear his name of accusations stemming from his involvement in the 1848 revolu-

tion proved fruitless. Kürnberger eventually decided to submit to the Austrian legal system and was jailed from 3 to 12 February 1867.

During the last twelve years of his life Kürnberger attained a certain degree of recognition. He was elected general secretary of the prestigious Schiller Foundation when it moved its headquarters to Vienna temporarily in 1866. Kürnberger served in this capacity until 1869, and his annual reports detailing the state of literature are well informed and balanced.

Whenever one of his provocative feuilletons appeared, it became the talk of the town. The essays were so successful that Kürnberger had them published in two collections: *Siegelringe* (Signet Rings, 1874), a compilation of political feuilletons, and *Literarische Herzenssachen* (Literary Matters of the Heart, 1877), a selection of book reviews and literary essays. In his political writings Kürnberger, who considered himself the nation's court jester, exposed and castigated the repressive tendencies of the postrevolutionary Austrian government and the church hierarchy by unmasking the ideological purpose of language. He considered much of Vienna's press the accomplice of the governing bureaucracy and did not tire of attacking its deceptive use of language and its lack of integrity. Kürnberger fought with all his might against "Phrasen-Prostitution" (prostitution of the phrase) and insisted that one should treat one's language the same way one treats one's honor. When the Wienerwald, the woods and mountain chain to the west of Vienna, was threatened with deforestation, Kürnberger helped save it by mobilizing public opinion.

In his book reviews and literary feuilletons Kürnberger criticized imitative writing and the use of clichés. He favored realistic and naturalistic writers and was one of the first critics to recognize the importance of Gottfried Keller, the Swiss proponent of Poetic Realism. Kürnberger was also a strong advocate of the works of the Russian realist Ivan Turgenev, whom he called the "Shakespeare der Skizze" (Shakespeare of the sketch.) It was partly due to Kürnberger's lucid review that Turgenev's works became widely known and appreciated in Austria and exerted a strong influence on such realist writers as Marie von Ebner-Eschenbach and Ferdinand von Saar.

In spite of his success as an essayist, Kürnberger became increasingly bitter and misanthropic. The daily struggle to make ends meet hindered his poetic production, and he felt that his true talents as a writer of fiction and, above all, of plays were not appreciated by the public. His play *Das Pfand der Treue* (The Pledge of Fidelity, 1873) was a failure, as was his novel *Der Haustyrann* (The Tyrant of the House, 1876). Kürnberger was no longer able to tolerate the oppressive and stifling Viennese atmosphere and left his hometown in the summer of 1877. He spent the last two years of his life shuttling restlessly among Graz, Bregenz, and Munich. In August 1879 he fell ill with pleurisy and pneumonia, and he died in Munich's General Hospital on 14 October 1879. He was buried in Mödling in the Wienerwald, the forest he had helped to save.

Letters:

Ferdinand Kürnbergers Briefe an eine Freundin (1859–1879), edited by Otto Erich Deutsch (Vienna: Verlag des Literarischen Vereins, 1907);

"Briefe Ferdinand Kürnbergers an Heinrich Laube," *Deutsche Rundschau*, 181 (October 1919): 144–152; (November 1919): 286–304;

Briefe eines politischen Flüchtlings, edited by Deutsch (Leipzig & Vienna: Tal, 1920).

References:

L. H. Bailey, "Ferdinand Kürnberger, Friedrich Schlögl and the Feuilleton in the Gründerzeit Vienna," *Forum for Modern Language Studies*, 13 (January 1977): 59–71;

Thomas Stockham Baker, *Lenau and Young Germany in America* (Philadelphia: Stockhausen, 1897);

Eduard Castle, "Amerikamüde: Lenau und Kürnberger," *Jahrbuch der Grillparzer-Gesellschaft*, 12 (1902): 15–42;

Manfred Durzak, "Traumbild und Trugbild Amerika: Zur literarischen Geschichte einer Utopie. Am Beispiel von Willkomms *Europamüden* und Kürnbergers *Amerika-Müdem*," in his *Das Amerika-Bild in der deutschen Gegenwartsliteratur: Historische Voraussetzungen und aktuelle Beispiele* (Stuttgart, Berlin, Cologne & Mainz: Kohlhammer, 1979), pp. 16–37;

Hannelore Ederer, *Die literarische Mimesis entfremdeter Sprache* (Cologne: Pahl-Rugenstein, 1979);

Wilmont Haacke, "Kürnberger als politischer Publizist," *Publizistik*, 14 (1969): 443–450;

Wilhelm Arthur Hammer, "Kürnberger und Platen: Nach ungedruckten Tagebuchblättern," *Jahrbuch der Grillparzer-Gesellschaft*, 24 (1913): 188–198;

Guy T. Hollyday, *Anti-Americanism in the German Novel 1841–1862* (Bern, Frankfurt am Main & Las Vegas: Lang, 1977);

Victor Klemperer, "Ferdinand Kürnberger als dramatischer Dichter und Kritiker," *Bühne und Welt*, 14 (1911): 349–357;

Werner Kohlschmidt, "Kürnbergers Lenauroman *Der Amerikamüde*: Zur Geschichte der deutschen Auseinandersetzung mit dem Amerikanismus," *Zeitschrift für deutsche Bildung*, 19 (1943): 26–38;

Wolf-Dieter Kühnel, *Ferdinand Kürnberger als Literaturtheoretiker im Zeitalter des Realismus* (Göppingen: Kümmerle, 1970);

Hubert Lengauer, "Zwischen Anpassung und Widerstand: Ferdinand Kürnberger," in his *Ästhetik und Liberale Opposition: Zur Rollenproblematik des Schriftstellers in der österreichischen Literatur um 1848* (Vienna & Cologne: Böhlau, 1989), pp. 203–242;

Hildegard Meyer, *Nord-Amerika im Urteil des deutschen Schrifttums bis zur Mitte des 19. Jahrhunderts: Eine Untersuchung über Kürnbergers "Amerika-Müden"* (Hamburg: Friederichsen, de Gruyter, 1929);

Peter Michelsen, "Americanism and Anti-Americanism in German Novels of the XIXth Century," *Arcadia*, 11, no. 3 (1976): 272–287;

George A. Mulfinger, "Ferdinand Kürnbergers Roman *Der Amerikamüde,* dessen Quellen und Verhältnis zu Lenaus Amerikareise," *German American Annals,* 1, no. 6 (1903): 315–346, 385–405;

Jeffrey L. Sammons, "Land of Limited Possibilities: America in the Nineteenth-Century German Novel," "The Lorenzo Da Ponte Episode in Ferdinand Kürnberger's *Der Amerika-Müde,*" in his *Imagination and History: Selected Papers on Nineteenth-Century German Literature* (New York, Bern, Frankfurt am Main & Paris: Lang, 1988), pp. 217–247;

Rudolf Schier, "Die Amerika-Erfahrung Lenaus als Paradigma: Parallele Darstellungen bei Kürnberger, Chateaubriand, Dickens und Mark Twain," *Lenau Forum,* 15 (1989): 43–58;

Hansgeorg Schmidt-Bergmann, "Über die Gegenwärtigkeit von Literatur in literarischen Werken: Leben und Werk Lenaus als Modell für Ferdinand Kürnberger, Peter Härtling und Gernot Wolfgruber," *Lenau Forum,* 16 (1990): 77–84;

Rüdiger Steinlein, "Ferdinand Kürnbergers *Der Amerikamüde*: Ein amerikanisches Kulturbild als Entwurf einer negativen Utopie," in *Amerika in der deutschen Literatur: Neue Welt − Nordamerika − USA,* edited by Sigrid Bauschinger, Horst Denkler, and Wilfried Malsch (Stuttgart: Reclam, 1975), pp 154–177;

Theo Trummer, "Zwischen Dichtung und Kritik: Ferdinand Kürnberger zum 100. Todestag," *Jahrbuch der Grillparzer-Gesellschaft,* 14 (1980): 49–62;

Andreas Wildhagen, *Das politische Feuilleton Kürnbergers: Themen und Technik einer literarischen Kleinform im Zeitalter des deutschen Liberalismus in Österreich* (Frankfurt am Main, Bern & New York: Lang, 1985).

Papers:

Ferdinand Kürnberger's papers are in the Vienna City Library.

Ferdinand Lassalle

(11 April 1825 – 31 August 1864)

John Hibberd
University of Bristol

BOOKS: *Meine Vertheidigungs-Rede wider die Anklage der Verleitung zum Cassetten-Diebstahl, gehalten am 11. August 1848 vor dem Königlichen Assisenhofe zu Cöln und den Geschwornen* (Cologne: Greven, 1848);

Der Criminal-Prozeß wider mich wegen Verleitung zum Cassetten-Diebstahl oder Die Anklage der moralischen Mitschuld: Ein Tendenz-Prozeß (Cologne: Greven, 1848);

Meine Assisen-Rede gehalten vor den Geschwornen zu Düsseldorf am 3. Mai 1849, gegen die Anklage die Bürger zur Bewaffnung gegen die königl. Gewalt aufgereizt zu haben (Düsseldorf: Schaub, 1849);

Die Philosophie Herakleitos des Dunklen von Ephesos: Nach einer neuen Sammlung seiner Bruchstücke und der Zeugnisse der Alten dargestellt, 2 volumes (Berlin: Duncker, 1858);

Franz von Sickingen: Eine historische Tragödie (Berlin: Duncker, 1859); translated by Daniel de Leon as *Franz von Sickingen: A Tragedy in Five Acts* (New York: New York Labor News, 1904);

Der italienische Krieg und die Aufgabe Preußens: Eine Stimme aus der Demokratie (Berlin: Duncker, 1859);

Das System der erworbenen Rechte: Eine Versöhnung des positiven Rechts und der Rechtsphilosophie, 2 volumes (Leipzig: Brockhaus, 1861);

Herr Julian Schmidt der Literarhistoriker, mit Setzer-Scholien herausgegeben (Berlin: Jansen, 1862);

Über den besonderen Zusammenhang der gegenwärtigen Geschichtsperiode mit der Idee des Arbeiterstandes: Ein Vortrag gehalten am 12. April 1862 im Berliner Handwerker-Verein der Oranienburger Vorstadt (Berlin: Nöhring, 1862); republished as *Arbeiterprogramm: Über den besondern Zusammenhang der gegenwärtigen Geschichtsperiode mit der Idee des Arbeiterstandes* (Zurich: Meyer & Zeller, 1863); translated by Edward Peters as *The Working Men's Programme* (London: Modern Press, 1884);

Ferdinand Lassalle

Über Verfassungswesen: Ein Vortrag gehalten in einem Berliner Bürger-Bezirks-Verein (Berlin: Jansen, 1862);

Die Philosophie Fichte's und die Bedeutung des deutschen Volksgeistes: Festrede gehalten bei der am 19. Mai 1862 von der Philosophischen Gesellschaft und dem Wissenschaftlichen Kunst-Verein im Arnim'schen Saale veranstalteten Fichte-Feier (Berlin: Jansen, 1862);

Was nun?: Zweiter Vortrag über Verfassungswesen (Zurich: Meyer & Zeller, 1863);

Die Wissenschaft und die Arbeiter: Eine Vertheidigungsrede vor dem Berliner Criminalgericht gegen die Anklage, die besitzlosen Klassen zum Haßund zur Verachtung gegen die Besitzenden öffentlich angereizt zu haben (Zurich: Meyer & Zeller, 1863); translated by Thorstein Veblen as *Science and the Working Men: An Argument in His Own Defense before the Criminal Court of Berlin on the Charge of Having Publicly Incited the Unpropertied Classes to Hatred and Contempt of the Propertied Classes* (New York: International Library Publishing, 1900);

Macht und Recht: Offnes Sendschreiben (Zurich: Meyer & Zeller, 1863);

Offnes Antwortschreiben an das Central-Comité zur Berufung eines allgemeinen deutschen Arbeitercongresses zu Leipzig (Zurich: Meyer & Zeller, 1863); translated by John Ehmann and Fred Bader as *Lassalle's Open Letter to the National Labor Association of Germany* (Cincinnati, 1879);

Statut des Allgemeinen Deutschen Arbeiter-Vereins (Berlin: Bittner, 1863);

Zur Arbeiterfrage: Lassalles Rede bei der am 16. April in Leipzig abgehaltenen Arbeiterversammlung (Leipzig: Published by the author, 1863);

Arbeiterlesebuch: Rede Lassalle's zu Frankfurt am Main am 17. und 19. Mai 1863, nach dem stenographischen Bericht (Frankfurt am Main: Baist, 1863);

Die indirekte Steuer und die Lage der arbeitenden Klassen: Eine Vertheidigungsrede vor dem Kgl. Kammergericht zu Berlin gegen die Anklage die besitzlosen Klassen zum Haßund zur Verachtung gegen die Besitzenden öffentlich angereizt zu haben (Zurich: Meyer & Zeller, 1863);

Die Feste, die Presse und der Frankfurter Abgeordnetentag: Drei Symptome des öffentlichen Geistes. Eine Rede, gehalten in den Versammlungen des Allgemeinen Deutschen Arbeiter-Vereins zu Barmen, Solingen und Düsseldorf (Düsseldorf: Schaub, 1863; Chicago: Ahrens, 1863);

An die Arbeiter Berlins: Eine Ansprache im Namen des Allgemeinen Deutschen Arbeitervereins (Berlin: Schlingmann, 1863);

Herr Bastiat-Schulze von Delitzsch, der ökonomische Julian, oder: Capital und Arbeit (Berlin: Schlingmann, 1864); excerpts from chapter 4 freely translated by F. Keddell as *What Is Capital?* (New York: International Publishing, 1899);

Die Agitation des Allgem. Deutschen Arbeitervereins und das Versprechen des Königs von Preußen: Eine Rede gehalten am Stiftungsfest des Allgemeinen Deutschen Arbeitervereins zu Ronsdorf am 22. Mai 1864 (Berlin: Schlingmann, 1864);

Prozeßgegen den Schriftsteller Herrn F. Lassalle, verhandelt zu Düsseldorf vor der korrektionellen Appellkammer am 27. Juni 1864: Separatabdruck aus der Düsseldorfer Zeitung Nr. 176, 177 und 178 (Düsseldorf: Stahl, 1864);

Ferdinand Lassalles Tagebuch, edited by Paul Lindau (Breslau: Schlesische Buchdruckerei, Kunst- und Verlags-Anstalt, 1891);

Ferdinand Lassalle's sämtliche Reden und Schriften, 3 volumes, edited by Georg Hotschick (New York: Wolff, 1882);

Gesammelte Reden und Schriften, 12 volumes, edited by Eduard Bernstein (Berlin: Cassirer, 1919–1920).

Ferdinand Lassalle, an admirer and onetime friend of Karl Marx, was one of the most colorful and romantic figures in nineteenth-century history, an energetic and self-assertive political activist whose ardent radical convictions inspired him to powerful oratory and to ambitious and reckless deeds. He was an idealist with a strong sense of justice and inordinately high hopes for the victory of democracy and socialism in his own time; but he was also a master of effective propaganda and a political realist who concentrated on immediate tasks. He first earned public notoriety for his personal campaign on behalf of a woman whom he defended as a representative victim of male prejudice and of an unjust society. He kept himself in the limelight in a series of political trials in which he propagated his ideas by turning his defense into an accusation of his accusers. Meteorlike he emerged from an inauspicious background to become an intellectual, a man of independent means and aristocratic tastes who founded the first social democratic party in Germany and was its charismatic and tyrannical leader. Drawing on Marx's doctrines but without Marx's approval, he awakened German workers to class consciousness and to the need to struggle for their rights. After his premature death Lassalle became a legend as a larger-than-life personality with an extraordinary ability to give his all to a cause and to fill the masses with revolutionary fervor. He wrote scholarly volumes and a play, but it was his political writings, mostly long, fervent speeches published as pamphlets, which made a mark: they inspired generations of socialists despite, or because of, the suspicion with which he was regarded by orthodox Marxists. His *Arbeiterprogramm* (1863; translated as *The Working Men's Programme,* 1884) was an important historical document and remains a classic of political literature.

Ferdinand Johann Gottlieb Lassal (he adopted the more aristocratic spelling *Lassalle* later) was born in Breslau, Silesia (now Wroclaw, Poland), on 11 April 1825 into a relatively prosperous Jewish family – his father, Heyman Lassal, was a silk merchant – assimilated into German culture in almost

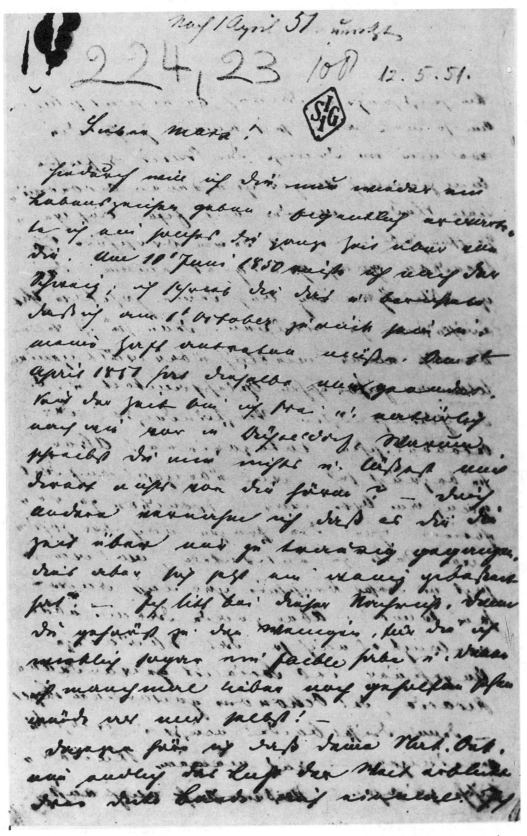

First page of a letter from Lassalle to Karl Marx (International Institute for Social History, Amsterdam)

all ways but religious belief and observance. The boy soon learned of anti-Semitic prejudice and violence and was determined to stand up for the rights of his people, whose passivity he despised. Indeed, he imagined himself as their savior, leading the Jews to liberty and dignity in Germany and even worldwide. Personal experiences of real and imagined injustice at the grammar school in Breslau evoked from him anger, tears of impotence, and oaths of vengeance. He believed that his true brilliance was not acknowledged by his teachers; in his family circle he was flattered as a youngster of outstanding intelligence, and he had no doubt that he was destined for great things. Heyman Lassal was a quick-tempered but fond and indulgent parent who involved his son as an ally in his disputes (which invariably ended in sentimental reconciliation) with his ever complaining wife, Rosalie Lassal, née Heitzfeld, and with Ferdinand's elder sister Friederike, whose tantrums and playacting the boy especially scorned. Rebuked by his father as a dandy and a spendthrift, he ran off to throw himself into the river; but his father restrained him. At the age of twelve he challenged another boy to a duel. Addicted to cards and billiards, he cultivated an image of himself as a man of the world and had precocious dreams of amorous conquests. He was a lazy and mutinous pupil but a voracious reader. To spare his parents shame, he forged their signatures on his school reports. In an attempt to avoid the discovery of his deceit he transferred at Easter 1840 to a commercial school in Leipzig, but he despised his teachers there even more. They thought him impertinent and big-headed and considered his behavior quite disgraceful. He quickly concluded that he would not devote his great talents to commerce.

His early vow to fight for the Jews was overtaken by an ambition to espouse the cause of human freedom. An admirer of the poet Heinrich Heine and the publicist Ludwig Börne, he hoped to use his pen to achieve a great, united, democratic Germany where all could proudly live in liberty. He returned to Breslau to prepare privately for the examination required for matriculation at a university. In March 1842 he was failed by the government inspector on the grounds of unorthodox ideas and poor punctuation. Knowing that the local examiners thought him an outstanding candidate, he characteristically wrote a forceful and clever letter of complaint to the Prussian minister of education, arguing that his failure violated the principle of individual freedom. A year later he retook and passed the examination.

Lassal brushed aside his father's expectation that he would study law or medicine, the usual paths for Jews, who were barred from the teaching profession. The works of the philosopher Georg Wilhelm Friedrich Hegel had convinced him that history was the most important of all subjects, because it was inextricably linked with progress toward liberty. For two years he alternated between the Universities of Breslau and Berlin but finally decided that the professors had nothing to teach him. Influenced by the ideals of the French Revolution, by early French socialists, and by reports of the plight of workers in England and France, and motivated by his impatience to see a better world than that of the age of reaction after the defeat of Napoleon, he undertook an intensive private study of Hegel that was to determine his later thought and action. He, like other so-called Young Hegelians, found in Hegel's philosophical system a key to the political and social problems of his time. In 1843 he declared himself a socialist. In 1844 he was prominent among the radical students who protested when the poet and democrat Hoffmann von Fallersleben was removed from his professorship at the University of Breslau, and he greeted the revolt of the Silesian weavers as the beginning of a war of the poor against the rich. In September 1844 he composed over three days a mammoth letter to his father in which he declared that industrialization was an important stage in the realization of individual freedom but also a triumph of materialism; it would be followed by communism, in which individual liberty would be reconciled with the authority of the state. He was planning an ambitious work to be titled "Philosophie des Geistes" (Philosophy of the Spirit) that would prepare the theoretical groundwork for revolution. His was an intellectual hatred of property as an obstacle to justice and the freedom of the human spirit; he himself meant to move in the highest circles and enjoy the good life. In Berlin he ruled over three disciples, young professional men several years his senior; for their benefit he wrote the ten-page "Kriegserklärung gegen die Welt" (Declaration of War on the World), an indictment of capitalist society as based on organized robbery. Yet until such robbery ceased, prudence dictated that he help his father and Friedrich Friedländer, his brother-in-law and cousin, set up gas companies in Breslau and Prague. But his prime aim was to establish a reputation for learning; without it his analyses of social ills would go unnoticed, and noticed he must be if he was to play the grand role in history that was his overwhelming ambition. He began studying the ancient Greek philosopher Heracleitus of Ephesus, a project that took him in the winter of 1845–1846 to the libraries of Paris. In

Paris he changed the spelling of his surname; there, too, he so impressed Heine that the aging poet dubbed him the messiah of the nineteenth century. Heine's letter of introduction opened the doors to the house of Karl and Rahel Varnhagen von Ense in Berlin, a center for liberal intellectuals and aristocrats. Lassalle was viewed by Alexander von Humboldt and others of considerable standing and influence as a young man of great brilliance but one lacking in tact and social graces.

In January 1846 Lassalle's career took a sudden turn when he met Sophie, Countess von Hatzfeldt, at the Varnhagens'. Twenty years older than Lassalle, she belonged to a rich and influential branch of the Prussian aristocracy and had been married for dynastic reasons in 1822, at the age of seventeen, to her cousin Count Edmund von Hatzfeldt-Wildenburg, one of the richest landowners on the lower Rhine. He disliked her, had affairs, squandered her money, and removed their children from her after she took a lover. Her family refused to support her in her claims against him. Lassalle perceived her as a victim of social prejudice who needed his services as a knight-errant standing up for justice and enlightenment. He was to devote eight years – half of his adult life – to her cause, fighting for her divorce and the restitution of her money and children. During those years he lived for long periods in the countess's house in Düsseldorf. He had resolved, he said, to combat lies with truth, rank with right, and the power of money with the power of the spirit. He quickly became a legal expert, a wily advocate, and a highly effective orator, and took center stage in an interminable series of scandalous court cases. For him the scandal was the injustice perpetrated by those in power on a defenseless woman; others saw the scandal in the association of a young provincial Jew with the illustrious and notorious countess. He convinced himself and her that her case was representative of a clash between the establishment, on the one hand, and the rights of women and the liberty of the individual, on the other. He importuned his acquaintances and his father for moral and financial support, since the countess's means were limited. He never regretted his commitment to her cause, even though his association with her was a hindrance to his subsequent political career. She was to reward him with lifelong devotion and, in due course, a handsome annuity.

No holds were barred in the Hatzfeldt campaign. Each side was supported by its own battalion of peasants from the Hatzfeldt estates, engaged in crude spying and grotesque intrigues, instigated libelous newspaper articles, and fought tooth and nail in the endless litigation. In August 1846 two of Lassalle's disciples from Berlin bungled an attempt to steal a casket, believed to contain incriminating evidence, from the count's mistress in Cologne. Early in 1848 he was charged with complicity in the theft and was in prison awaiting trial when revolutionary uprisings shook Vienna and Berlin in March. The trial in August was the occasion for his first great speech, *Meine Vertheidigungs-Rede wider die Anklage der Verleitung zum Cassetten-Diebstahl* (My Speech for the Defense against the Accusation of Incitement to Theft of a Casket, 1848), known as the "Kassettenrede" (Casket Speech), in which he employed sophistry and exaggerated pathos and played on the democratic sympathies of the Cologne jurymen. He was set free, and he and the countess, who declared herself a proletarian, were acclaimed by cheering crowds as heroes of the revolution. When they returned to Düsseldorf, the people unhitched the horses from their carriage and drew it through the streets.

Lassalle became involved with the left wing of the democrats in the Rhineland; prominent among them was Marx, whose friend and follower Lassalle became. Lassalle helped organize an armed citizens' guard; in November 1848 he was arrested for calling for violent insurrection and was kept in prison until his trial in May 1849. He had his speech in his defense, *Meine Assisen-Rede gehalten vor den Geschwornen zu Düsseldorf am 3. Mai 1849, gegen die Anklage die Bürger zur Bewaffnung gegen die königl. Gewalt aufgereizt zu haben* (Assizes Speech before the Jury in Düsseldorf on 3 May 1849 against the Accusation of Having Incited the Citizens to Take up Arms against the Royal Authority, 1849), published in advance. He proclaimed himself a democrat who defended the ideas of freedom promulgated by German liberals and a few socialists in 1848; he denied the legality of the Prussian constitution that had been imposed on the people and declared that it was the citizens' duty to fight against it. He listed the injustices committed in the name of law and order and prophesied worse to come. His mastery of logical rhetoric was rewarded: he was again set free by the jury. But this time the authorities did not concede defeat. He was tried again without a jury and sentenced to six months' imprisonment.

The main revolutionary events of 1848 and 1849 occurred while Lassalle was in prison. By the time he emerged, the Cologne communists who had not, like Marx, taken refuge abroad were about to be jailed. Lassalle could only lecture to workers' leaders in the Rhineland, comfort the dependents of those in prison, and try vainly to find a German publisher for Marx. He was, as he put it, "der letzte Mohikaner" (the Last of the Mohicans).

The Hatzfeldt affair dragged on and on, to be concluded in 1854 in a private settlement wrested from the count under a threat that was tantamount to blackmail. Lassalle became, thanks to the countess, a man of means (a kept man, in the opinion of many), who speculated on the stock exchange and conducted an affair with the daughter of a political intelligence agent who worked for many masters. He was under constant police surveillance. After moving mountains to obtain the right to live in Berlin, he set up a splendid establishment there in 1857 and entertained generously those members of society who were not afraid to accept his invitations. He completed the two-volume *Die Philosophie Herakleitos des Dunklen von Ephesos* (The Philosophy of Heracleitus the Obscure of Ephesus, 1858), most of which had been written by 1846. In Berlin intellectual circles the work was recognized as a remarkable achievement. He had added to the number of intelligible fragments of the pre-Socratic philosopher, researched his early reception, and discovered a consistent system where the Greeks themselves had found obscurity. The approbation of Marx was sought by the author but not given: to Friedrich Engels, Marx declared that this overlong study added nothing to what Hegel had said. Marx was impatient with Lassalle's Hegelianism, but also with his association with the countess; and the extravagant life-style he had adopted in Berlin did not recommend him to fellow socialists. Aided by his fine intellectual forehead and his aquiline profile, Lassalle was directing some of his compelling energy to the conquest of women, and he caused a stir when he thrashed a jealous official in a conflict over the affections of a married lady.

Lassalle's reflections on the failure of the 1848 revolution were summed up in his verse tragedy *Franz von Sickingen* (1859). Its hero fights for freedom and national unity in sixteenth-century Germany but fails because he has insufficient trust in the power of the idea of liberty and the revolutionary enthusiasm of the people. Marx and Engels disagreed with this interpretation of the Peasants' Revolt; their comments instigated a debate about the aesthetics of historical tragedy, a debate to which the literary critic György Lukács and the philosopher Ludwig Marcuse contributed in the twentieth century. But for that controversy this play, stronger in rhetoric than in characterization, would probably have been forgotten. The conflict it dramatizes between revolutionary passion and realistic

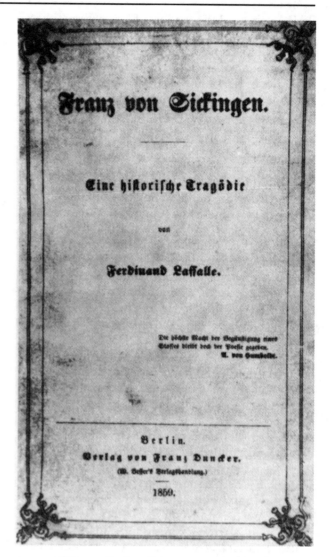

Title page for Lassalle's verse tragedy about the sixteenth-century Peasants' Revolt

opportunism did, however, prove central to Lassalle's career.

Lassalle judged that radical change in Germany could come only if the national liberation movement in Italy encouraged a Hungarian uprising and the disintegration of the Austrian Empire, leading to the creation of a united republic of German-speaking peoples. Unlike Marx, he saw that nationalism was a driving force in history. Multinational, reactionary Austria was, he thought, the prime obstacle to progress. The French emperor Napoleon III, widely seen as the great threat to democracy in Europe, he regarded as a passing phenomenon. His pamphlet *Der italienische Krieg und die Aufgabe Preußens* (The Italian War and Prussia's Task, 1859) advocates that Prussia refrain from war with France and assume leadership of a greater Germany. He explained to Marx that he aimed to make the Prussian government, which could not conceivably heed his advice, anathema to freedom-loving Germans.

Lassalle depended on Sophie von Hatzfeldt for emotional support; she continued to believe passionately in Lassalle the politician and man of ideas, but maintained that she regarded him as a son rather than a lover. She tolerated and even abetted his relations with younger women. A remarkable document to the Romantic religion of love and to Lassalle's belief in his historical mission is contained in the forty pages of a letter he wrote in French in 1860 to a nineteen-year-old Russian girl, Sophia Sontzov, whom he met while taking a cure at Aix-la-Chapelle (now Aachen). (It is generally thought that his recurrent complaints were due to syphilis.) She had told him that she did not return his love, but he was not to be deterred. He proposed marriage, declared the sacredness of love and of his own political task, and promised her a life of great and spiritually rewarding sacrifice. She, like many women, was fascinated by him; but, sensibly wary of this notorious "red," she did not rise to his challenge.

A second massive scholarly work by Lassalle, *Das System der erworbenen Rechte* (The System of Acquired Rights, 1861), showed that law, including property law, was subject to historical evolution; prophesied great imminent change; and held that only those rights that an individual had acquired by his own actions could not justly be removed by new legislation. History, he wrote, brings greater and greater limitation to private ownership. Existing laws often contradicted the idea of justice: the Prussian agrarian laws, for instance, legalized the robbery of the poor by the rich landowners.

Though Marx disapproved of a work that linked the evolution of law to the progress of the Hegelian Idea rather than material forces, Lassalle had not abandoned hope of working with him. But Lassalle's attempts to secure Marx's permanent return to Germany failed because Marx was considered a foreigner who was ineligible for an amnesty granted to political exiles. Lassalle's plan to edit a newspaper with him also came to nothing, for Marx did not intend to share decision making. In 1861 Lassalle visited Italy and tried to persuade Giuseppe Garibaldi to march on Austrian Venice.

Back in Berlin in 1862 he became friends with Lothar Bucher, a radical who had spent years of exile in England and was convinced that constitutional change alone could not alter society and that there was no popular basis for revolution in Ger-

many. Lassalle was not so easily discouraged, but he learned from Bucher to study carefully the realities of the political situation and to recognize that the masses needed the inspiration of a "gospel."

A constitutional crisis in Prussia in 1862 brought Lassalle's intervention into parliamentary politics and his decisive break with the Liberals. The Liberal majority in parliament refused to sanction the reorganization of the army demanded by the crown. In March the lower house of the Prussian parliament was dissolved and new elections were announced. In April Lassalle delivered two speeches, both masterpieces of their kind. *Über Verfassungswesen* (On the Nature of Constitutions, 1862) was given before Liberal voters in Berlin. Constitutions, said Lassalle, were not determined by words on paper but reflected the power structure in the land; the iniquitous Prussian three-class electoral system was an example. The power of public opinion, of the petite bourgeoisie and the workers, had yet to be organized. In the present situation the constitution would be altered in the interests either of the reactionary or of the democratic forces. His linking of legal right with power was greeted with malicious joy by the conservatives and made him unpopular with the Liberals, who believed in right as an abstract principle.

The other speech, *Über den besonderen Zusammenhang der gegenwärtigen Geschichtsperiode mit der Idee des Arbeiterstandes* (On the Special Connection of the Present Period of History with the Idea of the Working Class, 1862), given to a workers' group in the Berlin suburb of Oranienburg, soon became better known and was republished as the *Arbeiterprogramm*. It owes much to Marx and Engels's *Communist Manifesto* (1848), but in idealizing the dreams of the poor for justice, freedom, and dignity Lassalle provided the "gospel" that Bucher had declared necessary. He announced the claims of the masses, whose interests were represented neither by the king nor by the Liberals. As a political pamphlet the piece is to be judged less by the originality of its ideas or the truth of its statements than by its clarity, its passion, and its concentration on a tangible goal. It was excellent propaganda. Lassalle's sharply formulated survey of historical trends and present injustices, his overwhelmingly persuasive if biased statistics on indirect taxation and on the Prussian electoral system, under which one rich individual had the voting power of seventeen without property, underlined the need for direct universal male suffrage. With the vote the workers would gain a proper influence and abolish all privilege based on ownership of property. With the insight of the activist of genius Lassalle had seen the need to concentrate on one simple demand if Marxist principles were to become effective politics. He seemed to regard democracy and socialism as two sides of the same coin, and he derided Liberal laissez-faire doctrines. But he was careful not to alienate all middle-class democrats: they, too, could be classed as workers provided that they did not cling to political privilege. Violent revolution was not inevitable, though the alternative, peaceful reform, would be a slow process. Lassalle lauded the state, which he defined in Hegelian terms as the means by which individuals find their true value; he did not share Marx's notion that the state is an instrument of class domination.

Lassalle made little impression on the artisans to whom he addressed these ideas. The authorities found his speech much more worthy of attention. As soon as it was printed it was confiscated by the police and its author charged with endangering public order by stirring up class hatred. A visit in July to Marx in London showed that Lassalle could count on no support from there. Marx was embittered by his poverty and – influenced by Engels, who had always disliked Lassalle's arrogance – judged that Lassalle had stolen and twisted his ideas; Marx also gave undue credence to reports of Lassalle's betrayal of revolutionary principles. There were also petty disagreements, one of them over a loan Lassalle made to Marx.

Like his Hegelianism, Lassalle's patriotism reflected his indebtedness to a part of the German idealist tradition. His *Die Philosophie Fichte's und die Bedeutung des deutschen Volksgeistes* (The Philosophy of Fichte and the Meaning of the German National Spirit, 1862), delivered as a speech in May 1862, stresses the philosopher Johann Gottlieb Fichte's ideal of a German state based on the national spirit: Fichte had pointed out the evils of a Germany divided into many states and governed by a few ruling families, and he had posited a leading role for Germany in the advancement of freedom. Nationalism had stood alongside democracy on the platforms of the Liberals of 1848 but did not appeal to Marx, with whom Lassalle's relationship became more and more strained. Lassalle enjoyed his status as a man of learning in Berlin, where he addressed the Philosophical Society on the shortcomings of the Hegelian Johann Karl Friedrich Rosenkranz as measured against the master Hegel himself, while incidentally proclaiming the inevitability of progress from a monarchy to a republic.

In November 1862, in his speech *Was nun?* (What Now?, 1863), Lassalle called on the Liberals to expose the unconstitutionality of the situation in

Title page for the published version of a speech given by Lassalle to Berlin workers on 12 April 1862. The speech was republished the following year as the Arbeiterprogramm.

Prussia. They must withdraw from parliament; such a political strike would force the government to give way. Their horrified reaction made it clear that any hopes Lassalle still had of influencing them had little foundation. But in December the *Arbeiterprogramm* elicited a response from a group of workers in Leipzig who had asked Liberal leaders to consider support for direct universal suffrage and had met with a lukewarm response. Two of their representatives came to see Lassalle in Berlin when he was defending himself in court against the charge arising from the *Arbeiterprogramm*. He used the trial to repeat and reinforce the arguments of that work. At his clever and provocative best, reveling as always in the opportunity to reach a wide public with his ideas, he argued for four hours in his speech *Die Wissenschaft und die Arbeiter* (1863; translated as *Science and the Working Men,* 1900) that the *Arbeiterprogramm* was a work of scholarship and therefore immune from prosecution; in any case, it promoted social harmony, not hatred as the prosecution maintained. He embarrassed the prosecutor by quoting his father, the philosopher Friedrich Wilhelm Schelling. Lassalle demonstrated that he could run rings around the professional lawyers; nevertheless, he was sentenced to four months' imprisonment. Both he and the prosecution appealed the sentence. In February 1863, with his *Macht und Recht* (Might and Right), which the Liberal press had refused to print, he declared open war on the Liberals: right must be backed by might if injustice was to be overcome. He had concluded that the Liberals had abandoned democratic principles and that collaboration with them was impossible.

The last eighteen months of Lassalle's life were the most frantic of his career. At the beginning of 1863 he made public his response to the Leipzig workers; he dreamed that his *Offnes Antwortschreiben an das Central-Comité zur Berufung eines allgemeinen deutschen Arbeitercongresses zu Leipzig* (Open Letter to the Central Committee for the Summoning of a General German Workingmen's Conference at Leipzig; translated as *Lassalle's Open Letter to the National Labor Association of Germany*, 1879), which he composed in two weeks, would have an effect comparable to that of Martin Luther's theses of 1517. A companion piece to the *Arbeiterprogramm*, it presented the workers with revelations of the iniquities of free-market liberalism that they could relate to their own experience. Lassalle dismissed Liberal proposals for self-help: they could aid some individuals but could not solve the underlying problem. Workingmen, Lassalle argued, must be saved from capitalism by organizing themselves into a separate party and demanding universal direct suffrage. Universal suffrage was his slogan, and he called on the workers to make it theirs: they should repeat it day in day out, he wrote, and their words would call forth a tremendous echo and become an irresistible force. They should also demand the financial backing of the state for the establishment of workers' cooperatives. Lassalle advanced proposals that stood a real chance of acceptance. He knew that the majority of workers were not revolutionary hotheads; they must fight for their interests, he said, by legal and peaceful means. He explained to his friend, the radical economist Karl Rodbertus-Jagetzow, that his ultimate, (but publicly unexpressed), aim was a system under which prices, wages, and conditions of work would be laid down by the state; Rodbertus-Jagetzow, who believed in such state socialism, was not pleased by the open letter. Lassalle here laid himself open to the charge of opportunistically concealing his true stance to gain wide support.

In March the policies in the open letter were approved by the workers in Leipzig and then in a few other centers, though most labor associations chose to remain faithful to the Liberal party. The Allgemeiner Deutscher Arbeiter-Verein (General Association of German Workers [ADAV]) was founded in May with branches in eleven towns. Lassalle became its first president, with sweeping powers. He had no truck with democratic discussion: leave the talk shops and the bickering to the bourgeoisie, he said; we want action! There was nobody else in the movement with the intellect and character to challenge his leadership. Two lengthy sessions (seven hours in all) of oratory in Frankfurt am Main in May were published immediately as the *Arbeiterlesebuch* (The Working Man's Reader, 1863). Knowing that the word *Sozialismus* (socialism) would frighten many, he insisted that his principles were democratic.

In September 1863, speaking to workers in Barmen, Solingen, and Düsseldorf, he rounded on the Liberal press, frustrated that his party had no such means of reaching the public. In that speech, *Die Feste, die Presse und der Frankfurter Abgeordnetentag* (The Celebrations, the Press and the Meeting of Deputies in Frankfurt, 1863), he spoke of the Liberals as a crowd of old women and of Prussian prime minister Otto von Bismarck as a man to be respected. He was planning to use Bismarck, but he overestimated both his own ability to exert pressure on Bismarck and the pace of progress toward emancipation. His appearance in Solingen led to a confrontation between his supporters and the police, and Lassalle complained in a telegram to Bismarck that the Liberal authorities had acted illegally in breaking up the meeting. He also tried unsuccessfully to persuade three men who were sentenced to hard labor as a result of the confrontation to lodge an appeal to the king, a move that would have provided extra publicity and put further pressure on the government. Workers' demonstrations were not proving effective; public opinion was not being swayed fast enough; the Liberals, who claimed to be progressive but in his opinion were not, dominated the political opposition. An additional tactic was called for. For some months he had been in secret contact with Bismarck, offering himself and his party as allies in the battle against the Liberals and hoping that in return Bismarck would put Lassalle's ideas into practice. It was not an utterly unreasonable hope: in their attitudes toward the state they had some common ground, and Bismarck recognized the potential of the workers' votes – they would, he believed, be cast for the conservatives. He was considering both electoral reform and measures to alleviate the plight of the workers as means to outmaneuver the Liberal opposition.

In October 1863 the appeals arising from the *Arbeiterprogramm* case were heard. Again Lassalle published his defense as a pamphlet, *Die indirekte Steuer und die Lage der arbeitenden Klassen* (Indirect Taxation and the Condition of the Working Classes, 1863). How could it be said that the *Arbeiterprogramm* incited to hatred when it did not list the most horrifying examples of social injustice, which he proceeded to enumerate? His sentence was reduced to a small fine. It was a brilliant victory, but he complained to the countess that the working class took no notice of him.

In the winter of 1863–1864 Lassalle and Bismarck met on several occasions. Bismarck knew that he had the upper hand; Lassalle had said at the beginning of 1863 that the ADAV would be a power in the land as soon as it had one hundred thousand members, but during his lifetime, though he pretended otherwise, its membership was never much more than three or four thousand. Industrialized workers made up only a small fraction of the German labor force, and for all his energy and determination he could not overcome the traditional allegiance of many of them to the Liberal party. He made no headway with the workers of Berlin; they shouted him down.

Unfortunately for Lassalle, by 1864 the conflict with Denmark was taking all of Bismarck's attention, and he ignored Lassalle's advances. Within a year of the founding of the ADAV Lassalle desperately needed a tangible political victory to boost the morale of its members, and for all his talk of his army of socialists only the government could have delivered such a victory for him.

Herr Bastiat-Schulze von Delitzsch, der ökonomische Julian, oder: Capital und Arbeit (Mr. Bastiat-Schulze of Delitzsch, the Economic Julian; or, Capital and Labor, 1864; excerpts translated as *What Is Capital?*, 1899) is an attack on a leading Liberal economist who founded many workingmen's societies. Lassalle's chief work on economics, it is not a major work in the history of the subject and does not stand comparison with the writings of Marx. It is an eclectic piece with simplified and sometimes unsound analyses that makes much of a supposed iron law of wages according to which wages under capitalism can never rise above subsistence level. Nevertheless, it was effective propaganda because, again, Lassalle interpreted the plight of the workers in a way that made sense to them. In March 1864 he stood trial on a charge of treason arising from an address to Berlin workers

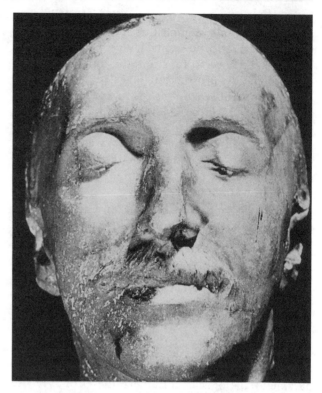

Death mask of Lassalle (International Institute for Social History, Amsterdam)

published the previous October. This charge conveniently blunted any suspicions within the labor movement that he was colluding with the class enemy; his discussions with Bismarck did not become public knowledge until after his death. He was acquitted. In May he was making extraordinary claims for the success of the ADAV on its first anniversary. At Ronsdorf in the Ruhr he gave a speech, published as *Die Agitation des Allgem. Deutschen Arbeitervereins und das Versprechen des Königs von Preußen* (The Campaign of the Gen. Association of German Workers and the King of Prussia's Promise, 1864), in which he not only inflated membership figures and boasted of branches that existed only on paper but also declared that the king had approved the introduction of state-subsidized workers' cooperatives. The king had, in fact, given only vague promises of help to a delegation of Silesian weavers who had no connection with the ADAV. Lassalle's words were, however, effective in one sense: he and Countess von Hatzfeldt made a tumultuous, triumphant procession through the Ruhr. He was seen by the workers as courageously defying the establishment, suffering persecution on their behalf, and leading them to a certain and immediate victory. In June he was once again standing trial in Düsseldorf for inciting class hatred. His sen-

Poster commemorating the unification of the Lassallean and Marxist movements at Gotha in 1875 to form the Social Democratic party of Germany (International Institute for Social History, Amsterdam)

tence of one year was reduced on appeal to six months.

A huge demonstration of workers acclaimed Lassalle as he left Düsseldorf. Yet it was an exhausted and severely depressed man who went to Switzerland in the early summer of 1864 for one of his frequent cures. His vocal cords had failed him more than once in the last months. He was also worn down by the repugnant task of grasping horny and grimy proletarian hands, for this revolutionary was a social snob. There had been discontent among officials of the ADAV over his dictatorial leadership and his high-society habit of disappearing to recuperate at a spa. The movement had not grown as he had hoped; he had expected supreme success within a year. He no longer faced the prospect of imprisonment with equanimity. He told the countess he was sick and tired of politics, since nothing could be achieved without power. But in Switzerland he met Helene von Dönniges, the beautiful, spirited, red-haired daughter of a Bavarian diplomat, who fired the impetuous, romantic lover in Lassalle. She wanted to elope to Egypt, but he in-

sisted that her parents should consent to their marriage. He would not take advantage of her passion and act in an ungentlemanly way; also, by forcing the parents to give their blessing he would score a great victory over social prejudice. Once she returned to them, however, Helene changed her mind. He insisted that she was being kept from him under duress and contrary to the law. He invoked principles of emancipation and justice and appealed for help to everyone he knew – asking Richard Wagner, for example, to use his influence at the Bavarian court. But Lassalle was left to fight alone, and his obsessive determination grew accordingly. Yanko von Jankowitz, a Romanian whom Helene's family regarded as her fiancé, was persuaded that her honor had been impugned; but it was Lassalle who insisted on fighting a duel. He made his will and refused to take pistol lessons. The duel took place on 26 August 1864; Lassalle was wounded, and he died five days later. The memorial service at the synagogue in Geneva was attended by four thousand sympathizers, among them such notable radicals as Aleksandr Herzen and Mikhail Bakunin. Sophie von Hatzfeldt took possession of his embalmed body and paraded it before the workers of the Rhineland before the authorities intervened and delivered it to the Lassal family for burial in the Jewish cemetery in Breslau.

The countess created an idealized myth of Lassalle as the great hero of the working classes. Future generations recognized that he had many faults, principally arrogance, but that much of what he declaimed as the truth for his time applied to subsequent history. Socialism became a power in German politics, though more slowly than Lassalle thought it would and not quite as he or Marx imagined. In 1875 the German Social Democratic party was founded from a union of the Lassallean and Marxist movements, and the former provided the official program for fifteen years and the unofficial code of practice until World War I. Photographs of Lassalle decorated many workers' living rooms. He, it was recalled, had not, like Marx, insisted that the proletarians knew no fatherland. And when the Communists and the Social Democrats went their separate ways in 1918, many of the latter looked to Lassalle for inspiration. Though uneasy about his flamboyant romanticism and his personal morals, they were happy that he had appeared to allow for an evolutionary rather than a revolutionary socialism. In 1864 it seemed that he had achieved little, but the ideas he expressed with such conviction and in such a dramatic manner took hold of people's minds.

Letters:

*Une page d'amour de Ferdinand Lassalle: récit, correspon-
dence, confession* (Leipzig: Brockhaus, 1878);
translated into German as *Eine Liebes-Episode
aus dem Leben Ferdinand Lassalle's: Tagebuch –
Briefwechsel – Bekenntnisse* (Leipzig: Brockhaus,
1878);

*Briefe von Ferdinand Lassalle an Carl Rodbertus-Jaget-
zow,* introduction by Adolph Wagner (Berlin:
Puttkammer & Mühlbrecht, 1878);

*Ferdinand Lassalles Briefe an Georg Herwegh, nebst Brie-
fen der Gräfin Sophie Hatzfeldt an Frau Emma Herwegh,* edited by Marcel Herwegh (Zurich: Müller, 1896);

*Aus dem literarischen Nachlaß von Karl Marx, Friedrich
Engels und Ferdinand Lassalle,* edited by Franz
Mehring, volume 4: *Briefe von Ferdinand Las-
salle an Karl Marx und Friedrich Engels* (Stuttgart:
Dietz, 1902);

Intime Briefe Ferdinand Lassalles an Eltern und Schwester,
edited by Eduard Bernstein (Berlin: Verlag
Buchhandlung Vorwärts, 1905);

"Lassalleana: Unbekannte Briefe Lassalles," edited
by Gustav Mayer, *Archiv für die Geschichte des
Sozialismus und der Arbeiterbewegung,* 1 (1910):
176–197;

"Briefe Lassalles an Dr. Otto Dammer in Leipzig,
Vizepräsident des ADAV," edited by Hermann Oncken, *Archiv für die Geschichte des Sozialismus und der Arbeiterbewegung,* 2 (1911): 380–
422;

"Briefe Lassalles an Dr. Moses Hess," edited by N.
Riasanoff, *Archiv für die Geschichte des Sozialismus
und der Arbeiterbewegung,* 3 (1912): 129–142;

"Ein Brief Lassalles an den Minister von Bodel-
schwingh," edited by Mayer, *Archiv für die
Geschichte des Sozialismus und der Arbeiterbewegung,* 4 (1914): 330–332;

"Neue Lassalle-Briefe, mitgeteilt von Hermann
Oncken," *Archiv für die Geschichte des Sozialismus
und der Arbeiterbewegung,* 4 (1914): 439–465;

"Briefe Ferdinand Lassalles an Ferdinand Freiligrath," edited by Mayer, *Archiv für die
Geschichte des Sozialismus und der Arbeiterbewegung,* 7 (1916): 431–445;

Ferdinand Lassalle, *Nachgelassene Briefe und Schriften,*
6 volumes, edited by Mayer (Stuttgart: Deutsche Verlagsanstalt, 1921–1925);

"Aus dem Briefwechsel Hans von Bülows und Lassalles," edited by Mayer, *Der Neue Merkur,* 7,
no. 6 (1924): 433–456;

*Bismarck und Lassalle: Ihr Briefwechsel und ihre Gesprä-
che,* edited by Mayer (Berlin: Dietz, 1928).

Bibliography:

Bert Andréas, "Bibliographie der Schriften von Ferdinand Lassalle und Auswahl der Literatur
über ihn," *Archiv für Sozialgeschichte,* 3 (1963):
331–423.

Biographies:

Hermann Oncken, *Lassalle: Eine politische Biographie,*
enlarged edition (Stuttgart & Berlin: Deutsche
Verlagsanstalt, 1920);

Konrad Haenisch, *Ferdinand Lassalle: Der Mensch und
Politiker in Selbstzeugnissen* (Leipzig: Kröner,
1925);

David Footman, *The Primrose Path: A Life of Ferdinand
Lassalle* (London: Cresset Press, 1946);

Gudrun von Uexküll, *Ferdinand Lassalle in Selbstzeugnissen und Bilddokumenten* (Reinbek: Rowohlt,
1974);

Hans Jürgen Friederici, *Ferdinand Lassalle: Eine politische Biographie* (Berlin: Dietz, 1985).

References:

Salo Wittmayer Baron, *Die politische Theorie Ferdinand Lassalles* (Leipzig: Hirschfeld, 1923);

Eduard Bernstein, *Ferdinand Lassalle as a Social Reformer* (London: Swan Sonnenschein / New York:
Scribners, 1893);

Georg Brandes, *Ferdinand Lassalle* (London: Heinemann / New York: Macmillan, 1911);

Edward Hallett Carr, "Lassalle meets Bismarck," in
his *Studies in Revolution* (London: Macmillan,
1950), pp. 72–87;

William Harbutt Dawson, *German Socialism and Fer-
dinand Lassalle: A Biographical History of German
Socialist Movements during This Century* (London:
Swan Sonnenschein, 1888);

H. Duncker, " 'Die Lassalle-Legende,' " *Internationale,* 8 (1925): 242–250;

Bernhard Harms, *Ferdinand Lassalle und seine Bedeutung für die deutsche Sozialdemokratie* (Jena:
Fischer, 1909);

Walter Höllerer, ed., *Sickingen-Debatte: Ein Beitrag
zur materialistischen Literaturtheorie* (Darmstadt:
Luchterhand, 1974);

Paul Kampffmeyer, *Lassalle, ein Erwecker der Arbeiterbewegung* (Berlin: Dietz, 1925);

Gustav Mayer, "Zum Verständnis der politischen
Aktion Lassalles," *International Review of Social
History,* 3 (1938): 89–104;

Franz Mehring, *Geschichte der deutschen Sozialdemokratie, Theil 1.: Von der Julirevolution bis zum
preußischen Verfassungsstreite. 1830 bis 1863,*
volume 1 of his *Gesammelte Schriften,* edited by

Thomas Höhle (Berlin: Dietz, 1960), pp. 478–491, 571–579, 587–620, 633–637, 652–695;

Susanne Miller, *Das Problem der Freiheit im Sozialismus: Freiheit, Staat und Revolution in der Programmatik der Sozialdemokratie von Lassalle bis zum Revisionismusstreit* (Frankfurt am Main: Europäische Verlags-Anstalt, 1964), pp. 25–54;

Hans Mommsen, "Lassalle, Ferdinand," in *Marxism, Communism and Western Society: A Comparative Encyclopedia,* volume 5, edited by Claus Dieter Kernig (New York: Herder & Herder, 1973), pp. 107–127;

Roger Morgan, *The German Social Democrats and the First International, 1864–72* (London: Cambridge University Press, 1965);

Schlomo Na'aman, *Ferdinand Lassalle* (Hannover: Verlag für Literatur und Zeitgeschehen, 1968);

Thilo Ramm, *Ferdinand Lassalle als Rechts- und Sozialphilosoph* (Meisenheim am Glan: Hain, 1953);

Ramm, "Lassalle und Marx," *Marxismus-Studien,* 3 (1960): 185–221;

Guenther Roth, *The Social Democrats in Imperial Germany: A Study in Working-Class Isolation and National Integration* (Totowa, N. J.: Bedminster, 1963);

Bertrand Russell, "Lecture II: Lassalle," in his *German Social Democracy* (London: Allen & Unwin, 1965), pp. 41–68;

Arnold Schirokauer, *Lassalle: the Power of Illusion and the Illusion of Power* (London: Allen & Unwin, 1931);

Ernest Antoine Aimé Léon, Baron Seillère, *Études sur Ferdinand Lassalle, fondateur du Parti Socialiste Allemand* (Paris: Plon, 1897);

Edmund Silberner, "Ferdinand Lassalle: From Maccabeism to Jewish Anti-Semitism," *Hebrew Union College Annual,* 24 (1953): 151–186;

Hartmut Stirner, *Die Agitation und Rhetorik Ferdinand Lassalles* (Marburg: Verlag Arbeiterbewegung und Gesellschaftswissenschaft, 1979);

Edmund Wilson, "Chapter 13: Lassalle," in his *To the Finland Station: A Study in the Writing and Acting of History* (London: Allen, 1940), pp. 228–259.

Papers:

Copies of many of Ferdinand Lassalle's letters are in the International Institute for Social History, Amsterdam; other materials are in the Archives of the Counts von Hatzfeldt, Castle Schönstein, Wissen/Sieg, Westerwald; the Bismarck-Archiv, Friedrichsruh; and the Bundesarchiv (Federal Archives), Frankfurt am Main.

Fanny Lewald

(24 March 1811 – 5 August 1889)

Irene Stocksieker Di Maio
Louisiana State University and A&M College

BOOKS: *Clementine,* anonymous (Leipzig: Brockhaus, 1842);

Jenny, anonymous, 2 volumes (Leipzig: Brockhaus, 1843);

Eine Lebensfrage: Roman, anonymous (Leipzig: Brockhaus, 1845);

Italienisches Bilderbuch, 2 volumes (Berlin: Duncker, 1847); translated by Rachel, Countess d'Avigdor, as *The Italians at Home* (London: Cautley, 1848);

Diogena: Roman von Iduna Gräfin H. . . H. . ., anonymous (Leipzig: Brockhaus, 1847);

Prinz Louis Ferdinand: Roman, 3 volumes (Breslau: Max, 1849); republished, with foreword, as *Prinz Louis Ferdinand: Ein Zeitbild,* 1 volume (Berlin: Hofmann, 1859); translated by Linda Rogols-Siegel as *Prinz Louis Ferdinand* (Lewiston, N.Y.: Mellen, 1988);

Erinnerungen aus dem Jahre 1848, 2 volumes (Brunswick: Vieweg, 1850);

Liebesbriefe: Aus dem Leben eines Gefangenen. Roman (Brunswick: Vieweg, 1850);

Auf rother Erde: Eine Novelle (Leipzig: Weber, 1850);

Dünen- und Berggeschichten: Erzählungen, 2 volumes (Brunswick: Vieweg, 1851);

England und Schottland: Reisetagebuch, 2 volumes (Brunswick: Vieweg, 1851–1852);

Wandlungen: Roman, 4 volumes (Brunswick: Vieweg, 1853);

Adele: Roman (Brunswick: Vieweg, 1855);

Die Kammerjungfer: Roman, 3 volumes (Brunswick: Vieweg, 1855);

Deutsche Lebensbilder: Erzählungen, 4 volumes (Brunswick: Vieweg, 1856) – comprises volume 1, *Die Hausgenossen: Erzählung;* volume 2, *Das große Loos: Erzahlung;* volume 3, *Kein Haus: Eine Dortgeschicte;* volume 4, *Die Tante: Erzählung;*

Die Reisegefährten: Roman, 2 volumes (Berlin: Guttentag, 1858);

Fanny Lewald (courtesy of Deutsche Staatsbibliothek in der Stiftung Preußischer Kulturbesitz, Berlin)

Neue Romane, 5 volumes (Berlin: Janke, 1859–1864) – comprises volume 1, *Der Seehof* (1859); translated by Nathaniel Greene as *Lake-House* (Boston: Ticknor & Fields, 1861); volume 2, *Schloß Tannenburg* (1859); volume 3, *Graf Joachim* (1859); volume 4, *Emilie* (1859); volume 5, *Der Letzte seines Stammes*;   *Mamsell Philippinens Philipp* (1864);

Das Mädchen von Hela: Ein Roman, 2 volumes (Berlin: Janke, 1860); translated by Mary M. Pleasants as *The Mask of Beauty: A Novel* (New York: Bonner, 1894);

Meine Lebensgeschichte, 3 volumes (Berlin: Janke, 1861–1862); translated and edited by Hanna Ballin Lewis as *The Education of Fanny Lewald* (Albany: State University of New York Press, 1992);

Gesammelte Novellen, 2 volumes (Berlin: Gerschel, 1862) – comprises volume 1, *Der dritte Stand: Novellistisches Zeitbild*; volume 2, *Ein armes Mädchen*;

Bunte Bilder: Gesammelte Erzählungen und Phantasiestücke (Berlin: Janke, 1862) – comprises "Der Stellvertreter," "Gräfin Marie," "Der Kunstteufel," "Der Nebel baut Nesterchen," "Tante Renate," "Eine alte Firma," "Berliner Kinder," "Das lebende Bild," "Der Domherr";

Osterbriefe für die Frauen (Berlin: Janke, 1863);

Von Geschlecht zu Geschlecht, 8 volumes (Berlin: Janke, 1864–1866) – comprises *Der Freiherr*, 3 volumes (1864); *Der Emporkömmling*, 5 volumes (1866);

Erzählungen, 3 volumes (Berlin: Grote, 1866–1868) – comprises volume 1, *Vornhme Welt*; *Das Mädchen von Oyas* (1866), translated anonymously as "The Aristocratic World" and "The Maid of Oyas," in *Stories and Novels, from the German of Fanny Lewald* (Chicago: Schick, 1885); volume 2, *Die Dilettanten* (1867); volume 3, *Jasch* (1868);

Villa Riunione: Erzählungen eines alten Tanzmeisters, 2 volumes (Berlin: Janke, 1869) – comprises volume 1, *Prinzessin Aurora*;   *Eine traurige Geschichte*; volume 2, *Ein Schiff aus Cuba*; *Domenico*;

Ein Winter in Rom, by Lewald and Adolf Stahr (Berlin: Guttentag, 1869);

Sommer und Winter am Genfersee: Ein Tagebuch (Berlin: Janke, 1869);

Für und wider die Frauen: Vierzehn Briefe (Berlin: Janke, 1870; second edition, with foreword, 1875);

Nella: Eine Weihnachtsgeschichte (Berlin: Janke, 1870);

Die Unzertrennlichen; Pflegeeltern: Zwei Erzählungen (Berlin: Janke, 1871);

Gesammelte Werke, 12 volumes (Berlin: Janke, 1871–1874) – comprises volumes 1–3, *Meine Lebensgeschichte*; volumes 4–7, *Von Geschlecht zu Geschlecht*; volume 8, *Clementine*; *Auf rother Erde*;

volume 9, *Jenny;* volume 10, *Eine Lebensfrage;* volumes 11–12, *Das Mädchen von Hela;*

Die Erlöserin: Roman, 3 volumes (Berlin: Janke, 1873); translated by Mrs. A. L. Wister as *Hulda; or, The Deliverer: A Romance* (Philadelphia: Lippincott, 1874);

Benedikt, 2 volumes (Berlin: Janke, 1874);

Benvenuto: Ein Roman aus der Künstlerwelt, 2 volumes (Berlin: Janke, 1875);

Neue Novellen (Berlin: Hertz, 1877) – comprises "Die Stimme des Blutes," "Ein Freund in der Not," "Martina";

Reisebriefe aus Deutschland, Italien und Frankreich, 1877–78 (Berlin: Janke, 1880);

Helmar: Roman (Berlin: Janke, 1880);

Zu Weihnachten: Drei Erzählungen (Berlin: Janke, 1880) – comprises "In Ragaz," "Der Magnetberg," "Dr. Melchior";

Vater und Sohn: Novelle (Stuttgart: Hallberger, 1881);

Vom Sund zum Posilipp!: Briefe aus den jahren 1879–1881 (Berlin: Janke, 1883);

Treue Liebe: Erzählung (Dresden: Minden, 1883);

Stella: Roman, 3 volumes (Berlin: Janke, 1883); translated by Beatrice Marshall as *Stella* (2 volumes, Leipzig: Tauchnitz, 1884; 1 volume, New York: Munro, 1885);

Im Abendroth: Kaleidoskopische Erzählung in sechzehn Briefen (Dresden: Minden, 1885);

Die Familie Darner: Roman, 3 volumes (Berlin: Duncker, 1887);

Josias: Eine Geschichte aus alter Zeit (Leipzig: Keil, 1888);

Zwölf Bilder aus dem Leben: Erinnerungen (Berlin: Janke, 1888);

Gefühltes und Gedachtes (1838–1888), edited by Ludwig Geiger (Dresden & Leipzig: Minden, 1900);

Römisches Tagebuch 1845/46, edited by Heinrich Spiero (Leipzig & Berlin: Klinkhardt & Biermann, 1927);

Freiheit des Herzens: Lebensgeschichte – Briefe – Erinnerungen, edited by Gerhard Wolf (Berlin: Buchverlag der Morgen, 1987).

Fanny Lewald was one of the most respected and successful German woman novelists of the mid nineteenth century. Contemporary critics praised her novels for their serious social, political, and ethical content. Today they serve as a rich mine for investigations of the struggle for enfranchisement, self-determination, and self-realization against barriers of gender, ethnicity, and class. Because Lewald was a keen observer with perceptive psychological insights, her autobiography, biographical sketches, travel books, and correspondence expand modern understanding of nineteenth-century European life.

As her works increased in scope to cover a wider spectrum of society at particular historical times, Lewald was criticized for being too ambitious: critics questioned whether any novel could effectively re-create an entire era, and her writing was faulted for its lack of detail. Lewald eschewed description for its own sake, however, focusing on the telling detail that reveals a character's thoughts or evokes the spirit of a particular time and place.

The Austrian writer Marie von Ebner-Eschenbach regarded Lewald as a model; the Swiss author Gottfried Keller found Lewald opinionated, but he respected her powers of reason, her perception, and her message; and the nineteenth-century German realist writer who is perhaps best known to English-language readers today, Theodor Fontane, confessed that he was indebted to Lewald for her suggestion that he restrict the number of characters in his novels. But as the naturalists supplanted the realists as literary innovators, the younger generation came to regard her work as outdated; and because the criteria of the modern literary canon were aesthetic rather than sociohistorical, Lewald's novels were pushed further into oblivion. In the early twentieth century, however, Lewald's writings enjoyed a revival in German academic circles: as women began to be admitted to universities, they often selected the writings of women authors as the subjects of their dissertations. But the takeover of the universities by the National Socialists in the 1930s put an end to feminist inquiries. Not until the 1960s, when scholars in both the German Democratic Republic and the Federal Republic of Germany looked to the nineteenth-century forebears of democratic, liberal, and revolutionary traditions and the second wave of feminists began to rediscover women's texts, did Lewald's writings arouse renewed interest.

Fanny Mathilde Auguste Markus was born on 24 March 1811 in Königsberg, Prussia (today Kaliningrad, Russia), to David Markus, a merchant, and Zipora ("Rosa") Assur Markus. She was the eldest of eight surviving children, six girls and two boys. Acculturated Jews, the Markuses did not observe Judaic ritual in their home.

At age six Fanny was enrolled in the Ulrich school, a private institution where boys and girls learned the same subjects except that in the afternoon the girls did needlework while the boys were instructed in classical languages. Tuition was on a sliding scale according to the parents' income, and the pupils could advance according to their abilities. As one of the gifted pupils, Fanny Markus had an extra tutorial in French. An examiner once told her that her head would sit better on a boy's shoulders. She reached the highest grade at age eleven (the norm was thirteen). She repeated the grade because there was no avenue for girls to continue their education; she would have repeated it again, but the school was closed. Thus ended her formal training. At home she reviewed old lessons and read and discussed with her father works by Johann Wolfgang von Goethe, Friedrich Schiller, and Immanuel Kant that he had selected based on moral considerations. She also had to spend hours practicing the piano, which she disliked intensely, for she had no musical talent. Later she took drawing and English lessons.

At age seventeen Markus fell in love with a young theology student, Leopold Bock. He introduced her to the patriotic, romantic poetry of Theodor Körner and awakened in her an idealism that supplemented the strict rationalism derived from her father; rationalism and common sense, however, are the predominant elements of the mature Lewald's approach to the world. Proud of her struggle to achieve independence, she later recognized the irony that all of her teachers had been men — her father, Bock, her brother Otto, and her husband.

Through a friend, Markus learned that her father had agreed that she and Bock could marry but had insisted that Bock not discuss marriage with her until he passed his second theological examination. She never knew why her father then abruptly stopped the courtship. After Bock died in 1830, she surmised that his family had objected to his marrying a Jew, and that her father wanted to shield her from being hurt.

As a form of consolation her father allowed her to convert to Lutheranism. He had refused her permission to do so the year before, when he had insisted that her younger brothers, Otto and Moritz, convert. In David Markus's view, conversion opened career avenues for a young man — in Prussia only Christians could be in the civil service, at that time the most prestigious career — whereas conversion might diminish a woman's chances to marry, the only "career" open to her. Conversion would cut a woman off from the Jewish marriage pool; should a Christian choose her for a wife, she could always convert at that point. While writing her confession of faith prior to her baptism and confirmation on 24 February 1830, Fanny realized that she did not believe in Christian dogma; she was ashamed of her sophistic, deliberately vague document. When Fanny was twenty years old, her father legally changed the family name to Lewald – a name that some relatives had assumed twenty years earlier – so that his children would not be labeled as Jews.

New horizons opened for Lewald when she accompanied her father on an extended business trip at age twenty-one. Her enthusiasm was replaced by humiliation when at the first stop, Berlin, she overheard her father express to a relative his hopes of finding a suitable match for her. But the sights in Frankfurt am Main, Heidelberg, and Strasbourg assuaged Lewald's hurt feelings. In Baden-Baden, where they joined her father's younger brother, Friedrich Jacob Lewald, and his family, Lewald felt honored when the liberal publicist Ludwig Börne asked her about political opinions in Königsberg. Her uncle took Lewald back with him to Breslau (today Wroclaw, Poland), where she spent the winter. Lewald thrived intellectually in Breslau: her relatives there were well off, and the women took advantage of their leisure to read widely. Lewald's reading was not as strictly supervised and censored as it had been in her father's house. The year 1832 was a time of literary revolution, and Lewald could read freely the writings of the French Romantics, of Heinrich Heine, and of Börne and other writers of Junges Deutschland (Young Germany).

That winter she met her cousin Heinrich Simon, whom she grew to love passionately, obsessively, and unrequitedly. Lewald clung so tenaciously to this love because the years following her return to Königsberg were bleak with respect to a meaningful use of her mind and energies. In 1834 she had a painful confrontation with her father when he tried to arrange a marriage with a suitor she deemed unworthy. Her father relented but was worried about how his daughters would be provided for. In 1839 Lewald learned that Simon had loved and renounced another woman, the aristocratic author Ida Gräfin von Hahn-Hahn. Lewald and Simon continued to correspond for a year, but Lewald finally realized that she needed to make a clean break.

In September 1840 Prussian subjects paid homage to their new king, Friedrich Wilhelm IV. Having appreciated Lewald's powers of description in their correspondence, her father's cousin August Lewald invited her to describe the ceremonies in Königsberg for his journal Europa. He encouraged

Lewald to develop her talent despite Otto's and her father's belittling remarks about her writing.

After submitting two short pieces to Europa, Lewald embarked on her first novel, Clementine (1842), which her father insisted be published anonymously. The work is partly an autobiographical response to her father about the issue of marriages of convenience, based on familial ambitions and economic concerns rather than love. After Clementine Frei's first love, Robert Thalberg (based on Simon), drifts away, she reluctantly agrees to marry an older man, Privy Councillor Meining. Meining treats her paternalistically, thwarts her attempts to confide in him, and becomes increasingly engrossed in his own career while Clementine remains unfulfilled and feels stifled by domestic obligations. Her dissatisfaction is thrown into relief when Thalberg returns, and she once again enjoys stimulating discussions about art and politics. Ideal love is defined in the novel as a man and woman's natural striving for fulfillment in harmonious union. But even though she and Robert may belong to each other in the natural order, Clementine renounces him after they declare their love because she views marriage as an eternal bond. Some scholars view Clementine's renunciation as a sign that Lewald was still under the influence of Goethe's novel Die Wahlverwandtschaften (1809; translated as "Elective Affinities," 1854), in which Ottilie renounces her lover and is transfigured; others focus on the narrator's statement that Clementine had made her peace, had found herself again, and conclude that Clementine's renunciation is an act of liberation for herself and the two men. None of the men in the novel views women as equal partners either in society or in intimate relationships: Meining says that politics and liberalism do not suit women; Robert claims that women's true position is one of dependence – they must share with men the ideal of liberty without wishing it for themselves; a painter flippantly indulges in sexual innuendo when remarking on the Saint-Simonian ideal liberated woman. Lest the reader think she does not pay a price for her erroneous acquiescence to marriage, Clementine reappears in Lewald's second novel, Jenny (1843), suffering from nervousness and insomnia. Lewald would examine the issue of a mismatched marriage again in her third novel, Eine Lebensfrage (A Question of Life and Death, 1845), where she defends divorce. From a feminist perspective, however, she treats the issue somewhat equivocally in this novel: a well-educated aristocrat decides that severe marital discord justifies his divorcing a wife who is less educated and of lower social standing.

Jenny is Lewald's only novel devoted exclusively to the issue of Jewish identity and emancipation, but Jewish characters play pivotal roles in all her major novels. Although the legal status of Jews differed from state to state, in most German states the emancipatory reforms resulting from the Napoleonic occupation were undercut by the Congress of Vienna in 1815 and Austrian chancellor Klemens Metternich's efforts to reestablish the old order after Napoleon's defeat. Measures directed against liberalization in general also negatively affected the Jews. Furthermore, although Enlightenment philosophy had pried open the ghetto in the eighteenth century, Jews had not won full social acceptance. By informing educated gentiles about Jewish life, depicting the devastating effects of prejudice, and pleading for the repeal of repressive laws, *Jenny* seeks to counteract attempts to isolate the Jews; it is both emancipatory and integrative in spirit.

With this novel Lewald joined the debate over whether Jewish identity was religious, national, or ethnic. The main protagonists, the Meiers, are acculturated Jews like the Lewalds; Jenny remarks that Jewish ritual is outmoded in a predominantly Christian society. The underlying argument is that ritual isolates its practitioners from the dominant Christian culture. The novel implicitly rebuts the argument that Jews had a separate national identity and could not be entrusted with full rights of citizenship. It points out that Jews are clannish and cherish family life because the majority culture views them as alien; oppression, exclusion, and the denial of rights have strengthened Jewish solidarity. The issue of ethnicity is treated in terms of physical appearance and language. Several Jewish characters are described as handsome or beautiful, but one character remarks that Jews could integrate more easily into German society, as they already have in France, if they did not look so different from the Germans. Speaking Yiddish and gesticulating in a pronounced manner are depicted as off-putting and déclassé. The suggested remedy for these practices, which are attributed to forced isolation of the Jews, is Bildung (education and acculturation). When *Jenny* was written, reformers still debated an issue that had its origin in the Enlightenment: should there be immediate political amelioration of the Jews' legal status or must this measure be preceded by moral regeneration through Bildung? Although the most respected Jews in the novel are the most acculturated, Lewald comes down on the side of immediate legal emancipation; she links the fate of the Jews to that of all oppressed peoples. The ideology of the novel flies in the face of the modern advocacy of cultural diversity: it implies that the eradication of differences of language, customs, and religious ritual would hasten the dominant culture's acceptance of the Jews.

Jenny is also a female bildungsroman. Jenny's process of self-formation consists of clarifying for herself matters of religious faith. While preparing for her conversion, Jenny defines her viewpoint as pantheistic deism. She goes through with the conversion, as did Lewald, but subsequently states in writing that she does not believe in Christian dogma. Lewald thus rectifies what she regarded as her own dishonesty during her conversion. The novel demonstrates that a Jewish woman has far less opportunity to develop her potential than a Jewish man, although she enjoys greater intellectual freedom than a Christian woman. Jenny's moment of liberation comes when she tells her fiancé, Reinhold, that she does not believe in Christian dogma, and he breaks off the engagement. Nevertheless, Jenny continues to live in her father's house, and, despite a lively interest in intellectual trends and politics, her only participation in public life is to perform small acts of charity. Jenny becomes the victim of prejudice when her second fiancé, an aristocrat who views her as an equal despite their class and ethnic differences, is slain in a duel with another aristocrat who has made disparaging remarks about Jenny's Jewishness. Jenny dies of a broken heart. Her brother Eduard, however, attends a university, joins a liberal fraternity, and becomes a respected physician, although he is denied the position of director of a hospital. When the state denies him permission to marry a Christian woman without converting, he joins like-minded men of all classes and of both faiths in the struggle for a liberal constitution.

Lewald had read drafts of *Jenny* to her mother, who was suffering from tuberculosis. She had completed only one-fourth of the manuscript when her mother died on 6 December 1841. (Lewald believed that her mother's health had been weakened by her giving birth to ten children, and she blamed her father's lack of self-restraint for her mother's frequent pregnancies.) Lewald and her sisters took turns managing the household, and during the next three years Lewald went to Berlin three times and to Breslau twice. In May 1844 Lewald and Simon met for the first time in almost twelve years and renewed their friendship, which lasted until Simon's death in 1860.

Lewald; sketch by Marie Meyer (courtesy of Deutsche Staatsbibliothek in der Stiftung Preußischer Kulturbesitz, Berlin)

In the winter of 1844–1845 Lewald realized that living in her father's house inhibited her writing, even though David Markus Lewald was proud of his daughter's accomplishments and had agreed that she no longer publish anonymously. In February 1845 she moved to Berlin and began taking Italian lessons in preparation for her first trip to Italy. Doors continued to open for her, particularly after she acknowledged that she was the author of *Jenny*. In Berlin she met Sarah Levy, Henriette Herz, and Karl August Varnhagen von Ense, who shared their memories of Berlin salons in the Romantic period, and the authors Henriette Paalzow, Luise Mühlbach, Theodor Mundt, Berthold Auerbach, and Therese von Bacheracht.

In June 1845 Lewald set out for Italy, arriving in Rome in October. There she visited the salons of Ottilie von Goethe, Adele Schopenhauer, and Sybille Mertens and also associated with a colony of artists that included Elisabeth Baumann and Louis Gurlitt, who later married Lewald's sister Elisabeth. Lewald's active social life that winter provided her with much material for future novels. At Mertens's salon she met Adolf Stahr, a professor of classics at the gymnasium in Oldenburg and a contributor to

Die Halleschen Jahrbücher (The Halle Yearbooks), a left-Hegelian journal. Stahr was on a year's sabbatical in Italy, seeking to heal a throat ailment. At the beginning of 1846 Lewald started to provide Stahr with small repasts to help him regain his strength, and she joined him and Hermann Hettner, a historian of art and literature, on their museum rounds. By February the friendship had flamed into mutual passion. Lewald tried to withdraw from the relationship because she knew that Stahr, who had had at least one previous affair, would eventually return to his wife, Marie, and their five children. But Stahr prevailed on her to let him be her lover and tutor during his remaining time in Rome. They parted in April with the intention of renouncing one another. Lewald headed south and in Naples received the devastating news that her father had died of a stroke on 9 May. She wrote two books about her year in Italy. *Italienisches Bilderbuch* (Italian Sketchbook, 1847; translated as *The Italians at Home*, 1848), reveals a lively interest in the Italian people and their customs and an open-minded readiness to appreciate the differences between the Italian and German cultures. It was her first work to be translated into English, and critics considered it to be better than Charles Dickens's account of his travels in Italy, also published in 1846. The story of her love affair with Stahr, *Römisches Tagebuch 1845/46* (Roman Diary, 1845/46, 1927) was published posthumously out of consideration for Marie Stahr. Lewald feared that her love letters would be published after their deaths, and she wanted to tell her version of the tale. It was difficult for Lewald to step out of bourgeois bounds; thus, she portrays their affair as one of extraordinary people destined by fate to support each other's intellectual endeavors.

Returning to Berlin in October 1846, Lewald continued to work diligently; even in times of adversity – indeed, particularly in those times – her motto was "Arbeiten, und nicht müde werden!" (Work, and don't get tired!). Having written three *Tendenzromane* (polemical novels), she turned to satire. The object of Lewald's scorn was the romantic excesses of aristocratic heroines in women's novels that imitated George Sand's works but lacked Sand's social message. The target of *Diogena: Roman von Iduna Gräfin H... H...* (Diogena: Novel by Iduna, Countess H... H..., 1847) was the work of one of Lewald's few equally successful female contemporaries, Ida Gräfin von Hahn-Hahn. (The countess had been Lewald's rival in love, but Lewald pointed out that when she wrote *Diogena* she already loved Stahr.) Not only was Lewald tired of heroines who had nothing to do but fall in love; she also objected to Hahn-Hahn's excessive, mannered use of French and of frenchified German.

Most of the novel is written in the form of Diogena's memoirs. Diogena traces her ancestry to Diogenes, the Greek Cynic philosopher who went about in daylight carrying a lantern and looking for a man of virtue. Diogenes' legacy to his female descendants is a coat of arms featuring a lantern and the charge to search for the ideal mate. Diogena is devoid of false modesty about her beauty – particularly her delicate hands and feet – and about her Faustian talents and ambitions. From the age of seventeen she has scoured the earth looking for the perfect lover, but she lacks the capacity to love. She drives her aristocratic lovers to suicide or death in duels or dismisses them if they momentarily turn their attention away. Diogena is most comfortable with a middle-class doctor, but the liaison dissolves when he makes the unforgivable mistake of falling asleep at her side after a hard day at the clinic.

Convinced that European men reason too much and Muslim men subjugate their women,

Diogena sets out for America, hoping to find a place where the relationship between the sexes is still in its natural state. Preparations for the expedition include reading all of James Fenimore Cooper's and Charles Sealsfield's novels, studying the Delaware language, and learning by heart the speeches of the heroine, Parthenia, in Friedrich Halm's *Der Sohn der Wildnis* (The Son of the Wilderness, 1843), a sentimental verse drama that advocates the amalgamation of diverse cultures. But fiction does not prepare Diogena for "reality." Shod in moccasins crafted by the best London cobbler, her body painted with a design of tiny lanterns, Diogena follows the Delaware chieftain Cœur de Lion to his wigwam. He fails to respond to her literary cues and utters not a line of Halm's verse. Nevertheless, he agrees to marry her, explaining that the countess will have the privilege of cooking and tending the fields. But after four days menial chores and living in nature have so aged Diogena that the chieftain rejects her.

Back in Europe, Diogena muses that the right man might live in the moon; she studies astronomy and makes inquiries about a hot-air balloon. Then she turns to the Bible, interprets the Apocalypse, and contemplates whether the Savior could be the right man. At the end of the memoirs Diogena sets out with the first trade expedition to China, saying, "Die Chinesen sind die wahren Aristokraten. Sie haben die kleinsten Füßchen, die soignirtesten Nägel, die magnifiksten Bärte und keine Spur von Liberalismus. Bei so viel ungemeinen Vorzügen muß auch die Liebe zu finden sein, die endlich meine Seele füllt" (The Chinese are the true aristocrats. They have the smallest feet, the most soigné fingernails, the most magnificent beards, and not a trace of liberalism. Surely among so many outstanding qualities, I shall be able to find the love that finally will fill my soul).

In the novel's epilogue, pride and egoism have driven Diogena mad. The doctor attributes her madness to the feminine selfishness that has reached its apex in German women's literature: imagining themselves to be exceptional, women love no one but themselves and then complain that they cannot find love. Lewald thus sensibly suggests that women will not be prepared for a loving partnership if they swallow whole the stuff of romantic novels. Even though Lewald is regarded as an early feminist, her satire reaffirms the division of labor in a bourgeois marriage: it is the husband's responsibility to work and participate in public affairs and the wife's duty to manage the home and cultivate the emotional sphere. Middle-class marriages in Lewald's novels do not disintegrate because of tyrannical or unfaithful husbands (only aristocrats and foreigners seem to make bad husbands); blame for marital discord is often laid at the feet of wives unable to manage a household or to comprehend their husband's intellectual endeavors. The claim that women's education was inadequate was well founded, and Lewald later suggested remedies for this situation in articles and letters. Finally, although Diogena's egoism may be misdirected, in her autobiography Lewald insists on the creative woman's need to be self-centered so that familial and societal expectations will not stifle her endeavors. Believing that a man had written the work, critics at first praised the parody; but when they learned that Lewald was the author, they found it unseemly. Lewald later regretted not giving Hahn-Hahn enough credit for her style and serious themes, and she never wrote another satire.

Lewald's next work was the historical novel *Prinz Louis Ferdinand* (Prince Louis Ferdinand, 1849; translated, 1988). The title character is the nephew of King Friedrich Wilhelm III of Prussia; the novel is set in 1800–1806, when Prussia tried to stay out of war with Napoleonic France through a series of ignominious treaties. Written in the late 1840s – a time of economic and political oppression in Prussia when the poor suffered famine and the liberals felt betrayed because the new king, Friedrich Wilhelm IV, had not presented them with a constitution – the novel is a scathing criticism of Friedrich Wilhelm III's political impotence. Lewald also re-creates the Berlin salon life of the Romantic period; her characters include Wilhelm von Humboldt, Friedrich Gentz, Dorothea and Friedrich Schlegel, and, above all, the brilliant Jewish *salonière* Rahel Levin. The characters represent all classes of society, and their common bond – from the lowliest shepherd to the prince – is that they are outsiders vis-à-vis the court; all are powerless victims of the time.

Lewald did extensive research for the novel, drawing on Levin's published letters, newspapers and documents, Friedrich Schlegel's novel *Lucinde* (1799; translated as *Lucinda,* 1913), and Karl August Varnhagen von Ense's biography of Louis Ferdinand (included in his *Gallerie von Bildnissen aus Rahel's Umgang und Briefwechsel* [Gallery of Portraits from Rahel's Circle and Correspondence, 1836]). In addition, Varnhagan (who had married Levin in 1814) lent Lewald the unpublished correspondence between the prince and one of his mistresses, Pauline Wiesel. Lewald struggled with the conflict between adherence to facts and the creation of poetic truth; the issue was particularly touchy because

many people who remembered the period were still alive. She decided to teach rather than merely describe, and she unleashed a storm of controversy by having Levin fall in love with Louis Ferdinand. Varnhagen and the Rahel cult that had arisen after her death in 1833 objected to Rahel being shown longing for the prince, who was infamous for his romantic and financial excesses. But those who objected most vociferously were anti-Jewish conservatives who deplored the depiction of a friendship between a Hohenzollern prince and a Jew. Furthermore, they were outraged that a Jewish woman author had appropriated the German monarchy in her fiction to promulgate her liberal ideas. No one had objected so vehemently to *Jenny:* it was fine for Jews to write about Jews, and women about women, but a Jewish woman dare not touch the hallowed monarchy. Lewald told Heine in 1850 that she would never write a historical novel again, and she never did make historical figures her main protagonists. Ironically, in 1859 *Prinz Louis Ferdinand* became Lewald's first novel to appear in a second edition.

Despite their intention of making their parting in Rome final, Lewald and Stahr continued their relationship. Lewald wrote to Stahr – and sometimes to Marie Stahr as well – several times a day, mailing a thick packet once a week. Stahr visited her in Berlin, they met in Hamburg and Bremen, and Lewald even went to Oldenburg with the notion that they would be able to arrange a ménage à trois.

On 28 February 1848 Lewald left Oldenburg for a trip to Paris with her friend Therese von Bacheracht. En route they received the news that revolution had broken out in Paris, and Lewald was excited to be able to learn firsthand about the event she and other liberals had long yearned for. Her observations on the revolutions in Paris and in Germany are recorded in *Erinnerungen aus dem Jahre 1848* (Memories From the Year 1848), published in 1850. Lewald relates accounts of the night the revolution began, summarizes the political debates, and vividly describes the demonstrations on the teeming Parisian streets. Parisian landmarks, permeated with the history of preceding revolutions, are once again transformed by revolutionary activity. When Lewald returns to Berlin, she is skeptical that the revolution, which has spread to German lands, will take hold. Compared to the self-assured manner with which the French handled their revolution, the Germans seem extremely insecure. In her observations on the struggle of the National Assembly in Frankfurt am Main to forge a constitution, her impatience with the conservative delegates' lack of courage and fear of bloodshed is expressed from the perspective of a woman: "und deutsche hochgelehrte Professoren, alte Staatsmänner, welche lange Bücher über Revolutionen und Staatsverfassungen geschrieben haben, sind außer sich darüber, daß bei uns gleiche Ursachen wenn auch hoffentlich nie gleiche, so doch ähnliche Folgen hervorrufen, daß Kampf und Sieg Opfer erheischen. Da ist doch jede junge Frau, die mit dem Blick auf ihre Mutter und Großmutter in ihr Wochenbett geht, mutiger und verständiger als diese Männer. Es kann ihr das Leben kosten, das Kind kann auch tot zur Welt kommen, kann sterben, nachdem sie all die Schmerzen erduldet hat; dennoch aber verzagt sie nicht, dennoch glaubt und hofft sie; denn übersteht sie es, so ist ein neues Leben geboren, und es haben es ja andere vor ihr überstanden" (and highly educated German professors, old statesmen, who have written lengthy books on revolutions and constitutions are beside themselves that in our country the same cause calls forth similar – albeit, one hopes, never the same – effects, that struggle and victory demand sacrifice. In this instance every young woman who, looking at her mother and grandmother, goes into childbirth is more courageous and reasonable than these men. It can cost her her life, the child can also be stillborn, can die, after she has suffered all the pain; but still she does not lose courage, still she believes and hopes; for if she endures, then a new life is born, and others before her have endured). *Erinnerungen aus dem Jahre 1848* combines vignettes of prominent political figures, including Simon and Lewald's left-liberal friends Moritz Hartmann and Johann Jacoby, with moving descriptions of the dignity of ordinary people during the revolutionary struggle.

Lewald treats the death throes of the revolution – the uprising in Baden in 1849 – in the novella *Auf rother Erde* (On Red Soil, 1850). In the summer of 1850 she traveled to England and Scotland; she was accompanied intermittently by Hartmann, who had gone into exile. She visited English and Scottish families, met authors and translators, and deepened her understanding of English literature. Lewald's record of this journey, *England und Schottland: Reisetagebuch* (England and Scotland: Travel Diary, 1851–1852), is a study of British political and social institutions, which had evolved differently from those on the Continent. Lewald was most interested in the manifestations of what she called "Sozialismus" (socialism), a term that encompassed organizations to care for orphans and the poor; communal baths, laundries, and kitchens; and schools for women. Even the uniform architectural style of London's row houses struck her as socialist.

In the fall of 1852 Adolf Stahr moved his family to Jena and rented a room near Lewald's Berlin apartment. Marie Stahr agreed to a divorce, and Lewald used her connections – including Duke Carl Alexander of Saxe-Weimar – to assist with legal and financial matters. The divorce became final on 24 March 1854, and Lewald and Stahr were married on 6 February 1855. The civil ceremony they would have preferred was not possible because Stahr was not a resident of Prussia. The couple took short trips to France, Switzerland, and northern Italy in the ensuing years and spent the winter of 1866–1867 in their beloved Rome. Lewald had found both meaningful work and personal contentment.

Wandlungen (Changes, 1853), Lewald's first major novel, can be viewed as a response to the revolution's failure; its theme is the inevitability of change. She examines the responses of men and women of all social classes – aristocrats, burghers, and workers – to historical change from shortly before the July 1830 revolution in France to the summer of 1848. By showing the development of individual characters in a particular historical period, with many references to events and intellectual trends that characterize the age, Lewald combines the bildungsroman and the Zeitroman (a novel critically analyzing the era in which it was written). The characters in the process of realizing themselves are not bound by class lines: a baron becomes a merchant in England, a seamstress becomes a famous opera singer, a carpenter's son becomes a classical archaeologist. The baron's daughter, Cornelie, after disentangling herself from a Pietist sect embroiled in a scandal like one that had actually occurred in Königsberg, moves to Paris, becomes a successful author under a pseudonym, and marries a middle-class Jewish doctor, the pivotal character of the novel. The story of the count who is too bound by convention to marry his mistress, a seamstress, is presumed to have inspired Fontane's *Irrungen, Wirrungen* (1888; translated as *Trials and Tribulations*, 1917).

The most widely read of Lewald's works today is her autobiography, *Meine Lebensgeschichte* (My Life Story, 1861–1862; translated as *The Education of Fanny Lewald*, 1992), which has served women's studies as a paradigm for the experience of a middle-class German woman in the first half of the nineteenth century. Modeled after Goethe's *Dichtung und Wahrheit* (Poetry and Truth, 1811–1813; translated as *Memoirs of Goethe*, 1824), it briefly covers the

Markus and Assur family histories from the time of Lewald's grandparents and then relates Lewald's own development up to her arrival in Italy in 1845. Even though it can be viewed as a gifted woman's success story, her autobiography also reveals — perhaps more than its author intended — how patriarchy stunted her development, how barriers to education and careers for women so long deprived her of meaningful work, and how stereotypes of femininity made her feel unloved. That the Markuses were Jews of only moderate means compounded the problem: David Markus Lewald, concerned about his children's social and economic survival, had to juggle the expectations of the majority and minority cultures. Yet for the young Fanny the strictures of gender were harsher than those of ethnicity. The autobiography also gives a broad picture of historical events, everyday life in Königsberg, trade, household management, education, and literary circles in Berlin.

Von Geschlecht zu Geschlecht (From Generation to Generation, 1864–1866) is Lewald's most ambitious novel, spanning the period from shortly before the outbreak of the French Revolution to the 1820s, the years of reconstruction following the German victory over the French in the Wars of Liberation. It treats a theme favored by German realists: the decline of the aristocracy and the rise of the middle classes. The novel's ideology creates problems of plot because the aristocrats' decline, which is supposed to be a historical necessity, results more from a lack of judgment or resolve than from economic or political conditions. Baron von Arten and his son Renatus lose their fortune and estates through overspending on the construction of a Catholic chapel in a Protestant village, hosting aristocratic French refugees, and keeping up appearances at court. Trade blockades and changes in the management of capital cause economic hardship, but the prudent, industrious middle-class characters are able to overcome these problems. At the end of the eight-volume novel the baron's bastard son, Paul Tremann, a self-made man who has earned a fortune in America, is the new owner of the von Arten estate. Proud of his own accomplishments, he refuses to assume the von Arten name and title but assures his Jewish wife, Davide, that their children will be happy in the castle if she helps him to teach them the value of work, freedom, and love of their fellow human beings.

In the 1860s Lewald became increasingly impatient with Prussian politics, particularly with the Progressive party's inability to assert itself vis-à-vis the king, and began to redirect her energies to the women's movement that was then gaining momentum. Two works of nonfiction describe women's sorry plight and suggest remedies to improve their lot. *Osterbriefe für die Frauen* (Easter Letters for Women, 1863) is concerned with the conditions of young women who move to the city from the provinces and seek employment as household help. Unlike their male counterparts, who have hostels to go to on their arrival, apprentice guilds to defend their rights, and associations where they can further their education, women are completely at the mercy of their employers. Their living conditions are dismal and often morally compromising, the pay miserly, and the training inadequate. Although the work is somewhat patronizing — Lewald calls on working-class men and middle-class women to assist the domestics — she offers practical suggestions for treating household help with dignity and for furthering their education during their leisure time. *Für und wider die Frauen* (For and Against Women, 1870) is concerned with educated middle-class women like Lewald herself. She emphasizes the wrongheadedness of the notion that middle-class women should be groomed for nothing but marriage, describing the psychological damage done to young women doomed to passively wait for men to choose them. Women must be educated and encouraged to choose useful work. Dual standards and moral convention should not prohibit women from working with male colleagues. Lewald does not drastically step beyond the bounds of bourgeois ideology about marriage and family: a young working woman can ease her father's burden by contributing to her own support; having learned to manage finances and saved up a dowry, she is a more attractive candidate for marriage; women with children should remain at home; if the husband dies, the family will not be suddenly destitute if the mother and daughters have learned a trade. Although the ideas of these treatises are not entirely original, both the feminist philosopher John Stuart Mill and Gertrud Bäumer, a turn-of-the-century feminist leader, considered them the best documents of the first feminist movement.

Adolf Stahr died in Wiesbaden on 3 October 1876. Lewald continued to travel, spending two more winters in Rome, and kept up her social and literary activities, but she never completely recovered from the loss. Her most popular novel, *Die Familie Darner* (The Darner Family, 1887), is a conciliatory and patriotic work that begins in 1803 and ends with Prussia's victory in the Wars of Liberation. Lewald considered the novel a tribute to recently achieved German unity; its depiction of the integration of Jewish characters into German society may have been a response to growing German anti-Semitism in the 1880s. The novel shows the impact of the French occupation and the liberation on the people of Königsberg. No well-known personages are portrayed; the reader merely hears what the people think about Napoleon, Czar Alexander, Friedrich Wilhelm III, and Queen Luise, each of whom is in Königsberg at some point. By eliminating the problem of fictionalizing historical figures, Lewald is free to concentrate on showing how the German people could flourish through emancipation from class and ethnic prejudice. Lorenz Darner, a mysterious and wealthy newcomer patterned after David Markus Lewald, quickly becomes the most powerful figure among the Königsberg merchants. Not until his son Frank's marriage to Justine Willberg, the niece and ward of the respected patrician Konrad Kollman, does Darner reveal that he was once an indentured servant who, after killing his master's son to defend his beloved, escaped to England and the Americas. It would have been more advantageous financially had Frank married the daughter of a Dutchman whose trade connections circle the globe. Kollman's son John marries Flora Lindheim, daughter of a successful and proud Jewish merchant, a match to which both Kollman and Lindheim are at first opposed. Darner's daughter Virginie weds a middle-class army captain of limited means. After an unhappy marriage to a wealthy Greek merchant in Venice, Virginie's twin, Dolores, is finally united with her first love, Baron Eberhard von Stromberg; their union is made possible when Eberhard relinquishes the entailed estate that keeps him in bondage because of the stipulation that its lord marry a woman of noble birth. Having learned financial management from Frank, Eberhard purchases and builds up an estate in Lithuania. *Die Familie Darner* is the fictional realization of Lewald's life project: the eradication of artificial barriers of gender, ethnicity, and class that thwarted individuals from developing their full potential.

Lewald died on 5 August 1889 in Dresden. She was buried next to Stahr in Wiesbaden.

Letters:

Aus Adolf Stahrs Nachlaß, edited by Ludwig Geiger (Oldenburg & Leipzig: Schulze, 1903);

"Der Briefwechsel Fanny Lewalds mit Paul Heyse," edited by Rudolf Göhler, *Deutsche Rundschau,* 183 (May 1920): 274–283; (June 1920): 410–441;

Kurd von Schlözer, *Amerikanische Briefe* (Stuttgart: Deutsche Verlagsanstalt, 1927), pp. 44–45, 86–88, 149–151, 155–156, 161;

"Aus dem Nachlaß von Fanny Lewald und Adolf Stahr," edited by Göhler, *Euphorion,* 31 (1930): 176–246;

Großherzog Carl Alexander und Fanny Lewald-Stahr in ihren Briefen 1848–1889, 2 volumes, edited by Göhler (Berlin: Mittler, 1932);

Johann Jacoby Briefwechsel: 1850–1877, edited by Edmund Silberner (Bonn: Neue Gesellschaft, 1978).

References:

Konstanze Bäumer, "Reisen als Moment der Erinnerung: Fanny Lewald's (1811–1889) 'Lehr- und Wanderjahre,' " in *Out of Line/Ausgefallen: The Paradox of Marginality in the Writings of Nineteenth-Century Women,* edited by Ruth-Ellen Boetcher Joeres and Marianne Burkhard (Amsterdam: Rodopi, 1989), pp. 137–157;

Kenneth Bruce Beaton, "Fontanes *Irrungen, Wirrungen* und Fanny Lewald," *Jahrbuch der Raabe-Gesellschaft* (1984): 208–224;

Jeannine Blackwell, "Bildungsroman mit Dame: The Heroine in the German Bildungsroman from 1770 to 1900," Ph.D. dissertation, Indiana University, 1982, pp. 255–274;

Gisela Brinker-Gabler, "Fanny Lewald," in *Frauen: Portraits aus zwei Jahrhunderten,* edited by Hans-Jürgen Schultz (Stuttgart: Kreuz, 1981), pp. 72–86;

Irene Stocksieker Di Maio, "Jewish Emancipation and Integration: Fanny Lewald's Narrative Strategies," in *Autoren damals und heute: Literaturgeschichtliche Beispiele veränderter Wirkungshorizonte,* edited by Gerhard P. Knapp (Amsterdam: Rodopi, 1991), pp. 273–301;

Di Maio, "Reclamation of the French Revolution: Fanny Lewald's Literary Response to the *Nachmärz* in *Der Seehof,*" in *Geist und Gesellschaft: Zur deutschen Rezeption der Französischen Revolution,* edited by Eitel Timm (Munich: Fink, 1990), pp. 149–164;

Katherine Goodman, *Dis/Closures: Women's Autobiography in Germany between 1790 and 1914* (New York: Lang, 1986), pp. 147–165, 181–185;

Deborah Hertz, "Work, Love, and Jewishness in the Life of Fanny Lewald," in *From East and West: Jews in a Changing Europe 1750–1870,* edited by Frances Malino and David Sorkin (Oxford: Blackwell, 1990), pp. 202–220;

Hanna Ballin Lewis, "Fanny Lewald and the Revolutions of 1848," in *Horizonte: Festschrift für Her-*

bert Lehnert zum 65. Geburtstag, edited by Hannelore Mundt, Egon Schwarz, and William J. Lillyman (Tübingen: Niemeyer, 1990), pp. 80–91;

Lewis, "The Misfits: Jews, Women, Soldiers and Princes in Fanny Lewald's *Prinz Louis Ferdinand,*" in *Crossings-Kreuzungen,* edited by R. Haymes (Columbia, S.C.: Camden House, 1990), pp. 104–114;

Lewis, "The Woman's Novel Parodied: Fanny Lewald's *Diogena,*" in *Continental, Latin-American and Francophone Women Writers,* edited by Eunice Myers and Ginette Adamson (Lanham, Md.: University Press of America, 1987), pp. 107–117;

Harriet E. Margolis, "The Ideal Marriage: Woman as Other in Three Lewald Novels," in *Continental, Latin-American and Francophone Women Writers,* pp. 119–127;

Renate Möhrmann, *Die andere Frau* (Stuttgart: Metzler, 1977), pp. 118–140;

Margarita Pazi, "Fanny Lewald: Das Echo der Revolution von 1848 in ihren Schriften," in *Juden im Vormärz und in der Revolution von 1848,* edited by Walter Grab and Julius Schoeps (Stuttgart: Burg, 1983), pp. 233–271;

Birgitta van Rheinberg, *Fanny Lewald: Geschichte einer Emanzipation* (Frankfurt am Main & New York: Campus, 1990);

Ruth Segebarth, "Fanny Lewald und ihre Auffassung von der Liebe und der Ehe," Ph.D. dissertation, University of Munich, 1922;

Marieluise Steinhauer, *Fanny Lewald, die deutsche George Sand: Ein Kapitel aus der Geschichte des Frauenromans im 19. Jahrhundert* (Berlin: Hoffmann, 1937);

Hans-Erich Teitge, "Unbekannte Briefe von Fanny Lewald und Adolf Stahr an Johann Jacoby: Aus dem Nachlaß Lewald/Stahr," *Studien zum Buch- und Bibliothekswesen,* 4 (1986): 78–101;

Regula Venska, "Discipline and Daydreaming in the Works of a Nineteenth-Century Woman Author, Fanny Lewald," in *German Women in the Eighteenth and Nineteenth Centuries,* edited by Joeres and Mary Jo Maynes (Bloomington: Indiana University Press, 1986), pp. 175–192;

Margaret E. Ward, "*Ehe* and *Entsagung:* Fanny Lewald's Early Novels and Goethe's Literary Paternity," *Women in German Yearbook,* 2 (1986): 57–77;

Marta Weber, *Fanny Lewald* (Rudolstadt: Rentsch, 1921).

Papers:

The Fanny Lewald/Adolf Stahr papers are in the manuscript division of the Deutsche Staatsbibliothek in der Stiftung Preußischer Kulturbesitz (German State Library in the Foundation for Prussian Cultural Property), Berlin.

Otto Ludwig

(12 February 1813 – 25 February 1865)

Gerald Opie
University of Exeter

BOOKS: *Dramatische Werke,* 2 volumes (Leipzig: Weber, 1853–1854) – comprises volume 1, *Der Erbförster,* translated by Paula Green as *The Forest Warden: A Tragedy in Five Acts* (Boston: Badger, 1913); volume 2, *Die Makkabäer;*

Zwischen Himmel und Erde: Erzählung (Frankfurt am Main: Meidinger, 1856); translated by William Metcalfe as *Between Heaven and Earth* (London & Glasgow: Gowans & Gray, 1911); translated by Muriel Almon as *Between Heaven and Earth* (New York: Ungar, 1965);

Thüringer Naturen: Charakter- und Sittenbilder in Erzählungen; Die Heiterethei und ihr Widerspiel. Zwei Erzählungen (Frankfurt am Main: Meidinger, 1857) – includes "Aus dem Regen in die Traufe";

Gesammelte Werke, 4 volumes, edited by Hermann Lücke (Berlin: Janke, 1870) – comprises in volume 1, *Der Erbförster, Das Fräulein von Scuderi;* in volume 2, *Die Makkabäer, Die Torgauer Heide, Der Engel von Augsburg, Tiberius Gracchus,* "Gedichte"; volume 3, *Die Heiterethei und ihr Widerspiel;* in volume 4, "Zwischen Himmel und Erde," "Reden oder Schweigen," "Todte von St. Anna's Kapelle";

Nachlaßschriften, 2 volumes, edited by Moritz Heydrich (Leipzig: Cnobloch, 1874) – comprises volume 1, *Skizzen und Fragmente;* volume 2, *Shakespeare-Studien;*

Das Märchen vom todten Kinde: Aus dem Nachlaß des Dichters (Berlin: Janke, 1877);

Die Rechte des Herzens (Paul und Eugenie): Trauerspiel (Berlin: Janke, 1877);

Gesammelte Schriften, 6 volumes, edited by Adolf Stern and Erich Schmidt (Leipzig: Grunow, 1891) – comprises in volume 1, "Gedichte," "Zwischen Himmel und Erde"; in volume 2, "Die Heiterethei," "Aus dem Regen in die Traufe," "Die wahrhaftige Geschichte von den drei Wünschen," "Aus einem alten Schulmei-

Otto Ludwig

sterleben," "Maria"; in volume 3, *Der Erbförster, Das Fräulein von Scuderi, Die Makkabäer, Die Pfarrose, Hanns Frei, Die Rechte des Herzens;* in volume 4, *Die Torgauer Heide, Der Jakobsstab, König Alfred, Der Engel von Augsburg, Agnes Bernauerin, Genoveva, Marino Falieri, Die Freunde von Imola, Die Kaufmannstochter von Messina, Tiberius Gracchus;* volume 5, *Studien und kritische Schriften: Erster Teil;* volume 6, *Studien und kritische Schriften: Zweiter Teil;*

Ludwigs Werke: Kritisch durchgesehene und erläuterte Ausgabe, 3 volumes, edited by Viktor Schweizer (Leipzig & Vienna: Bibliographisches Institut, 1898);

Werke, 6 volumes, edited by Adolf Bartels (Leipzig: Hesse, 1900);

Gedanken Otto Ludwigs: Aus seinem Nachlaß ausgewählt, edited by Cordelia Ludwig (Jena: Diederichs, 1903);

Sämtliche Werke, 6 volumes, edited by Paul Merker under the auspices of the Goethe- und Schiller-Archiv, Weimar (Munich: Müller, 1912–1922) – comprises volume 1 (1912), *Erzählungen* ("Das Hausgesinde," "Die Emanzipation der Domestiken," "Die wahrhaftige Geschichte von den drei Wünschen," "Maria," "Die Buschnovelle," "Das Märchen vom toten Kinde"); volume 2 (1912), *Die Heiteretei und ihr Widerspiel*; in volume 3 (1912), "Zwischen Himmel und Erde," "Novellenfragmente"; volume 4 (1922), *Gedichte*; in volume 5 (1922), "Die Torgauer Heide," "Die Rechte des Herzens," "Das Fräulein von Scuderi," "Die Pfarrrose"; volume 6 (1914), *Der Erbförster*;

Werke, 3 volumes, edited by Waltraut Leuschner-Meschke under the auspices of the Deutsche Akademie der Wissenschaften (Berlin: Akademie-Verlag, 1961–1969) – comprises volume 1 (1961), *Agnes-Bernauer-Dichtungen I: 1837–1847*; volume 2 (1965), *Agnes-Bernauer-Dichtungen II: 1854–1864*; volume 3 (1969), *Agnes-Bernauer-Dichtungen III: Entwürfe*;

Otto Ludwig: Romane und Romanstudien, edited by William J. Lillyman (Munich: Hanser, 1977).

In mid-nineteenth-century German literature, with its trend toward increasingly realistic fiction, Otto Ludwig occupies an important position both as a creative writer and a literary theorist. He is especially notable for his use of the term *Poetischer Realismus* (Poetic Realism), by which the dominant literary style of the period has come to be known. His realism, like that of many other regional writers of his time, represents a conservative rearguard action fought in defense of traditional moral and social values by middle-class authors; and in Ludwig's work, which has enjoyed a fluctuating critical reception, it is possible to observe clearly the ideological tensions of the age and the aesthetic transition from romanticism to realism. His work, uneven in quality and much of it fragmentary, has been compared at its best to that of Henrik Ibsen and Fyodor Dostoyevski in its rigorously realistic psychology, while at its worst it exhibits in both drama and fic-

tion – poetry constitutes a minor part of his literary output – the sentimental sensationalism of a debased and Gothic romanticism. He thought of himself principally as a dramatist, but his greatest works are in prose. In the stories *Zwischen Himmel und Erde* (1856; translated as *Between Heaven and Earth*, 1911) and "Die Heiterethei" (The Girl of Spirit, 1857) he achieves, in both the comic and the tragic modes, works of enduring worth that stand among the masterpieces of their time; and he is increasingly being recognized as a major contributor to the theories of drama and, perhaps even more notably, of fiction.

Like many literary figures of his time, Ludwig was a regional writer, although, like the best of his contemporaries, he transcends regionalism in his mature work. He is associated with Thuringia, whose countryside and people are immortalized in his fiction. His attachment to Eisfeld, a remote town of some twenty-five hundred souls at the time of Ludwig's birth, is exemplified by his practice of signing himself "Otto Ludwig von [of] Eisfeld" in later life. He was born into one of the town's leading families as the third of four children of the lawyer and Stadtsyndikus (chief magistrate) Ernst Ludwig and Sophie Christiane Ludwig, née Otto, on 12 February 1813. His education was first undertaken by Ludwig Ambrunn, his father's clerk, and continued at the local school.

In 1820 Ludwig's father was accused of embezzling municipal funds, and a fire that destroyed much of the town in 1822 was thought to have been started by arsonists protesting his acquittal. Feeling it his duty to make restitution, Ernst Ludwig considerably reduced the family fortune. The strain of the affair undermined his health, and he died in January 1825 at forty-six. The family, which had contracted, following the deaths of two other children, to Ludwig and his mother, was able to retain the large summer residence with garden, the "Gartenhaus," that Ernst Ludwig had acquired. Ludwig and his mother moved in with Sophie Ludwig's brother Christian Otto, a prosperous merchant, and Ludwig's first and only experience of the world of work was gained as an assistant in his uncle's business. In the spring of 1828 Ludwig was sent for a year to the gymnasium in nearby Hildburghausen, the ducal residence. A sickly, morbidly hypersensitive youth given to nocturnal rambles and hallucinations, he displayed a precocious musical talent under the tuition of a local organist.

Sophie Ludwig appears to have been a genteel and cultivated lady who introduced her son early in life to literature, and especially to the works of William Shakespeare, whose dramas were to become an abiding obsession with Ludwig. If she had a fault, it is that she was overprotective and indulged her son, fostering his innate sensitivity to the point where he was unequipped for the practicalities of the life that lay ahead of him. Christian Otto seems to have assumed a kindly interest in his nephew; but after Sophie Ludwig's death from tuberculosis in November 1831, life in his uncle's house became intolerable for Ludwig because of his uncle's mistress and housekeeper, a harridan who tyrannized and engaged in drunken brawls with Christian Otto. Domineering women are encountered frequently in Ludwig's fiction: Frau Bügel, the mother of the little tailor in "Aus dem Regen in die Traufe" (Out of the Frying Pan into the Fire, 1857), for instance. The search for harmony in human relations is a recurrent theme of Ludwig's work, often taking the form of sexual conflict; and although the question of the position of women was part of the public discourse of an age that was occupied with the idea of freedom in all its aspects, Ludwig's adolescent experiences may form the basis for the frequent treatment of the problem in his fiction. He was later to call his early life "ein fortgesetzter Kursus in der angewandten Psychologie und Pathologie" (an extended course in applied psychology and pathology).

For most of the year following his mother's death Ludwig lived in the Gartenhaus. In 1832 he enrolled at the grammar school in Saalfeld with a view to qualifying for university entrance; but the following year he was again living with his uncle in Eisfeld, with no definite plans for his future. It is not clear why he abandoned his studies, but an unhappy love affair has been suggested. He moved back into the Gartenhaus in 1834 to escape the tensions of his uncle's household. He shared the house with his friend Karl Schaller and devoted himself to musical composition and performance, indulged in local amateur dramatics, and took long walks to Coburg, Meiningen, and Hildburghausen to attend the opera. Modest, almost pathologically shy, careless of his appearance, and devoted to music and painting, he seemed to the inhabitants of Eisfeld a pathetic failure; the picture that emerges from the recollections of acquaintances is strongly reminiscent of the otherworldly, romantic heroes of E. T. A. Hoffmann, who, with Ludwig Tieck, was one of Ludwig's first literary models.

In 1839, with a grant from the duke of Meiningen, Ludwig went to Leipzig to study music with Felix Mendelssohn. His stay in Leipzig, like those in Hildburghausen and Saalfeld previously, lasted only a year. He thoroughly disliked the city, felt provincial and gauche, was plagued by illness because the climate did not suit him, despised what he saw as the corrupt and shallow sophistication of the city dwellers, and made few friends; finally, and shatteringly, his music was dismissed by Mendelssohn as thirty years out of date. He returned to Eisfeld, but he felt equally isolated there because his friend Schaller had married and moved to Wasungen. Toward the end of June 1842 he returned to Leipzig, his grant having been renewed on the recommendation of the writer Ludwig Bechstein to enable him to change direction in favor of literature.

The subsequent years Ludwig spent moving among Leipzig, Dresden, Meissen, and a mill in the hamlet of Niedergarsebach, near Meissen, which he discovered in the spring of 1844. From this time forward he devoted most of his energies to making his name as a dramatist, regarding fiction as hackwork that was useful for bringing in a little income. In the summer of 1842 he completed *Der Engel von Augsburg* (The Angel of Augsburg, 1870), the earliest version of which goes back to 1835. It is a historical play set in the fifteenth century and based on the story of Agnes Bernauer of Augsburg, a commoner who secretly married Albrecht, the heir to the throne, and was drowned in the Danube on the orders of the reigning duke. The drama underwent many revisions over the years without ever achieving the celebrity of Friedrich Hebbel's *Agnes Bernauer* (1855; translated, 1909) and was not published in its entirety until 1961. An attempt to get the play performed at the court theater in Dresden, which was at that time under the direction of Tieck, was unsuccessful. The other major dramatic work of this period, a play on Frederick the Great of Prussia, appears – unlike most of Ludwig's many massive projects – to have been completed; but only a fragment, *Die Torgauer Heide* (Torgau Heath, 1870), survives. Reminiscent of but inferior to Friedrich Schiller's *Wallensteins Lager* (1800; translated as *The Camp of Wallenstein*, 1830) and somewhat nationalistic in tone, it appeared in the *Zeitung für die elegante Welt* (Newspaper for the Elegant World) in 1844. Efforts to get the play accepted for performance at the theater in Leipzig failed. Other plays from this period of Ludwig's career, all published posthumously, are the comedy *Hanns Frei* (1891); the tragedies *Die Rechte des Herzens* (The Rights of the Heart, 1877) and *Die Pfarrose* (The Daughter of the Vicarage, 1891); and the drama *Das Fräulein von Scuderi* (The Maiden of Scuderi, 1870), a dramatic reworking of Hoffmann's tale of the jeweler Cardillac's murderous obsession with his artifacts. They are largely derivative pieces reminiscent of Schiller's early dramas and of Romantic fate tragedy, full of unnecessarily complicated intrigue and peopled with corrupt aristocrats who attempt to seduce innocent girls, who bewail their situation in moonlit graveyards. Yet in these early efforts it is possible to discern a realism that anticipates the later work, and modern readers may find even at this stage in Ludwig's development a surprisingly progressive attitude to the question of female emancipation. The liveliness of *Hanns Frei,* a comedy based on relations between the sexes, might, if it were better known, modify Ludwig's reputation as somber and humorless.

But it was with a tragedy, *Der Erbförster* (The Forest Warden), that he suddenly became a celebrity. Completed in the summer of 1849, it received its first performance on 4 March 1850 with Ludwig's erstwhile patron Eduard Devrient, the director of the Dresden court theater, in the title role; it was published in book form in 1853. The play's success secured Ludwig's acceptance into the literary circle in Dresden, where he had moved at the end of 1849. *Der Erbförster* presents the tragic fate of the forester Christian Ulrich, whose stubborn adherence to his conception of justice leads him, through a series of misunderstandings and coincidences, to shoot his own daughter. Ulrich refuses to accept the judgment of his employer, the industrialist and landowner Stein, that a certain tract of forest should be cleared. Ulrich, who is descended from several generations of foresters, believes that the proposal will be disastrous for the forest; he doggedly insists on what he sees as his right to make a professional decision, despite the threat of losing his position. Stein's son Robert is about to be betrothed to Ulrich's daughter Marie; but a chain of more or less plausible incidents leads Robert to be wrongly suspected of murdering the forester's son, Andres. Ulrich sets out in the darkness to seek his son's supposed murderer, but his daughter interposes herself between father and lover and receives the fatal shot. Filled with guilt and remorse, Ulrich turns his gun upon himself.

The play suffers, like Ludwig's earlier tragedies, from an element of melodrama, and the interaction of individual psychology with gratuitous external factors has attracted criticism. For all its weaknesses, however, *Der Erbförster* possesses a powerful atmosphere and some vivid character portrayals, notably in the central figure of the forester. The play's realistic evocation of region and social milieu anticipates the naturalism of the latter part of the nineteenth century, although its ethos owes more to the tradition of German idealism than to the fashionable radical philosophies of its own time. Socialist critics took Ludwig to task for making his name with such a politically reactionary piece so soon after the revolutions of 1848; Ludwig, however, was profoundly skeptical of the view that literature could or should be the handmaiden of politics. He deplored the emancipatory doctrines of his time, typified in the writings of the Young Germans, as destructive; although he hoped, like so many of his contemporaries, for a united Germany, for him the way forward led through the moral renewal of the individual, not through mass movements led by professional demagogues. Early in 1848 he wrote to Schaller: "Preise dich glücklich, daß du die gerühmte neue Literatur nicht in der Nähe siehst, ihr Charakter ist Charakterlosigkeit.... Die meisten heutigen Poeten sind keine gebornen, es sind geborne Politiker, Volksredner, Glücksritter.... Eine Rotte Bilderstürmer.... Die Literatur ist wirklich ein Markt geworden" (Count yourself fortunate that you are not in close touch with the vaunted new literature, for its character is lack of character.... Most poets today are not born poets, but born politicians, political orators, soldiers of fortune.... A rabble of iconoclasts.... Literature has become venal). Certainly *Der Erbförster* fails to make the kind of overt political statement desired by left-wing radicals, and one cannot imagine that it did much for the cause of capitalist entrepreneurs aspiring to political power. The play contains references to the civil disturbances of the time, but only fleetingly in the comments of Frei, the poacher, who looks forward to the collapse of law and order so that he may pursue his occupation unhindered by foresters; and Frei, like his associate Lindenschmied, who actually commits the murder on which the action of the play turns, is a totally negative caricature. The dramatist's concern is rather with the theme of eternal right and justice, but perhaps even more with the portrayal of human perversity. Ulrich is convinced of his natural right of inheritance, to which he has no legal title whatever; and this natural right is contrasted with the purchased right of Stein. The forester's right is conferred by knowledge and experience, Stein's by property alone. Ulrich has recourse to scriptural authority, invoking the eternal right of equality before divine authority against the secular and mutable law of his degenerate age. Characteristically, the conservative Ludwig's sympathy seems to lie with the forester, who is attempting to preserve nature against the foolish depredations of the industrial-

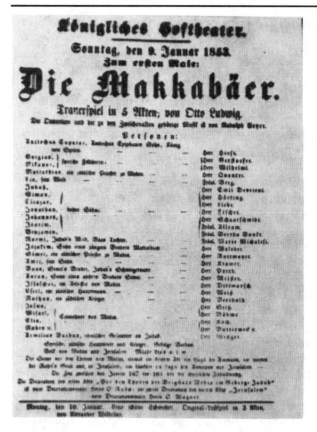

Poster for the premiere of Ludwig's tragedy about the Maccabean rebellion

ist – not least, as Ulrich is made to point out, to save Stein from the consequences of his own command, for the result will be the destruction of a large and valuable forest and commercial failure. Yet at the same time, Stein is no melodramatic villain but an essentially well-disposed man who does his best to retrieve the disaster into which the forester's behavior and his own foolish refusal to take advice have plunged him. As so often in Ludwig's work, the situation turns ultimately on the intransigence and perversity of individuals: tragedy arises from temperament.

Ludwig's disinclination to advocate political activism is apparent also in his only other completed play staged during his lifetime, *Die Makkabäer* (The Maccabees), which was first performed at the court theater in Dresden on 9 January 1853 and was published in 1854. The initial response was not enthusiastic, but later the play became part of the standard repertoire and achieved some success. The subject here is not individual insubordination but national revolt. Based on the account in the two apocryphal Books of the Maccabees and familiar also from George Frideric Handel's celebrated oratorio, it dramatizes the rebellion of the Jews led by

Judas Maccabaeus against Syrian domination. A somewhat turgid play, described as a tragedy but lacking tragic focus, it has sunk into obscurity. Its contemporary success sheds light on the aesthetic and intellectual climate of the post-1848 era: as an account of a nation's struggle for unity and independence, it is clearly relevant to its time. It would certainly not appeal to political activists, however. The rebellion succeeds because the Jews refuse to fight on the Sabbath. They are massacred; but the Syrian army, fearing the shame of being forced to perpetuate further butchery and dreading the vengeance of a deity who commands such absolute obedience, threatens mutiny if it is forced to renew the fray. The tragic fate of the protagonists is subordinated to the idea of obedience to the divine will: Judas's brother Eleazar, who collaborates with the Syrians in deference to the ambition of his mother, Lea, to see him king of the Jews as well as from his own ambition, finally elects to atone for his betrayal by going with his other brothers to the furnace prepared for them by the Syrian king Antiochus. In the final scene Lea persuades Judas to accept Antiochus's offer of peace. The final word is given to Judas, who proclaims that God has no need of the strong and that true strength – which here conveniently coincides with political advantage – lies in the abandonment of pride and personal vendetta. The play's political quietism, historical pageantry, and grandiose pathetic diction outweighed its perceived pro-Semitism to achieve a measure of success in conservative Vienna, where the director Heinrich Laube adopted it at the Burgtheater along with *Der Erbförster,* and where it received an annual performance until 1879.

Ludwig emerged as a writer of fiction with "Das Hausgesinde" (The Servants, 1912), which first appeared in 1840 in the Leipzig journal *Der Komet. Das Märchen vom todten Kinde* (The Fairy Tale of the Dead Child), also from the early 1840s, affords in its opening scene a glimpse of the fledgling realist but degenerates as it proceeds, despite some successful cameos of peasant types. It did not appear in print until 1877. The more substantial but structurally flawed "Die Emanzipation der Domestiken" (The Emancipation of the Domestics, 1912), which was apparently intended in part as a satire on the emancipatory social aims of the Young Germans, depicts the insubordination of a comic group of servants whose disregard for orders saves the day; it was first published in 1843 in the *Zeitung für die elegante Welt.* Two other works written in 1843, "Die wahrhaftige Geschichte von den drei Wünschen" (The True Story of the Three Wishes), a blend of Dickensian realism and Hoffmannesque fantasy set in contemporary Leipzig and recounting the adventures of an unsuccessful aspiring author who stumbles into the realm of Indian mythology in the midst of prosaic reality, and "Maria," on the delicate subject of imagined parthenogenesis familiar to readers of Heinrich von Kleist's "Die Marquise von O . . ." (1810; translated as "The Marquise of O . . . ," 1929), remained unpublished until 1891. "Die Buschnovelle" (The Bush Novella), which appeared in the *Neue Illustrierte Zeitschrift* (New Illustrated Magazine) in Stuttgart in 1846, was forgotten and was rediscovered only in 1912. It was written in 1844, the year Ludwig met and became engaged to Emilie Winkler of Meissen; they were married in 1852. A rambling, loosely constructed fairy tale in a realistic setting, it relates the romance of Pauline, an orphan who eventually proves to be an aristocrat by birth, and a disguised count who saves her from the attentions of a miser who has a financial hold over her. The count's melancholy is cured by his discovery of happiness in love. Of these early stories, "Die Emanzipation der Domestiken" and especially "Maria" prefigure the themes of Ludwig's mature fiction of the 1850s. The former concerns a young man and his intended fiancée, both extremely strong willed, who refuse to fulfill the terms of a testament enjoining their marriage. Circumstances throw them together in a situation where each is unaware of the other's identity, and they fall in love. A variation on the theme is found in the comedy *Hanns Frei,* where the reluctant lovers are brought together by their parents' device of forbidding them to see one another: as soon as the ban is imposed they perversely begin to find one another attractive, and they finally declare their love. The theme of the perversity of human nature is developed with more psychological subtlety in "Die Emanzipation der Domestiken," where the subconscious element is more fully treated. In "Maria," which is based on an actual occurrence, Ludwig displays his interest in more bizarre psychological states. Like the title character in Kleist's play *Prinz Friedrich von Homburg* (1821; translated as *Prince Frederick of Homburg,* 1875), Maria is a somnambulist. Her sleepwalking leads her to the bed of a visitor in her father's house, the young Herr Eisener. Eisener takes advantage of the situation, thinking in the darkness that Maria is the more sensual and flirtatious Julie, and Maria finds herself unaccountably pregnant. Ludwig develops the story in characteristically moralistic fashion. Eisener, thinking that Maria, who has lapsed into a coma, is dead, flees full of remorse to America; Maria, banished from

the parental home after recovering from her coma, goes to live with a relative of the family servant. The story details Maria's emotional struggle as she comes to terms with life as a single parent. Eventually Eisener returns and visits Maria. Although she does not know on a conscious level that he is the father of her child, she is strangely attracted to him, and the story ends with their union. A daring treatment of a delicate theme, it found little acceptance in its own time and has been largely neglected since.

Following the completion of *Die Makkabäer* Ludwig returned to fiction to earn money, for his marriage imposed increasing financial strain on his depleted resources. Four children were born to the couple: Otto in 1852; Reinhold in 1854; Alma, who failed to survive, in 1856; and Cordelia in 1858. Ludwig's friendship with the celebrated writer of tales of village life, Berthold Auerbach, whose acquaintance he had made in Dresden in 1850 and with whom he remained in contact until Auerbach's departure for Berlin ten years later, may also have influenced his decision to return to fiction. "Die Heiterethei," begun in 1853 and first published in serial form in the *Kölnische Zeitung* (Cologne Newspaper) in 1855, appeared in book form in 1857 alongside "Aus dem Regen in die Traufe"; *Zwischen Himmel und Erde* had been published the year before. In these three works Ludwig reaches maturity as a realist. All are set in the Thuringian milieu that he knew well and are peopled with credible characters drawn from life. The sentimentality that undermines his early work has been overcome and replaced by a healthy realism, both aesthetic and ethical.

"Die Heiterethei" takes up again the theme of reluctant courtship. Annedorle is a headstrong, robust village girl full of common sense who is used to the rigors of life and able to hold her own physically as well as in native wit with the men. Her antagonist, the farmer Holders-Fritz, is in his mid thirties but still behaves like a boorish and wild adolescent; he leads the pranks of the local lads, who admire him for his strength, fearlessness, and ability to hold his liquor. It is clear from the outset, when Annedorle reacts to some roadside teasing from Fritz by telling him in no uncertain terms her opinion of him and humiliating him before his friends, that the two are destined for each other: each is at heart an outsider by reason of his or her strength of personality and pride, for both are morally as well as physically superior to their fellows, and their only hope of happiness lies with each other. They resist each other to the end, and Ludwig is ingenious in devising a series of delaying

Otto Ludwig (engraving by A. Weger)

than its companion piece but is also a masterpiece of comic fiction; it is reminiscent of the work of Gottfried Keller, whom Ludwig greatly admired, although the compliment was not reciprocated. Again the plot turns on a courtship. Hannes Bügel, already familiar to readers of "Die Heiterethei," where he figures among the secondary characters, is a tailor; small of stature and lowly of status, he compensates for his shortcomings by a blustering attitude and by loud proclamation of his virtues. Tyrannized at home by his mother and contemptuous of Sannel, the servant girl who loves him despite his imperfections, he seeks a wife and becomes engaged to "die Schwarze" (the woman in black), who turns out to be a worse tyrant than Frau Bügel. Having insinuated herself into the household, she proves impossible to remove until the advent of a journeyman tailor who takes pity on Hannes and is cunning enough to beat "die Schwarze" at her own game. She exchanges the written promise of marriage that Hannes had been foolish enough to give her for a similar contract from the journeyman, only to discover after his departure that it is couched in such vague terms that it has no legal validity. Hannes is cured of his folly and learns to accept himself for what he is and Sannel for what she is, a loving and faithful companion who will gladly share his life. Frau Bügel, too, has received a salutary shock and realizes that her domineering ways, which she adopted at least partly to protect her inadequate son, have been largely responsible for the disaster that the family has narrowly escaped. Peace and harmony reign in the tailor's household.

The final work published during Ludwig's lifetime, the narrative *Zwischen Himmel und Erde,* justly remains the one by which he is chiefly known. Set in a small town in contemporary Thuringia, it is a powerful and somber tale of fraternal conflict and repressed sexual passion that is worked out with the inexorability of tragedy. Apollonius and Fritz Nettenmair are slaters and steeplejacks in the family business, which is dominated by the shadowy figure of their father. They are temperamental opposites: Apollonius is quiet, introverted, hypersensitive, obsessively tidy and orderly; Fritz is extroverted, wild, and irresponsible. Fritz is to speak on his brother's behalf to Christiane, whom Apollonius loves but is too shy to approach, although he has reason to think that she would not reject him; but Fritz, seeking to win her for himself, uses the opportunity to persuade Christiane that Apollonius despises her. Apollonius, not realizing the deception, departs for Cologne,

tactics to prolong his tale. His chief interest is the psychology of his two main characters, which he analyzes with extraordinary acuteness and sensitivity, displaying a sure grasp throughout of the psychology of the female protagonist in particular. Holders-Fritz represses his attraction to Annedorle for fear of ridicule by her and by the community, so that he is reduced to lying in wait for her by the roadside and prowling around her cottage at night; Annedorle, terrified of him and his reputation, almost drowns him by pushing him into the river in what she thinks is self-defense. As ever, Ludwig's concern is ultimately moral; but the moralizing never becomes heavy-handed. A strong element of social satire is introduced through the group of bigoted, arrogant, and patronizing local ladies who act as self-appointed vigilantes to protect Annedorle from the attentions of the presumed monster Holders-Fritz; and their comic discomfiture when Annedorle ejects them from her cottage carries the message that Annedorle's salvation lies in trusting her instincts, which have been clouded by fear and reliance on the judgment of her prejudiced social superiors.

"Aus dem Regen in die Traufe," thought to have been written in 1854, was published with "Die Heiterethei" in the volume *Thüringer Naturen* (Thuringian Types, 1857). It is shorter and slighter

where he spends some years learning his trade with a relative; by the time he returns, Christiane is married to Fritz. Apollonius is forced to live in the same house as the woman he still loves, who, as his sister-in-law, is forever beyond his reach and who hates him for having, as she thinks, scorned her. With masterly insight Ludwig traces the development of the psychological states of the three protagonists in the stifling emotional atmosphere of the Nettenmairs' house. Fritz's moral disintegration is matched by the emergence of Apollonius as a strong and responsible character whose moral constitution proves equal to every temptation. That constitution is tested to the limits of endurance, from Apollonius's realization that his brother has cheated him out of his chance at happiness to the moral struggle following the brothers' symbolic final encounter on the roof of the Church of Sankt Georg, whose spire dominates the work as an admonitory finger pointing heavenward. Apollonius, faced with the choice of falling to his death or moving aside to send his brother to equally certain death, allows Fritz to fall. The way is clear for Apollonius to claim Christiane, who has learned the truth about Fritz's deceit. Such is Apollonius's rectitude, however, that he cannot overcome the suspicion that revenge and the prospect of claiming his brother's widow were determining factors in his choice; consequently, he resigns himself to living out the remainder of his life alongside Christiane and taking care of her and his dead brother's son, thereby fulfilling what he sees as his duty to them, to the family honor, and ultimately to himself. This study of moral hypochondria is Ludwig's most subtle and impressive creation.

Ludwig's mature works of fiction combine realism of setting and individual psychology with moral idealism in a manner that fully realizes the concept of Poetic Realism that is virtually synonymous with Ludwig. His remaining years were plagued by failing health and financial difficulties so severe that, following his reluctant sale of the Gartenhaus, his friends organized a successful petition for a pension from the Deutsche Schillerstiftung (German Schiller Foundation). He continued his lifelong efforts to clarify his literary theories in a series of essays in which he analyzes novels by Charles Dickens – whose realism he admired as a contemporary continuation of that of Shakespeare – and works by Sir Walter Scott and George Eliot; his reflections on questions of narrative perspective and interior monologue place him among the precursors of modern theory and practice of the novel. Not systematic and not originally intended for publication, although Ludwig did contemplate the possibility as

the studies matured, the essays were published posthumously along with many other completed and fragmentary works, that never saw the light of day during Ludwig's lifetime. Shortly before his death in Dresden on 25 February 1865, following a long and painful illness that confined him to his house for the last five years of his life, he destroyed a large quantity of his manuscripts. Many of his projects, such as a planned cycle of dramas on the French Revolution and his social novels, were never completed. Nevertheless, he remains, on the strength of a slender and largely fragmentary oeuvre, one of the more significant writers of the period.

Letters:
Briefe, 1834–1847, edited by Kurt Vogtherr (Weimar: Böhlau, 1935).

Biographies:
Adolf Stern, *Otto Ludwig: Ein Dichterleben* (Leipzig: Grunow, 1906);
Wilhelm Greiner, *Otto Ludwig: Ein deutsches Dichterleben* (Weimar: Böhlau, 1938).

References:
Hans Baumeister, *Künstlerische Berufung und sozialer Status: Otto Ludwig* (Göttingen: Bautz, 1981);
Richard Brinkmann, *Wirklichkeit und Illusion: Studien über Gehalt und Grenzen des Begriffs Realismus für die erzählende Dichtung des neunzehnten Jahrhunderts* (Tübingen: Niemeyer, 1957);
Friedrich Christian Delius, *Der Held und sein Wetter* (Munich: Hanser, 1971);
Keith A. Dickson, " 'Die Moral von der Geschicht: Art and Artifice in 'Zwischen Himmel und Erde,' " *Modern Language Review,* 68 (January 1973): 115–128;
Ursula Jarvis, "Perspectives on Distance and Illusion: Otto Ludwig's Anticipations of Brecht," *Modern Language Quarterly,* 25 (September 1964): 308–321;
Gertrude Kolisko, "Syntactic Anomalies and Pronominal Ambiguity in Otto Ludwig's Narrative Prose," *Modern Language Review,* 60 (1965): 65–72;
William J. Lillyman, "The Function of the Leitmotifs in Otto Ludwig's 'Zwischen Himmel und Erde,' " *Monatshefte,* 57 (February 1965): 60–68;
Lillyman, "The Interior Monologue in James Joyce and Otto Ludwig," *Comparative Literature,* 23 (Winter 1971): 45–54;

Lillyman, *Otto Ludwig's "Zwischen Himmel und Erde":
A Study of Its Artistic Structure* (The Hague:
Mouton, 1967);

Fritz Martini, *Deutsche Literatur im bürgerlichen
Realismus, 1848-1898* (Stuttgart: Metzler,
1962);

William H. McClain, *Between Real and Ideal: The
Course of Otto Ludwig's Development as a Narrative
Writer* (Chapel Hill: University of North Caro-
lina Press, 1963);

McClain, "Otto Ludwig and the Problem of
Spannung in Fiction," *Modern Language Notes,* 80
(December 1965): 639-647;

Edward McInnes, "Analysis and Moral Insight in the
Novel: Otto Ludwig's Epische Studien," *Deutsche
Vierteljahrsschrift für Literaturwissenschaft und
Geistesgeschichte,* 46 (November 1972): 699-713;

McInnes, "Tragedy of the Everyday World: Otto
Ludwig's *Der Erbförster,*" *Neophilologus,* 59 (1975):
84-97;

Franz Mehring, "Otto Ludwig," *Die neue Zeit,* 31
(1913): 697-702;

Albert Meyer, *Die ästhetischen Anschauungen Otto Ludwigs* (Winterthur: Keller, 1957);

Gaston Raphaël, *Otto Ludwig: Ses Théories et ses
Oeuvres Romanesques* (Paris: Rieder, 1920);

Hans Heinrich Reuter, "Umriß eines mittleren
Erzählers: Anmerkungen zu Werk und
Wirkung Otto Ludwigs," *Jahrbuch der
Deutschen Schillergesellschaft,* 12 (1968): 318-
358;

Brigitte E. Schatzky, "Otto Ludwig's Conception of
Environment in Drama," *Modern Language Review,* 50 (July 1955): 298-306;

Jörg Schönert, "Otto Ludwig: *Zwischen Himmel und
Erde* (1856). Die Wahrheit des Wirklichen als
Problem poetischer Konstruktion," in *Romane
und Erzählungen des Bürgerlichen Realismus: Neue
Interpretationen,* edited by Horst Denkler (Stutt-
gart: Reclam, 1980), pp. 153-172;

Alfred Schwarz, "Otto Ludwig's Shakespearean
Criticism," in *Perspectives of Criticism,* edited by

Harry Levin (Cambridge: Harvard University
Press, 1950), pp. 85-101;

Walter Silz, "Otto Ludwig and the Process of Poetic
Creation," *Publications of the Modern Language
Association of America,* 60 (September 1945):
860-878;

Pramod Talgeri, *Otto Ludwig und Hegels Philosophie:
Die Widerspiegelung der Ästhetik Hegels im
poetischen Realismus Otto Ludwigs* (Tübingen:
Niemeyer, 1972);

Katherine Taylor and William H. McClain, "Otto
Ludwig's Use of Biblical References in *Der
Erbförster,*" *Modern Language Notes,* 84 (April
1969): 458-467;

Lionel Thomas, "Otto Ludwig's *Die Heiteretei und ihr
Widerspiel,*" *Forum for Modern Language Studies,* 6
(July 1970): 226-234;

Thomas, "Otto Ludwig's *Zwischen Himmel und Erde,*"
*Proceedings of the Leeds Philosophical and Literary
Society,* 16 (April 1975): 27-38;

Ida H. Washington, "Religious Symbolism in Otto
Ludwig's *Maria,*" *Modern Language Notes,* 85
(April 1970): 385-391;

Hermann John Weigand, "Zu Otto Ludwigs
Zwischen Himmel und Erde," *Monatshefte für den
deutschen Unterricht,* 38 (November 1946): 385-
402;

Heinz Wetzel, "Otto Ludwigs 'Zwischen Himmel
und Erde': Eine Säkularisierung der
christlichen Heilslehre," *Orbis Litterarum,* 27,
no. 2 (1972): 102-121;

Paul-Wolfgang Wührl, "Vergebliche Flucht in die
goldenen Haine von Gandhamadana: Otto
Ludwigs Montageerzählung *Die wahrhaftige
Geschichte von den drei Wünschen* und das
Hoffmannsche Wirklichkeitsmärchen,"
Mitteilungen der E. T. A. Hoffmann-Gesellschaft,
31 (1985): 69-76.

Papers:

Otto Ludwig's manuscripts are held by the Goethe-
und Schiller-Archiv, Weimar.

E. Marlitt
(Eugenie John)
(5 December 1825 – 22 June 1887)

Brent O. Peterson
Duquesne University

BOOKS: *Goldelse: Roman* (Leipzig: Keil, 1867);
translated by Annie Lee Wister as *Gold Elsie*
(Philadelphia: Lippincott, 1868);

Das Geheimniß der alten Mamsell, 2 volumes (Leipzig:
Keil, 1868); translated by Wister as *The Old
Mamsell's Secret* (Philadelphia: Lippincott,
1868);

Countess Gisela, translated by Wister (Philadelphia:
Lippincott, 1869); translated by Adolph Nah-
mer as *Countess Gisela* (New York: Harper,
1869); German version published as *Reichsgräfin Gisela,* 2 volumes (Leipzig: Keil, 1870);

Thüringer Erzählungen (Leipzig: Keil, 1869; New
York: Munro, 1882) – comprises "Die zwölf
Apostel," translated anonymously as "Magdalena," in *Magdalena: Translated from the German
of E. Marlitt; The Lonely Ones (The Solitaries):
Translated from the German of P. Heyse* (Philadelphia: Lippincott, 1870); "Der Blaubart,"
translated anonymously as *Over Yonder: A
Novelette* (Philadelphia: Lippincott, 1869);

Das Haideprinzeßchen: Roman, 2 volumes (Leipzig:
Keil, 1872); translated by Wister as *The Little
Moorland Princess* (Philadelphia: Lippincott,
1872);

Die zweite Frau: Roman, 2 volumes (Leipzig: Keil,
1874); translated by Wister as *The Second Wife:
A Romance* (Philadelphia: Lippincott, 1874);
translated by Annie Wood as *The Second Wife*
(3 volumes, London: Bentley, 1875; 1 volume,
New York: Burt, 1882);

At the Councillor's; or, A Nameless History, translated by
Wister (Philadelphia: Lippincott, 1876); Ger-
man version published as *Im Hause des Commerzienrathes: Roman,* 2 volumes (Leipzig: Keil,
1877);

In the Schillingscourt: A Romance, translated by Wister
(Philadelphia: Lippincott, 1879); translated by

E. Marlitt (Eugenie John)

Emily R. Steinestel as *In the Schillingscourt* (New
York: Munro, 1879); German version pub-
lished as *Im Schillingshof: Roman,* 2 volumes
(Leipzig: Keil, 1880);

Amtmanns Magd: Roman (Leipzig: Keil, 1881); translated by Wister as *The Bailiff's Maid: A Romance*
(Philadelphia: Lippincott, 1881);

Die Frau mit den Karfunkelsteinen: Roman (Leipzig: Keil, 1885); translated by Wister as *The Lady with the Rubies: A Novel* (Philadelphia: Lippincott, 1885).

Collections and Editions: *Gesammelte Romane und Novellen,* 10 volumes (Leipzig: Keil, 1888–1890); – includes as volume 9, *Das Eulenhaus,* completed by Wilhelmine Heimburg (Bertha Behrens) (1888); translated by Annie Lee Wister as *The Owl's Nest; A Romance* (Philadelphia: Lippincott, 1888); translated by Mary Stuart and G. Harrison Smith as *The Owl-House: A Posthumous Novel* (New York: Munro, 1888); as volume 10, *Thüringer Erzählungen* (1890) – comprises "Amtmanns Magd," "Die zwölf Apostel," "Der Blaubart," "Schulmeisters Marie," "Anhang: E. Marlitt, biographische Skizze";

Im Hause des Kommerzienrates, edited by Jochen Schulte-Sasse and Renate Werner (Munich: Fink, 1977);

Im Hause des Kommerzienrates (Hamburg: Deutscher Literatur-Verlag, 1981);

Das Geheimniß der alten Mamsell (Hamburg: Deutscher Literatur-Verlag, 1982);

Die zweite Frau (Hamburg: Deutscher Literatur-Verlag, 1982);

Die Frau mit den Karfunkelsteinen (Hamburg: Deutscher Literatur-Verlag, 1983);

Goldelse (Hamburg: Deutscher Literatur-Verlag, 1983);

Im Schillingershof (Hamburg: Deutscher Literatur-Verlag, 1984);

Reichsgräfin Gisela (Hamburg: Deutscher Literatur-Verlag, 1984);

Das Eulenhaus (Hamburg: Deutscher Literatur-Verlag, 1985);

Das Haideprinzeßchen (Hamburg: Deutscher Literatur-Verlag, 1987);

Goldelse (Berlin: Neues Leben, 1991);

Im Hause des Kommerzienrates (Berlin: Neues Leben, 1991);

Reichsgräfin Gisela (Berlin: Neues Leben, 1992);

Die zweite Frau (Berlin: Neues Leben, 1992).

Some of E. Marlitt's works were available in English, sometimes in two competing editions, even before they were published in book form in Germany. The dates are the result of the manner in which her works were originally published in German. E. Marlitt, the pen name of Eugenie John, was the star author in *Die Gartenlaube* (The Garden Bower), the most popular magazine in Germany during the second half of the nineteenth century.

Her novels generally appeared as books the year after being serialized in the magazine. So great was the demand for the latest Marlitt novel that translators worked from the magazine versions of her texts.

Although she was an immediate success with the German reading public, it took John a long time to develop her talents as a writer; her life was filled with detours on the way to her eventual vocation. She was born on 5 December 1825 in Arnstadt, a small town in Thuringia in south central Germany, to Ernst and Johanna John, née Böhm. At the time of his marriage Ernst John operated a private lending library; it eventually failed, he declared bankruptcy, and the family was forced to move from its comfortable – even imposing – house on the town's market square to a small cottage. Other unsuccessful occupations followed, until Ernst John settled into the not very rewarding profession of sign and portrait painting. Eugenie John seems to have felt obligated to try to help support the family. She succeeded admirably: in 1871, with the proceeds from the publication of her third novel, *Reichsgräfin Gisela* (1870; translated as *Countess Gisela,* 1869), she built in Arnstadt "Marlittsheim" (Marlitt's Home), a villa that was large enough to house herself, her elderly father, and her brother and his family – but such security was a long time in coming.

The family first pinned its hopes on her musical talent. Inspired by the town's choir director, who is reputed to have said that her voice was worth millions, Ernst John appealed to the local nobility for assistance. Princess Mathilde of Schwarzburg-Sondershausen, the wife of the ruling prince, was a patron of the arts, and in 1841 after she had been assured by one of the court musicians that the girl was genuinely talented, she brought the sixteen-year-old John to the palace at Sondershausen to begin serious musical training. By 1844 she had made enough progress for Princess Mathilde to send her to Vienna, the center of nineteenth-century musical culture, for two more years of study as an opera singer. John's debut in Leipzig in March 1847 was a disaster: stage fright struck, and she was unable to sing a note. She was more at ease on the smaller, more familiar stage in Sondershausen, but the princess's divorce soon put an end to her support for the arts. John made a series of appearances in Vienna, but her initial stage fright had been transformed into periods of virtual deafness that were almost certainly psychosomatic.

In 1853 Princess Mathilde employed John as a personal companion, secretary, and reader, and reading aloud to the princess seems to have honed

John's talents as a storyteller. During the ten years that she spent with the princess, John began to transform herself into E. Marlitt, a name that she apparently chose at random; it was during this period that she wrote her first work of fiction, a short story titled "Schulmeisters Marie" (Schoolmaster's Marie, 1890), which remained unpublished in her lifetime. Marie, the daughter of a village schoolteacher who has died before the story opens, seems too poor and too well educated to attract a man. Marie cannot believe that the rich young farmer she loves could possibly be interested in her, especially after her mother is jailed for stealing from the village pastor. Marie accidentally discovers the real thief, and because she possesses utter moral strength and an indomitable will to succeed, she marries the farmer.

In 1863 John left the service of Princess Mathilde and moved back to Arnstadt, where she lived with the family of her brother, a schoolteacher. She did needlework, gave piano and singing lessons, and continued to write. In 1865 she sent "Schulmeisters Marie" and a new story, "Die zwölf Apostel" (The Twelve Apostles, 1869; translated as *Magdalena*, 1870), to Ernst Keil, the publisher of *Die Gartenlaube*. With approximately 150,000 subscribers, *Die Gartenlaube* was the most widely read magazine in Germany. Although he rejected the first story on the grounds that it was too similar to the Dorfgeschichten (village tales) that were flooding the literary landscape as writers imitated Berthold Auerbach, Keil began serializing "Die zwölf Apostel" in September 1865 and offered to make Marlitt a regular contributor to the magazine. It was a wise decision. When Marlitt's fourth novel, *Das Haideprinzeßchen* (1872; translated as *The Little Moorland Princess*, 1872), was serialized there in 1871, *Die Gartenlaube* could claim 310,000 subscriptions and a readership of millions, most of them loyal Marlitt fans. So intense was their interest that an elderly woman on her deathbed is reported to have asked Keil for advance copies of the final two episodes of Marlitt's latest novel so that she could die in peace. Crowds lined up outside the magazine's offices in Leipzig on publication day, and servants sent off to purchase the week's issue were caught reading it first downstairs. Contemporaries such as Rudolf von Gottschall, Levin Schücking, and Gottfried Keller agreed that a significant narrative talent had arrived on the German literary scene. She would ultimately be judged differently by the conservative guardians of "high culture," but Marlitt's initial popularity was virtually universal.

The qualities that fascinated nineteenth-century readers are easy to find in all of Marlitt's novels, although her command of literary techniques improved considerably as she developed. In both "Die zwölf Apostel" and *Goldelse* (1867; translated as *Gold Elsie*, 1868) Marlitt takes far too long to set her plots in motion, and the reader is almost overwhelmed by details that are, in a manner uncharacteristic of the later Marlitt, ultimately superfluous. Susanna Hartmann, the old maid who appears in the opening scene of "Die zwölf Apostel" and is known as the "seejungfer" (dragonfly) on account of her peculiar gait, is interesting and well sketched, but her presence in such detail contributes nothing to the events that Marlitt goes on to narrate. The actual story — which concerns the troubled relationship of Hartmann's impoverished and reclusive niece, Magdalene Beroldo, with Werner Bauer, the scion of the town's leading merchant family — only begins in the second chapter of the threechapter novella. The plot is unduly complex; when the two finally marry, for example, it is against the wishes of Werner's aunt, who had once scorned Magdalene's impecunious uncle. What ultimately brings Werner and Magdalene together is their love of Italy and art and their refusal to be constrained by the social positions into which they were born. Magdalene is a Cinderella figure, while her "prince" is a bourgeois aesthete, similar to the heroes of Thomas Mann's early works, who scorns the pretensions of his class. The framing story of an old monastery with its rumored hidden treasure — twelve silver apostles in a secret passage — has nothing to do with the love story, which depends on the heroine gradually learning to understand her prospective husband's intentions. The work could have been written with far greater economy.

Goldelse suffers from the same kind of slow start, but once the novel gets going its myriad details fit together with a mastery that few of Marlitt's contemporaries were able to match. Marlitt's talents were more suited to the longer form of the novel than to the novella or the short story, and Keil was forced to serialize her works even though he had originally vowed to publish nothing that would not fit into a single issue of *Die Gartenlaube*. *Goldelse* began in the January 1866 issue and continued until the middle of the year, when it was followed by Marlitt's "Der Blaubart"(The Bluebeard, 1869; translated as *Over Yonder*, 1869). Thenceforth serialized novels, by Marlitt and others who followed in her footsteps, would become the magazine's standard fare.

Goldelse is another Cinderella story. Elisabeth ("Else") Ferber is related to the noble von Gnadewitz family through her mother, and it turns out that the Ferbers are also heirs to the von Gnadewitz title. In a society dominated by aristocratic titles, such an inheritance, though it brought little money with it, could transform the daughter of an impoverished officer-turned-bookkeeper into a suitable match for the local nobleman, Rudolf von Walde. (Else's father had begun his climb down the social ladder during the revolution of 1848, when he had refused to fire on the rebels, whom he regarded as his brothers.) Else steadfastly refuses to adopt the von Gnadewitz name; she does not want to be courted by a knight who might prefer the ancient name to the qualities that she possesses as a person. The decision is particularly incomprehensible to von Walde's cousin, a baroness of uncompromising pretension, who embarrasses herself by initially rejecting Else while simultaneously claiming an unfailing ability to detect aristocratic blood. Baroness Lessin also fires her daughter's governess for attempting to teach the child that nobility of the spirit, as evidenced by intelligence and compassion, is far more important than distinctions based on inherited titles. The baroness's son is a lout who disguises his inability to appreciate music or to carry on an intelligent conversation with a silence that only his shallow fellow aristocrats mistake for depth. Rudolf von Walde masks his dissatisfaction with the life of the court with a reserve that Else at first mistakes for rejection of her, and it is only when she discovers that Rudolf actually shares her disdain for the aristocracy that she is able to accept the love she instinctively feels for the handsome and intelligent young man. She learns that Rudolf's exterior actually does correspond to an inner nobility, just as he discovers that Goldelse's beauty is deeper and more lasting than that of the shimmering butterflies that are the source of her nickname.

Goldelse is set in the unspoiled forests of Marlitt's beloved home province of Thuringia, and Else is forever dashing off on treacherous mountain paths and running races with her admiring younger brother. Else's physical freedom contrasts starkly with Marlitt's own increasing frailness: since the early 1860s she had suffered from arthritis so severe that she spent most of the last two decades of her life confined to a wheelchair. As popular as her novels made her, Marlitt remained shy almost to the point of reclusiveness. Her brother handled her business affairs and shielded her from the outside world. She received almost no visitors and is only known to have been photographed twice. The social whirl that surrounds so many of her characters

must have been based on memories of the court at Sondershausen.

Her next two novels, *Das Geheimniß der alten Mamsell* (1868; translated as *The Old Mamsell's Secret*, 1868) and *Reichsgräfin Gisela*, lend credence to the accusation that Marlitt essentially wrote the same story over and over again. Both detail their heroines' early torment at the hands of tyrannical stepmothers; and both heroines are "rescued" by marriage to men who could easily have stepped from the pages of a fairy tale, except that the two "princes" are unapologetically middle-class. It is not surprising that *Gartenlaube,* whose program of bourgeois enlightenment was intended to wrest political power and social prestige from the feudal nobility, would publish these novels, for Marlitt constantly contrasted aristocratic corruption and hypocrisy with the honesty and integrity of the middle class. To be sure, in *Das Geheimniß der alten Mamsell* it takes hundreds of pages for Johannes Hellwig, a professor of medicine in Bonn, to recognize that Felizitas, whom his father had adopted as a young girl, has developed into a charming, well-educated young woman. Moreover, the members of the middle-class Hellwig family are anything but uniformly good. At first Johannes is proud and hard-hearted, while his mother is as prejudiced as any aristocrat – in large part because she represents another of Marlitt's favorite targets, religious intolerance. Frau Hellwig's power, however, which stems from her family's wealth and resultant social standing, is revealed to be based on fraud: the old Mamsell's secret is that Felizitas is not only the actual source of the Hellwig fortune but also a distant relative of the aristocratic Hirschsprung family. The novel concludes with the victory of the bourgeois values of family, propriety, and nobility of the mind, but only after Felizitas overcomes her own pride and recognizes and finally accepts the love Johannes offers her.

The imperial countess Gisela is also abandoned at an early age to a domineering and unloving stepmother; she renounces her inherited social position by marrying the industrialist Oliveira, a remarkable act for someone born so high in nineteenth-century German society. Like Goldelse and Felizitas, Gisela has to learn to read her prospective husband's words and gestures so as to decipher his true feelings and emotions, which often lie hidden behind a facade of sarcasm or indifference. Although Marlitt is sometimes accused of not letting her characters – particularly her heroines – develop, they stand in sharp contrast to the heroes of Karl May, the most important author of popular fiction for men and boys in the generation following

Marlitt: his characters arrive in the American West or the Middle East already able to read and understand the landscape and its inhabitants. The difficulty is not that Marlitt's female protagonists are static but that without exception they renounce their achievements – indeed, their very existence as free human beings – at the precise moment that they have almost succeeded in making independent lives for themselves. After emancipating themselves not only from the hated mores of the aristocracy but also from the patriarchal norms of bourgeois society, these intelligent, articulate, proud, and ambitious young women abandon the entire project of shaping their own lives in favor of subservience to a husband.

Middle-class empowerment and women's emancipation were among the most hotly debated issues in the decades following the failure of the revolution of 1848. Marlitt also spoke repeatedly in her works about the ill treatment of servants and the working class, and *Die zweite Frau* (1874; translated as *The Second Wife*, 1874), which was written at the height of the Kulturkampf (struggle between church and state), can be read as an endorsement of German chancellor Otto von Bismarck's anti-Catholicism. One of the novel's two villains is a hypocritical, immoral, and manipulative Jesuit priest who is more interested in satisfying his own lust and the Roman church's craving for power than in saving souls or doing good. This dark, secretive schemer, who is allied with a corrupt court that would like to impose its religion on an overwhelmingly Protestant population, represents all of the arguments used by Bismarck to justify the expulsion of the Jesuits from Germany in 1872. (An unauthorized Portuguese translation of the novel in 1878 transformed the heroine into a Catholic and her nemesis into an adherent of a conservative Lutheran sect.)

Im Hause des Commerzienrathes (1877; translated as *At the Councillor's*, 1876) offers the implicit message that home and family can serve as a refuge from the ravages wrought by social and economic change. Käthe, the orphaned granddaughter of an old miller, finds happiness with Doctor Bruck after she loses much of her fortune in the speculative fever that engulfed the greedy, unproductive citizens of the new German Empire – capitalists and aristocrats alike. The novel is about the conflict between these parvenus and speculators, on the one hand, and representatives of an older, more benign order, on the other. Käthe moves back and forth between the mill, where an organic community reminiscent of an earlier, unsullied age is still largely intact, and the sumptuous villa of the upstart councillor Römer. The rich descriptions of these opposing worlds show Marlitt at the height of her powers, even if some would argue that there is too much detail and that the plot is ultimately maudlin and predictable.

Even if they are excessive, the details in Marlitt's works allowed contemporary readers the illusion that they were actually experiencing the people and places depicted. Middle-class readers saw how the upper classes lived, and while satisfying their curiosity they also witnessed the failure of aristocratic claims. Unfortunately, recent versions of Marlitt's works, which are aimed at the consumers of romantic novels, have eliminated much of the richness of Marlitt's descriptions. In an edition of *Im Hause des Commerzienrathes* published in 1981, for example, the opening paragraph has been reduced from the 167 words in Marlitt's original text to 112.

So great was the public's demand for Marlitt's novels that Keil was constantly urging her to produce more. Marlitt was increasingly frail and unable to comply with his demands; as a result, novels that were promised for a particular volume of *Gartenlaube* were often delayed and appeared months or years later. A fall from a sedan chair incapacitated her for almost six months in 1883. Arthritis, recurring stomach disorders, and the prevailing medical opinion that women were weak meant that Marlitt spent much of her life resting. A case of pleurisy that she contracted in October 1886 incapacitated her for most of the winter, and she died in her bed at Marlittsheim on 22 June 1887. Her last novel, *Das Eulenhaus* (1888; translated as *The Owl's Nest*, 1888), was completed after her death by Bertha Behrens, whose career as one of the stable of popular novelists of *Gartenlaube* was the direct result of Marlitt having paved the way both for women writers and for the serialized novel. Marlitt's contribution to German literature should be reassessed; if nothing else, she changed both the form of the typical nineteenth-century novel and the size of its readership.

References:

Michael Andermatt, *Haus und Zimmer im Roman: Die Genese des erzählten Raums bei E. Marlitt, Th. Fontane und F. Kafka* (Frankfurt am Main: Lang, 1987);

Kirsten Belgum, "Interior Meaning: The Design of the Bourgeois Home in the Realist Novel," Ph.D. dissertation, University of Wisconsin – Madison, 1989, pp. 166–181;

Jeannine Blackwell, "Eugenie Marlitt," *Women Writers of Germany, Austria, and Switzerland: An Annotated Bio-Bibliographical Guide,* edited by Elke

Frederiksen (New York: Greenwood Press, 1989), pp. 152–154;

Ernest K. Bramsted, "Popular Literature and Philistinism," in his *Aristocracy and the Middle Classes in Germany: Social Types in German Literature 1830–1900* (Chicago: University of Chicago Press, 1937), pp. 200–227;

Ingrid Cella, "Die Genossen nannten sie die 'rote Marlitt': Minna Kautsky und die Problematik des sozialen Romans, aufgezeigt an 'Die Alten und die Neuen,'" *Österreich in Geschichte und Literatur mit Geographie,* 25, no. 1 (1981): 16–29;

Helmut Heissenbüttel, "Nicht Marlitt oder Anna Blum, sondern Marlitt *und* Anna Blum," *Deutsche Akademie für Sprache und Dichtung: Jahrbuch,* 2 (1981): 35–44;

Michael Kienzle, *Der Erfolgsroman: Zur Kritik seiner poetischen Ökonomie bei Gustav Freytag und Eugenie Marlitt* (Stuttgart: Metzler, 1975);

Kienzle, "Eugenie Marlitt: *Reichsgräfin Gisela* (1869). Zum Verhältnis zwischen Politik und Tagtraum," in *Romane und Erzählungen des bürgerlichen Realismus,* edited by Horst Denkler (Stuttgart: Reclam, 1980), pp. 217–230;

Ilse Langner, "Die Wahlverwandtschaften: Goethe und der Balzac der Gründerjahre: Eugenie Marlitt," *Frankfurter Hefte: Zeitschrift für Kultur und Politik,* 36 (March 1981): 53–60;

Leo Lensing, "The Caricatured Reader in *Im alten Eisen:* Raabe, Marlitt and the 'Familienblattroman,'" *German Life and Letters,* 31 (July 1988): 318–327;

George Mosse, "What Germans Really Read," in his *Masses and Man: Nationalist and Fascist Perceptions of Reality* (New York: Fertig, 1980), pp. 52–68;

Sigurd Parl Scheichel, "E. Marlitt," in *Erzählgattungen der Trivialliteratur,* edited by Zdenko Skreb and Uwe Baur (Innsbruck: Institut für Germanistik, Universität Innsbruck, 1984), pp. 67–112;

Herrad Schenk, *Die Rache der alten Mamsell: Eugenie Marlitts Lebensroman* (Düsseldorf: Claassen, 1986);

Jutta Schönberg, *Frauenrolle und Roman: Studien zu den Romanen der Eugenie Marlitt* (Frankfurt am Main: Lang, 1986);

Jochen Schulte-Sasse and Renate Werner, "E. Marlitts 'Im Hause des Kommerzienrates': Analyse eines Trivialromans in paradigmatischer Absicht," in Marlitt's *Im Hause des Kommerzienrates,* edited by Schulte-Sasse and Werner (Munich: Fink, 1977), pp. 389–434;

Katharina Seidel, " 'Das Geheimnis der alten Mamsell': Untersuchung eines 'klassischen' Trivialromans," *Blätter für den Deutschlehrer,* 32 (1988): 79–83;

Kirsten Søholm, " 'Goldelse': Ein populärer Roman von Marlitt," *Zeitschrift für Germanistik,* 11 (1990): 389–401;

Claudia Wilke, "Eugenie Marlitt vor 100 Jahren gestorben," *Neue Deutsche Hefte,* 34, no. 2 (1987): 331–347.

Papers:

E. Marlitt's papers are in the Rudolstadt City Archives, the Dortmund City Library, and the Arnstadt City Museum.

Karl Marx

(5 May 1818 – 14 March 1883)

Peter Morris-Keitel
Bucknell University

SELECTED BOOKS: *Die heilige Familie, oder Kritik der kritischen Kritik: Gegen Bruno Bauer und Consorten,* by Marx and Friedrich Engels (Frankfurt am Main: Literarische Anstalt [J. Rütten], 1845); translated by Richard Dixon and Clemens Dutt as *The Holy Family; or, Critique of Critical Critique* (Moscow: Foreign Languages Publishing House, 1956);

Misère de la Philosophie: Réponse à la philosophie de la misère de M. Proudhon (Paris: Franck / Brussels: Vogeler, 1847); translated by Harry Quelch as *The Poverty of Philosophy* (London: Twentieth Century Press, 1900; Chicago: Kerr, 1910);

Discours sur la question du libre échange: Prononcé à l'Association Démocratique du Bruxelles, dans la séance publique du 9 janvier 1848 (Brussels: L'Association Démocratique, 1848); translated by Florence Kelley Wischnewetzky as *Free Trade: A Speech Delivered before the Democratic Club, Brussels, Belgium, January 9, 1848* (Boston: Lea & Shepherd / New York: Dillingham, 1888);

Manifesto der kommunistischen Partei, by Marx and Engels (London: Office der "Bildungsgesellschaft für Arbeiter" von J. E. Burghard, 1848; Chicago: Hofmann, 1871); translated by Samuel Moore, edited by Engels as *Manifesto of the Communist Party* (London: Reeves, 1888; Chicago: Kerr, 1902);

Gesammelte Aufsätze, edited by Hermann Becker (Cologne: Becker, 1851);

Enthüllungen über den Kommunisten-Prozess zu Köln (Basel: Schabelitz, 1853; Boston: Neu-England-Zeitung, 1853); translated by Rodney Livingstone as "Revelations Concerning the Communist Trial in Cologne," in *The Cologne Communist Trial,* by Marx and Engels, edited and translated by Livingstone (London: Lawrence & Wishart, 1971; New York: International Publishers, 1971);

Zur Kritik der politischen Oekonomie (Berlin: Duncker, 1859); translated by Nahum Isaac Stone as *A*

Karl Marx in 1875

Contribution to the Critique of Political Economy (New York: International Publishing Co. / London: Kegan Paul, Trench, Trübner, 1904);

Herr Vogt (London: Petsch, 1860); translated by R. A. Archer as *Herr Vogt* (London: New Park Publications, 1982);

Address and Provisional Rules of the Working-Men's International Association: Established September 28, 1864, at a Public Meeting Held at St. Martin's

Hall, Longacre, London (London: Printed at the "Bee-Hive" Printing Office, 1864);

Das Kapital: Kritik der politischen Ökonomie. Erster Band. Buch I: Der Produktionsprocess des Kapitals (Hamburg: Meissner / New York: Schmidt, 1867); translated by Moore and Edward Aveling as *Capital: A Critical Analysis of Capitalist Production*, edited by Engels (2 volumes, London: Sonnenschein, Lowrey, 1887; 1 volume, New York: Appleton: 1889);

Der Achtzehnte Brumaire des Louis-Bonaparte (Hamburg: Meissner, 1869); translated by Daniel De Leon as *The Eighteenth Brumaire of Louis Bonaparte* (New York: International Publishing Co., 1898); translated by Eden and Cedar Paul as *The Eighteenth Brumaire of Louis Bonaparte* (London: Allen & Unwin, 1924; New York: International Publishers, 1926);

The Civil War in France: An Address of the General Council of the International Workingmen's Association (London: Truelove, 1871); translated by Engels as *Der Bürgerkrieg in Frankreich: Adresse des Generalraths der Internationalen Arbeiter-Association an alle Mitarbeiter in Europa und den Vereinigten Staaten* (Leipzig: Verlag der Expedition des "Volksstaat," 1871);

L'Alliance de la Démocratie Socialiste et l'Association Internationale des Travailleurs: Rapport et documents publiés par ordre du Congrès International de la Haye, by Marx, Engels, and Paul Lafargue (London: Darson / Hamburg: Meissner, 1873);

Lohnarbeit und Kapital (Breslau: Schlesische Volksbuchhandlung, 1881); translated by J. L. Joynes as *Wage-Labor and Capital* (London: Modern Press, 1885; Chicago: Kerr, 1891);

Das Kapital: Kritik der politischen Ökonomie. Zweiter Band. Buch II: Der Circulationsprocess des Kapitals, edited by Engels (Hamburg: Meissner, 1885); translated by Ernest Untermann as *Capital: A Critique of Political Economy. Volume 2: The Process of Circulation of Capital* (Chicago: Kerr, 1907);

Das Kapital: Kritik der politischen Ökonomie. Dritter Band. Buch III: Der Gesamtprocess der kapitalistischen Produktion, edited by Engels (Hamburg: Meissner, 1894); translated by Untermann as *Capital: A Critique of Political Economy. Volume 3: The Process of Capitalist Production as a Whole* (Chicago: Kerr, 1909);

Die Klassenkämpfe in Frankreich 1848 bis 1850 (Berlin: Glocke, 1895); translated by Henry Kuhn as *The Class Struggles in France, 1848-1850* (New York: New York Labor News, 1924; London: Lawrence, 1934);

The Eastern Question: A Reprint of Letters Written 1853-1856. Dealing with the Events of the Crimean War, edited by Eleanor Marx Aveling and Edward Aveling (London: Sonnenschein, 1897; New York: Franklin, 1968);

Value, Price and Profit: Addressed to Working Men, edited by Eleanor Marx Aveling (London: Sonnenschein, 1898; Chicago: Kerr, 1910);

Secret Diplomatic History of the Eighteenth Century, edited by Eleanor Marx Aveling (London: Sonnenschein, 1899);

The Story of the Life of Lord Palmerston, edited by Eleanor Marx Aveling (London: Sonnenschein, 1899);

Aus dem literarischen Nachlaß von Karl Marx, Friedrich Engels und Ferdinand Lassalle, 4 volumes, edited by Franz Mehring (Stuttgart: Dietz, 1902) — includes in volume 1, "Zur Judenfrage," pp. 399-431; translated by Helen Lederer as *On the Jewish Question* (Cincinnati: Hebrew Union College, Jewish Institute of Religion, 1958);

The Paris Commune, Including the "First Manifesto of the International on the Franco-Prussian War," the "Second Manifesto of the International on the Franco-Prussian War," "The Civil War in France," introduction by Engels, edited by Lucien Sanial (New York: New York Labor News, 1902);

Theorien über den Mehrwert: Aus dem nachgelassenen Manuskript "Zur Kritik der politischen Oekonomie," 4 volumes, edited by Karl Kautsky (Stuttgart: Dietz, 1905-1910); excerpts translated by G. A. Bonner and Emile Burns as *Theories of Surplus Value* (London: Lawrence & Wishart, 1951; New York: International Publishers, 1952);

Zur Kritik des sozialdemokratischen Programms von Gotha, edited by Karl Kreibich (Reichenberg: Runge, 1920); republished as *Randglossen zum Programm der Deutschen Arbeiter-Partei*, edited by Karl Korsch (Berlin: Vereinigung Internationaler Verlags-Anstalten, 1922); translated as *Critique of the Gotha Programme*, edited by E. Czobel (New York: International Publishers, 1933); edited by Dutt (London: Lawrence & Wishart, 1938);

The Essentials of Marx: The Communist Manifesto, by Karl Marx and Friedrich Engels; Wage-Labor and Capital; Value, Price and Profit, and Other Selections, by Karl Marx, edited by Algernon Lee (New York: Vanguard, 1926);

Selected Essays, translated by H. J. Stenning (London: Parsons, 1926; New York: International Publishers, 1926);

Karl Marx, Friedrich Engels: Historisch-kritische Gesamtausgabe, Werke, Schriften, Briefe, 12 volumes, edited by David Rjazanov (David Borisovich Goldendach) and Vladimir Viktorovich Adoratskij (Frankfurt am Main: Marx-Engels-Archiv, 1927-1935); – includes in volume 1, part 1 (1927), "Kritik des hegelschen Staatsrechts," pp. 401-553; translated by Annette Jolin and Joseph O'Malley as *Critique of Hegel's "Philosophy of Right"* (Cambridge: Cambridge University Press, 1970); in volume 5 (1932), "Die deutsche Ideologie: Kritik der neuesten deutschen Philosophie in ihren Repräsentanten, Feuerbach, B. Bauer und Stirner, und des deutschen Sozialismus in seinen verschiedenen Propheten 1845-1846," by Marx and Engels, pp. 3-532, "Thesen über Feuerbach," by Marx, pp. 533-535; translated by S. Ryazanskaya as *The German Ideology* (Moscow: Progress Publishers, 1964) – includes "Theses on Feuerbach";

Revolution in Spain, by Marx and Engels (New York: International Publishers, 1939);

Grundrisse der Kritik der politischen Ökonomie, 2 volumes (Moscow: Verlag für fremdsprachige Literatur, 1939-1941); translated by Martin Nicolaus as *Grundrisse: Foundations of the Critique of Political Economy* (New York: Random House, 1973; Harmondsworth, U.K. & Baltimore: Penguin, 1973);

Über Kunst und Literatur, by Marx and Engels, edited by Michail Lifschitz (Berlin: Henschel, 1948);

Die Revolution von 1848: Auswahl aus der "Neuen Rheinischen Zeitung," by Marx and Engels (Berlin: Dietz, 1949); translated by Ryazanskaya as *The Revolution of 1848-49: Articles from the Neue Rheinische Zeitung* (New York: International Publishers, 1972);

Marx on China, 1853-1869: Articles from the New York Daily Tribune, edited by Dona Torr (London: Lawrence & Wishart, 1951);

Karl Marx and Friedrich Engels on Britain (Moscow: Foreign Languages Publishing House, 1953);

Marx and Engels on Malthus: Selections from the Writings of Marx and Engels Dealing with the Theories of Thomas Robert Malthus, translated by Dorothea L. Meek and Ronald L. Meek, edited by Ronald L. Meek (London: Lawrence & Wishart, 1953);

Selected Writings in Sociology and Social Philosophy, edited by T. B. Bottomore and Maximilien Rubel, translated by Bottomore (London: Watts, 1956; New York: McGraw-Hill, 1964);

Karl Marx, Friedrich Engels: Werke [MEW], 43 volumes (Berlin: Dietz, 1956-1968);

K. Marx and F. Engels on Religion (Moscow: Foreign Languages Publishing House, 1957);

Basic Writings on Politics and Philosophy, by Marx and Engels, edited by Lewis S. Feuer (Garden City, N.Y.: Doubleday, 1959);

Economic and Philosophic Manuscripts of 1844, translated by Martin Milligan (Moscow: Foreign Languages Publishing House, 1959; New York: International Publishers, 1964);

On Colonialism, by Marx and Engels (Moscow: Foreign Languages Publishing House, 1960);

The Paris Commune, introduction by Engels, edited by Sanial (New York: New York Labor News, 1960);

Marx /Engels über Erziehung und Bildung, edited by Pavel N. Gruzdev (Berlin: Volk und Wissen, 1960);

Early Writings, edited and translated by Bottomore (London: Watts, 1963; New York: McGraw-Hill, 1964);

Karl Marx, Friedrich Engels, 4 volumes, edited by Iring Fetscher (Frankfurt am Main: Fischer, 1966);

Essential Writings of Karl Marx, edited by David Caute (London: MacGibbon & Kee, 1967);

Writings of the Young Marx on Philosophy and Society, edited and translated by Lloyd D. Easton and Kurt H. Guddat (Garden City, N.Y.: Doubleday, 1967);

Bildung und Erziehung: Studientexte zur Marxschen Bildungskonzeption, edited by Horst E. Wittig (Paderborn: Schöningh, 1968);

Über Kultur, Ästhetik, Literatur: Ausgewählte Texte, by Marx, Engels, and Vladimir I. Lenin, edited by Hans Koch (Leipzig: Reclam, 1969);

Birth of the Communist Manifesto: Full Text of the Manifesto, All Prefaces by Marx and Engels, Early Drafts by Engels and Other Supplementary Material, edited by Dirk J. Struik (New York: International Publishers, 1971);

Early Texts, edited and translated by David McLellan (New York: Barnes & Noble, 1971; Oxford: Blackwell, 1971);

Ireland and the Irish Question, by Marx and Engels, compiled by Lev Isaakovich Golman, V. E. Kunina, and M. A. Zhelnova, translated by Angela Clifford, K. Cook, R. Bean, and others, edited by Dixon (Moscow: Progress Publishers, 1971; New York: International Publishers, 1972);

On Revolution, edited and translated by Saul K. Padover (New York: McGraw-Hill, 1971);

Anarchism and Anarcho-Syndicalism, by Marx, Engels, and Lenin (New York: International Publishers, 1972);

The Ethnological Notebooks of Karl Marx, edited by Lawrence Krader (Assen: Van Gorcum, 1972);

The Marx-Engels Reader, edited by Robert C. Tucker (New York: Norton, 1972);

On America and the Civil War, edited and translated by Padover (New York: McGraw-Hill, 1972);

Die russische Kommune: Kritik eines Mythos, by Marx and Engels, edited by Rubel (Munich: Hanser, 1972);

Karl Marx, Friedrich Engels Gesamtausgabe [MEGA] (Berlin: Dietz, 1972–   );

Marx, Engels on Literature and Arts: A Selection of Writings, edited by Lee Baxandall and Stefan Morawski (Saint Louis: Telos, 1973; enlarged edition, New York: International General, 1974);

Political Writings, 3 volumes, edited by David Fernbach (London: Lane, 1973; New York: Random House, 1974);

Mathematische Manuskripte, edited by Wolfgang Endemann (Kronberg: Scriptor, 1974);

On Freedom of the Press and Censorship, edited and translated by Padover (New York: McGraw-Hill, 1974);

On Religion, edited and translated by Padover (New York: McGraw-Hill, 1974);

Über Sprache, Stil und Übersetzung, by Marx and Engels, edited by Heinz Ruschinski and Bruno Retzlaff-Kresse (Berlin: Dietz, 1974);

On Education, Women, and Children, edited and translated by Padover (New York: McGraw-Hill, 1975);

Texts on Method, edited and translated by Terrell Carver (New York: Barnes & Noble, 1975; Oxford: Blackwell, 1975);

Karl Marx, Friedrich Engels: Collected Works, 12 volumes, translated by Dixon and others (London: Lawrence & Wishart, 1975–1979; New York: International Publishers, 1975–1979);

Der Bürgerkrieg in den Vereinigten Staaten, by Marx and Engels, edited by Günter Wistozki and Manfred Tetzel (Berlin: Dietz, 1976);

Marx, Engels, Lenin: Über die Frau und die Familie, edited by the Bundesvorstand des Demokratischen Frauenbundes Deutschlands (Leipzig: Verlag für die Frau, 1976);

Marx and Engels on Ecology, edited by Howard L. Parsons (Westport, Conn.: Greenwood, 1977);

Love Poems of Karl Marx, edited and translated by Reinhard Lettau and Lawrence Ferlinghetti (San Francisco: City Lights Books, 1977);

Über Deutschland und die deutsche Arbeiterbewegung, by Marx and Engels (Berlin: Dietz, 1978);

The Essential Marx: The Non-Economic Writings, a Selection, edited and translated by Padover (New York: New American Library, 1979);

Karl Marx, Friedrich Engels, the Collected Writings in "The New York Daily Tribune," edited by A. Thomas Ferguson and Stephen J. O'Neil (New York: Urizen, 1980);

Droht der gemeinsame Untergang?: Marxismus und Ökologie. Originaltexte von Marx und Engels in Gegenüberstellung zu ihren aktuellen Kritikern (Hambuch: Buntbuch, 1980);

Marx und Engels über die sozialistische und kommunistische Gesellschaft: Die Entwicklung der marxistischen Lehre von der kommunistischen Umgestaltung, edited by Rolf Dlubek and Renate Merkel (Berlin: Dietz, 1981);

The Portable Karl Marx, edited by Eugene Kamenka (New York: Viking, 1983);

Unbekanntes von Friedrich Engels und Karl Marx, edited by Bert Andreas, Jacques Grandjonc, and Hans Pelger (Trier: Karl-Marx-Haus, 1986);

Über die Liebe, by Marx and Engels, edited by Heinrich and Hilde Gemkow (Berlin: Dietz, 1986);

Heiteres und Bissiges von Marx und Engels, edited by Käte Schubert (Berlin: Dietz, 1987);

Über den Kampf um Frieden und sozialen Fortschritt, by Marx, Engels, and Lenin (Berlin: Dietz, 1987);

Über den Sozialismus, by Marx, Engels, and Lenin (Berlin: Dietz, 1987).

OTHER: *Neue Rheinische Zeitung: Organ der Demokratie,* nos. 1–301, edited by Marx (1 June 1848– 19 May 1849);

Frank Mecklenburg and Manfred Stassen, eds., *German Essays on Socialism in the Nineteenth Century: Theory, History, and Political Organization, 1844– 1914,* contributions by Marx (New York: Continuum, 1990).

Karl Marx's writings have significantly influenced the course of international politics and culture since the 1840s. Together with Friedrich Engels he defined the concepts of scientific socialism, thereby contributing to the wide range of social theories that were developed in the nineteenth century. The popularization of these concepts has led to the application of its principles in the sciences and humanities, where it is known today as Marxism or, most recently, as neo-Marxism.

Karl Heinrich Marx was born on 5 May 1818 in Trier to Heinrich Marx, a lawyer, and Henriette Preßburg, both of whose fathers came from generations of rabbis. Because Jews were excluded from public office in Prussia after 1815, Heinrich Marx had been baptized as a Protestant in 1816 or 1817. Karl Marx was baptized on 26 August 1824.

Marx studied philosophy, history, and law at the Universities of Bonn and Berlin from October 1835 to March 1841. Central to his studies were the writings of Aristotle, Benedict de Spinoza, Gottfried Wilhelm Leibniz, David Hume, Immanuel Kant, and especially Gottfried Wilhelm Friedrich Hegel. In Berlin he joined the "Doctorklub," a group of students interested in philosophy, which also included Bruno Bauer and Karl Friedrich Köppen. This club, which centered around Arnold Ruge and his journal, the *Hallischen Jahrbücher* (Halle Yearbooks), formed the heart of the Young Hegelians, the leading philosophical and political avant-garde movement of the day. Engels occasionally attended the meetings, but without meeting Marx. On 15 April 1841 Marx received his doctorate on completing his dissertation, "Differenz der demokritischen und epikureischen Naturphilosophie" (Difference between the Philosophies of Nature of Democritus and Epicurus). At this early point in Marx's career the young communist Moses Hess wrote enthusiastically in a letter about the "einzig lebende Philosph" (only living philosopher): "Dr. Marx, so heißt mein Abgott, ist noch ein ganz junger Mann (etwa 24 Jahre höchstens alt), der der mittelalterlichen Religion und Politik den letzten Stoß versetzen wird; er verbindet mit dem tiefsten philosophischen Ernst den schneidendsten Witz; denk Dir Rousseau, Voltaire, Holbach, Lessing, Heine und Hegel in einer Person vereinigt, ich sage vereinigt, nicht zusammengeschmissen – so hast Du Dr. Marx" (Dr. Marx, for that is the name of my idol, is still a very young man [24 years old at the most] who will deal medieval religion and politics its final blow; he combines the deepest philosophical seriousness with the most cutting humor; think of Rousseau, Voltaire, Holbach, Lessing, Heine, and Hegel all rolled into one, and I mean integrated into one, not simply thrown together – then you have Dr. Marx).

On 15 October 1842 Marx assumed the position of editor in chief of the radical-liberal Cologne newspaper *Die Rheinische Zeitung*. This period marks the beginning of his preoccupation with economics and his analysis of communism. Because of Prussia's strict censorship laws, Marx did not think that the time was right for a presentation of communist

Cover for the call to revolution written by Marx and Engels for the Communist League

theory; he was primarily concerned with carving out a safe political position for the paper. When it was blacklisted in March 1843 despite his efforts, he accepted an offer from Arnold Ruge to move to Paris and edit his new journal, the *Deutsch-Französischen Jahrbücher* (German-French Yearbooks). It was in Cologne that Marx first met Engels. Their relationship was rather cool at first because Marx was skeptical about Engels's relationship to Young Hegelianism, a position Marx had already rejected. In June 1843 Marx married Jenny von Westphalen; they had four children: Jenny, Laura, Eleanor, and Edgar, who died at the age of eight.

In November 1843 Marx arrived in Paris, where he kept his distance from the eighty-five thousand exiled Germans living there. He devel-

First page of the first issue of the revolutionary newspaper edited by Marx in Cologne from 1 June 1848 until 18 May 1849

oped close friendships with only a few people, among them Hess, Ruge, the authors Heinrich Heine and Georg Herwegh, and the anarchist Mikhail Bakunin. Marx often visited French workers' meetings, which made a great impression on him: "Wenn die kommunistischen Handwerker sich vereinen, so gilt ihnen zunächst die Lehre, Propaganda etc. als Zweck. Aber zugleich eignen sie sich dadurch ein neues Bedürfnis, das Bedürfnis der Gemeinschaft, an, und was als Mittel erscheint, ist zum Zweck geworden. Diese praktische Bewegung kann man in ihren glänzendsten Resultaten anschauen, wenn man sozialistische französische ouvriers vereinigt sieht. Rauchen, Trinken, Essen etc. sind nicht mehr da, als Mittel der Verbindung, oder als verbindende Mittel. Die Gesellschaft, der Verein, die Unterhaltung, die wieder die Gesellschaft zum Zweck hat, reicht ihnen hin, die Brüderlichkeit der Menschen ist keine Phrase, sondern Wahrheit bei ihnen, und der Adel der Menschheit leuchtet uns aus den von der Arbeit verhärteten Gestalten entgegen" (When the communist craftsmen join together, their purpose is the teachings, propaganda, etc. But at the same time they create for themselves a new need, the need of community and what appears to be a means has become an end in itself. The glowing results of this practical movement can be seen when the socialist French workers unite. Smoking, drinking, eating, etc. are no longer a means of fraternizing. The society, the organization, the conversation which the society has as its purpose is enough for them, the brotherhood of man is no longer an empty phrase, but the truth. The nobility of mankind shines upon us from these figures hardened by work).

Marx spent the majority of his time in Paris expanding his understanding of philosophy and history. Through a critique of Hegel's understanding of law and with the help of Ludwig Feuerbach's philosophical writings and a thorough knowledge of the history of the French Revolution, as well as his study of the works of the French socialists, especially Pierre-Joseph Proudhon, Marx developed the concepts of communism. Communism for Marx was "such a necessary consequence of New Hegelian philosophy, that no opposition could keep it down," as Engels wrote at the time in the newspaper *New Moral World*. In his first essay for the *Deutsch-Französischen Jahrbücher* in 1844 Marx wrote that true democracy could only be achieved in a classless society. This ideal could only be realized by a revolution in which "die materielle Gewalt muß gestürzt werden durch materielle Gewalt, allein auch die Theorie wird zur materiellen Gewalt, sobald sie die Massen ergreift" (material force must be toppled by material force; even theory becomes a material force once it has taken hold among the masses). According to Marx, a revolution in Germany must come from below: "Die Emanzipation des Deutschen ist die Emanzipation des Menschen. Der Kopf dieser Emanzipation ist die Philosophie, ihr Herz das Proletariat" (The emancipation of the Germans is the emancipation of humankind. The head of this emancipation is philosophy, its heart the proletariat).

In 1844 Marx wrote "Zur Kritik der Nationalökonomie, mit einem Schlußkapitel über die Hegelsche Philosophie" (Critique of National Economy, with a Concluding Chapter on the Hegelian Philosophy), which was not published until it appeared in 1932 as a part of the first critical edition of his and Engels's works. Here Marx analyzes the situation of humanity of his day from the perspectives of philosophy, history, economics, and politics. Starting from Hegel's *Die Phänomenologie des Geistes*

Marx's wife, the former Jenny von Westphalen

(1807; translated as *The Phenomenology of Mind*, 1910), Marx redefines Hegel's categories of labor, reification, and alienation. Marx's critique is aimed at "alienated labor" — that is, work performed under economic compulsion rather than as a spontaneous expression of the human spirit — which results from the division of labor and ultimately from private property in the means of production. Only the abolition of private property would enable people to achieve a truly social existence. Communism is the only form of economic organization that corresponds to the essence and dignity of humanity.

At the end of May 1844 Marx and Engels met in Paris. Because of Engels's articles about capitalism and the condition of the working class in England that had been published in the *Deutsch-Französischen Jahrbücher,* Marx had come to consider Engels an ally. During Engels's ten-day visit the two met daily to discuss their theories, establishing a

collaboration and friendship that was to last until Marx's death.

In January 1845 Marx was expelled from Paris at the request of the Prussian government because of two anti-Prussian essays he had published in the Paris newspaper *Vorwärts* (Forward). With his family, he went to Brussels. To escape persecution by the Prussian authorities, Marx renounced his citizenship and never claimed another. He articulated his concept of history in 1845 and 1846 in "Die deutsche Ideologie" (translated as *The German Ideology,* 1964), written together with Engels, who had joined him in Brussels in April 1845. The work, which was not published until 1932, is a detailed analysis and critique of the philosophies of Feuerbach, Bauer, and Max Stirner, as well as of so-called true socialism, the emotionally laden version of communism prevalent at the time. Its interpretation of history, which Engels later termed historical materialism, is that the economic structure of society conditions the social, political, and intellectual aspects of human existence; a person's place in the relations of production determines his or her consciousness. Moreover, Marx and Engels maintained that the capitalist, or bourgeois, form of production was the final antagonistic form. From within bourgeois society forces of production would develop that would create the necessary material conditions for eradicating this antagonism. Marx became increasingly practice-oriented: "Die Philosophen haben die Welt nur verschieden interpretiert: es kommt darauf an, sie zu verändern" (Philosophers have only interpreted the world in various ways. What is really important, is to change it).

At its congress in November 1847 the London-based Communist League commissioned Marx and Engels to write its political statement. The *Manifest der kommunistischen Partei* (1848; translated as *Manifesto of the Communist Party,* 1888), generally known as *The Communist Manifesto,* contains a synopsis of Marx and Engels's insights in concise and understandable language and was intended as an incendiary call to revolution. The immediate reception, however, was relatively small; only about a thousand copies were printed in February 1848. Thus the revolutions that began that year on 24 February in Paris, on 13 March in Vienna, and on 18 March in Berlin were not directly inspired by the work. The *Manifesto* declares that the first priority for the communists and the bourgeoisie was to unite against the nobility; immediately following victory, the battle against the bourgeoisie must begin: "Auf Deutschland richten die Kommunisten ihre Hauptaufmerksamkeit, weil Deutschland am Vorabend einer bürgerlichen Revolution steht, und weil es diese Umwälzung unter fortgeschritteneren Bedingungen der europäischen Zivilisation überhaupt, und mit einem viel weiter entwickelteren Proletariat vollbringt als England im siebzehnten und Frankreich im achtzehnten Jahrhundert, die deutsche bürgerliche Revolution also nur das unmittelbare Vorspiel einer proletarischen Revolution sein kann" (The communists are watching Germany carefully, because Germany stands on the eve of a bourgeois revolution. This radical change is occurring under advanced conditions of European civilization and with a considerably better developed proletariat than had been the case in England in the seventeenth century and France in the eighteenth century. The German bourgeois revolution can only be understood as an overture to a proletarian revolution). In Germany, however, the proletarian class movement prescribed by Marx did not exist; only isolated radical groups were to be found.

When Marx arrived in Cologne at the beginning of April 1848, he concentrated his efforts on organizing the *Neue Rheinische Zeitung.* Its 301 issues were published from 1 June 1848 until 18 May 1849 with Marx as editor in chief. In collaboration with Engels and the authors Ernst Dronke, Georg Weerth, and Wilhelm Wolff, Marx created a revolutionary newspaper of the highest intellectual quality. The events of the German revolution were reported and commented on from the viewpoint of international politics.

The rapid strengthening of the counterrevolution quickly doused the fighting spirit of the revolutionaries. Marx was expelled from Germany on 16 May 1849 and fled via Paris to London, arriving at the end of August. In a series of articles titled "Die Klassenkämpfe in Frankreich 1848 bis 1850" (published in book form, 1895; translated as *The Class Struggles in France, 1848–1850,* 1924) for the Hamburg-based *Neue Rheinische Zeitung, politisch-oekonomische Revue* he conceded that the revolution had failed: "Die Revolution ist tot! Es lebe die Revolution!" (The revolution is dead! Long live the revolution!). After reading economic reports in the British newspaper the *Economist,* Marx concluded that the European revolution was made possible by the English commercial crisis of 1847 and its effects on the Continent. The economic recovery that began in 1849 crippled the revolutionary movement in every country. An economic crisis was, therefore, a precondition for revolution, and, according to Marx, a new crisis was bound to occur.

During his first years in London, Marx spent most of his time in the reading room of the British Museum studying economics. One of his publications in this period was *Der Achtzehnte Brumaire des Louis-Bonaparte* (1869; translated as *The Eighteenth Brumaire of Louis Bonaparte,* 1898), which originally appeared in the New York newspaper *Die Revolution,* edited by Joseph Weydemeyer, in 1852. In this article Marx sought to prove that the class struggle in France had led to conditions that enabled a mediocre and grotesque personage such as Napoleon III to play the role of a hero.

Between 1851 and 1862 Marx worked as a journalist for a variety of newspapers, including the Breslau *Neue Oder-Zeitung* in 1855, the Sheffield and London *Free Press* in 1855–1856, and the *People's Paper* and the *Wiener Presse* (Viennese Press) in 1861–1862. The most important paper was the *New York Daily Tribune,* for which Marx was the European correspondent. At that time the *Tribune* was the largest American newspaper representing a liberal-to-socialist position. More than one hundred articles appeared under Marx's name, but most were actually written by Engels. The articles dealt with contemporary events such as the Crimean War, unrest in Spain, and reoccurring economic crises. Special attention was paid to the commercial crisis of 1857, which began in the United States and spread to Europe.

The increasing industrialization of England, France, and Germany led to the founding of the International Working Men's Association – the "First International" – on 28 September 1864. While Marx soon assumed the leading role in this organization, the development of the German Workers' party went on without him. He had great misgivings about the party because he considered the leader of one of its two wings, Ferdinand Lassalle, a parvenu whose success was based on plagiarism of Marx's writings.

Marx, who was fluent in eight languages, established a new political catalyst with the International. Workers' organizations from various countries were united in this alliance, representing diverse political ideologies ranging from communist and socialist to anarchist. The program written by Marx and adopted by the International differed significantly from the *Manifesto*. Marx's thesis was that the destitution of the workers must necessarily lead to their emancipation. The workers had to gain political power by means of labor unions. Moreover, the absence of international connections had often contributed to the failure of the workers's interests to prevail. Consequently, at the congresses of the International between 1865 and 1872 Marx was concerned to establish a consensus of opinion among the workers of various countries. The International was, however, highly fractionalized, and Marx engaged in a long struggle against the anarchists and their leader, Mikhail Bakunin. The International was also subject to external threats: the uprising of the Paris workers – the Paris Commune of 18 March to 28 May 1871 – which Marx understood as an affirmation of the tenets of the International, was brutally crushed by the French army.

His work in the International convinced Marx that he had to finish the first volume of his magnum opus, *Das Kapital: Kritik der politischen Ökonomie* (Capital: Critique of Political Economy, 1867; translated as *Capital: A Critique of Capitalist Production*, 1887). Adopting the assumptions and principles of such bourgeois economists as Adam Smith and David Ricardo, Marx develops his theory of exploitation and

Marx (right) and Engels with Marx's daughters, (left to right) Laura, Eleanor, and Jenny, in 1864

surplus value. He constructs an ideal model of capitalism in which the capitalist pays full value for all resources used in the process of production. In the case of the workers, "full value" means what the worker needs to live and to raise his children (the next generation of workers) – in other words, a subsistence wage. The worker produces enough value to compensate the capitalist for this investment after working, say, eight hours. But the workday (in the second half of the nineteenth century) does not end at eight hours but goes on for several more hours. The extra value produced by the worker over and above the amount of the capitalist's investment in him is what Marx calls surplus value, and it is the source of the profits that drive the capitalist system. The worker is thus being exploited – he is producing more value than he is receiving; the surplus goes to the capitalist, who does nothing to produce it. Only the worker can produce surplus value and, hence, profit for the capitalist; in Marx's theoretical model the other factors of production, such as raw materials and machinery, reproduce only the value the capitalist invested in them before they are used up or wear out. But the pressure of competition forces the capitalist to cut prices and, hence, to reduce expenses; he lays off workers and replaces them with machines, which do not produce surplus value, and so his profits decline. To maintain his profits he lowers the wages of his remaining workers, driving them below subsistence level. As weaker businesses succumb in the competitive struggle, their former owners join the working class; thus, the bourgeoisie contracts and the proletariat increases. As the failed businesses are taken over by the successful ones, workers are brought together in larger and larger factories and begin to develop a consciousness of themselves as a class. The unemployed workers and those who are employed but are being paid less than a subsistence wage become unable to purchase the goods produced by the businesses; a business crisis (depression) results; more businesses fail, and their owners descend into the proletariat; finally prices fall, the excess goods are destroyed, and the process begins again. But the average rate of profit will continue to fall as more workers are replaced by machines, thus reducing the incentive of the capitalists. As means of transportation and communication are improved in the effort to acquire cheaper materials and open new markets, workers will be put in closer touch with each other, increasing their class consciousness still further. As crisis succeeds crisis, each one deeper than the last, the capitalists will extend their search for raw materials and markets overseas, thus bringing the entire world into the capitalist system. As the crises continue, the workers of the world, having become more and more impoverished and having arrived, with the help of certain bourgeois intellectuals (such as Marx himself), at an understanding of their situation, will seize control of the various governments from the bourgeois class and will abolish private property and institute socialism.

The first volume of *Das Kapital* contained only a fraction of Marx's lifelong work on economics. The remaining manuscripts were edited by Engels, who released the second volume of *Das Kapital* in 1885 (translated, 1907) and the third in 1894 (translated, 1909), and by Karl Kautsky, who between 1905 and 1910 edited four volumes titled *Theorien über den Mehrwert* (translated as *Theories of Surplus Value,* 1951). Further manuscripts were published in Moscow in 1939 and 1941 under the title *Grundrisse der Kritik der politischen Ökonomie* (translated as *Grundrisse: Foundations of the Critique of Political Economy,* 1973). Today it is generally acknowledged that Marx's mature conclusions had been formulated as early as the 1840s. Marx, who died in London on 14 March 1883, did not experience the triumph of his works among all European democratic mass parties in the 1880s and 1890s.

Letters:

Briefwechsel: Karl Marx, Friedrich Engels, 4 volumes, edited by the Marx-Engels-Institut, Moscow (Moscow: Verlagsgenossenschaft Ausländischer Arbeiter in der UdSSR, 1935–1939);

Karl Marx and Frederick Engels: Letters to Americans, 1848–1895, translated by Leonhard E. Mins (New York: International Publishers, 1953);

Briefe über "Das Kapital," by Engels, edited by the Marx-Engels-Lenin-Stalin-Institut beim ZK der SED (Berlin: Dietz, 1954);

The Letters of Karl Marx, edited and translated by Saul K. Padover (Englewood Cliffs, N. J.: Prentice-Hall, 1979).

Bibliographies:

Robert J. Usher, "The Bibliography of the *Communist Manifesto,*" *Bibliographical Society of America,* 5 (1910): 109–114;

Institut für Marxismus-Leninismus, *Die Erstdrucke der Werke von Marx und Engels: Bibliographie der Einzelausgaben* (Berlin: Dietz, 1955);

Maximilien Rubel, *Bibliographie des œuvres de Karl Marx* (Paris: Rivière, 1956);

Rubel, *Supplément à la Bibliographie des œuvres de Karl Marx* (Paris: Rivière, 1960);

R. L. Prager, *Marx, Engels, Lassalle: Eine Bibliographie des Sozialismus* (London: Slienger, 1977);

Franz Neubauer, *Marx-Engels Bibliographie* (Boppard: Boldt, 1979);

Dieter Zirnstein, *Verzeichnis der Werke von Karl Marx und Friedrich Engels: Herausgegeben von Verlagen nichtsozialistischer Länder in den Jahren 1945–1981* (Berlin, 1982);

Inge Kiesshauer, *Lebendiges Erbe der Klassiker: Auswahlbibliographie zum Karl-Marx-Jahr 1983* (Leipzig: Deutsche Bücherei, 1982);

Cecil L. Eubanks, *Karl Marx and Friedrich Engels: An Analytical Bibliography,* second edition (New York: Garland, 1984);

Hal Draper, *The Marx-Engels Register: A Complete Bibliography of Marx and Engels' Individual Writings* (New York: Schocken Books, 1985).

Biographies:

Franz Mehring, *Karl Marx: Geschichte seines Lebens* (Leipzig: Leipziger Buchdruckerei Aktiengesellschaft, 1918);

Otto Rühle, *Karl Marx: Leben und Werk* (Hellerau: Avalun, 1928); translated by Eden and Cedar

Paul as *Karl Marx: His Life and Work* (London: Allen & Unwin, 1929);

Boris Nicolaievsky and Otto Maenchen-Helfen, *Karl Marx: Man and Fighter* (London: Methuen, 1936; revised edition, London: Penguin, 1973);

Karl Korsch, *Karl Marx* (New York: Russell & Russell, 1963);

Robert Payne, *Karl Marx* (New York: Simon & Schuster, 1968);

Ernst Bloch, *On Karl Marx* (New York: Herder & Herder, 1971);

Petr Nikolaevich Fedoseyev and others, *Karl Marx: A Biography,* translated by Yuri Sdobnikov (Moscow: Progress Publishers, 1973);

David McLellan, *Karl Marx: His Life and Thought* (New York: Harper & Row, 1973);

Ferdinand Tönnies, *Karl Marx, His Life and Teachings* (East Lansing: Michigan State University Press, 1974);

Michael Evans, *Karl Marx* (Bloomington: Indiana University Press, 1975);

Fritz J. Raddatz, *Karl Marx: Der Mensch und seine Lehre* (Munich: Heine, 1977); translated by Richard Barry as *Karl Marx: A Political Philosophy* (Boston: Little, Brown, 1978);

Isaiah Berlin, *Karl Marx: His Life and Environment,* fourth edition (New York: Oxford University Press, 1978);

Saul K. Padover, *Karl Marx* (New York: McGraw-Hill, 1978);

Richard Friedenthal, *Karl Marx: Sein Leben und seine Zeit* (Munich: Piper, 1981);

Allen W. Wood, *Karl Marx* (Boston: Routledge & Kegan Paul, 1981);

Richard P. Appelbaum, *Karl Marx* (Beverly Hills, Cal.: Sage Publications, 1988).

References:

Edward J. Ahearn, *Marx and Modern Fiction* (New Haven, Conn.: Yale University Press, 1989);

Nelli Auerbach, *Marx und die Gewerkschaften* (Berlin: Kollektiv-Verlag, 1972);

Ernst Bloch, *Das Prinzip Hoffnung* (Frankfurt am Main: Suhrkamp, 1959);

Theodore Brameld, *A Philosophic Approach to Communism* (Chicago: University of Chicago Press, 1933);

Kevin M. Brien, *Marx, Reason, and the Art of Freedom* (Philadelphia: Temple University Press, 1987);

Alex Callinicos, *The Revolutionary Ideals of Karl Marx* (London: Bookmarks, 1983);

Marx's grave in Highgate Cemetery, London

Terrell Carver, *Marx and Engels: The Intellectual Relationship* (Bloomington: Indiana University Press, 1983);

Gerald Cohen, *Karl Marx's Theory of History: A Defense* (Princeton: Princeton University Press, 1978);

Henry Collins, *Karl Marx and the British Labour Movement: Years of the First International* (New York: St. Martin's Press, 1965);

Ian Cummings, *Marx, Engels, and National Movements* (New York: St. Martin's Press, 1980);

William Desmond, ed., *Hegel and His Critics: Philosophy in the Aftermath of Hegel* (Albany: State University of New York, 1989);

Raya Dunayevskaya, *Rosa Luxemburg, Women's Liberation, and Marx's Philosophy of Revolution,* second edition (Urbana: University of Illinois Press, 1991);

Andrew Feenberg, *Lukács, Marx, and the Sources of Critical Theory* (Totowa, N. J.: Rowman & Littlefield, 1981);

Iring Fetscher, *Marx and Marxism* (New York: Herder & Herder, 1971);

Herwig Förder, *Marx und Engels am Vorabend der Revolution: Die Ausarbeitung der politischen Richtlinien für die deutschen Kommunisten (1846–1848)* (Berlin: Akademie-Verlag, 1960);

Walter Bryce Gallie, *Philosophers of Peace and War: Kant, Clausewitz, Marx, Engels, and Tolstoy* (London & New York: Cambridge University Press, 1978);

Reiner Grundmann, *Marxism and Ecology* (New York: Oxford University Press, 1991);

Richard F. Hamilton, *The Bourgeois Epoch: Marx and Engels on Britain, France, and Germany* (Chapel Hill: University of North Carolina Press, 1991);

Oscar J. Hammen, *The Red '48ers: Karl Marx and Friedrich Engels* (New York: Scribners, 1969);

Robert Heister, *Political Identity: Thinking through Marx* (Cambridge: Blackwell, 1990);

Moses Hess, *Briefwechsel,* edited by Edmund Silburner (Berlin: Mouton: 1959), p. 80;

Institut für Marxistische Studien und Forschungen und Marx-Engels-Stiftung, eds., *". . . einen großen Hebel der Geschichte": Zum 100. Todestag von Karl Marx, Aktualität und Wirkung seines Werks* (Frankfurt am Main: IMSF, 1983);

John H. Jackson, *Marx, Proudhon, and European Socialism* (London: English Universities Press, 1957);

Hans-Peter Jaeck, *Die französische bürgerliche Revolution von 1789 im Frühwerk von Karl Marx (1843–1846)* (Vaduz: Topos, 1979);

Henri Lefebvre, *The Sociology of Marx* (New York: Columbia University Press, 1982);

Ernst Nolte, *Marxismus und industrielle Revolution* (Stuttgart: Klett-Cotta, 1983);

Siegbert S. Prawer, *Karl Marx and World Literature* (Oxford: Clarendon Press, 1976);

Zvi Rosen, *Moses Hess und Karl Marx: Ein Beitrag zur Entstehung der Marxschen Theorie* (Hamburg: Christians, 1983);

Adam Schaff, *Entfremdung als soziales Phänomen* (Vienna: Europa-Verlag, 1977);

Alfred Schmidt, *Der Begriff der Natur in der Lehre von Marx* (Frankfurt am Main: Europäische Verlagsanstalt, 1971);

Manfred Schneider, *Die kranke schöne Seele der Revolution: Heine, Börne, das "Junge Deutschland," Marx und Engels* (Frankfurt am Main: Syndikat, 1980);

Thomas Sowell, *Marxism, Philosophy, and Economics* (New York: Morrow, 1985);

Frank Trommler, *Sozialistische Literatur in Deutschland* (Stuttgart: Kröner, 1976);

Walter Tuchscheerer, *Bevor "Das Kapital" entstand: Die Entstehung der ökonomischen Theorien von Karl Marx* (Cologne: Rugenstein, 1968);

Axel van den Berg, *The Immanent Utopia: From Marxism on the State to the State of Marxism* (Princeton: Princeton University Press, 1988);

Lise Vogel, *Marxism and the Oppression of Women: Towards a Unitary Theory* (New Brunswick, N. J.: Rutgers University Press, 1983);

Robert Weiner, *Das Amerikabild von Karl Marx* (Bonn: Bouvier, 1982);

Lola Zahn, *Utopischer Sozialismus und Ökonomiekritik* (Berlin: Akademie-Verlag, 1984).

Papers:

Karl Marx's personal and political documents, correspondence, manuscripts, and notes form a single collection together with those of Friedrich Engels in the International Institute of Social History in Amsterdam. The Institute for Marxism-Leninism in Moscow has the largest part of the Marx-Engels papers, with photocopies of the Amsterdam collection.

Karl May

(25 February 1842 – 30 March 1912)

Karl W. Doerry
Northern Arizona University

BOOKS: *Das Buch der Liebe: Wissenschaftliche Darstellung der Liebe nach ihrem Wesen, ihrer Bestimmung, ihrer Geschichte und ihren geschlechtlichen Folgen, nebst eingehender Besprechung aller Geschlechts-, Frauen- und Kinderkrankheiten mit besonderer Berücksichtigung des Wochenbettes nebst Anleitung zur Heilung sämmtlicher Krankheiten,* anonymous (Dresden: Münchmeyer, 1876);

Auf hoher See gefangen (Philadelphia: Morwitz, 1879);

Weg mit den Grillen! (Berlin: Liebau, 1880);

Das Waldröschen oder Die Verfolgung rund um die Erde: Großer Enthüllungsroman über die Geheimnisse der menschlichen Gesellschaft, as Kapitain Ramon Diaz de la Escosura, 109 installments (Dresden: Münchmeyer, 1882–1884); republished as *Das Waldröschen oder Die Verfolgung rund um die Erde: Enthüllungsroman über die Geheimnisse der menschlichen Gesellschaft,* 6 volumes (Dresden: Münchmeyer, 1902–1903) – comprises volume 1, *Die Tochter des Granden* (1902); volume 2, *Der Schatz des Mixtekas* (1902); volume 3, *Matavase, der Fürst des Felsens* (1902); volumes 4–6, *Erkämpftes Glück* (1902–1903);

Die Liebe des Ulanen, 107 installments (Dresden: Münchmeyer, 1883–1885); republished as *Die Liebe des Ulanen: Original-Roman aus der Zeit des deutsch-französischen Krieges,* 3 volumes (Dresden: Münchmeyer, 1900–1901); enlarged as *Die Liebe des Ulanen,* 5 volumes (Dresden: Münchmeyer, 1905–1906) – comprises volume 1, *Die Herren von Königsau* (1905); volume 2, *Napoleons letzte Liebe* (1905); volume 3, *Der Kapitän der Kaisergarde* (1905); volume 4, *Der Spion von Ortry* (1905 or 1906); volume 5, *Durch Kampf zum Sieg* (1906);

Fürst und Leiermann: Eine Episode aus dem Leben des "alten Dessauer" (Lahr: Schauenburg, 1884);

Die Wüstenräuber: Erlebnisse einer Africa-Expedition durch die Sahara (Cologne: Bachem, 1885);

Karl May circa 1892

Der verlorene Sohn oder der Fürst des Elends, as Verfasser des *Waldröschen,* 101 installments (Dresden: Münchmeyer, 1885–1887); republished as *Der verlorene Sohn,* 5 volumes (Dresden: Münchmeyer, 1904–1905) – comprises volume 1, *Sklaven des Elends* (1904); volume 2, *Sklaven der Arbeit* (1905); volume 3, *Sklaven der Schande* (1905); volume 4, *Sklaven des Goldes* (1905); volume 5, *Sklaven der Ehre* (1905);

Deutsche Herzen – Deutsche Helden, as Verfasser des *Waldröschen* und *Der Fürst des Elends,* 109 installments (Dresden: Münchmeyer, 1885-1887); republished as *Deutsche Herzen und Helden,* 5 volumes (Dresden: Münchmeyer, 1901-1902) – comprises volume 1, *Eine deutsche Sultana: Roman. Illustrierte Ausgabe* (1901); volume 2, *Die Königin der Wüste: Roman. Illustrierte Ausgabe* (1901); volumes 3 and 4, *Der Fürst der Bleichgesichter: Roman. Illustrierte Ausgabe* (1901); volume 5, *Der Engel der Verbannten: Roman. Illustrierte Ausgabe* (1902);

Der Weg zum Glück, as Verfasser des *Waldröschen, Verlorener Sohn, Deutsche Herzen – Deutsche Helden,* 109 installments (Dresden: Münchmeyer, 1886-1887);

Die drei Feldmarschalls: Eine bisher unbekannte Episode aus dem Leben des "alten Dessauer" (Cologne: Bachem, 1888);

Die Helden des Westens, Band 1: Der Sohn des Bärenjägers (Stuttgart: Union, 1890);

Verwegene Thaten: Eine Erzählung aus dem Seeleben (Reutlingen: Bardtenschlager, 1890);

Der blau-rote Methusalem (Stuttgart: Union, 1892);

Gesammelte Reiseromane [title of series changes to *Gesammelte Reiseerzählungen* with volume 18], 33 volumes (Freiburg: Fehsenfeld, 1892-1904; reprinted, Bamberg: Karl-May-Verlag, 1982-1984) – comprises volume 1, *Durch Wüste und Harem: Reiseerlebnisse* (1892); republished as *Durch die Wüste* (Freiburg: Fehsenfeld, 1895); translated by F. Billerbeck-Gentz as *In the Desert* (Bamberg & New York: Ustad, 1955); volume 2, *Durchs wilde Kurdistan: Reiseerlebnisse* (1892); translated by Michael Shaw as *In the Desert: A Novel* [combined with translation of *Durch Wüste und Harem*] (New York: Seabury Press, 1977); volume 3, *Von Bagdad nach Stambul: Reiseerlebnisse* (1892); translated by Shaw as *The Caravan of Death: A Novel* (New York: Seabury Press, 1979); volume 4, *In den Schluchten des Balkan: Reiseerlebnisse* (1892); translated by Shaw as *The Secret Brotherhood: A Novel* (New York: Seabury Press, 1979); volume 5, *Durch das Land der Skipetaren: Reiseerlebnisse* (1892); translated by Shaw as *The Evil Saint: A Novel* (New York: Seabury Press, 1979); volume 6, *Der Schut: Reiseerlebnisse* (1892); translated by Shaw as *The Black Persian: A Novel* (New York: Seabury Press, 1979); volumes 7-9, *Winnetou, der rote Gentleman* (1893); translated by Shaw as *Winnetou: A Novel,* 2 volumes (New York: Seabury Press, 1977); volume 10, *Orangen und Datteln: Reisefrüchte aus dem Oriente* (1894 [i.e., 1893]); volume 11, *Am Stillen Ocean: Reiseerlebnisse* (1894); volume 12,

Am Rio de la Plata: Reiseerlebnisse (1894); volume 13, *In den Cordilleren: Reiseerlebnisse* (1894); volumes 14 and 15, *Old Surehand: Reiseerlebnisse* (1894-1895); volume 15 translated by Fred Gardner as *Captain Cayman* (London: Speaman, 1971); volumes 16-18, *Im Lande des Mahdi: Reiseerlebnisse* (1896); volume 19, *Old Surehand: Reiseerlebnisse* (1896); volumes 20-22, *Satan und Ischariot: Reiseerlebnisse,* (1896-1897); volume 23, *Auf fremden Pfaden: Reiseerlebnisse* (1897); volume 24, *"Weihnacht!": Reiseerzählung* (1897); volume 25, *Am Jenseits: Reiseerlebnisse* (1899); volumes 26-29, *Im Reiche des silbernen Löwen: Reiseerlebnisse* (1898-1903); volume 30, *Und Friede auf Erden!: Reiseerzählung* (1904); volumes 31 and 32, *Ardistan und Dschinnistan: Reiseerzählungen* (1909); translated by Shaw as *Ardistan and Djinnistan: A Novel,* 2 volumes (New York: Seabury Press, 1977); volume 33, *Winnetou: 4. Band* (1910);

Die Sklavenkarawane (Stuttgart: Union, 1893);

Der Karawanenwürger und andere Erzählungen: Erlebnisse und Abenteuer zu Wasser und zu Lande (Berlin: Liebau, 1894);

Die Rose von Kaïrwan: Erzählung aus drei Erdtheilen (Osnabrück: Wehberg, 1894);

Der Schatz im Silbersee (Stuttgart: Union, 1894);

Aus fernen Zonen: Erzählungen für die Jugend (Berlin: Liebau, 1894);

Das Vermächtnis des Inka (Stuttgart, Berlin & Leipzig: Union, 1895);

Der Oelprinz: Eine Erzählung für die reifere Jugend (Stuttgart: Union, 1897);

Ernste Klänge, Heft 1: Ave Maria: Vergiß mich nicht (Freiburg: Fehsenfeld, 1898);

Der schwarze Mustang (Stuttgart, Berlin & Leipzig: Union, 1899);

Himmelsgedanken: Gedichte (Freiburg: Fehsenfeld, 1900);

Wanda (Dresden: Münchmeyer, 1901);

Abu-Seif: Ein Reiseerlebnis (Stockholm: Billes, 1902);

Das Geheimnis des Stollens (Heilbronn: Weber, 1902);

Humoresken und Erzählungen (Dresden: Münchmeyer, 1902);

"Karl May als Erzieher" und "Die Wahrheit über Karl May" oder Die Gegner Karl Mays in ihrem eigenen Lichte, anonymous (Freiburg: Fehsenfeld, 1902);

Erzgebirgische Dorfgeschichten: Erstlingswerke (Dresden: Belletristischer Verlag, 1903);

Und Frieden auf Erden (Freiburg: Fehsenfeld, 1904);

Sonnenstrahlen aus Karl Mays Volksromanen (Dresden: Münchmeyer, 1904);

Der Weg zum Glück, 4 volumes (Dresden: Münch-
meyer, 1904) – comprises volume 1, *Die
Murenleni;* volume 2, *Der Wurz'nsepp;* volume 3,
Der Geldprotz; volume 4, *Der Krikelanton;*

Babel und Bibel: Arabische Fantasia in zwei Akten (Freiburg: Fehsenfeld, 1906);

Abdahn Effendi: Reiseerzählung (Stuttgart: Neues literarisches Institut, 1909);

Der Dukatenhof: Erzgebirgische Dorfgeschichte (Graz &
Vienna: Styria, 1909);

Mein Leben und Streben: Selbstbiographie (Freiburg:
Fehsenfeld, 1910);

Schamah: Reiseerzählung (Stuttgart: Neues literarisches Institut, 1911);

Gesammelte Werke, 65 volumes, edited by E. A.
Schmid and others (Radebeul: Karl-May-Verlag, 1913–1939);

Gesammelte Werke, 74 volumes, edited by E. A.
Schmid (Bamberg: Karl-May-Verlag, 1949–
1965);

*Karl Mays Werke: Historisch-kritische Ausgabe in 99 Bän-
den,* edited by Hermann Wiedenroth and
Hans Wollschläger (volumes 1–13, Nördlingen: Greno, 1987–1988; volumes 14– ,
Zurich: Haffmanns, 1989-).

OTHER: Gabriel Ferry, *Der Waldläufer: Für die
Jugend bearbeitet,* adapted by May (Stuttgart:
Neugebauer, 1879);

"Im fernen Westen," in *Zwei Erzählungen aus dem
Indianerleben für die Jugend,* by May and F. C.
von Wickede (Stuttgart: Neugebauer, 1879).

The work of Karl May is a cultural phenomenon that reflects many aspects of German civilization in the late nineteenth century – and beyond:
his works continue to attract mass audiences and
scholars alike. In terms of copies sold, May is easily
the most successful German author of all time; his
work sustains its own publishing house, the Karl-
May-Verlag, dedicated to bringing out new editions
of his writings and to the marketing of May-related
merchandise such as games, calendars, coloring
books, and T-shirts. By the time of May's death in
1912 his publisher Fehsenfeld alone had sold a million and a half volumes of his *Gesammelte Reiseromane*
(Collected Travel Novels, 1892–1904), a spectacular success by the standards of the time. By 1945
sales of the collected works had risen to nine million
volumes, all in handsome hardcover editions, and
by 1986 the Karl-May-Verlag had produced about
seventy million volumes of May's works. Since the
expiration of the copyright in 1962 bookstores have
been flooded with inexpensive editions from other

Cover for an installment of one of May's serial novels

publishers, so that the total number of May volumes far exceeds the production of the Karl-May-
Verlag.

His public appeal thus surpasses that of any
other German author in any literary category and is
not likely to be approached by many authors world-
wide. This success is all the more remarkable because it is not restricted to a particular class of readers. In addition to appealing to a mass audience,
May's works have always attracted the attention
and appreciation of highbrow readers as well. In
1876 the writer Peter Rosegger accepted, with high
praise, one of May's first short stories, "Die Rose
von Kahira" (The Rose of Kahira) for publication in
his magazine *Der Heimgarten* (The Home Garden).
Since then there have been testimonials from readers as diverse as Carl Zuckmayer, Albert Einstein,
Ernst Bloch, and Peter Handke. The first dissertation on May appeared in 1936, and scholarship on
his work has proliferated since the 1960s. The Karl-
May-Gesellschaft, founded in 1969, is the latest of a
series of literary societies devoted to the author.
With around four thousand members, it is not only

one of the largest but also one of the most comprehensive literary societies in the world: officers in 1991 included a law professor, civil servants, a literary scholar, and an author – a combination that accurately reflects the fascination that May's work continues to hold for a widely diverse audience.

The first thirty years of May's life gave no indication of his eventual success. Karl Friedrich May was born on 25 February 1842 to Heinrich August May and Christiane Wilhelmine May (née Weise) in Ernstthal, a town of some three thousand inhabitants near the city of Chemnitz in Saxony. He was the fifth of fourteen children and the only son among the five who survived early childhood. Like the majority of breadwinners in Ernstthal, his father was a weaver, a trade severely hurt by imports from textile factories in England. Eighty-hour workweeks for the weavers and piecework by their wives and children barely kept their families from starvation, and riots by weavers in this and other regions were common.

Shortly after birth May lost his eyesight because of an infection; he spent his first four years in blindness, listening to the stories and fairy tales of his paternal grandmother, to whom he always attributed a decisive influence. His mother, more practical and determined than his father, obtained certification as a midwife in 1845, and an operation performed by her professor restored May's eyesight in 1846. In later life May vividly recounted sewing gloves at home, begging for potato peels at the local inn, poor sanitation, and bitter poverty, and such scenes of social misery are depicted in some of his works.

With great sacrifice the family sent their only son to the village school, where he received a surprisingly extensive if disjointed education that included private instruction in foreign languages as well as piano, violin, and organ lessons. In addition, May claimed that his father made him memorize whole geography books, an exercise that may have contributed to May's predilection for faraway and wide-ranging locales for his stories. After school the boy set up bowling pins at the village inn, which also housed the local lending library, and May devoured its popular novels, romances, and adventure stories. In his autobiography, *Mein Leben und Streben* (My Life and Strife, 1910), he claims that his reading of romantic novels led him to run away from home "nach Spanien, dem Land der edlen Räuber, der Retter aus Armut" (to Spain, the land of noble robbers, the saviors from poverty) for a short time. While there is no independent confirmation of this incident, it anticipates a recurring motif of May's works: a hero

leaving his constricting existence at home for a life of freedom and adventure in exotic places.

The fourteen-year-old May was sent to a seminary in Waldenburg for training as an elementary-school teacher, which was not a particularly prestigious profession in nineteenth-century Germany but was far above the working-class status of his family. He entered a five-year training program, one quarter of which was devoted to religious instruction. Discipline was strict, and May was reprimanded repeatedly for infractions such as missing church service. In 1859 he was accused of stealing – he had taken six candles to his family for Christmas – and was expelled as morally unfit for his profession. He completed his training at a seminary in Plauen, but this punishment began an extended series of conflicts between May and society.

In 1861 he secured a position as assistant teacher in Glauchau but lost it twelve days later when he was accused of making advances to his landlord's wife. A second position ended, after a few weeks, in what May always considered the great catastrophe of his life: during Christmas vacation he took home a watch, a pipe, and a cigarette holder belonging to his absent roommate, who accused him of theft. May claimed that he had intended to return the items, but he was convicted, sentenced to six weeks in jail, and barred from teaching for life. It was probably during his imprisonment that May first thought of becoming a writer. He worked in the four-thousand-volume prison library and claimed to have left prison in 1862 with a stack of manuscripts, although no evidence exists that anything he might have written during that period was ever published.

May's activities from 1862 to 1864 are scantily documented. His autobiography describes these years sketchily as a time in which he was torn between "hellen und dunklen Stimmen" (voices of darkness and light) and dabbled in various occupations. In interviews and speeches he occasionally implied that he had traveled to America or the Orient in those years, claims which are patently false.

In March 1865 May was arrested in Leipzig; three months later he was sentenced to a four-year term of work detention in Zwickau. His sentence was reduced by seven months for good behavior, but shortly after his release in 1868 he was arrested and convicted again and received a second four-year term, this time in the penitentiary in Waldheim. Both convictions were for petty confidence schemes in which May exploited his victims' respect for authority and status by impersonating doctors, teachers, government officials, and the like.

While May was no doubt poor when he committed his crimes, financial gain does not seem to have been his main motivation. All his schemes yielded a total of not more than about one hundred talers over several years, about half the yearly salary of an assistant teacher. More important seems to have been the young man's need to present himself as a Respektsperson, a figure of authority, respect, and dignity. When he was released in 1874 he gave immigration to America as his plan for the future. He never did emigrate from Germany; but his frequent claim that years of travel in exotic places were the basis for his success, while not literally the case, does contain a core of truth: his tales of adventures in faraway lands proved to be the road to fame, fortune, and respectability for him.

A year after his release May accepted the position of editor with the publishing house of Heinrich Gotthold Münchmeyer in Dresden. Münchmeyer specialized in long pulp novels distributed in installments by traveling booksellers to mostly working-class readers, a booming market that had only recently developed with the arrival of universal schooling. Münchmeyer also published several magazines aimed at a working class eager to acquire the genteel attributes of the middle class. Put in charge of these magazines, May contributed short stories and homiletic editorials to them and also had stories published in magazines of other publishers. His employer tried to bind his editor to the family enterprise by getting May to marry his sister; but May had no inclination to take this step, and he quit after only eighteen months with the firm.

He took another job as a magazine editor but left after a year and never again held a salaried position. Until his death he lived on royalties from his steadily growing literary output. Between 1878 and 1882 May had a great variety of works published by various publishers, including his first novel set in the American West, "Im fernen Westen" (In the Far West, 1879), and Der Waldläufer (The Forest Man, 1879), an adaptation of Gabriel Ferry's popular French Western Le Coureur du Bois (1850). He achieved a certain degree of financial stability in 1879 when the Catholic family magazine Der Deutsche Hausschatz in Wort und Bild (The German Home Treasure in Word and Picture) offered to publish any of his manuscripts. Up to 1908 many of May's best-known novels would appear first in this magazine. By 1880 his income was sufficient to allow him to marry Emma Pollmer, a girl from his hometown.

Between 1882 and 1887 his former employer Münchmeyer published five huge serial novels by

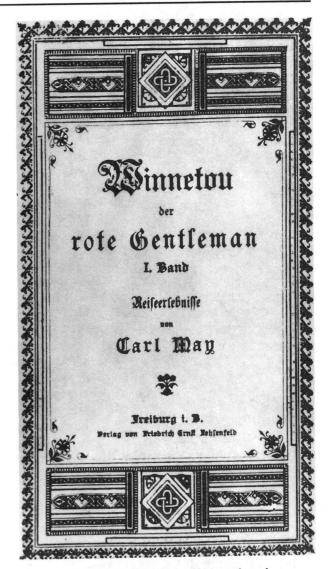

Title page for May's most widely read novel

May. Totaling more than ten thousand large-format pages, these five novels equal the quantity of all the rest of May's output during his life. The most successful was Das Waldröschen oder Die Verfolgung rund um die Erde: Großer Enthüllungsroman über die Geheimnisse der menschlichen Gesellschaft (The Forest Rose; or, The Pursuit around the World: Grand Novel Revealing the Secrets of Human Society, 1882–1884), but all five sold extremely well and made May financially comfortable for the first time in his life.

When the opportunity arose to write steadily for another magazine, Der gute Kamerad (The Good Friend), aimed at an adolescent readership, May severed his ties with Münchmeyer once more in 1887. Thus started his most fertile literary period,

May in costume as his characters Kara Ben Nemsi and Old Shatterhand

during which his best-known and most-enduring works were published. A series of loosely connected travel novels, they feature almost identical protagonists moving from adventure to adventure, mostly in the Orient or the American West. Based on skillful use of published reports, the novels show impressive accuracy in local detail and abundant talent for invention. Their main appeal derives from the reader's ability to experience vicariously a humane, just, educated, and intelligent German hero triumphing over both primitive savagery and a corrupt modern world.

May attracted the attention of a third publisher, F. E. Fehsenfeld, who offered to publish May's scattered works in a handsome hardbound edition with uniform design. May agreed, and in 1892 the first six volumes of his *Gesammelte Reiseromane* appeared in green bindings with a four-color cover illustration. This format – which is being continued today by the Karl-May-Verlag, the successor to the Fehsenfeld publishing house – made the

books suitable for display in the bookcases of respectable middle-class readers and was a decisive factor in the broad success of May's work. The series eventually grew to thirty-three volumes. Most were slightly revised versions of works that had appeared in magazines, but some were written especially for the Fehsenfeld edition. His revisions of his earlier works for the collected edition gave them a continuity and chronological progression that created the impression of two cycles of novels, one set in the American West and the other in the Middle East.

May's library contained a substantial number of both fiction and nonfiction books on the Islamic world, and he drew on these sources for his "Easterns." Most of these novels appeared originally in *Der Deutsche Hausschatz in Wort und Bild,* and six of them form a loosely connected cycle of about thirty-seven hundred pages held together by a recurring set of characters. Chief among these are the narrator, Kara Ben Nemsi (Karl the German), and his often comical Arab companion Hadschi Halef Omar. They experience a seemingly endless series of adventures as they pursue a band of murderous villains from Algeria to the Balkan peninsula. The adventures are a sequence of captures, escapes, battles, ambushes, deceptions, and court scenes skillfully interspersed with idyllic or comic interludes.

At the time of their appearance the novels appealed to middle-class readers' curiosity about locales that were often featured in contemporary news reports as Germany competed with the established colonial powers for territory. Readers could feel that they were not wasting their money and time on mere fiction but were learning useful facts about the world from the frequently surprisingly accurate descriptions of exotic landscapes and local customs, and May encouraged his readers to believe that they were reading eyewitness accounts. Over the years these attractions have diminished in importance, and the mythical and utopian dimension of May's work appears to explain its continuing appeal: it affords the reader vicarious fulfillment of wishes denied by reality. The thinly disguised alter ego of the author is free from money problems, is intellectually superior to the villains and the rest of the world, and has the power to right wrongs directly and autonomously. At the same time, he discovers himself to be in harmony with – indeed, a tool of – a benevolent providence that validates his decisions: seemingly unwise charity toward opponents is rewarded, and fate disposes of unrepentant villains through fatal accidents.

Many of the episodes seem to have provided May with personal wish fulfillment – for instance, the many court scenes in which the protagonist's accusers become the accused and the protagonist prevails triumphantly. But the continued success of the novels suggests that their utopia of individual power, moral justice, and freedom from economic oppression in a world that is rationally understandable and metaphysically meaningful has a timeless and broad appeal.

When May began to write, adventure stories set in the American West were already a well-established subgenre in German popular literature. James Fenimore Cooper's *Leatherstocking Tales* (1823–1841) had firmly established this tradition, which was continued by European authors. May not only worked in this tradition but also borrowed specific incidents and motifs from his German predecessors Charles Sealsfield and Friedrich Gerstäcker and from the French writer Ferry, as well as from Cooper.

May in his study at Villa Old Shatterhand, his home near Dresden, in 1896

Although "Western" settings appear in May's writing as early as 1876, in the story "Old Firehand" in the *Deutsches Familienblatt* (German Family Magazine), May's name is most closely associated with *Winnetou, der rote Gentleman* (Winnetou, the Red Gentleman, 1893; translated as *Winnetou,* 1977), by far the most widely read of all his novels. A major source for the setting and background has been shown to be George Catlin's writings about the American Indian, and the novel is suffused with Catlin's sympathy for his subjects and his melancholy over their doomed way of life.

Like his Oriental novels, May's Western novels feature as protagonists the author's German alter ego and a local companion; in *Winnetou, der rote Gentleman* they are "Old Shatterhand" – so called for his ability to knock out opponents with a single blow – and Winnetou, a young Apache chief, respectively. Again, one can see direct responses to May's experiences: there are many escapes from imprisonment and vindications of the initially despised or ridiculed protagonist. But the protagonist's triumphs are not just the result of his exceptional qualities; they are also a function of the conditions found in the West. Unlike Germany, which Old Shatterhand has left because of unspecified unpleasant conditions there, May's West recognizes and rewards natural ability and nobility and ignores or even penalizes privileges of birth, property, or other pretenses to excellence. This egalitarianism is a recurring motif in all of May's Western novels, which must be considered an important contribution to the image of America in popular German imagination.

At the same time, May contributes to a negative image of the United States as dominated by greed. Few of his positive characters are white Americans, but most of his villains are. They have typically come out West in pursuit of gold, oil, land, or other riches and are the corrupters of what is presented as a last precapitalist sanctuary. Old Shatterhand and his friends ally themselves with the Indians to defend this sanctuary, but Old Shatterhand sees that their victories can only be temporary. His long-term hope is to improve the Indians by teaching them the best of European culture so that they, in turn, can raise the rest of mankind to an exalted level that combines European culture with freedom from greed.

This utopian goal is best exemplified by Winnetou. When Old Shatterhand meets him, Winnetou has already read the great works of Western civilization, and has given up scalping and other barbaric practices; when he dies at the end of the third volume, he confesses that he has become a Christian. But he acquires these blessings of white civilization without succumbing to the white man's greed: he refuses to touch the gold deposits he knows about, and he takes the secret of their location to the grave. May thus continues the noble-savage motif but gives it a new dimension particularly attractive to an audience with a high regard for a genteel education and middle-class morality.

Winnetou and the other characters make frequent appearances in May's other novels and stories set in the American West. Often these works reuse earlier stories or parts of earlier novels. They all create a mythical American West in which the motifs of constant travel, capture, spying, escape, intrigue, crime, and the restoration of justice are repeated with hypnotic compulsiveness. In spite of superficial similarities to the American Western novel, May's West is profoundly different: deception is the rule, the prairie hides rather than reveals, the good characters are not easily distinguished from the bad, and the hero does not have to soil his hands with le-

thal violence, for providence provides the proper punishment.

The handsome edition of his Oriental and Western novels established May as a celebrity. Fan clubs formed, and in 1897 May entertained the Munich Karl-May-Club for three evenings by reading unpublished episodes from "his" adventures with Winnetou. For in the course of these years he convinced his fans, and to a degree himself, that he was identical with Old Shatterhand and his Oriental counterpart Kara Ben Nemsi and had experienced the adventures described in his novels. He built Villa Old Shatterhand near Dresden, where he showed visitors the weapons and other paraphernalia made famous by his novels and handed out photographs of himself in Western and Oriental costume. To write he would dress in the appropriate costume, lock himself in his study for several nights, and act out the scenes and dialogue of the novel. In his imagination he had experienced all the exotic adventures of his fiction, and it was a small step to claim that he had experienced them in actuality.

In 1899 and 1900 May finally made a voyage to the Orient. He came to realize the vast distance between his idealized fictional Orient and the reality. The journey to the Middle East and on to the Indonesian archipelago and through Turkey, Greece, and Italy produced a crisis and a redirection of his life and writing. It coincided with vicious attacks on May for having added the title "Doktor" to his name, for "pornographic" passages in the anonymous pulp novels of his early career, for being an ex-convict, and for pretending to have lived through adventures he had never experienced. In response to these charges May dropped the "Doktor," denounced any questionable passages as having been inserted by the publisher without his consent or knowledge, discarded the Old Shatterhand/Kara Ben Nemsi legend, and promoted a reinterpretation of his earlier works as allegories of humanity's progress from the lowlands of deception and error to the heights of spirituality – a progress he saw reflected in his personal journey from confidence man and convict to thinker and teacher. All of May's works written after this turning point are overtly symbolic or allegorical. There is, however, a consistency between the early travel stories and the later allegorical novels: they share a progress from darkness and confusion to clarity and insight, paralleled by a physical progress from desert or prairie lowlands to elevated terrain, with the climax typically occurring, after much hardship, on a mountaintop.

Thus, May could claim that he had always dramatized the story of humanity's rise from greed, violence, and materialism to the selfless spirituality of the "Reich des Edelmenschen" (Realm of the Noble Man), a progress achieved in a passage through suffering. This allegory with obvious religious overtones is worked out most clearly in *Ardistan und Dschinnistan* (1909; translated as *Ardistan and Djinnistan,* 1977). In this novel May gives up all pretense of an authentic setting and places the action on the star Sitara, although the names and setting retain a distinctly Oriental flavor. The narrator, Kara Ben Nemsi, and his familiar group of traveling companions land on the star in the ship *Wilahde* (Birth) and make their way from Ardistan, full of lowlands and deserts, toward Dschinnistan, a land of mountain peaks, fertility, purity, and beauty. Ardistan is populated by men of violence and materialism, Dschinnistan by Edelmenschen. Between these realms lies Märdistan, a hazardous terrain where a blacksmith forces travelers to pass painful tests and undergo acts of purification. Only those found worthy are allowed to proceed; the others are thrown back into the lowlands. Deliberate echoes of classical allegories such as Dante's *Divine Comedy* (1321) are unmistakable. In a series of adventures Kara Ben Nemsi saves the tyrant of Ardistan and converts him into a loving and humane ruler. The novel ends with Kara Ben Nemsi continuing his ascent into the mountains, suggesting that the pursuit of Dschinnistan is a continuous effort.

May had announced this novel as providing the answer to all questions facing humanity, including the question of world peace. While none of May's critics believes that the novel lives up to this ambitious claim, they have differed sharply on how respectable a failure it and the other works of his later years are. And while many of May's traditional readers, hungry for adventure stories, resented his new orientation, a smaller but intensely loyal part of the reading public welcomed the change.

May's artistic crisis and reorientation were paralleled by crises in his personal life. In 1903 his marriage broke up in a bitter divorce, in the course of which his wife at times allied herself with his opponents in May's many exhausting lawsuits. Three months after his divorce became final he married Klara Plöhn, the widow of a friend; but he remained embroiled in court battles to the end of his life. His autobiography was written in the context of these lawsuits and must be read in the light of May's need to defend his reputation as his criminal past was being exposed by his enemies.

May with his second wife, the former Klara Plöhn

During a lull in his court battles May and his wife took a long-postponed trip to the United States, arriving in New York City in September 1908. The couple visited Albany, Buffalo, and Niagara Falls. On 10 October May gave an enthusiastically received lecture to the German-Americans in Lawrence, Massachusetts, titled "Three Questions for Mankind: Who Are We? Where Do We Come From? Where Are We Going?" He made no effort to visit the locales of his Western novels, as if the shock of seeing the reality of his Oriental locations had destroyed all desire to risk such a confrontation again. By December, May and his wife were back in their home near Dresden to resume his legal battles.

On 22 March 1912 May was invited by the Vienna Academic Association for Literature and Music to give a lecture to an audience of several thousand people. For more than two hours he spoke on the topic "Empor ins Reich des Edelmenschen" (Rise to the Realm of the Man of Nobility). The text of his speech is not preserved, but the Vienna newspapers reported an enthusiastic response. He re-

May's tomb in the Radebeul cemetery

turned home with a cold and a fever; a week later, on 30 March, he died of heart failure.

While May tried his hand at a great variety of genres and subgenres from humorous anecdotes to local-color vignettes and short stories to symbolic drama and lyric poetry, even songs and musical compositions, he remains best known for tales of travel and adventure. Drawing on a well-established set of conventions, May did not need the personal experiences that had inspired his predecessors in the genre. His distance from the actual locales and events allowed him to stress the mythical or archetypal elements in his novels while maintaining the pretense of being instructive.

May's critics have deplored the predictability of his plots and the lack of variety and subtlety in his characters. But these qualities are typical not only of popular literature in general but especially of highly formal genres such as the romance. His admirers, on the other hand, praise May for the many subtle changes he rings on this limited set of patterns, and the enduring popularity of May's works with general readers as well as scholars sug-

gests that he continues to satisfy a deep need in the reading public.

The publication history of May's works is characterized by a low regard for textual authenticity, sometimes by May himself but more regularly by his publishers. One of May's many lawsuits, for instance, charged Münchmeyer with inserting salacious passages into the serial novels, and after May's death his widow authorized the Karl-May-Verlag to make any changes deemed necessary to maintain the works' appeal. The Karl-May-Verlag took liberal advantage of this permission, particularly with the later volumes of the collected works, which even include works not written by May.

Many works by May have been brought out by various other publishers, especially since the Karl-May-Verlag copyright expired in 1962. Ironically, some of these editions are more faithful to May's texts than the "official" publications by the Karl-May-Verlag. May's works have become part of German folklore: they are subject to all the changes and variations to which a culture subjects its collective consciousness.

Since the 1960s, several reprint series have begun to remedy the textual situation somewhat. From 1982 to 1984 the Karl-May-Verlag itself brought out a facsimile reprint of volumes 1 to 33 in the Fehsenfeld edition. Under the editorship of Hermann Wiedenroth and Hans Wollschläger the Greno publishing house in Nördlingen began a monumental historical-critical edition in 1987 that is projected to run to ninety-nine volumes; the edition is being continued by the Haffmanns firm in Zurich.

Bibliography:

Heiner Plaul, *Illustrierte Karl-May-Bibliographie* (Munich, London & New York: Sauer, 1989).

Biographies:

Hans Wollschläger, *Karl May: Grundriss eines gebrochenen Lebens* (Reinbek: Rowohlt, 1965);

Wollschläger, *Karl May in Selbstzeugnissen und Bilddokumenten* (Reinbek: Rowohlt, 1965; revised edition, Zurich: Diogenes, 1976);

Heiner Plaul, "Redakteur auf Zeit: Über Karl Mays Aufenthalt und Tätigkeit von Mai 1874 bis Dezember 1877," in *Jahrbuch der Karl-May-Gesellschaft* (Husum: Hansa, 1977), pp. 114–217;

Harald Eggebrecht, ed., *Karl May – der sächsische Phantast* (Frankfurt am Main: Suhrkamp, 1987);

Gerhard Klussmeier and Plaul, eds., *Der große Karl-May-Bildband* (Hildesheim & New York: Olms, 1987).

References:

R. H. Cacroft, "The American West of Karl May," Ph.D. dissertation, University of Utah, 1969;

Colleen Cook, "Germany's Wild West Author: A Researcher's Guide to Karl May," *German Studies Review*, 5 (February 1982): 67–86;

Margy Gerber, "Old Shatterhand Rides Again: The Rehabilitation of Karl May in the GDR," in *Studies in GDR Culture and Society 5: Selected Papers from the Tenth New Hampshire Symposium on the German Democratic Republic* (Lanham, Md., New York & London: University Press of America, 1985), pp. 237–250;

Martin Lowsky, *Karl May* (Stuttgart: Metzler, 1987);

Helmut Schmiedt, *Karl May Studien zu Leben, Werk und Wirkung eines Erfolgsschriftstellers* (Königstein, 1979; revised edition, Frankfurt am Main: Athenäum, 1987);

Schmiedt, ed., *Karl May Materialien* (Frankfurt am Main: Suhrkamp, 1983);

Heinz Hermann Stolte, *Der Volksschriftsteller Karl May* (Radebeul: Karl-May-Verlag, 1936);

text + kritik, special May issue, edited by Heinz Ludwig Arnold (1987);

Gert Ueding, ed., *Karl May-Handbuch* (Stuttgart: Kröner, 1987).

Papers:

Karl May's papers, letters, and surviving manuscripts are in the possession of the Karl-May-Verlag, Bamberg.

Conrad Ferdinand Meyer

(11 October 1825 – 28 November 1898)

Tiiu V. Laane
Texas A&M University

BOOKS: *Zwanzig Balladen von einem Schweizer,* anonymous (Stuttgart: Metzler, 1864); republished as *Balladen* (Leipzig: Haessel, 1867);

Romanzen und Bilder (Leipzig: Haessel, 1870 [i.e., 1869]);

Huttens letzte Tage: Eine Dichtung (Leipzig: Haessel, 1872 [i.e., 1871]; enlarged edition, 1881; revised edition, 1884);

Engelberg: Eine Dichtung (Leipzig: Haessel, 1872);

Das Amulett: Eine Novelle (Leipzig: Haessel, 1873); translated by George F. Folkers as "The Amulet (Das Amulett), 1872–73," in *The Complete Narrative Prose of Conrad Ferdinand Meyer,* 2 volumes (Lewisburg, Pa.: Bucknell University Press, 1976), I: 31–74;

Georg Jenatsch: Eine alte Bündnergeschichte (Leipzig: Haessel, 1876; revised, 1878); republished as *Jürg Jenatsch: Eine Bündnergeschichte* (Leipzig: Haessel, 1882); republished as *Jürg Jenatsch: Eine Bündnergeschichte* (Leipzig: Haessel, 1882); translated by David B. Dickens as "Jürg Jenatsch, 1874," in *The Complete Narrative Prose of Conrad Ferdinand Meyer,* I: 75–231;

Denkwürdige Tage: Zwei Novellen (Leipzig: Haessel, 1878) – comprises "Der Schuß von der Kanzel," translated by Folkers as "The Shot from the Pulpit (Der Schuss von der Kanzel), 1877," in *The Complete Narrative Prose of Conrad Ferdinand Meyer,* I: 233–269; "Das Amulett";

Der Heilige: Novelle (Leipzig: Haessel, 1880); republished as *König und Heiliger: Novelle* (Leipzig: Haessel, 1882); translated by M. V. Wendheim as *Thomas à Becket, the Saint: A Novel* (Leipzig: Haessel, 1885); translated by Mary J. Tabor as *The Chancellor's Secret: A Tale of the Twelfth Century* (New Bedford, Mass.: Lawton, 1887);

Kleine Novellen (Leipzig: Haessel, 1882) – comprises volume 1, *Der Schuß von der Kanzel;* volume 2, *Das Amulett;* volume 3, *Plautus im Nonnenkloster,* translated by William Guild Howard as "Plautus in the Convent," in *The German Classics of*

the Nineteenth and Twentieth Centuries, edited by Howard and Kuno Francke, volume 14 (New York: The German Publication Society, 1914), pp. 345–375; volume 4, *Gustav Adolfs Page,* translated by Dickens as "Gustav Adolf's Page (Gustav Adolfs Page), 1882," in *The Com-*

plete Narrative Prose of Conrad Ferdinand Meyer, II: 31–63;

Gedichte (Leipzig: Haessel, 1882; enlarged, 1887; enlarged, 1891; enlarged, 1892); selections translated by Charles Wharton Stork and Margarete Münsterberg as "Sowers' Song," "Do Thou Speak Now," "But the Sun is Ever Youthful," "The Dead Child," "Christmas in Ajaccio," "Schiller's Burial," "Again," "The Feet in the Fire," in *The German Classics of the Nineteenth and Twentieth Centuries,* volume 14, pp. 473–478;

Das Leiden eines Knaben: Novelle (Leipzig: Haessel, 1883); abridged and translated by E. M. Huggard as *The Tribulations of a Boy* (London: Harrap, 1949); translated by Dickens as "A Boy Suffers," in *The Complete Narrative Prose of Conrad Ferdinand Meyer,* II: 65–104;

Die Hochzeit des Mönchs: Novelle (Leipzig: Haessel, 1883); translated by Sarah Holland Adams as *The Monk's Wedding: A Novel* (Boston: Cupples & Hurd, 1887);

Die Richterin: Novelle (Leipzig: Haessel, 1885); translated by Marion W. Sonnenfeld as "The Judge (Die Richterin), 1885," in *The Complete Narrative Prose of Conrad Ferdinand Meyer,* II: 169–221;

Die Versuchung des Pescara: Novelle (Leipzig: Haessel, 1887); translated by Clara Bell as *The Tempting of Pescara* (New York: Gottsberger, 1890);

Angela Borgia: Novelle (Leipzig: Haessel, 1891); translated by Sonnenfeld as "Angela Borgia, 1891," in *The Complete Narrative Prose of Conrad Ferdinand Meyer,* II: 307–391;

Conrad Ferdinand Meyers unvollendete Prosadichtungen, 2 volumes, edited by Adolf Frey (Leipzig: Haessel, 1916);

Frühe Balladen, edited by Martin Bodmer (Leipzig: Haessel, 1922);

Sämtliche Werke, 4 volumes, edited by Robert Faesi (Berlin: Knauer, 1928);

Sämtliche Werke in sechs Teilen, 6 volumes, edited by Walther Linden (Berlin & Leipzig: Bong, 1928);

Conrad Ferdinand Meyers Gedichte an seine Braut Luise Ziegler, edited by Constanze Speyer (Zurich & New York: Oprecht, 1940);

Werke, 4 volumes, edited by Gustav Steiner (Basel: Birkhäuser, 1943);

Leuchtende Saat: Eine neue Sammlung von Gedichten und Sprüchen, edited by Friedrich Kempter (Engelberg: Verlag für Schöne Wissenschaft, 1951);

Sämtliche Werke: Historisch-kritische Ausgabe, 15 volumes projected, 13 volumes published, edited by Hans Zeller, Alfred Zäch, and Rätus Luck (Bern: Benteli, 1958–   ) – comprises volume 1, *Gedichte: Text* (1963); volume 2, *Gedichte: Bericht des Herausgebers. Apparat zu den Abteilungen I und II* (1964); volume 3, *Gedichte: Apparat zu den Abteilungen III und IV* (1967); volume 4, *Gedichte: Apparat zu den Abteilungen V, VI, und VII* (1975); volume 6, *Bilder und Balladen: Zwanzig Balladen; Romanzen und Bilder;* Text und Apparat (1988); volume 8, *Huttens letzte Tage: Eine Dichtung* (1970); volume 9, *Engelberg: Eine Dichtung* (1973); volume 10, *Jürg Jenatsch: Eine Bündnergeschichte* (1958); volume 11, *Novellen I: Das Amulett; Der Schuß von der Kanzel; Plautus im Nonnenkloster; Gustav Adolfs Page* (1959): volume 12, *Novellen II: Die Hochzeit des Mönchs; Das Leiden eines Knaben; Die Richterin* (1961); volume 13, *Der Heilige; Die Versuchung des Pescara* (1962); volume 14, *Angela Borgia: Novelle* (1966); volume 15, *Clara; Entwürfe; Kleine Schriften* (1985);

Werke in zwei Bänden, 2 volumes, edited by Hermann Engelhard (Stuttgart: Cotta, 1960);

Gedichte Conrad Ferdinand Meyers: Wege ihrer Vollendung, edited by Heinrich Henel, Deutsche Texte, no. 8 (Tübingen: Niemeyer, 1962);

Sämtliche Werke, edited by Hans Schmeer (Munich & Zurich: Knaur Klassiker, 1965);

Werke, 2 volumes, edited by Heinz Schöffler (Darmstadt: Temple, 1967);

Gesammelte Werke, 5 volumes, edited by Wolfgang Ingée (Munich: Nymphenberger, 1985).

Editions in English: *The Complete Narrative Prose of Conrad Ferdinand Meyer,* 2 volumes, translated by George F. Folkers, David B. Dickens, and Marion W. Sonnenfeld (Lewisburg, Pa.: Bucknell University Press, 1976).

TRANSLATIONS: Augustin Thierry, *Erzählungen aus den merowingischen Zeiten mit einleitenden Betrachtungen über die Geschichte Frankreichs* (Elberfeld: Friedrichs, 1855);

François Guizot, *Lady Russel: Eine geschichtliche Studie. Aus dem Französischen* (Zurich: Beyel, 1857);

Johann Jacob Ulrich, *La Suisse pittoresque* (Zurich, 1860).

SELECTED PERIODICAL PUBLICATIONS – UNCOLLECTED: "Autobiographische Skizze," *Die poetische Nationalliteratur der Schweiz,* 4 (1876): 106ff.;

"Ludwig Vulliemin," *Neue Züricher Zeitung,* 16–18 March 1878;

"Kleinstadt und Dorf um die Mitte des vorigen Jahrhunderts. Nach einem Manuscripte von Edmund Dorer mitgetheilt von C. Ferdinand Meyer," *Züricher Taschenbuch auf das Jahr 1881* (1881): 43–75;

"Mathilde Escher: Ein Portrait," *Züricher Taschenbuch auf das Jahr 1883* (1883): 1–18;

"Graf Ladislas Plater," *Neue Züricher Zeitung,* 22 April 1889;

"Erinnerungen an Gottfried Keller," *Deutsche Dichtung,* 9 (October 1890): 25–29;

"Mein Erstling 'Huttens letzte Tage,' " *Deutsche Dichtung,* 9 (January 1891): 172–174;

"Clara: Novelle," edited by Constanze Speyer, *Corona,* 8 (1938): 395–416.

The Swiss poet and prose writer Conrad Ferdinand Meyer ranks as one of the distinguished literary figures in German literature in the late nineteenth century. His cool and aristocratic art, wrought with meticulous attention to detail and with sharp objectivity, appeals to the educated reader. Unlike his Swiss literary compatriots Gottfried Keller and Jeremias Gotthelf, whose art originated from social and political engagement, Meyer drew the inspiration for his works from his own anguish and sense of isolation and rejection by society. His art was the result of great effort and years of painful and slow germination. Throughout his difficult life Meyer never lost faith that his calling to art was holy and that by giving aesthetic shape to his pain he could objectify and thus transcend it. He refined his works in a seemingly endless quest for perfection of form. Best known in his day for historical novellas that transpose his ambiguous and deeply pessimistic viewpoints into figures of grand past eras, Meyer carried the inherent tendency of Poetic Realism – with its aim of showing not merely the tangible in objects but also their felt meanings – to new heights in German literature. His lyrics make a transition from the confessional poetry of the Classical-Romantic tradition to a more objective and unemotional style; they are credited with paving the way for the German symbolists Stefan George, Hugo von Hofmannsthal, and Rainer Maria Rilke. Acknowledged as one of the finest of German stylists in prose and verse, Meyer was a virtuoso of the framework technique. His imagination tended toward the pictorial and dramatic, creating telling gestures and pervasive images. His refined and stylized manner of writing has been both criticized and lauded. Beginning with a virulent attack by Franz Ferdinand Baumgarten in 1917, critics have condemned Meyer as a cowardly aesthete who escaped to history and to the rarefied altar of art to evade his fear of the present and dislike of reality, and he has been accused of using his technical skills to veil a want of substance. More recently, however, Meyer's intricately shifting narrative perspectives and distinctive pictorial style have been seen as a means of giving voice to a most modern skepticism and relativism. His subtle manner of characterization has been regarded as a precursor of the psychological writing of the twentieth century. Meyer was a man of contrasts: he doubted the validity of grand metaphysical principles, yet he read the Bible daily. He partook of the spiritual precariousness of bourgeois society in the late nineteenth century and turned to the concrete form and beauty of art as a means to distill order out of his internal conflicts.

Meyer was born on 11 October 1825 in Zurich into a cultivated and relatively well-to-do patrician family. He was baptized Conrad after his maternal grandfather. His father, Ferdinand Meyer, was the privy councillor of the canton of Zurich, a student of law and languages, and a teacher of history at a gymnasium. Meyer's mother, Elisabeth Ulrich Meyer, was the only daughter of a bourgeois family that had a history of depression and hypochondria. Charming and highly intelligent, she was also puritanical and tormented by a sense of guilt that she countered by engaging in philanthropic activity and adhering to a rigid pietism. Meyer was healthy and lively until his sixth year, when his personality underwent a profound change after a bout of roseola: he began to oscillate between tantrums and listlessness and was overcome with feelings of guilt instilled in him by his mother.

The Meyer home was the setting for intellectual gatherings of politicians and professors from the University of Zurich after its founding in 1833. Their lively discussions provided Meyer with viewpoints counter to the provincialism of Zurich in the 1830s. Under his father's tutelage, Meyer learned about Frederick the Great, Frederick Barbarossa, and the German emperors, thus beginning his lifelong interest in history. Trips with his father in 1836 and 1838 through the canton of Graubünden introduced Meyer to the beauty and grandeur of the Alps, which were to play an important role in his stories and poems. Meyer excelled in school and made his first attempts at creative work, sketching and trying his hand at poems. His father's death from tuberculosis in 1840 was a severe blow.

After her husband's death, Meyer's mother succumbed to her nervous weaknesses and excessive piety, donning a gray cloak similar to a nun's habit that she wore for the rest of her life. She viewed any accident as a punishment from God and allowed Meyer and his younger sister Elisabeth (Betsy) no deviation from her own puritanical standards. Meyer, in turn, began to behave coarsely – at least in his mother's opinion – and became alternately arrogant and passive, often withdrawing from social contact altogether. He would burst inexplicably into tears and often became hyperactive. His mother despaired at what was to become of her "armen Conrad" (poor Conrad), who seemed to be taking too strong an interest in German literature instead of the classics. Meyer would transcribe the pain and humiliation of his youth into the figure of the mentally retarded Julian in his novella *Das Leiden eines Knaben* (1883; translated as *The Tribulations of a Boy,* 1949).

Meyer entered the Zurich Gymnasium in 1837. Unable to concentrate and prone to daydream, he acquired little but a thorough knowledge of the classical languages. Fearing a total degeneration of her son's behavior at the unruly school, Meyer's mother withdrew him in 1843 and sent him to Lausanne in the French-speaking sector of Switzerland. Away from his mother's influence, Meyer thrived. He lived in a *petit château* (little castle), a type of pension for young people, where he made stimulating friendships. He profited from his contact with the renowned translator and historian Louis Vulliemin, a friend of his father's, who was to remain a staunch supporter of his literary activity. Soon fluent in French, Meyer studied Italian and immersed himself in Jean Paul and in the French classics, especially the works of Molière and Alfred de Musset. In a more confident and happy mood, he composed poetry in a late-Romantic style.

It was with sadness that Meyer returned to Zurich in 1844 to take his final school examinations. Encouraged by Professor J. C. Bluntschli, a friend of his parents, Meyer enrolled at the University of Zurich to study law. He took little interest in the subject, however, and soon stopped attending classes. The belief that he was destined to become an artist had taken root in him in Lausanne. He took painting lessons from the painter H. J. Schweizer but soon realized his lack of talent for the graphic arts. Attempts at writing poetry produced equally unsatisfactory results. Sonnets written in the style of August von Platen were forced and inept, with awkward rhymes. Only poems that took their motifs from the plastic arts gave any hint of Meyer's finely crafted, mature "art poems." Increasingly concerned that her son was wasting his life by pursuing his writing in such a desultory fashion,

Meyer in 1841; drawing by Paul Deschwanden (from Gero von Wilpert, Deutsche Literatur in Bildern, *1965)*

Meyer's mother decided to force a decision. Unknown to Meyer, she sent a sample of his poems in 1844 to the Swabian writer Gustav Pfizer, the husband of a friend, requesting his opinion. Expecting a positive evaluation, she hung Pfizer's response in its unopened envelope on the Christmas tree. Pfizer failed to recognize Meyer's potential and suggested that the young man give up writing. Meyer was devastated. He withdrew from contact with people except for visits from friends such as Conrad Nüscheler and Johanna Heußer (who later became a writer of children's stories under the name Johanna Spyri). Except for Johanna, who cheered him with her lively and natural spirit, Meyer avoided the company of women.

As he became more and more isolated, Meyer's irritability increased. He submerged himself in the works of the German Romantic writers Ludwig Tieck, Novalis, and Friedrich Schlegel and studied writers admired by the Romantics, especially William Shakespeare and Pedro Calderón de la Barca. Of the newer literature, he favored the political poets Ferdinand Freiligrath and Georg Herwegh; Christian Grabbe; and the late Romantic Nikolaus Lenau. Writers of antiquity and the modern French writers Alphonse-Marie-Louis de Prat de Lamartine and George Sand caught his interest;

and he also delved into historical writings and chronicles, where he preferred to read about psychologically dark and ambiguous events. During these aimless years between 1845 and 1852 Meyer continued his attempts at writing, mostly of epic and dramatic fragments. He began a dramatization of the life of the Swiss hero Georg Jenatsch and wrote sketches about the medieval emperors and figures from ancient Rome and the Italian Renaissance. Betsy, who shared his interest in literature, supported his efforts. While literary historians have generally held that Meyer remained removed from the political events of the 1840s, Betsy later attested that her brother read the newspaper avidly and greeted the strivings for national unification in Germany and in Italy with enthusiasm. In spite of his liberal orientation, however, Meyer refrained from calling for the emancipation of the masses; he was too bound by his refined sense of culture and tradition.

As years passed with no tangible literary accomplishments, Meyer's spiritual crisis deepened; he began to engage in thoughts of suicide. An acute attack of neurosis was precipitated by Friedrich Theodor Vischer's *Kritische Gänge* (Critical Thrusts, 1844), which Meyer had sought out in the hope that it would guide him in his literary efforts. The book shocked him into a realization of the aimlessness of his existence and the illusory quality of his art. Vischer criticized the boundless fantasies of the Romantics so admired by Meyer, arguing for a realistic portrayal of the world. While Vischer's work would later help Meyer find his own style of realism, the immediate effect was to intensify his depression. Hinting to his family that he would commit suicide, he began to tempt fate by rowing to the middle of a lake, swimming away from the boat until it was out of sight, and then swimming back. Though an ardent swimmer and rower since his youth, Meyer could reach the safety of the vessel only by exerting himself to the ultimate. He mountain-climbed recklessly. When he overheard his mother say that he was "tot" (dead) for this world, he began to avoid daylight and was convinced that a stench emanated from his mouth; he did, in fact, suffer from gumboils. After catching a cold during a nighttime swim in July 1852 Meyer began to have fainting spells. His neuroses increased so severely that his mother took him to the Préfargier mental institution, directed by Dr. James Borrel, near Neuchâtel. It was determined that he was not mentally ill but suffering from an "irritation of the nerves." After a few weeks he was invited to live in Borrel's home, where he encountered an atmosphere of loving optimism and cheerful piety. Positive influence emanated most of all from Borrel's sister, Cécile, the head nurse, with whom Meyer formed an attachment beyond that of patient and caregiver. Dr. Borrel prescribed a regimen that included physical activity, and he encouraged Meyer to seek financial independence. He was well aware that Meyer needed to be away from his mother.

In January 1853 Meyer moved to a pension in Neuchâtel and two months later, against his mother's wishes, to Lausanne to study French. He hoped to become a French teacher at a gymnasium in Germany. He took up residence near Vulliemin, who became the decisive influence in Meyer's pathway to mental health and productive activity. A Calvinist, the noted historian gave Meyer a sense of morality, deepened his Protestantism, and provided many of the historical motifs of Meyer's later writings. Vulliemin procured a position for Meyer as a history teacher at the Hirzel Institute for the Blind in Lausanne. He also requested permission from the author Augustin Thierry for Meyer to translate Thierry's *Récits des temps Mérovingiens* (Tales from the Times of the Merovingians, 1840), Meyer's first serious encounter with Romance culture. Meyer delighted in the painstaking work, and his clear and concrete pictorial style has its roots in this early French influence. Blaise Pascal, Alexandre Vinet, François Fénelon, and Claude-Henri Saint-Simon also left an unmistakable French influence on Meyer's diction and sense of form. Gradually, Meyer began to participate in the intellectual environment provided by Vulliemin's home, where the historians Thierry, François-Auguste-Maire Mignet, and Jules Michelet, the literary critic Charles-Augustin Sainte-Beuve, and the poet Adam Mickiewicz were often guests. On Vulliemin's recommendation, Meyer became the secretary of the Research Society of Switzerland for General History in 1855. He considered studying French language and literature at the University of Zurich; he even hinted that he might marry a patrician lady from Bern, Constance von Rodt. (Out of jealousy, Meyer's mother had apparently splintered the developing relationship between her son and Cécile Borrel.) His mother persisted, in the meanwhile, in considering her son a failure and considered his five-hundred-page translation only a modest accomplishment. She hounded him with reprimands to keep his razor clean, to become a more pious Christian, and to renounce his creative activity.

With misgivings, but out of financial necessity, Meyer returned to his mother's home on 31 December 1853. In Zurich he felt rejected by bourgeois society and stigmatized by his mental illness. He rejoiced in the honorarium for his Thierry translation, which was published anonymously in 1855, and in the praise of the work by critics. A colorless novella, "Clara," written during this period but first published in 1938, gave no hint of Meyer's future greatness as a prose writer. It was followed by a translation, published in 1857, of François Guizot's historical essay *L'amour dans le mariage* (Love in a Marriage, 1855). During this time Meyer lived removed from social contacts. His mother's mental disintegration, in the meanwhile, became acute; she was taken to Préfargier, where she committed suicide on 27 September 1856. Her death brought Meyer grief and guilt but also relief. Simultaneously, Meyer and his sister were relieved of financial worries. A longtime boarder with the Meyers, Antonin Mallet, a mentally retarded member of an aristocratic Geneva family, had died shortly before Meyer's mother and had willed his considerable estate to the Meyer children.

In March 1857 Meyer set out for Paris to study law. He soon became distracted by the architecture of the city and the treasures in its museums, which he viewed with the eyes of a historian and art lover. The splendor of historical buildings such as the Louvre and Nôtre Dame captivated his imagination and helped form his sense of history. In art, he preferred the Italian masters of the Renaissance — Leonardo da Vinci, Raphael, Perugino, and Correggio — and the Spaniard Bartolomé Esteban Murillo to French artists. Except for Nicolas Poussin and Jean-Auguste-Dominique Ingres, Meyer found French artists superficial, theatrical, and lacking in warmth and nobility. His puritanical Protestant background caused him to become disenchanted with glittery, modern Paris, which he found dirty and frivolous. Meyer cut off his stay on 30 June 1857 and returned to Zurich. He was joined by Betsy, who had traveled to Germany during Meyer's absence to train to become a nurse for mental patients. That summer the two took a trip to Engelberg, the Alps in central Switzerland, where Meyer found the monumentalism he had encountered in the architecture of Paris repeated in the realm of nature. A short trip to the "art city" Munich followed in the fall; there Meyer concentrated, as he had in Paris, on visiting historical buildings and viewing artworks.

On 17 March 1858 Meyer and his sister left Zurich for a third trip. They traveled via Marseilles and Civitavecchia to Rome, where they remained until the middle of May. It was there that Meyer knew that he was destined to become a writer.

Rome, the scene of grand historical events, put him in a mood of euphoria. He was captivated by the beauty of the Italian landscapes and the vitality of the Italian people; the colorful pageantry of the Catholic church loosened his ascetic Protestantism; he was filled with awe for the magnificent Renaissance and Baroque architecture, the monuments of antiquity, and the treasures of the Vatican. All these impressions, however, were eclipsed by the works of Michelangelo, whose statues and frescoes in the Sistine Chapel became for Meyer the exemplifications of the ideal of art. Again and again Meyer was to try to duplicate Michelangelo's grandeur in his own writing. Michelangelo's ability to transform feeling, even agonized emotions, into cool and beautiful forms gave impetus to Meyer's passion to concentrate meaning into symbols. During this time Vischer's theories began to take root in Meyer's thinking, leading him to break with his Romantic concepts and to turn to realism.

On his way home Meyer visited in Florence Baron Bettino Ricasoli, who had been a guest of Meyer's mother in 1848 and who was to serve as the model for the great historical personalities in Meyer's writings. The aristocratic and immensely wealthy Ricasoli was a champion of Italian unification; a passive personality himself, Meyer was captivated by Ricasoli's passion for his cause. Strongwilled men of action capable of single-handedly changing the course of history — Jenatsch, Thomas Becket, Gustav Adolf, and Marqués de Pescara — were to stand at the center of Meyer's narratives.

On his return to Zurich at the end of June 1858 Meyer took up his work as a translator, this time from German into French. His translation of texts accompanying artworks in the luxury edition of Johann Jacob Ulrich's *Die Schweiz in Bildern* (Switzerland in Pictures) was published without his name in 1860. Other translations were begun but dropped when no publisher was found. Meyer longed for marriage, but when three women — Maria Burckhardt, Pauline Escher, and Clelia Weidmann — did not encourage his attachment, he fled to Lausanne in March 1860 to study French language and literature so that he could become a lecturer at the Polytechnic Institute in Zurich. He delved into the Epistles of Paul in the original Greek and began research on the relationship between Johann Wolfgang von Goethe and the Zurich physiognomist Johann Kaspar Lavater. More important, he reworked one hundred poems he had written after his trip to Rome and submitted them to the Leipzig publisher J. J. Weber in November 1860 under the title "Bilder und Balladen von Ulrich Meister" (Pictures and Ballads by Ulrich Meister). Weber declined to publish the work – perhaps fortunately for Meyer, since the majority of the poems were immature, too long, and lacked distinctive character. Weber suggested that Meyer seek another publisher, but Meyer held back for two years while he refined and polished his poems in what was to become his characteristic manner of artistic creation. Although he was aware that he needed advice, he forged no contact with the literary circles in Zurich on his return home from Lausanne in January 1861. His principal supporter and critic remained his sister, Betsy. An old friend from Neuchâtel, the librarian and theology professor Félix Bovet, also gave him counsel and encouragement.

In the spring of 1861 Meyer submitted twenty poems, mostly ballads, to the Stuttgart *Morgenblatt* (Morning Paper); they were rejected. In the spring of 1863 Betsy took the poems to Stuttgart to seek a publisher. Even though Pfizer had so bitterly dashed Meyer's literary hopes when Meyer was nineteen, she sought advice from him. Pfizer declined to critique the poems, but his wife made suggestions. Betsy convinced the Metzler firm in Stuttgart to publish the poems at Meyer's expense after Meyer agreed to further revisions. Under the pretext that he did not wish the work to be confused with that of another Swiss writer named Conrad Meyer, Meyer had the lyrics published anonymously in 1864 under the title *Zwanzig Balladen von einem Schweizer* (Twenty Ballads Written by a Swiss). They received little attention from critics, but Vuillemin's lengthy review in the *Bibliothèque Universelle* in November 1864 gave Meyer impetus for further literary activity and accorded him prestige among his friends and among the burghers in Zurich who had always held him in low esteem. While the poems are still rudimentary, they show some of the compactness of style that was to become characteristic of his later lyrics.

Pfizer became Meyer's mentor and succeeded in having the *Morgenblatt für gebildete Leser* (Morning Paper for Cultured Readers) in Stuttgart publish some of Meyer's poems in 1865; others followed in the Swiss periodical *Die Alpenrosen* in 1866 and 1867. Through Betsy, Meyer made the acquaintance in 1865 of the Leipzig publisher Hermann Haessel, who republished *Zwanzig Balladen* as *Balladen* (1867). Betsy took charge of the practical and financial aspects of their lives; her cheerful nature bolstered Meyer's self-confidence, and he dictated his works to her. They moved in 1868 to the "Seehof" (Lake House) in Küsnacht; the view of the Lake of Zurich with its surrounding mountains, the changing moods of the water in different seasons and weather conditions, and the steamships gave Meyer motifs for his poems and narratives. Meyer assumed the publishing costs for his next book, *Romanzen und Bilder* (Romances and Pictures, 1869), but was confident enough of his work to send copies to such literary notables as Vischer, Rudolf von Gottschall, Heinrich Laube, Emanuel Geibel, and Wolfgang Menzel. The book appeared under Meyer's own name, to which he added his father's name, Ferdinand. Divided into two parts, "Stimmung" (Mood), which contains thirty-three lyric poems, and "Erzählung" (Narrative), which encompasses twenty-one ballads, the collection received little critical recognition.

A circle of cultivated friends helped broaden Meyer's literary and cultural horizons. In addition to Bovet, Vuillemin, and Alfred Rochat, he associated with the art historian Johann Rudolf Rahn, the historian Georg von Wyß, and the Romantic poet and rhetorician Adolf Calmberg. His deepest friendship was with François and Eliza Wille, whose home, "Mariafeld," near Meilen, was a meeting place for the important musicians, performing artists, writers, and scholars of the era. There Meyer met the German writer Gottfried Kinkel, Richard Wagner's friend Mathilde Wesendonck, the architect Gottfried Semper, and, once, Keller. François Wille, who had been a Young German journalist in Hamburg, inspired Meyer with his fiery spirit. He became Meyer's mentor, critic, and patron. Meyer found the respect and acceptance from the intelligentsia that he needed in Wille's cultured circle. Discussion centered often on the unification of Germany and the glories of Prussia, providing Meyer the theme and impetus for the work that was to make him famous, *Huttens letzte Tage* (Hutten's Last Days, 1871).

A verse narrative, *Huttens letzte Tage* depicts the last days of the national hero Ulrich von Hutten, who fought for the Reformation and for a unified and powerful Germany free from the rule of papal Rome. Meyer thus took up a topic which appealed to a public enraptured with the founding of the German Empire. Written principally in the winter of 1870–1871, during the Franco-Prussian War, the tale is composed in iambic-pentameter couplets with a hard masculine rhyme that allows Meyer to voice Hutten's energetic manner rhythmically. The work is a cycle of eight parts: "Die Ufenau" (The Ufenau), "Das Buch der Vergangenheit" (The Book of the Past), "Einsamkeit" (Solitude), "Huttens Gast" (Hutten's Guest), "Menschen" (People), "Das

Todesurteil" (Death Sentence), "Dämonen" (Demons), and "Das Sterben" (Death). The cycle germinated from an unpublished poetic sketch, "Der sterbende Hutten" (The Dying Hutten, 1870), drafted as early as 1866, which describes the dying Hutten looking at the dimming sunset as a Holbeinian death figure cuts down a grape, golden with ripeness, from a vine in the arched window. The scene signified for Meyer that "Reif sein ist alles" (Ripeness is all). The cycle grasps the great political and cultural events of the time and vividly portrays the lake and its surroundings; it also takes up Meyer's concern with death and the loneliness that had tormented him since his youth, topics that were to form the nucleus of later narratives. In what was to become a characteristic feature of his writing, Meyer welds historical material to his personal experience. History offered Meyer an opportunity to reveal his innermost thoughts while distancing himself from his ambiguous feelings. In *Huttens letzte Tage* he captures his own elegiac mood and preoccupation with death through the life of a historical figure depicted in a series of lyrical pictures and dramatic memoirs. The work encapsulates past events into concentrated scenes, a structural technique much favored by Meyer. The narrative opens with the tired and dying Hutten's arrival on the island of Ufenau in Lake Constance and closes with his departure by boat for the land of the dead. The poems within this frame constitute a fragmented monologue by Hutten, recounting his life of action, his fight against death, and his eventual acceptance of it. Meyer's love of antithesis as a structural device is evident in the contrast of the fullness of life with the emptiness of death and in the opposition of the aesthetic world of the Italian Renaissance with the ethical world of the Reformation. Published by Haessel in October 1871, *Huttens letzte Tage* received accolades beyond Meyer's fondest dreams; it remains one of his most popular works even today. No other was more lovingly revised by Meyer, both in theme and style, than this one.

In high spirits, Meyer and Betsy began their second trip to Italy in November 1871. Passing through Munich, Innsbruck, and Verona, they took up residence for the winter in Venice, where Meyer deepened his impressions of Romance art and studied the art of the Renaissance. The works of the Basel historian Jakob Burckhardt, *Die Cultur der Renaissance in Italien* (The Culture of the Renaissance in Italy, 1860) and *Die Geschichte der Renaissance in Italien* (The History of the Renaissance in Italy, 1867), influenced Meyer profoundly. Above all, Meyer was impressed by the realism and color of Titian. He

began work on his verse epic *Engelberg* (1872), completing it on his return to Switzerland in March 1872. Written in four-stress rhymed iambics, the story is set in the mountains. In the original version an angel, Engel, comes down from heaven and experiences the joys and sorrows of earthly existence. The paintings of Giovanni Bellini with their graceful angels and Titian's *Assunta* gave impetus to the creation of the poem. Meyer's increasing wish to give a realistic character to his art, however, led him in the published version to turn Engel into an orphan girl who is passed off as an angel by a monk. Somber and realistic elements, including murder and suicide, clash with the original idyllic character of the story. The work takes up the dominant themes of Meyer's writing – love, conscience, and hate – and again shows his preoccupation with death. Meyer was later critical of his work, and it did not enjoy the success of its predecessor.

In 1872 Meyer and Betsy moved into another lake house in Meilen. Meyer's first historical novella, *Das Amulett* (1873; translated as "The Amulet," 1976), is set in the Reformation, a time of transition from a brutal era to a more civilized one. Like Burckhardt, Meyer found the beginnings here of the philosophical skepticism and ambiguous point of view characteristic of the nineteenth century. The visual impetus that set Meyer's poetic imagination into motion was a painting he had seen in Lausanne of the Saint Bartholomew's Day Massacre in Paris in 1572; later, in Paris, he had imagined the buildings of the Louvre splattered with the blood of the Huguenots. Based on Prosper Mérimée's *La Chronique du règne de Charles IX* (Chronicle of the Reign of Charles IX, 1829) and readings in the works of Michelet; Leopold von Ranke; Pierre de Bourdeille, seigneur de Brantôme, and Ludwig Häusser, *Das Amulett* is recounted by Hans Schadau, a Huguenot and staunch believer in the Calvinist doctrine of predestination. Meyer contrasts Schadau with the devout Catholic and Mariolater Wilhelm Boccard, who wears a medallion in gratitude to the Virgin Mary for having cured him of a childhood paralysis. The story shows how the amulet paradoxically fails to protect the believer but guards the nonbeliever. As the ambiguous qualities of the medallion become more pronounced, the events point to a seemingly irrational fate and throw divine omnipotence into question. Narrated with breathless speed and a strong sense of foreboding, the action is concentrated into pregnant scenes. The symbolic use of objects such as the amulet points to Meyer's inclination to portray his ideas in a concrete, visual manner. While the characters in *Das Amulett* are shadowy, the story is an important first step in Meyer's mastery of prose form. Published by Haessel in the fall of 1873, it was not a great success but did receive favorable reviews from Vulliemin, Calmberg, and Paul Wislicenus.

Meyer's mastery in transposing historical material into effective prose fiction was proven by his long historical novella *Jürg Jenatsch: Eine Bündnergeschichte* (1883; Jürg Jenatsch: A Story of Bünden; translated as "Jürg Jenatsch," 1976). Published first from 31 July to 25 December 1874 in the periodical *Die Literatur* under the title "Georg Jenatsch: Eine Geschichte aus der Zeit des Dreißigjährigen Krieges" (Georg Jenatsch: A Story from the Time of the Thirty Years' War), it is one of the most successful books ever written in Switzerland, receiving thirty editions in Meyer's lifetime. The story had a long germination period, during which Meyer delved into historical works, chronicles, reports, and biographies, even searching out pictures of characters in the Zurich library. Bruce Reber's *Georg Jenatsch, Graubündens Pfarrer und Held während des 30jährigen Krieges* (Georg Jenatsch, Graubünden's Pastor and Hero during the Thirty Years' War, 1860) served as the primary source for the story, while impressions gleaned from Meyer's trips to the Alps in Graubünden and to Venice formed the background. Meyer had devoted himself to "Georg Jenatsch" in 1866 and 1867 and in the winters of 1871–1872 and 1872–1873. At one point he had attempted to write the work as a drama, which he considered the highest art form, but his instinctive need for distancing himself from his material was incompatible with the immediacy of stage action. The work reveals his skill in condensing vast amounts of historical detail. Based on the life of the national hero Georg Jenatsch, who liberated Graubünden from Hapsburg and French domination in 1639 during the Thirty Years' War, the novella questions the compatibility of ethics and politics: Jenatsch is forced to sacrifice his morals for the welfare of his country. The work thus shares the pessimism of Burckhardt, who argued that political power itself was suspect. While Meyer was an admirer of the German chancellor Otto von Bismarck, the novella sheds light on Meyer's doubts about Bismarck's realpolitik.

Divided into three books, the novella compresses eighteen historical years into three short periods. The first book, "Die Reise des Herrn Waser" (The Trip of Mr. Waser), depicts Jenatsch's rise from humble beginnings to become a champion of Swiss independence. This section recounts the events of the Valtellina massacre of 1620, in which the Catholic majority of the Valtellina Valley murdered some five hundred of their Protestant fellows. The Protestant pastor Jenatsch becomes embroiled in the bloody events and rises to prominence as a soldier and politician. Supported by the French-Venetian party, he murders his enemy, Pompejus Planta, the leader of the Spanish party. The duality of Jenatsch's nature – his impetuousness and tenderness, spontaneity and cool cunning, love of country and personal ambition – is revealed by his deeds and through foils who either mirror or contrast with his personality. The second book, "Lucretia," deepens the ambiguity of Jenatsch's motives. In Venice in the winter of 1634–1635 Jenatsch joins the French army under the command of the Protestant Duke Rohan to help free Graubünden from Spanish rule. Jenatsch has loved Lucretia, Planta's daughter, since childhood; having been forced to kill Lucretia's father, he has sacrificed his personal happiness for the sake of his homeland. The second book amasses increasingly negative details about Jenatsch's motives and contrasts his ever-growing ambition to Lucretia's impeccable honesty. Book 3, "Der gute Herzog" (The Good Duke), contrasts Jenatsch and the highly ethical Duke Rohan. It covers events from 1635 to 1639, when Jenatsch commits his ultimate betrayal: he ruthlessly abandons Rohan and the French to win independence for Graubünden. This act leads to his death at the hands of Lucretia, who seeks to prevent him from falling prey to hubris.

Written in a rigorously objective style that avoids authorial commentary and direct psychological analysis, the novella is calculated to leave the motivation of the hero shrouded in mystery. In keeping with his basic artistic tenet that feelings are to be depicted through external symptoms, Meyer portrays Jenatsch through gestures and facial expressions and through the multiple perspectives of the other characters. He allows all points of view to be validated but also to be contradicted or made ambiguous, leaving the reader at an impasse. All of Meyer's stories force the reader to interpret the events on the basis of the given evidence; the contradictions in the narratives, however, leave the reader dangling.

Meyer dictated his works from nine o'clock in the morning to two o'clock in the afternoon to Betsy, who served as his secretary. On 5 October 1875 he married Luise Ziegler, who came from a patrician Zurich family. The newlyweds honeymooned in Corsica until January 1876. On their return home they lived first in Küsnacht and then bought a home in Kilchberg. They attended concerts, the theater, and other cultural events in accordance with Meyer's new position in society. A gracious host and an epicure, he became portly. In 1877 he legally adopted Ferdinand as his middle name.

Meyer's contentment is reflected in his humorous novella "Der Schuß von der Kanzel" (1878; translated as "The Shot from the Pulpit," 1976). Its protagonist, General Rudolf Wertmüller, had appeared in *Jürg Jenatsch* as an eccentric lieutenant. In this comedy, Wertmüller is an unorthodox and mercurial thinker who is contrasted with the self-righteous inhabitants of the fictitious town of Mythikon on the Au peninsula near Zurich. The limited point of view of the bourgeois citizens is spoofed in a delightful manner. While the story has a somber background of death and war, hinting at Meyer's dark side even in a happy period of his life, it reflects his talent for comedy. Although Meyer claimed that the story left a bitter taste in his mouth — unlike tragedy, which elevated and edified him — it has remained one of his most popular works.

A daughter, Luise Elisabetha Camilla, was born to the Meyers in 1879. (She would commit suicide in 1936 as a result of a schizophrenic depression.) Friction entered Meyer's life only through the growing tension between Betsy and his wife: Luise had no feeling for literary matters herself but was intensely jealous of Betsy's role in her brother's creative activities. In 1879 Betsy was replaced as Meyer's secretary by their young cousin Fritz Meyer.

Meyer's masterpiece, *Der Heilige* (The Saint, 1880; translated as *Thomas à Becket, the Saint*, 1885), represents the culmination of the style Meyer had forged over the years and is the best exemplification of his artistic ideals. His tendency toward the pictorial and dramatic; his striving for symbolization, concentration, and the grand gesture; and his demand for strict objectivity reach their epitome in this novella. Set in twelfth-century England, it is the tale of Thomas Becket, the elegant and worldly chancellor in the court of Henry II who was elevated to archbishop of Canterbury, suddenly became an ascetic, was murdered at Henry's behest in Canterbury Cathedral in 1170, and was canonized two years later. Having come across Becket in Thierry's *Histoire de la conquête de l'Angleterre par les Normands* (History of the Conquest of England by the Normans, 1825) perhaps as early as 1853, Meyer was tormented for years by the archbishop's mysterious transformation. The novella was completed by 1875, but Meyer held back publication for

Conrad Ferdinand Meyer

another four years while he painstakingly reworked every detail until stylistic perfection matched thematic complexity. Becket exemplified the type of enigmatic personality that had always captured Meyer's imagination. Meyer deepened the mystery of Becket's transformation by adding fictional elements and shifting the emphasis from historical events to the psychological level. By endowing Becket with Oriental blood and culture, Meyer set up a classic confrontation between humane, "modern" behavior and Henry's medieval brutality. Becket is a cool and intellectual aesthete, while Henry represents the robust physical side of human nature. Meyer also created a daughter for Becket to add stronger motivation for Becket's conversion: Grace is seduced by Henry and accidentally killed as her anguished father attempts to prevent the act. A strong element of revenge thus interweaves with Becket's spiritual conversion.

Drawn against a vivid historical panorama that illustrates the church-state conflicts, the ethics of government, and the relationships between the Norman conquerors and the vanquished Saxons, the story probes the human soul more deeply than any other of Meyer's creations. The story, Meyer insisted repeatedly, is intentionally ambiguous. By making pervasive use of irony and shifting perspectives, Meyer enshrouds Becket in a net of contradictions that becomes impenetrable. The ambiguity derives to a large extent from Meyer's masterful use of a framework.

The story is related by a psychologically complex narrator, Hans the crossbow maker, whose vantage point is nonomniscient and biased. Hans admits that he cannot fathom Becket; since the other characters' evaluations of the chancellor's motives are as unreliable as Hans's, the reader is left in a quandary, as Meyer intended. Adhering to his artistic ideal, which called for the visual representation of feelings, Meyer portrays Becket through stylized gestures, postures, symbolic artworks, and architectonically composed scenes that hint at the inner man. Antithetical motifs of the sun and the moon, heat and coolness, red blood and the purity of white symbolize Henry's passion and Becket's cool intellect, respectively. The images weave a dense and often contradictory pattern over the narrative and indicate the complexity of human existence. Becket avows the power of Christ and love, yet he extracts merciless revenge on Henry; the archbishop receives his death blow with a smile of triumph. Meyer poured all his uncertainties about human motivation into Becket's character. He spoke of the jewellike quality of his narrative: polished like a precious stone, it refracts light and casts shadows dark with ambiguity. To Meyer's dismay, the novella was criticized in Switzerland after its publication in the *Deutsche Rundschau* (German Review) from November 1879 to January 1880: led by an attack by Jakob Bächtold, the Swiss critics took offense at the seduction scene. The novella was popular during Meyer's lifetime, however, going through sixteen editions by the time of his death; but it was not until the twentieth century that *Der Heilige* was recognized as his masterpiece.

In 1880 Meyer received an honorary doctorate from the University of Zurich; he had the title embossed on his calling card and sometimes added it to his signature. The first of his Renaissance novellas, the ironically humorous *Plautus im Nonnenkloster* (translated as "Plautus in the Convent," 1914), was begun in December 1880 and completed about six months later. It appeared under the title "Das Brigittchen von Trogen" in the *Deutsche Rundschau* in November 1881, followed by a book edition the following year. Drawn freely from Meyer's imagination, the story is narrated by the Florentine human-

ist Poggio Bracciolini to the elegant Florentine court of Cosimo de' Medici. The sophisticated frame, which depicts the intellectually refined world of the Renaissance, abounds with cultural allusions. Meyer contrasts this climate with the Swiss milieu of the tale proper, which describes how Poggio uncovers a fraudulent miracle in a nunnery while searching for a lost codex by the Roman dramatist Titus Maccius Plautus, the author of lively and earthy comedies. Gertrude, a simple peasant girl with a strict conscience, is tricked into believing that she is carrying a heavy cross, which is actually hollow, to prove the power of piety. The girl is forced to take the veil, but she escapes when she learns of the deceit. The story portrays the three "types" of the Reformation: the aesthetically overrefined high clergy represented by Poggio, the bestial low clergy characterized by the Abbess Brigittchen von Trogen, and the simple "Volksnatur" (spirit of the people) embodied in Gertrude. Critically acclaimed in Meyer's time, it is one of his finest works; Meyer himself took delight in its perfect form and delicate nuances. His next novella, *Gustav Adolfs Page* (1882; translated as "Gustav Adolf's Page," 1976), did not reach the high standards of its predecessor and has received mixed reviews ever since its publication. Based on intense study of historical sources dealing with the Swedish king Gustav Adolf, a heroic symbol of devout Protestantism for Meyer, the tale depicts a fictitious episode in which a young girl, Auguste (Gustel) Leubelfing, poses as the king's page so that she can follow her hero into battle during the Thirty Years' War. The motif of the disguised girl derives from an early fragment of a play about Gustav Adolf by Laube, discussed by Laube in the introduction to his drama *Monaldeschi* (1845). Gustel is consumed with heedless devotion to her beloved, like Klärchen in Goethe's *Egmont* (1788; translated, 1848), another source of inspiration for Meyer. Passionately in love with the king, who remains unaware of her gender, the page revels in her closeness to him. Both she and the king are killed in the battle of Lützen. Although the action moves quickly, the plot is generally faulted for its contrived convolutions and overuse of chance.

Although Meyer repeatedly termed his poetry the subordinate side of his art, he had continued having poems published in more-or-less obscure magazines ever since the appearance of *Romanzen und Bilder*. After polishing, revising, and compressing his poems in an attempt to achieve perfection of form, he chose 191 of them to be published under the title *Gedichte* (Poems, 1882). The fifth, definitive edition of 1892 contained 231 poems. Heinrich

Henel's *The Poetry of Conrad Ferdinand Meyer* (1954) shows how Meyer worked at refining his art. Using manuscripts that Betsy salvaged before Meyer could destroy them, as was his custom once an old version of a poem had been superseded by a new one, Henel demonstrates how Meyer transformed mediocre poems into creations of original beauty. Unable to express his complex inner life through the forthright outpouring of emotion in the manner of classical and Romantic poets, Meyer put his feelings into objective shape; he thereby created a new type of poem, the Dinggedicht (object poem), in which a visual image assumes symbolic meaning. While weaker poems exhibit the danger of over-explicitness, his symbolist poems at their best blend scene and symbol into an exquisite and perfect whole. Nonconfessional and unemotional, they evoke profound feelings with a seeming ease and eloquence that belie Meyer's conscious manipulation of motifs and language. In creating this new type of poem Meyer became the precursor of symbolist poetry in Germany, the forerunner of Hofmannsthal, Rilke, and George. Since Meyer had no cognizance of the symbolist movement that had taken root in France with the works of Charles Baudelaire and Stéphane Mallarmé, his contribution must be considered an original one.

Gedichte is divided into nine cycles, each of which takes up an individual theme, motif, or form; the cycles combine architectonically into a whole. The work is introduced by "Vorsaal" (Antechamber), twenty-three poems that serve as a preview of the edifice to be constructed; they take up the themes of the collection: poetry, love, and death. The poems probe, as Henel has demonstrated, the mute stage of Meyer's life, the time when he lived in a dreamworld, unable to express his experiences. Sections 2 through 5 present Meyer's ever-widening personal life. Section 2, "Stunde" (Hour), moves from day to night and spring to winter. Its poems draw on motifs from the lake, the fields, and the woods, Meyer's immediate surroundings when he was a child. Some of Meyer's most original and beautiful symbolist poems, which express his sense of closeness with death, are found here. The motifs move within a limited range, often making use of traditional concepts – the fountain to express ever-flowing life, the reaper to symbolize death, the grape to depict the ripeness of time. Meyer often endowed common motifs with new and complex associations, turning them into private symbols. Elegant lake poems make use of some of Meyer's best-known motifs – the quietly drifting boat with oars at rest, dark and stagnating water, and sluggish bul-

rushes – to create scenes of eerie silence and a sense of painless unconcern in the face of death. Harvest poems portray fields of golden ripened wheat and the glowing setting sun to symbolize the end of life as its holy and supreme moment. Section 3, "In den Bergen" (In the Mountains), depicts Meyer's trips to the Alps; snowy peaks and pure air, the intensely blue heaven, mountain flowers, rushing water, ice, cliffs, and the sound of cowbells provide the motifs. The mountains, the borderline between heaven and earth, symbolize the limitless place where the soul is free and without pain, and the poems speak of the rejuvenation and healing to be gained from nature. Section 4, "Reise" (Travel), contains impressions of Meyer's trips to Italy, southern France, and Corsica. Paintings and sculptures often serve as motifs. Meyer's impressions of Venice are transcribed into an impressionistic blend of color and shade to signify life and death. Section 5, "Liebe" (Love), is the inner and most intimate sanctum of the volume. Here Meyer speaks of his deep feelings for his sister, mother, and wife and remembers, although never explicitly those who died young. The poems use luminous motifs – white blossoms at night evoking terror; heat lightning – to speak of the poet's love frustrated through death and distance. Footsteps disappearing in the rain symbolize the transience of life and portend the beloved's death.

Sections 6 through 9 expand the volume to the broader scene of European history and make more use of the ballad form. Section 6, "Götter" (Gods), takes up motifs of Greek and Roman antiquity; figures from mythology – Dionysus, Pentheus, Medusa, and Eros – reflect Meyer's fascination with the bacchanalian and tumultuous aspects of life. In contrast, polar mythological figures represent death. Section 7, "Frech und fromm" (Impudent and Pious), deals with the tension between piety and sensuality in the Middle Ages. Section 8, "Genie" (Genius), captures the grandeur of the Renaissance and its artistic achievements. "Männer" (Men), Section 9, encapsulates the Reformation with such heroic figures as Martin Luther and Huldruych Zwingli. The ballads are theatrical in nature and contain effective groupings and pregnantly drawn scenes; they have led critics to rank Meyer with Theodor Fontane and Detlev von Liliencron as an outstanding representative of the realistic and symbolist ballad form. Hofmannsthal, impatient with Meyer's dependency on historical costumes to express his thought, condemned Meyer's poems as allegories. Yet even he had to admit that Meyer had reached perfection in a few poems and placed Meyer among the few truly great German poets. Meyer's reputation as a lyricist has grown steadily since the publication of his *Gedichte,* which was praised by luminaries such as Keller and George.

The psychological novella *Das Leiden eines Knaben,* singled out by Keller with particular praise and recognized today as one of Meyer's finest works, is his most emotional story. In it, his intense association with the fictive events continually threatens to break his customary authorial objectivity. Begun in 1877 and worked on sporadically for the next six years, it is based loosely on *Mémoires complets et authentiques de duc de Saint-Simon sur le siècle de Louis XIV et la Régence* (The Complete Memoirs of the Duke of Saint-Simon from the Time of Louis XIV and His Regency, 1829–1830), one of Meyer's favorite books. A young boy, Julian Boufflers, suffers humiliation at the hands of a brutal Jesuit teacher and dies when his strict father fails to recognize his son's anguish. Enclosed within a framework in which the narrator and listeners react to each other emotionally, the story is told by Louis XIV's physician, Fagon. Fagon seeks to awaken the king's conscience but fails because the king persists in rigid, socially determined thinking. Meyer probes his own anguished youth and social isolation through the figure of Julian, who is mentally disabled and, like Meyer, ridiculed by society. Narrated with bitter irony and fine psychological detail, the story reflects the virulent anti-Jesuitism of the era as well as Meyer's own anti-Catholic tendencies. The Jesuit teacher, Père Tellier, is portrayed through a leitmotiv of wolf imagery that assumes demonic shape at the end of the story. The novella was first published in September 1883 in *Schorers Familienblatt* (Schorer's Family Paper) under the title "Julian Boufflers: Das Leiden eines Kindes."

The novella *Die Hochzeit des Mönchs* (1883; translated as *The Monk's Wedding,* 1887) is set in thirteenth-century Padua, at the court of the tyrant Ezzelino da Romano. The plot is based loosely on Niccolò Macchiavelli's *Istorie fiorentine* (Florentine Stories, 1825) and takes up the theme of the renegade monk, a recurring motif in Keller's narratives. Meyer's demand that every thought assume visible shape is more purposefully carried out here than in any other story. Written in a highly stylized, epigrammatic language in which each word assumes psychological significance, the narrative uses gestures, facial expressions, and scenic arrangements as symbols of psychological events. The framework here is considered to be one of the most complex uses of the device in the German novella.

Die Hochzeit des Mönchs is in the tradition of the old Italian novella of Giovanni Boccaccio, where a group of people pass the time telling stories. The events are narrated by the poet Dante, who invents the tale on the spot for the ruler of Verona, Cangrande della Scala, and his court. Ranging from mocking tones to capture human foibles to tragic irony, Dante derives the motif of the story from an epitaph: "Hier schlümmert der Mönch Astorre neben seiner Gattin Antiope. Beide begrub Ezzelin" (Here slumbers the monk Astorre next to his wife, Antiope. Ezzelino buried them both). He takes the names and external features of his characters from his audience, making them typifications of human passions. Cangrande's wife, the fair and proud Diana Pizzaguerra, a "northern" type, is juxtaposed antithetically to his dark-hued mistress, Antiope Canossa, a sensuous "southern" type. The two women vie in Dante's story for the love of the monk Astorre, the only main character invented by Dante. Astorre, the last of four sons of the Vicedomini family, is forced by his avaricious father to renounce his monastic vows and marry Diana to save the family's lineage. He soon becomes blinded by passion for Antiope and betrays Diana. Astorre's and Antiope's love ultimately leads to a breakdown of social order, leading to their tragic deaths at the end of the narrative.

As the story unfolds, the interaction between the frame and the narrative becomes increasingly intense. Dante interrupts the tale frequently and invites his listeners to comment on the characters' motivations and personalities. The plot of Dante's story and the framework begin to blend as Cangrande's wife and mistress start to take sides with their namesakes. Although he is the author of the story and theoretically omniscient, Dante repeatedly asserts his inability to fathom his characters' souls and refuses to judge their actions. His perplexing stance is emblematic of the enigmatic nature of human motivation and implicitly points to the inability of even the artist to comprehend life. The constant eruption of the dark forces of fate and chance in the story hints that Astorre's and Antiope's actions may be ruled by factors beyond their control; at the same time, the psychological details given show that their motivations are not entirely innocent. Justice prevails in the end, and the guilty are punished. Meyer's deep pessimism is reflected in the story, in which even positive factors such as love and friendship turn into aberrations. Critics were perplexed and fascinated by the novella. Julius Rodenberg, the editor of the *Deutsche Rundschau,* was captivated, while Paul

Heyse, Otto Brahm, and Adolf Frey expressed the fear that Meyer was beginning to succumb to mannerism, that form was becoming an end in itself for him. Haessel demanded a revision of the ending for the book publication. Meyer defended his novella but vowed to give up the framework technique since he had extracted all its subtleties and could bring it to no further development. Meyer's readers, in contrast to the critics, devoured the story. The work had gone into nine editions by 1892 and was translated into English and Italian by 1887. Subject to a variety of interpretations, it has never ceased to fascinate readers and critics and is recognized today as a German classic.

Meyer did abandon the framework technique in his next novella, *Die Richterin* (1885; translated as "The Judge," 1976). Written in a terse style without adjectives, the novella has vividly drawn expressionistic passages. Meyer drafted half of the work as a drama before switching to the novella form. Set in the untamed mountains of Graubünden in the ninth century, the novella depicts primordial characters in a tale of love, murder, deceit, justice, conscience, and incest. The work shows the influence of *Crime and Punishment* (1866), by Fyodor Dostoyevski, one of the authors whose work Meyer was reading avidly during this time. The judge, Stemma, is consumed by guilt because she killed her husband sixteen years ago, when she was pregnant with the child of another man. Her daughter, Palma, has languished to the point of death because of her seemingly incestuous love for her supposed half-brother, Wulfrin, who is actually the murdered man's son from a previous marriage. Overcome by her conscience, symbolized by the persistent sound of a magical horn calling for judgment, Stemma pronounces herself guilty and commits suicide. Stemma's confession of her crime releases Palma and Wulfrin from their torment. Meyer's psychological presentation of the repressed and subconscious lives of Palma and Wulfrin is powerfully depicted through erotic nature symbolism, which conjures up a world of chaos. The story so captivated Sigmund Freud that he chose *Die Richterin* for his first analysis of a literary text. Meyer himself called the work his "Liebling" (favorite one) and his best one and viewed it as a coming-to-terms with the whispers about his relationship with his sister: although his reasoning seems somewhat confused, he saw the novella as a vindication of the purity of their relationship. His fears that readers in bourgeois Switzerland would take exception to the incest theme did not materialize. Readers interpreted the novella as a vindication of conscience and an affirmation of justice.

Putting aside two large literary projects he had pursued during the 1880s – a novel, "Der Dynast" (The Dynast), and a drama, "Petrus Vinea" (both fragments were published in 1916 in *Conrad Ferdinand Meyers unvollendete Prosadichtungen* [Conrad Ferdinand Meyer's Unfinished Prose Works]) – Meyer turned for the third time to the Renaissance for his last major novella, *Die Versuchung des Pescara* (1887; translated as *The Tempting of Pescara,* 1890). Based on extensive readings in the works of the historians Ranke, Ferdinand Gregorovius, Alfred von Reumont, Friedrich Christoph Schlosser, and Paulus Jovius during 1886, the novella evinces Meyer's ever-deepening preoccupation with death. Fernando Avalos, the Marquis of Pescara, a Spanish general, was asked to join an Italian conspiracy against the Spanish emperor Charles V. The historical Pescara joined the collusion but then carried out the emperor's orders; he died, perhaps of wounds received in a battle in Pavia, in 1525. While the facts suggest a struggle between loyalty and betrayal, Meyer, after toying with the idea of free will as the theme of the novella, decided to make Pescara a dying man. Thus, unknown to the conspirators, Pescara is beyond temptation. Death is depicted as a state of rest, equilibrium, and escape from the unsolvable conflicts of life. Meyer cast his deepest feelings about death into the novella, which blends the pseudoreligious fatalism, escapism, and resignation so often found in his poems. Pescara is surrounded by a rich array of subordinate characters who represent the chaos and immorality of life as they try to convince – even force – him to commit betrayal. Meyer viewed the Renaissance as an age of amoral, power-hungry individuals and of aesthetic grandeur, and the novella casts ironic light on its dual and ambiguous nature. *Die Versuchung des Pescara* is Meyer's most formalized work, the one in which his manipulation of imagery, gestures, costumes, symbolic artworks, and elaborate scenic settings is worked out in the finest detail. It received mixed reviews.

Toward the end of 1887 Meyer fell into a depression and also began to suffer from an inflammation of the throat that led to shortness of breath, a sensation of choking, and excruciating pain. His heart and lungs became involved, and he developed an infection of the mucous membranes of the nose. Doctors could offer little help, but a stay at his family's Steinegg Castle in the woods near Thurgau offered some relief. The ensuing year was one of Meyer's most difficult. Attempts at work failed; he gave up his correspondence and avoided visitors. Receiving the Bavarian Order of Maximilian in December 1888 seemed to revive him. Late in 1889 he had recovered enough to become engrossed in his final work, the lengthy novella *Angela Borgia* (1891; translated as "Angela Borgia," 1976). Its completion was a heroic act of will: Meyer felt pushed to the limit by a deadline set by Rodenberg of the *Deutsche Rundschau* and caught in a struggle between Betsy, who had returned as his secretary, and his wife, who resented the toll that the work was taking on his health. The story reflects Meyer's return to traditional Christianity, brought about by his illness. Set in the court of Duke Alfonso d'Este of Ferrara in the fifteenth century, the story portrays once again the aesthetic opulence and the immorality of the Renaissance in scenes of bacchanalian frenzy and hideous mutilation. The influence of contemporary literature with its social engagement and psychologically analytical techniques can be felt clearly in the story: Meyer was reading Henrik Ibsen's *Hedda Gabler* (1890) and works by August Strindberg, Gerhart Hauptmann, Emile Zola, Dostoyevski, Ivan Turgenev, and Leo Tolstoy during this period. The stylistic influence of naturalism is evident in the bloody scenes of horror. The novella shows Meyer's turn away from the influence of French literature to Nordic and Russian models. The story centers on the beautiful and amoral Lucrezia Borgia, a woman with too little conscience, and her young cousin Angela, who has too much conscience, and takes up Meyer's usual themes of crime, revenge, love, hate, justice, and death. The novella shows a weakening of Meyer's control of form and lacks unity of action, and its positive ending is a wrenching attempt to stave off the darkness Meyer must have perceived closing in on his life. Angela passes through a stage of exaggerated moral severity to a life of Christian humility and self-sacrifice. Meyer's underlying fascination lay clearly, however, in the corrupt and seductive Lucrezia, a symbol of immorality and ever-threatening chaos.

Meyer's physical and psychological overexertion in writing *Angela Borgia* took its toll. At the end of 1891 he developed an infection of the eyes that forced him to give up reading and writing. In 1892 severe depression set in, and Meyer began to suffer from delusions. With his consent, he was taken on 7 July 1892 to the mental institution of Königsfelden in the canton of Aargau, where he was diagnosed as suffering from "senile melancholy." He had hallucinations, believing that he was being pursued by wild animals and not knowing in what century he lived. He was well enough to return to Kilchberg in September 1893, but his creative energies were spent. Betsy oversaw his correspondence and new editions of his works. Meyer was able only to write a few religious poems; he was aware that they lacked artistic value, and he did not allow their publication. He and his wife took occasional trips to Geneva, Strasbourg, and the Alps. The antagonism Meyer's wife had always felt toward Betsy flared during this time: she reproached Betsy for supporting Meyer's artistic endeavors, which Luise saw as the cause of his illness. The unending strife finally brought Meyer to condemn his sister. In the fall of 1898 his health took a sudden turn for the better, and he briefly regained his lively ways and mental clarity. He died suddenly of a heart attack on 28 November 1898 while reading the *Deutsche Rundschau*, which had introduced his works to posterity.

Letters:

"Conrad-Ferdinand Meyer et Louis Vuillemin," edited by Charles Vuillemin, *Bibliothèque universelle et Revue suisse,* 104, no. 16 (1899): 225–246, 532–553;

Louise von François und Conrad Ferdinand Meyer: Ein Briefwechsel, edited by Anton Bettelheim (Berlin: Reimer, 1905; revised edition, Berlin: Vereinigung wissenschaftlicher Verleger, 1920);

"Conrad Ferdinand Meyer und Friedrich Th. Vischer," edited by Robert Vischer, *Süddeutsche Monatshefte,* 3 (February 1906): 172–179;

Briefe Conrad Ferdinand Meyers: Nebst seinen Rezensionen und Aufsätzen, 2 volumes, edited by Adolf Frey (Leipzig: Haessel, 1908);

"Betty Paoli und Conrad Ferdinand Meyer: Zeugnisse einer Dichterfreundschaft in elf Briefen (1877–1886)," edited by A. Schaer, *Euphorion,* 16 (1909): 497–510;

"C. F. Meyers Briefe," edited by E. Bertram, *Mitteilungen der Literarischen Gesellschaft Bonn,* 7, no. 3 (1912);

Briefe von und an Heinrich Bulthaupt, edited by Heinrich Kraeger (Oldenburg & Leipzig: Schulze, 1912), pp. 470–475;

C.-F. Meyer: La Crise de 1852–1856. Lettres de C.-F. Meyer et de son entourage, edited by Robert d'Harcourt (Paris: Alcan, 1913);

Conrad Ferdinand Meyer und Julius Rodenberg: Ein Briefwechsel, edited by August Langmesser (Berlin: Paetel, 1918);

"Von Conrad Ferdinand Meyer und seinem Verleger," edited by Anton Reitler, *Jahrbuch der Literarischen Vereinigung,* 10 (1925): 5–20;

"Briefe von Conrad Ferdinand Meyer, Betsy Meyer und J. Hardmeyer-Jenny," edited by Otto Schultheß, *Neujahrsblätter der Literarischen Gesellschaft Bern,* new series, no. 5 (1927);

"Die Briefe C. F. Meyers an Mathilde Wesendonck," appendix to *Mathilde Wesendonck: Die Frau und die Dichterin,* edited by Friedrich Wilhelm Freiherr von Bissing (Essen: Essener Verlags-Anstalt, 1942);

Conrad Ferdinand Meyer und Gottfried Kinkel: Ihre persönlichen Beziehungen auf Grund ihres Briefwechsels, edited by Emil Bebler (Zurich: Rascher, 1949);

"Frau Anna von Doß über C. F. Meyer: Berichte und Briefe mit einem Nachwort von Hans Zeller," edited by Hans Zeller, *Euphorion,* 57 (1963): 370–410;

Johanna Spyri / Conrad Ferdinand Meyer: Briefwechsel 1877–1897. Mit einem Anhang: Briefe der Johanna Spyri an die Mutter und die Schwester C. F. Meyers 1853–1897, edited by Hans Zeller and Rosmarie Zeller (Kilchberg: Romano, 1977).

Bibliographies:

Joseph Weingartner, *Conrad Ferdinand Meyer nach seinem Leben und Dichten* (Halle, 1903);

Hans Corrodi, "C. F. Meyers Bild im Spiegel literaturwissenschaftlicher Erkenntnis," *Schweizerische Monatshefte für Politik und Kultur,* 3 (1923–1924): 442–453;

Rudolf Unger, "Moderne Strömungen in der deutschen Literaturwissenschaft: Über und um C. F. Meyer," *Die Literatur,* 26, no. 6 (1924): 321–324;

Friedrich Michael, "Conrad Ferdinand Meyers Werk und sein Echo: Ein Rückblick bei seinem 100. Geburtstag," *Die schöne Literatur,* 26 (December 1925): 443–447;

August Schröder, *Kritische Studien zu den Gedichten Conrad Ferdinand Meyers: Im Zusammenhang mit einer Kritik der bis 1926 über C. F. Meyer und sein Gedichtwerk erschienenen Literatur* (Cologne: Gehly, 1928);

Arthur Burkhard, "Conrad Ferdinand Meyer, 1825–1925," *Journal of English and Germanic Philology,* 27, no. 4 (1928): 486–495;

Fritz Eckardt, "Die Auflagen der Werke von Conrad Ferdinand Meyer," *Die schöne Literatur,* 29, no. 6 (June 1928): 279–282;

H. Kempert, "Conrad Ferdinand Meyer–Bibliographie," *Mitteilungen für Bücherfreunde,* 9 (1932);

Gustav Konrad, "C. F. Meyer. Ein Forschungsbericht," *Der Deutschunterricht,* 3, no. 2 (1951): 72–81;

Werner Oberle, "Conrad Ferdinand Meyer: Ein Forschungsbericht," *Germanisch-romanische Monatsschrift,* new series 6 (1956): 231–252;

Fritz Martini, "Forschungsbericht zur deutschen Literatur in der Zeit des Realismus," *Deutsche Vierteljahrsschrift,* 34 (1960): 657–666;

Roy C. Cowen, "Neunzehntes Jahrhundert (1830–1880)," in *Handbuch der deutschen Literaturgeschichte: Zweite Abteilung. Bibliographien 9,* volume 9 (Bern & Munich: Francke, 1970), pp. 170–175;

Helene Elisabeth Du Preez, *The Poetry of Conrad Ferdinand Meyer: A Bibliography* (Johannesburg: Department of Bibliography, Librarianship and Topography, University of Witwatersrand, 1974);

Gotthart Wunberg and Rainer Funke, *Deutsche Literatur des 19. Jahrhunderts (1830–1895). Erster Bericht: 1960–1975* (Bern, Frankfurt am Main & Las Vegas: Lang, 1980), pp. 159–160.

Biographies:

Adolf Frey, *Conrad Ferdinand Meyer: Sein Leben und seine Werke* (Stuttgart: Cotta, 1900);

Betsy Meyer, *C. F. Meyer in der Erinnerung seiner Schwester,* second edition (Berlin: Paetel, 1903);

August Langmesser, *Conrad Ferdinand Meyer: Sein Leben, seine Werke und sein Nachlaß,* third edition (Berlin: Wiegant & Grieben, 1905);

Robert d'Harcourt, *C.-F. Meyer: Sa vie, son oeuvre (1825–1898)* (Paris: Alcan, 1913);

Max Nußberger, *Conrad Ferdinand Meyer: Leben und Werke* (Frauenfeld: Huber, 1919);

Walther Linden, *Conrad Ferdinand Meyer: Entwicklung und Gestalt* (Munich: Beck, 1922);

Erich Everth, *Conrad Ferdinand Meyer: Dichtung und Persönlichkeit* (Dresden: Sibyll, 1924);

Harry Maync, *Conrad Ferdinand Meyer und sein Werk,* second edition (Frauenfeld: Huber, 1925; New York: AMS Press, 1969);

Karl Emanuel Lusser, *Conrad Ferdinand Meyer: Das Problem seiner Jugend* (Leipzig: Haessel, 1926);

Arthur Burkhard, *Conrad Ferdinand Meyer: The Style and the Man* (Cambridge, Mass.: Harvard University Press, 1932);

Lily Hohenstein, *Conrad Ferdinand Meyer* (Bonn: Athenäum, 1957);

S. A. Friebert, "A Chronicle of C. F. Meyer's Life with a Collection of His Comments on His Own Works," Ph.D. dissertation, University of Wisconsin, 1958;

Karl Fehr, *Conrad Ferdinand Meyer* (Stuttgart: Metzler, 1971; enlarged, 1980);

David A. Jackson, *Conrad Ferdinand Meyer in Selbst-zeugnissen und Bilddokumenten* (Reinbek: Rowohlt, 1975);

Fehr, *Conrad Ferdinand Meyer: Auf- und Niedergang seiner dichterischen Produktivität im Spannungsfeld von Erbanlagen und Umwelt* (Bern & Munich: Francke, 1983).

References:

Franz Ferdinand Baumgarten, *Das Werk Conrad Ferdinand Meyers: Renaissance-Empfinden und Stilkunst* (Munich: Beck, 1917);

Gustav Beckers, "Morone und Pescara: Proteisches Verwandlungsspiel und existentielle Metamorphose. Ein Beitrag zur Interpretation von C. F. Meyers Novelle *Die Versuchung des Pescara*," *Euphorion*, 63 (1969): 117–145;

Frederick J. Beharriell, "C. F. Meyer and the Origins of Psychoanalysis," *Monatshefte*, 47 (March 1955): 140–148;

W. P. Bridgwater, "C. F. Meyer and Nietzsche," *Modern Language Review*, 60 (October 1965): 568–583;

Hans-Dieter Brückner, *Heldengestaltung im Prosawerk Conrad Ferdinand Meyers* (Bern: Lang, 1970);

Georges Brunet, *C. F. Meyer et la nouvelle* (Paris: Didier, 1967);

Marianne Burkhard, *C. F. Meyer und die antike Mythologie* (Zurich: Atlantis, 1966);

Burkhard, *Conrad Ferdinand Meyer* (New York: Twayne, 1978);

Mary Crichton, "Zur Funktion der Gnade-Episode in C. F. Meyers *Der Heilige*," in *Lebendige Form: Interpretationen zur deutschen Literatur, Festschrift Henel*, edited by Jeffrey Sammons and Ernst Schürer (Munich: Fink, 1970), pp. 245–258;

Lena F. Dahme, *Women in the Life and Art of Conrad Ferdinand Meyer* (New York: Columbia University Press, 1936);

Tamara S. Evans, *Formen der Ironie in Conrad Ferdinand Meyers Novellen* (Bern & Munich: Francke, 1980);

Sigmund Freud, *Aus dem Anfängen der Psychoanalyse: Briefe an Wilhelm Fliess, Abhandlungen und Notizen aus den Jahren 1887-1902,* edited by Marie Bonaparte, Anna Freud, and Ernst Kris (London: Imago, 1950); translated by Eric Mosbacher and James Strachey as *The Origins of Psycho-analysis: Letters to Wilhelm Fliess, Drafts, and Notes, 1887-1902* (London: Imago, 1954; New York: Basic Books, 1954);

Heinrich Henel, *The Poetry of Conrad Ferdinand Meyer* (Madison: University of Wisconsin Press, 1954);

Gunter H. Hertling, *Conrad Ferdinand Meyers Epik: Traumbeseelung, Traumbesinnung und Traumbesitz* (Bern & Munich: Francke, 1973);

Valentin Herzog, *Ironische Erzählformen bei Conrad Ferdinand Meyer dargestellt am "Jürg Jenatsch"* (Bern: Francke, 1970);

Heinz Hillmann, "Conrad Ferdinand Meyer," in *Deutsche Dichter des 19. Jahrhunderts,* edited by Benno von Wiese (Berlin: Schmidt, 1969), pp. 463–486;

Hugo von Hofmannsthal, "C. F. Meyers Gedichte," *Wissen und Leben*, 29 (1925): 980–987;

David A. Jackson, "Conrad Ferdinand Meyer, 'Huttens letzte Tage' and the Liberal Ideal," *Oxford Germanic Studies*, 5 (1970): 67–89;

Manfred R. Jacobson, "The Narrator's Allusions to Art and Ambiguity: A Note on C. F. Meyer's *Der Heilige*," *Seminar*, 10 (November 1974): 265–273;

Erwin Kalischer, *C. F. Meyer in seinem Verhältnis zur italienischen Renaissance* (Berlin: Mayer & Müller, 1907);

Friedrich A. Kittler, *Der Traum und die Rede. Eine Analyse der Kommunikationssituation Conrad Ferdinand Meyers* (Bern & Munich: Francke, 1977);

Gerhard Knapp, *Conrad Ferdinand Meyer: Das Amulett. Historische Novellistik auf der Schwelle zur Moderne* (Paderborn, Munich, Vienna & Zurich: Schöningh, 1985);

Tiiu V. Laane, *Imagery in Conrad Ferdinand Meyer's Prose Works: Form, Motifs and Functions,* Germanic Studies in America, no. 47, edited by Katharina Mommsen (Bern: Lang, 1983);

Deborah S. Lund, *Ambiguity as Narrative Strategy in the Prose Work of C. F. Meyer,* North American Studies in Nineteenth-Century German Literature, no. 6, edited by Sammons (New York, Bern, Frankfurt am Main & Paris: Lang, 1990);

Dennis McCort, *States of Unconsciousness in Three Tales by C. F. Meyer* (London & Toronto: Associated University Presses, 1988);

Siegfried Mews, "Der fehlende Shakespeare: Betrachtungen zu C. F. Meyers *Der Schuß von der Kanzel*," *Seminar*, 9 (March 1973): 36–49;

Carlo Moos, *Dasein als Erinnerung: Conrad Ferdinand Meyer und die Geschichte* (Bern: Lang, 1973);

Robert Mühlher, "C. F. Meyer und der Manierismus," in *Dichtung der Krise: Mythos und Psychologie in der Dichtung des 19. und 20. Jahrhunderts* (Vienna: Herold, 1951), pp. 141–230;

Per Øhrgaard, *C. F. Meyer: Zur Entwicklung seiner Thematik* (Copenhagen: Munsksgaard, 1969);

Sjaak Onderdelinden, *Die Rahmenerzählungen Conrad Ferdinand Meyers* (Leiden: University Press, 1974);

George W. Reinhardt, "Two Romance Wordplays in C. F. Meyer's *Novellen*," *Germanic Review,* 46 (January 1971): 43–62;

Herbert Rowland, "Conscience and the Aesthetic in Conrad Ferdinand Meyer's *Plautus im Nonnenkloster,*" *Michigan Germanic Studies,* 11, no. 2 (1985): 152–181;

Christian Sand, *Anomie und Identität: Zur Wirklichkeitsproblematik in der Prosa von C. F. Meyer* (Stuttgart: Akademischer Verlag Hans-Dieter Heinz, 1980);

Beatrice Sandberg-Braun, *Wege zum Symbolismus: Zur Entstehungsgeschichte dreier Gedichte Conrad Ferdinand Meyers* (Zurich: Atlantis, 1969);

Michael Shaw, "C. F. Meyer's Resolute Heroes: A Study of Becket, Astorre and Pescara," *Deutsche Vierteljahrsschrift,* 40 (October 1966): 360–390;

Walter Silz, "Meyer: 'Der Heilige,'" in his *Realism and Reality: Studies in the German Novelle of Poetic Realism* (Chapel Hill: University of North Carolina Press, 1954), pp. 94–116;

Emil Staiger, "Im Spätboot: Zu Conrad Ferdinand Meyers Lyrik," in his *Die Kunst der Interpretation: Studien zur deutschen Literaturgeschichte,* fourth edition (Zurich: Atlantis, 1963), pp. 239–273;

Werner Stauffacher, "Lyrisches Ich, ins Bodenlose starrend," *Colloquium Helveticum* (1985): 51–61;

Martin Swales, "Fagon's Defeat: Some Remarks on C. F. Meyer's *Das Leiden eines Knaben,*" *Germanic Review,* 52 (January 1977): 29–43;

Marion Lee Taylor, *A Study of the Technique in C. F. Meyer's Novellen* (Chicago: University of Chicago Press, 1909);

Louis Wiesmann, *Conrad Ferdinand Meyer. Der Dichter des Todes und der Maske* (Bern: Francke, 1958);

William D. Williams, *The Stories of C. F. Meyer* (Oxford: Clarendon Press, 1962);

Alfred Zäch, *Conrad Ferdinand Meyer: Dichtkunst als Befreiung aus Lebenshemmnissen* (Frauenfeld & Stuttgart: Huber, 1973);

Rosmarie Zeller and Hans Zeller, "Conrad Ferdinand Meyer," in *Handbuch der deutschen Erzählung,* edited by Karl Konrad Polheim (Düsseldorf: Bagel, 1981), pp. 288–302.

Papers:

Conrad Ferdinand Meyer's papers are in the Zentralbibliothek (Central Library) in Zurich.

Balduin Möllhausen

(27 January 1825 – 28 May 1905)

Horst Dinkelacker
Rhodes College

BOOKS: *Tagebuch einer Reise vom Mississippi nach den Küsten der Südsee* (Leipzig: Mendelssohn, 1858); translated by Mrs. Percy Sinnett as *Diary of a Journey from the Mississippi to the Coasts of the Pacific with a United States Government Expedition* (London: Longman, Brown, Green, Longmans & Roberts, 1858); German version republished as *Wanderungen durch die Prairien und Wüsten des westlichen Nordamerika vom Mississippi nach den Küsten der Südsee, im Gefolge der von der Regierung der Vereinigten Staaten unter Lieutenant Whipple ausgesandten Expedition* (Leipzig: Mendelssohn, 1860);

Der Halbindianer: Erzählung aus dem westlichen Nord-Amerika, 4 volumes (Leipzig: Costenoble, 1861);

Der Flüchtling: Erzählung aus Neu-Mexico und dem angrenzenden Indianergebiet; im Anschluß an den "Halbindianer," 4 volumes (Jena: Costenoble, 1861);

Reisen in die Felsengebirge Nord-Amerikas bis zum Hochplateau von Neu-Mexiko, unternommen als Mitglied der im Auftrage der Regierung der Vereinigten Staaten ausgesandten Colorado-Expedition, 2 volumes (Leipzig: Mendelssohn, 1861);

Der Majordomo: Erzählung aus dem südlichen Kalifornien und Neu-Mexiko; im Anschluß an den "Halbindianer" und "Flüchtling," 4 volumes (Jena: Costenoble, 1863);

Palmblätter und Schneeflocken: Erzählungen aus dem fernen Westen, 2 volumes (Leipzig: Costenoble, 1863);

Das Mormonenmädchen: Eine Erzählung aus der Zeit des Kriegszuges der Vereinigten Staaten gegen die "Heiligen der Letzten Tage" im Jahre 1857–1858, 6 volumes (Jena: Costenoble, 1864);

Reliquien: Erzählungen und Schilderungen aus dem westlichen Nord-Amerika, 3 volumes (Berlin: Janke, 1865);

Die Mandanenwaise: Erzählung aus den Rheinlanden und dem Stromgebiet des Missouri, 4 volumes (Berlin: Janke, 1865);

Balduin Möllhausen in 1854

Der Meerkönig: Eine Erzählung in 3 Abtheilungen, 6 volumes (Jena: Costenoble, 1867);

Nord und Süd: Erzählungen und Schilderungen aus dem westlichen Nord-Amerika, 2 volumes (Jena: Costenoble, 1867);

Der Hochlandpfeifer: Erzählung, 6 volumes (Jena: Costenoble, 1868);

Das Hundertguldenblatt: Erzählung, 3 volumes (Berlin: Janke, 1870);

Der Piratenlieutenant: Roman, 4 volumes (Berlin: Janke, 1870);

Der Kesselflicker: Erzählung in 3 Abtheilungen, 5 volumes (Berlin: Hausfreund-Expedition, 1871);

Das Finkenhaus: Roman, 4 volumes (Berlin: Janke, 1872);

Die Einsiedlerinnen: Roman, 4 volumes (Berlin: Janke, 1873);

Westliche Fährten: Erzählungen und Schilderungen, 2 volumes (Berlin: Janke, 1873);

Das Monogramm: Roman, 4 volumes (Berlin: Janke, 1874);

Die Hyänen des Capitals: Roman, 4 volumes (Berlin: Janke, 1876);

Die Kinder des Sträflings: Roman, 4 volumes (Berlin: Janke, 1876);

Die Reiher: Roman, 3 volumes (Berlin: Janke, 1878);

Die Töchter des Consuls: Roman, 3 volumes (Berlin: Janke, 1880);

Vier Fragmente: Roman, 4 volumes (Berlin: Janke, 1880);

Der Schatz von Quivira: Roman, 3 volumes (Berlin: Janke, 1880);

Der Fanatiker: Roman, 3 volumes (Berlin: Janke, 1883);

Der Leuchtturm am Michigan und andere Erzählungen, introduction by Theodor Fontane (Stuttgart: Spemann, 1883);

Der Haushofmeister: Roman, 3 volumes (Jena: Costenoble, 1884);

Die Trader: Roman, 3 volumes (Berlin: Janke, 1884);

Wildes Blut: Erzählung, 3 volumes (Jena: Costenoble, 1886);

Das Geheimnis des Hulks, 4 volumes (Stuttgart: Spemann, 1886);

Das Loggbuch des Kapitains Eisenfinger: Roman, 3 volumes (Stuttgart: Union, 1887);

Die Familie Melville: Roman aus der Zeit des nordamerikanischen Bürgerkriegs, 3 volumes (Leipzig: Keil, 1889);

Der Fährmann am Kanadian: Roman, 3 volumes (Stuttgart: Union, 1890);

Haus Montague: Roman, 3 volumes (Jena: Costenoble, 1891);

Die beiden Yachten: Roman, 3 volumes (Stuttgart: Union, 1891);

Die Söldlinge: Roman, 3 volumes (Stuttgart: Union, 1892);

Kaptein Meerrose und ihre Kinder: Erzählung, 3 volumes (Berlin: Fontane, 1893);

Der Spion: Roman, 3 volumes (Stuttgart: Union, 1893);

Der Talisman: Roman, 2 volumes (Jena: Costenoble, 1894);

Die Dreilinden-Lieder (Berlin: Mittler, 1896);

Welche von Beiden? Roman, 2 volumes (Stuttgart: Union, 1897);

Der alte Korpsbursche: Roman (Berlin, Eisenach & Leipzig: Hillger, 1898);

Das Fegefeuer in Frappes Wigwam: Roman (Berlin, Eisenach & Leipzig: Hillger, 1900);

Die Verlorene; Die Bärenhaut: Zwei Erzählungen (Berlin, Eisenach & Leipzig: Hillger, 1903);

Bilder aus dem Reiche der Natur (Berlin: Reimer, 1904);

Sankt Elmsfeuer und andere Novellen (Berlin, Eisenach & Leipzig: Hillger, 1905);

Der Vaquero: Roman (Stuttgart: Union, 1905);

Illustrierte Romane, Reisen und Abenteuer, 30 volumes, edited by Dietrich Theden (Leipzig: List, 1906–1913).

SELECTED PERIODICAL PUBLICATIONS –
UNCOLLECTED: "Indianer auf dem Kriegspfad," *Die Gartenlaube,* 43 (1862): 325–327;

"Die Mission San Louis Obispo," *Deutsches Magazin zur Unterhaltung und Belehrung,* 3 (1863): 184–186;

"Monterey in Kalifornien," *Deutsches Magazin zur Unterhaltung und Belehrung,* 3 (1863): 340–342;

"Das Grab in der Steppe," *Illustrierte Welt,* 2 (1872): 29–31;

"Senior Demonio," *Westermann's Illustrierte Monatshefte,* 45 (1878/1879): 582–597;

"Die Flucht aus dem Rebellenlager," *Das neue Buch der Welt,* 1 (1879): 392–412;

"Ein Tag auf dem Ufer des Colorado," *Das neue Buch der Welt,* 1 (1879): 42–47;

"Mein gutmütiger Freund," *Westermann's Illustrierte Monatshefte,* 49 (1880): 145–165;

"Engelid," *Die Gartenlaube,* 22 (1882): 357–360; 23 (1882): 373–376; 24 (1882): 389–392; 25 (1882): 405–410; 26 (1882): 421–424;

"Der Chef des Vigilance Komitees," *Vom Fels zum Meer,* 2 (1883): 282–298, 442–456;

"Der Finkenkrug," *Großer Volkskalender des Lahrer Hinkenden Boten für das Jahr 1905* (1905): 129–148;

"Die alte Harfenistin," *Großer Volkskalender des Lahrer Hinkenden Boten für das Jahr 1906* (1906): 97–108.

Balduin Möllhausen was the most prolific and most widely read German exponent of the popular genre of travel and adventure literature, especially the Amerikaroman (transatlantic novel) in the sec-

A party of Sioux sketched by Möllhausen in 1851, during his first trip to America. The original drawing was destroyed in World War II (Staatliches Museum für Volkerkunde, Berlin).

ond half of the nineteenth century. This genre was inspired by James Fenimore Cooper, whose novels were an immediate success when they appeared on the European literary scene in the 1820s. In Germany it reached its apotheosis with the fanciful tales of Karl May at the turn of the century. Unlike May, Möllhausen and earlier, more realistic practitioners of the genre, such as Charles Sealsfield (pseudonym of Karl Postl), Friedrich Armand Strubberg, and Friedrich Gerstäcker, had firsthand experience of America and did much to popularize its image in Germany. The Amerikaroman fulfilled both escapist desires and a need for information, reflecting the manifold ties German readers of all classes had to the New World as a consequence of the mass emigration of the nineteenth century.

Möllhausen was born on 27 January 1825 in Bonn. His childhood was overshadowed by the death of his mother, née Elisabeth, Baroness von Falkenstein, in 1837 and the absence of his father, a Prussian artillery officer turned civil engineer, who sometime before had gone to Greece and never returned. Möllhausen and his two younger siblings were placed under the guardianship of Count Krassow and their education entrusted to an aunt, Adelheid von Falkenstein, on an estate in Mecklenburg. He was sent back to Bonn to attend the gym-

nasium, which, to his lifelong regret and resentment, he had to leave when he turned fourteen. Instead of allowing him to become a painter, as he had hoped, his aristocratic relatives summoned him back to Mecklenburg for a career in agriculture. He remained there until 1846, when he entered military service. Finally, in 1849, like so many of his countrymen, he sailed for America with his life's savings in his pocket. This decision seems to have been prompted not by any political motivations but by a dissatisfaction with the lack of direction in his life, as well as a longing for faraway lands inherited from his itinerant father and nurtured by the tales of Cooper and Washington Irving. For the next two years the footloose immigrant roamed the frontier in Illinois and Missouri, indulging his romantic fantasies and occasionally working as a sign painter or court clerk.

In the spring of 1851 Möllhausen met the daring and dashing Duke Paul Wilhelm von Württemberg, a scientific traveler who modeled himself on Alexander von Humboldt. Impressed by Möllhausen's breeding and manners, his artistic talents, but above all his courage, the duke took on the eager greenhorn as a scout and draftsman for his journey from the Mississippi River across the plains to Fort Laramie. The trip there went smoothly, but on the way back they were beset by a series of misfortunes, including a prairie fire and encounters with hostile Indians. When an early winter storm killed their horses they were left stranded on the prairie, facing death by starvation and cold. A mail coach appeared but could take only one of them back to civilization; the other would have to remain with their belongings until help could be sent. The lot favored the duke, and thus, on 25 November 1851 began Möllhausen's Robinsonade (Robinson Crusoe-like existence) on the banks of Sandy Hill Creek. Cold, hunger, wolves, and loneliness strained his physical and mental capacities to the limit; he also endured the moral agony of having to kill two Indians to save his own life. Finally, in early January 1852 a band of hunting Otoes rescued him. He only halfheartedly resisted their good-humored attempts to "Indianize" him. On his safe return, he spent an additional three months with the Omahas.

When the duke heard of his young companion's "miraculous" escape, he invited Möllhausen to his home in New Orleans. A few months later Möllhausen accepted an offer from the Prussian consul in Saint Louis to accompany a shipment of animals to the Berlin Zoo. In January 1853, after an absence of almost four years, Möllhausen returned home.

Through the director of the zoo he was introduced to Humboldt, in whose house he also met his future wife, Carolina Alexandra Seifert, who was supposedly the daughter of Humboldt's private secretary and majordomo. While it remains unresolved whether Carolina was actually the natural daughter of Humboldt, as was rumored, she did enjoy the old man's special favor, which was extended to her suitor. The universally respected Nestor of scientific travelers and natural philosophers, who was well into his eighties at the time, became Möllhausen's mentor and tireless patron, guiding his fledgling artistic talent, encouraging and helping to polish his first writing efforts, and introducing him at court. Under the experienced and influential hands of Humboldt, Möllhausen's life took shape intellectually, professionally, socially, and materially.

In April 1853, after Humboldt wrote a strong letter of recommendation for him, Möllhausen set out for Washington, D.C., to join the Whipple expedition, one of four charged with determining the most practicable railroad route from the Mississippi to the Pacific. They were to proceed from Fort Smith, Arkansas, along the thirty-fifth parallel to southern California. Möllhausen was appointed as topographer. On this mission, which lasted almost

eleven months, he perfected his artistic technique, tested his narrative skills by entertaining his companions around the campfire with stories of his exploits with Duke Paul Wilhelm, and gained a firsthand view of the Southwest and its Mexican and Indian inhabitants and culture.

In January 1855 Möllhausen was appointed custodian of the royal libraries in and around Potsdam, a sinecure that left him largely unencumbered to pursue his writing. On 6 February he married Carolina. His diary of the Whipple expedition, *Tagebuch einer Reise vom Mississippi nach den Küsten der Südsee* (1858; translated as *Diary of a Journey from the Mississippi to the Coasts of the Pacific,* 1858), was actively promoted in the right circles by Humboldt. It was well received, and even at this early stage in his career critics named him in the same breath with two artists with whom he was to be compared in the future: George Catlin, famed for his portraits of Indians and scenes of tribal life; and Cooper.

By the time these favorable reviews appeared, the author was on his way to accompany Lieutenant Ives, whom he had met on the Whipple expedition, on a mission to survey the Colorado River. Compared to his first excursion to the Southwest, the trip yielded only minimal results; accordingly, his account of that expedition, *Reisen in die Felsengebirge Nord-Amerikas* (Travels to the Rocky Mountains of North America, 1861), reveals a more somber mood. His most memorable experience on that often frustrating venture was his descent into the Grand Canyon, whose grandeur he was one of the first to capture in words and sketches. After the expedition disbanded in Albuquerque, he took a nostalgic journey across the prairie. On 1 September 1858, setting sail from New York, the thirty-three-year-old Möllhausen bade his final farewell to the land of his youthful dreams.

His journeyman years at an end, the formerly restless traveler settled into the writing career for which his American experiences and Humboldt's patronage had laid the foundation. For the next forty-seven years – the first twenty-eight in Potsdam, and after 1886 living in Berlin – he led the outwardly uneventful life of a solid burgher. Drawing inspiration from the memorabilia, drawings, and sketches from his travels, which surrounded him in his study in a careful arrangement, Möllhausen turned out an immense oeuvre. Its extent is difficult to ascertain, as he had works published in newspapers, magazines, and anthologies and by a variety of publishers. It is also difficult to classify, since he made no attempt to differentiate his tales according to genre; but novels constitute the bulk of

Fort Smith, Arkansas, from which the Whipple expedition set out in 1853 to find the most practicable railroad route from the Mississippi to the Pacific coast. This lithograph, from a sketch by Möllhausen, was included in the expedition's official report.

his works, which were highly popular between 1860 and 1880.

Möllhausen's first three novels – *Der Halbindianer* (The Half-breed, 1861), *Der Flüchtling* (The Refugee, 1861), and *Der Majordomo* (1863), which form a loose trilogy – as well as *Das Mormonenmädchen* (The Mormon Maiden, 1864) and *Die Mandanenwaise* (The Mandan Orphan, 1865) are set exclusively on American soil, primarily on the frontier in Missouri, Louisiana, New Mexico, and southern California. With *Der Meerkönig* (The Sea-King, 1867) Möllhausen found the characteristic formula for his novels, for the most part dividing each of them thenceforth evenly between the New World and the Old. Germany, Scotland, and Norway provided the backdrop for the European part of the action. This pattern was temporarily abandoned in his social novels *Das Monogramm* (1874), a diatribe against the Jesuits at the height of the Kulturkampf (the conflict between the German government under Chancellor Otto von Bismarck and the Roman Catholic church), and *Die Hyänen des Capitals* (The Hyenas of Capital, 1876), in which he bemoaned what he considered the excesses of American-style capitalism. In his late writings he again placed the action exclusively on the American continent, as in the Civil War novels *Die Familie*

Melville (The Melville Family, 1889) and *Welche von Beiden?* (Which of the Two?, 1897). Finally, in his swan song, *Der Vaquero* (The Cowboy, 1905), the protagonist uncharacteristically refuses to set foot on European soil despite the prospects of a rich inheritance and a rise into the ranks of the aristocracy.

"Erinnerungen, die niemals bleichen" (memories that never fade) constitute the main inspiration and impetus for Möllhausen's writings. Privileged to have experienced a world that already was rapidly vanishing, he felt it incumbent on himself to capture and preserve it, to remember and remind, to conjure up and warn. Möllhausen saw on the American frontier the unfolding of a drama of world-historic proportions that had to end with the victory of what he considered a higher civilization. This superiority, however, in his view, also entailed a higher moral responsibility toward the vanquished – natural as well as human – whose fervent and nostalgic spokesman Möllhausen remained throughout his writings. For example, the Indians deserve compassion, tolerance, and understanding; above all, they need help in rising to a higher level, and this help is symbolized in the frequent marriages between Indian women and white men in his works. The whites are almost always either uncouth

Painting by Möllhausen showing the Whipple expedition crossing the Colorado River (Whipple Collection, Oklahoma Historical Society)

French-Canadian mountain men who are unhampered by traditional social and sexual restrictions, or cultured and morally impeccable German immigrants who are setting an example for the often narrow-minded and calculating if not racist "Yankees." Throughout his oeuvre Möllhausen never ceased to raise his voice against any form of religious fanaticism, of which he particularly accuses the Mormons – for example, in *Das Mormonenmädchen* and *Der Fanatiker* (The Fanatic, 1883) – and especially of racism, condemning slavery as the worst of all institutions. Not surprisingly, the Civil War, of which he had no firsthand experience, occupies a prominent place in his writings. In addition to *Die Familie Melville* and *Welche von Beiden?*, works concerned with the war include the stories "Die Meermuschel" (The Sea Shell) and "Whip-poor-Will" in *Reliquien* (Relics, 1865) and "Alice Ludlow" in *Nord und Süd* (North and South, 1867) and the novels *Der Piratenlieutenant* (The Pirate Lieutenant, 1870), *Das Finkenhaus* (The House of Fink, 1872), and *Der Spion* (The Spy, 1893). Despite his lifelong preoccupation with this watershed period in American history, his treatment of it remained simplistic and superficial; his sympathies were unequivocally with the North.

Möllhausen was most at home with the trappers, hunters, mountain men, settlers, and pioneers who sought on the frontier the fulfillment of the American dream of freedom and opportunity. Probably reflecting the declining number of emigrants from Bismarck's Germany and the country's growing assertiveness and pride in the wake of national unification in 1871, Möllhausen often saw that promise closer to home: for many of his German characters, as well as for the author himself, the ulti-

mate destiny – and reward – was a return to the fatherland. Before they could settle there, however, they had to prove themselves in the New World, to which an unkind fate, conceited and scheming relatives, or vague romantic and politically naive notions had driven them. America's harsh realities dealt these wanderers a lesson in the practical school of life. After they had passed the test and met the challenge – or come into a nice inheritance when their true identity was revealed after many vicissitudes – they were allowed to return to the "center of civilization." In these vaguely educational novels the author envisioned for the Old and New Worlds a mutually beneficial division of labor in which "Germany sings, paints, composes and writes, America speculates and calculates," as a character remarks in *Der Haushofmeister* (The Majordomo, 1884). Möllhausen's image of America is a mixture of firsthand observations and traditional European clichés and is tinged with melancholy nostalgia as well as utopian optimism.

The author's repeatedly stated approach to his writings was the wish to combine information with entertainment. Thus, he intended his first novel as an illustration of his two travelogues; and in the foreword to its sequel he emphasized that by giving unadulterated portrayals of nature and of peoples and their customs he hoped to elevate his fiction above the level of mere entertainment literature. He only rarely achieved that aim in his novels, where the informative core is often buried under far-fetched and convoluted plots and the characters are one-dimensional and predictable. In many of his shorter tales and novellas, however, Möllhausen achieved that balance of information and entertain-

The Grand Canyon (lithograph after a sketch made by Möllhausen during the Whipple expedition)

ment with vivid, realistic, and insightful portrayals of frontier life and nature. Noteworthy examples, virtually all from the first two decades of his career, are the tales "Der Steppenbrand" (The Prairie Fire) and "Der Postläufer von Wisconsin" (The Mail Runner from Wisconsin), vignettes of the encounter of European and Indian values and expectations in his collection *Palmblätter und Schneeflocken* (Palm Leaves and Snow Flakes, 1863); "Der Hornfrosch" (The Horned Toad), "Die Castagnetten" (The Castanets), "Der Lederrock" (The Buckskin Coat), and "Der Tabaksbeutel" (The Tobacco Pouch), all of which revolve around a central object evoking memories of frontier life, in *Reliquien*; "Whip-poor-Will," a tragic love story set against the background of the Civil War in the same collection, which contains more memorable examples of his art than any other; "Der erste Baum zur Blockhütte" (The First Tree for the Log Cabin), where a nomadic hunter is elevated into the more settled existence of the pioneers, in *Nord und Süd*; "Fleur rouge" (Red Flower), humorously depicting the happy union of a trapper and his Indian wife, and "Der Fallensteller" (The Trapper), in *Westliche Fährten* (Western Tracks, 1873); and "Mein gutmütiger Freund" (My Good-Natured Friend, 1880), his best treatment of America's complex racial situation.

"Der Fallensteller," which was first published in the periodical *Der Hausfreund* (The Family Friend) in 1868, illustrates his best efforts. A romance and a story within a story, it treats Möllhausen's favorite theme of the conflict of nature and civilization by weaving together inspirations from Cooper's tales and his own experiences. On the Kansas frontier the itinerant author enjoys the hospitality of a group of pioneers who have fled to this remote corner in the hope of making their fourth and final home far from the encroachment of towns and railroads. The site they have selected is blocked by an immense oak tree, which, regrettably, has to make room for progress. But an old trapper arises from behind the old tree to defend nature and to demand respect for the beloved he had buried there forty-six years previously. To the reverently listening settlers he tells, in sometimes long-winded detail, the moving story of his unhappy love. He had spent a happy youth untouched by civilization but was later gently educated and polished by a young woman who had fled from the unsolicited advances of her lascivious cousin. Aptly named Tomaso Urbano, the latter destroyed their idyll when he murdered her out of jealousy.

The next morning, the pioneers pursue the work that must be done; but, deeply moved by the trapper's tale, they do so more thoughtfully and without their usual boisterousness and only cut down the tree after they have marked the grave and reserved a place next to it for him. The old trapper takes his leave, and "gesenkten Hauptes, die Büchse quer vor sich auf dem Sattel" (his head bowed, the musket in front of him across the saddle), he rides into the distance until he merges with the prairie.

Despite superficial resemblances to Cooper's Leatherstocking tales, "Der Fallensteller" bears Möllhausen's particular stamp. Characteristically, the author places himself between the backward-looking trapper and the future-oriented pioneers. Möllhausen the romantic realist sympathizes with both: he recognizes nature's and the old man's entitlement to respect and piety, and he feels at home among the optimistic settlers and their rightful expectations. To the latter he lends his helping hand, but his heart belongs to the wizened trapper. Thus Möllhausen harmonizes clashing demands and shies away, as he almost invariably does, from tragic conflict.

"Der Fallensteller" is both a personal and a literary self-portrait. Möllhausen appears as his own youthful self as well as in the guise of the old trapper, who, through the evocation of the past, tries to stem the tide of change. Despite the avoidance of tragedy, there is an underlying element of resignation, even futility.

Although he had never harbored any illusions about his artistic endeavors, in the last two decades of his life, when his fame began to wane and his popularity was eclipsed by May's, Möllhausen was increasingly beset by the feeling that he had outlived himself and that his writings would not stand the test of time. In *Der Vaquero* he asks his readers' indulgence for the great, even excessive number of works he had written – an acknowledgment that his prolific output may have come at the expense of quality. Nevertheless, his fellow author Theodor Fontane, in the introduction to Möllhausen's collection of stories *Der Leuchtturm am Michigan und andere Erzählungen* (The Lighthouse on Lake Michigan and Other Tales, 1883), praised him as an "Erzähler pur sang" (a pure-blooded narrator).

Möllhausen's innate optimism prevented him from following his literary alter ego in "Der Fallensteller" into self-imposed seclusion from the world. He was especially popular with the officers in Potsdam; joined a Masonic lodge in Berlin; and was a regular at the convivial gatherings of Prince Friedrich Karl von Preuen at his hunting refuge, Dreilinden, outside Berlin, where Möllhausen was appreciated as a raconteur and poet. With his flow-

ing white beard, the "Alte Trapper" (Old Trapper), as he was known, was also a familiar figure in the streets of Berlin. After his death on 28 May 1905 he was, following his wishes, buried in the old buckskin coat in which he claimed to have spent his happiest hours and from which he had drawn personal and artistic inspiration. Only the first of his two travelogues and none of his sketches, short stories, novellas, tales, and novels have been translated into English, although America is their central focus and the best not only can claim literary value but also would hold considerable cultural and historical interest for an American audience.

Biography:

Andreas Graf, *Der Tod der Wölfe: Das abenteuerliche und bürgerliche Leben des Romanschrifters und Amerikareisenden Balduin Möllhausen (1825–1905). Mit einem Dokumenten- und Briefanhang* (Berlin: Duncker & Humblot, 1991).

References:

D. L. Ashliman, "The American West in Nineteenth Century German Literature," Ph.D. dissertation, Rutgers University, 1969;

Preston A. Barba, *Balduin Möllhausen: The German Cooper,* Americana Germanica, no. 17 (Philadelphia: University of Pennsylvania Press, 1914);

Barba, "Cooper in Germany," *Indiana University Studies,* 2 (May 1914): 49–104;

Barba, "The North American Indian in German Fiction," *German American Annals,* 11 (1913): 143–174;

Rudolph Beissel, *Von Atala bis Winnetou: Die Väter des Western-Romans* (Brunswick: Graff, 1978);

Ray Allen Billington, *Land of Savagery, Land of Promise: The European Image of the American Frontier in the Nineteenth Century* (New York: Norton, 1981), pp. 39–40, 74;

Peter J. Brenner, "Ein Reisender und Romancier des 19. Jahrhunderts: Balduin Möllhausen," *Die Horen,* 31, no. 2 (1986): 74–78;

Horst Dinkelacker, *Amerika zwischen Traum und Desillusionierung im Leben und Werk des Erfolgsschriftstellers Balduin Möllhausen (1825–1905)* (New York: Lang, 1990);

William H. Goetzmann, *Exploration and Empire: The Explorer and the Scientist in the Winning of the American West* (New York: Knopf, 1966), pp. 289, 308;

Karl Gutzmer, "Balduin Möllhausen: Eine biographische Skizze," *Bonner Geschichtsblätter,* 34 (1982): 727–739;

Horst Hartmann, *Catlin und Möllhausen: Zwei Interpreten der Indianer und des Alten Westens,* second edition (Berlin: Reimer, 1984);

David H. Miller, "Balduin Möllhausen: A Prussian's Image of the American West," Ph.D. dissertation, University of New Mexico at Albuquerque, 1970;

Miller, "The Ives Expedition Revisited: A Prussian's Impressions," *Journal of Arizona History,* 13 (Spring 1972): 1-25;

Miller, "The Ives Expedition Revisited: Overland into the Grand Canyon," *Journal of Arizona History,* 13 (Autumn 1972): 177-196;

Miller, "A Prussian on the Plains: Balduin Möllhausen's Impressions," *Great Plains Journal,* 12 (Spring 1973): 175-193;

Volker Neuhaus, "Der Unterhaltungsroman im 19. Jahrhundert," in *Handbuch des deutschen Romans,* edited by Helmut Koopmann (Düsseldorf: Bagel, 1983), pp. 404-417;

Norbert Oellers, "Geschichte der Literatur in den Rheinlanden seit 1815," in *Rheinische Geschichte,* volume 3: *Wirtschaft und Kultur im 19. und 20. Jahrhundert,* edited by Franz Patri and Georg Droege (Düsseldorf: Schwann, 1979), pp. 611-612;

Hans Plischke, *Von Cooper bis Karl May: Eine Geschichte des völkerkundlichen Reise- und Abenteuerromans* (Düsseldorf: Droste, 1951);

Karl-Jürgen Roth, "Balduin Möllhausen: Vom Reiseschriftsteller zum Romanautor I," *Magazin für Abenteuer-, Reise- und Unterhaltungsliteratur,* 54 (1987): 39-43;

Roth, "Balduin Möllhausen: Vom Reiseschriftsteller zum Romanautor II," *Magazin für Abenteuer-, Reise- und Unterhaltungsliteratur,* 55 (1987): 4-18;

Helmut Schmiedt, "Balduin Möllhausen und Karl May: Reiseziel St. Louis," in *Karl May: Text und Kritik,* edited by Heinz Ludwig Arnold (Munich: Edition text + kritik, 1987), pp. 127-145;

Gustav Sichelschmidt, *Liebe, Mord und Abenteuer: Eine Geschichte der deutschen Unterhaltungsliteratur* (Berlin: Haude & Spener, 1970), pp. 174-175, 203;

Bernd Steinbrink, *Abenteuerliteratur des 19. Jahrhunderts in Deutschland: Studien zu einer vernachlässigten Gattung* (Tübingen: Niemeyer, 1983), pp. 158-168;

Robert Taft, "The Pictorial Record of the Old West: VI. Heinrich Balduin Möllhausen," *Kansas Historical Quarterly,* 16 (August 1948): 225-244;

Muriel H. Wright and George H. Shirk, "Artist Möllhausen in Oklahoma 1853," *Chronicles of Oklahoma,* 21 (Winter 1853-1854): 391-441.

Papers:
Letters by and about Balduin Möllhausen are in the Staatsbibliothek Preuischer Kulturbesitz (State Library of Prussian Cultural Property), Berlin; the Deutsches Archäologisches Institut (German Archaeological Institute), Berlin; the Germanisches Nationalmuseum (German National Museum), Nuremberg; the Hessische Landesbibliothek (Hessian Provincial Library), Wiesbaden; the Deutsches Literaturarchiv (German Literature Archives), Marbach; the Stadt- und Landesbibliothek (Municipal and Provincial Library), Dortmund; the Universitäts- und Stadtbibliothek (University and Municipal Library), Cologne; and the National Anthropological Archives of the Smithsonian Institution, Washington, D.C.

Friedrich Nietzsche

(15 October 1844 – 25 August 1900)

Adrian Del Caro
University of Colorado

BOOKS: *Die Geburt der Tragödie aus dem Geiste der Musik* (Leipzig: Fritzsch, 1872; revised, 1874); revised as *Die Geburt der Tragödie: Oder Griechenthum und Pessimismus. Neue Ausgabe mit dem Versuch einer Selbstkritik* (Leipzig: Fritzsch, 1886); translated by William A. Haussmann as *The Birth of Tragedy* (1909), volume 1 of *The Complete Works of Friedrich Nietzsche*, 18 volumes, edited by Oscar Levy (London: Foulis, 1909–1913);

Unzeitgemäße Betrachtungen. Erstes Stück: David Strauß der Bekenner und der Schriftsteller (Leipzig: Fritzsch, 1873); translated by Anthony Ludovici as "Thoughts out of Season: David Strauss the Confessor and the Writer," in volume 4 (1910) of *The Complete Works of Friedrich Nietzsche*;

Unzeitgemäße Betrachtungen. Zweites Stück: Vom Nutzen und Nachtheil der Historie für das Leben (Leipzig: Fritzsch, 1874); translated by Adrian Collins as "On the Use and Disadvantage of History," in volume 5 (1909) of *The Complete Works of Friedrich Nietzsche*;

Unzeitgemäße Betrachtungen. Drittes Stück: Schopenhauer als Erzieher (Chemnitz: Schmeitzner, 1874); translated by Collins as "Schopenhauer as Educator," in volume 5 (1909) of *The Complete Works of Friedrich Nietzsche*;

Unzeitgemäße Betrachtungen. Viertes Stück: Richard Wagner in Bayreuth (Chemnitz: Schmeitzner, 1876); translated by Ludovici as "Richard Wagner in Bayreuth," in volume 4 (1910) of *The Complete Works of Friedrich Nietzsche*;

Menschliches, Allzumenschliches: Ein Buch für freie Geister, 3 volumes (Chemnitz: Schmeitzner, 1878–1880) – includes as volume 2, *Menschliches, Allzumenschliches: Ein Buch für freie Geister. Anhang: Vermischte Meinungen und Sprüche* (1879); as volume 3, *Der Wanderer und sein Schatten* (1880); revised edition, 2 volumes (Leipzig: Fritzsch, 1886); translated by Helen Zimmern and Paul V. Cohn as *Human, All-Too-Human*,

Friedrich Nietzsche in 1887

volumes 6 and 7 (1909, 1911) of *The Complete Works of Friedrich Nietzsche*;

Morgenröthe: Gedanken über die moralischen Vorurtheile (Chemnitz: Schmeitzner, 1881; enlarged edition, Leipzig: Fritzsch, 1887); translated by Johanna Volz as *The Dawn of Day* (London: Unwin, 1903; New York: Macmillan, 1903);

Die fröhliche Wissenschaft (Chemnitz: Schmeitzner, 1882; enlarged edition, Leipzig: Fritzsch, 1887); translated by Thomas Common as *The Joyful Wisdom*, in volume 10 (1910) of *The Complete Works of Friedrich Nietzsche*;

Also sprach Zarathustra: Ein Buch für Alle und Keinen, 4 volumes (volumes 1–3, Chemnitz: Schmeitzner, 1883–1884; volume 4, Leipzig: Naumann, 1885); translated by Alexander Tille as *Thus Spake Zarathustra: A Book for All and None* (London: Henry, 1896; New York: Macmillan, 1896);

Jenseits von Gut und Böse: Vorspiel einer Philosophie der Zukunft (Leipzig: Naumann, 1886); translated by Zimmern as *Beyond Good and Evil,* volume 12 (1909) of *The Complete Works of Friedrich Nietzsche;*

Zur Genealogie der Moral: Eine Streitschrift (Leipzig: Naumann, 1887); translated by Haussmann as "A Genealogy of Morals," in *A Genealogy of Morals; Poems,* translated by Haussmann and John Gray (New York: Macmillan, 1897; London: Unwin, 1899);

Der Fall Wagner: Ein Musikanten-Problem (Leipzig: Naumann, 1888); translated by Common as "The Case of Wagner," in *The Case of Wagner, Nietzsche contra Wagner, The Twilight of the Idols, The Antichrist* (London: Henry, 1896; New York: Macmillan, 1896);

Götzen-Dämmerung oder Wie man mit dem Hammer philosophirt (Leipzig: Naumann, 1889); translated by Common as "The Twilight of the Idols," in *The Case of Wagner, Nietzsche contra Wagner, The Twilight of the Idols, The Antichrist;*

Nietzsche contra Wagner: Aktenstücke eines Psychologen (Leipzig: Naumann, 1889); translated by Common as "Nietzsche contra Wagner," in *The Case of Wagner, Nietzsche contra Wagner, The Twilight of the Idols, The Antichrist;*

Nietzsches Werke: Gesamtausgabe, edited by Peter Gast (Leipzig: Naumann, 1892–1894);

Nietzsches Werke: Großoktavausgabe, 15 volumes, edited by the Nietzsche Archive (Leipzig: Naumann, 1894–1904) – includes in volume 8 (1895), "Der Antichrist: Fluch auf das Christenthum," translated by Common as "The Antichrist," in *The Case of Wagner, Nietzsche contra Wagner, The Twilight of the Idols, The Antichrist;* in volume 15 (1901), "Der Wille zur Macht," translated by Ludovici as *The Will to Power,* volumes 15 and 16 (1909, 1910) of *The Complete Works of Friedrich Nietzsche;*

Gedichte und Sprüche, edited by Elisabeth Förster-Nietzsche (Leipzig: Naumann, 1908);

Ecce homo: Wie man wird, was man ist (Leipzig: Insel, 1908); translated by Ludovici as "Ecce Homo," in *The Complete Works of Friedrich Nietzsche,* volume 17 (1911);

Friedrich Nietzsche: Werke, 4 volumes, edited by Karl Schlechta (Munich: Hanser, 1954);

Kritische Gesamtausgabe, 30 volumes, edited by Giorgio Colli and Mazzino Montinari (Berlin: De Gruyter, 1967–1978);

Kritische Studienausgabe: Sämtliche Werke, 15 volumes, edited by Colli and Montinari (Berlin & Munich: De Gruyter & Deutscher Taschenbuch Verlag, 1980).

Editions in English: *The Complete Works of Friedrich Nietzsche,* 18 volumes, edited by Oscar Levy (New York: Macmillan, 1909–1911; Edinburgh & London: Foulis, 1909–1913);

The Portable Nietzsche, edited and translated by Walter Kaufmann (New York: Viking, 1954);

The Will to Power, edited by Kaufmann, translated by Kaufmann and R. J. Hollingdale (New York: Random House, 1967);

Basic Writings of Nietzsche, edited and translated by Kaufmann (New York: Modern Library, 1968);

The Gay Science, translated by Kaufmann (New York: Random House, 1974);

Daybreak: Thoughts on the Prejudices of Morality, translated by Hollingdale (Cambridge & New York: Cambridge University Press, 1982);

Untimely Meditations, translated by Hollingdale (Cambridge & New York: Cambridge University Press, 1983) – comprises *David Strauss, the Confessor and the Writer, On the Uses and Disadvantage of History for Life, Schopenhauer as Educator, Richard Wagner in Bayreuth;*

Human, All Too Human, translated by Hollingdale (Cambridge & New York: Cambridge University Press, 1986);

The Poetry of Friedrich Nietzsche, translated by Philip Grundlehner (New York: Oxford University Press, 1986).

Virtually unknown and ignored during his productive life, Friedrich Nietzsche lapsed into insanity in the first days of 1889 and only glimpsed the beginning of his rapid ascent to fame and controversy throughout the world. By 1900 Nietzsche's thoughts were resonating in the works of George Bernard Shaw, Hugo von Hofmannsthal, August Strindberg, and Thomas Mann. The writer who advocated bringing "Heroismus in die Erkenntnis" (heroism into knowledge) waged spirited campaigns against intellectual smugness, metaphysics, Christianity, romanticism, nationalism, idealism, and a host of modern society's chief ills. Nietzsche earned the distinction of being history's most eloquent wielder of the *anti* while, paradoxically, serving as a champion of life-affirmation. To a greater extent than any predecessor Nietzsche elevated philosophical expression to an art. His approach to issues was influenced by comparisons between ancients and moderns; his overriding concern for the condition of the modern individual, forced to come to terms with egalitarian institutions and principles, provides coherence to his writings, which he refused to systematize. Nietzsche rejected the age-old academic standard of comprehensive philosophical systems purporting to illuminate "reality" but resulting only in metaphors; the will to systematize, he said in his typically succinct style, shows a lack of integrity. After a hundred years of debate in a variety of disciplines, Nietzsche's mastery of language and his psychological insights continue to fascinate commentators and expand the horizons of art and theory.

Born on 15 October 1844 in the small town of Röcken, Friedrich Wilhelm Nietzsche (he was named for the Prussian king Friedrich Wilhelm IV, whose birthday he shared) was expected to follow in the footsteps of his father, the Lutheran pastor Karl Ludwig Nietzsche. The father's death in 1849 at thirty-five, due to a condition diagnosed as Gehirnerweichung (softening of the brain), left Nietzsche with his mother, Franziska (née Oehler); his younger sister, Elisabeth; and a brother, born in 1848, who died in 1850. The family resettled in 1850 in nearby Naumburg, where they lived with Nietzsche's grandmother Erdmuthe Nietzsche and two maiden aunts. In Naumburg, Nietzsche was tutored along with two other boys; one of them was Gustav Krug, whose father was a music patron and a friend of the composer Felix Mendelssohn-Bartholdy. Nietzsche's earliest exposure to music took place in this setting. His boyhood penchant for setting psalms to music and writing religious poems stands in stark contrast to his writing in 1888 of "Der Antichrist" (1895; translated as "The Antichrist," 1896). Beginning around his twelfth year Nietzsche was stricken by severe headaches; the condition grew worse as he aged.

After three years at the local gymnasium, Nietzsche transferred in 1858 to the Latin school Schulpforta, from which such notables as Friedrich Gottlieb Klopstock and Johann Gottlieb Fichte had graduated. There he received rigorous training in Latin, Greek, and German. Throughout his adolescence Nietzsche's major interests were music and literature; by the time he left Schulpforta for the University of Bonn in 1864 he was no longer committed to theological study, and a year later he informed his mother that he was switching to philology.

Nietzsche in 1861

Under the auspices of growing Prussian strength, Germany was on the road to nationhood at the same time that Nietzsche was entering adulthood; the sense of destiny fermenting within the diverse German lands was bound to infect Nietzsche's generation.

At Bonn, Nietzsche joined the Franconia, a fraternity popular among aspiring philologists, but demonstrated his independence by preferring lectures and discussions to the drinking and carousing of his peers. Nietzsche behaved more soberly and thoughtfully than other young men; his sense of responsibility probably resulted from being the only male in his family. During a visit to nearby Cologne in 1865 he engaged a guide to take him on a walking tour of the city; at the end of the tour he instructed the man to take him to a restaurant. Instead, Nietzsche found himself in a bordello, where, as he explained to his friend Paul Deussen the next day, he was at such a loss when surrounded by the scantily clad prostitutes that he instinctively approached the piano (the only creature in the place with a soul, he said), struck a few chords, and, as if liberated by the music, walked out. This incident was richly detailed and embellished by Thomas Mann in his

Nietzsche (second row, third from left, with hand on forehead) and other members of the fraternity Franconia at Bonn University in 1865

novel *Doktor Faustus* (1947; translated as *Doctor Faustus*, 1948), in which the protagonist, Adrian Leverkühn, is partly based on Nietzsche. It is possible that Nietzsche later visited a brothel and contracted syphilis: the disease that plunged him into madness may have resulted from an infection sustained during his student years.

When the prominent philologist Friedrich Ritschl left Bonn in 1865 for the University of Leipzig, Nietzsche also transferred to Leipzig and began a close association with Ritschl. Following Ritschl's advice, Nietzsche helped to establish a philology club at Leipzig. Beside the real mentor, Ritschl, stood a spiritual mentor who was to compete with the philologist for Nietzsche's attention: Arthur Schopenhauer, whose masterpiece, *Die Welt als Wille und Vorstellung* (1819; translated as *The World as Will and Idea,* 1883–1886), Nietzsche discovered in a secondhand bookstore. Nietzsche served a compulsory stint in the military from 1867 to 1868, but he injured himself while mounting his horse and required several weeks to convalesce. When he made the acquaintance of Richard Wagner in 1868, through a meeting arranged by Ritschl's wife, Sophie, the major ingredients of Nietzsche's future

philosophical thought were in place: philology, with a focus on Greek drama; philosophy in the manner of the Romantic Schopenhauer; and the music of Wagner, whom Nietzsche came to regard as the apotheosis of Schopenhauerian genius. Nietzsche's interest in literature and music had seduced him away from theology, and now a growing passion for philosophy and music was beginning to weaken his commitment to philology.

During his years at Leipzig, Nietzsche began to see himself as a continuator of the tradition of German idealism fueled by the philosophy of Immanuel Kant, promulgated in the highly idealistic writings of Friedrich Schiller and Schopenhauer, and culminating in Wagner's concept of the Gesamtkunstwerk (total work of art). Nietzsche was blessed with two powerful and influential patrons, each representing a different side of his character: Ritschl appealed to the scholar in Nietzsche, who was a gifted student of languages and an ardent admirer of ancient Greek culture; Wagner appealed to the artist in him and also satisfied his craving for philosophical substance, since Wagner was not only a composer but also a theorist and avowed Schopenhauerian. It began to seem to Nietzsche that

Nietzsche (seated at left) and other members of the philology club he helped found at the University of Leipzig

philology was too narrow a field for him, and he entertained the idea of writing a dissertation on the concept of the organic in philosophy since Kant.

Whatever wavering Nietzsche might have experienced came to an end in 1869, when Ritschl recommended him for a position at the University of Basel. Nietzsche had had articles published in a philology journal, but he had not written a dissertation; yet he became a professor of Greek language and literature in February 1869. In the spring he was awarded the doctoral degree by the University of Leipzig.

His teaching duties in Basel included advanced courses at the university on the literature and philosophy of the Greeks and language courses at the local gymnasium. He volunteered to serve in the Franco-Prussian War in 1870 but spent less than a month as a medical orderly before contracting diphtheria. After convalescing in Naumburg for a month he returned to Basel. Nietzsche's firsthand experience of the ravages of warfare would not keep him from claiming in *Also sprach Zarathustra* (1883–1885; translated as *Thus Spake Zarathustra,* 1896) that it is not the good cause that justifies war but the good war that justifies the cause — one of the many transvaluations or reversals of values that are signatures of his later philosophical writings.

The Basel years are considered Nietzsche's early Romantic phase; many of his writings from this period are devoted to Wagner's rising fame, Schopenhauerian philosophy, and Germany's emergence as a military and political power. Wagner was living in Tribschen, Switzerland, where Nietzsche frequently visited him. Nietzsche still felt constrained by his profession; his application in 1871 for a vacancy in philosophy at Basel was politely declined.

The tension that to Nietzsche was a fundamental principle of all life was at work in him before it surfaced in his writings, and he was fond of pointing out that his writings spoke only of things he had overcome. His first major published work, *Die Geburt der Tragödie aus dem Geiste der Musik* (The Birth of Tragedy from the Spirit of Music, 1872; translated as *The Birth of Tragedy,* 1909), embodied this tension and immediately gained notoriety for Nietzsche. The book, for which Wagner had secured his own publisher, is dedicated to Wagner and contains a panegyric foreword about him. Ostensibly a work of classical philology, the treatise combines Schopenhauerian, Wagnerian, and earlier theoretical Romantic elements in a complex argument intended to demonstrate the relationship between music and word that culminated among the early Greeks in the tragic dramas of Aeschylus and Sophocles. The relationship was represented in the worship of Dionysus, the god of wine, regeneration, death, madness, and resurrection. During the Dionysian festivals, revelers became free of their individual identities and merged with the Primal Unity, Nietzsche's metaphor for all-encompassing nature. The Dionysian principle represents the unrestrained and unbounded life force; on the other hand, the Apollinian principle derived from the worship of Apollo and the other Olympian deities represents the calm, individuated, and orderly perception of the universe. These principles interact to sustain a tension, and tragedy evolved from a form of worship into the highest expression of Greek art and a direct reflection of the Greek soul. In the tragedies of Aeschylus and Sophocles, but no longer in those of Euripides, Nietzsche saw the vitality and wisdom of mythology contributing to the Greeks' sophisticated understanding of the world as a fertile, burgeoning chaos. The triumphant sublimation momentarily reconciling the states of individuation and Primal Unity was celebrated in tragic drama, wherein the hero symbolizes the fate of Dionysus. Ultimately, Nietzsche argues for a rebirth of tragedy and a revitalization of modern culture through the music of Wagner. Nietzsche is writing in the tradition of German Romantic theory, which was sympathetic toward mythologically based cultures and their unifying spirit, as opposed to knowledge-based, optimistic, and theoretical cultures that contribute to fragmentation. In *Die Geburt der Tragödie* Nietzsche's main quarrel is with Socrates, whom he sees as a metaphor for the momentous historical shift from mythology to cognition: Nietzsche opposes the symbol of the dying Socrates, who sacrificed himself for knowledge, with the symbol of the music-playing Socrates, who acknowledged the importance of the Dionysian aspect of Greek culture by playing the flute. German writers, philosophers, and poets such as Fichte, Schiller, Friedrich Schlegel, and Friedrich Hölderlin had addressed themselves to the role that Germany and moderns in general would play in the wake of the French Revolution and the rapidly vanishing old world order. Nietzsche adopted the model of cultural unity suggested by the ancient Greeks at the precise time that Germany was unified and became a modern state with the establishment of the Second Reich in 1871.

Responses to the publication of *Die Geburt der Tragödie* were swift and emotional; by the time Nietzsche again received such attention he would be insane and thus unaware of it. Rivals attacked the work as a product of the imagination and ridiculed it as Wagnerian propaganda; Wagnerians and Nietzsche's friends came to its defense. But Nietzsche had not intended to win the favor of his colleagues; he wanted to make a case for the culture of antiquity as a rich source of inspiration for moderns who were increasingly falling under the yoke of utilitarian values, specialization, alienation, and fragmentation. He had presented the ancient Greek aesthetic through the eyes not only of the philologist but those of the philosopher Schopenhauer and the artist Wagner as well. One effect of this painful intellectual debut was a rift between Nietzsche and Ritschl, who dismissed the book as "geistreiche Schwiemelei" (genial dissipation). Nietzsche's resentment toward his profession and its constraints deepened; he also resented Wagner for having lured him into the dangerous zone of artistic metaphysics. Years later, when bitter enmity had developed between the two, Nietzsche would refer to Wagner as a clever old Minotaur who feasted on German youths delivered to him as human sacrifices. For his part, he would never again sacrifice his independence. His later theory of resentment as the motivating factor in "slave morality" carried, as usual, the bitter flavor of those obstacles that Nietzsche had had to overcome in himself.

The controversy surrounding *Die Geburt der Tragödie* subsided, but Nietzsche had become aware of the distance between himself and his society. Migraine headaches and their accompanying nausea continued to afflict him, and writing became a means of therapy. The four book-length essays collectively titled *Unzeitgemäße Betrachtungen* (Untimely Meditations, 1873–1876) were devoted to issues of the day rather than to classical philology. Nietzsche felt out of step with the times, but this feeling had been disguised in *Die Geburt der Tragödie* because of his devotion to Wagner. The age was rife with stirrings of nationalism and cultural chauvinism brought on by Prussia's decisive defeat of France and by the unification of Germany under Prussian hegemony. Nietzsche continued to visit Wagner and write favorably about him, but he observed with disdain that Wagner was allowing himself to become the symbol of a new Germany that represented a self-righteous blend of Christian and nationalistic sentiments. The Wagner to whom Nietzsche had devoted himself had been a cosmopolitan spirit struggling against the smugness of his age, a fellow Schopenhauerian whose aesthetic vision had been animated by respect for the culture of pagan Greece.

The most original and widely studied essay of *Unzeitgemäße Betrachtungen* is the second volume, *Vom Nutzen und Nachtheil der Historie für das Leben* (1874; translated as "On the Use and Disadvantage of History," 1909), a treatise on modern society's preoccupation with history. The health of individuals and of peoples, Nietzsche maintains, is determined not only by the historical sense, recollection, but also by the unhistorical sense, the ability to forget. Moreover, the unhistorical sense is more important because it is the foundation of human growth, enabling us to experience change unencumbered by the static effect of the past. The best sense, however, would be the suprahistorical: historical people look to the past and believe in progress, while unhistorical types concentrate on deeds and act without guidance from the past. The suprahistorical type would combine both, bringing together a healthy regard for deeds as well as the ability to bring memory to bear on great historical events. *Vom Nutzen und Nachtheil der Historie für das Leben* was clearly influenced by the writings of Johann Wolfgang von Goethe and the example he provided as an individual; Nietzsche says that the goal of humanity cannot lie at its end but only in its highest representatives, such as Goethe, Michelangelo, Julius Caesar, or William Shakespeare.

Since 1873 Nietzsche had suffered increasingly from migraines, and on the advice of his family and friends he decided to find a suitable spouse to look after him. In 1876 he proposed marriage to Mathilde Trampedach, a woman he had known for only a few hours, through an intermediary; she declined. That year his illness became severe; his sister Elisabeth had to care for him, as she had done on several occasions since 1873. In October he was granted a year's leave from the university.

The final volume of *Unzeitgemäße Betrachtungen, Richard Wagner in Bayreuth* (1876; translated, 1910), concerns the transformation of Bayreuth into a Wagnerian mecca and festival center, and Wagner's place in German cultural history. Though the work is favorable to the composer, Nietzsche's experiences at the first festival in 1876 were grueling and tiresome. Surrounded by Wagnerian devotees and the increasing nationalism of the German scene, he felt out of place.

When the first volume of *Menschliches, Allzumenschliches* (1878–1880; translated as *Human, All-Too-Human*, 1909, 1911) was published, Nietzsche's situation had changed considerably. First, the friendship with Wagner was over, and hostility would prevail between Wagner and Nietzsche until Wagner's death in 1883. *Menschliches, Allzumen-*

Nietzsche as a philology professor at the University of Basel, 1872

schliches announced his debut as a writer no longer affiliated with Wagner, since all the writings Nietzsche had undertaken between 1872 and 1876 had been devoted to Wagner or at least enjoyed Wagner's blessing. Second, Nietzsche had developed a new style: the essayistic works of the years 1872 to 1876 had yielded to a collection of philosophical aphorisms. Third, Nietzsche had wanted to retire from academic life since 1874, but he had to wait for a medical pension that was granted in 1879. Free of both Wagner and academe, he would never again be distracted from his vocation of writing. Another significant factor contributing to the new Nietzsche was his friendship with Paul Rée, a writer, and Peter Gast (pseudonym of Heinrich Köselitz), a struggling composer. Nietzsche had met them when they took courses at Basel. Having found a kindred spirit in Rée and an ardent disciple in Gast, Nietzsche could feel better about himself than the minuscule sale of his books would have allowed. The publication of *Menschliches, All-*

Lou Salomé in 1882, the year Nietzsche met her

zumenschliches, whose subtitle, *Ein Buch für freie Geister* (A Book for Free Spirits), was Nietzsche's gesture of independence. He would write in his foreword to the second edition (1886) that *Menschliches, Allzumenschliches* had been the chronicle of his anti-Romantic self-treatment, his declaration of independence and convalescence from his physical illness and from the insidious disease of romanticism that he had contracted from Wagner.

Menschliches, Allzumenschliches was not only Nietzsche's longest work to date, amounting to more than seven hundred pages, it was also the most baffling. The hundreds of aphorisms comprising each volume cover a wide range of concerns including metaphysics, the origin of morals, religious faith, cultural values, the state, democratic institutions, and the nature of the artist. *Menschliches, Allzumenschliches* is Nietzsche's first attempt to work out his philosophical priorities and spell out his agenda as a thinker no longer hemmed in by German concerns. Significant for this work and all those to follow was Nietzsche's solitary, nomadic life-style. Constantly searching for a comfortable climate and an abode that was not beyond his humble means, he lived at various times in Genoa; Sils-Maria, Switzer-

land; Nice; and Turin, and stayed for a few months at a time at other locations in southern Switzerland and northern Italy. Themes of wandering, homelessness, an unfettered existence, and exploration are hallmarks of his writings, and he once said that one must never trust a thought that originates from behind a desk. Nietzsche had given up his Prussian citizenship in 1869 to accept his position at Basel, and his Swiss citizenship had expired when he left Basel in 1879; thus, technically, Nietzsche was a man without a country.

The "freie Geister" (free spirits) whom Nietzsche invented as his spiritual allies were enlightened individuals who accepted nothing without close scrutiny, especially in the realm of values. They were opponents of Christianity and nationalism. They remained aloof from politics, disavowing nationalism, socialism, and causes in general. The dominant feature of the free spirits was an aversion to egalitarian principles and liberalism, which Nietzsche traced to decadent Christianity or "Platonismus fürs Volk" (Platonism for the people). *Menschliches, Allzumenschliches* contains Nietzsche's first reflections on the concepts of good, bad, and evil: in early tribal society the good were the powerful, and the bad were the powerless; the resentment of the powerless inspired them to create a new moral category, evil, which they ascribed to the powerful. In a similar way, Nietzsche analyzed other concepts whose origins had become dim. Revenge, for example, depends on a complicated set of circumstances including time for reflection, sufficient intelligence to feel offended, the need to restore honor, and the need to demonstrate lack of fear in restoring the balance between two parties. Justice is society's revenge on behalf of the individual. Viewing linear progress and an ultimate goal for humanity as biases of Socratic optimism, Nietzsche defined progress as "Veredelung" (ennoblement). For its spiritual and cultural ennoblement a society must be inoculated by the introduction of a pathogen that rallies the forces of the collective first to fight off and then eventually to embody the outsider. Nietzsche's consistent advocacy of the presence of artists to test the collective's stability through creative behavior was based on his understanding that society cannot thrive without tension.

In 1881 a collection of 575 aphorisms titled *Morgenröthe* (translated as *The Dawn of Day,* 1903) appeared. The subtitle, *Gedanken über die moralischen Vorurtheile* (Thoughts on Moral Prejudice), indicates the thrust of Nietzsche's late work: an aggressive, radical campaign against modern decadence. In *Morgenröthe* Nietzsche says that there are two basic denials of morality: first, one can deny that people's alleged motives actually contribute to their actions; second, one can deny that moral judgments are based on truth. Nietzsche opts for the second choice: he admits that many actions generally considered immoral should be avoided and that many actions considered moral should be encouraged; the challenge is to perform right actions and avoid wrong ones for different reasons than those that have proven to be in error. We have to learn anew in order to be able to feel anew later on. The words Nietzsche used to convey "learning anew" and "feeling anew" are *umlernen* and *umfühlen*. The prefix *um* indicates reversal of the action denoted by the stem verb, so that in these acts of relearning and refeeling Nietzsche is suggesting his later campaign to revaluate all values (Umwertung aller Werte). An aphorism near the conclusion of *Morgenröthe* expresses Nietzsche's philosophy of development: a snake that cannot shed its skin must die; minds that are not permitted to change their opinions cease to be minds.

In 1882 another collection of aphorisms, *Die fröhliche Wissenschaft* (The Gay Science; translated as *The Joyful Wisdom*, 1910), appeared. By this time Nietzsche had met Lou Salomé, a young Russian friend of Rée's. Nietzsche's attraction to her was profound and was both intellectual and sexual. Salomé, however, preferred Rée's company to Nietzsche's. As a result Nietzsche became embittered toward Rée and Salomé.

In his aphorism "Der tolle Mensch" (The Madman) Nietzsche depicts a madman who rushes about in broad daylight with a lantern, desperately trying to illuminate the way for humanity in the appalling darkness that follows the death of God. But the people are not aware of the darkness; they remain indifferent to the ravings of the madman and continue to act complacently. In the infancy of the species gods, and later God, provided life with meaning; but in the absence of belief in God, religion and its institutions are hollow. The nothingness that accumulates in the absence of God, in the absence of absolute meaning, is insidious but inevitable. Nietzsche uses the analogy of light traveling from distant stars to make his point: by the time we see starlight, it has been on its way for years; in time humanity will receive the awesome and devastating news that it has been worshipping a God who died years ago. Meanwhile, should we persist in going through the motions as if God were a living concept? Should we passively stand by while the foundations of faith erode, refusing to create new values because the old ones have not been questioned?

This intense focus on living well in the here and now is related in *Die fröhliche Wissenschaft* in a parable that became one of Nietzsche's most celebrated ideas. "Das größte Schwergewicht" (The Greatest Stress) presents a scenario in which an individual – Nietzsche uses the familiar pronoun *du* (you) – finds himself in the depths of abject depression. A demon pursues you into your isolation and utters a horrifying proposition: your entire life in every detail, including this very moment of horror, will recur eternally – there is no end to look forward to, no heaven, no hell, no oblivion, no redemption from the weight of the eternal recurrence of the same events. You must now live with the consequences of this knowledge. Do you curse the demon and sink deeper into misery and denial, or do you affirm your existence for all eternity? Nietzsche intended the parable of the eternal recurrence to lay the greatest possible stress on living in the here and now: if we believe that we will live the same life in every detail over and over, then it is incumbent on us to create a life that we can *will* to recur eternally.

In his advocacy of adding style to one's character, of achieving selfhood, and of living dangerously in the absence of God, Nietzsche had rounded the corner from the criticism of prevailing values to positing new ones. This development reaches fruition in *Also sprach Zarathustra*, a work that deviates from Nietzsche's usual aphoristic style.

In *Also sprach Zarathustra* dramatic, exuberant expression is given to Nietzsche's own experience of that fateful moment of affirmation called for by the demon in "Das größte Schwergewicht," so that the work is even more confessional than Nietzsche's earlier writings. Hymnic in tone, prophetic in vision, and brimming with metaphors, *Also sprach Zarathustra* defies all standards of philosophical discourse and blurs the distinction between philosophy and poetry. The protagonist of the work is the mythical prophet Zarathustra (German for Zoroaster), Nietzsche's alter ego. Zarathustra's experiences are not uniformly joyous, and, like most prophets, he is not accepted in his own land. Nietzsche animated his alter ego with the tensions of his own life, providing sometimes lyrical and sometimes biting testimony about the journey through suffering to affirmation. The tone of the book was influenced by his disappointment in Rée and Salomé: *Also sprach Zarathustra* is the work of a lonely and sometimes bitter man.

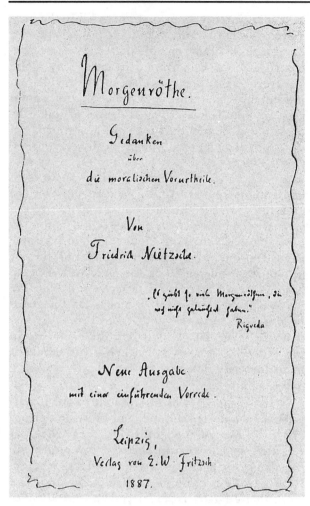

Nietzsche's design for the title page to the enlarged edition of his 1881 book of aphorisms (from Ivo Frenzel, ed., Friedrich Nietzsche in Selbstzeugnissen und Bilddokumenten, *1968)*

Nietzsche wrote volumes one through three, which appeared in 1883, in a matter of less than two weeks each. The final part was published in a private, limited edition in 1885. In *Ecce homo* (Behold the Man, 1908; translated, 1911) Nietzsche described the inspiration under which he wrote the work, explaining that revelation would be an appropriate term: suddenly, and with undeniable certainty, those things that had shaken and convulsed him on the inside became visible and audible. He heard but did not have to seek, he took but did not have to ask the source; thoughts flashed like lightning, by necessity, and without hesitation: "Ich habe nie eine Wahl gehabt" (I never had a choice). (Carl Gustav Jung devoted a seminar to a psychological analysis of *Also sprach Zarathustra,* claiming that during the hectic weeks of writing Nietzsche was taken over by the archetype represented by the wise old prophet.)

Also sprach Zarathustra is full of parables, proclamations, metaphors, and lyrical-hymnic writing. Zarathustra comes down the mountain after ten years of solitude to share his overabundant wisdom with the people. He learns on his way down that the people have not heard that God is dead, so his first message proclaims the death of all gods. In tandem with this news, however, he exhorts the people to prepare for the "Übermensch" (overman or superman), who represents an "Übergehen" (going over) from current man, hindered by misplaced faith, to a future man who will represent the fulfillment of man's destiny on earth. Humanity has historically perceived itself as a creation of a god and cast itself in the image of a god; it is now incumbent on humans to determine their own image, free of all gods. This existential mission requires the exploration of uncharted, dangerous territory: man, Zarathustra says, is a rope tied between animal and "overman," with an abyss below. The "going over" from one to the other will not occur overnight, it will not come about easily, and many will perish in the abyss before the hour of the great noon — the moment when, without the cover of shadow, man experiences the transition from Mensch (human) to overman. Nietzsche is adamant that mankind must face its condition without the false comfort of gods, ideals, and religions. The greatness of humanity is that we are a bridge, not a goal; mankind is a constant journey toward fulfillment.

The people, of course, reject or at best misunderstand Zarathustra's teachings. The prophet must tell even his disciples that they should strive to overcome their master and demonstrate their own growth by denying him. This commandment is a direct transvaluation of Matt. 10:24–25, 33: "The disciple is not above his master, nor the servant above his lord. / It is enough for the disciple that he be as his master, and the servant as his lord. / But whosoever shall deny me before men, him will I also deny before my Father which is in heaven." Throughout *Also sprach Zarathustra* there are allusions to the Bible because Zarathustra is diametrically opposed to Christ, who preached about the afterlife, renunciation, and humility and therefore contributed to man's inauthentic relation to the here and now. Nietzsche's alter ego voices his concerns about the rabble and its uninspired, unconscious life in speeches, tales, and parables. In one parable the three metamorphoses of the spirit are described: mankind's spirit is first a camel that allows itself to be burdened, and it is practiced in surviving in harsh climes; the camel becomes a lion and does battle against the dragon Thou Shalt, but the lion can only annihilate, it cannot create; finally, the lion becomes a child, representing a new beginning, a promise, and a potential once the field has been cleared of decadent obstacles.

All of the concepts of Nietzsche's later philosophy appear in *Also sprach Zarathustra*. The eternal recurrence appears in the third part, when Zarathustra summons the strength to affirm his own eternal existence. The will to power is presented in the context of self-overcoming: wherever Zarathustra finds life, he finds a will to power ceaselessly struggling to overcome itself. The concept of the Übermensch is presented early in the work and contrasted with that of the "letzter Mensch" (last man) who can no longer harbor ambitions but prefers to cultivate tiny virtues and remain happy. The first three parts of the work illustrate Zarathustra's inability to communicate with the people because the distance between his message and their spiritual condition is too great. In the fourth part, which is more pessimistic in tone than the hymnic early parts, Zarathustra no longer even tries to function among ordinary humans. The "höhere Menschen" (higher men) visit Zarathustra on his mountain, but they have not yet reached a high enough level of growth and enlightenment to have earned the privilege of staying with him. They rely too strongly on Zarathustra and take his words literally, so that they are not capable of surviving on their own in Zarathustra's harsh environment.

Though Nietzsche poured his heart into *Also sprach Zarathustra,* the work did not attract many readers; the fourth part was published in only forty copies. Undeterred by his failure to win a large readership for his works, or perhaps emboldened by the challenge of espousing his new philosophy against all odds, Nietzsche launched the final phase of his writing with *Jenseits von Gut und Böse* (1886; translated as *Beyond Good and Evil,* 1909). In this carefully structured, aphoristic work, which is divided into chapters, Nietzsche spells out the implications of ideas that had emerged with eruptive force in *Also sprach Zarathustra.* Many of the 296 aphorisms are a page or more in length; hence, they deviate from the traditional aphorism, which is a concise statement of a principle or a terse formulation of a truth. Nietzsche retained this style of single paragraphs of varying length in the remainder of his works, and beginning with *Jenseits von Gut und Böse* the paragraphs are more closely related than the aphorisms of the pre-*Zarathustra* works. This style afforded him both the conceptual rigor and the open-ended freedom that characterize his thought.

After *Also sprach Zarathustra* Nietzsche had little to say about the Übermensch, but he retained a vi-

Nietzsche with his mother after the onset of his insanity

sion of the emerging individual. The new philosopher, Nietzsche claimed, is one who prepares the way for a nonidealized consummation of life. In aphorism 212 of *Jenseits von Gut und Böse* he explains that the philosopher's work requires him to establish a presence in opposition to the times, to exist as the thorny question mark within a society that is losing the strength to ask questions. Modern society encourages narrowness, specialization, and lack of will disguised as objectivity; the philosopher should demonstrate strength of will, hardness, and the capacity for long-range decisions as a means of countering the nihilistic Christian values of renunciation, humility, and selflessness. The closing words of the aphorism summarize the fate of Nietzsche's alter ego Zarathustra, the prophet of the Übermensch: the greatest human being will be the one who is loneliest, most concealed, most deviant, living beyond good and evil as the master of his own virtues, overly rich in will, and capable of being as manifold as he is whole.

Nietzsche in his final year; charcoal sketch by Hans Olde (from Ronald Hayman, Nietzsche: A Critical Life, *1980)*

Nietzsche had taken legal action against his publisher, Ernst Schmeitzner, in 1884 to collect royalties from the sale of *Also sprach Zarathustra*. His old publisher, E. W. Fritzsch, bought the rights to *Menschliches, Allzumenschliches, Morgenröthe,* and *Die fröhliche Wissenschaft* from Schmeitzner in 1886, and also brought out a new edition of *Die Geburt der Tragödie*. For *Jenseits von Gut und Böse* and all the works that followed, Nietzsche paid for publication under an agreement with the publisher C. G. Naumann. By 1886 only sixty to seventy copies of *Also sprach Zarathustra* had been sold.

To supplement and clarify *Jenseits von Gut und Böse,* Nietzsche wrote *Zur Genealogie der Moral* (1887; translated as "A Genealogy of Morals," 1897). In number 260 (an "aphorism" of four pages) Nietzsche discusses the differences between "Herrenmoral" (master morality) and "Sklavenmoral" (slave morality). Master morality observes a distinction between noble and contemptible, calling the noble "good" and the contemptible "bad." The close-knit group of masters feels responsibilities only to itself. Modern slave morality, on the other hand, advocates sympathy, responsibility for others, and altruism. Slave morality is created by the oppressed, the victimized, the weak, and the disenfranchised. Of prime importance to this group is the alleviation of suffering, and it promotes virtues that contribute to making existence bearable. Slave morality applies the term *good* to whatever is not dangerous; wherever there is a preponderance of slave morality, language has a tendency to equate the word *good* with *stupid*. *Evil* is invented by the powerless and victimized, and those who arouse fear are regarded as evil. In master morality, on the other hand, those who arouse fear are regarded as good, because they are capable of inflicting harm and are therefore worthy of respect, while *bad* designates those who, being powerless, are contemptible. It is the ressentiment (resentment; Nietzsche preferred the French term) of the slaves toward the masters that drives them to invent the category of evil. The French Revolution was a triumph of ressentiment over the classical aristocratic ideals of seventeenth- and eighteenth-century France, "die letzte politische Vornehmheit, die es in Europa gab" (the last political noblesse that existed in Europe). The ideals of the French Revolution, which Nietzsche often vilified in the person of Jean-Jacques Rousseau, are the renunciatory values of slave morality; the appearance of the last great representative of the noble ideal, Napoleon, was the single factor that justified the revolution. Modern society is basically the society of Rousseau, the Enlightenment, and the French Revolution.

In November 1887 the influential Danish scholar and critic Georg Brandes, who had received a copy of *Jenseits von Gut und Böse* from Nietzsche's publisher in 1886, wrote to Nietzsche. Brandes expressed his admiration for Nietzsche, pointed out affinities between their views, and said he was surprised at not having learned of Nietzsche earlier. Nietzsche replied to Brandes in a letter of 2 December 1887: "Verehrter Herr, ein paar Leser, die man sich selbst in Ehren hält und sonst keine Leser – so gehört es in der Tat zu meinen Wünschen" (Dear Sir, a few readers whom I can hold in honor and otherwise no readers – this indeed is my wish). In 1888 Brandes gave the first lectures on Nietzsche's philosophy at the University of Copenhagen. By this time Nietzsche had endured much depression owing to his ill health; to his friend and former Basel colleague Franz Overbeck, Nietzsche explained that writing had become alchemy, a process whereby he turned the mud of his painful experiences into the gold of his works. Not only did Nietzsche have to contend with solitude and frail health; he was constantly feuding with his mother and sister, who meddled in his affairs at every opportunity.

Buoyed by the dialogue he enjoyed with Brandes and, through him, with Strindberg, Nietzsche experienced his most productive – and final – year of writing in 1888. *Der Fall Wagner* (1888; translated as "The Case of Wagner," 1896), a polemic detailing the differences between healthy taste and healthy values, on the one hand, and the decadence associated with romanticism in general and with Wagner as the personification of romanticism in particular, on the other hand, is much more than a debate about music. Wagner stands for the modern spirit and modern taste: frenetic, nervous, emotional, obscure, Germanic; in contrast, Georges Bizet is extolled as a representative of the healthy, lucid, light, and Mediterranean character – Nietzsche frequently praises the French at the expense of the Germans. "Der Antichrist: Fluch auf das Christenthum" (The Antichrist: A Curse on Christianity) was finished in 1888 but did not appear until 1895. The Germans are taken to task in this work for having sabotaged Europe's chances for a great cultural revival: the Renaissance revalued Christian values by offering its own aristocratic ones, but Martin Luther, concerned only with his own salvation, attacked the Catholic church and re-

stored its power at the same time. According to Nietzsche, Christianity was on the verge of collapsing at precisely the moment when Luther decided to save it; the corruption of the popes actually signaled a triumph of life's affirmative values.

Also written in 1888 was *Götzen-Dämmerung* (1889; translated as "The Twilight of the Idols," 1896), in which Nietzsche returns to his major concerns and makes final formulations of his positions; the title is yet another barb directed at Wagner, a play on Wagner's *Götterdämmerung* (1863; translated as *The Twilight of the Gods,* 1900). The critique of Socrates begun in *Die Geburt der Tragödie* concludes in *Götzen-Dämmerung:* the Socratic dialectic, aimed against aristocratic authority, represents the modern spirit of mob rule. By attacking the instincts and elevating the pursuit of knowledge through reason alone, Socrates took a step backwards, since ascending vitality is accompanied by an affirmation of the instincts. In *Götzen-Dämmerung* and other writings of 1888 Nietzsche referred to himself as "der letzte Jünger des Philosophen Dionysos" (the last disciple of the philosopher Dionysus), the deity symbolic of the values of ascending life and eternal recurrence.

Nietzsche contra Wagner (1889; translated, 1896) is a brief essay that continues Nietzsche's critique of Wagner; it relies heavily on passages from earlier works. *Ecce homo* is Nietzsche's ironic and self-parodistic autobiography; the title is the words Pontius Pilate used to indicate the flogged and humiliated Christ, and in the work Nietzsche distinguishes between his teachings and those of Christ. Nietzsche gives expression in *Ecce homo* to the euphoria he experienced in his last year of writing: "Wie sollte ich nicht meinem ganzen Leben dankbar sein? – Und so erzähle ich mir mein Leben" (How should I not be grateful to my whole life? – And so I will recount my life to myself). Nietzsche spent the latter part of 1888 in a condition of physical and mental exhaustion; he was also subject to uncontrollable facial contortions – grins and grimaces. His feelings of euphoria probably enabled him to work beyond his normal endurance. *Ecce homo* is frequently cited along with other late works as the product of madness, but it exhibits typical Nietzschean boldness. *Ecce homo* also offers Nietzsche's reviews of his own works, in which ample doses of arrogance are mixed with self-parody.

Nietzsche suffered a mental breakdown on 3 January 1889 in the Piazza Carlo Alberto in Turin. From 3 to 7 January he wrote brief, ecstatic notes to various people, signing himself "Der Gekreuzigte" (The Crucified One) to Gast and Brandes and "Dionysos" to Wagner's wife, Cosima, and the his-

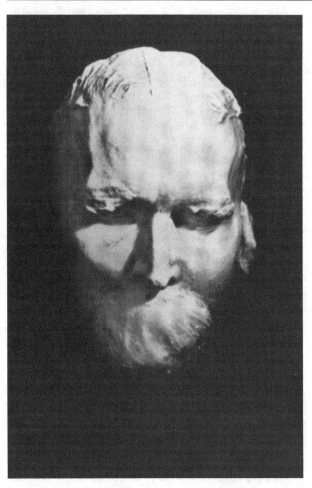

Death mask of Nietzsche (Nationale Forschungs- und Gedenkstätten der klassischen deutschen Literatur, Weimar)

torian Jakob Burckhardt. Burckhardt, a former colleague of Nietzsche's at Basel, also received a long, rambling letter dated 6 January that begins: "Lieber Herr Professor, zuletzt wäre ich sehr viel lieber Basler Professor als Gott; aber ich habe es nicht gewagt, meinen Privat-Egoismus so weit zu treiben, um seinetwegen die Schaffung der Welt zu unterlassen. Sie sehen, man muß Opfer bringen, wie und wo man lebt" (Dear Professor, ultimately I would much rather be a Basel professor than God, but I did not dare to push my private egoism so far as to neglect the creation of the world. You see, one has to make sacrifices however and wherever one lives). Burckhardt took the letter to Overbeck, who sped down to Turin by train to fetch Nietzsche and return him to Basel. He was diagnosed as suffering from progressive paralysis. On 17 January 1889 his mother and two orderlies took him to Jena, where he was committed to the psychiatric clinic at the university. In 1890 he was released to the care of his mother in Naumburg.

In 1885 Nietzsche's sister had married Dr. Bernhard Förster, an outspoken anti-Semite who had tried to establish a colony of "Aryans" in Paraguay and had committed suicide in 1889 when the colony collapsed financially. After Elisabeth Förster-Nietzsche returned from Paraguay in 1893, she devoted all her energy to acquiring sole possession and control of Nietzsche's literary estate. In 1894 Nietzsche's works finally began to bring in considerable royalties. Förster-Nietzsche manipulated Nietzsche's late unpublished writings and letters to present her own version of his ideas, and she represented herself as his greatest supporter. In 1896 she moved the Nietzsche archive to Weimar to profit from the association with the Goethe Archive located there. After their mother died in 1897, Förster-Nietzsche moved her brother to Weimar. Nietzsche never recovered from his total nervous breakdown. He died on 25 August 1900.

Nietzsche's madness and his sister's unprofessional behavior as the executor of his literary estate contributed to the myths, half-truths, and intrigues that swirled around his reputation. She dismissed Gast as editor of the first collected edition of Nietzsche's works even though he was infinitely better prepared to perform the work than those chosen by her. In 1901 she began to publish Nietzsche's notes from the 1880s, even though Nietzsche had already used this material in the published works. It was thus that "Der Wille zur Macht" (1901; translated as *The Will to Power*, 1909, 1910) was put together. Förster-Nietzsche claimed that her brother had intended to write such a work and had finished the first part, "Der Antichrist." Nietzsche had indeed referred to a work with that title, and to "Der Antichrist" as its first installment, but he frequently made plans for books that he later abandoned. The projected "Der Wille zur Macht" was never completed by Nietzsche, but his notes of the 1880s were published under that title by Förster-Nietzsche.

Nietzsche's works are difficult to translate, since he uses wordplay and coinages. The iconoclastic nature of the late writings, such as "Der Antichrist" and *Ecce homo,* caused the editors, frequently under the inept guidance of Förster-Nietzsche, to postpone their publication while instead publishing discarded notes that appeared more "philosophical." Nietzsche's reception in the English-speaking world was hampered by the fact that his late works were translated before the early ones; hence, his ideas were construed as unfounded and eccentric. An additional drawback was the poor quality of the English translations. Furthermore, Nietzsche's ideas were given an anti-Semitic, nationalistic, and prowar slant by Nazi propagandists. Nietzsche's message, then, reached the English-speaking world in a distorted form.

In the 1950s the American philosopher Walter Kaufmann began translating Nietzsche's major writings into English; Kaufmann also argued forcefully in his own publications against the misinterpretations of Nietzsche's thought. Today a consensus exists among philosophers, literary theorists, and historians of ideas that Nietzsche was a watershed figure of Western culture. His criticisms of metaphysics and values have influenced theorists who are committed to exposing bias, hypocrisy, and false assumptions. Deconstructionist followers of Jacques Derrida lionize Nietzsche for what they perceive as his disavowal of the "ideal" of meaning; other thinkers, however, claim that Nietzsche saw his task as a philosopher to be that of rescuing the concept of meaning from the chaos of collapsing values.

Letters:

Selected Letters of Friedrich Nietzsche, edited by Oscar Levy, translated by Anthony Ludovici (New York: Doubleday, 1921);

Selected Letters of Friedrich Nietzsche, translated and edited by Christopher Middleton (Chicago: University of Chicago Press, 1969);

Briefwechsel: Kritische Gesamtausgabe, 24 volumes, edited by Giorgio Colli and Mazzino Montinari (Berlin: De Gruyter, 1975–1984).

Bibliographies:

Herbert Reichert and Karl Schlechta, International Nietzsche Bibliography (Chapel Hill: University of North Carolina Press, 1960; revised and enlarged, 1968);

Reichert, "International Nietzsche Bibliography 1968–1971," Nietzsche-Studien, 2 (1973): 320–339;

Reichert, "International Nietzsche Bibliography 1972–1973," Nietzsche-Studien, 4 (1975): 351–373.

Biographies:

Lou Andreas-Salomé, Friedrich Nietzsche in seinen Werken (Vienna: Konegan, 1894); edited and translated by Siegfried Mandel as Nietzsche (Redding Ridge, Conn.: Black Swan, 1988);

Georg Brandes, Friedrich Nietzsche, translated by A. G. Chater (London: Heinemann, 1914);

Charles Andler, Nietzsche: Sa vie et sa pensée, 6 volumes (Paris: Bossard, 1920–1931);

Erich Podach, Nietzsches Zusammenbruch: Beiträge zu einer Biographie auf Grund unveröffentlichter Doku-

mente (Heidelberg: Kampmann, 1930); translated by Fritz August Voigt as The Madness of Nietzsche (New York: Putnam's, 1930);

Crane Brinton, Nietzsche (Cambridge, Mass.: Harvard University Press, 1941);

Frederick Copleston, Friedrich Nietzsche: Philosopher of Culture (London: Burns, Oates & Washbourne, 1942);

H. A. Reyburn, Nietzsche: The Story of a Human Philosopher (London: Macmillan, 1948);

Frederick Love, Young Nietzsche and the Wagnerian Experience (Chapel Hill: University of North Carolina Press, 1963);

R. J. Hollingdale, Nietzsche: The Man and His Philosophy (Baton Rouge: Louisiana State University Press, 1965);

Curt Paul Janz, Friedrich Nietzsche, 3 volumes (Munich: Hanser, 1978);

Ronald Hayman, Nietzsche: A Critical Life (London: Weidenfeld & Nicolson, 1980);

Sander L. Gilman, ed., Begegnungen mit Nietzsche, second edition (Bonn: Bouvier, 1985); translated by David J. Parent as Conversations with Nietzsche: A Life in the Words of His Contemporaries (Oxford: Oxford University Press, 1987);

Peter Bergmann, Nietzsche: "The Last Antipolitical German" (Bloomington: Indiana University Press, 1987);

Carl Pletsch, Young Nietzsche: Becoming a Genius (New York: Free Press, 1991).

References:

David Allison, ed., The New Nietzsche: Contemporary Styles of Interpretation (New York: Dell, 1977);

Ernst Behler, "Deconstruction versus Hermeneutics: Derrida and Gadamer on Text and Interpretation," Southern Humanities Review, 21 (Summer 1987): 201–223;

Behler, Derrida – Nietzsche, Nietzsche – Derrida (Munich: Schöningh, 1988);

Ernst Bertram, Nietzsche: Versuch einer Mythologie, eighth edition (Bonn: Bouvier, 1965);

Harold Bloom, ed., Friedrich Nietzsche (New York: Chelsea House, 1987);

William M. Calder III, "The Wilamowitz-Nietzsche Struggle: New Documentation and a Reappraisal," Nietzsche-Studien, 12 (1983): 214–254;

Adrian Del Caro, Nietzsche contra Nietzsche: Creativity and the Anti-Romantic (Baton Rouge: Louisiana State University Press, 1989);

Del Caro, "Reception and Impact: The First Decade of Nietzsche in Germany," Orbis Litterarum, 37, no. 1 (1982): 32–46;

Jacques Derrida, *Spurs: The Styles of Nietzsche,* translated by Barbara Howell (Chicago: University of Chicago Press, 1979);

Linda Duncan, "Heine and Nietzsche," *Nietzsche-Studien,* 19 (1990): 336–345;

Volker Dürr, Reinhold Grimm, and Kathy Harms, eds., *Nietzsche: Literature and Values* (Madison: University of Wisconsin Press, 1988);

Ivo Frenzel, ed., *Friedrich Nietzsche in Selbstzeugnissen und Bilddokumenten* (Hamburg: Rowohlt, 1968);

Michael A. Gillespie and Tracey B. Strong, eds., *Nietzsche's New Seas: Explorations in Philosophy, Aesthetics, and Politics* (Chicago: University of Chicago Press, 1988);

Reinhold Grimm, "Antiquity as Echo and Disguise," *Nietzsche-Studien,* 14 (1973): 201–249;

Martin Heidegger, *Nietzsche,* 2 volumes (Pfullingen: Neske, 1961); volume 1 translated by David Krell as *The Will to Power as Art* (New York: Harper & Row, 1979);

Erich Heller, *The Artist's Journey Into the Interior and Other Essays* (New York: Random House, 1965);

Heller, *The Disinherited Mind* (Philadelphia: Dufour & Saifer, 1952);

Heller, *The Importance of Nietzsche: Ten Essays* (Chicago: University of Chicago Press, 1988);

Carl G. Jung, *Nietzsche's Zarathustra: Notes of the Seminar Given in 1934–1939,* 2 volumes, edited by James L. Jarrett (Princeton: Princeton University Press, 1988);

Walter Kaufmann, *Nietzsche: Philosopher, Psychologist, Antichrist* (Princeton: Princeton University Press, 1950; revised, 1974);

Richard Krummel, *Nietzsche und der deutsche Geist* (Berlin: De Gruyter, 1974);

György Lukács, *Die Zerstörung der Vernunft* (Berlin: Aufbau, 1962);

Jürgen Manthey, ed., *Literaturmagazin XII: Nietzsche* (Reinbek: Rowohlt, 1980);

James C. O'Flaherty, ed., *Studies in Nietzsche and the Classical Tradition* (Chapel Hill: University of North Carolina Press, 1976);

John Pizer, "The Use and Abuse of 'Ursprung': On Foucault's Reading of Nietzsche," *Nietzsche-Studien,* 19 (1990): 462–478;

Matthias Politycki, *Umwertung aller Werte?: Deutsche Literatur im Urteil Nietzsches* (Berlin: De Gruyter, 1989);

Richard Schacht, *Nietzsche* (London: Routledge & Kegan Paul, 1985);

M. S. Silk and Joseph Peter Stern, *Nietzsche on Tragedy* (Cambridge: Cambridge University Press, 1981);

Joan Stambaugh, *Nietzsche's Thought of Eternal Recurrence* (Baltimore: Johns Hopkins University Press, 1972);

Wolfgang F. Taraba, "Friedrich Nietzsche," in *Deutsche Dichter der Moderne,* edited by Benno von Wiese, third edition (Berlin: Schmidt, 1975), pp. 11–26;

David S. Thatcher, *Nietzsche in England 1890–1914: The Growth of a Reputation* (Toronto: University of Toronto Press, 1970).

Papers:
Friedrich Nietzsche's papers are in the Goethe- und Schillerarchiv in Weimar.

Louise Otto-Peters

(26 March 1819 – 13 March 1895)

Ruth-Ellen Boetcher Joeres
University of Minnesota

BOOKS: *Ludwig der Kellner,* 2 volumes (Leipzig: Wienbrack, 1843);

Kathinka: Ein Roman, 2 volumes (Leipzig: Wienbrack, 1844);

Aus der neuen Zeit: Novellen und Erzählungen (Leipzig: Wienbrack, 1845);

Die Freunde: Roman, 3 volumes (Leipzig: Wienbrack, 1845);

Schloß und Fabrik: Roman, 3 volumes (Leipzig: Wienbrack, 1846);

Lieder eines deutschen Mädchens (Leipzig: Wienbrack, 1847);

Römisch und Deutsch: Roman, 4 volumes (Leipzig: Wienbrack, 1847);

Ein Bauernsohn: Eine Erzählung für das Volk aus der neuesten Zeit (Leipzig: Wienbrack, 1849);

Westwärts!: Lieder (Meissen: Klinckicht, 1850);

Buchenheim: Roman, 3 volumes (Leipzig: Wienbrack, 1851);

Vier Geschwister: Roman, 2 volumes (Dessau: Katz, 1852);

Die Kunst und unsere Zeit (Großenhain: Haffner, 1852);

Cäcilie Telville: Roman, 3 volumes (Leipzig: Hinze, 1852);

Die Nibelungen: Text zu einer großen heroischen Oper in 5 Akten (Gera: Hofmeister, 1852);

Andreas Halm: Roman, 3 volumes (Plauen: Schröter, 1856);

Zwei Generationen: Roman, 3 volumes (Leipzig: Hübner, 1857);

Eine Grafenkrone: Roman, 3 volumes (Leipzig: Hübner, 1857);

Heimische und Fremde: Ein Gemälde aus der Schweiz. Roman, 3 volumes (Leipzig: Hübner, 1858);

Nürnberg: Culturhistorischer Roman, 3 volumes (Prague: Kober & Markgraf, 1859);

Die Erben von Schloß Ehrenfels: Roman, 3 volumes (Leipzig: Hübner, 1860);

Aus der alten Zeit: Historische Erzählungen, 2 volumes (Leipzig: Hübner, 1860);

Louise Otto-Peters

Die Mission der Kunst mit besonderer Rücksicht auf die Gegenwart (Leipzig: Matthes, 1861);

Die Schultheißentöchter von Nürnberg: Culturhistorischer Roman, 3 volumes (Vienna: Markgraf, 1861);

Kunst und Künstlerleben: Novellen (Bromberg: Roskowski, 1863);

Neue Bahnen: Roman, 2 volumes (Vienna: Markgraf, 1864);

Mädchenbilder aus der Gegenwart: Novellen (Leipzig: Colditz, 1864);

Nebeneinander, 2 volumes (Duisburg: Nieten, 1864);

Zerstörter Friede: Roman, 2 volumes (Jena: Hermsdorf & Hoßfeld, 1866);

Das Recht der Frauen auf Erwerb: Blicke auf das Frauenleben der Gegenwart (Hamburg: Hoffmann & Campe, 1866);

Die Idealisten: Roman, 4 volumes (Jena: Hermsdorf, 1867);

Drei verhängnisvolle Jahre: Zeitroman, 2 volumes (Altona: Verlags-Bureau, 1867);

Die Dioskuren: Roman (Altona: Verlags-Bureau, 1868);

Gedichte (Leipzig: Rötschke, 1868);

Privatgeschichten der Weltgeschichte, 6 volumes (Leipzig: Matthes, 1868–1872) – comprises volume 1, *Geschichte mediatisirter deutscher Fürstenhäuser: Hannover, Kurhessen, Nassau, Thurn und Taxis, Hohenzollern-Sigmaringen, Hohenzollern-Hechingen, Ansbach, Baireuth und Arenberg* (1868); volume 2, *Merkwürdige und geheimnißvolle Frauen* (1868); volume 3, *Geistliche Fürsten und Herren in Deutschland bis zur Säkularisation 1803* (1869); volume 4, *Einflußreiche Frauen aus dem Volke* (1869); volume 5, *Neufranzösisches und Altdeutsches: Ein Beitrag zu den Ereignissen von 1870* (1871); volume 6, *Seltene Charaktere aus deutschen Adelsgeschlechtern* (1872);

Aus der Börsenwelt (Berlin: Behrend, 1869);

Der Genius des Hauses: Eine Gabe für Mädchen und Frauen (Pest, Vienna & Leipzig: Hartleben, 1869);

Victoria regia: Historische Novelle aus dem 18. Jahrhundert (Leipzig: Rötschke, 1869);

Rittersporn, 4 volumes (Leipzig: Rötschke, 1870);

Der Genius der Menschheit: Frauenwirken im Dienste der Humanität: Eine Gabe für Mädchen und Frauen (Pest, Vienna & Leipzig: Hartleben, 1870);

Musiker-Leiden und Freuden: Drei Novellen (Leipzig: Bibliographische Anstalt, 1871);

Der Genius der Natur: Harmonien der Natur zu dem Frauenleben der Gegenwart. Eine Gabe für Mädchen und Frauen (Vienna, Pest & Leipzig: Hartleben, 1871);

Deutsche Wunden: Zeitroman (1864–1871), 4 volumes (Bremen: Kühtmann, 1872) – comprises volume 1, *Kleinstaatliches;* volume 2, *Verbrüderungsfeste;* volume 3, *Deutscher Bruderkrieg;* volume 4, *Alldeutschland;*

Theodor Körner: Vaterländische Oper in fünf Akten und einem Vorspiel, Des Königs Aufruf (Munich: Wolf, 1872);

Die Stiftsherren von Straßburg: Historischer Roman aus dem dreizehnten Jahrhundert, 2 volumes (Leipzig: Schlicke, 1872);

Rom in Deutschland: Zeit-Roman, 3 volumes (Bremen: Kühtmann, 1873);

Weihe des Lebens: Ein Buch zur Erhebung und Erbauung des Geistes und Herzens (Leipzig: Schäfer, 1873);

Zwischen den Bergen: Erzählungen und Zeitbilder, 2 volumes (Bremen: Kühtmann, 1873);

Ein bedenkliches Geheimniß: Erzählung aus der Gegenwart (Leipzig: Theile, 1875);

Frauenleben im deutschen Reich: Erinnerungen aus der Vergangenheit mit Hinweis auf Gegenwart und Zukunft (Leipzig: Schäfer, 1876);

Einige deutsche Gesetz-Paragraphen über die Stellung der Frau: Herausgegeben vom Allgemeinen deutschen Frauenverein (Leipzig: Schäfer, 1876);

Aus vier Jahrhunderten: Historische Erzählungen, 2 volumes (Norden: Fischer, 1883);

Gräfin Lauretta: Historische Erzählung aus dem 14. Jahrhundert (Leipzig: Reißner, 1884);

Die Nachtigall von Werawag: Kulturhistorischer Roman, 4 volumes (Freiburg: Kiepert, 1887);

Das erste Vierteljahrhundert des Allgemeinen deutschen Frauenvereins, gegründet am 18. Oktober 1865 in Leipzig: Auf Grund der Protokolle mitgeteilt (Leipzig: Schäfer, 1890);

Mein Lebensgang: Gedichte aus fünf Jahrzehnten (Leipzig: Schäfer, 1893).

OTHER: "Mein Programm als Mitarbeiterin einer Frauenzeitung," in *Das Wesen der Ehe,* edited by Luise Dittmar (Leipzig: Wigand, 1849), pp. 19–22;

Quellen des Vergnügens: Die sinnigsten Spiele, nützlichsten Beschäftigungen und angenehmsten Unterhaltungen zur Erholung des Körpers und Geistes, edited by Otto-Peters and Auguste Schmidt (Leipzig: Schäfer, 1873);

Elfried von Taura: Erzählungen aus Sachsen- und Böhmerland, edited by Otto-Peters (Sondershausen: Expedition des "Deutschen," 1878);

"Zur Stellung der deutschen veheirateten und unverheirateten Frauen im Hause, in der Gesellschaft und in der Öffentlichkeit," in *Die Stellung der Frau im Leben* (Kiel & Leipzig: Lipsius & Tischer, 1891), pp. 19–23.

Louise Otto-Peters — who signed most of her books Louise Otto and was most commonly known by that name — was the founder of the bourgeois German women's movement that lumbered to life in the second half of the nineteenth century. She was a prolific producer of novels and also wrote novellas, short stories, opera librettos, and poetry. But her reputation rests on her polemical writings, which advocated women's rights and political liberalism. Like many of her liberal contemporaries, Otto-Peters seems to have written poetry and fiction to gain income to support her more controversial writings and activities. Generally acknowledged as the mother of German feminism, she was as active in politics as she was in the sphere – more socially acceptable for women – of poetic creativity. Thus, even her fictional writings, although they are often set in the past, tend to be filled with tendentious contemporary political messages. All of Otto-Peters's writings reflect her view that there is a vital connection between art and politics. Her public engagement in the social issues of her time did not permit her to hide for long behind a pseudonym: all of her contributions to Robert Blum's radical newspapers during the 1840s appeared under her own name, and only sporadically in the articles she contributed to Ernst Keil's newspapers did she conceal her identity behind a male name, Otto Stern.

Another element that binds her writings together is her interest in women's place in society, their rights and privileges, and their duties. This interest is overt in novels whose heroines struggle against great odds to achieve aims that do not always include marriage; in volumes of poetry with titles such as *Lieder eines deutschen Mädchens* (Songs of a German Girl, 1847); in the subtitles of the homiletic books *Der Genius der Menschheit: Frauenwirken im Dienste der Humanität* (The Spirit of the Human Race: The Work of Women in the Service of Humanity, 1870) and *Der Genius der Natur: Harmonien der Natur zu dem Frauenleben der Gegenwart* (The Spirit of Nature: The Harmonies of Nature in Contemporary Women's Lives, 1871); and in the marvelous, heavily autobiographical *Frauenleben im deutschen Reich: Erinnerungen aus der Vergangenheit mit Hinweis auf Gegenwart und Zukunft* (Women's Lives in the German Empire: Memoirs From the Past With References to the Present and Future, 1876). But there is also a gender-specific point of view in *Privatgeschichten der Weltgeschichte* (Private Stories of World History, 1868–1872), historical sketches that emphasize the women whose presence in world history has frequently been neglected and forgotten. The focus of the majority of Otto-Peters's polemical articles is a portrait of German women: how they were, how they are, and how they should be.

Louise Otto was born on 26 March 1819 in the provincial Saxon city of Meissen, noted then as now for its porcelain industry, to the court assessor Fürchtegott Wilhelm Otto and Charlotte Matthäi Otto. She grew up in a liberal middle-class household where there was much reading aloud, much talk of Bildung (cultural education) and of the great poets, and much discussion of the role of the citizen – female as well as male – in the state. An anec-

dote about Otto's father relates his delight in reporting to his daughters and wife the passing of a law in Saxony that would allow women to serve as executors of estates and his comment that his girls would no longer be as helpless as they had been before. In poetry describing her childhood, Otto-Peters speaks repeatedly of the two-pronged influence of poetry and politics on her intellectual formation.

Otto lost her sister Clementine in 1831, her mother in 1835, her father in 1836, and her fiancé, Wilhelm Müller, in 1841. Thus Otto found herself both bereft and free at the age of twenty-two. Rather than accede to her fate and join the ranks of unmarried middle-class women who eked out livings as governesses or as companions to wealthy ladies, Otto began to write; her first poems were published in a Meissen newspaper in 1842.

Otto approached Keil, a Leipzig publisher whose political views resembled her own, suggesting that he publish a volume of her poetry; he remarked that women wrote too much poetry and suggested that she write a prose work instead. Her first book was a two-volume novel, *Ludwig der Kellner* (Ludwig the Waiter, 1843).

Otto spent most of her life in Leipzig, where she moved in 1846, working as a writer, a publicist, an editor, and an organizer for women's rights. One of her best-known novels, and one that has continued to garner interest, is *Schloß und Fabrik* (Castle and Factory, 1846). In its depiction of tensions emerging during the industrialization of Germany in the 1840s it illustrates particularly well the early revolutionary phase of Otto's thinking. The work appeared at a time when the social novel was increasingly dominant not only in Germany but also in England and France. Its multiple but interweaving stories of the fates of members of various classes are full of stereotypes – the benevolent but impoverished aristocrats, the evil and scheming factory owners, the idealistic workers – but also of powerful female characters. Although the novel has a pat ending – involving the fiery destruction of the factory and the factory manager's estate, as well as the deaths of the worker-poet hero, Franz Thalheim, and the factory owner's daughter, Pauline Felchner, whom he loves – there is much in the way of local color and of the ideology of supporters of the revolutionary stirrings in the 1840s, in particular the women. What distinguishes Otto's social novel from those of her male compatriots such as Ernst Willkomm or Georg Weerth is its focus on the women who also played a role in the fermentation leading up to the revolution. Although Otto obliges expectations in her depiction of standard

Mein Zimmer, 1852 (My Room, 1852): sketch by Louise Otto (from Max Großmann, Und weiter fließt der Strom, 1966)

class rivalries, in seeing the poor (and occasionally the aristocracy) as unfairly treated, and in placing the blame for the conflict between the classes on the managerial class, the presence of stories interesting to women broadens the usual perspective and reflects an attempt to appeal to the rapidly growing group of women readers that emerged in Germany in the nineteenth century. The friendship between the aristocratic Elisabeth von Hohenthal and the middle-class Pauline Felchner and their determination to fight poverty are significant for showing the crossing of class boundaries, but it is equally important that these young women see their lives in terms of public service and activity. The more usual depiction of the oppression and helplessness of the poor is countered in Otto's novel by the presence of active and committed women.

Otto met the writer and publicist August Peters in 1849, not long before he was imprisoned for nine years because of his revolutionary activities. That year she founded the *Frauen-Zeitung* (Women's Newspaper), and, despite the growing reaction following the failure of the 1848 revolution, she kept it alive until 1852. In prose and poetry the paper po-

larized issues and offered powerful, persuasive arguments. The outspoken nature of the *Frauen-Zeitung* ultimately brought about its demise, but not until after Otto had established a widespread network of female supporters whose letters and contributions often showed a surprising political sophistication. The fiction in each weekly issue was alternately by Otto and by various contributors, male as well as female. It echoes the political messages of *Schloß und Fabrik* and Otto's many other socially critical novels of the 1840s, and the heroizing of women remains a prominent theme: the brave girl who sacrifices all and mounts the barricades only to be shot down by the evil representatives of a corrupt regime, for example.

In the 1850s, with the onset of widespread repression following the failed revolution, the zealous tone of Otto's writings of the 1840s had to be muted. Her idealism was expressed in more-subtle terms, as in the poem "Nebel" (Fog). Although it can be read as a harmless description of a natural phenomenon, it has a barely concealed political message. Two of the three stanzas describe fog and the unease that it produces in those who experience it: the missing sun, the silent landscape, the loneliness of a circling eagle, the apprehension felt by the human observer. But the third stanza offers a less than subtle message. Fog, Otto claims, resembles the times: there is no sunshine, and there is not even the chaos of a storm; the world is enveloped by a silent cloud. Then she breaks open her metaphor, calling the sun the sun of freedom and the silence the silence of the people. The exact date of the poem is unknown; it appears in Otto-Peters's last collection of poetry (1893) in the section "Aus der Gefängniszeit" (From the Period of Imprisonment): the section title refers on one level to the imprisonment of Peters and on another to the symbolic imprisonment of the German people. Politics also remains apparent in Otto's novels of this period. The historical novels she wrote during the 1850s do not contain open polemical statements, but they continued to express her liberal beliefs. Connections are almost always drawn between the historical era portrayed and more-recent times, most often the reactionary 1850s. Thus the tendentious message is not missing, even at a time when such comments could have been considered traitorous.

Otto and Peters were married on his release from prison in 1858. They spent their few years together writing and coediting various newspapers, the most important of which was the *Mitteldeutsche Volkszeitung* (Peoples' Newspaper for Central Germany). Peters died in 1864.

In 1865 Otto-Peters founded the Allgemeiner deutscher Frauenverein (General German Women's Organization), the first national women's group in Germany dedicated not to philanthropic purposes but to improving the social and political conditions of women. The journal *Neue Bahnen* (New Paths), founded by Otto-Peters as the organ of the Allgemeiner deutscher Frauenverein, is far more analytic, less spontaneous, and more sophisticated than the *Frauen-Zeitung*. Otto-Peters edited the journal from 1866 until shortly before her death. She not only established editorial policies that continued after her death but also wrote regularly and profusely for it – from occasional poetry to book reviews to obituaries to articles on both contemporary and historical topics. Her own biography is frequently apparent not only in accounts of her childhood and young adulthood but also in analytical discussions of such themes as women writers, education for women, and what sorts of employment and training are appropriate for women. There is a model who is almost always present: Otto-Peters measures the world on the basis of her own experience. She is not naive enough to represent that

Otto-Peters circa 1871

bourgeois experience as absolutely universal – she stresses, for example, the problems of the working class – but she nevertheless sees validity in using her own experiences as illustrative.

Otto-Peters's *Das Recht der Frauen auf Erwerb* (The Right of Women to Employment, 1866) served as a programmatic text for the early years of the bourgeois German women's movement. Once again, she illustrates her ideas by using herself as an example. Bourgeois ideals and an acknowledgment of working-class women characterize her book, which has attracted the attention of modern feminist scholars. Although Otto-Peters emphasizes the traditional role of women as wives and mothers, she also speaks of the need for women to be able to support themselves and to have access to professions and training – thereby reflecting the bourgeois feminist movement, which tended to concentrate on issues of education and employment in its efforts to improve the lot of German women. Although Otto-Peters leaves her discussion of working-class women to the end of her tract, making it appear as an afterthought, her words are sharp and uncompromising and reflect her lifelong concern for improvement in the lives of such women.

Otto-Peters's love of poetry remained constant throughout her life. She produced several volumes of verse and liberally sprinkled poetry in her two journals, and her last book was a collection of verse compiled from earlier publications and titled *Mein Lebensgang* (The Path of My Life, 1893). She never wrote a traditional autobiography, but this collection could be considered a last rebellious act, an autobiography that challenges the usual formal expectations of the genre. She sees her life as a series of momentous events and meaningful revelations, as the life of an active and engaged individual influenced by her intellectual and political environment but also affecting that environment. There are poems about those who influenced her, technological developments that changed her life, and the revolution that played such a galvanizing role in the shaping of her career. Full of optimism at the end of her long life, she leaves this testament of her continuing belief in progress. Otto-Peters died in Leipzig on 13 March 1895 and is buried there in the Johannisfriedhof, next to August Peters.

Despite having engaged in what were viewed in her time as rebellious activities, Otto-Peters can be judged now as having been no more than moderate in her political convictions, her social perceptions, and her writing. The social and political context must be taken into account in any analysis of her life and work: the fragmented and rigidly conservative society in which she grew up, the failed revolution in which she continued to believe, a middle class increasingly characterized by a strong patriarchal ideology, and role expectations that did not welcome women in the public sphere. All of these limitations had a powerful effect on Otto-Peters: her writings are marked by hesitancy combined with a degree of rebelliousness; by an adherence to role models such as Friedrich Schiller, whose attitude toward women writers and acceptable social roles for women was hardly liberal; and by difficulties in making her position clear. Like others of her class, her gender, and her liberal convictions, Otto-Peters reveals in her political activities sporadic radicalism muted by the effort to be acceptable to the patriarchal power structure. In her choice of literary forms — social novels, occasional poetry, and opera librettos — she followed the expectations for women writers of her day.

Her rebelliousness can, however, be seen in her polemical books, articles, and essays: the very choice of such forms is exceptional for a woman of her time and place. But the sentiments expressed in her polemics are most often not radical; they tend to appease while demurely calling for change. The ambivalence of Otto-Peters's writings reflects the difficulties inherent in being a politically engaged middle-class woman in an age that did not know how to accommodate even the slightest rebellion, particularly on the part of the female population. Unlike her contemporary Hedwig Dohm, who avoided formal involvement in the women's movement and confined her rebellion to her writings, Otto moved determinedly into a public world that was often contemptuous or suspicious of her. She thereby made her position infinitely more difficult. This difficulty is reflected in her writings, which both compromise and challenge, and in which she tried to conform while knowing that conformity was folly.

Biographies:

Auguste Schmidt and Hugo Rösch, *Louise Otto-Peters, die Dichterin und Vorkämpferin für Frauenrecht: Ein Lebensbild* (Leipzig: Voigtländer, 1898);

Hedda Zinner, *Nur eine Frau: Roman* (Berlin: Henschel, 1954);

Max Großmann, *Und weiter fließt der Strom: Historischer Roman,* second edition (Berlin: Verlag der Nation, 1966);

Cordula Koepcke, *Louise Otto-Peters: Die rote Demokratin* (Freiburg: Herder, 1981);

Ruth-Ellen Boetcher Joeres, *Die Anfänge der deutschen Frauenbewegung: Louise Otto-Peters* (Frankfurt am Main: Fischer, 1983);

Jeanne Berta Semmig, *Louise Otto-Peters: Lebensbild einer deutschen Kämpferin* (Berlin: Union Verlag, n.d.);

Siegfried Sieber, *Ein Romantiker wird Revolutionär: Lebensgeschichte des Freiheitskämpfers August Peters und seiner Gemahlin Louise Otto-Peters, der Vorkämpferin deutscher Frauenrechte* (Dresden: Ehlermann, n.d.).

References:

Hans Adler, *Soziale Romane im Vormärz: Literatursemiotische Studie* (Munich: Fink, 1980), pp. 115–147;

Gisela Brinker-Gabler, ed., *Frauenarbeit und Beruf* (Frankfurt am Main: Fischer, 1979), pp. 111–123;

Ika Freudenberg, *Wie die Frauenbewegung entstanden und gewachsen ist: Vortrag gehalten im Verein Frauenheil, Würzburg* (Würzburg: Verlagsdruckerei, 1899);

Ruth-Ellen Boetcher Joeres, "1848 from a Distance: German Women Writers on the Revolution," *Modern Language Notes,* 97 (April 1982): 590–614;

Joeres, "Frauenfrage und Belletristik: Zu Positionen deutscher sozialkritischer Schriftstellerinnen im 19. Jahrhundert," in *Frauen sehen ihre Zeit: Literaturausstellung des Landesfrauenbeirates Rheinland-Pfalz* (Mainz, 1984), pp. 21–40;

Joeres, "An Introduction to the Life and Times of Louise Otto," in *Woman as Mediatrix: Essays on Nineteenth-Century European Women Writers,* edited by Avriel H. Goldberger (New York, Westport, Conn. & London: Greenwood Press, 1987), pp. 111–121;

Joeres, "Louise Otto and Her Journals: A Chapter in Nineteenth-Century German Feminism," *Internationales Archiv für Sozialgeschichte der deutschen Literatur,* 4 (1979): 100–129;

Joeres, " 'Ein Nebel schließt uns ein': Social Comment in the Novels of German Women Writers, 1850–1870," *Women in German Yearbook,* 3 (1986): 101–122;

Joeres, "Self-Conscious Histories: Biographies of German Women in the Nineteenth Century," in *German Women in the Nineteenth Century: A Social History,* edited by John C. Fout (New York & London: Holmes & Meier, 1984), pp. 172–196;

Joeres and William H. McClain, "Three Unpublished Letters from Robert Schweichel to Louise Otto," *Monatshefte,* 72 (Winter 1980): 39–50;

Helene Lange and Gertrud Bäumer, eds., *Handbuch der Frauenbewegung,* volume 1: *Die Geschichte der Frauenbewegung in den Kulturländern* (Berlin: Moeser, 1901), pp. 34–38;

Frances Magnus-Hansen, "Ziel und Weg in der deutschen Frauenbewegung des XIX. Jahrhunderts," in *Deutscher Staat und Deutsche Parteien: Friedrich Meinecke Festschrift,* edited by Paul Wentzcke (Munich & Berlin: Oldenbourg, 1922), pp. 201–226;

Lore Mallachow, "Biographische Erläuterungen zu dem literarischen Werk von Louise Otto-Peters," *Weimarer Beiträge,* 9, no. 1 (1963): 150–155;

Jutta Menschik, *Feminismus, Geschichte, Theorie, Praxis* (Cologne: Pahl-Rugenstein, 1977), pp. 19–41;

Renate Möhrmann, *Die andere Frau: Emanzipationsansätze deutscher Schriftstellerinnen im Vorfeld der Achtundvierziger-Revolution* (Stuttgart: Metzler, 1977);

Catherine M. Prelinger, *Charity, Challenge, and Change: Religious Dimensions of the Mid-Nineteenth-Century Women's Movement in Germany* (New York, Westport, Conn. & London: Greenwood, 1987);

Prelinger, "Religious Dissent, Women's Rights, and the *Hamburger Hochschule für das weibliche Geschlecht* in Mid-Nineteenth-Century Germany," *Church History,* 35 (March 1976): 1–14;

Hermann Schneider, "Die Widerspiegelung des Weberaufstandes von 1844 in der zeitgenössischen Prosaliteratur," *Weimarer Beiträge,* 7, no. 2 (1961): 255–277;

Hannelore Schröder, ed., *Die Frau ist frei geboren: Texte zur Frauenemanzipation,* volume 1: *1789–1870* (Munich: Beck, 1979), pp. 218–239;

Margrit Twellmann, *Die deutsche Frauenbewegung: Ihre Anfänge und erste Entwicklung 1843–1889* (Meisenheim am Glan: Hain, 1972);

Else Wex, *Staatsbürgerliche Arbeit deutscher Frauen 1865–1928* (Berlin: Herbig, 1929), pp. 13–17;

Clara Zetkin, "Louise Otto-Peters," in *Zur Geschichte der proletarischen Frauenbewegung Deutschlands* (Frankfurt am Main: Roter Stern, 1971), pp. 218–239.

Papers:

Some of Louise Otto-Peters's papers are held by the Deutscher Staatsbürgerinnen-Verband (Union of German Women Citizens), Berlin.

Wilhelm Raabe

(8 September 1831 – 15 November 1910)

Jeffrey L. Sammons
Yale University

BOOKS: *Die Chronik der Sperlingsgasse,* as Jakob Corvinus (Berlin: Stage, 1857 [i.e., 1856]);

Ein Frühling, as Corvinus (Brunswick: Vieweg, 1857; revised edition, Berlin: Janke, 1872);

Die Kinder von Finkenrode, as Corvinus (Berlin: Schotte, 1859);

Halb Mähr, halb mehr!: Erzählungen, Skizzen und Reime, as Corvinus (Berlin: Schotte, 1859) – comprises "Der Weg zum Lachen," "Der Student von Wittenberg," "Weihnachtsgeister," "Lorenz Scheibenhart," "Einer aus der Menge";

Der heilige Born: Blätter aus dem Bilderbuche des sechzehnten Jahrhunderts, 2 volumes, as Corvinus (Vienna & Prague: Kober & Markgraf, 1861);

Nach dem großen Kriege: Eine Geschichte in zwölf Briefen (Berlin: Schotte, 1861);

Unseres Herrgotts Canzlei: Eine Erzählung in zwei Theilen, 2 volumes (Brunswick: Westermann, 1862);

Verworrenes Leben: Novellen und Skizzen (Glogau: Flemming, 1862) – comprises "Die alte Universität," "Der Junker von Denow," "Aus dem Lebensbuch des Schulmeisterleins Michel Haas," "Wer kann es wenden?," "Ein Geheimnis";

Die Leute aus dem Walde, ihre Sterne, Wege und Schicksale: Ein Roman, 3 volumes (Brunswick: Westermann, 1863);

Der Hungerpastor: Ein Roman in drei Bänden, 3 volumes (Berlin: Janke, 1864); translated by Arnold Congdon as *The Hunger-Pastor,* 2 volumes (London: Chapman & Hall, 1885);

Drei Federn (Berlin: Janke, 1865);

Ferne Stimmen: Erzählungen (Berlin: Janke, 1865) – comprises "Die schwarze Galeere," excerpt translated by Gertrude M. Cross as "How the *Black Galley* Took the *Andrea Doria,*" in *Great Sea Stories of All Nations,* edited by Henry Major Tomlinson (London: Harrap, 1930), pp. 947–953; "Eine Grabrede aus dem Jahre 1609," "Das letzte Recht," "Hollunderblüthe";

Abu Telfan oder Die Heimkehr vom Mondgebirge: Ein Roman in drei Theilen, 3 volumes (Stuttgart: Hallberger, 1868); translated by Sophie Delffs as *Abu Telfan; or, The Return from the Mountains of the Moon,* 3 volumes (London: Chapman & Hall, 1881);

Der Regenbogen: Sieben Erzählungen, 2 volumes (Stuttgart: Hallberger, 1869) – comprises in volume 1, "Die Hämelschen Kinder"; "Else von der Tanne," translated by James C. O'Flaherty and Janet K. King as *Elsa of the Forest* (University: University of Alabama Press, 1972); "Keltische Knochen," "Sankt Thomas," translated by John E. Woods as "Celtic Bones" and "St. Thomas," in *German Novellas of Realism,* volume 2, edited by Jeffrey L. Sammons (New York: Continuum, 1989), pp. 74–108, 29–73; "Die Gänse von Bützow"; "Gedelöcke"; "Im Siegeskranze";

Der Schüdderump, 3 volumes (Brunswick: Westermann, 1870);

Der Dräumling (Berlin: Janke, 1872);

Deutscher Mondschein: Vier Erzählungen (Stuttgart: Hallberger, 1873) – comprises "Deutscher Mondschein," "Der Marsch nach Hause," "Des Reiches Krone," "Thekla's Erbschaft";

Christoph Pechlin: Eine internationale Liebesgeschichte, 2 volumes (Leipzig: Günther, 1873);

Meister Autor oder Die Geschichten vom versunkenen Garten (Leipzig: Günther, 1874);

Horacker (Berlin: Grote, 1876); translated by Woods as "Horacker," in *Wilhelm Raabe: Novels,* edited by Volkmar Sander (New York: Continuum, 1983), pp. 1–153;

Krähenfelder Geschichten, 3 volumes (Brunswick: Westermann, 1879) – comprises in volume 1, "Zum wilden Mann," "Höxter und Corvey"; in volume 2, "Eulenpfingsten," "Frau Salome"; in volume 3, "Die Innerste," "Vom alten Proteus";

Wunnigel: Eine Erzählung (Brunswick: Westermann, 1879);

Alte Nester: Zwei Bücher Lebensgeschichten (Brunswick: Westermann, 1880);

Deutscher Adel: Eine Erzählung (Brunswick: Westermann, 1880);

Das Horn von Wanza: Eine Erzählung (Brunswick: Westermann, 1881);

Fabian und Sebastian: Eine Erzählung (Brunswick: Westermann, 1882);

Prinzessin Fisch: Eine Erzählung (Brunswick: Westermann, 1883);

Pfisters Mühle: Ein Sommerferienheft (Leipzig: Grunow, 1884);

Villa Schönow: Eine Erzählung (Brunswick: Westermann, 1884);

Unruhige Gäste: Ein Roman aus dem Saekulum (Berlin: Grote, 1886);

Im alten Eisen: Eine Erzählung (Berlin: Grote, 1887);

Der Lar: Eine Oster-, Pfingst-, Weihnachts- und Neujahrsgeschichte (Brunswick: Westermann, 1889);

Das Odfeld: Eine Erzählung (Leipzig: Elischer, 1889);

Stopfkuchen: Eine See- und Mordgeschichte (Berlin: Janke, 1891); translated by Woods and Barker Fairley as "Tubby Schaumann" in *Wilhelm Raabe: Novels*, pp. 155–311;

Gutmanns Reisen (Berlin: Janke, 1892);

Kloster Lugau (Berlin: Janke, 1894);

Die Akten des Vogelsangs (Berlin: Janke, 1896);

Gesammelte Erzählungen, 4 volumes (Berlin: Janke, 1896–1901);

Hastenbeck: Eine Erzählung (Berlin: Janke, 1899);

Altershausen, edited by Paul Wasserfall (Berlin: Janke, 1911);

Gesammelte Gedichte, edited by Wilhelm Brandes (Berlin: Janke, 1912);

Sämtliche Werke, 18 volumes (Berlin: Klemm, 1913–1920);

Werke, 4 volumes, edited by Karl Hoppe (Freiburg: Klemm, 1954);

Sämtliche Werke, 24 volumes to date, edited by Hoppe and others, revised edition (Göttingen: Vandenhoeck & Ruprecht, 1966–   ).

SELECTED PERIODICAL PUBLICATIONS –
UNCOLLECTED: "Berthold Auerbachs deutscher Volkskalender auf das Jahr 1859," *Westermanns illustrierte deutsche Monatshefte,* 6 (1859): 159;

"Auf dunklem Grunde: Eine Skizze," *Westermanns illustrierte deutsche Monatshefte,* 10, no. 58 (1861): 341–355;

"Kleist von Nollendorf," *Illustriertes Familien-Journal,* 17, no. 436 (1862): 216–220;

"Der alte Musäus," *Freya,* 7 (1867): 307–310;

Wilhelm Raabe

"Edmund Hoefer," *Über Land und Meer,* 20, no. 27 (1867/1868): 430;

"Auf dem Altenteil: Eine Sylvesterstimmung und Neujahrsgeschichte," *Deutsches Montagsblatt,* no. 52 (30 December 1878);

"Ein Besuch," *Illustrierte Zeitung,* 83, no. 2152 (1884): 316–317;

"Der gute Tag oder die Geschichte eines ersten Aprils," *Daheim,* 48, no. 17 (1912): 19–24; no. 18 (1912): 18–24;

"Aphorismen Raabes: Chronologisch geordnet," edited by Karl Hoppe, *Jahrbuch der Raabe-Gesellschaft* (1960): 94–139.

Wilhelm Raabe, after exceptional fluctuations in reputation, has come to be recognized as a major nineteenth-century German fiction writer; a rather sudden burgeoning of scholarship and interpretation has put understanding of him on an entirely new footing. Although a few of his works have been translated into foreign languages, he is little known outside the German-speaking countries; nevertheless, British, Canadian, and American scholars have played a major role in his modern rehabilitation. They have recognized him as a writer of the Victorian age who was a conscious successor to Charles Dickens and William Makepeace Thackeray, and as an experimenter in ironic narration whose techniques prefigure those of modern fiction. More recently, German scholars have sensed in him a subtle recorder of the psyche of the German bourgeoisie in the second half of the nineteenth century.

Raabe always resisted biography on the grounds that his life was of no interest; those wishing to know him, he said, should read his works. In part, this stance reflects an innate reticence that is also evident in his personal relationships and in his still unpublished diary, which he kept obsessively every day for more than fifty-three years beginning in 1857, yet which reveals little about his deeper feelings and reflections. But it is true also that his external life was singularly uneventful.

Wilhelm Karl Raabe was born on 8 September 1831 in Eschershausen, a small town in the duchy of Brunswick, to Gustav Raabe, a minor but rising judicial official, and Auguste Raabe, née Jeep. Owing to the father's transfers, the family moved a few weeks after his birth to the larger town of Holzminden and in 1842 to the smaller one of Stadtoldendorf. In 1845 the father died of acute appendicitis, leaving Raabe and his mother, brother, and sister in impoverished circumstances. They moved to Wolfenbüttel, where the mother had relatives. For some reason the highly intelligent and imaginative Raabe, who in his mature years would be of a notably studious nature, always had difficulty in school. He had particular trouble with Latin, even though he had a gift for languages: as an adult he was a competent Latinist, knew some Greek, read French with ease, taught himself a reading knowledge of English, and seems to have learned Italian as well. He also had a talent for drawing, and for a time it was thought that he might become an artist. While he did not take up this career, his drawings have always been regarded as an integral part of his creative work and have been much studied.

Although he failed to graduate from the gymnasium, he attended the University of Berlin as an auditor for four semesters. There, in November 1854, he began to write a novel, *Die Chronik der Sperlingsgasse* (The Chronicle of Sparrow Alley); when its appearance late in 1856 (with the date 1857 on the title page) was greeted with friendly reviews, he was encouraged to launch a career of writing fiction. For most of the rest of his life he did little else. By 1862 he felt sufficiently well established to marry Berthe Leiste, of a locally prominent Wolfenbüttel family. They had four daughters, whom he named for four different cultures – Greek, Hebrew, Latin, and Germanic: Margarethe, born in 1863; Elisabeth, born in 1868; Clara, born in 1872; and Gertrud, born in 1876.

On their wedding day the Raabes moved to Stuttgart, where Raabe hoped to find a livelier and less provincial environment. At first all went well; he made many friends, as he always did, despite his introversion. The most important of them were a young writer and journalist, Wilhelm Jensen, and his wife Marie. Jensen is remembered today almost exclusively for Sigmund Freud's analysis of his late novella "Gradiva" (1903); in his own time he was a prominent figure on the literary scene and in some ways a more successful writer than Raabe. Since both men knew that Raabe was the finer writer, this incongruity generated some edginess in their relationship. Marie Jensen was a sensitive reader and eloquent admirer of Raabe's writing. Those who perceive stress in Raabe's marriage see it as having been generated by his attraction to this pretty, vivacious, and artistic woman, who made no secret of her preference for his writing over her husband's. In any case, the Raabes and the Jensens remained friends for more than forty years, though the families, perhaps fortunately for the endurance of the friendship, came to live far from one another.

Otherwise, Raabe's gratification at his situation in Stuttgart was not sustained. His writing career, despite his immense efforts, flagged; he began to find the literary and social life around him shallow and withdrew from it. Most abrasive were political differences: he was a staunch nationalist, longing for the unification of Germany under Prussian leadership (since it could not otherwise be accomplished) and excluding Austria; the Catholic west, on the other hand, was wary of the hegemony of a militantly Protestant Prussia, unenthusiastic about unification, and inclined to sympathize with Austria. These differences led to confrontations, and at

Raabe's outline for his novel Der Hungerpastor *(from Raabe,* Werke, *edited by Karl Hoppe, volume 2, 1954)* the outbreak in 1870 of the Franco-Prussian War (which he greeted with immense enthusiasm) Raabe moved his family to the city of Brunswick, the capital of his homeland. There he lived for forty years without notable incident except for the death of his daughter Gertrud of meningitis at age sixteen. His last published novel, *Hastenbeck,* appeared in 1899. He once said that he was not made to be a twentieth-century writer; nevertheless, he began one more novel, *Altershausen* (1911), worked on it intermittently until 1902, then abandoned it. It is not clear that he ever intended it for publication.

His career is unusual for its time in one respect: Raabe's single-minded concentration on fiction. Most post-Romantic German professional writers were not so specialized. Jensen, for example, wrote not only novellas and novels but also lyric verse, epic poems, dramas, essays, and memoirs, and edited journals. He produced between twice and three times as much as Raabe in a career of about the same length. Raabe went through a phase in which he wrote verse, but he gave it up in recognition of his amateurishness; he thought about writing dramas but did not attempt one. He wrote a single book review and a couple of parochial, forgettable essays. He refused all editorial positions or other employment opportunities and avoided literary associations and, as far as possible, public life generally. He understood his vocation to be his sixty-eight stories, novellas, and novels, and nothing else. One reason German writers tended to be so diversified and prolific was that it was difficult to make money from literature. Raabe, however, was determined to earn his living from fiction. Doing so was not easy, especially for a writer increasingly perceived as demanding and eccentric. As he refined his art, he became conscious that he was developing into the major novelist in the German language, while at the same time his standing with the public was growing increasingly fragile. The consequence was not only a wearying struggle for financial stability but also an embittered and confrontational relationship with publishers and the public.

In the latter part of his life Raabe seemed to have achieved the fame for which he was ambitious. He was showered with honors and prizes. The Schiller Foundation awarded him a grant in 1864 and an annual stipend of one thousand marks beginning in 1886. In 1899 the kingdom of Bavaria decorated him with the Order of Maximilian as the successor to the deceased Swiss poet Conrad Ferdinand Meyer. On his elaborately celebrated seventieth birthday he received a gift of eighteen thousand marks, an honorary doctorate from the University of Tübingen, honorary citizenship of Escherhausen and Brunswick, and hundreds of congratulatory letters and telegrams. The Tiedge Foundation in Dresden awarded him a prize of three thousand marks in 1908, and in the same year Duke Johann Albrecht of Mecklenburg, who was regent in Brunswick, surprised him by having a bust of him placed in the museum. The University of Berlin awarded him an honorary doctorate of medicine in October 1910; the announcement brought the students to their feet, cheering. In his late years his earnings from republications of earlier works became considerable. But it all came too late; his feelings of having been neglected and denied his place in the life of the nation were never assuaged.

Owing to the resistance of the larger public and the taste-making critics Raabe became, much against his will, a coterie writer. In his personal life he avoided literary people and other intellectuals, spending most of his free time sipping wine in taverns surrounded by the bourgeois salt of the earth: officials, professional men, businessmen, schoolteachers, and clergymen. Raabe was well aware that these men had little sensitivity to his artistic acumen, his subtleties of perspective, or his narrative experiments, but he shared with them the mundane exterior surface of his personality and otherwise kept his own counsel.

Soon after his death on 15 November 1910 — the fifty-sixth anniversary of the day he had begun to write *Die Chronik der Sperlingsgasse* — some of these acquaintances formed the Society of the Friends of Wilhelm Raabe; with chapters throughout Germany and in some foreign countries, it became, after the Goethe Society, the second-largest German literary society, and for a generation it militantly managed Raabe's reputation. The society was determinedly unaesthetic and hostile to critical analysis. Its spokespersons portrayed their hero not as the probing, experimental, reflective, ironic, and satirical artist who is recognized today but as a wise man and guide to right thinking, an icon of petit bourgeois verities and nationalist sentiment. In the mid 1920s the society became thoroughly Nazified. Although it endeavored to reconstitute itself in total amnesia immediately after World War II, this course of events left Raabe's reputation severely compromised; among many who suffered through that period it remained unrevivable. The contemporary process of rehabilitation may be thought of as one of rescuing Raabe from his "friends."

These "friends," and the public generally, tended to prefer the earlier works, even though Raabe himself repudiated them as immature. The overall pattern of modern criticism has been to see his first work, *Die Chronik der Sperlingsgasse,* as a highly original creation looking forward to his later achievements; but the following period, until Raabe's move to Stuttgart, is considered a phase of more commonplace writing. Gropingly in Stuttgart and then more confidently in Brunswick he discovered his characteristic voice and manner, a process that culminated in his last and finest works.

Die Chronik der Sperlingsgasse constitutes a striking beginning to Raabe's career. The illegitimate son of a dissolute count and a mother who drowns herself marries a girl who has been courted by his friend, the narrator; after the death of the young man and his wife, the narrator raises their daughter and oversees her betrothal to another youth, who is also a descendant of the count. This plot is in the realm of the most conventional nineteenth-century storytelling: it includes sentiment, renunciation, loyalty in sorrow, poetic justice, and antiaristocratic class consciousness. The story is not told in linear fashion, however, but resides in the memory of the narrator, an elderly man reminiscing in an upper-story room on a narrow street in Berlin. The levels of time interpenetrate and reflect one another; contemporary political and social concerns are woven unobtrusively into the text; the story threatens to escape the narrator's control; a second narrator intervenes, impatient with the incompetence of the first, but is no better able to discipline the narration into normative form. The insecurities and meanderings of the fictional narrators are firmly in the control of the author.

After this success, Raabe did not immediately exploit what are now perceived as its virtues of narrative ingenuity but wrote works that were more conventional and conformed to reader expectations. As soon as he determined upon a writing career he was confronted with the problem of how to remain faithful to his creative vision while achieving success with the public. Not until the end of his career did he accept the likelihood that the problem was insoluble; for years he struggled with it in increasing bitterness and resentment. Thus, for several years after *Die Chronik der Sperlingsgasse* he not only wrote rapidly but tended toward two fairly conventional types of fiction: the historical adventure story and the more or less sentimental story of contemporary life. While approximately a third of Raabe's oeuvre consists of historical fiction, most of it is concentrated in the first half of his career; as it decreased in frequency, however, it increased in literary quality, though even the early works are competently told and often exciting. Some of them have become

Raabe in 1867

children's stories, like Robert Louis Stevenson's. An example is "Die schwarze Galeere" (The Black Galley, 1865; excerpt translated as "How the *Black Galley* Took the *Andrea Doria,*" 1930), a lively story of the revolt of the Netherlands against Spain at the end of the sixteenth century; it has long been a school text. A work that may have been underestimated is *Der heilige Born* (The Holy Spring, 1861), a complicated, somewhat lurid tale about a religious shrine in the Age of the Reformation. The novel is redeemed by a satiric edge; it also introduces one of Raabe's enduring themes, the harm done to Germany by the civil wars that created conditions exploited by foreign powers.

Among the early works of promise with contemporary settings are Raabe's third novel, *Die Kinder von Finkenrode* (The Children of Finkenrode, 1859), a parodic bildungsroman in which the narrator-hero does not get the girl and turns out to be rather a dunce; and the last novel he undertook in Wolfenbüttel, *Die Leute aus dem Walde* (The People from the Forest, 1863), a thoughtful work featuring two of Raabe's persistent motifs: the miseries suffered by children of dysfunctional families, and the "Kleeblatt" (cloverleaf) – three childhood friends whose relationship is followed into adulthood.

It was in Stuttgart that Raabe began to hit his stride as a writer. The best-known products of his eight years in that city are three ambitious novels referred to, from a remark at the end of the third and an extrapolation of the remark in a review by Jensen, as the "Stuttgart Trilogy," although nothing connects them except an increasingly pessimistic view of human possibilities in an obdurately inhumane society: *Der Hungerpastor* (1864; translated as *The Hunger-Pastor,* 1885), *Abu Telfan* (1868; translated, 1881), and *Der Schüdderump* ([the title is an untranslatable term for a sixteenth-century cart employed to transport the corpses of plague victims] 1870). *Der Hungerpastor,* like many of Raabe's works, was rather indifferently received upon publication but grew in acceptance over time; it came to be his best-known book. This reception was another misfortune for his reputation, for the novel has, especially by those who have not read it carefully, been considered anti-Semitic. It tells of the parallel careers of Hans Unwirrsch, an idealistic young man who, after a series of discouraging experiences, becomes pastor of an impoverished community of fishermen on the Baltic, and his Jewish schoolmate Moses Freudenstein, a brilliant scholar of languages whose heartless pursuit of power, status, and wealth leads him to become a Frenchified Catholic intellectual and a police spy and to ruin several women along the way. There is reason to believe that Raabe, though he normally ignored contemporary German letters, modeled this work on Gustav Freytag's *Soll und Haben* (1855; translated as *Debit and Credit,* 1855), a novel that was the great bestseller of mid-nineteenth-century Germany and remained widely read for nearly a hundred years; it, too, contrasts the youthful careers of an earnest, moral Gentile and an evil, conniving Jew. If this assumption is correct, it would be another symptom of Raabe's struggle for recognition by the public: he did not admire Freytag or his novel but registered the book's success and doubtless believed that he could improve on it. This belief was justified, for *Der Hungerpastor* is more thoughtful, more subtle, and more realistic than *Soll und Haben.*

Raabe's relationship to the Jews has been discussed for a long time; generally, the practice has been to show that *Der Hungerpastor* is not anti-Semitic in its intent, that other works by Raabe portray Jews in a sympathetic light (in some cases, per-

haps, these portrayals were motivated by his worry about the effect of *Der Hungerpastor*), and that he maintained good relations with Jews. He himself vociferously denied that he was anti-Semitic and became quite irritable whenever the issue was brought up. But regardless of Raabe's intent in writing the novel, the long popularity of *Der Hungerpastor* may, in some quarters, have been owing to a perception of it as anti-Semitic. Also, while Raabe's entourage included Jews, it also included anti-Semites. He was a national and class partisan and often expressed himself intolerantly about those thought to be alien, including, sometimes, the Jews. The best that can be said about such expressions is that they were customary at the time and that they were not pronounced features of Raabe's speech and writing.

Der Schüdderump is the gloomy story of an unachieved mésalliance between a well-meaning but tepid country nobleman, Hennig von Lauen, and an illegitimate orphan girl, Tonie Häussler. The girl's grandfather, a jovial, vigorous, utterly amoral man of wealth and prestige, tries to sell her to a dissolute Russian aristocrat; though he is balked in this attempt, he is unpunished for his deeds, is not much less pleased with himself at the end of the novel than at the beginning, and is throughout admired by the majority of the community. He represents Raabe's conviction, particularly pronounced at this time, about the absence of justice and empathy among the common run of people. The most pessimistic of his major works, *Der Schüdderump* is not highly regarded today, perhaps because its pervasive gloom is felt to be a regression to a form of sentimentality. More respected is the middle novel of the "Trilogy," *Abu Telfan,* a deft social and political satire about a man who returns to his hometown after ten years of slavery in Africa and finds himself even more out of phase with his community and family than he was when he left. The central character, Leonhard Hagebucher, is unheroic: he is maladroit and limited in his affects, and, as the reader comes to see, is himself infected by the maladies that debilitate human relations in the community and family. Raabe works across the grain of reader expectations, involving the reader in the imaginative process and making him or her a cocreator of the text. Few readers of his time, however, wanted to work that hard.

Although these three novels are the most prominent works of the Stuttgart period, at the same time Raabe was unobtrusively experimenting with the possibilities of first-person narration. His range in this regard is virtually unsurpassed in German fiction. In "Keltische Knochen" (1869; translated as "Celtic Bones," 1989) the narrator is the passive observer of the grotesquely comic efforts of two scholars to steal bones and artifacts from the excavations of the Hallstatt culture near Salzburg. (Raabe is underestimated as a comic writer. Traditionally he was referred to as a "Humorist," which in German usage denotes one who takes a calmly harmonious, idealistic posture elevated above worldly contradictions, and Raabe sometimes so denominated himself; but he was also capable of a range of comic effects from the elegant to the slapstick.) In "Sankt Thomas" (1869; translated as "St. Thomas," 1989), on the other hand, the narrator, a military chaplain who accompanies a futile Dutch siege of a Spanish-held island, is so affected by the horror he witnesses that he is driven to the edge of madness. "Else von der Tanne" (Elsa of the Fir, 1869; translated as *Elsa of the Forest*, 1972), set in the period after the Thirty Years' War, is about an innocent young girl who is stoned as a witch; it is told in the third person, but the narrative perspective is so close to the consciousness of the pastor who experiences the event, so subtly reveals his repressed and unacknowledged erotic stirrings, that it resembles a first-person technique. With "Im Siegeskranze" (In the Victory Wreath, 1869), Raabe tried his hand at a female narrator, a young girl who sets her insane stepsister free in defiance of their family; Raabe thus gives the Victorian motif of the "madwoman in the attic" an unusual twist.

His most original experiment in the Stuttgart period was *Drei Federn* (Three Pens, 1865), in which three narrators alternately relate the story from quite different perspectives. Raabe felt that with this novel he was learning his trade at last, and later he referred to it as his first independent work. Here Dickens begins to be displaced as a model by Thackeray. Raabe greatly admired Dickens, and one can detect elements of Dickens's tone and technique in several places, starting with *Die Chronik der Sperlingsgasse;* there are characters in *Drei Federn* who seem clearly derived from Wickfield and Uriah Heep in *David Copperfield* (1849–1850). But it was from Thackeray that Raabe learned about first person narration. He taught himself English to read *Pendennis* (1848–1850), and he was especially drawn to Thackeray's unreliable first–person narrators who cause satire and irony to double back on the narration itself. Raabe was to refine this technique in his most mature works. The public in no way acknowledged these efforts; and the critics complained regularly of Jean-Paulian mannerisms, a shorthand of the time for any deviation from four-square realism with the authorial voice completely suppressed.

Thus, when Raabe moved to Brunswick in 1870 he was discouraged concerning his career

Self-portrait of Marie Jensen, drawn in 1887. Jensen and her husband, Wilhelm, were friends of Raabe and his wife for more than forty years (Schleswig-Holsteinische Landesbibliothek, Kiel).

prospects. Nevertheless, he produced one work after another, year upon year. It would be inaccurate to suppose that this sequence was a steady progression to his late masterpieces; there are works from the Brunswick period that are imperfectly achieved or even routine. Nevertheless, the variety of which he was capable is striking. The novella "Zum wilden Mann" (At the Sign of the Wild Man, 1879) and the novel *Unruhige Gäste* (Restless Guests, 1886) are both set in the Harz Mountain region in the neighborhood of Bad Harzburg and have some overlapping characters. But they are quite different in type. "Zum wilden Mann" is a bizarre story in which a pharmacist owes his modest prosperity to the benefaction of an acquaintance who then disappears; thirty years later the acquaintance reappears with lurid tales of having been a hereditary executioner and henchman of Brazilian dictators, and he demands and receives the return of his gift with interest. *Unruhige Gäste,* on the other hand, is a somber tale of psychological realism in which the narrative voice is almost totally suppressed; it tells of a friendly, privileged young man who, through care-

Raabe in 1892; painting by Hans Fechner (from Gero von Wilpert,
Deutsche Literatur in Bildern, *1965)*

lessness and inattention, permanently upsets the equilibrium of a fine young woman who is religiously repressed but unconsciously ready for emancipation.

Der Dräumling (The Dräumling Swamp, 1872) and *Meister Autor* (Master Author, 1874) both touch on aspects of literary culture; the first portrays with kindly if uproarious satire the 1859 Friedrich Schiller Centennial in a backwater town, while the second views an aging, nearly forgotten author through the somewhat cynical eyes of a gentleman of society. "Deutscher Mondschein" (German Moonshine, 1873) portrays a man who is attacked by the moon in 1848 and becomes a literal lunatic, rebelling against authority and writing political verse; in "Frau Salome" (Madame Salome, 1879) the daughter of a mad sculptor is rescued from her father. "Vom alten Proteus" (Of Old Proteus, 1879) tells of moronically banal lovers who are aided in their purposes by a much brighter hermit and two highly entertaining ghosts. *Horacker* (1876; translated, 1983), a much-loved novel that may be the classic example of Raabe as a humorist, describes a town in terror of an escaped criminal; he turns out to be an undernourished nineteen-year-old who is much less frightening than the petty-

minded absence of human sympathy among the townspeople. *Pfisters Mühle* (Pfister's Mill, 1884), Raabe's only work that directly reflects public events of the time it was written, deals with water pollution. It has, therefore, enjoyed a considerable vogue in the late twentieth century. It is less an ecological tract, however, than an ironic probe into the social dilemmas of industrialization.

The culmination of Raabe's mature phase is generally thought to be his last two historical novels, *Das Odfeld* (The Odin Field, 1889) and *Hastenbeck*; the three social novels called by analogy the "Brunswick Trilogy," *Alte Nester* (Old Nests, 1880), *Stopfkuchen* (Stuffcake, 1891; translated as "Tubby Schaumann," 1983), and *Die Akten des Vogelsangs* (The Documents of the Birdsong, 1896); and the fragmentary novel *Altershausen*.

The two historical novels deal with the Seven Years' War, a conflict that occupied an important place in Raabe's consciousness and to which he returned several times. For him it was a civil war fought to no detectable benefit to the German people by princes who, for their own ends, invited foreign powers to ravage the land. Raabe, who was a considerable amateur student of history, wrote much about wars and their aftermath, but after passing through his youthful phase of adventure fiction he took little interest in heroism and glory; instead, he put much emphasis on the sufferings of ordinary people and the damage to humane, civilized values. *Das Odfeld* is set before, during, and after a battle that took place on 5 November 1761 on a heath near Raabe's birthplace not a major battle but a bloody, indecisive, and ultimately pointless skirmish. Noah Buchius, a timid, crotchety, superannuated teacher who has been left behind in an abandoned cloister school, shepherds a group of civilian refugees through the horrors of the day, a task at which he succeeds (though his favorite pupil, a high-spirited, rascally young man, is killed) owing to his scholar's curiosity and knowledge of the terrain. Thus, Raabe, as he often did, projects a transformation of aspects of his imagined self – here the neglected, peripheral bookworm – into a situation that tests and reveals his qualities. One much-discussed element of the text is a battle of ravens in the sky preceding the battle on the ground; Buchius rescues one of the ravens and takes it to his cell, but at the end of the story it escapes and flies to freedom. The battle between birds of the same species may symbolize the self-laceration of the Germans in their useless wars. Raabe, whose name means "raven" (his first five books were published under the pseudonym Jakob Corvinus, from *Corvus,* the Latin for "raven"), frequently employed ravens, blackbirds, jackdaws, and the like as images; they are another aspect of his ironic, self-reflexive narrative habits.

Hastenbeck takes place in the aftermath of a battle in July 1757; it concerns the rescue, in the midst of the chaos, of two young lovers, hardly more than children, by mentors who guide them to neutral territory. The boy is an unsoldierly conscript who has deserted and therefore must be hidden. By vocation he is a painter of figures on the porcelain manufactured at Fürstenberg; the delicate rococo decoration is meant to contrast with the miseries of war. The contrast is replicated by reference to the pastoral idylls of Salomon Gessner, a bloodstained copy of which is carried around by a wounded old Swiss warrior; the juxtaposition implies that the rococo idylls are a mendacious distraction from the sufferings of the real world. Raabe also develops at the narrative level a vision of the future well beyond the consciousness of the characters, with references to the beginnings of the coming great age of German classicism and romanticism. Thus, in the last work published in his lifetime he projects hopes for the German future – not the Germany of the empire, which disappointed him in many ways, but the Germany of the liberal imagination that drew on the humane achievements of literature and philosophy.

The novels of the "Brunswick Trilogy" are narrated by personalities whose perspectives require the interpreter to read not only with them but, sometimes, against them. The effect is least pronounced in *Alte Nester;* the narrator, Fritz Langreuter, stands – not always observantly – outside the other three characters' process of self-discovery and maturation, which involves outgrowing the sentimentally recollected idyll of childhood. Part of the story concerns the transformation of an aristocratic estate into a modern farm; symbolically, the stones of the ruined castle, which cannot be restored as one of the characters had wished, are employed to build a bridge. The resolution is achieved by a thoughtful but initially not very competent cousin of two of the young people, Just Everstein, who acquires confidence and sheds his German diffidence and submissiveness to authority through his experiences as a farmer in the United States.

Today *Alte Nester* is held in rather less regard by critics than the other two novels of the "trilogy," which are commonly assessed as the late masterpieces of Raabe's career. He himself thought *Stopfkuchen* his finest achievement: in no previous work is the relationship between narrator and subject so involved and intense. The narrator, called only Eduard, is a prosperous farmer in South Africa who is visiting his hometown in Germany. He goes to see a childhood acquaintance, Heinrich Schaumann, called "Stopfkuchen" from his gluttonous habits, who lives on a farm built within the fortifications of a redoubt from which the town was bombarded in the Seven Years' War. Schaumann becomes a secondary narrator, garrulously rolling over Eduard's attempts to say anything about himself. He recounts his own history as a victorious self-creation, from his youth as a despised fat boy struggling against horrible parents and malicious peers; through his taming of and marriage to a wild girl and his subduing of her savage father; to his inheritance of his father-in-law's property, on which his heart had been set from boyhood; after which he cut himself off from the community as far as possible. As persistently as Eduard tries to insist on his former friendship for Schaumann, just as relentlessly Schaumann includes Eduard among those who tormented him and his wife. Finally, Schaumann tells Eduard something that sends him fleeing back to South Africa. It happens to be the day of the funeral of a postman who had been Eduard's mentor; the postman had introduced him to the travel book that inspired Eduard to his wanderings. Schaumann reveals a discovery he has long kept secret: years before, the mild-mannered postman – under extreme provocation, to be sure – had killed a man and had allowed the suspicion to fall on the querulous, universally disliked misanthrope who was to become Schaumann's father-in-law. Eduard writes his story on board ship, and since he is concerned to exculpate himself from his complicity in the persecution of Schaumann and his family and to repress insights, his narrative must be read with uncommon alertness.

Stopfkuchen is not an easy novel to understand, and it has taken a long time to obtain adequate critical perspectives on it. In the past Eduard was perceived as a neutral, colorless narrator of no special importance to the story; only attentive reading reveals his implication in and distortive effect on the story he relates. Schaumann, on the other hand, was taken to have achieved complacency and unperturbed sovereignty above the crude world of common experience, and thus to be a projection of the author's ideal self. But Schaumann's claimed equilibrium is an illusion; he is still roiled by unappeased resentment and vengefulness. No other alter ego of Raabe is so militant or hostile or possesses such a violent imagination.

The narrator of *Die Akten des Vogelsangs,* Karl Krumhardt, is a great deal more searching and conscientious than the devious Eduard. A disciplined, orderly official following in the footsteps of his strict father, he begins to generate the "documents"

Raabe in 1901

of his life when he is informed by a childhood friend, the wealthy German-American Helene Mungo, née Trotzendorff, of the lonely death in Berlin of another friend, Velten Andres. Velten was the visionary son of a cheerful, tolerant, and unwaveringly supportive mother (like Raabe's own mother), and he spent his energies in quixotic pursuit of Helene. After she married an American millionaire, he let his life wind down to stasis in a fruitless effort to kill all feeling in himself. Krumhardt recognizes Velten as an alternative self, a path not taken, a symbol of unrealized possibilities of freedom and imagination in himself; he must endeavor to reintegrate himself by acknowledging this split in his psyche. Most critics have seen in this work a projection of an unresolved dichotomy in Raabe's own self, though they differ as to whether the novel, which caused him the most severe agonies of creation in his entire career, comes to a resolution. More recently the novel has been seen in sociopsychoanalytic terms, with Velten understood as the repressed, utopian, maternal alternative to the patriarchal, achievement-oriented, bourgeois Krumhardt. Velten's alternative is, however, not without dangers: though intelligent and competent, he is unable to realize himself in

any effective way; in his pursuit of Helene he refuses to respect her autonomy. The shaping of the self by the indulgent mother, though deeply gratifying, may not have been an unqualified advantage for Velten (and, by extension, for Raabe); his mother is contrite about it at the end of her life, while Velten, by masking his true circumstances from her, implicitly repudiates the harmony of mother and son. In one of the strangest scenes in Raabe's fiction, Velten burns some of his mother's belongings after her death and then opens her house to looting by neighbors and the members of a traveling circus before giving it away. The novel is certainly one of Raabe's finest and most challenging; the serious irony with which it treats the dichotomy of bourgeois rectitude and imaginative temperament has been thought to prefigure the work of Thomas Mann.

The fragmentary nature of the posthumously published *Altershausen* presents interpretive difficulties that may be insuperable insofar as it is difficult to see whither the novel is tending, and it is possible that Raabe himself lost his way in it. Begun when he was contemplating, with some anxiety, his seventieth birthday a couple of years hence, it opens with the narrator, the prestigious medical scientist Fritz Feyerabend, having survived a seventieth-birthday celebration of his own. Here Raabe undertakes a last experiment in narrative technique: the narration begins in the first person but continues in the third, a further device of the objectivization of the self. Feyerabend, retired, widowed, and childless, decides to reconnect himself with his origins by returning to his hometown, Altershausen, where he hopes to see a childhood friend, Ludchen Bock. To his horror he finds that Ludchen's development was arrested by a head injury when he was twelve; he is now a whiny old man teased by the townspeople, doing odd jobs for drinking money, and in the care of another childhood friend, a placid, nurturing woman. The text breaks off with Feyerabend in a conversation with her. Much interpretive ingenuity has been expended on what Feyerabend may or may not have recovered in his quest; the text has several intriguing features, including two dream scenes, one of them heavily laden with psychic stress. It may be that Raabe ran into insoluble difficulties in his characterization of Ludchen, for the retarded, disagreeable man can hardly serve as an icon of the recovery of past time or the successful closing of life's circle. Several other troubling features, such as a whiff of anti-Semitism, suggest that Raabe may have been wise in knowing when to retire from his creative career.

Raabe is a striking example of how discoveries may still be made in the most familiar precincts of literary history. A writer who within living memory was held in limited if not low regard by canonical criticism, who seemed to belong to a parochial German literature that had failed to penetrate its national borders, whose reputation was compromised by the complicity of his admirers in the atrocities of modern German history, has been rehabilitated by the capacity to read with fresh eyes and refined attentiveness. There is reason to think that an adequate evaluation and understanding of Raabe as a major nineteenth-century writer of European dimensions has just begun.

Letters:

"In alls gedultig": Briefe Wilhelm Raabes, edited by Wilhelm Fehse (Berlin: Grote, 1940);

Briefwechsel Raabe–Jensen, edited by Else Hoppe and Hans Oppermann, supplementary volume 3 of Raabe's *Sämtliche Werke* (Göttingen: Vandenhoeck & Ruprecht, 1970);

Briefe, edited by Karl Hoppe and Hans-Werner Peter, supplementary volume 2 of Raabe's *Sämtliche Werke* (Göttingen: Vandenhoeck & Ruprecht, 1975).

Bibliographies:

Hans Martin Schultz, *Raabe-Schriften: Eine systematische Darstellung* (Wolfenbüttel: Heckner, 1931);

Fritz Meyen, *Wilhelm Raabe Bibliographie,* second edition, supplementary volume 1 of Raabe's *Sämtliche Werke* (Göttingen: Vandenhoeck & Ruprecht, 1973);

Manfred R. W. Garzmann and Wolf-Dieter Schuegraf, eds., *Raabe-Verzeichnis: Bestände in Braunschweig, Marbach/Neckar und Wolfenbüttel* (Brunswick: Stadtarchiv und Städtische Bibliotheken, 1985).

Biographies:

Herman Anders Krüger, *Der junge Raabe: Jugendjahre und Erstlingswerke. Nebst einer Bibliographie der Werke Raabes und der Raabeliteratur* (Leipzig: Xenien-Verlag, 1911);

Wilhelm Fehse, *Wilhelm Raabes Leben* (Berlin: Klemm, 1928); revised and enlarged as *Wilhelm Raabe: Sein Leben und seine Werke* (Brunswick: Vieweg, 1937);

Jochen Meyer, *Wilhelm Raabe: Unter Demokraten, Hoflieferanten und Philistern. Eine Chronik seiner Stuttgarter Jahre* (Stuttgart: Fleischhauer & Spohn, 1981);

Raabe in 1906

Gespräche: Ein Lebensbild in Aufzeichnungen und Erinnerungen der Zeitgenossen, edited by Rosemarie Schillemeit, supplementary volume 4 of Raabe's *Sämtliche Werke,* edited by Karl Hoppe and others (Göttingen: Vandenhoeck & Ruprecht, 1983);

Horst Denkler, *Wilhelm Raabe: Legende – Leben – Literatur* (Tübingen: Niemeyer, 1989).

References:

Eduard Beaucamp, *Literatur als Selbstdarstellung: Wilhelm Raabe und die Möglichkeiten eines deutschen Realismus* (Bonn: Bouvier, 1968);

Margrit Bröhan, *Die Darstellung der Frau bei Wilhelm Raabe und ein Vergleich mit liberalen Positionen zur Emanzipation der Frau im 19. Jahrhundert* (Frankfurt am Main & Bern: Lang, 1981);

Horst S. Daemmrich, *Wilhelm Raabe* (Boston: Twayne, 1981);

Horst Denkler, *Neues über Wilhelm Raabe: Zehn Annäherungsversuche an einen verkannten Schriftsteller* (Tübingen: Niemeyer, 1988);

Paul Derks, *Raabe-Studien: Beiträge zur Anwendung psychoanalytischer Interpretationsmodelle. Stopfkuchen und Das Odfeld* (Bonn: Bouvier, 1976);

Heinrich Detering, *Theodizee und Erzählverfahren: Narrative Experimente mit religiösen Modellen im Werk Wilhelm Raabes* (Göttingen: Vandenhoeck & Ruprecht, 1990);

Irene Stocksieker Di Maio, *The Multiple Perspective: Wilhelm Raabe's Third-Person Narratives of the Braunschweig Period* (Amsterdam: Benjamins, 1981);

Ulf Eisele, *Der Dichter und sein Detektiv: Raabes "Stopfkuchen" und die Frage des Realismus* (Tübingen: Niemeyer, 1979);

Barker Fairley, *Wilhelm Raabe: An Introduction to His Novels* (Oxford: Clarendon Press, 1961);

Marilyn Sibley Fries, *The Changing Consciousness of Reality: The Image of Berlin in Selected German Novels from Raabe to Döblin* (Bonn: Bouvier, 1980);

Charlotte L. Goedsche, *Narrative Structures in Wilhelm Raabe's* Die Chronik der Sperlingsgasse (New York, Bern, Frankfurt am Main & Paris: Lang, 1989);

Uwe Heldt, *Isolation und Identität: Die Bedeutung des Idyllischen in der Epik Wilhelm Raabes* (Frankfurt am Main, Bern & Circencester, U.K.: Lang, 1980);

Hermann Helmers, *Die bildenden Mächte in den Romanen Wilhelm Raabes* (Weinheim: Beltz, 1960);

Helmers, *Wilhelm Raabe* (Stuttgart: Metzler, 1968);

Helmers, ed., *Raabe in neuer Sicht* (Stuttgart, Berlin, Cologne & Mainz: Kohlhammer, 1968);

Karl Hoppe, *Wilhelm Raabe als Zeichner* (Göttingen: Vandenhoeck & Ruprecht, 1960);

Hoppe, *Wilhelm Raabe: Beiträge zum Verständnis seiner Person und seiner Werke* (Göttingen: Vandenhoeck & Ruprecht, 1967);

Wolfgang Jehmüller, *Die Gestalt des Biographen bei Wilhelm Raabe* (Munich: Fink, 1975);

Fritz Jensch, *Wilhelm Raabes Zitatenschatz* (Wolfenbüttel: Heckner, 1925);

Nancy A. Kaiser, *Social Integration and Narrative Structure: Patterns of Realism in Auerbach, Freytag, Fontane, and Raabe* (New York, Bern & Frankfurt am Main: Lang, 1986);

Eduard Klopfenstein, *Erzähler und Leser bei Wilhelm Raabe: Untersuchungen zu einem Formelement der Prosaerzählung* (Bern: Haupt, 1969);

Hans Kolbe, *Wilhelm Raabe: Vom Entwicklungs- zum Desillusionierungsroman* (Berlin: Akademie-Verlag, 1981);

Rolf-Dieter Koll, *Raumgestaltung bei Wilhelm Raabe* (Bonn: Bouvier, 1977);

Leo A. Lensing, *Narrative Structure and the Reader in Wilhelm Raabe's* Im alten Eisen (Bern, Frankfurt am Main & Las Vegas: Lang, 1977);

Lensing and Hans-Werner Peter, eds., *Wilhelm Raabe: Studien zu seinem Leben und Werk* (Brunswick: pp-Verlag, 1981);

Gerhart Mayer, *Die geistige Entwicklung Wilhelm Raabes: Dargestellt unter besonderer Berücksichtigung seines Verhältnisses zur Philosophie* (Göttingen: Vandenhoeck & Ruprecht, 1960);

Hubert Ohl, *Bild und Wirklichkeit: Studien zur Romankunst Raabes und Fontanes* (Heidelberg: Stiehm, 1968);

Hans Oppermann, *Raabe* (Reinbek: Rowohlt, 1970);

Nicolaas Cornelis Adrianus Perquin, S. J., *Wilhelm Raabes Motive als Ausdruck seiner Weltanschauung* (Amsterdam: Paris, 1927);

Stanley Radcliffe, *Der Sonderling im Werk Wilhelm Raabes,* volume 2 of *Raabe-Forschungen,* edited by Hans-Werner Peter (Brunswick: pp-Verlag, 1984);

Irmgard Roebling, *Wilhelm Raabes doppelte Buchführung: Paradigma einer Spaltung* (Tübingen: Niemeyer, 1988);

Eugen Rüter, *Die Gesellschaft der Freunde Wilhelm Raabes: Rezeptionssteuerung als Programm* (Darmstadt: Thesen, 1977);

Jeffrey L. Sammons, *The Shifting Fortunes of Wilhelm Raabe: A History of Criticism as a Cautionary Tale* (Columbia, S.C.: Camden House, 1992);

Sammons, *Wilhelm Raabe: The Fiction of the Alternative Community* (Princeton: Princeton University Press, 1987);

Walter Schedlinsky, *Rolle und industriegesellschaftliche Entwicklung: Die literarische Vergegenständlichung eines sozialgeschichtlichen Phänomens im Werk Wilhelm Raabes* (Frankfurt am Main: Fischer, 1980);

William T. Webster, *Wirklichkeit und Illusion in den Romanen Wilhelm Raabes,* volume 1 of *Raabe-Forschungen,* edited by Peter (Brunswick: pp-Verlag, 1982).

Papers:

The Raabe Archive is in the Stadtarchiv und städtische Bibliothek (Municipal Archives and Library), Brunswick; there are also materials in the Niedersächsisches Staatsarchiv (Lower Saxon State Archives), Wolfenbüttel, and the Deutsches Literaturarchiv (German Literature Archives), Marbach am Neckar.

Fritz Reuter

(7 November 1810 – 12 July 1874)

Wulf Koepke
Texas A&M University

BOOKS: *Läuschen un Riemels: Plattdeutsche Gedichte heiteren Inhalts in mecklenburgisch-vorpommerscher Mundart* (Treptow: Selbstverlag, 1853; enlarged edition, Anclam: Dietze, 1856);

Polterabendgedichte in hochdeutscher und niederdeutscher Mundart (Treptow: Selbstverlag, 1855; enlarged edition, Schwerin: Hildebrand, 1863);

Dei Reis' nah Belligen: Poetische Erzählung in niederdeutscher Mundart (Treptow: Selbstverlag, 1855);

Der 1. April 1856 oder Onkel Jakob und Onkel Jochen: Lustspiel in 3 Acten; Blücher in Teterow: Dramatischer Schwank in 1 Act (Greifswald & Leipzig: Koch, 1857);

Abweisung der ungerechten Angriffe und unwahren Behauptungen, welche Dr. Klaus Groth in seinen Briefen über Plattdeutsch und Hochdeutsch gegen mich gerichtet hat (Berlin: Wagner, 1858);

Die drei Langhänse: Original-Lustspiel in drei Akten (Berlin: Guthschmidt, 1858);

Kein Hüsung (Greifswald: Koch, 1858);

Läuschen un Riemels: Neue Folge. Plattdeutsche Gedichte heiteren Inhalts in mecklenburgisch-vorpommerscher Mundart (Neubrandenburg: Selbstverlag, 1859);

Olle Kamellen, 7 volumes (Wismar & Ludwigslust: Hinstorff, 1859–1868) — comprises volume 1, *Twei lustige Geschichten: Woans ick tau 'ne Fru kam; Ut de Franzosentid* (1860 [i.e., 1859]); "Woans ick tau 'ne Fru kam" translated by Paul C. Glave as *How I Came by a Wife* (Denver: Echo, 1883); "Ut de Franzosentid" translated by Charles Lee Lewes as *In the Year '13: A Tale of Mecklenburg Life* (New York: Leypolt & Holt, 1867); translated by Carl F. Bayer Schmidt as *When the French Were Here* (Rutherford, Madison & Teaneck, N. J.: Fairleigh Dickinson University Press, 1984); volume 2, *Ut mine Festungstid* (1862); volumes 3–5, *Ut mine Stromtid* (1863–1864), translated anonymously as *Seed-time and Harvest; or, "During My Appren-*

Fritz Reuter; portrait by Wulff (from Kuno Francke and William Guild Howard, eds., The German Classics of the Nineteenth and Twentieth Centuries, *volume 8, 1914)*

ticeship" (Philadelphia: Lippincott, 1871); translated by M. W. Macdowall as *An Old Story of My Farming Days,* 3 volumes (Leipzig: Tauchnitz, 1878; London: Low, Marston, Searle & Rivington, 1878); volume 6, *Dörchläuchting* (1866); volume 7, *De meckelnbörgischen*

Montecchi un Capuletti oder De Reis' nah Konstanti-nopel (1868);

Hanne Nüte un de lütte Pudel: 'Ne Vagel- un Minschenge-schicht (Wismar & Ludwigslust: Hinstorff, 1860);

Schurr-Murr: Wat tausamen is schrapt ut de hochdütsche Schöttel, ut den plattdütschen Pott un den missing-schen Ketel (Wismar & Ludwigslust: Hinstorff, 1861);

Sämmtliche Werke, 15 volumes (Wismar: Hinstorff, 1869–1875; New York: Steiger, 1869–1875);

Manuscript eines Romans, edited by Rudolf Bender (Halle: Selbstverlag, 1930);

Einer selbander: Ungedrucktes Novellenfragment, edited by Wilhelm Greiner (Eisenach: Kühner, 1935);

Herr von Hakensterz und seine Leibeigenen: Roman, edited by Willi Finger (Rostock: Hinstorff, 1949);

Herr von Hakensterz und seine Tagelöhner: Manuskript eines Romans, edited by Kurt Batt (Leipzig: Reclam, 1961);

Gesammelte Werke und Briefe, 9 volumes, edited by Batt (Rostock: Hinstorff, 1966–1967);

Das Leben im Paradiese; Gezeiten des Lebens, translated into standard German by Friedrich and Barbara Minssen (Vienna & Munich: Langen/Müller, 1977).

OTHER: *Unterhaltungsblatt für beide Mecklenburg und Pommern*, edited by Reuter (April 1855–March 1856);

Alwine Wuthenow, *En poa Blomen ut Annmarick Schulten ehren Goahrn*, edited by Reuter (Greifswald & Leipzig: Koch, 1858);

Nige Blomen ut Annmarick Schulten ehren Goahr, edited by Reuter (Greifswald & Leipzig: Koch, 1861).

SELECTED PERIODICAL PUBLICATIONS–
UNCOLLECTED: "Die Feier des Geburtstages der regierenden Frau Gräfin, wie sie am 29. und 30. Mai 1842 in der Begüterung vor sich ging," "Erster Tag," *Mecklenburgisches Volksbuch für das Jahr 1846* (1846): 136–154;

"Hans Dumm, der kluge Bauer," "Offener Brief an die mecklenburgischen Landwirte," "Das Turnen," "Zweiter Tag," *Mecklenburg: Ein Jahrbuch für alle Stände* (1847): 140–143, 148–150, 167–169, 171–173;

"Von't Pird up den Esel," "Wenn't kümmt, denn kümmt mit Huupen," *Plattdütsche Volkskalenner* (1859): 22–29, 80–82;

"Wat bi 'ne Äwerraschung 'rute kamen kann," *Platt-dütsche Volkskalenner* (1860): 42–57;

"Ein Heimatloser in Mecklenburg," *Die Grenzboten*, 21 (1862): 501–516.

Fritz Reuter has a secure place as the classical writer of Low German prose in the nineteenth century, the writer who elevated Low German literature beyond regional entertainment. Starting out without much literary ambition, Reuter was soon taken seriously and is still counted among the foremost realists in Germany. His instant popularity and immense fame endured as long as there was a large enough audience to read and enjoy Low German stories. The dramatic population movements following World War II and the growing impact of mass communication have contributed to a considerable decrease in the number of Low German speakers, especially among the reading public. Thus, while Reuter's name is still familiar, and scholars and critics keep discussing his works, those works are much less accessible for a general audience than they used to be. Translations into standard German, even those by Reuter himself, are largely unsuccessful: the lifeblood of his tales is his idiom, the language that conveys vividness and authenticity. It was only after years of mediocre and unconvincing writing in standard German that Reuter found his own voice when he dared to switch to his native tongue.

Reuter was born on 7 November 1810 in Stavenhagen, a town of twelve hundred inhabitants in eastern Mecklenburg, northwest of Neubrandenburg. One of Reuter's ancestors was Christian Reuter, author of the entertaining and popular *Schelmuffskys Wahrhafftige curiöse und sehr gefährliche Reisebeschreibung zu Wasser und Land* (Schelmuffsky's Account of His Truly Strange and Dangerous Journey by Water and Land, 1696). His father, Georg Johann Reuter, the son of a minister, was mayor and municipal judge of Stavenhagen.

Georg Reuter was a demanding and stern public servant who had been raised in the spirit of the Enlightenment; a progressive and successful farmer and entrepreneur in addition to his public duties, he was prosperous in spite of the unfavorable conditions and general backwardness of the grand duchies of Mecklenburg. He demanded the same energy, dedication, business sense, and ambition from his only son, who had none of these qualities. Reuter's mother, Johanna Luise Oelpke Reuter, was paralyzed as a consequence of the difficult birth of Reuter's younger brother, who died before his second birthday; she used a wheelchair until her death in 1825. Reuter's father did not remarry but had two daughters out of wedlock, whom he adopted.

Reuter's education in Stavenhagen was largely left to friends and relatives. In 1824 he was sent to a gymnasium in Friedland, transferring in 1828 to one in Parchim. Anything but a good student, he was talented as an artist and enjoyed drawing and painting, liked sports, and was not averse to mathematics; but he was lazy, chronically late with his homework, and showed little interest. His father forbade an artistic career for him and insisted that he study law. In 1831 Reuter began his studies at the University of Rostock, at that time an institution of little distinction and few students. In the spring of 1832 he transferred to Jena University. He did not attend many lectures but got involved with the liberal student group Burschenschaft Germania. After a group of students and workers stormed the military guardhouse in Frankfurt am Main on 3 April 1833, the authorities reacted with extremely harsh measures: around two thousand students at various universities were arrested and sentenced to long years of imprisonment. Reuter left Jena and returned home. In the fall of 1833 he tried to register at the University of Leipzig but was rejected. In Berlin, where he also attempted to enter the university, he was arrested on 30 October. Reuter was not a Prussian citizen, he had never lived in Prussia, and his only "crime" was temporary membership in the Burschenschaft. The government of Mecklenburg made many attempts to achieve his extradition to his own country, where lenient treatment would have been guaranteed, but in 1836 the Berlin court sentenced him to death; the sentence was commuted to thirty years in prison and later reduced to eight years. Reuter spent the first year in Berlin, then more than two years in Silberberg in the Silesian mountains; from there he was transferred to Magdeburg and finally to Graudenz in East Prussia. His prison years, in spite of the humorous tone of his later autobiographical account *Ut mine Festungstid* (From My Time in the Fortress, 1862), were devastating for Reuter. He wasted the best years of his youth in damp and unhealthy cells, and he contracted many diseases. The worst effect of his imprisonment was dipsomania, an irresistible craving for alcohol that would befall Reuter every few months for the rest of his life and make him unfit for any regular career.

During his prison years he did some drawing; tried to study mathematics, agriculture, and other subjects; and wrote poems. In 1839 he was finally transferred to Mecklenburg, where he spent a year at the fortress of Dömitz. In 1840 the new Prussian king Friedrich Wilhelm IV granted a general amnesty. Reuter returned home, a sick and broken man with few prospects. He asked his father to allow him to turn to agronomy, but the father insisted on one more attempt to complete law school. A semester in Heidelberg in the fall of 1840 was a disaster. Finally, Reuter was allowed to gain practical knowledge of agriculture, but his hope of buying his own farm was dashed: when his father died in 1845, his will refused Reuter access to the capital of the inheritance and placed harsh conditions on his receiving even the interest. Reuter found refuge with his friend Fritz Peters, who administered the estate Talberg near Treptow. Also in 1845, he met Luise Kuntze, a governess, and began a long courtship of her.

Reuter's earliest published prose pieces are mostly satirical and betray the influence of Jean Paul and Heinrich Heine, as well as lesser and now forgotten writers of wit and satire. "Die Feier des Geburtstages der regierenden Frau Gräfin, wie sie am 29. und 30. Mai 1842 in der Begüterung vor sich ging" (The Celebration of the Birthday of the Governing Countess, as It Occurred on 29 and 30 May 1842 on the Estate) was probably written in 1845; it was published anonymously in 1846. The piece ridicules the nobility of Mecklenburg, the abject dependence of their subjects, and the anachronistic feudalism of the country. The perspective is that of a liberal onlooker; concern is mixed with arrogance. The satire is rather gross and aggressive, and the work has little literary merit.

Around 1847 Reuter began work on a novel that he abandoned in 1850. *Herr von Hakensterz und seine Leibeigenen* (Baron von Hakensterz and His Serfs, 1949) demonstrates the misery caused by serfdom, which had only been abolished in Mecklenburg in 1829, but Reuter also intended to allow his aristocratic landowner a process of education and enlightenment. In a balloon ride over Mecklenburg Reuter has one of his characters outline his ideas for liberal reforms.

Reuter was involved in the March 1848 Revolution; he was sent to a constitutional assembly as the delegate from Stavenhagen, and he was active in a democratic club. In Mecklenburg the revolution did change things: the privileges of the nobility were curtailed, and a legislature elected by the people was constituted. Reuter was no great politician; he soon turned to political journalism rather than politics proper, writing articles proposing progressive methods in agriculture. He still wanted to make his living in agriculture, but since he lacked the funds to lease an estate he turned to teaching. In 1850 he began giving private lessons in drawing, sports, and mathematics in Treptow. In 1851 he married Luise Kuntze, who joined him in Treptow and contributed to the family income by giving piano and French lessons. In his spare time Reuter turned many of the anecdotes and jokes that he liked to tell his friends into Low German poems. Unable to find a publisher, he borrowed money from a friend and published the poems in 1853, just in time for the Christmas market, as *Läuschen un Riemels* (Funny Stories and Rhymes). Reuter dared to print twelve hundred copies, and after the holidays they were gone. *Läuschen un Riemels* would always remain popular: most of the short, funny stories were already known to the audience, but they are told in a lively and concentrated form. They relate everyday events in Mecklenburg, usually in a somewhat exaggerated fashion, but they retain enough realism to sound authentic. They contain practical jokes and some violence but no sex, and they evoke mild laughter. One story is that of a shoemaker whose daughter runs away to become an actress and returns to town with a theater group. When the character she is portraying in the play kneels down and asks her father for forgiveness, the shoemaker goes up on the stage and declares that he will forgive her. There are also simple jokes, such as the one about the farm boy who asks the pharmacist for a headache remedy. The pharmacist treats the boy with smelling salts, but then the boy tells him that it is his master's daughter who has the headache. There are stories about horse trades, daughters who fight over an inheritance, stupid and wise judges, apprentices and servants who trick their masters, Jews and Christians. Even Field Marshal Gebhard Leberecht von Blücher, the popular hero of the Wars of Liberation against Napoleon, makes an appearance. Occasionally Reuter contrasts standard and Low German, and he also exploits the comic effects of "Missingsch," a hybrid of standard German vocabulary and Low German grammar that would later be made immortal by his character Inspektor Bräsig.

Läuschen un Riemels appeared at a time when there was special interest in dialect literature, and in Low German in particular. Klaus Groth's *Quickborn* (1853), a collection of lyrical and narrative poetry in Low German, had just been published; it would soon be followed by John Brinckman's novel *Kaspar Ohm un ik* (Caspar Ohm and I, 1855). In this atmosphere of heightened expectations Reuter's modest poems could easily be judged by unfair standards, and the critical response was scant and largely negative. Groth, who was to become a fan of Reuter's novels, condemned *Läuschen un Riemels* in his *Briefe über Hochdeutsch und Plattdeutsch* (Letters on Standard

German and Low German, 1858). Reuter's work seemed to Groth to reinforce the prejudice that Low German was only good for low topics and that low comedy and farce were all that Low-German-speaking people liked. Reuter's later works were directed to a middle-class audience, but he would never try to "ennoble" the language or the people; he remained a realist.

Reuter had written many humorous poems, skits, and dialogues for festive occasions; encouraged by the success of *Läuschen un Riemels,* he published a collection of them in 1855 as *Polterabendgedichte* (Poems for a Wedding Eve). The book was popular with Reuter's primary audience in Mecklenburg and Pomerania but is of little lasting value. Some of the dialogues and scenes in the collection indicate an inclination toward the drama, and Reuter was indeed thinking about conquering the stage. For the time being, however, he became the editor of the newly founded weekly *Unterhaltungsblatt für beide Mecklenburg und Pommern* (Family Journal for the Two Duchies of Mecklenburg and Pomerania). The journal, started in April 1855, lasted for about a year. Besides short stories and narrative poems, it carried news and readers' letters; it offered a mix of Low German and standard German material. The contributions from writers in the region turned out to be insufficient in quantity and quality, and Reuter was unable to provide the bulk of the material himself. Finally, he had to resort to reprinting already published material. In the course of his work Reuter made the acquaintance of several regional writers, among them Brinckman, but he was relieved when the journal ceased to exist. It never sold more than three hundred to four hundred copies.

In 1855 Reuter published another book at his own expense. A satire on newly rich peasants, *Dei Reis' nah Belligen* (The Trip to Belgium) is a verse narrative, a genre that was popular at the time. Reuter had started it in standard German in 1845 and had rewritten it in Low German in 1846 – his first use of the dialect. In 1854 he had returned to the work, enriching it with a love story and ameliorating the biting tone. It remains largely in the style of *Läuschen un Riemels,* dealing with peasants in a mode of low comedy. The farmers Swart (Black) and Witt (White) decide to take their sons to "Belligen" (Belgium) to educate them. Their wives are opposed to the idea – as is Swart's son Fritz, who is in love with the sexton's daughter – but the men are stubborn. They get passports and head south. Since they do not know the world and are not very bright, they have some unwelcome adventures and lose most of their money and possessions. In Neustrelitz they are thrown in jail after a brawl with some musicians; in Berlin they are completely bewildered. In the meantime, Swart's wife finds out that her son wants to marry the sexton's daughter; she is dead set against the marriage because the sexton's family does not have much money. But the girl saves Frau Swart's life when she falls into a creek, and she relents. In the end the men return, humiliated but richer in experience, and the wedding will take place. Enriching comedy with a love plot was a recipe that would work well for Reuter in his subsequent stories.

In 1856 the Reuters moved to Neubrandenburg, where Reuter would write his most important works. He completed three plays: *Der 1. April 1856 oder Onkel Jakob und Onkel Jochen* (The First of April 1856; or, Uncle Jacob and Uncle John), a comedy in three acts, and *Blücher in Teterow*, a one-act farce that was an expansion of the last anecdote in *Läuschen un Riemels,* were published together in 1857; they were followed by *Die drei Langhänse* (The Three Long Johns, 1858), another comedy in three acts. All three plays were performed, the last one in Berlin in March 1858, but none had lasting success. They are remarkable for Reuter's attempts to mix Low German and standard German for comic effect. Hardly any writer of the nineteenth century did not have a phase of dramatic ambition, which is understandable given the enormous importance of theater in German social life. But Reuter soon realized that in spite of his talent for lively dialogue, and although many of his tales can be called "dramatic," he had no real sense for the stage. He abandoned these dreams, and did not even include the plays in his collected works.

In 1858 Reuter's tragic verse tale *Kein Hüsung* (No Homestead), which he always considered his best work, was published. The young day laborer Jehann and his pregnant fiancée, Mariken, need the permission of Jehann's master, the baron, to marry. But the permission is denied because Jehann had angered the baron by saving a child from a burning house rather than caring for the baron's horses, and Mariken had rejected the baron's sexual advances. Jehann wants to immigrate to America, but Mariken cannot leave her sick old father. Jehann learns that his father had been in a similar situation with the baron's father: the old baron had taken the father's girlfriend, and Jehann's father had had to keep his mouth shut. Jehann will not take his master's arrogance with the same endurance. A dispute erupts, and Jehann kills the baron in self-defense and has to

flee. Mariken stays behind and gives birth to her child. But she is driven out of her hut after her father dies, and the child is to be taken away from her. She flees into hiding; later she loses her mind and drowns herself. The child is raised by a neighbor. Years later Jehann returns, claims his son, and takes him to freedom in America. There are lengthy arguments about the right to resist injustice and the question of moral guilt. The tale conveys a powerful message about conditions in backward Mecklenburg. Reuter did not return to the tragic mode, preferring conciliatory humor, but he never glossed over the problems in his homeland. It is clear in *Kein Hüsung,* however, that the social problems are primarily individual problems; they are caused by the remnants of feudal privileges, but it is the irresponsible behavior of the aristocrats that leads to the tragedy. Political freedom is needed, but it will not solve all the problems.

Reuter finally found a publisher who was willing and able to market his books effectively. Detloff Carl Hinstorff of Rostock was a businessman who did not know much about literature. No friendship ever developed between the two men; Reuter bargained hard for the best terms he could obtain, and Hinstorff took his revenge by printing pirated editions of Reuter's works. But Reuter was tired of acting as his own publisher, and Hinstorff handled the marketing well. It was not a difficult task, for Reuter's popularity was growing rapidly. Hinstorff brought out the fourth edition of *Läuschen un Riemels* in 1859, and in the same year he published a volume comprising two prose stories: "Woans ick tau 'ne Fru kam" (translated as *How I Came by a Wife,* 1883) and "Ut de Franzosentid" (From the Time of the French Occupation; translated as *In the Year '13,* 1867). The volume was titled *Olle Kamellen,* which means something like "Old Stories That Are Known to All but Almost Forgotten and Not That Important." The first story is a benign version of William Shakespeare's *The Taming of the Shrew:* the narrator tells how his uncle helps him to find a caring and obedient wife. The story has farcical elements and could be considered misogynistic; the narrator's kindhearted manner of telling the story is inconsistent with his actions in the story. Apparently Reuter was still shaking off the tradition of low comedy.

There is an enormous qualitative jump from that story to the novella or short novel "Ut de Franzosentid." Set in Stavenhagen and based on tales Reuter had heard as a child, the story includes Reuter's parents and many of his other relatives and friends among its characters. The town is vis-

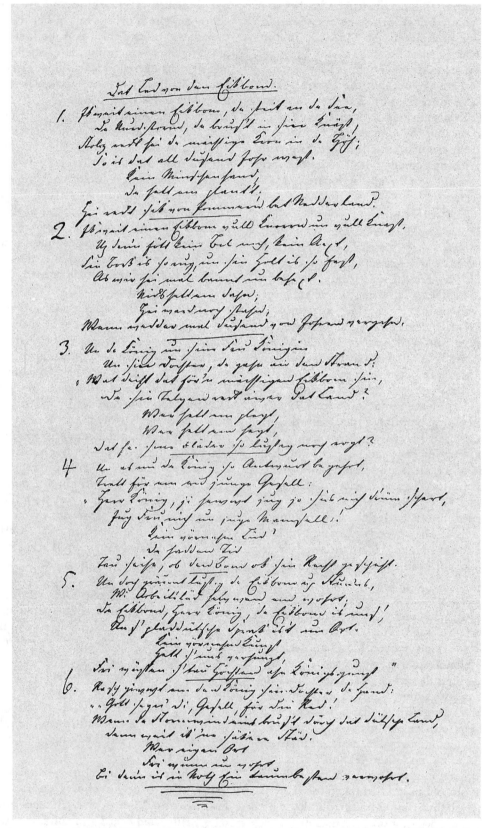

Page from the manuscript for Reuter's Hanne Nüte un de lütte Pudel *(from Friedrich Vogt and Max Koch,* Geschichte der deutschen Literatur von der ältesten Zeiten bis zur Gegenwart, *1910)*

ited by marauding French soldiers who try to take advantage of the chaos following the French defeat in Russia in 1812–1813. The townspeople get the soldiers' leader drunk to prevent him from confiscating property; but, through a series of misunderstandings, when the regular French troops arrive the town officials and the miller are accused of murdering him. After a series of fast-paced episodes and vivid descriptions of the atmosphere of the time, a happy ending is reached. If "Woans ick tau 'ne Fru kam" can be seen as misogynistic, "Ut de Franzosentid" takes the opposite viewpoint: the miller, who has a low opinion of women, is converted by the exceptional courage and intelligence of his daughter. The superpatriotism of 1813 is seen in an ironic light, while the inner conflicts of Germans serving in the French army are described sympathetically. The characters have human weaknesses, but they are generally upright and well intentioned. The narrator laughs with, not at his countrymen. The humor is conciliatory; while it by no means condones everything, it accepts the human condition. With this perspective, Reuter had found his true voice. Furthermore, "Ut de Franzosentid" is saturated with authentic details. It is not a string of episodes but a close-knit tale. Public and private events are given equal prominence, reflecting Reuter's populist view of history.

By this time Reuter's reputation had spread beyond the Low-German-speaking area, and literary critics took note of the new novelist. Even Groth relented and praised this volume and the following prose narratives. Reuter's undeniable strengths were his mastery of dialogue, the authenticity of his descriptions of milieu, and his realistic depiction of his characters. His plots were conventional, but he obviously delighted in describing scenes of country and small-town life and creating odd characters. Without the Low German idiom, these situations and characters turn flat; they live through the language and its connotations.

Hanne Nüte un de lütte Pudel: 'Ne Vagel- un Minschengeschicht (Hanne Nüte and the Little Poodle: A Story about People and Birds, 1860) is a verse epic in an idyllic mode. Johann Snut, nicknamed "Hanne Nüte," is the only son of a master blacksmith who is learning his father's trade and will inherit the shop. Fike Smidt, nicknamed "de lütte Pudel" (the Little Poodle), is the oldest daughter of a poor man with many children: she is not only pretty but exceptionally bright, responsible, and industrious. After an apprenticeship with his father,

Hanne must spend three years as a wandering journeyman. This is where the birds come in: to keep the budding love between Hanne and Fike intact, they save Hanne from the many temptations on the road, including the young and attractive widows of blacksmiths who would like to keep the handsome and hardworking man in their house. Reuter describes the bird society in human terms, except that there is more harmony and goodwill among the birds than among humans. In Cologne Hanne befriends an old Jewish woman whose son was murdered twenty years previously; the murderer was never caught. Then she is killed with Hanne's hammer, which had been missing from his toolbox. He is accused of the murder and jailed. The news reaches his native village, brought by a rich baker from the next town who has hired Fike as a maid. The baker makes advances to her and even proposes marriage; her mother pressures her to accept, so as to alleviate the family's abject poverty, but her father tells her to resist. In Cologne another smith, prompted by a bird, confesses to the murder of the old Jewish woman. Meanwhile, the vengeful baker accuses Fike of stealing silver spoons that he has hidden in her room. When the mayor and a councillor examine the case, they discover, thanks in part to half of a ring sent from Cologne and in part to the help of the birds, that the baker had murdered a Jew twenty years ago. Hanne and his lütte Pudel are reunited in the end.

The story is told in an engaging style, but there is, as Reuter himself realized, a problem with the two levels on which it operates: on the one hand, it is full of realistic details, including the rituals and language of the wandering journeymen; on the other hand, it is also a fairy tale. The murders of Jews and the mixture of realism and legend are reminiscent of the novella "Die Judenbuche" (The Jew Beech, 1842), by Annette von Droste-Hülshoff; but Droste-Hülshoff was much more successful in fusing the two levels. Reuter had tried something that was beyond his talent: to create a modern legend. Nevertheless, the story gained considerable popularity with readers and even among critics.

Schurr-Murr (1861), the following collection published by Hinstorff, was generated by contractual obligations: Reuter was supposed to deliver one volume per year. The book consists of three funny tales that had been published previously; "Abenteuer des Inspektor Bräsig (Adventures of Inspector Bräsig, a first-person narrative of some episodes that Reuter would later incorporate in *Ut mine Stromtid* (My Time as an Agricultural Apprentice,

1863–1864; translated as *Seed-time and Harvest,* 1871); and the autobiographical account "Meine Vaterstadt Stavenhagen" (My Hometown Stavenhagen) in standard German. *Schurr-Murr* means a mixture of uneven quality and with little unity, and that is exactly what this collection is.

"Meine Vaterstadt Stavenhagen" is the beginning of an autobiography that was never written, although *Ut mine Festungstid* supplies material from a later period in Reuter's life. Reuter starts with a description of the town and its surroundings as they were when he was a child, and contrasts it with the present. He goes on to tell stories about school, dancing lessons and balls, theater performances, country fairs, and the Jewish peddlers going from house to house. The work provides a lively and authentic picture of what it meant to grow up in a small town in Mecklenburg at the beginning of the nineteenth century. Reuter is at his best in the narration of funny scenes. This relatively short piece shows that Reuter was fully capable of writing stories in standard German as well as Low German although he found it impossible to translate his work from one idiom to the other.

Ut mine Festungstid was written in 1861 and published in 1862 as volume two of *Olle Kamellen;* a first version of some episodes in standard German had been published in 1855 in the *Unterhaltungsblatt für beide Mecklenburg und Pommern.* Reuter had a hard time coming to grips with this most painful part of his life, and for *Ut mine Festungstid* he chose the "best" part of his prison years, the time he spent in Graudenz. The story consists of mostly humorous incidents and describes the widespread corruption that made life easier for prisoners who had money. The prisoners are young; they think of love, they play practical jokes, they never lose hope. The commanders, officers, and guards are only human. Reuter suggests some cruel treatment but does not describe it. The reader comes away regarding both guards and prisoners as common victims of an irrational system.

Immediately after completing *Ut mine Festungstid* Reuter started on his crowning achievement, *Ut mine Stromtid.* Instead of offering an autobiographical view of the 1840s, when he tried to be a "Strom" (agricultural apprentice), he expanded the novel into a general view of conditions in Mecklenburg between 1830 and 1850. The book shows that Reuter was paying more attention to the literary trends of the period: he was aware of the work of Karl Leberecht Immermann, Jeremias Gotthelf, Berthold Auerbach, Wilhelm Raabe, Theodor Fontane, Charles Dickens, and especially Gustav Freytag's novel *Soll und Haben* (1855; translated as *Debit and Credit,* 1855) and Brinckman's *Kaspar Ohm un ik. Ut mine Stromtid,* which comprises volumes three to five of *Olle Kamellen,* is set in rural Mecklenburg and focuses on the nobility; the rural middle class of farmers with large homesteads, Lutheran ministers, and administrators of large estates; and the urban counterparts of the latter class: merchants, lawyers, doctors, and Jewish moneylenders. Political events such as the March 1848 Revolution are seen from the perspective of the village. Once more, Reuter depicts the individual sources of social movements. A moralist who would not accept the idea that human beings are determined by their milieu, he believed in individual responsibility.

The story begins in 1829 with the bankruptcy of the farm manager Hawermann, who, although he is a competent agronomist, cannot meet his financial obligations because of his betrayal by Pomuchelskopp, the owner of the farm. The bankruptcy and auctioning off of his property coincide with the sudden death of his wife, leaving him alone with his young daughter, Luise. His old friend Bräsig finds a place for him as an administrator on the estate of Pümpelhagen, which belongs to the Kammerrat (Counselor of the Exchequer) von Rambow. Pastor Behrens and his wife, who live nearby, take care of Luise. Hawermann is successful in his farming operation, but he cannot overcome the profligacy of the Kammerrat's wife and his son, Axel, a Prussian lieutenant. Hawermann gets two apprentices: the Kammerrat's nephew, Franz, and the pastor's nephew, Fritz.

After suffering a heart attack, the Kammerrat moves to Pümpelhagen. That winter he dies of a second heart attack. Axel quits the service, returns to the estate, and tries to improve it. Pomuchelskopp, who has designs on the estate; the unscrupulous notary Slusuhr; and the moneylender David know that Axel has gambling debts and will be easy prey. Axel trusts Pomuchelskopp more than he trusts Hawermann; when an account book and a sum of money disappear, Hawermann is wrongly accused and feels compelled to give up his post. He finds refuge with Mrs. Behrens, whose husband has died in the meantime. Bräsig investigates, and clears Hawermann's name. Bräsig is the protagonist in a subplot that shows how traces of the old feudal system still persisted in Mecklenburg: his aristocratic master had made Bräsig's pension conditional on his not marrying, and it takes some tenacious action to change the count's mind. During the March 1848 Revolution the laborers on Pomuchelskopp's estate, fed up with his harsh and arbitrary rule, chase him out of the country. Meanwhile, Axel von Rambow has died, leaving his widow saddled with debt to the moneylender Moses, David's father. Moses agrees to give her a chance to pay off the debt under the condition that she rehire Hawermann. Thus, Hawermann's reputation is restored. In the happy ending of another subplot, Franz von Rambow is engaged to Luise.

Reuter's villains are weak people who are seduced by greed and the lure of social standing; his heroes are those who stick to their principles. The real attractions of the book are its lively scenes, its dialogue and its cumulative depiction of a whole society through typical representatives. Reuter's optimistic view, which is not typical for the period of reaction after 1848, is reinforced by the epilogue set in the early 1860s: the narrator finds that people like Hawermann and Bräsig, both now deceased, have left a heritage of progress and public spirit that has visibly improved the countryside.

In 1863 Reuter received an honorary doctorate from the University of Rostock. He considered the honor a sign of his rehabilitation in the eyes of society. That year he moved to Eisenach in Thuringia, where he built a comfortable villa. He thereby cut himself off from the environment that was so vital for his inspiration. There is a consensus among critics that Reuter's works after *Ut mine Stromtid* show a decline in inspiration and creative powers. In *Dörchläuchting* (His Highness, 1866) and *De meckelnbörgischen Montecchi un Capuletti oder De Reis' nah Konstantinopel* (The Mecklenburg Montagues and Capulets; or, The Trip to Constantinople, 1868), volumes six and seven of *Olle Kamellen,* respectively, the plots are conventional and contrived, the characters and situations are repeats, and the messages are of little weight. The title character of *Dörchläuchting* is Duke Adolf Friedrich IV of Mecklenburg-Strelitz, the lesser of the two duchies of Mecklenburg. The duke is mortally afraid of ghosts, of work, of witches, of thunderstorms, and of women; he also has paranoid fears that he might be deposed. The other main characters are the duke's servant, Halsband, who wants to quit, marry, and take over his father-in-law's business; the Konrektor (assistant principal) Äpinus; and Äpinus's housekeeper, Dürten. The plot involves various pranks that take advantage of the duke's fears, and many episodes that show how much the other characters depend on the duke's whims; the "little people" prevail through cleverness and an accurate observation of the duke's weaknesses.

The reader has to decide whether to consider the arbitrary rule of such an unfit duke as simply ridiculous or outrageous.

De meckelnbörgischen Montecchi un Capuletti oder De Reis' nah Konstantinopel intertwines Reuter's favorite target, the newly rich; a love story; and a comic picture of tourism. Reuter had taken a trip to the Near East in 1864 and drew from this experience, though his descriptions of the sites are hardly memorable. A group of tourists from Mecklenburg includes a newly rich family, the Groterjahns. The love story is that of Helene Groterjahn and Karl Jahn, whose family is also among the tourists. Helene's socially ambitious mother, Jeannette Groterjahn, longs to have an aristocrat for her son-in-law, and thus is easy prey for an impostor who turns out to be a tailor who is on the run from the law. Reuter employs language contrasts to characterize the figures: Jeannette Groterjahn does not speak Low German, nor does she allow her children to speak it; the people with common sense use it without inhibition. The trip goes through Berlin, Vienna, Venice, and Corfu, to Istanbul; on the way back the drama unfolds in Verona, the setting of Shakespeare's *Romeo and Juliet.* The parody is not very daring. Reuter knew that it was not his best work, and he decided to stop writing. He had more than reached his goal: he was well off financially and had gained critical respect. He was fifty-eight years old, in poor health, and did not want to write mediocre books.

Reuter left one promising project unfinished. He had worked on "De Urgeschicht von Meckelnborg" (Earliest History of Mecklenburg) since 1859. The text, which breaks off at the end of the twelfth chapter, was published posthumously in 1874 in volume fourteen of his collected works. The introduction shows Reuter at his humorous best: he says that he found an old manuscript describing the history of Mecklenburg from the Creation to the year 1200, but while he was away on a trip his wife organized his papers and unwittingly threw away the invaluable manuscript. Fortunately, Reuter had already read it, and now he will restore it from memory. The rest of the fragment is a satirical view of the country and its backwardness. Creation was less than ideal, since God relied too much on the help of his lazy angels. The first inhabitants of Mecklenburg, which was originally a large swamp, were frogs and storks; from them descended the common people and the aristocrats, respectively. The text points out repeatedly that nothing has changed in Mecklenburg since the most primitive times, and nothing is likely to change. "Urgeschicht von Meckelnborg," which is spiced with many allusions to living persons, shows that there was a residue of aggression left in Reuter. In a less timid age, he could have developed his Swiftian vein.

Reuter was happy to see Schleswig-Holstein return to Germany in 1864, and he greeted the new German Empire in 1871 with patriotic verses. Even so, he maintained that he had not changed his political views, as many other liberals had. He received a flood of invitations to read from his works, but he shunned public appearances. Many actors and recitors, however, made their livings reading from Reuter's texts.

Reuter's collected works appeared from 1869 to 1875 in Germany and in the United States, where they were enjoyed by recent German immigrants. Reuter died on 12 July 1874. Until World War II his popularity remained intact; his image was largely that of an entertaining writer of funny stories. Reuter scholarship had a heavy dose of regional partisanship, including the defense of the beleaguered Low German dialects. The most serious attempt at a revaluation came after World War II in the German Democratic Republic, with an emphasis on Reuter's social criticism. Since then there have been movements to restore and preserve Low German as a literary medium, and Reuter remains the unsurpassed master of narrative prose in that language. Although it suffers from a stigma attached to Low German as a language of the lower classes, Reuter's oeuvre transcends the limitations of regionalism.

Letters:

Briefe von Fritz Reuter an seinen Vater (1827–1841), edited by Franz Engel (Brunswick: Westermann, 1896);

Briefe: Gesamtausgabe, edited by Otto Weltzien (Leipzig: Hesse & Becker, 1913);

Briefe Fritz Reuters an seinen Verleger Detloff Carl Hinstorff, edited by Arnold Hückstädt (Rostock: Hinstorff, 1971).

Bibliographies:

Wilhelm Seelmann, "Reuter-Bibliographie," *Jahrbuch des Vereins für niederdeutsche Sprachforschung,* 22 (1896): 102–107; 28 (1902): 87–95; 41 (1915): 62–68;

Ilse Barnikol, "Fritz-Reuter Bibliographie," in *Fritz Reuter: Eine Festschrift zum 150. Geburtstag,* edited by the Reuter-Komitee der Deutschen Demokratischen Republik (Rostock: Hinstorff, 1960), pp. 187–226;

Georg Günther, *Fritz Reuter Bibliographie,* edited by Walter Lehmbecker (Lübeck: Fritz-Reuter-Gesellschaft, 1971);

Heinz C. Christiansen, "Fritz Reuter-Auswahlbibliographie," in *Fritz Reuter Gedenkschrift,* edited by Hans C. Christiansen (Amsterdam: Rodopi, 1975), pp. 95–114.

Biographies:

Karl Theodor Gaedertz, *Fritz-Reuter-Reliquien* (Wismar: Hinstorff, 1885);

Wilhelm Trinius, *Erinnerungen an Fritz Reuter* (Wismar: Hinstorff, 1886);

Gaedertz, *Aus Fritz Reuters jungen und alten Tagen,* 3 volumes (Wismar: Hinstorff, 1896–1901);

Abraham Römer, *Fritz Reuter in seinem Leben und Schaffen: Mit Erinnerungen persönlicher Freunde des Dichters und anderen Überlieferungen* (Berlin: Mayer & Müller, 1896);

Gaedertz, *Im Reiche Reuters* (Leipzig: Wigand, 1905);

Gaedertz, *Fritz Reuter* (Leipzig: Reclam, 1906);

Wilhelm Seelmann, *Reuters Leben und Werke* (Leipzig: Bibliographisches Institut, 1908);

Kurt Batt, *Fritz Reuter: Leben und Werk* (Rostock: Hinstorff, 1967);

Michael Töteberg, *Fritz Reuter in Selbstzeugnissen und Bilddokumenten* (Reinbek: Rowohlt, 1978);

Arnold Hückstädt, *Wenn einer Augen hat zu sehen . . . Fritz Reuter: Sein Leben in Bildern und Texten* (Hamburg: Christians, 1986).

References:

Paul Bailleu, "Fritz Reuters Universitäts- und Festungszeit," *Deutsche Rundschau,* 43 (1885): 385–401;

Kurt Batt, "Fritz Reuters *Ut mine Stromtid,*" *Sinn und Form,* 19 (1967): 717–739;

Batt, "Reuter und die Folgen: Arbeitsnotizen zu einer wirkungsgeschichtlichen Skizze," in *Mecklenburg: Ein Lesebuch,* edited by Batt (Rostock: Hinstorff, 1977), pp. 289–314;

Hans Bunje, *Der Humor in der niederdeutschen Dichtung des Realismus* (Neumünster: Wachholtz, 1953);

Christian Bunners, *Fritz Reuter und der Protestantismus: Theologische Beiträge zu Fritz Reuter, seinem Werk und dessen Rezeption* (Berlin: Evangelische Verlagsanstalt, 1987);

Heinz C. Christiansen, *Fritz Reuter* (Stuttgart: Metzler, 1975);

Christiansen, ed., *Fritz Reuter-Gedenkschrift* (Amsterdam: Rodopi, 1975);

Hans-Dietrich Dahnke, "Fritz Reuter: Sein Werk und die Frage des Erbes," *Weimarer Beiträge:*

Zeitschrift für Deutsche Literaturgeschichte, 6, no. 3 (1960): 487–505;

Willi Finger-Hain, *Fritz Reuter in der Weltliteratur* (Flensburg: Wolf, 1970);

Lotte Foerste, "Fritz Reuter," in *Deutsche Dichter des 19. Jahrhunderts,* edited by Benno von Wiese (Berlin: Schmidt, 1969), pp. 412–439;

Fritz Reuter: Eine Festschrift zum 150. Geburtstag, edited by the Reuter-Komitee der Deutschen Demokratischen Republik (Rostock: Hinstorff, 1960);

Fritz-Reuter-Gedenkbuch zum 100. Geburtstag des Dichters (Allgemeiner Plattdeutscher Verband, 1910);

Karl Theodor Gaedertz, *Fritz-Reuter-Studien* (Wismar: Hinstorff, 1890);

Maria Hähner, *Der politische und kulturgeschichtliche Hintergrund in Fritz Reuters "Ut de Franzosentid": Ein Beitrag zur Reuterforschung* (Münster: Mulle, 1916);

Arnold Hückstädt, ed., *Fritz Reuter im Urteil der Literaturkritik seiner Zeit* (Rostock: Hinstorff, 1983);

Monika Jaeger, *Theorien der Mundartdichtung: Anspruch und Funktion* (Tübingen: Tübinger Vereinigung für Volkskunde, 1964);

Carl Friedrich Müller, *Reuter-Lexikon: Der plattdeutsche Sprachschatz in Fritz Reuters Schriften, gesammelt und alphabetisch geordnet* (Leipzig: Hesse & Becker, 1904);

Gustav Raatz, *Wahrheit und Dichtung in Fritz Reuters Werken: Urbilder bekannter Reuter-Gestalten* (Wismar: Hinstorff, 1895);

Friedrich Rothe, "Unkel Bräsig: Zur nachrevolutionären Erzählkunst im 19. Jahrhundert," *Deutsche Vierteljahrsschrift für Literaturwissenschaft und Geistesgeschichte,* 43 (June 1969): 260–273;

Wilhelm Seelmann, *Reuter-Forschungen* (Soltau: Norden, 1910).

Papers:

The most important collection of Fritz Reuter's papers is in the Goethe- und- Schiller-Archiv, Weimar; other collections are in the Reuter houses and museums in Eisenach, Stavenhagen, and Neubrandenburg.

Peter Rosegger
(31 July 1843 – 26 June 1918)

E. Allen McCormick
City University of New York

BOOKS: *Zither und Hackbrett: Gedichte in obersteiri-scher Mundart* (Graz: Pock, 1870 [i.e., 1869]);

Tannenharz und Fichtennadeln: Geschichten, Schwänke, Skizzen und Lieder in obersteierischer Mundart (Graz: Pock, 1870);

Sittenbilder aus dem steirischen Oberlande (Graz: Leykam, 1870);

Geschichten aus Steiermark (Pest: Heckenast, 1871);

Wanderleben: Skizzen (Pest: Heckenast, 1871);

In der Einöde: Eine Geschichte in zwei Büchern (Pest: Heckenast, 1872);

Gestalten aus dem Volke der österreichischen Alpenwelt (Pest: Heckenast, 1872);

Geschichten aus den Alpen, 2 volumes (Pest: Heckenast, 1872);

Aus dem Walde: Ausgewählte Geschichten für die reifere Jugend (Pest: Heckenast, 1873; enlarged edition, Vienna: Hartleben, 1892);

Die Schriften des Waldschulmeisters (Pest: Heckenast, 1875); translated by Frances E. Skinner as *The Forest Schoolmaster* (New York: Putnam's, 1901);

Sonderlinge aus dem Volke der Alpen, 3 volumes (Preßburg: Heckenast, 1875–1876);

Das Volksleben in Steiermark in Charakter- und Sittenbildern dargestellt, 2 volumes (Graz: Leykam-Josefsthal, 1875);

Aus Wäldern und Bergen: Stille Geschichten (Brunswick: Westermann, 1875);

Streit und Sieg: Novellen, 2 volumes (Preßburg: Heckenast, 1876);

Waldheimat: Erinnerungen aus der Jugendzeit (Preßburg: Heckenast, 1877); translated by Maude Egerton King, A. T. de Mattos, and others as *The Forest Farm: Tales of the Austrian Tyrol* (London: Fifield, 1912);

Wanderungen durch Steiermark und Kärnten, by Rosegger, Fritz Pichler, and A. von Rauschenfels (Stuttgart: Kröner, 1877–1880);

Peter Rosegger

Wie sie lieben und hassen: Erzählung (Berlin: Janke, 1878);

Lustige Geschichten (Vienna: Manz, 1879);

Mann und Weib: Liebesgeschichten, 2 volumes (Vienna: Manz, 1880);

326

Bilder von Defregger: Geschichten von Rosegger (Vienna: Manz, 1880);

Aus meinem Handwerkerleben: Beiträge zur Charakteristik der Älpler (Leipzig: Duncker & Humblot, 1880);

Die Älpler in ihren Wald- und Dorftypen geschildert (Vienna: Hartleben, 1881);

Vom Kreuzweg des Lebens: Novellistische Studien, as Hans Malser (Stuttgart: Levy & Müller, 1881);

Das Buch der Novellen, 3 volumes (Vienna: Hartleben, 1881–1882);

Ausgewählte Schriften, 12 volumes (Vienna: Hartleben, 1881);

Am Wanderstabe (Vienna: Hartleben, 1882);

Feierabende: Lustige und finstere Geschichten (Vienna: Hartleben, 1882);

Heidepeter's Gabriel: Eine Geschichte in zwei Büchern (Vienna: Hartleben, 1882);

Dorfsünden: Das Buch der Novellen, Band 4 (Vienna: Hartleben, 1883);

Meine Ferien (Vienna: Hartleben, 1883);

Der Gottsucher: Ein Roman, 2 volumes (Vienna: Hartleben, 1883); translated by Skinner as *The God Seeker: A Tale of Old Styria* (New York & London: Putnam's, 1901);

Sonntagsruhe: Ein Unterhaltungs- und Erbauungsbuch, enthaltend Gedichte in steirischer Mundart, hochdeutsche Gedichte, Aufsätze über Kinder, Parabeln, Legenden und Weltbetrachtungen (Vienna: Hartleben, 1883);

Neue Waldgeschichten (Vienna: Hartleben, 1884);

Stoansteirisch: Vorlesungen in steirischer Mundart (Graz: Leykam, 1885);

Bergpredigten: Gehalten auf der Höhe der Zeit unter freiem Himmel und zu Schimpf und Spott unseren Feinden, den Schwächen, Lastern und Irrthümern der Kultur gewidmet (Vienna: Hartleben, 1885);

Ein Sterben im Walde: Eine Erinnerung aus Kindertagen (Lahr: Schauenburg, 1885);

Das Geschichtenbuch des Wanderers: Neue Erzählungen aus Dorf und Berg, aus Wald und Welt, 2 volumes (Vienna: Hartleben, 1885);

Defregger-Album (Vienna: Bondy, 1886);

Ausgewählte Schriften: Miniaturausgaben, 19 volumes (Vienna: Hartleben, 1886–1894);

Höhenfeuer: Neue Geschichten aus den Alpen (Vienna: Hartleben, 1887);

Waldferien: Ländliche Geschichten für die Jugend gewählt (Vienna: Hartleben, 1887);

Allerhand Leute (Vienna: Hartleben, 1888);

Jakob der Letzte: Eine Waldbauerngeschichte aus unseren Tagen (Vienna: Hartleben, 1889);

Stoansteirisch: Vorlesungen in steirischer Mundart. Neue Folge (Graz: Leykam, 1889);

Martin der Mann: Erzählung (Vienna: Hartleben, 1889);

Deutsches Geschichtenbuch: Für die reifere Jugend gewählt aus den Schriften von P. K. Rosegger (Vienna: Hartleben, 1890);

Der Schelm aus den Alpen: Allerlei Geschichten und Gestalten, Schwänke und Schnurren, 2 volumes (Vienna: Hartleben, 1891);

Persönliche Erinnerungen an Robert Hamerling (Vienna: Hartleben, 1891);

Gedichte (Vienna: Hartleben, 1891);

Hoch vom Dachstein: Geschichten und Schildereien aus Steiermark (Vienna: Hartleben, 1891);

Am Tage des Gerichts: Volksschauspiel in vier Aufzügen (Vienna: Hartleben, 1892);

Allerlei Menschliches (Vienna: Hartleben, 1892);

Ernst und heiter und so weiter: Für die reifere Jugend gewählt aus den Schriften von P. K. Rosegger (Vienna: Hartleben, 1892);

Gute Kameraden: Persönliche Erinnerungen an berühmte und beliebte Zeitgenossen (Vienna: Hartleben, 1893);

Peter Mayr, der Wirt an der Mahr: Eine Geschichte aus deutscher Heldenzeit (Vienna: Hartleben, 1893);

Spaziergänge in der Heimat. Nebst einem Anhang: Ausflüge in die Fremde (Vienna: Hartleben, 1894);

Als ich jung noch war: Neue Geschichten aus der Waldheimat (Leipzig: Staackmann, 1895);

Aus Stadt und Land: Vier Erzählungen, by Rosegger and Hermine Möbius (Dresden: Köhler, 1895);

Schriften in steirischer Mundart, 3 volumes (Graz: Leykam, 1895–1896);

Schriften: Volksausgabe, 40 volumes (volumes 1–29, Vienna: Hartleben, 1895–1898; volumes 31–40, Leipzig: Staackmann, 1905–1907);

Alpengeschichten (Stuttgart: Krabbe, 1896);

Der Waldvogel: Neue Geschichten aus Berg und Thal (Leipzig: Staackmann, 1896);

Durch! und andere Geschichten aus den Alpen (Stuttgart: Krabbe, 1897);

Das ewige Licht: Erzählung aus den Schriften eines Waldpfarrers (Leipzig: Staackmann, 1897); translated anonymously as *The Light Eternal* (London: Unwin, 1907);

Waldjugend: Geschichten für junge Leute von 15 bis 70 Jahren. (Leipzig: Staackmann, 1898);

Das ewig Weibliche; Die Königsucher (Stuttgart: Krabbe, 1898);

Mein Weltleben oder Wie es dem Waldbauernbuben bei den Stadtleuten erging (Leipzig: Staackmann, 1898);

Idyllen aus einer untergehenden Welt (Leipzig: Staackmann, 1899);

Geschichten und Gestalten aus den Alpen (Leipzig: Reclam, 1899);

Erdsegen: Vertrauliche Sonntagsbriefe eines Bauernknechtes. Ein Kulturroman (Leipzig: Staackmann, 1900); translated by Skinner as *The Earth and the Fullness Thereof: A Romance of Modern Styria* (New York & London: Putnam's, 1902);

Als ich noch der Waldbauernbub' war: Für die Jugend ausgewählt aus den Schriften Roseggers vom Hamburger Jugendschriftenausschuß, 3 volumes (Leipzig: Staackmann, 1900–1902);

Mein Himmelreich: Bekenntnisse, Geständnisse und Erfahrungen aus dem religiösen Leben (Leipzig: Staackmann, 1901); translated by Elizabeth Lee as *My Kingdom of Heaven* (London: Hodder & Stoughton, 1907);

Das zu Grunde gegangene Dorf: Erzählung (Wiesbaden: Staadt, 1901);

Eine Standrede an die Deutschen (Hildesheim & Berlin: Mäßigkeits-Verlag, 1902);

Sonnenschein (Leipzig: Staackmann, 1902);

Der Höllbart: Erzählung (Leipzig: Hesse, 1903);

Arme Sünder und andere Geschichten (Berlin, Eisenach & Leipzig: Hillger, 1903);

Geschichten (Berlin, Eisenach & Leipzig: Hillger, 1903) – comprises "Die Wache der Knechtlin," "Der Mädeljäger," "Mann und Weib";

Steirische Geschichten (Graz: Styria, 1903);

Weltgift: Roman (Leipzig: Staackmann, 1903);

Das Sünderglöckel (Leipzig: Staackmann, 1904);

I. N. R. I. Frohe Botschaft eines armen Sünders (Leipzig: Staackmann, 1905); translated by Lee as *I. N. R. I.: A Prisoner's Story of the Cross* (New York: McClure, Phillips, 1905; London: Hodder & Stoughton, 1905);

Das Ereignis in der Schrun; 's Guderl; Die Nottaufe (Wiesbaden: Staadt, 1905);

Wildlinge (Leipzig: Staackmann, 1906);

Die Abelsberger Chronik: Den Schriften entnommene Sonderausgabe (Leipzig: Staackmann, 1907);

Nixnutzig Volk: Eine Bande paßloser Leute (Leipzig: Staackmann, 1907);

Die Försterbuben: Roman aus den steirischen Alpen (Leipzig: Staackmann, 1908);

Volksreden über Fragen und Klagen. Zagen und Wagen der Zeit (Berlin: Kantorowicz, 1908);

Alpensommer (Leipzig: Staackmann, 1909);

Die Ehestandspredigt (Munich: Callwey, 1910);

Lasset uns von Liebe reden: Letzte Geschichten (Leipzig: Staackmann, 1910);

Das Buch von den Kleinen: Den Eltern zur Freude, den liebenden zur Hoffnung, den Junggesellen zur Mahnung und den Weltweisen zur Lehre (Leipzig: Staackmann, 1911);

Mein Lied (Leipzig: Staackmann, 1911);

Die beiden Hänse: Ein Roman aus unserer Zeit (Leipzig: Staackmann, 1912);

Gesammelte Werke, 40 volumes, (Leipzig: Staackmann, 1913–1916; revised, 1922–1924);

Heimgärtners Tagebuch (Leipzig: Staackmann, 1913);

Steirischer Waffensegen, by Rosegger and Ottokar Kernstock (Graz: Leykam, 1916);

Das lichte Land und allerhand: Eine späte Nachlese aus Friedenszeiten (Leipzig: Staackmann, 1917);

Heimgärtners Tagebuch: Neue Folge (1912–1917) (Leipzig: Staackmann, 1917);

Abenddämmerung: Rückblicke auf den Schauplatz des Lebens (Leipzig: Staackmann, 1919);

Der Liebste ist mein Glaube!: Roman (Berlin: Hillger, 1920);

Frohe Vergangenheit: Launige Geschichten (Leipzig: Staackmann, 1921);

Der Herrensepp und andere Erzählungen (Leipzig: Koehler & Amelang, 1925);

Schneiderpeterl erzählt: Aus P. K. Roseggers unveröffentlichten Jugendschriften, edited by Moritz Mayer (Graz: Leykam, 1936);

Ausgewählte Werke, 4 volumes, edited by Kurt Eigl (Vienna: Kremayr & Scheriau, 1964–1965).

OTHER: *Volkslieder aus Steiermark mit Melodien*, edited by Rosegger and Richard Heuberger (Pest: Heckenast, 1872);

Das neue Jahr: Deutscher Volkskalender für Österreich-Ungarn, 8 volumes, edited by Rosegger (volumes 1–3, Pest: Heckenast, 1873–1875; volumes 4–6, Preßburg: Heckenast, 1876–1878; volumes 7–8, Vienna: Manz, 1879–1880);

Joseph Friedrich Lentner, *Geschichten aus Tirol und Oberbayern*, second edition, edited by Rosegger (Magdeburg: Baensch, 1876);

Heimgarten: Eine Monatsschrift, 35 volumes, edited by Rosegger (Graz: Leykam, 1876–1910).

Highly successful in a genre that is now generally out of favor, the Austrian Peter Rosegger wrote Dorfgeschichten (village tales) and novels about his native Styria with a prolixity unmatched by his predecessors and contemporaries in literary regionalism. More than five million copies of his novels and shorter fiction were sold by one publisher alone, and the popularity of this self-taught son of poor peasants has remained steady; along with Ludwig Anzengruber and Berthold Auerbach, Rosegger represents what is perhaps best and most typical of antiurbanism and antimaterialism in late-nineteenth- and early-twentieth-century German literature.

Petri Kettenfeier Rosegger was born in the mountain hamlet of Alpl near Krieglach in Upper Styria on 31 July 1843. He grew up without formal education and with no prospects; his frail constitution made farming impossible and, as a local clergyman told him, represented no special qualification for a life in the church. He was taught to read and write by an unemployed schoolmaster. At seventeen he was apprenticed to an itinerant tailor; for the next four years, while wandering about the province, he began writing poems, stories, and sketches, which he circulated among his friends.

In 1864 he submitted some dialect poems and other material to the *Grazer Tagespost* (Graz Daily Mail) and found in its editor, Dr. Adalbert Svoboda, an enthusiastic and lifelong supporter. Additional patrons were found who brought the young poet to Graz and offered aid in the form of money and books. An attempt to steer Rosegger toward a career as a bookseller proved misguided; a post offered him in 1864 with a book dealer in Laibach proved so uncongenial that Rosegger returned to Graz that same year. There, with Svoboda's help, he attended the business and trade college until 1869.

Alarmed by rumors of her son's dissolute ways in the city, Rosegger's mother journeyed to Graz in 1865 to check on her twenty-four-year-old son's behavior. Apparently her fears were allayed. Two years later the Rosegger farm had to be sold at auction, leaving the heavily indebted family with barely enough to survive. Rosegger's reaction to his family's ruin was: "Ich habe keine Heimat mehr. Den alten Eltern ist, Gott sei Dank, noch ein Plätzchen in der Hinterstube geblieben, für ihren Lebensrest zu wohnen und zu darben, uns Kindern ist die heilige Stätte verfallen" (I no longer have a home. There is still, thank God, a little place for my old parents in a back room where they can live out their days; we children have lost a sacred spot).

For Rosegger's first published collection of poems in Styrian dialect, *Zither und Hackbrett* (Zither and Cutting Board, 1869), the popular poet Robert Hamerling wrote a glowing introduction. A second collection, *Tannenharz und Fichtennadeln* (Pine Resin and Fir Needles), consisting of sketches, comic tales, and poems and also in dialect, appeared in 1870. From this time on hardly a year passed without the publication of at least one volume of poetry or stories. A grant from his home district allowed Rosegger to travel in Germany, Holland, Switzerland, and Italy from 1870 to 1872.

Rosegger's first major work, *Die Schriften des Waldschulmeisters* (Writings of the Forest Schoolmas-

Rosegger in 1903

ter, 1875; translated as *The Forest Schoolmaster,* 1901), establishes the basic elements and tone of much of his later writing: in a chatty, often anecdotal style Rosegger draws upon his surroundings, incidents from his childhood and youth, and his strong if somewhat unconventional religious bent to relate the story of Andreas Erdmann, the schoolmaster of a remote Alpine village. After fifty years of selfless service to an ideal, "den Menschen dienen und Gutes wirken" (to serve humanity and do good), Erdmann vanishes one day. Now an old man, the schoolmaster has followed a long-felt urge to see the world outside. He is discovered frozen to death on a high peak in the Styrian Alps, from which one can see the Adriatic in the far distance.

While *Die Schriften des Waldschulmeisters* contains much that is transparently autobiographical, it is above all the land itself with its simple, rough-hewn, and often highly eccentric peasants that represents the "protagonist." The central theme of the story, world withdrawal versus world affirmation, would remain a primary concern of virtually all Rosegger's later writings. The novel was written during Rosegger's brief but happy marriage to Anna Pichler, an admirer from Graz who had intended to visit the author's home during his absence but found him there. They were married in 1873; Anna died shortly after giving birth to their second child in 1875.

In 1876 Rosegger founded a monthly magazine devoted to entertainment and education. *Heimgarten* (Home Garden) offered original contributions on art, literature, nature, popular science, pedagogy, and Alpine life and culture, and brief reviews of recommended books. Despite its modest circulation of about six thousand, *Heimgarten* remained one of the more influential organs of Heimatkunst (regional art) for most of its nearly sixty years of existence. Much of the literary material was by Rosegger, but the list of additional contributors, all of them prominent in their day, is impressive; it included Anzengruber, Otto Julius Bierbaum, Alphonse Daudet, Marie von Ebner-Eschenbach, Paul Heyse, Gottfried Keller, Alexander Kielland, Karl May, Theodor Storm, Detlev von Liliencron, Ernst von Wildenbruch, and Gustav Freytag.

Rosegger's childhood reminiscences, the four-volume *Waldheimat* (Forest Home, 1877; translated as *The Forest Farm*, 1912) offers an example of his tendency to blend fact and fiction. In the late 1870s he built a home in Krieglach, courted the builder's daughter, and began to suffer from asthma. He married Anna Knauer in 1879 and moved to a new home in Graz. A twelve-volume edition of his selected works appeared in 1881.

It is necessary to separate achievements of real literary value from Rosegger's countless ephemeral stories and generally weaker novels of his later years. An important work is the novel *Heidepeter's Gabriel* (1882), the story of growing poverty and the gradual disintegration of a peasant family's way of life in the high Alpine region. Rosegger added a disclaimer to the 1912 edition of this enormously popular work: while conceding that he has borrowed colors from the palette of personal experience, he insists that he is not the protagonist, for "eine solche Selbstbespiegelung wäre geschmacklos bis zur Unanständigkeit" (such a self-mirroring would be tasteless to the point of indecency). His case is weak: as in *Waldheimat* and in the selection of tales published in 1900–1902 as *Als ich noch der Waldbauernbub' war* (When I Was Still the Backwoods Boy), the attempt to maintain artistic distance fails to conceal the main events of his own life – the father who cannot read or write and gradually sinks into bankruptcy; the old former schoolmaster who teaches Gabriel to read; Gabriel's departure for the city, where sponsors help with his education and

Rosegger in 1910 (photograph by Franz Josef Böhm)

the publication of his works; his courtship and marriage; and the death of his young wife. To this outline of his life Rosegger adds frequent lyrical descriptions of nature (influenced by Adalbert Stifter, whom Rosegger greatly admired); a deft account of daily life in the "Einöde" (wilderness), as he calls his region; and characterizations of the village types whose human frailties remind the reader of Gottfried Keller's Seldwya folk.

In this guided tour of a high Alpine farm community Rosegger maintains a fair balance between realism and what he calls his "dichterische Darstellung" (poetic presentation), lapsing occasionally into cloying sentiment but on the whole keeping the reader engaged and painfully aware of the threatened heritage of Alpine Austria. *Heidepeter's Gabriel* is a rags-to-riches story that exposes many of the author's technical weaknesses – unexpected summaries, sometimes disjointed narration in which the plot threatens to disappear, a failure to go beyond quaintness of character, frequent asides that take the form of sermonizing – but rarely causes the reader to lose interest in, and even love for, the simple, often infuriatingly obtuse peasants of the "wilderness."

Like so many writers of German regional fiction around the turn of the century – and their French, English, and American counterparts – Rosegger perceived the need to reflect and clarify important social issues while offering an antidote to the growing industrialization and standardization of the age. But at bottom he preferred the safety of a fiction of reminiscence to reportorial accuracy or social indignation; as a result, he often fails to grapple with the deeper problems besetting his characters in a time of decay and in a region caught up in too-rapid change. As he once said of himself, "ich nahm die Dinge besser, als sie an sich sein mögen" (I took things to be better than they might well have been); but in the struggle between Heimat (homeland) with its conservative religious values and the advent of capitalism, his heart and his pen were with the former.

Rosegger's introduction to his *Idyllen aus einer untergehenden Welt* (Idylls from a Disappearing World, 1899) makes his stand explicit and goes far in accounting for the limited thematic range of his novels and stories: "Am Ende des neunzehnten Jahrhunderts aber stehen wir vor einem Weltuntergange, der durchaus nicht ohne Wirkung auf unser Herz vorüberzieht. Wer in den Alpen wandert, der stößt von Stunde zu Stunde auf verfallende Höfe, auf Ruinen von Häusern und Hütten, an deren verwitterndem Gemäuer das Unkraut wuchert und die Eidechse rieselt" (At the end of the nineteenth century we are facing the end of the world, which does not at all pass by without producing an impression on our heart. Whoever wanders through the Alps encounters at any moment decaying farms, the ruins of houses and huts, on whose weathered walls weeds run rampant and the lizard scuttles). Rosegger supplies his damning answer to the question of what happened to a rich old world that once seemed as indestructible as nature itself: "Die neue Kultur! Die Maschinen, die Eisenbahnen haben den Erdball erschüttert, die Völker entwurzelt; ihr Einfluß zerstört auch in den Alpen allmählich ein Gemeinleben, das im Vergleiche zu anderen Bereichen eine wahre Idylle gewesen ist" (Modern civilization! Machines, railroads have shaken the globe, uprooted peoples; their influence in the Alps is also gradually destroying a communal way of life which, in comparison to other regions, has been a true idyll).

One of Rosegger's most important novels, *Jakob der Letzte* (Jacob the Last, 1889), explores this problem of destroyed idylls as decay attacks a village from within and without. Villagers have begun to sell their lands to "Kapitalisten" (capitalists), Rosegger's label for the monied outsiders, but one family doggedly hangs on to its land and tradition. The son is eventually forced to emigrate while the father, one of Rosegger's noble peasants who cling to ideals that are enfeebled and ultimately destroyed by this age of corruption, must resort to shooting wild animals that threaten to destroy his crops. Since the peasants have sold hunting rights to their lands, Jacob the Last is, in effect, forced to poach on his own soil. The end is predictable: surprised by the warden, Jacob shoots him, then drowns himself.

Rosegger presents flight and passive and, finally, tragic resistance not as solutions but simply as phenomena of a dying world. His essentially conservative outlook could not prevail in the face of a gloomy present in which he found chiefly decline and decay. Here and there one sees a protest against the loss of wilderness to tourists and hunters and the invasion of the high mountain landscape by telegraph wires, but for the most part Rosegger seems content to fictionalize his native region as a "Gegenstand der Sehnsucht" (subject of yearning).

Unlike other regionalists who were really outsiders posing as insiders in a rural setting, Rosegger belonged so completely to his region that his range of themes had to remain small. His subject matter was simply Rosegger, the "Waldbauernbub" in his little world, and his departures from this limited but highly effective autobiographical approach were generally unsuccessful.

From 1877 until his death Rosegger wintered in Graz and summered in Krieglach. Asthmatic attacks and catarrh plagued him intermittently after 1877. A serious bout with pneumonia in 1892 further undermined his health. One of his five children, Hans Ludwig, assumed the editorship of *Heimgarten* in 1910. Shortly before his seventy-fifth birthday, heaped with honors from universities and state and local governments and long recognized as one of Austria's best-loved sons, Rosegger was taken by special railway car from his residence in Graz to Krieglach. It was his wish "nur daheim, daheim zu sterben" (just to die at home, at home). He died on 26 June 1918 and was buried in Krieglach.

Letters:

Peter Rosegger: Das Leben in seinen Briefen, 4 volumes, edited by Otto Janda (Graz: Böhlau, 1943).

Biographies:

Hermine and Hugo Möbius, *Peter Rosegger* (Leipzig: Staackmann, 1903);

Theodore Kappstein, *Peter Rosegger* (Stuttgart: Greiner & Pfeiffer, 1905);

Richard Plattensteiner, *Peter Rosegger* (Leipzig: Staackmann, 1906);

Amebée Vulliod, *Peter Rosegger: Sein Leben und seine Werke,* translated from the French by Moriß Necker (Leipzig: Staackmann, 1913);

Ernst Decsey, *Peter Rosegger* (Bielefeld: Velhagen & Klasing, 1913);

Emil Ertl, *Peter Rosegger: Wie ich ihn kannte und liebte* (Leipzig: Staackmann, 1925);

Rudolf Latzke, *Peter Rosegger: Sein Leben und sein Schaffen,* 2 volumes (Graz: Böhlau, 1942–1953);

Adolf Haller, *Peter Rosegger: Die Geschichte seines Lebens* (Bern: Schweizerischer Verein abstinenter Lehrer und Lehrerinnen, 1947);

Paul Anton Keller, *Peter Rosegger: Sein Bild im Licht unserer Zeit. Zu seinem 120. Geburtstag* (Krems an der Donau: Heimatland, 1963).

References:

Josef Buchowiecki, "Peter Rosegger als Herold Adalbert Stifters: mit zwei unveröffentlichten Briefen," *Adalbert Stifter Institut des Landes Oberösterreich: Vierteljahrsschrift,* 11(1962): 31–32;

Wolfgang Bunte, *Peter Rosegger und das Judentum: Altes und Neues Testament, Antisemitismus, Judentum und Zionismus* (Hildesheim: Olms, 1977);

W. Diamond, "Peter Rosegger," *Monatshefte,* 20 (1928): 134–141;

James R. Dow and James P. Sandrock, "Peter Rosegger's *Erdsegen:* The Function of Folklore in the Work of an Austrian *Heimatdichter,*" *Journal of the Folklore Institute,* 13, no. 3 (1976): 227–239;

Emil Ertl, "Fernweh und Heimfreude. Persönliche Erinnerungen an Peter Rosegger," *Deutsche Rundschau,* 195 (1923): 123–190;

Emma Hackl, "Peter Rosegger und die Politik seiner Zeit." Ph.D. dissertation, University of Vienna, 1953;

Karl Kern, "Peter Rosegger," *Sudetenland,* 11 (1969): 200–205;

Jürgen Koppensteiner, " 'Der Waldbauernbub' in Amerika?: Ein verspäteter Beitrag zum Rosegger-Jahr," *Österreich-in-amerikanischer-Sicht,* 4 (1988): 23–27;

Gertrude Kümmel, "Landschaftszeichnung bei Peter Rosegger," Ph.D. dissertation, University of Vienna, 1960;

Edward Allen McCormick, "Decadence and 'Heimatdichtung': Peter Rosegger's *Jakob der Letzte,*" *Modern Austrian Literature,* 10, no. 2 (1977): 31–36;

Eva Philipoff, "Martin der Mann et Heidepeters Gabriel: Le Roman sentimental malgré lui," in *Le Roman sentimental,* edited by Ellen Constans (Limoges: University of Limoges, 1990), pp. 441–418;

Alfred Schneider, " '. . . unsere Seelen haben viel Gemeinsames!': Zum Verhältnis Peter Rosegger–Karl May," *Jahrbuch der Karl-May-Gesellschaft,* 1 (1975): 227–242;

Wolfgang Schober, "Roseggerforschung und Roseggerkult," *Österreich in Geschichte und Literatur* 25, no. 3 (1981): 156–167;

Henry Charles Sorg, *Rosegger's Religion: A Critical Study of his Works* (Washington: Catholic University of America, 1939);

Dean Stroud, "The *Axis Mundi* in the *Waldheimat,*" *Germanic Notes,* 17, no. 4 (1986): 53–54;

Franz Taucher, *Die Heimat und die Welt* (Vienna: Bergland, 1947);

Hans Vogelsang, "Peter Rosegger: Lebenslanger Autobiograph," *Österreich in Geschichte und Literatur,* 9 (1965): 373–385;

Karl Wagner, "Regionaler Eigensinn? Roseggers 'Waldheimatgeschichten,'" in his *Kontroversen, alte und neue,* volume 7: *Bildungsexklusivität und volkssprachliche Literatur* (Tübingen: Niemeyer, 1986), pp. 37–53.

Papers:

Most of Peter Rosegger's papers and manuscripts are in the Steiermärkische Landesbibliothek (Styrian Provincial Library) in Graz. The University of Vienna Library and the Rosegger Museum in Krieglach contain papers and memorabilia.

Joseph Viktor von Scheffel

(16 February 1826 – 9 April 1886)

Ulrich Scheck
Queen's University, Kingston, Canada

BOOKS: *Der Trompeter von Säckingen: Ein Sang vom Oberrhein* (Stuttgart: Metzler, 1854); translated by Mrs. Francis Brünnow as *The Trumpeter of Säkkingen: A Song from the Upper Rhine* (London: Chapman & Hall / New York: Scribner, Armstrong, 1877); translated by Jessie Beck and Louise Lorimer as *The Trumpeter: A Romance of the Rhine* (Edinburgh: Blackwood, 1893);

Ekkehard: Eine Geschichte aus dem zehnten Jahrhundert (Frankfurt am Main: Meidinger, 1855); translated by Sofie Delffs as *Ekkehard: A Tale of the Tenth Century*, 2 volumes (Leipzig: Tauchnitz, 1872; New York: Gottsberger, 1890);

Lieder aus dem Engern in Heidelberg (Lahr: Schauenburg, 1861; enlarged edition, Heidelberg: Meder, 1865);

Frau Aventiure: Lieder aus Heinrich von Ofterdingen's Zeit (Stuttgart: Metzler, 1863);

Juniperus: Geschichte eines Kreuzfahrers (Stuttgart: Metzler, 1867);

Gaudeamus!: Lieder aus dem Engeren und Weiteren (Stuttgart: Metzler, 1868); translated by Charles G. Leland as *Gaudeamus!: Humorous Poems* (London: Trübner, 1872; Boston: Osgood, 1872);

Bergpsalmen (Stuttgart: Metzler, 1870); translated by Brünnow as *Mountain Psalms* (London: Trübner, 1882);

Der Brautwillkomm auf der Wartburg: Lyrisches Festspiel (Weimar: Böhlau, 1873);

Waldeinsamkeit: Dichtung zu zwölf landschaftlichen Stimmungsbildern von Julius Marak (Vienna: Kaeser, 1878);

Das Gabelbachlied, der Gemeinde Gabelbach gewidmet (Ilmenau: Gabelbach, 1879);

Der Heini von Steier: Dichtung (Munich: Ackermann, 1883);

Hugideo: Eine alte Geschichte (Stuttgart: Bonz, 1884);

Festgedicht zum Jubiläum der Universität Heidelberg: 1386–1886 (Stuttgart: Bonz, 1886);

Fünf Dichtungen (Stuttgart: Bonz, 1887);

Reise-Bilder (Stuttgart: Bonz, 1887);

Gedichte aus dem Nachlaß (Stuttgart: Bonz, 1889);

Episteln (Stuttgart: Bonz, 1892);

Aus Heimat und Fremde: Lieder und Gedichte (Stuttgart: Bonz, 1892);

Gedenkbuch über stattgehabte Einlagerung auf Castell Toblino im Tridentinischen: Juli und August 1855 (Stuttgart: Bonz, 1900);

Gesammelte Werke, 6 volumes, edited by Johannes Proelß (Stuttgart: Bonz, 1907);

Nachgelassene Dichtungen: Gesamtausgabe, edited by Proelß (Stuttgart: Bonz, 1908);

Joseph Victor von Scheffels sämtliche Werke, 10 volumes, edited by Johannes Franke (Leipzig: Hesse & Becker, 1917);

Scheffels Werke, 4 volumes, edited by Friedrich Panzer (Leipzig: Bibliographisches Institut, 1919);

Irene von Spilimberg: Unvollendeter Roman, edited by Panzer (Karlsruhe: Deutscher Scheffelbund, 1930).

OTHER: *Waltharius: Lateinisches Gedicht des zehnten Jahrhunderts*, translated by Scheffel and Alfred Holder (Stuttgart: Metzler, 1874);

Wartburg-Sprüche, compiled by Scheffel and B. von Armswald, edited by Franz Lechleitner (Weimar: Böhlau, 1892).

The astonishing number of editions and copies of his works reveals that Joseph Viktor von Scheffel was one of the most popular German authors in the latter half of the nineteenth century; only Johann Wolfgang von Goethe and Friedrich Schiller found greater favor in the eyes of the reading public. Such was the extent of Scheffel's literary success that for decades his Stuttgart publisher, Adolf Bonz, employed a huge Schnellpresse (an especially fast press) solely for the purpose of printing his works. After he achieved his breakthrough as a writer in 1868 with *Gaudeamus!* (translated, 1872), an enormously popular collection of poems and songs, Scheffel's earlier works *Der Trompeter von Säckingen* (1854; translated as *The Trumpeter of Säkkingen*, 1877) and *Ekkehard* (1855; translated,

Joseph Viktor von Scheffel

1872) also became best-sellers. For decades Scheffel's reputation rested on these three books. He was admired by a large middle-class readership and celebrated by professional critics and fellow writers such as the noted novelist Theodor Fontane. At the turn of the century it was common for Scheffel's collected works to be given to children as confirmation gifts or as prizes to students who had performed well in high school. In the mid 1920s every educated German still knew and treasured *Der Trompeter von Säckingen* and *Ekkehard*, as well as many of Scheffel's songs about the joys and conviviality of student life.

Yet many today dismiss him as a second-rate writer whose success was deservedly short-lived. Some critics argue that Scheffel's prose is a mediocre concoction of Germanocentric ideas mixed with fragments of the classical education he had received at the humanistische Gymnasium, an institution cherished by the German bourgeoisie of his time. Others have criticized Scheffel for not developing enough dramatic action in his works, for employing an archaic style, for resorting to too many stylistic

mannerisms, and for relying heavily on historical sources but never attempting to be historically accurate. If they take notice at all of Scheffel, scholars today almost unanimously share in the verdict that he was a producer of trivial literature with a politically suspect ideology. With the exception of *Ekkehard,* none of Scheffel's works is in print; thus, the decline in critical acclaim has been paralleled by an almost complete loss of readership. Today hardly any educated German is familiar with Scheffel's life and work, and only a few know why their grandparents and great-grandparents admired and loved him.

Scheffel was most influenced by Johann Peter Hebel and Heinrich Heine; other writers who were important for him were Ludwig Börne, Goethe, William Shakespeare, and the Persian poet Hafez. Scheffel was most productive between 1850 and 1870, a period in German literature that can be characterized as a mosaic of classical, romantic, realistic, and "Biedermeier" (writing that emphasizes traditional values of comfort and domesticity and eschews grand passions) tendencies. The coexistence of these features in Scheffel's writing, along with allusions to the historical and literary past, made his texts palatable to middle-class readers and may partially explain his enormous success. Another reason for his popularity is that, although his works often take place in the distant past, the psychological makeup of their protagonists is that of nineteenth-century people; thus, his readers could easily identify with the main characters.

Scheffel was born in Karlsruhe, the capital of the Grand Duchy of Baden, on 16 February 1826. Karlsruhe was still untouched by industrialization, and its many trees and parks provided the city with a pleasant pastoral ambience; the Scheffel home bordered the Hardtwald and had a large garden. This idyllic setting made a strong impression on Scheffel, whose love of nature and hiking continued into his manhood and who in his later years preferred rural to urban life. His father, Philipp Jakob Scheffel, an energetic but somewhat pedantic man, was an engineer for the Badensian public works and a captain in the militia. His mother, Josephine Scheffel (née Krederer), was a witty and creative woman with a strong sense of social responsibility; in 1848 she founded the "Elisabethenverein," an organization that supported the families of pauperized workers. From her and from his grandmother, Katharina Krederer, Scheffel acquired a fondness for local history, legend, and folklore. And it was his mother who always believed in his talent for writing; she was herself an accomplished author of fairy tales and poems.

But Scheffel's great love was painting. He shared the desire to become a painter rather than a writer with many other nineteenth-century authors, such as Adalbert Stifter and Gottfried Keller. But since Philipp Jakob Scheffel hoped for an extraordinary career in the civil service for his highly talented son, who always was among the best students in school, Scheffel was supposed to study law. After he graduated from the lycée in Karlsruhe as *primus omnium* (first among his classmates) in 1843, he and his father reached a compromise: Scheffel began his legal studies in Munich, a city known as "Athens on the Isar" because of its many museums and vibrant atmosphere and the leading city in Germany for the fine arts. Studying in Munich gave Scheffel the opportunity to attend lectures on history and art as well as to visit the studios of such painters as Moritz von Schwind, Jean Baptist Kirner, and Feodor Dietz, all of whom were friends of his parents. In 1844 he transferred to the University of Heidelberg because he was enchanted by the city's history and scenic environment. After spending the winter term of 1845–1846 at the University of Berlin, Scheffel returned to the University of Heidelberg.

During his Heidelberg years Scheffel, like many of his fellow students, became involved in the emerging movement toward a democratic Germany. In the spring of 1848 he participated in student gatherings in Eisenach and at the Wartburg (the twelfth-century castle near Eisenach), and in May he traveled to Frankfurt am Main as second secretary to Karl Theodor Welcker, the representative from Baden in the newly formed German National Assembly.

Scheffel always favored a unified nation consisting of all German-speaking areas, but he was never a chauvinist. He hoped that the Frankfurt assembly would establish a democratic framework for a unified Germany, but he was soon disappointed.

In Heidelberg, Scheffel became an active member of the fraternities Alemannia, Teutonia, and Frankonia. During his student years he started to write poems and songs such as "Alt Heidelberg" (Old Heidelberg) and "Das große Faß zu Heidelberg" (The Big Barrel of Heidelberg). Many of them were later published in the magazine *Fliegende Blätter* (Pamphlets), in *Gaudeamus!,* and in the *Kommersbuch* (1858), a widely distributed booklet that contained the most popular student songs. One of the main themes in Scheffel's songs and poems is drinking, and one of his best-known characters is the dwarf Perkêo; every student at the time was familiar with this wine-loving eccentric. Scheffel is said to have coined the word *feuchtfröhlich* (wet and happy), which perfectly describes the atmosphere in a student pub. Scheffel was, in fact, never the beer-drinking joker many of his admirers liked to see in him. Rather, he cherished the convivial atmosphere and wit of his circle of friends. Fraternity life was, for him, a character-building experience and a forum for political debate.

During his student years Scheffel hiked through many areas of Germany, especially the southwestern part from the Palatinate to Lake Constance. Throughout his life he succumbed to his wanderlust, not only for health reasons but also to experience the beauty of nature and to educate himself about the history and culture of the regions through which he passed – "ambulando discimus" (we learn through travel) was his motto. His fondness for traveling and hiking resulted in letters and essays that describe the landscape, people, and history of many regions of central Europe.

Embarking without much enthusiasm on a career in the legal profession, in November 1848 he was appointed practitioner in the Superior Court of Heidelberg. Soon afterward he joined the "Engere" (Inner Circle), a group presided over by the historian Ludwig Häusser that met on Wednesday nights. Scheffel named a collection of poems he wrote during his Heidelberg years after this group: *Lieder aus dem Engern in Heidelberg* (Songs from the Inner Circle in Heidelberg, 1861). He received his doctoral degree in law summa cum laude from the University of Heidelberg in 1849.

After moving in 1850 to Säckingen, where he spent almost two years as a criminal investigator, he quit the civil service and traveled to Italy to acquire inspiration and training for his first love, painting. But he impressed the painters in the small German artists' colony near Rome with his narrative talents and finally had to accept that his real artistic strength was in writing. Early in 1853 he went to the island of Capri, where within six weeks he composed *Der Trompeter von Säckingen*. An epic poem in unrhymed trochaic verse set in the second half of the seventeenth century, it tells a story of love fulfilled. Werner Kirchhof, a young man skilled in playing the trumpet, hikes through the Black Forest region after abandoning his studies in Heidelberg and falls in love with Margareta, the daughter of a nobleman in Säckingen. Her father opposes their wedding plans, and only after a long separation and after the obstacle of Werner's lower social station is removed when he is ennobled by the pope can the wedding take place. This rather simple story is constantly interrupted by autobiographical references and by anecdotes and episodes involving entertaining and colorful minor characters. Hiddigeigei, the somewhat pompous, philosophizing tomcat, has among his illustrious predecessors such notable literary cats as Ludwig Tieck's Hinze and E. T. A. Hoffmann's Murr; Hiddigeigei, however, is modeled mostly after Heine's bear Atta Troll. The portrayal of Hiddigeigei best illustrates Scheffel's skeptical, sometimes satirical, occasionally pessimistic, but never cynical humor. Although the first edition of *Der Trompeter von Säckingen* did not receive much attention, it eventually became what would now be called a cult book: by 1921 it had reached its 322d printing. It appealed to middle-class readers mainly because of its humor and its affectionate description of the people, customs, and landscape of the Upper Rhine region.

Early in 1854 Scheffel started to do research for what was to become his second major work, the historical novel *Ekkehard*. The major source is the part of the chronicle of Saint Gall Abbey that was written by Ekkehard IV around the middle of the eleventh century and that recapitulates events that took place from 890 to 975. The novel is, again, a story of love – this time, however, of love unrequited. Duchess Hadwig of Swabia, the young and beautiful widow of Duke Burkhard II, follows the advice of her chambermaid Praxedis to visit Saint Gall Abbey, which is headed by Hadwig's cousin Cralo. Women, however, are not allowed to enter the abbey. This problem is solved by reasoning that Hadwig, as the territorial ruler, is equal to a man. She is carried over the threshold by Ekkehard, a young monk. Ekkehard is chosen later to tutor Hadwig in Latin and moves to her castle on the Hohentwiel mountain. He falls in love with her, but, as in *Der Trompeter von Säckingen,* the lower social station of the male protagonist is an obstacle. In *Ekkehard* the obstacle is not removed: the monk becomes a hermit, eventually conquers his passion, and achieves maturity. Thus, *Ekkehard* is not only a historical novel but also a bildungsroman. The narrator comments on the events, shifts perspectives at will, and distances himself from the events through irony and humor. Scheffel's translation of the tenth-century Latin epic poem *Waltharius manu fortis* (Walther with the Strong Hand) constitutes chapter 24 of the novel; Ekkehard writes the poem during his solitary life in the mountains and sends the manuscript to Hadwig as a gift. The poem is the story of Walther of Aquitaine and Hiltgunt of Burgundy, who grow up as hostages at the court of Attila the Hun. The inclusion of *Waltharius* and the addition of 1285 scholarly annotations at the end of the novel provided readers with the gratifying feeling that they were not only being entertained but were also being educated.

Scheffel's contemporaries had nothing but praise for the novel. Fontane counted *Ekkehard* one of the best books he had ever read, and the *Morgenblatt für gebildete Leser* (Morning Paper for Cultured Readers) said that it marked the beginning of a new era in the history of the novel. Through the first two decades of the twentieth century Scheffel was regarded by many as the writer who best captured the spirit of Germany in his works. Ekkehard's participation in a victorious battle against the invading Huns touched the right chord in readers who had experienced the Napoleonic Wars from 1805 to 1815. After the Franco-Prussian War of 1870–1871 and the founding of the German Empire under Chancellor Otto von Bismarck in 1871, the novel corresponded to the nationalist zeitgeist to such an extent that it was regarded as a classic. The nationalistic fervor sweeping the country in the 1870s needed festivities, songs, and poets celebrating Germany; Scheffel's book responded to this need, and he became for many the great poet of the Germans, something he had never wanted to be. By the time Scheffel died in 1886, ninety editions of *Ekkehard* had appeared.

Response to the novel is markedly different today. Scheffel's use of archaic language, for some modern readers and critics, borders on kitsch. Another criticism has been raised against Scheffel's use of historical sources. While the employment of the chronicle of Saint Gall Abbey gives the work a ring of authenticity, anachronisms occur when events from the chronicle are combined with allusions to other literary sources and to later occurrences such as Martin Luther's taking refuge with Frederick the Wise in the Wartburg in 1521–1522.

The novel's theme of rejected love was quite real for Scheffel. While he was working on the book the great love of his life, Emma Heim, married a merchant. Scheffel was devastated, and after weeks of feverish work to finish *Ekkehard* despite his grief he collapsed mentally and physically. At the age of twenty-nine he had reached the highest point of his literary activity. *Ekkehard* was followed by years of personal catastrophes and ill health. A trip to Italy in 1855 with the painter Anselm Feuerbach was interrupted by an outbreak of cholera in Venice, and in December of the same year Scheffel was struck by a mysterious illness. After he recovered he moved to Munich, where he became friends with many painters and with writers such as Felix Dahn and Paul Heyse. Late in 1856 his sister Marie joined him in Munich; on 19 February 1857 she died of typhoid. Scheffel felt responsible for bringing her to Munich and exposing her to the typhoid epidemic. His novella *Hugideo: Eine alte Geschichte* (Hugideo: An Old Tale), which appeared in the journal *Westermanns Monatshefte* in the fall of 1857 but was not published in book form until 1884, was dedicated to Marie. The work is set in the fifth century and is saturated with an atmosphere of doom. Hugideo lives in seclusion high above the Rhine. Except for worshipping a marble bust of the beautiful Benigna Serena, his former lover, his only activity is to help the fisherman Nebi with the recovery of dead bodies from the river. One day, while he is cleaning the sculpture, the bust falls to the ground and breaks into pieces, and he immediately knows that his life is coming to an end. Soon afterward he finds Benigna's corpse in the river and kills himself. *Hugideo* is both a veiled confession of guilt and a poetic expression of Scheffel's apprehension about his own future.

Title page for the book of poems that marked Scheffel's breakthrough as a writer

From 1857 until 1859 Scheffel worked as court librarian at the Fürstenberg library in Donaueschingen. During the next few years he worked on a novel about the Wartburg that was never finished; he only completed three fragments, which were published as separate works. The first of these fragments was the novella *Juniperus: Geschichte eines Kreuzfahrers* (Juniperus: The Tale of a Crusader, 1867), written in 1859. Two former friends want God to decide which of them will win the noble maiden Rothraut von Almishofen. They go on a suicidal ride over the dangerous falls of the river Rhine at Schaffhausen, and only Gottfried von Neuenhewen – nicknamed "Juniperus" by his fellow students because he often wears a juniper branch – survives. The abbot of Rheinau rules that this temptation of God was sinful. To atone for his sin, Gottfried has to join a crusade to the Holy Land and is prohibited from speaking for two years.

The other two segments of the Wartburg novel, *Frau Aventiure: Lieder aus Heinrich von Ofterdingen's Zeit* (Lady Aventiure: Songs from Heinrich of Ofterdingen's Times, 1863) and *Bergpsalmen* (1870; translated as *Mountain Psalms*, 1882) are collections of highly complex, sometimes

Scheffel in 1880

enigmatic poems. The poems in *Frau Aventiure* have intricate stanzas and are written in elevated and archaic language; they also contain many scientific, cultural, and historical allusions that were lost on most readers. Scheffel received the inspiration for *Frau Aventiure* from Moritz von Schwind's painting *Der Sängerkrieg auf der Wartburg* (The War of Poets on the Wartburg, 1844–1846). In some of the poems in *Frau Aventiure* Scheffel tries to imitate the complex meters of medieval love poetry. Other poems are about vagrants and the liberating effect of life on the road.

The poems in *Bergpsalmen* also focus on the motif of escape from societal restrictions. They display in hymnic stanzas the thoughts and perceptions of a former bishop who lives as a recluse in the mountains. Withdrawal from society is experienced as therapeutic; retreating to the natural environment of the mountains is seen not as an act of renunciation but as invigorating and re-creative. The poems in *Bergpsalmen* mirror Scheffel's yearning to break free from the constrictions of bourgeois existence. They are also a critique of urban life and the vanities of civilization. As was the case with *Frau*

Aventiure, Bergpsalmen, which consists of six songs of varied length and metric complexity, appealed only to a small readership. Scheffel modeled the collection loosely after Heine's poetic cycle "Die Nordsee" (The North Sea) in *Buch der Lieder* (1827; translated as *Heine's Book of Songs,* 1864).

After being rejected by several women, on 22 August 1864 Scheffel married Karoline von Malzen, the daughter of the Bavarian representative to the Badensian court; they settled in Karlsruhe. The marriage did not last long: the couple separated in September 1867, four months after their son, Victor, was born. Karoline moved with Victor to Salzburg and later to Munich.

The year 1868 marks the beginning of Scheffel's sudden rise to fame. The first edition of *Gaudeamus!* was sold out within four weeks. Many of the poems had been set to music by Christoph Schmezer years earlier, and by 1868 they had become popular with students all over Germany. In addition to the songs about the pleasures of drinking that provided Scheffel with the dubious reputation of being a "Saufpoet" (poet for boozers), the collection also contains satiric poems about academic research of the day, such as the scholarly inquiries into prehistoric times. A third group appears under the heading "kulturgeschichtlich" (pertaining to cultural history) and deals with historical, cultural, and autobiographical matters. The least-known poems in *Gaudeamus!,* they are beautiful, quiet, and intimate. The poems about "Wein, Weib und Gesang" (wine, women and song), however, were the ones that made Scheffel famous and ensured the success of his earlier works *Der Trompeter von Säckingen* and *Ekkehard.* The poems are, on the other hand, also responsible to a high degree for the distorted image of Scheffel that persists today. Scheffel could not have been happy that the more intricate and darker side of his oeuvre was completely ignored.

In 1869 Scheffel abducted Victor from a playground in Munich and brought him to Karlsruhe. Since his mother's death in 1865 Scheffel had also been looking after his brother Karl, who had been born in 1827 partially paralyzed because of brain damage. Husband and wife did not communicate until 1886, the year of Scheffel's death, when they finally reconciled their differences.

In 1871 Scheffel, who had long wanted to live in the Lake Constance area, decided to move to Radolfzell, where his publisher, Bonz, owned a summer home. His house, "Seehalde" (Lake Hillside), was completed in 1873.

Scheffel's literary production in his later years was scanty and much inferior to his earlier works. The lyrical drama *Der Brautwillkomm auf der Wartburg* (Welcoming the Bride on the Wartburg, 1873) and *Waldeinsamkeit* (Solitude in the Forest, 1878), texts for pictures by Julius Marak, were commissioned works that Scheffel wrote without much enthusiasm; the same is true of several poems he composed for festive occasions. A translation of *Waltharius* by Scheffel and Alfred Holder appeared in a bilingual edition, with commentary, in 1874.

Scheffel's fiftieth birthday on 16 February 1876 was a national event; the favorite author of the newly unified Germany received congratulations from all over the world. He was declared an honorary member of many societies, was honored by the kings of Bavaria and Württemberg and ennobled by Archduke Frederick of Baden, and received telegraphed congratulations from Chancellor Bismarck. He was also made an honorary citizen of the cities of Radolfzell, Karlsruhe, and Heidelberg, a distinction he had received from Säckingen in 1875.

Scheffel's last ten years were uneventful; he led a withdrawn life, trying to cure his many illnesses. His friends included such renowned writers as Berthold Auerbach and Friedrich von Spielhagen. On Scheffel's sixtieth birthday the castle in Heidelberg was illuminated in his honor, but he was unable to attend the event because he had fallen severely ill. Around seven o'clock in the evening of 9 April 1886 he died in his parents' house in Karlsruhe. Three days later he was buried next to his sister Marie. A huge crowd, including members of the nobility, attended the funeral, and all of Germany, Austria, and the German-speaking part of Switzerland mourned his death. Posthumously Scheffel was elevated by patriotic, antimodern, and Germanocentric groups to the status of German poet par excellence. This dubious honor remains an inseparable part of his reputation, eclipsing the ironic and satiric critic who is revealed in his travel descriptions and letters as a man who tried to escape the bureaucracy, vanities, and superficiality of urban life. He attacks everything from tourism to the English, from the railway to his favorite target, the city of Karlsruhe. The prevalent assessment of Scheffel as an opportunistic, ideologically suspect, and mediocre writer needs to be corrected: he was certainly not the great author his contemporaries believed him to be, but neither does he deserve the low ranking he gets from modern critics.

Letters:

Briefe Joseph Viktor von Scheffels an Schweizer Freunde, edited by Adolf Frey (Zurich: Schultheß, 1898);

Joseph Viktor von Scheffels Briefe an Karl Schwanitz nebst Briefen der Mutter Scheffels 1845–1886 (Leipzig: Merseburger, 1906);

Briefe von Joseph Victor von Scheffel an Anton von Werner 1863–1886, edited by Anton von Werner (Stuttgart: Bonz, 1915);

Briefe ins Elternhaus: 1843–1849, edited by Wilhelm Zentner (Karlsruhe: Deutscher Scheffelbund, 1926);

Briefwechsel zwischen Joseph Victor von Scheffel und Carl Alexander von Sachsen-Weimar-Eisenach 1857–1885, edited by Conrad Höfer (Karlsruhe: Deutscher Scheffelbund, 1928);

Scheffel in Italien: Briefe ins Elternhaus 1852–1853, edited by Zentner (Karlsruhe: Deutscher Scheffelbund, 1929);

Briefwechsel zwischen Joseph Victor von Scheffel und Paul Heyse 1853–1881, edited by Höfer (Karlsruhe: Deutscher Scheffelbund, 1932);

Vom Trompeter zum Ekkehard: Scheffels Briefe ins Elternhaus 1853–1855, edited by Zentner (Karlsruhe: Deutscher Scheffelbund, 1934);

Eine Studienfreundschaft: Scheffels Briefe an Friedrich Eggers 1844–1849, edited by Gerda Ruge (Karlsruhe: Deutscher Scheffelbund, 1936);

Zwischen Pflicht und Neigung: Scheffel in Donaueschingen: Briefe ins Elternhaus 1857–1859, edited by Zentner (Karlsruhe: Volksbund für Dichtung, 1946);

Wandern und Weilen: Scheffels Briefe ins Elternhaus 1860–1864, edited by Zentner (Karlsruhe: Volksbund für Dichtung, 1951).

Bibliographies:

Anton Breitner, *Joseph Viktor von Scheffel und seine Literatur: Prodromus einer Scheffel-Bibliographie* (Bayreuth: Seligsberg, 1912);

Ernst Carlebach, *Joseph Victor v. Scheffel: Erstausgaben-Scheffelliteratur: Zu seinem 100. Geburtstag am 16. Februar 1926,* Antiquarisches Verzeichnis, no. 341 (Heidelberg, 1926).

Biographies:

Hermann Pilz, *Viktor von Scheffel: Ein deutsches Dichterleben* (Leipzig: Knaur, 1887);

Johannes Proelß, *Scheffel's Leben und Dichten* (Berlin: Freund & Jeckel, 1887);

Alfred Ruhemann, *Joseph Viktor von Scheffel: Sein Leben und Dichten* (Stuttgart: Bonz, 1887);

Josef Stöckle, *Ich fahr' in die Welt: Joseph Victor von Scheffel, der Dichter des fröhlichen Wanderns und harmlosen Genießens* (Paderborn: Schöningh, 1888);

Proelß, *Scheffel – Ein Dichterleben* (Stuttgart: Bonz, 1902).

References:

Josef August Beringer, *Scheffel, der Zeichner und Maler* (Karlsruhe: Deutscher Scheffelbund, 1925);

Ernst Boerschel, *Josef Viktor von Scheffel und Emma Heim: Eine Dichterliebe* (Berlin: Hofmann, 1906);

Richard Clyde Ford, "Scheffel als Romandichter (Scheffel as a Novelist)," Ph.D. dissertation, University of Munich, 1900;

Manfred Fuhrmann, "Scheffels Erzählwerk: Bildungsbeflissenheit, Deutschtümelei," *Allmende,* 1 (1981): 60–69;

Reiner Haehling von Lanzenauer, *Dichterjurist Scheffel* (Karlsruhe: Gesellschaft für kulturhistorische Dokumentation, 1988);

Adolf Hausrath, "Joseph Victor von Scheffel und Anselm Feuerbach," *Deutsche Rundschau,* 52 (1887): 97–122;

Manfred Lechner, "Joseph Victor von Scheffel: Eine Analyse seines Werkes und seines Publikums," Ph.D. dissertation, University of Munich, 1962;

Friederike Liharzik, "Josef Viktor von Scheffels Stellung zum Mittelalter," Ph.D. dissertation, University of Vienna, 1935;

Günther Mahal, *Joseph Viktor von Scheffel: Versuch einer Revision* (Karlsruhe: Müller, 1986);

Friedrich Panzer, *Scheffels Romanentwurf "Irene von Spilimberg"* (Heidelberg: Winter, 1931);

Johannes Proelß, *Scheffels Leben: Biographische Einführung in die Werke des Dichters* (Stuttgart: Bonz, 1907);

Rolf Selbmann, *Dichterberuf im bürgerlichen Zeitalter: Joseph Viktor von Scheffel und seine Literatur* (Heidelberg: Winter, 1982);

Eugen Teucher, "Sterne am Himmel der älteren Literatur. Josef Viktor von Scheffel: *Der Trompeter von Säckingen,*" *Sprachspiegel,* 44 (February 1988): 10–11;

Eugen Wohlhaupt, "Josef Viktor von Scheffel," in *Dichterjuristen,* volume 3, edited by Horst Gerhard Seifert (Tübingen: Mohr, 1957), pp. 190–284;

Ludwig Wolf, *Der Anteil der Natur am Menschenleben bei Freytag und Scheffel* (Gießen: Münchow, 1923).

Papers:

The Joseph Viktor von Scheffel archive is in the Oberrheinisches Dichtermuseum (Upper Rhine Writers Museum) in Karlsruhe.

Wilhelm Scherer

(26 April 1841 – 6 August 1886)

Kurt R. Jankowsky
Georgetown University

BOOKS: *Über den Ursprung der deutschen Literatur: Vortrag gehalten an der K. K. Universität zu Wien am 7. März 1864* (Berlin: Reimer, 1864);

Jakob Grimm (Berlin: Reimer, 1865; revised and enlarged edition, Berlin: Weidmann, 1885);

Leben Willirams Abtes von Ebersberg in Baiern: Beitrag zur Geschichte des XI. Jahrhunderts (Vienna: Gerold, 1866);

Zur Geschichte der deutschen Sprache (Berlin: Duncker, 1868; enlarged edition, Berlin: Weidmann, 1878);

Deutsche Studien, 3 volumes (Vienna: K. K. Hof- und Staats-Druckerei, 1870–1878) – comprises volume 1, *Sperrvogel;* volume 2, *Die Anfänge des Minnesanges;* volume 3, *Dramen und Dramatiker;*

Geschichte des Elsasses von den ältesten Zeiten bis auf die Gegenwart: Bilder aus dem politischen und geistigen Leben der deutschen Westmark, 2 volumes, by Scherer and Ottokar Lorenz (Berlin: Duncker, 1871; revised, 1872);

Zum Gedächtnis Franz Grillparzers (Vienna: Rosner, 1872);

Vorträge und Aufsätze zur Geschichte des geistigen Lebens in Deutschland und Österreich (Berlin: Weidmann, 1874);

Geistliche Poeten der deutschen Kaiserzeit: Studien, 2 volumes (Strasbourg: Trübner, 1874–1875);

Geschichte der deutschen Dichtung im elften und zwölften Jahrhundert (Strasbourg: Trübner, 1875);

Die Anfänge des deutschen Prosaromans und Jörg Wickram von Colmar: Eine Kritik (Strasbourg: Trübner, 1877);

Aus Goethes Frühzeit: Bruchstücke eines Commentars zum jungen Goethe, by Scherer, Jacob Minor, Max Posner, and Erich Schmidt (Strasbourg: Trübner, 1879);

Geschichte der deutschen Literatur (Berlin: Weidmann, 1883); translated by Mrs. F. C. [Mary Emily] Conybeare as *A History of German Literature,* 2 volumes, edited by F. Max Müller (New York: Scribners, 1886; Oxford: Clarendon Press, 1886);

Mars Thingsus (Berlin: Reichsdruckerei, 1884);

Rede auf Geibel (Berlin: Weidmann, 1884);

Rede auf Jacob Grimm, gehalten in der Aula der Königlichen Friedrich-Wilhelms-Universität am 4. Januar 1885 (Berlin: Vogt, 1885);

Altdeutsche Segen (Berlin: Verlag der Königlichen Akademie, 1885);

Gedächtnißrede auf Karl Müllenhoff (Berlin: Verlag der Königlichen Akademie, 1885);

Aufsätze über Goethe, edited by Schmidt (Berlin: Weidmann, 1886);

Poetik, edited by Richard M. Meyer (Berlin: Weidmann, 1888);

Kleine Schriften, 2 volumes (Berlin: Weidmann, 1893) – comprises volume 1, *Kleine Schriften zur altdeutschen Philologie,* edited by Konrad Burdach; volume 2, *Kleine Schriften zur neueren Literatur, Kunst und Zeitgeschichte,* edited by Schmidt;

Karl Müllenhoff: Ein Lebensbild (Berlin: Weidmann, 1896);

Von Wolfram bis Goethe, edited by Josef Hofmiller (Munich: Langen, 1924);

Deutsche Bildnisse: Dichter- und Gelehrtenportraits, edited by Alexander Eggers (Berlin: Deutsche Bibliothek, n.d.).

Wilhelm Scherer in 1886

OTHER: *Denkmäler deutscher Poesie und Prosa aus dem VIII.–XII. Jahrhundert,* edited by Scherer and Karl Müllenhoff (Berlin: Weidmann, 1864);

Jacob Grimm, *Deutsche Grammatik,* 2 volumes, edited by Scherer (Berlin: Dümmler, 1869);

Notgers Psalmen, nach der Wiener Handschrift [Hs. 2681], edited by Scherer and Richard Heinzel (Strasbourg: Trübner, 1876);

Deutsche Drucke älterer Zeit in photolithographischer Nachbildung: Murners Schelmenzunft, selected by Scherer (Berlin: Burchard, 1881);

Bernhard Seuffert, ed., *Frankfurter Gelehrte Anzeigen vom Jahr 1772,* 2 volumes, introduction by Scherer (Heilbronn: Henninger, 1883);

Deutsche Drucke älterer Zeit in Nachbildungen, 2 volumes, edited by Scherer (Berlin: Grote, 1883–1884);

Mythologische Forschungen aus dem Nachlasse von Wilhelm Mannhardt, edited by Hermann Patzig, preface by Scherer (Strasbourg: Trübner, 1884; New York: Arno, 1978);

Goethes Werke: Herausgegeben im Auftrage der Großherzogin Sophie von Sachsen, 143 vol-

umes, edited by Scherer and others (Weimar: Böhlau, 1887–1919).

SELECTED PERIODICAL PUBLICATIONS – UNCOLLECTED: "Über das Nibelungenlied," *Preußische Jahrbücher,* 16 (1865): 253–271;

"Volksorthographie; Volksphonologie," *Zeitschrift für die österreichischen Gymnasien,* 17 (1866): 825–843;

"Pater Abraham a Sancta Clara," *Preußische Jahrbücher,* 19 (1867): 62–98;

Review of Ernst Windisch, *Der Heliand und seine Quellen,* in *Zeitschrift für die österreichischen Gymnasien,* 11 (1869): 847–853;

"Die deutsche Spracheinheit," *Preußische Jahrbücher,* 29 (1872): 1–22;

Review of William D. Whitney, *Die Sprachwissenschaft,* translated by Julius Jolly, *Preußische Jahrbücher,* 35 (1875): 106–111;

"Johann Christoph Adelung," *Allgemeine Deutsche Biographie,* 1 (1875): 80–84;

Review of Jost Winteler, *Die Kerenzer Mundart des Kantons Glarus in ihren Grundzügen dargestellt,* in

Anzeiger für deutsches Altertum und deutsche Literatur, 3 (1877): 57–70;

"Goethe's Iphigenie in Delphi," *Westermanns illustrierte deutsche Monatshefte*, 46 (1879): 73–78;

"Moritz Haupt," *Allgemeine Deutsche Biographie*, 11 (1880): 72–80;

"Satyros und Brey," *Goethe-Jahrbuch*, 1 (1880): 81–118;

"Gotthold Ephraim Lessing: Zum 15. Februar 1881," *Deutsche Rundschau*, 25 (1881): 272–299;

"Über die Anordnung Goethescher Schriften: I," *Goethe-Jahrbuch*, 3 (1882): 159–173;

"Karl Lachmann," *Allgemeine Deutsche Biographie*, 17 (1883): 471–481;

"Über die Anordnung Goethescher Schriften: II. Die vermischten Gedichte von 1789," *Goethe-Jahrbuch*, 4 (1883): 51–78;

"Über die Anordnung Goethescher Schriften: III. Die Gedichte von 1800 in den Neuen Schriften," *Goethe-Jahrbuch*, 5 (1884): 257–287;

"Hans Ferdinand Massmann," *Allgemeine Deutsche Biographie*, 20 (1884): 569–571;

"Achim von Arnim: Ein Vortrag aus dem Nachlasse von Wilhelm Scherer," edited by Erich Schmidt, *Deutsche Rundschau*, 65 (1891): 44–63;

"Wissenschaftliche Pflichten: Aus einer Vorlesung Wilhelm Scherers," edited by Schmidt, *Euphorion*, 1 (1894): 1–4.

Wilhelm Scherer practiced philology and literary criticism as two successive occupations. He was extremely successful, respected, and influential in his pursuit of linguistic interests; when he left Vienna for Strasbourg in 1872, literary criticism emerged as his primary concern and remained the center of his professional life until his death in 1886. Scherer's lasting influence is based on two important works, one from each field: *Zur Geschichte der deutschen Sprache* (On the History of the German Language, 1868) and *Geschichte der deutschen Literatur* (1883; translated as *A History of German Literature*, 1886).

Scherer was born on 26 April 1841 in Schönborn, Austria, near Vienna, to Wilhelm and Anna Scherer, née Rieck. His father, who was an administrator in the employ of the count of Schönborn, died when Scherer was four. Hardship for the family was avoided by his mother's marriage to an economist, A. Stadler, a friend of her first husband. The family moved several times before settling in Vienna, just in time for Scherer to enroll at the Akademische Gymnasium in 1854. This high school, specializing in classical Greek and Latin, profoundly influenced his outlook, academically as well as politically. Here the foundations were laid for his lifelong study of German language and literature as well as for his activism in favor of a unified Germany under Prussian leadership.

When Scherer entered the University of Vienna at age seventeen, his high expectations suffered a severe disappointment. While representatives of other disciplines, such as the classical scholars Hermann Bonitz and Johannes Vahlen and the Slavist Franz Ritter von Miklosich, captivated his interest, the efforts of the Germanist Franz Pfeiffer struck Scherer as totally unsatisfactory. Pfeiffer was a philologist who was never at ease with any linguistic or literary phenomenon that could not be directly tied to authentic manuscripts; he was not open to experimentation with new approaches. Scherer left Vienna after four semesters to study with Pfeiffer's adversary Karl Müllenhoff at the University of Berlin.

Scherer later acknowledged that he had profited greatly from most of his teachers in Berlin: the classical scholar and Germanist Moritz Haupt; Franz Bopp, the Indo-Europeanist and founder of the discipline of comparative linguistics; Karl Gustav Homeyer, professor of law, noted for his painstaking textual criticism of German legal source books; the Indologist Alfred Weber; the philosopher Adolf Trendelenburg; and the historian Leopold von Ranke. But the greatest influence was Müllenhoff, a disciple of Karl Lachmann who propagated his master's procedures for editing and interpreting classical and Old and Middle High German texts. In an entry on Lachmann for the journal *Allgemeine Deutsche Biographie* (General German Biography) in 1883 Scherer characterized the approach of the "Lachmann School": "Alle Feinheit des poetischen Nachempfindens, alles Stilgefühl, alle Auf-merksamkeit auf Silbenmass, Rhythmus und Reim, alles vielseitige Interesse an der klassischen, mittelalterlichen und modernen Literatur, wie es die Romantik pflegte, und dazu die neue Methode der historischen Schule, wie sie teils auf der Philosophie der Aufklärung, teils auf der im Gegensatz zur Aufklärung gekräftigten Ehrfurcht vor der Vergangenheit beruhte, dies alles stellte er in den Dienst der kritischen Philologie" (All sensitiveness of poetic empathy, all sense of style, all consideration for meter, rhythm, and rhyme, all multilayered interest in classical, medieval, and modern literature as cultivated in the Romantic period, and, in addition, the new method of the Historical School, based partly on the philosophy of the Enlightenment, partly on the reverence, nurtured in opposition to the Enlightenment, for the past – all this was utilized by him for the benefit of critical philology). In Müllenhoff he gained a lifelong friend who did not hesitate, after they had been acquainted for only a few months, to offer the twenty-year-old student the coeditorship of his *Denkmäler deutscher Poesie und Prosa aus dem VIII.–XII. Jahrhundert* (Monuments of German Poetry and Prose from the Eighth to the Twelfth Century, 1864).

In Berlin Scherer met the renowned philologist Jacob Grimm. He also came into contact with other students and young lecturers who were as gifted, as restless, and as enthusiastic as himself. He met with the art historian Hermann Friedrich Grimm, the historian Bernhard Erdmannsdörffer, the Romanist Adolf Tobler, the jurist Alfred Boretius, and the philosopher Wilhelm Dilthey at a café once a week. Erich Rothacker calls this circle "eines der wichtigsten Ausstrahlungszentren geisteswissenschaftlicher Ideen" (one of the most important centers of spreading scholarly ideas).

On his return to Vienna in 1862 Scherer obtained his Ph.D.; two years later he received his Habilitation, a second doctorate that was the prerequisite for being granted the *venia legendi* (permission to hold lectures at the university level). For both examinations his work on *Denkmäler deutscher Poesie und Prosa* provided the required thesis material. His professional career in Vienna had a bumpy start: his immediate superior was Pfeiffer, who could not forgive Scherer for joining the camp of his opponents, the Lachmann School. Scherer had to teach courses he did not want to teach and suffered restrictions of various other kinds. Nevertheless, from the beginning he was a successful teacher, and he immediately started producing scholarly publications that won him recognition in Germany and other European countries. In his 1865 biography of Jacob Grimm, in spite of his esteem for Grimm's pioneering achievements, he identifies the old philologist's shortcomings: Grimm's adherence to indistinct Romantic ideas, his lack of methodical rigor, and his reluctance to look for causal relationships. At the end of his life Scherer would suffer the same fate as Grimm: his research of the mid 1880s, still shaped by principles established in the mid 1860s, when his career got under way, would have greatly benefited from some of the trends that had emerged in the meantime.

When Pfeiffer died in 1868, Scherer was appointed his successor as Ordinarius (full professor). With the appearance of his *Zur Geschichte der deutschen Sprache* Scherer attained a level of accomplishment that eludes most linguists in a lifetime. The book triggered a highly stimulating reorienta-

tion of the way to view the development of language. For Scherer, the earliest stages and the most modern stages are parts of a continuous process; language changes in prehistoric times were no different from those occurring in more-recent periods. It is the task of the researcher to uncover the physical and psychological forces behind the changes. Scherer's belief in the necessity of a rigorous method of analysis did not preclude him from working with hypotheses that were characterized as of "etwas tumultuarischer Kühnheit" (somewhat tumultuous boldness). Thus, in the introduction to *Zur Geschichte der deutschen Sprache* he says that by an analysis of the sounds of the German language he will attempt to explain certain fundamental values of the German nation. In the second edition of 1878 this claim is modified by a footnote: "Diese Auffassung hat sich leider nicht bewährt" (This assumption can unfortunately not be upheld). The few hypotheses that proved untenable, however, are easily outweighed by the much larger number of assumptions that led to fruitful results.

Scherer increasingly ran into problems because of his political convictions. He openly criticized conditions in Austria and pointed to Prussia as a model for improvement. When, as a result of the annexation of Alsace-Lorraine by the newly founded German Empire, the University of Strasbourg opened its doors to German-speaking scholars, Scherer was invited in the fall of 1872 to join the faculty. One reason for the invitation may have been the publication in 1871 of *Geschichte des Elsasses von den ältesten Zeiten bis auf die Gegenwart* (History of Alsace from Earliest Times to the Present), co-authored by Scherer. In 1875 he declined to accept a call from the University of Berlin, only to give in when the invitation was repeated two years later, in 1877.

Soon after arriving in Berlin he married Maria Leeder, a fellow Austrian. His mother, who had accompanied her son to Strasbourg to manage his household, moved back to Vienna. Scherer and his wife had two children.

In the nation's capital Scherer became more and more absorbed in the study of modern literature; his foremost preoccupation was the work of Johann Wolfgang von Goethe. His greatest achievement in his "second life" as a literary historian, his *Geschichte der deutschen Literatur,* treats the development of German literature from its early beginnings to the death of Goethe. Scherer consistently tries to apply the principle of causality to literary phenomena. Literature, for him, is a manifestation of the intellectual development of a nation. The primary objective of its description and interpretation is to identify the forces that shape this development.

It was Müllenhoff who had advocated that the Prussian Ministry of Culture invite Scherer to Berlin; it was also Müllenhoff who saw to it that Scherer was made a member of the Preußische Akademie der Wissenschaften (Prussian Academy of Science) in 1884. In the same year, on his deathbed, Müllenhoff entrusted Scherer with the completion of his *Deutsche Alterthumskunde* (German Archaeology, 1870-1900); but Scherer did not have enough time left to live up to the commitment he made to his dying friend.

Scherer became the first vice president of the Goethe Society, which was established in Weimar in June 1885. Shortly thereafter, Grand Duchess Sophie of Saxony put him in charge of the preparatory work for the 143-volume edition of Goethe's works (1887-1919). He is credited with establishing and developing a "Goethe philology" that served as a model of scholarly perfection for several generations.

Scherer attracted large numbers of students at all three universities where he taught, many of whom went on to become university teachers themselves. He encouraged his most capable students to write treatises and theses and provided help in having them published. Together with Bernhard ten Brink, he established in 1874 the series Quellen und Forschungen zur Sprach- und Kulturgeschichte der germanischen Völker (Source Material and Investigations concerning the Linguistic and Cultural History of the Germanic Peoples). By the time of Scherer's death the series totaled fifty-nine books, most of them written at Scherer's instigation.

In the twenty-three years of professional life allotted to him Scherer produced an astonishingly large amount of research work. A bibliography of Scherer's writings lists 174 reviews and 87 contributions to the *Allgemeine Deutsche Biographie*. A contemporary observer remarks that Scherer did not have any use or time for ordinary entertainment: "Die gewöhnlichen Erholungen des Alltagslebens kannte er nicht" (The usual recreations of everyday life he did not know). Life and work were, for him, synonymous.

Scherer's formidable, self-inflicted work load had severe consequences for his health. He fell ill on many occasions but always bounced back to health. He suffered a stroke in the fall of 1885, from which he recovered during the ensuing months. He taught his regular course load in the summer semester of 1886 and was looking forward to joining his family and friends for a vacation in Sierning in the Austrian mountains. But on 6 August 1886 he suffered another stroke, this one resulting in immediate death.

Letters:

Briefwechsel zwischen Karl Müllenhoff und Wilhelm Scherer, im Auftrag der Preußischen Akademie der Wissenschaften, edited by Albert Leitzmann and Edward Schröder (Berlin: De Gruyter, 1937);

Ulrich Pretzel, "Briefe Klaus Groths an Wilhelm Scherer," in *Festgruß für Hans Pyritz zum 15.9.1955 aus dem Kreise der Hamburger Kollegen und Mitarbeiter* (Heidelberg: Winter, 1955), pp. 55-61;

Wilhelm Scherer – Erich Schmidt: Briefwechsel, edited by Werner Richter and Eberhard Lämmert (Berlin: Schmidt, 1963);

Wilhelm Scherer / Elias von Steinmeyer: Briefwechsel 1872-1886, edited by Horst Brunner and Joachim Helbig (Göppingen: Kümmerle, 1982).

Bibliographies:

Konrad Burdach, "Schriftenverzeichnis," in Wilhelm Scherer's *Kleine Schriften zur neueren Literatur, Kunst und Zeitgeschichte,* edited by Erich Schmidt (Berlin: Weidmann, 1893), pp. 391-415;

Josef Körner, *Bibliographie zu Scherer-Walzel, Geschichte der deutschen Literatur* (Berlin: Askanischer Verlag, 1921).

Biographies:

Wilhelm Dilthey, "Wilhelm Scherer zum persönlichen Gedächtnis," *Deutsche Rundschau,* 49 (October 1886): 132-146;

Richard M. Werner, "Wilhelm Scherer," *Zeitschrift für Allgemeine Geschichte, Kultur-, Literatur- und Kunstgeschichte,* 3 (1886): 862-867;

Julius Hoffory, "Wilhelm Scherer," *Westermanns Illustrierte Deutsche Monatshefte,* 62 (1887): 646-653;

Adalbert H. Horawitz, "Wilhelm Scherer: Ein Blatt der Erinnerung," *Monatsblätter des wissenschaftlicxhen Clubs in Wien,* 8, no. 3 (1887): 1-28;

Johannes Schmidt, "Gedächtnisrede auf Wilhelm Scherer," *Abhandlungen der Königlichen Akademie der Wissenschaften zu Berlin* (Berlin: Reimer, 1887);

Fritz Bechtel, "Wilhelm Scherer," *Beiträge zur Kunde der indogermanischen Sprachen,* 13 (1888): 163-172;

Erich Schmidt, "Wilhelm Scherer," *Goethe-Jahrbuch,* 9 (1888): 249-259;

Ludwig Speidel, "Wilhelm Scherer," in his *Persön-lichkeiten: Biographisch-literarische Essays* (Berlin: Meyer & Jessen, 1910), pp. 255–264;

Josef Körner, "Wilhelm Scherer (1841–1886): Zur 30. Wiederkehr seines Todestages," *Neue Jahr-bücher für das klassische Altertum, Geschichte und deutsche Literatur und für Pädagogik*, 37 (1916): 475–485;

Dietrich Seckel, "Wilhelm Scherer: Zu seinem 50. Todestag am 6. August," *Deutsche Rundschau*, 62 (1936): 111–115;

Ernst Leury, "Wilhelm Scherer," *Neophilologus*, 22 (1937): 169–170;

Julius Petersen, "Zum Gedächtnis Wilhelm Sche-rers," *Deutsche Rundschau*, 267 (1941): 78–83;

Herbert Cysarz, "Wilhelm Scherer," *Große Österrei-cher*, 13 (1959): 75–85;

Jürgen Sterndorff, *Wissenschaftskonstitution und Reichs-gründung: Die Entwicklung der Germanistik bei Wilhelm Scherer. Eine Biographie nach unveröffent-lichten Quellen* (Frankfurt am Main: Lang, 1979).

References:

Victor Basch, *Wilhelm Scherer et la philologie allemande* (Paris: Berger-Levrault, 1889);

Wilbur A. Benware, *The Study of Indo-European Vocal-ism in the 19th Century: From the Beginnings to Whitney and Scherer. A Critical-Historical Account* (Amsterdam: Benjamins, 1974);

Roberto Biscardo, *Wilhelm Scherer e la critica letteraria tedesca* (Rome: Abrighi, Segati, 1937);

Friedrich Bonn, *Ein Baustein zur Rehabilitierung der Schererschule: Zur 30. Wiederkehr von Berthold Litzmanns Todestag* (Emsdetten: Lechte, 1956);

Karl Brugmann and Hermann Osthoff, "Vorwort," in their *Morphologische Untersuchungen auf dem Gebiete der indogermanischen Sprachen*, volume 1 (Leipzig: Hirzel, 1878), pp. iii–xx;

Konrad Burdach, *Die Wissenschaft von deutscher Spra-che: Ihr Werden, ihr Weg, ihre Führer* (Berlin & Leipzig: De Gruyter, 1934);

Wilhelm M. A. Creizenach, *Wilhelm Scherer über die Entstehungsgeschichte von Goethe's Faust: Ein Bei-trag zur Geschichte des literarischen Humbugs* (Leip-zig: Grunow, 1887);

Herbert Cysarz, "Wilhelm Scherers Programmatik und Poetik," in *Worte und Werte: Bruno Mark-wardt zum 60. Geburtstag,* edited by Gustav A. Erdmann and Alfons Eichstaedt (Berlin: De Gruyter, 1961), pp. 42–50;

Wilhelm Fieber, "Wilhelm Scherers Ahnen," *Unsere Heimat: Monatsblatt des Vereins für Landeskunde*

von Niederösterreich und Wien, new series 18 (1947): 41–42;

Sander L. Gilman, "Die Wilhelm Scherer-Biblio-thek," *Jahrbuch für Internationale Germanistik*, 1, no. 1 (1969): 195–196;

Gilman, "The Wilhelm Scherer Library: A Bibliog-raphy of the Works Printed prior to 1700," *Archiv für das Studium der Neueren Sprachen*, 206 (April 1970): 433–446;

Dietrich Grohnert, "Die methodologische Konzep-tion in Wilhelm Scherers *Geschichte der deutschen Literatur*," *Wissenschaftliche Zeitschrift der Pädagogi-schen Hochschule Potsdam*, 9 (1965): 111–126;

Grohnert, "Untersuchungen zur literaturwissen-schaftlichen Methode Wilhelm Scherers," Ph.D. dissertation, University of Potsdam, 1963;

Richard Heinzel, "Rede auf Wilhelm Scherer," in his *Kleine Schriften*, edited by Max H. Jellinek and Carl von Kraus (Heidelberg: Winter, 1907), pp. 145–163;

Wolfgang Höppner, "Die Beziehung von Dichter und Publikum als Grundverhältnis des litera-rischen Verkehrs: Gedanken zu Wilhelm Scherers 'Poetik,'" *Weimarer Beiträge: Zeitschrift für Literaturwissenschaft, Ästhetik und Kulturwissen-schaft*, 35, no. 2 (1989): 208–232;

Höppner, "'Deutscher Geist' und 'japanisches Wesen': Das 'Fremde' im Konzept des literatur-wissenschaftlichen Positivismus der Scherer-Schule," *Zeitschrift für Germanistik*, 1, no. 1 (1991): 49–54;

Höppner, "Wilhelm Scherer, Erich Schmidt und die Gründung des Germanischen Seminars an der Berliner Universität," *Zeitschrift für Germanistik*, 9 (1988): 545–557;

Höppner, "Wilhelm Scherer und Jacob Grimm," in *Sprache, Mensch und Gesellschaft: Werk und Wir-kungen von Wilhelm von Humboldt und Jacob und Wilhelm Grimm in Vergangenheit und Gegenwart: Humboldt-Grimm-Konferenz, Berlin — 22.–25. Ok-tober 1985,* edited by Arwed Spreu and Wil-helm Bondizo, part 2 (Berlin: Humboldt-Uni-versität, Sektion Germanistik, 1986), pp. 279–287;

Kurt R. Jankowsky, *The Neogrammarians: A Re-evalu-ation of their Place in the Development of Linguistic Science* (The Hague: Mouton, 1972);

Jankowsky, "Wilhelm Scherer's *Zur Geschichte der deutschen Sprache*: A Milestone in 19th-Century Linguistics," in *Current Issues in Linguistic The-ory: Papers from the 6th International Conference on Historical Linguistics,* edited by Jacek Fisiak (Amsterdam: Benjamins, 1984), pp. 301–311;

Josef Körner, Review of Scherer's *Geschichte der deutschen Literatur,* in *Literaturblatt für germanische und romanische Philologie,* 40 (July–August 1919): 214–223;

Adalbert Kuhn, Review of Scherer's *Zur Geschichte der deutschen Sprache,* in *Zeitschrift für vergleichende Sprachforschung,* 18 (1869): 321–411;

Katherine Inez Lee, "Wilhelm Scherer's Goethe Criticism: An Investigation and Examination of Scherer's Critical Method," Ph.D. dissertation, Stanford University, 1971;

Lee, "Wilhelm Scherer's Two-fold Approach to Literature," *Germanic Review,* 51 (May 1976): 209–228;

Catherine LeGouis, "Three Versions of Positivism: Emile Hannequin, Wilhelm Scherer, Apollon Grigoriev," Ph.D. dissertation, Yale University, 1989;

Hermann Paul, Review of Scherer's *Zur Geschichte der deutschen Sprache,* in *Jenaer Literaturzeitung,* 1 (1879): 307–311;

S. B. Platner, "Wilhelm Scherer's Library," *New Englander,* 46 (1987): 383–386;

Gustav Roethe, Review of Scherer's *Kleine Schriften,* in *Anzeiger für deutsches Altertum und deutsche Literatur,* 24 (3 July 1898): 225–242;

Winthrop H. Root, "Naturalism's Debt to Wilhelm Scherer," *Germanic Review,* 11 (January 1936): 20–29;

Erich Rothacker, *Einleitung in die Geisteswissenschaften* (Tübingen: Mohr, 1930);

Peter Salm, "The Literary Theories of Scherer, Walzel and Staiger," Ph.D. dissertation, Yale University, 1959;

Salm, *Three Modes of Criticism: The Literary Theories of Scherer, Walzel, and Staiger* (Cleveland: The Press of Case Western Reserve University, 1968);

Siegfried Scheibe, "Die Chronologie von Goethes Faust I im Lichte der Forschung seit Wilhelm Scherer," Ph.D. dissertation, University of Leipzig, 1959;

Wieland Schmidt, "Scherers Goetheausgabe: Aus der geheimen Geschichte der Berliner Germanistik," in *Festgabe für Ulrich Pretzel,* edited by Werner Simon and others (Berlin: Schmidt, 1963), pp. 411–426;

Oskar Walzel, "Wilhelm Scherer und seine Nachwelt," *Zeitschrift für deutsche Philologie,* 55 (1930): 391–400;

Peter Wiesinger, "Jacob Grimm und Wilhelm Scherer als Sprachhistoriker," *Zeitschrift für Phonetik, Sprachwissenschaft und Kommunikationsforschung,* 38, no. 5 (1985): 519–532;

Otto Wirth, "Wilhelm Scherer, Josef Nadler, and Wilhelm Dilthey as Literary Historians," Ph.D. dissertation, University of Chicago, 1937.

Papers:

Wilhelm Scherer's papers are in the Zentralarchiv der Deutschen Akademie der Wissenschaften (Central Archive of the German Academy of Sciences), Berlin.

Friedrich Spielhagen

(24 February 1829 – 25 February 1911)

Katherine Roper
Saint Mary's College of California

BOOKS: *Clara Vere* (Hannover: Meyer, 1857); translated anonymously as *Lady Clara de Vere: A Story* (New York: Appleton, 1881);

Auf der Düne (Hannover: Meyer, 1858);

In der zwölften Stunde (Hannover: Meyer, 1860);

Problematische Naturen, 4 volumes (Berlin: Janke, 1861); translated by Maximilian Schele De Vere as *Problematic Characters: A Novel* (New York: Leypoldt & Holt, 1869);

Durch Nacht zum Licht, 4 volumes (Berlin: Janke, 1862); translated by De Vere as *Through Night to Light: A Novel* (New York: Leypoldt & Holt, 1870);

Kleine Romane, 5 volumes (Berlin: Janke, 1862–1864) – comprises *Auf der Düne,* 2 volumes (1862); *Clara Vere* (1862); *In der zwölften Stunde* (1863); *Röschen vom Hofe* (1864);

Die von Hohenstein, 4 volumes (Berlin: Janke, 1864); translated by De Vere as *The Hohensteins* (New York: Leypoldt & Holt, 1870);

Vermischte Schriften, 2 volumes (Berlin: Janke, 1864–1868);

Gesammelte Werke, 21 volumes (Berlin: Janke, 1866–1867);

In Reih' und Glied: Ein Roman in neun Büchern, 5 volumes (Berlin: Janke, 1867);

Faust und Nathan: Ein Vortrag gehalten im Saale des Berliner Handwerkervereins am 13. Dezember 1866 (Berlin: Duncker, 1867);

Hans und Grete: Eine Dorfgeschichte (Berlin: Janke, 1868);

Unter Tannen: Zwei Novellen (Berlin: Janke, 1868) – comprises "Die schönen Amerikanerinnen," "Der Vergnügungskommissar";

Hammer und Amboß: Roman in 5 Büchern, 5 volumes (Schwerin: Hildebrand, 1869); translated by William Hand Browne as *Hammer and Anvil: A Novel* (New York: Leypoldt & Holt, 1870);

Die Dorfcoquette: Eine Erzählung (Schwerin: Hildebrand, 1869); translated by J. L. Laird as *The Village Coquette* (London: Chapman, 1875);

Friedrich Spielhagen

Deutsche Pioniere: Eine Geschichte aus dem vorigen Jahrhundert (Berlin: Janke, 1870); translated by Ida Veramy as *The Block House on the Prairie, or, German Pioneers* (London: City of London Publishing Co., 1882); translated by Levi Sternberg as *The German Pioneers: A Tale of the Mohawk* (Chicago: Donohue, Henneberry, 1891);

Sämmtliche Werke, 10 volumes (Leipzig: Staackmann, 1871; enlarged, 15 volumes, 1877–1879);

Allzeit voran: Roman, 3 volumes (Leipzig: Staackmann, 1872);

Was die Schwalbe sang: Roman, 2 volumes (Leipzig: Staackmann, 1873); translated by Mary J. Safford as *What the Swallow Sang: A Novel* (New York: Holt & Williams, 1873);

Ultimo: Novelle (Leipzig: Staackmann, 1873);

Aus meinem Skizzenbuche (Leipzig: Staackmann, 1874);

Liebe für Liebe: Schauspiel in vier Acten (Leipzig: Staackmann, 1875);

Hans und Grete: Schauspiel in fünf Akten (Leipzig: Staackmann, 1876);

Der lustige Rath: Lustspiel in vier Acten (Leipzig: Staackmann, 1876);

Sturmflut: Roman in sechs Büchern, 3 volumes (Leipzig: Staackmann, 1877); translated by S. E. A. H. Stephenson as *The Breaking of the Storm* (London: Bentley, 1877);

Von Neapel bis Syrakus: Reiseskizzen (Leipzig: Staackmann, 1878);

Das Skelett im Hause: Novelle (Leipzig: Staackmann, 1878); translated by Safford as *The Skeleton in the House* (New York: Harlan, 1881);

Platt Land: Roman, 3 volumes (Leipzig: Staackmann, 1879);

Quisisana: Novelle (Leipzig: Staackmann, 1880); translated by H. E. Goldschmidt as *Quisisana; or, Rest at Last* (London: Nimmo & Bain, 1881; New York: Lovell, 1884);

Angela: Roman, 2 volumes (Leipzig: Staackmann, 1881);

Breite Schultern (Leipzig: Staackmann, 1881);

Skizzen, Geschichten und Gedichte (Leipzig: Staackmann, 1881);

Beiträge zur Theorie und Technik des Romans (Leipzig: Staackmann, 1883);

Uhlenhans: Roman, 2 volumes (Leipzig: Staackmann, 1884);

Gerettet: Schauspiel in vier Akten (Leipzig: Staackmann, 1884);

An der Heilquelle: Novelle (Leipzig: Staackmann, 1885);

Was will das werden?: Roman in neun Büchern, 3 volumes (Leipzig: Staackmann, 1887);

Die Philosophin: Schauspiel in vier Akten (Leipzig: Staackmann, 1887);

Noblesse Oblige: Roman in drei Büchern (Leipzig: Staackmann, 1888);

Ein neuer Pharao: Roman in vier Büchern (Leipzig: Staackmann, 1889);

Finder und Erfinder: Erinnerungen aus meinem Leben, 2 volumes (Leipzig: Staackmann, 1890);

Aus meiner Studienmappe: Beiträge zur litterarischen Aesthetik und Kritik (Berlin: Allgemeiner Verlag für Deutsche Literatur, 1891);

In eiserner Zeit: Trauerspiel in fünf Akten (Leipzig: Staackmann, 1891);

Gedichte (Leipzig: Staackmann, 1892);

Sonntagskind: Roman in sechs Büchern, 3 volumes (Leipzig: Staackmann, 1893);

Stumme des Himmels: Roman in vier Büchern, 2 volumes (Leipzig: Staackmann, 1895);

Susi: Eine Hofgeschichte, 2 volumes (Stuttgart: Engelhorn, 1895); translated by Hilda Skae as *Baroness Susi* (New York: Brentano's, 1905);

Sämmtliche Romane, 29 volumes (Leipzig: Staackmann, 1895–1904);

Selbstgerecht: Roman, 2 volumes (Stuttgart: Engelhorn, 1896);

Zum Zeitvertreib: Roman (Leipzig: Staackmann, 1897);

Mesmerismus – Alles fließt: Zwei Novellen (Leipzig: Staackmann, 1897);

Faustulus: Roman (Leipzig: Staackmann, 1898);

Neue Beiträge zur Theorie und Technik der Epik und Dramatik (Leipzig: Staackmann, 1898);

Herrin: Novelle (Leipzig: Staackmann, 1899; Chicago: Laird & Lee, 1899);

Neue Gedichte (Leipzig: Staackmann, 1899);

Opfer: Roman (Leipzig: Staackmann, 1900);

Frei geboren: Roman (Leipzig: Staackmann, 1900);

Am Wege: Vermischte Schriften (Leipzig: Staackmann, 1903).

OTHER: Wilhelm von Kaulbach, *Goethes Frauengestalten,* second edition, annotated by Spielhagen (Munich: Bruckmann, 1863).

TRANSLATIONS: George William Curtis, *Nil-Skizzen eines Howadji* (Hannover: Meyer, 1857);

Ralph Waldo Emerson, *Englische Charakterzüge* (Hannover: Meyer, 1857);

Amerikanische Gedichte (Leipzig: Staackmann, 1859);

Jules Michelet, *Die Liebe* (Leipzig: Weber, 1859);

Michelet, *Die Frau* (Leipzig: Weber, 1860);

Michelet, *Das Meer* (Leipzig: Weber, 1861);

William Roscoe, *Leben Lorenzo von Medici* (Leipzig: Senf, 1861);

Hjalmar Hjorth Boyesen, *Novellen* (Stuttgart: Engelhorn, 1885).

SELECTED PERIODICAL PUBLICATION – UNCOLLECTED: "Neues vom Ich-Roman," *Litterarisches Echo,* 2 (1900): 450–458.

Friedrich Spielhagen's first novel, *Problematische Naturen* (Problematic Natures, 1861; translated as *Problematic Characters,* 1869), catapulted him to literary fame. Over the next four decades twenty-one other novels followed, several of which achieved comparable renown. Together they constitute a massive fictional portrayal of the era surrounding German unification in 1871. Their popularity, manifested by abundant serializations, editions, and translations, was augmented by critical acclaim of Spielhagen as the master of the German novel. By the 1880s, however, outpourings of praise were being replaced by sharp attacks from a younger generation of naturalist writers who criticized his novels as ideologically tendentious and aesthetically inept. Such dismissive judgments of Spielhagen's work still prevail, obscuring its literary innovations and its cultural importance in the emergent German nation. As a novelist and literary theorist, Spielhagen significantly influenced the development of German realism. As a fervent democrat, he contributed to the tradition of literary engagement in German culture.

Keys to Spielhagen's values and personality can be found in the dichotomies that pervade his writings: hammer versus anvil, discovery versus invention, realism versus idealism, individual versus society, resoluteness versus compromise. Such themes of dichotomy also govern his account in his *Finder und Erfinder: Erinnerungen aus meinem Leben* (Discoverer and Inventor: Memories from My Life, 1890) of his childhood and youth, which he describes in terms of the deadening weight of provincial tradition versus liberating stimuli for flight from social conformity and political indifference.

One of the six children of Friedrich August Wilhelm Spielhagen and Wilhelmine Listemann Spielhagen (née Robrahn), Spielhagen was born in the Lower Saxon town of Magdeburg on 24 February 1829. He grew up in the still more provincial Baltic port of Stralsund, where his family moved when he was six. Two liberating influences in this provincial atmosphere came from defining traits Spielhagen cherished in his father: an intense love of nature that the elder Spielhagen inherited from his own father, a Thuringian forester, and a powerful work ethic that drew him from forestry into the civil service, where he rose to the position of waterworks inspector in Stralsund. His father, according to Spielhagen, was a self-made man in the best sense of the word because he exemplified the ability of an individual to mold his destiny through effort and will, unaided by aristocratic title, academic degree, wealth, or connections. These qualities, however, were offset in Spielhagen's mind by his growing perception of his father as a hidebound bureaucrat whose unquestioning subservience to authority robbed him of freedom and creativity. A complete

indifference to culture and politics was another disturbing paternal attribute. The relationship between father and son thus developed tensions.

Similar tensions grew between young Spielhagen and his wider environment. Spielhagen's education at the local preparatory school and then at the gymnasium allowed for no discussion of current political issues, and the rote study of Greek, Latin, and German classics did not inspire him; nevertheless, the gymnasium was the indispensable preparation for his literary pursuits. Stralsund was a cultural and political backwater, lacking even a daily newspaper. The nearby island of Rügen, dominated by a culturally lethargic aristocracy, was even worse. Contacts with the Pomeranian nobility, although they resulted in some close friendships, instigated Spielhagen's lifelong hatred of aristocratic privilege. On the other hand, the Baltic shore and windswept countryside provided a splendid natural setting that Spielhagen later celebrated in countless descriptive passages. Such conflicting experiences in Pomerania contributed to the prolonged inner turmoil that troubled him through his twenties.

Spielhagen began his studies at the University of Berlin in 1847 in a state of dreamy melancholy that left him oblivious to the mounting crisis in Europe. He left Berlin literally on the eve of the March 1848 revolution there, and when he matriculated at the University of Bonn he was, by his account, only an interested observer of the political ferment around him. He immersed himself in reading, especially the works of Homer, William Shakespeare, and Johann Wolfgang von Goethe – a triad of authors from whose works he drew both literary inspiration and the guiding principles for his later literary theories. Although some of this study was academic, much of it was self-designed; and as his lack of progress toward his examinations became more evident, tensions with his father grew. Additional semesters in Berlin and Greifswald, at the behest of the impatient and perplexed parent, still failed to result in a degree.

In 1851 Spielhagen abandoned plans for a scholarly career to try a succession of other middle-class pursuits: a year in the army, a stint as a tutor on a Pomeranian estate, and, finally, to his family's relief, a respectable position as an English teacher at a Leipzig gymnasium in 1854. During this period he worked his way through the writings of Benedict de Spinoza, Friedrich Schlegel, and Friedrich Schleiermacher in search of deeper philosophical and literary understanding. A hopeless romantic passion in the early 1850s became the impetus for his first novella, titled *Clara Vere* (1857; translated as *Lady Clara de Vere,* 1881) after Alfred Tennyson's poem. His entry into publishing came gradually during his six years in Leipzig: first a few essays and then translations of works by Ralph Waldo Emerson, other American authors, and Jules Michelet. Finally, in 1857 he received word that the tattered manuscript for *Clara Vere* had found a publisher.

A copy of the novella reached Ehrenreich Eichholz, editor of the liberal *Zeitung für Norddeutschland* (Newspaper for North Germany) in Hannover, who invited Spielhagen to contribute to his newspaper. When Spielhagen sent him the manuscript for a second novella, *Auf der Düne* (On the Dune, 1858), Eichholz reacted with cautious praise, querying what he identified as a shift from idealism to realism. Far from discouraging him, Eichholz's misgivings strengthened Spielhagen's conviction that he must defy conventional literary idealism and create characters of flesh and blood in a recognizable social and physical milieu. Eichholz published the novella in his paper, solicited other works, and offered Spielhagen the position of feuilleton editor. Spielhagen moved to Hannover in 1860; his newfound financial security allowed him to marry an Erfurt widow, Therese Wittich (née Boûtin).

During the 1850s the reactionary atmosphere in Germany had reinforced Spielhagen's political indifference; politics, he had assumed, was merely the pursuit of selfish interests. But the liberal circle that surrounded the *Zeitung für Norddeutschland* drew the new editor into their discussions of the prospects for political liberation and German unification, transforming Spielhagen into a committed democrat by convincing him that his ideal of individual self-determination could thrive only in an environment of political and social freedom.

Spielhagen's *Problematische Naturen* became a clear expression of his literary and social aims. He later compared the novel to Goethe's *Die Leiden des jungen Werthers* (1774; translated as *The Sorrows of Werther,* 1779), saying that each book allowed the author to work through his own inner torment while giving literary expression to the turmoil of a whole generation. The title came from Goethe's term for people who are so inadequate to any situation that they are destined to be consumed by misery. In intricately constructed episodes Spielhagen entwines such characters in a tangle of social hypocrisy, snobbery, and corruption. *Problematische Naturen* depicts them in the context of rural Pomerania of the "Vormärz" (pre-March – the period before the German revolutions of 1848), a society of outmoded hereditary privilege in an age of moral and intellectual confusion. The sequel, written after Spielhagen's arrival in Hannover, proposes

resolution in the form of social action. Its title, *Durch Nacht zum Licht* (1862; translated as *Through Night to Light,* 1870), signifies not individual redemption but the liberation of humanity. The concluding scenes at the barricades in Berlin clearly announce Spielhagen's own political engagement.

The protagonist of the two novels, Oswald Stein, personifies the title of the first novel, and his personal odyssey drives both works. The parallels between Oswald and Spielhagen exemplify Spielhagen's conviction that an author must write from firsthand experience. *Problematische Naturen* opens with Oswald arriving, as Spielhagen had, to take a position as tutor in the household of a Pomeranian nobleman. Oswald's "problematic nature" reflects Spielhagen's own impetuous romantic passions, his middle-class resentment of aristocratic privilege, and the collision of his poetic nature with the mundane outlooks of those around him. Unlike Spielhagen, however, Oswald proves unable to resolve his inner conflicts.

Problematische Naturen and *Durch Nacht zum Licht* display another Spielhagen hallmark: a determination to portray objective reality by largely banishing the authorial voice in favor of dialogue and action. Oswald relates his personal history in a conversation; his perspectives are revealed through internal monologues; another character expounds on Goethe's passage about problematic natures; and a relatively minor character uses a bridal toast to proclaim the importance of social action.

The physical setting of each episode manifests Spielhagen's aim of directly linking the characters with their environment. Descriptions of surroundings, such as the layout of the estate, floor plans, furnishings, and portraits on the walls usually occur as Oswald or another character moves into each location. The Pomeranian landscape is first seen through Oswald's eyes as he marvels at the contrast between the vast natural panoramas and the densely built-up Berlin from which he has just come. Such vivid depictions of natural landscapes became characteristic of Spielhagen novels, as did references to the weather to indicate the emotional tenor of an episode. In structure each of the two novels builds toward a denouement in which growing tensions explode, and each achieves a resolution that looks toward the future. The first novel culminates when Oswald's clash with aristocratic insolence ends in a duel that forces him off the estate and into the wider world. The second depicts Oswald's confused wanderings and ends in Berlin, where he and other characters sublimate their problematic natures into political action. The climax comes with the revolution of March 1848, when poetic justice is meted out at the barricades. The differing outcomes of the various problematic natures, Spielhagen says in his autobiography, were intended to demonstrate the necessity of such qualities as humility, moderation, and patience for individual redemption. The last scene, however, shifts the focus away from individuals to the implications of the revolution. A public funeral honoring the dead is the occasion for what became a Spielhagen convention: a eulogy enunciating the novel's social message. Here the speaker charges Germans to ensure that the "night" of reactionary tyranny never returns. They must educate themselves politically so that they can work toward genuine liberation – a goal to which Spielhagen devoted the rest of his literary career.

Some critics charged that the political emphasis of *Problematische Naturen*, the title applied to both novels in later editions, violated aesthetic principles of literature. But these voices were muffled by a chorus of admirers who declared that Spielhagen's characters had achieved a startling resonance with contemporary reality (so much so that trying to guess the models for them became a popular pastime). The multitude of readers who testified to the novels' impact included such prominent figures as the progressive politician Rudolf von Bennigsen, the Prussian minister-president Otto von Bismarck, the literary theorist Julian Schmidt, the young Friedrich Nietzsche, and even Crown Prince Friederich, who took the occasion of an encounter with Spielhagen to discuss the novel knowledgeably.

After his literary triumph Spielhagen left his editorship in Hannover to settle in Berlin with his family, which included Jenny, a daughter from his wife's previous marriage, whom Speilhagen adopted and Antonie (Toni), the Spielhagens' daughter. His activities in Berlin included editorship of the widely read literary periodical *Westermanns illustrierte deutsche Monatshefte* (Westermann's Illustrated German Monthly) from 1878 to 1884 and the publication of essays, cultural critiques, poems, dramas, travel writings, and a rapid succession of novels.

Spielhagen's enunciation of his literary theory, in six volumes of essays published between 1864 and 1898, made him a prominent participant in the intense debate in Germany over the form and purposes of the novel. The theory combines three fundamental elements: aesthetic principles, a theory of literary realism, and a logic that commits the novelist to social engagement.

The aesthetic principles of Spielhagen's theory stem from his resistance to Friedrich Schiller's belittlement of the novelist as the half brother of the poet. In the writings of Wilhelm von Humboldt, Spielhagen discovered the foundations of a theory that would raise the novel to an aesthetic status equal to that of drama, which Aristotle had characterized as the height of poetry. The highest purpose of art, Humboldt wrote, was the representation of reality by a Bild (image) that sparked immediate recognition in the viewer. In the case of the written word, such representation meant using language to impart an objective reality completely removed from the author's subjectivity. Drama achieved this goal by conveying action directly, without narrational mediation; but the most complete representation of reality, Humboldt argued, was the epic, which also conveyed action directly but portrayed a total world rather than drama's single tragic conflict. Spielhagen characterized the novel as the modern counterpart of the Homeric epic: it, too, should communicate to society the totality of that society's shared experience. The epic form used by Homer, however, emerged from the oral tradition of a simpler age; the complex modern world could be represented only through the novel's intricate network of events and characters.

The relationship between the novelist and reality was explained by Spielhagen in terms of another favorite dichotomy: discoverer versus inventor. The novelist must be both the discoverer of an objective reality and the inventor of an artistic form by which to convey that reality. Discovery resided in the novelist's Erlebnis (experience) of reality; and invention emerged in the transformation of that experience by the epische Phantasie (epic imagination). Thus, every novel, of necessity, began as autobiography; but subjective experience would be transformed into art only insofar as the story sparked in readers the recognition of a total reality. Like the epic, the novel must be grounded in objectivity; its reality must emerge directly through characters' actions, without authorial reflection. The dialectic of discovery and invention also lay behind Spielhagen's idea that the hero had to personify the unifying idea of the novel. To be grounded in objectivity, the hero had to be "discovered" by the author in a flesh-and-blood model such as the Baltic sea captain, described by Spielhagen in an 1877 essay, who became the model for Reinhold Schmidt, the hero of *Sturmflut* (Storm Flood, 1877; translated as *The Breaking of the Storm,* 1877). The "invention" emerges as the writer gives aesthetic form to the character, connects his life with the events of the story, and constructs these elements into an artistic whole.

Spielhagen's logic of social engagement derived from what he saw as a distinctively modern purpose behind the goal of objectivity. Modern humanity, he averred, wanted to understand the natural and social forces that molded its destiny in order to gain a measure of control over that destiny. By conveying such understanding, the novelist would help humanity determine its fate. This notion is the basis of Spielhagen's commitment to using literature to further the cause of freedom. Spielhagen's attempts to justify these theoretical assumptions and to translate them into practice both reflected and contributed to dilemmas in German realism.

The tension between the goal of portraying an objective reality and that of conveying social understanding is evident in Spielhagen's *Die von Hohenstein* (1864; translated as *The Hohensteins,* 1870). The novel's depiction of revolutionary and counterrevolutionary events in the Rhineland during 1848–1849 contains such a blatant political purpose that many admirers of Spielhagen, including Nietzsche, expressed disappointment in the work. By depicting an array of political motives, tactics, and strategies through characters extending over the whole social spectrum, Spielhagen searched for an explanation of the defeat of the revolution and for lessons that would allow for the future triumph of revolutionary hopes. Bismarckian politics and diplomacy were gathering momentum, and the novel's portrayals of political discussions, of rapid economic change, and of the new social consciousness all contributed to Spielhagen's purpose of using his work to inject democratic ideals into the cultural arena of the emergent German nation.

Spielhagen's next novel, *In Reih' und Glied* (In Rank and File, 1867), reveals a similar purpose by depicting the years surrounding 1848 as a time of rapid change. Instead of focusing on the revolution, the work first portrays an explosion of provincial violence in Thuringia in late 1847 and then skips to the reactionary aftermath in the mid 1850s. A deteriorating feudal society and an emergent German capitalism are the context for tangled political intrigues. Like most Spielhagen novels, the work has a double setting: a remote Thuringian estate surrounded by impoverished mountain villages; and Berlin, depicted as a cauldron for monarchical, liberal, and radical politics. Reacting to the many signs of social crisis, myriad political characters – including the protagonist, as a self-styled people's tribune; a reform-minded baron; a liberal novelist; a radical ideologue; and the Prussian king – exemplify Spielhagen's search throughout the political spectrum for a means of liberating the German nation. Episode by episode, the novel shows the impossibility of any single leader, political party, or ideology

fostering the needed transformation. The answer, as the title suggests, must be a national effort that unites oppressed masses and reform-minded leaders in a genuinely popular movement.

In Reih' und Glied calls for a German revolution quite different from the one being orchestrated by Bismarck. A historical legacy for this revolution is suggested by allusions to the peasant wars of the sixteenth century, but the nature of this legacy is unclear. What is clear is Spielhagen's conviction that the forthcoming revolution must achieve both spiritual liberation and economic justice. The novel suggests through its portrayal of peasant and working-class violence in the Thuringian villages that a revolution based on purely economic goals will be disastrous.

Through the failures of Leo Gutmann, his protagonist, Spielhagen cautions against attempts to bring the revolution from above. Modeled after the socialist leader Ferdinand Lassalle, Leo is contemptuous of what he sees as liberals' lethargy and incompetence. His own attempt to manipulate the power of the monarchy, however, enmeshes him in corrupt intrigues; his advice to the workers results only in ill-conceived action and violent defeat; and his tumultuous personal relationships lead him to a fatal duel.

Although many episodes disparage liberalism, two liberal characters survive the panorama of ruination and death, suggesting that Spielhagen saw liberalism as the genuine hope for Germany. One of these characters is a novelist who endures a prison sentence for writing a politically explosive novel but remains committed to using literature to attack social ills. The second is a liberal Jewish physician who explicates the novel's title in a toast invoking images of the German people marching in columns toward liberation. The novel received widespread acclaim for its call to a new generation to march together rather than succumb to being "problematic natures" or rely on famous leaders.

A distinctive stylistic feature of *In Reih' und Glied* is the pervasive dream imagery with which Spielhagen emphasizes the contrast between the romantic inclinations of the age and the social realities. The frequent recounting of characters' dreams also suggests his pre-Freudian conviction that dreams are representations of psychological states, for he uses them to give insight into troubled souls. The image takes on a political dimension when one character refers to Leo as the "Traumdeuter" (dream interpreter) for the king, explaining that he articulates the king's ideals and tries to turn them into action. The vision of humanity marching toward liberation remains here an unrealized dream.

First two pages from the manuscript for Spielhagen's novel Sturmflut *(from Hans Henning,* Friedrich Spielhagen, *1910)*

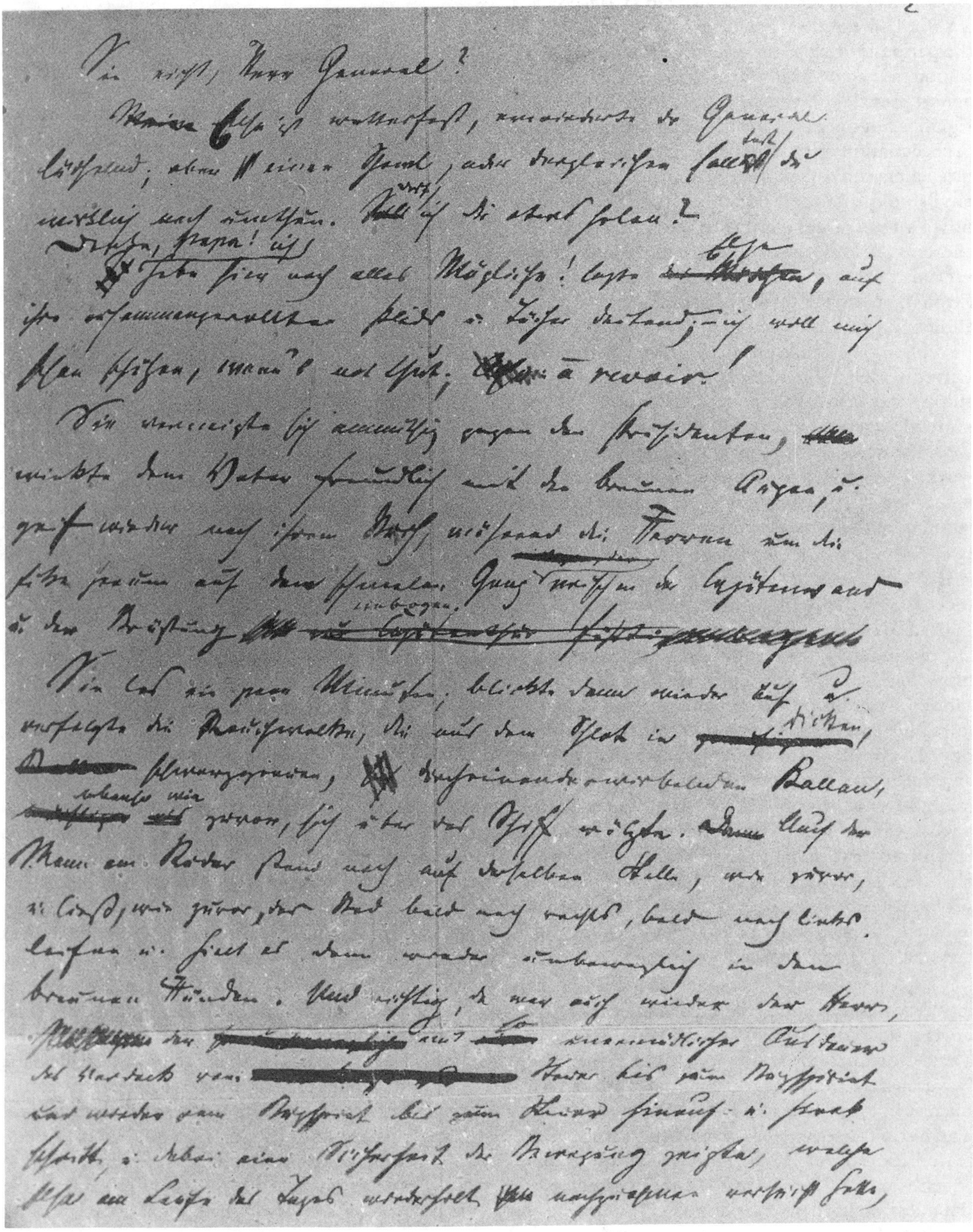

Hammer und Amboß (1869; translated as *Hammer and Anvil,* 1870) extended Spielhagen's horizons back to the period leading to the rise of German industrialization in the mid 1840s. The hammer-and-anvil imagery, prevalent throughout Spielhagen's writings, signifies not only an industrializing age but also his preoccupation with whether individuals and peoples hammer out their own destinies or submit, like anvils, to the pounding of external influences. The novel's hero, Georg Hartwig, personifies this dichotomy. A prototype of the self-made man, Georg ascends to a position as a successful factory owner through energetic, intelligent effort, but only after enduring youthful ordeals. At the beginning of the novel he is a gymnasium student who becomes involved with a nobleman's smuggling operation, resulting in a seven-year prison sentence. A reform-minded warden acts as a hammer, remolding Georg's waywardness to the discipline of hard work. The warden also expounds a vision of a humanity beyond the unidirectional hammer-anvil relation of master and slave.

Some critics hailed the author of *Hammer und Amboß* as a German Charles Dickens. Those who took issue with the comparison, however, noted the limitations of his techniques of realism. Whereas Dickens directly depicted prison and factory conditions, Spielhagen's characters have erudite conversations about them. More important, Spielhagen allowed his goal of objectivity to be overrun by ideology. The portrayal of Georg's transformation from an impetuous adventurer to a humane industrialist, critics asserted, was moralizing that had no place in a work of art. Spielhagen, however, was becoming convinced that he had to convey understanding. His ideal of the novelist as schoolmaster, or even prophet, to the nation contributed to the growing debate in German criticism over notions of artistic creation and social engagement.

Spielhagen's most successful attempt at combining art with social criticism unfolded in *Sturmflut.* The novel sustains the image of the storm on two levels: as a catastrophic Baltic flood modeled after the one of November 1872 and as the financial crash of 1873. Each storm brings death, destruction, and heroism. The historical setting for the man-made storm is the period immediately following German unification, which came to be known as the Gründerjahre (founders' era). The term referred to the founding not just of the German empire but of the financial empires that burgeoned in the wake of the huge war indemnity France paid to Germany. Spielhagen uses frenzied struggles over a Baltic railway and a harbor project to characterize the era as one of scramble for fortune,

Spielhagen in 1890

rampant corruption, and triumph of greed over national interest. The collapse of the project unleashes the storm that lays waste to the social landscape. Interpreting the crash of 1873 as a national moral failure, Spielhagen conveys overtones of cosmic judgment. This depiction of the Gründerjahre was echoed by other writers for decades.

Reinhold Schmidt, the hero of *Sturmflut,* is Spielhagen's most sustained paean to middle-class idealism. Planted firmly in the chaos of the newly unified Germany and with no hint of a "problematic nature," Reinhold is a positive counterpart to the many self-serving, manipulative, and corrupt characters around him. Having risen to the post of Baltic sea captain through competence and devotion to duty, he has sacrificed his position to serve in the Franco-Prussian War. In the aftermath he is a pillar of reason, stability, humility, and courage, navigating as a principled commoner through the shoals of wealth and privilege. His unerring warnings about the follies of the harbor project and his heroic actions in the story result in his being called at the end

Spielhagen on his seventieth birthday

of the novel to a high government post, where he will presumably bring his much-needed talents to bear on building Germany. He will also wed the daughter of a titled Prussian general. Thus Spielhagen, despite his disdain for aristocratic privilege, uses his hero to build a fictional bridge between the middle class and aristocracy — a link he believed essential to achieving social harmony.

A strong theme of crisis in middle-class values resounds in *Sturmflut*. The rigidities of the traditional Bürger (middle-class citizen) are counterposed to the recklessness and greed of the newly emerged capitalist bourgeoisie. The two groups are personified in Ernst Schmidt — Reinhold's uncle — and his son Philipp. Uncle Ernst is a veteran of the barricades of 1848 who has since built a successful marble works in Berlin. In him the ideals of 1848 have become petrified in the notion that the highest value is a principled refusal to compromise. He automatically stiffens in the presence of the despised aristocracy; he scoffs at the thought of negotiating

with striking workers; he despises Bismarck for what he sees as opportunistic concessions; and he refuses to contemplate a Germany that is not republican. Philipp Schmidt, on the other hand, knows no ideals other than pursuit of profit. In the atmosphere of the Gründerjahre he builds an immense fortune and acquires a lavish mansion on Berlin's prestigious Wilhelmstraße. The splendor collapses with the crash, and, pursued by the police over millions in missing funds, Philipp commits suicide.

A unique stylistic moment for Spielhagen occurs in a passage in which he unleashes his outrage over the sins of the Gründerjahre in unaccustomed fury. The usual third-person narration ends abruptly when the storm and the crash simultaneously break over Berlin. Amid the howling winds, the narrator assumes the voice of an anonymous, bitter Berliner watching the wealthy run for cover after their victimization of the common people. A few paragraphs later the narration switches again, becoming the sarcastic voice of a guest observing the social ambition and hypocrisy at a ball at Philipp's mansion. This narrator vanishes when a fulsome toast to Philipp collapses into apocalyptic chaos as the police arrive to arrest him, and the guests disperse into the furious storm.

Sturmflut soon became Spielhagen's best-known work. Along with his other epic novels, it overshadowed his work in other genres, including his twenty novellas. Even he tended to regard the novellas as merely a pause between novels, and he paid the genre only slight attention in his theoretical writings. The distinctive characteristic of the novella, as Spielhagen saw it, was its focus on a small segment of human experience as opposed to the novel's panoramic totality. Moreover, the characters of the novella were not to be developed; they simply found themselves in a situation and reacted to it, much as would the characters in a drama. In practice, however, Spielhagen showed himself to be unclear about the differences. Not only did some works he designated as novellas run to hundreds of pages, but he relabeled his first three novellas as novels in a collected edition and as novellas again in a later one.

Perhaps because of the lack of self-imposed pressure to create a social totality, Spielhagen often seemed freer in his novellas than in his novels. He used them to experiment with humor, as in *Das Skelett im Hause* (1878; translated as *The Skeleton in the House*, 1881); to present psychological studies, as in *Quisisana*, (1880; translated, 1881); and to address philosophical concerns, as in *Faustulus* (1898). He sometimes came closer to achieving his ideal of objectivity in his novellas than in his novels: in the novellas he showed a trend away from authorial narration; his tendency to moralize was lessened by his avoidance of political emphases; and presenting characters in specific situations made him less likely to idealize them.

Far less successful were Spielhagen's six dramas, even though his first literary efforts had taken the form of plays he wrote and produced as a child for his family; he had tried acting briefly in his twenties; his lifelong love of the theater resulted in countless drama critiques, and, of course, his ideal of objectivity was closely tied to his notion of dramatic representation. But even Hans Henning, his admiring biographer, conceded that Spielhagen's dramas lacked the forcefulness of his novels. Whatever literary deficiencies were evident, however, there was another cause for Spielhagen's relative eclipse as a dramatist: as he put it in a letter to a friend, his dramas fell victim to the murderous assault of a younger literary generation.

In fact, more than the dramas were attacked: the ascendancy of literary naturalism in the mid 1880s was accompanied by the naturalists' rejection of Spielhagen's novels. The most concerted attack came from the brothers Heinrich and Julius Hart, who in 1884 devoted an issue of their literary journal *Kritische Waffengänge* (Critical Warfare) to Spielhagen. His works, they announced, exemplified all that was wrong with the preceding epoch of German novels. The Harts' most fundamental objection concerned Spielhagen's equating the novel with the epic. This equation, they argued, grounded the novel in idealism rather than realism: the epic writer, who rendered heroic deeds of the social elite, was an idealist; but the novelist must be a realist, committed to portraying the everyday reality of the times. Spielhagen's aloofness from the lower classes, as they saw it, was representative of a generation whose social horizons were limited to the salons. Another indication of Spielhagen's confusion between idealism and realism was his pervasive didacticism, which had turned his novels from works of art into tendentious pamphlets: a realist must allow readers to discover any moral message themselves through the objective portrayal of social reality.

Such criticism, however, points to the link rather than the disparity between Spielhagen's realism and literary naturalism. For all their virulence, the Harts were essentially criticizing Spielhagen for violating his own principles of realism. They drew from his novels myriad examples of unwarranted narrational reflections, of characters who were mere social types, of an improbable High German in the speech of all the characters, of a reliance on dialogue about social conditions rather than portrayal of them, and of preoccupation with the propertied classes. But the Harts' insistence that the writer must remain free of social moralizing would prove as difficult for naturalist writers as it was for their predecessors. Moreover, their battle cry of objectivity differed only in degree from Spielhagen's principles. Their call for more literary attention to the language and situation of the lower classes accorded completely with Spielhagen's unrealized goal of depicting a social totality. Spielhagen thus had some cause for bewilderment when the naturalists declared him their enemy rather than a comrade fighting for the same literary goals.

With his epic novel *Was will das werden?* (What Will Come of This?, 1887) Spielhagen implicitly answered the Harts' criticism by reasserting the moral role of the novelist. Through the biblical title, taken from a passage in the Book of Acts, Spielhagen identified the era of German unification with the confusion experienced by Christians immediately after the Crucifixion. A spectrum of characters responds in multifarious ways to the novel's insistent questioning about what direction Germany should take. The question is answered by a reaffirmation of the position of previous novels: that a German revolution must forge a society based on social harmony and justice. The artist-hero, surrounded by messianic imagery, is charged with communicating these truths through literary works that will speak to the age.

A more explicit counterattack against the naturalists emerged in the novels *Ein neuer Pharao* (The New Pharaoh, 1889) and *Sonntagskind* (Sunday's Child, 1893). The first gives a pessimistic portrayal of Bismarckian Germany at the end of the 1870s; the title refers to the passage in Exodus describing the coming of a "new pharaoh" who does not recognize the loyalty and service of Joseph and his descendants. By the end of the novel the protagonist, a disillusioned participant in the 1848 revolutions, is leaving a Germany he believes has failed to recognize the democratic legacy of that era. In his last speech he lashes out at the naturalists for having spurned social ideals and for thereby providing a dangerous example to social groups suffering under the injustices of modern society. *Sonntagskind* extends the attack by portraying the frustrations of an idealistic dramatist whose art defies the new literary direction. At the close he nevertheless vows to continue the literary struggle for the liberation of his society.

These conflicts abated to some extent as Spielhagen became an elder literary statesman. On the occasion of his seventieth birthday in 1899 a published "album" poured forth tributes from literati of all ages. For his eightieth birthday Max Kretzer, one of Germany's most prominent naturalists, composed an affectionate poem hailing Spielhagen as a towering influence on his generation. And indeed, Spielhagen's prolific literary production had laid the foundations for future literary engagement in Germany: his probing questions about the relationships of idealism, literary realism, and society would continue to form part of the cultural discourse, and his commitment to democracy would contribute a much-needed legacy to German civilization.

By the turn of the century, however, Spielhagen's popularity was waning. Although his writings continued to be published in large editions, none of his later works enjoyed the popular success of the early novels. The naturalist attacks accounted only partially for this decline. The discrediting of liberalism during the Bismarckian era diminished popular tolerance for Spielhagen's devotion to the ideals of 1848. In addition, Spielhagen was showing signs of failing imagination; his contin-

Spielhagen in 1909 (photograph by Filip Kester)

ued use of familiar themes and character types and his often cumbersome language discouraged all but the most fervent Spielhagen devotees.

Spielhagen never really recovered from the death of his wife in 1900. His weariness and resignation are reflected in those of the heroine who narrates his last novel, *Frei geboren* (Born Free, 1900). Nevertheless, her impassioned affirmation of freedom testifies to Spielhagen's unyielding commitment to this ideal. After Spielhagen died on 25 February 1911 the writer Hermann Sudermann delivered a eulogy worthy of a Spielhagen novel in which he called on his fellow Germans to commit themselves to the struggle for freedom that had so long engaged their dead hero.

Biographies:
Ludwig Ziemmsen, *Friedrich Spielhagen* (Breslau: Deutsche Bücherei, 1883);

Gustav Karpeles, *Friedrich Spielhagen: Ein literarischer Essay* (Leipzig, 1889);

Hans Henning, *Friedrich Spielhagen* (Leipzig: Staackmann, 1910).

References:

Paul Colonge, "*Sturmflut,* de Friedrich Spielhagen, représentation romanesque de l'Ère des Fondateurs,'" in his *Images de l'Allemagne* (Toulouse: Mirail, 1990), pp. 111–125;

Joseph Dresch, *Le roman social en Allemagne (1850–1900): Gutzkow – Freytag – Spielhagen – Fontane* (Paris: Alcan, 1913);

Andrea Fischbacher-Bosshardt, *Anfänge der modernen Erzählkunst: Untersuchungen zu Friedrich Spielhagens theoretischem und literarischem Werk* (Bern: Lang, 1988);

Friedrich Spielhagen: Dem Meister des deutschen Romans zu seinem 70. Geburtstage (Leipzig: Staackmann, 1899);

Rolf Geissler, "Verspielte Realitätserkenntnis: Zum Problem der objektiven Darstellung in Friedrich Spielhagens *Hammer und Amboß,*" *Deutsche Vierteljahrsschrift für Literaturwissenschaft und Geistesgeschichte,* 52 (September 1978): 496–510;

Martha Geller, *Friedrich Spielhagens Theorie und Praxis des Romans* (Berlin: Grote, 1917);

Alfred F. Goessl, "Die Darstellung des Adels im Prosaschaffen Friedrich Spielhagens," Ph.D. dissertation, Tulane University, 1966;

Il-Sop Han, "Spielhagens Ich-Roman-Theorie," Ph.D. dissertation, University of Hamburg, 1977;

Heinrich and Julius Hart, *Friedrich Spielhagen und der Roman der Gegenwart, Kritishce Waffengänge,* 6 (Leipzig: Wigand, 1884);

Winfried Hellmann, "Objektivität, Subjektivität und Erzählkunst: Zur Romantheorie Friedrich Spielhagens," in *Deutsche Romantheorien: Beiträge zu einer historischen Poetik des Romans in Deutschland,* edited by Reinhold Grimm (Frankfurt am Main: Athenäum, 1968), pp. 165–217;

Rainer L. Hempel, "Objektivität in 'Witiko': Eine Untersuchung der Ästhetik und Ethik im Vergleich zu Spielhagens 'Problematische Naturen' und Flauberts 'Salammbo,' " Ph.D. dissertation, University of British Columbia, 1973;

Arthur H. Hughes, "Wilhelm von Humboldt's Influence on Spielhagen's Esthetics," *Germanic Review,* 5 (July 1930): 211–224;

Dieter Kafitz, *Figurenkonstellation als Mittel der Wirklichkeitserfassung: Dargestellt an Romanen der zweiten Hälfte des 19. Jahrhunderts* (Kronberg: Athenäum, 1978);

Victor Klemperer, *Die Zeitromane Friedrich Spielhagens und ihre Wurzeln* (Weimar: Duncker, 1913);

Leo Löwenthal, "Friedrich Spielhagen – der bürgerliche Idealismus," in his *Erzählkunst und Gesellschaft: Die Gesellschaftsproblematik in der deutschen Literatur des 19. Jahrhunderts* (Neuwied & Berlin: Luchterhand, 1971), pp. 137–175;

Christa Müller-Donges, *Das Novellenwerk Friedrich Spielhagens in seiner Entwicklung zwischen 1851 und 1899* (Marburg: Elwert, 1970);

Bernd Neumann, "Friedrich Spielhagen: *Sturmflut* (1877): Die 'Gründerjahre' als die 'Signatur des Jahrhunderts,' " in *Romane und Erzählungen des Bürgerlichen Realismus: Neue Interpretationen,* edited by Horst Denkler (Stuttgart: Reclam, 1980), pp. 260–273;

Gregor H. Pompen, "Dichtung und Wahrheit: Spielhagen auf den Spuren Fontanes" in *Festgabe des deutschen Instituts der Universität Nijmwegen, Paul B. Wessels zum 65. Geburtstag,* edited by Hans Pörnbacher (Nijmwegen: Dekker & van de Vegt, 1974), pp. 112–130;

Günter Rebing, *Der Halbbruder des Dichters: Friedrich Spielhagens Theorie des Romans* (Frankfurt am Main: Athenäum Verlag, 1972);

Wilhelm Scherer, *Kleine Schriften zur neueren Litteratur, Kunst und Zeitgeschichte,* volume 2 (Berlin: Weidmann, 1893), pp. 159–170, 280–281;

Hermann Schierding, *Untersuchungen über die Romantechnik Friedrich Spielhagens* (Borna: Noske, 1914);

Julian Schmidt, "Friedrich Spielhagen," *Westermanns Monatshefte,* 29 (1870/1871): 422–449;

Thomas Tyrrell, "Theodor Fontanes 'Effi Briest' und Friedrich Spielhagens 'Zum Zeitvertreib': Zwei Dichtungen zu einer Wirklichkeit," Ph.D. dissertation, Rice University, 1986.

Papers:

A collection of Friedrich Spielhagen's manuscripts is at the Stadtarchiv (City Archives) in Magdeburg. His letters are scattered among many archives, including the Deutsche Staatbibliothek (German State Library) in Berlin, the Deutsches Literaturarchiv (German Literature Archives) in Marbach, and the Stadtbibliothek (Municipal Library) in Hannover.

Carl Spitteler
(24 April 1845 – 29 December 1924)

Malcolm J. Pender
University of Strathclyde

BOOKS: *Prometheus und Epimetheus: Ein Gleichnis,* as Carl Felix Tandem, 2 volumes (Aarau: Sauerländer, 1880–1881); translated by James F. Muirhead as *Prometheus and Epimetheus* (London: Jarrolds, 1931);

Extramundana: Kosmische Dichtungen, as Tandem (Leipzig: Haessel, 1883; revised edition, Jena: Diederichs, 1905);

Der Parlamentär: Lustspiel in vier Akten (Basel: Gassmann, 1889);

Schmetterlinge, as Tandem (Hamburg: Verlagsanstalt und Druckerei Aktien Gesellschaft, 1889);

Friedli der Kolderi (Zurich: Müller, 1891);

Der Ehrgeizige: Lustspiel in vier Aufzügen (Bern: Lack & Scheim, 1892);

Gustav: Ein Idyll (Zurich: Müller, 1892);

Literarische Gleichnisse (Zurich: Müller, 1892);

Balladen (Zurich: Müller, 1896);

Der Gotthard (Frauenfeld: Huber, 1897);

Lachende Wahrheiten: Gesammelte Essays (Florence & Leipzig: Diederichs, 1898); translated by Muirhead as *Laughing Truths* (London & New York: Putnam's, 1927);

Conrad der Leutenant: Eine Darstellung (Berlin: Verlag der Romanwelt, 1898);

Olympischer Frühling: Epos, 4 volumes (Leipzig & Jena: Diederichs, 1900–1905) – comprises volume 1, *Die Auffahrt: Ouvertüre*; volume 2, *Hera die Braut*; volume 3, *Die hohe Zeit*; volume 4, *Ende und Wende*; revised, 2 volumes (1910);

Glockenlieder: Gedichte (Jena: Diederichs, 1906);

Imago (Jena: Diederichs, 1906);

Gerold und Hansli, die Mädchenfeinde: Kindergeschichte (Jena: Diederichs, 1907); republished as *Die Mädchenfeinde: Eine Kindergeschichte* (Jena: Diederichs, 1920); translated by Vicomtesse de la Roquette-Buisson as *Two Little Misogynists* (New York: Holt, 1922);

Meine Beziehungen zu Nietzsche (Munich: Süddeutsche Monatshefte, 1908);

Meine frühesten Erlebnisse (Jena: Diederichs, 1914);

Carl Spitteler

Unser Schweizer Standpunkt: Vortrag (Zurich: Rascher, 1915);

Gottfried-Keller-Rede, in Luzern gehalten am 26. Juli 1919 (Lucerne: Wicke, 1919); republished as *Gottfried Keller: Eine Rede* (Jena: Diederichs, 1920);

Warum ich meinen Prometheus umgearbeitet habe: Vortrag (Zurich: Rascher, 1923);

Prometheus der Dulder (Jena: Diederichs, 1924);

Gesammelte Werke, 11 volumes, edited by Gottfried Bohnenblust, Wilhelm Altwegg, and Robert Faesi (Zurich: Artemis, 1945–1958).

Edition in English: *Selected Poems of Carl Spitteler,* translated by Ethel Colburn Mayne and James

F. Muirhead (London & New York: Putnam's, 1928; New York: Macmillan, 1928).

OTHER: "Eugenia, eine Dichtung," in Carl Meißner, *Carl Spitteler* (Jena: Diederichs, 1912), pp. 108–132.

A generation younger than Gottfried Keller and Conrad Ferdinand Meyer, the best-known nineteenth-century writers of German-speaking Switzerland, Carl Spitteler sits uneasily in the literary tradition his two older compatriots did so much to establish. Spitteler was inspired by a belief in the writer as a visionary, a notion that stood at odds with the pragmatic Swiss ethos. In Spitteler's view, it was precisely the contemporary belief in unfettered progress, with its emphasis on the practical application of the sciences, that helped to demystify and trivialize life. Spitteler is, therefore, associated less with the German-Swiss narrative literary tradition than with the cultural pessimism proclaimed by the German philosophers Arthur Schopenhauer and Friedrich Nietzsche. In his chosen medium of the epic poem – a form he revived as the only one compatible with his high calling – Spitteler drew on classical mythology to depict the suffering and folly of humanity within a misbegotten creation. The major redeeming feature in these somber works is the noble figure whose singleness of purpose in the face of humiliation and deprivation bears witness to an ideal beyond anything entertained by the common herd.

Spitteler's was an elitist view that set itself against contemporary styles such as realism and naturalism and against the genre of the novel. Yet, because the form and content of his major works do not appeal to a wide public, he is today better known for the narratives in the realist and modern manner that he undertook as mere exercises. Despite his undoubted literary strengths and his keen awareness, reflected in many essays, of the most significant forces at work in the contemporary world, Spitteler is a somewhat anachronistic figure in the German-speaking literary scene of the last two decades of the nineteenth century and the first two of the twentieth.

The first child of Karl and Anna Dorothea (Brodbeck) Spitteler, Carl Georg Friedrich Spitteler was born on 24 April 1845 in the small town of Liestal, some thirty miles southeast of Basel. In 1849 Karl Spitteler was appointed federal treasurer in the wake of the reforms that set up the Swiss Federation in 1848, and the family, which by this time included a second son, moved to Bern. The boys attended primary and secondary school in Bern until the return of the family to Liestal in 1857, when Spitteler was sent as a boarder to the Humanistisches Gymnasium (Classical High School) in Basel. There he received instruction from Wilhelm Wackernagel, the first incumbent of the chair of German at the University of Basel, and from the great art historian Jacob Burckhardt, whose pessimistic views were an important influence on Spitteler.

In 1860 Spitteler made the acquaintance of the artistically and musically gifted Widmann family; the son, Joseph Viktor, was to remain a lifelong friend and a tireless campaigner for recognition of Spitteler as a writer. Spitteler's contacts with the family furthered his talents for art and music, but he decided in the autumn of 1862, after a period of inner turmoil he later called "das entscheidende Jahr" (the decisive year), that he would devote himself to the high calling of "Dichter" (poet). Almost twenty years were to elapse, however, before his first publication, *Prometheus und Epimetheus* (1880–1881; translated as *Prometheus and Epimetheus,* 1931).

Difficulties in his relationship with his practical-minded father were the first substantial obstacle to the realization of Spitteler's literary goals. Under paternal pressure, after graduating from the gymnasium in 1863 he studied law at the University of Basel for two semesters; but he suffered a complete physical and mental collapse in early 1864. In the autumn of that year Spitteler fled to friends in Lucerne, where he remained for almost a year. On his return home it was agreed as a compromise that Spitteler would study theology at the University of Zurich. Four semesters, characterized by increasing involvement with his own literary projects, ensued. Two semesters at the University of Heidelberg completed Spitteler's formal preparation for his final examinations, which he failed in the autumn of 1869. After some fifteen months of study, mainly in Basel, he was successful, and he was awarded the authority to preach in the spring of 1871. But in the summer he accepted an offer of a post as tutor to a noble family in Saint Petersburg, Russia.

Spitteler remained in Russia as a tutor for almost eight years, changing his employer in 1873. During this period he ceaselessly reworked the material that was to yield his first publication. Prior to his studies in Zurich, Spitteler had sought to give dramatic form to the travails of a rugged individualist in a uniform world through a portrayal of the biblical figure of Saul. He had abandoned this attempt in favor of another figure who set himself against all manner of vicissitudes, the legendary titan Prometheus, and it was in Russia, after many false starts in Zurich and Heidelberg, that the painful fashioning of the story in classical epic form took place. Spitteler's determination to overcome his problems with the material and the form was sustained in these difficult years by his high notion of the calling to which he had chosen to devote himself. That Spitteler was prepared to make the sacrifices demanded of a poet was further underlined by the outcome of his love affair with his cousin Ellen Brodbeck during a short visit to Switzerland in 1876: his renunciation of the relationship, which he saw as deflecting him from his true path, would achieve literary form in the novel *Imago* (1906).

Spitteler returned to Switzerland in 1879. His father had died the previous year, and his financial situation was by no means secure. His friend Widmann, who had become headmaster of a girls' school in Bern, was able to help by offering him a post. The job lasted a year, and thereafter Spitteler was obliged to take temporary teaching positions. In 1880 his journalistic work began as a result of Widmann becoming literary editor of the influential Bern newspaper *Der Bund* (The Federation). Spitteler was at that time negotiating for the publication of *Prometheus und Epimetheus*; the two volumes appeared at his own expense in 1880 and 1881.

Prometheus und Epimetheus depicts an ignoble world in which the kingdom of God on earth fails to offer a counterweight to the baseness and falsity represented by the monster Behemoth. When the work opens, the angel of God has offered the throne of the kingdom to Prometheus on the condition that he renounce his allegiance to his soul and accept instead the rulings of his conscience, the repository of generally prevailing views. Prometheus has refused the offer, and it is his brother Epimetheus, compliant to law and custom, who has been chosen as king. Prometheus has been humiliated and banished. The shortcomings of Epimetheus are revealed when Behemoth seeks to abduct the children of God in the king's care and Epimetheus feebly yields to the aggressor. At this point Doxa, the companion of the angel of God, appeals to Prometheus, who intervenes. The last child of God is rescued, and the enemy hosts vanish; but Prometheus, spent after his efforts and his years of exile, declines the offered crown; the future of the kingdom remains uncertain.

As Spitteler pointed out, the two brothers represent two contrary principles: Prometheus seeks to order his life in accord with the highest of ideals, and Epimetheus acquiesces in the ways of the world; the first battles relentlessly with contrary forces, and the second settles for the line of least re-

Spitteler in 1864, the year he suffered a mental and physical collapse

sistance. The Prometheus figure, as well as having parallels to Spitteler's self-perception, owes much to Burckhardt's notion of historical greatness and to the prominent figures in history evoked in the writings of Meyer. But the metrically rhythmic prose and musical structures of *Prometheus und Epimetheus* impart a unique quality to it. Signed with the pseudonym Carl Felix Tandem, the work elicited practically no response from the critics or the public, despite Widmann's best efforts on his friend's behalf.

In the spring of 1881 Spitteler began teaching at a high school in La Neuveville, northwest of Bern in the French-speaking part of Switzerland. His second book, *Extramundana* (1883), was a collection of myths pertaining to the creation of the world; the author did not receive a fee for it, but he was not required to pay for its publication. Also in 1883 Spitteler married Marie Op den Hooff, a Dutch woman who had been his pupil at the girls' school

First page of the manuscript for a poem that was written for, but not included in, Spitteler's collection Schmetterlinge *(from Spitteler,* Gesammelte Werke, *edited by Wilhelm Altwegg, volume 3, 1945)*

in Bern. The couple had two daughters: Anna, born in 1886; and Marie Adèle, born in 1891.

Spitteler moved to Basel in the autumn of 1885 to take a job with the newspaper *Grenzpost* (Border Post). For almost two years he reviewed books, wrote articles on the arts, and commented on politics in Switzerland and elsewhere in Europe. The *Grenzpost* ran into financial difficulties, necessitating Spitteler's dismissal. Almost three years of insecurity followed, during which short periods of employment as a literary journalist filling in for absent staff members supplemented the fees he earned from his free-lance stories (some of which drew on his Russian experiences), essays on literature and aesthetics, and book reviews. Spitteler was slowly establishing a reputation in the literary world, and journeys to Germany and Austria brought him into contact with editors of leading reviews. Keller, the grand old man of Swiss letters, had been prevailed upon by Widmann to read *Prometheus und Epimetheus* and *Extramundana*; he had reacted favorably to the former but less so to the latter. In neither case, however, had there been public support for Spitteler from Keller. In 1887 Nietzsche, who had succeeded Spitteler's teacher Wackernagel in the chair of German at the University of Basel, was impressed by a collection of Spitteler's essays sent to him by Widmann. Nietzsche recommended Spitteler to Ferdinand Avenarius, who was about to launch *Kunstwart* (Curator), a Munich periodical that was to become highly influential and that for many years would publish Spitteler's contributions. In 1889 Spitteler's *Schmetterlinge* (Butterflies) appeared, once more at his own expense. In this collection of poems the butterfly is symbolic both of the fate of humanity in an evilly disposed world and of the beauty and ephemerality of human love. By the end of 1889 Spitteler had acquired sufficient standing for the respected and influential daily *Neue Zürcher Zeitung* (New Zurich Newspaper) to offer him a post in the literary and cultural section.

Spitteler worked in Zurich from the beginning of 1890 to the middle of 1892. His contacts in the world of literature increased and became firmer. He was able, by means of his reviews and essays in the leading newspaper of German-speaking Switzerland, to contribute to public standards of taste and judgment; and he was able to encourage talented writers by publishing their work in the columns for which he was responsible. When Meyer withdrew from a commitment to write a play for the reopening of the Zurich City Theater after its destruction by fire, Spitteler was approached; he accepted, and his play, *Der Ehrgeizige* (Greedy for Honor, 1892),

was performed in 1891. The following year brought the publication of two books. *Gustav,* a short story in an idyllic small-town setting about a young man who, after initial reverses and with the help of a devoted woman, gains confidence in his talents as a composer, has parallels with Spitteler's situation. The cycle of poems *Literarische Gleichnisse* (Literary Parables) presents in parable form the forces against which he had struggled for so long: the belittling of idealism, the restrictiveness of the much-vaunted realist style, the self-regarding nature of literary society, and the derivativeness of much of what it produced.

The deaths in Lucerne, within a year of one another, of Spitteler's mother-in-law and sister-in-law left his ailing and wealthy father-in-law alone. Thus, in 1892 Spitteler and his family moved to Lucerne so that Spitteler could administer his father-in-law's affairs. Spitteler's reputation to that point was based on his work as an essayist and critic; freedom from financial care would permit him to return to realizing the high ideals envisaged in the vows of "the decisive year."

Thus, although his financial situation would have permitted him to relax, Spitteler's last thirty-two years were characterized by ceaseless activity. He participated in the cultural life of his adopted city, of which he received the honorary citizenship in 1909; he traveled widely; he accepted many invitations to lecture; and he attended conscientiously to a huge correspondence. But his major concern continued to be the composition of his poetic works.

Three publications from the early Lucerne years demonstrate Spitteler's range. *Balladen* (Ballads, 1896) again evinces his independent attitude toward genre and fashion. The poems are by no means all ballads in any accepted sense of the term; the majority are revisions of dramatic and epic fragments; and many draw on mythology and legend. Neither in form nor in content do they relate to contemporary German poetry. *Lachende Wahrheiten* (1898; translated as *Laughing Truths,* 1927) is a collection of essays, mainly on literary and aesthetic subjects. *Conrad der Leutenant* (Conrad the Lieutenant, 1898) is one of the stories Spitteler regarded as exercises in writing in the realist manner; he wanted to show that his failure to depict the real world in the work he regarded as his major contribution to literature was by choice and not from inability. The presentation of the clash between a father and a son over the management of a village inn verges at times on caricature, and the tragic death of the son does not seem properly motivated.

The work regarded by Spitteler as his magnum opus, *Olympischer Frühling* (Olympic Spring), appeared in four volumes between 1900 and 1905; it was republished in revised form in two volumes in 1910. Like *Prometheus und Epimetheus, Olympischer Frühling* is set in a cosmic landscape and draws on mythology for its characters, all of which is a device permitting Spitteler to present his view of the determinants of human behavior. The rhythmical prose of the earlier epic has been replaced by rhyming couplets.

The former generation of gods has been deposed by Ananke, who represents unalterable necessity. A new generation of gods rises from the underworld and makes its way to Olympus, the sundrenched peak in whose shadow the humans live. In the course of the two-day journey from Hades the gods simultaneously witness and represent the forces governing the world, thereby portraying the senselessness of human fate. At Olympus the god who succeeds in winning Hera, the queen, will become king of the gods. Competitions in singing, running, chariot racing, and interpretation of dreams and prophecy are organized. The victor is Apollo, the god of the spirit and most noble of all heroes; but his victory does not matter, for Zeus, the taciturn, ruthless man of action, has not deigned to participate. Zeus becomes king of Olympus by winning Hera, the dominating, intriguing woman who ensnares men, and inherits her matriarchal empire. To celebrate the union of Zeus and Hera, the goddess Moira suspends time; an Olympian spring takes place, during which the gods descend to earth to experience adventures that have a symbolic content. Pallas rebels against death as a destroyer but is eventually reconciled to it as beneficial and just; Apollo, who drives the chariot of the sun, has to contend with the foolishness of those who seek to impose a new sun on him; Dionysius, the visionary youth, is a symbol of religious experience; Poseidon, representing the foolish man of strength, vainly expends his energies in seeking to cause water to flow uphill; Aphrodite, with her grace and beauty, enslaves men and drives them to every form of folly on her behalf. The rule of Ananke is confirmed by the mindless behavior of the great mass of humans, whose lack of dignity and spiritual independence is symbolized by the figure of the automaton. The gods are summoned back to Olympus by Zeus, who has decided to go to the land of humans himself. There he discovers that they revere an ape dressed as a king. Enraged at this blindness and stupidity, Zeus resolves to exterminate the human race; but he relents and decides to help the humans. He prepares Heracles for the task of redeeming humanity, and the epic poem closes with the young man who obeys his own soul – a cardinal distinction between Heracles and the generality of humans – leaving to begin his mission. His departure is linked to the opening of the epic and so to the hopefulness of a new beginning, but it is also attended by the knowledge that the redemption of humans as they have been depicted in the course of the poem will pose a challenge verging on the insurmountable.

Like Spitteler's earlier epic, *Olympischer Frühling* is pessimistic. The world is deeply flawed and in thrall to death and violence. Human behavior is governed by pride, greed, foolishness, and shortsightedness, whose control over the great majority of people makes a mockery of the concept of free will. Only a few great figures stand above the soulless, mindless herd, but because they are perceived to be different they are cast out. Although *Olympischer Frühling* met with the critical acclaim that Spitteler had so much wanted and had not received for *Prometheus und Epimetheus,* it did not sell in significant quantities. But it did attract the attention of influential people such as the Austrian musician and composer Felix Weingartner; Weingartner became active on Spitteler's behalf in Germany, where the distance of the work from daily reality and from disturbing modern literary trends appealed to a certain middle-class readership. Thus, *Olympischer Frühling* was a breakthrough for Spitteler to the wider German-speaking audience beyond Switzerland; gained him his first literary prize, Austria's Bauernfeld Foundation prize, in 1904; and established his reputation. But the works with which Spitteler struggled hardest and longest and by which he set most store were much less widely read than those he regarded as mere literary exercises, and this situation has not substantially changed since his death.

The year 1906 brought the publication of *Glockenlieder* (Bell Songs), Spitteler's last book of lyric poems, devoted to the role of the bell in human life; and *Imago,* which Spitteler, for whom writing was never easy, described as the most difficult text he ever fashioned. It is his final reckoning with his love affair of the late 1870s with Ellen Brodbeck. The narrator, Viktor, a writer, returns to a small town where, four years previously, the impact of his meeting with a young woman named Theuda caused her to become in his eyes "Imago," the incarnation of the power of his "Strenge Herrin" (exacting mistress), his poetic muse. But Theuda, because she has married a pillar of local society, has become "Pseuda" (the false one), and Viktor has returned to avenge her perfidy. The incomprehensibility in bourgeois eyes of this undertaking is shown by the reaction of Frau Steinbach, a young widow in love with Viktor, who cannot believe that the imagination can so influence real life; but for Viktor the imaginative powers, through the medium of art, have a point of reference beyond society and its interpretation of reality. Viktor resolves to convert to his own values the society represented by Pseuda. To this end, he participates in the activities of the "Idealia," a cultural circle of which Pseuda is the honorary president and which Viktor holds in extreme contempt. Viktor's illusion that Pseuda is coming to regard him with increasing warmth is shattered when Frau Steinbach discloses that Pseuda is relating to her friends, for their amusement, Viktor's disclosures to her. Outraged, Viktor leaves the town, taking with him the manuscript he has been writing during his stay. He resolves henceforth to dedicate himself solely to the service of his "Strenge Herrin," of whom he has a vision at the railway station. In his excitement he fails to see Frau Steinbach, who has come to say a sad farewell.

The story presents, in a middle-class setting, the Prometheus theme of renunciation and humiliation endured on behalf of a higher calling, and the satirical manner of its telling makes it one of Spitteler's most accessible texts today. The historical perspective of the novel is also of interest: on the one hand, Viktor subscribes to a bygone notion of the calling of the writer, which only his financial independence permits him to sustain; on the other hand, the novel points forward by showing the extent to which the mass dissemination of print and picture was standardizing cultural expectation and response. Ironically, in view of Spitteler's dislike of professional psychologists, who in his view contributed to the shallowness of the modern age, Sigmund Freud in 1912 named his journal for the application of psychoanalysis to the humanities *Imago* after the novel.

By 1908 Spitteler was sufficiently well known to be invited to write for *Kunstwart* a long essay titled "Mein Schaffen und meine Werke" (My Creative Work and My Books). The possibility of an autobiography was mooted, but only his remarkable evocation of his infancy, *Meine frühesten Erlebnisse* (My Earliest Experiences, 1914), was published. The major task of Spitteler's last years was the revision of his first publication, *Prometheus und Epimetheus.*

Shortly after the outbreak of World War I Spitteler carried out what is frequently characterized as the one overtly political act of his life. His speech of December 1914, published as *Unser Schweizer Standpunkt* (Our Swiss Standpoint, 1915),

Carl Spitteler

had both immediate and enduring consequences. In his hour-long discourse Spitteler provided the classic modern definition of Swiss neutrality: he urged his German- and French-speaking compatriots to recognize that, despite the cultural ties created by common languages, Germany and France were politically separate from Switzerland; and that the German- and French-speaking parts of Switzerland, for all their differences with each other, constituted a political unity. His formulation of the cultural and political paradox of being Swiss was a response to the divisive identification with German and French war aims then prevalent in the German- and French-speaking parts of Switzerland, respectively. The speech cost Spitteler some of his contemporary Swiss and all of his German popularity, but it provided for his countrymen a vision of Switzerland that would offer guidance and succor throughout both World Wars.

During his years in Lucerne, Spitteler came to be regarded in Switzerland as the main living figure in German-Swiss letters. In 1905 he had been awarded an honorary doctorate by the University of Zurich, and his seventieth and seventy-fifth birthdays were publicly celebrated. In the autumn of

1920 he was awarded the Nobel Prize for Literature for 1919; Spitteler is to date the only native-born Swiss to have gained this distinction.

Spitteler's last published work, *Prometheus der Dulder* (Prometheus the Endurer, 1924), is a revision of his first. The story line remains, in broad terms, that of the first work, but there are changes of emphasis that are reflected in the changed title. Prometheus, uncompromisingly certain of his mission, stands out more prominently as the repository of the values of the soul in contrast to those of conscience, the ineffectiveness of which are again underscored by the pusillanimity and failure of Epimetheus. The conflict between the kingdom of God and the world of Behemoth is stripped of all that is extraneous; its resolution, upon the intervention of Prometheus, is more restrained than in the earlier work; and Prometheus, his mission accomplished, reconciles the individualistic aspects of the soul with its obligations to the human community. *Prometheus der Dulder,* written in rhyming hexameters, may have been even less suited to the tastes of its time than *Prometheus und Epimetheus* had been nearly half a century previously.

Spitteler's sense of mission persisted to the end. Plagued by circulatory disorders and the disabilities of age, he had, with help, completed correcting the proofs of *Prometheus der Dulder* at the end of October 1924. He was able to receive the first copies of the book and to read reviews of it before he died on 29 December 1924.

Biographies:

Werner Stauffacher, *Carl Spitteler: Biographie* (Zurich & Munich: Artemis, 1973);

Justus Hermann Wetzel, *Carl Spitteler: Ein Lebens- und Schaffensbericht* (Bern & Munich: Francke, 1973).

References:

Gottfried Bohnenblust, *Carl Spitteler: Dichter und Heimat* (Bern: Haupt, n.d.);

Robert Faesi, *Spittelers Weg und Werk* (Frauenfeld & Leipzig: Huber, 1933);

Werner Günther, *Dichter der neueren Schweiz,* volume 1 (Bern & Munich: Francke, 1963), pp. 228–280;

Margaret McHaffie, "Prometheus and Viktor: Carl Spitteler's *Imago,*" *German Life and Letters,* 31 (October 1977): 67–77;

McHaffie and J. H. Ritchie, "Narrative Technique in Spitteler's *Conrad der Leutnant,*" *German Life and Letters,* 14 (October 1960): 45–51;

Otto Rommel, *Spittelers Olympischer Frühling und seine epische Form* (Bern & Munich: Francke, 1965).

Papers:

Carl Spitteler's papers are in the Landesbibliothek (National Library), Bern.

Max Stirner
(Johann Kaspar Schmidt)
(25 October 1806 – 25 June 1856)

Kurt R. Jankowsky
Georgetown University

BOOKS: *Der Einzige und sein Eigenthum* (Leipzig: Wigand, 1845 [i.e., 1844]); translated by Steven T. Byington as *The Ego and His Own* (New York: Tucker, 1907; London: Fifield, 1907);

Geschichte der Reaction, 2 volumes (Berlin: Allgemeine Deutsche Verlags-Anstalt, 1852) – comprises volume 1, *Die Vorläufer der Reaction*; volume 2, *Die moderne Reaction*;

Max Stirner's kleinere Schriften und seine Entgegnungen auf die Kritik seines Werkes: "Der Einzige und sein Eigenthum." Aus den Jahren 1842–1847, edited by John Henry Mackay (Berlin: Schuster & Loeffler, 1898); revised and enlarged as *Max Stirner's kleinere Schriften und seine Entgegnungen auf die Kritik seines Werkes: "Der Einzige und sein Eigenthum," aus den Jahren 1842–1848* (Treptow: Zack, 1914);

Stirnerbrevier: Die Stärke des Einsamen. Max Stirner's Individualismus und Egoismus mit seinen eigenen Worten wiedergegeben, edited by Anselm Ruest (Berlin: Seemann, 1906);

Max Stirner über Schulgesetze (1834), edited by Rolf Engert (Dresden: Verlag des Dritten Reiches, 1921);

Das unwahre Prinzip unserer Erziehung, oder Der Humanismus und Realismus (Charlottenburg: Selbstverlag, 1911); edited by Willy Storer (Basel: Verlag für Freies Geistesleben, 1926); translated by Robert H. Beebe as *The False Principle of Our Education: or, Humanism and Realism,* edited by James J. Martin (Colorado Springs: Myles, 1967);

Parerga, Kritiken, Repliken / Max Stirner, edited by Bernd A. Laska (Nuremberg: LSR-Verlag, 1986).

OTHER: *Die National-Oekonomen der Franzosen und Engländer,* 10 volumes, edited and translated by Stirner (Leipzig: Wigand, 1845–1847).

Max Stirner (Johann Kaspar Schmidt); pencil sketch by Friedrich Engels, drawn from memory in 1902 (from Karl Marx/Friedrich Engels Collected Works, *volume 5, edited by Georgi Bagaturia and others, 1975)*

Max Stirner's main treatise, *Der Einzige und sein Eigenthum* (1844; translated as *The Ego and His Own,* 1907), is an outrageous book, designed to call into question, if not to destroy, conventional values. And yet, from the first day of its existence, the book has created and sustained an almost inescapable fascination for many people.

Caricature by Engels of a meeting of "Die Freien" at Hippel's Wine Room in Berlin; left to right: Arnold Ruge, Ludwig Buhl, Karl Nauwerk, Bruno Bauer, Otto Wigand, Edgar Bauer, Stirner (smoking cigarette), Eduard Meyen, two unidentified individuals, and Karl Friedrich Köppen (from Karl Marx, Friedrich Engels Correspondence, *volume 1, 1971)*

Its impact is only to some extent explainable by the outrageousness of Stirner's message. His contention that only the ego counts undoubtedly hit a nerve; the time was ripe for casting doubt on values that had been regarded as sacrosanct. While Stirner could not expect his efforts to meet with general approval, he was successful in arousing serious interest in many of the points he addressed. His work was passionately discussed not only in his native country but all over Europe, the Americas, and even in Asia. Apart from Germanistics, the areas primarily affected were those of philosophy, political science, and sociology. The controversy regarding his work is still alive today.

Stirner was born Johann Kaspar Schmidt on 25 October 1806 in Bayreuth, Bavaria, to a fairly well-to-do lower-middle-class Lutheran family. His father, Albert Christian Heinrich Schmidt, was a craftsman who made musical instruments; he died when Johann Kaspar was eighteen months old. A few years later his mother, Sophia Eleonora, married Heinrich Friedrich Ludwig Ballerstedt, a pharmacist.

The parents left Bayreuth in 1809 and settled in Culm on the Vistula; the boy was left behind with relatives, then joined his parents in 1810. In 1818 he was sent back to Bayreuth to stay with his father's elder sister, Anna Marie, and her husband, Johann Caspar Martin Sticht. He attended the Altsprachliche Gymnasium, a high school specializing in classical Greek and Latin. There he acquired a nickname that he liked so much that he discarded his commonplace given name, which would be equivalent in English to "John Smith." Because of his unusually high forehead – in German, *Stirn* – his fellow students called him *Stirner*. After graduating in 1826 as number three in a class of twenty-five, he attended the University of Berlin for two years; his teachers included the theologian Friedrich Schleiermacher and the philosopher Georg Wilhelm Friedrich Hegel. As was customary at the time, he also studied at other universities. In Erlangen he still devoted all of his time to theology and philosophy; whereas in Königsberg (today Kaliningrad, Russia), where he enrolled in the fall of 1829, he does not seem to have done any studying at all. Perhaps the reason was that he was spending his time caring for his ailing mother, who was suffering from mental disease. He returned to the University of Berlin in 1832 and formally completed his studies two years later.

The marginal quality of his final examination resulted in his being awarded a conditional *facultas docendi,* which gave him permission to teach only at the high school level. He married Clara Kunigunde Burtz, the daughter of his landlady, in December 1837. She died about a year later, after giving birth to a stillborn baby. It was not until 1839 that he was able to obtain a teaching position at a girls' high school in Berlin, where he offered classes in history and literature.

In 1841 he began meeting with a group of young intellectuals who called themselves "Die Freien" (The Free Ones). Intensely critical of the existing society, all of them had been influenced by Hegel. They met fairly regularly at Hippel's Weinstube (Wine Room) in the Friedrichstraße. Karl Marx and Friedrich Engels occasionally joined in the discussions, but the principal members were Bruno Bauer, a Lutheran theologian who had lectured at Berlin University until 1841, when he was removed from the faculty because of his criticism of the Bible; his brother Edgar, who was equally critical of traditional religion; Arnold Ruge, a former collaborator of Marx; Otto Wigand, the publisher of some of Hegel's writings; Karl Friedrich Köppen; and Karl Nauwerk. The poets Georg Herwegh and Heinrich Hoffmann von Fallersleben were infrequent visitors. Ruge, who soon broke with the group, wrote to a friend that he had come to know "die Berliner Freien als die ekelhaftesten Renommisten, die Gott oder vielmehr ihre eigene Blasiertheit geschaffen hat. . . . Sie schrieen, schimpften und prügelten sich in der Weinstube" (the Berliner Free Ones as the most disgusting braggarts that God or rather their own blasé attitude has created. . . . They screamed, abused each other, and beat each other up in the tavern). Stirner usually did not participate in the loud and lively debates; he preferred to listen to the exchanges while thinking his own thoughts with an enigmatic smile.

Another occasional visitor at Hippel's Weinstube was Marie Wilhelmine Dähnhardt, who liked the free life-style of the group. She and Stirner were married in October 1843.

The life of a schoolteacher could not remain attractive for long to a man with aspirations like those silently cultivated by Stirner. He hoped that the publication of his book would bring him material success in addition to acclaim by the intellectual community. Furthermore, his wife had come into an inheritance of some thirty thousand talers, a fortune at that time. For those reasons he felt that it was time for him to stop being a salaried employee, and he resigned from his teaching position when his

magnum opus, *Der Einzige und sein Eigenthum,* appeared in the fall of 1844 (with the date 1845 on the title page).

The first edition of the work, which was published by Wigand, consisted of 1,000 copies. Immediately 250 copies were confiscated by the authorities in Leipzig; this act of censorship was soon reversed by the Interior Ministry of Saxony, whose officials believed that the book was too outrageous to be taken seriously by anyone.

The motto "Ich hab' mein' Sach' auf Nichts gestellt" (I have founded my affair on nothing), placed at the beginning and the end of *Der Einzige und sein Eigenthum,* is taken from Johann Wolfgang von Goethe's poem "Vanitas! Vanitatum Vanitas." Stirner's theories had precedents, some of which he may not have known about. Sophistic philosophy in ancient Greece occasionally featured similar arguments; his stance against the authority of state and church could draw on a long list of previous antagonists; even his fight against any values to which the individual has to subscribe is not without precedence. But Stirner's radicalism places him in a class by himself. He rejects all conventional values, moral norms, and religious concepts; others had merely questioned, cast doubt on, or renounced a few notions held in esteem by society. Ludwig Feuerbach, for instance, more radical than anyone before Stirner in his rejection of theism, "gibt uns nur eine theologische Befreiung von der Theologie und Religion" (gives us merely a theological liberation from theology and religion), Stirner complains, "aber lässt das Göttliche, lässt die Prädikate Gottes unangefochten bestehen" (but retains undisputed [the notion of] the divine, the attributes of God). In his *Das Wesen des Christenthums* (1841; translated as *The Essence of Christianity,* 1854) Feuerbach had used Hegel's concept of "Entfremdung" (alienation) to analyze the traditional concept of God as an imaginary projection of the human essence; in worshiping God, according to Feuerbach, people were unknowingly worshiping humanity itself. Feuerbach proposed that such worship be made explicit in a "Religion der Humanität" (religion of humanity). He continued, however, to believe in the reality of moral values. Stirner left no room for any compromise. His attack was aimed at all forces that place restrictions on the "Ich" (I or ego). Not only God but all moral concepts, such as altruism, chastity, and natural rights, as well as abstractions such as "humanity," that demand obedience or allegiance from individuals are, according to Stirner, "Spuke" (spooks) with no objective reality. In allowing our lives to be dominated and controlled by such no-

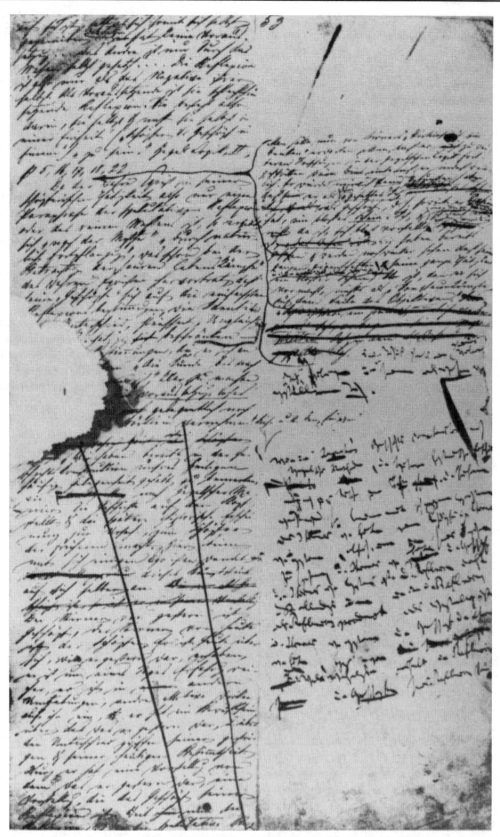

Page from the manuscript for the chapter on Stirner in Marx and Engels's Die deutsche Ideologie *(from* Karl Marx/Friedrich Engels
Collected Works, *volume 5, edited by Georgi Bagaturia and others, 1975)*

tions, we are bowing down to our creations. The Ich should not be concerned with the divine, nor with the human, nor with what is good, true, or right; it should only concern itself with what is its own: "Das Göttliche ist Gottes Sache, das Menschliche Sache 'des Menschen.' Meine Sache ist weder das Göttliche noch das Menschliche, ist nicht das Wahre, Gute, Rechte, Freie u.s.w., sondern allein das Meinige, und sie ist keine allgemeine, sondern ist – einzig, wie Ich einzig bin. Mir geht nichts über Mich" (The divine is God's concern; the human, man's. My concern is neither the divine nor the human, not the true, good, just, free, etc., but solely what is *mine,* and it is not a general one, but is – unique, as I am unique. Nothing is more to me than myself). Stirner's radicalism remained purely cerebral; he demanded for the individual the unrestrained exercise of every power, but in his own life he deployed little initiative in any practical matter.

Stirner was surprised by the harsh reaction to his book by the members of Die Freien. All but Bruno Bauer were appalled at the radicalism they encountered in the work. They obviously had not had any inkling as to the contents of the book, since he had apparently kept his thoughts to himself.

In 1845–1846 Marx and Engels composed a scathing diatribe of several hundred pages, in which they analyzed and critiqued Stirner's work virtually line by line; titled "Der hl. Max" (Saint Max), their attack remained unknown to Stirner because it was not published until 1902–1903. It constitutes the longest part of their *Die deutsche Ideologie* (The German Ideology) but is omitted from almost all editions of this work; only the much briefer sections directed against Feuerbach and Bruno Bauer are usually reprinted. The amount of effort they devoted to demolishing Stirner's book indicates that at that time, at least, they considered it important. In later years Engels, referring to the early 1840s, said, "We were all Feuerbachians then"; David McLellan has argued that it was Stirner's more radical work that broke Marx away from his attachment to Feuerbach and led to the first formulation of his theory of historical materialism, which occurred at this time. Before reading Stirner, Marx espoused an idealistic version of communism based on such philosophical notions as the human essence; afterward he eschewed such ideas in favor of more "scientific" concepts. As Marx said later, he and Engels were content to leave the manuscript of *Die deutsche Ideologie* "to the gnawing criticism of the mice" because it had been written primarily to clarify their own thinking.

The majority of even the harshest critics are complimentary about the styleof Stirner's book. Ruge, for example, said: "Viele Parthieen sind ganz meisterhaft, und die Wirkung des Ganzen kann nur befreiend sein. Es ist das erste leserliche philosophische Buch in Deutschland" (Many sections are truly masterful, and the effect of it all can only be liberating. It is the first readable philosophical book in Germany). The literary historian Eduard Engel said of the book in 1907: "Geschrieben aber ist es, wie in Deutschland ungemein selten geschrieben wird: mit einer packenden Lebendigkeit, im ungekünstelten Gesprächsstil und mit einer Sprachreinheit, die ans Wunderbare grenzt." (But it is written, as books are written in Germany extremely rarely: with a thrilling sprightliness, in the natural conversational style and with a purity of language bordering on the marvelous).

Stirner was eager to enter into the great debate he expected to be triggered by the publication of his book. The immediate reaction from those sections of society that felt attacked was intense, but the firestorm died down as quickly as it had been unleashed; Stirner's responses could do little to keep the lagging interest alive. By 1847 Stirner's moment of glory had melted away. Stirner the philosopher ceased to exist; he was replaced by Stirner the writer of uninspiring books on education and on the conservative reaction to the revolutions of 1848 and Stirner the translator of the works of French and British free-market economists.

Stirner's wife had left him in 1846; when Stirner's biographer John Henry Mackay (who, in spite of his name, was German) interviewed her in London fifty years later, he found her still to be extremely bitter toward her former husband. With her departure Stirner's financial security had vanished. The meager income from his writing as well as from occasional short-lived business ventures barely kept him alive. On two occasions in 1853–1854 he spent time in prison for defaulting on loans. He was sustained for the last two years of his life by advance payments on the sale of property belonging to his mother, who had been moved to a mental institution in Berlin in 1837. She died there in 1859, three years after her son.

The circumstances of Stirner's death are as dismal as those of most of his adult life. He was stung on the neck by a flying insect and died within a month, on 25 June 1856, from the resulting blood infection. Only a few friends and former associates accompanied him three days later on his last journey. Among them were Bruno Bauer and Ludwig Buhl, editor of the *Berliner Monatsschrift*

(Berlin Monthly), which, after being prevented from appearing in Berlin in 1843 by government censors, had been published for the first and last time two years later in Mannheim. The issue had contained two essays by Stirner: "Einiges Vorläufige vom Liebesstaat" (Some Preliminary Remarks on the State of Love) and a review of Eugène Sue's novel *Les Mystères de Paris"* (The Mysteries of Paris, 1842–1843). Also present was Mrs. Weiss, a widow in whose house he had rented two rooms for the last three years of his life and who bestowed on him motherly care. The few newspapers that mentioned his death did not go beyond a few dim references to the passions he had aroused with his work a decade earlier. As Mackay put it in his biography, Johann Caspar Schmidt was dead; Max Stirner had died before him.

A Stirner revival began about ten years after his death. Johann Eduard Erdmann seems to have been the first to stress the need for looking at Stirner again in his *Grundriß der Geschichte der Philosophie* (Outline of the History of Philosophy, 1866). The philosopher Eduard von Hartmann dealt fairly extensively with Stirner in his *Philosophie des Unbewußten* (1869; translated as *Philosophy of the Unconscious*, 1931), *Phänomenologie des sittlichen Bewußtseins* (Phenomenology of the Moral Consciousness, 1879), and *Ethische Studien* (Ethical Studies, 1898). Of special importance is his article on Friedrich Nietzsche, "Neue Moral" (New Morality, 1891), where he argues that Stirner's and Nietzsche's thoughts show many affinities and that Stirner is philosophically the more important of the two. According to Hartmann, while Nietzsche takes great pains to mask the true extent of his radicalism, Stirner hides behind no shield. Hence, he is potentially more dangerous than Nietzsche but also more accessible to direct criticism. Since Hartmann, many writers have compared Stirner to Nietzsche (who was, coincidentally, born within a month of the publication of *Der Einzige und sein Eigenthum*); but Jules Lévy showed in 1904 that there is no evidence that Nietzsche was influenced by Stirner's work.

The book was translated into French in 1900 and into English in 1907; it has also appeared in Italian and Russian. Among those who have praised Stirner's work are the Norwegian playwright Henrik Ibsen, the Danish critic Georg Brandes, and the American critic James G. Huneker. In his *Egoists* (1909) Huneker called the book "the most dangerous ever written . . . dangerous in every sense of the word – to socialism, to politicians, to hypocrisy." In fact, the work has not had much practical effect, although the Marxist scholar Hans G. Helms tried to

prove in his *Die Ideologie der anonymen Gesellschaft* (The Ideology of the Anonymous Society, 1966) that Stirner was responsible for the rise of Italian and German fascism – a belief system that could not be more opposed to Stirner's anarchistic individualism: such "spooks" as political parties, the State, and the Fatherland are particular objects of his attack.

The danger of Stirner's *Der Einzige und sein Eigenthum* is real to this day. A world full of Stirnerian egoists would probably be intolerable, most particularly for weak individuals like Stirner himself. On the other hand, however, Stirner's cold-eyed analysis of illusory ideals could be regarded as therapeutic. It is difficult to imagine a reader who has been persuaded by Stirner's arguments becoming a member of a religious cult, persecuting racial or ethnic minorities, or blindly following a demagogue into war.

Biographies:

Karl Joël, "Stirner," *Neue Deutsche Rundschau,* 9 (1898): 995–1015;

John Henry Mackay, *Max Stirner: Sein Leben und sein Werk* (Berlin: Schuster & Loeffler, 1898);

Moritz Kronenberg, "Max Stirner," in his *Moderne Philosophen: Porträts und Charakteristiken* (Munich: Beck, 1899), pp. 181–213;

Max Messer, *Max Stirner* (Berlin: Bard, Marquardt, 1907);

Miguel Gimenez Igualada, *Stirner, 26* [sic] *de octubre de 1806–23* [sic] *de junio de 1856* (Mexico City: Costa-Amic, 1968).

References:

Georg Adler, "Stirners anarchistische Sozialtheorie," in *Festgabe für Wilhelm Lexis zum 70. Geburtstag* (Jena: Fischer, 1907), pp. 3–46;

Yngve Ahlberg, *Gudsbegrepp och sprakkritik: En idéhistorisk undersökning av ett avsnitt unghegeliansk ateism och därtill hörande sprakkritik i anslutning till Max Stirners Der Einzige und sein Eigentum* (Stockholm: Svenska bokforlaget, 1967);

Bettina von Arnim, "Die Auflösung des Einzigen durch den Menschen," *Epigonen,* 4 (1847): 189–251;

Henri Arvon, "L'actualité de la pensée de Max Stirner," in *Anarchici e anarchia nel mondo contemporaneo* (Turin: Fondazione Luigi Einaudi, 1971), pp. 285–292;

Arvon, *Aux sources de l'existentialisme: Max Stirner* (Paris: Presses Universitaires de France, 1954);

Arvon, *Max Stirner; ou, L'experience du néant: Présentation, choix de textes, bibliographie* (Paris: Seghers, 1973);

Arvon, "Une polémique inconnue: Marx et Stirner," *Les temps modernes*, 7 (September 1951): 509–536;

Victor Basch, *L'Individualisme anarchiste: Max Stirner* (Paris: Alcan, 1904);

Fabio Bazzani, *Weitling e Stirner: Filosofia e storia, 1838–1845* (Milan: Angeli, 1985);

Gerhard Beck, "Die Stellung des Menschen zu Staat und Recht bei Max Stirner," Ph.D. dissertation, University of Cologne, 1965;

Alfredo Maria Bonanno, *Max Stirner* (Catania: Edizioni della rivista Anarchismo, 1977);

Gerhard Bückling, "Der Einzelne und der Staat bei Stirner und Marx: Eine quellenkritische Untersuchung zur Geschichte des Anarchismus und Sozialismus," *Schmollers Jahrbuch für Gesetzgebung, Verwaltung und Volkswirtschaft im deutschen Reiche*, 4 (1920): 1071–1116;

John Carroll, *Break-out from the Crystal Palace: The Anarcho-Psychological Critique. Stirner, Nietzsche, Dostoevsky* (London & Boston: Routledge & Kegan Paul, 1974);

Claudio Cesa, "Le idee politiche di Max Stirner," in *Anarchici e anarchia nel mondo contemporaneo*, pp. 307–319;

Alfred Cless, *Max Stirners Lehre: Mit einem Auszug aus "Der Einzige und sein Eigentum,"* edited by A. Martin (Leipzig: Wigand, 1906);

Philip Breed Dematteis, *Individuality and the Social Organism: The Controversy between Max Stirner and Karl Marx* (New York: Revisionist Press, 1976);

Diederik Dettmeijer, ed., *Max Stirner: Ou la Première confrontation entre Karl Marx et la pensée anti-autoritaire*, translated by A. Sauge (Lausanne: Edition L'Age d'homme, 1979);

Eugen Dietzgen, "An Illustration of the Proletarian Method of Research and Conception of the World: Max Stirner and Josef Dietzgen," appendix to *Streifzüge eines Sozialisten in das Gebiet der Erkenntnislehre*, by Josef Dietzgen (Hottingen-Zurich: Volksbuchhandlung, 1877);

Julius Duboc, *Das Ich und die Übrigen: Für und wider Max Stirner. Ein Beitrag zur Philosophie des Fortschritts* (Leipzig: Wigand, 1897);

Carl August Emge, *Max Stirner: Eine geistig nicht bewältigte Tendenz* (Mainz: Akademie der Wissenschaften und der Literatur, 1964);

Horst Engert, *Das historische Denken Max Stirners* (Leipzig: Wigand, 1911);

Rolf Engert, ed., *Die Freiwirtschaft: Ein praktischer Ausdruck der Stirnerschen Philosophie* (Erfurt: Freiland-Freigeld, 1921);

Engert, ed., *Neue Beiträge zur Stirner-Forschung*, 4 volumes (Dresden: Verlag des Dritten Reiches, 1921–1924);

Johann Eduard Erdmann, *Grundriß der Geschichte der Philosophie*, volume 2 (Berlin: Hertz, 1866); pp. 684–685;

Wolfgang Essbach, *Die Bedeutung Max Stirners für die Genese des historischen Materialismus: Zur Rekonstruktion der Kontroverse zwischen Karl Marx, Friedrich Engels und Max Stirner* (Göttingen, 1978);

Essbach, *Gegenzüge: Der Materialismus des Selbst und seine Ausgrenzung aus dem Marxismus. Eine Studie über die Kontroverse zwischen Max Stirner und Karl Marx; mit einem Anhang, Sexualität und Gesellschaftstheorie* (Frankfurt am Main: Materialis, 1982);

Essbach, "A Language without a Master: Max Stirner's Influence on B. Traven," in *B. Traven: Life and Work*, edited by Ernst Schürer and Philip Jenkins (University Park & London: Pennsylvania State University Press, 1987), pp. 101–119;

Iring Fetscher, "Die Bedeutung Max Stirners für die Entwicklung des historischen Materialismus," *Zeitschrift für philosophische Forschung*, 6 (1952): 425–426;

Ludwig Feuerbach, "Das Wesen des Christenthums in Beziehung auf den 'Einzigen und sein Eigenthum,'" *Wigands Vierteljahrsschrift*, 2 (1845): 193–205; reprinted in his *Sämtliche Werke*, volume 7, edited by Wilhelm Bolin and Friedrich Jodl (Stuttgart & Bad Cannstatt: Frommann-Holzboog, 1960), pp. 294–310;

Bernd Fischer, "Stirner im Dschungel: Zum 'proletarischen' Kulturbegriff in B. Traven's *Caoba-Zyklus*," in *Erkundungen: Beiträge zu einem erweiterten Literaturbegriff: Helmut Kreuzer zum sechzigsten Geburtstag*, edited by Jens Malte Fischer, Karl Prümm, and Helmut Scheuer (Göttingen: Vandenhoeck & Ruprecht, 1987), pp. 182–206;

Kuno Fischer, "Ein Apologet der Sophistik und ein 'philosophischer Reaktionär,'" *Epigonen*, 4 (1847): 152–165;

Fischer, "Moderne Sophisten," *Epigonen*, 5 (1848): 247–316;

Hervé Marie Forest, *Marx au miroir de Stirner* (Paris: Le Sycomore, 1979);

W. Friedensburg, "Zur Sittengeschichte der neuesten Philosophie: Max Stirner, Der Einzige und sein Eigenthum," *Die Grenzboten,* 1 (1845): 239–241;

Jin Haimin, *Der Einzige und sein Eigenttum:* Max Stirners Werk in chinesischer Übersetzung; eine Untersuchung zur Transposition deutscher idealistischer Philosophie in dem kulturellen Kontext Chinas," Ph.D. dissertation, University of Trier, 1987;

Eduard von Hartmann, "Neue Moral," *Preußische Jahrbücher,* 67 (1891): 504–521;

Hartmann, *Phänomenologie des sittlichen Bewußtseins* (Berlin: Duncker, 1879);

Hartmann, *Philosophie des Unbewußten: Versuch einer Weltanschauung* (Berlin: Duncker, 1869); translated by William Chatterton as *Philosophy of the Unconscious: Speculative Results according to the Inductive Method of Physical Science* (London: Routledge & Kegan Paul, 1931);

Hartmann, "Stirners Verherrlichung des Egoismus," in his *Ethische Studien* (Leipzig: Haacke, 1898), pp. 70–90;

Hans G. Helms, *Die Ideologie der anonymen Gesellschaft: Max Stirners "Einziger" und der Fortschritt des demokratischen Selbstbewußtseins vom Vormärz bis zur Bundesrepublik* (Cologne: DuMont Schauberg, 1966);

Moses Hess, *Die letzten Philosophen* (Darmstadt: Leske, 1845);

Wolfram Hogrebe, *Deutsche Philosophie im XIX. Jahrhundert: Kritik der idealistischen Vernunft; Schelling, Schleiermacher, Schopenhauer, Stirner, Kierkegaard, Engels, Marx, Dilthey, Nietzsche* (Munich: Fink, 1987);

Christine Hohnschopp, "Der 'Eigene' im Prokrustesbett des Marxismus: Über die T'-Rezeption in der DDR," in *B. Traven,* edited by Heinz Ludwig Arnold (Munich: Edition text + kritik, 1989), pp. 50–59;

Hans Heinz Holz, ed., *Die abenteuerliche Rebellion: Bürgerliche Protestbewegungen in der Philosophie: Stirner, Nietzsche, Sartre, Marcuse, Neue Linke* (Darmstadt & Neuwied: Luchterhand, 1976);

Ewald Horn, *Max Stirners ethischer Egoismus: Eine Säkular-Rede* (Berlin: Simion, 1907);

James Gibbons Huneker, *Egoists, a Book of Supermen: Stendhal, Baudelaire, Flaubert, Anatole France, Huysmans, Barres, Nietzsche, Blake, Ibsen, Stirner, and Ernest Hello* (New York: Scribners, 1909);

Friedrich Jodl, "Max Stirner und Ludwig Feuerbach," in his *Gesammelte Vorträge und Aufsätze,* volume 1, edited by Wilhelm Börner (Stuttgart: Cotta, 1916), pp. 275–286;

Pere Juan i Tous, "Vom Ich-Kult zur vaterländischen Empörung: Baroja und der individuali-stische Anarchismus um die Jahrhundertwende," *Romanische Literaturbeziehungen im 19. und 20. Jahrhundert: Festschrift für Franz Rauhut zum 85. Geburtstag,* edited by Angel San Miguel (Tübingen: Narr, 1985), pp. 169–184;

Howard Harold Judson, "The Concept of Freedom in Anarchist Thought," Ph.D. dissertation, University of California, Santa Barbara, 1977;

Bernd Kast, *Die Thematik des "Eigners" in der Philosophie Max Stirners: Sein Beitrag zur Radikalisierung der anthropologischen Fragestellung* (Bonn: Bouvier, 1979);

Martin Kessel, "Der Einzige und die Milchwirtschaft," *Berliner Hefte,* 2 (1947): 418–428;

Mikhail Kurtschinsky, *Der Apostel des Egoismus: Max Stirner und seine Philosophie der Anarchie,* translated from the Russian by Gregor von Glasenapp (Berlin: Prager, 1923);

Benedict Lachmann, *Protagoras, Nietzsche, Stirner: Ein Beitrag zur Philosophie des Individualismus und Egoismus* (Berlin: Simion, 1914);

Dieter Lehner, *Individualanarchismus und Dadaismus: Stirnerrezeption und Dichterexistenz* (Frankfurt am Main: Lang, 1988);

Albert Lévy, *Stirner et Nietzsche* (Paris: Société nouvelle de librairie et d'édition, 1904);

Henri Lichtenberger, "L'anarchisme en Allemagne: Max Stirner," *La nouvelle revue,* 89 (July 1894): 235–241;

Matteo Johannes Paul Lucchesi, *Die Individualitätsphilosophie Max Stirners* (Leipzig: Hoffmann, 1897);

Lucchesi, "Max Stirner als logischer, sozialer und ethischer Anarchist: Ein Nietzsche vor Nietzsche," *Jahresbericht der Lausitzer Prediger-Gesellschaft zu Leipzig,* 25 (1900): 3–20;

Angelika Machinek, *B. Traven und Max Stirner: Der Einfluß Stirners auf Ret Marut / B. Traven: Eine literatursoziologische Untersuchung zur Affinität ihrer Weltanschauungen* (Göttingen: David, 1986);

John Henry Mackay, *Die Anarchisten: Kulturgemälde aus dem Ende des XIX. Jahrhunderts* (Zurich: Schabelitz, 1891); translated by George Schumm as *The Anarchists: A Picture of Civilization at the Close of the Nineteenth Century* (Boston: Tucker, 1891);

Anton Martin, *Max Stirners Lehre* (Leipzig: Wigand, 1906);

Jürgen Maruhn, *Die Kritik an der Stirnerschen Ideologie im Werke von Karl Marx und Friedrich Engels: Max Stirners "Einziger" als Dokument des kleinbürgerlichen Radikalismus* (Frankfurt am Main: Fischer, 1982);

Karl Marx and Friedrich Engels, "Der hl. Max," excerpts in *Dokumente des Sozialismus,* edited by Eduard Bernstein (Stuttgart, 1903–1904); published in full in *Karl Marx / Friedrich Engels Historisch-kritische Gesamtausgabe: Werke-Schriften-Briefe,* volume 5 (Vienna: Verlag für Literatur und Politik, 1932);

Kurt Adolf Mautz, *Die Philosophie Max Stirners im Gegensatz zum Hegelschen Idealismus* (Berlin: Junker & Dünnhaupt, 1936);

David McLellan, *The Young Hegelians and Karl Marx* (London: Macmillan, 1969);

Benito Mussolini, *Opera Omnia* (Florence: La Fenice, 1951–1963), volume 4 (1952), p. 258; volume 14 (1954), pp. 193–194;

Theodor Opitz, *Bruno Bauer und seine Gegner: Vier kritische Artikel* (Breslau: Trewendt, 1846);

Paolo Orano, "Max Stirner in Italia: L'unicismo," *Rivista di Filosofia e Scienze Affini,* 5–6 (1903): 348–373;

Ronald William K. Paterson, *The Nihilistic Egoist Max Stirner* (London, New York & Toronto: Oxford University Press, 1971);

Giorgio Penzo, *Max Stirner: La rivolta esistenziale* (Turin: Marietti Editori, 1972);

Pierre Ramus, *Mutterschutz und Liebesfreiheit* (Berlin: Kommunistische Verlagsanstalt, 1907);

Albrecht Rau, *Harnack, Goethe, D. Strauss und L. Feuerbach über das Wesen des Christentums* (Delitzsch: Walter, 1903);

Rau, "Ludwig Feuerbach und Max Stirner," *Magazin für die Literatur des In- und Auslandes,* 41 (1888): 643–646;

Herbert Read, "Max Stirner," in his *The Tenth Muse: Essays in Criticism* (New York: Grove, 1958), pp. 74–82;

Anselm Ruest, *Max Stirner: Leben, Weltanschauung, Vermächtnis* (Berlin: Seemann, 1906);

Arnold Ruge, *Briefwechsel und Tagebuchblätter aus den Jahren 1825–1880,* edited by Paul Nerrlich (Berlin: Weidmann, 1886);

Henry C. Rutherford, *The Sovereign Self through Max Stirner* (Richmond, U.K.: New Atlantis Foundation, 1956);

Robert Schellwien, *Max Stirner und Friedrich Nietzsche: Erscheinungen des modernen Geistes und das Wesen des Menschen* (Leipzig: Pfeffer, 1892);

Schellwien, "Der Wille und Max Stirner," *Pädagogische Studien,* 2–3 (1899): 89–99; 109–113;

Hermann Schultheiss, *Stirner: Grundlagen zum Verständnis des Werkes "Der Einzige und sein Eigenthum"* (Ratibor: Lindner, 1906);

Ernst Schultze, "Stirner'sche Ideen in einem paranoischen Wahnsystem," *Archiv für Psychiatrie und Nervenkrankheiten,* 36 (1903): 793–818;

Gerhard G. Senft, *Die Schatten des Einzigen: Die Geschichte des Stirnerschen Individual-Anarchismus* (Vienna: Verlag Monte Verita, 1988);

Alberto Signorini, *L'antiumanesimo di Max Stirner* (Milan: Giuffre, 1974);

Ulrich Simon, "Zur Kritik der Philosophie Max Stirners," Ph.D. dissertation, University of Frankfurt, 1982;

Willy Storrer, ed., *"In memoriam Max Stirner": Max Stirner, Das unwahre Prinzip unserer Erziehung; oder, Der Humanismus und Realismus* (Basel: Verlag für freies Geistesleben, 1926);

Herbert Stourzh, *Max Stirners Philosophie des Ich* (Berlin: Paetel, 1926);

Georg Strugurescu, *Max Stirner: Der Einzige und sein Eigenthum* (Munich: Beck, 1911);

Peter Suren, *Max Stirner über Nutzen und Schaden der Wahrheit: Eine philosophische Untersuchung nebst einer Einleitung und einem Anhang mit ergänzenden Betrachtungen* (Frankfurt am Main: Lang, 1991);

Hans Sveistrup, "Stirner als Soziologe," in *Von Büchern und Bibliotheken,* edited by Gustav Abb (Berlin: Struppe & Winckler, 1928), pp. 103–123;

Sveistrup, *Stirners drei Egoismen: Wider Karl Marx, Othmar Spann und die Fysiokraten* (Lauf: Zitzman, 1932);

F. Szeliga, " 'Der Einzige und sein Eigenthum' von Max Stirner," *Norddeutsche Blätter für Kritik, Literatur und Unterhaltung,* 10 (March 1845): 1–34;

René S. Taube, "Das Bild Max Stirners in der deutschen Literatur um die Mitte des 19. Jahrhunderts," Ph.D. dissertation, Ohio State University, 1958;

Ernie Thomson, "Feuerbach, Marx, and Stirner: An Investigation into Althusser's Epistemological Break Thesis," Ph.D. dissertation, University of California, Santa Barbara, 1991;

Miriama Widakowich-Weyland, *La filosofia de Max Stirner: historia de su controversia con Marx* (Buenos Aires: Fundacion para la Educacion, la Ciencia y la Cultura, 1981);

Achim von Winterfeld, *Max Stirner* (Gautzsch: Dietrich, 1911);

Ettore Zoccoli, *I gruppi anarchici degli Stati Uniti e l'opera di Max Stirner* (Modena: Vincenzi, 1901).

Theodor Storm

(14 September 1817 – 4 July 1888)

A. Tilo Alt
Duke University

BOOKS: *Liederbuch dreier Freunde,* by Storm, Theodor Mommsen, and Tycho Mommsen (Kiel: Schwers, 1843);

Sommer-Geschichten und Lieder (Berlin: Duncker, 1851) – includes *Immensee,* translated by Helen Clark as *Immensee, or the Old Man's Reverie* (Münster: Brunn, 1863);

Gedichte (Kiel: Schwers, 1852; enlarged edition, Berlin: Schindler, 1856; enlarged, 1864; revised edition, Brunswick: Westermann, 1868; revised edition, Berlin: Paetel, 1875; enlarged, 1885);

Im Sonnenschein: Drei Sommergeschichten (Berlin: Duncker, 1854) – comprises "Im Sonnenschein"; "Marthe und ihre Uhr"; "Im Saal," translated anonymously as *In the Great Hall* (London: Educational Book, 1923);

Ein grünes Blatt: Zwei Sommergeschichten (Berlin: Schindler, 1855) – comprises "Angelika," "Ein grünes Blatt";

Hinzelmeier: Eine nachdenkliche Geschichte (Berlin: Paetel, 1857);

In der Sommer-Mondnacht: Novellen (Berlin: Schindler, 1860) – comprises "Auf dem Staatshof," "Wenn die Äpfel reif sind," "Posthuma";

Drei Novellen (Berlin: Schindler, 1861) – comprises "Veronica," "Späte Rosen," "Drüben am Markt";

Im Schloß (Münster: Brunn, 1863);

Auf der Universität (Münster: Brunn, 1863); republished as *Lenore* (Münster: Brunn, 1865);

Zwei Weihnachtsidyllen (Berlin: Schindler, 1865) – comprises "Unter dem Tannenbaum," "Abseits";

Drei Märchen (Hamburg: Mauke, 1866); republished as *Geschichten aus der Tonne* (Berlin: Paetel, 1873) – comprises "Die Regentrude," "Bulemann's Haus," "Der Speigel des Cyprianus";

Theodor Storm in 1887

Von Jenseit des Meeres: Novelle (Schleswig: Schulbuchhandlung, 1867);

In St. Jürgen (Schleswig: Schulbuchhandlung, 1868);

Novellen (Schleswig: Schulbuchhandlung, 1868) – comprises "In St. Jürgen," "Von Jenseit des Meeres," "Eine Malerarbeit";

Sämmtliche Schriften, 19 volumes (Brunswick: Westermann, 1868-1869); enlarged as *Sämmtliche*

Werke, 12 volumes (Brunswick: Westermann, 1898–1916);

Zerstreute Kapitel (Berlin: Paetel, 1873);

Novellen und Gedenkblätter (Brunswick: Westermann, 1874) – comprises "Viola tricolor," "Beim Vetter Christian," "Von heut' und ehedem";

Waldwinkel; Pole Poppenspäler: Novellen (Brunswick: Westermann, 1875);

Ein stiller Musikant; Psyche; Im Nachbarhause links: Drei Novellen (Brunswick: Westermann, 1876);

Aquis submersus: Novelle (Berlin: Paetel, 1877); translated by Geoffrey Skelton as *Beneath the Flood* (London: New English Library, 1962);

Carsten Curator (Berlin: Paetel, 1878); translated by Frieda Voigt as *Curator Carsten* (London: Calder, 1956);

Renate (Berlin: Paetel, 1878); translated by James Millar as *Renate* (London: Gowans & Gray, 1909);

Eekenhof; Im Brauer-Hause: Zwei Novellen (Berlin: Paetel, 1880); "Eekenhof," translated by Millar as *Eekenhof* (London: Gowans & Gray, 1908);

Zur "Wald- und Wasserfreude": Novelle (Berlin: Paetel, 1880);

Der Herr Etatsrat; Die Söhne des Senators: Novellen (Berlin: Paetel, 1881); "Die Söhne des Senators," translated by E. M. Huggard as *The Senator's Sons* (London: Harrap, 1947);

Hans und Heinz Kirch (Berlin: Paetel, 1883);

Schweigen (Berlin: Paetel, 1883);

Zur Chronik von Grieshuus (Berlin: Paetel, 1884);

John Riew'; Ein Fest auf Haderslevhuus: Zwei Novellen (Berlin: Paetel, 1885);

Bötjer Basch: Eine Geschichte (Berlin: Paetel, 1887);

Ein Doppelgänger: Novelle (Berlin: Paetel, 1887);

Ein Bekenntniß: Novelle (Berlin: Paetel, 1888);

"Es waren zwei Königskinder" (Berlin: Paetel, 1888);

Der Schimmelreiter (Berlin: Paetel, 1888); translated by Muriel Almon as "The Rider of the Pale Horse," in *The German Classics of the Nineteenth and Twentieth Centuries*, volume 11 (New York: German Publication Society, 1914), pp. 225–342.

Editions in English: *Viola Tricolor, The Little Stepmother*, translated by Bayard Quincy Morgan; *Curator Carston*, translated by Frieda M. Voigt (London: Calder, 1956; New York: Ungar, 1956);

The Rider on the White Horse, and Selected Stories, translated by James Wright (New York: New American Library, 1964) – comprises "In the Great Hall," "Immensee," "A Green Leaf," "In the Sunlight," "Veronika," "In St. Jürgen," "Aquis Submersus," "The Rider on the White Horse."

OTHER: *Deutsche Liebeslieder seit Johann Christian Günther: Eine Codification*, edited by Storm (Berlin: Schindler, 1859);

Hausbuch aus deutschen Dichtern seit Claudius: Eine kritische Anthologie, edited by Storm (Hamburg: Mauke, 1870).

Theodor Storm is a prominent representative of the group of European writers known as "poetic" or "bourgeois" realists. The majority of his tales are set in his native region of Schleswig-Holstein, some of them in his hometown of Husum. His lyrical poetry also treats regional themes and motifs. This regionalism, however, is merely Storm's vehicle for treating themes of national and human significance. In his 1930 essay on Storm, Thomas Mann said that Storm's thematic innovations and craftsmanship were equal to those of such European contemporaries as Ivan Turgenev, Charles Dickens, and Gottfried Keller. Storm's novellas *Immensee* (Bee's Lake, 1851; translated as *Immensee*, 1863) and *Der Schimmelreiter* (1888; translated as "The Rider of the Pale Horse," 1914) are still widely known, and the line "die graue Stadt am Meer" (the gray town by the sea) from his poem "Die Stadt" (The Town, 1851) has entered the German language as a synonym for the poet's hometown. His major themes are love, family, death, and the transience of all things. Some of his stories have been adapted as films and television plays, and many of his poems have been set to music by eminent composers.

Storm's friend Ferdinand Tönnies outlined in his classic sociological text *Gemeinschaft und Gesellschaft* (Community and Society, 1887) the dilemma of the individual in postagrarian, industrial German society of the late nineteenth century. Storm was aware of this loss of community and the isolation of the individual in the impersonal, abstract organization of the body politic, and he turns to near-absolute love or to an idyllic past to counteract isolation and loneliness. He also points to the psychological stress that the impersonal society of isolated individuals has caused.

Theodor Woldsen Storm was born in Husum in the duchy of Schleswig on 14 September 1817, the son of Johann Kasimir Storm and his wife, Lucie Woldsen Storm. Since Schleswig then belonged to Denmark, Storm was a Danish citizen. On his mother's side he was descended from one of Husum's old patrician families, and the stately rococo house of his maternal grandparents made a lasting impression on him; the vignettes *Im Sonnenschein* (1854; translated as "In the Sunlight," 1964) and *Im Saal* (1854; translated as *In the Great Hall*, 1923), which take place in the middle of the eighteenth century, were inspired by memories of his youth in the Woldsen house. On his father's side Storm was descended from a long line of millers and farmers. His father was a highly respected lawyer who had been decorated by the Danish king. The beauty of idyllic Westermühlen, his paternal grandparents' village, survives in many of Storm's poems.

Storm's secondary education at the Gelehrtenschule in Husum and the Katharineum in Lübeck was followed by his admission to the law school at the University of Kiel in 1837. His earliest attempts at writing poetry date from his student days, when he was under the influence of the lyrics of Heinrich Heine, Eduard Mörike, and Joseph von Eichendorff. Storm left Kiel after a year to join his friend Ferdinand Röse at the University of Berlin. Röse had introduced Storm to Johann Wolfgang von Goethe's *Faust* (1808, 1832) and to German poetry. Through Röse he met Emanuel Geibel, who was destined to become Germany's most celebrated poet in the nineteenth century and whom Storm in his later years was to call his poetic antithesis. In Berlin, Storm attended only the lectures of the jurist Karl von Savigny.

Röse's departure in 1839 prompted Storm to return to the University of Kiel, where he became a member of the circle around Theodor Mommsen, who was to become Germany's foremost classical historian and the world's first Nobel laureate in literature, and Mommsen's brother Tycho.

In 1842 Storm was admitted to the bar and went to work in his father's law office in Husum; the same year Bertha von Buchan, whom he had loved since his high-school days, refused his proposal of marriage. His poems reflecting his feelings for Bertha mark the point at which Storm found his individual style as a writer of love poetry. Some of the poems were included in *Liederbuch dreier Freunde* (Book of Songs by Three Friends, 1843), by Storm and the Mommsen brothers. Few of his poems in the book were included by him in his first separate collection of poetry.

Storm set up his own law practice in Husum in 1843. In 1846 he married his cousin Konstanze Esmarch, the daughter of the mayor of Seegeberg in Holstein and of the sister of Storm's mother. Many of Storm's twelve siblings and Konstanze's ten also intermarried, so that Storm's extended family was large indeed. Storm's views on family life were determined by this background: he saw the family as a bastion in a world that was becoming increasingly impersonal, isolating the individual from the traditional certainties of community life and religion. Nevertheless, during the first two years of his marriage Storm had an affair with Dorothea Jensen, who inspired some of his most outspoken love lyrics and also poems of remorse; some of these sexually daring poems were not published until after his death. So as not to endanger his marriage, Dorothea left Husum in 1848. Storm confessed his infidelity to his wife, who magnanimously told him that if she should predecease him he should marry Dorothea. He also confessed to his friends Hartmuth and Laura Brinkmann in what came to be known posthumously as his "Beichtbrief" (Confessional Letter).

Storm's first prose work of note was *Immensee,* a tale of unfulfilled love that also concerns the separation of art and life and the middle-class valorization of austerity and frugality. It is a lyrical novella rich in poetic imagery and descriptive detail, especially about the psychological states of the protagonist. An atmosphere of tragic resignation permeates the story. In the frame of the novella Reinhard, an aging poet, is sitting in his lonely study remembering Elisabeth, his childhood companion and later his only love. In the main story Elisabeth's mother decides that the impractical Reinhard will never earn an adequate living, and Elisabeth is obliged to marry Erich, whom she does not love. Two years later Reinhard is invited to visit Erich and Elisabeth at their estate, Immensee. One evening Reinhard and his hosts are singing folk songs; Elisabeth's reaction to one of the songs reveals that she still loves him. The song's opening lines recall the reason for Elisabeth's marriage to Erich: "Meine Mutter hat's gewollt / Den andern ich, nehmen sollt" (My mother willed it / The other one I had to wed). In a gesture of utter hopelessness Elisabeth gets up and turns her back on the two men. Erich and Elisabeth must resign themselves to their unhappy marriage just as Reinhard and Elisabeth must accept their separate destinies. This state of affairs is symbolized by Reinhard's attempt to fetch a water lily in the Immen Lake: swimming toward it, he gets entangled in the stalks of the plants and has to turn back. Elisabeth, as delicate and beautiful as the water lily, is equally unattainable for him. When Reinhard takes his leave, Elisabeth realizes that he will never return.

The first separate edition of Storm's poetry, titled simply *Gedichte* (Poems, 1852), reflects the lyrical creed he was to elaborate later in his correspondence and in his two anthologies of German poetry. Storm has been regarded as the last of the great poets of the Sturm und Drang tradition that began in the eighteenth century. The poems in *Gedichte* are meant to be read consecutively, from cover to cover, for full effect; they were selected according to a set of criteria that included the requirement that a poem be the product of specific experience and be accompanied by a strong emotion. Storm favored the folk-song stanza, alternating rhyme schemes, and the iambic meter; he emphasized the untrammeled expression of an experience or subject matter and rejected intellectual or reflective lyrics. He also rejected the popular products of the Munich neoclassical school of poets, led by Geibel and Paul Heyse, as exercises in formalism. The themes of his poetry include love, nature, transiency, and death. The work includes "Die Stadt," the poem that made him famous and immortalized his hometown of Husum.

Storm's poetry at this point reflects his materialistic view of life, combined with a desire for a spiritual concept that would lend meaning to prosaic reality. This concept is that of absolute love, including love for the family and for one's native region. A materialistic philosophy brings into relief the transitory nature of all things, explaining the dominance of the motif of transiency in Storm's poems as well as in his prose. It is an entirely modern consciousness that stems from the loss of the anchor provided by commonly held religious beliefs. For Storm, sexual love is a substitute for divine love. "Schließe mir die Augen beide" (Close both my eyes), Storm's ultimate love poem, depicts a mystical union of two individuals that replaces the traditional Pietistic *unio mystica* with God.

On occasion, his poems violate the classical tenet of the exclusion of the aesthetically ugly from a work of art. The poem "Geh' nicht hinein" (Do Not Enter), for example, describes a dead body in vivid detail. To Storm it is the truth of art as measured against reality that gives it importance and provides aesthetic satisfaction.

Storm's political lyrics were based on his feeling of union with his homeland. Like absolute love, the homeland was to Storm a bastion against an impersonal and isolating universe; his political poems concern "verletztes Heimatgefühl" (violated sense of home). The struggle for independence from Denmark during the revolution of 1848 moved the poet deeply. Yet his poems are far from being tendentious or programmatic; rather, they are expressions of rage over the loss of personal freedom. He fa-

Storm in 1857; painting by Hans Nikolai Sunde (private collection)

vored a semidemocratic order based on representation by the social estates, as was the tradition in Schleswig-Holstein. He loathed the unbridled power of the developing nation-state of his day. In addition, he could not abide the arrogance of the German aristocracy and their ideological allies, the clergy.

The duchies were reoccupied and reclaimed by Denmark in 1851. As an outspoken foe of Danish rule, Storm was denied renewal of his law license. In 1853, although unfamiliar with Prussian law, he became an assistant judge at the district court in Potsdam; since the position was unpaid, he had to depend on his and his wife's parents for financial support. In Potsdam he made the acquaintance of one of his poetic mentors, the Romantic poet Eichendorff, as well as the writers Heyse and Fontane and the painter Adolph Menzel. He joined two literary societies, Der Tunnel über der Spree (The Tunnel over the River Spree) and Rütli. In

Potsdam he also found an outlet for his novellas and poems in the literary journal *Argo*, edited by Fontane. In 1855 Storm traveled to Heidelberg and Stuttgart with his parents. In Stuttgart they met Eduard Mörike, another of Storm's poetic mentors.

In 1856 Storm was offered a judgeship at the district court in Heiligenstadt, a provincial backwater in Thuringia. He founded a choir in the town, in which he sang. In Heiligenstadt Storm prepared his important anthology of lyrical poetry, *Deutsche Liebeslieder seit Johann Christian Günther: Eine Codification* (German Love Lyrics since Johann Christian Günther: A Codification, 1859). The work aims to educate the reading public in the tradition of the lyric of personal experience that began in the eighteenth century, the tradition to which Storm's own poetic products belong. The book was intended to counteract the influence of the many anthologies on the market that advanced the kind of sentimental love poetry that Storm considered inferior.

It was also in Heiligenstadt that he entered the second phase of his prose-writing activity, in which he produced novellas focused on psychological problems. In his earlier works he had developed isolated situations taken from everday life into short vignettes. The novella *Im Schloß* (Inside the Chateau, 1863) concerns the then frequently treated theme of the love of an aristocratic young woman for her brother's tutor. A comparison has been made by scholars and by Storm himself of his story with Friedrich Spielhagen's novel *Problematische Naturen* (1861; translated as *Problematic Characters*, 1869). Both works attack the unwarranted status and power of the aristocracy, but Hinrich Arnold, Storm's self-assured protagonist, is proud of his humble origins, whereas Spielhagen's Oswald Stein suffers from inferiority feelings because of his middle-class background. Since, however, Stein turns out to be the natural offspring of Baron von Grenwitz and thus a close relative of his aristocratic employer, Spielhagen defuses his social criticism and preaches what Storm calls the mystery of two kinds of blood. Spilehagen's protagonist dies on the barricades during the 1848 revolution; Storm did not feel that such an overly dramatic tragic ending was justified. For him the realities of the 1860s dictated that the middle class seek equality with the aristocracy by compromise rather than by forcibly removing the aristocracy from power. Storm shows a gradual process of ideological change within the characters toward a "reines Menschentum" (pure humanity). Thus, Anna's love for Arnold must be

openly acknowledged; she cannot conceal her feelings for the sake of a convention that makes a liaison between the aristocracy and the bourgeoisie unsuitable. Predictably, the novella was received enthusiastically by middle-class readers and rejected by aristocratic ones.

In 1863 and 1864 Storm turned to the writing of fairy tales. The best of these tales is "Die Regentrude" (The Rain Maiden, 1866) which develops the theme of the interdependence of humanity and nature.

The Dano-Prussian war of 1863–1864 resulted in Schleswig-Holstein becoming a Prussian province. The people of Husum needed a replacement for the pro-Danish chief of police, who also held the office of judge. Because of his father's reputation in the area Storm was elected Landvogt (county provost), an ancient office combining police and judicial powers. He and his family moved to Husum in March 1864. The office of Landvogt was abolished by the Prussian government in 1867; Storm turned down a high administrative post that was offered him to become a lower court judge once again, a position he preferred because of the greater degree of independence it afforded. In 1865 Konstanze died after the birth of their seventh child. Later that year Storm traveled to Baden-Baden to meet the Russian novelist Turgenev, with whom he shared literary interests. In 1866 he married Dorothea Jensen. A child was born to them the following year. In 1868–1869 Storm's collected works were published by the firm of George Westermann in Brunswick.

In 1870 Storm's second anthology of lyrical poetry, *Hausbuch aus deutschen Dichtern seit Claudius: Eine kritische Anthologie* (Book for the Home of German Poets since Claudius: A Critical Anthology), was published. Unlike most anthologies popular at the time, Storm's book included only selections that met his personal criteria for lyrical poetry; it was also organized chronologically rather than thematically, with the intention of enabling his readers to arrive at their own conclusions about a poem (hence the words "Critical Anthology" in the title). It also contained biographical and bibliographical information on the poets whose works were included.

In *Von Jenseit des Meeres* (From across the Sea, 1867) Storm introduces the theme of the threat to the absolute values of family and home. Marriage and the family, he holds, are cultural inventions rather than natural law; as such, they are a counterpoise to the natural extinction of the individual. These institutions are inherently unstable and endangered. The protagonist of *Von Jenseit des Meeres*

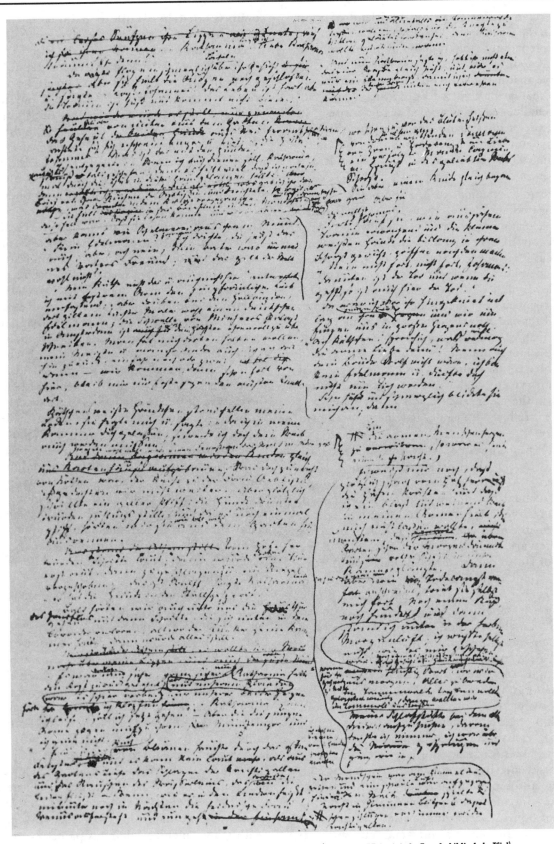

Page from the first draft for Storm's novella Aquis Submersis *(Schleswig-Holsteinische Landesbibliothek, Kiel)*

is a German businessman on the island of Saint Croix in the Caribbean. The novella is a racist tale of miscegenation in the tradition of nineteenth-century colonialism based on social Darwinism. The primitive instincts with which the natives are imbued threaten the civilized Europeans, whose culture is challenged by unbridled sexual instinct. In the end the businessman takes Jenni, the offspring of his liaison with a black woman, to Germany; there she will be raised as a European in control of her instincts.

Storm's reaction to the outbreak of the Franco-Prussian War of 1870–1871 was that the primitive instincts of humanity are given an outlet in such wars. He wrote his son Ernst on 3 August 1870 that he believed that the stronger always devours the weaker, and since humanity has no predator to devour it, it devours itself. His ideology of social Darwinism even superseded Storm's contempt for the Prussian state: he considered the defense of the German way of life against a non-German way, to him, a moral imperative. Storm, however, did not rejoice in the Prussian victory; he feared that his countrymen might come to savor "gloire" (glory) in the manner of Napoleon. He hated war because it reduced humanity to a mere instrument of nature.

In 1877 appeared what was subsequently hailed as Storm's best prose effort to date, *Aquis submersus* (translated as *Beneath the Flood*, 1962). This novella is one of the so-called chronicle novellas or novellas of tragic fate, frame tales that were Storm's only genre in the last decade of his life. They are set in the fairly distant past in the duchy of Holstein. As a boy, the narrator of *Aquis submersus* had seen in a village church a seventeenth-century painting of a pastor and a boy holding a water lily. The picture was captioned "CPAS," an abbreviation of the Latin *culpa patris aquis submersus* (drowned through the fault of the father). As a student in search of a room, the narrator comes to a house that attracts his attention because of an inscription in Low German above the doorway: "Geliek as Rook un Stof verswindt, Also sind ook de Minschenkind" (Just as smoke and dust vanish, So does the human being). He enters and sees the same painting. The owner produces a seventeenth-century manuscript that contains the autobiographical account of the painter, Johannes. Johannes, a commoner, grew up on the estate of Squire Gerhardus, a friend of his dead father, with the squire's children, Wulf and Katharina. After the squire's death Johannes returns from a five-year apprenticeship in Holland and is

commissioned by Wulf to paint a portrait of Katharina, who is about to be married to von der Risch, a country squire. During the sittings for the portrait the two fall in love. An encounter of Johannes, Wulf, and von der Risch in a tavern leads to an argument, and Wulf's bloodhounds pursue the painter back to the estate. Johannes finds refuge in Katharina's bedchamber, and he stays in the arms of his beloved until daybreak. He had been seen entering her room, and to head off scandal he asks Wulf for his sister's hand in marriage. Wulf's answer is a shot from his pistol. Badly wounded, Johannes flees and spends many weeks in the care of a friend. On his return he learns that von der Risch has married someone else, and that Katharina has vanished without a trace. Johannes and Katharina meet again when he is asked to paint the portrait of a pastor who turns out to be Katharina's husband; she had been forced to marry him because she was expecting Johannes's child. The painter and his beloved meet in the garden of the rectory; their child is playing nearby. As Johannes and Katharina embrace, the child drowns in the garden pond. At the pastor's request, Johannes adds the dead child to the picture of the pastor and places a water lily in his hand. Under the painting he places the letters *C.P.A.S.* After reporting Wulf's violent end from the bite of a rabid dog and of the passing of the estate into the hands of strangers, Johannes concludes his story. In the closing frame the narrator converts the motif of drowning into a metaphor of oblivion: Johannes's biography, he says, is nowhere to be found outside the autobiographical manuscript. Even in his native region he is not remembered; he is "aquis submersus," he has vanished in the flood.

The novella is a critique of an anachronistic feudal order that, according to Storm, destroys whatever is human and beautiful and, hence, justified. The aristocracy regards the artist as a mere servant. Storm's anticlerical stance also stands out in the negative characterization of Katharina's husband. In a comment on his novella Storm emphasized that he had not intended to locate tragic guilt in the passionate union of Johannes and Katharina; rather, guilt lies with the inherited power of the landed gentry, the force that drives the couple into each other's arms. Another important motif is that of heredity; the science of genetics was just emerging at the time of the novella's composition. Wulf's negative traits can be traced to a female ancestor beneath whose picture Johannes paints Katharina's portrait; the ancestor's picture periodically casts a pall over the otherwise happy sessions. The overarching motif of the novella is articulated by the epigraph above the doorway: the transitoriness of all things and the demise of the individual.

A conscientious worker, Storm rose in the Prussian judicial hierarchy. In 1880 he built a house in the village of Hademarschen in Holstein, where he retired in 1881.

Storm's view that the family forms a bastion against the forces that threaten the individual extends to the state: ideally, the latter is the natural extension of the family. Political power, however, should be communal, not usurped as in a feudal or despotic state. Storm's contempt for the Prussian government was well known. Between 1877 and 1882 he wrote three novellas that deal with the collapse of the family because of hereditary factors, social values, and the Prussian state's perversion of the idea of community. Storm suffered from guilt because of the alcoholism of his eldest son, Hans; in the last decade of his life a "culpa patris" motif runs through his correspondence as well as some of his novellas and poems. In *Carsten Curator* (1878; translated as *Curator Carsten*, 1956) the middle-aged Carsten Carstens, a solid citizen, marries the young and beautiful Juliane, his opposite in all essentials. She lends charm and excitement to his staid middle-class existence; but she dies when giving birth to their son, Heinrich, who turns out to be as morally weak, irresponsible, and reckless as his mother and ultimately drags his father down with him. An ineluctable hereditary mechanism destroys the family. Carsten's moral convictions demand that he stand by his son, no matter the consequences, and chaos overwhelms his world of middle-class prosperity and order. Anna, Carsten's foster child, although fully aware of Heinrich's irresponsible and morally weak character, accepts his marriage proposal. At the end of the story Heinrich is missing in a flood and has bankrupted his father. Carsten's house is auctioned off, and he, Anna, and her child are living in poverty. The novella ends on a hopeful note, however, since Heinrich's son resembles his grandfather and mother, thus promising the continuation of the middle-class traits that Storm and his age admired: trust, responsible behavior, self-reliance, and honesty.

In "Der Herr Etatsrat" (The State Councilor, 1881) the father is the destructive force in the family. Etatsrat Sternow, a Prussian government official in Schleswig-Holstein, destroys his wife, his son, his daughter, and his grandchild. The story is told in humorous tones; its tragic and horrific dimensions become manifest only gradually. The traits exhibited by this official are those that Storm had noted

Storm in 1879

about the Prussian government in general: condescension toward the citizens, arbitrary decisions, and a general indifference toward people. The state is the extension of the family; but the Prussian state, as an extension of Sternow's family, is inhuman. In part, the fault lies with a perversion of the patriarchal order. Storm's ideal was the family governed by paternal love. The family is a bulwark against the untamed forces of nature, and traditionally the father is best suited to lead the family because of the middle-class tradition that prepares him for this duty. In the Sternow family the mother has died, and the masculinization of the family is a reflection of the heartlessness of a masculinized society. Presiding over this "Familie in der Zerstörung" (family in a state of disintegration), as Storm put it, is death. The Etatsrat has an altar to death in a large cabinet; at the foot of the black cross formed by the door frame of the cabinet lie a skull and crossbones carved from boxwood with horrifying realism. The Prussian state as symbolized by Sternow is life-destroying. To be sure, Prussia turned its death cult into one of positive value: to die for one's country was regarded as noble. To Storm, death signifies nothingness. Archimedes, Sternow's university-student son, has no sense of self; it has been destroyed by his father. Archimedes has adopted the habits of the enemy of humanity: the repetitious phrases typical of the Prussian officer class and the paraphernalia and rituals of the militant student fraternities. Phia, the weak and vulnerable daughter, has been seduced by her father's villainous assistant Käfer (the name means beetle or bug) and is expecting his child. She commits suicide and thereby destroys the weakest member of the family, her unborn baby. The entire society lives for the mindless pleasures of dancing and drinking. Archimedes' handmade patent leather shoes are a symbol of waste: he has had dozens of pairs of them made, using funds that were supposed to go for his studies. Archimedes relentlessly consumes alcohol, in keeping with the habits of the male members of the ruling classes in his society; he finally dies from the habit. He is unlamented by his father; Sternow's sole concern is with his son's debts, which he refuses to pay. In the end Sternow dies and Käfer disappears, and the townspeople scarcely remember them.

In *Hans und Heinz Kirch* (1883) a father is guilty of the demise of his son. The story is set in a small Baltic seaport where the father, Hans Kirch, is the owner and captain of a small merchantman; his son, Heinz, is a deckhand on the ship. The town is a middle-class cultural void whose sole interest is commerce. Patient, thrifty, hardworking, and devoted to his family, Hans embodies the ideals of his social class. There is, however, a tragic flaw in his character: his irascibility, which ultimately proves the undoing of both father and son. Wieb, the illegitimate daughter of a sailor and a washerwoman, was Heinz's childhood sweetheart, and they are now lovers. Wieb's family background is detrimental to Hans's plans for his son, which involve the accumulation of sufficient wealth to be accepted by the patrician families and become a senator. He forbids Heinz to continue his relationship with Wieb. Heinz does not reply, nor does he return to his father's ship; instead, he takes service on another ship. The father-son conflict turns into a contest of wills. The father expects the son to make the first move toward reconciliation, in keeping with the fourth commandment. At the end of two years a letter arrives with postage due; Hans refuses to accept it. Wieb offers to pay for it, but Hans remains adamant. Fifteen years later, Hans's wife has died of grief for her lost son, and Wieb has married a sailor. Hans hears that a man answering to the name of John Smidt and living in a cheap boarding house in Hamburg is Heinz. Hans decides to bring his son home. But Heinz is different from what his family remembers: there are smallpox scars on his face; his manner is coarse; his speech is punctuated with English and Spanish phrases; and the anchor tattooed on his arm has disappeared. No reconciliation between father and son takes place, and rumors circulate that the man in Hans's house is not really his son. Hans leaves an envelope with a modest sum of money in Heinz's room and tells him to leave. On a stormy night some time after Heinz's departure, Hans has a vision of his son's death at sea. He remembers his wife's pleas not to reject their son's letter, and he seeks Wieb's company as an act of atonement for his wrongs. His death, his son-in-law's succession to his fortune, the arrival of a grandson, and his son-in-law's prospects of becoming a senator are listed laconically, and the narrator concludes the novella by saying that the question of Heinz's whereabouts remains unanswered.

Storm went to Berlin in 1884 at the invitation of many of his friends and admirers, including Theodor Mommsen, Fontane, Menzel, and Alexander von Wussow the former administrative head of the region around Heiligenstadt and then a high official in the Prussian ministry of culture. In 1886 he traveled to Weimar, accompanied by Tönnies, to take his daughter Elsabe to the school of music there; to visit with the writer Wilhelm Raabe, whose works he held in high esteem; and to accept invitations by the Goethe Gesellschaft (Goethe Society) and the grand duke of Saxe-Weimar. On both occasions, Storm was celebrated as one of Germany's outstanding writers. His son Hans, who was serving as a ship's doctor, died as a result of alcoholism in 1886.

In the winter of 1886–1887 Storm suffered his first bout with abdominal cancer. The protagonist of his novella *Ein Bekenntnis* (A Confession, 1888) is the gynecologist Franz Jebe, who loves his wife passionately and devotedly. She is suffering from cancer of the uterus. Unaware of a newly discovered method of treating that form of cancer, he gives her a lethal injection at her request. This act of euthanasia makes him guilty in a metaphysical sense: life is a sacred mystery, and no man of science has the right to end it. Jebe can only atone for his deed by serving life; no church or court of law can acquit him. Jebe renounces possible happiness with Hilda Rosen, the daughter of a woman he cures using the new procedure, and becomes a medical missionary in Africa. Jebe's confession to his friend, the narrator just before his departure for Africa, is devoid of sentimentality or self-pity. Thirty years later, the narrator learns that Jebe had died in Africa in an epidemic. In Heyse's "Auf Tod und Leben" (A Matter of Life and Death, 1886), which also deals with euthanasia, the protagonist is reintegrated into society through understanding and love. The problem in Heyse's story is psychological rather than ethical, as it is in Storm's work.

On his seventieth birthday Storm was made an honorary citizen of Husum. Although he was seriously ill, Storm finished his last and most significant work, *Der Schimmelreiter*. The novella is based on a legend Storm had read in his youth; an early reference to it can be found in an 1843 letter from Storm to Theodor Mommsen. It is his longest novella; not only its length but also its concentration on the development of the hero rather than on a central event, as is typical of the novella genre, would justify the label "character novel" for this narrative.

The novella has three frames: the author recalls a tale he heard in his grandmother's house, in which a traveler in the 1830s took refuge from a storm with a schoolmaster who, in turn, told him the eighteenth-century story that forms the core of the narrative. Even as a youth Hauke Haien maintained that the construction of the dike protecting his village from the North Sea was faulty. Hauke enters the service of Tede Volkerts, the Deichgraf (dike reeve), as a handyman; he is able to make many suggestions for the improvement of the dike. It is no secret in the village that Volkerts was made Deichgraf because of his wealth rather than his ability; he comes to rely more and more on Hauke as his accountant and engineer. Hauke is promoted to foreman and marries Elke, Volkerts's daughter. When Volkerts dies, Hauke is appointed the new Deichgraf; his marriage to Elke brought him sufficient property to qualify for the position. Hauke draws up plans for a new dike and land-reclamation project, which are finally approved by the head Deichgraf. On the same day he acquires an emaciated white horse from a swarthy Slovak. Through patient care the horse is restored to health; it becomes inseparable from its new master and will tolerate no other rider. Hauke's men have a superstitious fear of the animal, because it is rumored to have risen from a horse's skeleton on a sandbar off the coast; the skeleton had disappeared after Hauke's purchase of the horse.

To construct the new dike, Hauke has to struggle against the prejudice of the villagers, who are opposed to innovation and resent his superior

intelligence. Hauke drives himself and his workers hard, and the dike is completed the following year. In a weakened state after an illness, however, he allows himself to be persuaded to carry out only superficial repairs on the old dike. During a severe storm in October 1756 he discovers a breach where he should have insisted on much more extensive repairs. His wife and child have gone out in the storm to look for him; he sees them driving toward the dike but cannot stop them. The waters rush through the gap in the old dike and carry them away. In despair he forces his horse into the waves, where both perish. Since that time, the villagers claim, the horse's skeleton has reappeared on the shoal; and during storms a ghostly figure on a white horse is seen riding on the dikes. After the schoolmaster finishes his story and the storm raging outside dies down, the traveler rides away across the Hauke Haien Dike.

Storm strikes a balance between the legendary character of the story and its realistic setting through a technique of deliberate ambiguity. Without committing himself, he presents reason and unreason, intelligence and ignorance, enlightenment and superstition in constant juxtaposition. He involves himself in the opening frame to indicate the importance he attaches to the search for a redemptive force, which he sees in the combining of reason, represented by the construction of the dike, and myth, represented by the legend to which Hauke's life and death have given rise. The novella is Storm's crowning achievement and ranks with the best literature of his country and time.

On 4 July 1888, four months after the completion of the novella, Storm died of abdominal cancer. He was buried in the family crypt in Husum. At his request, neither a priest nor a friend spoke at his grave. It was his ultimate acknowledgment that there is no answer to the power of death.

Letters:

"Briefwechsel zwischen Theodor Storm und Emil Kuh," edited by Paul R. Kuh, *Westermanns illustrierte deutsche Monatshefte*, 67 (1889–1890); 99–107, 264–274, 363–378, 541–554;

Briefe in die Heimat aus den Jahren 1853–64, edited by Gertrud Storm (Berlin: Curtius, 1907);

Briefe an seine Braut, edited by Storm (Brunswick: Westermann, 1915);

Briefe an seine Frau, edited by Storm (Brunswick: Westermann, 1915);

Briefe an seine Kinder, edited by Storm (Brunswick: Westermann, 1916);

Theodor Storms Briefwechsel mit Theodor Mommsen, edited by Hans-Erich Teitge (Weimar: Böhlau, 1966);

Theodor Storm und Iwan Turgenjew: Persönliche und literarische Beziehungen, Einflüsse, Briefe, Bilder, edited by Karl-Ernst Laage (Heide: Boyens, 1967);

Der Briefwechsel zwischen Theodor Storm und Gottfried Keller, edited by Peter Goldammer (Berlin: Aufbau, 1967);

Theodor Storm – Paul Heyse: Briefwechsel, 3 volumes, edited by Clifford A. Bernd (Berlin: Schmidt, 1969–1974);

Theodor Storm – Erich Schmidt: Briefwechsel, 2 volumes, edited by Laage (Berlin: Schmidt, 1972–1976);

"Theodor Storm und Hieronymus Lorm: Unveröffentlichte Briefe," edited by Arthur Tilo Alt, *Schriften der Theodor-Storm-Gesellschaft*, 27 (1978) 26–36;

Theodor Storm – Eduard Mörike; Theodor Storm – Margareth Mörike: Briefwechsel, mit Storms "Meine Erinnerungen an Eduard Mörike," edited by Hildburg and Werner Kohlschmidt (Berlin: Schmidt, 1978);

Theodor Storm – Ernst Esmarch: Briefwechsel, edited by Alt (Berlin: Schmidt, 1979);

Theodor Storm – Theodor Fontane: Briefwechsel, edited by Jacob Steiner (Berlin: Schmidt, 1981);

Theodor Storm – Wilhelm Petersen, Briefwechsel, edited by Brian Coghlan (Berlin: Schmidt, 1984);

Theodor Storm – Hartmuth und Laura Brinkmann: Briefwechsel, edited by August Stahl (Berlin: Schmidt, 1986);

Theodor Fontane über den "Eroticismus" und die "Husumerei" Storms: Fontanes Briefwechsel mit Hedwig Büchting, edited by Dieter Lohmeier, *Schriften der Theodor-Storm-Gesellschaft*, 39 (1990): 26–45;

Theodor Storm – Klaus Groth: Briefwechsel, edited by Boy Hinrichs (Berlin: Schmidt, 1990).

Bibliographies:

Hans-Erich Teitge, ed., *Theodor Storm Bibliographie* (Berlin: Deutsche Staatsbibliothek, 1967);

Kurt Meyer, "Storm Bibliographie: 1967–1973," *Schriften der Theodor-Storm-Gesellschaft*, 23 (1974): 72–81;

Meyer, "Storm Bibliographie: Neuerscheinungen," *Schriften der Theodor-Storm-Gesellschaft*, 24 (1975): 105–108;

Margarethe Draheim, "Storm Bibliographie: Neuerscheinungen," *Schriften der Theodor-Storm-Gesellschaft*, 25 (1976) 79–81; 26 (1977): 87–89; 27 (1978): 66–68; 28 (1979): 132–134; 29 (1980): 73–76; 30 (1981): 89–91; 31 (1982): 69–72; 32 (1983): 79–83; 33 (1984): 86–88; 34 (1985): 77–80; 35 (1986): 55–59; 36 (1987): 91–96;

Elke Jacobsen, "Storm Bibliographie: Neuerscheinungen," *Schriften der Theodor-Storm-Gesellschaft*, 38 (1989): 11–118; 39 (1990): 80–89; 40 (1991): 87–92.

Biographies:

Gertrud Storm, *Theodor Storm: Ein Bild seines Lebens*, 2 volumes (Berlin: 1912–1913);

Franz Stuckert, *Theodor Storm: Sein Leben und seine Welt* (Bremen: Schünemann, 1955);

Fritz Böttger, *Theodor Storm in seiner Zeit* (Berlin: Verlag der Nation, 1959).

References:

Arthur Tilo Alt, *Theodor Storm* (New York: Twayne, 1973);

Lore Amlinger, "Von 'Immensee' zum 'Schimmelreiter': Zur Entwicklung des Stormschen Helden," *Schriften der Theodor-Storm-Gesellschaft*, 38 (1989): 63–72;

David Artiss, *Theodor Storm: Studies in Ambivalence. Symbol and Myth in his Narrative Fiction* (Amsterdam: Benjamins, 1978);

Ralf Bartoleit, "Das Verhältnis von Ferdinand Tönnies' 'Gemeinschaft und Gesellschaft' zu Theodor Storm's Erzählwerk: Über die Fragwürdigkeit einer naheliegenden Interpretation," *Schriften der Theodor-Storm-Gesellschaft*, 36 (1987): 69–82;

Moritz Baßler, "Die ins Haus heimgeholte Transzendenz": Theodor Storms Liebesauffassung vor dem Hintergrund der Philosophie Ludwig Feuerbachs," *Schriften der Theodor-Storm-Gesellschaft*, 36 (1987): 43–60;

Clifford Bernd, *Theodor Storm's Craft of Fiction* (Chapel Hill: University of North Carolina Press, 1966);

Georg Bollenbeck, "Theodor Storm, verengter Horizont und vertiefter Blick," *Schriften der Theodor-Storm-Gesellschaft*, 39 (1990): 15–25;

Robert M. Browning, "Association and Disassociation in Storm's Novellen: A Study on the Meaning of the Frame," *PMLA*, 66 (June 1951): 381–404;

Ernst Feise, "Theodor Storm's 'Aquis submersus,'" in his *Xenion: Themes, Forms and Ideas in German Literature* (Baltimore: Johns Hopkins University Press, 1950), pp. 226–240;

Günter Häntzschel, "Storm als Anthologie-Herausgeber," *Schriften der Theodor-Storm-Gesellschaft*, 38 (1989): 39–51;

Lee B. Jennings, "Shadows from the Void in Theodor Storm's Novellen," *Germanic Review*, 37 (May 1962): 174–189;

Karl Ernst Laage, *Theodor Storm: Studien zu seinem Leben und Werk mit einem Handschriftenkatalog* (Berlin: Schmidt, 1985);

Ernst Loeb, *Faust ohne Transzendenz: Theodor Storms Schimmelreiter* (Saint Louis: Washington University Press, 1963);

Thomas Mann, "Theodor Storm: 1930," in his *Adel des Geistes: Sechzehn Versuche zum Problem der Humanität* (Stockholm: Bermann-Fischer, 1945), pp. 518–542;

Allen McCormick, *Theodor Storm's Novellen: Essays on Literary Technique* (Chapel Hill: University of North Carolina Press, 1964);

Eckart Pastor, *Die Sprache der Erinnerung: Zu den Novellen von Theodor Storm* (Frankfurt am Main: Athenäum, 1988);

Willy Schumann, "Theodor Storm und Thomas Mann: Gemeinsames und Unterschiedliches," *Schriften der Theodor-Storm-Gesellschaft*, 13 (1964): 28–44;

Friedrich Sengle, "Storms lyrische Eigenleistung," *Schriften der Theodor-Storm-Gesellschaft*, 28 (1979): 9-33;

Walter Silz, "Theodor Storm: Three Poems," *Germanic Review*, 42 (November 1967): 293–300;

Silz, "Theodor Storm's *Schimmelreiter*," *PMLA*, 61 (September 1946): 762–783;

Silz, "Theodor Storm's "Über die Heide," in *Studies in German Literature of the Nineteenth and Twentieth Centuries: Festschrift for Frederic E. Coenen*, edited by Siegfried Mews (Chapel Hill: University of North Carolina Press, 1970), pp. 105–110;

Lloyd Wedberg, *The Theme of Loneliness in Theodor Storm's Novellen* (The Hague: Mouton, 1964);

Benno von Wiese, "Theodor Storm: Hans und Heinz Kirch," in his *Die deutsche Novelle von Goethe bis Kafka*, volume 2 (Düsseldorf: Bagel, 1964), pp. 216–235;

Elmer Wooley, *Studies in Theodor Storm* (Bloomington: Indiana University Press, 1943);

Wooley, *Theodor Storm's World in Pictures* (Bloomington: Indiana University Press, 1954).

Papers:

Theodor Storm's papers are in the Schleswig-Holsteinische Landesbibliothek (Schleswig-Holstein Provincial Library), Kiel; and the Storm-Haus, Husum.

Richard Wagner

(22 May 1813 – 13 February 1883)

Gerda Jordan
University of South Carolina

BOOKS: *Rienzi, der Letzte der Tribunen: Große tragische
Oper in fünf Akten* (Dresden: Meser, 1842);
translated by Oliver Huchel as *Rienzi, a Dramatic Poem* (New York: Crowell, 1914);

*Der fliegende Holländer: Romantische Oper in drei Aufzü-
gen* (Dresden: Meser, 1843); translated by J.
Troutbeck as *The Flying Dutchman* (London:
Novello, Ewer, 1877);

*Tannhäuser und der Sängerkrieg auf Wartburg: Großer
romantische Oper in drei Akten* (Dresden: Meser,
1845); translated by John P. Jackson as *Tannhäuser and the Tournament of Song on the Wartburg*
(London & New York: 1875);

Die Kunst und die Revolution (Leipzig: Wigand, 1849);

Die Wibelungen: Weltgeschichte aus der Sage (Leipzig:
Wigand, 1850);

Das Kunstwerk der Zukunft (Leipzig: Wigand, 1850);

*Drei Operndichtungen nebst einer Mittheilung an seine
Freunde als Vorwort* (Leipzig: Breitkopf & Härtel, 1851);

Ein Theater in Zürich (Zurich: Schulthess, 1851);

Zwei Briefe (Leipzig: Matthes, 1852);

Lohengrin: Romantische Oper in drei Akten (Leipzig:
Breitkopf & Härtel, 1852); translated anonymously as *Lohengrin: A Romantic Opera* (London: Hope, 1857);

Oper und Drama, 3 volumes (Leipzig: Weber, 1852)
– comprises volume 1, *Die Oper und das Wesen
der Musik;* volume 2, *Das Schauspiel und das
Wesen der dramatischen Dichtkunst;* volume 3,
Dichtkunst und Tonkunst im Drama der Zukunft;

Ein Brief über Franz Liszt's symphonische Dichtungen
(Leipzig: Kahnt, 1857);

Tristan und Isolde (Leipzig: Breitkopf & Härtel,
1859); translated by H. and F. Corder as *Tristan and Isolde: Lyric Drama in 3 Acts* (Leipzig:
Breitkopf & Härtel, 1889); translated by Stewart Robb as *Tristan and Isolde* (New York: Dutton, 1965);

*"Zukunftsmusik": Brief an einen französischen Freund als
Vorwort zu einer Prosa-Übersetzung seiner Operndichtungen* (Leipzig: Weber, 1861); translated

*Richard Wagner in 1860 (photograph by Petit
et Trinquart, Paris)*

by Edward Dannreuther as *The Music of the
Future: A Letter* (London: Scott, 1873; New
York: Schirmer, 1873);

Die Meistersinger von Nürnberg (Mainz: Schott, 1862);
translated by Jackson as *The Master-Singers of
Nuremberg* (New York: Jackson, 1892);

Das Wiener Hofoperntheater (Vienna: Gerold, 1863);

*Der Ring des Nibelungen: Ein Bühnenfestspiel für 3 Tage
und 1 Vorabend* (Leipzig: Weber, 1863) – com-
prises *Das Rheingold, Die Walküre, Siegfried, Göt-
terdämmerung;* translated by Alfred Forman as
*The Nibelung's Ring: A Festival Play for Three
Days and a Fore-evening* (London & Mainz:
Schott, 1877) – comprises *The Rhinegold, The
Valkyrie, Siegfried, The Twilight of the Gods;*

Bericht an Seine Majestät den König Ludwig II. von Bayern über eine in München zu errichtende deutsche Musikschule (Munich: Kaiser, 1865);

Deutsche Kunst und deutsche Politik (Leipzig: Weber, 1868);

Herr Eduard Devrient und sein Styl: Eine Studie über dessen "Erinnerungen an Felix Mendelssohn-Bartholdy," as Wilhelm Drach (Munich: Fritzsch, 1869);

Das Judenthum in der Musik (Leipzig: Weber, 1869);

Über das Dirigiren (Leipzig: Kahnt, 1870); translated by Dannreuther as *On Conducting: A Treatise on Style in the Execution of Classical Music* (London: Reeves, 1887);

Beethoven (Leipzig: Fritzsch, 1870); translated by Albert L. Parsons as *Beethoven* (Indianapolis: Benham, 1872);

Über die Aufführung des Bühnenfestspieles "Der Ring des Nibelungen": Eine Mittheilung und Aufforderung an die Freunde seiner Kunst (Leipzig: Fritzsch, 1871);

Über die Bestimmung der Oper: Ein akademischer Vortrag (Leipzig: Fritzsch, 1871);

Lehr- und Wanderjahre: Autobiographisches (Leipzig: Wagner, 1871);

Gesammelte Schriften und Dichtungen, 10 volumes (Leipzig: Fritzsch, 1871–1883);

Über Schauspieler und Sänger (Leipzig: Fritzsch, 1872);

Über Staat und Religion (Leipzig: Fritzsch, 1873);

Parsifal: Ein Bühnenweihfestspiel (Mainz: Schott, 1877); translated by H. L. and F. Corder as *Parsifal: A Festival Drama* (Mainz: Schott, 1879); translated by Forman as *Parsifal* (London: Macmillan, 1899);

Offener Brief an Ernst von Weber, Verfasser der "Folterkammern der Wissenschaft": Über die Vivisection (Berlin & Leipzig: Schneider, 1880);

Was ist Deutsch? (Berlin, 1881);

Lebens-Bericht (Leipzig: Schlömp, 1884);

Entwürfe, Gedanken, Fragmente: Aus nachgelassenen Papieren zusammengestellt (Leipzig: Breitkopf & Härtel, 1885);

Jesus von Nazareth: Ein dichterischer Entwurf aus dem Jahre 1848 (Leipzig: Breitkopf & Härtel, 1887);

Die Feen (Mannheim, 1888); translated by A. V. Sinclair as *The Fairies: A Romantic Opera in Three Acts* (New York, 1894; London, 1906);

Nachgelassene Schriften und Dichtungen (Leipzig: Breitkopf & Härtel, 1895);

Gedichte (Berlin: Grote, 1905);

Entwürfe zu: Die Meistersinger von Nürnberg, Tristan und Isolde, Parsifal, edited by Hans von Wolzogen (Leipzig: Siegel, 1907);

Aus Richard Wagners Pariser Zeit: Aufsätze und Kunstberichte des Meisters aus Paris 1841, 2 volumes, edited by Richard Sternfeld (Berlin: Deutsche Bücherei, 1907);

Mein Leben, 2 volumes (Munich: Bruckmann, 1911); translated anonymously as *My Life* (New York: Dodd, Mead, 1939);

Sämtliche Schriften und Dichtungen: Volksausgabe, 16 volumes (Leipzig: Breitkopf & Härtel, 1911–1914);

Gesammelte Schriften und Dichtungen, 10 volumes, edited by Wolfgang Golther (Berlin: Bong, 1914);

Das Liebesverbot oder Die Novize von Palermo (Leipzig: Breitkopf & Härtel, 1922); translated by Edward Dent as *The Ban on Love: Text after Shakespeare's "Measure for Measure"* (Leipzig: Breitkopf & Härtel, 1922);

Die Hauptschriften, edited by Ernst Bucken (Leipzig: Kroner, 1937);

Sämtliche Werke, edited by Carl Dahlhaus (Mainz: Schott, 1970);

Die Musikdramen, edited by Joachim Kaiser (Hamburg: Hoffmann & Campe, 1971);

Das braune Buch: Tagebuchaufzeichnungen, 1865–1882, edited by Joachim Bergfeld (Zurich: Atlantis, 1975); translated by George Bird as *The Diary of Richard Wagner 1865–1882: The Brown Book* (London & New York: Cambridge University Press, 1980).

Editions in English: *Art, Life and Theories,* edited and translated by Edward L. Burlingame (New York: Holt, 1875) – comprises "Autobiography," "The Love-Veto, the Story of the First Performance of an Opera," "A Pilgrimage to Beethoven," "An End in Paris," "Der Freischütz in Paris," "The Music of the Future," "Account of the Production of 'Tannhäuser' in Paris," "The Purpose of the Opera," "Musical Criticism," "Extracts of a Letter," "The Legend of the Nibelungen," "The Opera-House at Bayreuth";

Prose Works, 8 volumes, translated by William Ashton Ellis (London: Kegan Paul, Trench, Trubner, 1893–1899; New York: Broude, 1966) – comprises volume 1, *The Art-Work of the Future;* volume 2, *Opera and Drama;* volume 3, *The Theatre;* volume 4, *Art and Politics;* volume 5, *Actors and Singers;* volume 6, *Religion and Art;* volume 7, *In Paris and Dresden;* volume 8, *Posthumous;*

Judaism in Music: Unabridged English Translation, translated anonymously (Hollywood, Cal.: Sons of Liberty, 1966; London: Britons, 1966);

Wagner's Aesthetics, translated by Derek Fogg and Jim Ford, edited by Carl Dahlhaus (Bayreuth: Edition Musica, 1972);

Wagner Writes from Paris: Stories, Essays and Articles by the Young Composer, edited and translated by Robert L. Jacobs and Geoffrey Skelton (London: Allen & Unwin, 1973; New York: Day, 1973);

Stories and Essays, edited by Charles Osborne (La Salle, Ill.: Library Press, 1973; London: Owen, 1973);

The Ring, translated by Andrew Porter (Folkstone, U.K.: Dawson, 1976); republished as *The Ring of the Nibelung* (New York: Norton, 1977).

SELECTED PERIODICAL PUBLICATIONS –
UNCOLLECTED: "Über deutsche Musik," *Revue et Gazette Musicale* (12 July 1840); (26 July 1840);

"Der Virtuose und der Künstler," *Revue et Gazette Musicale* (18 October 1840);

"Eine Pilgerfahrt zu Beethoven," *Revue et Gazette Musicale* (19 November 1840); (22 November 1840); (29 November 1840); (3 December 1840);

"Ein Ende in Paris," *Revue et Gazette Musicale* (31 January 1841): 65–68; (7 February 1841): 83–84; (11 February 1841): 91–94;

"Der Künstler und die Öffentlichkeit," *Revue et Gazette Musicale* (1 April 1841): 203–204;

"Ein glücklicher Abend," *Revue et Gazette Musicale* (24 October 1841); (7 November 1841);

"Autobiographische Skizze," *Zeitung für die Elegante Welt* (1 February 1843); (8 February 1843);

"Kunst und Klima," *Deutsche Monatsschrift für Politik, Wissenschaft, Kunst und Leben,* 4 (23 February 1850): 1–11;

"Über die Benennung *Musikdrama,*" *Musikalisches Wochenblatt,* 46 (8 November 1872): 719–721;

"Modern," *Bayreuther Blätter,* 3 (April 1878): 59–63;

"Publikum und Popularität," *Bayreuther Blätter,* no. 4 (April 1878): 85–92; no. 6 (June 1878): 171–177; no. 8 (August 1878): 213–222;

"Über das Dichten und Komponieren," *Bayreuther Blätter,* no. 7 (July 1878): 185–196;

"Das Publikum in Zeit und Raum," *Bayreuther Blätter,* no. 10 (October 1878): 277–285;

"Ein Rückblick auf die Bühnenfestspiele des Jahres 1876," *Bayreuther Blätter,* no. 12 (December 1878): 341–351;

"Wollen wir hoffen?," *Bayreuther Blätter,* no. 5 (May 1879): 121–135;

"Über die Anwendung der Musik auf das Drama," *Bayreuther Blätter,* no. 11 (November 1879): 313–325;

"Religion und Kunst," *Bayreuther Blätter,* no. 10 (October 1880): 269–300;

"Heldentum und Christentum," *Bayreuther Blätter,* no. 9 (September 1881): 249–258.

Almost a hundred years after Richard Wagner's death the noted musicologist Marcel Prawy wrote, "Richard Wagner wurde am 22. Mai 1813 geboren und ist niemals gestorben" (Richard Wagner was born on May 22, 1813, and he never died). Ten of his thirteen musical-dramatic works are still performed to packed houses in Europe and America; he is now as much as ever a topic of controversy. He has been called both a "monster" and "the ventriloquist of God." During his life the debate was about the outlandish claims he made for his works and for music and drama in general, about his never-before-heard musical idiom, about his political views, about his extravagances, and about his sexual relationships. Since then his alleged anti-Semitism has been seen as the root of that of Adolf Hitler, who adored Wagner's music but understood none of his dramas; if he had, he would have banned them from the stage. Today there is controversy over the productions of Wagner's works that update them from the distant past, where Wagner set them, to the present or the future: for example, the thirteenth-century minnesinger Tannhäuser has been depicted as a televangelist, and *Der Ring des Nibelungen* (1863; translated as *The Nibelung's Ring,* 1877) has been set in a post-nuclear-war age.

One of the three or four original geniuses in music history, Wagner left to the world an innovative theater in Bayreuth, where the festival dedicated to him is attended every year by fifty-seven thousand music lovers while around two hundred thousand applicants for tickets are turned down. The ninth child of the police official Karl Friedrich Wagner and Johanna Rosine Wagner, née Pätz, Wagner was born in Leipzig on 22 May 1813. Saxony was then being reoccupied by Napoleon, whose fortunes were crumbling elsewhere. The battle of Leipzig in October 1813 was the indirect cause of Karl Friedrich Wagner's death: he succumbed to typhus in November because the hospitals were overcrowded with wounded and could not care for him. His friend Ludwig Geyer, an actor and painter, devoted himself to the Wagner children and to Johanna, whom he married on 28 August 1814 – a bit too soon after Karl Friedrich Wagner's death and yet not soon enough, for Wagner's half sister Cäcilie was born six months after the wedding. There is no foundation for the popular speculation that Geyer may have been Wagner's father.

The relative stability provided by Geyer in Dresden, where he was court player and supplemented his income with painting, lasted only until 1821, when he died of tuberculosis. Wagner was put with relatives in various places before he rejoined his family in Dresden and was enrolled in the Kreuzschule in December 1822. He revealed no talent for anything other than schoolboy pranks until the day he wrote down the music to Carl Maria von Weber's *Lützows wilde Jagd* (Lutzow's Wild Hunt, 1814) after hearing it once. He wrote a gory play about knights for a puppet theater Geyer had given him; he also used it to stage his idol Weber's opera *Der Freischütz* (The Shooting Contest, 1821). Yet piano lessons led nowhere, and at school Wagner neglected everything except the study of Greek mythology, Greek history, and the works of William Shakespeare. He suffered from facial erysipelas, which was to plague him all his life. As a teenager he became an insatiable reader. In 1827 his first political opinion was shaped when he developed an admiration for the Burschenschaften, the student fraternities founded in opposition to the restraints the German Federation was exerting on the German states. In the same year he embarked on a tragedy inspired by Johann Wolfgang von Goethe's play *Götz von Berlichingen* (1773) and the works of Shakespeare. Years later he remarked about this first dramatic attempt, "Leubald und Adelaide," that since all the characters had died by the middle of the play he had to make them return as ghosts in order to bring about a conclusion. During the three months of writing he had neglected his schoolwork to such an extent that he could not return to the Kreuzschule. He rejoined his family, then residing again in Leipzig, and was enrolled at the Nicolaischule with the loss of one grade. His uncle Adolf Wagner, a scholar, translator, poet, and literary critic, introduced him to Dante and the German classics and shared his love for Shakespeare. But he disapproved of "Leubald und Adelaide," and Wagner came to the conclusion that the play needed music similar to that which Ludwig van Beethoven had provided for Goethe's *Egmont* (1788) in 1810. He contracted the first of the many debts he would incur during his life when he kept a book on composition methods he had borrowed from a lending library for so long that he could not pay the fee with his allowance. He took music lessons in secret but found them dry and in opposition to his idea that

music springs from words, as E. T. A. Hoffmann had claimed for opera in *Die Serapions-Brüder* (1819–1821; translated as *The Serapion Brothers,* 1886–1892). His reading of Hoffmann's work also acquainted him with the earliest source for his *Die Meistersinger von Nürnberg* (1862; translated as *The Master-Singers of Nuremberg,* 1892), Johann Christian Wagenseil's *Von der Meister-Singer holdseligen Kunst* (Of the Mastersingers' Delightful Art, 1697); with the Wartburg poetic circle; and with the legendary characters Heinrich von Ofterdingen, Parzival, and Clinschor. This material was much more exciting than the dull lessons in harmony. In 1829 he began his own unsystematic musical studies by immersing himself in Beethoven scores. A performance of *Fidelio* (1805) with the singing actress Wilhelmine Schröder-Devrient convinced him even more that ideal music can exist only in combination with words. Meanwhile, he honed his skills by writing piano scores for Beethoven's Ninth Symphony and Haydn's 103rd, an overture to Friedrich Schiller's *Die Braut von Messina* (1803; translated as *The Bride of Messina,* 1837), an overture in C major, and one in B-flat major that was actually performed and stunned the audience because of a recurring drumbeat every fifth bar. In 1831 Wagner enrolled at the University of Leipzig, where he participated in student life in the taverns. In August 1832 he began taking instruction in composition from Theodor Weinlig, cantor at Saint Thomas Church in Leipzig; at the end of six months Weinlig declared that he could teach Wagner nothing more. Wagner's Overture in D minor was performed at the Gewandhaus, followed by his C-major symphony. Then he drafted the libretto for his first opera, "Die Hochzeit" (The Wedding), of which his sister Rosalie disapproved so heartily that all but a septet ended in the wastebasket. A new friend in Leipzig, Heinrich Laube, who later gained fame as director of the Burgtheater in Vienna, introduced Wagner to the Junges Deutschland (Young Germany) movement; Wagner embraced some of their ideals – the promotion of a united free Germany and the ousting of Austrian foreign minister Klemens Wenzel Nepomuk Lothar Metternich and his repressive policies – but rejected their debunking of his classical idols. Laube tried to interest him in composing music for his libretto *Koscinszko;* but Wagner even then could not set another's words to music, and he was at work on a libretto of his own based on Carlo Gozzi's *La donna serpente* (The Serpent Lady, 1792). In this tale a mortal marries a beautiful fairy; after years of wedded bliss he asks a forbidden question, upon which she, their children, and the castle disappear. The hero undergoes and fails a series of tests, but, with the help of magicians, spirits, his lyre, and song, he is reunited with his wife; they are now both immortal, redeemed from the troubled world through love. Wagner's first completed opera, *Die Feen* (1888; translated as *The Fairies,* 1894), was never staged during his lifetime. He had worked on it while filling a temporary position at the Würzburg theater as chorus master and jack-of-all-trades.

While he was trying to get this opera, which was in the tradition of German romanticism, produced, he turned toward an Italianate style. By the summer of 1834 he had designed the scenario for his second opera, *Das Liebesverbot* (1922; translated as *The Ban on Love,* 1922), based on Shakespeare's *Measure for Measure.* In sixteenth-century Palermo a German governor, Friedrich, is in charge of enforcing the moral laws. Friedrich closes the places of entertainment and condemns to death Claudio, who has loved a girl despite her parents' disapproval. Claudio's friend Luzio persuades Claudio's sister Isabella, a novice in the convent, to speak to the governor on her brother's behalf. Isabella bids farewell to her friend Marianne, who had entered the convent to forget her faithless lover – the governor himself. In a private audience with Friedrich, Isabella pleads for her brother; he is willing to show mercy, but at the price of her love. Horrified, she shouts the offer out of the window at the crowd below, but Friedrich informs her that he will deny everything. After a moment's despair she hits on an idea; she promises to spend the night with him after the upcoming carnival, then sends Marianne in her stead. The meeting of parties in masks takes place, and after a series of mix-ups, outbursts of jealousy, and accusations, three happy couples emerge: Friedrich and Marianne, Claudio and his beloved, and Isabella and Luzio.

In 1834 Wagner was offered the musical directorship of the Magdeburg theater company. He found the conditions there so bad that he declined the offer; but as he was leaving he met the actress Minna Planer. Smitten, he changed his mind. At Magdeburg he gained experience in conducting, staging, and mounting concerts. He completed the composition of *Das Liebesverbot* in January 1836; its production in March of that year was a failure. The theater closed for financial reasons shortly thereafter.

Wagner followed Minna to Königsberg (today Kaliningrad, Russia), where she was performing; they were married in November 1836. Her illegitimate daughter, Natalie, lived with them as her sis-

ter. Not long after their marriage Minna briefly ran off with another man after she and Wagner quarreled.

In April 1837 Wagner became musical director of the Königsberg theater; a better offer came from Riga, and the Wagners moved there in August. His conducting of the twenty-four-piece orchestra was highly praised. His reading at Riga included Heinrich Heine's "Aus den Memoiren des Herren von Schnabelewopski" (From the Memoirs of Mr. Schnabelewopski, 1835), containing the legend of the Flying Dutchman, and Edward Bulwer-Lytton's *Rienzi* (1835), about the fourteenth-century Italian hero Niccolò Cola di Rienzo, whose ambition had been to restore Rome to its old glory. Wagner wrote *Rienzi, der Letzte der Tribunen* (Rienzi, the Last of the Tribunes, 1842; translated as *Rienzi, a Dramatic Poem,* 1914) in the summer of 1838.

The opera begins with the attempted abduction of Rienzi's sister Irene by the noble Orsini faction. The son of the rival faction, Adriano Colonna, saves Irene and falls in love with her. The feuding nobles have endangered the peace of Rome, and the people agree with the papal notary Rienzi to ban both the Orsinis and the Colonnas from the city. Rienzi wins Adriano over to the people's cause. The grateful populace would name him emperor, but he chooses the title "tribune." The nobles are allowed to return; they bow down to Rienzi, but they are plotting his death. Rienzi receives ambassadors, whom he offends with the declaration that a united Italy should have a say in the election of the Holy Roman emperor. During a festive dance Orsini tries to stab Rienzi. The nobles are arrested, tried by a quickly assembled court of justice, and condemned, but Rienzi gives in to the pleas of Adriano and Irene and pardons them. They persist in their enmity toward Rienzi, arm themselves, and are about to attack. Rienzi calls the people to arms and promises no more pardons. The Romans go off to fight, returning victorious with the corpses of the leaders of both families. Adriano vows revenge for his father's death and incites the people into opposition. Rienzi and Irene are isolated in their house. As the mob advances, Adriano attempts to pull Irene out of danger. But firebrands are thrown, the house catches fire, and Rienzi, Irene, and Adriano perish.

Because of a previous arrangement by the theater director in Riga, Wagner was replaced in 1839. He decided to go to Paris. Biographers have made much of the Wagners' adventurous flight from creditors in Riga; the facts are that a friend advised Wagner not to pay off all his debts but to keep a financial cushion for Paris; he could not get a passport without a public notice, which would have attracted the creditors' attention, appearing in the newspaper. Therefore, the Wagners sneaked across the border. During their voyage a storm in the Skagerrak brought the legend of the Flying Dutchman back to Wagner's mind. The Wagners arrived in Paris on 9 September 1839.

Wagner made friends in Paris, but they were uninfluential and just as impecunious as he. Laube came in November and introduced him to Heine, who became his literary model. A theater that had accepted *Das Liebesverbot* for staging went bankrupt. Laube obtained a small subsidy for Wagner from Leipzig, and Wagner did hackwork for music journals. From 1840 and 1841 date the seven essaylike short stories he titled "Ein deutscher Musiker in Paris" (A German Musician in Paris). They are connected by a fictional young musician, obviously based on Wagner himself. The first story, "Eine Pilgerfahrt zu Beethoven" (translated as "A Pilgrimage to Beethoven," 1875), describes the young musician's hike to Vienna to meet the great man. Beethoven becomes the mouthpiece of Wagner's emerging ideas about music drama: he dislikes his own opera, *Fidelio,* because it does not conform to what music drama should be; there should be no division into arias, duets, trios, and the like. But no one nowadays would go to see a true music drama, and its creator would be considered a fool. The human voice must be regarded as an instrument, essential to utter the inner workings of the human heart and supplemental to the instruments of the orchestra. But where to find the poetry? In the second story, "Ein Ende in Paris" (translated as "An End in Paris," 1875), the young man comes to Paris filled with hope, knocks at closed doors, and literally starves to death in an antechamber because no one is interested in new ideas. Before he dies he confesses his — that is, Wagner's — credo to a friend: he believes in God, Wolfgang Amadeus Mozart, Beethoven, the Holy Ghost, the truth of the one indivisible art, and in a Last Judgment that would condemn all those who dared to exploit this chaste and noble art for the sake of sensual pleasure. In "Ein glücklicher Abend" (A Happy Evening) the young musician's friend remembers a conversation they had had about the value of program music. The other four pieces in the collection are critical essays a friend claims to have found in the papers of the musician. "Über deutsches Musikwesen" (On German Music) makes the observation that opera in Germany is really an import; that with the exceptions of the choral works of the great Johann Sebastian Bach and Protestant hymns, Germans have produced more instrumental music because it met the innate need of the people. Opera came to Germany from Italy; then, with Mozart's truly German *Die Zauberflöte* (The Magic Flute, 1791) and Weber's *Freischütz,* the German operatic repertoire seemed exhausted. The French influence on the German operatic scene is to be welcomed, for the two nations complement each other. "Der Virtuose und der Künstler" (The Virtuoso and the Artist) treats the preference by French audiences for the virtuoso over the true artist, and the beauty of the music goes unnoticed. "Der Künstler und die Öffentlichkeit" (The Artist and the Public) says that the artist exposes his work to the public to communicate, not for material success. In "Rossini's *Stabat Mater*" Wagner makes fun of the values of the Paris audience who felt cheated when they were offered Mozart's *Requiem* instead of the piece by Gioacchino Rossini they had expected.

Life for the Wagners in Paris was one of poverty and a daily struggle for existence, on the one hand; on the other hand, it was a time of development for Wagner. Among his readings were Pierre-Joseph Proudhon's *Qu'est-ce que la propriété?* (What Is Property?, 1840), precipitations of which are to be found in *Der Ring des Nibelungen;* the just-published *Das Wesen des Christentums* (1842; translated as *The Essence of Christianity,* 1854), by Ludwig Feuerbach; Heine's "Tannhäuser, eine Legende" (1837); and Professor C. T. L. Lukas's "Über den Krieg von Wartburg" (On the Wartburg War, 1838), which gave him material for *Tannhäuser und der Sängerkrieg auf Wartburg* (1845; translated as *Tannhäuser and the Tournament of Song on the Wartburg,* 1875) and also contains the legend of Lohengrin. In June 1841 *Rienzi* was accepted by the Dresden theater, but its preparation dragged on. One reason for the delay was censorship: Wagner had to change the word *päpstlich* (papal) to *römisch* (Roman) by order of the Catholic Saxon court, for example. Wagner became anxious to return to Dresden.

Before departing from Paris he finished composing the music for *Der fliegende Holländer* (1843; translated as *The Flying Dutchman,* 1877); he had completed the libretto in May 1841. Heine's story in "Aus den Memoiren des Herren von Schnabelewopski" had been preceded by other versions of the Scottish legend in dramatic form; the redemption of the Dutchman through the love of a faithful woman was new in Heine's work, where it is treated in rather tongue-in-cheek fashion. Wagner takes the theme seriously. Long ago a captain had sworn that nothing would stop him from sailing around a cape; Satan heard him and punished him by condemning

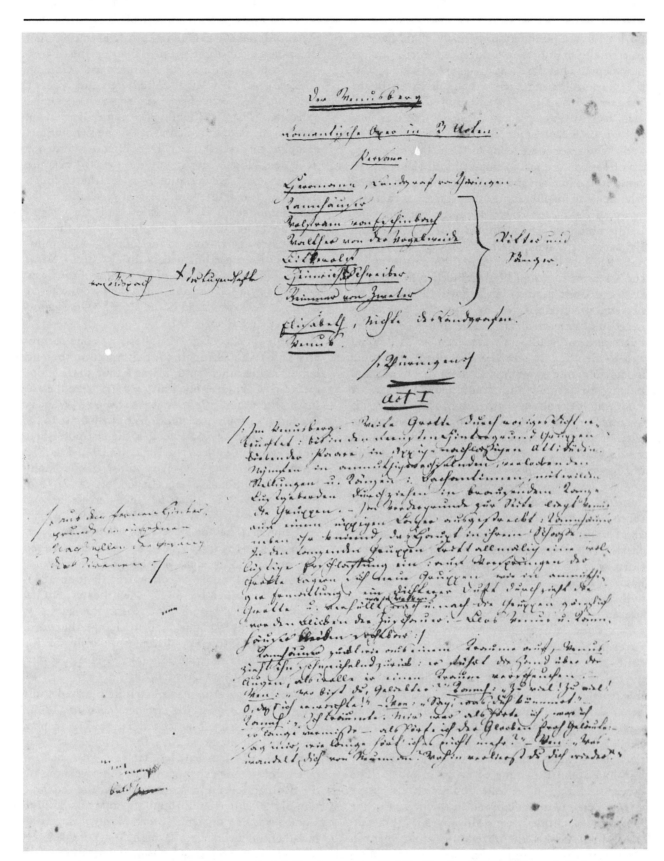

First page of the manuscript for the prose sketch for Tannhäuser, *then titled "Der Venusberg" (Richard Wagner Archive)*

him to sail on eternally. Every seven years he is permitted to come ashore to search for a faithful woman whose love can save him from this fate, but the search is always in vain. When the opera opens a seven-year period has ended; the Dutchman steps on land and meets the Norwegian captain Daland. He impresses Daland with his gold and jewels, and Daland invites him to his home as a possible son-in-law. Daland's daughter Senta has long been fascinated by the legend of the Dutchman, and when she sees him at her threshold, her empathy turns to love. The Dutchman is attracted to her, but he is unsure whether what he feels is love or longing for salvation. Senta, committed to saving the Dutchman's soul, refuses the attentions of Erik, who had taken it for granted that she belongs to him. The Dutchman overhears their conversation; he believes that Senta is unfaithful, and he leaves. Senta throws herself off a cliff into the sea, faithful unto death; her action redeems the Dutchman. His ship sinks, and his and Senta's transfigured shapes ascend to heaven in the rising sun. This work was the first manifestation of Wagner's obsession with the redemptive power of a woman's love.

In *Der fliegende Holländer* Wagner reveals himself as the master of the choral scene with his robust sailors, his chattering girls at their spinning wheels, and the ghostly crew of the Dutchman's ship. It is still an opera of set numbers, but Wagner begins the move away from this form by integrating the orchestral accompaniment of the recitatives into the dramatic action. Italian melodies are linked to the uncomprehending realists Daland and Erik, whereas Wagner's own musical idiom is given to Senta and the Dutchman. The fusion of dramatic and musical movement was something totally new, and the dramatic content was far superior to the general operatic fare of the time.

The premiere of *Rienzi* in Dresden on 20 October 1842 was an unmitigated success: after the five-hour performance the applause lasted for fifteen minutes. The premiere on 2 January 1843 of *Der fliegende Holländer,* however, found the Dresden audience unprepared. Wagner's evolution toward the "Wagnerian" sound was considered by critics such as Laube as a step backward; the composer Robert Schumann said that Wagner could not write four consecutive bars of beautiful music. Wagner made the mistake of responding to the criticism rather than relying on his inner conviction that he was right.

In February 1843 he accepted the post of royal court kapellmeister in Dresden. He was praised as the first conductor who read the composers' inten-

tions with care. The Dresden audiences were exposed to meticulously prepared performances and heard familiar works in an entirely new way.

He completed *Tannhäuser und der Sängerkrieg auf Wartburg* in May 1843. In addition to the material he knew from his Paris days he used Hoffmann's "Sängerkrieg auf der Wartburg" (Singers' Contest at the Wartburg), where he found the basis for his second act, and he was probably familiar with the collection of Thuringian legends edited by Ludwig Bechstein, *Die Sagen von Eisenach und der Wartburg, dem Hörselberg und Reinhardsbrunn* (The Sagas of Eisenach and the Wartburg, the Hörselberg, and Reinhardsbrunn, 1835), containing the song contest and placing Tannhäuser in the time and at the court of Hermann of Thuringia. Hermann's historical daughter-in-law Elisabeth became the love interest in Wagner's opera.

The minnesinger Tannhäuser leaves the court of the landgrave Hermann because his bold poetry was not appreciated there and wanders into the grotto of Venus in the Hörselberg. Venus lavishes her favors on him to the point that he becomes disgusted. He leaves, and she curses him. His fellow minnesingers at the Wartburg welcome their long-lost friend, and the landgrave's niece Elisabeth declares her love for him. She is to be the prize for the singer who can best define the nature of love. Wolfram von Eschenbach opens the contest with the assertion that pure love is a distant bliss one must not touch. Tannhäuser disagrees: the full enjoyment of love makes it endless, and that is its true nature. Elisabeth is about to applaud but holds back when no one else does. Walther von der Vogelweide and the others agree with Wolfram that touching the object of love would render it worthless. Tannhäuser persists in his view, and the heated argument is about to turn into a fight when Tannhäuser blurts out his secret: to find out what love really is, he says, they should visit Venus, as he has. Everyone is shocked; Elisabeth is concerned for her beloved's soul. It is decided that he should join a group of pilgrims who are traveling to Rome and ask forgiveness from the pope. Months pass; the pilgrims return, but Tannhäuser is not among them. Elisabeth, heartbroken, prays for him and dies. Tannhäuser returns and tells Wolfram of his painful experience in Rome: the pope had decreed that his sin was too great to be forgiven, that Tannhäuser's salvation was no more possible than that the staff in the pope's hand would grow leaves. There is nothing left for him but to return to Venus. Wolfram tells him that Elisabeth has gone to heaven to plead for him. As Tannhäuser sinks down and dies over her

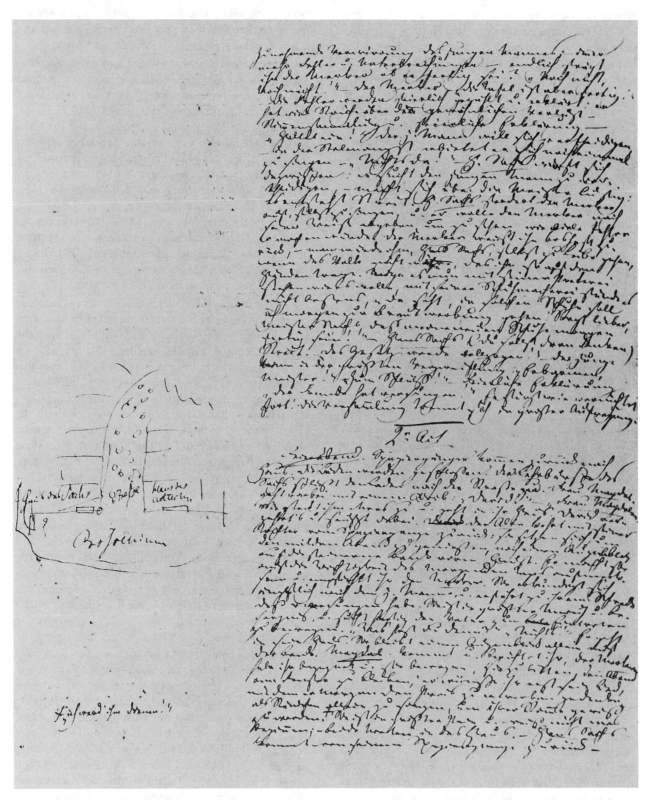

Third page of the manuscript, completed in 1845, for the prose sketch for Die Meistersinger von Nürnberg *(Richard Wagner Archive)*

bier, a young pilgrim carries in the pope's staff with freshly sprouted leaves. Once again a woman's selfless love has saved a man's soul.

It is generally believed that Venus and Elisabeth are the embodiments of sinful and pure love, respectively, the latter triumphing over the former; but Elisabeth displays a sensual love that is revealed by her impulse to applaud Tannhäuser's song and in her prayer asking forgiveness for her sinful desire. The work premiered in Dresden on 19 October 1845. Only from the third performance was it a success; Wagner's demand that acting be given priority over singing was rejected at first by the public. The *Tannhäuser* given nowadays is the modified "Paris" version, with an expanded overture and an abridged song contest. Wagner was never completely satisfied with the opera; shortly before he died, he said he still owed the world a *Tannhäuser*.

Beginning in 1844, Wagner, under the influence of August Röckel, his assistant kapellmeister, became increasingly interested in current events. Röckel had become a socialist and democrat during an extended stay in France and England, and he awakened Wagner's liberal political awareness. But a few years of feverish artistic activity were to go by before Wagner could think of any definite engagement in politics.

For a vacation at Marienbad in the summer of 1845 he supplied himself — against doctor's orders — with reading material: Georg Gottfried Gervinus's *Geschichte der poetischen Nationalliteratur der Deutschen* (History of German National Poetry, 1835–1842), Karl Joseph Simrock's 1842 translation of Wolfram von Eschenbach's thirteenth-century epics *Parzival* and *Titurel*, and the anonymous *Lohengrin* epic of 1260, edited by Joseph Görres (1813). At Marienbad he sketched the plot for *Die Meistersinger von Nürnberg* after reading about Hans Sachs in Gervinus's work and pulling from memory a street brawl he had witnessed in Nuremberg in 1835. Then he sketched out *Lohengrin* (1852; translated, 1857), finishing it in November. It and *Rienzi* are his only truly tragic works.

King Heinrich I is traveling in the German duchies in an effort to gather a force to fight the invading Magyars in the east. In Brabant he finds strife over the disappearance of the duke's heir, who has supposedly been murdered by his sister Elsa. Before he can recruit an army, Heinrich must sit in judgment. Upon Elsa's prayer for a defender of her innocence, Lohengrin appears, they fall in love, and he asks to marry her. She must agree never to ask whence he came. Lohengrin defeats Elsa's accuser, Friedrich von Telramund; his pagan

wife, Ortrud, gets revenge by persuading Elsa to ask the forbidden question. Lohengrin is forced to reveal that he is the son of the Grail King Parzival; having divulged this information, he cannot stay. Before he departs he restores Elsa's lost brother, whom Ortrud had turned into a swan. Wagner completed the score in April 1848, and the Dresden theater accepted the work for production. But Wagner had to wait thirteen years to see it performed.

The repercussions of the French revolution in 1848 stirred up unrest in Saxony. King Friedrich August II made concessions such as abolishment of feudal rights, institution of trial by jury, and a promise of electoral reforms. There were rumors that the subsidies for the theater would be cut; Wagner designed a plan for the theater's reorganization, but it was rejected. When the German National Assembly convened in May 1848 in Frankfurt, Wagner sent proposals for replacing the German Federation with the National Assembly, concluding an alliance with France, and abolishing states with fewer than six million inhabitants. He spoke out against the power of money and the privileges of the rich but did not embrace communism. For a time he was totally absorbed in politics; he expected the revolution to bring about a rebirth of art because of his belief that bad political conditions cannot produce decent artistic conditions. Later in 1848 he returned to a project he had begun two years before, a five-act play about Friedrich Barbarossa, the hero-emperor of the twelfth century. Studies into Barbarossa's background led him to the Nibelungen myth; he combined the two in *Die Wibelungen: Weltgeschichte aus der Sage* (The Wibelungs: World History from Myth, 1850), which is etymological and historical nonsense but represents a stage in the process of fermentation of the vast Nibelungen material he was digesting. A few weeks later he wrote another essay, "Der Nibelungen-Mythus, als Entwurf zu einem Drama" (The Nibelungen Myth as a Sketch for a Drama; published in his *Gesammelte Schriften und Dichtungen* [Collected Writings and Poetry], 1871–1883); it contains the basic material for what turned out to be the four dramas comprising *Der Ring des Nibelungen*. At this time the only planned drama was "Siegfrieds Tod" (Siegfried's Death), which was completed in November 1848. The changes it underwent before it became *Götterdämmerung* (translated as *The Twilight of the Gods*, 1877) in 1852 were made because of new insights; for example, absent in 1848 is what was to become the driving force in the entire *Der Ring des Nibelungen*, the power of love. Already apparent,

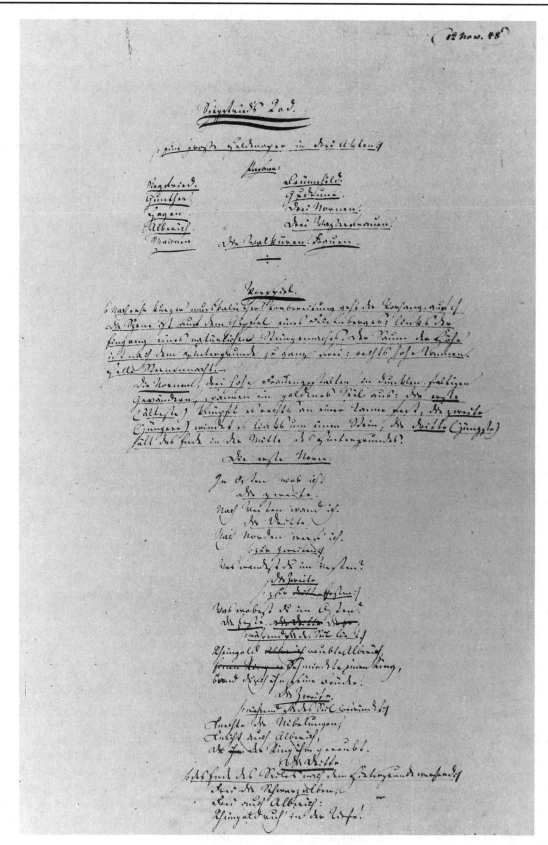

First page of the manuscript for "Siegfrieds Tod," completed in November 1848. Wagner later adapted "Siegfrieds Tod"
into Götterdämmerung *(Richard Wagner Archive).*

however, is Wagner's skillful interweaving of tales from various sources.

Another project that engrossed him for a while in this eventful year was a drama titled *Jesus von Nazareth;* conceived under the influence of Feuerbach and the theologian David Friedrich Strauß, it would have depicted Jesus as a man and a victim of the Roman world, dying a self-sacrificial death. Nothing more than plans, which were published in 1887, came of this idea. The court theater refused to produce *Lohengrin,* perhaps because it promoted German unity. Röckel beckoned with more-exciting and more-pressing needs: there were articles to be written, speeches to be made, and questions to be asked: why, after the promises made in March, did privilege still reign supreme? Why had an archconservative minister been appointed? A new friend entered Wagner's life: the Russian anarchist Mikhail Bakunin was in Dresden under an assumed name, and he and Wagner became inseparable.

In *Mein Leben* (1911; translated as *My Life,* 1939) Wagner downplays his participation in the events of May 1849; the autobiography was written by a liberal-turned-conservative for a conservative audience. In reality, he was in the midst of things. The Saxon parliament had adopted the new imperial constitution from Frankfurt, but the king had not; conservative government was completely restored in April 1849. From Prussia came assurance of aid in case of a revolt; the revolt started on 3 May. Wagner appropriated the private gun collection of his tenor, Joseph Tichatschek, to arm his friends against the Prussians. The throngs in the streets were fired on by the royal infantry, but the troops were stoned into retreat. The king fled the next day, and a provisional proconstitutional government was formed. Wagner saw his cause as trying to induce the royal army to join the revolutionaries in repelling the Prussians and forcing the king to accept the Frankfurt constitution. He had leaflets printed asking "Seid Ihr mit uns gegen fremde Truppen?" (Are you with us against foreign troops?) and handed them out to the soldiers, oblivious to the gunfire all around him. On 5 May he helped reinforce barricades and supervised the construction of new ones; then he climbed the steeple of the Kreuzkirche to observe troop movements. On 6 May the Prussians arrived. The provisional government prepared to leave, Wagner took Minna to safety in Chemnitz, and Röckel was arrested at the head of a platoon of insurgents. Wagner returned to Dresden on 8 May but saw that the situation was hopeless and took a coach to Freiberg. By a quirk of fate he missed the coach he had planned

to take to Chemnitz with the provisional government and thereby escaped the trap that had been set for them. Franz Liszt, an acquaintance from the Paris days, took him in at Weimar until a search warrant was issued for him, then helped him get to Paris and on to Zurich, where Minna joined him. A period of voracious reading and of reflection began.

Wagner's enormous need for communication resulted in his Zurich essays. Under the influence of his recent experiences and of the works of Proudhon and Feuerbach he wrote *Die Kunst und die Revolution* (Art and Revolution, 1849). He goes back to the origins of art as stemming from the needs of the Volk, its manifestation in ancient Greece, and its subsequent suffocation by Christianity. Art was suppressed until the Renaissance again brought forth honest, true art; but then it sold itself to industry and became entertainment. Along the way, Greek tragedy dissolved into its component parts — rhetoric, sculpture, painting, music, and so on — and no artist dares put them back together to create the "Gesamtkunstwerk" (total artwork) lest he starve. The artist has become a slave in the service of the rich and powerful, like the factory worker. Art must be reborn, but first humanity must undergo a revolution that restores brotherly love. Only love can understand beauty; only beauty shapes art. The prerequisite for love is freedom from worry, and that freedom is brought about by a social revolution.

In *Das Kunstwerk der Zukunft* (1850; translated as *The Art-Work of the Future* in Wagner's *Prose Works,* 1893–1899) Wagner says that the artwork of the future is to satisfy not desire for luxury, as art does now, but people's real needs. But only after the conditions that permit art as luxury are abolished can art go back to life and nature directly and create the total work of art. The artwork of the future must be all-inclusive; drama, however, will lead the other arts. The artist of the future will not be the poet or the painter or the actor or the sculptor, but the people. They will be driven by the Schiller-Beethoven sentiment "Freude! Seid umschlungen, Millionen!" (O joy! Be embraced, you millions!) because they have the need for the artwork in their hearts. The essay ends with a sketch for a three-act drama, "Wieland der Schmied" (Wieland the Smith), about a mythological smith who became inventive from a real need and designed wings that freed him from slavery. It remains a sketch.

In "Kunst und Klima" (Art and Climate, 1850) Wagner declares that the power that unites people and gives them true freedom is love. He gives a definition of love to which he adhered all his life and which is the basic motivation in *Der fliegende Holländer, Tannhäuser, Lohengrin, Der Ring des Nibelungen,* and *Parsifal* (1877; translated, 1879): "Die Mittlerin zwischen Kraft und Freiheit, die Erlöserin, ohne welche die Kraft Roheit, die Freiheit aber Willkür bleibt, ist somit – die Liebe; nicht jedoch jene geoffenbarte, von oben herein uns verkündete, gelehrte und anbefohlene, – deshalb auch nie wirklich gewordene – wie die christliche, sondern die Liebe, die aus der Kraft der unentstellten, wirklichen, menschlichen Natur hervorgeht; die in ihrem Ursprunge nichts anderes als die tätigste Lebensäußerung dieser Natur ist, die sich in reiner Freude am sinnlichen Dasein ausspricht, und, von der Geschlechtsliebe ausgehend, durch die Kindes-, Bruder- und Freundesliebe bis zur allgemeinen Menschenliebe fortschreitet" (The mediator between strength and freedom, the redeemer, without which strength remains barbarism and freedom remains whim, is love. Not, however, the love revealed and preached to us from above, taught and commanded to be practiced – for which reason it never became a reality – such as Christian love, but the love that proceeds from the strength of undistorted, real human nature, which in its origin is nothing other than nature's most active manifestation of life, expressed in the pure joy of sensuous existence, and, beginning with sexual love, continues by way of love for children, brotherly love, and love for friends onto general love for all mankind). The person who loves – his or her mate, children, friends, whomever – has the potential to love all humanity. The various manifestations of love are one and the same to Wagner. His villains are incapable of love; his heroes are all love.

One article of his Zurich days, "Das Judentum in der Musik" (Judaism in Music), published in the *Neue Zeitschrift für Musik* (New Journal for Music) in September 1850, stamped him as anti-Semitic. In the twentieth century the work has taken on a significance it did not have at the time, and it is mild compared to what Martin Luther, Voltaire, Immanuel Kant, and others had to say about Judaism. Wagner's frame of mind in 1850 was one of depression over the failure of the revolution; his exile; the general state of the theaters, which catered to entertainment and the superficial tastes of the monied public; his isolation from the production of his own work; and a dry spell in his creativity. What prompted the article was the phrase "hebräischer Kunstgeschmack" (Hebraic taste in art), used in the *Neueste Zeitschrift für Musik* (Latest Journal for Music) in connection with the success of Giacomo Meyerbeer's *Le Prophète* (The Prophet), a success

Wagner circa 1864–1865, oil portrait by Friedrich Pecht, commissioned by Wagner's patron, King Ludwig II of Bavaria. A bust of Ludwig can be seen in the upper right corner (Metropolitan Museum of Art, New York).

Meyerbeer had insured by bribing the critics. Wagner was outraged when the public hailed this shallow work, which was so unlike his own efforts. He says that Jewish speech, mannerisms, and interests are alien. That Jews deal mainly in money is not their fault but that of the Christians, but they have become the kings of creditors and will remain so as long as money is in power. The Jew is an outsider, yet he dictates our public tastes. He has no roots in our culture. He may be able to imitate our art, but he cannot create it; he cannot compose from an inner need because music is a luxury to him. The formerly noble and sublime melodies of the synagogue have become gargling, yodeling chatter that sneaks into his compositions along with the superficialities of ours, which he mistakes for their essence. An example is the talented and well-educated Felix Mendelssohn-Bartholdy, whose music does not affect the soul deeply; he is at his best when he melancholically seems to recognize his shortcomings. The "famous Jewish opera composer" – Wagner unmistakably means Meyerbeer – caters to the tastes of a superficial public that seeks relief from boredom, and he deceives it with another kind of boredom: his operas. At the bottom of all this is the hopelessness of our artistic period: the public makes no demands, for its inner core is dead; it is a wormy corpse, and outside forces have taken hold of it and will disintegrate it. Wagner mentions Heine admiringly because Heine mocked the hollowness of modern poetry; but he, too, fell prey to self-deception. Ludwig Börne has Wagner's full respect because Börne set being human above all else and thus stopped being an outsider. He did so with pain and suffering, setting an example of how the distinction between Jew and non-Jew can be eradicated through assimilation. Wagner calls on Jews to follow Börne's example, to stamp out the distinction and to become one with all humanity.

The longest of Wagner's theoretical works of the Zurich period is the three-volume *Oper und Drama* (1852; translated as *Opera and Drama* in Wagner's *Prose Works*, 1893-1899). It marks the point at which his future direction had become clear to him; its thesis is that the artwork of the future is possible in the combination of music and drama. After an outline of the development of opera he pinpoints the reasons why nothing new has been created in that genre recently: the means of expression, music, has become the end, and the end of expression, drama, has become the means. The total work of art – which is not, as some critics imagine, a Goethe novel read in an art gallery while Beethoven's Ninth Symphony is played – is the offspring of a marriage of poetry and music. The poet's intention is the sperm that fertilizes the music to produce the total work of art. In such a perfect union the orchestra assumes the language of the unspeakable, of innermost thought, that is, the musical expression carries poetic content. "melodische Momente" – what the musicologist Hans von Wolzogen would later name Leitmotiv – with poetic meaning are to serve as reminders or presages; they are direction pointers for the spectator's feelings throughout the drama. They complement the poetry and give coherence to the whole. Wagner had used musical themes attached to characters, objects, events, and emotions in *Rienzi, Der fliegende Holländer, Tannhäuser,* and *Lohengrin* to remind the listener of something or to signal an event. In the *Ring* cycle they take on an existence of their own and undergo changes. For example, the "nature" motif as a simple major chord represents life and growth, but in a minor key and turned upside down it implies death and decay. Another rule Wagner set for himself in *Oper und Drama* is that of finally abandoning a structure of separate "numbers": the drama must flow uninterrupted.

In a 144-page letter, "Eine Mitteilung an meine Freunde" (A Communication to My Friends), Wagner traces his development, his views, his in-

tentions, his hopes, and his visions of the future. His research on Barbarossa, he writes, led him to discover the Germanic idol Siegfried, in whom he found the true human being unencumbered by history or convention and unhampered by reflection. He had no thought of ever seeing "Siegfrieds Tod" performed until his friend Eduard Devrient pointed out its possibilities if the many obscure allusions to past events were clarified. This suggestion prompted a second drama, "Der junge Siegfried" (Young Siegfried), to precede "Siegfrieds Tod." Then plans emerged for another drama, *Die Walküre* (translated as *The Valkyrie,* 1877), to precede "Der junge Siegfried," and yet another, *Das Rheingold* (translated as *The Rhinegold,* 1877), as a prelude going back to the beginning of time, the four parts were to be performed on consecutive evenings. Since no existing theater can take on such a task, Wagner writes, he has no idea whether this dream will come true. In a footnote he says that he no longer writes operas; his works henceforth are music dramas. The letter was published in 1851 as the foreword to a collection that comprises *Der fliegende Holländer, Tannhäuser,* and *Lohengrin.*

During 1851-1852 Wagner rewrote "Der junge Siegfried" as *Siegfried;* he wrote *Die Walküre* and *Das Rheingold;* and he reworked "Siegfrieds Tod" into *Götterdämmerung.* When he was asked about the sources he used for this vast tetralogy, he listed ten; he drew the basic material from the Norse Eddas and Völsungensaga and used the others for added details. He invented little, and when he did it was always based on some hint in mythology. To illustrate the power that gold has over human beings he invested the ring, which in mythology has no such consequences, with the power to give its owner rule over everyone; this idea was taken from an otherwise unimportant mention in the nineteenth adventure of the *Nibelungenlied* of a little golden rod in Siegfried's hoard that had such power. Wagner combined and interwove the stories he found to serve his intentions: to tell the story of humanity from beginning to end, to show that love and the lust for power are mutually exclusive, to expose the complete range of the human psyche, to hold a mirror up to society, to show the destruction of the concept of the state through love, and to depict the voluntary negation of the will.

The prelude, *Das Rheingold,* establishes a loveless world where lust for power reigns. After wooing the Rhine Maidens in vain, the frustrated Nibelung dwarf Alberich curses love and steals the pure gold guarded by the maidens. His incapacity for love enables him to forge a ring from it, and with its magic he enslaves his fellow Nibelungs and forces them to amass a hoard of gold. With this treasure he plans to buy the world and be master of it. Meanwhile, the god Wotan stands at the beginning of his rule. His symbol of lawful power is the castle Walhalla, built by the giants Fasolt and Fafner, to whom he has promised Freia, the goddess of love and eternal youth, in payment. But Wotan has no intention of parting with Freia, and therewith with his own immortality, and has sent the demigod Loge in search of a substitute for Freia. Loge finds Alberich and his gold, and the giants agree to accept the gold in place of Freia; but until it is delivered, they take her hostage. Wotan and Loge descend to the netherworld, where they trick the boastful Alberich into changing himself into a toad to illustrate the power of his invention, the Tarnhelm (magic cap); they capture him and bring him up from the depths as their prisoner. Alberich relinquishes his hoard except for the ring, with which he can amass more gold. Wotan, infected by lust for power, snatches the ring from him. Alberich curses the ring and whoever may come to own it: everyone will be greedy for it; no one will enjoy it; everyone will be a slave to it. Alberich adds that he will not rest until he holds it again. Wotan is the ring's owner for only a short time; the giants will not release Freia unless the ring is part of the payment, and the primeval goddess Erda warns Wotan of a shameful end for the gods if he persists in his greed. Wotan decides to rule lawfully and parts with the ring. Freia is restored, and the gods become young again. In awe, they watch Alberich's curse at work: Fasolt seizes the ring and is slain by Fafner. Wotan realizes that something must be done to prevent Alberich from regaining the ring.

Seen as social criticism, *Das Rheingold* is a portrayal of Wagner's world: Wotan is one of the petty German princes, helpless without his clever minister Loge; two other gods, Froh and Donner, are the toadies of the court; Alberich is the slave-driving factory owner; and the giants Fasolt and Fafner are the self-reliant workers insisting on their rights. In the scheme of the *Ring* tetralogy *Das Rheingold* sets the stage for a loveless world into which love comes by accident and takes over slowly, eventually overpowering even Wotan so that he relinquishes his rule.

Wagner attaches melodische Momente to Wotan's spear, to Loge, to Walhalla, to the gold in its pure state and in its impure state as the ring, and so on. He thereby conveys meanings that are not contained in the words alone. For example, nowhere does he say that Freia, the goddess of youth

and immortality, is also the symbol of love; but in 1968 Deryck Cooke analyzed the "flight" motif of her first appearance, when she flees from the giants, and discovered that it is a fast version of the "love" motif in *Die Walküre*. This dimension of Freia emphasizes the lovelessness of the world during her absence and explains Wotan's greed and incapacity to feel compassion.

Wotan cannot recapture the ring from Fafner, but he knows that Alberich must be prevented at all costs from getting it back. When *Die Walküre* opens, he has devised and put into action a plan to accomplish this goal. He learned from Erda that Alberich is planning to arm his fellow Nibelungs to attack Walhalla and that he has bought a woman and begotten a son to aid him. Erda bore Wotan a daughter, Brünnhilde, one of the nine valkyries who bring fallen heroes from the battlefield to defend Walhalla. Then Wotan begat a twin son and daughter with a mortal woman. The boy, Siegmund, is to be his instrument. Wotan separated Siegmund from his sister, Sieglinde, and prepared him for the battle with Fafner, who has transformed himself into a dragon with the aid of the Tarnhelm. Siegmund is then left to his own devices, but Wotan leads him to a sword he had implanted into a tree at Sieglinde's house. Wotan's plans go awry when Siegmund and Sieglinde fall in love on their first meeting. Siegmund abducts Sieglinde from her oppressive husband and thus angers Fricka, the wife of Wotan and goddess of marriage. She demands that Wotan not protect his son in the forthcoming fight between Siegmund and the husband and that he instruct Brünnhilde to protect the husband. But Brünnhilde, overwhelmed by the depth of love that unites Siegmund and Sieglinde, disobeys her father's command and protects Siegmund. Wotan has to interfere and let his son be killed. Brünnhilde whisks Sieglinde away, for she carries Siegmund's child.

Wotan must punish Brünnhilde. He dismisses her reasons for disobedience as folly and womanish self-indulgence. He plans to put her to sleep and allow any passerby who wakes her to marry her. She begs him to surround her sleeping place with fire, so that only the greatest hero can claim her as a bride. She is thinking of Sieglinde's son; Wotan cries out that he wants nothing to do with that brood, unaware that by doing so he has created the condition for the independent hero he needs. Brünnhilde's pleading ignites in Wotan an understanding of the force of love and changes him. The power-wielding god of the beginning of the drama feels love for the first time. The love of Siegmund and Sieglinde, an unexpected nuisance, has a chain-reaction effect: its spark goes to Brünnhilde, and from her to Wotan.

The first two acts of *Siegfried* are devoted to the growing up of the boy to whom Sieglinde gave birth in the woods near the smithy of Mime, Alberich's brother. She died in childbirth, and Mime has raised Siegfried for the sole purpose of someday killing the dragon Fafner; then the hoard and the ring will be Mime's. But the skilled smith cannot forge a sword that Siegfried does not smash to pieces, nor can he forge one from the pieces of Siegmund's sword, the only legacy Sieglinde left her son. Siegfried forges it himself in an unconventional manner. Mime takes Siegfried to Fafner's cave, and the fearless boy kills the dragon. As he licks the blood off his finger, he is able to read in a bird's song that Mime plans to poison him. He kills the dwarf, then follows the bird's instruction to take the ring and the Tarnhelm from Fafner's hoard. The bird leads him to a beautiful woman sleeping on a rock surrounded by fire. On the way he meets Wotan, who is roaming the world in the guise of a wanderer. Wotan has resolved to surrender the rule of the world to the young, and he blocks Siegfried's path with his spear to find out whether this decision was wise. Siegfried shatters the weapon and thus fulfills Wotan's prediction that only one who is fearless of the spear should find his way through the fire to Brünnhilde. Wotan picks up the pieces and vanishes, leaving Siegfried, unaware that he has just destroyed a world order, free to pursue love. He wakes Brünnhilde – literally at first, then also sexually – and the drama ends with perfect love between man and woman.

In *Götterdämmerung* Wotan has retired to Walhalla; the old world order has passed, but a new one not yet come into being. The Norns, the goddesses of fate, no longer grasp what is going on; they vanish. Meanwhile, Siegfried and Brünnhilde's wedded bliss must come to an end because the professional hero must venture out into the world. He gives Brünnhilde the ring as a token of his love, and it restores the superhuman strength she lost when she became a mortal woman. In return she gives him all of her wisdom, after which she no longer possesses it; but Siegfried does not know how to use it.

At the court of the Gibichungs, Siegfried meets Gunther, the king; his sister, Gutrune; and their half brother, Hagen. Hagen's father is Alberich, who has kept his son informed of the whereabouts of the ring. Gutrune gives Siegfried a potion that makes him forget Brünnhilde. Siegfried offers to help Gunther acquire Brünnhilde in exchange for being given Gutrune for his wife. The magic of the Tarnhelm having been explained to him by Hagen, Siegfried appears to Brünnhilde in Gunther's form, overpowers her, and robs her of the ring. Subconsciously she recognizes him through the disguise, for only the greatest hero could overcome her superhuman strength. Being honorable, he lays his sword between them during the night. He then returns to Gibichung Hall to plan his wedding to Gutrune. When Gunther arrives with the heartbroken Brünnhilde, she sees her ring on Siegfried's finger and demands an explanation; Siegfried cannot give one because he is under the influence of the potion; Brünnhilde is helpless because she has given her wisdom away. The only one with the solution to the mystery is Hagen. Brünnhilde claims that Siegfried is her husband, and everyone understands her to mean that he betrayed Gunther's trust the night before. Hagen calls for Siegfried's death; during a hunt the next day he plunges his spear into Siegfried's back. Siegfried's death restores Brünnhilde's wisdom, and she recognizes the treachery of which she and Siegfried had been victims. She joins him on the funeral pyre; the pyre ignites Gibichung Hall, and the flames reach Walhalla. The end of the gods has arrived. On Brünnhilde's finger the ring has been cleansed from its curse by fire; her all-encompassing love has freed the world from corruption. The Rhine Maidens arrive on the crest of the overflowing river, take the ring from the ashes, and return it as pure gold to the cliff whence it was stolen.

During the years of gestation the ending underwent several changes; Wagner's first sketch brought Siegfried and Brünnhilde, united in death, to live with Wotan in Walhalla; the second left the world, without a ruler, to the rule of love; the third depicted the end of the world. In the final version the music at the end implies a cleansed world, a new beginning; the text, however, leaves Alberich unaccounted for and the Rhine Maidens still in existence. Wagner has left the ending open; the possibility of a repetition of the events is stressed in modern productions.

Wagner discovered Arthur Schopenhauer's philosophy two years after he had reworked the text of *Götterdämmerung*. It elated him that his Wotan practices Schopenhauer's negation of the will; in fact, he said that only through Schopenhauer could he really understand Wotan.

He proceeded to compose the music for the first two dramas, completing the score for *Das Rheingold* in 1854 and that for *Die Walküre* in 1856, and began work on the score for *Siegfried;* but a combination of circumstances caused him to stop in 1857. He became convinced that the magnitude of the cycle would prevent its performance; he was unhappy in exile, especially after a petition for amnesty was denied by the Saxon king; and he hoped that a smaller, more manageable project would bring in sorely needed funds. After finishing the score for the second act of *Siegfried,* he put the work aside and began *Tristan und Isolde* (1859; translated as *Tristan and Isolde,* 1889).

It turned out not to be the small item Wagner planned but one of enormous consequence; it has been called the "birth of the modern." Wagner reshaped Gottfried von Straßburg's medieval epic poem of stolen love, intrigue, deception, and bliss: he made Gottfried's lecherous, deceived husband, King Marke of Cornwall, into a kindly, understanding man and combined the many obsequious courtiers in the poem into the character of Melot. The essentials of Gottfried's background – the earlier meeting of Tristan and Isolde, Isolde's healing of his wound, and Tristan's return to woo her for his uncle, Marke, to which Wagner adds the suppressed love between Tristan and Isolde – are related by Isolde to her confidante Brangäne aboard the ship that is taking her, escorted by Tristan, to wed Marke. The love potion is not a careless mix-up by a servant, as in Gottfried's poem, but a deliberate attempt by Brangäne to save Isolde's life after Isolde orders her to prepare poison for her and Tristan. Thomas Mann points out that the effect would have been the same had they drunk water: they expected to die and believe they have found each other in death – "Weltentronnen, du mir gewonnen" (Escaped from the world, you are mine) – only to be cruelly awakened to the arrival on shore and Isolde's upcoming wedding to Marke. Wagner reduces Gottfried's many subsequent trysts to one. After rejoicing over being together again, they reflect on what separates them: it is the day and all that it implies – honor, duty, the court, and so on – and they long for the night of death that will unite them forever. They are so lost in one another that they exchange identities, and they do not heed Brangäne's warning song. When they are discovered in the midst of their lovemaking, Tristan attempts suicide by challenging his betrayer, Melot, then dropping his sword and allowing his adversary to wound him. Tristan's servant brings his comatose master home. When Tristan awakens he is delirious; he calls wildly for Isolde, then raves against the light of day and longs for death. Brangäne has revealed the truth to Marke, and he has released Isolde to come to Tristan. When the ship arrives,

Tristan tears off his bandages, rushes into her arms, and dies. Isolde then wills her own death. Wagner invented a new musical language of harmonies, dissonances, and unresolved chords to characterize the unfulfilled longing of the lovers and the otherworldliness in which they exist.

Tristan und Isolde reflects Wagner's relationship with Mathilde Wesendonck. The Wagners had moved into a house on the grounds of the estate of their friends and benefactors Otto and Mathilde Wesendonck. The Wagner marriage had been shaky almost from the beginning: Wagner had not provided Minna with the comfortable life of the wife of a famous composer she had hoped for. Instead, he had subjected her to poverty in Paris and life as a refugee. She never let him forget her disappointment. She was unable to share her husband's flights of fancy and could not understand why he wrote theoretical works instead of devoting himself to lucrative composing. Nor could Minna give Wagner what he desperately needed: adulation and support of his ideas. Mathilde Wesendonck adored not only the music but also the man, and he reciprocated her feelings. *Die Walküre* was composed with her in mind, and they were together daily during his work on *Tristan und Isolde,* which was even more directly inspired by her. She wrote poems, and he set them to music; he played and sang for her, and she listened for hours. The affair was broken up when Minna intercepted a letter containing a declaration of love. Wagner went to Italy to finish the score for *Tristan und Isolde;* Minna went to a spa to be treated for a heart condition. The friendship with the Wesendoncks continued, but coolly. Although Wagner belittled Mathilde later in *Mein Leben,* he told a friend in 1863 that she was his first and only love – and there is *Tristan und Isolde* to prove it.

In 1860 Wagner set out to try his luck in Paris once more, this time with a production of *Tannhäuser.* Among the difficulties he had to overcome in Paris were a bout with typhoid fever, a demand to write a ballet into the second act, and an attack by French patriots who were resentful of the favors shown the German. But he made new friends, including the composers Charles Gounod and Camille Saint-Saëns, painters, critics, and politicians. In Germany partial amnesty was granted him, with the stipulation that he not travel to Saxony. The poet Charles Baudelaire paid tribute to him in a letter that foreshadowed *wagnérisme,* saying that he was carried to a state of religious ecstasy by Wagner's music. The performances of *Tannhäuser,* however, were ruined by laughter, jeers, and whistling from the political Jockey Club, and Wagner withdrew the work.

After the Paris fiasco, he explored, in Karlsruhe and then in Vienna, the possibility of having *Tristan und Isolde* performed; in Vienna he saw *Lohengrin* for the first time and wept. *Tristan und Isolde* was considered unsingable, and the *Ring* cycle was still incomplete. Wagner decided to write a short, funny, and performable opera to make some money; it became *Die Meistersinger von Nürnberg.* He pulled out his sketch of 1845, immersed himself in Jacob Grimm's *Über den altdeutschen Meistergesang* (On the Old German Mastersong, 1811), and reread Wagenseil's *Von der Meister-Singer holdseligen Kunst.* The text was finished in 1862. He settled in Biebrich, where Minna joined him one last time. They separated permanently after ten unpleasant days together; but they corresponded, and during the few years she had left to live Wagner never fell short in his financial support of her, no matter in what straits he was himself.

The Meistersinger carried on the tradition of the minnesingers after courtly culture died out. They set up strict rules according to which a song had to be composed; their intention was to perpetuate their art, but instead they stifled it. In Wagner's opera the young knight Walter is in love with Eva, the master goldsmith's daughter, who is to be the prize at a song contest the next day. But she can marry only a man who belongs to the mastersingers' guild. Walter has no training, does not know the rules, and miserably fails the audition. He and Eva decide to elope that night. Hans Sachs, master shoemaker and poetaster, overhears their plot and foresees dire consequences; he liked Walter's unruly song and wants to help him and Eva, but he must prevent the elopement. He cleverly incites a riot, during which he whisks Walter away to his house. The next morning Walter tells Sachs a dream he had during the night, and the dream serves as the basis for the song he will sing at the contest. Sachs makes the song fit the rules without losing its spontaneity; Walter sings it at the festival and wins Eva. There are humorous side plots and witty lines. Many Wagnerians consider *Die Meistersinger von Nürnberg* his best work, one that could be performed successfully as straight drama.

He began composing the score right away, but the work did not go well. He had no home and no real love, although he did have several affairs; and his debts were mounting. He made a Russian tour, then traveled to Vienna and Zurich. In November 1863 he went to Berlin to see Hans von Bülow con-

Wagner with his second wife, Cosima, in Vienna, 1872

duct, and on this occasion he and Bülow's wife, Cosima, the daughter of Liszt, fell in love. But his spirits did not lift; he was physically ill with heart spasms, and he contemplated suicide. Life had become unbearable to him, and he had become unbearable to others. He had the most high-flown opinions of his work; he became demanding. He had always had a sense of mission, but he had borne the world's misunderstanding with the confidence that he would be appreciated someday. He had become impatient. His meanderings found him in Stuttgart in May 1864, and it was there that Hofrat (Privy Councillor) Franz Seraph von Pfistermeier tracked him down after a two-week search. Pfistermeier had been sent by Bavaria's new king, Ludwig II, to find him at any cost.

Ludwig had been deeply moved by Wagner's works since seeing *Lohengrin* three years before, and he supported Wagner from the time he became king at age eighteen. First he financed the completion of *Die Meistersinger von Nürnberg* and *Der Ring des*

Wahnfried, Wagner's home in Bayreuth

Nibelungen. A strange relationship arose between the two men, to which their correspondence bears witness. Addresses such as Ludwig's "Heiliger" (Holy One), "Ein und All" (One and All), and "Gott meines Lebens" (God of my life) were matched by Wagner's "Angebeteter, engelgleicher Freund" (Adored, Angelic Friend) and so on.

Wagner was installed in a house near Starnberg and saw the king almost daily. The Bülows were to visit; but Cosima and her two small daughters came a week early, and the affair between Cosima and Wagner began. Ludwig wished to know whether Wagner's attitude toward revolution had changed: the answer was the essay *Über Staat und Religion* (On State and Religion, 1873), in which he belittles his part in the revolution of 1849 on the grounds that he was too preoccupied with his Nibelungen studies to have been deeply involved. He sees the state as a contract for the protection of individuals from exploitation; its aim is stability; the guarantor of its basic laws is the monarch, who is above party politics. Religion is separate from the state.

Hans von Bülow was appointed to the Munich theater; Wagner continued work on *Siegfried* and oversaw the rehearsals for *Tristan und Isolde*. Bülow

and the tenor Ludwig Schnorr von Carolsfeld understood the work fully, and the premiere on 10 June 1865 was a great success. Three weeks later Schnorr died after a brief illness, perpetuating the legend that the role of Tristan was impossible to sing.

Wagner was drawn into Bavarian politics. The people disapproved of his demands for reorganization of all cultural affairs, his plan for a festival theater, his private "court" of friends, and his extravagances. Rival factions sought out his influence with the king, a battle was fought in the press, and in December 1865 he had to leave Munich on the grounds that he had estranged the monarch from his people. He took up his peregrinations again; news of Minna's death on 25 January 1866 reached him in Marseilles.

In Munich, Cosima had kept up the appearance of her pseudomarriage to Bülow who, being a slave to Wagner, had acted as if unaware; he always acknowledged Isolde, born in April 1865, as his child. In March 1866 Cosima visited Wagner in Geneva, and they found their future home at Tribschen, near Lucerne. Their second child, Eva, was born in February 1867. In October 1868 Wagner and Friedrich Nietzsche met for the first time. They saw kindred spirits in each other, and Nietzsche thrived on the intellectual laughter in the Wagner household: "Schopenhauer, Goethe, Aischylus und Pindar leben noch" (Schopenhauer, Goethe, Aeschylus, and Pindar are alive), he wrote to a friend. The atmosphere of scholarly delight led him to his concept of the Dionysian temperament. Cosima commuted from Munich until she moved to Tribschen in November 1868, by which time their third child, Siegfried, was on the way; he was born in June 1869. Bülow divorced Cosima on 18 July 1870, and she and Wagner were married on 25 August.

Wagner's old dream of building his own theater, where the four *Ring* dramas could be performed together, returned. On a trip to Bayreuth he and Cosima found the theater there to have the large stage he needed, but it was otherwise not suitable. They liked the town, however, and moved there in April 1872. Bayreuth donated the site, and the arduous task of raising money for the theater began. Construction was begun on Wagner's fifty-ninth birthday. The opening had to wait until 1876 for monetary reasons; what Wagner had dreamed of as a festival for everyone turned out to be one for the privileged, and still it was a financial loss.

As early as spring 1872 Cosima had noticed that Nietzsche was becoming unusually reticent. But when the Wagners left Tribschen for Bayreuth that year, there was no rift. Suffering from migraine headaches, Nietzsche fled the *Ring* rehearsals and the bustle of overcrowded Bayreuth in the summer heat of 1876, but he returned for the performances in August. There was still no sign of a break in the friendship when they met in Sorrento in November 1876, and Nietzsche said that he was looking forward to *Parsifal*. The real estrangement came about — it is believed today — when Nietzsche discovered a letter from Wagner to Nietzsche's doctor, Dr. Eiser, suggesting excessive masturbation as a possible cause of Nietzsche's eye trouble. As ludicrous as such an idea seems today, it was then fashionable to attribute various nervous disorders to masturbation, and Wagner made the suggestion out of genuine concern for his friend's health. Deeply hurt — especially since he assumed that Cosima, whom he revered, knew of the matter — Nietzsche broke with Wagner.

In 1877 Wagner completed the text of *Parsifal*. Its source, Wolfram von Eschenbach's *Parzival,* was one of the books he had taken with him to Marienbad in 1845; it is the epic of the perfect knight who, after a series of adventures during which he matures, attains the highest honors at King Arthur's court and becomes king of the realm of the Holy Grail. Wagner reduces the adventures to the significant ones. His Parsifal starts out, like Wolfram's, innocent of life, roaming to learn about the world. He chances to arrive at the castle of the Holy Grail, where the ailing king Amfortas is tended by the Grail knights. Only "durch Mitlied wissend, der reine Tor" (a pure fool, insightful through compassion) can retrieve the spear Amfortas lost to the warlock Klingsor while he rested in a woman's arms, and only the touch of this spear can heal the wound. The hermit Gurnemanz tells aspiring knights about the Grail: it is the chalice from which Christ drank at the Last Supper; the same chalice collected the blood of Christ on the cross. Along with the spear that pierced Christ's side, it was entrusted to Titurel, Amfortas's father. Titurel built the castle to house the Grail and protected it with his knights. Klingsor had wanted to be one of them, but his sinfulness was too great. He castrated himself and planned revenge; he received magic powers, built a garden in the desert, and populated it with beautiful women who lie in wait to lead Grail knights astray. When Amfortas set out to destroy Klingsor, he became one of their victims. Gurnemanz senses that Parsifal may be the chosen "pure fool"; Amfortas, in great pain, performs the ceremony of unveiling the Grail while Parsifal looks on, dazed and moved but uttering no word of compassion, and Gurnemanz pushes him away. In the magic garden Klingsor also suspects Parsifal to be the one who will save Amfortas; he must prevent Parsifal from doing so because he wants to be the Grail king himself. He orders Kundry to ensnare Parsifal as she had Amfortas. She refuses, but his magic overpowers her. Her flower maidens beset Parsifal; he resists them and is about to flee when Kundry calls his name. He had not heard it since he left home; it stops him, and he listens to Kundry's tale of how his mother died of heartache over him. She suggests to the grief-stricken Parsifal that he should console himself with her, but her kiss has the effect of making him clairvoyant. In his confusion of sexuality, love, and motherly love he feels Amfortas's wound in his own heart and reproaches himself bitterly for not having perceived it before. He also realizes that Kundry was Amfortas's seductress. Kundry begs for his compassion; she has been condemned to suffer eternal life because she laughed at Christ, and Parsifal can be her savior if only he will grant her an hour of love. When he rejects her, she calls on Klingsor for help; Klingsor flings the spear at Parsifal, and he catches it. After a long time Parsifal finds his way to Gurnemanz's hut

Wagner's Festival Theater in Bayreuth in 1876, the year it opened

again; Kundry is also there. Gurnemanz is overjoyed at the sight of Parsifal and the spear. Amfortas has not been tending to his duty of unveiling the life-giving Grail; today is Good Friday, and he has promised to do so for the last time. Kundry washes Parsifal's feet in a symbolic gesture, he baptizes her, and she weeps for the first time. At the Grail castle, Amfortas, longing for death, is reluctant to unveil the shrine, for this act will prolong his life; but then Parsifal appears and closes the wound with the spear. Amfortas's sins are forgiven, Kundry dies, and all present are sustained by the power of the Grail and the power of compassion.

Parsifal is Wagner's most solemn and concentrated work; it is not a step in his progress but a summation of all preceding works. It is regarded as his loftiest achievement in music and poetry. *Parsifal* premiered in Bayreuth 26 July 1882.

Wagner continued to spew forth ideas and opinions until the day he died. The student of Wagner has to deal with sometimes quite contradictory essays or with contradictions between Wagner's written opinions and his actions. A prime example is his ambivalence on the Jewish matter. Early in 1869 he had *Das Judenthum in der Musik* published in book form; this act lost him several friends, among them the novelist Gustav Freytag. In subsequent essays he brought up again and again his conviction that a foreign element was introduced into the German Volk (nation) by the Jews,

on whom he blamed the growing materialism of the day. Yet he had several close Jewish friends, and he entrusted *Parsifal* to the conductor Hermann Levi, the son of a rabbi. He had no use for anti-Semites such as Bernhard Förster (Nietzsche's brother-in-law) and Eugen Dühring, and he opposed the anti-Semitic theories of Joseph-Arthur de Gobineau; when he and Gobineau first met, in February 1881, the topic did not arise; and at their second meeting, in May of the same year, they clashed violently.

In 1877 Wagner established the *Bayreuther Blätter: Deutsche Zeitschrift im Geiste Richard Wagners* (Pages from Bayreuth: A German Journal in the Spirit of Richard Wagner), with Wolzogen as editor, as a forum for his ideas as well as those of others. It appeared until 1938; Wagner's last essays were published in it.

In the last years of his life Wagner idolized Greek antiquity more than ever. The ideal artist, he said, is one who created great art imperceptibly, as Miguel de Cervantes did in *Don Quixote* (1605–1615) and Goethe did in *Die Leiden des jungen Werthers* (1774; translated as *The Sorrows of Werther,* 1779), as in Beethoven's melodies, Shakespearean scenes, and Bach's fugues. He hated big cities and their rabble; he hated parliamentary government. In the essay "Modern" (1878) he denigrates the modernistic trend of the Young Germans – of whom he once was one – because it contributes to the corruption of the theater; he finds the age of psychology frightening, apparently unaware that his own work, beginning with *Der fliegende Holländer,* probes the human psyche; and he opposes technology, social criticism, progress, the economic upswing, and the rule of money. He had been a democrat in his younger years; later, he supported the conservative Prussian chancellor Otto von Bismarck and the unification of Germany. But he became disillusioned with the militarism of the Second German Empire, founded in 1871, and its expansion into Alsace-Lorraine. The poverty of the country folk around Bayreuth appalled him. In 1880 he revived plans he had had in 1854 and 1859 for a concert tour in America. Disgusted with German materialism and shoddy artistic workmanship, he dreamed of building a drama school in Minnesota and dedicating *Parsifal* to the Americans.

In "Religion und Kunst" (Religion and Art, 1880) he proposes that since religion has not been able to redeem suffering humanity, maybe art can. "Heldentum und Christentum" (Heroism and Christianity, 1881) seems to contradict this idea: heroes let their intellects rule over their passions; the highest stage of the ladder of humanity, exemplified by Christ, is the capacity to suffer consciously; true Christianity, not enlightened morality, should be the basis for the equality of peoples and a flowering of the arts.

An Italian sojourn in 1882 was cut short by recurring heart spasms. He attended the performances of *Parsifal,* but they exhausted him. During the third act at the final performance he took the baton from Levi, conducted the orchestra to the end of the work, and thus bade farewell to the Bayreuth ensemble. The family went to Venice in September. Among the many visitors were Liszt, Levi, and the composer Engelbert Humperdinck. Wagner knew that he was close to death, but he had occasional bursts of energy during which he wrote on vivisection, on Proudhon, and on the feminine in the human being. On 13 February 1883 Cosima found him slumped over his desk. The last words he had written were "Liebe – Tragödie" (Love – tragedy).

Wagner was a model of notoriety, a target for criticism, caricature, and satire. People everywhere asked each other, "What do you think of Wagner?" Everyone knew who he was. While he never doubted that his art would ennoble humanity, he had doubts about his ability: "Als reiner Musiker tauge ich nicht viel" (As a pure musician, I don't amount to much); "Ich bin kein Dichter" (I'm no poet); "Wenn Mendelssohn mich komponieren sähe, würde er die Hände über dem Kopf zusammenschlagen" (If Men-

Drawing of Wagner by Paul von Joukovsky. The inscription by Cosima Wagner reads "R. reading, 12 Febr. 1883." Wagner died the next day (Richard Wagner Archive).

delssohn could see me compose, he would have a fit). He was not a wordsmith; his texts, without the music – unless he read them aloud and instilled them with emotion – fall short as poetry. But the words alone are less than half the totality that is completed by the perfect dramatic structure and the meaning carried by the music. The *Liebestod* (Love-Death) music in *Tristan und Isolde* is a literary idea; the *Rheingold* prelude is "acoustic thought"; the orchestra functions as a Greek chorus. The melodies came to Wagner while he was on walks or engaged in other banal activities, and he stored them in his memory until the time came to apply them. He was sometimes amazed by what he had written. He found the composing of *Die Walküre* exceedingly painful; he felt that he was being punished for artistically trifling with the sorrows and suffering of the world. His productive life was fraught with disasters, feuds, emotional outbursts, and grotesque incidents, whether of his making or not; his most sublime music does not reveal that it was composed under such trying circumstances.

Since a Munich psychiatrist, Dr. Theodor Puschmann, started the trend in 1872, a series of psychological speculations have been published about Wagner; he has been diagnosed as neurotic, hysterical, overwrought through physical exhaustion, a megalomaniac, and egocentrically pugnacious. He was, in fact, volatile, capricious, arrogant at times, and quick-tempered; but he was also witty, sensitive, gentle, compassionate, a charming companion, loyal to his friends, effervescent, and loving. His life has attracted many negative interpretations – for example, he is accused of stealing his best friend's wife when actually Cosima threw herself at him. But whatever shortcomings Wagner may have had as a man, he was unquestionably one of the greatest musical geniuses of all time.

Letters:

Fünfzehn Briefe von Richard Wagner nebst Erinnerungen und Erläuterungen, edited by Eliza Wille (Berlin: Paetel, 1894);

Richard Wagners Briefe nach Zeitfolge und Inhalt, edited by Wilhelm Altmann (Leipzig: Breitkopf & Härtel, 1905);

Richard Wagners Bayreuther Briefe, edited by Carl Friedrich Glasenapp (Berlin & Leipzig: Schuster & Loeffler, 1907);

Richard Wagner an seine Künstler, edited by Erich Kloss (Berlin & Leipzig: Schuster & Loeffler, 1908);

Richard Wagners Briefwechsel mit seinen Verlegern, edited by Altmann (Leipzig: Breitkopf & Härtel / Mainz: Schott, 1911);

An Freunde und Zeitgenossen, edited by Kloss (Leipzig: Schuster & Loeffler, 1912);

Richard Wagners gesammelte Briefe, edited by Julius Kapp and Emerich Kastner (Leipzig: Hesse & Becker, 1914);

Richard Wagner an Mathilde und Otto Wesendonck: Tagebuchblätter und Briefe (Leipzig: Hesse & Becker, 1915);

Richard Wagners Briefe an Hans Richter, edited by Ludwig Karpath (Berlin, Vienna & Leipzig: Zsolnay, 1924);

Richard Wagners Briefe, 2 volumes, edited by Altmann (Leipzig: Bibliographisches Institut, 1925); translated by M. M. Bozman as *Letters of Richard Wagner* (New York: Dutton, 1927);

König Ludwig II. und Richard Wagner: Briefwechsel, 5 volumes, edited by Otto Strobel (Karlsruhe: Braun, 1936–1939);

Richard Wagner: Ausgewählte Schriften und Briefe, edited by Alfred Lorenz (Berlin: Hahnefeld, 1938);

Letters of Richard Wagner: The Collection Burrell, edited by John N. Burk (New York: Macmillan, 1950);

Richard Wagners Sämtliche Briefe, 15 volumes projected, 4 volumes published, edited by Gertrud Strobel and Werner Wolf (Leipzig & Mainz: Deutscher Verlag für Musik, 1967–);

Richard Wagners Briefe, edited by Hanjo Kesting (Munich: Piper, 1983).

Bibliographies:

Herbert Barth, ed., *Internationale Wagner-Bibliographie 1945–1955* (Bayreuth: Edition Musica Bayreuth, 1956);

Henrik Barth, ed., *Internationale Wagner-Bibliographie 1956–1960* (Bayreuth: Edition Musica Bayreuth, 1961);

Henrik Barth, ed., *Internationale Wagner-Bibliographie 1961–1966* (Bayreuth: Edition Musica Bayreuth, 1968);

Hans Martin Plesske, *Richard Wagner in der Dichtung: Bibliographie deutschsprachiger Veröffentlichungen* (Bayreuth: Edition Musica Bayreuth, 1971);

Herbert Barth, ed., *Internationale Wagner-Bibliographie 1967–1978* (Bayreuth: Mühl'scher Universitätsverlag, 1979).

Biographies:

Mary Burrell, *Richard Wagner: His Life and Works from 1813–1834* (London: Wyan, 1898);

William Ashton Ellis, *Life of Richard Wagner,* 6 volumes (London: Kegan Paul, 1900–1908);

Max Koch, *Richard Wagner,* 3 volumes (Berlin: Hofmann, 1918);

Paul Bekker, *Wagner: Das Leben im Werke* (Stuttgart: Deutsche Verlagsanstalt, 1924);

William Wallace, *Richard Wagner as He Lived* (New York: Harper, 1925);

Ernest Newman, *The Life of Richard Wagner,* 4 volumes (New York: Knopf, 1937);

Houston Stewart Chamberlain, *Richard Wagner* (Munich: Bruckmann, 1942);

Willi Reich, *Richard Wagner: Leben, Fühlen, Schaffen* (Olten: Walter, 1948);

Otto Strobel, *Richard Wagner: Leben und Schaffen, eine Zeittafel* (Bayreuth: Verlag der Festspielleitung, 1952);

Zdenko von Kraft, *Richard Wagner: Ein dramatisches Leben* (Munich & Vienna: Andermann, 1953);

Ludwig Marcuse, *Das denkwürdige Leben des Richard Wagner* (Munich: Szczesny, 1953);

Curt von Westernhagen, *Richard Wagner: Sein Werk, sein Wesen, seine Welt* (Zurich: Atlantis, 1956);

Walter G. Armando, *Richard Wagner: Eine Biographie* (Hamburg: Rütten & Loening, 1962);

Walter Panofsky, *Wagner: Eine Bildbiographie* (Munich: Kindler, 1963); translated by Richard Ricket as *Wagner: A Pictorial Biography* (London: Thames & Hudson, 1964);

Robert Jacobs, *Wagner* (London: Dent, 1965);

Chapell White, *An Introduction to the Life and Works of Richard Wagner* (Englewood Cliffs, N. J.: Prentice-Hall, 1967);

Robert W. Gutman, *Richard Wagner: The Man, His Mind, and His Music* (New York: Time, 1968);

Curt von Westernhagen, *Wagner* (Zurich & Freiburg: Atlantis, 1968);

Carl Friedrich Glasenapp, *Das Leben Richard Wagners,* 6 volumes (Walluf: Sändig, 1976);

John Chancellor, *Wagner* (Boston: Little, Brown, 1978);

John Culshaw, *Wagner: The Man and His Music* (New York: Dutton, 1978);

Dietrich Mack and Egon Voss, *Richard Wagner: Leben und Werke in Daten und Bildern* (Frankfurt am Main: Insel, 1978);

Hans Mayer, *Richard Wagner: Mitwelt und Nachwelt* (Stuttgart: Belser, 1978);

Horst Althaus, *Richard Wagner: Genie und Ärgernis* (Bergisch-Gladbach: Lübbe, 1980);

Martin Gregor-Dellin, *Richard Wagner: Sein Leben, sein Werk, sein Jahrhundert* (Munich: Piper, 1980); translated by J. Maxwell Brownjohn as *Richard Wagner: His Life, His Work, His Century* (San Diego, New York & London: Harcourt Brace Jovanovich, 1983);

Rudolph Sabor, *The Real Wagner* (Worcester: Baylis, 1987).

References:

Theodor Adorno, *Versuch über Wagner* (Frankfurt am Main: Suhrkamp, 1952);

Martin van Amerongen, *Wagner: A Case History* (New York: Braziller, 1984);

Oskar Andree, *Ein Geistesruf für unsere Zeit in Richard Wagners "Meistersingern"* (Stuttgart: Mellinger, 1974);

Andree, *Richard Wagners "Ring des Nibelungen"* (Stuttgart: Mellinger, 1976);

Robert C. Bagar, *Wagner and His Music Dramas* (New York: Grosset & Dunlap, 1950);

Herbert Barth, *Der Festspielhügel: Richard Wagners Werk in Bayreuth 1876-1976* (Munich: Deutscher Taschenbuchverlag, 1976);

Barth, ed., *Richard Wagner: Life, Work, Festspielhaus* (Bayreuth: Verlag der Festspielleitung, 1952);

Barth, ed., *Richard Wagner und Bayreuth in Karikatur und Anekdote* (Bayreuth: Edition Musica Bayreuth, 1970);

Barth, Dietrich Mack, and Egon Voss, eds., *Wagner: A Documentary Study* (London: Thames & Hudson, 1975);

Jacques Barzun, *Darwin, Marx, Wagner: Critique of a Heritage* (Garden City, N.Y.: Doubleday, 1958);

Hans Bélart, *Richard Wagner in Zürich 1849-1858,* 2 volumes (Leipzig: Seeman, 1900-1901);

Joachim Bergfeld, *Wagners Werk und unsere Zeit* (Berlin: Hesse, 1963);

Johannes Bertram, *Mythos, Symbol, Idee in Richard Wagners Musikdramen* (Hamburg: Kultur, 1957);

Dieter Borchmeyer, *Das Theater Richard Wagners: Idee-Dichtung-Wirkung* (Stuttgart: Reclam, 1982);

Maurice Boucher, *The Political Concepts of Richard Wagner* (New York: M & H Publications, 1950);

Clyde Robert Bulla, *The Ring and the Fire: Stories from Wagner's Nibelung Operas* (New York: Crowell, 1962);

Peter Burbridge and Richard Sutton, eds., *The Wagner Companion* (London & Boston: Faber & Faber, 1979);

Houston Stewart Chamberlain, *Das Drama Richard Wagners: Eine Anregung* (Walluf: Sändig, 1973);

Chamberlain, *Die Grundlagen des 19. Jahrhunderts,* 2 volumes (Munich: Bruckmann, 1932);

Deryck Cooke, *An Introduction to* Der Ring des Nibelungen (London: Decca Record Co., 1968);

Cooke, *I Saw the World End: A Study of Wagner's "Ring"* (London: Oxford University Press, 1979);

Cooke, *The Language of Music* (London: Oxford University Press, 1959);

John Culshaw, *Reflections on Wagner's "Ring"* (London: Secker & Warburg, 1976);

Carl Dahlhaus, *Richard Wagner: Werk und Wirkung* (Regensburg: Bosse, 1971);

Dahlhaus, *Richard Wagners Musikdramen* (Velber: Friedrich, 1971); translated by Mary Whittall as *Richard Wagner's Music Dramas* (Cambridge, U.K.: Cambridge University Press, 1979);

Dahlhaus, *Wagners Konzeption des musikalischen Dramas* (Regensburg: Bosse, 1971);

Dahlhaus, ed., *Das Drama Richard Wagners als musikalisches Kunstwerk* (Regensburg: Bosse, 1970);

Dahlhaus, ed., *Wagners Ästhetik* (Bayreuth: Edition Musica Bayreuth, 1971); translated by Derek Fogg and Jim Ford as *Wagner's Aesthetics* (Bayreuth: Edition Musica Bayreuth, 1972);

Claude David, *Von Richard Wagner zu Bertolt Brecht: Eine Geschichte der neueren deutschen Literatur* (Frankfurt am Main & Hamburg: Fischer, 1964);

Marcel Doisy, *Der Mensch im Werke Richard Wagners* (Bayreuth: Nierenheim, 1952);

Robert Donington, *Wagner's "Ring" and Its Symbols* (New York: St. Martin's Press, 1963);

Erich Ebermayer, *Magisches Bayreuth: Legende und Wirklichkeit* (Stuttgart: Steingrüben, 1951);

Manfred Eger, *Wagner und die Juden: Fakten und Hintergründe* (Bayreuth: Druckhaus Bayreuth, 1985);

Walter Einbeck, *Der religiös-philosophische Gehalt in Richard Wagners Musikdramen* (Würzburg: Zettner, 1956);

Stephen Fay and Roger Wood, *The "Ring": Anatomy of an Opera* (Dover, N.H.: Longwood Press, 1985);

Henry Theophilus Finck, *Wagner and His Works,* 2 volumes (New York: Scribners, 1904);

Dietrich Fischer-Dieskau, *Wagner und Nietzsche: Der Mystagoge und sein Abtrünniger* (Stuttgart: Deutsche Verlags-Anstalt, 1974);

Leo Fremgen, *Richard Wagner heute: Wesen, Werk, Verwicklichung, ein Triptychon* (Hensenstamm: Heimreiter, 1977);

Richard Fricke, *Bayreuth vor dreißig Jahren: Erinnerungen an Wahnfried und aus dem Festspielhaus* (Dresden: Bertling, 1906);

Carl Albert Friedenreich, *Richard Wagner: Eine geisteswissenschaftliche Studie über Wesen und Aufgabe seiner Musik* (Freiburg: Die Kommenden, 1967);

Hans Gal, *Richard Wagner: Versuche einer Würdigung* (Frankfurt am Main & Hamburg: Fischer, 1963);

Hugh Frederick Garten, *Wagner the Dramatist* (London: Calder, 1977);

Lawrence Gilman, *Wagner's Operas* (New York: Farrar & Rinehart, 1937);

Karl Gjellerup, *Richard Wagner in seinem Hauptwerke "Der Ring des Nibelungen"* (Leipzig: Reinboth, 1891);

Carl Friedrich Glasenapp, *Wagner-Encyklopedie: Haupterscheinungen der Kunst- und Kulturgeschichte im Lichte der Anschauungen Richard Wagners,* 2 volumes (Leipzig: Fritzsch, 1891);

Victor Gollancz, *The "Ring" at Bayreuth and Some Thoughts on Operatic Production* (New York: Dutton, 1964);

Wolfgang Golther, *Die sagengeschichtlichen Grundlagen der Ringdichtung Richard Wagners* (Charlottenburg: Lehsten, 1909);

Marie Haefliger Graves, "Schiller and Wagner: A Study of Their Dramatic Theory and Technique," Ph.D. dissertation, University of Michigan, 1938;

Martin Gregor, *Wagner und kein Ende: Richard Wagner im Spiegel von Thomas Manns Prosawerk* (Bayreuth: Edition Musica Bayreuth, 1958);

Martin Gregor-Dellin, *Das kleine Wagnerbuch* (Salzburg: Residenz, 1969);

Gregor-Dellin, *Richard Wagner: Die Revolution als Oper* (Munich: Hanser, 1973);

Gregor-Dellin, ed., *Cosima Wagner: Die Tagebücher,* 2 volumes (Munich: Piper, 1976–1977); translated by Geoffrey Skelton as *Cosima Wagner's Diaries* (New York: Harcourt Brace Jovanovich, 1978);

Hermann Hakel, *Richard der Einzige: Satire, Parodie, Karikatur* (Vienna: Forum, 1963);

Bertita Leonarz Harding, *Magic Fire: Scenes around Richard Wagner* (Indianapolis: Bobbs-Merrill, 1953; London: Harrap, 1954);

Otto Julius Hartmann, *Die Esoterik im Werk Richard Wagners* (Freiburg: Die Kommenden, 1960);

Hartmann, *Die geistigen Hintergründe der Musikdramen Richard Wagners* (Schaffhausen: Novalis, 1976);

Ruth Henry and Walter Mönch, *Richard Wagner und Frankreich* (Bayreuth: Edition Musica Bayreuth, 1977);

Phillip Hodson, *Who's Who in Wagner* (New York: Macmillan, 1984);

Herbert Hubert, *Richard Wagner: Der Ring des Nibelungen. Nach seinem mythologischen, theologischen und philosophischen Gehalt Vers für Vers erklärt* (Weinheim: Acta humaniora, 1988);

Martin Hürlimann, ed., *Richard Wagner in Selbstzeugnissen und im Urteil der Zeitgenossen* (Zurich: Manesse, 1972);

Karl Ipser, *Richard Wagner in Italien* (Salzburg: Das Bergland-Buch, 1951);

Paul Walter Jacob, *Taten der Musik: Richard Wagner und seine Werke* (Regensburg: Bosse, 1952);

Ute Jung, *Die Rezeption der Kunst Richard Wagners in Italien* (Regensburg: Bosse, 1974);

Julius Kapp, *Richard Wagner und die Frauen* (Berlin: Hesse, 1951);

Erich Kloss, *Wagnertum in Vergangenheit und Gegenwart* (Berlin: Hofmann, 1909);

Annette Kolb, *König Ludwig II. von Bayern und Richard Wagner* (Amsterdam: Querido, 1947);

Zdenko von Kraft, *Das Festspielhaus in Bayreuth: Zur Geschichte seiner Idee, seines Werdeganges und seiner Vollendung* (Bayreuth: Verlag der Festspielleitung, 1958);

Kraft, *Welt und Wahn: Barrikaden-Liebestod-Wahnfried* (Heidelberg: Kayser, 1954);

Robert Tallant Landon, *Sources of the Wagnerian Synthesis: A Study of the Franco-German Tradition in Nineteenth-Century Opera* (Regensburg: Bosse, 1979);

David C. Large and William Weber, eds., *Wagnerism in European Culture and Politics* (Ithaca, N.Y. & London: Cornell University Press, 1984);

Helmut Loos and Günther Massenkeil, eds., *Zu Richard Wagner* (Bonn: Bouvier Verlag Herbert Grundmann, 1984);

Paul Arthur Loos, *Richard Wagner: Vollendung und Tragik der deutschen Romantik* (Bern: Francke, 1952);

Alfred Lorenz, *Das Geheimnis der Form bei Richard Wagner,* 4 volumes (Tutzing: Schneider, 1966);

Lore Lucas, *Die Festspiel-Idee Richard Wagners* (Regensburg: Bosse, 1973);

Dietrich Mack, *Bayreuther Festspiele: Die Idee, der Bau, die Aufführungen* (Bayreuth: Verlag der Festspielleitung, 1974);

Mack, ed., *Richard Wagner: Das Betroffensein der Nachwelt. Beiträge zur Wirkungsgeschichte* (Darmstadt: Wissenschaftliche Buchgesellschaft, 1984);

Bryan Magee, *Aspects of Wagner* (New York: Stein & Day, 1968);

Raymond Mander and Joe Mitchenson, eds., *The Wagner Companion* (London: Allen, 1977);

Erika Mann, ed., *Wagner und unsere Zeit: Aufsätze, Betrachtungen, Briefe* (Frankfurt am Main: Fischer, 1963);

Thomas Mann, "Leiden und Größe Richard Wagners," in his *Schriften und Reden zur Literatur, Kunst und Philosophie,* volume 2 (Frankfurt am Main: Fischer, 1968);

Gerhard Mattern, *Die große Bedeutung des Rechts in den Bühnendichtungen Richard Wagners: Ein Wegweiser zum Verständnis seiner Werke* (Bayreuth: Edition Musica Bayreuth, 1973);

Hans Mayer, *Anmerkungen zu Richard Wagner* (Frankfurt am Main: Suhrkamp, 1966);

Mayer, *Richard Wagner in Bayreuth: 1876–1976* (Stuttgart & Zurich: Belser, 1976);

Mayer, *Richard Wagners geistige Entwicklung* (Düsseldorf & Hamburg: Progress, 1954);

Josef Meinertz, *Richard Wagner und Bayreuth: Zur Psychologie des Schaffens und Erlebens von Wagners Werken* (Berlin: Hesse, 1961);

Barry Millington, ed., *The Wagner Compendium: A Guide to Wagner's Life and Music* (New York: Schirmer, 1992);

Andrea Mork, *Richard Wagner als politischer Schriftsteller: Weltanschauung und Wirkungsgeschichte* (Frankfurt am Main: Campus, 1990);

Sir Oswald Mosley, *Wagner and Shaw: A Synthesis* (London: Sanctuary Press, 1956);

Edwin Müller and Gottfried Ginter, *Richard Wagner als Welterneuerungslehrer: Der Ideengehalt der Bayreuther Weihespiele nach des Meisters eigenen Worten* (Bühl & Baden: Konkordia, 1953);

Angelo Neumann, *Erinnerungen an Richard Wagner* (Leipzig: Staackmann, 1907); translated by Edith Livemore as *Personal Recollections of Wagner* (New York: Holt, 1908);

Ernest Newman, *Fact and Fiction about Wagner* (New York: Knopf, 1931; London: Cassell, 1931);

Newman, *A Study of Wagner* (New York: Vienna House, 1974);

Newman, *Wagner as Man and Artist* (New York: Tudor, 1946);

Newman, *The Wagner Operas* (New York: Knopf, 1972);

Friedrich Nietzsche, *Der Fall Wagner; Götzen-Dämmerung; Nietzsche contra Wagner* (Munich: Goldmann, 1964);

Nietzsche, *Wagner in Bayreuth* (Leipzig: Neumann, 1876);

Friedrich Oberkogler, *Richard Wagner: Vom Ring zum Gral. Wiedergewinnung seines Werkes aus Musik und Mythos* (Stuttgart: Verlag Freies Geistesleben, 1978);

Nikolaus Oesterlein, *Katalog einer Richard-Wagner-Bibliothek,* 4 volumes (Wiesbaden: Sändig, 1970);

Charles Osborne, *Wagner and His World* (London: Thames & Hudson, 1977);

Kurt Overhoff, *Die Musikdramen Richard Wagners: Eine thematisch-musikalische Interpretation* (Salzburg: Pustet, 1967);

Overhoff, *Richard Wagners germanisch-christlicher Mythos: Einführung in den "Ring des Nibelungen" und "Parsifal"* (Dinkelsbühl: Kronos, 1955); translated by Rosamond Chapin as *The Germanic-Christian Myth of Richard Wagner* (Dinkelsbühl: Kronos, 1955);

Overhoff, *Wagners Nibelungentetralogie: Eine zeitgemäße Betrachtung* (Salzburg & Munich: Pustet, 1971);

Hans Perthes, *Richard Wagner sachlich und nüchtern gesehen* (Brunswick: Serger & Hempel, 1948);

Ernst von Pidde, *Wagners Musikdrama "Der Ring des Nibelungen" im Lichte des deutschen Strafrechts* (Hamburg: Hoffmann & Campe, 1979);

Richard Pohl, *Richard Wagner: Studien und Kritiken* (Walluf: Sändig, 1977);

Guy de Pourtales, *Richard Wagner: Histoire d'un artiste* (Zurich: Arche, 1957); translated by Lewis May as *Richard Wagner: The Story of an Artist* (Westport, Conn.: Greenwood, 1972);

Marcel Prawy, *Nun sei bedankt* (Munich: Goldmann, 1982);

Emil Preetorius, *Wagner: Bild und Vision* (Godesberg: Küpper, 1949);

Robert Raphael, *Richard Wagner* (New York: Twayne, 1969);

Robert Saitschick, *Götter und Menschen in Richard Wagners "Ring des Nibelungen": Eine Lebensdeutung* (Tübingen: Katzmann, 1957);

George Bernard Shaw, *The Perfect Wagnerite* (Chicago: Stone, 1899);

Shaw, *Wagner in Bayreuth* (London: Broadsheet King, 1976);

Leroy Shaw, Nancy Cirillo, and Marion S. Miller, eds., *Wagner in Retrospect: A Centennial Reappraisal* (Amsterdam: Rodopi, 1987);

John Shearer, *Music and Drama: A Commentary on Wagner and Shakespeare* (Nedlands, W.A.: Shearer, 1972);

Skelton, *Wagner at Bayreuth: Experiment and Tradition* (London: Barrie & Rockliff, 1965);

Monroe Stearns, *Richard Wagner: Titan of Music* (New York: Watts, 1969);

Herbert von Stein, *Dichtung und Musik im Werk Richard Wagners* (Berlin: De Gruyter, 1962);

Jack Madison Stein, *Richard Wagner and the Synthesis of the Arts* (Detroit: Wayne State University Press, 1960);

Leon Stein, *The Racial Thinking of Richard Wagner* (New York: Philosophical Library, 1950);

Wilhelm Tappert, *Richard Wagner im Spiegel der Kritik* (Leipzig: Siegel, 1903);

Ernst Uehli, *Richard Wagners mythisches Lebensbild* (Ahrweiler: Are, 1953);

Egon Voss, ed., *Richard Wagner Schriften: Ein Schlüssel zu Leben, Werk und Zeit* (Frankfurt am Main: Fischer Taschenbuch Verlag, 1978);

Voss, ed., *Richard Wagner: Schriften eines revolutionären Genies* (Munich & Vienna: Langen/Müller, 1976);

Peter Wapnewski, *Richard Wagner: Die Szene und ihr Meister* (Munich: Beck, 1978);

Wapnewski, *Der traurige Gott: Richard Wagner in seinen Helden* (Munich: Beck, 1978);

Wapnewski, *Tristan der Held Richard Wagners* (Berlin: Severin & Siedler, 1981);

Curt von Westernhagen, *Gespräche um Wagner* (Bayreuth: Edition Musica Bayreuth, 1961): translated by Desmond Clayton as *Discussions on Wagner* (Bayreuth: Edition Musica Bayreuth, 1961);

Westernhagen, *Richard Wagners Dresdener Bibliothek 1842–1849* (Bayreuth: Edition Musica Bayreuth, 1966);

Westernhagen, *Vom Holländer zum Parsifal: Neue Wagner-Studien* (Freiburg: Atlantis, 1962);

Opal Wheeler, *Adventures of Richard Wagner* (London: Faber & Faber, 1961);

Georg Gustav Wieszner, *Richard Wagner, der Theaterreformer: Vom Werden des deutschen Nationaltheaters im Geiste des Jahres 1848* (Emsdetten: Lechte, 1951);

Franz Emil Winkler, ed., *For Freedom Destined: Mysteries of Man's Evolution in Wagner's "Ring" Operas and "Parsifal"* (Garden City, N.Y.: Waldorf Press, 1974);

Hans von Wolzogen, *Erinnerungen an Richard Wagner* (Leipzig: Reclam, 1892);

Wolzogen, *Thematischer Leitfaden durch die Musik zu Richard Wagners Festspiel "Der Ring des Nibelungen"* (Leipzig: Schloemp, 1876);

Wolzogen, *Wagneriana: Gesammelte Aufsätze über Richard Wagners Werke vom Ring bis zum Gral* (Waluff: Sändig, 1977);

Hartmut Zelinsky, *Richard Wagner: Ein deutsches Thema. Eine Dokumentation zur Wirkungsgeschichte Richard Wagners 1876–1976* (Frankfurt am Main: Zweitausendeins, 1976).

Papers:

The Richard Wagner Archive is at the Nationalarchiv der Richard-Wagner-Stiftung (National Archives of the Richard Wagner Foundation), Bayreuth.

Georg Weerth

(17 February 1822 – 30 July 1856)

Jo-Jacqueline Eckardt
New York University

BOOKS: *Leben und Taten des berühmten Ritters Schnapphahnski: Roman* (Hamburg: Hoffmann & Campe, 1849);

Gedichtsammlung, edited by Franz Leschnitzer (Engels: Deutscher Staatsverlag, 1936);

Ausgewählte Werke, edited by Bruno Kaiser (Berlin: Volk und Welt, 1948);

Humoristische Skizzen aus dem deutschen Handelsleben, edited by Kaiser (Berlin: Volk und Welt, 1949);

Das Blumenfest der englischen Arbeiter und andere Skizzen, edited by Kurt Kanzog (Leipzig: Reclam, 1954);

Englische Reisen, edited by Kaiser (Berlin: Rütten & Loening, 1954);

Die ersten Gedichte der Arbeiterbewegung, edited by Harry Pross (Stierstadt: Eremiten-Presse, 1956);

Sämtliche Werke, 5 volumes, edited by Kaiser (Berlin: Aufbau, 1956–1957) – comprises volume 1, *Gedichte* (1956); volume 2, *Prosa des Vormärz* (1956); volume 3, *Skizzen aus dem sozialen und politischen Leben der Briten* (1957); volume 4, *Prosa 1848/49* (1957); volume 5, *Briefe* (1957);

Weerths Werke, 2 volumes, edited by Kaiser (Weimar: Volksverlag Weimar, 1963);

Fragment eines Romans, introduction by Siegfried Unseld (Frankfurt am Main: Insel, 1965);

Blödsinn deutscher Zeitungen und Anderes, edited by Dietger Pforte (Steinbach: Anabas, 1970);

Vergessene Texte, 2 volumes, edited by Jürgen-Wolfgang Goette, Jost Hermand, and Rolf Schloesser (Cologne: Europäische Verlagsanstalt, 1975–1976);

Gedichte, edited by Winfried Hartkopf (Stuttgart: Reclam, 1976).

Georg Weerth

Edition in English: *A Young Revolutionary in Nineteenth-Century England: Selected Writings of Georg*

Weerth, edited by Ingrid and Peter Kuczynski (Berlin: Seven Seas, 1971).

Georg Weerth is one of the important literary figures of the so-called Vormärz (Pre-March) period before the German Revolutions of March 1848. Yet, for nearly one hundred years after his death, Weerth was almost completely forgotten. His political poetry, satiric and journalistic writing, and active political commitment helped shape the critical consciousness of the German bourgeoisie and contributed to the uprising of 1848; Friedrich Engels praised Weerth as the first and most important poet of the German proletariat. But his poems and narratives are more than political propaganda. No other author in nineteenth-century Germany, with the exception of Heinrich Heine, exhibits a similar command of the satiric and "feuilletonistic" style. The few critics who have interpreted Weerth's work have suggested that his style anticipates that of the twentieth-century playwright and poet Bertolt Brecht.

There are various reasons why Weerth received so little recognition in the century following his death. He had only one book of satire published in his lifetime; his other texts appeared in newspapers and in a few anthologies and thus were not easily accessible until his collected works were edited and published in 1956–1957. A second reason is that Weerth himself put little emphasis on preparing his work for posterity. When a friend criticized poems that Weerth had intended for a collection of poetry, he immediately dropped the project and never looked at the poems again. A third reason for Weerth's limited literary reputation may be his friendships with Engels and Karl Marx and his outspoken commitment to their communist cause, which he never renounced. It was probably on these grounds that the bourgeois critics of successive generations passed over his literary work in silence.

Weerth was born on 17 February 1822 in Detmold, Westphalia, to Georg Ludwig Weerth, a Protestant clergyman, and Wilhelmine Weerth, née Burgmann. Christian Dietrich Grabbe and Ferdinand Freiligrath also came from Detmold. The three poets lived within one hundred yards of each other, went to the same school, and were taught by the same teacher.

Weerth was sent to nearby Elberfeld as a business apprentice in 1836, the year his father died. His mother, with whom Weerth always remained close, would have preferred for her son to pursue a religious career, in line with the family's tradition. But while his pietistic upbringing might have influenced the development of Weerth's strong social consciousness, it certainly did not produce an inclination toward spirituality – quite the opposite. Later in life, his antireligious attitude would be reinforced by reading the work of the philosopher Ludwig Feuerbach.

Weerth took an immediate liking to the world of business. From 1840 until 1842 he worked as a bookkeeper in Cologne. His professional enthusiasm did not keep him from enjoying the pleasures the big city had to offer, however; the Cologne carnival inspired his first poems. In 1842 he moved to Bonn to become private secretary to his uncle, Friedrich aus'm Weerth, a clothing manufacturer who was also a liberal politician. Weerth sat in on lectures by August Wilhelm von Schlegel at Bonn University. He also became acquainted with poets and intellectuals such as Gottfried Kinkel and Karl Simrock. Soon, his first poems, praising the joys of love and wine, appeared in local newspapers. While his poetry would later become more critical and politicized, Weerth always remained appreciative of the pleasures of a comfortable existence. Nor did his hedonistic attitude hinder his social conscience from developing. In 1843 he unmasked the mayor of Bonn for publicly supporting the emancipation of Jews but secretly counteracting it. The scandal resulted in Weerth's expulsion from the city. His uncle suggested that he go to England, and he found a clerical position with a German firm in Bradford, a rapidly growing industrial town in Yorkshire. His stay in England turned out to be a pivotal experience in several ways: it was the start of a career as a specialist in international trade; in his creative work it led to a shift from poetry to prose. England also confronted Weerth with a more advanced stage of industrialism than that in Germany.

Bradford was described by the Health of Towns Commission in 1846 as "the dirtiest city in the kingdom," with garbage piling up in the streets and the water supply serving as a breeding ground for disease. The average life expectancy of the working population in Bradford was seventeen years. On the other hand, the textile factories, which were quickly becoming more modern and specialized, brought in huge profits for the upper and middle classes in Bradford.

Weerth, fascinated, took it all in. He accompanied a friend, a Scottish doctor, on his nightly calls to the town's squalid workers' quarters. He participated in union meetings and observed poor-law hearings. The Poor Law of 1834, the latest in a series of acts dating from the twelfth century that tried to control poverty and unemployment in the kingdom, separated "potent" from "impotent" workers and sent the latter to the workhouses. But Weerth also socialized with the German industrialists in Bradford, who probably had no inkling of his interest in the poor. Weerth's most important experience in England was his friendship with Engels, who had come to work in Manchester in 1842. By talking to Engels, immersing himself in the study of economics, and observing industrial England, Weerth shaped his critical and political ideas.

His impressions and observations are well captured in *Skizzen aus dem sozialen und politischen Leben der Briten* (Sketches of the Social and Political Life of the British, 1957). Travel literature had been in vogue for some time, and Heine's work in this genre was widely copied. Weerth's sketches reveal Heine's influence in their heterogeneous, open, and experimental form: there are satirical and critical passages, witty and sometimes personal comments, and romantic images. At the time, only individual chapters were published in periodicals; *Skizzen aus dem sozialen und politischen Leben der Briten* as a whole was not available until Weerth's collected works appeared in the 1950s.

Weerth was familiar with Charles Dickens's work, the satirical magazine *Punch,* recent workers' literature, and most of all the writings of British philosophers and economists such as Robert Owen and Adam Smith. Consequently, his travel impressions are more focused and more direct than Heine's "Englische Fragmente" (English Fragments, 1831). The central theme in his varied vignettes is always the struggle of the working class. Whether describing hectic urban life in London, a flower festival in Bradford, or the history of the British Chartist movement, he never fails to make England a symbol of industrialism and exploitation.

Weerth began another literary work in England that he never completed; it was published in 1965 as *Fragment eines Romans* (Fragment of a Novel). Less satiric than Weerth's later prose, the fragment attempts to draw a picture of society as a whole. The story takes place in Germany, with three major sets of characters representing the three classes: aristocracy, bourgeoisie, and workers. Mr. Preiss, a powerful and wealthy businessman modeled on Weerth's uncle, embodies all the capitalistic characteristics that Weerth despised, such as ruthlessness and a belief in trade protectionism. His name indicates a preoccupation with money: the German word *Preis* means price. Mr. Preiss's sons, however, represent other facets of the bourgeoisie. One is an

unworldly "philosopher" who never takes part in the narrative; another son falls in love with the daughter of an impoverished aristocrat – later Weerth would describe the aristocracy in less idealized terms. Preiss's third son, August, discovers that his heart lies with the working class. He is secretly in love with Marie Martin, a young woman working in his father's factory. But it is Marie's brother, Eduard, who is the true hero of the novel. He has just returned from England full of stories of indignation, strikes, and rebellion. Eduard Martin may well be the first "proletarian" hero in German literature. Unfortunately, the fragment ends before his character becomes central to the story.

In April 1846 Weerth moved to Brussels, a center of exile and communist activity. The Congress on Free Trade met there the following year; Weerth, Marx, and Engels were among the participants. Marx and Engels did not speak, but Weerth did. The congress participants were stunned by his radical ideas: never before had anyone publicly championed the working class. Weerth became internationally famous overnight. His commitment to the cause did not go as deep as that of Marx and Engels, however; he never became an active member of the Communist party, and theory was not his calling.

In 1848 the revolution broke out in Paris. Weerth went there immediately and joined in the demonstrations; an enthusiastic letter to his mother from Paris ends with the words "Vive la République!"

The revolution swept into Germany in March, and Weerth returned with it. He settled in Cologne, where Marx and Engels had just arrived and were planning to publish a daily newspaper. The *Neue Rheinische Zeitung* (New Rhenish Newspaper) appeared from 1 June 1848 until 19 May 1849. The newspaper was soon internationally recognized and boasted a relatively wide circulation. Weerth took over the feuilleton section, which in most newspapers contained literary and entertaining pieces. Weerth and Freiligrath, who had also joined the paper, filled the space with political and social satire.

Two of Weerth's prose pieces that appeared in the *Neue Rheinische Zeitung* became particularly well known. *Humoristische Skizzen aus dem deutschen Handelsleben* (Humorous Sketches from the German Business Life) appeared between November 1847 and July 1848 in the *Kölnische Zeitung* (Cologne Newspaper) and continued in the *Neue Rheinische Zeitung* from 1 June until 6 July 1848; it was published in book form in 1949. The sketches offer a "humor-

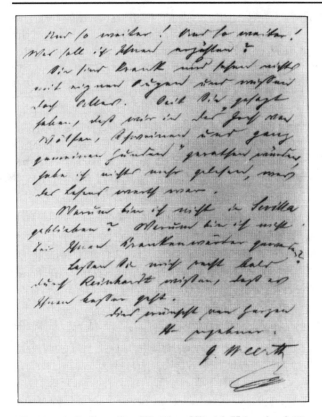

Last page of a letter from Weerth to Heinrich Heine, dated 12 April 1851 (Heinrich Heine Institute, Düsseldorf)

ous" glimpse of the nineteenth-century business world and its values and principles. Weerth's considerable knowledge of the field enabled him to draw a vivid, accurate picture of life and work in a successful business. The industrialist Mr. Preiss appears again; his selfish and unscrupulous behavior is more exaggerated than in the earlier *Fragment eines Romans*. Mr. Preiss regularly preaches to his employees the value and the "Moral" (morality) of money. To attain as much money as possible, Mr. Preiss lies, cheats, and dupes his customers as well as his business partners. He never shows a trace of bad conscience, since, after all, those are the tricks of the game. Among the characteristics that Mr. Preiss respects in his employees are thriftiness, vanity, subservience, and opportunism. Mr. Preiss and a few protegés accumulate more and more wealth, while most of his employees are left out in the cold. Mr. Preiss does not show the least inclination to accept any social responsibility for the latter; for example, he does not hesitate to fire old Sassafraß, who has devotedly served him for thirty-five years. Sassafraß accepts his fate; thus Weerth not only blames the capitalist system for the uneven distribution of wealth but also criticizes the working class for tolerating this inequity.

The events surrounding the 1848 revolution are also captured in *Humoristische Skizzen aus dem deutschen Handelsleben*. Laws guaranteeing freedom of the press were passed, and elections were held to establish a parliament in Frankfurt am Main. But before the parliament could effect major changes, it was dissolved through the counterrevolution. Weerth was bitterly disappointed and blamed the bourgeoisie for abandoning its goal of a democratic Germany. *Humoristische Skizzen aus dem deutschen Handelsleben* ends with Mr. Preiss's negotiating with the counterrevolutionary aristocratic and capitalistic forces: realizing that politics can lead to profit, he begins to deal in arms and is offered the position of secretary of state.

Weerth's other well-known prose work published in the *Neue Rheinische Zeitung* is an attack on the aristocracy: *Leben und Taten des berühmten Ritters Schnapphahnski* (Life and Deeds of the Famous Knight Schnapphahnski) appeared from 8 August 1848 to 21 January 1849. It is generally considered Germany's first feuilletonistic novel. Schnapphahnski, the paradigm of a vain, corrupt, lazy, hypocritical, and utterly incompetent nobleman, uses women, cheats, lies, and plots. In the first chapter he seduces and runs away with the Countess S. Count S. overtakes them on the road; the cowardly Schnapphahnski runs from the scene, abandoning the countess. He goes from one such incident to another, eventually touring all of Europe.

Critics noted that as unbelievable as they seemed, most of Schnapphahnski's adventures were based on events in the life of Prince Felix Lichnowsky. Readers recognized the veiled subject of the satire immediately; Heine had ridiculed the prince in his verse epic *Atta Troll* (1847; translated, 1876) and had also called his character Schnapphahnski. At the end of his tour, Weerth's Schnapphahnski appears to be humiliated and ruined; but he launches a career as a politician and quickly rises to power, just as the real Lichnowsky did as an ultraconservative member of the Frankfurt parliament.

Leben und Taten des berühmten Ritters Schnapphahnski has been praised as Weerth's best work. It has also been criticized for its confused heterogeneity, its mannerism, and its failure to attack the aristocracy as a whole. In no other work did Weerth achieve such stylistic mastery, but Schnapphahnski's behavior is too ridiculous to stand for a whole class or a whole era.

In 1848, while *Leben und Taten des berühmten Ritters Schnapphahnski* was being published in the newspaper, Prince Lichnowsky was killed by a street mob. Weerth was arrested for libel. To prove that he had not intended to insult the prince, he wrote additional episodes that had nothing to do with Schnapphahnski and had the whole series published in book form by Heine's publisher, Hoffman und Campe, in 1849. Only in the last chapter does Weerth regain his sharp analytical sense. He completely shifts focus to give a satiric account of the six hundredth anniversary of the laying of the foundation of the Cologne Cathedral. Representatives from most German states had been invited to this historic celebration, which took place on 12 August 1848. By depicting it as empty and pompous and the participants as greedy and dumb, the author creates a hilarious image of parliamentary Germany just prior to the restoration. The effort, however, had little effect on the courts. Weerth was sentenced to three months in prison and a loss of his civil rights for five years. The judgment marked a turning point in his life and career. Rather than escaping to exile as other writers had, Weerth entered Cologne's Klingelpütz prison on 25 February 1850. While going to jail enabled Weerth to remain in Germany and resume his business career, it meant the end of Weerth as a writer at age twenty-eight.

During the last six years of his life Weerth was a successful businessman. He traveled all over Europe, and in 1852 he moved to Saint Thomas in the Virgin Islands and toured most of Central and South America. Letters from those years to his family, to Marx and Engels, and to Heine – whom Weerth had finally met in Paris in 1851 – are fascinating travel accounts; what is astonishing, however, in light of Weerth's earlier writing, is his failure to mention the plight of the poor, especially of the Indians and the African slaves, except in passing. Declining solicitations from Marx and Engels as well as from newspapers for literary or political commentary, he said: "den vaterländischen Fratzen ein blödes Lächeln abzulocken – ich kenne nichts Erbärmlicheres!" (To secure a stupid grin from my countrymen – I know of nothing more pathetic!).

Evidently, Weerth was depressed by social and political developments. In addition, a more personal disappointment overshadowed his life during this period. He had been unhappily in love with a distant relative, Betty Tendering, since 1852. She appears as Dortchen Schönfund in Gottfried Keller's novel *Der grüne Heinrich* (1854–1855; translated as *Green Henry*, 1960); Keller was also in love with Tendering. After a final meeting with Tendering in Marseilles in 1855, Weerth returned to Saint Thomas and undertook long trips in the Americas

that could have been attempts to recover from her rejection of him. Weerth's letters to Tendering are some of his most beautiful texts; he says that not even his adventurous escapades in the highest mountains and thickest jungles could make him forget her. Before he could regain his enthusiasm for life or art, he caught malaria and died in Havana on 30 July 1856.

Letters:

Briefwechsel mit Betty Tendering, edited by Bruno Kaiser (Berlin & Weimar: Aufbau, 1972);

Sämtliche Briefe, 2 volumes, edited by Jürgen-Wolfgang Goette (Frankfurt am Main & New York: Campus, 1989).

Bibliographies:

Ernst Fleischhack, "Georg-Weerth-Bibliographie," *Lippische Mitteilungen aus Geschichte und Landeskunde,* 41 (1972): 191–227;

Bernd Füllner, "Georg Weerth: Ein Forschungsbericht," in *Georg Weerth: Neue Studien,* edited by Füllner (Bielefeld: Aisthesis, 1988), pp. 1–43.

Biographies:

Karl Weerth, *Georg Weerth: Der Dichter des Proletariats: Ein Lebensbild* (Leipzig: Hirschfeld, 1930);

Heinrich Leber, *Freiligrath; Herwegh; Weerth* (Leipzig: VEB Bibliographisches Institut, 1973);

Uwe Zemke, *Georg Weerth: 1822–1856. Ein Leben zwischen Literatur, Politik und Handel* (Düsseldorf: Droste, 1989).

References:

Akademie der Wissenschaften der DDR, eds., *Georg Weerth: Werk und Wirkung* (Berlin: Akademie-Verlag, 1974);

Rosemary Ashton, "Three Communist Clerks: Engels, Weerth and Freiligrath in Manchester, Bradford and London," in her *Little Germany: Exile and Asylum in Victorian England* (Oxford & New York: Oxford University Press, 1986), pp. 56–138;

Hans Bender, "Versuch über Georg Weerths 'Schnapphahnski,'" *Akzente,* 22 (June 1975): 276–287;

Horst Bunke, *Georg Weerth, 1822–1856: Ein Überblick über sein Leben und Wirken* (Frankfurt an der Oder: Neuer Tag, 1956);

Walter Dietze, "Georg Weerths geistige Entwicklung und künstlerische Meisterschaft," in his *Reden, Vorträge, Essays* (Leipzig: Reclam, 1972), pp. 128–169;

A. L. Dymschiz, "Georg Weerth," *Kunst und Literatur,* 4 (1956): 591–607;

Jo-Jacqueline Eckardt, *Angriff, Rückzug und Zuversicht: Satirisches Erzählen bei Bonaventura, Jean Paul, E. T. A. Hoffmann, Heinrich Heine und Georg Weerth* (Bern: Lang, 1989);

Bernd Füllner, ed., *Georg Weerth: Neue Studien* (Bielefeld: Aisthesis, 1988);

Jürgen-Wolfgang Goette, "Zur Edition sämtlicher Briefe von und an Georg Weerth," *Grabbe-Jahrbuch,* 7 (1988): 126–142;

Karl Hotz, *Georg Weerth – Ungleichzeitigkeit und Gleichzeitigkeit im literarischen Vormärz* (Stuttgart: Klett, 1976);

Ludwig Krapf, "Zur politischen Satire Georg Weerths: Überlegungen zu den 'Humoristischen Skizzen aus dem deutschen Handelsleben,' " *Der Deutschunterricht,* 31, no. 2 (1979): 95–106;

Juan Marinello, "Georg Weerth: The Early Prophet," *Granma,* 9, no. 11 (17 March 1974): 2;

Florian Vaßen, *Georg Weerth: Ein politischer Dichter des Vormärz und der Revolution von 1848/49* (Stuttgart: Metzler, 1971);

Uwe Zemke, "Georg Weerth – Friend of Marx and Engels," *Marxism Today,* 16, no. 16 (1972): 187–191;

Zemke, "Von Detmold nach Havanna: Vorbereitung und Zusammenstellung der Georg-Weerth-Ausstellung 1989," *Grabbe-Jahrbuch,* 9 (1990): 149–169.

Papers:

The International Institute of Social History, Amsterdam, has most of Georg Weerth's manuscripts and letters. Some papers are also in the Weerth-Archiv, Landesbibliothek (Provincial Library) Detmold. The Institute for Marxism-Leninism, Moscow, holds most of Weerth's letters to Karl Marx and Friedrich Engels.

Wilhelm Weitling

(5 October 1808 – 25 January 1871)

Keith Bullivant
University of Florida

BOOKS: *Die Menschheit, wie sie ist und wie sie sein sollte,* anonymous (Paris: Bund der Gerechten, 1838); republished, as Weitling (New York: Druckerei der "Republik der Arbeiter," 1854);

Garantien der Harmonie und Freiheit (Vivis: Weitling, 1842); republished as *Des seligen Schneider's Weitling Lehre vom Sozialismus und Communismus* (New York: Deutsche Verlagsanstalt, 1879);

Das Evangelium des armen Sünders (Bern: Jenni, 1844; enlarged, 1844; New York: Weitling, 1847);

Kerkerpoesien (Hamburg: Hoffmann & Campe, 1844);

Ein Nothruf an die Männer der Arbeit (New York: Weitling, 1847);

Die Bibliothek der Arbeiter: Enthaltend Wilhelm Weitlings sämmtliche Werke, nebst einer Auswahl der bekanntesten und wirksamsten aller in diesem Geiste erschienenen Schriften, 3 volumes (New York: Druckerei des Arbeiterbundes, 1854);

Der bewegende Urstoff in seinen kosmo-electro-magnetischen Wirkungen: Ein Bild des Weltalls (New York: Druckerei der "Republik der Arbeiter," 1856; Kiel: Mühlau, 1931);

Gerechtigkeit: Ein Studium in 500 Tagen. Bilder der Wirklichkeit und Betrachtungen des Gefangenen, edited by Ernst Barnikol (Kiel: Mühlau, 1929);

Klassifikation des Universums: Eine frühsozialistische Weltanschauung. Nebst: Weitlings "Adressbuch" und Hamburger Versammlungsreden 1848–1849, edited by Barnikol (Kiel: Mühlau, 1931).

OTHER: Hugues Félicité de Lamennais, *Das Buch des Volkes,* translated by Weitling (1838);

Der Hülferuf der deutschen Jugend, renamed *Die junge Generation* in 1842, edited by Weitling (September 1840 – December 1842);

Volksklänge: Eine Sammlung patriotischer Lieder, edited by F. W. G. Mäurer, contributions by Weitling (Paris: Wittersheim, 1841);

Der Urwähler, nos. 1–5, edited by Weitling (1848);

Die Republik der Arbeiter, edited by Weitling (15 January 1850 – 21 July 1855).

Wilhelm Weitling

Wilhelm Weitling, although considerably less well known than his fellow poets of the Vormärz (the period from 1840 up to the German revolutions of March 1848), such as Georg Herwegh, Ferdinand Freiligrath, and Hoffmann von Fallersleben, exemplifies more than any of them the convergence of political theory, activism, and literary practice in the 1840s. He is widely considered to be the first communist theoretician.

Wilhelm Christian Weitling was born in Magdeburg on 5 October 1808, the illegitimate son of a seamstress, Christine Weitling, and Guillaume Terijou, a soldier in the French occupying force. After completing school Weitling was apprenticed to a tailor; as a journeyman he moved to Leip-

Weitling's wife, the former Dorothea Caroline Louise Toedt, and their first two children in a daguerreotype she gave Weitling on his fiftieth birthday. Mrs. Weitling was twenty-four years younger than her husband (from Carl Wittke, The Utopian Communist: A Biography of Wilhelm Weitling, *1950)*

zig in 1830, to Dresden in 1832, to Vienna in 1834, and to Paris in 1837.

In Paris he was one of the founders of a German socialist organization, the Bund der Geächteten (League of Outlaws); later the organization was called the Bund der Gerechten (League of the Just) and, after that, the Bund der Kommunisten (Communist League). In France he came under the influence of utopian socialists such as Etienne Cabet, François-Noël Babeuf, and Hugues Félicité Robert de Lamennais, and he translated the latter's *Livre du peuple* (Book of the People) into German in 1838. His first work, *Die Menschheit, wie sie ist und wie sie sein sollte* (The Human Race, as It Is and as It Should Be, 1838) offered a utopian socialism based on a revolutionary interpretation of the Bible. The involvement of the League of the Just in the insurrection of the "société des saisons" (society of the seasons) in 1839 forced him to flee to Zurich. There, in 1840, he founded the periodical *Der Hülferuf der deutschen Jugend* (The Cry of German Youth for Help), which was renamed *Die junge Generation* (The Young Generation) in 1842. His *Garantien der Harmonie und Freiheit* (Guarantees of Harmony and Freedom,

1842) revealed the emergence in Weitling of a proletarian class consciousness. His next book led to his prosecution for blasphemy in 1843 on the basis of the prospectus through which Weitling had tried to solicit subscriptions; he was sentenced to ten months' imprisonment and subsequent banishment from Switzerland for five years. The book itself, *Das Evangelium des armen Sünders* (The Gospel of the Poor Sinner), was published the following year. It is an interpretation of the Bible in which Christ – "der revolutionäre Zimmermann" (the revolutionary carpenter) – is portrayed as a communist preaching the abolition of private property. Weitling holds that the contradiction in contemporary society between a nominal Christianity and "die Macht des Mammons" (the power of Mammon) results from a misunderstanding of the teachings of Christ; Christ "war . . . ein Kommunist" (was . . . a communist) who regarded property as inherently evil: "Das Prinzip der Lehre Jesu ist die Gemeinschaft der Arbeiten und Genüsse" (the principle of Christ's message is the communality of work and of pleasure). The spectacular nature of Weitling's trial and the publication of the poems he wrote while in prison as *Kerkerpoesien* (Prison Poems, 1844) generated great interest in radical circles. Released from imprisonment, he arrived in London in August 1844. Unlike many of his colleagues in the League of the Just, he found it difficult to get involved in British working-class politics and had little patience with the new, "scientific" direction that communist thought was taking.

In 1846 he moved to Brussels, where Karl Marx and Friedrich Engels were becoming increasingly prominent in the Belgian branch of the League of the Just; but after losing a confrontation with Marx that established the victory of "wissenschaftlicher Sozialismus" (scientific socialism) over "Gefühlssozialismus" (intuitive socialism) he became increasingly isolated. He immigrated to New York at the beginning of 1847, returning to Germany in 1848 as the representative of the New York lodge of the Befreiungsbund (Union of Liberation). That year he founded a weekly newspaper, *Der Urwähler* (The Archetypal Voter), in Berlin, but it quickly collapsed. It rapidly became clear that Weitling was out of place on the German revolutionary scene. Nevertheless, he continued to be hounded by the authorities and fled back to New York, via London, in 1849. He edited and published the utopian socialist journal *Republik der Arbeiter* (Workers' Republic) from 1850 to 1855, and he was involved for a time in attempts to establish a workers' cooperative bank and a communist settlement in Communia, Iowa.

In 1854 he married the twenty-two-year-old Dorothea Caroline Louise Toedt, who had immigrated to the United States with her parents two years previously. The Weitlings had five sons and a daughter.

The publishing firm connected with his *Republik der Arbeiter* republished most of his early writings, but after his first treatise on cosmology appeared in 1856 (the second was not published until 1931) his publishing ventures collapsed. He was forced to return to tailoring and spent years fighting a patent battle with the Singer Sewing Company over buttonhole and embroidery machines he had invented. He became an American citizen in 1867. He died of a stroke on 5 January 1871, the day after he attended a banquet of the Workers' International.

Recent attention to Weitling, particularly in the former German Democratic Republic, has centered on his relationship to Marx and Engels and his theoretical writings, which are seen as important in the development of early socialist thought. His literary work, which has received little attention, consists of twelve poems in the collection *Volksklänge* (Sounds of the People, 1841) and his *Kerkerpoesien*. Like his theoretical writings, the poetry in *Volksklänge* demonstrates the changes that mark off the Vormärz from Young Germany (the socially engaged writers of the 1830s, represented by Theodor Mundt, Ludwig Wienbarg, and Karl Gutzkow). Instead of vague cries for German unity and freedom and instead of the rejection of absolutism in non-class-specific terms, Weitling's watchword is "Gleichheit" (equality), which has more-explicit political connotations. His verses on the Rhine crisis (France's threat in 1840 to extend its borders east of the Rhine) express hope for the establishment in Germany of a free and equal society that will be an example to the rest of the world. "Das Geld" (Money) and "Klage und Hoffnung" (Lament and Hope) focus on the existing distribution of wealth as the main impediment to social and material equality. This ideal is one that was "von den Brüdern Jesu Christs verstanden" (understood by brothers in Jesus Christ). The principles of Christian socialism – the constant theme of Weitling's theoretical writings – find particularly vigorous expression in "Jakob von Hutten," a hymn of praise to the sixteenth-century Anabaptist leader Jakob

Huter, who set an example for the present by establishing a social order based on the communality of goods. The poems have little intrinsic merit; the simple rhyme patterns and the hymnlike forms, with frequent use of refrains, indicate that they were meant to be sung in the exile craftsmen's clubs in France, Switzerland, Belgium, and England, as well as in the political underground in Germany, as a means of raising consciousness and reinforcing a political message; in many cases Weitling indicates the particular folk tune to which the poem is set. They constitute the tip of an iceberg of poems, songs, pamphlets, and other ephemera that were published in the late 1830s and 1840s and, as such, afford an insight into these stormy years. *Kerkerpoesien* is fascinating for its account of his anguish in jail but lacks the emotive force of the comparable poems of his contemporary, the English poet-activist Thomas Cooper, published two years later.

Biography:

Carl Wittke, *The Utopian Communist: A Biography of Wilhelm Weitling, Nineteenth-Century Reformer* (Baton Rouge: Louisiana State University Press, 1950).

References:

Werner Bellmann, "Heines Begegnung mit Schneider Weitling," *Heine-Jahrbuch,* 20 (1981): 158–162;

Wolfram von Moritz, *Wilhelm Weitling: Religiöse Problematik und literarische Form* (Frankfurt am Main: Lang, 1981);

Wolfgang Schieder, "Wilhelm Weitling und die deutsche politische Handwerkerlyrik im Vormärz," *International Review of Social History,* 5, no. 2 (1960): 265–290;

George Schulz-Behrend, "Communia, Iowa: A Nineteenth-Century German Utopia," *Iowa Journal of History and Politics,* 48, no. 1 (1950): 27–54;

Waltraud Seidel-Höppner, *Wilhelm Weitling, der erste deutsche Theoretiker und Agitator des Kommunismus* (Berlin: Dietz, 1961);

Carl Wittke, "Wilhelm Weitling's Literary Efforts," *Monatshefte,* 40 (February 1948): 63–68.

Papers:

Some of Wilhelm Weitling's papers are in the Zurich Staatsarchiv (State Archives). The Library of Congress, Washington, D.C., has a few of Weitling's papers.

Adolf von Wilbrandt

(24 August 1837 – 10 June 1911)

Glen W. Gadberry
University of Minnesota – Twin Cities

BOOKS: *Heinrich von Kleist* (Nördlingen: Beck, 1863);

Geister und Menschen: Roman, 3 volumes (Nördlingen: Beck, 1864);

Der Licentiat: Roman, 3 volumes (Nordhausen: Büchting, 1868);

Novellen (Berlin: Hertz, 1869) – comprises "Die Brüder," "Heimat," "Reseda";

Neue Novellen (Berlin: Hertz, 1870) – comprises "Narciß," "Die Geschwister von Portovenere," "Johann Ohlerich," "Die Reise nach Freienwalde";

Dramatische Schriften, 2 volumes (Berlin: Lassar, 1870) – comprises volume 1, *Unerreichbar*; volume 2, *Der Graf von Hammerstein*;

Jugendliebe: Lustspiel in einem Aufzuge (Vienna: Rosner, 1872);

Die Vermählten: Lustspiel in drei Aufzügen (Vienna: Rosner, 1872);

Die Maler: Lustspiel in drei Aufzügen (Vienna: Rosner, 1872);

Gracchus, der Volkstribun: Trauerspiel in fünf Aufzügen (Vienna: Rosner, 1872);

Der Kampf ums Dasein: Lustspiel in drei Aufzügen (Vienna: Rosner, 1873);

Arria und Messalina: Trauerspiel in fünf Aufzügen (Vienna: Rosner, 1874);

Giordano Bruno: Trauerspiel in drei Aufzügen (Vienna: Rosner, 1874);

Durch die Zeitung: Lustspiel in einem Aufzug (Vienna: Rosner, 1874);

Gedichte (Vienna: Rosner, 1874);

Ein neues Novellenbuch: Dritte Sammlung der Novellen (Vienna: Rosner, 1875) – comprises "Dämonen," "Die Bande des Bluts," "Die Königin von Castilien," "Unser Rechtsbewußtsein," "Das Märchen vom ersten Menschen"; republished as *Dämonen und andere Geschichten* (Stuttgart & Berlin: Cotta, 1908);

Fridolins heimliche Ehe: Nach Erinnerungen und Mitteilungen erzählt (Vienna: Rosner, 1875); translated by Clara Bell as *Fridolin's Mystical Marriage: A Study of an Original, Founded on Reminiscences of a Friend* (New York: Gottsberger, 1884);

Nero: Trauerspiel in fünf Aufzügen (Vienna: Rosner, 1876);

Die Wege des Glücks: Lustspiel in fünf Aufzügen (Vienna: Rosner, 1876);

Kriemhild: Trauerspiel in drei Aufzügen (Vienna: Rosner, 1877);

Die Reise nach Riva: Lustspiel in drei Aufzügen (Vienna: Rosner, 1877);

Der Thurm in der Stadtmauer: Lustspiel in drei Aufzügen (Vienna: Rosner, 1879);

Meister Amor: Roman, 2 volumes (Vienna: Rosner, 1880);

Robert Kerr: Tragödie in fünf Aufzügen (Vienna: Rosner, 1880);

Novellen aus der Heimath, 2 volumes (Breslau: Schottländer, 1882) – comprises "Der Lotsenkommandeur," translated as "The Pilot Captain," in *Masterpieces of German Fiction* (Chicago: Schick, 1890); "Der Gast vom Abendstern"; "Am heiligen Damm"; "Der Mitschuldige";

Assunta Leoni: Schauspiel in fünf Aufzügen (Vienna: Rosner, 1883);

Die Tochter des Herrn Fabricius: Schauspiel in drei Aufzügen (Vienna: Rosner, 1883);

Der Verwalter; Die Verschollenen: Novellen (Breslau: Schottländer, 1884);

Der Wille zum Leben; Untrennbar: Novellen (Stuttgart: Engelhorn, 1885);

Marianne: Lustspiel in vier Aufzügen (Berlin: Sittenfeld, 1889);

Gespräche und Monologe: Sammlung vermischter Schriften (Stuttgart: Cotta, 1889) – comprises "Ein Gespräch, das fast nur Biographie wird," "Für Schleswig-Holstein! Wie den Schleswig-Holsteinern zu helfen ist, und was uns allen not thut," "Shakespeare's Coriolanus," "Mein Freund Scaevola: Ein Gespräch," "Hölderlin, der Dichter des Pantheismus," "Wie 'Arria und Messalina' entstand: Ein Gespräch," "Platos Verteidigungsrede des Sokrates," "Er und ich: Ein Gespräch," "Meister Amor," "Fritz Reuters Leben und Werke," "Drei Nächte: Ein Gespräch," "Johannes Kugler";

Neue Gedichte (Stuttgart: Cotta, 1889);

Der Meister von Palmyra: Dramatische Dichtung in fünf Aufzügen (Stuttgart: Cotta, 1889); translated by Harriott S. Olive as *The Master of Palmyra: A Dramatic Poem,* in *Poet Lore,* 13, no. 2 (1901): 161-248; translated by Charles Wharton Stork as *The Master of Palmyra,* in *The German Classics of the Nineteenth and Twentieth Centuries,* volume 16, edited by Kuno Francke and William G. Howard (New York: German Publishing Society, 1914), pp. 10-99;

Adams Söhne: Roman (Berlin: Hertz, 1890);

Friedrich Hölderlin; Fritz Reuter: Zwei Biographieen, volume 2 of *Führende Geister,* edited by Anton Bettelheim (Dresden: Ehlermann, 1890);

Hermann Ifinger: Roman (Stuttgart: Cotta, 1892);

Der Dornenweg: Roman (Stuttgart: Cotta, 1894);

Die Osterinsel: Roman (Stuttgart: Cotta, 1895); translated by Angelo Solomon Rappoport as *A New Humanity; or, The Easter Island* (London: Maclaren, 1905);

Beethoven (Stuttgart: Cotta, 1895);

Die Rothenburger: Roman (Stuttgart: Cotta, 1895);

Vater und Sohn und andere Geschichten (Stuttgart: Cotta, 1896) – comprises "Vater und Sohn," "Die gute Lorelei," "Hütchen";

Die Eidgenossen: Schauspiel in fünf Aufzügen (Berlin: Sittenfeld, 1895);

Hildegard Mahlmann: Roman (Stuttgart: Cotta, 1897);

Schleichendes Gift: Roman (Stuttgart: Cotta, 1897);

Die glückliche Frau: Roman (Stuttgart: Cotta, 1898);

Vater Robinson: Roman (Stuttgart: Cotta, 1899);

Der Sänger: Roman (Stuttgart: Cotta, 1899);

Hairan: Dramatische Dichtung in fünf Aufzügen (Stuttgart: Cotta, 1900);

Erika; Das Kind: Erzählungen (Stuttgart: Cotta, 1900);

Feuerblumen: Roman (Stuttgart: Cotta, 1900);

Timandra: Trauerspiel in fünf Aufzügen (Berlin: Sittenfeld, 1900);

Franz: Roman (Stuttgart: Cotta, 1901);

Das lebende Bild und andere Geschichten (Stuttgart: Cotta, 1901) – comprises "Das lebende Bild," "Der Mörder," "Zwei Tagebücher," "Das Urteil des Paris";

Ein Mecklenburger: Roman (Stuttgart: Cotta, 1901);

Villa Maria: Roman (Stuttgart: Cotta, 1902);

Der Rosengarten: Novelle (Leipzig: Keil, 1903);

Familie Roland: Roman (Stuttgart: Cotta, 1903);

Große Zeiten und andere Geschichten (Stuttgart & Berlin: Cotta, 1904) – comprises "Große Zeiten," "Der Rosengarten," "Das freie Kloster," "Drinnen und Draußen";

Fesseln: Roman (Stuttgart & Berlin: Cotta, 1904);

Erinnerungen (Stuttgart & Berlin: Cotta, 1905);

Irma: Roman (Stuttgart: Cotta, 1905);

Die Schwestern: Roman (Stuttgart: Cotta, 1906);

Lieder und Bilder (Stuttgart & Berlin: Cotta, 1907) – includes "Beethoven," "Indische Liedchen," "Tiziano und Giorgine";

Sommerfäden: Roman (Stuttgart: Cotta, 1907);

Aus der Werdezeit: Erinnerungen. Neue Folge (Stuttgart & Berlin: Cotta, 1907);

König Teja: Trauerspiel in fünf Aufzügen, biographical introduction by Karl Vogt (Leipzig: Reclam, 1908);

Am Strom der Zeit: Roman (Stuttgart: Cotta, 1908);

Rund ums Mittelmeer: Reisebriefe an einen Freund (Stuttgart & Berlin: Cotta, 1909);

Opus 23 und andere Geschichten (Stuttgart & Berlin: Cotta, 1909) – comprises "Opus 23," "Das Kind von Goslar," "Anneli," "Nach dem Ende";

Hiddensee: Roman (Stuttgart, Berlin & Leipzig: Union, 1910);

Die Tochter: Roman (Stuttgart: Cotta, 1911);

Adonis, und andere Geschichten (Stuttgart: Cotta, 1911) – comprises "Adonis," "Meineidig," "Junggesellen," "Zwischen den Ufern," "Das Vorbild."

OTHER: *Sophokles und Euripides: Ausgewählte Dramen,* 2 volumes, translated by Wilbrandt (Nördlingen: Beck, 1866) – comprises *König Oedipus, Oedipus in Kolonos, Antigone, Kyclops*;

William Shakespeare, *Viel Lärmen um Nichts,* translated by Wilbrandt, volume 5 of *Shakespeare's dramatische Werke,* edited by Friedrich Bodenstedt, (Leipzig: Brockhaus, 1867);

Shakespeare, *Coriolanus,* translated by Wilbrandt, volume 11 of *Shakespeare's dramatische Werke,* edited by Bodenstedt (Leipzig: Brockhaus, 1867);

Fritz Reuter, *Sämtliche Werke,* volume 1, introduction by Wilbrandt (Berlin: Knauer, 1874);

Reuter, *Nachgelassene Schriften,* 2 volumes, edited with biography by Wilbrandt (Wismar, Rostock & Ludwigslust: Hinstorff, 1874, 1875);

"Heinrich von Kleist's Leben," in Kleist's *Werke,* volume 1 (Berlin: Hempel, 1879), pp. 3–64;

Reuter, *Sämtliche Werke: Volksausgabe in sieben Bänden,* 7 volumes, edited by Wilbrandt (Wismar: Hinstorff, 1888);

Aristophanes, *Frauenherrschaft: Lustspiel in vier Aufzügen, nach Aristophanes' "Ekklesiazusen" und "Lysistrate,"* translated and adapted by Wilbrandt (Berlin: Sittenfeld, 1892);

Georg Christoph Lichtenberg, *Ausgewählte Schriften,* edited by Wilbrandt (Stuttgart: Cotta, 1893);

Johann Wolfgang von Goethe, *Faust: Tragödie von Goethe,* adapted by Wilbrandt (Vienna: Breitenstein, 1895);

Sophokles: Ausgewählte Tragödien, translated by Wilbrandt (Munich: Beck, 1903) – comprises *König Oedipus, Oedipus in Kolonos, Antigone, Elektra*;

Pedro Calderón de la Barca, *Der Richter von Zalamea: Schauspiel in drei Aufzügen,* translated by Wilbrandt (Stuttgart & Berlin: Cotta, 1903);

Ulrich Bräker, *Das Leben und die Abentheuer des armen Mannes im Tockenburg, von ihm selbst erzählt,* edited by Wilbrandt (Berlin: Meyer & Jesser, 1910);

Calderón, *Dame Kobold: Lustspiel in drei Aufzügen,* translated by Wilbrandt (Leipzig: Reclam, 1920).

SELECTED PERIODICAL PUBLICATIONS – UNCOLLECTED: "Die Lerche," *Deutsche Rundschau,* 87 (1888): 338–341;

"Georg Christoph Lichtenberg," *Allgemeine Zeitung* (Munich), no. 81 (1893), supplement;

"Friedrich Hessing, der Meister der mechanischen Heilkunst," *Vom Fels zum Meer,* 12 (1893): 60;

"Franz von Lenbach," *Neue Freie Presse* (Vienna), 12 April 1903;

"Ulrich Bräker: Der arme Mann in Tockenburg," *Monatsblätter für deutsche Literatur,* 7 (1903): 263–266, 325–339;

"Hugo Bertsch und Bob der Sonderling," *Allgemeine Zeitung* (Munich), no. 265 (1905), supplement.

Adolf von Wilbrandt catered to the literary interests of the nineteenth-century liberal bourgeoisie and seldom challenged the prevailing ideology. He was a welcome addition to social salons where knowledge of new directions in current affairs, art, science, and philosophy was much prized, especially if combined with a sense of proportion and humor. His literary success was often due to his ability to refer to these shifting intellectual interests. As the critic Max Behr observed in his obituary of the author, Wilbrandt's work shows more breadth than depth. He touched on hypnotism and spiritualism, socialism and woman's rights, naturalism and theosophy. He developed thinly disguised portraits of the cultural figures of the age in his novels and plays—the painter Johannes Kugler in *Die Maler* (The Painters, 1872), the art historian Friedrich Eggers in *Fridolins heimliche Ehe* (1875; translated as *Fridolin's Mystical Marriage,* 1884), the Viennese painter Hans Makart and the Munich patron Count Adolf Friedrich von Schack in *Hermann Ifinger* (1892), the poet Johanna Ambrosius in *Hildegard Mahlmann* (1897), the "cure" celebrity Friedrich Hessing in *Die Rothenburger* (The Rothenburgers, 1895), and the philosopher Friedrich Nietzsche in *Osterinsel* (1895; Easter Island; translated as *A New Humanity,* 1905). But there is little analysis of these individuals or their contributions. They provide comfortable and timely settings for his Bildungsliteratur (dramas and narratives that offer popular personal instruction). His central figures typically achieve social and personal satisfaction after false starts or wrong choices. Wilbrandt thus reinforced the nineteenth century's preoccupation with self-education. He criticized Christianity for its intolerance and seemed to prefer a more humanistic deism. Politically, Wilbrandt argued for the creation of a united and enlightened German state to end local repression and guarantee individual freedom and to bring an advance in German culture. He came to revere Otto von Bismarck; one of his most memorable experiences was the 1895 visit with the former chancellor recounted in "Beim Fürsten Bismarck in Friedrichsruh" (With Prince Bismarck in Friedrichsruh) in his *Erinnerungen* (Memoirs, 1905). Wilbrandt had limited sympathy for revolutionary social movements or for the radical or avant-garde aesthetics of naturalism and symbolism, which appeared at the close of the century. Social advance and personal contentment were possible through will power and education; this was, after all, the path his own life had taken. His social advice, expressed in "Mein Freund Scaevola" (My Friend Scaevola, 1877), a dialogue on art and life, was that one should become a whole human being through study of ennobling models from history and contemporary life. True virtue and art are found in eternal human values, not in the mundane or the merely popular. Wilbrandt developed this commonplace philosophy with some artistry and usually with an engaging sense of humor. He claimed that his Mecklenburg heritage prompted his optimistic view that seeming misfortune is actually a means to change for the better.

One of nine children, Wilbrandt was born on 24 August 1837 in Rostock to Christian Wilbrandt, a professor of aesthetics and modern literature, and Charlotte Wendhausen Wilbrandt; both parents were from established families of educators, ministers, and landowners. Wilbrandt inherited his father's respect for classical education and democratic ideals. Active in state politics, Christian Wilbrandt was indicted in the wave of political reaction following the revolutions of 1848 and endured two years of house arrest. Wilbrandt wrote poems and songs of freedom in his father's defense. He also started to write plays at this time: Wilbrandt's youthful attraction to the theater was nurtured, as the young Johann Wolfgang von Goethe's had been, by the gift of a puppet theater. He regularly attended the local theater and fell in love with a young actress. The theater would figure predominantly in his subsequent career as dramatist, artistic director of the Vienna Burgtheater, and translator and adapter of dramatic literature; it would also shape his novels: critics such as Viktor Klemperer

have noted Wilbrandt's dependence on dramatic structures, characters, and settings, and several of his novels depend principally on dialogue. Wilbrandt was also prone to the populist weaknesses of the nineteenth-century stage – melodramatic effects, rhetorical excess, and unrealistic motivation for characters and events.

After graduating from the gymnasium in March 1856 Wilbrandt attended the Universities of Rostock, Berlin, and Munich. He began by studying law but soon switched to ancient and modern languages, literature, history, and philosophy. In Berlin he studied Egyptology under Karl Lepsius and art history under Franz Kugler and Friedrich Eggers. Kugler and Eggers brought him onto the student staff of their artistic newspaper, the *Kunstblatt,* and into their aesthetic circle, which included the writers Theodor Fontane, Otto Roquette, and Paul Heyse, and the painters Franz Lenbach and Arnold Böcklin. In Munich he studied history under Heinrich Sybel and broadened his artistic friendships. He returned to Rostock to take his doctoral examination in May 1859; because of an exemplary oral examination, a doctoral dissertation was thought unnecessary. He was granted both a master of fine arts and a doctorate.

He returned to Munich and joined the poets' circle "Krokodil" (Crocodile Society), which included his friend Heyse, the poet Emanuel Geibel, the writer Friedrich von Bodenstedt, and the artistic patron Count von Schack. The immensely popular Heyse would be the major influence on his novellas and comedies, and Bodenstedt would include Wilbrandt's translations in his edition of the works of Shakespeare. In 1859 Wilbrandt helped found the nationalist *Süddeutsche Zeitung* (South German Newspaper) and served as its translator, critic, and political commentator. He agitated for a constitution for Mecklenburg that would limit the prerogatives of the ruler and argued for the civil rights of the German population of Schleswig-Holstein, then in danger of being absorbed by Denmark. Revolutionary fervor, inspired by patriotism and his father's political beliefs, was redefined as a love of fatherland. Nationalist sympathies in his work would contribute to their success, but often to the detriment of their literary quality.

Wilbrandt left the newspaper in 1861 to work on the critical biography *Heinrich von Kleist* (1863), which portrays Kleist's inner torment as the essential component of his creativity; his biographies of the writers Friedrich Hölderlin and Fritz Reuter would appear in 1890. Kleist's romantic persona and Goethe's novel *Wilhelm Meisters Lehrjahre* (1795–

1796; translated as *Wilhelm Meister's Apprenticeship,* 1824) informed Wilbrandt's three-volume novel *Geister und Menschen* (Spirits and Men, 1864). The mature author would reject the work as an ill-conceived and formless product of an overpoliticized youth; it was his most experimental work, a passionate mixture of obvious literary models and contemporary events. While working on both projects, Wilbrandt reluctantly agreed to go to Frankfurt am Main to report on the German states' debate on the status and future of Schleswig-Holstein for the *Süddeutsche Zeitung.* By this time he was in a state of complete exhaustion and suffering from nervous ailments that would reappear in the physical makeup of some of his characters. He observed his own symptoms with as much care as he observed the artistic personalities around him. When he returned to Munich in 1864, some of his friends convinced him to take a trip to Italy with them to restore his health.

During his stay in Rome and other cities he studied the works of Charles Darwin and the natural sciences; read the plays of Sophocles, Euripides, and Shakespeare; and conceived his Roman tragedies. After he returned to Munich in 1865, he completed his first volumes of novellas (1869) and poems (1874). The latter contained his adolescent works; translations from the works of Sappho, William Shakespeare, and other poets; and an epic patriotic poem in seven parts, *König Otto's Haus* (King Otto's House). He then turned to the drama; his restored health and innate Mecklenburg sense of humor yielded light comedies of love and intrigue that mixed comic situations with amusing dialogue. *Die Vermählten* (The Newlyweds, 1872), the first of these plays to be produced, was staged in Munich in 1868. The comedy reverses the Romeo and Juliet theme: a young English couple falls out of love when their families force them to marry, but all ends happily. Eleven of his other comedies were produced but were not printed. In June 1871 Wilbrandt went to Vienna for the opening of *Die Vermählten* at the Burgtheater, the Austrian national theater, which was then under the direction of Franz Dingelstedt; he returned in October for the premiere of *Die Maler.* The favorable reception of his plays in Vienna and the city's cultural heritage were great attractions, as was the actress Auguste Baudius, who had appeared in *Die Vermählten.* Wilbrandt moved to Vienna at the end of the year and married Baudius in 1873. His only regret, as he said in his autobiography covering his first thirty years, *Aus der Werdezeit: Erinnerungen* (From the Years of Growth: Memoirs, 1907), was leaving his newly united Germany.

Portrait of Wilbrandt by Franz von Lenbach (from Kuno Francke and William G. Howard, eds., The German Classics of the Nineteenth and Twentieth Centuries, *volume 16, 1914)*

Vienna was Wilbrandt's home for the next sixteen years and the site of his greatest honors and challenges. He secured a local publisher, Ludwig Rosner, and his plays premiered at the Burgtheater and occasionally at its competitor, the Stadttheater. In November 1872 his Kleistian history play *Graf von Hammerstein* (Count von Hammerstein, 1870), set in the eleventh century, opened at the Stadttheater; two days later the verse tragedy *Gracchus, der Volkstribun* (Gracchus, Tribune of the People, 1872) premiered at the Burgtheater. *Gracchus, der Volkstribun* was among his most frequently produced serious plays; it was influenced by Shakespeare's *Coriolanus,* which Wilbrant had translated in 1867. The revolutionary possibilities of the play – Gaius Gracchus as the representative of the people in conflict with a repressive oligarchy – were diminished by Wilbrandt's focus on a personal revenge plot; but its avoidance of radicalism enabled it to receive the Austrian Grillparzer Prize in 1875. In 1878 his Nibelungen tragedy *Kriemhild* (1877) received the Schiller Prize from Emperor Wilhelm I; Victorian-Wilhelminian moderation and "good taste" tempered and weakened the powerful Germanic source. The play premiered in Vienna in 1880 and opened in Berlin in 1882. In 1884 King Ludwig II of Bavaria awarded Wilbrandt the Maximilian Order for service to German literature and bestowed personal nobility on him; from then on he was known as Adolf *von* Wilbrandt.

The Burgtheater circle of artists and aristocratic enthusiasts continued to be his principal audience and inspiration. He was welcomed as a house playwright of charm and wit and, after his marriage, as one of the family. In 1880 Dingelstedt produced Wilbrandt's first major success, *Die Tochter des Herrn Fabricius* (The Daughter of Mr. Fabricius, 1883). A peripheral critique of the treatment of former-convicts, the play features a tearful reunion of daughter and father. Sentimentality combined with strong central roles and a happy ending brought wide and lasting success; the play was produced in German in New York in 1889 with the renowned actor Ernst Possart and in 1902 with the equally well known Adolf Sonnenthal. The drama reveals the successful Wilbrandt formula of using topical material to frame what would otherwise be a shallow, sentimental plot; audiences received an emotional story tempered with a social message.

When Dingelstedt died in 1881, Wilbrandt emerged as the compromise candidate for artistic director of the Burgtheater. Because he was reluctant to sacrifice his writing for a lifetime commitment to managing the most important theater in Austria, he negotiated an open-ended contract. Promising to keep the trivial from the repertoire, the untruthful from the stage, and deficit from the ticket office, he selected the plays and worked with the actors on the understanding of texts; other production details were left to his stage directors. He used the opportunity to produce his adaptations of Sophocles' *Electra* (1903) and of Euripides' *Cyclops* (1866), which opened together on 10 February 1882, and, most successfully, of *Oedipus the King* (1866), which premiered on 29 December 1886. His translations of plays by Pedro Calderón de la Barca and Shakespeare were well received, as was a three-evening adaptation of Goethe's *Faust* (1895), which premiered on 2–4 January 1883. Some of his translations were produced but not published, including his versions of Euripides' *Philoctetes* and *Medea*. During his years at the Burgtheater, Wilbrandt gave little attention to serious contemporary German playwriting and was forced to feature lightweight French and German comedies. Unable to upgrade the repertoire and keep an audience, and disappointed by internal arguments, he resigned in 1887.

Wilbrandt returned to Rostock with his wife and their son, Robert, who had been born in 1875.

He set about revising his metaphysical dramatic masterpiece, *Der Meister von Palmyra* (1889; translated as *The Master of Palmyra,* 1901), which premiered in Munich in 1889 and opened in Vienna in 1892; it brought him his second Grillparzer Prize in 1890. *Der Meister von Palmyra* was Wilbrandt's most widely read play and went through twelve editions by 1907. It is a vast allegoric history, spanning the third and fourth centuries, as the Roman Empire shifted from paganism to Christianity. The master architect Apelles is granted eternal life and ultimately learns that this gift is a curse. Eternal life means eternal pain and separation from loved ones, but it is particularly reprehensible because it interferes with a larger divine plan that has not been understood by Christianity: the soul must be allowed to grow to perfection through death and reincarnation. To help Apelles – and the audience – understand the reality of metempsychosis, another soul accompanies him through five generations; one actress takes fives roles in the course of the play as she is reborn five times. When Apelles finally recognizes the truth of reincarnation and the divine pattern, he is allowed to die. Derived from Gotthold Ephraim Lessing's treatise *Die Erziehung des Menschengeschlechts* (1780; translated as *The Education of the Human Race,* 1858), the play's metaphysics, combined with an exotic Roman-era, Middle-Eastern setting, assured its success, at least for theaters large enough to produce it. Reviewers – including Mark Twain, who saw it in Vienna in 1898 – were impressed with its grand ideas and theatrical scope. Wilbrandt's similarly metaphysical *Hairan* (1900), dedicated to his son, premiered in March 1897 at the Berliner Theater. Set in Antioch in 24 B.C. *Hairan* is a passion play for a new faith. A moral teacher preaches enlightened ideas of brotherhood, love, religious tolerance, and a passion for life. But Hairan is rejected and killed by the mob – the time is not ripe for a humanistic synthesis of pagan and Christian virtues. Prussian censors closed the play after two performances because Hairan too closely resembled Christ, who could not be used as a stage character.

Wilbrandt's final Rostock years were devoted to the novel: twenty-two were published between 1890 and 1911, along with an occasional play, novella, or poem. The novels provide technically proficient portraits of the Zeitgeist, and several derive from Wilbrandt's close connections to the arts. He had begun to portray the theater in *Meister Amor* (Master Amor, 1880): a character actor trains an actress to technical excellence, but she is unable to animate her roles. She needs emotional passion, which comes after she falls in love with a young student. The novel is important to theater history as an informed commentary on conservative nineteenth-century acting theory and practice. Among the more mature Rostock arts novels, *Hermann Ifinger* portrays Vienna's modish painter Makart and Wilbrandt's friends from the Munich circle of artists; *Hildegard Mahlmann* (1897) explores the romantic Kleistian notion that poetic creation is a product of the pain of living; *Der Sänger* (The Singer, 1899) depicts the career of a successful opera star. The title character in *Irma* (1905) finds a proper teacher and a successful career in the opera; she achieves personal satisfaction by marrying an old boyfriend whose doctorate has led him into theater criticism. Despite their sentimentality, these novels register Wilbrandt's knowing observations of the art world.

His other novels portray the larger society but lack equivalent authenticity. *Adams Söhne* (Adam's Sons, 1890) is the most political of these novels, portraying a full range of ideologies from fanatical anarchism to radical nationalism. It also expresses Wilbrandt's social imperatives: cultivate the individual, educate the masses, and provide a minimal level of social welfare. *Der Dornenweg* (The Way of Thorns, 1894) is set in 1880, before those social-welfare programs were enacted. The Bismarck party is depicted as the champion of an ideal Germany, fighting against reactionary financial and political corruption in Berlin. The novel betrays Wilbrandt's continued admiration for Bismarck, who had been dismissed as chancellor in 1890.

Wilbrandt's most popular and provocative novels appeared in 1895. In *Die Rothenburger* a brilliant doctor, modeled on the society orthopedist Friedrich Hessing, builds a marvelous spa, combining a Greek gymnasium and the romantic charm of the medieval walled town Rothenburg ob der Tauber. He achieves medical success through love and strength of will, despite interference from institutional Christianity and southern German provincialism. The sentimentality – the doctor weds the crippled daughter of the woman he loved and lost – contributed to its popularity; it went through eight printings by 1910.

In *Osterinsel* Professor Helmut Adler has a vision of a phoenix rising from its ashes. He interprets the vision as the promise of a reborn and godlike humanity ("Göttermenschen") who will inherit the earth. The present breed of humans has been weakened by the Christian dogma of meekness and egalitarianism and by the increased power of the rabble. Darwin had shown that evolution was continuous; present humanity could evolve into a new humanity

that would be as far above present humans as those humans are above the ape. Adler hopes to hasten evolution through selective breeding; he announces his plans in a series of volumes titled *Der Phönix* (The Phoenix). He will assemble a group of resolute, strong, and noble-minded individuals to occupy and populate an isolated territory. Easter Island is ideal because it is remote, fertile, and defensible – Adler knows that his new beings will need to protect themselves against an envious world of increasingly backward humans. The island is no longer populated due to the raids of slave ships, and there will be no immigration to contaminate his eugenic mission; if the original islanders try to return, they will be cast back into the sea. After hundreds of years Easter Island will be the home of superior beings who will go forth to rule the earth. Like the philosopher of the "Übermensch" (superman), Nietzsche, on whom he is modeled, Adler suffers from nervous disorders and finally madness – in his case, exacerbated by morphine. Adler dies, but his teachings continue to inspire: his disciples will not isolate themselves on a distant island but will live as islands of perfection in the broad mass of people. They must find each other and produce a better humanity.

Helmut Adler – his name means "courageous eagle" – is a hero who combines the author's vision of the best of the German past: he resembles Frederick the Great of Prussia and Goethe. But Adler is flawed by the romantic scope of his dreams, by his addiction, and by his insensitivity not only to the original residents of Easter Island but also to his own daughters, who, he feels, cannot serve his mission. *Osterinsel* is one of many literary works that fed popular interest in Nietzsche's antidemocratic, anti-Christian doctrine of the Übermensch. There is the same frustration in the novel as in Nietzsche's philosophy with a German world gone awry as the highest human aspirations and possibilities were being dissipated by weakness and indecision. Wilbrandt provides a compelling story but once again occasionally succumbs to the sentimental and romantic. On the whole, *Osterinsel* is a sympathetic and fascinating reconfiguration of the Nietzschean assault on the decaying values of the nineteenth century.

After 1900 Wilbrandt's recurring nationalism turned into a dangerous chauvinism as he envisioned a greater German empire in the novels *Franz* (1901), *Familie Roland* (The Roland Family, 1903), and *Fesseln* (Chains, 1904). *Franz* is the most extreme of these novels: a Germanic messiah develops a new religion for the new "auserwähltes Volk" (chosen people), complete with a nationalistic Lord's Prayer. Patriotism, an iron will, and love of earthly life were Wilbrandt's prescriptions for Germany in the twentieth century. *Ein Mecklenburger* (1901), a more genial work, taps Wilbrandt's Rostock heritage. The indigenous optimism of Mecklenburg carries the picaresque hero through danger and adventure, including an episode in the Nevada gold mines that is reminiscent of the works of Bret Harte or Mark Twain.

Wilbrandt maintained a rigorous and structured writing schedule from his youth until the last weeks of his life, interrupted only by his directorship of the Burgtheater. In 1911 his final works, the novel *Die Tochter* (The Daughter) and *Adonis, und andere Geschichten* (Adonis, and Other Stories), his twelfth collection of novellas, were published. Like his novels, Wilbrandt's novellas range over European politics, history, philosophy, and cultural personalities, all topics of interest to the German bourgeoisie. He was as successful in this form as he was in the drama and the novel.

In June, while on a trip to Schwerin to visit a relative, Wilbrandt fell ill. He weakened rapidly, developed pneumonia and other complications, and died on 10 June 1911. He was buried in Rostock on 14 June. Auguste Wilbrandt-Baudius lived until 1937; her memoirs, *Aus Kunst und Leben: Erinnerungen einer alten Burgschauspielerin* (Out of Art and Life: Memories of an Old Burgtheater Actress, 1919), covers her career and her marriage until 1887. Robert Wilbrandt became a professor of economics; his publications include *Mein Vater Adolf Wilbrandt* (My Father, Adolf Wilbrandt, 1937).

Wilbrandt's popularity did not survive World War I. His works are of interest principally for their populist interpretations of the complex social and artistic pressures on the new Germany and the Austro-Hungarian Empire. His works for the theater and his narrative prose amused and educated their readers but lack depth or social impact. He mirrored the times and did not suspect the upheavals which would come to central Europe in the twentieth century.

References:

Adolf Wilbrandt: Zum 24. August 1907. Von seinen Freunden (Stuttgart & Berlin: Cotta, 1907);

Max Behr, "Adolf Wilbrandt und die Grundlagen seines Schaffens," *Hochland,* 8 (August 1911): 572–582;

Heinrich Glücksmann, ed., *Zu Adolf Wilbrandts 100. Geburtstag: Festschrift* (Vienna: Horn, 1937);

Viktor Klemperer, *Adolf Wilbrandt: Eine Studie über seine Werke* (Stuttgart & Berlin: Cotta, 1907);

Gerhard Köhler, "Adolf Wilbrandts Dramen am Burgtheater," Ph.D. dissertation, University of Vienna, 1970;

Max Lederer, "Einige Bemerkungen zu Adolf Wilbrandts *Der Meister von Palmyra,*" *Modern Language Notes,* 61 (December 1946): 551–555;

Eduard Scharrer-Santen, *Adolf Wilbrandt als Dramatiker* (Munich & Leipzig: Haist, 1912);

Thomas C. van Stockum, "Ein vergessenes deutsches Drama: Adolf Wilbrandts 'Der Meister von Palmyra,' " in his *Von Friedrich Nicolai bis Thomas Mann: Aufsätze zur deutschen und vergleichenden Literaturgeschichte* (Groningen: Wolters, 1962), pp. 254–273;

Mark Twain, "About Play-Acting: *Master of Palmyra* at the Burg Theatre in Vienna," *Forum,* 26 (October 1898): 143–151;

Robert Wilbrandt, *Mein Vater Adolf Wilbrandt: Zu seinem 100. Geburtstag* (Berlin & Vienna: Österreichischer Wirtschaftsverlag, 1937);

Auguste Wilbrandt-Baudius, *Aus Kunst und Leben: Erinnerungen einer alten Burgschauspielerin* (Zurich: Amalthea, 1919).

Papers:

The major collections of Adolf von Wilbrandt's papers are in the theater collection of the Österreichische Nationalbibliothek (Austrian National Library) and the Haus- und Hofarchiv (House and Home Archives), Vienna; several adaptations and scripts are at the Burgtheater Archiv in Vienna. Materials relating to his relationship with his publisher are in the Cotta Archiv of the Schiller Nationalmuseum und Literaturarchiv, Marbach am Neckar; additional materials are in the Literatur und Germanistik Bibliothek (Literature and Germanistics Library) of the University of Rostock.

Checklist of Further Readings

Alker, Ernst. *Die deutsche Literatur im 19. Jahrhundert (1832–1914),* second edition. Stuttgart: Kröner, 1962.

Auerbach, Erich. *Mimesis: The Representation of Reality in Western Literature,* translated by Willard Trask. Princeton: Princeton University Press, 1953.

Aust, Hugo. *Literatur des Realismus.* Stuttgart: Metzler, 1981.

Bark, Joachim. *Biedermeier–Vormärz: Bürgerlicher Realismus,* volume 3 of *Geschichte der deutschen Literatur,* edited by Bark and others. Stuttgart: Klett, 1984.

Berman, Russel. *The Rise of the Modern German Novel: Crisis and Charisma.* Cambridge, Mass.: Harvard University Press, 1986.

Bernd, Clifford. *German Poetic Realism.* Boston: Twayne, 1987.

Boeschenstein, Hermann. *German Literature of the Nineteenth Century.* New York: St. Martin's Press, 1969; London: Arnold, 1969.

Bramstedt, Ernest K. *Aristocracy and the Middle Classes in Germany: Social Types in German Literature, 1830–1900.* Chicago: University of Chicago Press, 1964.

Brinkmann, Richard, ed. *Begriffsbestimmung des literarischen Realismus,* third edition, enlarged. Darmstadt: Wissenschaftliche Buchgesellschaft, 1987.

Bucher, Max, and others, eds. *Realismus und Gründerzeit: Manifeste und Dokumente zur deutschen Literatur 1848–1880,* 2 volumes. Stuttgart: Metzler, 1976.

Cowen, Roy. *Der Poetische Realismus: Kommentar zu einer Epoche.* Munich: Winkler, 1985.

Craig, Gordon A. *Germany, 1866–1945.* Oxford: Clarendon Press, 1978.

Daemmrich, Horst S. "Realismus," in *Geschichte der deutschen Literatur,* volume 3: *Vom Realismus bis zur Gegenwartsliteratur,* edited by Ehrhard Bahr and Otto F. Best. Tübingen: Francke, 1988, pp. 1–87.

David, Claude. *Geschichte der deutschen Literatur: Zwischen Romantik und Symbolismus, 1820–1885.* Gütersloh: Mohn, 1966.

Denkler, Horst, ed. *Romane und Erzählungen des Bürgerlichen Realismus: Neue Interpretationen.* Stuttgart: Reclam, 1980.

Eggert, Hartmut. *Studien zur Wirkungsgeschichte des deutschen historischen Romans 1850–1875.* Frankfurt am Main: Klostermann, 1971.

Ellis, John. *Narration in the German Novelle: Theory and Interpretation.* London: Cambridge University Press, 1974.

Fehr, Karl. *Der Realismus in der schweizerischen Literatur.* Bern: Francke, 1965.

Finney, Gail. "Poetic Realism: Theodor Storm (1817–1888), Gottfried Keller (1819–1890), Conrad Ferdinand Meyer (1825–1898)," in *European Writers,* volume 6: *The Romantic Century,* edited by Jacques Barzun. New York: Scribners, 1985, pp. 913–942.

Frederiksen, Elke, ed. *Die Frauenfrage in Deutschland: 1865–1915. Texte und Dokumente.* Stuttgart: Reclam, 1981.

Fuerst, Norbert. *The Victorian Age of German Literature: Eight Essays.* University Park: Pennsylvania State University Press, 1966.

Himmel, Hellmuth. *Geschichte der deutschen Novelle.* Bern: Francke, 1963.

Holub, Robert C. *Reflections of Realism: Paradox, Norm, and Ideology in Nineteenth-Century German Prose.* Detroit: Wayne State University Press, 1991.

Huyssen, Andreas, ed. *Bürgerlicher Realismus.* Stuttgart: Reclam, 1974.

Jansen, Josef, and others. *März-Revolution. Reichsgründung und die Anfänge des Imperialismus,* volume 2 of *Einführung in die deutsche Literatur des 19. Jahrhunderts,* edited by Jansen and Jürgen Hein. Opladen: Westdeutscher Verlag, 1984.

Just, Klaus Günther. *Von der Gründerzeit bis zur Gegenwart: Geschichte der deutschen Literatur seit 1871.* Bern & Munich: Francke, 1973.

Kaiser, Nancy. "Realism," in *A Concise History of German Literature to 1900,* edited by Kim Vivian. Columbia, S.C.: Camden House, 1992, pp. 262–288.

Kaiser. *Social Integration and Narrative Structure: Patterns of Realism in Auerbach, Freytag, Fontane, and Raabe.* Bern: Lang, 1986.

Killy, Walther. *Wirklichkeit und Kunstcharakter: Neun Romane des 19. Jahrhunderts.* Munich: Beck, 1963.

Kinder, Hermann. *Poesie als Synthese: Ausbreitung eines deutschen Realismusverständnisses in der Mitte des 19. Jahrhunderts.* Frankfurt am Main: Athenäum, 1973.

Löwith, Karl. *From Hegel to Nietzsche: The Revolution in Nineteenth-Century Thought,* translated by David E. Green. New York: Holt, Rinehart & Winston, 1964.

Martini, Fritz. *Deutsche Literatur im bürgerlichen Realismus 1848–1898,* fourth edition. Stuttgart: Metzler, 1981.

McInnes, Edward. *Das deutsche Drama des 19. Jahrhunderts.* Berlin: Schmidt, 1983.

Müller, Klaus-Detlef. *Bürgerlicher Realismus: Grundlagen und Interpretationen.* Königstein: Athenäum, 1981.

Plumpe, Gerhard, ed. *Theorie des bürgerlichen Realismus: Eine Textsammlung.* Stuttgart: Reclam, 1985.

Prawer, Siegbert Salomon. *German Lyric Poetry: A Critical Analysis of Selected Poems from Klopstock to Rilke.* New York: Barnes & Noble, 1965.

Sagarra, Eda. *Tradition and Revolution: German Literature and Society, 1830–1890.* New York: Basic Books, 1971.

Silz, Walter. *Realism and Reality: Studies in the German Novelle of Poetic Realism.* Chapel Hill: University of North Carolina Press, 1954.

Stern, Joseph P. *Idylls and Realities: Studies in Nineteenth-Century German Literature*. London: Methuen, 1971.

Stern. *Re-Interpretations: Seven Studies in Nineteenth-Century German Literature*. London: Thames & Hudson, 1964.

Swales, Martin W. *The German Novelle*. Princeton: Princeton University Press, 1977.

Widhammer, Helmuth. *Die Literaturtheorie des deutschen Realismus, 1848–1860*. Stuttgart: Metzler, 1977.

Widhammer. *Realismus und klassizistische Tradition: Zur Theorie der Literatur in Deutschland 1848–1860*. Tübingen: Niemeyer, 1972.

Widhammer and Hans-Joachim Ruckhäberle, eds. *Roman und Romantheorie des deutschen Realismus: Darstellung und Dokumente*. Kronberg: Athenäum, 1977.

Wiese, Benno von. *Die deutsche Novelle von Goethe bis Kafka: Interpretationen*, 2 volumes. Düsseldorf: Bagel, 1956.

Zeman, Herbert. *Die österreichische Literatur: Ihr Profil im 19. Jahrhundert (1830–1880)*. Graz: Akademische Druck- und Verlagsanstalt, 1982.

Contributors

A. Tilo Alt .... *Duke University*
Keith Bullivant .... *University of Florida*
Adrian Del Caro .... *University of Colorado*
Horst Dinkelacker .... *Rhodes College*
Karl W. Doerry .... *Northern Arizona University*
Jo-Jacqueline Eckardt .... *New York University*
Glen W. Gadberry .... *University of Minnesota – Twin Cities*
Mark H. Gelber .... *Ben-Gurion University*
Glenn A. Guidry .... *Nashville, Tennessee*
Gail K. Hart .... *University of California, Irvine*
Charles H. Helmetag .... *Villanova University*
John Hibberd .... *University of Bristol*
Kurt R. Jankowsky .... *Georgetown University*
Ruth-Ellen Boetcher Joeres .... *University of Minnesota*
Calvin N. Jones .... *University of South Alabama*
Gerda Jordan .... *University of South Carolina*
Nancy Kaiser .... *University of Wisconsin – Madison*
Wulf Koepke .... *Texas A&M University*
Jill Anne Kowalik .... *University of California, Los Angeles*
Tiiu V. Laane .... *Texas A&M University*
William H. McClain .... *Johns Hopkins University*
E. Allen McCormick .... *City University of New York*
Siegfried Mews .... *University of North Carolina at Chapel Hill*
Helen G. Morris-Keitel .... *Bucknell University*
Peter Morris-Keitel .... *Bucknell University*
Gerald Opie .... *University of Exeter*
Malcolm J. Pender .... *University of Strathclyde*
Brent O. Peterson .... *Duquesne University*
Otto Pflanze .... *Bard College*
Katherine Roper .... *Saint Mary's College of California*
Jeffrey L. Sammons .... *Yale University*
Ulrich Scheck .... *Queen's University, Kingston, Canada*
Karl Ludwig Stenger .... *University of South Carolina – Aiken*
Irene Stocksieker Di Maio .... *Louisiana State University and A&M College*
Reinhard K. Zachau .... *University of the South*

Cumulative Index

Dictionary of Literary Biography, Volumes 1-129
Dictionary of Literary Biography Yearbook, 1980-1992
Dictionary of Literary Biography Documentary Series, Volumes 1-10

Cumulative Index

DLB before number: *Dictionary of Literary Biography,* Volumes 1-129
Y before number: *Dictionary of Literary Biography Yearbook,* 1980-1992
DS before number: *Dictionary of Literary Biography Documentary Series,* Volumes 1-10

A

D

G

H

I

J

Cumulative Index

N

O

P

S

U

V

ISBN 0-8103-5388-1

(Continued from front endsheets)

Documentary Series

Yearbooks